D1537039

F^{mini}rench_{dictionary}

French > English   English > French

mini
French
dictionary

French > English   English > French

This edition published exclusively for WHSmith
Greenbridge Road, Swindon SN3 3LD

www.WHSmith.co.uk

in 2003 by Collins, an imprint of
HarperCollins*Publishers*
Westerhill Road, Bishopbriggs, Glasgow G64 2QT
Great Britain

© HarperCollins Publishers 2003

Latest reprint 2004

ISBN 0-00-712816-9

A catalogue record for this book
is available from the British Library.

Typeset by Morton Word Processing Ltd,
Scarborough, England

Printed by Legoprint S.P.A.

TABLE DES MATIÈRES

CONTENTS

INTRODUCTION

Nous sommes très heureux que vous ayez décidé d'acheter ce dictionnaire et espérons que vous aimerez l'utiliser et que vous en tirerez profit au lycée, à la maison, en vacances ou au travail.

Cette introduction a pour but de vous donner quelques conseils sur la meilleure façon d'utiliser au mieux votre dictionnaire, en vous référant non seulement à son importante nomenclature mais aussi aux informations contenues dans chaque entrée. Ceci vous aidera à lire et à comprendre, mais aussi à communiquer et à vous exprimer en anglais contemporain.

Le dictionnaire commence par la liste des abréviations utilisées dans le texte et par la transcription des sons par des symboles phonétiques. À la fin vous trouverez des tables de verbes français ainsi que la liste des verbes irréguliers en anglais, suivis d'une section finale sur les nombres et sur les expressions de temps.

COMMENT UTILISER VOTRE DICTIONNAIRE

Ce dictionnaire offre une masse d'informations et use de divers formes et tailles de caractères, symboles, abréviations, parenthèses et crochets. Les conventions et symboles utilisés sont expliqués dans les sections qui suivent.

Entrées

Les mots que vous cherchez dans le dictionnaire (les 'entrées') sont classés par ordre alphabétique. Ils sont imprimés en **caractères gras** pour pouvoir être repérés rapidement. Les deux entrées figurant en haut de page indiquent le premier et le dernier mot qui apparaissent sur la page en question.

Des informations sur l'usage ou sur la forme de certaines entrées sont données entre parenthèses, après la transcription phonétique. Ces indications apparaissent sous forme abrégée et en italiques (ex (*fam*), (*COMM*)).

Dans les cas appropriés, les mots apparentés aux entrées sont regroupés sous la même entrée (**ronger, rongeur; accept,**

acceptance) et apparaissent en caractères gras, légèrement plus petits que ceux de l'entrée.

Les expressions courantes dans lesquelles apparaît l'entrée sont indiquées par des caractères romains gras différents (ex **avoir du retard**).

Transcription phonétique

La transcription phonétique de chaque entrée (indiquant sa prononciation) est indiquée entre crochets immédiatement après l'entrée (ex **fumer** [fyme]; **knead** [ni:d]). Une liste de ces symboles figure à la page xiv.

Traductions

Les traductions des entrées apparaissent en caractères ordinaires et, lorsque plusieurs sens ou usages coexistent, ces traductions sont séparées par un point-virgule. Vous trouverez souvent entre parenthèses d'autres mots en italiques qui précèdent les traductions. Ces mots fournissent souvent certains des contextes dans lesquels l'entrée est susceptible d'être utilisée (ex **rough** (*voice*) ou (*weather*)) ou offrent des synonymes (ex **rough** (*violent*)).

'Mots-clés'

Une importance particulière est accordée à certains mots français et anglais qui sont considérés comme des "mots-clés" dans chacune des langues. Cela peut être dû à leur utilisation très fréquente ou au fait qu'ils ont divers types d'usages (ex **vouloir, plus; get, that**). Une combinaison de losanges et de chiffres vous aident à distinguer différentes catégories grammaticales et différents sens. D'autres renseignements utiles apparaissent en italiques et entre parenthèses dans la langue de l'utilisateur.

Données grammaticales

Les catégories grammaticales sont données sous forme abrégée et en italiques après la transcription phonétique des entrées (ex *vt, adv, conj*).

Les genres des noms français sont indiqués de la manière suivante: *nm* pour un nom masculin et *nf* pour un nom féminin. Le féminin et le pluriel irréguliers de certains noms sont également indiqués (**directeur, -trice; cheval, -aux**).

Le masculin et le féminin des adjectif sont indiqués lorsque ces deux formes sont différentes (ex **noir, e**). Lorsque l'adjectif a un féminin ou un pluriel irrégulier, ces formes sont clairement indiquées (ex **net, nette**). Les pluriels irréguliers des noms, et les formes irréguliers des verbes anglais sont indiqués entre parenthèses, avant la catégorie grammaticale (ex **man** ... (*pl* **men**) *n*; **give** (*pt* **gave**, *pp* **given**) *vt*).

INTRODUCTION

We are delighted you have decided to buy this dictionary and hope you will enjoy and benefit from using it at school, at home, on holiday or at work.

This introduction gives you a few tips on how to get the most out of your dictionary — not simply from its comprehensive wordlist but also from the information provided in each entry. This will help you to read and understand modern French, as well as communicate and express yourself in the language.

The dictionary begins by listing the abbreviations used in the text and illustrating the sounds shown by the phonetic symbols. You will find French verb tables and English irregular verbs at the back, followed by a final section on numbers and time expressions.

USING YOUR DICTIONARY

A wealth of information is presented in the dictionary, using various typefaces, sizes of type, symbols, abbreviations and brackets. The conventions and symbols used are explained in the following sections.

Headwords

The words you look up in a dictionary — "headwords" — are listed alphabetically. They are printed in **bold type** for rapid identification. The two headwords appearing at the top of each page indicate the first and last word dealt with on the page in question.

Information about the usage or form of certain headwords is given in brackets after the phonetic spelling. This usually appears in abbreviated form and in italics (e.g. (*fam*), (*COMM*)).

Where appropriate, words related to headwords are grouped in the same entry (**ronger, rongeur; accept, acceptance**) in a slightly smaller bold type than the headword.

Common expressions in which the headword appears are shown in a different bold roman type (e.g. **avoir du retard**).

Phonetic spellings

The phonetic spelling of each headword (indicating its pronunciation) is given in square brackets immediately after the headword (e.g. **fumer** [fyme]; **knead** [ni:d]). A list of these symbols is given on page xiv.

Translations

Headword translations are given in ordinary type and, where more than one meaning or usage exists, these are separated by a semi-colon. You will often find other words in italics in brackets before the translations. These offer suggested contexts in which the headword might appear (e.g. **rough** (*voice*) or (*weather*)) or provide synonyms (e.g. **rough** (*violent*)).

"Key" words

Special status is given to certain French and English words which are considered as "key" words in each language. They may, for example, occur very frequently or have several types of usage (e.g. **vouloir, plus; get, that**). A combination of lozenges and numbers helps you to distinguish different parts of speech and different meanings. Further helpful information is provided in brackets and in italics in the relevant language for the user.

Grammatical information

Parts of speech are given in abbreviated form in italics after the phonetic spellings of headwords (e.g. *vt, adv, conj*).

Genders of French nouns are indicated as follows: *nm* for a masculine and *nf* for a feminine noun. Feminine and irregular plural forms of nouns are also shown (**directeur, -trice; cheval, -aux**).

Adjectives are given in both masculine and feminine forms where these forms are different (e.g. **noir, e**). Clear information is provided where adjectives have an irregular feminine or plural form (e.g. **net, nette**).

ABRÉVIATIONS

ABBREVIATIONS

abréviation	**ab(b)r**	abbreviation
adjectif, locution adjective	**adj**	adjective, adjectival phrase
adverbe, locution adverbiale	**adv**	adverb, adverbial phrase
administration	**ADMIN**	administration
agriculture	**AGR**	agriculture
anatomie	**ANAT**	anatomy
architecture	**ARCHIT**	architecture
article défini	**art déf**	definite article
article indéfini	**art indéf**	indefinite article
l'automobile	**AUT(O)**	the motor car and motoring
aviation, voyages aériens	**AVIAT**	flying, air travel
biologie	**BIO(L)**	biology
botanique	**BOT**	botany
anglais de Grande-Bretagne	**BRIT**	British English
chimie	**CHEM**	chemistry
commerce, finance, banque	**COMM**	commerce, finance, banking
comparatif	**compar**	comparative
informatique	**COMPUT**	computing
conjonction	**conj**	conjunction
construction	**CONSTR**	building
nom utilisé comme adjectif	**cpd**	compound element
cuisine, art culinaire	**CULIN**	cookery
article défini	**def art**	definite article
déterminant: article; adjectif démonstratif ou indéfini etc	**dét**	determiner: article, demonstrative etc
diminutif	**dimin**	diminutive
économie	**ECON**	economics
électricité, électronique	**ELEC**	electricity, electronics
exclamation, interjection	**excl**	exclamation, interjection
féminin	**f**	feminine
langue familière (! emploi vulgaire)	**fam (!)**	colloquial usage (! particularly offensive)
emploi figuré	**fig**	figurative use
(verbe anglais) dont la particule est inséparable du verbe	**fus**	(phrasal verb) where the particle cannot be separated from main verb
généralement	**gén, gen**	generally
géographie, géologie	**GEO**	geography, geology
géométrie	**GEOM**	geometry
impersonnel	**impers**	impersonal
article indéfini	**indef art**	indefinite article
langue familière (! emploi vulgaire)	**inf(!)**	colloquial usage (! particularly offensive)
infinitif	**infin**	infinitive
informatique	**INFORM**	computing
invariable	**inv**	invariable
irrégulier	**irrég, irreg**	irregular

ABRÉVIATIONS

ABBREVIATIONS

domaine juridique	JUR	law
grammaire, linguistique	LING	grammar, linguistics
masculin	m	masculine
mathématiques, algèbre	MATH	mathematics, calculus
médecine	MÉD MED	medical term, medicine
masculin ou féminin, suivant le sexe	m/f	masculine or feminine depending on sex
domaine militaire, armée	MIL	military matters
musique	MUS	music
nom	n	noun
navigation, nautisme	NAVIG, NAUT	sailing, navigation
adjectif ou nom numérique	num	numeral adjective or noun
	o.s.	oneself
péjoratif	péj, pej	derogatory, pejorative
photographie	PHOT(O)	photography
physiologie	PHYSIOL	physiology
pluriel	pl	plural
politique	POL	politics
participe passé	pp	past participle
préposition	prép, prep	preposition
pronom	pron	pronoun
psychologie, psychiatrie	PSYCH	psychology, psychiatry
temps du passé	pt	past tense
quelque chose	qch	
quelqu'un	qn	
religions, domaine ecclésiastique	REL	religions, church service
	sb	somebody
enseignement, système scolaire et universitaire	SCOL	schooling, schools and universities
singulier	sg	singular
	sth	something
subjonctif	sub	subjunctive
sujet (grammatical)	su(b)j	(grammatical) subject
superlatif	superl	superlative
techniques, technologie	TECH	technical term, technology
télécommunications	TEL	telecommunications
télévision	TV	television
typographie	TYP(O)	typography, printing
anglais des USA	US	American English
verbe (auxiliaire)	vb (aux)	(auxiliary) verb
verbe intransitif	vi	intransitive verb
verbe transitif	vt	transitive verb
zoologie	ZOOL	zoology
marque déposée	®	registered trademark
indique une équivalence culturelle	≃	introduces a cultural equivalent

TRANSCRIPTION PHONÉTIQUE

CONSONNES

NB. **p, b, t, d, k, g** sont suivis d'une aspiration en anglais.

CONSONANTS

NB. **p, b, t, d, k, g** are not aspirated in French.

French	IPA	English
poupée	p	*puppy*
bombe	b	*baby*
tente thermal	t	*tent*
dinde	d	*daddy*
coq qui képi	k	*cork kiss chord*
gag bague	g	*gag guess*
sale ce nation	s	*so rice kiss*
zéro rose	z	*cousin buzz*
tache chat	ʃ	*sheep sugar*
gilet juge	ʒ	*pleasure beige*
	tʃ	*church*
	dʒ	*judge general*
fer phare	f	*farm raffle*
valve	v	*very rev*
	θ	*thin maths*
	ð	*that other*
lent salle	l	*little ball*
rare rentrer	R	
	r	*rat rare*
maman femme	m	*mummy comb*
non nonne	n	*no ran*
agneau vigne	ɲ	
	ŋ	*singing bank*
hop!	h	*hat reheat*
yeux paille pied	j	*yet*
nouer oui	w	*wall bewail*
huile lui	ɥ	
	x	*loch*

DIVERS

pour l'anglais: le r final se prononce en liaison devant une voyelle

MISCELLANEOUS

ʳ	in French wordlist: no liaison

pour l'anglais: précède la syllabe accentuée

ˈ	in French transcription: no liaison

xiv

PHONETIC TRANSCRIPTION

VOYELLES

NB. La mise en équivalence de certains sons n'indique qu'une ressemblance approximative.

VOWELS

NB. The pairing of some vowel sounds only indicates approximate equivalence.

ici vie lyre	i i:	heel bead
	ɪ	hit pity
jouer été	e	
lait jouet merci	ɛ	set tent
plat amour	a æ	bat apple
bas pâte	ɑ ɑ:	after car calm
	ʌ	fun cousin
le premier	ə	over above
beurre peur	œ	
peu deux	ø ə:	urn fern work
or homme	ɔ	wash pot
mot eau gauche	o ɔ:	born cork
genou roue	u	full soot
	u:	boon lewd
rue urne	y	

DIPHTONGUES

DIPHTHONGS

ɪə	beer tier
ɛə	tear fair there
eɪ	date plaice day
aɪ	life buy cry
au	owl foul now
əu	low no
ɔɪ	boil boy oily
uə	poor tour

NASALES

NASAL VOWELS

matin plein	ɛ̃
brun	œ̃
sang an dans	ɑ̃
non pont	ɔ̃

FRANÇAIS – ANGLAIS
FRENCH – ENGLISH

A, a

a [a] *vb voir* **avoir**

MOT-CLÉ

à [a] (*à + le* = **au**, *à + les* = **aux**) *prép* **1**
(*endroit, situation*) at, in; **être à Paris/
au Portugal** to be in Paris/Portugal;
être à la maison/à l'école to be at
home/at school; **à la campagne** in
the country; **c'est à 10 km/20
minutes (d'ici)** it's 10 km/20 minutes
away

2 (*direction*) to; **aller à Paris/au Portugal** to go to Paris/Portugal; **aller à la
maison/à l'école** to go home/to
school; **à la campagne** to the country

3 (*temps*): **à 3 heures/minuit** at 3
o'clock/midnight; **au printemps/mois
de juin** in the spring/the month of
June

4 (*attribution, appartenance*) to; **le livre
est à Paul/à lui/à nous** this book is
Paul's/his/ours; **donner qch à qn** to
give sth to sb

5 (*moyen*) with; **se chauffer au gaz** to
have gas heating; **à bicyclette** on a *ou*
by bicycle; **à la main/machine** by
hand/machine

6 (*provenance*) from; **boire à la bouteille** to drink from the bottle

7 (*caractérisation, manière*): **l'homme
aux yeux bleus** the man with the blue
eyes; **à la russe** the Russian way

8 (*but, destination*): **tasse à café** coffee
cup; **maison à vendre** house for sale

9 (*rapport, évaluation, distribution*): **100
km/unités à l'heure** 100 km/units per
ou an hour; **payé à l'heure** paid by the
hour; **cinq à six** five to six

---

abaisser [abese] *vt* to lower, bring
down; (*manette*) to pull down; **s'~** *vi*
to go down; (*fig*) to demean o.s.

abandon [abādɔ̃] *nm* abandoning; giving up; withdrawal; **être à l'~** to be in
a state of neglect

abandonner [abādɔne] *vt* (*personne*)
to abandon; (*projet, activité*) to abandon, give up; (*SPORT*) to retire *ou* withdraw from; (*céder*) to surrender; **s'~ à**
(*paresse, plaisirs*) to give o.s. up to

abasourdir [abazurdir] *vt* to stun,
stagger

abat-jour [abaʒur] *nm inv* lampshade

abats [aba] *nmpl* (*de bœuf, porc*) offal
sg; (*de volaille*) giblets

abattement [abatmã] *nm*: **~ fiscal** ≈
tax allowance

abattoir [abatwar] *nm* slaughterhouse

abattre [abatr] *vt* (*arbre*) to cut down,
fell; (*mur, maison*) to pull down; (*avion,
personne*) to shoot down; (*animal*) to
shoot, kill; (*fig*) to wear out, tire out; to
demoralize; **ne pas se laisser ~** to keep one's spirits
up, not to let things get one down; **s'~
sur** to beat down on; (*fig*) to rain
down on

abbaye [abei] *nf* abbey

abbé [abe] *nm* priest; (*d'une abbaye*)
abbot

abcès [apsɛ] *nm* abscess

abdiquer [abdike] *vi* to abdicate

abdominaux [abdɔmino] *nmpl*: **faire
des ~** to do exercises for one's abdominals, do one's abdominals

abeille [abej] *nf* bee

aberrant, e [aberã, ãt] *adj* absurd

aberration [aberasjɔ̃] *nf* aberration

abêtir [abetir] *vt* to make morons of
(*ou* a moron of)

abîme [abim] nm abyss, gulf

abîmer [abime] vt to spoil, damage; **s'~** vi to get spoilt ou damaged

ablation [ablasjɔ̃] nf removal

aboiement [abwamɑ̃] nm bark, barking

abois [abwa] nmpl: **aux ~** at bay

abolir [abɔlir] vt to abolish

abominable [abɔminabl] adj abominable

abondance [abɔ̃dɑ̃s] nf abundance

abondant, e [abɔ̃dɑ̃, ɑ̃t] adj plentiful, abundant, copious; **abonder** vi to abound, be plentiful; **abonder dans le sens de qn** to concur with sb

abonné, e [abɔne] nm/f subscriber; season ticket holder

abonnement [abɔnmɑ̃] nm subscription; (transports, concerts) season ticket

abonner [abɔne] vt: **s'~ à** to subscribe to, take out a subscription to

abord [abɔr] nm: **au premier ~** at first sight, initially; **~s** nmpl (environs) surroundings; **d'~** first

abordable [abɔrdabl] adj (prix) reasonable; (personne) approachable

aborder [abɔrde] vi to land ♦ vt (sujet, difficulté) to tackle; (personne) to approach; (rivage etc) to reach

aboutir [abutir] vi (négociations etc) to succeed; **~ à** to end up at; **n'~ à rien** to come to nothing

aboyer [abwaje] vi to bark

abréger [abreʒe] vt to shorten

abreuver [abrœve] vt: **s'~** vi to drink; **abreuvoir** nm watering place

abréviation [abrevjasjɔ̃] nf abbreviation

abri [abri] nm shelter; **être à l'~** to be under cover; **se mettre à l'~** to shelter

abricot [abriko] nm apricot

abriter [abrite] vt to shelter; **s'~** vi to shelter, take cover

abrupt, e [abrypt] adj sheer, steep; (ton) abrupt

abruti, e [abryti] adj stunned, dazed ♦

nm/f (fam) idiot, moron; **~ de travail** overworked

absence [apsɑ̃s] nf absence; (MÉD) blackout; **avoir des ~s** to have mental blanks

absent, e [apsɑ̃, ɑ̃t] adj absent ♦ nm/f absentee; **absenter: s'absenter** vi to take time off work; (sortir) to leave, go out

absolu, e [apsɔly] adj absolute; **absolument** adv absolutely

absorbant, e [apsɔrbɑ̃, ɑ̃t] adj absorbent

absorber [apsɔrbe] vt to absorb; (gén MÉD: manger, boire) to take

abstenir [apstənir] vb: **s'~ de qch/de faire** to refrain from sth/from doing

abstraction [apstraksjɔ̃] nf abstraction

abstrait, e [apstre, et] adj abstract

absurde [apsyrd] adj absurd

abus [aby] nm abuse; **~ de confiance** breach of trust; **abuser** vi to go too far, overstep the mark; **abuser de** (duper) to take advantage of; **abusif, -ive** adj exorbitant; (punition) excessive

acabit [akabi] nm: **de cet ~** of that type

académie [akademi] nf academy; (SCOL: circonscription) ≃ regional education authority

---

Académie française

The Académie française was founded by Cardinal Richelieu in 1635 during the reign of Louis XIII. It consists of forty elected scholars and writers who are known as "les Quarante" or "les Immortels". One of the Académie's functions is to regulate the development of the French language and its recommendations are frequently the subject of lively public debate. It has produced several editions of its famous dictionary and awards various literary prizes.

---

acajou [akaʒu] nm mahogany

acariâtre [akaʀjɑtʀ] *adj* cantankerous

accablant, e [akablɑ̃, ɑ̃t] *adj* (*chaleur*) oppressive; (*témoignage, preuve*) overwhelming

accablement [akabləmɑ̃] *nm* despondency

accabler [akable] *vt* to overwhelm, overcome; **~ qn d'injures** to heap *ou* shower abuse on sb

accalmie [akalmi] *nf* lull

accaparer [akapaʀe] *vt* to monopolize; (*suj: travail etc*) to take up (all) the time *ou* attention of

accéder [aksede]: **~ à** *vt* (*lieu*) to reach; (*accorder: requête*) to grant, accede to

accélérateur [akseleʀatœʀ] *nm* accelerator

accélération [akseleʀasjɔ̃] *nf* acceleration

accélérer [akseleʀe] *vt* to speed up ♦ *vi* to accelerate

accent [aksɑ̃] *nm* accent; (*PHONÉTIQUE, fig*) stress; **mettre l'~ sur** (*fig*) to stress; **~ aigu/grave/circonflexe** acute/grave/circumflex accent; **accentuer** [aksɑ̃tɥe] *vt* (*LING*) to accent; (*fig*) to accentuate, emphasize; **s'accentuer** *vi* to become more marked *ou* pronounced

acceptation [akseptasjɔ̃] *nf* acceptance

accepter [aksepte] *vt* to accept; **~ de faire** to agree to do

accès [akse] *nm* (*à un lieu*) access; (*MÉD: de toux*) fit; (: *de fièvre*) bout; **d'~** **facile** easily accessible; **facile d'~** easy to get to; **~ de colère** fit of anger; **accessible** *adj* accessible; (*livre, sujet*): **accessible à qn** within the reach of sb

accessoire [akseswaʀ] *adj* secondary; incidental ♦ *nm* accessory; (*THÉÂTRE*) prop

accident [aksidɑ̃] *nm* accident; **par ~** by chance; **~ de la route** road accident; **~ du travail** industrial injury *ou* accident; **accidenté, e** *adj* damaged; injured; (*relief, terrain*) uneven; hilly; **accidentel, le** *adj* accidental

acclamations [aklamasjɔ̃] *nfpl* cheers

acclamer [aklame] *vt* to cheer, acclaim

acclimater [aklimate]: **s'~** *vi* (*personne*) to adapt (o.s.)

accolade [akɔlad] *nf* (*amicale*) embrace; (*signe*) brace

accommodant, e [akɔmɔdɑ̃, ɑ̃t] *adj* accommodating, easy-going

accommoder [akɔmɔde] *vt* (*CULIN*) to prepare; **s'~ de** *vt* to put up with; (*se contenter de*) to make do with

accompagnateur, -trice [akɔ̃paɲatœʀ, tʀis] *nm/f* (*MUS*) accompanist; (*de voyage: guide*) guide; (*de voyage organisé*) courier

accompagner [akɔ̃paɲe] *vt* to accompany, be *ou* go *ou* come with; (*MUS*) to accompany

accompli, e [akɔ̃pli] *adj* accomplished

accomplir [akɔ̃pliʀ] *vt* (*tâche, projet*) to carry out; (*souhait*) to fulfil; **s'~** *vi* to be fulfilled

accord [akɔʀ] *nm* agreement; (*entre des styles, tons etc*) harmony; (*MUS*) chord; **d'~!** OK!; **se mettre d'~** to come to an agreement; **être d'~ (pour faire qch)** to agree (to do sth)

accordéon [akɔʀdeɔ̃] *nm* (*MUS*) accordion

accorder [akɔʀde] *vt* (*faveur, délai*) to grant; (*harmoniser*) to match; (*MUS*) to tune; **s'~** *vi* to get on together; to agree

accoster [akɔste] *vt* (*NAVIG*) to draw alongside ♦ *vi* to berth

accotement [akɔtmɑ̃] *nm* verge (*BRIT*), shoulder

accouchement [akuʃmɑ̃] *nm* delivery, (child)birth; labour

accoucher [akuʃe] *vi* to give birth, have a baby; **~ d'un garçon** to give birth to a boy; **accoucheur** *nm*: (**médecin**) **accoucheur** obstetrician

accouder [akude]: **s'~** *vi* to rest one's elbows on/against; **accoudoir** *nm* armrest

accoupler [akuple] *vt* to couple; (*pour*

la reproduction) to mate; **s'~** vt to mate

accourir [akuRiR] vi to rush ou run up

accoutrement [akutRəmã] (péj) nm (tenue) outfit

accoutumance [akutymãs] nf (gén) adaptation; (MÉD) addiction

accoutumé, e [akutyme] adj (habituel) customary, usual

accoutumer [akutyme] vt: **s'~ à** to get accustomed ou used to

accréditer [akRedite] vt (nouvelle) to substantiate

accroc [akRo] nm (déchirure) tear; (fig) hitch, snag

accrochage [akRɔʃaʒ] nm (AUTO) collision; (dispute) clash, brush

accrocher [akRɔʃe] vt (fig) to catch, attract; **s'~** (se disputer) to have a clash ou brush; **~ qch à** (suspendre) to hang sth (up) on; (attacher: remorque) to hitch sth (up) to; **~ qch à** (déchirer) to catch sth (on); **~ un passant** (heurter) to hit a pedestrian; **s'~** (rester pris à) to catch on; (agripper, fig) to hang on ou cling to

accroissement [akRwasmã] nm increase

accroître [akRwatR]: **s'~** vi to increase

accroupir [akRupiR]: **s'~** vi to squat, crouch (down)

accru, e [akRy] pp de **accroître**

accueil [akœj] nm welcome; **comité d'~** reception committee; **accueillir** vt to welcome; (aller chercher) to meet, collect

acculer [akyle] vt: **~ qn à** ou **contre** to drive sb back against

accumuler [akymyle] vt to accumulate, amass; **s'~** vi to accumulate; to pile up

accusation [akyzasjɔ̃] nf (gén) accusation; (JUR) charge; (partie): **l'~** the prosecution

accusé, e [akyze] nm/f accused; defendant; **~ de réception** acknowledgement of receipt

accuser [akyze] vt to accuse; (fig) to emphasize, bring out; to show; **~ qn de** to accuse sb of; (JUR) to charge sb with; **~ réception de** to acknowledge receipt of

acerbe [asɛRb] adj caustic, acid

acéré, e [asere] adj sharp

acharné, e [aʃaRne] adj (efforts) relentless; (lutte, adversaire) fierce, bitter

acharner [aʃaRne] vb: **s'~ contre** to set o.s. against; (suj: malchance) to dog; **s'~ à faire** to try doggedly to do; (persister) to persist in doing

achat [aʃa] nm purchase; **faire des ~s** to do some shopping; **faire l'~ de qch** to purchase sth

acheminer [aʃ(ə)mine] vt (courrier) to forward, dispatch; **s'~ vers** to head for

acheter [aʃ(ə)te] vt to buy, purchase; (soudoyer) to buy; **~ qch à** (marchand) to buy ou purchase sth from; (ami etc: offrir) to buy sth for; **acheteur, -euse** nm/f buyer; shopper; (COMM) buyer

achever [aʃ(ə)ve] vt to complete, finish; (blessé) to finish off; **s'~** vi to end

acide [asid] adj sour, sharp; (CHIMIE) acid(ic) ♦ nm (CHIMIE) acid; **acidulé, e** adj slightly acid

acier [asje] nm steel; **aciérie** nf steelworks sg

acné [akne] nf acne

acolyte [akɔlit] (péj) nm associate

acompte [akɔ̃t] nm deposit

à-côté [akote] nm side-issue; (argent) extra

à-coup [aku] nm: **par ~~s** by fits and starts

acoustique [akustik] nf (d'une salle) acoustics pl

acquéreur [akeRœR] nm buyer, purchaser

acquérir [akeRiR] vt to acquire

acquis, e [aki, iz] pp de **acquérir** ♦ nm (accumulated) experience; **son aide nous est ~e** we can count on her help

acquit [aki] vb voir **acquérir** ♦ nm (quittance) receipt; **par ~ de conscience** to set one's mind at rest

acquitter [akite] vt (JUR) to acquit; (facture) to pay, settle; **s'~ de** vt (devoir) to discharge; (promesse) to fulfil

âcre [ɑkʀ] adj acrid, pungent

acrobate [akʀɔbat] nm/f acrobat; **acrobatie** nf acrobatics sg

acte [akt] nm act, action; (THÉÂTRE) act; **prendre ~ de** to note, take note of; **faire ~ de candidature** to apply; **faire ~ de présence** to put in an appearance; **~ de naissance** birth certificate

acteur [aktœʀ] nm actor

actif, -ive [aktif, iv] adj active ♦ nm (COMM) assets pl; (fig): **avoir à son ~** to have to one's credit; **population active** working population

action [aksjɔ̃] nf (gén) action; (COMM) share; **une bonne ~** a good deed; **actionnaire** nm/f shareholder; **actionner** vt (mécanisme) to activate; (machine) to operate

activer [aktive] vt to speed up; **s'~** vi to bustle about; to hurry up

activité [aktivite] nf activity; **en ~** (volcan) active; (fonctionnaire) in active life

actrice [aktʀis] nf actress

actualiser [aktɥalize] vt to bring up to date

actualité [aktɥalite] nf (d'un problème) topicality; (événements): **l'~** current events; **les ~s** nfpl (CINÉMA, TV) the news; **d'~** topical

actuel, le [aktɥɛl] adj (présent) present; (d'actualité) topical; **à l'heure ~le** at the present time; **actuellement** adv at present, at the present time

acuité [akɥite] nf acuteness

acupuncture [akypɔ̃ktœʀ] nm acupuncturist

acupuncture [akypɔ̃ktyʀ] nf acupuncture

adaptateur [adaptatœʀ] nm (ÉLEC) adapter

adapter [adapte] vt to adapt; **s'~ (à)** (suj: personne) to adapt (to); **~ qch à** (approprier) to adapt sth to (fit); **~ qch sur/dans/à** (fixer) to fit sth on/into/to

additif [aditif] nm additive

addition [adisjɔ̃] nf addition; (au café) bill; **additionner** vt to add (up)

adepte [adɛpt] nm/f follower

adéquat, e [adekwa, at] adj appropriate, suitable

adhérent, e [adeʀɑ̃, ɑ̃t] nm/f member

adhérer [adeʀe]: **~ à** vt (coller) to adhere ou stick to; (se rallier à) to join; **adhésif, -ive** adj adhesive, sticky; **ruban adhésif** sticky ou adhesive tape; **adhésion** nf joining; (fait d'être membre) membership; (accord) support

adieu, x [adjø] excl goodbye ♦ nm farewell

adjectif [adʒɛktif] nm adjective

adjoindre [adʒwɛ̃dʀ] vt: **~ qch à** to attach sth to; (ajouter) to add sth to; **s'~** vt (collaborateur etc) to take on, appoint; **adjoint, e** nm/f assistant; **adjoint au maire** deputy mayor; **directeur adjoint** assistant manager

adjudant [adʒydɑ̃] nm (MIL) warrant officer

adjuger [adʒyʒe] vt (prix, récompense) to award; (lors d'une vente) to auction (off); **s'~** vt to take for o.s.

adjurer [adʒyʀe] vt: **~ qn de faire** to implore ou beg sb to do

admettre [admɛtʀ] vt (laisser entrer) to admit; (candidat: SCOL) to pass; (tolérer) to allow, accept; (reconnaître) to admit, acknowledge

administrateur, -trice [administʀatœʀ, tʀis] nm/f (COMM) director; (ADMIN) administrator

administration [administʀasjɔ̃] nf administration; **l'A~** ≈ the Civil Service

administrer [administʀe] vt (firme) to manage, run; (biens, remède, sacrement etc) to administer

admirable [admiʀabl] adj admirable, wonderful

admirateur, -trice [admiʀatœʀ, tʀis] nm/f admirer

admiration [admiʀasjɔ̃] nf admiration

admirer [admiʀe] vt to admire

admis, e [admi, iz] *pp de* **admettre**

admissible [admisibl] *adj* (candidat) eligible; (comportement) admissible, acceptable

admission [admisjɔ̃] *nf* admission; acknowledgement; **demande d'~** application for membership

ADN *sigle m* (= acide désoxyribonucléique) DNA

adolescence [adɔlesɑ̃s] *nf* adolescence

adolescent, e [adɔlesɑ̃, ɑ̃t] *nm/f* adolescent, teenager

adonner [adɔne]: **s'~ à** *vt* (sport) to devote o.s. to; (boisson) to give o.s. over to

adopter [adɔpte] *vt* to adopt; **adoptif, -ive** *adj* (parents) adoptive; (fils, patrie) adopted

adorable [adɔʀabl] *adj* delightful, adorable

adorer [adɔʀe] *vt* to adore; (REL) to worship

adosser [adose] *vt*: **~ qch à** *ou* **contre** to stand sth against; **s'~ à** *ou* **contre** to lean with one's back against

adoucir [adusiʀ] *vt* (goût, température) to make milder; (avec du sucre) to sweeten; (peau, voix) to soften; (caractère) to mellow

adresse [adʀɛs] *nf* (domicile) address; (dextérité) skill, dexterity

adresser [adʀese] *vt* (lettre: expédier) to send; (: écrire l'adresse sur) to address; (injure, compliments) to address; **s'~ à** (parler à) to speak to, address; (s'informer auprès de) to go and see; (: bureau) to enquire at; (suj: livre, conseil) to be aimed at; **~ la parole à** to speak to, address

adroit, e [adʀwa, wat] *adj* skilful, skilled

adulte [adylt] *nm/f* adult, grown-up ♦ *adj* (chien, arbre) fully-grown, mature; (attitude) adult, grown-up

adultère [adyltɛʀ] *nm* (acte) adultery

advenir [advəniʀ] *vi* to happen

adverbe [advɛʀb] *nm* adverb

adversaire [advɛʀsɛʀ] *nm/f* (SPORT, gén) opponent, adversary

adverse [advɛʀs] *adj* opposing

aération [aeʀasjɔ̃] *nf* airing; (circulation de l'air) ventilation

aérer [aeʀe] *vt* to air; (fig) to lighten; **s'~** *vi* to get some (fresh) air

aérien, ne [aeʀjɛ̃, jɛn] *adj* (AVIAT) air *cpd*, aerial; (câble, métro) overhead; (fig) light; **compagnie ~ne** airline

aéro... [aeʀɔ] *préfixe*: **aérobic** *nm* aerobics *sg*; **aérogare** *nf* airport (buildings); (en ville) air terminal; **aéroglisseur** *nm* hovercraft; **Aéronavale** *nf* ≈ Fleet Air Arm (BRIT), ≈ Naval Air Force (US); **aérophagie** *nf* (MÉD) wind, aerophagia (MÉD); **aéroport** *nm* airport; **aéroporté, e** *adj* airborne, airlifted; **aérosol** *nm* aerosol

affable [afabl] *adj* affable

affaiblir [afebliʀ]: **s'~** *vi* to weaken

affaire [afɛʀ] *nf* (problème, question) matter; (criminelle, judiciaire) case; (scandaleuse etc) affair; (entreprise) business; (marché, transaction) deal; business *no pl*; (occasion intéressante) bargain; **~s** *nfpl* (intérêts publics et privés) affairs; (activité commerciale) business *sg*; (effets personnels) things, belongings; **ce sont mes ~s** (cela me concerne) that's my business; **ça fera l'~** that will do (nicely); **se tirer d'~** to sort it *ou* things out for o.s.; **avoir ~ à** (être en contact) to be dealing with; **les A~s étrangères** Foreign Affairs; **affairer: s'affairer** *vi* to busy o.s., bustle about

affaisser [afese]: **s'~** *vi* (terrain, immeuble) to subside, sink; (personne) to collapse

affaler [afale] *vb*: **s'~ (dans/sur)** to collapse *ou* slump (into/onto)

affamé, e [afame] *adj* starving

affectation [afɛktasjɔ̃] *nf* (nomination) appointment; (manque de naturel) affectation

affecter [afɛkte] *vt* to affect; **~ qch à** to allocate *ou* allot sth to; **~ qn à** to appoint sb to; (diplomate) to post sb to

affectif, -ive [afεktif, iv] adj emotional

affection [afεksjɔ̃] nf affection; (mal) ailment; **affectionner** vt to be fond of; **affectueux, -euse** adj affectionate

affermir [afεrmir] vt to consolidate, strengthen; (muscles) to tone up

affichage [afiʃaʒ] nm billposting; (électronique) display

affiche [afiʃ] nf poster; (officielle) notice; (THÉÂTRE) bill

afficher [afiʃe] vt (affiche) to put up; (réunion) to put up a notice about; (électroniquement) to display; (fig) to exhibit, display; **"défense d'~"** "stick no bills"

affilée [afile]: **d'~** adv at a stretch

affiler [afile] vt to sharpen

affilier [afilje]: **s'~ à** vt (club, société) to join

affiner [afine] vt to refine

affirmatif, -ive [afirmatif, iv] adj affirmative

affirmation [afirmasjɔ̃] nf assertion

affirmer [afirme] vt to assert

affligé, e [afliʒe] adj distressed, grieved; **~ de** (maladie, tare) afflicted with

affliger [afliʒe] vt (peiner) to distress, grieve

affluence [aflyɑ̃s] nf crowds pl; **heures d'~** rush hours; **jours d'~** busiest days

affluent [aflyɑ̃] nm tributary

affluer [aflye] vi (secours, biens) to flood in, pour in; (sang) to rush, flow

affolant, e [afɔlɑ̃, ɑ̃t] adj frightening

affolement [afɔlmɑ̃] nm panic

affoler [afɔle] vt to throw into a panic; **s'~** vi to panic

affranchir [afrɑ̃ʃir] vt to put a stamp ou stamps on; (à la machine) to frank (BRIT), meter (US); (fig) to free, liberate; **affranchissement** nm postage

affréter [afrete] vt to charter

affreux, -euse [afrø, øz] adj dreadful, awful

affront [afrɔ̃] nm affront; **affronte-**

-ment nm clash, confrontation

affronter [afrɔ̃te] vt to confront, face

affubler [afyble] (péj) vt: **~ qn de** to rig ou deck sb out in

affût [afy] nm: **à l'~ (de)** (gibier) lying in wait (for); (fig) on the look-out (for)

affûter [afyte] vt to sharpen, grind

afin [afε̃]: **~ que** conj so that, in order that; **~ de faire** in order to do, so as to do

africain, e [afrikε̃, εn] adj, nm/f African

Afrique [afrik] nf: **l'~** Africa; **l'~ du Sud** South Africa

agacer [agase] vt to irritate

âge [aʒ] nm age; **quel ~ as-tu?** how old are you?; **prendre de l'~** to be getting on (in years); **âgé, e** adj old, elderly; **âgé de 10 ans** 10 years old

agence [aʒɑ̃s] nf agency, office; (succursale) branch; **~ de voyages** travel agency; **~ immobilière** estate (BRIT) ou real estate (US) agent's (office)

agencer [aʒɑ̃se] vt to put together; (local) to arrange, lay out

agenda [aʒε̃da] nm diary

agenouiller [aʒ(ə)nuje]: **s'~** vi to kneel (down)

agent [aʒɑ̃, ɑ̃t] nm/f (aussi: **~(e) de police**) policeman (policewoman); (ADMIN) official, officer; **~ d'assurances** insurance broker

agglomération [aglɔmerasjɔ̃] nf town; built-up area; **l'~ parisienne** the urban area of Paris

aggloméré [aglɔmere] nm (bois) chipboard

aggraver [agrave]: **s'~** vi to worsen

agile [aʒil] adj agile, nimble

agir [aʒir] vi to act; **il s'agit de** (ça traite de) it is about; (il est important de) it's a matter ou question of

agitation [aʒitasjɔ̃] nf (hustle and) bustle; (trouble) agitation, excitement; (politique) unrest, agitation

agité, e [aʒite] adj fidgety, restless; (troublé) agitated, perturbed; (mer) rough

agiter [aʒite] vt (bouteille, chiffon)

shake; (*bras*) to wave; (*préoccuper, exciter*) to perturb; **s'~** *vi* (*enfant*) to fidget

agneau, x [aɲo] *nm* lamb

agonie [agɔni] *nf* mortal agony, death pangs *pl*; (*fig*) death throes *pl*

agrafe [agʀaf] *nf* (*de vêtement*) hook, fastener; (*de bureau*) staple; **agrafer** *vt* to fasten; to staple; **agrafeuse** *nf* stapler

agrandir [agʀɑ̃diʀ] *vt* to enlarge; **s'~** *vi* (*ville, famille*) to grow, expand; (*trou, écart*) to get bigger; **agrandissement** *nm* (*PHOTO*) enlargement

agréable [agʀeabl] *adj* pleasant, nice

agréé, e [agʀee] *adj*: **concessionnaire ~** registered dealer

agréer [agʀee] *vt* (*requête*) to accept; **~ à** to please, suit; **veuillez ~ ...** (*formule épistolaire*) yours faithfully

agrégation [agʀegasjɔ̃] *nf* highest teaching diploma in France; **agrégé, e** *nm/f* holder of the *agrégation*

agrément [agʀemɑ̃] *nm* (*accord*) consent, approval; **agrémenter** *vt* to embellish, adorn

agresser [agʀese] *vt* to attack; **agresseur** *nm* aggressor, attacker; (*POL, MIL*) aggressor; **agressif, -ive** *adj* aggressive

agricole [agʀikɔl] *adj* agricultural; **agriculteur** *nm* farmer; **agriculture** *nf* agriculture, farming

agripper [agʀipe] *vt* to grab, clutch; **s'~ à** to cling (on) to, clutch, grip

agroalimentaire [agʀoalimɑ̃tɛʀ] *nm* farm-produce industry

agrumes [agʀym] *nmpl* citrus fruit(s)

aguerrir [ageʀiʀ] *vt* to harden

aguets [agɛ] *nmpl*: **être aux ~** to be on the look out

aguicher [agiʃe] *vt* to entice

ahuri, e [ayʀi] *adj* (*stupéfait*) flabbergasted

ai [e] *vb voir* **avoir**

aide [ɛd] *nm/f* assistant; carer ♦ *nf* assistance, help; (*secours financier*) aid; **à l'~ de** (*avec*) with the help *ou* aid of; ap-

peler (qn) à l'~ to call for help (from sb); **~ familiale** home help, mother's help; **~ judiciaire** ♦ *nf* legal aid; **~ sociale** ♦ *nf* (*assistance*) state aid; **aide-éducateur, -trice** *nm/f* classroom assistant; **aide-mémoire** *nm inv* memoranda pages *pl*; (*key facts*) handbook; **aide-soignant, e** *nm/f* auxiliary nurse

aider [ede] *vt* to help; **s'~ de** (*se servir de*) to use, make use of

aie *etc* [ɛ] *vb voir* **avoir**

aïe [aj] *excl* ouch!

aïeul, e [ajœl] *nm/f* grandparent, grandfather(-mother)

aïeux [ajø] *nmpl* grandparents; (*ancêtres*) forebears, forefathers

aigle [ɛgl] *nm* eagle

aigre [ɛgʀ] *adj* sour, sharp; (*fig*) sharp, cutting; **aigre-doux, -ce** *adj* (*sauce*) sweet and sour; **aigreur** *nf* sourness; sharpness; **aigreurs d'estomac** heartburn *sg*; **aigrir** *vt* (*personne*) to embitter; (*caractère*) to sour

aigu, ë [egy] *adj* (*objet, douleur*) sharp; (*son, voix*) high-pitched, shrill; (*note*) high(-pitched)

aiguille [egɥij] *nf* needle; (*de montre*) hand; **~ à tricoter** knitting needle

aiguiller [egɥije] *vt* (*orienter*) to direct; **aiguilleur du ciel** *nm* air-traffic controller

aiguillon [egɥijɔ̃] *nm* (*d'abeille*) sting; **aiguillonner** *vt* to spur *ou* goad on

aiguiser [egize] *vt* to sharpen; (*fig*) to stimulate; (*: sens*) to excite

ail [aj, o] *nm* garlic

aile [ɛl] *nf* wing; **aileron** *nm* (*de requin*) fin; **ailier** *nm* winger

aille *etc* [aj] *vb voir* **aller**

ailleurs [ajœʀ] *adv* elsewhere, somewhere else; **partout/nulle part ~** everywhere/nowhere else; **d'~** (*du reste*) moreover, besides; **par ~** (*d'autre part*) moreover, furthermore

aimable [ɛmabl] *adj* kind, nice

aimant [ɛmɑ̃] *nm* magnet

aimer [eme] *vt* to love; (*d'amitié, affec-*

tion, par goût) to like; *(souhait)*: **j'~ais ...** I would like ...; **bien ~ qn/qch** to like sb/sth; **j'~ais mieux faire** I'd much rather do

aine [ɛn] *nf* groin

aîné, e [ene] *adj* elder, older; *(le plus âgé)* eldest, oldest ♦ *nm/f* eldest child *ou* one, oldest boy *ou* son/girl *ou* daughter

ainsi [ɛ̃si] *adv (de cette façon)* like this, in this way, thus; *(ce faisant)* thus ♦ *conj* thus, so; **~ que** *(comme)* (just) as; *(et aussi)* as well as; **pour ~ dire** so to speak; **et ~ de suite** and so on

aïoli [ajɔli] *nm* garlic mayonnaise

air [ɛʀ] *nm (mélodie)* tune; *(expression)* look, air; **prendre l'~** to get some (fresh) air; **avoir l'~** *(sembler)* to look, appear; **avoir l'~ de** to look like; **avoir l'~ de faire** to look as though one is doing, appear to be doing; **en l'~** *(promesses)* empty

aisance [ɛzɑ̃s] *nf* ease; *(richesse)* affluence

aise [ɛz] *nf* comfort; **être à l'~** *ou* **à son ~** to be comfortable; *(pas embarrassé)* to be at ease; *(financièrement)* to be comfortably off; **se mettre à l'~** to make o.s. comfortable; **être mal à l'~** to be uncomfortable; *(gêné)* to be ill at ease; **en faire à son ~** to do as one likes; **aisé, e** *adj* easy; *(assez riche)* well-to-do, well-off

aisselle [ɛsɛl] *nf* armpit

ait [ɛ] *vb voir* **avoir**

ajonc [aʒɔ̃] *nm* gorse *no pl*

ajourner [aʒuʀne] *vt (réunion)* to adjourn; *(décision)* to defer, postpone

ajouter [aʒute] *vt* to add

ajusté, e [aʒyste] *adj*: **bien ~** *(robe etc)* close-fitting

ajuster [aʒyste] *vt (régler)* to adjust; *(vêtement)* to alter; *(coup de fusil)* to aim; *(cible)* to aim at; *(TECH, adapter)*: **~ qch à** to fit sth to

alarme [alaʀm] *nf* alarm; **donner l'~** to give *ou* raise the alarm; **alarmer** *vt*

to alarm; **s'alarmer** *vi* to become alarmed; **alarmiste** *adj, nm/f* alarmist

album [albɔm] *nm* album

albumine [albymin] *nf* albumin; **avoir de l'~** to suffer from albuminuria

alcool [alkɔl] *nm*: **l'~** alcohol; **un ~** a spirit, a brandy; **bière sans ~** non-alcoholic *ou* alcohol-free beer; **~ à brûler** methylated spirits *(BRIT)*, wood alcohol *(US)*; **~ à 90°** surgical spirit; **alcoolique** *adj, nm/f* alcoholic; **alcoolisé, e** *adj* alcoholic; **une boisson non alcoolisée** a soft drink; **alcoolisme** *nm* alcoholism; **alcootest** ® *nm* Breathalyser ®; *(test)* breath-test

aléas [alea] *nmpl* hazards; *(INFORM)* random; **aléatoire** *adj* uncertain; *(INFORM)* random

alentour [alɑ̃tuʀ] *adv* around, round about; **~s** *nmpl (environs)* surroundings; **aux ~s de** in the vicinity *ou* neighbourhood of, round about; *(temps)* round about

alerte [alɛʀt] *adj* agile, nimble; brisk, lively ♦ *nf* alert; warning; **~ à la bombe** bomb scare; **alerter** *vt* to alert

algèbre [alʒɛbʀ] *nf* algebra

Alger [alʒe] *n* Algiers

Algérie [alʒeʀi] *nf*: **l'~** Algeria; **algérien, ne** *adj* Algerian ♦ *nm/f*: **Algérien, ne** Algerian

algue [alg] *nf (gén)* seaweed *no pl*; *(BOT)* alga

alibi [alibi] *nm* alibi

aliéné, e [aljene] *nm/f* insane person, lunatic *(péj)*

aligner [aliɲe] *vt* to align, line up; *(idées, chiffres)* to string together; *(adapter)*: **~ qch sur** to bring sth into alignment with; **s'~** *(soldats etc)* to line up; **s'~ sur** *(POL)* to align o.s. on

aliment [alimɑ̃] *nm* food; **alimentaire** *adj*: **denrées alimentaires** foodstuffs; **alimentation** *nf (commerce)* food trade; *(magasin)* grocery store; *(régime)* diet; *(en eau etc, de moteur)* supplying; *(INFORM)* feed; **alimenter** *vt* to feed; *(TECH)*: **alimenter (en)** to supply (with);

to feed (with); (fig) to sustain, keep going

alinéa [alinea] nm paragraph

aliter [alite]: **s'~** vi to take to one's bed

allaiter [alete] vt to (breast-)feed, nurse; (suj: animal) to suckle

allant [alã] nm drive, go

alléchant, e [aleʃɑ̃, ɑ̃t] adj (odeur) mouth-watering; (offre) enticing

allécher [aleʃe] vt: **~ qn** to make sb's mouth water; to tempt ou entice sb

allée [ale] nf (de jardin) path; (en ville) avenue, drive; **~s et venues** comings and goings

allégé, e [aleʒe] adj (yaourt etc) low-fat

alléger [aleʒe] vt (voiture) to make lighter; (chargement) to lighten; (souffrance) to alleviate, soothe

allègre [a(l)lɛgʀ] adj lively, cheerful

alléguer [a(l)lege] vt to put forward (as proof ou an excuse)

Allemagne [alman] nf: **l'~** Germany; **allemand, e** adj German ♦ nm/f: **Allemand, e** German ♦ nm (LING) German

aller [ale] nm (trajet) outward journey; (billet: aussi: **~ simple**) single (BRIT) ou one-way (US) ticket ♦ vi (gén) to go; **~ à** (convenir) to suit; (suj: forme, pointure etc) to fit; **~ (bien) avec** (couleurs, style etc) to go (well) with; **je vais y ~/me fâcher** I'm going to go/to get angry; **~ voir** to go and see; to go to see; **allez!** come on!; **allons!** come now!; **comment allez-vous?** how are you?; **comment ça va?** how are you?; (affaires etc) how are things?; **il va bien/mal** he's well/not well, he's fine/ill; **ça va bien/mal** (affaires etc) it's going well/not going well; **~ mieux** to be better; **s'en ~** (partir) to be off, go, leave; (disparaître) to go away; **~ retour** return journey (BRIT), round trip (US); (billet) return (ticket) (BRIT), round trip ticket (US)

allergique [alɛʀʒik] adj: **~ à** allergic to

alliage [aljaʒ] nm alloy

alliance [aljɑ̃s] nf (MIL, POL) alliance; (bague) wedding ring

allier [alje] vt (POL, gén) to ally; (fig) to combine; **s'~** to become allies; to combine

allô [alo] excl hullo, hallo

allocation [alɔkasjɔ̃] nf allowance; **~ (de) chômage** unemployment benefit; **~s familiales** ≈ child benefit

allocution [a(l)lɔkysjɔ̃] nf short speech

allonger [alɔ̃ʒe] vt to lengthen, make longer; (étendre: bras, jambe) to stretch (out); (étendre: bras, jambe) to stretch (out); **s'~** vi to get longer; (se coucher) to lie down, stretch out; **~ le pas** to hasten one's step(s)

allouer [alwe] vt to allocate, allot

allumage [alymaʒ] nm (AUTO) ignition

allume-cigare [alymsigaʀ] nm inv cigar lighter

allumer [alyme] vt (lampe, phare, radio) to put ou switch on; (pièce) to put the light(s) on in; (feu) to light; **s'~** vi (lumière, lampe) to come ou go on

allumette [alymɛt] nf match

allure [alyʀ] nf (vitesse) speed, pace; (démarche) walk; (aspect, air) look; **avoir de l'~** to have style; **à toute ~** at top speed

allusion [a(l)lyzjɔ̃] nf allusion; (sousentendu) hint; **faire ~ à** to allude ou to hint at

MOT-CLÉ

alors [alɔʀ] adv **1** (à ce moment-là) then, at that time; **il habitait alors à Paris** he lived in Paris at that time
2 (par conséquent) then; **tu as fini? alors je m'en vais** have you finished? I'm going then; **et alors?** so what?
alors que conj **1** (au moment où) when, as; **il est arrivé alors que je partais** he arrived as I was leaving
2 (pendant que) while, when; **alors qu'il était à Paris, il a visité ...** while ou when he was in Paris, he visited ...
3 (tandis que) whereas, while; **alors**

que son frère travaillait dur, lui se reposait while his brother was working hard, HE would rest

alouette [alwɛt] nf (sky)lark
alourdir [aluʀdiʀ] vt to weigh down, make heavy
aloyau [alwajo] nm sirloin
Alpes [alp] nfpl: **les ~** the Alps
alphabet [alfabɛ] nm alphabet; (livre) ABC (book); **alphabétique** adj alphabetical; **alphabétiser** vt to teach to read and write; (pays) to eliminate illiteracy in
alpinisme [alpinism] nm mountaineering, climbing; **alpiniste** nm/f mountaineer, climber
Alsace [alzas] nf Alsace; **alsacien, ne** adj Alsatian ♦ nm/f: **Alsacien, ne** Alsatian
altérer [alteʀe] vt (vérité) to distort; **s'~** vi to deteriorate
alternateur [altɛʀnatœʀ] nm alternator
alternatif, -ive [altɛʀnatif, iv] adj alternating; **alternative** nf (choix) alternative; **alternativement** adv alternately; **alterner** vi to alternate
Altesse [altɛs] nf Highness
altitude [altityd] nf altitude, height
alto [alto] nm (instrument) viola
aluminium [alyminjɔm] nm aluminium (BRIT), aluminum (US)
amabilité [amabilite] nf kindness
amadouer [amadwe] vt to mollify, soothe
amaigrir [amegʀiʀ] vt to make thin(ner); **amaigrissant, e** adj (régime) slimming
amalgame [amalgam] (péj) nm (strange) mixture
amande [amɑ̃d] nf (de l'amandier) almond; **amandier** nm almond (tree)
amant [amɑ̃] nm lover
amarrer [amaʀe] vt (NAVIG) to moor; (gén) to make fast
amas [amɑ] nm heap, pile; **amasser** vt

to amass; **s'amasser** vi (foule) to gather
amateur [amatœʀ] nm amateur; **en ~** (péj) amateurishly; **~ de musique/sport** etc music/sport etc lover
amazone [amazon] nf: **en ~** side-saddle
ambassade [ɑ̃basad] nf embassy; **l'~ de France** the French Embassy; **ambassadeur, -drice** nm/f ambassador (-dress)
ambiance [ɑ̃bjɑ̃s] nf atmosphere
ambiant, e [ɑ̃bjɑ̃, ɑ̃t] adj (air, milieu) surrounding; (température) ambient
ambigu, ë [ɑ̃bigy] adj ambiguous
ambitieux, -euse [ɑ̃bisjø, jøz] adj ambitious
ambition [ɑ̃bisjɔ̃] nf ambition
ambulance [ɑ̃bylɑ̃s] nf ambulance; **ambulancier, -ière** nm/f ambulance man(-woman) (BRIT), paramedic (US)
ambulant, e [ɑ̃bylɑ̃, ɑ̃t] adj travelling, itinerant
âme [ɑm] nf soul
amélioration [ameljɔʀasjɔ̃] nf improvement
améliorer [ameljɔʀe] vt to improve; **s'~** vi to improve, get better
aménager [amenaʒe] vt (agencer, transformer) to fit out; to lay out; (: quartier, territoire) to develop; (installer) to fix up, put in; **ferme aménagée** converted farmhouse
amende [amɑ̃d] nf fine; **faire ♦ honorable** to make amends
amener [am(ə)ne] vt to bring; (causer) to bring about; **s'~** vi to show up (fam), turn up
amenuiser [amənɥize]: **s'~** vi (chances) to grow slimmer, lessen
amer, amère [amɛʀ] adj bitter
américain, e [ameʀikɛ̃, ɛn] adj American ♦ nm/f: **A~,** e American
Amérique [ameʀik] nf: **l'~** America; **l'~ centrale/latine** Central/Latin America; **l'~ du Nord/du Sud** North/South America

amertume [amɛʀtym] *nf* bitterness

ameublement [amœbləmɑ̃] *nm* furnishing; *(meubles)* furniture

ameuter [amøte] *vt (peuple)* to rouse

ami, e [ami] *nm/f* friend; *(amant/maîtresse)* boyfriend/girlfriend ♦ *adj*: **pays/groupe ~** friendly country/group

amiable [amjabl]: **à l'~** *adv (JUR)* out of court; *(gén)* amicably

amiante [amjɑ̃t] *nm* asbestos

amical, e, -aux [amikal, o] *adj* friendly; **amicalement** *adv* in a friendly way; *(formule épistolaire)* regards

amidon [amidɔ̃] *nm* starch

amincir [amɛ̃siʀ] *vt*: **~ qn** to make sb thinner ou slimmer; *(suj: vêtement)* to make sb look slimmer

amincissant, e [amɛ̃sisɑ̃, ɑ̃t] *adj*: **régime ~** (slimming) diet; **crème ~e** slimming cream

amiral, -aux [amiʀal, o] *nm* admiral

amitié [amitje] *nf* friendship; **prendre en ~** to befriend; **~s, Christèle** best wishes, Christèle; **présenter ses ~s à qn** to send sb one's best wishes

ammoniaque [amɔnjak] *nf* ammonia (water)

amnistie [amnisti] *nf* amnesty

amoindrir [amwɛ̃dʀiʀ] *vt* to reduce

amollir [amɔliʀ] *vt* to soften

amonceler [amɔ̃s(ə)le] *vt* to pile ou heap up; **s'~** *vi* to pile ou heap up; *(fig)* to accumulate

amont [amɔ̃]: **en ~** *adv* upstream

amorce [amɔʀs] *nf (sur un hameçon)* bait; *(explosif)* cap; primer; priming; *(fig: début)* beginning(s), start; **amorcer** *vt* to start

amorphe [amɔʀf] *adj* passive, lifeless

amortir [amɔʀtiʀ] *vt (atténuer: choc)* to absorb, cushion; *(bruit, douleur)* to deaden; *(COMM: dette)* to pay off; **~ un achat** to make a purchase pay for itself; **amortisseur** *nm* shock absorber

amour [amuʀ] *nm* love; **faire l'~** to

make love; **amouracher: s'amouracher de** *(péj)* *vt* to become infatuated with; **amoureux, -euse** *adj (regard, tempérament)* amorous; *(vie, problèmes)* love *cpd*; *(personne)* amorous; **amoureux (de qn)** in love (with sb) ♦ *nmpl* courting couple(s); **amour-propre** *nm* self-esteem, pride

amovible [amɔvibl] *adj* removable, detachable

ampère [ɑ̃pɛʀ] *nm* amp(ere)

amphithéâtre [ɑ̃fiteɑtʀ] *nm* amphitheatre; *(d'université)* lecture hall ou theatre

ample [ɑ̃pl] *adj (vêtement)* roomy, ample; *(gestes, mouvement)* broad; *(ressources)* ample; **amplement** *adv*: **c'est amplement suffisant** that's more than enough; **ampleur** *nf (de dégâts, problème)* extent

amplificateur [ɑ̃plifikatœʀ] *nm* amplifier

amplifier [ɑ̃plifje] *vt (fig)* to expand, increase

ampoule [ɑ̃pul] *nf (électrique)* bulb; *(de médicament)* phial; *(aux mains, pieds)* blister; **ampoulé, e** *(péj)* *adj* pompous, bombastic

amputer [ɑ̃pyte] *vt (MÉD)* to amputate; *(fig)* to cut ou reduce drastically

amusant, e [amyzɑ̃, ɑ̃t] *adj (divertissant, spirituel)* entertaining, amusing; *(comique)* funny, amusing

amuse-gueule [amyzgœl] *nm inv* appetizer, snack

amusement [amyzmɑ̃] *nm (divertissement)* amusement; *(jeu etc)* pastime, diversion

amuser [amyze] *vt (divertir)* to entertain, amuse; *(égayer, faire rire)* to amuse; **s'~** *vi (jouer)* to play; *(se divertir)* to enjoy o.s., have fun; *(fig)* to mess around

amygdale [amidal] *nf* tonsil

an [ɑ̃] *nm* year; **avoir quinze ~s** to be fifteen (years old); **le jour de l'~, le premier de l'~, le nouvel ~** New

Year's Day

analogique [analɔʒik] *adj* (INFORM, montre) analog

analogue [analɔg] *adj*: ~ **(à)** analogous (to), similar (to)

analphabète [analfabɛt] *nm/f* illiterate

analyse [analiz] *nf* analysis; (MÉD) test; **analyser** *vt* to analyse; to test

ananas [anana(s)] *nm* pineapple

anarchie [anarʃi] *nf* anarchy

anatomie [anatɔmi] *nf* anatomy

ancêtre [ɑsɛtʀ] *nm/f* ancestor

anchois [ɑʃwa] *nm* anchovy

ancien, ne [ɑsjɛ̃, jɛn] *adj* old; (de jadis, de l'antiquité) ancient; (précédent, ex-) former, old; (par l'expérience) senior ♦ *nm/f* (dans une tribu) elder; **~ combattant** *nm* war veteran; **ancienneté** *nf* (ADMIN) (length of) service; (privilèges obtenus) seniority

ancre [ɑkʀ] *nf* anchor; **jeter/lever l'~** to cast/weigh anchor; **ancrer** *vt* (CONSTR: câble etc) to anchor; (fig) to fix firmly

Andorre [ɑdɔʀ] *nf* Andorra

andouille [ɑduj] *nf* (CULIN) sausage made of chitterlings; (fam) clot, nit

âne [ɑn] *nm* donkey, ass; (péj) dunce

anéantir [aneɑtiʀ] *vt* to annihilate, wipe out; (fig) to obliterate, destroy

anémie [anemi] *nf* anaemia; **anémique** *adj* anaemic

ânerie [anʀi] *nf* stupidity; (parole etc) stupid ou idiotic comment etc

anesthésie [anɛstezi] *nf* anaesthesia; **faire une ~ locale/générale à qn** to give sb a local/general anaesthetic

ange [ɑʒ] *nm* angel; **être aux ~s** to be over the moon

angélus [ɑʒelys] *nm* angelus; (cloches) evening bells *pl*

angine [ɑʒin] *nf* throat infection; **~ de poitrine** angina

anglais, e [ɑgle, ɛz] *adj* English ♦ *nm/f*: **A~, e** Englishman(-woman) ♦ *nm* (LING) English; **les A~** the English; **filer à l'~e**

to take French leave

angle [ɑgl] *nm* angle; (coin) corner; **~ droit** right angle

Angleterre [ɑgletɛʀ] *nf*: **l'~** England

anglo... [ɑglɔ] *préfixe* Anglo-, anglo(-); **anglophone** *adj* English-speaking

angoisse [ɑgwas] *nf* anguish, distress; **angoissé, e** *adj* (personne) distressed; **angoisser** *vt* to harrow, cause anguish to ♦ *vi* to worry, fret

anguille [ɑgij] *nf* eel

anicroche [anikʀɔʃ] *nf* hitch, snag

animal, e, -aux [animal, o] *adj, nm* animal

animateur, -trice [animatœʀ, tʀis] *nm/f* (de télévision) host; (de groupe) leader, organizer

animation [animasjɔ̃] *nf* (voir animé) busyness; liveliness; (CINÉMA: technique) animation; **~s culturelles** cultural activities

animé, e [anime] *adj* (lieu) busy, lively; (conversation, réunion) lively, animated

animer [anime] *vt* (ville, soirée) to liven up; (mener) to lead; **s'~** *vi* to liven up

anis [ani(s)] *nm* (CULIN) aniseed; (BOT) anise

ankyloser [ɑkiloze]: **s'~** *vi* to get stiff

anneau, x [ano] *nm* (de rideau, bague) ring; (de chaîne) link

année [ane] *nf* year

annexe [anɛks] *adj* (problème) related; (document) appended; (salle) adjoining ♦ *nf* (bâtiment) annex(e); (jointe à une lettre) enclosure

anniversaire [anivɛʀsɛʀ] *nm* birthday; (d'un événement, bâtiment) anniversary

annonce [anɔ̃s] *nf* announcement; (signe, indice) sign; (aussi: ~ **publicitaire**) advertisement; **les petites ~s** the classified advertisements, the small ads

annoncer [anɔ̃se] *vt* to announce; (être le signe de) to herald; **s'~ bien/difficile** to look promising/difficult; **annonceur, -euse** *nm/f* (publicitaire) advertiser; (TV, RADIO: speaker) announcer

annuaire [anɥɛR] *nm* yearbook, annual; **~ téléphonique** (telephone) directory, phone book

annuel, le [anɥɛl] *adj* annual, yearly

annuité [anɥite] *nf* annual instalment

annulation [anylasjɔ̃] *nf* cancellation

annuler [anyle] *vt* (rendez-vous, voyage) to cancel, call off; (jugement) to quash (BRIT), repeal (US); (MATH, PHYSIQUE) to cancel out

anodin, e [anɔdɛ̃, in] *adj* (blessure) harmless; (détail) insignificant, trivial

anonymat [anɔnima] *nm* anonymity

anonyme [anɔnim] *adj* anonymous; (fig) impersonal

ANPE *sigle f* (= Agence nationale pour l'emploi) national employment agency

anorak [anɔrak] *nm* anorak

anormal, e, -aux [anɔrmal, o] *adj* abnormal

anse [ɑ̃s] *nf* (de panier, tasse) handle

antan [ɑ̃tɑ̃]: **d'~** *adj* of long ago

antarctique [ɑ̃tarktik] *adj* Antarctic ♦ *nm*: **l'A~** the Antarctic

antécédents [ɑ̃tesedɑ̃] *nmpl* (MÉD etc) past history *sg*

antenne [ɑ̃tɛn] *nf* (de radio) aerial; (d'insecte) antenna, feeler; (poste avancé) outpost; (succursale) sub-branch; **passer à l'~** to go on the air

antérieur, e [ɑ̃terjœR] *adj* (d'avant) previous, earlier; (de devant) front

anti... [ɑ̃ti] *préfixe* anti...; **antialcoolique** *adj* anti-alcohol; **antiatomique** *adj*: **abri antiatomique** fallout shelter; **antibiotique** *nm* antibiotic; **antibogue** *adj* debugging ♦ *nm* debugging device; **antibrouillard** *adj*: **phare antibrouillard** fog lamp (BRIT) ou light (US)

anticipation [ɑ̃tisipasjɔ̃] *nf*: **livre/film d'~** science fiction book/film

anticipé, e [ɑ̃tisipe] *adj*: **avec mes remerciements ~s** thanking you in advance ou anticipation

anticiper [ɑ̃tisipe] *vt* (événement, coup) to anticipate, foresee

anti...: anticonceptionnel, le *adj* con-

traceptive; **anticorps** *nm* antibody; **antidote** *nm* antidote; **antigel** *nm* antifreeze; **antihistaminique** *nm* antihistamine

antillais, e [ɑ̃tije, ɛz] *adj* West Indian, Caribbean ♦ *nm/f*: **A~, e** West Indian, Caribbean

Antilles [ɑ̃tij] *nfpl*: **les ~** the West Indies

antilope [ɑ̃tilɔp] *nf* antelope

anti...: antimite(s) *adj, nm*: (produit) **antimite(s)** mothproofer; moth repellent; **antimondialisation** *nf* antiglobalization; **antipathique** *adj* unpleasant, disagreeable; **antipelliculaire** *adj* anti-dandruff

antipodes [ɑ̃tipɔd] *nmpl* (fig): **être aux ~ de** to be the opposite extreme of

antiquaire [ɑ̃tikɛR] *nm/f* antique dealer

antique [ɑ̃tik] *adj* antique; (très vieux) ancient, antiquated; **antiquité** *nf* (objet) antique; **l'Antiquité** Antiquity; **magasin d'antiquités** antique shop

anti...: antirabique *adj* rabies *cpd*; **antirouille** *adj inv* anti-rust *cpd*; **antisémite** *adj* anti-Semitic; **antiseptique** *adj, nm* antiseptic; **antivol** *adj, nm*: (dispositif) **antivol** anti-theft device

antre [ɑ̃tR] *nm* den, lair

anxiété [ɑ̃ksjete] *nf* anxiety

anxieux, -euse [ɑ̃ksjø, jøz] *adj* anxious, worried

AOC *sigle f* (= appellation d'origine contrôlée) label guaranteeing the quality of wine

août [u(t)] *nm* August

apaiser [apeze] *vt* (colère, douleur) to soothe; (personne) to calm (down), worried pacify; **s'~** *vi* (*tempête, bruit*) to die down, subside; (*personne*) to calm down

apanage [apanaʒ] *nm*: **être l'~ de** to be the privilege *ou* prerogative of

aparté [aparte] *nm* (*entretien*) private conversation; **en ~** in an aside

apathique [apatik] *adj* apathetic

apatride [apatrid] *nm/f* stateless person

apercevoir [apɛʀsəvwaʀ] *vt* to see; **s'~ de** to notice; **s'~ que** to notice that

aperçu [apɛʀsy] *nm* (*vue d'ensemble*) general survey

apéritif [aperitif] *nm* (*boisson*) aperitif; (*réunion*) drinks *pl*

à-peu-près [apøpʀɛ] (*péj*) *nm inv* vague approximation

apeuré, e [apœʀe] *adj* frightened, scared

aphte [aft] *nm* mouth ulcer

apiculture [apikyltyʀ] *nf* beekeeping, apiculture

apitoyer [apitwaje] *vt* to move to pity; **s'~ (sur)** to feel pity (for)

aplanir [aplaniʀ] *vt* to level; (*fig*) to smooth away, iron out

aplatir [aplatiʀ] *vt* to flatten; **s'~** to become flatter; (*écrasé*) to be flattened; **s'~ devant qn** (*fig*: *s'humilier*) to crawl to sb

aplomb [aplɔ̃] *nm* (*équilibre*) balance, equilibrium; (*fig*) self-assurance; nerve; **d'~** steady

apogée [apɔʒe] *nm* (*fig*) peak, apogee

apologie [apɔlɔʒi] *nf* vindication, praise

a posteriori [apɔsteʀjɔʀi] *adv* after the event

apostrophe [apɔstʀɔf] *nf* (*signe*) apostrophe

apostropher [apɔstʀɔfe] *vt* (*interpeller*) to shout at, address sharply

apothéose [apɔteoz] *nf* pinnacle (of achievement); (*MUS*) grand finale

apôtre [apotʀ] *nm* apostle

apparaître [apaʀɛtʀ] *vi* to appear

apparat [apaʀa] *nm*: **tenue d'~** ceremonial dress

appareil [apaʀɛj] *nm* (*outil, machine*) piece of apparatus, device; (*électrique, ménager*) appliance; (*avion*) (aero)plane, aircraft *inv*; (*téléphonique*) phone; (*dentier*) brace (*BRIT*), braces (*US*); **"qui est à l'~?"** "who's speaking?"; **dans le plus simple ~** in one's birthday suit; **appareiller** *vi* (*NAVIG*) to cast off, get under way ♦ *vt* (*assortir*) to match up; **appareil(-photo)** *nm* camera

apparemment [apaʀamɑ̃] *adv* apparently

apparence [apaʀɑ̃s] *nf* appearance; **en ~** apparently

apparent, e [apaʀɑ̃, ɑ̃t] *adj* visible; (*évident*) obvious; (*superficiel*) apparent

apparenté, e [apaʀɑ̃te] *adj*: **~ à** related to; (*fig*) similar to

apparition [apaʀisjɔ̃] *nf* appearance; (*surnaturelle*) apparition

appartement [apaʀtəmɑ̃] *nm* flat (*BRIT*), apartment (*US*)

appartenir [apaʀtəniʀ]: **~ à** *vt* to belong to; **il lui appartient de** it is his duty to

apparu, e [apaʀy] *pp de* **apparaître**

appât [apa] *nm* (*PÊCHE*) bait; (*fig*) lure, bait; **appâter** *vt* to lure

appauvrir [apovʀiʀ] *vt* to impoverish

appel [apɛl] *nm* (*nominal*) roll call; (*: SCOL*) register; (*MIL*: *recrutement*) call-up; **faire ~ à** (*invoquer*) to appeal to; (*avoir recours à*) to call on; (*nécessiter*) to call for, require; **faire ~** (*JUR*) to appeal; **faire l'~** to call the roll; to call the register; **sans ~** (*fig*) final, irrevocable; **~ d'offres** (*COMM*) invitation to tender; **faire un ~ de phares** to flash one's headlights; **~ (téléphonique)** (tele)phone call

appelé [ap(ə)le] *nm* (*MIL*) conscript

appeler [ap(ə)le] *vt* to call; (*faire venir: médecin etc*) to call, send for; **s'~** *vi*: **elle s'appelle Gabrielle** her name is Gabrielle, she's called Gabrielle;

comment ça s'appelle? what is it called?; **être appelé à** (fig) to be destined to

appendice [apɛ̃dis] nm appendix; **appendicite** nf appendicitis

appentis [apɑ̃ti] nm lean-to

appesantir [apəzɑ̃tir]: **s'~** vi to grow heavier; **s'~ sur** (fig) to dwell on

appétissant, e [apetisɑ̃, ɑ̃t] adj appetizing, mouth-watering

appétit [apeti] nm appetite; **bon ~!** enjoy your meal!

applaudir [aplodir] vt to applaud ♦ vi to applaud, clap; **applaudissements** nmpl applause sg, clapping sg

application [aplikasjɔ̃] nf application

applique [aplik] nf wall lamp

appliquer [aplike] vt to apply; (loi) to enforce; **s'~** vi (élève etc) to apply o.s.; **s'~ à** to apply to

appoint [apwɛ̃] nm (extra) contribution ou help; **chauffage d'~** extra heating

appointements [apwɛ̃tmɑ̃] nmpl salary sg

apport [apɔr] nm (approvisionnement) supply; (contribution) contribution

apporter [apɔrte] vt to bring

apposer [apoze] vt (signature) to affix

appréciable [apresjabl] adj appreciable

apprécier [apresje] vt to appreciate; (évaluer) to estimate, assess

appréhender [apreɑ̃de] vt (craindre) to dread; (arrêter) to apprehend; **appréhension** nf apprehension, anxiety

apprendre [aprɑ̃dr] vt to learn; (événement, résultats) to learn of, hear of; **~ qch à qn** (informer) to tell sb (of) sth; (enseigner) to teach sb sth; **~ à faire qch** to learn to do sth; **~ à qn à faire qch** to teach sb to do sth; **apprenti, e** nm/f apprentice; **apprentissage** nm learning; (COMM, SCOL: période) apprenticeship

apprêté, e [aprete] adj (fig) affected

apprêter [aprete] vt: **s'~ à faire qch** to get ready to do sth

appris, e [apri, iz] pp de **apprendre**

apprivoiser [aprivwaze] vt to tame

approbation [aprɔbasjɔ̃] nf approval

approchant, e [aprɔʃɑ̃, ɑ̃t] adj similar; **quelque chose d'~** something like that

approche [aprɔʃ] nf approach

approcher [aprɔʃe] vi to approach, come near ♦ vt to approach; (rapprocher): **~ qch (de qch)** to bring ou put sth near (to sth); **s'~ de** to approach, go ou come near to; **~ de** (lieu, but) to draw near to; (quantité, moment) to approach

approfondir [aprɔfɔ̃dir] vt to deepen; (question) to go further into

approprié, e [aprɔprije] adj: **~ (à)** appropriate (to), suited to

approprier [aprɔprije]: **s'~** vt to appropriate, take over

approuver [apruve] vt to agree with; (trouver louable) to approve of

approvisionner [aprɔvizjɔne] vt to supply; (compte bancaire) to pay funds into; **s'~ en** to stock up with

approximatif, -ive [aprɔksimatif, iv] adj approximate, rough; (termes) vague

appt abr = **appartement**

appui [apɥi] nm support; **prendre ~ sur** to lean on; (objet) to rest on; **l'~ de la fenêtre** the windowsill, the window ledge; **appui(e)-tête** nm inv headrest

appuyer [apɥije] vt (poser): **~ qch sur/contre** to lean ou rest sth on/against; (soutenir: personne, demande) to support, back (up) ♦ vi: **~ sur** (bouton, frein) to press, push; (mot, détail) to stress, emphasize; **s'~ sur** to lean on; (fig: compter sur) to rely on

âpre [ɑpr] adj acrid, pungent; **~ au gain** grasping

après [apre] prép after ♦ adv afterwards; **2 heures ~** 2 hours later; **~ qu'il est ou soit parti** after he left; **~ avoir fait** after having done; **d'~** (selon) according to; **~ coup** after the event, afterwards; **~ tout** (au fond) after all; **et (puis) ~?** so what?; **après-demain** adv the day after tomorrow; **après-guerre** nm post-war years pl; **après-midi** nm ou nf inv afternoon; **après-rasage** nm inv aftershave; **après-shampooing** nm inv conditioner; **après-ski** nm inv snow boot

à-propos [apʀopo] nm (d'une remarque) aptness; **faire preuve d'~~** to show presence of mind

apte [apt] adj capable; (MIL) fit

aquarelle [akwaʀɛl] nf watercolour

aquarium [akwaʀjɔm] nm aquarium

arabe [aʀab] adj Arabic; (désert, cheval) Arabian; (nation, peuple) Arab ♦ nm/f: **A~** Arab ♦ nm (LING) Arabic

Arabie [aʀabi] nf: **l'~ (Saoudite)** Saudi Arabia

arachide [aʀaʃid] nf (plante) groundnut (plant); (graine) peanut, groundnut

araignée [aʀeɲe] nf spider

arbitraire [aʀbitʀɛʀ] adj arbitrary

arbitre [aʀbitʀ] nm (SPORT) referee; (: TENNIS, CRICKET) umpire; (fig) arbiter, judge; (JUR) arbitrator; **arbitrer** vt to referee; to umpire; to arbitrate

arborer [aʀbɔʀe] vt to bear, display

arbre [aʀbʀ] nm tree; (TECH) shaft; **~ généalogique** family tree

arbuste [aʀbyst] nm small shrub

arc [aʀk] nm (arme) bow; (GÉOM) arc; (ARCHIT) arch; **en ~ de cercle** semi-circular

arcade [aʀkad] nf arch(way); **~s** nfpl (série) arcade sg, arches

arcanes [aʀkan] nmpl mysteries

arc-boutant [aʀkbutɑ̃] nm flying buttress

arceau, x [aʀso] nm (métallique etc) hoop

arc-en-ciel [aʀkɑ̃sjɛl] nm rainbow

arche [aʀʃ] nf arch; **~ de Noé** Noah's Ark

archéologie [aʀkeɔlɔʒi] nf arch(a)eology; **archéologue** nm/f arch(a)eologist

archet [aʀʃɛ] nm bow

archevêque [aʀʃəvɛk] nm archbishop

archi... [aʀʃi] (fam) préfixe tremendously; **archicomble** (fam) adj chock-a-block; **archiconnu, e** (fam) adj enormously well-known

archipel [aʀʃipɛl] nm archipelago

architecte [aʀʃitɛkt] nm architect

architecture [aʀʃitɛktyʀ] nf architecture

archives [aʀʃiv] nfpl (collection) archives

arctique [aʀktik] adj Arctic ♦ nm: **l'A~** the Arctic

ardemment [aʀdamɑ̃] adv ardently, fervently

ardent, e [aʀdɑ̃, ɑ̃t] adj (soleil) blazing; (amour) ardent, passionate; (prière) fervent

ardeur [aʀdœʀ] nf ardour (BRIT), ardor (US); (du soleil) heat

ardoise [aʀdwaz] nf slate

ardu, e [aʀdy] adj (travail) arduous; (problème) difficult

arène [aʀɛn] nf arena; **~s** nfpl (amphithéâtre) bull-ring sg

arête [aʀɛt] nf (de poisson) bone; (d'une montagne) ridge

argent [aʀʒɑ̃] nm (métal) silver; (monnaie) money; **~ de poche** pocket money; **~ liquide** ready money, (ready) cash; **argenté, e** adj (couleur) silver, silvery; **en métal argenté** silver-plated; **argenterie** nf silverware

argentin, e [aʀʒɑ̃tɛ̃, in] adj Argentinian, Argentine

Argentine [aʀʒɑ̃tin] nf: **l'~** Argentina, the Argentine

argile [aʀʒil] nf clay

argot [aʀgo] nm slang; **argotique** adj slang cpd; (très familier) slangy

argument [aʀgymɑ̃] nm argument

argumentaire [aʀgymɑ̃tɛʀ] nm sales leaflet

argumenter [aʀgymɑ̃te] vi to argue

argus [aʀgys] nm guide to second-hand car etc prices

aride

aride [aʀid] *adj* arid

aristocratie [aʀistɔkʀasi] *nf* aristocracy; **aristocratique** *adj* aristocratic

arithmétique [aʀitmetik] *adj* arithmetic(al) ♦ *nf* arithmetic

armateur [aʀmatœʀ] *nm* shipowner

armature [aʀmatyʀ] *nf* framework; (*de tente etc*) frame; **soutien-gorge à/ sans ~** underwired/unwired bra

arme [aʀm] *nf* weapon; **~s** *nfpl* (~ment) weapons, arms; (*blason*) (coat of) arms; **~ à feu** firearm

armée [aʀme] *nf* army; **~ de l'air** Air Force; **~ de terre** Army

armement [aʀməmɑ̃] *nm* (*matériel*) arms *pl*, weapons *pl*

armer [aʀme] *vt* to arm; (*arme à feu*) to cock; (*appareil-photo*) to wind on; **~ qch de** to reinforce sth with; **s'~ de** to arm o.s. with

armistice [aʀmistis] *nm* armistice; **l'A~** ≈ Remembrance (*BRIT*) *ou* Veterans (*US*) Day

armoire [aʀmwaʀ] *nf* (*tall*) cupboard; (*penderie*) wardrobe (*BRIT*), closet (*US*)

armoiries [aʀmwaʀi] *nfpl* coat *sg* of arms

armure [aʀmyʀ] *nf* armour *no pl*, suit of armour; **armurier** *nm* gunsmith

arnaque [aʀnak] (*fam*) *nf* swindling; **c'est de l'~** it's a rip-off; **arnaquer** (*fam*) *vt* to swindle

aromates [aʀɔmat] *nmpl* seasoning *sg*, herbs (and spices)

aromathérapie [aʀɔmateʀapi] *nf* aromatherapy

aromatisé, e [aʀɔmatize] *adj* flavoured

arôme [aʀom] *nm* aroma

arpenter [aʀpɑ̃te] *vt* (*salle, couloir*) to pace up and down

arpenteur [aʀpɑ̃tœʀ] *nm* surveyor

arqué, e [aʀke] *adj* arched; (*jambes*) bandy

arrache-pied [aʀaʃpje]: **d'~-~** *adv* relentlessly

arracher [aʀaʃe] *vt* to pull out; (*page etc*) to tear off, tear out; (*légumes,*

arrière

herbe) to pull up; (*bras etc*) to tear off; **s'~** *vt* (*article recherché*) to fight over; **~ qch à qn** to snatch sth from sb; (*fig*) to wring sth out of sb

arraisonner [aʀɛzɔne] *vt* (*bateau*) to board and search

arrangeant, e [aʀɑ̃ʒɑ̃, ɑ̃t] *adj* accommodating, obliging

arrangement [aʀɑ̃ʒmɑ̃] *nm* agreement, arrangement

arranger [aʀɑ̃ʒe] *vt* (*gén*) to arrange; (*réparer*) to fix, put right; (*régler: différend*) to settle, sort out; (*convenir à*) to suit, be convenient for; **s'~** *vi* (*se mettre d'accord*) to come to an agreement; **je vais m'~** I'll manage; **ça va s'~** it'll sort itself out

arrestation [aʀɛstasjɔ̃] *nf* arrest

arrêt [aʀe] *nm* stopping; (*de bus etc*) stop; (*JUR*) judgment, decision; **à l'~** stationary; **tomber en ~ devant** to stop short in front of; **sans ~** (*sans interruption*) non-stop; (*très fréquemment*) continually; **~ de travail** stoppage (of work); **~ maladie** sick leave

arrêté [aʀete] *nm* order, decree

arrêter [aʀete] *vt* to stop; (*chauffage etc*) to turn off, switch off; (*fixer: date etc*) to appoint, decide on; (*criminel, suspect*) to arrest; **s'~** *vi* to stop; **~ de faire** to stop doing

arrhes [aʀ] *nfpl* deposit *sg*

arrière [aʀjɛʀ] *nm* back; (*SPORT*) fullback ♦ *adj inv*: **siège/roue ~** back *ou* rear seat/wheel; **à l'~** behind, at the back; **en ~** behind; (*regarder*) back, behind; (*tomber, aller*) backwards; **arriéré, e** *adj* (*péj*) backward ♦ *nm* (*d'argent*) arrears *pl*; **arrière-goût** *nm* aftertaste; **arrière-grand-mère** *nf* great-grandmother; **arrière-grand-père** *nm* great-grandfather; **arrière-pays** *nm inv* hinterland; **arrière-pensée** *nf* ulterior motive; mental reservation; **arrière-plan** *nm* background; **arrière-saison** *nf* late autumn; **arrière-train** *nm* hindquarters *pl*

arrimer [aʀime] vt to secure; (cargaison) to stow

arrivage [aʀivaʒ] nm consignment

arrivée [aʀive] nf arrival; (ligne d'~) finish

arriver [aʀive] vi to arrive; (survenir) to happen, occur; **il arrive à Paris à 8h** he gets to ou arrives in Paris at 8; ~ **à** (atteindre) to reach; ~ **à faire qch** to succeed in doing sth; **en** ~ **à** (finir par) to come to; **il arrive que** it happens that; **il lui arrive de faire** he sometimes does; **arriviste** nm/f go-getter

arrobase [aʀɔbaz] nf(INFORM) @, 'at' sign

arrogance [aʀɔgɑ̃s] nf arrogance

arrogant, e [aʀɔgɑ̃, ɑ̃t] adj arrogant

arrondir [aʀɔ̃diʀ] vt (forme, objet) to round; (somme) to round off

arrondissement [aʀɔ̃dismɑ̃] nm (ADMIN) ≈ district

arroser [aʀoze] vt to water; (victoire) to celebrate (over a drink); (CULIN) to baste; **arrosoir** nm watering can

arsenal, -aux [aʀsənal, o] nm (NAVIG) naval dockyard; (MIL) arsenal; (fig) gear

art [aʀ] nm art

artère [aʀtɛʀ] nf (ANAT) artery; (rue) main road

arthrite [aʀtʀit] nf arthritis

artichaut [aʀtiʃo] nm artichoke

article [aʀtikl] nm article; (COMM) item, article; **à l'~ de la mort** at the point of death; **~s de luxe** luxury goods

articulation [aʀtikylasjɔ̃] nf articulation; (ANAT) joint

articuler [aʀtikyle] vt to articulate

artifice [aʀtifis] nm device, trick

artificiel, le [aʀtifisjɛl] adj artificial

artisan [aʀtizɑ̃] nm artisan, (self-employed) craftsman; **artisanal, e, -aux** adj of ou made by craftsmen; (péj) cottage industry cpd; **de fabrication artisanale** home-made; **artisanat** nm arts and crafts pl

artiste [aʀtist] nm/f artist; (de variétés) entertainer; (musicien etc) performer; **artistique** adj artistic

as¹ [a] vb voir **avoir**

as² [as] nm ace

ascendance [asɑ̃dɑ̃s] nf (origine) ancestry

ascendant, e [asɑ̃dɑ̃, ɑ̃t] adj upward ♦ nm influence

ascenseur [asɑ̃sœʀ] nm lift (BRIT), elevator (US)

ascension [asɑ̃sjɔ̃] nf ascent; (de montagne) climb; **l'A~** (REL) the Ascension

---

Ascension

La fête de l'Ascension is a French public holiday, usually in May. As it falls on a Thursday, many people take Friday off work and enjoy a long weekend; see also faire le **pont**.

---

aseptisé, e (péj) adj sanitized

aseptiser [asɛptize] vt (ustensile) to sterilize; (plaie) to disinfect

asiatique [azjatik] adj Asiatic, Asian ♦ nm/f: **A~** Asian

Asie [azi] nf: **l'~** Asia

asile [azil] nm (refuge) refuge, sanctuary; (POL): **droit d'~** (political) asylum; ~ **(de vieillards)** old people's home

aspect [aspɛ] nm appearance, look; (fig) aspect, side; **à l'~ de** at the sight of

asperge [aspɛʀʒ] nf asparagus no pl

asperger [aspɛʀʒe] vt to spray, sprinkle

aspérité [aspeʀite] nf bump, protruding bit (of rock etc)

asphalte [asfalt] nm asphalt

asphyxier [asfiksje] vt to suffocate, asphyxiate; (fig) to stifle

aspirateur [aspiʀatœʀ] nm vacuum cleaner; **passer l'~** to vacuum

aspirer [aspiʀe] vt (air) to inhale; (liquide) to suck (up); (suj: appareil) to suck up; ~ **à** to aspire to

aspirine [aspiʀin] nf aspirin

assagir [asaʒiʀ]: **s'~** vi to quieten down, settle down

assaillir [asajiʀ] vt to assail, attack

assainir [aseniʀ] vt (logements) to clean

up; (eau, air) to purify
assaisonnement [asezɔnmã] nm seasoning
assaisonner [asezɔne] vt to season
assassin [asasɛ̃] nm murderer; assassin;
assassiner [asasine] vt to murder; (esp POL) to
assassinate
assaut [aso] nm assault, attack; **prendre d'~** to storm, assault; **donner l'~**
to attack
assécher [asefe] vt to drain
assemblage [asãblaʒ] nm (action) as-
sembling; (de couleurs, choses) collection
assemblée [asãble] nf (réunion) meeting; (assistance) gathering; (POL) assembly
assembler [asãble] vt (joindre, monter)
to assemble, put together; (amasser) to
gather, collect (together); **s'~** vi to gather
assener, asséner [asene] vt: **~ un
coup à qn** to deal sb a blow
assentiment [asãtimã] nm assent,
consent
asseoir [aswar] vt (malade, bébé) to sit
up; (personne debout) to sit down;
(autorité, réputation) to establish; **s'~**
to sit (o.s.) down
assermenté, e [asɛrmãte] adj sworn,
on oath
asservir [asɛrvir] vt to subjugate, en-
slave
assez [ase] adv (suffisamment) enough,
sufficiently; (passablement) rather,
quite, fairly; **~ de pain/livres** enough
ou sufficient bread/books; **vous en
avez ~?** have you got enough?; **j'en ai
~!** I've had enough!
assidu, e [asidy] adj (appliqué) assidu-
ous, painstaking; (ponctuel) regular
assied etc [asje] vb voir **asseoir**
assiéger [asjeʒe] vt to besiege
assiérai etc [asjere] vb voir **asseoir**
assiette [asjɛt] nf plate; (contenu)
plate(ful); **il n'est pas dans son ~**
he's not feeling quite himself; **~ à des-**

sert dessert plate; **~ anglaise** assorted
cold meats; **~ creuse** (soup) dish, soup
plate; **~ plate** (dinner) plate
assigner [asiɲe] vt: **~ qch à** (poste,
part, travail) to assign sth to
assimiler [asimile] vt to assimilate, absorb; (comparer): **~ qch/qn à** to liken
ou compare sth/sb to
assis, e [asi, iz] pp de **asseoir** ♦ adj sitting (down), seated; **assise** nf (fig) basis, foundation; **assises** nfpl (JUR) assizes
assistance [asistãs] nf (public) audience; (aide) assistance; **enfant de l'A~
publique** child in care
assistant, e [asistã, ãt] nm/f assistant;
(d'université) probationary lecturer; **~(e)
social(e)** social worker
assisté, e [asiste] adj (AUTO) power assisted; **~ par ordinateur** computer-
assisted
assister [asiste] vt (aider) to assist; **~ à**
(scène, événement) to witness; (conférence, séminaire) to attend, be at; (spectacle, match) to be at, see
association [asɔsjasjɔ̃] nf association
associé, e [asɔsje] nm/f associate;
(COMM) partner
associer [asɔsje] vt to associate; **s'~**
(entreprise) to join together; **s'~ à qn pour faire**
to join (forces) with sb to do; **s'~ à**
(couleurs, qualités) to be combined
with; (opinions, joie de qn) to share in;
~ qn à (profits) to give sb a share of;
(affaire) to make sb a partner in; (joie,
triomphe) to include sb in; **~ qch à**
(allier à) to combine sth with
assoiffé, e [aswafe] adj thirsty
assombrir [asɔ̃brir] vt to darken; (fig)
to fill with gloom
assommer [asɔme] vt (étourdir, abrutir)
to knock out, stun
Assomption [asɔ̃psjɔ̃] nf: **l'~** the Assomption

Assomption

La fête de l'Assomption on August

15 is a French national holiday. Traditionally, large numbers of holidaymakers set out on this date, frequently causing chaos on the roads; see also faire le **pont**.

---

assorti, e [asɔʀti] *adj* matched, matching; (*varié*) assorted; ~ **à** matching; **assortiment** *nm* assortment, selection

assortir [asɔʀtiʀ] *vt* to match; ~ **qch à** to match sth with; ~ **qch de** to accompany sth with

assoupi, e [asupi] *adj* dozing, sleeping

assoupir [asupiʀ]: **s'~** *vi* to doze off

assouplir [asupliʀ] *vt* to make supple; (*fig*) to relax; **assouplissant** *nm* (fabric) softener

assourdir [asuʀdiʀ] *vt* (*bruit*) to deaden, muffle; (*suj: bruit*) to deafen

assouvir [asuviʀ] *vt* to satisfy, appease

assujettir [asyʒetiʀ] *vt* to subject

assumer [asyme] *vt* (*fonction, emploi*) to assume, take on

assurance [asyʀɑ̃s] *nf* (*certitude*) assurance; (*confiance en soi*) (self-)confidence; (*contrat*) insurance (policy); (*secteur commercial*) insurance; ~ **maladie** health insurance; ~ **tous risques** (*AUTO*) comprehensive insurance; **~s sociales** ≃ National Insurance (*BRIT*), ≃ Social Security (*US*); **assurance-vie** *nf* life assurance ou insurance

assuré, e [asyʀe] *adj* (*certain: réussite, échec*) certain, sure; (*air*) assured; (*pas*) steady ♦ *nm/f* insured (person); **assurément** *adv* assuredly, most certainly

assurer [asyʀe] *vt* (*FIN*) to insure; (*victoire etc*) to ensure; (*frontières, pouvoir*) to make secure; (*service*) to provide, operate; **s'~** (**contre**) (*COMM*) to insure o.s. (against); **s'~ de/que** (*vérifier*) to make sure of/that; **s'~ de** (*aide de qn*) to secure; ~ **à qn que** to assure sb that; ~ **qn de** to assure sb of; **assureur** *nm* insurer

asthmatique [asmatik] *adj, nm/f* asthmatic

asthme [asm] *nm* asthma

asticot [astiko] *nm* maggot

astiquer [astike] *vt* to polish, shine

astre [astʀ] *nm* star

astreignant, e [astʀɛɲɑ̃, ɑ̃t] *adj* demanding

astreindre [astʀɛ̃dʀ] *vt*: ~ **qn à faire** to compel ou force sb to do; **s'~ à faire** to force o.s. to do

astrologie [astʀɔlɔʒi] *nf* astrology

astronaute [astʀonot] *nm/f* astronaut

astronomie [astʀonɔmi] *nf* astronomy

astuce [astys] *nf* shrewdness, astuteness; (*truc*) trick, clever way; **astucieux, -euse** *adj* clever

atelier [atalje] *nm* workshop; (*de peintre*) studio

athée [ate] *adj* atheistic ♦ *nm/f* atheist

Athènes [atɛn] *n* Athens

athlète [atlɛt] *nm/f* (*SPORT*) athlete; **athlétisme** *nm* athletics *sg*

atlantique [atlɑ̃tik] *adj* Atlantic ♦ *nm*: **l'(océan) A~** the Atlantic (Ocean)

atlas [atlɑs] *nm* atlas

atmosphère [atmɔsfɛʀ] *nf* atmosphere

atome [atom] *nm* atom; **atomique** *adj* atomic, nuclear

atomiseur [atɔmizœʀ] *nm* atomizer

atout [atu] *nm* trump; (*fig*) asset

âtre [ɑtʀ] *nm* hearth

atroce [atʀɔs] *adj* atrocious

attabler [atable]: **s'~** *vi* to sit down at (the) table

attachant, e [ataʃɑ̃, ɑ̃t] *adj* engaging, lovable, likeable

attache [ataʃ] *nf* clip, fastener; (*fig*) tie

attacher [ataʃe] *vt* to tie up; (*étiquette*) to attach, tie on; (*ceinture*) to fasten ♦ *vi* (*poêle, riz*) to stick; **s'~ à** (*par affection*) to become attached to; **s'~ à faire** to endeavour to do; ~ **qch à** to attach sth to

attaque [atak] *nf* attack; (*cérébrale*) stroke; (*d'épilepsie*) fit; ~ **à main armée** armed attack

attaquer [atake] *vt* to attack; (*en jus-*

tice) to bring an action against, sue ♦ *vi* to attack; **s'~ à** ♦ *vt (personne)* to attack; *(problème)* to tackle

attardé, e [atarde] *adj (enfant)* backward; *(passants)* late

attarder [atarde]: **s'~** *vi* to linger

atteindre [atɛ̃dʀ] *vt* to reach; *(blesser)* to hit; *(émouvoir)* to affect; **atteint, e** *adj* (MÉD): **être atteint de** to be suffering from; **atteinte** *nf*: **hors d'atteinte** out of reach; **porter atteinte à** to strike a blow at

atteler [at(ə)le] *vt (cheval, bœufs)* to hitch up; **s'~ à** *(travail)* to buckle down to

attelle [atɛl] *nf* splint

attenant, e [at(ə)nɑ̃, ɑ̃t] *adj*: **~ (à)** adjoining

attendant [atɑ̃dɑ̃] *adv*: **en ~** meanwhile, in the meantime

attendre [atɑ̃dʀ] *vt (gén)* to wait for; *(être destiné ou réservé à)* to await, be in store for ♦ *vi* to wait; **s'~ à (ce que)** to expect (that); **~ un enfant** to be expecting a baby; **~ de faire/d'être** to wait until one does/is; **attendez qu'il vienne** wait until he comes; **~ qch de** to expect sth of

attendrir [atɑ̃dʀiʀ] *vt* to move (to pity); *(viande)* to tenderize; **attendrissant, e** *adj* moving, touching

attendu, e [atɑ̃dy] *adj (visiteur)* expected; *(événement)* long-awaited; **~ que** considering that, since

attentat [atɑ̃ta] *nm* assassination attempt; **~ à la bombe** bomb attack; **~ à la pudeur** indecent assault *no pl*

attente [atɑ̃t] *nf* wait; *(espérance)* expectation

attenter [atɑ̃te]: **~ à** *vt (liberté)* to violate; **~ à la vie de qn** to make an attempt on sb's life

attentif, -ive [atɑ̃tif, iv] *adj (auditeur)* attentive; *(examen)* careful; **~ à** careful to

attention [atɑ̃sjɔ̃] *nf* attention; *(prévenance)* attention, thoughtfulness *no pl*;

à l'~ de for the attention of; **faire ~ (à)** to be careful (of); **faire ~ (à ce) que** to be *ou* make sure that; **~!** carefully, watch out!; **attentionné, e** *adj* thoughtful, considerate

atténuer [atenye] *vt (douleur)* to alleviate, ease; *(couleurs)* to soften

atterrer [atere] *vt* to dismay, appal

atterrir [ateʀiʀ] *vi* to land; **atterrissage** *nm* landing

attestation [atɛstasjɔ̃] *nf* certificate

attester [atɛste] *vt* to testify to

attirail [atiʀaj] *(fam) nm* gear; *(péj)* paraphernalia

attirant, e [atiʀɑ̃, ɑ̃t] *adj* attractive, appealing

attirer [atiʀe] *vt* to attract; *(appâter)* to lure, entice; **~ qn dans un coin** to draw sb into a corner; **~ l'attention de qn** to attract sb's attention; **~ l'attention de qn sur** to draw sb's attention to; **s'~ des ennuis** to bring trouble upon o.s., get into trouble

attiser [atize] *vt (feu)* to poke (up)

attitré, e [atitʀe] *adj (habituel)* regular, usual; *(agréé)* accredited

attitude [atityd] *nf* attitude; *(position du corps)* bearing

attouchements [atuʃmɑ̃] *nmpl (sexuels)* fondling *sg*

attraction [atʀaksjɔ̃] *nf (gén)* attraction; *(de cabaret, cirque)* number

attrait [atʀɛ] *nm* appeal, attraction

attrape-nigaud [atʀapnigo] *(fam) nm* con

attraper [atʀape] *vt (gén)* to catch; *(habitude, amende)* to get, pick up; *(fam: duper)* to con; **se faire ~** *(fam)* to be told off

attrayant, e [atʀɛjɑ̃, ɑ̃t] *adj* attractive

attribuer [atʀibɥe] *vt (prix)* to award; *(rôle, tâche)* to allocate, assign; *(imputer)*: **~ qch à** to attribute sth to; **s'~** *vt (s'approprier)* to claim for o.s.; **attribut** *nm* attribute

attrister [atʀiste] *vt* to sadden

attroupement [atʀupmɑ̃] *nm* crowd

attrouper [atʀupe]: **s'~** vi to gather

au [o] prép +dét = à +le

aubaine [oben] nf godsend

aube [ob] nf dawn, daybreak; **à l'~** at dawn ou daybreak

aubépine [obepin] nf hawthorn

auberge [obeʀʒ] nf inn; **~ de jeunesse** youth hostel

aubergine [obeʀʒin] nf aubergine

aubergiste [obeʀʒist] nm/f inn-keeper, hotel-keeper

aucun, e [okœ̃, yn] dét no, tournure négative +any; (positif) any; **(positif)** any; pron none, tournure négative +any; any(one); **sans ~ doute** without any doubt; **plus qu'~ autre** more than any other; **~ des deux** neither of the two; **~ d'entre eux** none of them; **aucunement** in no way, not in the least

audace [odas] nf daring, boldness; (péj) audacity; **audacieux, -euse** adj daring, bold

au-delà [od(ə)la] adv beyond ♦ nm: **l'~~** the hereafter; **~~ de** beyond

au-dessous [od(ə)su] adv underneath; below; **~~ de** under(neath); below; (limite, somme etc) below; under; (dignité, condition) below

au-dessus [odsy] adv above; **~~ de** above

au-devant [od(ə)vɑ̃]: **~~ de** prép: **aller ~~ de** (personne, danger) to go (out) and meet; (souhaits de qn) to anticipate

audience [odjɑ̃s] nf audience; (JUR: séance) hearing

audimat ® [odimat] nm (taux d'écoute) ratings pl

audio-visuel, le [odjovizɥɛl] adj audio-visual

auditeur, -trice [oditœʀ, tʀis] nm/f listener

audition [odisjɔ̃] nf (ouïe, écoute) hearing; (JUR: de témoins) examination; (MUS, THÉÂTRE: épreuve) audition

auditoire [oditwaʀ] nm audience

auge [oʒ] nf trough

augmentation [ɔgmɑ̃tasjɔ̃] nf increase; **~ (de salaire)** rise (in salary) (BRIT), (pay) raise (US)

augmenter [ɔgmɑ̃te] vt (gén) to increase; (salaire, prix) to increase, raise, put up; (employé) to increase the salary of ♦ vi to increase

augure [ogyʀ] nm: **de bon/mauvais ~** of good/ill omen; **augurer** vt: **augurer bien de** to augur well for

aujourd'hui [oʒuʀdɥi] adv today

aumône [omon] nf inv alms sg; **aumônier** nm chaplain

auparavant [oparavɑ̃] adv before(hand)

auprès [opʀɛ]: **~ de** prép next to, close to; (recourir, s'adresser) to; (en comparaison de) compared with

auquel [okɛl] prép +pron = **à +lequel**

aurai etc [ɔʀe] vb voir **avoir**

auréole [ɔʀeɔl] nf halo; (tache) ring

aurons etc [ɔʀɔ̃] vb voir **avoir**

aurore [ɔʀɔʀ] nf dawn, daybreak

ausculter [ɔskylte] vt to sound (the chest of)

aussi [osi] adv (également) also, too; (de comparaison) as ♦ conj therefore, consequently; **~ fort que** as strong as; **moi ~** me too

aussitôt [osito] adv straight away, immediately; **~ que** as soon as

austère [ostɛʀ] adj austere

austral, e [ostʀal] adj southern

Australie [ostʀali] nf: **l'~** Australia; **australien, ne** adj Australian ♦ nm/f: **Australien, ne** Australian

autant [otɑ̃] adv so much; (comparatif): **~ (que)** as much as; (nombre): as many (as); **~ (de)** so much (ou many); as much (ou many); **~ partir** we (ou you etc) may as well leave; **~ dire que ...** one might as well say that ...; pour **~ for** all that; **d'~ plus/mieux (que)** all the more/the better (since)

autel [otɛl] nm altar

auteur [otœʀ] nm author

authenticité [otɑ̃tisite] nf authenticity

authentique [otɑ̃tik] adj authentic,

genuine

auto [oto] *nf* car

auto...: autobiographie *nf* autobiography; **autobronzant** *nm* self-tanning cream (or lotion *etc*); **autobus** *nm* bus; **autocar** *nm* coach

autochtone [ɔtɔktɔn] *nm/f* native

auto...: autocollant, e *adj* self-adhesive; (*enveloppe*) self-seal ♦ *nm* sticker; **auto-couchettes** *adj*: **train auto-couchettes** car sleeper train; **autocuiseur** *nm* pressure cooker; **autodéfense** *nf* self-defence; **autodidacte** *nm/f* self-taught person; **auto-école** *nf* driving school; **autographe** *nm* autograph

automate [ɔtɔmat] *nm* (*machine*) (automatic) machine

automatique [ɔtɔmatik] *adj* automatic ♦ *nm*: **l'~** direct dialling; **automatiquement** *adv* automatically; **automatiser** *vt* to automate

automne [ɔtɔn] *nm* autumn (BRIT), fall (US)

automobile [ɔtɔmɔbil] *adj* motor *cpd* ♦ *nf* (motor) car; **automobiliste** *nm/f* motorist

autonome [ɔtɔnɔm] *adj* autonomous; **autonomie** *nf* autonomy

autopsie [ɔtɔpsi] *nf* post-mortem (examination), autopsy

autoradio [otoradjo] *nm* car radio

autorisation [ɔtɔrizasjɔ̃] *nf* permission, authorization; (*papiers*) permit

autorisé, e [ɔtɔrize] *adj* (*opinion, sources*) authoritative

autoriser [ɔtɔrize] *vt* to give permission for, authorize; (*fig*) to allow (of)

autoritaire [ɔtɔritɛr] *adj* authoritarian

autorité [ɔtɔrite] *nf* authority; **faire ~** to be authoritative

autoroute [otorut] *nf* motorway (BRIT), highway (US)

auto-stop [otostɔp] *nm*: **faire de l'~** to hitch-hike; **prendre qn en ~** to give sb a lift; **auto-stoppeur, -euse** *nm/f* hitch-hiker

autour [otur] *adv* around; **~ de** around; **tout ~** all around

autre [otr] *adj* **1** (*différent*) other, different; **je préférerais un autre verre** I'd prefer another *ou* a different glass

2 (*supplémentaire*) other; **je voudrais un autre verre d'eau** I'd like another glass of water

3: **autre chose** something else; **autre part** somewhere else; **d'autre part** on the other hand

♦ *pron*: **un autre** another (one); **nous/vous autres** us/you; **d'autres** others; **l'autre** the other (one); **les autres** the others; (*autrui*) others; **l'un et l'autre** both of them; **se détester l'un l'autre/les uns les autres** to hate each other *ou* one another; **d'une semaine à l'autre** from one week to the next; (*incessamment*) any week now; **entre autres** among other things

autrefois [otrəfwa] *adv* in the past

autrement [otrəmɑ̃] *adv* differently; (*d'une manière différente*) in another way; (*sinon*) otherwise; **~ dit** in other words

Autriche [otriʃ] *nf*: **l'~** Austria; **autrichien, ne** *adj* Austrian ♦ *nm/f*: **Autrichien, ne** Austrian

autruche [otryʃ] *nf* ostrich

autrui [otrɥi] *pron* others

auvent [ovɑ̃] *nm* canopy

aux [o] *prép* +*dét* = **à +les**

auxiliaire [ɔksiljɛr] *adj, nm/f* auxiliary

auxquelles [okɛl] *prép* +*pron* = **à +lesquelles**

auxquels [okɛl] *prép* +*pron* = **à +lesquels**

avachi, e [avaʃi] *adj* limp, flabby

aval [aval] *nm*: **en ~** downstream, downriver

avalanche [avalɑ̃ʃ] *nf* avalanche

avaler [avale] *vt* to swallow

avance [avɑ̃s] nf (de troupes etc) advance; (progress; (d'argent) advance; (sur un concurrent) lead; **~s** nfpl (amoureuses) advances; (être) en **~** (to be) early; (sur un programme) (to be) ahead of schedule; **à l'~, d'~** in advance

avancé, e [avɑ̃se] adj advanced; (travail) well on, well under way

avancement [avɑ̃smɑ̃] nm (professionnel) promotion

avancer [avɑ̃se] vt to move forward, advance; (projet, travail) to make progress; (montre, réveil) to be fast; to gain ♦ vt to move forward, advance; (argent) to advance; (montre, pendule) to put forward; **s'~** vi to move forward, advance; (fig) to commit o.s.

avant [avɑ̃] prép, adv before ♦ adj inv: **siège/roue ~** front seat/wheel ♦ nm (d'un véhicule, bâtiment) front; (SPORT: joueur) forward; **~ qu'il (ne) fasse/de faire** before he does/doing; **~ tout** (surtout) above all; **à l'~** (dans un véhicule) in (the) front; **en ~** forward(s); **en ~ de** in front of

avantage [avɑ̃taʒ] nm advantage; **~s sociaux** fringe benefits; **avantager** vt (favoriser) to favour; (embellir) to flatter; **avantageux, -euse** adj (prix) attractive

avant...: avant-bras nm inv forearm; **avantcoureur** adj inv: **signe avant-coureur** advance indication ou sign; **avant-dernier, -ière** adj, nm/f next to last, last but one; **avant-goût** nm foretaste; **avant-guerre** nm pre-war years; **avant-hier** adv the day before yesterday; **avant-première** nf (de film) preview; **avant-projet** nm (preliminary) draft; **avant-propos** nm foreword; **avant-veille** nf: **l'avant-veille** two days before

avare [avar] adj miserly, avaricious ♦ nm/f miser; **~ de** (compliments etc) sparing of

avarié, e [avarje] adj (aliment) rotting

avaries [avari] nfpl (NAVIG) damage sg

avec [avɛk] prép with; (à l'égard de) to(wards), with; **et ~ ça?** (dans magasin) anything else?

avenant, e [av(ə)nɑ̃, ɑ̃t] adj pleasant; **à l'~** in keeping

avènement [avɛnmɑ̃] nm (d'un changement) advent, coming

avenir [avniʀ] nm future; **à l'~** in future; **politicien d'~** politician with prospects ou a future

aventure [avɑ̃tyʀ] nf adventure; (amoureuse) affair; **aventurer: s'aventurer** vi to venture; **aventureux, -euse** adj adventurous, venturesome; (projet) risky, chancy

avenue [avny] nf avenue

avérer: s'~ vb +attrib to prove (to be)

averse [avɛʀs] nf shower

averti, e [avɛʀti] adj (well-)informed

avertir [avɛʀtiʀ] vt: **~ qn (de qch/que)** to warn sb (of sth/that); (renseigner) to inform sb (of sth/that); **avertissement** nm warning; **avertisseur** nm horn, siren

aveu, x [avø] nm confession

aveugle [avœgl] adj blind ♦ nm/f blind man/woman; **aveuglément** adv blindly; **aveugler** vt to blind

aviateur, -trice [avjatœʀ, tʀis] nm/f aviator, pilot

aviation [avjasjɔ̃] nf aviation; (sport) flying; (MIL) air force

avide [avid] adj eager; (péj) greedy, grasping

avilir [aviliʀ] vt to debase

avion [avjɔ̃] nm (aero)plane (BRIT), (air)plane (US); **aller (quelque part) en ~** to go (somewhere) by plane, fly (somewhere); **par ~** by airmail; **~ à réaction** jet (plane)

aviron [avirɔ̃] nm oar; (sport): **l'~** rowing

avis [avi] nm opinion; (notification) notice; **à mon ~** in my opinion; **changer d'~** to change one's mind; **jusqu'à nouvel ~** until further notice

avisé, e [avize] *adj* sensible, wise; **bien/mal ~** de well-/ill-advised to

aviser [avize] *vt* (*informer*): **~ qn de/que** to advise *ou* inform sb of/that ♦ *vi* to think about things, assess the situation; **nous ~ons sur place** we'll work something out once we're there; **s'~ de qch/que** to become suddenly aware of sth/that; **s'~ de faire** to take it into one's head to do

avocat, e [avɔka, at] *nm/f* (JUR) barrister (BRIT), lawyer ♦ *nm* (CULIN) avocado (pear); **~ de la défense** counsel for the defence; **~ général** assistant public prosecutor

avoine [avwan] *nf* oats *pl*

MOT-CLÉ

avoir [avwaR] *nm* assets *pl*, resources *pl*; (COMM) credit
♦ *vt* **1** (*posséder*) to have; **elle a 2 enfants/une belle maison** she has (got) 2 children/a lovely house; **il a les yeux bleus** he has (got) blue eyes
2 (*âge, dimensions*) to be; **il a 3 ans** he is 3 (years old); **le mur a 3 mètres de haut** the wall is 3 metres high; *voir aussi* **faim**; **peur** *etc*
3 (*fam: duper*) to do, have; **on vous a eu!** you've been done *ou* had!
4: en avoir contre qn to have a grudge against sb; **en avoir assez** to be fed up; **j'en ai pour une demi-heure** it'll take me half an hour
♦ *vb aux* **1** to have; **avoir mangé/dormi** to have eaten/slept
2 (*avoir +à +infinitif*): **avoir à faire qch** to have to do sth; **vous n'avez qu'à lui demander** you only have to ask him
♦ *vb impers* **1**: **il y a 1** (+ *singulier*) there is; (+ *pluriel*) there are; **qu'y-a-t-il?, qu'est-ce qu'il y a?** what's the matter?, what is it?; **il doit y avoir une explication** there must be an explanation; **il n'y a qu'à ...** we (*ou* you *etc*) will just have to ...

2 (*temporel*): **il y a 10 ans** 10 years ago; **il y a 10 ans/longtemps que je le sais** I've known it for 10 years/a long time; **il y a 10 ans qu'il est arrivé** it's 10 years since he arrived

avoisiner [avwazine] *vt* to be near *ou* close to; (*fig*) to border *ou* verge on

avortement [avɔrtəmɑ̃] *nm* abortion

avorter [avɔrte] *vi* (MÉD) to have an abortion; (*fig*) to fail

avoué, e [avwe] *adj* avowed ♦ *nm* (JUR) ≈ solicitor

avouer [avwe] *vt* (*crime, défaut*) to confess (to); **~ avoir fait/que** to admit *ou* confess to having done/that

avril [avril] *nm* April

poisson d'avril

The traditional prank on April 1 in France is to stick a cut-out paper fish, known as a **poisson d'avril**, *to someone's back without being caught.*

axe [aks] *nm* axis; (*de roue etc*) axle; (*fig*) main line; **axer** *vt*: **axer qch sur** to centre sth on

ayons *etc* [ejɔ̃] *vb voir* **avoir**

azote [azɔt] *nm* nitrogen

B, b

baba [baba] *nm*: **~ au rhum** rum baba

babines [babin] *nfpl* chops

babiole [babjɔl] *nf* (*bibelot*) trinket; (*vétille*) trifle

bâbord [babɔr] *nm*: **à ~** to port, on the port side

baby-foot [babifut] *nm* table football

baby-sitting [babisitiŋ] *nm*: **faire du ~** to baby-sit

bac [bak] *abr m* = **baccalauréat** ♦ *nm* (*récipient*) tub

baccalauréat [bakalɔrea] *nm* high school diploma

baccalauréat

In France the **baccalauréat** *or* **bac** *is the school-leaving certificate taken at a lycée at the age of seventeen or eighteen, enabling entry to university. Different subject combinations built from the broad subject range studied.*

bâche [bɑʃ] nf tarpaulin

bachelier, -ière [baʃəlje, jɛʀ] nm/f holder of the baccalauréat

bâcler [bɑkle] vt to botch (up)

badaud, e [bado, od] nm/f idle onlooker, stroller

badigeonner [badiʒɔne] vt (barbouiller) to daub

badiner [badine] vi: ~ **avec qch** to treat sth lightly

baffe [baf] (fam) nf slap, clout

baffle [bafl] nm speaker

bafouer [bafwe] vt to deride, ridicule

bafouiller [bafuje] vi, vt to stammer

bâfrer [bɑfʀe] (fam) vi to guzzle

bagages [bagaʒ] nmpl luggage sg; ~ **à main** hand-luggage

bagarre [bagaʀ] nf fight, brawl; **bagarrer: se bagarrer** vi to have a fight ou scuffle, fight

bagatelle [bagatɛl] nf trifle

bagne [baɲ] nm penal colony

bagnole [baɲɔl] (fam) nf car

bagout [bagu] nm: **avoir du ~** to have the gift of the gab

bague [bag] nf ring; ~ **de fiançailles** engagement ring

baguette [bagɛt] nf stick; (cuisine chinoise) chopstick; (de chef d'orchestre) baton; (pain) stick of (French) bread; ~ **magique** magic wand

baie [bɛ] nf (GÉO) bay; (fruit) berry; ~ **(vitrée)** picture window

baignade [bɛɲad] nf bathing; "~ interdite" "no bathing"

baigner [beɲe] vt (bébé) to bath; **se ~** vi to have a swim, go swimming ou bathing; **baignoire** nf bath(tub)

bail, baux [baj, bo] (pl baux) nm lease

bâillement [bɑjmɑ̃] nm yawn

bâiller [bɑje] vi to yawn; (être ouvert) to gape; **bâillonner** vt to gag

bain [bɛ̃] nm bath; **prendre un ~** to have a bath; **se mettre dans le ~** (fig) to get into it ou things; ~ **de soleil: prendre un ~ de soleil** to sunbathe; ~**s de mer** sea bathing sg; **bain-marie** nm: **faire chauffer au bain-marie** (boîte etc) to immerse in boiling water

baiser [beze] nm kiss ♦ vt (main, front) to kiss; (fam!) to screw (!)

baisse [bes] nf fall, drop; **être en ~** to be falling, be declining

baisser [bese] vt to lower; (radio, chauffage) to turn down ♦ vi to fall, drop, go down; (vue, santé) to fail, dwindle; **se ~** vi to bend down

bal [bal] nm dance; (grande soirée) ball; ~ **costumé** fancy-dress ball

balade [balad] (fam) nf (à pied) walk, stroll; (en voiture) drive; **balader** (fam): **se balader** vi to go for a walk ou stroll; to go for a drive; **baladeur** nm personal stereo, Walkman ®

balafre [balafʀ] nf (cicatrice) scar

balai [bale] nm broom, brush; **balai-brosse** nm (long-handled) scrubbing brush

balance [balɑ̃s] nf scales pl; (signe): **la B~** Libra

balancer [balɑ̃se] vt to swing; (fam: lancer) to fling, chuck; (: jeter) to chuck out; **se ~** vi to swing, rock; **se ~ de** (fam) not to care about; **balançoire** nf swing; (sur pivot) seesaw

balayer [baleje] vt (feuilles etc) to sweep up, brush up; (pièce) to sweep; (objections) to sweep aside; (suj: radar) to scan; **balayeur, -euse** nm/f roadsweeper

balbutier [balbysje] vi, vt to stammer

balcon [balkɔ̃] nm balcony; (THÉÂTRE) dress circle

baleine [balɛn] *nf* whale

balise [baliz] *nf* (NAVIG) beacon; (marker) buoy; (AVIAT) runway light, beacon; (AUTO, SKI) sign, marker; **baliser** *vt* to mark out (with lights *etc*)

balivernes [balivɛRn] *nfpl* nonsense *sg*

ballant, e [balɑ̃, ɑ̃t] *adj* dangling

balle [bal] *nf* (de fusil) bullet; (de sport) ball; (fam: franc) franc

ballerine [bal(ə)Rin] *nf* (danseuse) ballet dancer; (chaussure) ballet shoe

ballet [balɛ] *nm* ballet

ballon [balɔ̃] *nm* (de sport) ball; (jouet, AVIAT) balloon; ~ **de football** football

ballot [balo] *nm* bundle; (péj) nitwit

ballottage [balɔtaʒ] *nm* (POL) second ballot

ballotter [balɔte] *vt*: **être ballotté** to be thrown about

balnéaire [balneɛR] *adj* seaside *cpd*; **station ~** seaside resort

balourd, e [baluR, uRd] *adj* clumsy

balustrade [balystRad] *nf* railings *pl*, handrail

bambin [bɑ̃bɛ̃] *nm* little child

bambou [bɑ̃bu] *nm* bamboo

ban [bɑ̃] *nm*: **mettre au ~ de** to outlaw from; **~s** *nmpl* (de mariage) banns

banal, e [banal] *adj* banal, commonplace; (péj) trite; **banalité** *nf* banality

banane [banan] *nf* banana; (sac) waist-bag, bum-bag

banc [bɑ̃] *nm* seat, bench; (de poissons) shoal; ~ **d'essai** (fig) testing ground

bancaire [bɑ̃kɛR] *adj* banking; (chèque, carte) bank *cpd*

bancal, e [bɑ̃kal] *adj* wobbly

bandage [bɑ̃daʒ] *nm* bandage

bande [bɑ̃d] *nf* (de tissu etc) strip; (MÉD) bandage; (motif) stripe; (magnétique etc) tape; (groupe) band; (: péj) bunch; **faire ~ à part** to keep to o.s.; ~ **dessinée** comic strip; ~ **sonore** sound track

bande dessinée

The **bande dessinée** *or* **BD** *enjoys a huge following in France amongst*

adults as well as children. An international show takes place at Angoulême in January every year. Astérix, Tintin, Lucky Luke and Gaston Lagaffe are among the most famous cartoon characters.

---

bandeau, x [bɑ̃do] *nm* headband; (sur les yeux) blindfold

bander [bɑ̃de] *vt* (blessure) to bandage; ~ **les yeux à qn** to blindfold sb

banderole [bɑ̃dRɔl] *nf* banner, streamer

bandit [bɑ̃di] *nm* bandit; **banditisme** *nm* violent crime, armed robberies *pl*

bandoulière [bɑ̃duljɛR] *nf*: **en ~** (slung *ou* worn) across the shoulder

banlieue [bɑ̃ljø] *nf* suburbs *pl*; **lignes/ quartiers de ~** suburban lines/areas; **trains de ~** commuter trains

banlieusard, e [bɑ̃ljøzaR, aRd] *nm/f* (suburban) commuter

bannière [banjɛR] *nf* banner

bannir [baniR] *vt* to banish

banque [bɑ̃k] *nf* bank; (activités) banking; ~ **d'affaires** merchant bank; **banqueroute** *nf* bankruptcy

banquet [bɑ̃kɛ] *nm* dinner; (d'apparat) banquet

banquette [bɑ̃kɛt] *nf* seat

banquier [bɑ̃kje] *nm* banker

banquise [bɑ̃kiz] *nf* ice field

baptême [batɛm] *nm* christening, baptism; ~ **de l'air** first flight

baptiser [batize] *vt* to baptize, christen

baquet [bakɛ] *nm* tub, bucket

bar [baR] *nm* bar

baraque [baRak] *nf* shed; (fam) house; (fam) tape; **baraqué, e** (fam) *adj* well-built, hefty; **baraquements** *nmpl* (provisoires) huts

baratin [baRatɛ̃] *nm* smooth talk, patter; **baratiner** *vt* to chat up

barbare [baRbaR] *adj* barbaric; **barbarie** *nf* barbarity

barbe [baRb] *nf* beard; **la ~!** (*fam*)

damn it!; **quelle ~!** (*fam*) what a drag
ou bore!; **à la ~ de qn** under sb's nose;
~ à papa candy-floss (*BRIT*), cotton candy (*US*)

barbelé [baʀbəle] *adj, nm*: **(fil de fer) ~**
barbed wire *no pl*

barber [baʀbe] (*fam*) *vt* to bore stiff

barbiturique [baʀbityʀik] *nm* barbitu-
rate

barboter [baʀbɔte] *vi* (*enfant*) to paddle

barbouiller [baʀbuje] *vt* to daub;
avoir l'estomac barbouillé to feel
queasy

barbu, e [baʀby] *adj* bearded

barda [baʀda] (*fam*) *nm* kit, gear

barder [baʀde] (*fam*) *vi*: **ça va ~**
sparks will fly, things are going to get
hot

barème [baʀɛm] *nm* (*SCOL*) scale; (*table
de référence*) table

baril [baʀi(l)] *nm* barrel; (*poudre*) keg

bariolé, e [baʀjɔle] *adj* gaudily-
coloured

baromètre [baʀɔmɛtʀ] *nm* barometer

baron, ne [baʀɔ̃] *nm/f* baron(ess)

baroque [baʀɔk] *adj* (*ART*) baroque;
(*fig*) weird

barque [baʀk] *nf* small boat

barquette [baʀkɛt] *nf* (*pour repas*) tray;
(*pour fruits*) punnet

barrage [baʀaʒ] *nm* dam; (*sur route*)
roadblock, barricade

barre [baʀ] *nf* bar; (*NAVIG*) helm; (*écrite*)
line, stroke

barreau, x [baʀo] *nm* bar; (*JUR*): **le ~**
the Bar

barrer [baʀe] *vt* (*route etc*) to block;
(*mot*) to cross out; (*chèque*) to cross
(*BRIT*); (*NAVIG*) to steer; **se ~** (*fam*) *vi* to
clear off

barrette [baʀɛt] *nf* (*pour cheveux*) (hair)
slide (*BRIT*) *ou* clip (*US*)

barricader [baʀikade]: **se ~** *vi* to barricade o.s.

barrière [baʀjɛʀ] *nf* fence; (*obstacle*)
barrier; (*porte*) gate

barrique [baʀik] *nf* barrel, cask

bar-tabac [baʀtaba] *nm* bar (which sells
tobacco and stamps)

bas, basse [ba, bas] *adj* low ♦ *nm* bottom, lower part; (*vêtement*) stocking ♦
adv low; (*parler*) softly; **au ~ mot** at the
lowest estimate; **en ~** down below;
(*d'une liste, d'un mur etc*) at/to the bottom; (*dans une maison*) downstairs; **en
~ de** at the bottom of; **un enfant en ~
âge** a young child; **à ~ ...!** I down with
...!; **~ morceaux** *nmpl* (*viande*) cheap
cuts

basané, e [bazane] *adj* tanned

bas-côté [bakote] *nm* (*de route*) verge
(*BRIT*), shoulder (*US*)

bascule [baskyl] *nf*: **(jeu de) ~** seesaw; **(balance à) ~** scales *pl*; **fauteuil
à ~** rocking chair

basculer [baskyle] *vi* to fall over, topple (over); (*benne*) to tip up ♦ *vt* (*contenu*) to tip out; (*benne*) to tip up

base [baz] *nf* base; (*POL*) rank and file;
(*fondement, principe*) basis; **de ~** basic;
à ~ de café *etc* coffee *etc* -based; **~ de
données** database; **baser** *vt* to base;
se baser sur *vt* (*preuves*) to base one's
argument on

bas-fond [baf5] *nm* (*NAVIG*) shallow; **~
-s** *nmpl* (*fig*) dregs

basilic [bazilik] *nm* (*CULIN*) basil

basket [basket] *nm* trainer (*BRIT*), sneak-
er (*US*); (*aussi*: **~-ball**) basketball

basque [bask] *adj, nm/f* Basque

basse [bas] *adj voir* **bas** ♦ *nf* (*MUS*) bass;
basse-cour *nf* farmyard

bassin [basɛ̃] *nm* (*pièce d'eau*) pond,
pool; (*de fontaine, GÉO*) basin; (*ANAT*)
pelvis; (*portuaire*) dock

bassine [basin] *nf* (*ustensile*) basin;
(*contenu*) bowl(ful)

basson [bas5] *nm* bassoon

bas-ventre [bavɑ̃tʀ] *nm* (lower part of)
the stomach

bat [ba] *vb voir* **battre**

bataille [bataj] *nf* (*MIL*) battle; (*rixe*)
fight; **batailler** *vi* to fight

bâtard, e [batar, ard] *nm/f* illegitimate child, bastard (*pej*)

bateau, x [bato] *nm* boat; ship; **bateau-mouche** *nm* passenger pleasure boat (*on the Seine*)

bâti, e [bati] *adj*: **bien ~** well-built

batifoler [batifɔle] *vi* to frolic about

bâtiment [batimɑ̃] *nm* building; (NAVIG) ship, vessel; (*industrie*) building trade

bâtir [batir] *vt* to build

bâtisse [batis] *nf* building

bâton [batɔ̃] *nm* stick; **à ~s rompus** informally

bats [ba] *vb voir* **battre**

battage [bataʒ] *nm* (*publicité*) (hard) plugging

battant, e [batɑ̃, ɑ̃t] *nm*: **porte à double ~** double door

battement [batmɑ̃] *nm* (*de cœur*) beat; (*intervalle*) interval; **10 minutes de ~** 10 minutes to spare

batterie [batri] *nf* (MIL, ÉLEC) battery; (MUS) drums *pl*, drum kit; **~ de cuisine** pots and pans *pl*, kitchen utensils *pl*

batteur [batœr] *nm* (MUS) drummer; (*appareil*) whisk

battre [batr] *vt* to beat; (*blé*) to thresh; (*passer au peigne fin*) to scour; (*cartes*) to shuffle ♦ *vi* (*cœur*) to beat; (*volets etc*) to bang, rattle; **se ~** *vi* to fight; **~ la mesure** to beat time; **~ son plein** to be at its height, be going full swing; **~ des mains** to clap one's hands

battue [baty] *nf* (*chasse*) beat; (*policière etc*) search, hunt

baume [bom] *nm* balm

baux [bo] *nmpl de* **bail**

bavard, e [bavar, ard] *adj* (very) talkative; gossipy; **bavarder** *vi* to chatter; (*commérer*) to gossip; (*divulguer un secret*) to blab

bave [bav] *nf* dribble; (*de chien etc*) slobber; (*d'escargot*) slime; **baver** *vi* to dribble; (*chien*) to slobber; **en baver** (*fam*) to have a hard time (of it); **baveux, -euse** *adj* (*omelette*) runny; **ba-**

voir *nm* bib

bavure [bavyr] *nf* smudge; (*fig*) hitch; (*policière etc*) blunder

bayer [baje] *vi*: **~ aux corneilles** to stand gaping

bazar [bazar] *nm* general store; (*fam*) jumble; **bazarder** (*fam*) *vt* to chuck out

BCBG *sigle adj* (= *bon chic bon genre*) preppy, smart and trendy

BCE *sigle f* (= *Banque centrale européenne*) ECB

BD *sigle f* = **bande dessinée**

bd *abr* = **boulevard**

béant, e [beɑ̃, ɑ̃t] *adj* gaping

béat, e [bea, at] *adj*: **~ d'admiration** struck dumb with admiration; **béatitude** *nf* bliss

beau (bel), belle [bo, bel] (*mpl* **beaux**) *adj* beautiful, lovely; (*homme*) handsome; (*femme*) beautiful ♦ *adv*: **il fait beau** the weather's fine; **un ~jour** one (fine) day; **de plus belle** more than ever, even more; **on a ~essayer** however hard we try; **bel et bien** well and truly

---
MOT-CLÉ
---

beaucoup [boku] *adv* **1** a lot; **il boit beaucoup** he drinks a lot; **il ne boit pas beaucoup** he doesn't drink much *ou* a lot
2 (*suivi de plus, trop etc*) much, a lot, far; **il est beaucoup plus grand** he is much *ou* a lot *ou* far taller
3: **beaucoup de** (*nombre*) many, a lot of; (*quantité*) a lot of; **beaucoup d'étudiants/de touristes** a lot of *ou* many students/tourists; **beaucoup de courage** a lot of courage; **il n'a pas beaucoup d'argent** he hasn't got much *ou* a lot of money
4: **de beaucoup** by far

beau...: **beau-fils** *nm* son-in-law; (*remariage*) stepson; **beau-frère** *nm* brother-in-law; **beau-père** *nm* fatherin-law; (remariage) stepfather

beauté [bote] nf beauty; **de toute ~** beautiful; **finir qch en ~** to complete sth brilliantly

beaux-arts [bozaR] nmpl fine arts

beaux-parents [boparã] nmpl wife's/ husband's family, in-laws

bébé [bebe] nm baby

bec [bɛk] nm beak, bill; (de théière) spout; (de casserole) lip; (fam) mouth; **~ de gaz** (street) gaslamp

bécane [bekan] (fam) nf bike

bec-de-lièvre [bɛkdəljɛvʀ] nm harelip

bêche [bɛʃ] nf spade; **bêcher** vt to dig

bécoter [bekɔte]: **se ~** vi to smooch

becqueter [bɛkte] (fam) vt to eat

bedaine [bədɛn] nf paunch

bedonnant, e [bədɔnã, ãt] adj pot-bellied

bée [be] adj: **bouche ~** gaping

beffroi [befʀwa] nm belfry

bégayer [begeje] vt, vi to stammer

bègue [bɛg] nm/f: **être ~** to have a stammer

beige [bɛʒ] adj beige

beignet [bɛɲɛ] nm fritter

bel [bɛl] adj voir **beau**

bêler [bele] vi to bleat

belette [bəlɛt] nf weasel

belge [bɛlʒ] adj Belgian ♦ nm/f: **B~** Belgian

Belgique [bɛlʒik] nf: **la ~** Belgium

bélier [belje] nm ram; (signe): **le B~** Aries

belle [bɛl] adj voir **beau** ♦ nf (SPORT) decider; **belle-fille** nf daughter-in-law; (remariage) stepdaughter; **belle-mère** nf mother-in-law; stepmother; **belle-sœur** nf sister-in-law

belliqueux, -euse [belikø, øz] adj aggressive, warlike

belvédère [bɛlvedɛʀ] nm panoramic viewpoint (or small building there)

bémol [bemɔl] nm (MUS) flat

bénédiction [benediksjɔ̃] nf blessing

bénéfice [benefis] nm (COMM) profit; (avantage) benefit; **bénéficier: bénéfi-**

cier de vt to enjoy; (situation) to benefit by ou from; **bénéfique** adj beneficial

bénévole [benevɔl] adj voluntary, unpaid

bénin, -igne [benɛ̃, iɲ] adj minor, mild; (tumeur) benign

bénir [beniʀ] vt to bless; **bénit, e** adj consecrated; **eau bénite** holy water

benjamin, e [bɛ̃ʒamɛ̃, in] nm/f youngest child

benne [bɛn] nf skip; (de téléphérique) (cable) car; **~ basculante** tipper (BRIT), dump truck (US)

BEP sigle m (= brevet d'études professionnelles) technical school certificate

béquille [bekij] nf crutch; (de bicyclette) stand

berceau, x [bɛʀso] nm cradle, crib

bercer [bɛʀse] vt to rock, cradle; (suj: musique etc) to lull; **~ qn de** (promesses etc) to delude sb with; **berceuse** nf lullaby

béret (basque) [beʀɛ(bask(ə))] nm beret

berge [bɛʀʒ] nf bank

berger, -ère [bɛʀʒe, ɛʀ] nm/f shepherd(-ess); **~ allemand** alsatian (BRIT), German shepherd

berlingot [bɛʀlɛ̃go] nm (bonbon) boiled sweet, humbug (BRIT)

berlue [bɛʀly] nf: **j'ai la ~** I must be seeing things

berner [bɛʀne] vt to fool

besogne [bəzɔɲ] nf work no pl, job

besoin [bəzwɛ̃] nm need; **avoir ~ de qch/faire qch** to need sth/to do sth; **au ~** if need be; **le ~** (pauvreté) need, want; **être dans le ~** to be in need ou want; **faire ses ~s** to relieve o.s.

bestiaux [bɛstjo] nmpl cattle

bestiole [bɛstjɔl] nf (tiny) creature

bétail [betaj] nm livestock, cattle pl

bête [bɛt] nf animal; (bestiole) insect, creature ♦ adj stupid, silly; **il cherche la petite ~** he's being pernickety ou overfussy; **~ noire** pet hate

bêtement [bɛtmɑ̃] *adv* stupidly

bêtise [betiz] *nf* stupidity; *(action)* stupid thing (to say *ou* do)

béton [betɔ̃] *nm* concrete; **(en) ~** *(alibi, argument)* cast iron; **~ armé** reinforced concrete; **bétonnière** *nf* cement mixer

betterave [bɛtʀav] *nf* beetroot *(BRIT)*, beet *(US)*; **~ sucrière** sugar beet

beugler [bøgle] *vi* to low; *(radio etc)* to blare ♦ *vt (chanson)* to bawl out

Beur [bœʀ] *nm/f* person of North African origin living in France

beurre [bœʀ] *nm* butter; **beurrer** *vt* to butter; **beurrier** *nm* butter dish

beuverie [bøvʀi] *nf* drinking session

bévue [bevy] *nf* blunder

Beyrouth [beʀut] *n* Beirut

bi... [bi] *préfixe* bi..., two-

biais [bjɛ] *nm (moyen)* device, expedient; *(aspect)* angle; **en ~, de ~** *(obliquement)* at an angle; **par le ~ de** by means of; **biaiser** *vi (fig)* to sidestep the issue

bibelot [biblo] *nm* trinket, curio

biberon [bibʀɔ̃] *nm (feeding)* bottle; **nourrir au ~** to bottle-feed

bible [bibl] *nf* bible

biblio... [biblo] *préfixe*: **bibliobus** *nm* mobile library van; **bibliographie** *nf* bibliography; **bibliothécaire** *nm/f* librarian; **bibliothèque** *nf* library; *(meuble)* bookcase

bic ® [bik] *nm* Biro ®

bicarbonate [bikaʀbɔnat] *nm*: **~ (de soude)** bicarbonate of soda

biceps [bisɛps] *nm* biceps

biche [biʃ] *nf* doe

bichonner [biʃɔne] *vt* to pamper

bicolore [bikɔlɔʀ] *adj* two-coloured

bicoque [bikɔk] *nf (péj)* shack

bicyclette [bisiklɛt] *nf* bicycle

bide [bid] *nm (fam) (ventre)* belly; *(THÉÂTRE)* flop

bidet [bidɛ] *nm* bidet

bidon [bidɔ̃] *nm* can ♦ *adj inv (fam)* phoney

bidonville [bidɔ̃vil] *nm* shanty town

bidule [bidyl] *(fam) nm* thingumajig

MOT-CLÉ

---

bien [bjɛ̃] *nm* 1 *(avantage, profit)*: **faire du bien à qn** to do sb good; **dire du bien de** to speak well of; **c'est pour son bien** it's for his own good

2 *(possession, patrimoine)* possession, property; **son bien le plus précieux** his most treasured possession; **avoir du bien** to have property; **biens (de consommation** *etc)* (consumer *etc)* goods

3 *(moral)*: **le bien** good; **distinguer le bien du mal** to tell good from evil

♦ *adv* 1 *(de façon satisfaisante)* well; **elle travaille/mange bien** she works/ eats well; **croyant bien faire, je/il** ... thinking I/he was doing the right thing, I/he ...; **c'est bien fait!** it serves him *(ou her etc)* right!

2 *(valeur intensive)* quite; **bien jeune** quite young; **bien assez** quite enough; **bien mieux** (very) much better; **j'espère bien y aller** I do hope to go; **je veux bien le faire** *(concession)* I'm quite willing to do it; **il faut bien le faire** it has to be done

3: **bien du temps/des gens** quite a time/a number of people

♦ *adj inv* 1 *(en bonne forme, à l'aise)*: **je me sens bien** I feel fine; **je ne me sens pas bien** I don't feel well; **on est bien dans ce fauteuil** this chair is very comfortable

2 *(joli, beau)* good-looking; **tu es bien dans cette robe** you look good in that dress

3 *(satisfaisant)* good; **elle est bien, cette maison/secrétaire** it's a good house/she's a good secretary

4 *(moralement)* right; *(: personne)* good, nice; *(respectable)* respectable; **ce n'est pas bien de ...** it's not right to ...; **elle est bien, cette femme** she's a nice woman, she's a good sort; **des gens biens** respectable people

5 (en bons termes): **être bien avec qn** to be on good terms with sb
♦ préfixe: **bien-aimé, e** adj, nm/f beloved; **bien-être** nm well-being; **bienfaisance** nf charity; **bienfaisant, e** adj (chose) beneficial; **bienfait** nm act of generosity, benefaction; (de la science etc) benefit; **bienfaiteur, -trice** nm/f benefactor/benefactress; **bienfondé** nm soundness; **bien-fonds** nm property; **bienheureux, -euse** adj happy; (REL) blessed, blest; **bien que** conj (al)though; **bien sûr** adv certainly

bienséant, e [bjɛ̃seã, ãt] adj seemly

bientôt [bjɛ̃to] adv soon; **à ~** see you soon

bienveillant, e [bjɛ̃vejã, ãt] adj kindly

bienvenu, e [bjɛ̃vny] adj welcome; **bienvenue nf: souhaiter la bienvenue à** to welcome; **bienvenue à** welcome to

bière [bjɛʀ] nf (boisson) beer; (cercueil) bier; ~ **(à la) pression** draught beer; ~ **blonde** lager; ~ **brune** brown ale

biffer [bife] vt to cross out

bifteck [biftɛk] nm steak

bifurquer [bifyʀke] vi (route) to fork; (véhicule) to turn off

bigarré, e [bigaʀe] adj multicoloured; (disparate) motley

bigorneau, x [bigɔʀno] nm winkle

bigot, e [bigo, ɔt] (péj) adj bigoted

bigoudi [bigudi] nm curler

bijou, x [biʒu] nm jewel; **bijouterie** nf jeweller's (shop); **bijoutier, -ière** nm/f jeweller

bikini [bikini] nm bikini

bilan [bilã] nm (fig) (net) outcome; (: de victimes) toll; (COMM) balance sheet(s); **un ~ de santé** a (medical) checkup; **faire le ~ de** to assess, review; **déposer son ~** to file a bankruptcy statement

bile [bil] nf bile; **se faire de la ~** (fam) to worry o.s. sick

bilieux, -euse [biljø, øz] adj bilious; (fig: colérique) testy

bilingue [bilɛ̃g] adj bilingual

billard [bijaʀ] nm (jeu) billiards sg; (table) billiard table; ~ **américain** pool

bille [bij] nf (gén) ball; (du jeu de ~s) marble

billet [bijɛ] nm (aussi: ~ **de banque**) (bank)note; (de cinéma, de bus etc) ticket; (courte lettre) note; ~ **Bige** cheap rail ticket for under-26s; **billetterie** nf ticket office; (distributeur) ticket machine; (BANQUE) cash dispenser

billion [biljɔ̃] nm billion (BRIT), trillion (US)

billot [bijo] nm block

bimensuel, le [bimãsɥɛl] adj bimonthly

binette [binɛt] nf hoe

bio... [bjo] préfixe bio...; **biochimie** nf biochemistry; **biodiversité** nf biodiversity; **bioéthique** nf bioethics sg; **biographie** nf biography; **biologie** nf biology; **biologique** adj biological; (produits, aliments) organic; **biologiste** nm/f biologist; **bioterroriste** nm/f bioterrorist

Birmanie [biʀmani] nf Burma

bis [bis] adv: **12 ~** 12a ou A ♦ excl, nm encore

bisannuel, le [bizanɥɛl] adj biennial

biscornu, e [biskɔʀny] adj twisted

biscotte [biskɔt] nf toasted bread (sold in packets)

biscuit [biskɥi] nm biscuit; ~ **de savoie** sponge cake

bise [biz] nf (fam: baiser) kiss; (vent) North wind; **grosses ~s (de)** (sur lettre) love and kisses (from)

bisou [bizu] (fam) nm kiss

bissextile [bisɛkstil] adj: **année ~** leap year

bistro(t) [bistʀo] nm bistro, café

bitume [bitym] nm asphalt

bizarre [bizaʀ] adj strange, odd

blafard, e [blafaʀ, aʀd] adj wan

blague [blag] nf (propos) joke; (farce)

trick; **sans ~!** no kidding!; **blaguer** vi to joke

blaireau, x [blɛʀo] nm (ZOOL) badger; (brosse) shaving brush

blairer [blɛʀe] (fam) vt: **je ne peux pas le ~** I can't bear ou stand him

blâme [blɑm] nm blame; (sanction) reprimand; **blâmer** vt to blame

blanc, blanche [blɑ̃, blɑ̃ʃ] adj white; (non imprimé) blank ♦ nm/f white, white man(-woman) ♦ nm (couleur) white; (espace non écrit) blank; (aussi: ~ d'œuf) (egg-)white; (aussi: ~ de poulet) breast, white meat; (aussi: vin ~) white wine; **~ cassé** off-white; **chèque en ~** blank cheque; **à ~** (chauffer) white-hot; (tirer, charger) with blanks; **blanche** nf (MUS) minim (BRIT), half-note (US); **blancheur** nf whiteness

blanchir [blɑ̃ʃiʀ] vt (gén) to whiten; (linge) to launder; (CULIN) to blanch; (fig: disculper) to clear ♦ vi to grow white; (cheveux) to go white; **blanchisserie** nf laundry

blason [blazɔ̃] nm coat of arms

blasphème [blasfɛm] nm blasphemy

blazer [blazɛʀ] nm blazer

blé [ble] nm wheat; **~ noir** buckwheat

bled [blɛd] (péj) nm hole

blême [blɛm] adj pale

blessant, e [blesɑ̃, ɑ̃t] adj (offensant) hurtful

blessé, e [blese] adj injured ♦ nm/f injured person, casualty

blesser [blese] vt to injure; (délibérément) to wound; (offenser) to hurt; **se ~** to injure o.s.; **se ~ au pied** to injure one's foot; **blessure** nf (accidentelle) injury; (intentionnelle) wound

bleu, e [blø] adj blue; (bifteck) very rare ♦ nm (couleur) blue; (contusion) bruise; (vêtement: aussi: **~s**) overalls pl; **~ marine** navy blue; **bleuet** nm cornflower; **bleuté, e** adj blue-shaded

blinder [blɛ̃de] vt to armour; (fig) to harden

bloc [blɔk] nm (de pierre etc) block; (de papier à lettres) pad; (ensemble) group, block; **serré à ~** tightened right down; **en ~** as a whole; **~ opératoire** operating ou theatre block; **~ sanitaire** toilet block; **blocage** nm (des prix) freezing; (PSYCH) hang-up; **bloc-notes** nm note pad

blocus [blɔkys] nm blockade

blond, e [blɔ̃, blɔ̃d] adj fair, blond; (sable, blés) golden; **~ cendré** ash blond; **blonde** nf (femme) blonde; (bière) lager; (cigarette) Virginia cigarette

bloquer [blɔke] vt (passage) to block; (pièce mobile) to jam; (crédits, compte) to freeze; **se ~** to jam; (PSYCH) to have a mental block

blottir [blɔtiʀ]: **se ~** vi to huddle up

blouse [bluz] nf overall

blouson [bluzɔ̃] nm blouson jacket; **~ noir** (fig) ≈ rocker

blue-jean [bludʒin] nm (pair of) jeans

bluff [blœf] nm bluff; **bluffer** vi to bluff

bobard [bɔbaʀ] (fam) nm tall story

bobine [bɔbin] nf reel; (ÉLEC) coil

bocal, -aux [bɔkal, o] nm jar

bock [bɔk] nm glass of beer

body [bɔdi] nm body(suit); (SPORT) leotard

bœuf [bœf] nm ox; (CULIN) beef

bof! [bɔf] (fam) excl don't care!; (pas terrible) nothing special

bogue [bɔg] nm: **le ~ de l'an 2000** the millennium bug

bohème [bɔɛm] adj happy-go-lucky, unconventional; **bohémien, ne** nm/f gipsy

boire [bwaʀ] vt to drink; (s'imprégner de) to soak up; **~ un coup** (fam) to have a drink

bois [bwa] nm wood; **de ~, en ~** wooden; **boisé, e** adj woody, wooded

boisson [bwasɔ̃] nf drink

boîte [bwat] nf box; (fam: entreprise) firm; **aliments en ~** canned ou tinned (BRIT) foods; **~ aux lettres** letter box;

d'allumettes box of matches; (vide) matchbox; **~ (de conserve)** can ou tin (BRIT) (of food); **~ de nuit** night club; **~ de vitesses** gear box; **~ postale** PO Box; **~ vocale** (TEL) voice mail

boiter [bwate] vi to limp; (fig: raisonnement) to be shaky

boîtier [bwatje] nm case

boive etc [bwav] vb voir **boire**

bol [bɔl] nm bowl; **un ~ d'air** a breath of fresh air; **j'en ai ras le ~** (fam) I'm fed up with this; **avoir du ~** (fam) to be lucky

bolide [bɔlid] nm racing car; **comme un ~** at top speed, like a rocket

bombardement [bɔ̃bardəmɑ̃] nm bombing

bombarder [bɔ̃barde] vt to bomb; **~ qn de** (cailloux, lettres) to bombard sb with

bombe [bɔ̃b] nf bomb; (atomiseur) (aerosol) spray; **bombé, e** adj (forme) rounded; **bomber** vt: **bomber le torse** to swell out one's chest

---MOT-CLÉ---

bon, bonne [bɔ̃, bɔn] adj 1 (agréable, satisfaisant) good; **un bon repas/restaurant** a good meal/restaurant; **être bon en maths** to be good at maths

2 (charitable): **être bon (envers)** to be good (to)

3 (correct) right; **le bon numéro/moment** the right number/moment

4 (souhaits): **bon anniversaire** happy birthday; **bon voyage** have a good trip; **bonne chance** good luck; **bonne année** happy New Year; **bonne nuit** good night

5 (approprié, apte): **bon à/pour** fit to/ for

6: **bon enfant** adj inv accommodating, easy-going; **bonne femme** (péj) woman; **de bonne heure** early; **bon marché** adj inv cheap ♦ adv cheap; **bon mot** witticism; **bon sens** common

sense; **bon vivant** jovial chap; **bonnes œuvres** charitable works, charities

♦ nm 1 (billet) voucher; (aussi: **bon cadeau**) gift voucher; **bon d'essence** petrol coupon; **bon du Trésor** Treasury bond

2: **avoir du bon** to have its good points; **pour de bon** for good

♦ adv: **il fait bon** it's ou the weather is fine; **sentir bon** to smell good; **tenir bon** to stand firm

♦ excl good!; **ah bon?** really?; voir aussi **bonne**

bonbon [bɔ̃bɔ̃] nm (boiled) sweet

bonbonne [bɔ̃bɔn] nf demijohn

bond [bɔ̃] nm leap; **faire un ~** to leap in the air

bondé, e [bɔ̃de] adj packed (full)

bondir [bɔ̃diʀ] vi to leap

bonheur [bɔnœʀ] nm happiness; **porter ~ (à qn)** to bring (sb) luck; **au petit ~** haphazardly; **par ~** fortunately

bonhomie [bɔnɔmi] nf goodnaturedness

bonhomme [bɔnɔm] (pl **bonshommes**) nm fellow; **~ de neige** snowman

bonifier [bɔnifje] vt to improve

boniment [bɔnimɑ̃] nm patter no pl

bonjour [bɔ̃ʒuʀ] excl, nm hello; (selon l'heure) good morning/afternoon; **c'est simple comme ~** it's as easy as pie!

bonne [bɔn] adj voir **bon** ♦ nf (domestique) maid; **bonnement** adv: **tout bonnement** quite simply

bonnet [bɔnɛ] nm hat; (de soutiengorge) cup; **~ de bain** bathing cap

bonshommes [bɔ̃zɔm] nmpl de **bonhomme**

bonsoir [bɔ̃swaʀ] excl good evening

bonté [bɔ̃te] nf kindness no pl

bonus [bɔnys] nm no-claims bonus

bord [bɔʀ] nm (de table, verre, falaise) edge; (de rivière, lac) bank; (de route) side; **(monter) à ~** (to go) on board

jeter par-dessus ~ to throw overboard; **le commandant de/les hommes du ~** the ship's master/crew; **au ~ de la mer** at the seaside; **être au ~ des larmes** to be on the verge of tears

bordeaux [bɔʀdo] *nm* Bordeaux (wine) ♦ *adj inv* maroon

bordel [bɔʀdɛl] *nm* brothel; (*fam!*) bloody mess (*!*)

bordelais, e [bɔʀdəlɛ, ɛz] *adj of ou* from Bordeaux

border [bɔʀde] *vt* (*être le long de*) to line; (*qn dans son lit*) to tuck up; (*garnir*): ~ **qch de** to edge with

bordereau, x [bɔʀdəʀo] *nm* (*formulaire*) slip

bordure [bɔʀdyʀ] *nf* border; **en ~ de** on the edge of

borgne [bɔʀɲ] *adj* one-eyed

borne [bɔʀn] *nf* boundary stone; (*aussi*: ~ **kilométrique**) kilometre-marker; ≃ milestone; ~**s** *nfpl* (*fig*) limits; **dépasser les ~s** to go too far

borné, e [bɔʀne] *adj* (*personne*) narrow-minded

borner [bɔʀne] *vt*: **se ~ à faire** (*se contenter de*) to content o.s. with doing; (*se limiter à*) to limit o.s. to doing

bosquet [bɔskɛ] *nm* grove

bosse [bɔs] *nf* (*de terrain etc*) bump; (*enflure*) lump; (*du bossu, du chameau*) hump; **avoir la ~ des maths** *etc* to have a gift for maths *etc*; **il a roulé sa ~** (*fam*) he's been around

bosser [bɔse] (*fam*) *vi* (*travailler*) to work; (*travailler dur*) to slave (away)

bossu, e [bɔsy] *nm/f* hunchback

botanique [bɔtanik] *nf* botany ♦ *adj* botanic(al)

botte [bɔt] *nf* (*soulier*) (high) boot; (*gerbe*): ~ **de paille** bundle of straw; ~ **de radis** bunch of radishes; ~**s de caoutchouc** wellington boots; **botter** *vt*: **ça me botte** (*fam*) I fancy that

bottin [bɔtɛ̃] *nm* directory

bottine [bɔtin] *nf* ankle boot

bouc [buk] *nm* goat; (*barbe*) goatee; ~ **émissaire** scapegoat

boucan [bukɑ̃] (*fam*) *nm* din, racket

bouche [buʃ] *nf* mouth; **rester ~ bée** to stand open-mouthed; **le ~ à ~** the kiss of life; ~ **d'égout** manhole; ~ **d'incendie** fire hydrant; ~ **de métro** métro entrance

bouché, e [buʃe] *adj* (*temps, ciel*) overcast; **c'est ~** there's no future in it

bouchée [buʃe] *nf* mouthful; ~**s à la reine** chicken vol-au-vents

boucher, -ère [buʃe] *nm/f* butcher ♦ *vt* (*trou*) to fill up; (*obstruer*) to block (up); **se ~** *vi* (*tuyau etc*) to block up, get blocked up; **j'ai le nez bouché** my nose is blocked; **se ~ le nez** to hold one's nose; **boucherie** *nf* butcher's (shop); (*fig*) slaughter

bouche-trou [buʃtʀu] *nm* (*fig*) stop-gap

bouchon [buʃɔ̃] *nm* stopper; (*de tube*) top; (*en liège*) cork; (*fig: embouteillage*) holdup; (*PÊCHE*) float

boucle [bukl] *nf* (*forme, figure*) loop; (*objet*) buckle; ~ (**de cheveux**) curl; ~ **d'oreille** earring

bouclé, e [bukle] *adj* (*cheveux*) curly

boucler [bukle] *vt* (*fermer: ceinture etc*) to fasten; (*terminer*) to finish off; (*fam: enfermer*) to shut away; (*quartier*) to seal off ♦ *vi* to curl

bouclier [buklije] *nm* shield

bouddhiste [budist] *nm/f* Buddhist

bouder [bude] *vi* to sulk ♦ *vt* to stay away from

boudin [budɛ̃] *nm*: ~ (**noir**) black pudding; ~ **blanc** white pudding

boue [bu] *nf* mud

bouée [bwe] *nf* buoy; ~ (**de sauvetage**) lifebuoy

boueux, -euse [bwø, øz] *adj* muddy

bouffe [buf] (*fam*) *nf* grub (*Brit*), food

bouffée [bufe] *nf* (*de cigarette*) puff; **une ~ d'air pur** a breath of fresh air

bouffer [bufe] (*fam*) *vi* to eat

bouffi, e [bufi] *adj* swollen

bougeoir [buʒwar] nm candlestick

bougeotte [buʒɔt] nf: **avoir la ~** (fam) to have the fidgets

bouger [buʒe] vi to move; (dent etc) to be loose; (s'activer) to get moving ♦ vt to move; **les prix/les couleurs n'ont pas bougé** prices/colours haven't changed

bougie [buʒi] nf candle; (AUTO) spark(ing) plug

bougon, ne [bugɔ̃, ɔn] adj grumpy

bougonner [bugɔne] vi, vt to grumble

bouillabaisse [bujabɛs] nf type of fish soup

bouillant, e [bujɑ̃, ɑ̃t] adj (qui bout) boiling; (très chaud) boiling (hot)

bouillie [buji] nf (de bébé) cereal; **en ~** (fig) crushed

bouillir [bujir] vi, vt to boil; **~ d'impatience** to seethe with impatience

bouilloire [bujwar] nf kettle

bouillon [bujɔ̃] nm (CULIN) stock ou pl; **bouillonner** vi to bubble; (fig: idées) to bubble up

bouillotte [bujɔt] nf hot-water bottle

boulanger, -ère [bulɑ̃ʒe, ɛr] nm/f baker; **boulangerie** nf bakery; **boulangerie-pâtisserie** nf baker's and confectioner's (shop)

boule [bul] nf (gén) ball; **~s** nfpl (jeu) bowls; **se mettre en ~** (fig: fam) to fly off the handle, to blow one's top; **jouer aux ~s** to play bowls; **~ de neige** snowball

bouleau, x [bulo] nm (silver) birch

bouledogue [buldɔg] nm bulldog

boulet [bulɛ] nm (aussi: **~ de canon**) cannonball

boulette [bulɛt] nf (de viande) meatball

boulevard [bulvar] nm boulevard

bouleversant, e [bulvɛrsɑ̃, ɑ̃t] adj (scène, récit) deeply moving

bouleversement [bulvɛrsəmɑ̃] nm upheaval

bouleverser [bulvɛrse] vt (émouvoir) to overwhelm; (causer du chagrin) to distress; (pays, vie) to disrupt; (papiers,

objets) to turn upside down

boulon [bulɔ̃] nm bolt

boulot, te [bulo, ɔt] adj plump, tubby ♦ nm (fam: travail) work

boum [bum] nm bang ♦ nf (fam) party

bouquet [bukɛ] nm (de fleurs) bunch (of flowers), bouquet; (de persil etc) bunch; **c'est le ~!** (fam) that takes the biscuit!

bouquin [bukɛ̃] (fam) nm book; **bouquiner** (fam) vi to read; **bouquiniste** nm/f bookseller

bourbeux, -euse [burbø, øz] adj muddy

bourbier [burbje] nm (quag)mire

bourde [burd] (fam) nf (erreur) howler; (gaffe) blunder

bourdon [burdɔ̃] nm bumblebee; **bourdonner** vi to buzz

bourg [bur] nm small market town

bourgeois, e [burʒwa, waz] (péj) adj ≈ (upper) middle class; **bourgeoisie** nf ≈ upper middle classes pl

bourgeon [burʒɔ̃] nm bud

Bourgogne [burgɔɲ] nf: **la ~** Burgundy ♦ nm: **b~** burgundy (wine)

bourguignon, ne [burgiɲɔ̃, ɔn] adj of ou from Burgundy, Burgundian

bourlinguer [burlɛ̃ge] (fam) vi to knock about a lot, get around a lot

bourrade [burad] nf shove, thump

bourrage [buraʒ] nm: **~ de crâne** brainwashing; (SCOL) cramming

bourrasque [burask] nf squall

bourratif, -ive [buratif, iv] (fam) adj filling, stodgy (péj)

bourré, e [bure] adj (fam: ivre) plastered, tanked up (BRIT); (rempli): **~ de** crammed full of

bourreau, x [buro] nm executioner; (fig) torturer; **~ de travail** workaholic

bourrelet [burlɛ] nm fold ou roll (of flesh)

bourrer [bure] vt (pipe) to fill; (poêle) to pack; (valise) to cram (full)

bourrique [burik] nf (âne) ass

bourru, e [bury] adj surly, gruff

bourse [buʀs] *nf* (*subvention*) grant; (*porte-monnaie*) purse; **la B~** the Stock Exchange

boursier, -ière [buʀsje, jɛʀ] *nm/f* (*étudiant*) grant holder

boursoufler [buʀsufle]: **se ~** *vi* to swell (up)

bous [bu] *vb voir* **bouillir**

bousculade [buskylad] *nf* (*hâte*) rush; (*cohue*) crush; **bousculer** *vt* (*heurter*) to knock into; (*fig*) to push, rush

bouse [buz] *nf* dung *no pl*

bousiller [buzije] (*fam*) *vt* (*appareil*) to wreck

boussole [busɔl] *nf* compass

bout [bu] *vb voir* **bouillir** ♦ *nm* bit; (*d'un bâton etc*) tip; (*d'une ficelle, table, rue, période*) end; **au ~ de** at the end of, after; **pousser qn à ~** to push sb to the limit; **venir à ~ de** to manage to finish

boutade [butad] *nf* quip, sally

boute-en-train [butɑ̃tʀɛ̃] *nm inv* (*fig*) live wire

bouteille [butɛj] *nf* bottle; (*de gaz butane*) cylinder

boutique [butik] *nf* shop

bouton [butɔ̃] *nm* button; (*sur la peau*) spot; (*BOT*) bud; **~ d'or** buttercup; **boutonner** *vt* to button up; **boutonnière** *nf* buttonhole; **bouton-pression** *nm* press stud

bouture [butyʀ] *nf* cutting

bovins [bɔvɛ̃] *nmpl* cattle *pl*

bowling [bulin] *nm* (*tenpin*) bowling; (*salle*) bowling alley

box [bɔks] *nm* (*d'écurie*) loose-box; (*JUR*): **~ des accusés** dock

boxe [bɔks] *nf* boxing; **boxeur** *nm* boxer

boyaux [bwajo] *nmpl* (*viscères*) entrails, guts

BP *abr* = **boîte postale**

bracelet [bʀaslɛ] *nm* bracelet

braconnier [bʀakɔnje] *nm* poacher

brader [bʀade] *vt* to sell off; **braderie** *nf* cut-price shop/stall

braguette [bʀagɛt] *nf* fly *ou* flies *pl* (*BRIT*), zipper (*US*)

brailler [bʀaje] *vi* to bawl, yell

braire [bʀɛʀ] *vi* to bray

braise [bʀɛz] *nf* embers *pl*

brancard [bʀɑ̃kaʀ] *nm* (*civière*) stretcher; **brancardier** *nm* stretcher-bearer

branchages [bʀɑ̃ʃaʒ] *nmpl* boughs

branche [bʀɑ̃ʃ] *nf* branch

branché, e [bʀɑ̃ʃe] (*fam*) *adj* trendy

brancher [bʀɑ̃ʃe] *vt* to connect (up); (*en mettant la prise*) to plug in

brandir [bʀɑ̃diʀ] *vt* to brandish

branle [bʀɑ̃l] *nm*: **mettre en ~** to set in motion; **branle-bas** *nm inv* commotion

braquer [bʀake] *vi* (*AUTO*) to turn (the wheel) ♦ *vt* (*revolver etc*): **~ qch sur** to aim sth at, point sth at; (*mettre en colère*): **~ qn** to put sb's back up

bras [bʀa] *nm* arm; **~ dessus, ~ dessous** arm in arm; **se retrouver avec qch sur les ~** (*fam*) to be landed with sth; **~ droit** (*fig*) right hand man; **~ de fer** arm wrestling

brasier [bʀazje] *nm* blaze, inferno

bras-le-corps [bʀalkɔʀ] *adv*: **à ~~~** (a)round the waist

brassard [bʀasaʀ] *nm* armband

brasse [bʀas] *nf* (*nage*) breast-stroke

brassée [bʀase] *nf* armful

brasser [bʀase] *vt* to mix; **~ l'argent/ les affaires** to handle a lot of money/ business

brasserie [bʀasʀi] *nf* (*restaurant*) café-restaurant; (*usine*) brewery

brave [bʀav] *adj* (*courageux*) brave; (*bon, gentil*) good, kind

braver [bʀave] *vt* to defy

bravo [bʀavo] *excl* bravo ♦ *nm* cheer

bravoure [bʀavuʀ] *nf* bravery

break [bʀɛk] *nm* (*AUTO*) estate car

brebis [bʀəbi] *nf* ewe; **~ galeuse** black sheep

brèche [bʀɛʃ] *nf* breach, gap; **être toujours sur la ~** (*fig*) to be always on the go

bredouille [brəduj] *adj* empty-handed

bredouiller [brəduje] *vi*, *vt* to mumble, stammer

bref, brève [brɛf, ɛv] *adj* short, brief ♦ *adv* in short; **d'un ton ~** sharply, curtly; **en ~** in short, in brief

Brésil [brezil] *nm* Brazil; **brésilien, -ne** *adj* Brazilian ♦ *nm/f*: **B~, ne** Brazilian

Bretagne [brətaɲ] *nf* Brittany

bretelle [brətɛl] *nf* (*de vêtement, de sac*) strap; (*d'autoroute*) slip road (*BRIT*), entrance/exit ramp (*US*); **~s** *nfpl* (*pour pantalon*) braces (*BRIT*), suspenders (*US*)

breton, -ne [brətɔ̃, ɔn] *adj* Breton ♦ *nm/f*: **B~, ne** Breton

breuvage [brœvaʒ] *nm* beverage, drink

brève [brɛv] *adj voir* **bref**

brevet [brəvɛ] *nm* diploma, certificate; **~ (d'invention)** patent; **breveté, e** *adj* patented

bribes [brib] *nfpl* (*de conversation*) snatches; **par ~** piecemeal

bricolage [brikɔlaʒ] *nm*: **le ~** do-it-yourself

bricole [brikɔl] *nf* (*babiole*) trifle

bricoler [brikɔle] *vi* (*petits travaux*) to do DIY jobs; (*passe-temps*) to potter about ♦ *vt* (*réparer*) to fix up; **bricoleur, -euse** *nm/f* handyman(-woman), DIY enthusiast

bride [brid] *nf* bridle; **tenir qn en ~** to keep a tight rein on sb

bridé, e [bride] *adj*: **yeux ~s** slit eyes

bridge [bridʒ] *nm* (*CARTES*) bridge

brièvement [brijɛvmɑ̃] *adv* briefly

brigade [brigad] *nf* (*POLICE*) squad; (*MIL*) brigade; **brigadier** *nm* sergeant

brigandage [brigɑ̃daʒ] *nm* robbery

briguer [brige] *vt* to aspire to

brillamment [brijamɑ̃] *adv* brilliantly

brillant, e [brijɑ̃, ɑ̃t] *adj* (*remarquable*) bright; (*luisant*) shiny, shining

briller [brije] *vi* to shine

brimer [brime] *vt* to bully

brin [brɛ̃] *nm* (*de laine, ficelle etc*) strand; (*fig*): **un ~ de** a bit of; **~ d'herbe** blade of grass; **~ de muguet** sprig of lily of the valley

brindille [brɛ̃dij] *nf* twig

brio [brijo] *nm*: **avec ~** with panache

brioche [brijɔʃ] *nf* brioche (bun); (*fam: ventre*) paunch

brique [brik] *nf* brick; (*de lait*) carton

briquer [brike] *vt* to polish up

briquet [brike] *nm* (*cigarette*) lighter

brise [briz] *nf* breeze

briser [brize] *vt* to break; **se ~** *vi* to break

britannique [britanik] *adj* British ♦ *nm/f*: **B~** British person, Briton; **les B~s** the British

brocante [brɔkɑ̃t] *nf* junk, second-hand goods *pl*; **brocanteur, -euse** *nm/f* junkshop owner; junk dealer

broche [brɔʃ] *nf* brooch; (*CULIN*) spit; (*MÉD*) pin; **à la ~** spit-roasted

broché, e [brɔʃe] *adj* (*livre*) paper-backed

brochet [brɔʃɛ] *nm* pike *inv*

brochette [brɔʃɛt] *nf* (*ustensile*) skewer; (*plat*) kebab

brochure [brɔʃyr] *nf* pamphlet, brochure, booklet

broder [brɔde] *vt* to embroider ♦ *vi* to embroider the facts; **broderie** *nf* embroidery

broncher [brɔ̃ʃe] *vi*: **sans ~** without flinching, without turning a hair

bronches [brɔ̃ʃ] *nfpl* bronchial tubes; **bronchite** *nf* bronchitis

bronze [brɔ̃z] *nm* bronze

bronzer [brɔ̃ze] *vi* to get a tan; **se ~** to sunbathe

brosse [brɔs] *nf* brush; **coiffé en ~** with a crewcut; **~ à cheveux** hairbrush; **~ à dents** toothbrush; **~ à habits** clothesbrush; **brosser** *vt* (*nettoyer*) to brush; (*fig: tableau etc*) to paint; **se brosser les dents** to brush one's teeth

brouette [bruɛt] *nf* wheelbarrow

brouhaha [bruaa] *nm* hubbub

brouillard [bʀujaʀ] nm fog

brouille [bʀuj] nf quarrel

brouiller [bʀuje] vt (œufs, message) to scramble; (idées) to mix up; (rendre trouble) to cloud; (désunir: amis) to set at odds ♦ vi (vue) to cloud over; **se ~** vi (vue) to cloud over; (gens) to fall out

brouillon, ne [bʀujɔ̃, ɔn] adj (sans soin) untidy; (qui manque d'organisation) disorganized ♦ nm draft; (papier) ~ rough paper

broussailles [bʀusaj] nfpl undergrowth sg; **broussailleux, -euse** adj bushy

brousse [bʀus] nf: **la ~** the bush

brouter [bʀute] vi to graze

broutille [bʀutij] nf trifle

broyer [bʀwaje] vt to crush; **~ du noir** to be down in the dumps

bru [bʀy] nf daughter-in-law

brugnon [bʀyɲɔ̃] nm (BOT) nectarine

bruiner [bʀɥine] vb impers: **il bruine** it's drizzling, there's a drizzle

bruire [bʀɥiʀ] vi (feuilles) to rustle

bruit [bʀɥi] nm: **un ~** a noise, a sound; (fig: rumeur) a rumour; **le ~** noise; **sans ~** without a sound, noiselessly; **~ de fond** background noise; **bruitage** nm sound effects pl

brûlant, e [bʀylɑ̃, ɑ̃t] adj burning; (liquide) boiling (hot)

brûlé, e [bʀyle] adj (fig: démasqué) blown ♦ nm: **odeur de ~** smell of burning

brûle-pourpoint [bʀylpuʀpwɛ̃]: **à ~~** adv point-blank

brûler [bʀyle] vt to burn; (suj: eau bouillante) to scald; (consommer: électricité, essence) to use; (feu rouge, signal) to go through ♦ vi to burn; (jeu): **tu brûles!** you're getting hot!; **se ~** to burn o.s.; (s'ebouillanter) to scald o.s.

brûlure [bʀylyʀ] nf (lésion) burn; **~s d'estomac** heartburn sg

brume [bʀym] nf mist; **brumisateur** nm atomizer

brun, e [bʀœ̃, bʀyn] adj (gén, bière) dark;

---

brown; (cheveux, tabac) dark; **elle est ~e** she's got dark hair

brunch [bʀɛntʃ] nm brunch

brunir [bʀyniʀ] vi to get a tan

brushing [bʀœʃiŋ] nm blow-dry

brusque [bʀysk] adj abrupt; **brusquer** vt to rush

brut, e [bʀyt] adj (minerai, soie) raw; (diamant) rough; (COMM) gross; (pétrole) **~** crude (oil)

brutal, e, aux [bʀytal, o] adj brutal; **brutaliser** vt to handle roughly, manhandle

Bruxelles [bʀysɛl] n Brussels

bruyamment [bʀɥijamɑ̃] adv noisily

bruyant, e [bʀɥijɑ̃, ɑ̃t] adj noisy

bruyère [bʀɥijɛʀ] nf heather

BTS sigle m (= brevet de technicien supérieur) vocational training certificate taken at the end of a higher education course

bu, e [by] pp de **boire**

buccal, e, -aux [bykal, o] adj: **par voie ~e** orally

bûche [byʃ] nf log; **prendre une ~** (fig) to come a cropper; **~ de Noël** Yule log

bûcher [byʃe] nm (funéraire) pyre; (supplice) stake ♦ vi (fam) to swot (BRIT), slave (away) ♦ vt (fam) to swot up (BRIT), slave away at; **bûcheron** nm woodcutter; **bûcheur, -euse** (fam) adj hard-working

budget [bydʒɛ] nm budget

buée [bɥe] nf (sur une vitre) mist

buffet [byfɛ] nm (meuble) sideboard; (de réception) buffet; **~ (de gare)** (station) buffet, snack bar

buffle [byfl] nm buffalo

buis [bɥi] nm box tree; (bois) box(wood)

buisson [bɥisɔ̃] nm bush

buissonnière [bɥisɔnjɛʀ] adj: **faire l'école ~** to skip school

bulbe [bylb] nm (BOT, ANAT) bulb

Bulgarie [bylgaʀi] nf Bulgaria

bulle [byl] nf bubble

bulletin [byltɛ̃] nm (communiqué, jour-

nal) bulletin; (*SCOL*) report; **~ d'informations** news bulletin; **~ de salaire** pay-slip; **~ (de vote)** ballot paper; **~ météorologique** weather report

bureau, x [byʀo] *nm* (*meuble*) desk; (*pièce, service*) office; **~ de change** (foreign) exchange office *ou* bureau; **~ de poste** post office; **~ de tabac** tobacconist's (shop); **~ de vote** polling station; **bureaucratie** [byʀokʀasi] *nf* bureaucracy

burin [byʀɛ̃] *nm* cold chisel; (*ART*) burin

burlesque [byʀlɛsk] *adj* ridiculous; (*LITTÉRATURE*) burlesque

bus¹ [by] *vb voir* **boire**

bus² [bys] *nm* bus

busqué, e [byske] *adj* (*nez*) hook(ed)

buste [byst] *nm* (*torse*) chest; (*seins*) bust

but¹ [by] *vb voir* **boire**

but² [by(t)] *nm* (*cible*) target; (*fig*) goal, aim; (*FOOTBALL etc*) goal; **de ~ en blanc** point-blank; **avoir pour ~ de faire** to aim to do; **dans le ~ de** with the intention of

butane [bytan] *nm* (*camping*) butane; (*usage domestique*) Calor gas ®

buté, e [byte] *adj* stubborn, obstinate

buter [byte] *vi*: **~ contre** (*cogner*) to bump into; (*trébucher*) to stumble against; **se ~** *vi* to get obstinate, dig in one's heels; **~ contre une difficulté** (*fig*) to hit a snag

butin [bytɛ̃] *nm* booty, spoils *pl*; (*d'un vol*) loot

butiner [bytine] *vi* (*abeilles*) to gather nectar

butte [byt] *nf* mound, hillock; **être en ~ à** to be exposed to

buvais *etc* [byvɛ] *vb voir* **boire**

buvard [byvaʀ] *nm* blotter

buvette [byvɛt] *nf* bar

buveur, -euse [byvœʀ, øz] *nm/f* drinker

C, c

c' [s] *dét voir* **ce**

CA *sigle m* = **chiffre d'affaires**

ça [sa] *pron* (*pour désigner*) this; (: *plus loin*) that; (*comme sujet indéfini*) it; **comment ~ va?** how are you?; **~ va?** (*d'accord?*) OK?, all right?; **où ~?** where's that?; **qui ~?** who's that?; **~ alors!** well really!; **~ fait 10 ans (que)** it's 10 years (since); **c'est ~** that's right; **~ y est** that's it

çà [sa] *adv*: **~ et là** here and there

cabane [kaban] *nf* hut, cabin

cabaret [kabaʀɛ] *nm* night club

cabas [kaba] *nm* shopping bag

cabillaud [kabijo] *nm* cod *inv*

cabine [kabin] *nf* (*de bateau*) cabin; (*de piscine etc*) cubicle; (*de camion, train*) cab; (*d'avion*) cockpit; **~ d'essayage** fitting room; **~ (téléphonique)** call *ou* (tele)phone box

cabinet [kabinɛ] *nm* (*petite pièce*) closet; (*de médecin*) surgery (*BRIT*), office (*US*); (*de notaire etc*) office; (: *clientèle*) practice; (*POL*) Cabinet; **~s** *nmpl* (*w.-c.*) toilet *sg*; **~ d'affaires** business consultancy; **~ de toilette** toilet

câble [kɑbl] *nm* cable

cabosser [kabɔse] *vt* to dent

cabrer [kabʀe]: **se ~** *vi* (*cheval*) to rear up

cabriole [kabʀijɔl] *nf*: **faire des ~s** to caper about

cacahuète [kakaɥɛt] *nf* peanut

cacao [kakao] *nm* cocoa

cache [kaʃ] *nm* mask, card (for masking)

cache-cache [kaʃkaʃ] *nm*: **jouer à ~~** to play hide-and-seek

cachemire [kaʃmiʀ] *nm* cashmere

cache-nez [kaʃne] *nm inv* scarf, muffler

cacher [kaʃe] *vt* to hide, conceal; **se ~** *vi* (*volontairement*) to hide; (*être caché*) to be hidden *ou* concealed; **~ qch à qn** to hide *ou* conceal sth from sb

cachet [kaʃɛ] *nm* (*comprimé*) tablet; (*de la poste*) postmark; (*rétribution*) fee; (*fig*) style, character; **cacheter** *vt* to seal

cachette [kaʃɛt] *nf* hiding place; **en ~** on the sly, secretly

cachot [kaʃo] *nm* dungeon

cachotterie [kaʃɔtʀi] *nf*: **faire des ~** to be secretive

cactus [kaktys] *nm* cactus

cadavre [kadɑvʀ] *nm* corpse, (dead) body

Caddie ®, **caddy** [kadi] *nm* (super-market) trolley

cadeau, x [kado] *nm* present, gift; **faire un ~ à qn** to give sb a present *ou* gift; **faire ~ de qch à qn** to make a present of sth to sb, give sb sth as a present

cadenas [kadna] *nm* padlock

cadence [kadɑ̃s] *nf* (*tempo*) rhythm; (*de travail etc*) rate; **en ~** rhythmically

cadet, te [kadɛ, ɛt] *adj* younger; (*le plus jeune*) youngest ♦ *nm/f* youngest child *ou* one

cadran [kadʀɑ̃] *nm* dial; **~ solaire** sun-dial

cadre [kadʀ] *nm* frame; (*environne-ment*) surroundings *pl* ♦ *nm/f* (ADMIN) managerial employee, executive; **dans le ~ de** (*fig*) within the framework *ou* context of

cadrer [kadʀe] *vi*: **~ avec** to tally *ou* correspond with ♦ *vt* to centre

cafard [kafaʀ] *nm* cockroach; **avoir le ~** (*fam*) to be down in the dumps

café [kafe] *nm* coffee; (*bistro*) café ♦ *adj inv* coffee(-coloured); **~ au lait** white coffee; **~ noir** black coffee; **~ tabac** to-bacconist's *ou* newsagent's serving coffee and spirits; **cafetière** *nf* (*pot*) coffee-pot

cafouiller [kafuje] (*fam*) *vi* to get into a shambles

cage [kaʒ] *nf* cage; **~ d'escalier** (stair)well; **~ thoracique** rib cage

cageot [kaʒo] *nm* crate

cagibi [kaʒibi] (*fam*) *nm* (*débarras*) box-room

cagnotte [kaɲɔt] *nf* kitty

cagoule [kagul] *nf* (*passe-montagne*) balaclava

cahier [kaje] *nm* notebook; **~ de brouillons** roughbook, jotter; **~ d'exercices** exercise book

cahot [kao] *nm* jolt, bump

caïd [kaid] *nm* big chief, boss

caille [kaj] *nf* quail

cailler [kaje] *vi* (*lait*) to curdle; **ça caille** (*fam*) it's freezing; **caillot** [kajo] (*blood*) clot

caillou, x [kaju] *nm* (little) stone; **cail-louteux, -euse** *adj* (*route*) stony

Caire [kɛʀ] *nm*: **le ~** Cairo

caisse [kɛs] *nf* box; (*tiroir où l'on met la recette*) till; (*où l'on paye*) cash desk (BRIT), check-out; (*de banque*) cashier's desk; **~ d'épargne** savings bank; **~ de retraite** pension fund; **~ enregistreu-se** cash register; **caissier, -ière** *nm/f* cashier

cajoler [kaʒɔle] *vt* (*câliner*) to cuddle; (*amadouer*) to wheedle, coax

cake [kɛk] *nm* fruit cake

calandre [kalɑ̃dʀ] *nf* radiator grill

calanque [kalɑ̃k] *nf* rocky inlet

calcaire [kalkɛʀ] *nm* limestone ♦ *adj* (*eau*) hard; (GÉO) limestone *cpd*

calciné, e [kalsine] *adj* burnt to ashes

calcul [kalkyl] *nm* calculation; **le ~** (SCOL) arithmetic; **~ (biliaire)** (gall)stone; **calculatrice** *nf* calculator; **calculer** *vt* to calculate, work out; **cal-culette** *nf* pocket calculator

cale [kal] *nf* (*de bateau*) hold; (*en bois*) wedge; **~ sèche** dry dock

calé, e [kale] (*fam*) *adj* clever, bright

caleçon [kalsɔ̃] *nm* (*d'homme*) boxer shorts; (*de femme*) leggings

calembour [kalɑ̃buʀ] *nm* pun

calendrier [kalɑ̃dʀije] *nm* calendar; (*fig*) timetable

calepin [kalpɛ̃] *nm* notebook

caler [kale] vt to wedge ♦ vi (moteur, véhicule) to stall

calfeutrer [kalføtʀe] vt to (make) draughtproof; **se ~** vi to make o.s. snug and comfortable

calibre [kalibʀ] nm calibre

califourchon [kalifuʀʃɔ̃]: **à ~** adv astride

câlin, e [kɑlɛ̃, in] adj cuddly, cuddlesome; (regard, voix) tender; **câliner** vt to cuddle

calmant [kalmɑ̃] nm tranquillizer, sedative; (pour la douleur) painkiller

calme [kalm] adj calm, quiet ♦ nm calm(ness), quietness; **calmer** vt to calm (down); (douleur, inquiétude) to ease, soothe; **se calmer** vi to calm down

calomnie [kalɔmni] nf slander; (écrite) libel; **calomnier** vt to slander; to libel

calorie [kalɔʀi] nf calorie

calotte [kalɔt] nf (coiffure) skullcap; (fam: gifle) slap; **~ glaciaire** (GÉO) icecap

calquer [kalke] vt to trace; (fig) to copy exactly

calvaire [kalvɛʀ] nm (croix) wayside cross, calvary; (souffrances) suffering

calvitie [kalvisi] nf baldness

camarade [kamaʀad] nm/f friend, pal; (POL) comrade; **camaraderie** nf friendship

cambouis [kɑ̃bwi] nm dirty oil ou grease

cambrer [kɑ̃bʀe]: **se ~** vi to arch one's back

cambriolage [kɑ̃bʀijɔlaʒ] nm burglary; **cambrioler** vt to burgle (BRIT), burglarize (US); **cambrioleur, -euse** nm/f burglar

camelote [kamlɔt] (fam) nf rubbish, trash, junk

caméra [kameʀa] nf (CINÉMA, TV) camera; (d'amateur) cine-camera

caméscope ® [kameskɔp] nm camcorder ®

camion [kamjɔ̃] nm lorry (BRIT), truck; **~**

de dépannage breakdown (BRIT) ou tow (US) truck; **camion-citerne** nm tanker; **camionnette** nf (small) van; **camionneur** nm (chauffeur) lorry (BRIT) ou truck driver; (entrepreneur) haulage contractor (BRIT), trucker (US)

camisole [kamizɔl] nf: **~ (de force)** straitjacket

camomille [kamɔmij] nf camomile; (boisson) camomile tea

camoufler [kamufle] vt to camouflage; (fig) to conceal, cover up

camp [kɑ̃] nm camp; (fig) side; **~ de vacances** children's holiday camp (BRIT), summer camp (US)

campagnard, e [kɑ̃paɲaʀ, aʀd] adj country cpd

campagne [kɑ̃paɲ] nf country, countryside; (MIL, POL, COMM) campaign; **à la ~** in the country

camper [kɑ̃pe] vi to camp ♦ vt to sketch; **se ~ devant** to plant o.s. in front of; **campeur, -euse** nm/f camper

camping [kɑ̃piŋ] nm camping; (terrain de) **~** campsite, camping site; **faire du ~** to go camping; **camping-car** nm camper, motorhome (US); **camping-gaz** ® nm inv camp(ing) stove

Canada [kanada] nm: **le ~** Canada; **canadien, ne** adj Canadian ♦ nm/f: **Canadien, ne** Canadian; **canadienne** nf (veste) fur-lined jacket

canaille [kanɑj] (péj) nf scoundrel

canal, -aux [kanal, o] nm canal; (naturel) channel; **canalisation** nf (tuyau) pipe; **canaliser** vt to canalize; (fig) to channel

canapé [kanape] nm settee, sofa

canard [kanaʀ] nm duck; (fam: journal) rag

canari [kanaʀi] nm canary

cancans [kɑ̃kɑ̃] nmpl (malicious) gossip sg

cancer [kɑ̃sɛʀ] nm cancer; (signe): **le C~** Cancer; **~ de la peau** skin cancer

cancre [kɑ̃kʀ] nm dunce

candeur [kɑ̃dœʀ] nf ingenuousness,

guilelessness

candidat, e [kɑ̃dida, at] nm/f candidate; (à un poste) applicant, candidate; **candidature** nf (POL) candidature; (à poste) application; **poser sa candidature à un poste** to apply for a job

candide [kɑ̃did] adj ingenuous, guileless

cane [kan] nf (female) duck

caneton [kantɔ̃] nm duckling

canette [kanɛt] nf (de bière) (flip-top) bottle

canevas [kanva] nm (COUTURE) canvas

caniche [kaniʃ] nm poodle

canicule [kanikyl] nf scorching heat

canif [kanif] nm penknife, pocket knife

canine [kanin] nf canine (tooth)

caniveau, x [kanivo] nm gutter

canne [kan] nf (walking) stick; **~ à pêche** fishing rod; **~ à sucre** sugar cane

cannelle [kanɛl] nf cinnamon

canoë [kanɔe] nm canoe; (sport) canoeing

canon [kanɔ̃] nm (arme) gun; (HISTOIRE) cannon; (d'une arme: tube) barrel; (fig: norme) model; (MUS) canon

canot [kano] nm ding(h)y; **~ de sauvetage** lifeboat; **~ pneumatique** inflatable ding(h)y; **canotier** nm boater

cantatrice [kɑ̃tatris] nf (opera) singer

cantine [kɑ̃tin] nf canteen

cantique [kɑ̃tik] nm hymn

canton [kɑ̃tɔ̃] nm district consisting of several communes; (en Suisse) canton

cantonade [kɑ̃tɔnad]: **à la ~** adv to everyone in general

cantonner [kɑ̃tɔne]: **se ~ à** vt to confine o.s. to

cantonnier [kɑ̃tɔnje] nm roadmender

canular [kanylaʀ] nm hoax

caoutchouc [kautʃu] nm rubber

cap [kap] nm (GÉO) cape; (promontoire) headland; (fig: tournant) watershed; (NAVIG): **changer de ~** to change course; **mettre le ~ sur** to head ou steer for

CAP sigle m (= Certificat d'aptitude professionnelle) vocational training certificate taken at secondary school

capable [kapabl] adj able, capable; **~ de qch/faire** capable of sth/doing

capacité [kapasite] nf (compétence) ability; (JUR, contenance) capacity

cape [kap] nf cape, cloak; **rire sous ~** to laugh up one's sleeve

CAPES [kapɛs] sigle m (= Certificat d'aptitude pédagogique à l'enseignement secondaire) teaching diploma

capillaire [kapilɛʀ] adj (soins, lotion) hair cpd; (vaisseau etc) capillary

capitaine [kapitɛn] nm captain

capital, e, -aux [kapital, o] adj (œuvre) major; (question, rôle) fundamental ♦ nm capital; (fig) stock; **d'une importance ~e** of prime importance; voir aussi **capitaux**; **~ (social)** authorized capital; **capitale** nf (ville) capital; (lettre) capital (letter); **capitalisme** nm capitalism; **capitaliste** adj, nm/f capitalist; **capitaux** nmpl (fonds) capital sg

capitonné, e [kapitɔne] adj padded

caporal, -aux [kapɔʀal, o] nm lance corporal

capot [kapo] nm (AUTO) bonnet (BRIT), hood (US)

capote [kapɔt] nf (de voiture) hood (BRIT), top (US); (fam) condom

capoter [kapɔte] vi (négociations) to founder

câpre [kɑpʀ] nf caper

caprice [kapʀis] nm whim, caprice; **faire des ~s** to make a fuss; **capricieux, -euse** adj (fantasque) capricious, whimsical; (enfant) awkward

Capricorne [kapʀikɔʀn] nm: **le ~** Capricorn

capsule [kapsyl] nf (de bouteille) cap; (BOT etc, spatiale) capsule

capter [kapte] vt (ondes radio) to pick up; (fig) to win, attract

captivant, e [kaptivɑ̃, ɑ̃t] adj captivating

captivité [kaptivite] nf captivity

capturer [kaptyʀe] vt to capture

capuche [kapyʃ] nf hood

capuchon [kapyʃɔ̃] nm hood; (de stylo) cap, top

capucine [kapysin] nf (BOT) nasturtium

caquet [kakɛ] nm: **rabattre le ~ à qn** (fam) to bring sb down a peg or two

caqueter [kakte] vi to cackle

car [kaʀ] nm coach ♦ conj because, for

carabine [kaʀabin] nf rifle

caractère [kaʀaktɛʀ] nm (gén) character; **avoir bon/mauvais ~** to be good-/ill-natured; **en ~s gras** in bold type; **en petits ~s** in small print; **~s d'imprimerie** (block) capitals; **caractériel, le** adj (traits) (of) character; (enfant) emotionally disturbed

caractérisé, e [kaʀakteʀize] adj sheer, downright

caractériser [kaʀakteʀize] vt to be characteristic of

caractéristique [kaʀakteʀistik] adj, nf characteristic

carafe [kaʀaf] nf (pour eau, vin ordinaire) carafe

caraïbe [kaʀaib] adj Caribbean ♦ n: **les C~s** the Caribbean (Islands)

carambolage [kaʀɑ̃bɔlaʒ] nm multiple crash, pileup

caramel [kaʀamɛl] nm (bonbon) caramel, toffee; (substance) caramel

carapace [kaʀapas] nf shell

caravane [kaʀavan] nf caravan; **caravaning** nm caravanning

carbone [kaʀbɔn] nm carbon; (double) carbon (copy); **carbonique** adj: **gaz carbonique** carbon dioxide; **neige carbonique** dry ice; **carbonisé, e** adj charred

carburant [kaʀbyʀɑ̃] nm (motor) fuel

carburateur [kaʀbyʀatœʀ] nm carburettor

carcan [kaʀkɑ̃] nm (fig) yoke, shackles pl

carcasse [kaʀkas] nf carcass; (de véhicule etc) shell

cardiaque [kaʀdjak] adj cardiac, heart

cpd ♦ nm/f heart patient; **être ~** to have heart trouble

cardigan [kaʀdigɑ̃] nm cardigan

cardiologue [kaʀdjɔlɔg] nm/f cardiologist, heart specialist

carême [kaʀɛm] nm: **le C~** Lent

carence [kaʀɑ̃s] nf (manque) deficiency

caresse [kaʀɛs] nf caress

caresser [kaʀese] vt to caress; (animal) to stroke

cargaison [kaʀgɛzɔ̃] nf cargo, freight

cargo [kaʀgo] nm cargo boat, freighter

caricature [kaʀikatyʀ] nf caricature

carie [kaʀi] nf: **la (dentaire)** tooth decay; **une ~** a bad tooth

carillon [kaʀijɔ̃] nm (air, de pendule) chimes pl

caritatif, -ive [kaʀitatif, iv] adj: **organisation caritative** charity

carnassier, -ière [kaʀnasje, jɛʀ] adj carnivorous

carnaval [kaʀnaval] nm carnival

carnet [kaʀnɛ] nm (calepin) notebook; (de tickets, timbres etc) book; **~ de chèques** cheque book; **~ de notes** school report

carotte [kaʀɔt] nf carrot

carpette [kaʀpɛt] nf rug

carré, e [kaʀe] adj square; (fig: franc) straightforward ♦ nm (MATH) square; **mètre/kilomètre ~** square metre/kilometre

carreau, x [kaʀo] nm (par terre) (floor) tile; (au mur) (wall) tile; (de fenêtre) (window) pane; (motif) check, square; (CARTES: couleur) diamonds pl; **tissu à ~x** checked fabric

carrefour [kaʀfuʀ] nm crossroads sg

carrelage [kaʀlaʒ] nm (sol) (tiled) floor

carrelet [kaʀlɛ] nm (poisson) plaice

carrément [kaʀemɑ̃] adv (franchement) straight out, bluntly; (sans hésiter) straight; (intensif) completely; **c'est ~ impossible** it's completely impossible

carrière [kaʀjɛʀ] nf (métier) career; (de roches) quarry; **militaire de ~** professional soldier

carrossable [kaʀɔsabl] *adj* suitable for (motor) vehicles

carrosse [kaʀɔs] *nm* (horse-drawn) coach

carrosserie [kaʀɔsʀi] *nf* body, coachwork *no pl*

carrure [kaʀyʀ] *nf* build; (*fig*) stature, calibre

cartable [kaʀtabl] *nm* satchel, (school)bag

carte [kaʀt] *nf* (*de géographie*) map; (*marine, du ciel*) chart; (*d'abonnement, à jouer*) card; (*au restaurant*) menu; (*aussi*: **~ de visite**) (visiting) card; **à la ~** (*au restaurant*) à la carte; **donner ~ blanche à qn** to give sb a free rein; **~ bancaire** cash card; **~ de crédit** credit card; **~ de fidélité** loyalty card; **~ d'identité** identity card; **~ de séjour** residence permit; **~ grise** (AUTO) ≈ (car) registration book, logbook; **~ postale** postcard; **~ routière** road map; **~ téléphonique** phonecard

carter [kaʀtɛʀ] *nm* sump

carton [kaʀtɔ̃] *nm* (*matériau*) cardboard; (*boîte*) (cardboard) box; **faire un ~** (*fam*) to score a hit; **~ (à dessin)** portfolio; **carton-pâte** *nm* pasteboard

cartouche [kaʀtuʃ] *nf* cartridge; (*de cigarettes*) carton

cas [kɑ] *nm* case; **ne faire aucun ~ de** to take no notice of; **en aucun ~** on no account; **au ~ où** in case; **en ~ de** in case of, in the event of; **en ~ de besoin** if need be; **en tout ~** in any case, at any rate

casanier, -ière [kazanje, jɛʀ] *adj* stay-at-home

cascade [kaskad] *nf* waterfall, cascade; (*fig*) stream, torrent; **cascadeur, -euse** *nm/f* stuntman(-girl)

case [kɑz] *nf* (*hutte*) hut; (*compartiment*) compartment; (*sur un formulaire, de mots croisés etc*) box

caser [kaze] (*fam*) *vt* (*placer*) to put (away); (*loger*) to put up; **se ~** *vi* (*se marier*) to settle down; (*trouver un em-*

ploi) to find a (steady) job

caserne [kazɛʀn] *nf* barracks *pl*

cash [kaʃ] *adv*: **payer ~** to pay cash down

casier [kazje] *nm* (*pour courrier*) pigeon-hole; (*compartiment*) compartment; (*à clef*) locker; **~ judiciaire** police record

casino [kazino] *nm* casino

casque [kask] *nm* helmet; (*chez le coiffeur*) (hair-)drier; (*pour audition*) (head-)phones *pl*, headset

casquette [kaskɛt] *nf* cap

cassant, e [kasɑ̃, ɑ̃t] *adj* brittle; (*fig: ton*) curt, abrupt

cassation [kasasjɔ̃] *nf*: **cour de ~** final court of appeal

casse [kɑs] (*fam*) *nf* (*pour voitures*): **mettre à la ~** to scrap; (*dégâts*): **il y a eu de la ~** there were a lot of breakages; **casse-cou** *adj inv* daredevil, reckless; **casse-croûte** *nm inv* snack; **casse-noix** *nm inv* nutcrackers *pl*; **casse-pieds** (*fam*) *adj inv*: **il est casse-pieds** he's a pain in the neck

casser [kase] *vt* to break; (*JUR*) to quash; **se ~** *vi* to break; **~ les pieds à qn** (*fam: irriter*) to get on sb's nerves; **se ~ la tête** (*fam*) to go to a lot of trouble

casserole [kasʀɔl] *nf* saucepan

casse-tête [kastɛt] *nm inv* (*difficultés*) headache (*fig*)

cassette [kasɛt] *nf* (*bande magnétique*) cassette; (*coffret*) casket

casseur [kasœʀ] *nm* hooligan

cassis [kasis] *nm* blackcurrant

cassoulet [kasulɛ] *nm* bean and sausage hot-pot

cassure [kasyʀ] *nf* break, crack

castor [kastɔʀ] *nm* beaver

castrer [kastʀe] *vt* (*mâle*) to castrate; (*: cheval*) to geld; (*femelle*) to spay

catalogue [katalɔg] *nm* catalogue

cataloguer [katalɔge] *vt* to catalogue, to list; (*péj*) to put a label on

catalyseur [katalizœʀ] *nm* catalyst; **catalytique** *adj*: **pot catalytique** catalytic convertor

catastrophe [katastʁɔf] nf catastrophe, disaster; **catastrophé, e** (fam) adj stunned

catch [katʃ] nm (all-in) wrestling

catéchisme [kateʃism] nm catechism

catégorie [kategɔʁi] nf category; **catégorique** adj categorical

cathédrale [katedʁal] nf cathedral

catholique [katɔlik] adj, nm/f (Roman) Catholic; **pas très ~** a bit shady ou fishy

catimini [katimini]: **en ~** adv on the sly

cauchemar [koʃmaʁ] nm nightmare

cause [koz] nf cause; (JUR) lawsuit, case; **à ~ de** because of, owing to; **pour ~ de** on account of; **(et) pour ~** and for (a very) good reason; **être en ~** (intérêts) to be at stake; **remettre en ~** to challenge; **causer** vt to cause ♦ vi to chat, talk; **causerie** nf (conférence) talk; **causette** nf: **faire la causette** to have a chat

caution [kosjɔ̃] nf guarantee, security; (JUR) bail (bond); (fig) backing, support; **libéré sous ~** released on bail; **cautionner** vt (répondre de) to guarantee; (soutenir) to support

cavalcade [kavalkad] nf (fig) stampede

cavalier, -ière [kavalje, jɛʁ] adj (désinvolte) offhand ♦ nm/f rider; (au bal) partner ♦ nm (ÉCHECS) knight

cave [kav] nf cellar

caveau, x [kavo] nm vault

caverne [kavɛʁn] nf cave

CCP sigle m = **compte chèques postaux**

CD sigle m (= compact disc) CD

CD-ROM [sederɔm] sigle nm CD-ROM

CE n abr (= Communauté Européenne) EC

MOT-CLÉ

ce, cette [sə, sɛt] (devant nm **cet** + voyelle ou h aspiré, pl **ces**) dét (proximité) this; these pl; (non-proximité) that; those pl;

cette maison(-ci/là) this/that house; cette nuit (qui vient) tonight; (passée) last night

♦ pron 1: c'est c'est ou it is; c'est un peintre he's ou he is a painter; ce sont des peintres they're ou they are painters; c'est le facteur (à la porte) it's the postman; qui est-ce? who is it?; (en désignant) who is he/she?; qu'est-ce? what is it?

2: ce qui, ce que pron (chose qui): il est bête, ce qui me chagrine he's stupid, which saddens me; tout ce qui bouge everything that ou which moves; tout ce que je sais all I know; ce dont j'ai parlé what I talked about; ce que c'est grand! it's so big!; voir aussi -ci; est-ce que; n'est-ce pas; c'est-à-dire

ceci [səsi] pron this

cécité [sesite] nf blindness

céder [sede] vt (donner) to give up ♦ vi (chaise, barrage) to give way; (personne) to give in; **~ à** to yield to, to give in to

CEDEX [sedɛks] sigle m (= courrier d'entreprise à distribution exceptionnelle) postal service for bulk users

cédille [sedij] nf cedilla

cèdre [sedʁ] nm cedar

CEI sigle f (= Communauté des États Indépendants) CIS

ceinture [sɛ̃tyʁ] nf belt; (taille) waist; **~ de sécurité** safety ou seat belt

cela [s(ə)la] pron that; (comme sujet indéfini) it; **quand/où ~?** when/where (was that?)

célèbre [selɛbʁ] adj famous; **célébrer** vt to celebrate

céleri [sɛlʁi] nm: **~(-rave)** celeriac; **~ (en branche)** celery

célibat [seliba] nm (homme) bachelorhood; (femme) spinsterhood; (prêtre) celibacy; **célibataire** adj single, unmarried ♦ nm bachelor ♦ nf unmarried woman

celle(s) [sɛl] *pron voir* **celui**

cellier [selje] *nm* storeroom (for wine)

cellule [selyl] *nf* (*gén*) cell

cellulite [selylit] *nf* excess fat, cellulite

MOT-CLÉ
---

celui, celle [səlɥi, sɛl] (*mpl* **ceux**, *fpl* **celles**) *pron* 1: **celui-ci/là**, **celle-ci/là** this one/that one; **ceux-ci, celles-ci** these (ones); **ceux-là, celles-là** those (ones); **celui de mon frère** my brother's; **celui du salon/du dessous** the one in the lounge/below 2: **celui qui bouge** the one which *ou* that moves; (*personne*) the one who moves; **celui que je vois** the one (which *ou* that) I see; **celui dont je parle** the one (whom) I'm talking about 3 (*valeur indéfinie*): **celui qui veut** whoever wants

---

cendre [sɑ̃dʀ] *nf* ash; **~s** *nfpl* (*d'un défunt*) ashes; **sous la ~** (*CULIN*) in (the) embers; **cendrier** *nm* ashtray

cène [sɛn] *nf*: **la ~** (Holy) Communion

censé, e [sɑ̃se] *adj*: **être ~ faire** to be supposed to do

censeur [sɑ̃sœʀ] *nm* (*SCOL*) deputy-head (*BRIT*), vice-principal (*US*)

censure [sɑ̃syʀ] *nf* censorship; **censurer** *vt* (*CINÉMA, PRESSE*) to censor; (*POL*) to censure

cent [sɑ̃] *num* a hundred, one hundred ♦ *nm* (*US, Canada etc*) cent; (*partie de l'euro*) cent; **centaine** *nf*: **une centaine (de)** about a hundred, a hundred *ou* so; **des centaines (de)** hundreds (of); **centenaire** *adj* hundred-year-old ♦ *nm* (*anniversaire*) centenary; **centième** *num* hundredth; **centigrade** *nm* centigrade; **centilitre** *nm* centilitre; **centime** *nm* centime; **centime d'euro** cent; **centimètre** *nm* centimetre; (*ruban*) tape measure, measuring tape

central, e, -aux [sɑ̃tʀal, o] *adj* central ♦ *nm*: **~ (téléphonique)** (telephone)

exchange; **centrale** *nf* power station

centre [sɑ̃tʀ] *nm* centre; **~ commercial** shopping centre; **~ d'appels** call centre; **~ de loisirs** leisure centre; **centre-ville** *nm* town centre, downtown (area) (*US*)

centuple [sɑ̃typl] *nm*: **le ~ de qch** a hundred times sth; **au ~** a hundredfold

cep [sɛp] *nm* (vine) stock

cèpe [sɛp] *nm* (edible) boletus

cependant [s(ə)pɑ̃dɑ̃] *adv* however

céramique [seʀamik] *nf* ceramics *sg*

cercle [sɛʀkl] *nm* circle

cercueil [sɛʀkœj] *nm* coffin

céréale [seʀeal] *nf* cereal; **~s** *nfpl* breakfast cereal

cérémonie [seʀemɔni] *nf* ceremony

cerf [sɛʀ] *nm* stag

cerfeuil [sɛʀfœj] *nm* chervil

cerf-volant [sɛʀvɔlɑ̃] *nm* kite

cerise [s(ə)ʀiz] *nf* cherry; **cerisier** *nm* cherry (tree)

cerne [sɛʀn] *nm*: **avoir des ~s** to have shadows *ou* dark rings under one's eyes

cerner [sɛʀne] *vt* (*MIL etc*) to surround; (*fig: problème*) to delimit, define

certain, e [sɛʀtɛ̃, ɛn] *adj* certain ♦ *dét* certain; **d'un ~ âge** past one's prime, not so young; **un ~ temps** (quite) some time; **~s** ♦ *pron* some; **certainement** *adv* (*probablement*) most probably *ou* likely; (*bien sûr*) certainly, of course

certes [sɛʀt] *adv* (*sans doute*) admittedly; (*bien sûr*) of course

certificat [sɛʀtifika] *nm* certificate

certifier [sɛʀtifje] *vt*: **~ qch à qn** to assure sb of sth; **copie certifiée conforme** certified copy of the original

certitude [sɛʀtityd] *nf* certainty

cerveau, x [sɛʀvo] *nm* brain

cervelas [sɛʀvəla] *nm* saveloy

cervelle [sɛʀvɛl] *nf* (*ANAT*) brain; (*CULIN*) brains

ces [se] *dét voir* **ce**

CES *sigle m* (= *Collège d'enseignement*

secondaire) ≃ (junior) secondary school (*BRIT*)

cesse [sɛs]: **sans ~** *adv* (*tout le temps*) continually, constantly; (*sans interruption*) continuously; **il n'a eu de ~ que** he did not rest until; **cesser** *vt* to stop ♦ *vi* to stop, cease; **cesser de faire** to stop doing; **cessez-le-feu** *nm inv* ceasefire

c'est-à-dire [sɛtadiʀ] *adv* that is (to say)

cet, cette [sɛt] *dét voir* **ce**

ceux [sø] *pron voir* **celui**

CFC *abr* (= *chlorofluorocarbon*) CFC

CFDT *sigle f* (= *Confédération française démocratique du travail*) French trade union

CGT *sigle f* (= *Confédération générale du travail*) French trade union

chacun, e [ʃakœ̃, yn] *pron* each; (*indéfini*) everyone, everybody

chagrin [ʃagʀɛ̃] *nm* grief, sorrow; **avoir du ~** to be grieved; **chagriner** *vt* to grieve

chahut [ʃay] *nm* uproar; **chahuter** *vt* to rag, bait ♦ *vi* to make an uproar

chaîne [ʃɛn] *nf* chain; (*RADIO, TV: stations*) channel; **~s** *nfpl* (*AUTO*) (snow) chains; **travail à la ~** production line work; (*de montage*) production ou assembly line; **~ de montagnes** mountain range; **~ (hi-fi)** hi-fi system; **~ laser** CD player; **~ (stéréo)** stereo (system); **chaînette** *nf* (small) chain

chair [ʃɛʀ] *nf* flesh; **avoir la ~ de poule** to have goosepimples ou gooseflesh; **bien en ~** plump, well-padded; **en ~ et en os** in the flesh; **~ à saucisse** sausage meat

chaire [ʃɛʀ] *nf* (*d'église*) pulpit; (*d'université*) chair

chaise [ʃɛz] *nf* chair; **~ longue** deckchair

châle [ʃal] *nm* shawl

chaleur [ʃalœʀ] *nf* heat; (*fig: accueil*) warmth; **chaleureux, -euse** *adj* warm

chaloupe [ʃalup] *nf* launch; (*de sauve-*

tage) lifeboat

chalumeau, x [ʃalymo] *nm* blowlamp, blowtorch

chalutier [ʃalytje] *nm* trawler

chamailler [ʃamaje]: **se ~** *vi* to squabble, bicker

chambouler [ʃãbule] (*fam*) *vt* to disrupt, turn upside down

chambre [ʃãbʀ] *nf* bedroom; (*POL, COMM*) chamber; **faire ~ à part** to sleep in separate rooms; **~ à air** (*de pneu*) (inner) tube; **~ à coucher** bedroom; **~ à un lit/deux lits** (*à l'hôtel*) single-/twin-bedded room; **~ d'amis** spare ou guest room; **~ noire** (*PHOTO*) dark room; **chambrer** *vt* (*vin*) to bring to room temperature

chameau, x [ʃamo] *nm* camel

chamois [ʃamwa] *nm* chamois

champ [ʃã] *nm* field; **~ de bataille** battlefield; **~ de courses** racecourse; **~ de tir** rifle range

champagne [ʃãpaɲ] *nm* champagne

champêtre [ʃãpɛtʀ] *adj* country *cpd*, rural

champignon [ʃãpiɲɔ̃] *nm* mushroom; (*terme générique*) fungus; **~ de Paris** button mushroom

champion, ne [ʃãpjɔ̃, jɔn] *adj, nm/f* champion; **championnat** *nm* championship

chance [ʃãs] *nf*: **la ~** luck; **~s** *nfpl* (*possibilités*) chances; **avoir de la ~** to be lucky; **il a des ~s de réussir** he's got a good chance of passing

chanceler [ʃãs(ə)le] *vi* to totter

chancelier [ʃãsəlje] *nm* (*allemand*) chancellor

chanceux, -euse [ʃãsø, øz] *adj* lucky

chandail [ʃãdaj] *nm* (thick) sweater

Chandeleur [ʃãdlœʀ] *nf*: **la ~** Candlemas

chandelier [ʃãdəlje] *nm* candlestick

chandelle [ʃãdɛl] *nf* (*tallow*) candle; **dîner aux ~s** candlelight dinner

change [ʃãʒ] *nm* (*devises*) exchange

changement [ʃãʒmã] *nm* change;

de vitesses gears pl

changer [ʃɑ̃ʒe] vt (modifier) to change, alter; (remplacer, COMM) to change ♦ vi to change, alter; **se ~** vi to change (o.s.); **~ de** (remplacer: adresse, nom, voiture etc) to change one's; (échanger: place, train etc) to change; **~ d'avis** to change one's mind; **~ de vitesse** to change gear

chanson [ʃɑ̃sɔ̃] nf song

chant [ʃɑ̃] nm song; (art vocal) singing; (d'église) hymn

chantage [ʃɑ̃taʒ] nm blackmail; **faire du ~** to use blackmail

chanter [ʃɑ̃te] vt, vi to sing; **si cela lui chante** (fam) if he feels like it; **chanteur, -euse** nm/f singer

chantier [ʃɑ̃tje] nm (building) site; (sur une route) roadworks pl; **mettre en ~** to put in hand; **~ naval** shipyard

chantilly [ʃɑ̃tiji] nf voir **crème**

chantonner [ʃɑ̃tɔne] vi, vt to sing to oneself, hum

chanvre [ʃɑ̃vʁ] nm hemp

chaparder [ʃapaʁde] (fam) vt to pinch

chapeau, x [ʃapo] nm hat; **~!** well done!

chapelet [ʃaplɛ] nm (REL) rosary

chapelle [ʃapɛl] nf chapel

chapelure [ʃaplyʁ] nf (dried) breadcrumbs pl

chapiteau, x [ʃapito] nm (de cirque) marquee, big top

chapitre [ʃapitʁ] nm chapter

chaque [ʃak] dét each, every; (indéfini) every

char [ʃaʁ] nm (MIL): **~ (d'assaut)** tank; **~ à voile** sand yacht

charabia [ʃaʁabja] (péj) nm gibberish

charade [ʃaʁad] nf riddle; (mimée) charade

charbon [ʃaʁbɔ̃] nm coal; **~ de bois** charcoal

charcuterie [ʃaʁkytʁi] nf (magasin) pork butcher's shop and delicatessen; (produits) cooked pork meats pl; **charcutier, -ière** nm/f pork butcher

chardon [ʃaʁdɔ̃] nm thistle

charge [ʃaʁʒ] nf (fardeau) load, burden; (explosif, ÉLEC, MIL, JUR) charge; (rôle, mission) responsibility; **~s** nfpl (du loyer) service charges; **à la ~ de** (dépendant de) dependent upon; (aux frais de) chargeable to; **prendre en ~** to take charge of; (suj: véhicule) to take on; (dépenses) to take care of; **~s sociales** social security contributions

chargé, e [ʃaʁʒe] adj (emploi du temps, journée) full, heavy

chargement [ʃaʁʒəmɑ̃] nm (objets) load

charger [ʃaʁʒe] vt (voiture, fusil, caméra) to load; (batterie) to charge ♦ vi (MIL etc) to charge; **se ~ de** to see to; **~ qn de (faire) qch** to put sb in charge of (doing) sth

chariot [ʃaʁjo] nm trolley; (charrette) waggon

charité [ʃaʁite] nf charity

charmant, e [ʃaʁmɑ̃, ɑ̃t] adj charming

charme [ʃaʁm] nm charm; **charmer** vt to charm

charnel, le [ʃaʁnɛl] adj carnal

charnière [ʃaʁnjɛʁ] nf hinge; (fig) turning-point

charnu, e [ʃaʁny] adj fleshy

charpente [ʃaʁpɑ̃t] nf frame(work); **charpentier** nm carpenter

charpie [ʃaʁpi] nf: **en ~** (fig) in shreds ou ribbons

charrette [ʃaʁɛt] nf cart

charrier [ʃaʁje] vt (entraîner: fleuve) to carry (along); (transporter) to cart, carry

charrue [ʃaʁy] nf plough (BRIT), plow (US)

charter [ʃaʁtɛʁ] nm (vol) charter flight

chasse [ʃas] nf hunting; (au fusil) shooting; (poursuite) chase; (aussi: **~ d'eau**) flush; **~ gardée** private hunting grounds pl; **prendre en ~** to give chase to; **tirer la ~ (d'eau)** to flush the toilet, pull the chain; **~ à courre** hunting; **chasse-neige** nm inv snowplough (BRIT), snowplow (US); **chasser** vt to hunt; (*expulser*) to chase away *ou* out, drive away *ou* out; **chasseur, -euse** *nm/f* hunter ♦ *nm* (*avion*) fighter

châssis [ʃasi] *nm* (AUTO) chassis; (*cadre*) frame

chat [ʃa] *nm* cat

châtaigne [ʃatɛɲ] *nf* chestnut; **châtaignier** *nm* chestnut (tree)

châtain [ʃatɛ̃] *adj inv* (*cheveux*) chestnut (brown); (*personne*) chestnut-haired

château, x [ʃato] *nm* (*forteresse*) castle; (*résidence royale*) palace; (*manoir*) mansion; ~ **d'eau** water tower; ~ **fort** stronghold, fortified castle

châtier [ʃatje] *vt* to punish; **châtiment** *nm* punishment

chaton [ʃatɔ̃] *nm* (ZOOL) kitten

chatouiller [ʃatuje] *vt* to tickle; **chatouilleux, -euse** *adj* ticklish; (*fig*) touchy, over-sensitive

chatoyer [ʃatwaje] *vi* to shimmer

châtrer [ʃatʀe] *vt* (*mâle*) to castrate; (: *cheval*) to geld; (*femelle*) to spay

chatte [ʃat] *nf* (she-)cat

chaud, e [ʃo, ʃod] *adj* (*gén*) warm; (*très* ~) hot; **il fait** ~ it's warm; it's hot; **avoir** ~ to be warm; to be hot; **ça me tient** ~ it keeps me warm; **rester au** ~ to stay in the warm

chaudière [ʃodjɛʀ] *nf* boiler

chaudron [ʃodʀɔ̃] *nm* cauldron

chauffage [ʃofaʒ] *nm* heating; ~ **central** central heating

chauffard [ʃofaʀ] *nm* (*péj*) reckless driver

chauffe-eau [ʃofo] *nm inv* water-heater

chauffer [ʃofe] *vt* to heat ♦ *vi* to heat up, warm up; (*trop*: *moteur*) to overheat; **se** ~ *vi* (*au soleil*) to warm o.s

chauffeur [ʃofœʀ] *nm* driver; (*privé*) chauffeur

chaume [ʃom] *nm* (*du toit*) thatch; **chaumière** *nf* (thatched) cottage

chaussée [ʃose] *nf* road(way)

chausse-pied [ʃospje] *nm* shoe-horn

chausser [ʃose] *vt* (*bottes, skis*) to put on; (*enfant*) to put shoes on; ~ **du 38/**

42 to take size 38/42

chaussette [ʃosɛt] *nf* sock

chausson [ʃosɔ̃] *nm* slipper; (*de bébé*) bootee; ~ **(aux pommes)** (apple) turnover

chaussure [ʃosyʀ] *nf* shoe; ~**s à talon** high-heeled shoes; ~**s de marche** walking shoes/boots; ~**s de ski** ski boots

chauve [ʃov] *adj* bald; **chauve-souris** *nf* bat

chauvin, e [ʃovɛ̃, in] *adj* chauvinistic

chaux [ʃo] *nf* lime; **blanchi à la** ~ whitewashed

chavirer [ʃaviʀe] *vi* to capsize

chef [ʃɛf] *nm* head, leader; (*de cuisine*) chef; ~ **d'accusation** charge; ~ **d'entreprise** company head; ~ **d'état** head of state; ~ **de famille** head of the family; ~ **de gare** station master; ~ **d'orchestre** conductor; ~ **de service** department head; **chef-d'œuvre** *nm* masterpiece; **chef-lieu** *nm* county town

chemin [ʃ(ə)mɛ̃] *nm* path; (*itinéraire, direction, trajet*) way; **en** ~ on the way; ~ **de fer** railway (BRIT), railroad (US); **par** ~ **de fer** by rail

cheminée [ʃ(ə)mine] *nf* chimney; (*à l'intérieur*) chimney piece, fireplace; (*de bateau*) funnel

cheminement [ʃ(ə)minmã] *nm* progress

cheminot [ʃ(ə)mino] *nm* railwayman

chemise [ʃ(ə)miz] *nf* shirt; (*dossier*) folder; ~ **de nuit** nightdress

chemisier [ʃ(ə)mizje, jɛʀ] *nm* blouse

chenal, -aux [ʃənal, o] *nm* channel

chêne [ʃɛn] *nm* oak (tree); (*bois*) oak

chenil [ʃ(ə)nil] *nm* kennels *pl*

chenille [ʃ(ə)nij] *nf* (ZOOL) caterpillar

chèque [ʃɛk] *nm* cheque (BRIT), check (US); ~ **sans provision** bad cheque; ~ **de voyage** traveller's cheque; **chéquier** [ʃekje] *nm* cheque book

cher, -ère [ʃɛʀ] *adj* (*aimé*) dear; (*coûteux*) expensive, dear ♦ *adv*: **ça**

coûte ~ it's expensive

chercher [ʃɛʀʃe] vt to look for; (gloire etc) to seek; **aller** ~ to go for, go and fetch; ~ **à faire** to try to do; **chercheur, -euse** nm/f researcher, research worker

chère [ʃɛʀ] adj voir **cher**

chéri, e [ʃeʀi] adj beloved, dear; **(mon)** ~ darling

chérir [ʃeʀiʀ] vt to cherish

cherté [ʃɛʀte] nf: **la ~ de la vie** the high cost of living

chétif, -ive [ʃetif, iv] adj (enfant) puny

cheval, -aux [ʃ(ə)val, o] nm horse; (AUTO): ~ **(vapeur)** horsepower no pl; **faire du** ~ to ride; **à** ~ on horseback; **à** ~ **sur** astride; (fig) overlapping; ~ **de course** racehorse

chevalet [ʃ(ə)valɛ] nm easel

chevalier [ʃ(ə)valje] nm knight

chevalière [ʃ(ə)valjɛʀ] nf signet ring

chevalin, e [ʃ(ə)valɛ̃, in] adj: **boucherie** ~ horse-meat butcher's

chevaucher [ʃ(ə)voʃe] vi (aussi: **se** ~) to overlap (each other) ♦ vt to be astride, straddle

chevaux [ʃ(ə)vo] nmpl de **cheval**

chevelu, e [ʃəv(ə)ly] adj (péj) long-haired

chevelure [ʃəv(ə)lyʀ] nf hair no pl

chevet [ʃ(ə)vɛ] nm: **au ~ de qn** at sb's bedside; **lampe de** ~ bedside lamp

cheveu, x [ʃ(ə)vø] nm hair; ~**x** nmpl (chevelure) hair sg; **avoir les ~x courts** to have short hair

cheville [ʃ(ə)vij] nf (ANAT) ankle; (de bois) peg; (pour une vis) plug

chèvre [ʃɛvʀ] nf (she-)goat

chevreau, x [ʃəvʀo] nm kid

chèvrefeuille [ʃɛvʀəfœj] nm honeysuckle

chevreuil [ʃəvʀœj] nm roe deer inv; (CULIN) venison

chevronné, e [ʃəvʀɔne] adj seasoned

MOT-CLÉ

chez [ʃe] prép **1** (à la demeure de) at;
(: direction) to; **chez qn** at/to sb's house ou place; **chez moi** at home; (direction) home
2 (+profession) at; (: direction) to; **chez le boulanger/dentiste** at/to the baker's/dentist's
3 (dans le caractère, l'œuvre de) in; **chez les renards/Racine** in foxes/Racine

chez-soi [ʃeswa] nm inv home

chic [ʃik] adj inv chic, smart; (fam: généreux) nice, decent ♦ nm stylishness; ~ **(alors)!** (fam) great!; **avoir le ~ de** to have the knack of

chicane [ʃikan] nf (querelle) squabble; **chicaner** vi (ergoter): **chicaner sur** to quibble about

chiche [ʃiʃ] adj niggardly, mean ♦ excl (à un défi) you're on!

chichis [ʃiʃi] nmpl fuss sg

chicorée [ʃikɔʀe] nf (café) chicory; (salade) endive

chien [ʃjɛ̃] nm dog; ~ **de garde** guard dog; **chien-loup** nm wolfhound

chiendent [ʃjɛ̃dɑ̃] nm couch grass

chienne [ʃjɛn] nf dog, bitch

chier [ʃje] (fam!) vi to crap (!)

chiffon [ʃifɔ̃] nm (piece of) rag; **chiffonner** vt to crumple; (fam: tracasser) to concern

chiffre [ʃifʀ] nm (représentant un nombre) figure, numeral; (montant, total) total, sum; **en ~s ronds** in round figures; ~ **d'affaires** turnover; **chiffrer** vt (dépense) to put a figure to, assess; (message) to (en)code, cipher; **se chiffrer à** to add up to, amount to

chignon [ʃiɲɔ̃] nm chignon, bun

Chili [ʃili] nm: **le** ~ Chile; **chilien, ne** adj Chilean ♦ nm/f: **Chilien, ne** Chilean

chimie [ʃimi] nf chemistry; **chimique** adj chemical; **produits chimiques** chemicals

chimpanzé [ʃɛ̃pɑ̃ze] nm chimpanzee

Chine [ʃin] nf: **la** ~ China; **chinois, e** adj Chinese ♦ nm/f: **Chinois, e** Chinese

♦ *nm* (LING) Chinese

chiot [ʃjo] *nm* pup(py)

chiper [ʃipe] (*fam*) *vt* to pinch

chipoter [ʃipɔte] (*fam*) *vi* (*ergoter*) to quibble

chips [ʃips] *nfpl* crisps (BRIT), (potato) chips (US)

chiquenaude [ʃiknod] *nf* flick, flip

chirurgical, e, -aux [ʃiRyRʒikal, o] *adj* surgical

chirurgie [ʃiRyRʒi] *nf* surgery; **~ esthétique** plastic surgery; **chirurgien, ne** *nm/f* surgeon

chlore [klɔR] *nm* chlorine

choc [ʃɔk] *nm* (*heurt*) impact, shock; (*collision*) crash; (*moral*) shock; (*affrontement*) clash

chocolat [ʃɔkɔla] *nm* chocolate; **~ au lait** milk chocolate; **~ (chaud)** hot chocolate

chœur [kœR] *nm* (*chorale*) choir; (OPÉRA, THÉÂTRE) chorus; **en ~** in chorus

choisir [ʃwaziR] *vt* to choose, select

choix [ʃwa] *nm* choice, selection; **avoir le ~** to have the choice; **premier ~** (COMM) class one; **de ~** choice, selected; **au ~** as you wish

chômage [ʃomaʒ] *nm* unemployment; **mettre au ~** to make redundant, put out of work; **être au ~** to be unemployed *ou* out of work; **chômeur, -euse** *nm/f* unemployed person

chope [ʃɔp] *nf* tankard

choper [ʃɔpe] (*fam*) *vt* (*objet, maladie*) to catch

choquer [ʃɔke] *vt* (*offenser*) to shock; (*deuil*) to shake

chorale [kɔRal] *nf* choir

choriste [kɔRist] *nm/f* choir member; (OPÉRA) chorus member

chose [ʃoz] *nf* thing; **c'est peu de ~** it's nothing really

chou, x [ʃu] *nm* cabbage; **mon petit ~** (my) sweetheart; **~ à la crème** choux bun; **~x de Bruxelles** Brussels sprouts; **chouchou, te** (*fam*) *nm/f* darling; (SCOL) teacher's pet; **choucroute** *nf*

sauerkraut

chouette [ʃwet] *nf* owl **♦** *adj* (*fam*) great, smashing

chou-fleur [ʃuflœR] *nm* cauliflower

choyer [ʃwaje] *vt* (*dorloter*) to cherish; (: *excessivement*) to pamper

chrétien, ne [kRetjɛ̃, jɛn] *adj, nm/f* Christian

Christ [kRist] *nm*: **le ~** Christ; **christianisme** *nm* Christianity

chrome [kRom] *nm* chromium; **chromé, e** *adj* chromium-plated

chronique [kRɔnik] *adj* chronic **♦** *nf* (*de journal*) column, page; (*historique*) chronicle; (RADIO, TV): **la ~ sportive** the sports review

chronologique [kRɔnɔlɔʒik] *adj* chronological

chronomètre [kRɔnɔmɛtR] *nm* stopwatch; **chronométrer** *vt* to time

chrysanthème [kRizɑ̃tɛm] *nm* chrysanthemum

chuchotement [ʃyʃɔtmɑ̃] *nm* whisper

chuchoter [ʃyʃɔte] *vt, vi* to whisper

chut [ʃyt] *excl* sh!

chute [ʃyt] *nf* fall; (*déchet*) scrap; **faire une ~ (de 10 m)** to fall (10 m); **~ (d'eau)** waterfall; **la ~ des cheveux** hair loss; **~ libre** free fall; **~s de pluie/neige** rain/snowfalls

Chypre [ʃipR] *nm/f* Cyprus

-ci [si] *adv voir* **par ♦** *dét*: **ce garçon-~/-là** this/that boy; **ces femmes-~/-là** these/those women

cible [sibl] *nf* target

ciboulette [sibulet] *nf* (small) chive

cicatrice [sikatRis] *nf* scar; **cicatriser** *vt* to heal

ci-contre [sikɔ̃tR] *adv* opposite

ci-dessous [sidəsu] *adv* below

ci-dessus [sidəsy] *adv* above

cidre [sidR] *nm* cider

Cie *abr* (= *compagnie*) Co.

ciel [sjɛl] *nm* sky; (REL) heaven; **cieux** *nmpl* (REL) heaven *sg*; **à ~ ouvert** open-air; (*mine*) open-cast

cierge [sjɛRʒ] *nm* candle

cieux [sjø] *nmpl de* **ciel**

cigale [sigal] *nf* cicada

cigare [sigaʀ] *nm* cigar

cigarette [sigaʀɛt] *nf* cigarette

ci-gît [siʒi] *adv +vb* here lies

cigogne [sigɔɲ] *nf* stork

ci-inclus, e [siɛ̃kly, yz] *adj, adv* enclosed

ci-joint, e [siʒwɛ̃, ɛt] *adj, adv* enclosed

cil [sil] *nm* (eye)lash

cime [sim] *nf* top; (*montagne*) peak

ciment [simɑ̃] *nm* cement

cimetière [simtjɛʀ] *nm* cemetery; (*d'église*) churchyard

cinéaste [sineast] *nm/f* film-maker

cinéma [sinema] *nm* cinema; **cinématographique** *adj* film *cpd*, cinema *cpd*

cinglant, e [sɛ̃glɑ̃, ɑ̃t] *adj* (*remarque*) biting

cinglé, e [sɛ̃gle] (*fam*) *adj* crazy

cinq [sɛ̃k] *num* five; **cinquantaine** [sɛ̃kɑ̃tɛn] *nf*: **une cinquantaine (de)** about fifty; **avoir la cinquantaine** (*âge*) to be around fifty; **cinquante** *num* fifty; **cinquantenaire** *adj, nm/f* fifty-year-old; **cinquième** *num* fifth

cintre [sɛ̃tʀ] *nm* coat-hanger

cintré, e [sɛ̃tʀe] *adj* (*chemise*) fitted

cirage [siʀaʒ] *nm* (shoe) polish

circonflexe [siʀkɔ̃flɛks] *adj*: **accent ~** circumflex accent

circonscription [siʀkɔ̃skʀipsjɔ̃] *nf* district; **~ électorale** (*d'un député*) constituency

circonscrire [siʀkɔ̃skʀiʀ] *vt* (*sujet*) to define, delimit; (*incendie*) to contain

circonstance [siʀkɔ̃stɑ̃s] *nf* circumstance; (*occasion*) occasion; **~s atténuantes** mitigating circumstances

circuit [siʀkɥi] *nm* (*ÉLEC, TECH*) circuit; (*trajet*) tour, (round) trip

circulaire [siʀkylɛʀ] *adj, nf* circular

circulation [siʀkylasjɔ̃] *nf* circulation; (*AUTO*): **la ~** (the) traffic

circuler [siʀkyle] *vi* (*sang, devises*) to circulate; (*véhicules*) to drive (along); (*passants*) to walk along; (*train, bus*) to

run; **faire ~** (*nouvelle*) to spread (about), circulate; (*badauds*) to move on

cire [siʀ] *nf* wax; **ciré** *nm* oilskin; **cirer** *vt* to wax, polish

cirque [siʀk] *nm* circus; (*fig*) chaos, bedlam; **quel ~!** what a carry-on!

cisaille(s) [sizaj] *nf(pl)* (gardening) shears *pl*

ciseau, x [sizo] *nm*: **~ (à bois)** chisel; **~x** *nmpl* (*paire de ~x*) (pair of) scissors

ciseler [siz(ə)le] *vt* to chisel, carve

citadin, e [sitadɛ̃, in] *nm/f* city dweller

citation [sitasjɔ̃] *nf* (*d'auteur*) quotation; (*JUR*) summons *sg*

cité [site] *nf* town; (*plus grande*) city; **~ universitaire** students' residences *pl*

citer [site] *vt* (*un auteur*) to quote (from); (*nommer*) to name; (*JUR*) to summon

citerne [sitɛʀn] *nf* tank

citoyen, ne [sitwajɛ̃, jɛn] *nm/f* citizen

citron [sitʀɔ̃] *nm* lemon; **~ vert** lime; **citronnade** *nf* still lemonade

citrouille [sitʀuj] *nf* pumpkin

civet [sivɛ] *nm*: **~ de lapin** rabbit stew

civière [sivjɛʀ] *nf* stretcher

civil, e [sivil] *adj* (*mariage, poli*) civil; (*non militaire*) civilian; **en ~** in civilian clothes; **dans la ~** in civilian life

civilisation [sivilizasjɔ̃] *nf* civilization

clair, e [klɛʀ] *adj* (*pièce*) light, bright; (*eau, son, fig*) clear ♦ *adv*: **voir ~** to see clearly; **tirer qch au ~** to clear sth up, clarify sth; **mettre au ~** (*notes etc*) to tidy up; **~ de lune** ♦ *nm* moonlight; **clairement** *adv* clearly

clairière [klɛʀjɛʀ] *nf* clearing

clairon [klɛʀɔ̃] *nm* bugle; **claironner** *vt* (*fig*) to trumpet, shout from the rooftops

clairsemé, e [klɛʀsəme] *adj* sparse

clairvoyant, e [klɛʀvwajɑ̃, ɑ̃t] *adj* perceptive, clear-sighted

clandestin, e [klɑ̃dɛstɛ̃, in] *adj* clandestine, secret; (*mouvement*) underground; (*travailleur*) illegal; **passager ~**

stowaway

clapier [klapje] *nm* (rabbit) hutch

clapoter [klapɔte] *vi* to lap

claque [klak] *nf* (*gifle*) slap; **claquer** *vi* (*porte*) to bang, slam; (*fam: mourir*) to snuff it ♦ *vt* (*porte*) to slam, bang; (*doigts*) to snap; (*fam: dépenser*) to blow; **il claquait des dents** his teeth were chattering; **être claqué** (*fam*) to be dead tired; **se claquer un muscle** to pull *ou* strain a muscle; **claquettes** *nfpl* tap-dancing *sg*; (*chaussures*) flip-flops

clarinette [klarinɛt] *nf* clarinet

clarté [klarte] *nf* (*luminosité*) brightness; (*d'un son, de l'eau*) clearness; (*d'une explication*) clarity

classe [klas] *nf* class; (SCOL: *local*) class(room); (: *leçon, élèves*) class; **aller en ~** to go to school; **classement** *nm* (*rang*: SCOL) place; (: SPORT) placing; (*liste*: SCOL) class list (in order of merit); (: SPORT) placings *pl*

classer [klase] *vt* (*idées, livres*) to classify; (*papiers*) to file; (*candidat, concurrent*) to grade; (JUR: *affaire*) to close; **se ~ premier/dernier** to come first/last; (SPORT) to finish first/last; **classeur** *nm* (*cahier*) file

classique [klasik] *adj* classical; (*sobre: coupe etc*) classic(al); (*habituel*) standard, classic

clause [kloz] *nf* clause

clavecin [klav(ə)sɛ̃] *nm* harpsichord

clavicule [klavikyl] *nf* collarbone

clavier [klavje] *nm* keyboard

clé [kle] *nf* key; (MUS) clef; (*de mécanicien*) spanner (BRIT), wrench (US); **prix ~s en main** (*d'une voiture*) on-the-road price; **~ anglaise** (monkey) wrench; **~ de contact** ignition key

clef [kle] *nf* = **clé**

clément, e [klemɑ̃, ɑ̃t] *adj* (*temps*) mild; (*indulgent*) lenient

clerc [klɛr] *nm*: **~ de notaire** solicitor's clerk

clergé [klɛrʒe] *nm* clergy

cliché [kliʃe] *nm* (*fig*) cliché; (*négatif*) negative; (*photo*) print

client, e [klijɑ̃, klijɑ̃t] *nm/f* (*acheteur*) customer, client; (*d'hôtel*) guest, patron; (*du docteur*) patient; (*de l'avocat*) client; **clientèle** *nf* (*du magasin*) customers *pl*, clientèle; (*du docteur, de l'avocat*) practice

cligner [kliɲe] *vi*: **~ des yeux** to blink (one's eyes); **~ de l'œil** to wink; **clignotant** *nm* (AUTO) indicator; **clignoter** *vi* (*étoiles etc*) to twinkle; (*lumière*) to flicker

climat [klima] *nm* climate

climatisation [klimatizasjɔ̃] *nf* air conditioning; **climatisé, e** *adj* air-conditioned

clin d'œil [klɛ̃dœj] *nm* wink; **en un ~** in a flash

clinique [klinik] *nf* private hospital

clinquant, e [klɛ̃kɑ̃, ɑ̃t] *adj* flashy

clip [klip] *nm* (*boucle d'oreille*) clip-on; (*vidéo*) **~** (-pop) video

cliqueter [klik(ə)te] *vi* (*ferraille*) to jangle; (*clés*) to jingle

clochard, e [klɔʃar, ard] *nm/f* tramp

cloche [klɔʃ] *nf* (*d'église*) bell; (*fam*) clot; **cloche-pied: à cloche-pied** *adv* on one leg, hopping (along); **clocher** *nm* church tower; (*en pointe*) steeple ♦ *vi* (*fam*) to be *ou* go wrong; **de clocher** (*péj*) parochial

cloison [klwazɔ̃] *nf* partition (wall)

cloître [klwatr] *nm* cloister; **cloîtrer**: **se cloîtrer** to shut o.s. up *ou* away

cloque [klɔk] *nf* blister

clore [klɔr] *vt* to close; **clos, e** *adj* (*voir* **maison**; **huis**

clôture [klotyr] *nf* closure; (*barrière*) enclosure; **clôturer** *vt* (*terrain*) to enclose; (*débats*) to close

clou [klu] *nm* nail; **~s** *nmpl* (*passage ~té*) pedestrian crossing; **pneus à ~s** studded tyres; **le ~ du spectacle** the highlight of the show; **~ de girofle** clove; **clouer** *vt* to nail down *ou* up; **clouer le bec à qn** (*fam*) to shut sb up

clown [klun] *nm* clown

club [klœb] *nm* club

CMU *sigle f* (= *couverture maladie universelle*) system of free health care for those on low incomes

CNRS *sigle m* (= *Centre nationale de la recherche scientifique*) ≃ SERC (*BRIT*), ≃ NSF (*US*)

coaguler [kɔagyle] *vt, vi* (*aussi*: **se ~**: *sang*) to coagulate

coasser [kɔase] *vi* to croak

cobaye [kɔbaj] *nm* guinea-pig

coca [kɔka] *nm* Coke ®

cocaïne [kɔkain] *nf* cocaine

cocasse [kɔkas] *adj* comical, funny

coccinelle [kɔksinɛl] *nf* ladybird (*BRIT*), ladybug (*US*)

cocher [kɔʃe] *vt* to tick off

cochère [kɔʃɛʀ] *adj f*: **porte ~** carriage entrance

cochon, ne [kɔʃɔ̃, ɔn] *nm* pig ♦ *adj* (*fam*) dirty, smutty; **~ d'Inde** guinea pig; **cochonnerie** (*fam*) *nf* (*saleté*) filth; (*marchandise*) rubbish, trash

cocktail [kɔktɛl] *nm* cocktail; (*réception*) cocktail party

coco [kɔko] *nm voir* **noix**

cocorico [kɔkɔʀiko] *excl, nm* cock-a-doodle-do

cocotier [kɔkɔtje] *nm* coconut palm

cocotte [kɔkɔt] *nf* (*en fonte*) casserole; **~ (-minute)** pressure cooker; **ma ~** (*fam*) sweetie (pie)

cocu [kɔky] (*fam*) *nm* cuckold

code [kɔd] *nm* code ♦ *adj*: **phares ~s** dipped lights; **(se mettre en ~(s)** to dip one's (head)lights; **~ à barres** bar code; **~ civil** Common Law; **~ de la route** highway code; **~ pénal** penal code; **~ postal** (*numéro*) post (*BRIT*) ou zip (*US*) code

cœur [kœʀ] *nm* heart; (*CARTES: couleur*) hearts *pl*; (: *carte*) heart; **avoir bon ~** to be kind-hearted; **avoir mal au ~** to feel sick; **par ~** by heart; **de bon ~** willingly; **cela lui tient à ~** that's (very) close to his heart

coffre [kɔfʀ] *nm* (*meuble*) chest; (*d'auto*) boot (*BRIT*), trunk (*US*); **coffre(-fort)** *nm* safe; **coffret** *nm* casket

cognac [kɔɲak] *nm* brandy, cognac

cogner [kɔɲe] *vi* to knock; **se ~ la tête** to bang one's head

cohérent, e [kɔeʀɑ̃, ɑ̃t] *adj* coherent; consistent

cohorte [kɔɔʀt] *nf* troop

cohue [kɔy] *nf* crowd

coi, coite [kwa, kwat] *adj*: **rester ~** to remain silent

coiffe [kwaf] *nf* headdress

coiffé, e [kwafe] *adj*: **bien/mal ~** with tidy/untidy hair

coiffer [kwafe] *vt* (*fig: surmonter*) to cover, top; **se ~** *vi* to do one's hair; **~ qn** to do sb's hair; **coiffeur, -euse** *nm/f* hairdresser; **coiffeuse** *nf* (*table*) dressing table; **coiffure** *nf* (*cheveux*) hairstyle, hairdo; (*art*): **la coiffure** hairdressing

coin [kwɛ̃] *nm* corner; (*pour ~cer*) wedge; **l'épicerie du ~** the local grocer; **dans le ~** (*aux alentours*) in the area, around about; (*habiter*) locally; **je ne suis pas du ~** I'm not from here; **au ~ du feu** by the fireside; **regard en ~** sideways glance

coincé, e [kwɛ̃se] *adj* stuck, jammed; (*fig: inhibé*) inhibited, hung up (*fam*)

coincer [kwɛ̃se] *vt* to jam; (*fam: attraper*) to pinch

coïncidence [kɔɛ̃sidɑ̃s] *nf* coincidence

coïncider [kɔɛ̃side] *vi* to coincide

coing [kwɛ̃] *nm* quince

col [kɔl] *nm* (*de chemise*) collar; (*encolure, cou*) neck; (*de montagne*) pass; **~ de l'utérus** cervix; **~ roulé** polo-neck

colère [kɔlɛʀ] *nf* anger; **une ~** a fit of anger; **(se mettre) en ~** (to get) angry; **coléreux, -euse** *adj*, **colérique** *adj* quick-tempered, irascible

colifichet [kɔlifiʃɛ] *nm* trinket

colimaçon [kɔlimasɔ̃] *nm*: **escalier en**

~ spiral staircase

colin [kɔlɛ̃] nm hake

colique [kɔlik] nf diarrhoea

colis [kɔli] nm parcel

collaborateur, -trice [kɔ(l)labɔʀatœʀ, tʀis] nm/f (aussi POL) collaborator; (d'une revue) contributor

collaborer [kɔ(l)labɔʀe] vi to collaborate; ~ à to collaborate on; (revue) to contribute to

collant, e [kɔlɑ̃, ɑ̃t] adj sticky; (robe etc) clinging, skintight; (péj) clinging ♦ nm (bas) tights pl; (de danseur) leotard

collation [kɔlasjɔ̃] nf light meal

colle [kɔl] nf glue; (à papiers peints) (wallpaper) paste; (fam: devinette) teaser, riddle; (SCOL: fam) detention

collecte [kɔlɛkt] nf collection; **collectif, -ive** adj collective; (visite, billet) group cpd

collection [kɔlɛksjɔ̃] nf collection; (ÉDITION) series; **collectionner** vt to collect; **collectionneur, -euse** nm/f collector

collectivité [kɔlɛktivite] nf group; ~s **locales** (ADMIN) local authorities

collège [kɔlɛʒ] nm (école) (secondary) school; (assemblée) body; **collégien** nm schoolboy; **collégienne** nf school-girl

---
| collège |

The collège is a state secondary school for children aged between eleven and fifteen. Pupils follow a nationally prescribed curriculum consisting of a common core and various options. Before leaving the collège, pupils are assessed by examination and course work for their **brevet des collèges**.

---

collègue [kɔ(l)lɛg] nm/f colleague

coller [kɔle] vt (papier, timbre) to stick (on); (affiche) to stick up; (enveloppe) to stick down; (morceaux) to stick ou glue

together; (fam: mettre, fourrer) to stick, shove; (SCOL: fam) to keep in ♦ vi (être collant) to be sticky; (adhérer) to stick; ~ à to stick to; **être collé à un examen** (fam) to fail an exam

collet [kɔlɛ] nm (piège) snare, noose; (cou): **prendre qn au ~** to grab sb by the throat

collier [kɔlje] nm (bijou) necklace; (de chien, TECH) collar

collimateur [kɔlimatœʀ] nm: **avoir qn/qch dans le ~** (fig) to have sb/sth in one's sights; **être dans le ~ de qn** to be in sb's sights

colline [kɔlin] nf hill

collision [kɔlizjɔ̃] nf collision, crash; **entrer en ~ (avec)** to collide (with)

colloque [kɔ(l)lɔk] nm symposium

collyre [kɔliʀ] nm eye drops

colmater [kɔlmate] vt (fuite) to seal off; (brèche) to plug, fill in

colombe [kɔlɔ̃b] nf dove

Colombie [kɔlɔ̃bi] nf: **la ~** Colombia

colon [kɔlɔ̃] nm settler

colonie [kɔlɔni] nf colony; ~ **(de vacances)** holiday camp (for children)

colonne [kɔlɔn] nf column; **se mettre en ~ par deux** to get into twos; ~ **(vertébrale)** spine, spinal column

colorant [kɔlɔʀɑ̃, ɑ̃t] nm colouring

colorer [kɔlɔʀe] vt to colour

colorier [kɔlɔʀje] vt to colour (in)

coloris [kɔlɔʀi] nm colour, shade

colporter [kɔlpɔʀte] vt to hawk, peddle

colza [kɔlza] nm rape(seed)

coma [kɔma] nm coma; **être dans le ~** to be in a coma

combat [kɔ̃ba] nm fight, fighting no pl; ~ **de boxe** boxing match; **combattant** nm: **ancien combattant** war veteran; **combattre** vt to combat, fight; (épidémie, ignorance) to combat, fight against

combien [kɔ̃bjɛ̃] adv (quantité) how much; (nombre) how many; ~ **de** (quantité) how much; (nombre) how many; ~ **de temps** how long; ~ **ça coûte/pèse?** how much does it cost/

weigh?; **on est le ~ aujourd'hui?** *(fam)* what's the date today?

combinaison [kɔ̃binɛz3] *nf* combination; *(astuce)* scheme; *(de femme)* slip; *(de plongée)* wetsuit; *(de travail)* boiler suit *(BRIT)*, coveralls *pl (US)*

combine [kɔ̃bin] *nf* trick; *(péj)* scheme, fiddle *(BRIT)*

combiné [kɔ̃bine] *nm (aussi: ~ télé- phonique)* receiver

combiner [kɔ̃bine] *vt (grouper)* to combine; *(plan, horaire)* to work out, devise

comble [kɔ̃bl] *adj (salle)* packed (full) ♦ *nm (du bonheur, plaisir)* height; **~s** *nmpl (CONSTR)* attic *sg*, loft *sg*; **c'est le ~!** that beats everything!

combler [kɔ̃ble] *vt (trou)* to fill in; *(be- soin, lacune)* to fill; *(déficit)* to make good; *(satisfaire)* to fulfil

combustible [kɔ̃bystibl] *nm* fuel

comédie [kɔmedi] *nf* comedy; *(fig)* playacting *no pl*; **faire la ~** *(fam)* to make a fuss; **~ musicale** musical; **co- médien, ne** *nm/f* actor(-tress)

Comédie française

Founded in 1680 by Louis XIV, the Comédie française is the French national theatre. Subsidized by the state, the company performs mainly in the Palais Royal in Paris and stages mainly classical French plays.

---

comestible [kɔmestibl] *adj* edible

comique [kɔmik] *adj (drôle)* comical; *(THÉÂTRE)* comic ♦ *nm (artiste)* comic, comedian

comité [kɔmite] *nm* committee; **~ d'entreprise** works council

commandant [kɔmɑ̃dɑ̃] *nm (gén)* commander, commandant; *(NAVIG, AVIAT)* captain

commande [kɔmɑ̃d] *nf (COMM)* order; **~s** *nfpl (AVIAT etc)* controls; **sur ~** to order; **commandement** *nm* command; *(REL)* commandment; **commander** *vt (COMM)* to order; *(diriger, ordonner)* to

command; **commander à qn de faire** to command *ou* order sb to do

commando [kɔmɑ̃do] *nm* commando (squad)

MOT-CLÉ

comme [kɔm] *prép* **1** *(comparaison)* like; **tout comme son père** just like his father; **fort comme un bœuf** as strong as an ox; **joli comme tout** ever so pretty

2 *(manière)* like; **faites-le comme ça** do it like this, do it this way; **comme ci, comme ça** so-so, middling

3 *(en tant que)* as a; **donner comme prix** to give as a prize; **travailler comme secrétaire** to work as a secretary

♦ *conj* **1** *(ainsi que)* as; **elle écrit comme elle parle** she writes as she talks; **comme si** as if

2 *(au moment où, alors que)* as; **il est parti comme j'arrivais** he left as I arrived

3 *(parce que, puisque)* as; **comme il était en retard, il ...** as he was late, he ...

♦ *adv*: **comme il est fort/c'est bon!** he's so strong/it's so good!

---

commémorer [kɔmemɔre] *vt* to commemorate

commencement [kɔmɑ̃smɑ̃] *nm* beginning, start

commencer [kɔmɑ̃se] *vt, vi* to begin, start; **~ à** *ou* **de faire** to begin *ou* start doing

comment [kɔmɑ̃] *adv* how; **~?** *(que dites-vous)* pardon?

commentaire [kɔmɑ̃tɛʀ] *nm (remar- que)* comment, remark; *(exposé)* commentary

commenter [kɔmɑ̃te] *vt (jugement, événement)* to comment (up)on; *(RADIO, TV: match, manifestation)* to cover

commérages [kɔmeʀaʒ] *nmpl* gossip *sg*

commerçant, e [kɔmɛrsɑ̃, ɑ̃t] nm/f shopkeeper, trader

commerce [kɔmɛrs] nm (activité) trade, commerce; (boutique) business; ~ **électronique** e-commerce; **commercial, e, -aux** adj commercial, trading; (péj) commercial; **les commerciaux** the sales people; **commercialiser** vt to market

commère [kɔmɛr] nf gossip

commettre [kɔmɛtr] vt to commit

commis [kɔmi] nm (de magasin) (shop) assistant; (de banque) clerk

commissaire [kɔmisɛr] nm (de police) ≈ (police) superintendent; **commissaire-priseur** nm auctioneer; **commissariat** nm police station

commission [kɔmisjɔ̃] nf (comité, pourcentage) commission; (message) message; (course) errand; ~**s** nfpl (achats) shopping sg

commode [kɔmɔd] adj (pratique) convenient, handy; (facile) easy; (personne): **pas ~** awkward (to deal with) ♦ nf chest of drawers; **commodité** nf convenience

commotion [kɔmosjɔ̃] nf: ~ **(cérébrale)** concussion; **commotionné, e** adj shocked, shaken

commun, e [kɔmɛ̃, yn] adj common; (pièce) communal, shared; (effort) joint; **ça sort du ~** it's out of the ordinary; **le ~ des mortels** the common run of people; **en ~** (faire) jointly; **mettre en ~** to pool, share; voir aussi **communs**

communauté [kɔmynote] nf community

commune [kɔmyn] nf (ADMIN) commune, ≈ district; (: urbaine) ≈ borough

communicatif, -ive [kɔmynikatif, iv] adj (rire) infectious; (personne) communicative

communication [kɔmynikasjɔ̃] nf communication; ~ **(téléphonique)** (telephone) call

communier [kɔmynje] vi (REL) to receive communion

communion [kɔmynjɔ̃] nf communion

communiquer [kɔmynike] vt (nouvelle, dossier) to pass on, convey; (peur etc) to communicate ♦ vi to communicate; **se ~ à** (se propager) to spread to

communisme [kɔmynism] nm communism; **communiste** adj, nm/f communist

communs [kɔmɛ̃] nmpl (bâtiments) outbuildings

commutateur [kɔmytatœr] nm (ÉLEC) (change-over) switch, commutator

compact, e [kɔpakt] adj (dense) dense; (appareil) compact

compagne [kɔpaɲ] nf companion

compagnie [kɔpaɲi] nf (firme, MIL) company; **tenir ~ à qn** to keep sb company; **fausser ~ à qn** to give sb the slip, slip ou sneak away from sb; ~ **aérienne** airline (company)

compagnon [kɔpaɲɔ̃] nm companion

comparable [kɔparabl] adj: ~ **(à)** comparable (to)

comparaison [kɔparɛzɔ̃] nf comparison

comparaître [kɔparɛtr] vi: ~ **(devant)** to appear (before)

comparer [kɔpare] vt to compare; ~ **qch/qn à** ou **et** (pour choisir) to compare sth/sb with ou and; (pour établir une similitude) to compare sth/sb to

compartiment [kɔpartimɑ̃] nm compartment

comparution [kɔparysjɔ̃] nf (JUR) appearance

compas [kɔpa] nm (GÉOM) (pair of) compasses pl; (NAVIG) compass

compatible [kɔpatibl] adj compatible

compatir [kɔpatir] vi to sympathize

compatriote [kɔpatrijɔt] nm/f compatriot

compensation [kɔpɑ̃sasjɔ̃] nf compensation

compenser [kɔpɑ̃se] vt to compensate for, make up for

compère [kɔpɛr] nm accomplice

compétence [kɔpetɑ̃s] nf competence

compétent, e [kɔ̃petɑ̃, ɑ̃t] adj (apte) competent, capable

compétition [kɔ̃petisjɔ̃] nf (gén) competition; (SPORT: épreuve) event; **la ~ automobile** motor racing

complainte [kɔ̃plɛ̃t] nf lament

complaire [kɔ̃plɛʀ]: **se ~** vi: **se ~ dans** to take pleasure in

complaisance [kɔ̃plɛzɑ̃s] nf kindness; **pavillon de ~** flag of convenience

complaisant, e [kɔ̃plɛzɑ̃, ɑ̃t] adj (aimable) kind, obliging

complément [kɔ̃plemɑ̃] nm complement; (reste) remainder; **~ d'information** (ADMIN) supplementary ou further information; **complémentaire** adj complementary; (additionnel) supplementary

complet, -ète [kɔ̃plɛ, ɛt] adj complete; (plein: hôtel etc) full ♦ nm (aussi: ~-veston) suit; **pain ~** wholemeal bread; **complètement** adv completely; **compléter** vt (porter à la quantité voulue) to complete; (augmenter: connaissances, études) to complement, supplement; (: garde-robe) to add to; **se compléter** (caractères) to complement one another

complexe [kɔ̃plɛks] adj, nm complex; **complexé, e** adj relaxed-up, hung-up

complication [kɔ̃plikasjɔ̃] nf complexity, intricacy; (difficulté, ennui) complication

complice [kɔ̃plis] nm accomplice; **complicité** nf complicity

compliment [kɔ̃plimɑ̃] nm (louange) compliment; **~s** nmpl (félicitations) congratulations

compliqué, e [kɔ̃plike] adj complicated, complex; (personne) complicated; **compliquer** vt to complicate; **se ~** to become complicated

complot [kɔ̃plo] nm plot

comportement [kɔ̃pɔʀtəmɑ̃] nm behaviour

comporter [kɔ̃pɔʀte] vt (consister en) to consist of, comprise; (inclure) to

have; **se ~** vi to behave

composant [kɔ̃pozɑ̃] nm, **composante** [kɔ̃pozɑ̃t] nf component

composé [kɔ̃poze] nm compound

composer [kɔ̃poze] vt (musique, texte) to compose; (mélange, équipe) to make up; (numéro) to dial; (constituer) to make up, form ♦ vi (transiger) to come to terms; **se ~ de** to be composed of, be made up of; **compositeur, -trice** nm/f (MUS) composer; **composition** nf composition; (SCOL) test

composter [kɔ̃pɔste] vt (billet) to punch

compote [kɔ̃pɔt] nf stewed fruit no pl; **~ de pommes** stewed apples

compréhensible [kɔ̃pʀeɑ̃sibl] adj comprehensible; (attitude) understandable

compréhensif, -ive [kɔ̃pʀeɑ̃sif, iv] adj understanding

comprendre [kɔ̃pʀɑ̃dʀ] vt to understand; (se composer de) to comprise, consist of

compresse [kɔ̃pʀɛs] nf compress

compression [kɔ̃pʀesjɔ̃] nf compression; (de personnes) reduction

comprimé [kɔ̃pʀime] nm tablet

comprimer [kɔ̃pʀime] vt to compress; (fig: crédit etc) to reduce, cut down

compris, e [kɔ̃pʀi, iz] pp de **comprendre** ♦ adj (inclus) include; (situé) contained between; **l'électricité ~e/non ~e, y/non ~ l'électricité** including/excluding electricity; **100 F tout ~** 100 F all inclusive ou all-in

compromettre [kɔ̃pʀɔmɛtʀ] vt to compromise; **compromis** nm compromise

comptabilité [kɔ̃tabilite] nf (activité) accounting, accountancy; (comptes) accounts pl, books pl; (service) accounts office

comptable [kɔ̃tabl] nm/f accountant

comptant [kɔ̃tɑ̃] adv: **payer ~** to pay cash; **acheter ~** to buy for cash

compte [kɔ̃t] nm count; (total, mon-

tant) count, (right) number; *(bancaire, facture)* account; **~s** nmpl *(FINANCE)* accounts, books; *(fig)* explanation *sg*; **en fin de ~** all things considered; **s'en tirer à bon ~** to get off lightly; **pour le ~ de** on behalf of; **pour son propre ~** for one's own benefit; **tenir ~ de** to take account of; **travailler à son ~** to work for oneself; **rendre ~ (à qn) de qch** to give (sb) an account of sth; *voir aussi* **rendre ~ à rebours** countdown; **~ chèques postaux** Post Office account; **~ courant** current account; **~ rendu** report; *(de film, livre)* review; **compte-gouttes** nm inv dropper

compter [kɔ̃te] vt to count; *(facturer)* to charge for; *(avoir à son actif, comporter)* to have; *(prévoir)* to allow, reckon; *(penser, espérer)* ♦ **réussir** to expect to succeed ♦ vi to count; *(être économe)* to economize; *(figurer)*: **~ parmi** to be *ou* rank among; **~ sur** to count (up)on; **~ avec qch/qn** to reckon with *ou* take account of sth/sb; **sans ~ que** besides which

compteur [kɔ̃tœr] nm meter; **~ de vitesse** speedometer

comptine [kɔ̃tin] nf nursery rhyme

comptoir [kɔ̃twar] nm *(de magasin)* counter; *(bar)* bar

compulser [kɔ̃pylse] vt to consult

comte [kɔ̃t] nm count; **comtesse** nf countess

con, ne [kɔ̃, kɔn] *(fam!)* adj damned *ou* bloody *(BRIT)* stupid (!)

concéder [kɔ̃sede] vt to grant; *(défaite, point)* to concede

concentré, e [kɔ̃sɑ̃tre] adj *(lait)* condensed ♦ nm: **~ de tomates** tomato purée

concentrer [kɔ̃sɑ̃tre] vt to concentrate; **se ~** vi to concentrate

concept [kɔ̃sɛpt] nm concept

conception [kɔ̃sɛpsjɔ̃] nf conception; *(d'une machine etc)* design; *(d'un problème, de la vie)* approach

concerner [kɔ̃sɛrne] vt to concern; **en ce qui me concerne** as far as I am concerned

concert [kɔ̃sɛr] nm concert; **de ~** *(décider)* unanimously; **concerter: se concerter** vi to put their *etc* heads together

concession [kɔ̃sesjɔ̃] nf concession; **concessionnaire** nm/f agent, dealer

concevoir [kɔ̃s(ə)vwar] vt *(idée, projet)* to conceive (of); *(comprendre)* to understand; *(enfant)* to conceive; **bien/mal conçu** well-/badly-designed

concierge [kɔ̃sjɛrʒ] nm/f caretaker

conciliabules [kɔ̃siljabyl] nmpl (private) discussions, confabulations

concilier [kɔ̃silje] vt to reconcile; **se ~** vt to win over

concis, e [kɔ̃si, iz] adj concise

concitoyen, ne [kɔ̃sitwajɛ̃, jɛn] nm/f fellow citizen

concluant, e [kɔ̃klyɑ̃, ɑ̃t] adj conclusive

conclure [kɔ̃klyr] vt to conclude; **conclusion** nf conclusion

conçois etc [kɔ̃swa] vb voir **concevoir**

concombre [kɔ̃kɔ̃br] nm cucumber

concorder [kɔ̃kɔrde] vi to tally, agree

concourir [kɔ̃kurir] vi *(SPORT)* to compete; **~ à** *(effet etc)* to work towards

concours [kɔ̃kur] nm competition; *(SCOL)* competitive examination; *(assistance)* aid, help; **~ de circonstances** combination of circumstances; **~ hippique** horse show

concret, -ète [kɔ̃krɛ, ɛt] adj concrete; **concrétiser: se ~** vi to materialize

conçu, e [kɔ̃sy] pp de **concevoir**

concubinage [kɔ̃kybinaʒ] nm *(JUR)* cohabitation

concurrence [kɔ̃kyrɑ̃s] nf competition; **faire ~ à** to be in competition with; **jusqu'à ~ de** up to

concurrent, e [kɔ̃kyrɑ̃, ɑ̃t] nm/f *(SPORT, ÉCON etc)* competitor; *(SCOL)* candidate

condamner [kɔ̃dane] vt *(blâmer)* to

condemn; (JUR) to sentence; (porte, ouverture) to fill in, block up; **~ qn à 2 ans de prison** to sentence sb to 2 years' imprisonment

condensation [kɔ̃dɑ̃sasjɔ̃] nf condensation

condenser [kɔ̃dɑ̃se] vt to condense; se **~** vi to condense

condisciple [kɔ̃disipl] nm/f fellow student

condition [kɔ̃disjɔ̃] nf condition; **~s** nfpl (tarif, prix) terms; (circonstances) conditions; **à ~ de** ou **que** provided that; **conditionnel, le** nm conditional (tense)

conditionnement [kɔ̃disjɔnmã] nm (emballage) packaging

conditionner [kɔ̃disjɔne] vt (déterminer) to determine; (COMM: produit) to package; **air conditionné** air conditioning

condoléances [kɔ̃dɔleɑ̃s] nfpl condolences

conducteur, -trice [kɔ̃dyktœr, tris] nm/f driver ♦ nm (ÉLEC etc) conductor

conduire [kɔ̃dɥir] vt to drive; (délégation, troupeau) to lead; se **~** vi to behave; **~ à** to lead to; **~ qn quelque part** to take sb somewhere; to drive sb somewhere

conduite [kɔ̃dɥit] nf (comportement) behaviour; (d'eau, de gaz) pipe; **sous la ~ de** led by; **~ à gauche** left-hand drive

cône [kon] nm cone

confection [kɔ̃fɛksjɔ̃] nf (fabrication) making; (COUTURE): **la ~** the clothing industry

confectionner [kɔ̃fɛksjɔne] vt to make

conférence [kɔ̃ferɑ̃s] nf conference; (exposé) lecture; **~ de presse** press conference; **conférencier, -ière** nm/f speaker, lecturer

confesser [kɔ̃fese] vt to confess; se **~** vi (REL) to go to confession; **confession** nf confession; (culte: catholique etc) denomination

confiance [kɔ̃fjɑ̃s] nf (en l'honnêteté de qn) confidence, trust; (en la valeur de qch) faith; **avoir ~ en** to have confidence ou faith in, trust; **faire ~ à qn** to trust sb; **mettre sa ~ en** to win sb's trust; **~ en soi** self-confidence

confiant, e [kɔ̃fjɑ̃, jɑ̃t] adj confident; trusting

confidence [kɔ̃fidɑ̃s] nf confidence; **confidentiel, le** adj confidential

confier [kɔ̃fje] vt: **~ à qn** (objet, travail) to entrust to sb; (secret, pensée) to confide to sb; se **~ à qn** to confide in sb

confins [kɔ̃fɛ̃] nmpl: **aux ~ de** on the borders of

confirmation [kɔ̃firmasjɔ̃] nf confirmation

confirmer [kɔ̃firme] vt to confirm

confiserie [kɔ̃fizri] nf (magasin) confectioner's ou sweet shop; **~s** nfpl (bonbons) confectionery sg

confisquer [kɔ̃fiske] vt to confiscate

confit, e [kɔ̃fi, it] adj: **fruits ~s** crystallized fruits ♦ nm: **~ d'oie** conserve of goose

confiture [kɔ̃fityr] nf jam; **~ d'oranges** (orange) marmalade

conflit [kɔ̃fli] nm conflict

confondre [kɔ̃fɔ̃dr] vt (jumeaux, faits) to confuse, mix up; (témoin, menteur) to confound; se **~** vi to merge; se **~ en excuses** to apologize profusely; **confondu, e** adj (stupéfait) speechless, overcome

conforme [kɔ̃fɔrm] adj: **~ à** (loi, règle) in accordance with; **conformément** adv: **conformément à** in accordance with; **conformer** vt: se **conformer à** to conform to

confort [kɔ̃fɔr] nm comfort; **tout ~** (COMM) with all modern conveniences; **confortable** adj comfortable

confrère [kɔ̃frɛr] nm colleague

confronter [kɔ̃frɔ̃te] vt to confront

confus, e [kɔ̃fy, yz] adj (vague) confused; (embarrassé) embarrassed; **confusion** nf (voir confus) confusion;

embarrassment; (*voir* confondre) confusion, mixing up

congé [kɔ̃ʒe] *nm* (*vacances*) holiday; **en ~** on holiday; **semaine de ~** week off; **prendre ~ de qn** to take one's leave of sb; **donner son ~ à** to give in one's notice to; **~ de maladie** sick leave; **~ de maternité** maternity leave; **~s payés** paid holiday

congédier [kɔ̃ʒedje] *vt* to dismiss

congélateur [kɔ̃ʒelatœʀ] *nm* freezer

congeler [kɔ̃ʒ(ə)le] *vt* to freeze; **les produits congelés** frozen foods

congestion [kɔ̃ʒɛstjɔ̃] *nf* congestion; **~ cérébrale** stroke; **congestionner** *vt* (*rue*) to congest; (*visage*) to flush

congrès [kɔ̃gʀɛ] *nm* congress

conifère [kɔnifɛʀ] *nm* conifer

conjecture [kɔ̃ʒɛktyʀ] *nf* conjecture

conjoint, e [kɔ̃ʒwɛ̃, wɛ̃t] ♦ *adj* joint ♦ *nm/f* spouse

conjonction [kɔ̃ʒɔ̃ksjɔ̃] *nf* (LING) conjunction

conjonctivite [kɔ̃ʒɔ̃ktivit] *nf* conjunctivitis

conjoncture [kɔ̃ʒɔ̃ktyʀ] *nf* circumstances *pl*; **la ~ actuelle** the present (economic) situation

conjugaison [kɔ̃ʒygɛzɔ̃] *nf* (LING) conjugation

conjuguer [kɔ̃ʒyge] *vt* (LING) to conjugate; (*efforts etc*) to combine

conjuration [kɔ̃ʒyʀasjɔ̃] *nf* conspiracy

conjurer [kɔ̃ʒyʀe] *vt* (*sort, maladie*) to avert; (*implorer*) to beseech, entreat

connaissance [kɔnɛsɑ̃s] *nf* (*savoir*) knowledge *no pl*; (*personne connue*) acquaintance; **être sans ~** to be unconscious; **perdre/reprendre ~** to lose/regain consciousness; **à ma/sa ~** to (the best of) my/his knowledge; **faire la ~ de qn** to meet sb

connaisseur [kɔnɛsœʀ, øz] *nm* connoisseur

connaître [kɔnɛtʀ] *vt* to know; (*éprouver*) to experience; (*avoir: succès*) to have, enjoy; **~ de nom/vue** to know

by name/sight; **ils se sont connus à Genève** they (first) met in Geneva; **s'y ~ en qch** to know a lot about sth

connecter [kɔnɛkte] *vt* to connect

connerie [kɔnʀi] (*fam!*) *nf* stupid thing (to do/say)

connu, e [kɔny] *adj* (*célèbre*) well-known

conquérir [kɔ̃keʀiʀ] *vt* to conquer; **conquête** *nf* conquest

consacrer [kɔ̃sakʀe] *vt* (*employer*) to devote, dedicate; (REL) to consecrate

conscience [kɔ̃sjɑ̃s] *nf* conscience; **avoir/prendre ~ de** to be/become aware of; **perdre ~** to lose consciousness; **avoir bonne/mauvaise ~** to have a clear/guilty conscience; **consciencieux, -euse** *adj* conscientious; **conscient, e** *adj* conscious

conscrit [kɔ̃skʀi] *nm* conscript

consécutif, -ive [kɔ̃sekytif, iv] *adj* consecutive; **~ à** following upon

conseil [kɔ̃sɛj] *nm* (*avis*) piece of advice; (*assemblée*) council; **des ~s** advice; **prendre ~ (auprès de qn)** to take advice (from sb); **~ d'administration** board (of directors); **le ~ des ministres** ≃ the Cabinet; **~ municipal** town council

conseiller, -ère [kɔ̃seje, ɛʀ] *nm/f* adviser ♦ *vt* (*personne*) to advise; (*méthode, action*) to recommend, advise; **~ à qn de** to advise sb to; **~ municipal** town councillor

consentement [kɔ̃sɑ̃tmɑ̃] *nm* consent

consentir [kɔ̃sɑ̃tiʀ] *vt* to agree, consent

conséquence [kɔ̃sekɑ̃s] *nf* consequence; **en ~** (*donc*) consequently; (*de façon appropriée*) accordingly; **conséquent, e** *adj* logical, rational; (*fam: important*) substantial; **par conséquent** consequently

conservateur, -trice [kɔ̃sɛʀvatœʀ, tʀis] *nm/f* (POL) conservative; (*de musée*) curator ♦ *nm* (*pour aliments*) preservative

conservatoire [kɔ̃sɛrvatwar] nm academy

conserve [kɔ̃sɛrv] nf (gén pl) canned ou tinned (BRIT) food; **en ~** canned, tinned (BRIT) to preserve

conserver [kɔ̃sɛrve] vt (faculté) to retain, keep; (amis, livres) to keep; (préserver, aussi CULIN) to preserve

considérable [kɔ̃siderabl] adj considerable, significant, extensive

considération [kɔ̃siderasjɔ̃] nf consideration; (estime) esteem

considérer [kɔ̃sidere] vt to consider; ~ qch comme to regard sth as

consigne [kɔ̃siɲ] nf (de gare) left luggage (office) (BRIT), checkroom (US); (ordre, instruction) instructions pl; ~ **(automatique)** left-luggage locker; **consigner** vt (note, pensée) to record; (punir: élève) to put in detention; (COMM) to put a deposit on

consistant, e [kɔ̃sistɑ̃, ɑ̃t] adj (mélange) thick; (repas) solid

consister [kɔ̃siste] vi: ~ **en/à faire** to consist of/in doing

consœur [kɔ̃sœr] nf (lady) colleague

console [kɔ̃sɔl] nf: ~ **de jeux** games console

consoler [kɔ̃sɔle] vt to console

consolider [kɔ̃sɔlide] vt to strengthen; (fig) to consolidate

consommateur, -trice [kɔ̃sɔmatœr, tris] nm/f (ÉCON) consumer; (dans un café) customer

consommation [kɔ̃sɔmasjɔ̃] nf (boisson) drink; (ÉCON) consumption

consommer [kɔ̃sɔme] vt (suj: personne) to eat ou drink, consume; (: voiture, machine) to use, consume; (mariage) to consummate ♦ vi (dans un café) to (have a) drink

consonne [kɔ̃sɔn] nf consonant

conspirer [kɔ̃spire] vi to conspire

constamment [kɔ̃stamɑ̃] adv constantly

constant, e [kɔ̃stɑ̃, ɑ̃t] adj constant, firm; (personne) steadfast

constat [kɔ̃sta] nm (de police, d'accident) report; ~ **(à l')amiable** jointly-agreed statement for insurance purposes; ~ **d'échec** acknowledgement of failure

constatation [kɔ̃statasjɔ̃] nf (observation) (observed) fact, observation

constater [kɔ̃state] vt (remarquer) to note; (ADMIN, JUR: attester) to certify

consterner [kɔ̃stɛrne] vt to dismay

constipé, e [kɔ̃stipe] adj constipated

constitué, e [kɔ̃stitɥe] adj: ~ **de** made up ou composed of

constituer [kɔ̃stitɥe] vt (équipe) to set up; (dossier, collection) to put together; (suj: éléments: composer) to make up, constitute; (représenter, être) to constitute; **se ~ prisonnier** to give o.s. up; **constitution** nf (composition) composition; (santé, POL) constitution

constructeur [kɔ̃stryktœr] nm manufacturer, builder

constructif, -ive [kɔ̃stryktif, iv] adj constructive

construction [kɔ̃stryksjɔ̃] nf construction, building

construire [kɔ̃strɥir] vt to build, construct

consul [kɔ̃syl] nm consul; **consulat** nm consulate

consultant, e [kɔ̃syltɑ̃, ɑ̃t] adj, nm consultant

consultation [kɔ̃syltasjɔ̃] nf consultation; ~**s** nfpl (POL) talks; **heures de ~** (MÉD) surgery (BRIT) ou office (US) hours

consulter [kɔ̃sylte] vt to consult ♦ vi (médecin) to hold surgery (BRIT), be in (the office) (US); **se ~** vi to confer

consumer [kɔ̃syme] vt to consume; **se ~** vi to burn

contact [kɔ̃takt] nm contact; **au ~ de** (air, peau) on contact with; (gens) through contact with; **mettre/couper le ~** (AUTO) to switch on/off the ignition; **entrer en** ou **prendre ~ avec** to get in touch ou contact with; **contacter** vt to contact, get in touch with

contagieux, -euse [kɔ̃taʒjø, jøz] adj infectious; (par le contact) contagious

contaminer [kɔ̃tamine] vt to contaminate

conte [kɔ̃t] nm tale; ~ **de fées** fairy tale

contempler [kɔ̃tɑ̃ple] vt to contemplate, gaze at

contemporain, e [kɔ̃tɑ̃pɔʀɛ̃, ɛn] adj, nm/f contemporary

contenance [kɔ̃t(ə)nɑ̃s] nf (d'un récipient) capacity; (attitude) bearing, attitude; **perdre** ~ to lose one's composure

conteneur [kɔ̃t(ə)nœʀ] nm container

contenir [kɔ̃t(ə)niʀ] vt to contain; (avoir une capacité de) to hold; **se** ~ vi to contain o.s.

content, e [kɔ̃tɑ̃, ɑ̃t] adj pleased, glad; ~ **de** pleased with; **contenter** vt to satisfy, please; **se contenter de** to content o.s. with

contentieux [kɔ̃tɑ̃sjø] nm (COMM) litigation; (service) litigation department

contenu [kɔ̃t(ə)ny] nm (d'un récipient) contents pl; (d'un texte) content

conter [kɔ̃te] vt to recount, relate

contestable [kɔ̃tɛstabl] adj questionable

contestation [kɔ̃tɛstasjɔ̃] nf (POL) protest

conteste [kɔ̃tɛst]: **sans** ~ adv unquestionably, indisputably; **contester** vt to question ♦ vi (POL, gén) to rebel (against established authority)

contexte [kɔ̃tɛkst] nm context

contigu, ë [kɔ̃tigy] adj: ~ **(à)** adjacent (to)

continent [kɔ̃tinɑ̃] nm continent

continu, e [kɔ̃tiny] adj continuous; **faire la journée** ~**e** to work without taking a full lunch break; **(courant)** ~ direct current, DC

continuel, le [kɔ̃tinɥɛl] adj (qui se répète) constant, continual; (continu) continuous

continuer [kɔ̃tinɥe] vt (travail, voyage etc) to continue (with), carry on (with),

go on (with); (prolonger: alignement, rue) to continue ♦ vi (vie, bruit) to continue, go on; ~ **à** ou **de faire** to go on ou continue doing

contorsionner [kɔ̃tɔʀsjɔne]: **se** ~ vi to contort o.s., writhe about

contour [kɔ̃tuʀ] nm outline, contour; **contourner** vt to go round; (difficulté) to get round

contraceptif, -ive [kɔ̃tʀasɛptif, iv] adj, nm contraceptive; **contraception** nf contraception

contracté, e [kɔ̃tʀakte] adj tense

contracter [kɔ̃tʀakte] vt (muscle etc) to tense, contract; (maladie, dette) to contract; (assurance) to take out; **se** ~ vi (muscles) to contract

contractuel, le [kɔ̃tʀaktɥɛl] nm/f (agent) traffic warden

contradiction [kɔ̃tʀadiksjɔ̃] nf contradiction; **contradictoire** adj contradictory, conflicting

contraignant, e [kɔ̃tʀɛɲɑ̃, ɑ̃t] adj restricting

contraindre [kɔ̃tʀɛ̃dʀ] vt: ~ **qn à faire** to compel sb to do; **contrainte** nf constraint

contraire [kɔ̃tʀɛʀ] adj, nm opposite; ~ **à** contrary to; **au** ~ on the contrary

contrarier [kɔ̃tʀaʀje] vt (personne: irriter) to annoy; (fig: projets) to thwart, frustrate; **contrariété** nf annoyance

contraste [kɔ̃tʀast] nm contrast

contrat [kɔ̃tʀa] nm contract; ~ **de travail** employment contract

contravention [kɔ̃tʀavɑ̃sjɔ̃] nf parking ticket

contre [kɔ̃tʀ] prép against; (en échange) (in exchange) for; **par** ~ on the other hand

contrebande [kɔ̃tʀəbɑ̃d] nf (trafic) contraband, smuggling; (marchandise) contraband, smuggled goods pl; **faire la** ~ **de** to smuggle; **contrebandier, -ière** nm/f smuggler

contrebas [kɔ̃tʀəba]: **en** ~ adv (down) below

contrebasse [kɔ̃trəbas] *nf* (double) bass

contre...: contrecarrer *vt* to thwart; **contrecœur: à contrecœur** *adv* (be)grudgingly, reluctantly; **contrecoup** *nm* repercussions *pl*; **contredire** *vt* (*personne*) to contradict; (*faits*) to refute

contrée [kɔ̃tre] *nf* (*région*) region; (*pays*) land

contrefaçon [kɔ̃trəfasɔ̃] *nf* forgery

contrefaire [kɔ̃trəfɛr] *vt* (*document, signature*) to forge, counterfeit

contre...: contre-indication (*pl* **contre-indications**) *nf* (MÉD) contra-indication; **"contre-indication en cas d'eczéma"** "should not be used by people with eczema"; **contre-indiqué, e** *adj* (MÉD) contraindicated; (*déconseillé*) unadvisable, ill-advised; **contre-jour: à contre-jour** *adv* against the sunlight

contremaître [kɔ̃trəmɛtr] *nm* foreman

contrepartie [kɔ̃trəparti] *nf*: **en ~** in return

contre-pied [kɔ̃trəpje] *nm*: **prendre le ~~ de** (*opinion*) to take the opposing view of; (*action*) to take the opposite course to

contre-plaqué [kɔ̃trəplake] *nm* plywood

contrepoids [kɔ̃trəpwa] *nm* counterweight, counterbalance

contrepoison [kɔ̃trəpwazɔ̃] *nm* antidote

contrer [kɔ̃tre] *vt* to counter

contresens [kɔ̃trəsɑ̃s] *nm* (*erreur*) misinterpretation; (*de traduction*) mistranslation; **à ~** the wrong way

contretemps [kɔ̃trətɑ̃] *nm* hitch; **à ~** (*fig*) at an inopportune moment

contrevenir [kɔ̃trəv(ə)nir] : **~ à** *vt* to contravene

contribuable [kɔ̃tribɥabl] *nm/f* taxpayer

contribuer [kɔ̃tribɥe] : **~ à** *vt* to contribute towards; **contribution** *nf* contribution; **contributions directes/indirectes** direct/indirect taxation; **mettre à contribution** to call upon

contrôle [kɔ̃trol] *nm* checking *ou* id, check; (*des prix*) monitoring, control; (*test*) test, examination; **perdre le ~ de** (*véhicule*) to lose control of; **~ continu** (SCOL) continuous assessment; **~ d'identité** identity check

contrôler [kɔ̃trole] *vt* (*vérifier*) to check; (*surveiller: opérations*) to supervise; (: *prix*) to monitor, control; (*maîtriser*, COMM: *firme*) to control; **se ~** *vi* to control o.s.; **contrôleur, -euse** *nm/f* (*de train*) (ticket) inspector; (*de bus*) (bus) conductor(-tress)

contrordre [kɔ̃trɔrdr] *nm*: **sauf ~** unless otherwise directed

controversé, e [kɔ̃trɔverse] *adj* (*personnage, question*) controversial

contusion [kɔ̃tyzjɔ̃] *nf* bruise, contusion

convaincre [kɔ̃vɛkr] *vt*: **~ qn (de qch)** to convince sb (of sth); **~ qn (de faire)** to persuade sb (to do)

convalescence [kɔ̃valesɑ̃s] *nf* convalescence

convenable [kɔ̃vnabl] *adj* suitable; (*assez bon, respectable*) decent

convenance [kɔ̃vnɑ̃s] *nf*: **à ma/votre ~** to my/your liking; **~s** *nfpl* (*normes sociales*) proprieties

convenir [kɔ̃vnir] *vi* to be suitable; **~ à** to suit; **~ de** (*bien-fondé de qch*) to admit (to), acknowledge; (*date, somme etc*) to agree upon; **~ que** (*admettre*) to admit that; **~ de faire** to agree to do

convention [kɔ̃vɑ̃sjɔ̃] *nf* convention; **~s** *nfpl* (*convenances*) convention *sg*; **~ collective** (ÉCON) collective agreement; **conventionné, e** *adj* (ADMIN) applying charges laid down by the state

convenu, e [kɔ̃vny] *pp de* **convenir** ♦ *adj* agreed

conversation [kɔ̃versasjɔ̃] *nf* conversation

convertir [kɔ̃vɛrtir] vt: ~ qn (à) to convert sb (to); se ~ (à) to be converted (to); ~ qch en to convert sth into

conviction [kɔ̃viksjɔ̃] nf conviction

convienne etc [kɔ̃vjɛn] vb voir **convenir**

convier [kɔ̃vje] vt: ~ qn à (dîner etc) to (cordially) invite sb to

convive [kɔ̃viv] nm/f guest (at table)

convivial, e, -aux [kɔ̃vivjal, jo] adj (INFORM) user-friendly

convocation [kɔ̃vɔkasjɔ̃] nf (document) notification to attend; (: JUR) summons sg

convoi [kɔ̃vwa] nm convoy; (train) train

convoiter [kɔ̃vwate] vt to covet

convoquer [kɔ̃vɔke] vt (assemblée) to convene; (subordonné) to summon; (candidat) to ask to attend

convoyeur [kɔ̃vwajœr] nm: ~ de fonds security guard

coopération [kɔɔperasjɔ̃] nf cooperation; (ADMIN): **la C~** ≈ Voluntary Service Overseas (BRIT), ≈ Peace Corps (US)

coopérer [kɔɔpere] vi: ~ (à) to cooperate (in)

coordonnées [kɔɔrdɔne] nfpl: donnez-moi vos ~ (fam) can I have your details please?

coordonner [kɔɔrdɔne] vt to coordinate

copain [kɔpɛ̃] (fam) nm mate, pal; (petit ami) boyfriend

copeau, x [kɔpo] nm shaving

copie [kɔpi] nf copy; (SCOL) script, paper; **copier** vt, vi to copy; **copier sur** to copy from; **copieur** nm (photo)copier

copieux, -euse [kɔpjø, jøz] adj copious

copine [kɔpin] (fam) nf mate, pal; (petite amie) girlfriend

copropriété [kɔprɔprijete] nf coownership, joint ownership

coq [kɔk] nm cock, rooster; **coq-à-**

l'âne nm inv abrupt change of subject

coque [kɔk] nf (de noix, mollusque) shell; (de bateau) hull; **à la ~** (CULIN) (soft-)boiled

coquelicot [kɔkliko] nm poppy

coqueluche [kɔklyʃ] nf whooping-cough

coquet, te [kɔkɛ, ɛt] adj appearance-conscious; (logement) smart, charming

coquetier [kɔk(ə)tje] nm egg-cup

coquillage [kɔkijaʒ] nm (mollusque) shellfish inv; (coquille) shell

coquille [kɔkij] nf shell; (TYPO) misprint; **~ St Jacques** scallop

coquin, e [kɔkɛ̃, in] adj mischievous, roguish; (polisson) naughty

cor [kɔr] nm (MUS) horn; (MÉD): ~ (au pied) corn

corail, -aux [kɔraj, o] nm coral no pl

Coran [kɔrɑ̃] nm: **le ~** the Koran

corbeau, x [kɔrbo] nm crow

corbeille [kɔrbɛj] nf basket; ~ **à papier** waste paper basket ou bin

corbillard [kɔrbijar] nm hearse

corde [kɔrd] nf rope; (de violon, raquette) string; **usé jusqu'à la ~** threadbare; ~ **à linge** washing ou clothes line; ~ **à sauter** skipping rope; **~s vocales** vocal cords

cordée nf (d'alpinistes) rope, roped party

cordialement [kɔrdjalmɑ̃] adv (formule épistolaire) (kind) regards

cordon [kɔrdɔ̃] nm cord, string; ~ **ombilical** umbilical cord; ~ **sanitaire/de police** sanitary/police cordon

cordonnerie [kɔrdɔnri] nf shoe repairer's (shop); **cordonnier** nm shoe repairer

Corée [kɔre] nf: **la ~ du Sud/du Nord** South/North Korea

coriace [kɔrjas] adj tough

corne [kɔrn] nf horn; (de cerf) antler

cornée [kɔrne] nf cornea

corneille [kɔrnɛj] nf crow

cornemuse [kɔrnəmyz] nf bagpipes pl

cornet [kɔrnɛ] nm (paper) cone; (de

glace) cornet, cone

corniche [kɔrniʃ] *nf (route)* coast road

cornichon [kɔrniʃɔ̃] *nm* gherkin

Cornouailles [kɔrnwaj] *nf* Cornwall

corporation [kɔrpɔrasjɔ̃] *nf* corporate body

corporel, le [kɔrpɔrɛl] *adj* bodily; *(punition)* corporal

corps [kɔr] *nm* body; **à ~ perdu** headlong; **prendre ~** to take shape; **~ à ~** ♦ *adv* hand-to-hand ♦ *nm* clinch; **le ~ électoral** the electorate; **le ~ enseignant** the teaching profession

corpulent, e [kɔrpylɑ̃, ɑ̃t] *adj* stout

correct, e [kɔrɛkt] *adj* correct; *(fam: acceptable: salaire, hôtel)* reasonable, decent; **correcteur, -trice** *nm/f (SCOL)* examiner; **correction** *nf (voir corriger)* correction; *(voir correct)* correctness; *(coups)* thrashing; **correctionnel, le** *adj (JUR)*: **tribunal correctionnel** ≃ criminal court

correspondance [kɔrɛspɔ̃dɑ̃s] *nf* correspondence; *(de train, d'avion)* connection; **cours par ~** correspondence course; **vente par ~** mail-order business

correspondant, e [kɔrɛspɔ̃dɑ̃, ɑ̃t] *nm/f* correspondent; *(TÉL)* person phoning *(ou* being phoned)

correspondre [kɔrɛspɔ̃dr] *vi* to correspond, tally; **~ à** to correspond to; **~ avec qn** to correspond with sb

corrida [kɔrida] *nf* bullfight

corridor [kɔridɔr] *nm* corridor

corrigé [kɔriʒe] *nm (SCOL: d'exercice)* correct version

corriger [kɔriʒe] *vt (devoir)* to correct; *(punir)* to thrash; **~ qn de** *(défaut)* to cure sb of

corroborer [kɔrɔbɔre] *vt* to corroborate

corrompre [kɔrɔ̃pr] *vt* to corrupt; *(acheter: témoin etc)* to bribe

corruption [kɔrypsjɔ̃] *nf* corruption; *(de témoins)* bribery

corsage [kɔrsaʒ] *nm* bodice; *(chemisier)* blouse

corsaire [kɔrsɛr] *nm* pirate

corse [kɔrs] *adj, nm/f* Corsican ♦ *nf:* **la C~** Corsica

corsé, e [kɔrse] *adj (café)* full-flavoured; *(sauce)* spicy; *(problème)* tough

corset [kɔrsɛ] *nm* corset

cortège [kɔrtɛʒ] *nm* procession

cortisone [kɔrtizɔn] *nf* cortisone

corvée [kɔrve] *nf* chore, drudgery *no pl*

cosmétique [kɔsmetik] *nm* beauty care product

cosmopolite [kɔsmɔpɔlit] *adj* cosmopolitan

cossu, e [kɔsy] *adj (maison)* opulent(-looking)

costaud, e [kɔsto, od] *(fam) adj* strong, sturdy

costume [kɔstym] *nm (d'homme)* suit; *(de théâtre)* costume; **costumé, e** *adj* dressed up; **bal costumé** fancy dress ball

cote [kɔt] *nf (en Bourse)* quotation; **~ d'alerte** danger *ou* flood level

côte [kot] *nf (rivage)* coast(line); *(pente)* hill; *(ANAT)* rib; *(d'un tricot, tissu)* rib, ribbing *no pl;* **~ à ~** side by side; **la C~ (d'Azur)** the (French) Riviera

coté, e [kɔte] *adj:* **être bien ~** to be highly rated

côté [kote] *nm (gén)* side; *(direction)* way, direction; **de chaque ~ (de)** on each side (of); **de tous les ~s** from all directions; **de quel ~ est-il parti?** which way did he go?; **de ce/de l'autre ~** this/the other way; **du ~ de** *(provenance)* from; *(direction)* towards; *(proximité)* near; **de ~** *(regarder)* sideways; *(mettre)* aside; **mettre de l'argent de ~** to save some money; **à ~** *(right)* nearby; *(voisins)* next door; **à ~ de** beside, next to; *(en comparaison)* compared to; **être aux ~s de** to be by the side of

coteau, x [kɔto] *nm* hill

côtelette [kotlɛt] *nf* chop

côtier, -ière [kotje, jɛr] *adj* coastal

cotisation [kɔtizasjɔ̃] nf subscription, dues pl; (pour une pension) contributions pl

cotiser [kɔtize] vi: ~ (à) to pay contributions (to); **se** ~ vi to club together

coton [kɔtɔ̃] nm cotton; ~ **hydrophile** cotton wool (BRIT), absorbent cotton (US); **Coton-Tige** ® nm cotton bud

côtoyer [kotwaje] vt (fréquenter) to rub shoulders with

cou [ku] nm neck

couchant [kuʃɑ̃] adj: **soleil** ~ setting sun

couche [kuʃ] nf layer; (de peinture, vernis) coat; (de bébé) nappy (BRIT), diaper (US); ~ **d'ozone** ozone layer; ~**s sociales** social levels ou strata

couché, e [kuʃe] adj lying down; (au lit) in bed

coucher [kuʃe] nm (du soleil) setting ♦ vt (personne) to put to bed; (: loger) to put up; (objet) to lay on its side ♦ vi to sleep; **se** ~ vi (pour dormir) to go to bed; (pour se reposer) to lie down; (soleil) to set; ~ **de soleil** sunset

couchette [kuʃet] nf couchette; (pour voyageur, sur bateau) berth

coucou [kuku] nm cuckoo

coude [kud] nm (ANAT) elbow; (de tuyau, de la route) bend; ~ **à** ~ shoulder to shoulder, side by side

coudre [kudʀ] vt (bouton) to sew on ♦ vi to sew

couenne [kwan] nf (de lard) rind

couette [kwet] nf duvet, quilt; ~**s** nfpl (cheveux) bunches

couffin [kufɛ̃] nm Moses basket

couler [kule] vi to flow, run; (fuir: stylo, récipient) to leak; (nez) to run; (sombrer: bateau) to sink ♦ vt (cloche, sculpture) to cast; (bateau) to sink; (faire échouer: personne) to bring down

couleur [kulœʀ] nf colour (BRIT), color (US); (CARTES) suit; **film/télévision en** ~**s** colo(u)r film/television

couleuvre [kulœvʀ] nf grass snake

coulisse [kulis] nf: ~**s** nfpl (THÉÂTRE) wings; (fig): **dans les** ~**s** behind the scenes; **coulisser** vi to slide, run

couloir [kulwaʀ] nm corridor, passage; (d'avion) aisle; (de bus) gangway; ~ **aérien/de navigation** air/shipping lane

coup [ku] nm (heurt, choc) knock; (affectif) blow, shock; (agressif) blow; (avec arme à feu) shot; (de l'horloge) stroke; (tennis, golf) stroke; (boxe) blow; (fam: fois) time; ~ **de coude** nudge (with the elbow); ~ **de tonnerre** clap of thunder; ~ **de sonnette** ring of the bell; **donner un** ~ **de balai** to give the floor a sweep; **boire un** ~ (fam) to have a drink; **être dans le** ~ to be in on it; **du** ~ ... as a result; **d'un seul** ~ (subitement) suddenly; (à la fois) at one go; **du premier** ~ first time; **du même** ~ at the same time; **à tous les** ~**s** (fam) every time; **tenir le** ~ to hold out; **après** ~ afterwards; **à** ~ **sûr** definitely, without fail; **sur le** ~ outright; **sous le** ~ **de** (surprise etc) under the influence of; **en** ~ **de vent** in a tearing hurry; ~ **de chance** stroke of luck; ~ **de couteau** stab (of a knife); ~ **d'État** coup; ~ **de feu** shot; ~ **de fil** (fam) phone call; ~ **de frein** (sharp) braking no pl; ~ **de main**: **donner un** ~ **de main à qn** to give sb a (helping) hand; ~ **d'œil** glance; ~ **de pied** kick; ~ **de poing** punch; ~ **de soleil** sunburn no pl; ~ **de téléphone** phone call; ~ **de tête** (fig) (sudden) impulse

coupable [kupabl] adj guilty ♦ nm/f (gén) culprit; (JUR) guilty party

coupe [kup] nf (verre) goblet; (à fruits) dish; (SPORT) cup; (de cheveux, de vêtement) cut; (graphique, plan) (cross) section

coupe-papier [kuppapje] nm inv paper knife

couper [kupe] vt to cut; (retrancher) to cut (out); (route, courant) to cut off; (appétit) to take away; (vin à table) to dilute ♦ vi to cut; (prendre un raccourci) to take a short-cut; **se ~** vi (se blesser) to cut o.s.; **~ la parole à qn** to cut sb short

couple [kupl] nm couple

couplet [kuplɛ] nm verse

coupole [kupɔl] nf dome

coupon [kupɔ̃] nm (ticket) coupon; (reste de tissu) remnant; **coupon-réponse** nm reply coupon

coupure [kupyʀ] nf cut; (billet de banque) note; (de journal) cutting; **~ de courant** power cut

cour [kuʀ] nf (de ferme, jardin) (court)yard; (d'immeuble) back yard; (JUR, royale) court; **faire la ~ à qn** to court sb; **~ d'assises** court of assizes; **~ de récréation** playground; **~ martiale** court-martial

courage [kuʀaʒ] nm courage, bravery; **courageux, -euse** adj brave, courageous

couramment [kuʀamɑ̃] adv commonly; (parler) fluently

courant, e [kuʀɑ̃, ɑ̃t] adj (fréquent) common; (COMM, gén: normal) standard; (en cours) current ♦ nm current; (fig) movement; (: d'opinion) trend; **être au ~ (de)** (fait, nouvelle) to know (about); **mettre qn au ~ (de)** to tell sb (about); (nouveau travail etc) to teach sb the basics (of); **se tenir au ~ (de)** (techniques etc) to keep o.s. up-to-date (on); **dans le ~ de** (pendant) in the course of; **le 10 ~** (COMM) the 10th inst.; **~ d'air** draught; **~ électrique** (electric) current, power

courbature [kuʀbatyʀ] nf ache

courbe [kuʀb] adj curved ♦ nf curve; **courber** vt to bend; **se courber** vi (personne) to bend (down), stoop

coureur, -euse [kuʀœʀ, øz] nm/f (SPORT) runner (ou driver); (péj) womanizer; manhunter; **~ automobile** racing driver

courge [kuʀʒ] nf (CULIN) marrow; **courgette** nf courgette (BRIT), zucchini (US)

courir [kuʀiʀ] vi to run ♦ vt (SPORT: épreuve) to compete in; (risque) to run; (danger) to face; **~ les magasins** to go round the shops; **le bruit court que** the rumour is going round that

couronne [kuʀɔn] nf crown; (de fleurs) wreath, circlet

courons etc [kuʀɔ̃] vb voir **courir**

courrier [kuʀje] nm mail, post; (lettres à écrire) letters pl; **~ électronique** E-mail

courroie [kuʀwa] nf strap; (TECH) belt

courrons etc [kuʀɔ̃] vb voir **courir**

cours [kuʀ] nm (leçon) class; (: particulier) lesson; (série de leçons, cheminement) course; (écoulement) flow; (COMM: de devises) rate; (: de denrées) price; **donner libre ~ à** to give free expression to; **avoir ~** (SCOL) to have a class ou lecture; **en ~** (année) current; (travaux) in progress; **en ~ de route** on the way; **au ~ de** in the course of, during; **~ d'eau** waterway; **~ du soir** night school; **~ intensif** crash course

course [kuʀs] nf (action) running; (SPORT: épreuve) race; (d'un taxi) journey, trip; (commission) errand; **~s** nfpl (achats) shopping sg; **faire des ~s** to do some shopping

court, e [kuʀ, kuʀt(ə)] adj short ♦ adv short ♦ nm: **~ (de tennis)** (tennis) court; **à ~ de** short of; **prendre qn de court** to catch sb unawares; **court-circuit** nm short-circuit

courtier, -ère [kuʀtje, jɛʀ] nm/f broker

courtiser [kuʀtize] vt to court, woo

courtois, e [kuʀtwa, waz] adj courteous; **courtoisie** nf courtesy

couru, e [kuʀy] pp de **courir**

cousais etc [kuze] vb voir **coudre**

couscous [kuskus] nm couscous

cousin, e [kuzɛ̃, in] nm/f cousin

coussin [kusɛ̃] nm cushion

cousu, e [kuzy] pp de **coudre**

coût [ku] nm cost; **le ~ de la vie** the cost of living; **coûtant** adj m: **au prix coûtant** at cost price

couteau, x [kuto] nm knife

coûter [kute] vt, vi to cost; **combien ça coûte?** how much is it?, what does it cost?; **coûte que coûte** at all costs; **coûteux, -euse** adj costly, expensive

coutume [kutym] nf custom

couture [kutyʀ] nf sewing; (profession) dressmaking; (points) seam; **couturier** nm fashion designer; **couturière** nf dressmaker

couvée [kuve] nf brood, clutch

couvent [kuvã] nm (de sœurs) convent; (de frères) monastery

couver [kuve] vt to hatch; (maladie) to be coming down with ♦ vi (feu) to smoulder; (révolte) to be brewing

couvercle [kuvɛʀkl] nm lid; (de bombe aérosol etc, qui se visse) cap, top

couvert, e [kuvɛʀ, ɛʀt] pp de **couvrir** ♦ adj (ciel) overcast ♦ nm (place setting); (place à table) place; **~s** nmpl (ustensiles) cutlery sg; **~ de** covered with ou in; **mettre le ~** to lay the table

couverture [kuvɛʀtyʀ] nf blanket; (de livre, assurance, fig) cover; (presse) coverage; **~ chauffante** electric blanket

couveuse [kuvøz] nf (de maternité) incubator

couvre-feu [kuvʀəfø] nm curfew

couvre-lit [kuvʀəli] nm bedspread

couvreur [kuvʀœʀ] nm roofer

couvrir [kuvʀiʀ] vt to cover; **se ~** vi (s'habiller) to cover up; (se coiffer) to put on one's hat; (ciel) to cloud over

cow-boy [koboj] nm cowboy

crabe [kʀab] nm crab

cracher [kʀaʃe] vi, vt to spit

crachin [kʀaʃɛ̃] nm drizzle

crack [kʀak] nm (fam: as) ace

craie [kʀɛ] nf chalk

craindre [kʀɛ̃dʀ] vt to fear, be afraid of; (être sensible à: chaleur, froid) to be easily damaged by

crainte [kʀɛ̃t] nf fear; **de ~ de/que** for fear of/that; **craintif, -ive** adj timid

cramoisi, e [kʀamwazi] adj crimson

crampe [kʀãp] nf cramp

crampon [kʀãpɔ̃] nm (de chaussure de football) stud; (de chaussure de course) spike; (d'alpinisme) crampon; **cramponner**: **se cramponner (à)** to hang ou cling on (to)

cran [kʀã] nm (entaille) notch; (de courroie) hole; (fam: courage) guts pl; **~ d'arrêt** safety catch

crâne [kʀɑn] nm skull

crâner [kʀɑne] (fam) vi to show off

crapaud [kʀapo] nm toad

crapule [kʀapyl] nf villain

craquement [kʀakmã] nm crack, snap; (du plancher) creak, creaking no pl

craquer [kʀake] vi (bois, plancher) to creak; (fil, branche) to snap; (couture) to come apart; (fig: accusé) to break down; (: fam) to crack up ♦ vt (allumette) to strike; **j'ai craqué** (fam) I couldn't resist it

crasse [kʀas] nf grime, filth; **crasseux, -euse** adj grimy, filthy

cravache [kʀavaʃ] nf (riding) crop

cravate [kʀavat] nf tie

crawl [kʀol] nm crawl; **dos ~é** backstroke

crayon [kʀɛjɔ̃] nm pencil; **~ à bille** ball-point pen; **~ de couleur** crayon, colouring pencil; **crayon-feutre** (pl **crayons-feutres**) nm felt(-tip) pen

créancier, -ière [kʀeãsje, jɛʀ] nm/f creditor

création [kʀeasjɔ̃] nf creation

créature [kʀeatyʀ] nf creature

crèche [kʀɛʃ] nf (de Noël) crib; (garderie) crèche, day nursery

crédit [kʀedi] nm (gén) credit; **~s** nmpl (fonds) funds; **payer/acheter à ~** to pay/buy on credit ou on easy terms; **faire ~ à qn** to give sb credit; **créditer** vt: **créditer un compte (de)** to credit an account (with)

crédule [kʀedyl] adj credulous, gullible

créer [kʀee] vt to create

crémaillère [kʀemajɛʀ] nf: **pendre la ~** to have a house-warming party

crématoire [kʀematwaʀ] adj: **four ~**

crematorium

crème [kʀɛm] nf cream; (entremets) cream dessert ♦ adj inv cream(-coloured); **un (café) ~** ≃ a white coffee; **~ anglaise** (egg) custard; **~ chantilly** whipped cream; **~ fouettée** ≃ crème chantilly; **crémerie** nf dairy; **crémeux, -euse** adj creamy

créneau, x [kʀeno] nm (de fortification) crenel(le); (dans marché) gap, niche; (AUTO): **faire un ~** to reverse into a parking space (between two cars alongside the kerb)

crêpe [kʀɛp] nf (galette) pancake ♦ nm (tissu) crêpe; (de cheveux) backcombed; **crêperie** nf pancake shop ou restaurant

crépiter [kʀepite] vi (friture) to sputter, splutter; (fire) to crackle

crépu, e [kʀepy] adj frizzy, fuzzy

crépuscule [kʀepyskyl] nm twilight, dusk

cresson [kʀesɔ̃] nm watercress

crête [kʀɛt] nf (de coq) comb; (de vague, montagne) crest

creuser [kʀøze] vt (trou, tunnel) to dig; (sol) to dig a hole in; (fig) to go (deeply) into; **ça creuse** that gives you a real appetite; **se ~ la cervelle** (fam) to rack one's brains

creux, -euse [kʀø, kʀøz] adj hollow ♦ nm hollow; **heures creuses** slack periods; (électricité, téléphone) off-peak periods; **avoir un ~** (fam) to be hungry

crevaison [kʀəvɛzɔ̃] nf puncture

crevasse [kʀəvas] nf (dans le sol, la peau) crack; (de glacier) crevasse

crevé, e [kʀəve] (fam) adj (fatigué) all in, exhausted

crever [kʀəve] vt (ballon) to burst ♦ vi (pneu) to burst; (automobiliste) to have a puncture (BRIT) ou a flat (tire) (US); (fam) to die

crevette [kʀəvɛt] nf: **~ (rose)** prawn; **~ grise** shrimp

cri [kʀi] nm cry, shout; (d'animal: spécifique) cry, call; **c'est le dernier ~** (fig)

it's the latest fashion

criant, e [kʀijɑ̃, kʀijɑ̃t] adj (injustice) glaring

criard, e [kʀijaʀ, kʀijaʀd] adj (couleur) garish, loud; (voix) yelling

crible [kʀibl] nm riddle; **passer qch au ~** (fig) to go over sth with a fine-tooth comb; **criblé, e** adj: **criblé de** riddled with; (de dettes) crippled with

cric [kʀik] nm (AUTO) jack

crier [kʀije] vi (pour appeler) to shout, cry (out); (de douleur etc) to scream, yell ♦ vt (injure) to shout (out), yell (out)

crime [kʀim] nm crime; (meurtre) murder; **criminel, le** nm/f criminal; (assassin) murderer

crin [kʀɛ̃] nm (de cheval) hair no pl

crinière [kʀinjɛʀ] nf mane

crique [kʀik] nf creek, inlet

criquet [kʀikɛ] nm grasshopper

crise [kʀiz] nf crisis; (MÉD) attack; (: d'épilepsie) fit; **piquer une ~ de nerfs** to go hysterical; **~ cardiaque** heart attack; **~ de foie** bilious attack

crisper [kʀispe] vt (poings) to clench; **se ~** (visage) to tense; (personne) to get tense

crisser [kʀise] vi (neige) to crunch; (pneu) to screech

cristal, -aux [kʀistal, o] nm crystal; **cristallin, e** adj crystal-clear

critère [kʀitɛʀ] nm criterion

critiquable [kʀitikabl] adj open to criticism

critique [kʀitik] adj critical ♦ nm/f (de théâtre, musique) critic ♦ nf criticism; (THÉÂTRE etc: article) review

critiquer [kʀitike] vt (dénigrer) to criticize; (évaluer) to assess, examine (critically)

croasser [kʀoase] vi to caw

Croatie [kʀɔasi] nf Croatia

croc [kʀo] nm (dent) fang; (de boucher) hook; **croc-en-jambe** nm: **faire un croc-en-jambe à qn** to trip sb up

croche [kʀɔʃ] nf (MUS) quaver (BRIT),

eighth note (US); **croche-pied** nm = **croc-en-jambe**

crochet [kʁɔʃɛ] nm hook; (détour) detour; (TRICOT: aiguille) crochet hook; (: technique) crochet; **vivre aux ~s de qn** to live ou sponge off sb

crochu, e [kʁɔʃy] adj (nez) hooked; (doigts) claw-like

crocodile [kʁɔkɔdil] nm crocodile

croire [kʁwaʁ] vt to believe; **se ~ fort** to think one is strong; **~ que** to believe ou think that; **~ à, ~ en** to believe in

crois [kʁwa] vb voir **croître**

croisade [kʁwazad] nf crusade

croisé, e [kʁwaze] adj (veste) double-breasted

croisement [kʁwazmɑ̃] nm (carrefour) crossroads sg; (BIO) crossing; (: résultat) crossbreed

croiser [kʁwaze] vt (personne, voiture) to pass; (route) to cross, cut across; (BIO) to cross; **se ~** vi (personnes, véhicules) to pass each other; (routes, lettres) to cross; (regards) to meet; **~ les jambes/bras** to cross one's legs/ fold one's arms

croisière [kʁwazjɛʁ] nf cruise

croissance [kʁwasɑ̃s] nf growth

croissant [kʁwasɑ̃] nm (à manger) croissant; (motif) crescent

croître [kʁwatʁ] vi to grow

croix [kʁwa] nf cross; **~ gammée** swastika; **la C~ Rouge** the Red Cross

croque-monsieur [kʁɔkmɔsjø] nm inv toasted ham and cheese sandwich

croquer [kʁɔke] vt (manger) to crunch; (: manger) to munch; (dessiner) to sketch; **chocolat à ~** plain dessert chocolate

croquis [kʁɔki] nm sketch

cross [kʁɔs] nm: **faire du ~ (à pied)** to do cross-country running

crosse [kʁɔs] nf (de fusil) butt; (de revolver) grip

crotte [kʁɔt] nf droppings pl; **crotté, e** adj muddy, mucky; **crottin** nm dung, manure; (fromage) (small round) cheese (made of goat's milk)

crouler [kʁule] vi (s'effondrer) to collapse; (être délabré) to be crumbling

croupe [kʁup] nf rump; **en ~** pillion

croupir [kʁupiʁ] vi to stagnate

croustillant, e [kʁustijɑ̃, ɑ̃t] adj crisp

croûte [kʁut] nf crust; (du fromage) rind; (MÉD) scab; **en ~** (CULIN) in pastry

croûton [kʁutɔ̃] nm (CULIN) crouton; (bout du pain) crust, heel

croyable [kʁwajabl] adj credible

croyant, e [kʁwajɑ̃, ɑ̃t] nm/f believer

CRS sigle fpl (= Compagnies républicaines de sécurité) state security police force ♦ sigle m member of the CRS

cru, e [kʁy] pp de **croire** ♦ adj (non cuit) raw; (lumière, couleur) harsh; (paroles) crude ♦ nm (vignoble) vineyard; (vin) wine; **un grand ~** a great vintage; **jambon ~** Parma ham

crû [kʁy] pp de **croître**

cruauté [kʁyote] nf cruelty

cruche [kʁyʃ] nf pitcher, jug

crucifix [kʁysifi] nm crucifix; **crucifixion** nf crucifixion

crudités [kʁydite] nfpl (CULIN) salads

crue [kʁy] nf (inondation) flood

cruel, le [kʁyɛl] adj cruel

crus etc [kʁy] vb voir **croire**; **croître**

crûs etc [kʁy] vb voir **croître**

crustacés [kʁystase] nmpl shellfish

Cuba [kyba] nf Cuba; **cubain, e** adj Cuban ♦ nm/f: **Cubain, e** Cuban

cube [kyb] nm cube; (jouet) brick; **mètre ~** cubic metre; **2 au ~** = 2 cubed

cueillette [kœjɛt] nf picking; (quantité) crop, harvest

cueillir [kœjiʁ] vt (fruits, fleurs) to pick, gather; (fig) to catch

cuiller [kɥijɛʁ], **cuillère** [kɥijɛʁ] nf spoon; **~ à café** coffee spoon; (CULIN) teaspoonful; **~ à soupe** soup-spoon; (CULIN) tablespoonful; **cuillerée** nf spoonful

cuir [kɥiʁ] nm leather; **~ chevelu** scalp

cuire [kɥiʁ] vt (aliments) to cook; (au four) to bake ♦ vi to cook; **bien cuit** (viande) well done; **trop cuit** overdone

cuisant, e [kɥizɑ̃, ɑ̃t] *adj (douleur)* stinging; *(fig: souvenir, échec)* bitter

cuisine [kɥizin] *nf (pièce)* kitchen; *(art culinaire)* cookery, cooking; *(nourriture)* cooking, food; **faire la ~** to cook; **cuisiné, e** *adj:* **plat cuisiné** ready-made meal *ou* dish; **cuisiner** *vt* to cook; *(fam)* to grill ♦ *vi* to cook; **cuisinier, -ière** *nm/f* cook; **cuisinière** *nf (poêle)* cooker

cuisse [kɥis] *nf* thigh; *(CULIN)* leg

cuisson [kɥisɔ̃] *nf* cooking

cuit, e [kɥi, kɥit] *pp de* **cuire**

cuivre [kɥivʀ] *nm* copper; **les ~s** *(MUS)* the brass

cul [ky] *(fam!)* *nm* arse (!)

culbute [kylbyt] *nf (jeu)* somersault; *(accidentelle)* tumble, fall

culminant, e [kylminɑ̃, ɑ̃t] *adj:* **point ~** highest point

culminer [kylmine] *vi* to reach its highest point

culot [kylo] *(fam)* *nm (effronterie)* cheek

culotte [kylɔt] *nf (de femme)* knickers *pl (BRIT)*, panties *pl*

culpabilité [kylpabilite] *nf* guilt

culte [kylt] *nm (religion)* religion; *(hommage, vénération)* worship; *(protestant)* service

cultivateur, -trice [kyltivatœʀ, tʀis] *nm/f* farmer

cultivé, e [kyltive] *adj (personne)* cultured, cultivated

cultiver [kyltive] *vt* to cultivate; *(légumes)* to grow, cultivate

culture [kyltyʀ] *nf* cultivation; *(connaissances etc)* culture; **les ~s intensives** intensive farming; **~ physique** physical training; **culturel, le** *adj* cultural; **culturisme** *nm* body-building

cumin [kymɛ̃] *nm* cumin

cumuler [kymyle] *vt (emplois)* to hold concurrently; *(salaires)* to draw concurrently

cupide [kypid] *adj* greedy, grasping

cure [kyʀ] *nf (MÉD)* course of treatment

curé [kyʀe] *nm* parish priest

cure-dent [kyʀdɑ̃] *nm* toothpick

cure-pipe [kyʀpip] *nm* pipe cleaner

curer [kyʀe] *vt* to clean out

curieusement [kyʀjøzmɑ̃] *adv* curiously

curieux, -euse [kyʀjø, jøz] *adj (indiscret)* curious, inquisitive; *(étrange)* strange, curious ♦ *nmpl (badauds)* onlookers; **curiosité** *nf* curiosity; *(site)* unusual feature

curriculum vitae [kyʀikylɔmvite] *nm inv* curriculum vitae

curseur [kyʀsœʀ] *nm (INFORM)* cursor

cutané, e [kytane] *adj* skin

cuti-réaction [kytiʀeaksjɔ̃] *nf (MÉD)* skin-test

cuve [kyv] *nf* vat; *(à mazout etc)* tank

cuvée [kyve] *nf* vintage

cuvette [kyvet] *nf (récipient)* bowl, basin; *(GÉO)* basin

CV *sigle m (AUTO)* = **cheval vapeur**; *(COMM)* = **curriculum vitae**

cyanure [sjanyʀ] *nm* cyanide

cybercafé [sibɛʀkafe] *nm* cybercafé

cyclable [siklabl] *adj:* **piste ~** cycle track

cycle [sikl] *nm* cycle; **cyclisme** *nm* cycling; **cycliste** *nm/f* cyclist ♦ *adj* cycle *cpd;* **coureur cycliste** racing cyclist

cyclomoteur [siklomotœʀ] *nm* moped

cyclone [siklon] *nm* hurricane

cygne [siɲ] *nm* swan

cylindre [silɛ̃dʀ] *nm* cylinder; **cylindrée** *nf (AUTO)* (cubic) capacity

cymbale [sɛ̃bal] *nf* cymbal

cynique [sinik] *adj* cynical

cystite [sistit] *nf* cystitis

D, d

d' [d] *prép voir* **de**

dactylo [daktilo] *nf (aussi: ~graphe)* typist; *(aussi: ~graphie)* typing; **dactylographier** *vt* to type (out)

dada [dada] *nm* hobby-horse

daigner [deɲe] *vt* to deign

daim [dɛ̃] nm (fallow) deer inv; (cuir suédé) suede

dalle [dal] nf paving stone, slab

daltonien, ne [daltɔnjɛ̃, jɛn] adj colour-blind

dam [dã] nm: **au grand ~ de** much to the detriment (ou annoyance) of

dame [dam] nf lady; (CARTES, ÉCHECS) queen; **~s** nfpl (jeu) draughts sg (BRIT), checkers sg (US)

damner [dɑne] vt to damn

dancing [dãsiŋ] nm dance hall

Danemark [danmark] nm Denmark

danger [dɑ̃ʒe] nm danger; **~s** nfpl danger; **dangereux, -euse** adj dangerous

danois, e [danwa, waz] adj Danish ♦ nm/f: **D~, e** Dane ♦ nm (LING) Danish

MOT-CLÉ

dans [dã] prép 1 (position) in; (à l'intérieur de) inside; **c'est dans le tiroir/le salon** it's in the drawer/lounge; **dans la boîte** in ou inside the box; **marcher dans la ville** to walk about the town

2 (direction) into; **elle a couru dans le salon** she ran into the lounge

3 (provenance) out of, from; **je l'ai pris dans le tiroir/salon** I took it out of ou from the drawer/lounge; **boire dans un verre** to drink out of ou from a glass

4 (temps) in; **dans 2 mois** in 2 months, in 2 months' time

5 (approximation) about; **dans les 20 F** about 20F

danse [dãs] nf: **la ~** dancing; **une ~** a dance; **la ~ classique** ballet; **danser** vi, vt to dance; **danseur, -euse** nm/f ballet dancer; (au bal etc) dancer; (: cavalier) partner

dard [dar] nm (d'animal) sting

date [dat] nf date; **de longue ~** long-standing; **~ de naissance** date of birth; **~ de péremption** expiry date; **~ limite** deadline; **dater** vt, vi to date;

dater de to date from; **à dater de** (as) from

datte [dat] nf date

dauphin [dofɛ̃] nm (ZOOL) dolphin

davantage [davãtaʒ] adv more; (plus longtemps) longer; **~ de** more

MOT-CLÉ

de, d' [də] (de + le = du, de + les = des) prép 1 (appartenance) of; **le toit de la maison** the roof of the house; **la voiture d'Ann/de mes parents** Ann's/my parents' car

2 (provenance) from; **il vient de Londres** he comes from London; **elle est sortie du cinéma** she came out of the cinema

3 (caractérisation, mesure): **un mur de brique/bureau d'acajou** a brick wall/mahogany desk; **un billet de 50 F** a 50F note; **une pièce de 2 m de large** ou **large de 2 m** a room 2m wide, a 2m-wide room; **un bébé de 10 mois** a 10-month-old baby; **12 mois de crédit/travail** 12 months' credit/work; **augmenter de 10 F** to increase by 10F; **de 14 à 18** from 14 to 18

♦ dét 1 (phrases affirmatives) some (souvent omis); **du vin, de l'eau, des pommes** (some) wine, (some) water, (some) apples; **des enfants sont venus** some children came; **pendant des mois** for months

2 (phrases interrogatives et négatives) any; **a-t-il du vin?** has he got any wine?; **il n'a pas de pommes/d'enfants** he hasn't (got) any apples/children, he has no apples/children

dé [de] nm (à jouer) die ou dice; (aussi: ~ **à coudre**) thimble

dealer [dilœr] (fam) nm (drug) pusher

déambuler [deãbyle] vi to stroll about

débâcle [debɑkl] nf rout

déballer [debale] vt to unpack

débandade [debãdad] nf (dispersion) scattering

débarbouiller [debaʀbuje] *vt* to wash; **se ~** *vi* to wash (one's face)

débarcadère [debaʀkadɛʀ] *nm* wharf

débardeur [debaʀdœʀ] *nm* (*maillot*) tank top

débarquer [debaʀke] *vt* to unload, land ♦ *vi* to disembark; (*fig: fam*) to turn up

débarras [debaʀɑ] *nm* (*pièce*) lumber room; (*placard*) junk cupboard; **bon ~!** good riddance!; **débarrasser** *vt* to clear; **se débarrasser de** *vt* to get rid of; **débarrasser qn de** (*vêtements, paquets*) to relieve sb of

débat [deba] *nm* discussion, debate; **débattre** *vt* to discuss, debate; **se débattre** *vi* to struggle

débaucher [deboʃe] *vt* (*licencier*) to lay off, dismiss; (*entraîner*) to lead astray, debauch

débile [debil] (*fam*) *adj* (*idiot*) dim-witted

débit [debi] *nm* (*d'un liquide, fleuve*) flow; (*d'un magasin*) turnover (of goods); (*élocution*) delivery; (*bancaire*) debit; **~ de boissons** drinking establishment; **~ de tabac** tobacconist's; **débiter** *vt* (*compte*) to debit; (*couper: bois, viande*) to cut up; (*péj: dire*) to churn out; **débiteur, -trice** *nm/f* debtor ♦ *adj* in debit; (*compte*) debit *cpd*

déblayer [debleje] *vt* to clear

débloquer [deblɔke] *vt* (*prix, crédits*) to free

déboires [debwaʀ] *nmpl* setbacks

déboiser [debwaze] *vt* to deforest

déboîter [debwate] *vt* (*AUTO*) to pull out; **se ~ le genou** *etc* to dislocate one's knee *etc*

débonnaire [debɔnɛʀ] *adj* easy-going, good-natured

débordé, e [debɔʀde] *adj*: **être ~ (de)** (*travail, demandes*) to be snowed under (with)

déborder [debɔʀde] *vi* to overflow; (*lait etc*) to boil over; **~ (de) qch** (*dépasser*) to extend beyond sth

débouché [debuʃe] *nm* (*pour vendre*) outlet; (*perspective d'emploi*) opening

déboucher [debuʃe] *vt* (*évier, tuyau etc*) to unblock; (*bouteille*) to uncork ♦ *vi*: **~ de** to emerge from; **~ sur** (*études*) to lead on to

débourser [debuʀse] *vt* to pay out

déboussolé, e [debusɔle] (*fam*) *adj* disorientated

debout [d(ə)bu] *adv*: **être ~** (*personne*) to be standing, stand; (: *levé, éveillé*) to be up; **se mettre ~** to stand up; **se tenir ~** to stand; **~!** stand up!; (*du lit*) get up!; **cette histoire ne tient pas ~** this story doesn't hold water

déboutonner [debutɔne] *vt* to undo, unbutton

débraillé, e [debʀaje] *adj* slovenly, untidy

débrancher [debʀɑ̃ʃe] *vt* to disconnect; (*appareil électrique*) to unplug

débrayage [debʀɛjaʒ] *nm* (*AUTO*) clutch; **débrayer** *vi* (*AUTO*) to declutch; (*cesser le travail*) to stop work

débris [debʀi] *nmpl* fragments; **des ~ de verre** bits of glass

débrouillard, e [debʀujaʀ, aʀd] (*fam*) *adj* smart, resourceful

débrouiller [debʀuje] *vt* to disentangle, untangle; **se ~** *vi* to manage; **débrouillez-vous** you'll have to sort things out yourself

début [deby] *nm* beginning, start; **~s** *nmpl* (*de carrière*) début; **~ juin** in early June; **débutant, e** *nm/f* beginner, novice; **débuter** *vi* to begin, start; (*faire ses débuts*) to start out

deçà [dəsa]: **en ~ de** *prép* this side of

décadence [dekadɑ̃s] *nf* decline

décaféiné, e [dekafeine] *adj* decaffeinated

décalage [dekalaʒ] *nm* gap; **~ horaire** time difference

décaler [dekale] *vt* to shift

décalquer [dekalke] *vt* to trace

décamper [dekɑ̃pe] (*fam*) *vi* to clear out *ou* off

décaper [dekape] vt (surface peinte) to strip

décapiter [dekapite] vt to behead; (par accident) to decapitate

décapotable [dekapɔtabl] adj convertible

décapsuleur [dekapsylœʀ] nm bottle-opener

décarcasser [dekaʀkase]: **se ~** (fam) vi to flog o.s. to death

décédé, e [desede] adj deceased

décéder [desede] vi to die

déceler [des(ə)le] vt (trouver) to discover, detect

décembre [desɑ̃bʀ] nm December

décemment [desamɑ̃] adv decently

décennie [deseni] nf decade

décent, e [desɑ̃, ɑ̃t] adj decent

déception [desɛpsjɔ̃] nf disappointment

décerner [desɛʀne] vt to award

décès [dese] nm death

décevant, e [des(ə)vɑ̃, ɑ̃t] adj disappointing

décevoir [des(ə)vwaʀ] vt to disappoint

déchaîner [deʃene] vt (violence) to unleash; (enthousiasme) to arouse; **se ~** (tempête) to rage; (personne) to fly into a rage

déchanter [deʃɑ̃te] vi to become disillusioned

décharge [deʃaʀʒ] nf (dépôt d'ordures) rubbish tip ou dump; (électrique) electrical discharge; **décharger** vt (marchandise, véhicule) to unload; (tirer) to discharge; **se décharger** vi (batterie) to go flat; **décharger qn de** (responsabilité) to release sb from

décharné, e [deʃaʀne] adj emaciated

déchausser [deʃose] vt (skis) to take off; **se ~** vi to take off one's shoes; (dent) to come ou work loose

déchéance [deʃeɑ̃s] nf (physique) degeneration; (morale) decay

déchet [deʃɛ] nm (reste) scrap; **~s** nmpl (ordures) refuse sg, rubbish sg; **~s nucléaires** nuclear waste

déchiffrer [deʃifʀe] vt to decipher

déchiqueter [deʃik(ə)te] vt to tear ou pull to pieces

déchirant, e [deʃiʀɑ̃, ɑ̃t] adj heart-rending

déchirement [deʃiʀmɑ̃] nm (chagrin) wrench, heartbreak; (gén pl: conflit) rift, split

déchirer [deʃiʀe] vt to tear; (en morceaux) to tear up; (arracher) to tear out; (fig: conflit) to tear (apart); **se ~** vi to tear, rip; **se ~ un muscle** to tear a muscle

déchirure [deʃiʀyʀ] nf (accroc) tear, rip; **~ musculaire** torn muscle

déchoir [deʃwaʀ] vi (personne) to lower o.s., demean o.s.

déchu, e [deʃy] adj (roi) deposed

décidé, e [deside] adj (personne, air) determined; **c'est ~** it's decided; **décidément** adv really

décider [deside] vt: **~ qch** to decide on sth; **se ~** (à faire) to decide (to do), make up one's mind (to do); **se ~ pour** to decide on ou in favour of; **~ de faire/que** to decide to do/that; **~ qn (à faire qch)** to persuade sb (to do sth)

décimal, e, -aux [desimal, o] adj decimal; **décimale** nf decimal

décimètre [desimɛtʀ] nm decimetre

décisif, -ive [desizif, iv] adj decisive

décision [desizjɔ̃] nf decision

déclaration [deklaʀasjɔ̃] nf declaration; (discours: POL etc) statement; **~ (d'impôts)** ≈ tax return

déclarer [deklaʀe] vt to declare; (décès, naissance) to register; **se ~** vi (feu) to break out

déclencher [deklɑ̃ʃe] vt (mécanisme etc) to release; (sonnerie) to set off; (attaque, grève) to launch; (provoquer) to trigger off; **se ~** vi (mécanisme) to go off

déclic [deklik] nm (bruit) click

décliner [dekline] vi to decline ♦ vt (invitation) to decline; (nom, adresse) to state

décocher [dekɔʃe] vt (coup de poing) to throw; (flèche, regard) to shoot

décoiffer [dekwafe] vt: ~ **qn** to mess up sb's hair; **je suis toute décoiffée** my hair is in a real mess

déçois etc [deswa] vb voir **décevoir**

décollage [dekɔlaʒ] nm (AVIAT) takeoff

décoller [dekɔle] vt to unstick ♦ vi (avion) to take off; **se ~** vi to come unstuck

décolleté, e [dekɔlte] adj low-cut ♦ nm low neck(line); (plongeant) cleavage

décolorer [dekɔlɔRe]: **se ~** vi to fade; **se faire ~ les cheveux** to have one's hair bleached

décombres [dekɔ̃bR] nmpl rubble sg, debris sg

décommander [dekɔmɑ̃de] vt to cancel; **se ~** vi to cry off

décomposé, e [dekɔ̃poze] adj (pourri) decomposed; (visage) haggard, distorted

décompte [dekɔ̃t] nm deduction; (facture) detailed account

déconcerter [dekɔ̃sɛRte] vt to disconcert, confound

déconfit, e [dekɔ̃fi, it] adj crestfallen

décongeler [dekɔ̃ʒ(ə)le] vt to thaw

déconner [dekɔne] vi (fam) to talk rubbish

déconseiller [dekɔ̃seje] vt: ~ **qch** (à **qn**) to advise (sb) against sth; **c'est déconseillé** it's not recommended

décontracté, e [dekɔ̃tRakte] adj relaxed, laid-back (fam)

décontracter [dekɔ̃tRakte]: **se ~** vi to relax

déconvenue [dekɔ̃v(ə)ny] nf disappointment

décor [dekɔR] nm décor; (paysage) scenery; **~s** nmpl (THÉÂTRE) scenery sg, décor sg; (CINÉMA) set sg; **décorateur** nm (interior) decorator; **décoration** nf decoration; **décorer** vt to decorate

décortiquer [dekɔRtike] vt to shell; (fig: texte) to dissect

découcher [dekuʃe] vi to spend the night away from home

découdre [dekudR]: **se ~** vi to come unstitched

découler [dekule] vi: ~ **de** to ensue ou follow from

découper [dekupe] vt (papier, tissu etc) to cut up; (viande) to carve; (article) to cut out; **se faire ~ sur** to stand out against

décourager [dekuRaʒe] vt to discourage; **se ~** vi to lose heart, become discouraged

décousu, e [dekuzy] adj unstitched; (fig) disjointed, disconnected

découvert, e [dekuvɛR, ɛRt] adj (tête) bare, uncovered; (lieu) open, exposed ♦ nm (bancaire) overdraft; **découverte** nf discovery; **faire la découverte de** to discover

découvrir [dekuvRiR] vt to discover; (enlever ce qui couvre) to uncover; (dévoiler) to reveal; **se ~** vi (chapeau) to take off one's hat; (vêtement) to take something off; (ciel) to clear

décret [dekRe] nm decree; **décréter** vt to decree

décrié, e [dekRije] adj disparaged

décrire [dekRiR] vt to describe

décrocher [dekRɔʃe] vt (détacher) to take down; (téléphone) to take off the hook; (: pour répondre) to lift the receiver; (fam: contrat etc) to get, land ♦ vi (fam: abandonner) to drop out; (: cesser d'écouter) to switch off

décroître [dekRwatR] vi to decrease, decline

décrypter [dekRipte] vt to decipher

déçu, e [desy] pp de **décevoir**

décupler [dekyple] vt, vi to increase tenfold

dédaigner [dedeɲe] vt to despise, scorn; (négliger) to disregard, spurn; **dédaigneux, -euse** adj scornful, disdainful; **dédain** nm scorn, disdain

dédale [dedal] nm maze

dedans [dədɑ̃] adv inside; (pas en plein air) indoors, inside ♦ nm inside; **au ~** inside

dédicacer [dedikase] vt: ~ (à qn) to sign (for sb), autograph (for sb)

dédier [dedje] vt to dedicate

dédire [dediʀ]: se ~ vi to go back on one's word, retract

dédommagement [dedɔmaʒmɑ̃] nm compensation

dédommager [dedɔmaʒe] vt: ~ qn (de) to compensate sb (for)

dédouaner [dedwane] vt to clear through customs

dédoubler [deduble] vt (classe, effectifs) to split (into two)

déduire [deduiʀ] vt: ~ qch (de) (ôter) to deduct sth (from); (conclure) to deduce ou infer sth (from)

déesse [dees] nf goddess

défaillance [defajɑ̃s] nf (syncope) blackout; (fatigue) (sudden) weakness no pl; (technique) fault, failure; ~ **cardiaque** heart failure

défaillir [defajiʀ] vi to feel faint; (mémoire etc) to fail

défaire [defɛʀ] vt to undo; (installation) to take down, dismantle; se ~ vi to come undone; se ~ **de** to get rid of

défait, e [defɛ, ɛt] adj (visage) haggard, ravaged; **défaite** nf defeat

défalquer [defalke] vt to deduct

défaut [defo] nm (moral) fault, failing, defect; (tissus) fault, flaw; (manque, carence): ~ **de** shortage of; **prendre qn en** ~ to catch sb out; **faire** ~ (manquer) to be lacking; **à** ~ **de** for lack ou want of

défavorable [defavɔʀabl] adj unfavourable (BRIT), unfavorable (US)

défavoriser [defavɔʀize] vt to put at a disadvantage

défection [defɛksjɔ̃] nf defection, failure to give support

défectueux, -euse [defɛktyø, øz] adj faulty, defective

défendre [defɑ̃dʀ] vt to defend; (interdire) to forbid; se ~ vi to defend o.s.; ~ **à qn qch/de faire** to forbid sb sth/to do; **il se défend** (fam: se débrouille) he

can hold his own; se ~ **de/contre** (se protéger) to protect o.s. from/against; se ~ **de** (se garder de) to refrain from

défense [defɑ̃s] nf defence; (d'éléphant etc) tusk; "~ **de fumer**" "no smoking"

déférer [defeʀe] vt (JUR) to refer; ~ **à** (requête, décision) to defer to

déferler [defɛʀle] vi (vagues) to break; (fig: foule) to surge

défi [defi] nm challenge; **lancer un** ~ **à qn** to challenge sb; **sur un ton de** ~ defiantly

déficit [defisit] nm (COMM) deficit; **déficitaire** adj in deficit

défier [defje] vt (provoquer) to challenge; (mort, autorité) to defy

défigurer [defigyʀe] vt to disfigure

défilé [defile] nm (GÉO) (narrow) gorge ou pass; (soldats) parade; (manifestants) procession, march; ~ **de mode** fashion parade

défiler [defile] vi (troupes) to march past; (sportifs) to parade; (manifestants) to march; (visiteurs) to pour, stream; se ~ vi: **il s'est défilé** (fam) he wriggled out of it

définir [definiʀ] vt to define

définitif, -ive [definitif, iv] adj (final) final, definitive; (pour longtemps) permanent, definitive; (refus) definite; **définitive** nf: **en définitive** eventually; (somme toute) in fact; **définitivement** adv (partir, s'installer) for good

défoncer [defɔ̃se] vt (porte) to smash in ou down; se ~ (fam) vi (travailler) to work like a dog; (drogué) to get high

déformer [defɔʀme] vt to put out of shape; (pensée, fait) to distort; se ~ vi to lose its shape

défouler [defule]: se ~ vi to unwind, let off steam

défraîchir [defʀeʃiʀ]: se ~ vi to fade

défricher [defʀiʃe] vt to clear (for cultivation)

défunt, e [defœ̃, œ̃t] nm/f deceased

dégagé, e [degaʒe] adj (route, ciel) clear; **sur un ton** ~ casually

dégagement [degaʒmɑ̃] nm: **voie de ~** slip road

dégager [degaʒe] vt (exhaler) to give off; (délivrer) to free, extricate; (désencombrer) to clear; (isoler: idée, aspect) to bring out; **se ~** vi (passage, ciel) to clear

dégarnir [degaʀniʀ] vt (vider) to empty, clear; **se ~** vi (tempes, crâne) to go bald

dégâts [dega] nmpl damage sg

dégel [deʒel] nm thaw; **dégeler** vt to thaw (out)

dégénérer [deʒenere] vi to degenerate

dégingandé, e [deʒɛ̃gɑ̃de] adj gangling

dégivrer [deʒivre] vt (frigo) to defrost; (vitres) to de-ice

dégonflé, e [degɔ̃fle] adj (pneu) flat

dégonfler [degɔ̃fle] vt (pneu, ballon) to let down, deflate; **se ~** vi (fam) to chicken out

dégouliner [deguline] vi to trickle, drip

dégourdi, e [degurdi] adj smart, resourceful

dégourdir [degurdir] vt: **se ~ les jambes** to stretch one's legs (fig)

dégoût [degu] nm disgust, distaste; **dégoûtant, e** adj disgusting; **dégoûté, e** adj disgusted; **dégoûté de** sick of; **dégoûter** vt to disgust; **dégoûter qn de qch** to put sb off sth

dégrader [degrade] vt (MIL: officier) to degrade; (abîmer) to damage, deface; **se ~** vi (relations, situation) to deteriorate

dégrafer [degrafe] vt to unclip, unhook

degré [dəgre] nm degree

dégressif, -ive [degresif, iv] adj on a decreasing scale

dégringoler [degrɛ̃gɔle] vi to tumble (down)

dégrossir [degrosir] vt (fig: projet) to work out roughly

déguenillé, e [deg(ə)nije] adj ragged, tattered

déguerpir [degerpir] vi to clear off

dégueulasse [degœlas] (fam) adj disgusting

dégueuler [degœle] (fam) vi to throw up

déguisement [degizmɑ̃] nm (pour s'amuser) fancy dress

déguiser [degize]: **se ~** vi (se costumer) to dress up; (pour tromper) to disguise o.s.

dégustation [degystasjɔ̃] nf (de fromages etc) sampling; **~ de vins** wine-tasting session

déguster [degyste] vt (vins) to taste; (fromages etc) to sample; (savourer) to enjoy, savour

dehors [dəɔr] adv outside; (en plein air) outdoors ♦ nm outside ♦ nmpl (apparences) appearances; **mettre ou jeter ~** (expulser) to throw out; **au ~** outside; **au ~ de** outside; **en ~ de** (hormis) apart from

déjà [deʒa] adv already; (auparavant) before, already

déjeuner [deʒœne] vi to (have) lunch; (le matin) to have breakfast ♦ nm lunch

déjouer [deʒwe] vt (complot) to foil

delà [dəla] adv: **en ~ (de), au ~ (de)** beyond

délabrer [delabre]: **se ~** vi to fall into decay, become dilapidated

délacer [delase] vt (chaussures) to undo

délai [dele] nm (attente) waiting period; (sursis) extension of time; (temps accordé) time limit; **sans ~** without delay; **dans les ~s** within the time limit

délaisser [delese] vt to abandon, desert

délasser [delase] vt to relax; **se ~** vi to relax

délavé, e [delave] adj faded

délayer [deleje] vt (CULIN) to mix (with water etc); (peinture) to thin down

delco [delko] nm (AUTO) distributor

délecter [delekte]: **se ~** vi to revel ou delight in

délégué   81   démettre

délégué, e [delege] *nm/f* representative

déléguer [delege] *vt* to delegate

délibéré, e [delibere] *adj* (*conscient*) deliberate

délibérer [delibere] *vi* to deliberate

délicat, e [delika, at] *adj* delicate; (*plein de tact*) tactful; (*attention*) thoughtful; **délicatement** *adv* delicately; (*avec douceur*) gently

délice [delis] *nm* delight

délicieux, -euse [delisjø, jøz] *adj* (*au goût*) delicious; (*sensation*) delightful

délimiter [delimite] *vt* (*terrain*) to delimit, demarcate

délinquance [delɛ̃kɑ̃s] *nf* criminality; **délinquant, e** *adj, nm/f* delinquent

délirant, e [delirɑ̃, ɑ̃t] (*fam*) *adj* wild

délirer [delire] *vi* to be delirious; **tu délires!** (*fam*) you're crazy!

délit [deli] *nm* (*criminal*) offence

délivrer [delivre] *vt* (*prisonnier*) to (set) free, release; (*passeport*) to issue

déloger [deloʒe] *vt* (*objet coincé*) to dislodge

déloyal, e, -aux [delwajal, o] *adj* (*ami*) disloyal; (*procédé*) unfair

deltaplane [deltaplan] *nm* hang-glider

déluge [delyʒ] *nm* (*pluie*) downpour; (*biblique*) Flood

déluré, e [delyre] (*péj*) *adj* forward, pert

demain [d(ə)mɛ̃] *adv* tomorrow

demande [d(ə)mɑ̃d] *nf* (*requête*) request; (*revendication*) demand; (*d'emploi*) application; (ÉCON): **la ~** demand; **"~s d'emploi"** (*annonces*) "situations wanted"; **~ en mariage** proposal (of marriage)

demandé, e [d(ə)mɑ̃de] *adj* (*article etc*): **très ~** (very) much in demand

demander [d(ə)mɑ̃de] *vt* to ask for; (*chemin, heure etc*) to ask; (*nécessiter*) to require, demand; **se ~ si/pourquoi etc** to wonder whether/why *etc*; **~ qch à qn** to ask sb for sth; **~ un service à qn** to ask sb a favour; **~ à qn de faire** to ask sb to do; **demandeur, -euse**

nm/f: **demandeur d'emploi** job-seeker

démangeaison [demɑ̃ʒɛzɔ̃] *nf* itching; **avoir des ~s** to be itching

démanger [demɑ̃ʒe] *vi* to itch

démanteler [demɑ̃t(ə)le] *vt* to break up

démaquillant [demakijɑ̃] *nm* make-up remover

démaquiller [demakije] *vt*: **se ~** to remove one's make-up

démarche [demarʃ] *nf* (*allure*) gait, walk; (*intervention*) step; (*fig*: *intellectuelle*) thought processes *pl*; **faire les ~s nécessaires (pour obtenir qch)** to take the necessary steps (to obtain sth)

démarcheur, -euse [demarʃœr, øz] *nm/f* (COMM) door-to-door salesman/woman

démarque [demark] *nf* (*article*) markdown

démarrage [demaraʒ] *nm* start

démarrer [demare] *vi* (*conducteur*) to start (up); (*véhicule*) to move off; (*travaux*) to get moving; **démarreur** *nm* (AUTO) starter

démêlant [demelɑ̃] *nm* conditioner

démêler [demele] *vt* to untangle; **démêlés** *nmpl* problems

déménagement [demenaʒmɑ̃] *nm* move; **camion de ~** removal van

déménager [demenaʒe] *vt* (*meubles*) to (re)move ♦ *vi* to move (house); **déménageur** *nm* removal man

démener [dem(ə)ne]: **se ~** *vi* (*se dépenser*) to exert o.s.; (*pour obtenir qch*) to go to great lengths

dément, e [demɑ̃, ɑ̃t] *adj* (*fou*) mad, crazy; (*fam*) brilliant, fantastic

démentiel, le [demɑ̃sjɛl] *adj* insane

démentir [demɑ̃tir] *vt* to refute; **~ que** to deny that

démerder [demerde] (*fam*): **se ~** *vi* to sort things out for o.s.

démesuré, e [dem(ə)zyre] *adj* immoderate

démettre [demetr] *vt*: **~ qn de** (*fonction, poste*) to dismiss sb from; **se ~**

l'épaule *etc* to dislocate one's shoulder *etc*

demeurant [d(ə)mœrã]: **au ~** *adv* for all that

demeure [d(ə)mœr] *nf* residence; **demeurer** *vi* (*habiter*) to live; (*rester*) to remain

demi, e [dəmi] *adj* half ♦ *nm* (*bière*) ≈ half-pint (*0,25 litres*) ♦ *préfixe*: **~...** half-, semi-..., demi-; **trois heures/bouteilles et ~es** three and a half hours/bottles, three hours/bottles and a half; **il est 2 heures et ~e/midi et ~** it's half past 2/half past 12; **à ~** (*heure*) on the half-hour; **à la ~e** (*heure*) on the half-hour; **demi-cercle** *nm* semicircle; **en demi-cercle** ♦ *adj* semicircular ♦ *adv* in half circle; **demi-douzaine** *nf* half-dozen, half a dozen; **demi-finale** *nf* semifinal; **demi-frère** *nm* half-brother; **demi-heure** *nf* half-hour, half an hour; **demi-journée** *nf* half-day, half a day; **demi-litre** *nm* half-litre, half a litre; **demi-livre** *nf* half-pound, half a pound; **demi-mot** *adv*: **à demi-mot** without having to spell things out; **demi-pension** *nf* (*à l'hôtel*) half-board; **demi-pensionnaire** *nm/f*: **être demi-pensionnaire** to take school lunches; **demi-place** *nf* half-fare

démis, e [demi, iz] *adj* (*épaule etc*) dislocated

demi-sel [dəmisɛl] *adj inv* (*beurre, fromage*) slightly salted

demi-sœur [dəmisœr] *nf* half-sister

démission [demisjɔ̃] *nf* resignation; **donner sa ~** to give *ou* hand in one's notice; **démissionner** *vi* to resign

demi-tarif [dəmitarif] *nm* half-price; **voyager à ~~** to travel half-fare

demi-tour [dəmitur] *nm* about-turn; **faire ~~** to turn (and go) back

démocratie [demɔkrasi] *nf* democracy; **démocratique** *adj* democratic

démodé, e [demɔde] *adj* old-fashioned

demoiselle [d(ə)mwazɛl] *nf* (*jeune fille*) young lady; (*célibataire*) single lady,

maiden lady; **~ d'honneur** bridesmaid

démolir [demɔlir] *vt* to demolish

démon [demɔ̃] *nm* (*enfant turbulent*) devil, demon; **le D~** the Devil

démonstration [demɔ̃strasjɔ̃] *nf* demonstration

démonté, e [demɔ̃te] *adj* (*mer*) raging, wild

démonter [demɔ̃te] *vt* (*machine etc*) to take down, dismantle

démontrer [demɔ̃tre] *vt* to demonstrate

démordre [demɔrdr] *vi*: **ne pas ~ de** to refuse to give up, stick to

démouler [demule] *vt* to turn out

démuni, e [demyni] *adj* (*sans argent*) impoverished; **~ de** without

démunir [demynir] *vt*: **~ qn de** to deprive sb of; **se ~ de** to part with, give up

dénaturer [denatyre] *vt* (*goût*) to alter; (*pensée, fait*) to distort

dénicher [denife] *vt* (*fam*) (*objet*) to unearth; (*restaurant etc*) to discover

dénier [denje] *vt* to deny

dénigrer [denigre] *vt* to denigrate, run down

dénivellation [denivelasjɔ̃] *nf* (*pente*) slope

dénombrer [denɔ̃bre] *vt* to count

dénomination [denɔminasjɔ̃] *nf* designation, appellation

dénommé, e [denɔme] *adj*: **un ~ Dupont** a certain Mr Dupont

dénoncer [denɔ̃se] *vt* to denounce

dénouement [denumã] *nm* outcome

dénouer [denwe] *vt* to unknot, undo; **se ~** *vi* (*nœud*) to come undone

dénoyauter [denwajote] *vt* to stone

denrée [dãre] *nf*: **~s (alimentaires)** foodstuffs

dense [dãs] *adj* dense; **densité** *nf* density

dent [dã] *nf* tooth; **~ de lait/sagesse** milk/wisdom tooth; **dentaire** *adj* dental

dentelé, e [dãt(ə)le] *adj* jagged, indented

dentelle [dɑ̃tɛl] *nf* lace *no pl*
dentier [dɑ̃tje] *nm* denture
dentifrice [dɑ̃tifʀis] *nm* toothpaste
dentiste [dɑ̃tist] *nm/f* dentist
dentition [dɑ̃tisjɔ̃] *nf* teeth
dénuder [denyde] *vt* to bare
dénué, e [denye] *adj*: ~ **de** devoid of;
dénuement *nm* destitution
déodorant [deɔdɔʀɑ̃] *nm* deodorant
déontologie [deɔ̃tɔlɔʒi] *nf* code of
practice
dépannage [depanaʒ] *nm*: **service de
~** (AUTO) breakdown service
dépanner [depane] *vt* (*voiture, télévision*) to fix, repair; (*fig*) to bail out, help
out; **dépanneuse** *nf* breakdown lorry
(BRIT), tow truck (US)
dépareillé, e [depaʀeje] *adj* (*collection, service*) incomplete; (*objet*) odd
départ [depaʀ] *nm* departure; (SPORT)
start; **au ~** at the start; **la veille de
son ~** the day before he leaves/left
départager [depaʀtaʒe] *vt* to decide
between
département [depaʀtəmɑ̃] *nm* department

---
département

France is divided into 96 administrative units called **départements**.
These local government divisions are headed by a state-appointed **préfet**, *and administered by an elected* **Conseil général**. *Départements are usually named after prominent geographical features such as rivers or mountain ranges; see also* **DOM-TOM**.

---

dépassé, e [depase] *adj* superseded,
outmoded; **il est complètement ~**
he's completely out of his depth, he
can't cope
dépasser [depase] *vt* (*véhicule, concurrent*) to overtake; (*endroit*) to pass, go
past; (*somme, limite*) to exceed; (*fig: en
beauté etc*) to surpass, outshine ♦ *vi* (*ju-*

pon etc) to show
dépaysé, e [depeize] *adj* disoriented
dépaysement [depeizmɑ̃] *nm* (*changement*) change of scenery
dépecer [depase] *vt* to joint, cut up
dépêche [depɛʃ] *nf* dispatch
dépêcher [depeʃe]: **se ~** *vi* to hurry
dépeindre [depɛ̃dʀ] *vt* to depict
dépendance [depɑ̃dɑ̃s] *nf* dependence; (*bâtiment*) outbuilding
dépendre [depɑ̃dʀ]: **~ de** *vt* to depend
on; (*financièrement etc*) to be dependent on
dépens [depɑ̃] *nmpl*: **aux ~ de** at the
expense of
dépense [depɑ̃s] *nf* spending *no pl*, expense, expenditure *no pl*; **dépenser**
vt to spend; (*énergie*) to expend, use up;
se dépenser *vi* to exert o.s.; **dépensier, -ière** *adj*: **il est dépensier** he's a
spendthrift
dépérir [depeʀiʀ] *vi* (*personne*) to
waste away; (*plante*) to wither
dépêtrer [depetʀe] *vt*: **se ~** to extricate o.s. from
dépeupler [depœple]: **se ~** *vi* to become depopulated
dépilatoire [depilatwaʀ] *adj* depilatory, hair-removing
dépister [depiste] *vt* to detect; (*voleur*)
to track down
dépit [depi] *nm* vexation, frustration;
en ~ de in spite of; **en ~ du bon sens**
contrary to all good sense; **dépité, e**
adj vexed, frustrated
déplacé, e [deplase] *adj* (*propos*) out of
place, uncalled-for
déplacement [deplasmɑ̃] *nm* (*voyage*)
trip, travelling *no pl*
déplacer [deplase] *vt* (*table, voiture*) to
move, shift; **se ~** *vi* to move; (*voyager*)
to travel; **se ~ une vertèbre** to slip a
disc
déplaire [deplɛʀ] *vt*: **ça me déplaît** I
don't like this, I dislike this; **se ~** *vi* to
be unhappy; **déplaisant, e** *adj* disagreeable

dépliant
84
dériver

dépliant [deplijã] *nm* leaflet

déplier [deplije] *vt* to unfold

déplorer [deplɔʀe] *vt* to deplore

déployer [deplwaje] *vt* (*carte*) to open out; (*ailes*) to spread; (*troupes*) to deploy

déporter [depɔʀte] *vt* (*exiler*) to deport; (*dévier*) to carry off course

déposer [depoze] *vt* (*gén: mettre, poser*) to lay *ou* put down; (*à la banque, à la consigne*) to deposit; (*passager*) to drop (off), set down; (*roi*) to depose; (*plainte*) to lodge; (*marque*) to register; **se ~** *vi* to settle; **dépositaire** *nm/f* (*COMM*) agent; **déposition** *nf* statement

dépôt [depo] *nm* (*à la banque, sédiment*) deposit; (*entrepôt*) warehouse, store

dépotoir [depɔtwaʀ] *nm* dumping ground, rubbish dump

dépouiller [depuje] *vt* (*documents*) to go through, peruse; **~ qn/qch de** to strip sb/sth of; **~ le scrutin** to count the votes

dépourvu, e [depuʀvy] *adj:* **~ de** lacking in, without; **prendre qn au ~** to catch sb unprepared

déprécier [depʀesje]: **se ~** *vi* to depreciate

dépression [depʀesjɔ̃] *nf* depression; **~ (nerveuse)** (nervous) breakdown

déprimant, e [depʀimã, ãt] *adj* depressing

déprimer [depʀime] *vi* to be/get depressed

MOT-CLÉ

depuis [dəpɥi] *prép* **1** (*point de départ dans le temps*) since; **il habite Paris depuis 1983/l'an dernier** he has been living in Paris since 1983/last year; **depuis quand le connaissez-vous?** how long have you known him?

2 (*temps écoulé*) for; **il habite Paris depuis 5 ans** he has been living in Paris for 5 years; **je le connais depuis**

3 ans I've known him for 3 years

3 (*lieu*): **il a plu depuis Metz** it's been raining since Metz; **elle a téléphoné depuis Valence** she rang from Valence

4 (*quantité, rang*) from; **depuis les plus petits jusqu'aux plus grands** from the youngest to the oldest

♦ *adv* (*temps*) since (then); **je ne lui ai pas parlé depuis** I haven't spoken to him since (then)

depuis que *conj* (ever) since; **depuis qu'il m'a dit ça** (ever) since he said that to me

---

député, e [depyte] *nm/f* (*POL*) ≃ Member of Parliament (*BRIT*), ≃ Member of Congress (*US*)

députer [depyte] *vt* to delegate

déraciner [deʀasine] *vt* to uproot

dérailler [deʀaje] *vi* (*train*) to be derailed; **faire ~** to derail

déraisonner [deʀɛzɔne] *vi* to talk nonsense, rave

dérangement [deʀãʒmã] *nm* (*gêne*) trouble; (*gastrique etc*) disorder; **en ~** (*téléphone, machine*) out of order

déranger [deʀãʒe] *vt* (*personne*) to trouble, bother; (*projets*) to disrupt, upset; (*objets, vêtements*) to disarrange; **se ~** *vi*: **surtout ne vous dérangez pas pour moi** please don't put yourself out on my account; **est-ce que cela vous dérange si ...?** do you mind if ...?

déraper [deʀape] *vi* (*voiture*) to skid; (*personne, semelles*) to slip

dérégler [deʀegle] *vt* (*mécanisme*) to put out of order; (*estomac*) to upset

dérider [deʀide]: **se ~** *vi* to brighten up

dérision [deʀizjɔ̃] *nf:* **tourner en ~** to deride; **dérisoire** *adj* derisory

dérive [deʀiv] *nf:* **aller à la ~** (*NAVIG, fig*) to drift

dérivé, e [deʀive] *nm* (*TECH*) byproduct

dériver [deʀive] *vt* (*MATH*) to derive;

(*cours d'eau etc*) to divert ♦ *vi* (*bateau*) to drift; **~ de** to derive from

dermatologue [dɛʀmatɔlɔg] *nm/f* dermatologist

dernier, -ière [dɛʀnje, jɛʀ] *adj* last; (*le plus récent*) latest, last; **lundi/le mois ~** last Monday/month; **c'est le ~ cri** it's the very latest thing; **en ~** last; **ce ~, cette dernière** the latter; **dernièrement** *adv* recently

dérobé, e [deʀɔbe] *adj*: **à la ~e** surreptitiously

dérober [deʀɔbe] *vt* to steal; **se ~** *vi* (*s'esquiver*) to slip away; **se ~ à** (*justice, regards*) to hide from; (*obligation*) to shirk

dérogation [deʀɔgasjɔ̃] *nf* (special) dispensation

déroger [deʀɔʒe]: **~ à** *vt* to go against, depart from

dérouiller [deʀuje] *vt*: **se ~ les jambes** to stretch one's legs (*fig*)

déroulement [deʀulmɑ̃] *nm* (*d'une opération etc*) progress

dérouler [deʀule] *vt* (*ficelle*) to unwind; **se ~** *vi* (*avoir lieu*) to take place; (*se passer*) to go (off); **tout s'est déroulé comme prévu** everything went as planned

dérouter [deʀute] *vt* (*avion, train*) to reroute, divert; (*étonner*) to disconcert, throw (out)

derrière [dɛʀjɛʀ] *adv, prép* behind ♦ *nm* (*d'une maison*) back; (*postérieur*) behind, bottom; **les pattes de ~** the back ou hind legs; **par ~** from behind; (*fig*) behind one's back

des [de] *dét voir* **de** ♦ *prép* +*dét* = **de** +**les**

dès [dɛ] *prép* from; **~ que** as soon as; **~ son retour** as soon as he was (*ou* is) back

désabusé, e [dezabyze] *adj* disillusioned

désaccord [dezakɔʀ] *nm* disagreement; **désaccordé, e** *adj* (*MUS*) out of tune

désaffecté, e [dezafɛkte] *adj* disused

désagréable [dezagʀeabl] *adj* unpleasant

désagréger [dezagʀeʒe]: **se ~** *vi* to disintegrate, break up

désagrément [dezagʀemɑ̃] *nm* annoyance, trouble *no pl*

désaltérer [dezalteʀe] *vt*: **se ~** to quench one's thirst

désapprobateur, -trice [dezapʀɔbatœʀ, tʀis] *adj* disapproving

désapprouver [dezapʀuve] *vt* to disapprove of

désarmant, e [dezaʀmɑ̃, ɑ̃t] *adj* disarming

désarroi [dezaʀwa] *nm* disarray

désastre [dezastʀ] *nm* disaster; **désastreux, -euse** *adj* disastrous

désavantage [dezavɑ̃taʒ] *nm* disadvantage; **désavantager** *vt* to put at a disadvantage

descendre [desɑ̃dʀ] *vt* (*escalier, montagne*) to go (*ou* come) down; (*valise, paquet*) to take *ou* get down; (*étagère etc*) to lower; (*fam: abattre*) to shoot down ♦ *vi* (*ou* come) down; (*passager: s'arrêter*) to get out, alight; **~ à pied/en voiture** to walk/drive down; **~ du train** to get out of *ou* get off the train; **~ de cheval** to dismount; **~ à l'hôtel** to stay at a hotel

descente [desɑ̃t] *nf* descent, going down; (*chemin*) way down; (*SKI*) downhill (race); **~ de lit** bedside rug; **~ (de police)** (police) raid

description [dɛskʀipsjɔ̃] *nf* description

désemparé, e [dezɑ̃paʀe] *adj* bewildered, distraught

désemplir [dezɑ̃pliʀ] *vi*: **ne pas ~** to be always full

déséquilibre [dezekilibʀ] *nm* (*position*): **en ~** unsteady; (*fig: des forces, du budget*) imbalance; **déséquilibré, e** *nm/f* (*PSYCH*) unbalanced person; **déséquilibrer** *vt* to throw off balance

désert, e [dezɛʀ, ɛʀt] *adj* deserted ♦ *nm* desert; **déserter** *vi, vt* to desert; **désertique** *adj* desert *cpd*

désespéré, e [dezɛspeʀe] *adj* desperate

désespérer [dezɛspeʀe] *vi*: ~ **(de)** to despair (of); **désespoir** *nm* despair; **en désespoir de cause** in desperation

déshabiller [dezabije] *vt* to undress; **se ~** *vi* to undress (o.s.)

déshériter [dezeʀite] *vt* to disinherit; **déshérités** *nmpl*: **les déshérités** the underprivileged

déshonneur [dezɔnœʀ] *nm* dishonour

déshydraté, e [dezidʀate] *adj* dehydrated

desiderata [dezideʀata] *nmpl* requirements

désigner [deziɲe] *vt* (*montrer*) to point out, indicate; (*dénommer*) to denote; (*candidat etc*) to name

désinfectant, e [dezɛ̃fɛktɑ̃, ɑ̃t] *adj, nm* disinfectant

désinfecter [dezɛ̃fɛkte] *vt* to disinfect

désintégrer [dezɛ̃tegʀe] *vt*: **se ~** *vi* to disintegrate

désintéressé, e [dezɛ̃teʀese] *adj* disinterested, unselfish

désintéresser [dezɛ̃teʀese] *vt*: **se ~ (de)** to lose interest (in)

désintoxication [dezɛ̃tɔksikasjɔ̃] *nf*: **faire une cure de ~** to undergo treatment for alcoholism (*ou* drug addiction)

désinvolte [dezɛ̃vɔlt] *adj* casual, offhand; **désinvolture** *nf* casualness

désir [deziʀ] *nm* wish; (*sensuel*) desire; **désirer** [deziʀe] *vt* to want, wish for; (*sexuellement*) to desire; **je désire ...** (*formule de politesse*) I would like ...

désister [deziste]: **se ~** *vi* to stand down, withdraw

désobéir [dezɔbeiʀ] *vi*: ~ **(à qn/qch)** to disobey (sb/sth); **désobéissant, e** *adj* disobedient

désobligeant, e [dezɔbliʒɑ̃, ɑ̃t] *adj* disagreeable

désodorisant [dezɔdɔʀizɑ̃] *nm* air freshener, deodorizer

désœuvré, e [dezœvʀe] *adj* idle

désolé, e [dezɔle] *adj* (*paysage*) desolate; **je suis ~** I'm sorry

désoler [dezɔle] *vt* to distress, grieve

désopilant, e [dezɔpilɑ̃, ɑ̃t] *adj* hilarious

désordonné, e [dezɔʀdɔne] *adj* untidy

désordre [dezɔʀdʀ] *nm* disorder(liness), untidiness; (*anarchie*) disorder; **en ~** in a mess, untidy

désorienté, e [dezɔʀjɑ̃te] *adj* disorientated

désormais [dezɔʀmɛ] *adv* from now on

désossé, e [dezɔse] *adj* (*viande*) boned

desquelles [dekɛl] *prép +pron* = **de +lesquelles**

desquels [dekɛl] *prép +pron* = **de +lesquels**

desséché, e [deseʃe] *adj* dried up

dessécher [deseʃe] *vt* to dry out

dessein [desɛ̃] *nm*: **à ~** intentionally, deliberately

desserrer [deseʀe] *vt* to loosen; (*frein*) to release

dessert [desɛʀ] *nm* dessert, pudding

desserte [desɛʀt] *nf* (*table*) side table; (*transport*): **la ~ du village est assurée par autocar** there is a coach service to the village

desservir [desɛʀviʀ] *vt* (*ville, quartier*) to serve; (*débarrasser*): ~ **(la table)** to clear the table

dessin [desɛ̃] *nm* (*œuvre, art*) drawing; (*motif*) pattern, design; ~ **animé** cartoon (film); ~ **humoristique** cartoon; **dessinateur, -trice** *nm/f* drawer; (*de bandes dessinées*) cartoonist; (*industriel*) draughtsman(-woman) (*BRIT*), draftsman(-woman) (*US*); **dessiner** *vt* to draw; (*concevoir*) to design

dessous [d(ə)su] *adv* underneath, beneath ♦ *nm* underside ♦ *nmpl* (*sousvêtements*) underwear *sg*; **en ~, par ~** underneath; **au-~** (*ci*) below; (*peu digne de*) beneath; **avoir le ~** to get the worst of it; **les voisins du ~** the downstairs neighbours; **dessous-deplat** *nm inv* tablemat

dessus [d(ə)sy] *adv* on top; (*collé, écrit*)

on it ♦ *nm* top; **en ~** above; **par ~** ♦ *adv* over it ♦ *prép* over; **au-~ (de)** above; **avoir le ~** to get the upper hand; **dessus-de-lit** *nm inv* bedspread

destin [dɛstɛ̃] *nm* fate; (*avenir*) destiny

destinataire [dɛstinatɛR] *nm/f* (*POSTES*) addressee; (*d'un colis*) consignee

destination [dɛstinasjɔ̃] *nf* (*lieu*) destination; (*usage*) purpose; **à ~ de** bound for, travelling to

destinée [dɛstine] *nf* fate; (*existence, avenir*) destiny

destiner [dɛstine] *vt*: **~ qch à qn** (*envisager de donner*) to intend sb to have sth; (*adresser*) to intend sth for sb; **être destiné à** (*usage*) to be meant for

désuet, -ète [dezɥɛ, ɛt] *adj* outdated, outmoded

détachant [detaʃɑ̃] *nm* stain remover

détachement [detaʃmɑ̃] *nm* detachment

détacher [detaʃe] *vt* (*enlever*) to detach, remove; (*délier*) to untie; (*ADMIN*): **~ qn (auprès de** *ou* **à)** to post sb (to); **se ~** *vi* (*se séparer*) to come off; (: *page*) to come out; (*se défaire*) to come undone; **se ~ sur** to stand out against; **se ~ de** (*se désintéresser*) to grow away from

détail [detaj] *nm* detail; (*COMM*): retail; **en ~** in detail; **au ~** (*COMM*) retail; **détaillant** *nm* retailer; **détaillé, e** *adj* (*plan, explications*) detailed; (*facture*) itemized; **détailler** *vt* (*expliquer*) to explain in detail

détaler [detale] (*fam*) *vi* (*personne*) to take off

détartrant [detaRtRɑ̃] *nm* scale remover

détaxé, e [detakse] *adj*: **produits ~s** tax-free goods

détecter [detɛkte] *vt* to detect

détective [detɛktiv] *nm*: **~ (privé)** private detective

déteindre [detɛ̃dR] *vi* (*au lavage*) to run, lose its colour

détendre [detɑ̃dR] *vt* (*corps, esprit*) to

relax; **se ~** *vi* (*ressort*) to lose its tension; (*personne*) to relax

détenir [det(ə)niR] *vt* (*record, pouvoir, secret*) to hold; (*prisonnier*) to detain, hold

détente [detɑ̃t] *nf* relaxation

détention [detɑ̃sjɔ̃] *nf* (*d'armes*) possession; (*captivité*) detention; **~ préventive** custody

détenu, e [det(ə)ny] *nm/f* prisoner

détergent [detɛRʒɑ̃] *nm* detergent

détériorer [deteRjɔRe] *vt* to damage; **se ~** *vi* to deteriorate

déterminé, e [detɛRmine] *adj* (*résolu*) determined; (*précis*) specific, definite

déterminer [detɛRmine] *vt* (*fixer*) to determine; **se ~ à faire qch** to make up one's mind to do sth

déterrer [deteRe] *vt* to dig up

détestable [detɛstabl] *adj* foul, detestable

détester [detɛste] *vt* to hate, detest

détonner [detɔne] *vi* (*fig*) to clash

détour [detuR] *nm* detour; (*tournant*) bend, curve; **ça vaut le ~** it's worth the trip; **sans ~** (*fig*) plainly

détourné, e [detuRne] *adj* (*moyen*) roundabout

détournement [detuRnəmɑ̃] *nm*: **~ d'avion** hijacking

détourner [detuRne] *vt* to divert; (*par la force*) to hijack; (*yeux, tête*) to turn away; (*de l'argent*) to embezzle; **se ~** *vi* to turn away

détracteur, -trice [detRaktœR, tRis] *nm/f* disparager, critic

détraquer [detRake] *vt* to put out of order; (*estomac*) to upset; **se ~** *vi* (*machine*) to go wrong

détrempé, e [detRɑ̃pe] *adj* (*sol*) sodden, waterlogged

détresse [detRɛs] *nf* distress

détriment [detRimɑ̃] *nm*: **au ~ de** to the detriment of

détritus [detRity(s)] *nmpl* rubbish *sg*, refuse *sg*

détroit [detRwa] *nm* strait

détromper [detʀɔpe] vt to disabuse

détruire [detʀɥiʀ] vt to destroy

dette [dɛt] nf debt

DEUG sigle m (= diplôme d'études universitaires générales) diploma taken after 2 years at university

deuil [dœj] nm (perte) bereavement; (période) mourning; **être en ~** to be in mourning

deux [dø] num two; **tous les ~** both; **ses ~ mains** both his hands, his two hands; **~ fois** twice; **deuxième** num second; **deuxièmement** adv secondly; **deux-pièces** nm inv (tailleur) two-piece suit; (de bain) two-piece (swimsuit); (appartement) two-roomed flat (BRIT) ou apartment (US); **deux-points** nm inv colon sg; **deux-roues** nm inv two-wheeled vehicle

devais etc [dəvɛ] vb voir devoir

dévaler [devale] vt to hurtle down

dévaliser [devalize] vt to rob, burgle

dévaloriser [devalɔʀize] vt to depreciate; **se ~** vi to depreciate

dévaluation [devalɥasjɔ̃] nf devaluation

devancer [dəvɑ̃se] vt (coureur, rival) to get ahead of; (arriver) to arrive before; (prévenir: questions, désirs) to anticipate

devant [dəvɑ̃] adv in front; (à distance: en avant) ahead ♦ prép in front of; (en avant) ahead of; (avec mouvement: passer) past; (en presence de) before, in front of; (étant donné) in view of ♦ nm front; **prendre les ~s** to make the first move; **les pattes de ~** the front legs, the forelegs; **par ~** (boutonner) at the front; (entrer) the front way; **aller au-~ de qn** to go out to meet sb; **aller au-~ de** (désirs de qn) to anticipate

devanture [dəvɑ̃tyʀ] nf (étalage) display; (vitrine) (shop) window

déveine [devɛn] (fam) nf rotten luck no pl

développement [dev(ə)lɔpmɑ̃] nm development; **pays en voie de ~** developing countries

développer [dev(ə)lɔpe] vt to develop; **se ~** vi to develop

devenir [dəv(ə)niʀ] vb +attrib to become; **que sont-ils devenus?** what has become of them?

dévergondé, e [devɛʀgɔ̃de] adj wild, shameless

déverser [devɛʀse] vt (liquide) to pour (out); (ordures) to tip (out); **se ~ dans** (fleuve) to flow into

dévêtir: se ~ [devetiʀ] vi to undress

devez etc [dəve] vb voir devoir

déviation [devjasjɔ̃] nf (AUTO) diversion (BRIT), detour (US)

devienne etc [dəvjɛn] vb voir devenir

dévier [devje] vt (fleuve, circulation) to divert; (coup) to deflect ♦ vi to veer (off course)

devin [dəvɛ̃] nm soothsayer, seer

deviner [d(ə)vine] vt to guess; (apercevoir) to distinguish; **devinette** nf riddle

devins etc [dəvɛ̃] vb voir devenir

devis [d(ə)vi] nm estimate, quotation

dévisager [devizaʒe] vt to stare at

devise [dəviz] nf (formule) motto, watchword; **~s** nfpl (argent) currency sg

deviser [dəvize] vi to converse

dévisser [devise] vt to unscrew, undo

dévoiler [devwale] vt to unveil

devoir [d(ə)vwaʀ] nm duty; (SCOL) homework no pl; (: en classe) exercise ♦ vt (argent, respect): **~ qch (à qn)** to owe (sb) sth; (+infin: obligation): **il doit le faire** he has to do it, he must do it; (: intention): **le nouveau centre commercial doit ouvrir en mai** the new shopping centre is due to open in May; (: probabilité): **il doit être tard** it must be late

dévolu [devɔly] nm: **jeter son ~ sur** to fix one's choice on

dévorer [devɔre] vt to devour

dévot, e [devo, ɔt] adj devout, pious; **dévotion** nf devoutness

dévoué, e [devwe] adj devoted

dévouement [devumɑ̃] nm devotion

dévouer [devwe]: **se ~** vi (se sacrifier): **se ~ (pour)** to sacrifice o.s. (for); (se consacrer): **se ~ à** to devote ou dedicate o.s. to

dévoyé, e [devwaje] adj delinquent

devrai etc [dəvʀe] vb voir **devoir**

diabète [djabɛt] nm diabetes sg; **diabétique** nm/f diabetic

diable [djabl] nm devil

diabolo [djabɔlo] nm (boisson) lemonade with fruit cordial

diagnostic [djagnɔstik] nm diagnosis sg; **diagnostiquer** vt to diagnose

diagonal, e, -aux [djagɔnal, o] adj diagonal; **diagonale** nf diagonal; **en diagonale** diagonally

diagramme [djagʀam] nm chart, graph

dialecte [djalɛkt] nm dialect

dialogue [djalɔg] nm dialogue

diamant [djamɑ̃] nm diamond

diamètre [djamɛtʀ] nm diameter

diapason [djapazɔ̃] nm tuning fork

diaphragme [djafʀagm] nm diaphragm

diapo [djapo] (fam) nf slide

diapositive [djapozitiv] nf transparency, slide

diarrhée [djaʀe] nf diarrhoea

dictateur [diktatœʀ] nm dictator; **dictature** nf dictatorship

dictée [dikte] nf dictation

dicter [dikte] vt to dictate

dictionnaire [diksjɔnɛʀ] nm dictionary

dicton [diktɔ̃] nm saying, dictum

dièse [djɛz] nm sharp

diesel [djezɛl] nm diesel ♦ adj inv diesel

diète [djɛt] nf (jeûne) starvation diet; (régime) diet; **diététique** adj: **magasin diététique** health food shop

dieu, x [djø] nm god; **D~** God; **mon D~!** good heavens!

diffamation [difamasjɔ̃] nf slander; (écrite) libel

différé [difeʀe] nm (TV): **en ~** (pre-recorded

différemment [difeʀamɑ̃] adv differently

différence [difeʀɑ̃s] nf difference; **à la ~ de** unlike; **différencier** vt to differentiate; **différend** nm difference (of opinion), disagreement

différent, e [difeʀɑ̃, ɑ̃t] adj (dissemblable) different; **~ de** different from; (divers) different, various

différer [difeʀe] vt to postpone, put off ♦ vi: **~ (de)** to differ (from)

difficile [difisil] adj difficult; (exigeant) hard to please; **difficilement** adv with difficulty

difficulté [difikylte] nf difficulty; **en ~** (bateau, alpiniste) in difficulties

difforme [difɔʀm] adj deformed, misshapen

diffuser [difyze] vt (chaleur) to diffuse; (émission, musique) to broadcast; (nouvelle) to circulate; (COMM) to distribute

digérer [diʒeʀe] vt to digest; (fam: accepter) to stomach, put up with; **digestif** nm (after-dinner) liqueur; **digestion** nf digestion

digne [diɲ] adj dignified; **~ de** worthy of; **~ de foi** trustworthy; **dignité** nf dignity

digue [dig] nf dike, dyke

dilapider [dilapide] vt to squander

dilemme [dilɛm] nm dilemma

dilettante [diletɑ̃t] nm/f: **faire qch en ~** to dabble in sth

diligence [diliʒɑ̃s] nf stagecoach

diluer [dilɥe] vt to dilute

diluvien, ne [dilyvjɛ̃, jɛn] adj: **pluie ~ne** torrential rain

dimanche [dimɑ̃ʃ] nm Sunday

dimension [dimɑ̃sjɔ̃] nf (grandeur) size; (~s) dimensions

diminué, e [diminɥe] adj: **il est très ~ depuis son accident** he's not at all the man he was since his accident

diminuer [diminɥe] vt to reduce, decrease; (ardeur etc) to lessen; (dénigrer) to belittle ♦ vi to decrease, diminish;

diminutif nm (surnom) pet name; **diminution** nf decreasing, diminishing

dinde [dɛ̃d] nf turkey

dindon [dɛ̃dɔ̃] nm turkey

dîner [dine] nm dinner ♦ vi to have dinner

dingue [dɛ̃g] (fam) adj crazy

dinosaure [dinɔzɔʀ] nm dinosaur

diplomate [diplɔmat] adj diplomatic ♦ nm diplomat; (fig) diplomatist; **diplomatie** nf diplomacy

diplôme [diplom] nm diploma; **avoir des ~s** to have qualifications; **diplômé, e** adj qualified

dire [diʀ] nm: **au ~ de** according to ♦ vt to say; (secret, mensonge, heure) to tell; **~ qch à qn** to tell sb sth; **~ à qn qu'il fasse** ou **de faire** to tell sb to do; **on dit que** they say that; **ceci dit** that being said; **si cela lui dit** (plaire) if he fancies it; **que dites-vous de** (penser) what do you think of; **on dirait que** it looks (ou sounds etc) as if; **dis/dites (donc)!** I say!

direct, e [diʀɛkt] adj direct ♦ nm (TV): **en ~** live; **directement** adv directly

directeur, -trice [diʀɛktœʀ, tʀis] nm/f (d'entreprise) director; (de service) manager(-eress); (d'école) head(teacher) (BRIT), principal (US)

direction [diʀɛksjɔ̃] nf (sens) direction; (d'entreprise) management; (AUTO) steering; **"toutes ~s"** "all routes"

dirent [diʀ] vb voir **dire**

dirigeant, e [diʀiʒɑ̃, ɑ̃t] adj (classe) ruling ♦ nm/f (d'un parti etc) leader

diriger [diʀiʒe] vt (entreprise) to manage, run; (véhicule) to steer; (orchestre) to conduct; (recherches, travaux) to supervise; **se ~** vi (s'orienter) to find one's way; **se ~ vers** ou **sur** to make ou head for

dis [di] vb voir **dire**

discernement [disɛʀnəmɑ̃] nm (bon sens) discernment, judgement

discerner [disɛʀne] vt to discern, make out

discipline [disiplin] nf discipline; **discipliner** vt to discipline

discontinu, e [diskɔ̃tiny] adj intermittent

discontinuer [diskɔ̃tinɥe] vi: **sans ~** without stopping, without a break

discordant, e [diskɔʀdɑ̃, ɑ̃t] adj discordant

discothèque [diskɔtɛk] nf (boîte de nuit) disco(thèque)

discours [diskuʀ] nm speech

discret, -ète [diskʀɛ, ɛt] adj discreet; (parfum, maquillage) unobtrusive; **discrétion** nf discretion; **à discrétion** as much as one wants

discrimination [diskʀiminasjɔ̃] nf discrimination; **sans ~** indiscriminately

disculper [diskylpe] vt to exonerate

discussion [diskysjɔ̃] nf discussion

discutable [diskytabl] adj debatable

discuté, e [diskyte] adj controversial

discuter [diskyte] vt (débattre) to discuss; (contester) to question, dispute ♦ vi to talk; (protester) to argue; **~ de** to discuss

dise etc [diz] vb voir **dire**

diseuse [dizøz] nf: **~ de bonne aventure** fortuneteller

disgracieux, -euse [disgʀasjø, jøz] adj ungainly, awkward

disjoindre [disʒwɛ̃dʀ] vt to take apart; **se ~** vi to come apart

disjoncteur [disʒɔ̃ktœʀ] nm (ÉLEC) circuit breaker

disloquer [dislɔke]: **se ~** vi (parti, empire) to break up

disons [dizɔ̃] vb voir **dire**

disparaître [dispaʀɛtʀ] vi to disappear; (se perdre: traditions etc) to die out; **faire ~** (tache) to remove; (douleur) to get rid of

disparition [dispaʀisjɔ̃] nf disappearance; **espèce en voie de ~** endangered species

disparu, e [dispaʀy] nm/f missing person ♦ adj: **être porté ~** to be reported missing

dispensaire [dispɑ̃sɛʀ] nm community clinic

dispenser [dispɑ̃se] vt: ~ **qn de** to exempt sb from; **se ~ de** vt (corvée) to get out of

disperser [dispɛʀse] vt to scatter; **se ~** vi to break up

disponibilité [disponibilite] nf availability; **disponible** adj available

dispos [dispo] adj m: **(frais et) ~** fresh (as a daisy)

disposé, e [dispoze] adj: **bien/mal ~** (humeur) in a good/bad mood; **~ à** (prêt à) willing ou prepared to

disposer [dispoze] vt to arrange ♦ vi: **vous pouvez ~** you may leave; **~ de** to have (at one's disposal); **se ~ à faire** to prepare to do, be about to do

dispositif [dispozitif] nm device; (fig) system, plan of action

disposition [dispozisjɔ̃] nf (arrangement) arrangement, layout; (humeur) mood; **prendre ses ~s** to make arrangements; **avoir des ~s pour la musique** etc to have a special aptitude for music etc; **à la ~ de qn** at sb's disposal; **je suis à votre ~** I am at your service

disproportionné, e [dispʀopɔʀsjɔne] adj disproportionate, out of all proportion

dispute [dispyt] nf quarrel, argument; **disputer** vt (match) to play; (combat) to fight; **se disputer** vi to quarrel

disquaire [diskɛʀ] nm/f record dealer

disqualifier [diskalifje] vt to disqualify

disque [disk] nm (MUS) record; (forme, pièce) disc; (SPORT) discus; **~ compact** compact disc; **~ dur** hard disk; **disquette** nf floppy disk, diskette

disséminer [disemine] vt to scatter

disséquer [diseke] vt to dissect

dissertation [disɛʀtasjɔ̃] nf (SCOL) essay

dissimuler [disimyle] vt to conceal

dissipé, e [disipe] adj (élève) undisciplined, unruly

dissiper [disipe] vt to dissipate; (for-

tune) to squander; **se ~** vi (brouillard) to clear, disperse

dissolvant [disɔlvɑ̃] nm nail polish remover

dissonant, e [disɔnɑ̃, ɑ̃t] adj discordant

dissoudre [disudʀ] vt to dissolve; **se ~** vi to dissolve

dissuader [disɥade] vt: **~ qn de faire** to dissuade sb from doing; **dissuasion** nf: **force de dissuasion** deterrent power

distance [distɑ̃s] nf distance; (fig: écart) gap; **à ~** at ou from a distance; **distancer** vt to outdistance

distant, e [distɑ̃, ɑ̃t] adj (réservé) distant; **~ de** (lieu) far away from

distendre [distɑ̃dʀ]: **se ~** vi to distend

distillerie [distilʀi] nf distillery

distinct, e [distɛ̃(kt), ɛ̃kt] adj distinct; **distinctement** adv distinctly, clearly; **distinctif, -ive** adj distinctive

distingué, e [distɛ̃ge] adj distinguished

distinguer [distɛ̃ge] vt to distinguish

distraction [distʀaksjɔ̃] nf (inattention) absent-mindedness; (passe-temps) distraction, entertainment

distraire [distʀɛʀ] vt (divertir) to entertain, divert; (déranger) to distract; **se ~** to amuse ou enjoy o.s.; **distrait, e** adj absent-minded

distrayant, e [distʀɛjɑ̃, ɑ̃t] adj entertaining

distribuer [distʀibɥe] vt to distribute, hand out; (CARTES) to deal (out); (courrier) to deliver; **distributeur** nm (COMM) distributor; (automatique) (vending) machine; (: de billets) (cash) dispenser; **distribution** nf distribution; (postale) delivery; (choix d'acteurs) casting, cast

dit, e [di, dit] pp de **dire** ♦ adj (fixé): **le jour ~** the arranged day; (surnommé): **X, ~ Pierrot** X, known as Pierrot

dites [dit] vb voir **dire**

divaguer [divage] vi to ramble; (fam) to rave

divan [divã] *nm* divan

diverger [diverʒe] *vi* to diverge

divers, e [diver, ers] *adj* (*varié*) diverse, varied; (*différent*) different, various; **~es personnes** various *ou* several people

diversifier [diversifje] *vt* to vary

diversité [diversite] *nf* (*variété*) diversity

divertir [divertir]: **se ~** *vi* to amuse *ou* enjoy o.s.; **divertissement** *nm* distraction, entertainment

divin, e [divɛ̃, in] *adj* divine

diviser [divize] *vt* to divide; **division** *nf* division

divorce [divɔrs] *nm* divorce; **divorcé, e** *nm/f* divorcee; **divorcer** *vi* to get a divorce, get divorced

divulguer [divylge] *vt* to disclose

dix [dis] *num* ten; **dixième** *num* tenth

dizaine [dizɛn] *nf*: **une ~ (de)** about ten, ten *ou* so

do [do] *nm* (*note*) C; (*en chantant la gamme*) do(h)

docile [dɔsil] *adj* docile

dock [dɔk] *nm* dock; **docker** *nm* docker

docteur [dɔktœr] *nm* doctor; **doctorat** *nm* doctorate; **doctoresse** *nf* lady doctor

doctrine [dɔktrin] *nf* doctrine

document [dɔkymã] *nm* document; **documentaire** *adj, nm* documentary; **documentaliste** *nm/f* (*SCOL*) librarian; **documentation** *nf* documentation, literature; **documenter** *vt*: **se documenter (sur)** to gather information (on)

dodo [dodo] *nm* (*langage enfantin*): **aller faire ~** to go to beddy-byes

dodu, e [dɔdy] *adj* plump

dogue [dɔg] *nm* mastiff

doigt [dwa] *nm* finger; **à deux ~s de** within an inch of; **~ de pied** toe; **doigté** *nm* (*MUS*) fingering; (*fig: habileté*) diplomacy, tact

doit *etc* [dwa] *vb voir* **devoir**

doléances [dɔleãs] *nfpl* grievances

dollar [dɔlar] *nm* dollar

domaine [dɔmɛn] *nm* estate, property; (*fig*) domain, field

domestique [dɔmɛstik] *adj* domestic ♦ *nm/f* servant, domestic; **domestiquer** *vt* to domesticate

domicile [dɔmisil] *nm* home, place of residence; **à ~** at home; **livrer à ~** to deliver; **domicilié, e** *adj*: **"domicilié à ..."** "address ..."

dominant, e [dɔminã, ãt] *adj* (*opinion*) predominant

dominer [dɔmine] *vt* to dominate; (*sujet*) to master; (*surpasser*) to outclass, surpass; (*surplomber*) to tower above, dominate ♦ *vi* to be in the dominant position; **se ~** *vi* to control o.s.

domino [dɔmino] *nm* domino

dommage [dɔmaʒ] *nm*: **~s** (*dégâts*) damage *no pl*; **c'est ~!** what a shame!; **c'est ~ que** it's a shame *ou* pity that; **dommages-intérêts** *nmpl* damages

dompter [dɔ̃(p)te] *vt* to tame; **dompteur, -euse** *nm/f* trainer

DOM-TOM [dɔmtɔm] *sigle m* (= *départements et territoires d'outre-mer*) French overseas departments and territories

don [dɔ̃] *nm* gift; (*charité*) donation; **avoir du ~s pour** to have a gift *ou* talent for; **elle a le ~ de m'énerver** she's got a knack of getting on my nerves

donc [dɔ̃k] *conj* therefore, so; (*après une digression*) so, then

donjon [dɔ̃ʒɔ̃] *nm* keep

donné, e [dɔne] *adj* (*convenu: lieu, heure*) given; (*pas cher: fam*): **c'est ~** it's a gift; **étant ~ ...** given ...; **données** *nfpl* data

donner [dɔne] *vt* to give; (*vieux habits etc*) to give away; (*spectacle*) to put on; **~ qch à qn** to give sb sth, give sth to sb; **~ sur** (*suj: fenêtre, chambre*) to look (out) onto; **ça donne soif/faim** it makes you (feel) thirsty/hungry; **se ~ à fond** to give one's all; **se ~ du mal** to take (great) trouble; **s'en ~ à cœur**

joie (fam) to have a great time

MOT-CLÉ
---

dont [dɔ̃] pron relatif **1** (appartenance: objets) whose, of which; (appartenance: êtres animés) whose; **la maison dont le toit est rouge** the house the roof of which is red, the house whose roof is red; **l'homme dont je connais la sœur** the man whose sister I know

2 (parmi lesquel(le)s): **2 livres, dont l'un est ...** 2 books, one of which is ...; **il y avait plusieurs personnes, dont Gabrielle** there were several people, among them Gabrielle; **10 blessés, dont 2 grièvement** 10 injured, of which 2 of them seriously

3 (complément d'adjectif, de verbe): **le fils dont il est si fier** the son he's so proud of; **ce dont je parle** what I'm talking about

doré, e [dɔʀe] adj golden; (avec dorure) gilt, gilded

dorénavant [dɔʀenavɑ̃] adv henceforth

dorer [dɔʀe] vt to gild; (faire) ~ (CULIN) to brown

dorloter [dɔʀlɔte] vt to pamper

dormir [dɔʀmiʀ] vi to sleep; (être endormi) to be asleep

dortoir [dɔʀtwaʀ] nm dormitory

dorure [dɔʀyʀ] nf gilding

dos [do] nm back; (de livre) spine; "**voir au ~**" "see over"; **de ~** from the back

dosage [dozaʒ] nm mixture

dose [doz] nf dose; **doser** vt to measure out; **il faut savoir doser ses efforts** you have to be able to pace yourself

dossard [dosaʀ] nm number (worn by competitor)

dossier [dosje] nm (documents) file; (de chaise) back; (PRESSE) feature; **un ~ scolaire** a school report

dot [dɔt] nf dowry

doter [dɔte] vt: ~ **de** to equip with

douane [dwan] nf customs pl; **douanier, -ière** adj customs cpd ♦ nm customs officer

double [dubl] adj, adv double ♦ nm (2 fois plus): **le ~ (de)** twice as much (ou many) (as); (autre exemplaire) duplicate, copy; (sosie) double; (TENNIS) doubles sg; **en ~ (exemplaire)** in duplicate; **faire ~ emploi** to be redundant

double-cliquer [dublklike] vi (INFORM) to double-click

doubler [duble] vt (multiplier par 2) to double; (vêtement) to line; (dépasser) to overtake, pass; (film) to dub; (acteur) to stand in for ♦ vi to double

doublure [dublyʀ] nf lining; (CINÉMA) stand-in

douce [dus] adj voir doux; **douceâtre** adj sickly sweet; **doucement** adv gently; (lentement) slowly; **doucereux, -euse** (péj) adj sugary; **douceur** nf softness; (de quelqu'un) gentleness; (de climat) mildness

douche [duʃ] nf shower; **doucher: se doucher** vi to have ou take a shower

doudoune [dudun] nf padded jacket

doué, e [dwe] adj gifted, talented; **être ~ pour** to have a gift for

douille [duj] nf (ÉLEC) socket

douillet, te [dujɛ, ɛt] adj cosy; (péj: à la douleur) soft

douleur [dulœʀ] nf pain; (chagrin) grief, distress; **douloureux, -euse** adj painful

doute [dut] nm doubt; **sans ~** no doubt; (probablement) probably; **sans aucun ~** without a doubt; **douter** vt to doubt; **douter de** (sincérité de qn) to have (one's) doubts about; (réussite) to be doubtful of; **se douter de qch/que** to suspect sth/that; **je m'en doutais** I suspected as much; **douteux, -euse** adj (incertain) doubtful; (péj) dubious-looking

Douvres [duvʀ] n Dover

doux, douce [du, dus] adj soft; (sucré) sweet; (peu fort: moutarde, clément: cli-

mat) mild; *(pas brusque)* gentle

douzaine [duzɛn] *nf (12) dozen; (environ 12):* **une ~ (de)** a dozen or so

douze [duz] *num* twelve; **douzième** *num* twelfth

doyen, ne [dwajɛ̃, jɛn] *nm/f (en âge)* most senior member; *(de faculté)* dean

dragée [draʒe] *nf* sugared almond

dragon [dragɔ̃] *nm* dragon

draguer [drage] *vt (rivière)* to dredge; *(fam)* to try to pick up

dramatique [dramatik] *adj* dramatic; *(tragique)* tragic ♦ *nf (TV)* (television) drama

dramaturge [dramatyrʒ] *nm* dramatist, playwright

drame [dram] *nm* drama

drap [dra] *nm (de lit)* sheet; *(tissu)* woollen fabric

drapeau, x [drapo] *nm* flag

drap-housse [draus] *nm* fitted sheet

dresser [drese] *vt (mettre vertical, monter)* to put up, erect; *(liste)* to draw up; *(animal)* to train; **se ~** *vi (obstacle)* to stand; *(personne)* to draw o.s. up; **~ qn contre qn** to set sb against sb; **~ l'oreille** to prick up one's ears

drogue [drɔg] *nf* drug; **la ~** drugs *pl*; **drogué, e** *nm/f* drug addict; **droguer** *vt (victime)* to drug; **se droguer** *vi (aux stupéfiants)* to take drugs; *(péj: de médicaments)* to dose o.s. up; **droguerie** *nf* hardware shop; **droguiste** *nf* keeper/ owner of a hardware shop

droit, e [drwa, drwat] *adj (non courbe)* straight; *(vertical)* upright, straight; *(fig: loyal)* upright, straight(forward); *(opposé à gauche)* right, right-hand ♦ *adv* straight ♦ *nm (prérogative)* right; *(taxe)* duty, tax; *(: d'inscription)* fee; *(JUR):* **le ~** law; **avoir le ~ de** to be allowed to; **avoir ~ à** to be entitled to; **être dans son ~** to be within one's rights; **à ~e** on the right; *(direction)* to the right; **~s d'auteur** royalties; **~s de l'homme** human rights; **~ d'inscription** enrolment fee; **droite** *nf (POL):* **la droite**

right; *(wing)*; **droitier, -ière** *nm/f* right-handed person; **droiture** *nf* uprightness, straightness

drôle [drol] *adj* funny; **une ~ d'idée** a funny idea; **drôlement** *(fam) adv (très)* terribly, awfully

dromadaire [drɔmadɛr] *nm* dromedary

dru, e [dry] *adj (cheveux)* thick, bushy; *(pluie)* heavy

du [dy] *dét voir* **de** ♦ *prép +dét =* **de + le**

dû, due [dy] *vb voir* **devoir** ♦ *adj (somme)* owing, owed; *(causé par):* **~ à** due to ♦ *nm* due

duc [dyk] *nm* duke; **duchesse** *nf* duchess

dûment [dymɑ̃] *adv* duly

dune [dyn] *nf* dune

Dunkerque [dɛ̃kɛrk] *n* Dunkirk

duo [dɥo] *nm (MUS)* duet

dupe [dyp] *nf* dupe ♦ *adj:* **(ne pas) être ~ de** (not) to be taken in by

duplex [dyplɛks] *nm (appartement)* split-level apartment, duplex

duplicata [dyplikata] *nm* duplicate

duquel [dykɛl] *prép +pron =* **de +lequel**

dur, e [dyr] *adj (pierre, siège, travail, problème)* hard; *(viande, climat)* harsh; *(sévère)* hard, harsh; *(cruel)* hard(-hearted); *(porte, col)* stiff; *(viande)* tough ♦ *adv* hard ♦ *nm (fam: meneur)* tough nut; **~ d'oreille** hard of hearing

durant [dyrɑ̃] *prép (au cours de)* during; *(pendant)* for; **des mois ~** for months

durcir [dyrsir] *vt, vi* to harden; **se ~** *vi* to harden

durée [dyre] *nf* length; *(d'une pile etc)* life; **de courte ~** *(séjour)* short

durement [dyrmɑ̃] *adv* harshly

durer [dyre] *vi* to last

dureté [dyrte] *nf* hardness; harshness; stiffness; toughness

durit ® [dyrit] *nf (car radiator)* hose

dus *etc* [dy] *vb voir* **devoir**

duvet [dyvɛ] *nm* down; *(sac de couchage)* down-filled sleeping bag

DVD sigle m (= digital versatile disc) DVD

dynamique [dinamik] adj dynamic; **dynamisme** nm dynamism

dynamite [dinamit] nf dynamite

dynamo [dinamo] nf dynamo

dyslexie [disleksi] nf dyslexia, word-blindness

E, e

eau, x [o] nf water; **~x** nfpl (MÉD) waters; **prendre l'~** to leak, let in water; **tomber à l'~** (fig) to fall through; **~ courante** running water; **~ de Javel** bleach; **~ de toilette** toilet water; **~ douce** fresh water; **~ gazeuse** sparkling (mineral) water; **~ minérale** mineral water; **~ plate** still water; **~ potable** drinking water; **eau-de-vie** nf brandy; **eau-forte** nf etching

ébahi, e [ebai] adj dumbfounded

ébattre [ebatʀ]: **s'~** vi to frolic

ébaucher [eboʃe] vt to sketch out, outline; **s'~** vi to take shape

ébène [eben] nf ebony; **ébéniste** nm cabinetmaker

éberlué, e [ebeʀlɥe] adj astounded

éblouir [ebluiʀ] vt to dazzle

éborgner [ebɔʀɲe] vt to blind in one eye

éboueur [ebwœʀ] nm dustman (BRIT), garbageman (US)

ébouillanter [ebujɑ̃te] vt to scald; (CULIN) to blanch

éboulement [ebulmɑ̃] nm rock fall

ébouler [ebule]: **s'~** vi to crumble, collapse; **éboulis** nmpl fallen rocks

ébouriffé, e [eburife] adj tousled

ébranler [ebʀɑ̃le] vt to shake; (fig) to weaken; **s'~** vi (partir) to move off

ébrécher [ebʀeʃe] vt to chip

ébriété [ebʀijete] nf: **en état d'~** in a state of intoxication

ébrouer [ebʀue]: **s'~** vi to shake o.s.

ébruiter [ebʀɥite] vt to spread, disclose

ébullition [ebylisjɔ̃] nf boiling point

écaille [ekaj] nf (de poisson) scale; (matière) tortoiseshell; **écailler** vt (poisson) to scale; **s'écailler** vi to flake ou peel (off)

écarlate [ekaʀlat] adj scarlet

écarquiller [ekaʀkije] vt: **~ les yeux** to stare wide-eyed

écart [ekaʀ] nm gap; à l'~ out of the way; à l'~ de away from; **faire un ~** (voiture) to swerve; **~ de conduite** misdemeanour

écarté, e [ekaʀte] adj (lieu) out-of-the-way, remote; (ouvert): **les jambes ~es** legs apart; **les bras ~s** arms outstretched

écarter [ekaʀte] vt (séparer) to move apart, separate; (éloigner) to push back, move away; (ouvrir: bras, jambes) to spread, open; (: rideau) to draw (back); (éliminer: candidat, possibilité) to dismiss; **s'~** vi to part; (s'éloigner) to move away; **s'~ de** to wander from

écervelé, e [esεʀvəle] adj scatterbrained, featherbrained

échafaud [eʃafo] nm scaffold

échafaudage [eʃafodaʒ] nm scaffolding

échafauder [eʃafode] vt (plan) to construct

échalote [eʃalɔt] nf shallot

échancrure [eʃɑ̃kʀyʀ] nf (de robe) scoop neckline

échange [eʃɑ̃ʒ] nm exchange; **en ~ de** in exchange ou return for; **échanger** vt: **échanger qch (contre)** to exchange sth (for); **échangeur** nm (AUTO) interchange

échantillon [eʃɑ̃tijɔ̃] nm sample

échappement [eʃapmɑ̃] nm (AUTO) exhaust

échapper [eʃape]: **~ à** vt (gardien) to escape (from); (punition, péril) to escape; **s'~** vi to escape; **~ à qn** (détail, sens) to escape sb; (objet qu'on tient) to slip out of sb's hands; **laisser ~** (cri etc) to let out; **l'~ belle** to have a narrow escape

écharde [eʃaʀd] nf splinter (of wood)

écharpe [eʃaʀp] nf scarf; **avoir le bras en ~** to have one's arm in a sling

échasse [eʃas] nf stilt

échassier [eʃasje] nm wader

échauffer [eʃofe] vt (moteur) to overheat; **s'~** vi (SPORT) to warm up; (dans la discussion) to become heated

échéance [eʃeɑ̃s] nf (d'un paiement: date) settlement date; (: date butoir, fig) deadline; **à brève ~** in the short term; **à longue ~** in the long run

échéant [eʃeɑ̃]: **le cas ~** adv if the case arises

échec [eʃɛk] nm failure; (ÉCHECS): **~ et mat/au roi** checkmate/check; **~s** nmpl (jeu) chess sg; **tenir en ~** to hold in check

échelle [eʃɛl] nf ladder; (fig, d'une carte) scale

échelon [eʃ(ə)lɔ̃] nm (d'échelle) rung; (ADMIN) grade; **échelonner** vt to space out

échevelé, e [eʃəv(ə)le] adj tousled, dishevelled

échine [eʃin] nf backbone, spine

échiquier [eʃikje] nm chessboard

écho [eko] nm echo; **échographie** nf: **passer une échographie** to have a scan

échoir [eʃwaʀ] vi (dette) to fall due; (délais) to expire; **~ à** to fall to

échouer [eʃwe] vi to fail; **s'~** vi to run aground

échu, e [eʃy] pp de **échoir**

éclabousser [eklabuse] vt to splash

éclair [eklɛʀ] nm (d'orage) flash of lightning, lightning no pl; (gâteau) éclair

éclairage [eklɛʀaʒ] nm lighting

éclaircie [eklɛʀsi] nf bright interval

éclaircir [eklɛʀsiʀ] vt to lighten; (fig: mystère) to clear up; (: point) to clarify; **s'~** vi (ciel) to clear; **s'~ la voix** to clear one's throat; **éclaircissement** nm (sur un point) clarification

éclairer [eklɛʀe] vt (lieu) to light (up);

(personne: avec une lampe etc) to light the way for; (fig: problème) to shed light on ♦ vi: **~ mal/bien** to give a poor/good light; **s'~ à la bougie** to use candlelight

éclaireur, -euse [eklɛʀœʀ, øz] nm/f (scout) (boy) scout/(girl) guide ♦ nm (MIL) scout

éclat [ekla] nm (de bombe, de verre) fragment; (du soleil, d'une couleur etc) brightness, brilliance; (d'une cérémonie) splendour; (scandale): **faire un ~** to cause a commotion; **~s de voix** shouts; **~ de rire** roar of laughter

éclatant, e [eklatɑ̃, ɑ̃t] adj brilliant

éclater [eklate] vi (pneu) to burst; (bombe) to explode; (guerre) to break out; (groupe, parti) to break up; **~ en sanglots/de rire** to burst out sobbing/laughing

éclipser [eklipse]: **s'~** vi to slip away

éclore [eklɔʀ] vi (œuf) to hatch; (fleur) to open (out)

écluse [eklyz] nf lock

écœurant, e [ekœʀɑ̃, ɑ̃t] adj (gâteau etc) sickly; (fig) sickening

écœurer [ekœʀe] vt: **~ qn** (nourriture) to make sb feel sick; (conduite, personne) to disgust sb

école [ekɔl] nf school; **aller à l'~** to go to school; **~ maternelle/primaire** nursery/primary school; **~ publique** state school; **écolier, -ière** nm/f schoolboy(-girl)

école maternelle

Nursery school (l'école maternelle) is publicly funded in France and, though not compulsory, is attended by most children between the ages of two and six. Statutory education begins with primary school (l'école primaire) from the age of six to ten or eleven.

écologie [ekɔlɔʒi] nf ecology; **écologique** adj environment-friendly; **écolo-**

giste nm/f ecologist

éconduire [ekɔ̃dɥir] vt to dismiss

économe [ekɔnɔm] adj thrifty ♦ nm/f (de lycée etc) bursar (BRIT), treasurer (US)

économie [ekɔnɔmi] nf economy; (gain: d'argent, de temps etc) saving; (science) economics sg; **~s** nfpl (pécule) savings; **économique** adj (avantageux) economical; (ÉCON) economic; **économiser** vt, vi to save; **économiseur** nm: **économiseur d'écran** screen saver

écoper [ekɔpe] vi to bale out; **~ de 3 ans de prison** (fig: fam) to get sentenced to 3 years

écorce [ekɔrs] nf bark; (de fruit) peel

écorcher [ekɔrʃe] vt: **s'~ le genou/la main** to graze one's knee/one's hand; **écorchure** nf graze

écossais, e [ekɔsɛ, ɛz] adj Scottish ♦ nm/f: **É~, e** Scot

Écosse [ekɔs] nf: **l'~** Scotland

écosser [ekɔse] vt to shell

écoulement [ekulmɑ̃] nm (d'eau) flow

écouler [ekule] vt (marchandise) to sell; **s'~** vi (eau) to flow (out); (jours, temps) to pass (by)

écourter [ekurte] vt to curtail, cut short

écoute [ekut] nf (RADIO, TV): **temps/heure d'~** listening (ou viewing) time/hour; **rester à l'~** (de) to stay tuned in (to); **~s téléphoniques** phone tapping sg

écouter [ekute] vt to listen to; **écouteur** nm (TÉL) receiver; (RADIO) headphones pl, headset

écoutille [ekutij] nf hatch

écran [ekrɑ̃] nm screen; **petit ~** television; **~ total** sunblock

écrasant, e [ekrazɑ̃, ɑ̃t] adj overwhelming

écraser [ekraze] vt to crush; (piéton) to run over; **s'~** vi to crash; **s'~ contre** to crash into

écrémé, e [ekreme] adj (lait) skimmed

écrevisse [ekrəvis] nf crayfish inv

écrier [ekrije]: **s'~** vi to exclaim

écrin [ekrɛ̃] nm case, box

écrire [ekrir] vt to write; **s'~** to write to each other; **ça s'écrit comment?** how is it spelt?; **écrit** nm (examen) written paper; **par écrit** in writing

écriteau, x [ekrito] nm notice, sign

écriture [ekrityr] nf writing; **l'É~, les É~s** the Scriptures

écrivain [ekrivɛ̃] nm writer

écrou [ekru] nm nut

écrouer [ekrue] vt to imprison

écrouler [ekrule]: **s'~** vi to collapse

écru, e [ekry] adj off-white, écru

ECU [eky] sigle m ECU

écueil [ekœj] nm reef; (fig) pitfall

éculé, e [ekyle] adj (chaussure) down-at-heel; (fig: péj) hackneyed

écume [ekym] nf foam; **écumer** vt (CULIN) to skim; **écumoire** nf skimmer

écureuil [ekyrœj] nm squirrel

écurie [ekyri] nf stable

écusson [ekysɔ̃] nm badge

écuyer, -ère [ekɥije, jɛr] nm/f rider

eczéma [ɛgzema] nm eczema

édenté, e [edɑ̃te] adj toothless

EDF sigle f (= Électricité de France) national electricity company

édifice [edifis] nm edifice, building

édifier [edifje] vt to build, erect; (fig) to edify

Édimbourg [edɛ̃bur] n Edinburgh

éditer [edite] vt (publier) to publish; (annoter) to edit; **éditeur, -trice** nm/f publisher; **édition** nf edition; (industrie du livre) publishing

édredon [edrədɔ̃] nm eiderdown

éducateur, -trice [edykatœr, tris] nm/f teacher; (in special school) instructor

éducatif, -ive [edykatif, iv] adj educational

éducation [edykasjɔ̃] nf education; (familiale) upbringing; (manières) (good) manners pl; **~ physique** physical education

édulcorant [edylkɔrɑ̃] nm sweetener

éduquer [edyke] vt to educate; (élever)

to bring up

effacé, e [efase] *adj* unassuming

effacer [efase] *vt* to erase, rub out; **s'~** *vi* (*inscription etc*) to wear off; (*pour laisser passer*) to step aside

effarant, e [efarɑ̃, ɑ̃t] *adj* alarming

effarer [efare] *vt* to alarm

effaroucher [efaruʃe] *vt* to frighten *ou* scare away

effectif, -ive [efɛktif, iv] *adj* real ♦ *nm* (SCOL) (*pupil*) numbers *pl*; (*entreprise*) staff, workforce; **effectivement** *adv* (*réellement*) actually, really; (*en effet*) indeed

effectuer [efɛktɥe] *vt* (*opération*) to carry out; (*trajet*) to make

efféminé, e [efemine] *adj* effeminate

effervescent, e [efɛrvesɑ̃, ɑ̃t] *adj* effervescent

effet [efɛ] *nm* effect; (*impression*) impression; **~s** *nmpl* (*vêtements etc*) things; **faire ~** (*médicament*) to take effect; **faire bon/mauvais ~ sur qn** to make a good/bad impression on sb; **en ~** indeed; (*en réalité*) in fact

efficace [efikas] *adj* (*personne*) efficient; (*action, médicament*) effective; **efficacité** *nf* efficiency; effectiveness

effilocher [efilɔʃe]: **s'~** *vi* to fray

efflanqué, e [eflɑ̃ke] *adj* emaciated

effleurer [eflœre] *vt* to brush (against); (*sujet*) to touch upon; (*suj: idée, pensée*) **ça ne m'a pas effleuré** it didn't cross my mind

effluves [eflyv] *nmpl* exhalation(s)

effondrer [efɔ̃dre]: **s'~** *vi* to collapse

efforcer [efɔrse]: **s'~ de** *vt*: **s'~ de faire** to try hard to do

effort [efɔr] *nm* effort

effraction [efraksjɔ̃] *nf*: **s'introduire par ~ dans** to break into

effrayant, e [efrɛjɑ̃, ɑ̃t] *adj* frightening

effrayer [efreje] *vt* to frighten, scare

effréné, e [efrene] *adj* wild

effriter [efrite]: **s'~** *vi* to crumble

effroi [efrwa] *nm* terror, dread *no pl*

effronté, e [efrɔ̃te] *adj* cheeky

effroyable [efrwajabl] *adj* horrifying, appalling

effusion [efyzjɔ̃] *nf* effusion; **sans ~ de sang** without bloodshed

égal, e, -aux [egal, o] *adj* equal; (*constant: vitesse*) steady ♦ *nm/f* equal; **être ~ à** (*prix, nombre*) to be equal to; **ça lui est ~** it's all the same to him, he doesn't mind; **sans ~** matchless, unequalled; **d'~ à ~** as equals; **également** *adv* equally; (*aussi*) too, as well

égaler [egale] *vt* to equal; **égaliser** *vt* (*sol, salaires*) to level (out); (*chances*) to equalize ♦ *vi* (SPORT) to equalize; **égalité** *nf* equality; **être à égalité** to be level

égard [egar] *nm*: **~s** consideration *sg*; **à cet ~** in this respect; **par ~ pour** out of consideration for; **à l'~ de** towards

égarement [egarmɑ̃] *nm* distraction

égarer [egare] *vt* to mislay; **s'~** *vi* to get lost, lose one's way; (*objet*) to go astray

égayer [egeje] *vt* to cheer up; (*pièce*) to brighten up

églantine [eglɑ̃tin] *nf* wild *ou* dog rose

églefin [egləfɛ̃] *nm* haddock

église [egliz] *nf* church; **aller à l'~** to go to church

égoïsme [egɔism] *nm* selfishness; **égoïste** *adj* selfish

égorger [egɔrʒe] *vt* to cut the throat of

égosiller [egozije]: **s'~** *vi* to shout o.s. hoarse

égout [egu] *nm* sewer

égoutter [egute] *vi* to drip; **s'~** *vi* to drip; **égouttoir** *nm* draining board; (*mobile*) draining rack

égratigner [egratiɲe] *vt* to scratch; **égratignure** *nf* scratch

Égypte [eʒipt] *nf*: **l'~** Egypt; **égyptien, ne** *adj* Egyptian ♦ *nm/f*: **Égyptien, ne** Egyptian

eh [e] *excl* hey!; **~ bien** well

éhonté, e [eɔ̃te] *adj* shameless, brazen

éjecter [eʒɛkte] vt (TECH) to eject; (fam) to kick ou chuck out

élaborer [elabɔʀe] vt to elaborate; (projet, stratégie) to work out; (rapport) to draft

élan [elɑ̃] nm (ZOOL) elk, moose; (SPORT) run up; (fig: de tendresse etc) surge; **prendre de l'~** to gather speed

élancé, e [elɑ̃se] adj slender

élancement [elɑ̃smɑ̃] nm shooting pain

élancer [elɑ̃se]: **s'~** vi to dash, hurl o.s.

élargir [elaʀʒiʀ] vt to widen; **s'~** vi to widen; (vêtement) to stretch

élastique [elastik] adj elastic ♦ nm (de bureau) rubber band; (pour la couture) elastic no pl

électeur, -trice [elɛktœʀ, tʀis] nm/f elector, voter

élection [elɛksjɔ̃] nf election

électorat [elɛktɔʀa] nm electorate

électricien, ne [elɛktʀisjɛ̃, jɛn] nm/f electrician

électricité [elɛktʀisite] nf electricity; **allumer/éteindre l'~** to put on/off the light

électrique [elɛktʀik] adj electric(al)

électrocuter [elɛktʀɔkyte] vt to electrocute

électroménager [elɛktʀomenaʒe] adj, nm: **appareils ~s, l'~** domestic (electrical) appliances

électronique [elɛktʀɔnik] adj electronic ♦ nf electronics sg

électrophone [elɛktʀɔfɔn] nm record player

élégance [elegɑ̃s] nf elegance

élégant, e [elegɑ̃, ɑ̃t] adj elegant

élément [elemɑ̃] nm element; (pièce) component, part; **~s de cuisine** kitchen units; **élémentaire** adj elementary

éléphant [elefɑ̃] nm elephant

élevage [el(ə)vaʒ] nm breeding; (de bovins) cattle rearing; **truite d'~** farmed trout

élévation [elevasjɔ̃] nf (hausse) rise

élevé, e [el(ə)ve] adj high; **bien/mal ~** well-/ill-mannered

élève [elɛv] nm/f pupil

élever [el(ə)ve] vt (enfant) to bring up, raise; (animaux) to breed; (hausser: taux, niveau) to raise; (édifier: monument) to put up, erect; **s'~** vi (avion) to go up; (niveau, température) to rise; **s'~ à** (suj: frais, dégâts) to amount to, add up to; **s'~ contre qch** to rise up against sth; **~ la voix** to raise one's voice; **éleveur, -euse** nm/f breeder

élimé, e [elime] adj threadbare

éliminatoire [eliminatwaʀ] nf (SPORT) heat

éliminer [elimine] vt to eliminate

élire [eliʀ] vt to elect

elle [ɛl] pron (sujet) she; (: chose) it; (complément) her; it; **~s** (sujet) they; (complément) them; **~-même** herself; itself; **~s-mêmes** themselves; voir aussi **il**

élocution [elɔkysjɔ̃] nf delivery; **défaut d'~** speech impediment

éloge [elɔʒ] nm (gén no pl) praise; **faire l'~ de** to praise; **élogieux, -euse** adj laudatory, full of praise

éloigné, e [elwaɲe] adj distant, far-off; (parent) distant; **éloignement** nm (distance, aussi fig) distance

éloigner [elwaɲe] vt (échéance) to put off, postpone; (soupçons, danger) to ward off; (objet): **~ qch (de)** to move ou take sth away (from); (personne): **~ qn (de)** to take sb away ou remove sb (from); **s'~ (de)** (personne) to go away (from); (véhicule) to move away (from); (affectivement) to become estranged (from); **ne vous éloignez pas!** don't go far away!

élu, e [ely] pp de **élire** ♦ nm/f (POL) elected representative

éluder [elyde] vt to evade

Élysée [elize] nm: **(le palais de) l'~** the Élysée Palace (the French president's residence)

émacié, e [emasje] *adj* emaciated

émail [emaj, o] *nm* enamel

e-mail [imel] *nm* e-mail; **envoyer qch par ~** to e-mail sth

émaillé, e [emaje] *adj* (*fig*): **~ de** dotted with

émanciper [emɑ̃sipe]: **s'~** *vi* (*fig*) to become emancipated *ou* liberated

émaner [emane]: **~ de** *vt* to come from

emballage [ɑ̃balaʒ] *nm* (*papier*) wrapping; (*boîte*) packaging

emballer [ɑ̃bale] *vt* to wrap (up); (*dans un carton*) to pack (up); (*fig: fam*) to thrill (to bits); **s'~** *vi* (*moteur*) to race; (*cheval*) to bolt; (*fig: personne*) to get carried away

embarcadère [ɑ̃baʀkadɛʀ] *nm* wharf, pier

embarcation [ɑ̃baʀkasjɔ̃] *nf* (*small*) boat, (*small*) craft *inv*

embardée [ɑ̃baʀde] *nf*: **faire une ~** to swerve

embarquement [ɑ̃baʀkəmɑ̃] *nm* (*de passagers*) boarding; (*de marchandises*) loading

embarquer [ɑ̃baʀke] *vt* (*personne*) to embark; (*marchandise*) to load; (*fam*) to cart off ♦ *vi* (*passager*) to board; **s'~** *vi* to board; **s'~ dans** (*affaire, aventure*) to embark upon

embarras [ɑ̃baʀa] *nm* (*gêne*) embarrassment; **mettre qn dans l'~** to put sb in an awkward position; **vous n'avez que l'~ du choix** the only problem is choosing

embarrassant, e [ɑ̃baʀasɑ̃, ɑ̃t] *adj* embarrassing

embarrasser [ɑ̃baʀase] *vt* (*encombrer*) to clutter (up); (*gêner*) to hinder, hamper; **~ qn** to put sb in an awkward position; **s'~ de** to burden o.s. with

embauche [ɑ̃boʃ] *nf* hiring; **embaucher** *vt* to take on, hire

embaumer [ɑ̃bome] *vt*: **~ la lavande** *etc* to be fragrant with lavender *etc*

embellie [ɑ̃beli] *nf* brighter period

embellir [ɑ̃beliʀ] *vt* to make more attractive; (*une histoire*) to embellish ♦ *vi* to grow lovelier *ou* more attractive

embêtements [ɑ̃bɛtmɑ̃] *nmpl* trouble *sg*

embêter [ɑ̃bete] *vt* to bother; **s'~** *vi* (*s'ennuyer*) to be bored

emblée [ɑ̃ble]: **d'~** *adv* straightaway

embobiner [ɑ̃bɔbine] *vt* (*fam*) to get round

emboîter [ɑ̃bwate] *vt* to fit together; **s'~ (dans)** to fit (into); **~ le pas à qn** to follow in sb's footsteps

embonpoint [ɑ̃bɔ̃pwɛ̃] *nm* stoutness

embouchure [ɑ̃buʃyʀ] *nf* (*GÉO*) mouth

embourber [ɑ̃buʀbe]: **s'~** *vi* to get stuck in the mud

embourgeoiser [ɑ̃buʀʒwaze]: **s'~** *vi* to become middle-class

embouteillage [ɑ̃butɛjaʒ] *nm* traffic jam

emboutir [ɑ̃butiʀ] *vt* (*heurter*) to crash into, ram

embranchement [ɑ̃bʀɑ̃ʃmɑ̃] *nm* (*routier*) junction

embraser [ɑ̃bʀaze]: **s'~** *vi* to flare up

embrassades [ɑ̃bʀasad] *nfpl* hugging and kissing

embrasser [ɑ̃bʀase] *vt* to kiss; (*sujet, période*) to embrace, encompass; **s'~** to kiss (each other)

embrasure [ɑ̃bʀazyʀ] *nf*: **dans l'~ de la porte** in the door(way)

embrayage [ɑ̃bʀɛjaʒ] *nm* clutch

embrayer [ɑ̃bʀeje] *vi* (*AUTO*) to let in the clutch

embrocher [ɑ̃bʀɔʃe] *vt* to put on a spit

embrouiller [ɑ̃bʀuje] *vt* to muddle up; (*fils*) to tangle (up); **s'~** *vi* (*personne*) to get in a muddle

embruns [ɑ̃bʀœ̃] *nmpl* sea spray *sg*

embûches [ɑ̃byʃ] *nfpl* pitfalls, traps

embué, e [ɑ̃bye] *adj* misted up

embuscade [ɑ̃byskad] *nf* ambush

éméché, e [emeʃe] *adj* tipsy, merry

émeraude [em(ə)ʀod] *nf* emerald

émerger [emɛʀʒe] *vi* to emerge; (*faire*

saillie, aussi fig) to stand out

émeri [em(ə)ʀi] nm: **toile** *ou* **papier ~** emery paper

émerveillement [emɛʀvɛjmã] nm wonder

émerveiller [emɛʀveje] vt to fill with wonder; **s'~ de** to marvel at

émettre [emɛtʀ] vt (*son, lumière*) to give out, emit; (*message etc: RADIO*) to transmit; (*billet, timbre, emprunt*) to issue; (*hypothèse, avis*) to voice, put forward ♦ vi to broadcast

émeus *etc* [emø] *vb voir* **émouvoir**

émeute [emøt] nf riot

émietter [emjete] vt to crumble

émigrer [emigʀe] vi to emigrate

émincer [emɛ̃se] vt to cut into thin slices

éminent, e [eminã, ãt] adj distinguished

émission [emisjɔ̃] nf (*RADIO, TV*) programme, broadcast; (*d'un message*) transmission; (*de timbre*) issue

emmagasiner [ãmagazine] vt (*amasser*) to store up

emmanchure [ãmãʃyʀ] nf armhole

emmêler [ãmele] vt to tangle (up); (*fig*) to muddle up; **s'~** vi to get in a tangle

emménager [ãmenaʒe] vi to move in; **~ dans** to move into

emmener [ãm(ə)ne] vt to take (with one); (*comme otage, capture*) to take away; **~ qn au cinéma** to take sb to the cinema

emmerder [ãmɛʀde] (*fam!*) vt to bug, bother; **s'~** vi to be bored stiff

emmitoufler [ãmitufle]: **s'~** vi to wrap up (warmly)

émoi [emwa] nm commotion

émotif, -ive [emɔtif, iv] adj emotional

émotion [emɔsjɔ̃] nf emotion

émousser [emuse] vt to blunt; (*fig*) to dull

émouvoir [emuvwaʀ] vt to move; **s'~** vi to be moved; (*s'indigner*) to be roused

empailler [ãpaje] vt to stuff

empaqueter [ãpakte] vt to parcel up

emparer [ãpaʀe]: **s'~ de** vt (*objet*) to seize, grab; (*comme otage, MIL*) to seize; (*suj: peur etc*) to take hold of

empâter [ãpate]: **s'~** vi to thicken out

empêchement [ãpɛʃmã] nm (*unexpected*) obstacle, hitch

empêcher [ãpɛʃe] vt to prevent; **~ qn de faire** to prevent *ou* stop sb (from) doing; **il n'empêche que** nevertheless; **il n'a pas pu s'~ de rire** he couldn't help laughing

empereur [ãpʀœʀ] nm emperor

empester [ãpɛste] vi to stink, reek

empêtrer [ãpetʀe] vt: **s'~ dans** (*fils etc*) to get tangled up in

emphase [ãfaz] nf pomposity, bombast

empiéter [ãpjete] vi: **~ sur** to encroach upon

empiffrer [ãpifʀe]: **s'~** (*fam*) vi to stuff o.s.

empiler [ãpile] vt to pile (up)

empire [ãpiʀ] nm empire; (*fig*) influence

empirer [ãpiʀe] vi to worsen, deteriorate

emplacement [ãplasmã] nm site

emplettes [ãplɛt] nfpl shopping sg

emplir [ãpliʀ] vt to fill; **s'~ (de)** to fill (with)

emploi [ãplwa] nm use; (*COMM, ÉCON*) employment; (*poste*) job, situation; **mode d'~** directions for use; **~ du temps** timetable, schedule

employé, e [ãplwaje] nm/f employee; **~ de bureau** office employee *ou* clerk

employer [ãplwaje] vt to use; (*ouvrier, main-d'œuvre*) to employ; **s'~ à faire** to apply *ou* devote o.s. to doing; **employeur, -euse** nm/f employer

empocher [ãpɔʃe] vt to pocket

empoigner [ãpwaɲe] vt to grab

empoisonner [ãpwazɔne] vt to poison; (*empester: air, pièce*) to stink out; (*fam*): **~ qn** to drive sb mad

emporté, e [ɑ̃pɔrte] *adj* quick-tempered

emporter [ɑ̃pɔrte] *vt* to take (with one); *(en dérobant ou enlevant, emmener: blessés, voyageurs)* to take away; *(entraîner)* to carry away; **s'~** *vi (de colère)* to lose one's temper; **l'~ (sur)** to get the upper hand (of); **plats à ~** take-away meals

empreint, e [ɑ̃prɛ̃, ɛ̃t] *adj:* **~ de** *(regret, jalousie)* marked with; **empreinte** *nf:* **empreinte (de pas)** footprint; **empreinte (digitale)** fingerprint

empressé, e [ɑ̃prese] *adj* attentive

empressement [ɑ̃prɛsmɑ̃] *nm (hâte)* eagerness

empresser [ɑ̃prese]: **s'~** *vi:* **s'~ auprès de qn** to surround sb with attentions; **s'~ de faire** *(se hâter)* to hasten to do

emprise [ɑ̃priz] *nf* hold, ascendancy

emprisonnement [ɑ̃prizɔnmɑ̃] *nm* imprisonment

emprisonner [ɑ̃prizɔne] *vt* to imprison

emprunt [ɑ̃prœ̃] *nm* loan

emprunté, e [ɑ̃prœ̃te] *adj (fig)* ill-at-ease, awkward

emprunter [ɑ̃prœ̃te] *vt* to borrow; *(itinéraire)* to take, follow

ému, e [emy] *pp de* **émouvoir** ♦ *adj (gratitude)* touched; *(compassion)* moved

---

MOT-CLÉ

en [ɑ̃] *prép* **1** *(endroit, pays)* in; *(direction)* to; **habiter en France/ville** to live in France/town; **aller en France/ville** to go to France/town

2 *(moment, temps)* in; **en été/juin** in summer/June

3 *(moyen)* by; **en avion/taxi** by plane/taxi

4 *(composition)* made of; **c'est en verre** it's (made of) glass; **un collier en argent** a silver necklace

5 *(description, état)*: **une femme (ha-**

billée) en rouge a woman (dressed) in red; **peindre qch en rouge** to paint sth red; **en T/étoile** T/star-shaped; **en chemise/chaussettes** in one's shirt-sleeves/socks; **en soldat** as a soldier; **cassé en plusieurs morceaux** broken into several pieces; **en réparation** being repaired, under repair; **en vacances** on holiday; **en deuil** in mourning; **le même en plus grand** the same but *ou* only bigger

6 *(avec gérondif)* while, on, by; **en dormant** while sleeping, as one sleeps; **en sortant** on going out, as he *etc* went out; **sortir en courant** to run out

♦ *pron* **1** *(indéfini)*: **j'en ai/veux** I have/want some; **en as-tu?** have you got any?; **je n'en veux pas** I don't want any; **j'en ai 2** I've got 2; **combien y en a-t-il?** how many (of them) are there?; **j'en ai assez** I've got enough (of it *ou* them); *(j'en ai marre)* I've had enough

2 *(provenance)* from there; **j'en viens** I've come from there

3 *(cause)*: **il est malade/perd le sommeil** he is ill/can't sleep because of it

4 *(complément de nom, d'adjectif, de verbe)*: **j'en connais les dangers** I know its *ou* the dangers; **j'en suis fier/ai besoin** I am proud of it/need it

---

ENA *sigle f* = *École Nationale d'Administration)* one of the Grandes Écoles

encadrement [ɑ̃kadrəmɑ̃] *nm (cadres)* managerial staff

encadrer [ɑ̃kadre] *vt (tableau, image)* to frame; *(fig: entourer)* to surround; *(personnel, soldats etc)* to train

encaissé, e [ɑ̃kese] *adj (vallée)* steep-sided; *(rivière)* with steep banks

encaisser [ɑ̃kese] *vt (chèque)* to cash; *(argent)* to collect; *(fam: coup, défaite)* to take

encart [ɑ̃kar] *nm* insert

en-cas [ɑ̃ka] *nm* snack

encastré, e [ɑ̃kastre] *adj:* **four ~** built-in-oven

enceinte [ɑ̃sɛ̃t] *adj f:* **~ (de 6 mois)** (6 months) pregnant ♦ *nf (mur)* wall; *(espace)* enclosure; *(aussi:* **~ acoustique)** (loud)speaker

encens [ɑ̃sɑ̃] *nm* incense

encercler [ɑ̃sɛrkle] *vt* to surround

enchaîner [ɑ̃ʃene] *vt* to chain up; *(mouvements, séquences)* to link (together) ♦ *vi* to carry on

enchanté, e [ɑ̃ʃɑ̃te] *adj (ravi)* delighted; *(magique)* enchanted; **~ (de faire votre connaissance)** pleased to meet you

enchantement [ɑ̃ʃɑ̃tmɑ̃] *nm* delight; *(magie)* enchantment

enchère [ɑ̃ʃɛr] *nf* bid; **mettre/vendre aux ~s** to put up (for sale by)/sell by auction

enchevêtrer [ɑ̃ʃ(ə)vetre]: **s'~** *vi* to get in a tangle

enclencher [ɑ̃klɑ̃ʃe] *vt (mécanisme)* to engage; **s'~** *vi* to engage

enclin, e [ɑ̃klɛ̃, in] *adj:* **~ à** inclined *ou* prone to

enclos [ɑ̃klo] *nm* enclosure

enclume [ɑ̃klym] *nf* anvil

encoche [ɑ̃kɔʃ] *nf* notch

encoignure [ɑ̃kɔɲyr] *nf* corner

encolure [ɑ̃kɔlyr] *nf (cou)* neck

encombrant, e [ɑ̃kɔ̃brɑ̃, ɑ̃t] *adj* cumbersome, bulky

encombre [ɑ̃kɔ̃br]: **sans ~** *adv* without mishap *ou* incident; **encombrement** *nm:* **être pris dans un encombrement** to be stuck in a traffic jam

encombrer [ɑ̃kɔ̃bre] *vt* to clutter (up); *(gêner)* to hamper; **s'~ de** *(bagages etc)* to load *ou* burden o.s. with

encontre [ɑ̃kɔ̃tr]: **à l'~ de** *prép* against, counter to

MOT-CLÉ

encore [ɑ̃kɔr] *adv* **1** *(continuation)* still; **il y travaille encore** he's still working on it; **pas encore** not yet

2 *(de nouveau)* again; **j'irai encore demain** I'll go again tomorrow; **encore une fois** (once) again; **encore deux jours** two more days

3 *(intensif)* even, still; **encore plus fort/mieux** even louder/better, louder/better still

4 *(restriction)* even so *ou* then, only; **encore pourrais-je le faire si ...** even so, I might be able to do it if ...; **si encore** if only

encore que *conj* although

encouragement [ɑ̃kuraʒmɑ̃] *nm* encouragement

encourager [ɑ̃kuraʒe] *vt* to encourage

encourir [ɑ̃kurir] *vt* to incur

encrasser [ɑ̃krase] *vt* to make filthy

encre [ɑ̃kr] *nf* ink; **encrier** *nm* inkwell

encroûter [ɑ̃krute]: **s'~** *(fam) vi (fig)* to get into a rut, get set in one's ways

encyclopédie [ɑ̃siklopedi] *nf* encyclopaedia

endetter [ɑ̃dete]: **s'~** *vi* to get into debt

endiablé, e [ɑ̃djable] *adj (danse)* furious

endimanché, e [ɑ̃dimɑ̃ʃe] *adj* in one's Sunday best

endive [ɑ̃div] *nf* chicory *no pl*

endoctriner [ɑ̃dɔktrine] *vt* to indoctrinate

endommager [ɑ̃dɔmaʒe] *vt* to damage

endormi, e [ɑ̃dɔrmi] *adj* asleep

endormir [ɑ̃dɔrmir] *vt* to put to sleep; *(suj: chaleur etc)* to send to sleep; *(MÉD: dent, nerf)* to anaesthetize; *(fig: soupçons)* to allay; **s'~** *vi* to fall asleep, go to sleep

endosser [ɑ̃dose] *vt (responsabilité)* to take, shoulder; *(chèque)* to endorse; *(uniforme, tenue)* to put on, don

endroit [ɑ̃drwa] *nm* place; *(opposé à l'envers)* right side; **à l'~** *(vêtement)* the right way out; *(objet posé)* the right way round

enduire [ɑ̃dɥiʀ] vt to coat

enduit [ɑ̃dɥi] nm coating

endurance [ɑ̃dyʀɑ̃s] nf endurance

endurant, e [ɑ̃dyʀɑ̃, ɑ̃t] adj tough, hardy

endurcir [ɑ̃dyʀsiʀ] : **s'~** vi (physiquement) to become tougher; (moralement) to become hardened

endurer [ɑ̃dyʀe] vt to endure, bear

énergétique [enɛʀʒetik] adj (aliment) energy-giving

énergie [enɛʀʒi] nf (PHYSIQUE) energy; (TECH) power; (morale) vigour, spirit; **énergique** adj energetic, vigorous; (mesures) drastic, stringent

énervant, e [enɛʀvɑ̃, ɑ̃t] adj irritating, annoying

énerver [enɛʀve] vt to irritate, annoy; **s'~** vi to get excited, get worked up

enfance [ɑ̃fɑ̃s] nf childhood

enfant [ɑ̃fɑ̃] nm/f child; **~ de chœur ♦** nm (REL) altar boy; **enfantillage** (péj) nm childish behaviour no pl; **enfantin, e** adj (puéril) childlike; (langage, jeu etc) children's cpd

enfer [ɑ̃fɛʀ] nm hell

enfermer [ɑ̃fɛʀme] vt to shut up; (à clef, interner) to lock up

enfiévré, e [ɑ̃fjevʀe] adj feverish

enfiler [ɑ̃file] vt (vêtement) to slip on, slip into; (perles) to string; (aiguille) to thread

enfin [ɑ̃fɛ̃] adv at last; (en énumérant) lastly; (toutefois) still; (pour conclure) in a word; (somme toute) after all

enflammer [ɑ̃flame] : **s'~** vi to catch fire; (MÉD) to become inflamed

enflé, e [ɑ̃fle] adj swollen

enfler [ɑ̃fle] vi to swell (up)

enfoncer [ɑ̃fɔ̃se] vt (clou) to drive in; (faire pénétrer) : **qch dans** to push (ou drive) sth into; (forcer: porte) to break open; **s'~** vi to sink; **s'~ dans** to sink into; (forêt, ville) to disappear into

enfouir [ɑ̃fwiʀ] vt (dans le sol) to bury; (dans un tiroir etc) to tuck away

enfourcher [ɑ̃fuʀʃe] vt to mount

enfreindre [ɑ̃fʀɛ̃dʀ] vt to infringe, break

enfuir [ɑ̃fɥiʀ] : **s'~** vi to run away ou off

enfumer [ɑ̃fyme] vt (pièce) to fill with smoke

engageant, e [ɑ̃gaʒɑ̃, ɑ̃t] adj attractive, appealing

engagement [ɑ̃gaʒmɑ̃] nm commitment

engager [ɑ̃gaʒe] vt (embaucher) to take on; (: artiste) to engage; (commencer) to start; (lier) to bind, commit; (impliquer) to involve; (investir) to invest, lay out; (inciter) to urge; (introduire: clé) to insert; **s'~** vi (promettre) to commit o.s.; (MIL) to enlist; (débuter: conversation etc) to start (up); **s'~ à faire** to undertake to do; **s'~ dans** (rue, passage) to enter into; (fig: affaire, discussion) to enter into, embark on

engelures [ɑ̃ʒlyʀ] nfpl chilblains

engendrer [ɑ̃ʒɑ̃dʀe] vt to breed, create

engin [ɑ̃ʒɛ̃] nm machine; (outil) instrument; (AUT) vehicle; (AVIAT) aircraft inv

englober [ɑ̃glɔbe] vt to include

engloutir [ɑ̃glutiʀ] vt to swallow up

engoncé, e [ɑ̃gɔ̃se] adj: **~ dans** cramped in

engorger [ɑ̃gɔʀʒe] vt to obstruct, block

engouement [ɑ̃gumɑ̃] nm (sudden) passion

engouffrer [ɑ̃gufʀe] vt to swallow up, devour; **s'~ dans** to rush into

engourdir [ɑ̃guʀdiʀ] vt to numb; (fig) to dull, blunt; **s'~** vi to go numb

engrais [ɑ̃gʀɛ] nm manure; **~ (chimique)** (chemical) fertilizer

engraisser [ɑ̃gʀese] vt to fatten (up)

engrenage [ɑ̃gʀənaʒ] nm gears pl, gearing; (fig) chain

engueuler [ɑ̃gœle] (fam) vt to bawl at

enhardir [ɑ̃aʀdiʀ] : **s'~** vi to grow bolder

énigme [enigm] nf riddle

enivrer [ɑ̃nivʀe] vt: **s'~** to get drunk

enjambée [ɑ̃ʒɑ̃be] nf stride

enjamber [ãʒãbe] vt to stride over

enjeu, x [ãʒø] nm stakes pl

enjôler [ãʒole] vt to coax, wheedle

enjoliver [ãʒolive] vt to embellish; **enjoliveur** nm (AUTO) hub cap

enjoué, e [ãʒwe] adj playful

enlacer [ãlase] vt (étreindre) to embrace, hug

enlaidir [ãledir] vt to make ugly ♦ vi to become ugly

enlèvement [ãlɛvmã] nm (rapt) abduction, kidnapping

enlever [ãl(ə)ve] vt (ôter: gén) to remove; (: vêtement, lunettes) to take off; (emporter: ordures etc) to take away; (kidnapper) to abduct, kidnap; (obtenir: prix, contrat) to win; (prendre): ~ qch à qn to take sth (away) from sb

enliser [ãlize]: s'~ vi to sink, get stuck

enneigé, e [ãneʒe] adj (route, maison) snowed-up; (paysage) snowy

ennemi, e [ɛnmi] adj hostile; (MIL) enemy cpd ♦ nm/f enemy

ennui [ãɥi] nm (lassitude) boredom; (difficulté) trouble no pl; **avoir des ~s** to have problems; **ennuyer** vt to bother; (lasser) to bore; **s'ennuyer** vi to be bored; **ennuyeux, -euse** adj boring, tedious; (embêtant) annoying

énoncé [enõse] nm (de problème) terms pl

énoncer [enõse] vt (faits) to set out, state

enorgueillir [ãnɔrgœjir]: s'~ de vt to pride o.s. on

énorme [enɔrm] adj enormous, huge; **énormément** adv enormously; **énormément de neige/gens** an enormous amount of snow/number of people; **énormité** nf (propos) outrageous remark

enquérir [ãkerir]: s'~ de vt to inquire about

enquête [ãkɛt] nf (de journaliste, de police) investigation; (judiciaire, administrative) inquiry; (sondage d'opinion) survey; **enquêter** vi to investigate

enquiers etc [ãkje] vb voir **enquérir**

enquiquiner [ãkikine] (fam) vt to annoy, irritate, bother

enracine, e [ãrasine] adj deep-rooted

enragé, e [ãraʒe] adj (MÉD) rabid, with rabies; (fig) fanatical

enrageant, e [ãraʒã, ãt] adj infuriating

enrager [ãraʒe] vi to be in a rage

enrayer [ãreje] vt to check, stop

enregistrement [ãr(ə)ʒistrəmã] nm recording; ~ **des bagages** (à l'aéroport) baggage check-in

enregistrer [ãr(ə)ʒistre] vt (MUS etc) to record; (fig: mémoriser) to make a mental note of; (bagages: à l'aéroport) to check in

enrhumer [ãryme] vt: s'~, **être enrhumé** to catch a cold

enrichir [ãriʃir] vt to make rich(er); (fig) to enrich; s'~ vi to get rich(er)

enrober [ãrɔbe] vt: ~ **qch de** to coat sth with

enrôler [ãrole] vt to enlist; s'~ **(dans)** to enlist (in)

enrouer [ãrwe]: s'~ vi to go hoarse

enrouler [ãrule] vt (fil, corde) to wind (up)

ensanglanté, e [ãsãglãte] adj covered with blood

enseignant, e [ãsɛɲã, ãt] nm/f teacher

enseigne [ãsɛɲ] nf sign; ~ **lumineuse** neon sign

enseignement [ãsɛɲ(ə)mã] nm teaching; (ADMIN) education

enseigner [ãsɛɲe] vt, vi to teach; ~ **qch à qn** to teach sb sth

ensemble [ãsãbl] adv together ♦ nm (groupement) set; (vêtements) outfit; (totalité): l'~ **du/de la** the whole ou entire; (unité, harmonie) unity; **impression/idée d'~** overall ou general impression/idea; **dans l'~** (en gros) on the whole

ensemencer [ãs(ə)mãse] vt to sow

ensevelir [ãsəv(ə)lir] vt to bury

ensoleillé, e [ãsoleje] adj sunny

ensommeillé, e [ɑ̃sɔmeje] *adj* drowsy

ensorceler [ɑ̃sɔʁsəle] *vt* to enchant, bewitch

ensuite [ɑ̃sɥit] *adv* then, next; (*plus tard*) afterwards, later

ensuivre [ɑ̃sɥivʁ]: **s'~** *vi* to follow, ensue; **et tout ce qui s'ensuit** and all that goes with it

entaille [ɑ̃taj] *nf* cut; (*sur un objet*) notch

entamer [ɑ̃tame] *vt* (*pain, bouteille*) to start; (*hostilités, pourparlers*) to open

entasser [ɑ̃tase] *vt* (*empiler*) to pile up, heap up; **s'~** *vi* (*s'amonceler*) to pile up; **s'~ dans** (*personnes*) to cram into

entendre [ɑ̃tɑ̃dʁ] *vt* to hear; (*comprendre*) to understand; (*vouloir dire*) to mean; **s'~** *vi* (*sympathiser*) to agree; (*se mettre d'accord*) to agree; **j'ai entendu dire que** I've heard (it said) that

entendu, e [ɑ̃tɑ̃dy] *adj* (*réglé*) agreed; (*au courant: air*) knowing; **(c'est) ~** all right, agreed; **bien ~** of course

entente [ɑ̃tɑ̃t] *nf* understanding; (*accord, traité*) agreement; **à double ~** (*sens*) with a double meaning

entériner [ɑ̃teʁine] *vt* to ratify, confirm

enterrement [ɑ̃teʁmɑ̃] *nm* (*cérémonie*) funeral, burial

enterrer [ɑ̃teʁe] *vt* to bury

entêtant, e [ɑ̃tetɑ̃, ɑ̃t] *adj* heady

entêté, e [ɑ̃tete] *adj* stubborn

en-tête [ɑ̃tɛt] *nm* heading; **papier à ~** ~ headed notepaper

entêter [ɑ̃tete]: **s'~** *vi*: **s'~ (à faire)** to persist in doing

enthousiasme [ɑ̃tuzjasm] *nm* enthusiasm; **enthousiasmer** *vt* to fill with enthusiasm; **s'enthousiasmer (pour qch)** to get enthusiastic (about sth); **enthousiaste** *adj* enthusiastic

enticher [ɑ̃tiʃe]: **s'~ de** *vi* to become infatuated with

entier, -ère [ɑ̃tje, jɛʁ] *adj* whole; (*total: satisfaction etc*) complete; (*fig: caractère*) unbending ♦ *nm* (*MATH*) whole; **en ~** totally; **lait ~** full-cream milk; **en-**

tièrement *adv* entirely, wholly

entonner [ɑ̃tɔne] *vt* (*chanson*) to strike up

entonnoir [ɑ̃tɔnwaʁ] *nm* funnel

entorse [ɑ̃tɔʁs] *nf* (*MÉD*) sprain; (*fig*): **~ au règlement** infringement of the rule

entortiller [ɑ̃tɔʁtije] *vt* (*enrouler*) to twist, wind; (*fam: cajoler*) to get round

entourage [ɑ̃tuʁaʒ] *nm* circle; (*famille*) circle of family/friends; (*ce qui enclôt*) surround

entourer [ɑ̃tuʁe] *vt* to surround; (*apporter son soutien à*) to rally round; **~ de** to surround with

entracte [ɑ̃tʁakt] *nm* interval

entraide [ɑ̃tʁɛd] *nf* mutual aid; **s'~r** *vi* to help each other

entrain [ɑ̃tʁɛ̃] *nm* spirit; **avec/sans ~** spiritedly/half-heartedly

entraînement [ɑ̃tʁɛnmɑ̃] *nm* training

entraîner [ɑ̃tʁene] *vt* (*charrier*) to carry *ou* drag along; (*TECH*) to drive; (*emmener: personne*) to take (off); (*influencer*) to lead; (*SPORT*) to train; (*impliquer*) to entail; **s'~** *vi* (*SPORT*) to train; **s'~ à qch/à faire** to train o.s. for sth/to do; **~ qn à faire** (*inciter*) to lead sb to do; **entraîneur, -euse** *nm/f* (*SPORT*) coach, trainer ♦ *nm* (*HIPPISME*) trainer

entraver [ɑ̃tʁave] *vt* (*action, progrès*) to hinder

entre [ɑ̃tʁ] *prép* between; (*parmi*) among(st); **l'un d'~ eux/nous** one of them/us; **~ eux** among(st) themselves; **entrebâillé, e** *adj* half-open, ajar; **entrechoquer: s'entrechoquer** *vi* to knock *ou* bang together; **entrecôte** *nf* entrecôte *ou* rib steak; **entrecouper** *vt*: **entrecouper qch de** to intersperse sth with; **entrecroiser: s'entrecroiser** *vi* to intertwine

entrée [ɑ̃tʁe] *nf* entrance; (*accès: au cinéma etc*) admission; (*billet*) (admission) ticket; (*CULIN*) first course

entre...: entrefaites: sur ces entrefaites *adv* at this juncture; **entrefilet** *nm* paragraph (*short article*); **entrejam-**

bes nm crotch; **entrelacer** vt to intertwine; **entremêler: s'entremêler** vi to become entangled; **entremets** nm (cream) dessert; **entremise** nf intervention; **par l'entremise de** through

entreposer [ɑ̃trəpoze] vt to store, put into storage

entrepôt [ɑ̃trəpo] nm warehouse

entreprenant, e [ɑ̃trəprənɑ̃, ɑ̃t] adj (actif) enterprising; (trop galant) forward

entreprendre [ɑ̃trəprɑ̃dr] vt (se lancer dans) to undertake; (commencer) to begin ou start (upon)

entrepreneur [ɑ̃trəprənœr, øz] nm: **~ (en bâtiment)** (building) contractor

entreprise [ɑ̃trəpriz] nf (société) firm, concern; (action) undertaking, venture

entrer [ɑ̃tre] vi to go (ou come) in, enter ♦ vt (INFORM) to enter, input; (faire) **~ qch dans** to get sth into; **~ dans** (gén) to enter; (pièce) to go (ou come) into, enter; (club) to join; (heurter) to run into; **~ à l'hôpital** to go into hospital; **faire ~** (visiteur) to show in

entresol [ɑ̃trəsɔl] nm mezzanine

entre-temps [ɑ̃trətɑ̃] adv meanwhile

entretenir [ɑ̃trət(ə)nir] vt to maintain; (famille, maîtresse) to support, keep; **~ qn (de)** to speak to sb (about)

entretien [ɑ̃trətjɛ̃] nm maintenance; (discussion) discussion, talk; (pour un emploi) interview

entrevoir [ɑ̃trəvwar] vt (à peine) to make out; (brièvement) to catch a glimpse of

entrevue [ɑ̃trəvy] nf (audience) interview

entrouvert, e [ɑ̃truvɛr, ɛrt] adj half-open

énumérer [enymere] vt to list

envahir [ɑ̃vair] vt to invade; (suj: inquiétude, peur) to come over; **envahissant, e** (péj) adj (personne) intrusive

enveloppe [ɑ̃v(ə)lɔp] nf (de lettre) envelope; (crédits) budget; **envelopper** vt to wrap; (fig) to envelop, shroud

envenimer [ɑ̃v(ə)nime] vt to aggravate

envergure [ɑ̃vɛrgyr] nf (fig) scope; (personne) calibre

enverrai etc [ɑ̃vere] vb voir **envoyer**

envers [ɑ̃vɛr] prép towards, to, ♦ nm other side; (d'une étoffe) wrong side; **à l'~** (verticalement) upside down; (pull) back to front; (chaussettes) inside out

envie [ɑ̃vi] nf (sentiment) envy; (souhait) desire, wish; **avoir ~ de (faire)** to feel like (doing); (plus fort) to want (to do); **avoir ~ que** to wish that; **cette glace me fait ~** I fancy some of that ice cream; **envier** vt to envy; **envieux, -euse** adj envious

environ [ɑ̃virɔ̃] adv: **~ 3 h/2 km** (around) about 3 o'clock/2 km; voir aussi **environs**

environnant, e [ɑ̃virɔnɑ̃, ɑ̃t] adj surrounding

environnement [ɑ̃virɔnmɑ̃] nm environment

environs [ɑ̃virɔ̃] nmpl surroundings; **aux ~ de** (round) about

envisager [ɑ̃vizaʒe] vt to contemplate, envisage; **~ de faire** to consider doing

envoi [ɑ̃vwa] nm (paquet) parcel, consignment; **coup d'~** (SPORT) kick-off

envoler [ɑ̃vɔle]: **s'~** vi (oiseau) to fly away ou off; (avion) to take off; (papier, feuille) to blow away; (fig) to vanish (into thin air)

envoûter [ɑ̃vute] vt to bewitch

envoyé, e [ɑ̃vwaje] nm/f (POL) envoy; (PRESSE) correspondent

envoyer [ɑ̃vwaje] vt to send; (lancer) to hurl, throw; **~ chercher** to send for; **~ promener qn** (fam) to send sb packing

Éole [eɔl] sigle m (= est-ouest-liaison-express) Paris high-speed, east-west subway service

épagneul, e [epaɲœl] nm/f spaniel

épais, se [epɛ, ɛs] adj thick; **épaisseur** nf thickness

épancher [epɑ̃ʃe]: **s'~** vi to open one's heart

épanouir [epanwir]: **s'~** vi (fleur) to

bloom, open out; (*visage*) to light up; (*personne*) to blossom

épargne [eparɲ] *nf* saving

épargner [eparɲe] *vt* to save; (*ne pas tuer ou endommager*) to spare ♦ *vi* to save; ~ **qch à qn** to spare sb sth

éparpiller [eparpije] *vt* to scatter; **s'~** *vi* to scatter; (*fig*) to dissipate one's efforts

épars, e [epar, ars] *adj* scattered

épatant, e [epatɑ̃, ɑ̃t] (*fam*) *adj* super

épater [epate] (*fam*) *vt* (*étonner*) to amaze; (*impressionner*) to impress

épaule [epol] *nf* shoulder

épauler [epole] *vt* (*aider*) to back up, support; (*arme*) to raise (to one's shoulder) ♦ *vi* to (take) aim

épaulette [epolɛt] *nf* (MIL) epaulette; (*rembourrage*) shoulder pad

épave [epav] *nf* wreck

épée [epe] *nf* sword

épeler [ep(ə)le] *vt* to spell

éperdu, e [eperdy] *adj* distraught, overcome; (*amour*) passionate

éperon [eprɔ̃] *nm* spur

épervier [epervje] *nm* sparrowhawk

épi [epi] *nm* (*de blé, d'orge*) ear; (*de maïs*) cob

épice [epis] *nf* spice

épicé, e [epise] *adj* spicy

épicer [epise] *vt* to spice

épicerie [episri] *nf* grocer's shop; (*denrées*) groceries *pl*; ~ **fine** delicatessen; **épicier, -ière** *nm/f* grocer

épidémie [epidemi] *nf* epidemic

épiderme [epidɛrm] *nm* skin

épier [epje] *vt* to spy on, watch closely

épilepsie [epilɛpsi] *nf* epilepsy

épiler [epile] *vt* (*jambes*) to remove the hair from; (*sourcils*) to pluck

épilogue [epilɔg] *nm* (*fig*) conclusion, dénouement; **épiloguer sur** to hold forth on

épinards [epinar] *nmpl* spinach *sg*

épine [epin] *nf* thorn, prickle; (*d'oursin etc*) spine; ~ **dorsale** backbone; **épineux, -euse** *adj* thorny

épingle [epɛ̃gl] *nf* pin; ~ **à cheveux** hairpin; ~ **de nourrice** *ou* **de sûreté** safety pin; **épingler** *vt* (*badge, décoration*): **épingler qch sur** to pin sth on(to); (*fam*) to catch, nick

épique [epik] *adj* epic

épisode [epizɔd] *nm* episode; **film/ roman à ~s** serial; **épisodique** *adj* occasional

éploré, e [eplɔre] *adj* tearful

épluche-légumes [eplyʃlegym] *nm inv* (potato) peeler

éplucher [eplyʃe] *vt* (*fruit, légumes*) to peel; (*fig*) to go over with a fine-tooth comb; **épluchures** *nfpl* peelings

éponge [epɔ̃ʒ] *nf* sponge; **éponger** *vt* (*liquide*) to mop up; (*surface*) to sponge; (*fig: déficit*) to soak up

épopée [epɔpe] *nf* epic

époque [epɔk] *nf* (*de l'histoire*) age, era; (*de l'année, la vie*) time; **d'~** (*meuble*) period *cpd*

époumoner [epumɔne]: **s'~** *vi* to shout o.s. hoarse

épouse [epuz] *nf* wife; **épouser** *vt* to marry

épousseter [epuste] *vt* to dust

époustouflant, e [epustuflɑ̃, ɑ̃t] (*fam*) *adj* staggering, mind-boggling

épouvantable [epuvɑ̃tabl] *adj* appalling, dreadful

épouvantail [epuvɑ̃taj] *nm* scarecrow

épouvante [epuvɑ̃t] *nf* terror; **film d'~** horror film; **épouvanter** *vt* to terrify

époux [epu] *nm* husband ♦ *nmpl* (*married*) couple

éprendre [eprɑ̃dr]: **s'~ de** *vt* to fall in love with

épreuve [eprœv] *nf* (*d'examen*) test; (*malheur, difficulté*) trial, ordeal; (*PHOTO*) print; (*TYPO*) proof; (*SPORT*) event; **à toute** ~ unfailing; **mettre à l'~** to put to the test

épris, e [epri, iz] *pp de* **éprendre**

éprouvant, e [epruvɑ̃, ɑ̃t] *adj* trying, testing

éprouver [epruve] *vt* (*tester*) to test;

(marquer, faire souffrir) to afflict, distress; *(ressentir)* to experience

éprouvette [epʀuvɛt] *nf* test tube

épuisé, e [epɥize] *adj* exhausted; *(livre)* out of print; **épuisement** *nm* exhaustion

épuiser [epɥize] *vt (fatiguer)* to exhaust, wear ou tire out; *(stock, sujet)* to exhaust; **s'~** *vi* to wear ou tire o.s. out, exhaust o.s.

épuisette [epɥizɛt] *nf* shrimping net

épurer [epyʀe] *vt (liquide)* to purify; *(parti etc)* to purge

équateur [ekwatœʀ] *nm* equator; **(la république de) l'É~** Ecuador

équation [ekwasjɔ̃] *nf* equation

équerre [ekɛʀ] *nf (à dessin)* (set) square

équilibre [ekilibʀ] *nm* balance; **garder/perdre l'~** to keep/lose one's balance; **être en ~** to be balanced; **équilibré, e** *adj* well-balanced; **équilibrer** *vt* to balance; **s'équilibrer** *vi (poids)* to balance; *(fig: défauts etc)* to balance each other out

équipage [ekipaʒ] *nm* crew

équipe [ekip] *nf* team

équipé, e [ekipe] *adj*: **bien/mal ~** well-poorly-equipped; **équipée** *nf* escapade

équipement [ekipmɑ̃] *nm* equipment; **~s** *nmpl (installations)* amenities, facilities

équiper [ekipe] *vt* to equip; **~ qn/qch de** to equip sb/sth with

équipier, -ière [ekipje, jɛʀ] *nm/f* team member

équitable [ekitabl] *adj* fair

équitation [ekitasjɔ̃] *nf* (horse-)riding; **faire de l'~** to go riding

équivalent, e [ekivalɑ̃, ɑ̃t] *adj, nm* equivalent

équivaloir [ekivalwaʀ]: **~ à** *vt* to be equivalent to

équivoque [ekivɔk] *adj* equivocal, ambiguous; *(louche)* dubious ♦ *nf (incertitude)* doubt

érable [eʀabl] *nm* maple

érafler [eʀɑfle] *vt* to scratch; **éraflure** *nf* scratch

éraillé, e [eʀɑje] *adj (voix)* rasping

ère [ɛʀ] *nf* era; **en l'an 1050 de notre ~** in the year 1050 A.D.

érection [eʀɛksjɔ̃] *nf* erection

éreinter [eʀɛ̃te] *vt* to exhaust, wear out; *(critiquer)* to pull to pieces

ériger [eʀiʒe] *vt (monument)* to erect

ermite [ɛʀmit] *nm* hermit

éroder [eʀɔde] *vt* to erode

érotique [eʀɔtik] *adj* erotic

errer [eʀe] *vi* to wander

erreur [eʀœʀ] *nf* mistake, error; **faire ~** to be mistaken; **par ~** by mistake; **~ judiciaire** miscarriage of justice

érudit, e [eʀydi, it] *adj* erudite, learned

éruption [eʀypsjɔ̃] *nf* eruption; *(MÉD)* rash

es [ɛ] *vb voir* **être**

ès [ɛs] *prép:* **licencié ~ lettres/sciences** ≈ Bachelor of Arts/Science

escabeau, x [ɛskabo] *nm (tabouret)* stool; *(échelle)* stepladder

escadron [ɛskadʀɔ̃] *nm* squadron

escalade [ɛskalad] *nf* climbing *no pl*; *(POL etc)* escalation; **escalader** *vt* to climb

escale [ɛskal] *nf (NAVIG: durée)* call; *(endroit)* port of call; *(AVIAT)* stop(over); **faire ~ à** *(NAVIG)* to put in at; *(AVIAT)* to stop over at; **vol sans ~** nonstop flight

escalier [ɛskalje] *nm* stairs *pl*; **dans l'~** on the stairs; **~ roulant** escalator

escamoter [ɛskamɔte] *vt (esquiver)* to get round, evade; *(faire disparaître)* to conjure away

escapade [ɛskapad] *nf:* **faire une ~** to go on a jaunt; *(s'enfuir)* to run away ou off

escargot [ɛskaʀgo] *nm* snail

escarpé, e [ɛskaʀpe] *adj* steep

escarpin [ɛskaʀpɛ̃] *nm* low-fronted shoe, court shoe (BRIT)

escient [ɛsjɑ̃] *nm:* **à bon ~** advisedly

esclaffer [ɛsklafe]: **s'~** *vi* to guffaw

esclandre [ɛsklɑ̃dʀ] nm scene, fracas

esclavage [ɛsklavaʒ] nm slavery

esclave [ɛsklav] nm/f slave

escompte [ɛskɔ̃t] nm discount; **escompter** vt (fig) to expect

escorte [ɛskɔʀt] nf escort; **escorter** vt to escort

escrime [ɛskʀim] nf fencing

escrimer [ɛskʀime]: **s'~** vi: **s'~ à faire** to wear o.s. out doing

escroc [ɛskʀo] nm swindler, conman; **escroquer** [ɛskʀɔke] vt: **escroquer qch (à qn)** to swindle sth (out of sb); **escroquerie** nf swindle

espace [ɛspas] nm space

espacer [ɛspase] vt to space out; **s'~** vi (visites etc) to become less frequent

espadon [ɛspadɔ̃] nm swordfish inv

espadrille [ɛspadʀij] nf rope-soled sandal

Espagne [ɛspaɲ] nf: **l'~** Spain; **espagnol, e** adj Spanish ♦ nm/f: **Espagnol, e** Spaniard ♦ nm (LING) Spanish

escouade [ɛskwad] nf squad

espèce [ɛspɛs] nf (BIO, BOT, ZOOL) species inv; (gén: sorte) sort, kind, type; (péj): **~ de maladroit!** you clumsy oaf!; **~s** nfpl (COMM) cash sg; **en ~** in cash

espérance [ɛspeʀɑ̃s] nf hope; **~ de vie** life expectancy

espérer [ɛspeʀe] vt to hope for; **j'espère (bien)** I hope so; **~ que/faire** to hope that/to do

espiègle [ɛspjɛgl] adj mischievous

espion, ne [ɛspjɔ̃, jɔn] nm/f spy; **espionnage** nm espionage, spying; **espionner** vt to spy (up)on

esplanade [ɛsplanad] nf esplanade

espoir [ɛspwaʀ] nm hope

esprit [ɛspʀi] nm (intellect) mind; (humour) wit; (mentalité, d'une loi etc, fantôme etc) spirit; **faire de l'~** to be witty; **reprendre ses ~s** to come to; **perdre l'~** to lose one's mind

esquimau, de, x [ɛskimo, od] adj Eskimo ♦ nm/f: **E~, de** Eskimo ♦ nm: **E~** ® ice lolly (BRIT), popsicle (US)

esquinter [ɛskɛ̃te] (fam) vt to mess up

esquisse [ɛskis] nf sketch; **esquisser** vt to sketch; **esquisser un sourire** to give a vague smile

esquiver [ɛskive] vt to dodge; **s'~** vi to slip away

essai [ɛsɛ] nm (tentative) attempt, try; (de produit) testing; (RUGBY) try; (LITTÉRATURE) essay; **~s** nmpl (AUTO) trials; **~ gratuit** (COMM) free trial; **à l'~** on a trial basis

essaim [ɛsɛ̃] nm swarm

essayer [ɛseje] vt to try; (vêtement, chaussures) to try on; (méthode, voiture) to try (out) ♦ vi to try; **~ de faire** to try ou attempt to do

essence [ɛsɑ̃s] nf (de voiture) petrol (BRIT), gas(oline) (US); (extrait de plante) essence; (espèce: d'arbre) species inv

essentiel, le [ɛsɑ̃sjɛl] adj essential; **c'est l'~** (ce qui importe) that's the main thing; **l'~ de** the main part of

essieu, x [ɛsjø] nm axle

essor [ɛsɔʀ] nm (de l'économie etc) rapid expansion

essorer [ɛsɔʀe] vt (en tordant) to wring (out); (par la force centrifuge) to spin-dry; **essoreuse** nf spin-dryer

essouffler [ɛsufle]: **s'~** vi to get out of breath

essuie-glace [ɛsɥiglas] nm inv windscreen (BRIT) ou windshield (US) wiper

essuyer [ɛsɥije] vt to wipe; (fig: échec) to suffer; **s'~** vi (après le bain) to dry o.s.; **~ la vaisselle** to dry up

est[1] [e] vb voir **être**

est[2] [ɛst] nm east ♦ adj inv east; (région) east(ern); **à l'~** in the east; (direction) to the east, east(wards); **à l'~ de** (to the) east of

estampe [ɛstɑ̃p] nf print, engraving

est-ce que [ɛskə] adv: **~ c'est cher/c'était bon?** is it expensive/was it good?; **quand est-ce qu'il part?** when does he leave?, when is he leaving?; voir aussi **que**

esthéticienne [ɛstetisjɛn] nf beautician

esthétique [estetik] *adj* attractive

estimation [estimasjɔ̃] *nf* valuation; (*chiffre*) estimate

estime [estim] *nf* esteem, regard; **estimer** *vt* (*respecter*) to esteem; (*expertiser: bijou etc*) to value; (*évaluer: coût etc*) to assess, estimate; (*penser*): **estimer que/être** to consider that/o.s. to be

estival, e, -aux [estival, o] *adj* summer *cpd*

estivant, e [estivɑ̃, ɑ̃t] *nm/f* (summer) holiday-maker

estomac [estɔma] *nm* stomach

estomaqué, e [ɛstɔmake] (*fam*) *adj* flabbergasted

estomper [estɔ̃pe] **s'~** *vi* (*sentiments*) to soften; (*contour*) to become blurred

estrade [estrad] *nf* platform, rostrum

estragon [estragɔ̃] *nm* tarragon

estuaire [estɥɛr] *nm* estuary

et [e] *conj* and; ~ **lui?** what about him?; ~ **alors!** so what!

étable [etabl] *nf* cowshed

établi [etabli] *nm* (work)bench

établir [etablir] *vt* (*papiers d'identité, facture*) to make out; (*liste, programme*) to draw up; (*entreprise*) to set up; (*réputation, usage, fait, culpabilité*) to establish; **s'~** *vi* to be established; **s'~ (à son compte)** to set up in business; **s'~ à/près de** to settle in/near

établissement [etablismɑ̃] *nm* (*entreprise, institution*) establishment; ~ **scolaire** school, educational establishment

étage [eta3] *nm* (*d'immeuble*) storey, floor; **à l'~** upstairs; **au 2ème ~** on the 2nd (*BRIT*) *ou* 3rd (*US*) floor

étagère [eta3ɛr] *nf* (*rayon*) shelf; (*meuble*) shelves *pl*

étai [ete] *nm* stay, prop

étain [etɛ̃] *nm* pewter *no pl*

étais *etc* [etɛ] *vb voir* **être**

étal [etal] *nm* stall

étalage [etala3] *nm* display; (*devanture*) display window; **faire ~ de** to show

off, parade

étaler [etale] *vt* (*carte, nappe*) to spread (out); (*peinture*) to spread; (*échelonner: paiements, vacances*) to spread, stagger; (*marchandises*) to display; (*connaissances*) to parade; **s'~** *vi* (*liquide*) to spread out; (*fam*) to fall flat on one's face; **s'~ sur** (*suj: paiements etc*) to be spread out over

étalon [etalɔ̃] *nm* (*cheval*) stallion

étanche [etɑ̃ʃ] *adj* (*récipient*) watertight; (*montre, vêtement*) waterproof; **étancher** *vt*: **étancher sa soif** to quench one's thirst

étang [etɑ̃] *nm* pond

étant [etɑ̃] *vb voir* **être**; **donné**

étape [etap] *nf* stage; (*lieu d'arrivée*) stopping place; (: *CYCLISME*) staging point

état [eta] *nm* (*POL, condition*) state; **en mauvais ~** in poor condition; **en ~ (de marche)** in (working) order; **remettre en ~** to repair; **hors d'~** out of order; **être en ~/hors d'~ de faire** to be in a/in no fit state to do; **être dans tous ses ~s** to be in a state; **faire ~ de** (*alléguer*) to put forward; **l'É~** the State; ~ **civil** civil status; ~ **des lieux** inventory of fixtures; **étatiser** *vt* to bring under state control; **état-major** *nm* (*MIL*) staff; **États-Unis** *nmpl*: **les États-Unis** the United States

étau, x [eto] *nm* vice (*BRIT*), vise (*US*)

étayer [eteje] *vt* to prop *ou* shore up

etc. [ɛtsetera] *adv* etc.

et c(a)etera [ɛtsetera] *adv* et cetera, and so on

été [ete] *pp de* **être** ♦ *nm* summer

éteindre [etɛ̃dr] *vt* (*lampe, lumière, radio*) to turn *ou* switch off; (*cigarette, feu*) to put out, extinguish; **s'~** *vi* (*feu, lumière*) to go out; (*mourir*) to pass away; **éteint, e** *adj* (*fig*) lacklustre, dull; (*volcan*) extinct

étendard [etɑ̃dar] *nm* standard

étendre [etɑ̃dr] *vt* (*pâte, liquide*) to spread; (*carte etc*) to spread out; (*linge*) and so on to hang up; (bras, jambes) to stretch out; (fig: agrandir) to extend; **s'~** vi (augmenter, se propager) to spread; (terrain, forêt etc) to stretch; (s'allonger) to stretch out; (se coucher) to lie down; (fig: expliquer) to elaborate

étendu, e [etɑ̃dy] adj extensive; **étendue** nf (d'eau, de sable) stretch, expanse; (importance) extent

éternel, le [etɛʀnɛl] adj eternal

éterniser [etɛʀnize]: **s'~** vi to last for ages; (visiteur) to stay for ages

éternité [etɛʀnite] nf eternity; **ça a duré une ~** it lasted for ages

éternuement [etɛʀnymɑ̃] nm sneeze

éternuer [etɛʀnɥe] vi to sneeze

êtes [ɛt(z)] vb voir **être**

éthique [etik] adj ethical

ethnie [ɛtni] nf ethnic group

éthylisme [etilism] nm alcoholism

étiez [etje] vb voir **être**

étinceler [etɛ̃s(ə)le] vi to sparkle

étincelle [etɛ̃sɛl] nf spark

étiqueter [etik(ə)te] vt to label

étiquette [etikɛt] nf label; (protocole): **l'~** etiquette

étirer [etiʀe]: **s'~** vi (personne) to stretch; (convoi, route): **s'~ sur** to stretch out over

étoffe [etɔf] nf material, fabric

étoffer [etɔfe] vt to fill out

étoile [etwal] nf star; **à la belle ~** in the open; **~ de mer** starfish; **~ filante** shooting star; **étoilé, e** adj starry

étonnant, e [etɔnɑ̃, ɑ̃t] adj amazing

étonnement [etɔnmɑ̃] nm surprise, amazement

étonner [etɔne] vt to surprise, amaze; **s'~ que/de** to be amazed that/at; **cela m'~ait (que)** (j'en doute) I'd be very surprised (if)

étouffant, e [etufɑ̃, ɑ̃t] adj stifling

étouffée [etufe]: **à l'~** adv (CULIN: légumes) steamed; (: viande) braised

étouffer [etufe] vt to suffocate; (bruit) to muffle; (scandale) to hush up ♦ vi to suffocate; **s'~** vi (en mangeant etc) to

choke; **on étouffe** it's stifling

étourderie [etuʀdəʀi] nf (caractère) absent-mindedness no pl; (faute) thoughtless blunder

étourdi, e [etuʀdi] adj (distrait) scatter-brained, heedless

étourdir [etuʀdiʀ] vt (assommer) to stun, daze; (griser) to make dizzy ou giddy; **étourdissement** nm dizzy spell

étourneau, x [etuʀno] nm starling

étrange [etʀɑ̃ʒ] adj strange

étranger, ère [etʀɑ̃ʒe, ɛʀ] adj foreign; (pas de la famille, non familier) strange ♦ nm/f foreigner; stranger ♦ nm: **à l'~** abroad

étrangler [etʀɑ̃gle] vt to strangle; **s'~** vi (en mangeant etc) to choke

---

MOT-CLÉ

être [ɛtʀ] nm being; **être humain** human being

♦ vb +attrib **1** (état, description) to be; **il est instituteur** he's a teacher; **vous êtes grand/intelligent/fatigué** you are ou you're tall/clever/tired

2 (+à: appartenir) to be; **le livre est à Paul** the book is Paul's ou belongs to Paul; **c'est à moi/eux** it's mine/theirs

3 (+de: provenance): **il est de Paris** he is from Paris; (: appartenance): **il est des nôtres** he is one of us

4 (date): **nous sommes le 10 janvier** it's the 10th of January (today)

♦ vi to be; **je ne serai pas ici demain** I won't be here tomorrow

♦ vb aux **1** to have; to be; **être arrivé/allé** to have arrived/gone; **il est parti** he has left, he has gone

2 (forme passive) to be; **être fait par** to be made by; **il a été promu** he has been promoted

3 (+à: obligation): **c'est à réparer** it needs repairing; **c'est à essayer** it should be tried

♦ vb impers **1**: **il est** +adjectif it is +adjectif; **il est impossible de le faire** it's impossible to do it

2 (heure, date): **il est 10 heures, c'est 10 heures** it is ou it's 10 o'clock

3 (emphatique): **c'est moi** it's me; **c'est à lui de le faire** it's up to him to do it

étreindre [etʀɛ̃dʀ] *vt* to clutch, grip; (amoureusement, amicalement) to embrace; **s'~** *vi* to embrace

étrenner [etʀene] *vt* to use (ou wear) for the first time; **étrennes** *nfpl* Christmas box *sg*

étrier [etʀije] *nm* stirrup

étriqué, e [etʀike] *adj* skimpy

étroit, e [etʀwa, wat] *adj* narrow; (vêtement) tight; (fig: liens, collaboration) close; **à l'~** cramped; **~ d'esprit** narrow-minded

étude [etyd] *nf* studying; (ouvrage, rapport) study; (SCOL: salle de travail) study room; **~s** *nfpl* (SCOL) studies; **être à l'~** (projet etc) to be under consideration; **faire des ~s (de droit/médecine)** to study (law/medicine)

étudiant, e [etydjɑ̃, jɑ̃t] *nm/f* student

étudier [etydje] *vt, vi* to study

étui [etɥi] *nm* case

étuve [etyv] *nf* steamroom

étuvée [etyve] *nf*: **à l'~** braised

eu, eue [y] *pp de* avoir

euh [ø] *excl* er

euro [øʀo] *nm* euro

Euroland [øʀolɑ̃d] *nm* Euroland

Europe [øʀɔp] *nf*: **l'~** Europe; **européen, ne** *adj* European ♦ *nm/f*: **Européen, ne** European

eus *etc* [y] *vb voir* avoir

eux [ø] *pron* (sujet) they; (objet) them

évacuer [evakɥe] *vt* to evacuate

évader [evade]: **s'~** *vi* to escape

évaluer [evalɥe] *vt* (expertiser) to appraise, evaluate; (juger approximativement) to estimate

évangile [evãʒil] *nm* gospel

évanouir [evanwiʀ]: **s'~** *vi* to faint; (disparaître) to vanish, disappear; **éva-**

nouissement *nm* (syncope) fainting fit

évaporer [evapɔʀe]: **s'~** *vi* to evaporate

évasé, e [evaze] *adj* (manches, jupe) flared

évasif, -ive [evazif, iv] *adj* evasive

évasion [evazjɔ̃] *nf* escape

évêché [eveʃe] *nm* bishop's palace

éveil [evɛj] *nm* awakening; **être en ~** to be alert; **éveillé, e** *adj* awake; (vif) alert, sharp; **éveiller** *vt* to (a)waken; (soupçons etc) to arouse; **s'éveiller** *vi* to (a)waken; (fig) to be aroused

événement [evenmɑ̃] *nm* event

éventail [evãtaj] *nm* fan; (choix) range

éventaire [evãtɛʀ] *nm* stall, stand

éventer [evãte] *vt* (secret) to uncover; **s'~** *vi* (parfum) to go stale

éventualité [evãtɥalite] *nf* eventuality; possibility; **dans l'~ de** in the event of

éventuel, le [evãtɥɛl] *adj* possible; **éventuellement** *adv* possibly

évêque [evɛk] *nm* bishop

évertuer [evɛʀtɥe]: **s'~** *vi*: **s'~ à faire** to try very hard to do

éviction [eviksjɔ̃] *nf* (de locataire) eviction

évidemment [evidamɑ̃] *adv* (bien sûr) of course; (certainement) obviously

évidence [evidãs] *nf* obviousness; (fait) obvious fact; **de toute ~** quite obviously ou evidently; **être en ~** to be clearly visible; **mettre en ~** (fait) to highlight; **évident, e** *adj* obvious, evident; **ce n'est pas évident!** (fam) it's not that easy!

évider [evide] *vt* to scoop out

évier [evje] *nm* (kitchen) sink

évincer [evɛ̃se] *vt* to oust

éviter [evite] *vt* to avoid; **~ de faire** to avoid doing; **~ qch à qn** to spare sb sth

évolué, e [evɔlɥe] *adj* advanced

évoluer [evɔlɥe] *vi* (enfant, maladie) to develop; (situation, moralement) to evolve, develop; (aller et venir) to move about; **évolution** *nf* development, evolution

évoquer [evɔke] *vt* to call to mind, evoke; (*mentionner*) to mention

ex... [ɛks] *préfixe* ex-

exact, e [ɛgza(kt), ɛgzakt] *adj* exact; (*correct*) correct; (*ponctuel*) punctual; **l'heure ~e** the right *ou* exact time; **exactement** *adv* exactly

ex aequo [ɛgzeko] *adj* equally placed; **arriver ~** to finish neck and neck

exagéré, e [ɛgzaʒeRe] *adj* (*prix etc*) excessive

exagérer [ɛgzaʒeRe] *vt* to exaggerate ♦ *vi* to exaggerate; (*abuser*) to go too far

exalter [ɛgzalte] *vt* (*enthousiasmer*) to excite, elate

examen [ɛgzamɛ̃] *nm* examination; (*SCOL*) exam, examination; **à l'~** under consideration

examinateur, -trice [ɛgzaminatœR, tRis] *nm/f* examiner

examiner [ɛgzamine] *vt* to examine

exaspérant, e [ɛgzaspeRɑ̃, ɑ̃t] *adj* exasperating

exaspérer [ɛgzaspeRe] *vt* to exasperate

exaucer [ɛgzose] *vt* (*vœu*) to grant

excédent [ɛksedɑ̃] *nm* surplus; **en ~** surplus; **~ de bagages** excess luggage

excéder [ɛksede] *vt* (*dépasser*) to exceed; (*agacer*) to exasperate

excellent, e [ɛksɛlɑ̃, ɑ̃t] *adj* excellent

excentrique [ɛksɑ̃tRik] *adj* eccentric

excepté, e [ɛksɛpte] *adj, prép*: **les élèves ~s, ~ les élèves** except for the pupils

exception [ɛksɛpsjɔ̃] *nf* exception; **à l'~ de** except for, with the exception of; **d'~** (*mesure, loi*) special, exceptional; **exceptionnel, le** *adj* exceptional; **exceptionnellement** *adv* exceptionally

excès [ɛksɛ] *nm* surplus ♦ *nmpl* excesses; **faire des ~** to overindulge; **~ de vitesse** speeding *no pl*; **excessif, -ive** *adj* excessive

excitant, e [ɛksitɑ̃, ɑ̃t] *adj* exciting ♦ *nm* stimulant; **excitation** *nf* (*état*)

excitement

exciter [ɛksite] *vt* to excite; (*suj: café etc*) to stimulate; **s'~** *vi* to get excited

exclamation [ɛksklamasjɔ̃] *nf* exclamation

exclamer [ɛksklame]: **s'~** *vi* to exclaim

exclure [ɛksklyR] *vt* (*faire sortir*) to expel; (*ne pas compter*) to exclude, leave out; (*rendre impossible*) to exclude, rule out; **il est exclu que** it's out of the question that ...; **il n'est pas exclu que ...** it's not impossible that ...; **exclusif, -ive** *adj* exclusive; **exclusion** *nf* exclusion; **à l'exclusion de** with the exclusion *ou* exception of; **exclusivité** *nf* (*COMM*) exclusive rights *pl*; **film passant en exclusivité** à film showing only at

excursion [ɛkskyRsjɔ̃] *nf* (*en autocar*) excursion, trip; (*à pied*) walk, hike

excuse [ɛkskyz] *nf* excuse; **~s** *nfpl* (*regret*) apology *sg*, apologies; **excuser** *vt* to excuse; **s'excuser (de)** to apologize (for); **"excusez-moi"** "I'm sorry", (*pour attirer l'attention*) "excuse me"

exécrable [ɛgzekRabl] *adj* atrocious

exécuter [ɛgzekyte] *vt* (*tuer*) to execute; (*tâche etc*) to execute, carry out; (*MUS: jouer*) to perform, execute; **s'~** *vi* to comply; **exécutif, -ive** *adj, nm* (*POL*) executive; **exécution** *nf* execution; **mettre à exécution** to carry out

exemplaire [ɛgzɑ̃plɛR] *nm* copy

exemple [ɛgzɑ̃pl] *nm* example; **par ~** for instance, for example; **donner l'~** to set an example

exempt, e [ɛgzɑ̃, ɑ̃(p)t] *adj*: **~ de** (*dispensé de*) exempt from; (*sans*) free from

exercer [ɛgzɛRse] *vt* (*pratiquer*) to exercise, practise; (*influence, contrôle*) to exert; (*former*) to exercise, train; **s'~** *vi* (*sportif, musicien*) to practise

exercice [ɛgzɛRsis] *nm* exercise

exhaustif, -ive [ɛgzostif, iv] *adj* exhaustive

exhiber [ɛgzibe] vt (montrer: papiers, certificat) to present, produce; (péj) to display, flaunt; **s'~** vi to parade; (suj: exhibitionniste) to expose o.s; **exhibitionniste** [ɛgzibisjɔnist] nm/f flasher

exhorter [ɛgzɔʀte] vt to urge

exigeant, e [ɛgziʒɑ̃, ɑ̃t] adj demanding; (péj) hard to please

exigence [ɛgziʒɑ̃s] nf demand, requirement

exiger [ɛgziʒe] vt to demand, require

exigu, ë [ɛgzigy] adj cramped, tiny

exil [ɛgzil] nm exile; **exiler** vt to exile; **s'exiler** to go into exile

existence [ɛgzistɑ̃s] nf existence

exister [ɛgziste] vi to exist; **il existe un/des** there is a/are (some)

exonérer [ɛgzɔneʀe] vt: **~ de** to exempt from

exorbitant, e [ɛgzɔʀbitɑ̃, ɑ̃t] adj exorbitant

exorbité, e [ɛgzɔʀbite] adj: **yeux ~s** bulging eyes

exotique [ɛgzɔtik] adj exotic; **yaourt aux fruits ~s** tropical fruit yoghurt

expatrier [ɛkspatʀie] vt: **s'~** to leave one's country

expectative [ɛkspɛktativ] nf: **être dans l'~** to be still waiting

expédient [ɛkspedjɑ̃, jɑ̃t] (péj) nm: **vivre d'~s** to live by one's wits

expédier [ɛkspedje] vt (lettre, paquet) to send; (troupes) to dispatch; (fam: travail etc) to dispose of, dispatch; **expéditeur, -trice** nm/f sender; **expédition** nf sending; (scientifique, sportive, MIL) expedition

expérience [ɛkspeʀjɑ̃s] nf (de la vie) experience; (scientifique) experiment

expérimenté, e [ɛkspeʀimɑ̃te] adj experienced

expérimenter [ɛkspeʀimɑ̃te] vt to test out, experiment with

expert, e [ɛkspɛʀ, ɛʀt] adj, nm expert; **expert-comptable** nm ≈ chartered accountant (BRIT), ≈ certified public accountant (US)

expertise [ɛkspɛʀtiz] nf (évaluation) expert evaluation

expertiser [ɛkspɛʀtize] vt (objet de valeur) to value; (voiture accidentée etc) to assess damage to

expier [ɛkspje] vt to expiate, atone for

expirer [ɛkspiʀe] vi (prendre fin, mourir) to expire; (respirer) to breathe out

explicatif, -ive [ɛksplikatif, iv] adj explanatory

explication [ɛksplikasjɔ̃] nf explanation; (discussion) discussion; (dispute) argument; **~ de texte** (SCOL) critical analysis

explicite [ɛksplisit] adj explicit

expliquer [ɛksplike] vt to explain; **s'~** to explain (o.s.); **s'~ avec qn** (discuter) to explain o.s to sb; **son erreur s'explique** one can understand his mistake

exploit [ɛksplwa] nm exploit, feat; **exploitant, e** nm/f: **exploitant (agricole)** farmer

exploitation nf exploitation; (d'une entreprise) running; **~ agricole** farming concern; **exploiter** vt (personne, don) to exploit; (entreprise, ferme) to run, operate; (mine) to exploit, work

explorer [ɛksplɔʀe] vt to explore

exploser [ɛksploze] vi to explode, blow up; (engin explosif) to go off; (personne: de colère) to flare up; **explosif, -ive** adj, nm explosive; **explosion** nf explosion

exportateur, -trice [ɛkspɔʀtatœʀ, tʀis] adj export cpd, exporting ♦ nm exporter

exportation [ɛkspɔʀtasjɔ̃] nf (action) exportation; (produit) export

exporter [ɛkspɔʀte] vt to export

exposant [ɛkspozɑ̃] nm exhibitor

exposé, e [ɛkspoze] nm talk ♦ adj: **~ au sud** facing south

exposer [ɛkspoze] vt (marchandise) to display; (peinture) to exhibit, show; (parler de) to explain, set out; (mettre en danger, orienter, PHOTO) to expose;

exposition *nf* (*manifestation*) exhibition; (*PHOTO*) exposure

exprès[1] [ɛkspʀɛ] *adv* (*délibérément*) on purpose; (*spécialement*) specially

exprès[2], **-esse** [ɛksprɛs] *adj* (*ordre, défense*) express, formal ♦ *adj inv* (*PTT*) express ♦ *adv* express

express [ɛkspres] *adj, nm*: **(café) ~** espresso (coffee); **(train) ~** fast train

expressément [ɛkspresemã] *adv* (*spécialement*) specifically

expressif, -ive [ɛkspresif, iv] *adj* expressive

expression [ɛkspresjɔ̃] *nf* expression

exprimer [ɛksprime] *vt* (*sentiment, idée*) to express; (*jus, liquide*) to press out; **s'~** *vi* (*personne*) to express o.s

exproprier [ɛksprɔprije] *vt* to buy up by compulsory purchase, expropriate

expulser [ɛkspylse] *vt* to expel; (*locataire*) to evict; (*SPORT*) to send off

exquis, e [ɛkski, iz] *adj* exquisite

extase [ɛkstaz] *nf* ecstasy; **extasier: s'extasier sur** *vt* to go into raptures over

extension [ɛkstãsjɔ̃] *nf* (*fig*) extension

exténuer [ɛkstenɥe] *vt* to exhaust

extérieur, e [ɛksterjœr] *adj* (*porte, mur etc*) outer, outside; (*au dehors: escalier, w.-c.*) outside; (*commerce*) foreign; (*influences*) external; (*apparent: calme, gaieté etc*) surface *cpd* ♦ *nm* (*d'une maison, d'un récipient etc*) outside, exterior; (*apparence*) exterior ♦ **à l'~** outside; (*à l'étranger*) abroad; **extérieurement** *adv* on the outside; (*en apparence*) on the surface

exterminer [ɛkstɛrmine] *vt* to exterminate, wipe out

externat [ɛkstɛrna] *nm* day school

externe [ɛkstɛrn] *adj* external, outer ♦ *nm/f.* (*MÉD*) non-resident medical student (*BRIT*), extern (*US*); (*SCOL*) day pupil

extincteur [ɛkstɛ̃ktœr] *nm* (fire) extinguisher

extinction [ɛkstɛ̃ksjɔ̃] *nf*: **~ de voix** loss of voice

extorquer [ɛkstɔrke] *vt* to extort

extra [ɛkstra] *adj inv* first-rate; (*fam*) fantastic ♦ *nm inv* extra help

extracommunautaire [ɛkstrakɔmynotɛr] *adj* non-EU

extrader [ɛkstrade] *vt* to extradite

extraire [ɛkstrɛr] *vt* to extract; **extrait** *nm* extract

extraordinaire [ɛkstraɔrdinɛr] *adj* extraordinary; (*POL: mesures etc*) special

extravagant, e [ɛkstravagã, ãt]· *adj* extravagant

extraverti, e [ɛkstraverti] *adj* extrovert

extrême [ɛkstrɛm] *adj, nm* extreme; **extrêmement** *adv* extremely; **extrême-onction** *nf* last rites *pl*; **Extrême-Orient** *nm* Far East

extrémité [ɛkstremite] *nf* end; (*situation*) straits *pl*, plight; (*geste désespéré*) extreme action; **~s** *nfpl* (*pieds et mains*) extremities

exubérant, e [ɛgzyberã, ãt] *adj* exuberant

exutoire [ɛgzytwar] *nm* outlet, release

F, f

F *abr* = **franc**

fa [fa] *nm inv* (*MUS*) F; (*en chantant la gamme*) fa

fable [fɑbl] *nf* fable

fabricant [fabrikã, ãt] *nm* manufacturer

fabrication [fabrikasjɔ̃] *nf* manufacture

fabrique [fabrik] *nf* factory; **fabriquer** *vt* to make; (*industriellement*) to manufacture; (*fig*): **qu'est-ce qu'il fabrique?** (*fam*) what is he doing?

fabulation [fabylasjɔ̃] *nf* fantasizing

fac [fak] (*fam*) *abr f* (*SCOL*) = **faculté**

façade [fasad] *nf* front, façade

face [fas] *nf* (*gén*) face; (*fig: aspect*) side; **le côté ~** heads; **en ~ de** opposite; (*fig*) in front of; **de ~** (*voir*) face on; **à** (*fig*) faced with, in the face of; **faire ~ à** to face; **~ à ~** *adv* facing

each other ♦ *nm inv* encounter
fâché, e [faʃe] *adj* angry; (*désolé*) sorry
fâcher [faʃe] *vt* to anger; **se ~** *vi* to get angry; **se ~ avec** (*se brouiller*) to fall out with
fâcheux, -euse [faʃø, øz] *adj* unfortunate, regrettable
facile [fasil] *adj* easy; (*caractère*) easy-going; **facilement** *adv* easily
facilité *nf* easiness; (*disposition, don*) aptitude; **facilités de paiement** easy terms; **faciliter** *vt* to make easier
façon [fasɔ̃] *nf* (*manière*) way; (*d'une robe etc*) making-up, cut; **~s** *nfpl* (*péj*) fuss *sg*; **de ~ à/à ce que** so as to/that; **de toute ~** anyway, in any case; **façonner** [fasɔne] *vt* (*travailler: matière*) to shape, fashion
facteur, -trice [faktœr, tris] *nm/f* postman(-woman) (*BRIT*), mailman(-woman) (*US*) ♦ *nm* (*MATH, fig: élément*) factor
factice [faktis] *adj* artificial
faction [faksjɔ̃] *nf* faction; **être de ~** to be on guard (duty)
facture [faktyr] *nf* (*à payer: gén*) bill; invoice; **facturer** *vt* to invoice
facultatif, -ive [fakyltatif, iv] *adj* optional
faculté [fakylte] *nf* (*intellectuelle, d'université*) faculty; (*pouvoir, possibilité*) power
fade [fad] *adj* insipid
fagot [fago] *nm* bundle of sticks
faible [fɛbl] *adj* weak; (*voix, lumière, vent*) faint; (*rendement, revenu*) low ♦ *nm* (*pour quelqu'un*) weakness, soft spot; **faiblesse** *nf* weakness; **faiblir** *vi* to weaken; (*lumière*) to dim; (*vent*) to drop
faïence [fajɑ̃s] *nf* earthenware *no pl*
faignant, e [fɛɲɑ̃, ɑ̃t] *nm/f* = **fainéant, e**
faille [faj] *vb voir* **falloir** ♦ *nf* (*GÉO*) fault; (*fig*) flaw, weakness
faillir [fajir] *vi*: **j'ai failli tomber** I almost *ou* very nearly fell

faillite [fajit] *nf* bankruptcy
faim [fɛ̃] *nf* hunger; **avoir ~** to be hungry; **rester sur sa ~** (*aussi fig*) to be left wanting more
fainéant, e [feneɑ̃, ɑ̃t] *nm/f* idler, loafer

MOT-CLÉ

---

faire [fɛr] *vt* **1** (*fabriquer, être l'auteur de*) to make; **faire du vin/une offre/un film** to make wine/an offer/a film; **faire du bruit** to make a noise

2 (*effectuer: travail, opération*) to do; **que faites-vous?** (*quel métier etc*) what do you do?; (*quelle activité: au moment de la question*) what are you doing?; **faire la lessive** to do the washing

3 (*études*) to do; (*sport, musique*) to play; **faire du droit/du français** to do law/French; **faire du rugby/piano** to play rugby/the piano

4 (*simuler*): **faire le malade/l'ignorant** to act the invalid/the fool

5 (*transformer, avoir un effet sur*): **faire de qn un frustré/avocat** to make sb frustrated/a lawyer; **ça ne me fait rien** (*m'est égal*) I don't care *ou* mind; (*me laisse froid*) it has no effect on me; **ça ne fait rien** it doesn't matter; **faire que** (*impliquer*) to mean that

6 (*calculs, prix, mesures*): **2 et 2 font 4** 2 and 2 are *ou* make 4; **ça fait 10 m/15 F** it's 10 m/15F; **je vous le fais 10 F** I'll let you have it for 10F

7: **qu'a-t-il fait de sa valise?** what has he done with his case?

8: **ne faire que**: **il ne fait que critiquer** (*sans cesse*) all he (ever) does is criticize; (*seulement*) he's only criticizing

9 (*dire*) to say; **"vraiment?" fit-il** "really?" he said

10 (*maladie*) to have; **faire du diabète** to have diabetes *sg*

♦ *vi* **1** (*agir, s'y prendre*) to act, do; **il faut faire vite** we (*ou* you *etc*) must act quickly; **comment a-t-il fait pour?** how did he manage to?; **faites** comme chez vous make yourself at home

2 *(paraître)* to look; **faire vieux/ démodé** to look old/old-fashioned; **ça fait bien** it looks good

♦ *vb substitut* to do; **ne le casse pas comme je l'ai fait** don't break it as I did; **je peux le voir? - faites!** can I see it? - please do!

♦ *vb impers* 1: **il fait beau** *etc* the weather is fine *etc*; *voir aussi* **jour**; **froid** *etc*

2 *(temps écoulé, durée)*: **ça fait 2 ans qu'il est parti** it's 2 years since he left; **ça fait 2 ans qu'il y est** he's been there for 2 years

♦ *vb semi-aux* 1: **faire** +*infinitif (action directe)* to make; **faire tomber/bouger qch** to make sth fall/move; **faire démarrer un moteur/chauffer de l'eau** to start up an engine/heat some water; **cela fait dormir** it makes you sleep; **faire travailler les enfants** to make the children work *ou* get the children to work

2 *(indirectement, par un intermédiaire)*: **faire réparer qch** to get *ou* have sth repaired; **faire punir les enfants** to have the children punished; **se faire** *vi* 1 *(vin, fromage)* to mature

2: **cela se fait beaucoup/ne se fait pas** it's done a lot/not done

3: **se faire** +*nom ou pron*: **se faire une jupe** to make o.s. a skirt; **se faire des amis** to make friends; **se faire du souci** to worry; **il ne s'en fait pas** he doesn't worry

4: **se faire** +*adj (devenir)*: **se faire vieux** to be getting old; *(délibérément)*: **se faire beau** to do o.s. up

5: **se faire à** *(s'habituer)* to get used to; **je n'arrive pas à me faire à la nourriture/au climat** I can't get used to the food/climate

6: **se faire** +*infinitif*: **se faire examiner la vue/opérer** to have one's eyes tested/to have an operation; **se faire**

couper les cheveux to get one's hair cut; **il va se faire tuer/punir** he's going to get himself killed/get (himself) punished; **il s'est fait aider** he got somebody to help him; **il s'est fait aider par Simon** he got Simon to help him; **se faire faire un vêtement** to get a garment made for o.s.

7 *(impersonnel)*: **comment se fait-il/ faisait-il que?** how is it/was it that?

faire-part [fɛʀpaʀ] *nm inv* announcement *(of birth, marriage etc)*

faisable [fəzabl] *adj* feasible

faisan, e [fəzɑ̃, an] *nm/f* pheasant; **faisandé, e** *adj* high *(bad)*

faisceau, x [fɛso] *nm (de lumière etc)* beam

faisons [fəzɔ̃] *vb voir* **faire**

fait, e [fɛ, fɛt] *adj (mûr: fromage, melon)* ripe ♦ *nm (événement)* event, occurrence; *(réalité, donnée)* fact; **être au ~ (de)** to be informed (of); **au ~ (à propos)** by the way; **en venir au ~** to get to the point; **du ~ de ceci/qu'il a menti** because of *ou* on account of this/his having lied; **de ce ~** for this reason; **en ~** in fact; **prendre qn sur le ~** to catch sb in the act; **~ divers** news item

faîte [fɛt] *nm* top; *(fig)* pinnacle, height

faites [fɛt] *vb voir* **faire**

faitout [fɛtu] *nm*, **fait-tout** [fɛtu] *nm inv* stewpot

falaise [falɛz] *nf* cliff

falloir [falwaʀ] *vb impers*: **il faut qu'il parte/a fallu qu'il parte** *(obligation)* he has to *ou* must leave/had to leave; **il a fallu le faire** it had to be done; **il faut faire attention** you have to be careful; **il me faudrait 100 F** I would need 100 F; **il vous faut tourner à gauche après l'église** you have to turn left past the church; **nous avons ce qu'il (nous) faut** we have what we need; **s'en ~: il s'en est fallu de 100 F/5 minutes** we/they *etc* were 100 F short/5 minutes late (*ou* early); **il s'en faut de beaucoup qu'il soit** he is far from being; **il s'en est fallu de peu que cela n'arrive** it very nearly happened

falsifier [falsifje] *vt* to falsify, doctor

famé, e [fame] *adj*: **mal ~** disreputable, of ill repute

famélique [famelik] *adj* half-starved

fameux, -euse [famø, øz] *adj* (*illustre*) famous; (*bon*: *repas, plat etc*) first-class; (*valeur intensive*) real, downright

familial, e, -aux [familjal, -jo] *adj* family *cpd*

familiarité [familjaʀite] *nf* familiarity; **~s** *nfpl* (*privautés*) familiarities

familier, -ère [familje, jɛʀ] *adj* (*connu*) familiar; (*atmosphère*) informal, friendly; (*LING*) informal, colloquial ♦ *nm* regular (visitor)

famille [famij] *nf* family; **il a de la ~ à Paris** he has relatives in Paris

famine [famin] *nf* famine

fanatique [fanatik] *adj* fanatical ♦ *nm/f* fanatic; **fanatisme** *nm* fanaticism

faner [fane]: **se ~** *vi* to fade

fanfare [fɑ̃faʀ] *nf* (*orchestre*) brass band; (*musique*) fanfare

fanfaron, ne [fɑ̃faʀɔ̃, ɔn] *nm/f* braggart

fantaisie [fɑ̃tezi] *nf* (*spontanéité*) fancy, imagination; (*caprice*) whim ♦ *adj*: **bijou ~** costume jewellery; **fantaisiste** (*péj*) *adj* unorthodox, eccentric

fantasme [fɑ̃tasm] *nm* fantasy

fantasque [fɑ̃task] *adj* whimsical, capricious

fantastique [fɑ̃tastik] *adj* fantastic

fantôme [fɑ̃tom] *nm* ghost, phantom

faon [fɑ̃] *nm* fawn

farce [faʀs] *nf* (*viande*) stuffing; (*blague*) (practical) joke; (*THÉÂTRE*) farce; **farcir** (*viande*) to stuff

fardeau, x [faʀdo] *nm* burden

farder [faʀde]: **se ~** *vi* to make (o.s.) up

farfelu, e [faʀfəly] *adj* hare-brained

farine [faʀin] *nf* flour; **farineux, -euse** *adj* (*sauce, pomme*) floury

farouche [faʀuʃ] *adj* (*timide*) shy, timid

fart [faʀt] *nm* (ski) wax

fascicule [fasikyl] *nm* volume

fascination [fasinasjɔ̃] *nf* fascination

fasciner [fasine] *vt* to fascinate

fascisme [faʃism] *nm* fascism

fasse *etc* [fas] *vb voir* **faire**

faste [fast] *nm* splendour

fastidieux, -euse [fastidjø, jøz] *adj* tedious, tiresome

fastueux, -euse [fastɥø, øz] *adj* sumptuous, luxurious

fatal, e [fatal] *adj* fatal; (*inévitable*) inevitable; **fatalité** (*destin*) fate; (*coïncidence*) fateful coincidence

fatidique [fatidik] *adj* fateful

fatigant, e [fatigɑ̃, ɑ̃t] *adj* tiring; (*agaçant*) tiresome

fatigue [fatig] *nf* tiredness, fatigue; **fatigué, e** *adj* tired; **fatiguer** *vt* to tire, make tired; (*fig*: *agacer*) to annoy ♦ *vi* (*moteur*) to labour, strain; **se fatiguer** to get tired

fatras [fatʀa] *nm* jumble, hotchpotch

faubourg [fobuʀ] *nm* suburb

fauché, e [foʃe] (*fam*) *adj* broke

faucher [foʃe] *vt* (*herbe*) to cut; (*champs, blés*) to reap; (*fig*: *véhicule*) to mow down; (*fam*: *voler*) to pinch

faucille [fosij] *nf* sickle

faucon [fokɔ̃] *nm* falcon, hawk

faudra [fodʀa] *vb voir* **falloir**

faufiler [fofile]: **se ~** *vi*: **se ~ dans** to edge one's way into; **se ~ parmi/entre** to thread one's way among/between

faune [fon] *nf* (*ZOOL*) wildlife, fauna

faussaire [fosɛʀ] *nm* forger

fausse [fos] *adj voir* **faux**; **faussement** *adv* (*accuser*) wrongly, wrongfully; (*croire*) falsely

fausser [fose] *vt* (*objet*) to bend, buckle; (*fig*) to distort; **~ compagnie à qn** to give sb the slip

faut [fo] *vb voir* **falloir**

faute [fot] *nf* (*erreur*) mistake, error; (*mauvaise action*) misdemeanour; (FOOTBALL *etc*) offence; (TENNIS) fault; **c'est de sa/ma ~** it's his/my fault; **être en ~** to be in the wrong; **~ de** (*temps, argent*) for *ou* through lack of; **sans ~** without fail; **~ de frappe** typing error; **~ de goût** error of taste; **~ professionnelle** professional misconduct *no pl*

fauteuil [fotœj] *nm* armchair; **~ roulant** wheelchair

fauteur [fotœr] *nm*: **~ de troubles** trouble-maker

fautif, -ive [fotif, iv] *adj* (*responsable*) at fault, in the wrong; (*incorrect*) incorrect, inaccurate; **il se sentait ~** he felt guilty

fauve [fov] *nm* wildcat ♦ *adj* (*couleur*) fawn

faux¹ [fo] *nf* scythe

faux², fausse [fo, fos] *adj* (*inexact*) wrong; (*voix*) out of tune; (*billet*) fake, forged; (*sournois, postiche*) false ♦ *adv* (MUS) out of tune ♦ *nm* (*copie*) fake, forgery; (*opposé au vrai*): **le ~** falsehood; **faire ~ bond à qn** to stand sb up; **fausse alerte** false alarm; **fausse couche** miscarriage; **~ frais** *nmpl* extras, incidental expenses; **~ pas** tripping *no pl*; (*fig*) faux pas; **~ témoignage** (*délit*) perjury; **faux-filet** *nm* sirloin; **faux-monnayeur** *nm* counterfeiter, forger

faveur [favœr] *nf* favour; **traitement de ~** preferential treatment; **en ~ de** in favour of

favorable [favɔrabl] *adj* favourable

favori, te [favɔri, it] *adj, nm/f* favourite

favoriser [favɔrize] *vt* to favour

fax [faks] *nm* fax; **faxer** *vt* to fax

fébrile [febril] *adj* feverish, febrile

fécond, e [fekɔ̃, ɔ̃d] *adj* fertile; **féconder** *vt* to fertilize; **fécondité** *nf* fertility

fécule [fekyl] *nf* potato flour; **féculent** *nm* starchy food

fédéral, e, -aux [federal, o] *adj* fed-eral

fédération [federasjɔ̃] *nf* federation; **la F~ française de football** the French football association

fée [fe] *nf* fairy; **féerique** *adj* magical, fairytale *cpd*

feignant, e [fɛɲɑ̃, ɑ̃t] *nm/f* = **fainéant, e**

feindre [fɛ̃dr] *vt* to feign; **~ de faire** to pretend to do

feinte [fɛ̃t] *nf* (SPORT) dummy

fêler [fele] *vt* to crack

félicitations [felisitasjɔ̃] *nfpl* congratulations

féliciter [felisite] *vt*: **~ qn (de)** to congratulate sb (on)

félin, e [felɛ̃, in] *nm* (big) cat

fêlure [felyr] *nf* crack

femelle [fəmɛl] *adj, nf* female

féminin, e [feminɛ̃, in] *adj* feminine; (*sexe*) female; (*équipe, vêtements etc*) women's ♦ *nm* (LING) feminine; **féministe** [feminist] *adj* feminist

femme [fam] *nf* woman; (*épouse*) wife; **~ au foyer** housewife; **~ de chambre** chambermaid; **~ de ménage** cleaning lady

fémur [femyr] *nm* femur, thighbone

fendre [fɑ̃dr] *vt* (*couper en deux*) to split; (*fissurer*) to crack; (*traverser: foule, air*) to cleave through; **se ~** *vi* to crack

fenêtre [f(ə)nɛtr] *nf* window

fenouil [fənuj] *nm* fennel

fente [fɑ̃t] *nf* (*fissure*) crack; (*de boîte à lettres etc*) slit

fer [fɛr] *nm* iron; **~ à cheval** horseshoe; **~ (à repasser)** iron; **~ forgé** wrought iron

ferai *etc* [fəre] *vb voir* **faire**

fer-blanc [fɛrblɑ̃] *nm* tin(plate)

férié, e [ferje] *adj*: **jour ~** public holiday

ferions *etc* [fərjɔ̃] *vb voir* **faire**

ferme [fɛrm] *adj* firm ♦ *adv* (*travailler etc*) hard ♦ *nf* (*exploitation*) farm; (*maison*) farmhouse

fermé, e [fɛrme] *adj* closed, shut; (*gaz, eau etc*) off; (*fig: milieu*) exclusive

fermenter [fɛʀmɑ̃te] vi to ferment

fermer [fɛʀme] vt to close, shut; (cesser l'exploitation de) to close down, shut down; (eau, électricité, robinet) to turn off, turn off; (aéroport, route) to close ♦ vi to close, shut; (magasin: définitivement) to close down, shut down; **se ~** vi to close, shut

fermeté [fɛʀməte] nf firmness

fermeture [fɛʀmətyʀ] nf closing; (dispositif) catch; **heures de ~** closing times; **~ éclair** ® zip (fastener) (BRIT), zipper (US)

fermier [fɛʀmje, jɛʀ] nm farmer; **fermière** nf woman farmer; (épouse) farmer's wife

fermoir [fɛʀmwaʀ] nm clasp

féroce [feʀɔs] adj ferocious, fierce

ferons [fəʀɔ̃] vb voir **faire**

ferraille [feʀaj] nf scrap iron; **mettre à la ~** to scrap

ferrer [feʀe] vt (cheval) to shoe

ferronnerie [feʀɔnʀi] nf ironwork

ferroviaire [feʀɔvjɛʀ] adj rail(way) cpd (BRIT), rail(road) cpd (US)

ferry(boat) [feʀe(bot)] nm ferry

fertile [fɛʀtil] adj fertile; **~ en incidents** eventful, packed with incidents

féru, e [feʀy] adj: **~ de** with a keen interest in

fesse [fɛs] nf buttock; **fessée** nf spanking

festin [fɛstɛ̃] nm feast

festival [fɛstival] nm festival

festivités [fɛstivite] nfpl festivities

festoyer [fɛstwaje] vi to feast

fêtard [fɛtaʀ, aʀd] (fam) nm high liver, merry-maker

fête [fɛt] nf (religieuse) feast; (publique) holiday; (réception) party; (kermesse) fête, fair; (du nom) feast day, name day; **faire la ~** to live it up; **faire ~ à qn** to give sb a warm welcome; **les ~s** (de fin d'année) the festive season; **la salle des ~s** the village hall; **~ foraine** (fun) fair; **fêter** vt to celebrate; (personne) to have a celebration for

feu, x [fø] nm (gén) fire; (signal lumi-

neux) light; (de cuisinière) ring; **~x** nmpl (AUTO) (traffic) lights; **au ~!** (incendie) fire!; **à ~ doux/vif** over a slow/brisk heat; **à petit ~** (CULIN) over a gentle heat; (fig) slowly; **faire ~** to fire; **prendre ~** to catch fire; **mettre le ~ à** to set fire to; **faire du ~** to make a fire; **avez-vous du ~?** (pour cigarette) have you (got) a light?; **~ arrière** rear light; **~ d'artifice** (spectacle) fireworks pl; **~ de joie** bonfire; **~ rouge/vert/orange** red/green/amber (BRIT) ou yellow (US) light; **~x de brouillard** fog-lamps; **~x de croisement** dipped (BRIT) ou dimmed (US) headlights; **~x de position** sidelights; **~x de route** headlights

feuillage [fœjaʒ] nm foliage, leaves pl

feuille [fœj] nf (d'arbre) leaf; (de papier) sheet; **~ de maladie** medical expenses claim form; **~ de paie** pay slip

feuillet [fœjɛ] nm leaf

feuilleté, e [fœjte] adj: **pâte ~** flaky pastry

feuilleter [fœjte] vt (livre) to leaf through

feuilleton [fœjtɔ̃] nm serial

feutre [føtʀ] nm felt; (chapeau) felt hat; (aussi: **stylo-~**) felt-tip pen; **feutré, e** adj (atmosphère) muffled

fève [fɛv] nf broad bean

février [fevʀije] nm February

FF abr (= franc français) FF

FFF sigle f = **Fédération française de football**

fiable [fjabl] adj reliable

fiançailles [fjɑ̃saj] nfpl engagement sg

fiancé, e [fjɑ̃se] nm/f fiancé(e) ♦ adj: **être ~ (à)** to be engaged (to)

fiancer [fjɑ̃se]: **se ~** vi to become engaged

fibre [fibʀ] nf fibre; **~ de verre** fibreglass, glass fibre

ficeler [fis(ə)le] vt to tie up

ficelle [fisɛl] nf string no pl; (morceau) piece ou length of string

fiche [fiʃ] nf (pour fichier) (index) card; (formulaire) form; (ÉLEC) plug

ficher 122 **fin**

ficher [fiʃe] vt (dans un fichier) to file; (POLICE) to put on file; (fam: faire) to do; (: donner) to give; (: mettre) to stick ou shove; **se ~ de** (fam: se gausser) to make fun of; **fiche-(moi) le camp** (fam) clear off; **fiche-moi la paix** (fam) leave me alone; **je m'en fiche!** (fam) I don't care!

fichier [fiʃje] nm file

fichu, e [fiʃy] pp de **ficher** (fam) ♦ adj (fam: fini, inutilisable) bust, done for; (: intensif) wretched, darned ♦ nm (foulard) (head)scarf; **mal ~** (fam) feeling lousy

fictif, -ive [fiktif, iv] adj fictitious

fiction [fiksjɔ̃] nf fiction; (fait imaginé) invention

fidèle [fidɛl] adj faithful ♦ nm/f (REL): **les ~s** à l'église the congregation sg; **fidélité** nf fidelity

fier¹ [fje]: **se ~ à** vt to trust

fier², fière [fjɛʀ] adj proud; **fierté** nf pride

fièvre [fjɛvʀ] nf fever; **avoir de la ~/39 de ~** to have a high temperature/a temperature of 39ºC; **fiévreux, -euse** adj feverish

figé, e [fiʒe] adj (manières) stiff; (société) rigid; (sourire) set

figer [fiʒe]: **se ~** vi (huile) to congeal; (personne) to freeze

fignoler [fiɲole] (fam) vt to polish up

figue [fig] nf fig; **figuier** nm fig tree

figurant, e [figyʀɑ̃, ɑ̃t] nm/f (THÉÂTRE) walk-on; (CINÉMA) extra

figure [figyʀ] nf (visage) face; (forme, personnage) figure; (illustration) picture, diagram

figuré, e [figyʀe] adj (sens) figurative

figurer [figyʀe] vi to appear ♦ vt to represent; **se ~ que** to imagine that

fil [fil] nm (brin, fig: d'une histoire) thread; (électrique) wire; (d'un couteau) edge; **au ~ des années** with the passing of the years; **au ~ de l'eau** with the stream ou current; **coup de ~** (fam) phone call; **~ à coudre** (sewing)

thread; **~ de fer** wire; **~ de fer barbelé** barbed wire

filament [filamɑ̃] nm (ÉLEC) filament

filandreux, -euse [filɑ̃dʀø, øz] adj stringy

filature [filatyʀ] nf (fabrique) mill; (policière) shadowing no pl, tailing no pl

file [fil] nf line; (AUTO) lane; **en ~ indienne** in single file; **à la ~** (d'affilée) in succession; **~ (d'attente)** queue (BRIT), line (US)

filer [file] vt (tissu, toile) to spin; (prendre en filature) to shadow, tail; (fam: donner): **~ qch à qn** to slip sb sth ♦ vi (bas: runner, liter, vite) to fly past; (fam: partir) to make ou be off; **~ doux** to toe the line

filet [filɛ] nm net; (CULIN) fillet; (d'eau, de sang) trickle; **~ (à provisions)** string bag

filiale [filjal] nf (COMM) subsidiary

filière [filjɛʀ] nf (carrière) path; **suivre la ~** (dans sa carrière) to work one's way up (through the hierarchy)

filiforme [filifɔʀm] adj spindly

filigrane [filigʀan] nm (d'un billet, timbre) watermark

fille [fij] nf girl; (opposé à fils) daughter; **vieille ~** old maid; **fillette** nf (little) girl

filleul, e [fijœl] nm/f godchild, godson/daughter

film [film] nm (pour photo) (roll of) film; (œuvre) film, picture, movie; **~ d'épouvante** horror film; **~ policier** thriller

filon [filɔ̃] nm vein, lode; (fig) lucrative line, money spinner

fils [fis] nm son; **~ à papa** daddy's boy

filtre [filtʀ] nm filter; **filtrer** vt to filter; (fig: candidats, visiteurs) to screen

fin¹ [fɛ̃] nf end; **~s** nfpl (but) ends; **prendre ~** to come to an end; **mettre ~ à** to put an end to; **à la ~** in the end, eventually; **en ~ de compte** in the end; **sans ~** endless; **~ juin** at the end of June

fin², e [fɛ̃, fin] adj (papier, couche, fil)

thin; (*cheveux, visage*) fine; (*taille*) neat, slim; (*esprit, remarque*) subtle ♦ *adv* (*couper*) finely; ~ **prêt** quite ready; **~es herbes** mixed herbs

final, e [final, o] *adj* final ♦ *nm* (MUS) finale; **finale** *nf* final; **quarts de finale** quarter finals; **finalement** *adv* finally, in the end; (*après tout*) after all

finance [finãs]: **~s** *nfpl* (*situation*) finances; (*activités*) finance *sg*; **moyennant ~** for a fee; **financer** *vt* to finance; **financier, -ière** *adj* financial

finaud, e [fino, od] *adj* wily

finesse [fines] *nf* thinness; (*raffinement*) fineness; (*subtilité*) subtlety

fini, e [fini] *adj* finished; (MATH) finite ♦ *nm* (*d'un objet manufacturé*) finish

finir [finiʀ] *vt* to finish ♦ *vi* to finish, end; ~ **par faire** to end up *ou* finish up doing; ~ **de faire** to finish doing; (*cesser*) to stop doing; **il finit par m'agacer** he's beginning to get on my nerves; **en ~ avec** to be *ou* have done with; **il va mal ~** he will come to a bad end

finition [finisjɔ̃] *nf* (*résultat*) finish

finlandais, e [fēlãdɛ, ɛz] *adj* Finnish ♦ *nm/f*: **F~, e** Finn

Finlande [fēlãd] *nf*: **la ~** Finland

fiole [fjɔl] *nf* phial

firme [fiʀm] *nf* firm

fis [fi] *vb voir* **faire**

fisc [fisk] *nm* tax authorities *pl*; **fiscal, e, -aux** *adj* tax *cpd*, fiscal; **fiscalité** *nf* tax system

fissure [fisyʀ] *nf* crack; **fissurer** *vt* to crack; **se fissurer** *vi* to crack

fiston [fistɔ̃] (*fam*) *nm* son, lad

fit [fi] *vb voir* **faire**

fixation [fiksasjɔ̃] *nf* (*attache*) fastening; (PSYCH) fixation

fixe [fiks] *adj* fixed; (*emploi*) steady, regular ♦ *nm* (*salaire*) basic salary; **à heure ~** at a set time; **menu à prix ~** set menu

fixé, e [fikse] *adj*: **être ~ (sur)** (*savoir à quoi s'en tenir*) to have made up one's

mind (about)

fixer [fikse] *vt* (*attacher*): ~ **qch (à/sur)** to fix *ou* fasten sth (to/onto); (*déterminer*) to fix, set; (*regarder*) to stare at; **se ~** *vi* (*s'établir*) to settle down; **se ~ sur** (*suj: attention*) to focus on

flacon [flakɔ̃] *nm* bottle

flageoler [flaʒɔle] *vi* (*jambes*) to sag

flageolet [flaʒɔlɛ] *nm* (CULIN) dwarf kidney bean

flagrant, e [flagʀã, ãt] *adj* flagrant, blatant; **en ~ délit** in the act

flair [flɛʀ] *nm* sense of smell; (*fig*) intuition; **flairer** *vt* (*humer*) to sniff (at); (*détecter*) to scent

flamand, e [flamã, ãd] *adj* Flemish ♦ *nm* (LING) Flemish ♦ *nm/f*: **F~, e** Fleming; **les F~s** the Flemish

flamant [flamã] *nm* flamingo

flambant [flãbã, ãt] *adv*: ~ **neuf** brand new

flambé, e [flãbe] *adj* (CULIN) flambé

flambeau, x [flãbo] *nm* (flaming) torch

flambée [flãbe] *nf* blaze; (*fig: des prix*) explosion

flamber [flãbe] *vi* to blaze (up)

flamboyer [flãbwaje] *vi* to blaze (up)

flamme [flam] *nf* flame; (*fig*) fire, fervour; **en ~s** on fire, ablaze

flan [flã] *nm* (CULIN) custard tart *ou* pie

flanc [flã] *nm* side; (*mil*) flank

flancher [flãʃe] (*fam*) *vi* to fail, pack up

flanelle [flanɛl] *nf* flannel

flâner [flane] *vi* to stroll; **flânerie** *nf* stroll

flanquer [flãke] *vt* to flank; (*fam: mettre*) to chuck, shove; (: *jeter*): ~ **par terre/à la porte** to fling to the ground/chuck out

flaque [flak] *nf* (*d'eau*) puddle; (*d'huile, de sang etc*) pool

flash [flaʃ] (*pl* **~es**) *nm* (PHOTO) flash; ~ **(d'information)** newsflash

flasque [flask] *adj* flabby

flatter [flate] *vt* to flatter; **se ~ de qch** to pride o.s. on sth; **flatterie** *nf* flattery *no pl*; **flatteur, -euse** *adj* flattering

fléau, x [fleo] *nm* scourge

flèche [flεʃ] *nf* arrow; (*de clocher*) spire; **monter en ~** (*fig*) to soar, rocket; **partir en ~** to be off like a shot; **fléchette** *nf* dart

fléchir [fleʃiʀ] *vt* (*corps, genou*) to bend; (*fig*) to sway, weaken ♦ *vi* (*fig*) to weaken, flag

flemmard, e [flemaʀ, aʀd] (*fam*) *nm/f* lazybones *sg*, loafer

flemme [flεm] *nf* (*fam*) laziness; **j'ai la ~ de le faire** I can't be bothered doing it

flétrir [fletʀiʀ]: **se ~** *vi* to wither

fleur [flœʀ] *nf* flower; (*d'un arbre*) blossom; **en ~** (*arbre*) in blossom; **à ~s** flowery

fleuri, e [flœʀi] *adj* (*jardin*) in flower *ou* bloom; (*tissu, papier*) flowery

fleurir [flœʀiʀ] *vi* (*rose*) to flower; (*arbre*) to blossom; (*fig*) to flourish ♦ *vt* (*tombe*) to put flowers on; (*chambre*) to decorate with flowers

fleuriste [flœʀist] *nm/f* florist

fleuve [flœv] *nm* river

flexible [flεksibl] *adj* flexible

flic [flik] *nm* (*fam: péj*) cop

flipper [flipœʀ] *nm* pinball (machine)

flirter [flœʀte] *vi* to flirt

flocon [flɔkɔ̃] *nm* flake

flopée [flɔpe] (*fam*) *nf*: **une ~ de** loads of, masses of

floraison [flɔʀεzɔ̃] *nf* flowering

flore [flɔʀ] *nf* flora

florissant, e [flɔʀisɑ̃, ɑ̃t] *adj* (*économie*) flourishing

flot [flo] *nm* flood, stream; **~s** *nmpl* (*de la mer*) waves; **être à ~** (*NAVIG*) to be afloat; **entrer à ~s** to stream *ou* pour in

flottant, e [flɔtɑ̃, ɑ̃t] *adj* (*vêtement*) loose

flotte [flɔt] *nf* (*NAVIG*) fleet; (*fam: eau*) water; (: *pluie*) rain

flottement [flɔtmɑ̃] *nm* (*fig*) wavering, hesitation

flotter [flɔte] *vi* to float; (*nuage, odeur*) to drift; (*drapeau*) to fly; (*vêtements*) to

hang loose; (*fam: pleuvoir*) to rain; **faire ~** to float; **flotteur** *nm* float

flou, e [flu] *adj* fuzzy, blurred; (*fig*) woolly, vague

fluctuation [flyktɥasjɔ̃] *nf* fluctuation

fluet, te [flɥε, εt] *adj* thin, slight

fluide [flɥid] *adj* fluid; (*circulation etc*) flowing freely ♦ *nm* fluid

fluor [flyɔʀ] *nm*: **dentifrice au ~** fluoride toothpaste

fluorescent, e [flyɔʀεsɑ̃, ɑ̃t] *adj* fluorescent

flûte [flyt] *nf* flute; (*verre*) flute glass; (*pain*) long loaf; **~! drat it!; ~ à bec** recorder

flux [fly] *nm* incoming tide; (*écoulement*) flow; **le ~ et le reflux** the ebb and flow

FM *sigle f* (= *fréquence modulée*) FM

foc [fɔk] *nm* jib

foi [fwa] *nf* faith; **digne de ~** reliable; **être de bonne/mauvaise ~** to be sincere/insincere; **ma ~ ...** well ...

foie [fwa] *nm* liver; **crise de ~** stomach upset

foin [fwε̃] *nm* hay; **faire du ~** (*fig: fam*) to kick up a row

foire [fwaʀ] *nf* fair; (*fête foraine*) (fun) fair; **faire la ~** (*fig: fam*) to whoop it up; (*exposition*) trade fair

fois [fwa] *nf* time; **une/deux ~** once/twice; **2 ~ 2** 2 times 2; **une ~** (*passé*) once; (*futur*) sometime; **une ~ pour toutes** once and for all; **une ~ que** once; **des ~** (*parfois*) sometimes; **à la ~** (*ensemble*) at once

foison [fwazɔ̃] *nf*: **à ~** in plenty; **foisonner** *vi* to abound

fol [fɔl] *adj voir* **fou**

folie [fɔli] *nf* (*d'une décision, d'un acte*) madness, folly; (*état*) madness, insanity; **la ~ des grandeurs** delusions of grandeur; **faire des ~s** (*en dépenses*) to be extravagant

folklorique [fɔlklɔʀik] *adj* folk *cpd*; (*fam*) weird

folle [fɔl] *adj, nf voir* **fou**; **follement**

adv (très) madly, wildly

foncé, e [fɔ̃se] *adj* dark

foncer [fɔ̃se] *vi* to go darker; *(fam: aller vite)* to° tear *ou* belt along; **~ sur** to charge at

foncier, -ère [fɔ̃sje, jɛʁ] *adj (honnêteté etc)* basic, fundamental; *(COMM)* real estate *cpd*

fonction [fɔ̃ksjɔ̃] *nf* function; *(emploi, poste)* post, position; **~s** *nfpl (professionnelles)* duties; **voiture de ~** company car; **en ~ de** *(par rapport à)* according to; **faire ~ de** to serve as; **la ~ publique** the state *ou* civil *(BRIT)* service; **fonctionnaire** *nm/f* state employee, local authority employee; *(dans l'administration)* ≃ civil servant; **fonctionner** *vi* to work, function

fond [fɔ̃] *nm (d'un récipient, trou)* bottom; *(d'une salle, scène)* back; *(d'un tableau, décor)* background; *(opposé à la forme)* content; *(SPORT)*: **le ~** long distance (running); **au ~ de** at the bottom of; at the back of; **à ~** *(connaître, soutenir)* thoroughly; *(appuyer, visser)* right down *ou* home; **à ~ (de train)** *(fam)* full tilt; **dans le ~, au ~** *(en somme)* basically, really; **de ~ en comble** from top to bottom; *voir aussi* **fonds; ~ de teint** foundation (cream)

fondamental, e, -aux [fɔ̃damɑ̃tal, o] *adj* fundamental

fondant, e [fɔ̃dɑ̃, ɑ̃t] *adj (neige)* melting; *(poire)* that melts in the mouth

fondateur, -trice [fɔ̃datœʀ, tʀis] *nm/f* founder

fondation [fɔ̃dasjɔ̃] *nf* founding; *(établissement)* foundation; **~s** *nfpl (d'une maison)* foundations

fondé, e [fɔ̃de] *adj (accusation etc)* well-founded; **être ~ à** to have grounds for *ou* good reason to

fondement [fɔ̃dmɑ̃] *nm*: **sans ~** *(rumeur etc)* groundless, unfounded

fonder [fɔ̃de] *vt* to found; *(fig)* to base; **se ~ sur** *(suj: personne)* to base o.s. on

fonderie [fɔ̃dʀi] *nf* smelting works *sg*

fondre [fɔ̃dʀ] *vt (aussi:* **faire ~)** to melt; *(dans l'eau)* to dissolve; *(fig: mélanger)* to merge, blend ♦ *vi (à la chaleur)* to melt; *(dans l'eau)* to dissolve; *(fig)* to melt away; *(se précipiter)*: **~ sur** to swoop down on; **~ en larmes** to burst into tears

fonds [fɔ̃] *nm (COMM)*: **~ (de commerce)** business ♦ *nmpl (argent)* funds

fondu, e [fɔ̃dy] *adj (beurre, neige)* melted; *(métal)* molten; **fondue** *(CULIN)* fondue

font [fɔ̃] *vb voir* **faire**

fontaine [fɔ̃tɛn] *nf* fountain; *(source)* spring

fonte [fɔ̃t] *nf* melting; *(métal)* cast iron; **la ~ des neiges** the (spring) thaw

foot [fut] *(fam) nm* football

football [futbol] *nm* football, soccer; **footballeur** *nm* footballer

footing [futiŋ] *nm* jogging; **faire du ~** to go jogging

for [fɔʀ] *nm*: **dans son ~ intérieur** in one's heart of hearts

forain, e [fɔʀɛ̃, ɛn] *adj* fairground *cpd* ♦ *nm (marchand)* stallholder; *(acteur)* fairground entertainer

forçat [fɔʀsa] *nm* convict

force [fɔʀs] *nf* strength; *(PHYSIQUE, MÉCANIQUE)* force; **~s** *nfpl (physiques)* strength *sg*; *(MIL)* forces; **à ~ d'insister** by dint of insisting; as he *(ou* I *etc)* kept on insisting; **de ~** forcibly, by force; **les ~s de l'ordre** the police

forcé, e [fɔʀse] *adj* forced; **c'est ~** *(fam)* it's inevitable; **forcément** *adv* inevitably; **pas forcément** not necessarily

forcené, e [fɔʀsəne] *nm/f* maniac

forcer [fɔʀse] *vt* to force; *(voix)* to strain ♦ *vi (SPORT)* to overtax o.s.; **~ la dose** *(fam)* to overdo it; **se ~ (à faire)** to force o.s. (to do)

forcir [fɔʀsiʀ] *vi (grossir)* to broaden out

forer [fɔʀe] *vt* to drill, bore

forestier, -ère [fɔʀɛstje, jɛʀ] *adj* forest

cpd

forêt [fɔʀɛ] *nf* forest

forfait [fɔʀfɛ] *nm* (COMM) all-in deal *ou* price; **forfaitaire** *adj* inclusive

forge [fɔʀʒ] *nf* forge, smithy; **forger** *vt* to forge; (*fig: prétexte*) to contrive, make up; **forgeron** *nm* (black)smith

formaliser [fɔʀmalize]: **se ~** *vi*: **se ~ (de)** to take offence (at)

formalité [fɔʀmalite] *nf* formality; **simple ~** mere formality

format [fɔʀma] *nm* size; **formater** *vt* (*disque*) to format

formation [fɔʀmasjɔ̃] *nf* (*développement*) forming; (*apprentissage*) training; **~ permanente** continuing education; **~ professionnelle** vocational training

forme [fɔʀm] *nf* (*gén*) form; (*d'un objet*) shape, form; **~s** *nfpl* (*bonnes manières*) proprieties; (*d'une femme*) figure *sg*; **être en ~** (SPORT *etc*) to be on form; **en bonne et due ~** in due form

formel, le [fɔʀmɛl] *adj* (*catégorique*) definite, positive; **formellement** *adv* (*absolument*) positively; **formellement interdit** strictly forbidden

former [fɔʀme] *vt* to form; (*éduquer*) to train; **se ~** *vi* to form

formidable [fɔʀmidabl] *adj* tremendous

formulaire [fɔʀmylɛʀ] *nm* form

formule [fɔʀmyl] *nf* (*gén*) formula; (*expression*) phrase; **~ de politesse** polite phrase; (*en fin de lettre*) letter ending; **formuler** *vt* (*émettre*) to formulate

fort, e [fɔʀ, fɔʀt] *adj* strong; (*intensité, rendement*) high, great; (*corpulent*) stout; (*doué*) good, able ♦ *adv* (*serrer, frapper*) hard; (*parler*) loud(ly); (*beaucoup*) greatly, very much; (*très*) very ♦ *nm* (*édifice*) fort; (*point ~*) strong point, forte; **~e tête** rebel; **forteresse** *nf* stronghold

fortifiant [fɔʀtifjɑ̃, ɑ̃t] *nm* tonic

fortifier [fɔʀtifje] *vt* to strengthen

fortiori [fɔʀsjɔʀi]: **à ~** *adv* all the more so

fortuit, e [fɔʀtɥi, it] *adj* fortuitous, chance *cpd*

fortune [fɔʀtyn] *nf* fortune; **faire ~** to make one's fortune; **de ~** makeshift; **fortuné, e** *adj* wealthy

fosse [fos] *nf* (*grand trou*) pit; (*tombe*) grave

fossé [fose] *nm* ditch; (*fig*) gulf, gap

fossette [fosɛt] *nf* dimple

fossile [fosil] *nm* fossil

fossoyeur [foswajœʀ] *nm* gravedigger

fou(fol), folle [fu, fɔl] *adj* mad; (*déréglé etc*) wild, erratic; (*fam: extrême, très grand*) terrific, tremendous ♦ *nm/f* madman(-woman) ♦ *nm* (*du roi*) jester; **être ~de** to be mad *ou* crazy about; **avoir le ~rire** to have the giggles

foudre [fudʀ] *nf*: **la ~** lightning

foudroyant, e [fudʀwajɑ̃, ɑ̃t] *adj* (*progrès*) lightning; (*succès*) stunning; (*maladie, poison*) violent

foudroyer [fudʀwaje] *vt* to strike down; **être foudroyé** to be struck by lightning; **~ qn du regard** to glare at sb

fouet [fwɛ] *nm* whip; (CULIN) whisk; **de plein ~** (*se heurter*) head on; **fouetter** *vt* to whip; (*crème*) to whisk

fougère [fuʒɛʀ] *nf* fern

fougue [fug] *nf* ardour, spirit; **fougueux, -euse** *adj* fiery

fouille [fuj] *nf* search; **~s** *nfpl* (*archéologiques*) excavations; **fouiller** *vt* to search; (*creuser*) to dig ♦ *vi* to rummage; **fouillis** *nm* jumble, muddle

fouiner [fwine] (*péj*) *vi*: **~ dans** to nose around *ou* about in

foulard [fulaʀ] *nm* scarf

foule [ful] *nf* crowd; **la ~** crowds *pl*; **une ~ de** masses of

foulée [fule] *nf* stride

fouler [fule] *vt* to press; (*sol*) to tread upon; **se ~ la cheville** to sprain one's ankle; **ne pas se ~** not to overexert o.s.; **il ne se foule pas** he doesn't put himself out; **foulure** *nf* sprain

four [fuʀ] *nm* oven; (*de potier*) kiln;

(THÉÂTRE: échec) flop

fourbe [furb] adj deceitful

fourbu, e [furby] adj exhausted

fourche [furʃ] nf pitchfork

fourchette [furʃɛt] nf fork; (STATISTIQUE) bracket, margin

fourgon [furgɔ̃] nm van; (RAIL) wag(g)on; **fourgonnette** nf (small) van

fourmi [furmi] nf ant; **~s** nfpl (fig) pins and needles; **fourmilière** nf ant-hill; **fourmiller** vi to swarm

fournaise [furnɛz] nf blaze; (fig) furnace, oven

fourneau, x [furno] nm stove

fournée [furne] nf batch

fourni, e [furni] adj (barbe, cheveux) thick; (magasin): **bien ~ (en)** well stocked (with)

fournir [furnir] vt to supply; (preuve, exemple) to provide, supply; (effort) to put in; **fournisseur, -euse** nm/f supplier; (INTERNET): **fournisseur d'accès à Internet** (Internet) service provider, ISP; **fourniture** nf supply(ing); **fournitures scolaires** school stationery

fourrage [furaʒ] nm fodder

fourré, e [fure] adj (bonbon etc) filled; (manteau etc) fur-lined ♦ nm thicket

fourrer [fure] (fam) vt to stick, shove; **se ~ dans/sous** to get into/under; **fourre-tout** nm inv (sac) holdall; (fig) rag-bag

fourrière [furjɛr] nf pound

fourrure [furyr] nf fur; (sur l'animal) coat

fourvoyer [furvwaje]: **se ~** vi to go astray, stray

foutre [futr] (fam!) vt = **ficher**; **foutu, e** (fam!) adj = **fichu, e**

foyer [fwaje] nm (maison) home; (famille) family; (de cheminée) hearth; (de jeunes etc) (social) club; (résidence) hostel; (salon) foyer; **lunettes à double ~** bi-focal glasses

fracas [fraka] nm (d'objet qui tombe) crash; **fracassant, e** adj (succès) thun-

dering; **fracasser** vt to smash

fraction [fraksjɔ̃] nf fraction; **fractionner** vt to divide (up), split (up)

fracture [fraktyr] nf fracture; **~ du crâne** fractured skull; **fracturer** vt (coffre, serrure) to break open; (os, membre) to fracture

fragile [fraʒil] adj fragile, delicate; (fig) frail; **fragilité** nf fragility

fragment [fragmɑ̃] nm (d'un objet) fragment, piece

fraîche [frɛʃ] adj voir **frais**; **fraîcheur** nf coolness; (d'un aliment) freshness; **fraîchir** vi to get cooler; (vent) to freshen

frais, fraîche [frɛ, frɛʃ] adj fresh; (froid) cool ♦ adv (récemment) newly, fresh(ly) ♦ nm: **mettre au ~** to put in a cool place ♦ nmpl (gén) expenses; (COMM) costs; **il fait ~** it's cool; **servir ~** serve chilled; **prendre le ~** to take a breath of cool air; **faire des ~** to go to a lot of expense; **~ de scolarité** school fees (BRIT), tuition (US); **~ généraux** overheads

fraise [frɛz] nf strawberry; **~ des bois** wild strawberry

framboise [frɑ̃bwaz] nf raspberry

franc, franche [frɑ̃, frɑ̃ʃ] adj (personne) frank, straightforward; (visage) open; (net: refus) clear; (: coupure) clean; (intensif) downright ♦ nm franc

français, e [frɑ̃sɛ, ɛz] adj French ♦ nm/f: **F~, e** Frenchman(-woman) ♦ nm (LING) French; **les F~** the French

France [frɑ̃s] nf: **la ~** France

franche [frɑ̃ʃ] adj voir **franc**; **franchement** adv frankly; (nettement) definitely; (tout à fait: mauvais etc) downright

franchir [frɑ̃ʃir] vt (obstacle) to clear, get over; (seuil, ligne, rivière) to cross; (distance) to cover

franchise [frɑ̃ʃiz] nf frankness; (douanière) exemption; (ASSURANCES) excess

franc-maçon [frɑ̃masɔ̃] nm freemason

franco [frɑ̃ko] adv (COMM): **~ (de port)**

postage paid

francophone [fʀɑ̃kɔfɔn] adj French-speaking

franc-parler [fʀɑ̃paʀle] nm inv outspokenness; **avoir son ~~** to speak one's mind

frange [fʀɑ̃ʒ] nf fringe

frangipane [fʀɑ̃ʒipan] nf almond paste

franquette [fʀɑ̃kɛt]: **à la bonne ~** adv without any fuss

frappant, e [fʀapɑ̃, ɑ̃t] adj striking

frappé, e [fʀape] adj iced

frapper [fʀape] vt to hit, strike; (étonner) to strike; **~ dans ses mains** to clap one's hands; **frappé de stupeur** dumbfounded

frasques [fʀask] nfpl escapades

fraternel, le [fʀatɛʀnɛl] adj brotherly, fraternal; **fraternité** nf brotherhood

fraude [fʀod] nf fraud; (SCOL) cheating; **passer qch en ~** to smuggle sth in (ou out); **~ fiscale** tax evasion; **frauder** vi, vt to cheat; **frauduleux, -euse** adj fraudulent

frayer [fʀeje] vt to open up, clear ♦ vi to spawn; **se ~ un chemin dans la foule** to force one's way through the crowd

frayeur [fʀejœʀ] nf fright

fredonner [fʀədɔne] vt to hum

freezer [fʀizœʀ] nm freezing compartment

frein [fʀɛ̃] nm brake; **mettre un ~ à** (fig) to curb, check; **~ à main** handbrake; **freiner** vi to brake ♦ vt (progrès etc) to check

frêle [fʀɛl] adj frail, fragile

frelon [fʀəlɔ̃] nm hornet

frémir [fʀemiʀ] vi (de peur, d'horreur) to shudder; (de colère) to shake; (feuillage) to quiver

frêne [fʀɛn] nm ash

frénétique [fʀenetik] adj frenzied, frenetic

fréquemment [fʀekamɑ̃] adv frequently

fréquent, e [fʀekɑ̃, ɑ̃t] adj frequent

fréquentation [fʀekɑ̃tasjɔ̃] nf frequenting; **~s** nfpl (relations) company sg

fréquenté, e [fʀekɑ̃te] adj: **très ~** (very) busy; **mal ~** patronized by disreputable elements

fréquenter [fʀekɑ̃te] vt (lieu) to frequent; (personne) to see; **se ~** to see each other

frère [fʀɛʀ] nm brother

fresque [fʀɛsk] nf (ART) fresco

fret [fʀɛ(t)] nm freight

frétiller [fʀetije] vi (poisson) to wriggle

fretin [fʀətɛ̃] nm: **menu ~** small fry

friable [fʀijabl] adj crumbly

friand, e [fʀijɑ̃, fʀijɑ̃d] adj: **~ de** very fond of ♦ nm: **~ au fromage** cheese puff

friandise [fʀijɑ̃diz] nf sweet

fric [fʀik] (fam) nm cash, bread

friche [fʀiʃ]: **en ~** adj, adv (lying) fallow

friction [fʀiksjɔ̃] nf (massage) rub, rub-down; (TECH, fig) friction; **frictionner** vt to rub (down)

frigidaire ® [fʀiʒidɛʀ] nm refrigerator

frigide [fʀiʒid] adj frigid

frigo [fʀigo] (fam) nm fridge

frigorifié, e [fʀigɔʀifje] (fam) adj: **être ~** to be frozen stiff

frigorifique [fʀigɔʀifik] adj refrigerating

frileux, -euse [fʀilø, øz] adj sensitive to (the) cold

frime [fʀim] (fam) nf: **c'est de la ~** it's a lot of eyewash; it's all put on; **frimer** (fam) vi to show off

frimousse [fʀimus] nf (sweet) little face

fringale [fʀɛ̃gal] (fam) nf: **avoir la ~** to be ravenous

fringant, e [fʀɛ̃gɑ̃, ɑ̃t] adj dashing

fringues [fʀɛ̃g] (fam) nfpl clothes

fripé, e [fʀipe] adj crumpled

fripon, ne [fʀipɔ̃, ɔn] adj roguish, mischievous ♦ nm/f rascal, rogue

fripouille [fʀipuj] nf scoundrel

frire [fʀiʀ] vt, vi: **faire ~** to fry

frisé, e [fʀize] adj (cheveux) curly; (personne) curly-haired

frisson [fʀisɔ̃] nm (de froid) shiver; (de peur) shudder; **frissonner** vi (de fièvre, froid) to shiver; (d'horreur) to shudder

frit, e [fʀi, fʀit] pp de **frire**; **frite** nf: **(pommes) frites** chips (BRIT), French fries; **friteuse** nf chip pan; **friture** nf (huile) (deep) fat; (plat): **friture (de poissons)** fried fish

frivole [fʀivɔl] adj frivolous

froid, e [fʀwa, fʀwad] adj, nm cold; **il fait ~** it's cold; **avoir/prendre ~** to be/catch cold; **être en ~ avec** to be on bad terms with; **froidement** adv (accueillir) coldly; (décider) coolly

froideur [fʀwadœʀ] nf coldness

froisser [fʀwase] vt to crumple (up), crease; (fig) to hurt, offend; **se ~** vi to crumple, crease; (personne) to take offence; **se ~ un muscle** to strain a muscle

frôler [fʀole] vt to brush against; (suj: projectile) to skim past; (fig) to come very close to

fromage [fʀɔmaʒ] nm cheese; **~ blanc** soft white cheese

froment [fʀɔmɑ̃] nm wheat

froncer [fʀɔ̃se] vt to gather; **~ les sourcils** to frown

frondaisons [fʀɔ̃dɛzɔ̃] nfpl foliage sg

front [fʀɔ̃] nm forehead, brow; (MIL) front; **de ~** (se heurter) head-on; (rouler) together (i.e. 2 or 3 abreast); (simultanément) at once; **faire ~ à** to face up to

frontalier, -ère [fʀɔ̃talje, jɛʀ] adj border cpd, frontier cpd

frontière [fʀɔ̃tjɛʀ] nf frontier, border

frotter [fʀɔte] vi to rub, scrape ♦ vt to rub; (pommes de terre, plancher) to scrub; **~ une allumette** to strike a match

fructifier [fʀyktifje] vi to yield a profit

fructueux, -euse [fʀyktɥø, øz] adj fruitful

frugal, e, -aux [fʀygal, o] adj frugal

fruit [fʀɥi] nm fruit gen no pl; **~ de la passion** passion fruit; **~s de mer** seafood(s); **~s secs** dried fruit sg; **fruité, e** adj fruity; **fruitier, -ère** adj: **arbre fruitier** fruit tree

fruste [fʀyst] adj unpolished, uncultivated

frustrer [fʀystʀe] vt to frustrate

FS abr (= franc suisse) SF

fuel(-oil) [fjul(ɔjl)] nm fuel oil; (domestique) heating oil

fugace [fygas] adj fleeting

fugitif, -ive [fyʒitif, iv] adj (lueur) fleeting ♦ nm/f fugitive

fugue [fyg] nf: **faire une ~** to run away, abscond

fuir [fɥiʀ] vt to flee from; (éviter) to shun ♦ vi to run away; (gaz, robinet) to leak

fuite [fɥit] nf flight; (écoulement, divulgation) leak; **être en ~** to be on the run; **mettre en ~** to put to flight

fulgurant, e [fylgyʀɑ̃, ɑ̃t] adj lightning cpd, dazzling

fulminer [fylmine] vi to thunder forth

fumé, e [fyme] adj (CULIN) smoked; (verre) tinted; **fumée** nf smoke

fumer [fyme] vi to smoke; (soupe) to steam ♦ vt to smoke

fûmes etc [fym] vb voir **être**

fumet [fymɛ] nm aroma

fumeur, -euse [fymœʀ, øz] nm/f smoker

fumeux, -euse [fymø, øz] (péj) adj woolly, hazy

fumier [fymje] nm manure

fumiste [fymist] nm/f (péj: paresseux) shirker

funèbre [fynɛbʀ] adj funeral cpd; (fig: atmosphère) gloomy

funérailles [fyneʀaj] nfpl funeral sg

funeste [fynɛst] adj (erreur) disastrous

fur [fyʀ]: **au ~ et à mesure** adv as one goes along; **au ~ et à mesure que** as

furet [fyʀɛ] nm ferret

fureter [fyʀ(ə)te] (péj) vi to nose about

fureur [fyʀœʀ] nf fury; **être en ~** to

be infuriated; **faire ~** to be all the rage

furibond, e [fyʀibɔ̃, ɔ̃d] *adj* furious

furie [fyʀi] *nf* fury; *(femme)* shrew, vixen; **en ~** *(mer)* raging; **furieux, -euse** *adj* furious

furoncle [fyʀɔ̃kl] *nm* boil

furtif, -ive [fyʀtif, iv] *adj* furtive

fus [fy] *vb voir* **être**

fusain [fyzɛ̃] *nm* (ART) charcoal

fuseau, x [fyzo] *nm* (*pour filer*) spindle; (*pantalon*) (ski) pants; **~ horaire** time zone

fusée [fyze] *nf* rocket; **~ éclairante** flare

fuser [fyze] *vi* (*rires etc*) to burst forth

fusible [fyzibl] *nm* (ÉLEC: *fil*) fuse wire; (: *fiche*) fuse

fusil [fyzi] *nm* (*de guerre, à canon rayé*) rifle, gun; (*de chasse, à canon lisse*) shotgun, gun; **fusillade** *nf* gunfire *no pl*, shooting *no pl*; **fusiller** *vt* to shoot; **fusil-mitrailleur** *nm* machine gun

fusionner [fyzjɔne] *vi* to merge

fut [fy] *vb voir* **être**

fût [fy] *vb voir* **être ♦** *nm* (*tonneau*) barrel, cask

futé, e [fyte] *adj* crafty; **Bison ~** ® *TV and radio traffic monitoring service*

futile [fytil] *adj* futile; frivolous

futur, e [fytyʀ] *adj, nm* future

fuyant, e [fɥijã, ãt] *vb voir* **fuir ♦** *adj* (*regard etc*) evasive; (*lignes etc*) receding

fuyard, e [fɥijaʀ, aʀd] *nm/f* runaway

G, g

gâcher [ɡaʃe] *vt* (*gâter*) to spoil; (*gaspiller*) to waste; **gâchis** *nm* waste *no pl*

gadoue [ɡadu] *nf* sludge

gaffe [ɡaf] *nf* blunder; **faire ~** (*fam*) to be careful

gage [ɡaʒ] *nm* (*dans un jeu*) forfeit; (*fig: de fidélité, d'amour*) token

gageure [ɡaʒyʀ] *nf*: **c'est une ~** it's attempting the impossible

gagnant, e [ɡaɲã, ãt] *nm/f* winner

gagne-pain [ɡaɲpɛ̃] *nm inv* job

gagner [ɡaɲe] *vt* to win; (*somme d'argent, revenu*) to earn; (*aller vers, atteindre*) to reach; (*envahir: sommeil, peur*) to overcome; (: *mal*) to spread to **♦** *vi* to win; (*fig*) to gain; **~ du temps/de la place** to gain time/save space; **~ sa vie** to earn one's living

gai, e [ɡe] *adj* cheerful; (*un peu ivre*) merry; **gaiement** *adv* cheerfully; **gaieté** *nf* cheerfulness; **de gaieté de cœur** with a light heart

gaillard, e [ɡajaʀ, aʀd] *nm* (*strapping*) fellow

gain [ɡɛ̃] *nm* (*revenu*) earnings *pl*; (*bénéfice: gén pl*) profits *pl*

gaine [ɡɛn] *nf* (*corset*) girdle; (*fourreau*) sheath

gala [ɡala] *nm* official reception; **de ~** (*soirée etc*) gala

galant, e [ɡalã, ãt] *adj* (*courtois*) courteous, gentlemanly; (*entreprenant*) flirtatious, gallant; (*scène, rendez-vous*) romantic

galère [ɡalɛʀ] *nf* galley; **quelle ~!** (*fam*) it's a real grind!; **galérer** (*fam*) *vi* to slog away, work hard; (*rencontrer les difficultés*) to have a hassle

galerie [ɡalʀi] *nf* gallery; (THÉÂTRE) circle; (*de voiture*) roof rack; (*fig: spectateurs*) audience; **~ de peinture** (*private*) art gallery; **~ marchande** shopping arcade

galet [ɡalɛ] *nm* pebble

galette [ɡalɛt] *nf* flat cake; **~ des Rois** *cake eaten on Twelfth Night*

galipette [ɡalipɛt] *nf* somersault

Galles [ɡal] *nfpl*: **le pays de ~** Wales; **gallois, e** *adj* Welsh **♦** *nm* (LING) Welsh **♦** *nm/f*: **Gallois, e** Welshman(-woman)

galon [ɡalɔ̃] *nm* (MIL) stripe; (*décoratif*) piece of braid

galop [ɡalo] *nm* gallop; **galoper** *vi* to gallop

galopin [ɡalɔpɛ̃] *nm* urchin, ragamuffin

gambader [ɡãbade] *vi* (*animal, enfant*)

to leap about

gambas [gãbas] *nfpl* Mediterranean prawns

gamin, e [gamɛ̃, in] *nm/f* kid ♦ *adj* childish

gamme [gam] *nf* (MUS) scale; (*fig*) range

gammé, e [game] *adj*: **croix ~e** swastika

gang [gãg] *nm* (*de criminels*) gang

gant [gã] *nm* glove; **~ de toilette** face flannel (*BRIT*), face cloth

garage [garaʒ] *nm* garage; **garagiste** *nm/f* garage owner; (*employé*) garage mechanic

garantie [garãti] *nf* guarantee; (**bon de**) **~** guarantee *ou* warranty slip

garantir [garãtir] *vt* to guarantee

garce [gars] (*fam*) *nf* bitch

garçon [garsɔ̃] *nm* boy; (*célibataire*): **vieux ~** bachelor; (*serveur*): **~ (de café)** waiter; **~ de courses** messenger; **~ d'honneur** best man; **garçonnière** *nf* bachelor flat

garde [gard(ə)] *nm* (*de prisonnier*) guard; (*de domaine etc*) warden; (*soldat, sentinelle*) guardsman ♦ *nf* (*soldats*) guard; **de ~** on duty; **monter la ~** to stand guard; **mettre en ~** to warn; **prendre ~ (à)** to be careful (of); **~ champêtre** ♦ *nm* rural policeman; **~ du corps** ♦ *nm* bodyguard; **~ des enfants** ♦ *nm* (*après divorce*) custody of the children; **~ à vue** ♦ *nf* (*JUR*) ≈ police custody; **garde-à-vous** *nm*: **être/se mettre au garde-à-vous** to be at/ stand to attention; **garde-barrière** *nm/f* level-crossing keeper; **garde-boue** *nm inv* mudguard; **garde-chasse** *nm* gamekeeper; **garde-malade** *nf* home nurse; **garde-manger** *nm inv* (*armoire*) meat safe; (*pièce*) pantry, larder

garder [garde] *vt* (*conserver*) to keep; (*surveiller: enfants*) to look after; (: *immeuble, lieu, prisonnier*) to guard; **se ~** *vi* (*aliment: se conserver*) to keep; **se ~**

de faire to be careful not to do; **~ le lit/la chambre** to stay in bed/indoors; **pêche/chasse gardée** private fishing/ hunting (ground)

garderie [gardəri] *nf* day nursery, crèche

garde-robe [gardərɔb] *nf* wardrobe

gardien, ne [gardjɛ̃, jɛn] *nm/f* (*garde*) guard; (*de prison*) warder; (*de domaine, réserve*) warden; (*de musée etc*) attendant; (*de phare, cimetière*) keeper; (*d'immeuble*) caretaker; (*fig*) guardian; **~ de but** goalkeeper; **~ de la paix** policeman; **~ de nuit** night watchman

gare [gar] *nf* station; **~ routière** bus station

garer [gare] *vt* to park; **se ~** *vi* to park

gargariser [gargarize]: **se ~** *vi* to gargle

gargote [gargɔt] *nf* cheap restaurant

gargouille [garguj] *nf* gargoyle

gargouiller [garguje] *vi* to gurgle

garnement [garnəmã] *nm* rascal, scallywag

garni, e [garni] *adj* (*plat*) served with vegetables (*and chips or rice etc*)

garnison [garnizɔ̃] *nf* garrison

garniture [garnityr] *nf* (*CULIN*) vegetables *pl*; **~ de frein** brake lining

gars [ga] (*fam*) *nm* guy

Gascogne [gaskɔɲ] *nf* Gascony; **le golfe de ~** the Bay of Biscay

gas-oil [gazɔjl] *nm* diesel (oil)

gaspiller [gaspije] *vt* to waste

gastronome [gastrɔnɔm] *nm/f* gourmet; **gastronomie** *nf* gastronomy; **gastronomique** *adj* gastronomic

gâteau, x [gato] *nm* cake; **~ sec** biscuit

gâter [gate] *vt* to spoil; **se ~** *vi* (*dent, fruit*) to go bad; (*temps, situation*) to change for the worse

gâterie [gatri] *nf* little treat

gâteux, -euse [gatø, øz] *adj* senile

gauche [goʃ] *adj* left, left-hand; (*maladroit*) awkward, clumsy ♦ *nf* (*POL*) left; (*BOXE*) left (wing); **le bras ~** the left arm; **le côté ~** the left-hand side; **à ~** on the left;

(direction) (to the) left; **gaucher, -ère** adj left-handed; **gauchiste** nm/f leftist

gaufre [gofʀ] nf waffle

gaufrette [gofʀɛt] nf wafer

gaulois, e [golwa, waz] adj Gallic ♦ nm/f: **G~, e** Gaul

gaver [gave] vt to force-feed; **se ~ de** to stuff o.s. with

gaz [gaz] nm inv gas

gaze [gaz] nf gauze

gazer [gaze] (fam) vi: **ça gaze?** how's things?

gazette [gazɛt] nf news sheet

gazeux, -euse [gazø, øz] adj (boisson) fizzy; (eau) sparkling

gazoduc [gazodyk] nm gas pipeline

gazon [gazɔ̃] nm (herbe) grass; (pelouse) lawn

gazouiller [gazuje] vi to chirp; (enfant) to babble

geai [ʒɛ] nm jay

géant, e [ʒeɑ̃, ɑ̃t] adj gigantic; (COMM) giant-size ♦ nm/f giant

geindre [ʒɛ̃dʀ] vi to groan, moan

gel [ʒɛl] nm frost; **~ douche** shower gel

gélatine [ʒelatin] nf gelatine

gelée [ʒ(ə)le] nf jelly; (gel) frost

geler [ʒ(ə)le] vt, vi to freeze; **il gèle** it's freezing

gélule [ʒelyl] nf (MÉD) capsule

gelures [ʒəlyʀ] nfpl frostbite sg

Gémeaux [ʒemo] nmpl: **les ~** Gemini

gémir [ʒemiʀ] vi to groan, moan

gênant, e [ʒɛnɑ̃, ɑ̃t] adj (irritant) annoying; (embarrassant) embarrassing

gencive [ʒɑ̃siv] nf gum

gendarme [ʒɑ̃daʀm] nm gendarme; **gendarmerie** nf military police force in countryside and small towns; their police station or barracks

gendre [ʒɑ̃dʀ] nm son-in-law

gêné, e [ʒene] adj embarrassed

gêner [ʒene] vt (incommoder) to bother; (encombrer) to be in the way; (embarrasser): **~ qn** to make sb feel ill-at-ease

général, e, -aux [ʒeneʀal, o] adj, nm general; **en ~** usually, in general; **gé-**

nérale nf: (répétition) **générale** final dress rehearsal; **généralement** adv generally; **généraliser** vt, vi to generalize; **se généraliser** vi to become widespread; **généraliste** nm/f general practitioner, G.P.

génération [ʒeneʀasjɔ̃] nf generation

généreux, -euse [ʒeneʀø, øz] adj generous

générique [ʒeneʀik] nm (CINÉMA) credits pl

générosité [ʒeneʀozite] nf generosity

genêt [ʒ(ə)nɛ] nm broom no pl (shrub)

génétique [ʒenetik] adj genetic; **génétiquement** adv: **~ment modifié** genetically modified, GM

Genève [ʒ(ə)nɛv] n Geneva

génial, e, -aux [ʒenjal, jo] adj of genius; (fam: formidable) fantastic, brilliant

génie [ʒeni] nm genius; (MIL): **le ~** the Engineers pl; **~ civil** civil engineering

genièvre [ʒənjɛvʀ] nm juniper

génisse [ʒenis] nf heifer

génital, e, -aux [ʒenital, o] adj genital; **les parties ~es** the genitals

génoise [ʒenwaz] nf sponge cake

genou, x [ʒ(ə)nu] nm knee; **à ~x** on one's knees; **se mettre à ~x** to kneel down

genre [ʒɑ̃ʀ] nm kind, type, sort; (LING) gender; **avoir bon ~** to look a nice sort; **avoir mauvais ~** to be coarselooking; **ce n'est pas son ~** it's not like him

gens [ʒɑ̃] nmpl (f in some phrases) people pl

gentil, le [ʒɑ̃ti, ij] adj kind; (enfant: sage) good; (endroit etc) nice; **gentillesse** nf kindness; **gentiment** adv kindly

géographie [ʒeɔgʀafi] nf geography

geôlier, jer [ʒolje, jɛʀ] nm jailer

géologie [ʒeɔlɔʒi] nf geology

géomètre [ʒeɔmɛtʀ] nm/f (arpenteur) (land) surveyor

géométrie [ʒeɔmetʀi] nf geometry; **géométrique** adj geometric

gérant, e [ʒeʀɑ̃, ɑ̃t] nm/f manager(-

eress)

gerbe [ʒɛrb] *nf* (*de fleurs*) spray; (*de blé*) sheaf

gercé, e [ʒɛrse] *adj* chapped

gerçure [ʒɛrsyr] *nf* crack

gérer [ʒere] *vt* to manage

germain, e [ʒɛrmɛ̃, ɛn] *adj*: **cousin ~** first cousin

germe [ʒɛrm] *nm* germ; **germer** *vi* to sprout; (*semence*) to germinate

geste [ʒɛst] *nm* gesture

gestion [ʒɛstjɔ̃] *nf* management

ghetto [geto] *nm* ghetto

gibet [ʒibɛ] *nm* gallows *pl*

gibier [ʒibje] *nm* (*animaux*) game

giboulée [ʒibule] *nf* sudden shower

gicler [ʒikle] *vi* to spurt, squirt

gifle [ʒifl] *nf* slap (in the face); **gifler** *vt* to slap (in the face)

gigantesque [ʒigɑ̃tɛsk] *adj* gigantic

gigogne [ʒigɔɲ] *adj*: **lits ~s** truckle (*BRIT*) *ou* trundle beds

gigot [ʒigo] *nm* leg (of mutton *ou* lamb)

gigoter [ʒigɔte] *vi* to wriggle (about)

gilet [ʒilɛ] *nm* waistcoat; (*pull*) cardigan; **~ de sauvetage** life jacket

gin [dʒin] *nm* gin; **~-tonic** gin and tonic

gingembre [ʒɛ̃ʒɑ̃br] *nm* ginger

girafe [ʒiraf] *nf* giraffe

giratoire [ʒiratwar] *adj*: **sens ~** roundabout

girofle [ʒirɔfl] *nf*: **clou de ~** clove

girouette [ʒirwɛt] *nf* weather vane *ou* cock

gitan, e [ʒitɑ̃, an] *nm/f* gipsy

gîte [ʒit] *nm* (*maison*) home; (*abri*) shelter; **~ (rural)** holiday cottage *ou* apartment

givre [ʒivr] *nm* (hoar) frost; **givré, e** *adj* covered in frost; (*fam*: fou) nuts; **orange givrée** brange sorbet (*served in peel*)

glace [glas] *nf* ice; (*crème glacée*) ice cream; (*miroir*) mirror; (*de voiture*) window

glacé, e [glase] *adj* (*mains, vent, pluie*) freezing; (*lac*) frozen; (*boisson*) iced

glacer [glase] *vt* to freeze; (*gâteau*) to ice; (*fig*): **~ qn** (*intimider*) to chill sb; (*paralyser*) to make sb's blood run cold

glacial, e [glasjal, jo] *adj* icy

glacier [glasje] *nm* (*GÉO*) glacier; (*marchand*) ice-cream maker

glacière [glasjɛr] *nf* icebox

glaçon [glasɔ̃] *nm* icicle; (*pour boisson*) ice cube

glaïeul [glajœl] *nm* gladiolus

glaise [glɛz] *nf* clay

gland [glɑ̃] *nm* acorn; (*décoration*) tassel

glande [glɑ̃d] *nf* gland

glander [glɑ̃de] (*fam*) *vi* to fart around (!)

glauque [glok] *adj* dull blue-green

glissade [glisad] *nf* (*par jeu*) slide; (*chute*) slip; **faire des ~s sur la glace** to slide on the ice

glissant, e [glisɑ̃, ɑ̃t] *adj* slippery

glissement [glismɑ̃] *nm*: **~ de terrain** landslide

glisser [glise] *vi* (*avancer*) to glide on, slide along; (*coulisser, tomber*) to slide; (*déraper*) to slip; (*être glissant*) to be slippery ♦ *vt* to slip; **se ~ dans** to slip into

global, e, -aux [glɔbal, o] *adj* overall

globe [glɔb] *nm* globe

globule [glɔbyl] *nm* (*du sang*) corpuscle

globuleux, -euse [glɔbylø, øz] *adj*: **yeux ~** protruding eyes

gloire [glwar] *nf* glory; **glorieux, -euse** *adj* glorious

glousser [gluse] *vi* to cluck; (*rire*) to chuckle; **gloussement** *nm* cluck; chuckle

glouton, ne [glutɔ̃, ɔn] *adj* gluttonous

gluant, e [glyɑ̃, ɑ̃t] *adj* sticky, gummy

glucose [glykɔz] *nm* glucose

glycine [glisin] *nf* wisteria

goal [gol] *nm* goalkeeper

GO *sigle* (= *grandes ondes*) LW

gobelet [gɔblɛ] *nm* (*en étain, verre, ar-*

gent) tumbler; (d'enfant, de pique-nique) beaker; (à dés) cup

gober [gɔbe] vt to swallow (whole)

godasse [gɔdas] (fam) nf shoe

godet [gɔde] nm pot

goéland [gɔelɑ̃] nm (sea)gull

goélette [gɔelɛt] nf schooner

gogo [gɔgo]: à ~ adv galore

goguenard, e [gɔg(ə)naʀ, aʀd] adj mocking

goinfre [gwɛ̃fʀ] nm glutton

golf [gɔlf] nm golf; (terrain) golf course

golfe [gɔlf] nm gulf; (petit) bay

gomme [gɔm] nf (à effacer) rubber (BRIT), eraser; **gommer** vt to rub out (BRIT), erase

gond [gɔ̃] nm hinge; **sortir de ses ~s** (fig) to fly off the handle

gondoler [gɔ̃dɔle]: **se** ~ vi (planche) to warp; (métal) to buckle

gonflé, e [gɔ̃fle] adj swollen; **il est** ~ (fam: courageux) he's got some nerve; (impertinent) he's got a nerve

gonfler [gɔ̃fle] vt (pneu, ballon: en soufflant) to blow up; (: avec une pompe) to pump up; (nombre, importance) to inflate ♦ vi to swell (up); (CULIN: pâte) to rise; **gonfleur** nm pump

gonzesse [gɔ̃zes] (fam) nf chick, bird (BRIT)

goret [gɔʀe] nm piglet

gorge [gɔʀʒ] nf (ANAT) throat; (vallée) gorge

gorgé, e [gɔʀʒe] adj: ~ **de** filled with; (eau) saturated with; **gorgée** nf (petite) sip; (grande) gulp

gorille [gɔʀij] nm gorilla; (fam) bodyguard

gosier [gozje] nm throat

gosse [gɔs] (fam) nm/f kid

goudron [gudʀɔ̃] nm tar; **goudronner** vt to tar(mac) (BRIT), asphalt (US)

gouffre [gufʀ] nm abyss, gulf

goujat [guʒa] nm boor

goulot [gulo] nm neck; **boire au** ~ to drink from the bottle

goulu, e [guly] adj greedy

gourd, e [guʀ, guʀd] adj numb (with cold)

gourde [guʀd] nf (récipient) flask; (fam) (clumsy) clot ou oaf ♦ adj oafish

gourdin [guʀdɛ̃] nm club, bludgeon

gourer [guʀe] (fam): **se** ~ vi to boob

gourmand, e [guʀmɑ̃, ɑ̃d] adj greedy; **gourmandise** [guʀmɑ̃diz] nf greed; (bonbon) sweet

gourmet [guʀme] nm gourmet

gourmette [guʀmet] nf chain bracelet

gousse [gus] nf: ~ **d'ail** clove of garlic

goût [gu] nm taste; **avoir bon** ~ to taste good; **de bon** ~ tasteful; **de mauvais** ~ tasteless; **prendre** ~ **à** to develop a taste ou a liking for

goûter [gute] vt (essayer) to taste; (apprécier) to enjoy ♦ vi to have (afternoon) tea ♦ nm (afternoon) tea

goutte [gut] nf drop; (MÉD) gout; (alcool) brandy; **tomber** ~ **à** ~ to drip; **goutte-à-goutte** nm (MÉD) drip

gouttelette [gut(ə)let] nf droplet

gouttière [gutjeʀ] nf gutter

gouvernail [guvɛʀnaj] nm rudder; (barre) helm, tiller

gouvernante [guvɛʀnɑ̃t] nf governess

gouvernement [guvɛʀnəmɑ̃] nm government

gouverner [guvɛʀne] vt to govern

grabuge [gʀabyʒ] (fam) nm mayhem

grâce [gʀɑs] nf (charme) grace; (faveur) favour; (JUR) pardon; (REL) grace sg; **faire** ~ **à qn de qch** to spare sb sth; **rendre** ~(**s**) **à** to give thanks to; **demander** ~ to beg for mercy; ~ **à** thanks to; **gracier** vt to pardon; **gracieux, -euse** adj graceful

grade [gʀad] nm rank; **monter en** ~ to be promoted

gradin [gʀadɛ̃] nm tier; step; ~**s** nmpl (de stade) terracing sg

gradué, e [gʀadɥe] adj: **verre** ~ measuring jug

graduel, le [gʀadɥel] adj gradual

graduer [gʀadɥe] vt (effort etc) to increase gradually; (règle, verre) to graduate

graffiti [grafiti] nmpl graffiti

grain [grɛ̃] nm (gén) grain; (NAVIG) squall; ~ **de beauté** beauty spot; ~ **de café** coffee bean; ~ **de poivre** peppercorn; ~ **de poussière** speck of dust; ~ **de raisin** grape

graine [grɛn] nf seed

graissage [gresaʒ] nm lubrication, greasing

graisse [grɛs] nf fat; (lubrifiant) grease; **graisser** vt to lubricate, grease; (tacher) to make greasy; **graisseux, -euse** adj greasy

grammaire [gra(m)mɛr] nf grammar; **grammatical, e, -aux** adj grammatical

gramme [gram] nm gramme

grand, e [grɑ̃, grɑ̃d] adj (haut) tall; (gros, vaste, large) big, large; (long) long; (plus âgé) big; (adulte) grown-up; (sens abstrait) great ♦ adv: ~ **ouvert** wide open; **au ~ air** in the open (air); **les ~s blessés** the severely injured; ~ **ensemble** housing scheme; ~ **magasin** department store; ~ **personne** grown-up; ~**e surface** hypermarket; ~**es écoles** prestige schools of university level; ~**es lignes** (RAIL) main lines; ~ **vacances** summer holidays; **grand-chose** [grɑ̃ʃoz] nm/f inv: **pas grand-chose** not much; **Grande-Bretagne** nf (Great) Britain; **grandeur** nf (dimension) size; **grandeur nature** life-size; **grandiose** adj imposing; **grandir** vi to grow ♦ vt: **grandir qn** (suj: vêtement, chaussure) to make sb look taller; **grand-mère** nf grandmother; **grandmesse** nf high mass; **grand-peine**: **à grand-peine** adv with difficulty; **grand-père** nm grandfather; **grandroute** nf main road; **grands-parents** nmpl grandparents

grange [grɑ̃ʒ] nf barn

granit(e) [granit] nm granite

graphique [grafik] adj graphic ♦ nm graph

grappe [grap] nf cluster; ~ **de raisin** bunch of grapes

gras, se [gra, gras] adj (viande, soupe) fatty; (personne) fat; (surface, main) greasy; (plaisanterie) coarse; (TYPO) bold ♦ nm (CULIN) fat; **faire la ~se matinée** to have a lie-in (BRIT), sleep late (US); **grassement** adv: **grassement payé** handsomely paid; **grassouillet, te** adj podgy, plump

gratifiant, e [gratifjɑ̃, ɑ̃t] adj gratifying, rewarding

gratin [gratɛ̃] nm (plat) cheese-topped dish; (croûte) cheese topping; **gratiné, e** adj (CULIN) au gratin

gratis [gratis] adv free

gratitude [gratityd] nf gratitude

gratte-ciel [gratsjɛl] nm inv skyscraper

gratte-papier [gratpapje] (péj) nm inv penpusher

gratter [grate] vt (avec un outil) to scrape; (enlever: avec un outil) to scrape off; (: avec un ongle) to scratch; (enlever avec un ongle) to scratch off ♦ vi (irriter) to be scratchy; (démanger) to itch; **se ~** to scratch (o.s.)

gratuit, e [gratɥi, ɥit] adj (entrée, billet) free; (fig) gratuitous

gravats [grava] nmpl rubble sg

grave [grav] adj (maladie, accident) serious, bad; (sujet, problème) serious, grave; (air) grave, solemn; (voix, son) deep, low-pitched; **gravement** adv seriously; (parler, regarder) gravely

graver [grave] vt to engrave

gravier [gravje] nm gravel no pl; **gravillons** nmpl loose chippings ou gravel sg

gravir [gravir] vt to climb (up)

gravité [gravite] nf (de maladie, d'accident) seriousness; (de sujet, problème) gravity

graviter [gravite] vi to revolve

gravure [gravyr] nf engraving; (reproduction) print

gré [gre] nm: **de bon ~** willingly; **contre le ~ de qn** against sb's will; **de**

son (plein) ~ of one's own free will; **bon ~ mal ~** like it or not; **de ~ ou de force** whether one likes it or not; **savoir ~ à qn de qch** to be grateful to sb for sth

grec, grecque [gʁɛk] *adj* Greek; (*classique: vase etc*) Grecian ♦ *nm/f:* **G~, Grecque** Greek ♦ *nm* (LING) Greek

Grèce [gʁɛs] *nf:* **la ~** Greece

greffe [gʁɛf] *nf* (BOT, MÉD: *de tissu*) graft; (MÉD: *d'organe*) transplant; **greffer** *vt* (BOT, MÉD: *tissu*) to graft; (MÉD: *organe*) to transplant

greffier [gʁefje, jɛʁ] *nm* clerk of the court

grêle [gʁɛl] *adj* (very) thin ♦ *nf* hail; **grêler** *vb impers:* **il grêle** it's hailing; **grêlon** [gʁɛlɔ̃] *nm* hailstone

grelot [gʁəlo] *nm* little bell

grelotter [gʁələte] *vi* to shiver

grenade [gʁənad] *nf* (*explosive*) grenade; (BOT) pomegranate; **grenadine** *nf* grenadine

grenat [gʁəna] *adj inv* dark red

grenier [gʁənje] *nm* attic; (*de ferme*) loft

grenouille [gʁənuj] *nf* frog

grès [gʁɛ] *nm* sandstone; (*poterie*) stoneware

grésiller [gʁezije] *vi* to sizzle; (RADIO) to crackle

grève [gʁɛv] *nf* (*d'ouvriers*) strike; (*plage*) shore; **se mettre en/faire ~** to go on/be on strike; **~ de la faim** hunger strike; **~ du zèle** work-to-rule (BRIT), slowdown (US); **~ sauvage** wildcat strike

gréviste [gʁevist] *nm/f* striker

gribouiller [gʁibuje] *vt* to scribble, scrawl

grièvement [gʁijɛvmã] *adv* seriously

griffe [gʁif] *nf* claw; (*de couturier*) label; **griffer** *vt* to scratch

griffonner [gʁifɔne] *vt* to scribble

grignoter [gʁiɲɔte] *vt* (*personne*) to nibble at; (*souris*) to gnaw at ♦ *vi* to nibble

gril [gʁil] *nm* steak *ou* grill pan; **faire cuire au ~** to grill; **grillade** *nf* (*viande etc*) grill

grillage [gʁijaʒ] *nm* (*treillis*) wire netting; (*clôture*) wire fencing

grille [gʁij] *nf* (*clôture*) wire fence; (*portail*) (metal) gate; (*d'égout*) (metal) grate; (*fig*) grid

grille-pain [gʁijpɛ̃] *nm inv* toaster

griller [gʁije] *vt* (*pain*) to toast; (*viande*) to grill; (*fig: ampoule etc*) to blow; **faire ~** to toast; to grill; (*châtaignes*) to roast; **~ un feu rouge** to jump the lights

grillon [gʁijɔ̃] *nm* cricket

grimace [gʁimas] *nf* grimace; (*pour faire rire*) funny face; **faire des ~s** to pull *ou* make faces

grimper [gʁɛ̃pe] *vi, vt* to climb

grincer [gʁɛ̃se] *vi* (*objet métallique*) to grate; (*plancher, porte*) to creak; **~ des dents** to grind one's teeth

grincheux, -euse [gʁɛ̃ʃø, øz] *adj* grumpy

grippe [gʁip] *nf* flu, influenza; **grippé, e** *adj:* **être grippé** to have flu

gris, e [gʁi, gʁiz] *adj* grey; (*ivre*) tipsy

grisaille [gʁizaj] *nf* greyness, dullness

griser [gʁize] *vt* to intoxicate

grisonner [gʁizɔne] *vi* to be going grey

grisou [gʁizu] *nm* firedamp

grive [gʁiv] *nf* thrush

grivois, e [gʁivwa, waz] *adj* saucy

Groenland [gʁɔɛnlãd] *nm* Greenland

grogner [gʁɔɲe] *vi* to growl; (*fig*) to grumble; **grognon, ne** *adj* grumpy

groin [gʁwɛ̃] *nm* snout

grommeler [gʁɔm(ə)le] *vt* to mutter to o.s.

gronder [gʁɔ̃de] *vi* to rumble; (*fig: révolte*) to be brewing ♦ *vt* to scold; **se faire ~** to get a telling-off

groom [gʁum] *nm* bellboy

gros, se [gʁo, gʁos] *adj* big, large; (*obèse*) fat; (*travaux, dégâts*) extensive; (*épais*) thick; (*rhume, averse*) heavy

♦ *adv*: **risquer/gagner ~** to risk/win a lot ♦ *nm/f* fat man/woman ♦ *nm* (COMM): **le ~** the wholesale business; **prix de ~** wholesale price; **par ~ temps/grosse mer** in rough weather/ heavy seas; **en ~** roughly; (COMM) wholesale; **~ lot** jackpot; **~ mot** coarse word; **~ plan** (PHOTO) close-up; **~ sel** cooking salt; **~ titre** headline; **~se caisse** big drum

groseille [gʀozɛj] *nf*: **~ (rouge/ blanche)** red/white currant; **~ à maquereau** gooseberry

grosse [gʀos] *adj voir* **gros**; **grossesse** *nf* pregnancy; **grosseur** *nf* size; (*tumeur*) lump

grossier, -ière [gʀosje, jɛʀ] *adj* coarse; (*insolent*) rude; (*dessin*) rough; (*travail*) roughly done; (*imitation, instrument*) crude; (*évident: erreur*) gross; **grossièrement** *adv* (*sommairement*) roughly; (*vulgairement*) coarsely; **grossièretés** *nfpl*: **dire des grossièretés** to use coarse language

grossir [gʀosiʀ] *vi* (*personne*) to put on weight ♦ *vt* (*exagérer*) to exaggerate; (*au microscope*) to magnify; (*suj: vêtement*): **~ qn** to make sb look fatter

grossiste [gʀosist] *nm/f* wholesaler

grosso modo [gʀosomodo] *adv* roughly

grotesque [gʀotɛsk] *adj* (*extravagant*) grotesque; (*ridicule*) ludicrous

grotte [gʀot] *nf* cave

grouiller [gʀuje] *vi*: **~ de** to be swarming with; **se ~** (*fam*) ♦ *vi* to get a move on; **grouillant, e** *adj* swarming

groupe [gʀup] *nm* group; **le ~ des 8** Group of 8; **~ de parole** support group; **~ sanguin** blood group; **groupement** *nm* (*action*) grouping; (*groupe*) group; **grouper** *vt* to group; **se grouper** *vi* to gather

grue [gʀy] *nf* crane

grumeaux [gʀymo] *nmpl* lumps

grumeleux, -euse *adj voir* **grumeaux**

guenilles [gənij] *nfpl* rags

guenon [gənɔ̃] *nf* female monkey

guépard [gepaʀ] *nm* cheetah

guêpe [gɛp] *nf* wasp

guêpier [gepje] *nm* (*fig*) trap

guère [gɛʀ] *adv* (*avec adjectif, adverbe*): **ne ... ~** hardly; (*avec verbe*): **ne ... ~** (*pas beaucoup*) tournure négative +*much*; (*pas souvent*) hardly ever; (*pas longtemps*) tournure négative +(*very*) *long*; **il n'y a ~ que/de** there's hardly anybody (*ou* anything) but/hardly any; **ce n'est ~ difficile** it's hardly difficult; **nous n'avons ~ de temps** we have hardly any time

guéridon [geʀidɔ̃] *nm* pedestal table

guérilla [geʀija] *nf* guerrilla warfare

guérillero [geʀijeʀo] *nm* guerrilla

guérir [geʀiʀ] *vt* (*personne, maladie*) to cure; (*membre, plaie*) to heal ♦ *vi* (*malade, maladie*) to be cured; (*blessure*) to heal; **guérison** *nf* (*de maladie*) curing; (*de membre, plaie*) healing; (*de malade*) recovery; **guérisseur, -euse** *nm/f* healer

guerre [gɛʀ] *nf* war; **~ civile** civil war; **en ~** at war; **faire la ~ à** to wage war against; **guerrier, -ière** *adj* warlike ♦ *nm/f* warrior

guet [gɛ] *nm*: **faire le ~** to be on the look-out; **guet-apens** [gɛtapɑ̃] *nm* ambush; **guetter** *vt* (*épier*) to watch (intently); (*attendre*) to watch (*out*) for; (*hostilement*) to be lying in wait for

gueule [gœl] *nf* (*d'animal*) mouth; (*fam: figure*) face; (: *bouche*) mouth; **ta ~!** (*fam*) shut up!; **~ de bois** (*fam*) hangover; **gueuler** (*fam*) *vi* to bawl; **gueuleton** (*fam*) *nm* blow-out

gui [gi] *nm* mistletoe

guichet [giʃɛ] *nm* (*de bureau, banque*) counter; **les ~s** (*à la gare, au théâtre*) the ticket office *sg*; **~ automatique** cash dispenser (BRIT), automatic telling machine (US)

guide [gid] *nm* guide ♦ *nf* (*éclaireuse*) girl guide; **guider** *vt* to guide

guidon [gidɔ̃] *nm* handlebars *pl*

guignol [giɲɔl] *nm* ≈ Punch and Judy

show; (fig) clown

guillemets [gijmɛ] nmpl: **entre ~** in inverted commas

guillotiner [gijɔtine] vt to guillotine

guindé, e [gɛ̃de] adj (personne, air) stiff, starchy; (style) stilted

guirlande [giʀlɑ̃d] nf (fleurs) garland; **~ de Noël** tinsel garland; **~ lumineuse** string of fairy lights; **~ de papier** paper chain

guise [giz] nf: **à votre ~** as you wish ou please; **en ~ de** by way of

guitare [gitaʀ] nf guitar

gym [ʒim] nf (exercices) gym; **gymnase** nm gym(nasium); **gymnaste** nmf gymnast; **gymnastique** nf gymnastics sg; (au réveil etc) keep-fit exercises pl

gynécologie [ʒinekɔlɔʒi] nf gynaecology; **gynécologique** adj gynaecological; **gynécologue** nmf gynaecologist

H, h

habile [abil] adj skilful; (malin) clever; **habileté** [abilte] nf skill, skilfulness; cleverness

habillé, e [abije] adj dressed; (chic) dressy

habillement [abijmɑ̃] nm clothes pl

habiller [abije] vt to dress; (fournir en vêtements) to clothe; **s'~** vi to dress (o.s.); (se déguiser, mettre des vêtements chic) to dress up

habit [abi] nm outfit; **~s** nmpl (vêtements) clothes; **(de soirée)** evening dress; (pour homme) tails pl

habitant, e [abitɑ̃, ɑ̃t] nm/f inhabitant; (d'une maison) occupant; **loger chez l'~** to stay with the locals

habitation [abitasjɔ̃] nf house; **~s à loyer modéré** (block of) council flats

habiter [abite] vt to live in ♦ vi: **~ à/ dans** to live in

habitude [abityd] nf habit; **avoir l'~ de faire** to be in the habit of doing; (expérience) to be used to doing; **d'~**

usually; **comme d'~** as usual

habitué, e [abitye] nm/f (de maison) regular visitor; (de café) regular (customer)

habituel, le [abityɛl] adj usual

habituer [abitye] vt: **~ qn à** to get sb used to; **s'~ à** to get used to

'hache [ʹaʃ] nf axe

'hacher [ʹaʃe] vt (viande) to mince; (persil) to chop; **'hachis** nm mince no pl; **hachis Parmentier** ≈ shepherd's pie

'hachisch [ʹaʃiʃ] nm hashish

'hachoir [ʹaʃwaʀ] nm (couteau) chopper; (appareil) (meat) mincer; (planche) chopping board

hagard, e [ʹagaʀ, aʀd] adj wild, distraught

'haie [ʹɛ] nf hedge; (SPORT) hurdle

'haillons [ʹajɔ̃] nmpl rags

'haine [ʹɛn] nf hatred

'haïr [ʹaiʀ] vt to detest, hate

'hâlé, e [ʹale] adj (sun)tanned, sunburnt

haleine [alɛn] nf breath; **hors d'~** out of breath; **tenir en ~** (attention) to hold spellbound; (incertitude) to keep in suspense; **de longue ~** long-term

'haleter [ʹalte] vt to pant

'hall [ʹol] nm hall

'halle [ʹal] nf (covered) market; **~s** nfpl (d'une grande ville) central food market sg

hallucinant, e [alysinɑ̃, ɑ̃t] adj staggering

hallucination [alysinasjɔ̃] nf hallucination

'halte [ʹalt] nf stop, break; (endroit) stopping place ♦ excl stop!; **faire ~** to stop

haltère [altɛʀ] nm dumbbell, barbell; **~s** nmpl: **(poids et) ~s** (activité) weightlifting sg; **haltérophilie** nf weightlifting

'hamac [ʹamak] nm hammock

'hamburger [ʹɑ̃buʀgœʀ] nm hamburger

'hameau, x [ʹamo] nm hamlet

hameçon [amsɔ̃] nm (fish) hook

'hanche [ʹɑ̃ʃ] nf hip

'hand-ball ['ādbal] *nm* handball
handicapé, e ['ādikape] *nm/f* physically (*ou* mentally) handicapped person; **~ moteur** spastic
hangar ['āgar] *nm* shed; (AVIAT) hangar
hanneton ['ant5] *nm* cockchafer
hanter ['āte] *vt* to haunt
hantise ['ātiz] *nf* obsessive fear
happer ['ape] *vt* to snatch; (*suj: train etc*) to hit
haras ['arɑ] *nm* stud farm
harassant, e ['arasā, āt] *adj* exhausting
harcèlement ['arsɛlmā] *nm* harassment; **~ sexuel** sexual harassment
harceler ['arsəle] *vt* to harass; **~ qn de questions** to plague sb with questions
hardi, e ['ardi] *adj* bold, daring
hareng ['arā] *nm* herring
hargne ['arɲ] *nf* aggressiveness; **hargneux, -euse** *adj* aggressive
haricot ['ariko] *nm* bean; **~ blanc** haricot bean; **~ vert** green bean; **~ rouge** kidney bean
harmonica [armɔnika] *nm* mouth organ
harmonie [armɔni] *nf* harmony; **harmonieux, -euse** *adj* harmonious, (*couleurs, couple*) well-matched
harnacher ['arnaʃe] *vt* to harness
harnais ['arnɛ] *nm* harness
harpe ['arp] *nf* harp
harponner ['arpɔne] *vt* to harpoon; (*fam*) to collar
hasard ['azar] *nm*: **le ~** chance, fate; **un ~** a coincidence; **au ~** (*aller*) aimlessly; (*choisir*) at random; **par ~** by chance; **à tout ~** (*en cas de besoin*) just in case; (*en espérant trouver ce qu'on cherche*) on the off chance; **'hasarder** *vt* (*mot*) to venture; **se hasarder à faire** to risk doing
'hâte ['ɑt] *nf* haste; **à la ~** hurriedly, hastily; **en ~** posthaste, with all possible speed; **avoir ~ de** to be eager *ou* anxious to; **'hâter** *vt* to hasten; **se hâter** *vi* to hurry; **'hâtif, -ive** *adj* (*tra-*

**vail*) hurried; (*décision, jugement*) hasty
'hausse ['os] *nf* rise, increase; **être en ~** to be going up; **'hausser** *vt* to raise; **hausser les épaules** to shrug (one's shoulders)
'haut, e ['o, 'ot] *adj* high; (*grand*) tall ♦ *adv* high ♦ *nm* top (part); **de 3 m de ~** 3 m high, 3 m in height; **des ~s et des bas** ups and downs; **en ~ lieu** in high places; **à ~e voix, (tout) ~** aloud, out loud; **du ~ de** from the top of; **de ~ en bas** from top to bottom; **plus ~** higher up, further up; (*dans un texte*) above; (*parler*) louder; **en ~** (*être/aller*) at/to the top; (*dans une maison*) upstairs; **en ~ de** at the top of
'hautain, e ['otɛ̃, ɛn] *adj* haughty
hautbois ['obwa] *nm* oboe
haut-de-forme ['odfɔrm] *nm* top hat
hauteur ['otœr] *nf* height; **à la ~ de** (*accident*) near; (*fig: tâche, situation*) equal to; **à la ~** (*fig*) up to it
'haut...: 'haut-fourneau *nm* blast *ou* smelting furnace; **'haut-le-cœur** *nm inv* retch, heave; **'haut-parleur** *nm* (loud)speaker
'havre ['avr] *nm* haven
'Haye ['ɛ] *n*: **la ~** the Hague
'hayon ['ɛjɔ̃] *nm* hatchback
hebdo [ɛbdo] (*fam*) *nm* weekly
hebdomadaire [ɛbdɔmadɛr] *adj, nm* weekly
hébergement [ebɛrʒəmɑ̃] *nm* accommodation
héberger [ebɛrʒe] *vt* (*touristes*) to accommodate, lodge; (*amis*) to put up; (*réfugiés*) to take in
hébété, e [ebete] *adj* dazed
hébreu, x [ebrø] *adj m, nm* Hebrew
hécatombe [ekatɔ̃b] *nf* slaughter
hectare [ɛktar] *nm* hectare
hein ['ɛ̃] *excl* eh?
hélas ['elɑs] *excl* alas! ♦ *adv* unfortunately
héler ['ele] *vt* to hail
hélice [elis] *nf* propeller
hélicoptère [elikɔptɛr] *nm/m* helicopter

helvétique [ɛlvetik] *adj* Swiss

hématome [ematom] *nm* nasty bruise

hémicycle [emisikl] *nm* (POL): **l'~** ≃ the benches (of the Commons) (BRIT), ≃ the floor (of the House of Representatives) (US)

hémisphère [emisfɛr] *nm*: **l'~ nord/ sud** the northern/southern hemisphere

hémorragie [emɔraʒi] *nf* bleeding *no pl*, haemorrhage

hémorroïdes [emɔrɔid] *nfpl* piles, haemorrhoids

'hennir ['enir] *vi* to neigh, whinny; **'hennissement** *nm* neigh, whinny

hépatite [epatit] *nf* hepatitis

herbe [ɛrb] *nf* grass; (CULIN, MÉD) herb; **~s de Provence** mixed herbs; **en ~** unripe; (*fig*) budding; **herbicide** *nm* weed-killer; **herboriste** *nm/f* herbalist

'hère ['ɛr] *nm*: **pauvre ~** poor wretch

héréditaire [erediter] *adj* hereditary

'hérisser ['erise] *vt*: **~ qn** (*fig*) to ruffle sb; **se ~** *vi* to bristle, bristle up; **'hérisson** *nm* hedgehog

héritage [eritaʒ] *nm* inheritance; (*coutumes, système*) heritage, legacy

hériter [erite] *vi*: **~ de qch (de qn)** to inherit sth (from sb); **héritier, -ière** [eritje, jɛr] *nm/f* heir(-ess)

hermétique [ɛrmetik] *adj* airtight; watertight; (*fig: obscur*) abstruse; (*: impénétrable*) impenetrable

hermine [ɛrmin] *nf* ermine

'hernie ['ɛrni] *nf* hernia

héroïne [erɔin] *nf* heroine; (*drogue*) heroin

héroïque [erɔik] *adj* heroic

'héron ['erɔ̃] *nm* heron

'héros ['ero] *nm* hero

hésitant, e [ezitɑ̃, ɑ̃t] *adj* hesitant

hésitation [ezitasjɔ̃] *nf* hesitation

hésiter [ezite] *vi*: **~ (à faire)** to hesitate (to do)

hétéroclite [eterɔklit] *adj* heterogeneous; (*objets*) sundry

hétérogène [eterɔʒɛn] *adj* heterogeneous

hétérosexuel, le [eterɔsɛkɥel] *adj* heterosexual

'hêtre ['ɛtr] *nm* beech

heure [œr] *nf* hour; (SCOL) period; (*moment*) time; **c'est l'~** it's time; **quelle ~ est-il?** what time is it?; **2 ~s (du matin)** 2 o'clock (in the morning); **être à l'~** to be on time; (*montre*) to be right; **mettre à l'~** to set right; **à une ~ avancée (de la nuit)** at a late hour of the night; **à toute ~** at any time; **24 ~s sur 24** round the clock, 24 hours a day; **à l'~ qu'il est** at this time (of day); by now; **sur l'~** at once; **~ de pointe** rush hour; (*téléphone*) peak period; **~ d'affluence** rush hour; **~s creuses** slack periods; (*pour électricité, téléphone etc*) off-peak periods; **~s supplémentaires** overtime *sg*

heureusement [œrøzmɑ̃] *adv* (*par bonheur*) fortunately, luckily

heureux, -euse [œrø, øz] *adj* happy; (*chanceux*) lucky, fortunate

heurter ['œrte] *vt* (*mur*) to strike, hit; (*personne*) to collide with; **se ~ à** *vt* (*fig*) to come up against

heurts ['œr] *nmpl* (*fig*) clashes

hexagone [ɛgzagɔn] *nm* hexagon; (*la France*) France (*because of its shape*)

hiberner [ibɛrne] *vi* to hibernate

'hibou, x ['ibu] *nm* owl

'hideux, -euse ['idø, øz] *adj* hideous

hier [jɛr] *adv* yesterday; **~ soir** last night, yesterday evening; **toute la journée d'~** all day yesterday; **toute la matinée d'~** all yesterday morning

'hiérarchie ['jerarʃi] *nf* hierarchy

'hi-fi ['ifi] *adj inv* hi-fi ♦ *nf* hi-fi

hilare [ilar] *adj* mirthful

hindou, e [ɛ̃du] *adj* Hindu ♦ *nm/f*: **H~, e** Hindu

hippique [ipik] *adj* equestrian, horse *cpd*; **un club ~** a riding centre; **un concours ~** a horse show; **hippisme** *nm* (horse)riding

hippodrome [ipɔdrom] *nm* racecourse

hippopotame [ipɔpɔtam] *nm* hippopotamus

hirondelle [iʀɔ̃dɛl] *nf* swallow

hirsute [iʀsyt] *adj (personne)* shaggy-haired; *(barbe)* shaggy; *(tête)* tousled

'hisser ['ise] *vt* to hoist, haul up; **se ~** *vi* to heave o.s. up

histoire [istwaʀ] *nf (science, événements)* history; *(anecdote, récit, mensonge)* story; *(affaire)* business *no pl*; **~s** *nfpl (chichis)* fuss *no pl*; *(ennuis)* trouble *sg*; **historique** *adj* historical; *(important)* historic

'hit-parade ['itpaʀad] *nm*: **le ~~** the charts

hiver [iveʀ] *nm* winter; **hivernal, e, -aux** *adj* winter *cpd*; *(glacial)* wintry; **hiverner** *vi* to winter

HLM *nm ou f (= habitation à loyer modéré)* council flat; **des HLM** council housing

'hobby ['ɔbi] *nm* hobby

'hocher ['ɔʃe] *vt*: **la tête** to nod; *(signe négatif ou dubitatif)* to shake one's head

'hochet ['ɔʃe] *nm* rattle

'hockey ['ɔke] *nm*: **~ (sur glace/gazon)** (ice/field) hockey

'hold-up ['ɔldœp] *nm inv* hold-up

hollandais, e ['ɔlɑ̃dɛ, ɛz] *adj* Dutch ♦ *nm (LING)* Dutch ♦ *nm/f*: **H~, e** Dutchman(-woman); **les H~** the Dutch

'Hollande ['ɔlɑ̃d] *nf*: **la ~** Holland

'homard ['ɔmaʀ] *nm* lobster

homéopathique [ɔmeɔpatik] *adj* homœopathic

homicide [ɔmisid] *nm* murder; **~ involontaire** manslaughter

hommage [ɔmaʒ] *nm* tribute; **~s** *nmpl*: **présenter ses ~s** to pay one's respects; **rendre ~ à** to pay tribute *ou* homage to

homme [ɔm] *nm* man; **~ d'affaires** businessman; **~ d'État** statesman; **~ de main** hired man; **~ de paille** stooge; **~ politique** politician; **homme-grenouille** *nm* frogman

homo...: homogène *adj* homogeneous; **homologue** *nm/f* counterpart; **homologué, e** *adj (SPORT)* ratified; *(tarif)* authorized; **homonyme** *nm (LING)* homonym; *(d'une personne)* namesake; **homosexuel, le** *adj* homosexual

'Hongrie ['ɔ̃gʀi] *nf*: **la ~** Hungary; **'hongrois, e** *adj* Hungarian ♦ *nm/f*: **Hongrois, e** Hungarian ♦ *nm (LING)* Hungarian

honnête [ɔnɛt] *adj (intègre)* honest; *(juste, satisfaisant)* fair; **honnêtement** *adv* honestly; **honnêteté** *nf* honesty

honneur [ɔnœʀ] *nm* honour; *(mérite)* credit; **en l'~ de** in honour of; *(événement)* on the occasion of; **faire ~ à** *(engagements)* to honour; *(famille)* to be a credit to; *(fig: repas etc)* to do justice to

honorable [ɔnɔʀabl] *adj* worthy, honourable; *(suffisant)* decent

honoraire [ɔnɔʀɛʀ] *adj* honorary; **professeur ~** professor emeritus; **honoraires** [ɔnɔʀɛʀ] *nmpl* fees *pl*

honorer [ɔnɔʀe] *vt* to honour; *(estimer)* to hold in high regard; *(faire honneur à)* to do credit to; **honorifique** [ɔnɔʀifik] *adj* honorary

'honte ['ɔ̃t] *nf* shame; **avoir ~ de** to be ashamed of; **faire ~ à qn** to make sb (feel) ashamed; **'honteux, -euse** *adj* ashamed; *(conduite, acte)* shameful, disgraceful

hôpital, -aux [ɔpital, o] *nm* hospital

'hoquet ['ɔke] *nm*: **avoir le ~** to have (the) hiccoughs; **'hoqueter** *vi* to hiccough

horaire [ɔʀɛʀ] *adj* hourly ♦ *nm* timetable, schedule; **~s** *nmpl (d'employé)* hours; **~ souple** flexitime

horizon [ɔʀizɔ̃] *nm* horizon

horizontal, e, -aux [ɔʀizɔ̃tal, o] *adj* horizontal

horloge [ɔʀlɔʒ] *nf* clock; **l'~ parlante** the speaking clock; **horloger, -ère**

'hormis *nm/f* watchmaker; clockmaker

'hormis ['ɔrmi] *prép* save

horoscope [ɔrɔskɔp] *nm* horoscope

horreur [ʀɔɛʀ] *nf* horror; **quelle ~!** how awful!; **avoir ~ de** to loathe ou detest; **horrible** *adj* horrible; **horrifier** *vt* to horrify

horripiler [ɔʀipile] *vt* to exasperate

hors ['ɔʀ] *prép* : **~ de** out of; **~ pair** outstanding; **~ de propos** inopportune; **être ~ de soi** to be beside o.s.; **~ d'usage** out of service; **'hors-bord** *nm inv* speedboat (with outboard motor); **'hors-d'œuvre** *nm inv* hors d'œuvre; **'hors-jeu** *nm inv* offside; **'hors-la-loi** *nm inv* outlaw; **'hors-taxe** *adj* (boutique, articles) duty-free

hortensia [ɔʀtɑ̃sja] *nm* hydrangea

hospice [ɔspis] *nm* (de vieillards) home

hospitalier, -ière [ɔspitalje, jɛʀ] *adj* (accueillant) hospitable; (MÉD: service, centre) hospital *cpd*

hospitaliser [ɔspitalize] *vt* to take/send to hospital, hospitalize

hospitalité [ɔspitalite] *nf* hospitality

hostie [ɔsti] *nf* host (REL)

hostile [ɔstil] *adj* hostile; **hostilité** *nf* hostility

hosto [ɔsto] (fam) *nm* hospital

hôte [ot] *nm* (maître de maison) host; (invité) guest

hôtel [otɛl] *nm* hotel; **aller à l'~** to stay in hotels; **~ de ville** town hall; **~ (particulier)** (private) mansion; **hôtelier, -ière** *adj* hotel *cpd* ♦ *nm/f* hotelier; **hôtellerie** *nf* hotel business

hôtesse [otɛs] *nf* hostess; **~ de l'air** air stewardess; **~ (d'accueil)** receptionist

'hotte ['ɔt] *nf* (panier) basket (carried on the back); **~ aspirante** cooker hood

houblon ['ublɔ̃] *nm* (BOT) hop; (pour la bière) hops *pl*

'houille ['uj] *nf* coal; **~ blanche** hydroelectric power

'houle ['ul] *nf* swell; **'houleux, -euse** *adj* stormy

'houligan ['uligɑ̃] *nm* hooligan

'hourra ['uʀa] *excl* hurrah!

'houspiller ['uspije] *vt* to scold

'housse ['us] *nf* cover

'houx ['u] *nm* holly

hublot ['yblo] *nm* porthole

'huche ['yʃ] *nf* : **~ à pain** bread bin

'huer ['ɥe] *vt* to boo

huile [ɥil] *nf* oil; **~ solaire** suntan oil; **huiler** *vt* to oil; **huileux, -euse** *adj* oily

huis [ɥi] *nm* : **à ~ clos** in camera

huissier [ɥisje] *nm* usher; (JUR) ≈ bailiff

'huit ['ɥi(t)] *num* eight; **samedi en ~ a** week on Saturday; **dans ~ jours** in a week; **'huitaine** *nf* : **une huitaine (de jours)** a week or so; **'huitième** *num* eighth

huître [ɥitʀ] *nf* oyster

humain, e [ymɛ̃, ɛn] *adj* human; (compatissant) humane ♦ *nm* human (being); **humanitaire** *adj* humanitarian; **humanité** *nf* humanity

humble [œ̃bl] *adj* humble

humecter [ymɛkte] *vt* to dampen

humer ['yme] *vt* (plat) to smell; (parfum) to inhale

humeur [ymœʀ] *nf* mood; **de bonne/mauvaise ~** in a good/bad mood

humide [ymid] *adj* damp; (main, yeux) moist; (climat, chaleur) humid; (saison, route) wet

humilier [ymilje] *vt* to humiliate

humilité [ymilite] *nf* humility, humbleness

humoristique [ymɔristik] *adj* humorous

humour [ymuʀ] *nm* humour; **avoir de l'~** to have a sense of humour; **~ noir** black humour

'huppé, e ['ype] (fam) *adj* posh

'hurlement ['yʀləmɑ̃] *nm* howling *no pl*, howl, yelling *no pl*, yell

'hurler ['yʀle] *vi* to howl, yell

hurluberlu [yʀlybɛʀly] (péj) *nm* crank

'hutte ['yt] *nf* hut

hybride [ibʀid] *adj*, *nm* hybrid

hydratant, e [idʀatɑ̃, ɑ̃t] *adj (crème)* moisturizing

hydraulique [idʀolik] *adj* hydraulic

hydravion [idʀavjɔ̃] *nm* seaplane

hydrogène [idʀɔʒɛn] *nm* hydrogen

hydroglisseur [idʀɔɡlisœʀ] *nm* hydroplane

hyène [jɛn] *nf* hyena

hygiénique [iʒenik] *adj* hygienic

hymne [imn] *nm* hymn; **~ national** national anthem

hypermarché [ipɛʀmaʀʃe] *nm* hypermarket

hypermétrope [ipɛʀmetʀɔp] *adj* long-sighted

hypertension [ipɛʀtɑ̃sjɔ̃] *nf* high blood pressure

hypertexte [ipɛʀtɛkst] *nm (INFORM)* hypertext

hypnose [ipnoz] *nf* hypnosis; **hypnotiser** *vt* to hypnotize; **hypnotiseur** *nm* hypnotist

hypocrisie [ipɔkʀizi] *nf* hypocrisy; **hypocrite** *adj* hypocritical

hypothèque [ipɔtɛk] *nf* mortgage

hypothèse [ipɔtɛz] *nf* hypothesis

hystérique [isteʀik] *adj* hysterical

I, i

iceberg [ajsbɛʀɡ] *nm* iceberg

ici [isi] *adv* here; **jusqu'~** as far as this; *(temps)* so far; **d'~ demain** by tomorrow; **d'~ là** by then, in the meantime; **d'~ peu** before long

icône [ikon] *nf* icon

idéal, e, -aux [ideal, o] *adj* ideal ♦ *nm* ideal; **idéaliste** *adj* idealistic ♦ *nm/f* idealist

idée [ide] *nf* idea; **avoir dans l'~ que** to have an idea that; **~ fixe** obsession; **~ reçue** generally accepted idea

identifier [idɑ̃tifje] *vt* to identify; **s'~ à** *(héros etc)* to identify with

identique [idɑ̃tik] *adj*: **~ (à)** identical (to)

identité [idɑ̃tite] *nf* identity

idiot, e [idjo, idjɔt] *adj* idiotic ♦ *nm/f* idiot; **idiotie** *nf* idiotic thing

idole [idɔl] *nf* idol

if [if] *nm* yew

igloo [iɡlu] *nm* igloo

ignare [iɲaʀ] *adj* ignorant

ignifugé, e [iɲifyʒe] *adj* fireproof

ignoble [iɲɔbl] *adj* vile

ignorant, e [iɲɔʀɑ̃, ɑ̃t] *adj* ignorant

ignorer [iɲɔʀe] *vt* not to know; *(personne)* to ignore

il [il] *pron* he; *(animal, chose, en tournure impersonnelle)* it; **~s** they; *voir* **avoir**

île [il] *nf* island; **l'~ Maurice** Mauritius; **les ~s anglo-normandes** the Channel Islands; **les ~s Britanniques** the British Isles

illégal, e, -aux [i(l)legal, o] *adj* illegal

illégitime [i(l)leʒitim] *adj* illegitimate

illettré, e [i(l)letʀe] *adj, nm/f* illiterate

illimité, e [i(l)limite] *adj* unlimited

illisible [i(l)lizibl] *adj* illegible; *(roman)* unreadable

illogique [i(l)lɔʒik] *adj* illogical

illumination [i(l)lyminasjɔ̃] *nf* illumination; *(idée)* flash of inspiration

illuminer [i(l)lymine] *vt* to light up; *(monument, rue: pour une fête)* to illuminate; *(: au moyen de projecteurs)* to floodlight

illusion [i(l)lyzjɔ̃] *nf* illusion; **se faire des ~s** to delude o.s.; **faire ~** to delude *ou* fool people; **illusionniste** *nm/f* conjuror

illustration [i(l)lystʀasjɔ̃] *nf* illustration

illustre [i(l)lystʀ] *adj* illustrious

illustré, e [i(l)lystʀe] *adj* illustrated ♦ *nm* comic

illustrer [i(l)lystʀe] *vt* to illustrate; **s'~** to become famous, win fame

îlot [ilo] *nm* small island, islet

ils [il] *pron voir* **il**

image [imaʒ] *nf (gén)* picture; *(métaphore)* image; **~ de marque** brand image; *(fig)* public image; **imagé, e** *adj (texte)* full of imagery; *(langage)* colourful

imaginaire [imaʒinɛʀ] adj imaginary

imagination [imaʒinasjɔ̃] nf imagination; **avoir de l'~** to be imaginative

imaginer [imaʒine] vt to imagine; (*inventer, expédient*) to devise, think up; **s'~** vt (*se figurer: scène etc*) to imagine, picture; **s'~ que** to imagine that

imbattable [ɛ̃batabl] adj unbeatable

imbécile [ɛ̃besil] adj idiotic ♦ nm/f idiot; **imbécillité** nf idiocy; (*action*) idiotic thing; (*film, livre, propos*) rubbish

imbiber [ɛ̃bibe] vt to soak; **s'~ de** to become saturated with

imbu, e [ɛ̃by] adj: **~ de** full of

imbuvable [ɛ̃byvabl] adj undrinkable; (*personne: fam*) unbearable

imitateur, -trice [imitatœʀ, tʀis] nm/f (*gén*) imitator; (*MUSIC-HALL*) impersonator

imitation [imitasjɔ̃] nf imitation; (*de personnalité*) impersonation

imiter [imite] vt to imitate; (*contrefaire*) to forge; (*ressembler à*) to look like

immaculé, e [imakyle] adj (*linge, surface, réputation*) spotless; (*blancheur*) immaculate

immangeable [ɛ̃mɑ̃ʒabl] adj inedible

immatriculation [imatʀikylasjɔ̃] nf registration

immatriculer [imatʀikyle] vt to register; **faire/se faire ~** to register

immédiat, e [imedja, at] adj immediate ♦ nm: **dans l'~** for the time being; **immédiatement** adv immediately

immense [i(m)mɑ̃s] adj immense

immerger [imɛʀʒe] vt to immerse, submerge

immeuble [imœbl] nm building; (*à usage d'habitation*) block of flats

immigration [imigʀasjɔ̃] nf immigration

immigré, e [imigʀe] nm/f immigrant

imminent, e [iminɑ̃, ɑ̃t] adj imminent

immiscer [imise]: **s'~** vi: **s'~ dans** to interfere in ou with

immobile [i(m)mɔbil] adj still, motion-

less

immobilier, -ière [imɔbilje, jɛʀ] adj property cpd ♦ nm: **l'~** the property business

immobiliser [imɔbilize] vt (*gén*) to immobilize; (*circulation, véhicule, affaires*) to bring to a standstill; **s'~** (*personne*) to stand still; (*machine, véhicule*) to come to a halt

immonde [i(m)mɔ̃d] adj foul

immoral, e, -aux [i(m)mɔʀal, o] adj immoral

immortel, le [imɔʀtɛl] adj immortal

immuable [imɥabl] adj unchanging

immunisé, e [im(m)ynize] adj: **~ contre** immune to

immunité [imynite] nf immunity

impact [ɛ̃pakt] nm impact

impair, e [ɛ̃pɛʀ] adj odd ♦ nm faux pas, blunder

impardonnable [ɛ̃paʀdɔnabl] adj unpardonable, unforgiving

imparfait, e [ɛ̃paʀfɛ, ɛt] adj imperfect

impartial, e, -aux [ɛ̃paʀsjal, jo] adj impartial, unbiased

impasse [ɛ̃pas] nf dead end, cul-de-sac; (*fig*) deadlock

impassible [ɛ̃pasibl] adj impassive

impatience [ɛ̃pasjɑ̃s] nf impatience

impatient, e [ɛ̃pasjɑ̃, jɑ̃t] adj impatient; **impatienter: s'impatienter** vi to get impatient

impeccable [ɛ̃pekabl] adj (*parfait*) perfect; (*propre*) impeccable; (*fam*) smashing

impensable [ɛ̃pɑ̃sabl] adj (*événement hypothétique*) unthinkable; (*événement qui a eu lieu*) unbelievable

imper [ɛ̃pɛʀ] (*fam*) nm raincoat

impératif, -ive [ɛ̃peʀatif, iv] adj imperative ♦ nm (*LING*) imperative; **~s** nmpl (*exigences: d'une fonction, d'une charge*) requirements; (: *de la mode*) demands

impératrice [ɛ̃peʀatʀis] nf empress

imperceptible [ɛ̃pɛʀsɛptibl] adj imperceptible

impérial, e, -aux [ɛperjal, jo] *adj* impérial; **impériale** *nf* top deck

impérieux, -euse [ɛperjø, jøz] *adj* (*caractère, ton*) imperious; (*obligation, besoin*) pressing, urgent

impérissable [ɛperisabl] *adj* undying

imperméable [ɛpermeabl] *adj* waterproof; (*fig*): **~ à** impervious to ♦ *nm* raincoat

impertinent, e [ɛpertinɑ̃, ɑ̃t] *adj* impertinent

imperturbable [ɛpertyrbabl] *adj* (*personne, caractère*) unperturbable; (*sangfroid, gaieté, sérieux*) unshakeable

impétueux, -euse [ɛpetɥø, øz] *adj* impetuous

impitoyable [ɛpitwajabl] *adj* pitiless, merciless

implanter [ɛplɑ̃te] *vt* to be set up

impliquer [ɛplike] *vt* to imply; **~ qn (dans)** to implicate sb (in)

impoli, e [ɛpɔli] *adj* impolite, rude

impopulaire [ɛpɔpylɛr] *adj* unpopular

importance [ɛpɔrtɑ̃s] *nf* importance; **sans ~** unimportant

important, e [ɛpɔrtɑ̃, ɑ̃t] *adj* important; (*en quantité: somme, retard*) considerable, sizeable; (: *dégâts*) extensive; (*péj: airs, ton*) self-important ♦ *nm*: **l'~** the important thing

importateur, -trice [ɛpɔrtatœr, tris] *nm/f* importer

importation [ɛpɔrtasjɔ̃] *nf* importation; (*produit*) import

importer [ɛpɔrte] *vt* (*COMM*) to import; (*maladies, plantes*) to introduce ♦ *vi* (*être important*) to matter; **il importe qu'il fasse** it is important that he should do; **peu m'importe** (*je n'ai pas de préférence*) I don't mind; (*je m'en moque*) I don't care; **peu importe (que)** it doesn't matter (if); *voir aussi* **n'importe**

importun, e [ɛpɔrtœ̃, yn] *adj* irksome, importunate; (*arrivée, visite*) inopportune, ill-timed ♦ *nm* intruder; **importuner** *vt* to bother

imposable [ɛpozabl] *adj* taxable

imposant, e [ɛpozɑ̃, ɑ̃t] *adj* imposing

imposer [ɛpoze] *vt* (*taxer*) to tax; **s'~** (*être nécessaire*) to be imperative; **~ qch à qn** to impose sth on sb; **en ~ à** to impress; **s'~ comme** to emerge as; **s'~ par** to win recognition through

impossibilité [ɛposibilite] *nf* impossibility; **être dans l'~ de faire qch** to be unable to do sth

impossible [ɛposibl] *adj* impossible; **il m'est ~ de le faire** it is impossible for me to do it, I can't possibly do it; **faire l'~** to do one's utmost

imposteur [ɛpostœr] *nm* impostor

impôt [ɛpo] *nm* tax; **~s** *nmpl* (*contributions*) (income) tax; **payer 1000 F d'~s** to pay 1,000F in tax; **~ foncier** land tax; **~ sur le chiffre d'affaires** corporation (*BRIT*) *ou* corporate (*US*) tax; **~ sur le revenu** income tax

impotent, e [ɛpotɑ̃, ɑ̃t] *adj* disabled

impraticable [ɛpratikabl] *adj* (*projet*) impracticable, unworkable; (*piste*) impassable

imprécis, e [ɛpresi, iz] *adj* imprecise

imprégner [ɛprene] *vt* (*tissu*) to impregnate; (*lieu, air*) to fill; **s'~ de** (*fig*) to absorb

imprenable [ɛprənabl] *adj* (*forteresse*) impregnable; **vue ~** unimpeded outlook

imprésario [ɛpresarjo] *nm* manager

impression [ɛpresjɔ̃] *nf* impression; (*d'un ouvrage, tissu*) printing; **faire bonne ~** to make a good impression; **impressionnant, e** *adj* (*imposant*) impressive; (*bouleversant*) upsetting; **impressionner** *vt* (*frapper*) to impress; (*bouleverser*) to upset

imprévisible [ɛprevizibl] *adj* unforeseeable

imprévoyant, e [ɛprevwajɑ̃, ɑ̃t] *adj* lacking in foresight; (*en matière d'argent*) improvident

imprévu, e [ɛprevy] *adj* unforeseen, unexpected ♦ *nm* (*incident*) unexpected incident; **des vacances pleines d'~** holidays full of surprises; **en cas d'~** if anything unexpected happens; **sauf ~** unless anything unexpected crops up

imprimante [ɛ̃pʀimɑ̃t] *nf* printer

imprimé [ɛ̃pʀime] *nm* (*formulaire*) printed form; (*POSTES*) printed matter *no pl*; (*tissu*) printed fabric; **à fleur** floral print

imprimer [ɛ̃pʀime] *vt* to print; (*publier*) to publish; **imprimerie** *nf* printing; (*établissement*) printing works *sg*; **imprimeur** *nm* printer

impromptu, e [ɛ̃pʀɔ̃pty] *adj* (*repas, discours*) impromptu; (*départ*) sudden; (*visite*) surprise

impropre [ɛ̃pʀɔpʀ] *adj* inappropriate; **~ à** unfit for

improviser [ɛ̃pʀɔvize] *vt, vi* to improvise

improviste [ɛ̃pʀɔvist]: **à l'~** *adv* unexpectedly, without warning

imprudence [ɛ̃pʀydɑ̃s] *nf* (*d'une personne, d'une action*) carelessness *no pl*; (*d'une remarque*) imprudence *no pl*; **commettre une ~** to do something foolish

imprudent, e [ɛ̃pʀydɑ̃, ɑ̃t] *adj* (*conducteur, geste, action*) careless; (*remarque*) unwise, imprudent; (*projet*) foolhardy

impudent, e [ɛ̃pydɑ̃, ɑ̃t] *adj* impudent

impudique [ɛ̃pydik] *adj* shameless

impuissant, e [ɛ̃pɥisɑ̃, ɑ̃t] *adj* helpless; (*sans effet*) ineffectual; (*sexuellement*) impotent

impulsif, -ive [ɛ̃pylsif, iv] *adj* impulsive

impulsion [ɛ̃pylsjɔ̃] *nf* (*ÉLEC, instinct*) impulse; (*élan, influence*) impetus

impunément [ɛ̃pynemɑ̃] *adv* with impunity

inabordable [inabɔʀdabl] *adj* (*cher*) prohibitive

inacceptable [inakseptabl] *adj* unacceptable

inaccessible [inaksesibl] *adj* inacces-

sible

inachevé, e [inaʃ(ə)ve] *adj* unfinished

inactif, -ive [inaktif, iv] *adj* inactive; (*remède*) ineffective; (*BOURSE: marché*) slack ♦ *nm*: **les ~s** the non-working population

inadapté, e [inadapte] *adj* (*gén*): **~ à** not adapted to, unsuited to; (*PSYCH*) maladjusted

inadéquat, e [inadekwa(t), kwat] *adj* inadequate

inadmissible [inadmisibl] *adj* inadmissible

inadvertance [inadvɛʀtɑ̃s]: **par ~** *adv* inadvertently

inaltérable [inalteʀabl] *adj* (*matière*) stable; (*fig*) unfailing; **~ à** unaffected by

inanimé, e [inanime] *adj* (*matière*) inanimate; (*évanoui*) unconscious; (*sans vie*) lifeless

inanition [inanisjɔ̃] *nf*: **tomber d'~** to faint with hunger (and exhaustion)

inaperçu, e [inapɛʀsy] *adj*: **passer ~** to go unnoticed

inapte [inapt] *adj*: **~ à** incapable of; (*MIL*) unfit for

inattaquable [inatakabl] *adj* (*texte, preuve*) irrefutable

inattendu, e [inatɑ̃dy] *adj* unexpected

inattentif, -ive [inatɑ̃tif, iv] *adj* inattentive; **~ à** (*dangers, détails*) heedless of; **inattention** *nf*: **faute d'inattention** careless mistake

inauguration [inogyʀasjɔ̃] *nf* inauguration

inaugurer [inogyʀe] *vt* (*monument*) to unveil; (*exposition, usine*) to open; (*fig*) to inaugurate

inavouable [inavwabl] *adj* shameful; (*bénéfices*) undisclosable

incalculable [ɛ̃kalkylabl] *adj* incalculable

incandescence [ɛ̃kɑ̃desɑ̃s] *nf*: **porter à ~** to heat white-hot

incapable [ɛ̃kapabl] *adj* incapable; **~ de faire** incapable of doing; (*empêché*)

unable to do
incapacité [ɛ̃kapasite] nf (incompétence) incapability; (impossibilité) incapacity; **dans l'~ de faire** unable to do
incarcérer [ɛ̃karsere] vt to incarcerate, imprison
incarné, e [ɛ̃karne] adj (ongle) ingrown
incarner [ɛ̃karne] vt to embody, personify; (THÉÂTRE) to play
incassable [ɛ̃kɑsabl] adj unbreakable
incendiaire [ɛ̃sɑ̃djɛr] adj incendiary; (fig: discours) inflammatory
incendie [ɛ̃sɑ̃di] nm fire; **~ criminel** arson no pl; **~ de forêt** forest fire; **incendier** vt (mettre le feu à) to set fire to, set alight; (brûler complètement) to burn down; **se faire incendier** (fam) to burn up a rocket
incertain, e [ɛ̃sɛrtɛ̃, ɛn] adj uncertain; (temps) unsettled; (imprécis: contours) indistinct, blurred; **incertitude** nf uncertainty
incessamment [ɛ̃sesamɑ̃] adv very shortly
incident [ɛ̃sidɑ̃, ɑ̃t] nm incident; **~ de parcours** minor hitch ou setback; **~ technique** technical difficulties pl
incinérer [ɛ̃sinere] vt (ordures) to incinerate; (mort) to cremate
incisive [ɛ̃siziv] nf incisor
inciter [ɛ̃site] vt: **~ qn à (faire) qch** to encourage sb to do sth; (à la révolte etc) to incite sb to do sth
inclinable [ɛ̃klinabl] adj: **siège à dossier ~** reclining seat
inclinaison [ɛ̃klinɛzɔ̃] nf (déclivité: d'une route etc) incline; (: d'un toit) slope; (état penché) tilt
inclination [ɛ̃klinasjɔ̃] nf (penchant) inclination; **~ de (la) tête** nod (of the head); **~ (de buste)** bow
incliner [ɛ̃kline] vt (pencher) to tilt ♦ vi: **~ à qch/à faire** to incline towards sth/doing; **s'~ (devant)** to bow (before); (céder) to give in ou yield (to); **~ la tête** to give a slight bow

inclure [ɛ̃klyr] vt to include; (joindre à un envoi) to enclose; **jusqu'au 10 mars inclus** until 10th March inclusive
incognito [ɛ̃kɔɲito] adv incognito ♦ nm: **garder l'~** to remain incognito
incohérent, e [ɛ̃kɔerɑ̃, ɑ̃t] adj (comportement) inconsistent; (geste, langage, texte) incoherent
incollable [ɛ̃kɔlabl] adj (riz) non-stick; **il est ~** (fam) he's got all the answers
incolore [ɛ̃kɔlɔr] adj colourless
incommoder [ɛ̃kɔmɔde] vt (chaleur, odeur): **~ qn** to bother sb
incomparable [ɛ̃kɔ̃parabl] adj incomparable
incompatible [ɛ̃kɔ̃patibl] adj incompatible
incompétent, e [ɛ̃kɔ̃petɑ̃, ɑ̃t] adj incompetent
incomplet, -ète [ɛ̃kɔ̃plɛ, ɛt] adj incomplete
incompréhensible [ɛ̃kɔ̃preɑ̃sibl] adj incomprehensible
incompris, e [ɛ̃kɔ̃pri, iz] adj misunderstood
inconcevable [ɛ̃kɔ̃s(ə)vabl] adj inconceivable
inconciliable [ɛ̃kɔ̃siljabl] adj irreconcilable
inconditionnel, le [ɛ̃kɔ̃disjɔnɛl] adj unconditional; (partisan) unquestioning ♦ nm/f (d'un homme politique) ardent supporter; (d'un écrivain, d'un chanteur) ardent admirer; (d'une activité) fanatic
inconfort [ɛ̃kɔ̃fɔr] nm discomfort; **inconfortable** adj uncomfortable
incongru, e [ɛ̃kɔ̃gry] adj unseemly
inconnu, e [ɛ̃kɔny] adj unknown ♦ nm/f stranger ♦ nm: **l'~** the unknown; **inconnue** nf unknown factor
inconsciemment [ɛ̃kɔ̃sjamɑ̃] adv unconsciously
inconscient, e [ɛ̃kɔ̃sjɑ̃, ɑ̃t] adj unconscious; (irréfléchi) thoughtless, reckless; (sentiment) subconscious ♦ nm (PSYCH): **l'~** the unconscious; **~ de** unaware of
inconsidéré, e [ɛ̃kɔ̃sidere] adj ill-

considered

inconsistant, e [ɛ̃kɔ̃sistɑ̃, ɑ̃t] *adj* (*fig*) flimsy, weak

inconsolable [ɛ̃kɔ̃sɔlabl] *adj* inconsolable

incontestable [ɛ̃kɔ̃testabl] *adj* indisputable

incontinent, e [ɛ̃kɔ̃tinɑ̃, ɑ̃t] *adj* incontinent

incontournable [ɛ̃kɔ̃turnabl] *adj* unavoidable

incontrôlable [ɛ̃kɔ̃trolabl] *adj* unverifiable; (*irrépressible*) uncontrollable

inconvenant, e [ɛ̃kɔ̃v(ə)nɑ̃, ɑ̃t] *adj* unseemly, improper

inconvénient [ɛ̃kɔ̃venjɑ̃] *nm* disadvantage, drawback; **si vous n'y voyez pas d'~** if you have no objections

incorporer [ɛ̃kɔrpɔre] *vt*: ~ **(à)** to mix in (with); ~ **(dans)** (*paragraphe etc*) to incorporate (in); (*MIL: appeler*) to recruit (into); **il a très bien su s'~ à notre groupe** he was very easily incorporated into our group

incorrect, e [ɛ̃kɔrɛkt] *adj* (*impropre, inconvenant*) improper; (*défectueux*) faulty; (*inexact*) incorrect; (*impoli*) impolite; (*déloyal*) underhand

incorrigible [ɛ̃kɔriʒibl] *adj* incorrigible

incrédule [ɛ̃kredyl] *adj* incredulous; (*REL*) unbelieving

increvable [ɛ̃krəvabl] *adj* (*fam*) tireless

incriminer [ɛ̃krimine] *vt* (*personne*) to incriminate; (*action, conduite*) to bring under attack; (*bonne foi, honnêteté*) to call into question

incroyable [ɛ̃krwajabl] *adj* incredible

incruster [ɛ̃kryste] *vt* (*ART*) to inlay; **s'~ vi** (*invité*) to take root

inculpé, e [ɛ̃kylpe] *nm/f* accused

inculper [ɛ̃kylpe] *vt*: ~ **(de)** to charge (with)

inculquer [ɛ̃kylke] *vt*: ~ **qch à** to inculcate sth in *ou* instil sth into

inculte [ɛ̃kylt] *adj* uncultivated; (*esprit, peuple*) uncultured

Inde [ɛ̃d] *nf*: **l'~** India

indécent, e [ɛ̃desɑ̃, ɑ̃t] *adj* indecent

indéchiffrable [ɛ̃deʃifrabl] *adj* indecipherable

indécis, e [ɛ̃desi, iz] *adj* (*par nature*) indecisive; (*temporairement*) undecided

indéfendable [ɛ̃defɑ̃dabl] *adj* indefensible

indéfini, e [ɛ̃defini] *adj* (*imprécis, incertain*) undefined; (*illimité, LING*) indefinite; **indéfiniment** *adv* indefinitely; **indéfinissable** *adj* indefinable

indélébile [ɛ̃delebil] *adj* indelible

indélicat, e [ɛ̃delika, at] *adj* tactless

indemne [ɛ̃dɛmn] *adj* unharmed; **indemniser** *vt*: **indemniser qn (de)** to compensate sb (for)

indemnité [ɛ̃dɛmnite] *nf* (*dédommagement*) compensation *no pl*; (*allocation*) allowance; **indemnité de licenciement** redundancy payment

indépendamment [ɛ̃depɑ̃damɑ̃] *adv* independently; ~ **de** (*abstraction faite de*) irrespective of; (*en plus de*) over and above

indépendance [ɛ̃depɑ̃dɑ̃s] *nf* independence

indépendant, e [ɛ̃depɑ̃dɑ̃, ɑ̃t] *adj* independent; ~ **de** independent of

indescriptible [ɛ̃deskriptibl] *adj* indescribable

indésirable [ɛ̃dezirabl] *adj* undesirable

indestructible [ɛ̃destryktibl] *adj* indestructible

indétermination [ɛ̃determinasjɔ̃] *nf* (*irrésolution: chronique*) indecision; (*: temporaire*) indecisiveness

indéterminé, e [ɛ̃detɛrmine] *adj* (*date, cause, nature*) unspecified; (*forme, longueur, quantité*) indeterminate

index [ɛ̃dɛks] *nm* (*doigt*) index finger; (*d'un livre etc*) index; **mettre à l'~** to blacklist; **indexé, e** *adj* (*ÉCON*): **indexé (sur)** index-linked (to)

indic [ɛ̃dik] *nm* (*fam*) *nm* (*POLICE*) grass

indicateur [ɛ̃dikatœr] *nm* (*POLICE*) informer; (*TECH*) gauge, indicator

indicatif, -ive [ɛ̃dikatif, iv] *adj*: **à titre**

~ for (your) information ♦ *nm* (LING) indicative; (RADIO) theme *ou* signature
tune; (TÉL) dialling code

indication [ɛ̃dikasjɔ̃] *nf* indication;
(*renseignement*) information *no pl*; ~**s**
nfpl (*directives*) instructions

indice [ɛ̃dis] *nm* (*marque, signe*) indication, sign; (POLICE: *lors d'une enquête*)
clue; (JUR: *présomption*) piece of evidence; (SCIENCE, ÉCON, TECH) index

indicible [ɛ̃disibl] *adj* inexpressible

indien, ne [ɛ̃djɛ̃, jɛn] *adj* Indian ♦ *nm/f*:
I~, ne Indian

indifféremment [ɛ̃diferamɑ̃] *adv*
(*sans distinction*) equally (well)

indifférence [ɛ̃diferɑ̃s] *nf* indifference

indifférent, e [ɛ̃diferɑ̃, ɑ̃t] *adj* (*peu intéressé*) indifferent; **ça m'est ~** it
doesn't matter to me; **elle m'est ~e** I
am indifferent to her

indigence [ɛ̃diʒɑ̃s] *nf* poverty

indigène [ɛ̃diʒɛn] *adj* native, indigenous; (*des gens du pays*) local ♦ *nm/f*
native

indigeste [ɛ̃diʒɛst] *adj* indigestible

indigestion [ɛ̃diʒɛstjɔ̃] *nf* indigestion
no pl

indigne [ɛ̃diɲ] *adj* unworthy

indigner [ɛ̃diɲe] *vt*: **s'~ (de** *ou* **contre)**
to get indignant (at)

indiqué, e [ɛ̃dike] *adj* (*date, lieu*)
agreed; (*traitement*) appropriate; (*conseillé*) advisable

indiquer [ɛ̃dike] *vt* (*suj: pendule, aiguille*) to show; (: *étiquette, panneau*) to
show, indicate; (*renseigner sur*) to point
out, tell; (*déterminer: date, lieu*) to give,
state; (*signaler, dénoter*) to indicate,
point to; ~ **qch/qn à qn** (*montrer du
doigt*) to point sth/sb out to sb; (*faire
connaître: médecin, restaurant*) to tell sb
of sth/sb

indirect, e [ɛ̃dirɛkt] *adj* indirect

indiscipliné, e [ɛ̃disipline] *adj* undisciplined

indiscret, -ète [ɛ̃diskrɛ, ɛt] *adj* indiscreet

indiscutable [ɛ̃diskytabl] *adj* indisputable

indispensable [ɛ̃dispɑ̃sabl] *adj* indispensable, essential

indisposé, e [ɛ̃dispoze] *adj* indisposed

indisposer [ɛ̃dispoze] *vt* (*incommoder*)
to upset; (*déplaire à*) to antagonize;
(*énerver*) to irritate

indistinct, e [ɛ̃distɛ̃(kt), ɛ̃kt] *adj* indistinct; **indistinctement** *adv* (*voir, prononcer*) indistinctly; (*sans distinction*) indiscriminately

individu [ɛ̃dividy] *nm* individual; **indi-
viduel, le** *adj* (*gén*) individual; (*responsabilité, propriété, liberté*) personal;
chambre individuelle single room;
maison individuelle detached house

indolore [ɛ̃dɔlɔr] *adj* painless

indomptable [ɛ̃dɔ̃(p)tabl] *adj* untame-
able; (*fig*) invincible

Indonésie [ɛ̃dɔnezi] *nf* Indonesia

indu, e [ɛ̃dy] *adj*: **à une heure ~e** at
some ungodly hour

induire [ɛ̃dɥir] *vt*: ~ **qn en erreur** to
lead sb astray, mislead sb

indulgent, e [ɛ̃dylʒɑ̃, ɑ̃t] *adj* (*parent,
regard*) indulgent; (*juge, examinateur*)
lenient

industrialisé, e [ɛ̃dystrijalize] *adj* in-
dustrialized

industrie [ɛ̃dystri] *nf* industry; **industriel, le** *adj* industrial ♦ *nm* industrialist

inébranlable [inebrɑ̃labl] *adj* (*masse,
colonne*) solid; (*personne, certitude, foi*)
unshakeable

inédit, e [inedi, it] *adj* (*correspondance,
livre*) hitherto unpublished; (*spectacle,
moyen*) novel, original; (*film*) unreleased

ineffaçable [inefasabl] *adj* indelible

inefficace [inefikas] *adj* (*remède, moyen*) ineffective; (*machine, employé*)
inefficient

inégal, e, -aux [inegal, o] *adj* unequal;
(*irrégulier*) uneven; **inégalable** *adj*
matchless; **inégalé, e** *adj* (*record*) unequalled; (*beauté*) unrivalled; **inégalité**
nf inequality

inépuisable [inepɥizabl] *adj* inexhaustible

inerte [inɛʁt] *adj* (*immobile*) lifeless; (*sans réaction*) passive

inespéré, e [inɛspeʁe] *adj* unexpected, unhoped-for

inestimable [inɛstimabl] *adj* priceless; (*fig: bienfait*) invaluable

inévitable [inevitabl] *adj* unavoidable; (*fatal, habituel*) inevitable

inexact, e [inɛgza(kt), akt] *adj* inaccurate

inexcusable [inɛkskyzabl] *adj* unforgivable

inexplicable [inɛksplikabl] *adj* inexplicable

in extremis [inɛkstʁemis] *adv* at the last minute ♦ *adj* last-minute

infaillible [ɛ̃fajibl] *adj* infallible

infâme [ɛ̃fɑm] *adj* vile

infarctus [ɛ̃faʁktys] *nm*: ~ **(du myocarde)** coronary (thrombosis)

infatigable [ɛ̃fatigabl] *adj* tireless

infect, e [ɛ̃fɛkt] *adj* revolting; (*personne*) obnoxious; (*temps*) foul

infecter [ɛ̃fɛkte] *vt* (*atmosphère, eau*) to contaminate; (*MÉD*) to infect; **s'~** to become infected *ou* septic; **infection** *nf* infection; (*puanteur*) stench

inférieur, e [ɛ̃feʁjœʁ] *adj* lower; (*en qualité, intelligence*) inferior; ~ **à** (*somme, quantité*) less *ou* smaller than; (*moins bon que*) inferior to

infernal, e, -aux [ɛ̃fɛʁnal, o] *adj* (*insupportable: chaleur, rythme*) infernal; (*: enfant*) horrid; (*satanique, effrayant*) diabolical

infidèle [ɛ̃fidɛl] *adj* unfaithful

infiltrer [ɛ̃filtʁe] *vb*: **s'~ dans** to get into; (*liquide*) to seep through; (*fig: groupe, ennemi*) to infiltrate

infime [ɛ̃fim] *adj* minute, tiny

infini, e [ɛ̃fini] *adj* infinite ♦ *nm* infinity; **à l'~** endlessly; **infiniment** *adv* infinitely; **infinité** *nf*: **une infinité de** an infinite number of

infinitif [ɛ̃finitif, iv] *nm* infinitive

infirme [ɛ̃fiʁm] *adj* disabled ♦ *nm/f* disabled person

infirmerie [ɛ̃fiʁməʁi] *nf* medical room

infirmier, -ière [ɛ̃fiʁmje] *nm/f* nurse; **infirmière chef** sister

infirmité [ɛ̃fiʁmite] *nf* disability

inflammable [ɛ̃flamabl] *adj* (in)flammable

inflation [ɛ̃flasjɔ̃] *nf* inflation

infliger [ɛ̃fliʒe] *vt*: ~ **qch (à qn)** to inflict sth (on sb); (*amende, sanction*) to impose sth (on sb)

influençable [ɛ̃flyɑ̃sabl] *adj* easily influenced

influence [ɛ̃flyɑ̃s] *nf* influence; **influencer** *vt* to influence; **influent, e** *adj* influential

informateur, -trice [ɛ̃fɔʁmatœʁ, tʁis] *nm/f* (*POLICE*) informer

informaticien, ne [ɛ̃fɔʁmatisjɛ̃, jɛn] *nm/f* computer scientist

information [ɛ̃fɔʁmasjɔ̃] *nf* (*renseignement*) piece of information; (*PRESSE, TV: nouvelle*) item of news; (*diffusion de renseignements , INFORM*) information; (*JUR*) inquiry, investigation; **~s** *nfpl* (*TV*) news *sg*

informatique [ɛ̃fɔʁmatik] *nf* (*technique*) data processing; (*science*) computer science ♦ *adj* computer *cpd*; **informatiser** *vt* to computerize

informe [ɛ̃fɔʁm] *adj* shapeless

informer [ɛ̃fɔʁme] *vt*: ~ **qn (de)** to inform sb (of); **s'~ (de/si)** to inquire *ou* find out (about/whether *ou* if)

infos [ɛ̃fo] *nfpl*: **les** ~ the news *sg*

infraction [ɛ̃fʁaksjɔ̃] *nf* offence; ~ **à** violation *ou* breach of; **être en ~** to be in breach of the law

infranchissable [ɛ̃fʁɑ̃ʃisabl] *adj* impassable; (*fig*) insuperable

infrarouge [ɛ̃fʁaʁuʒ] *adj/nf* infrared

infrastructure [ɛ̃fʁastʁyktyʁ] *nf* (*AVIAT, MIL*) ground installations *pl*; (*ÉCON: touristique etc*) infrastructure

infuser [ɛ̃fyze] *vt, vi* (*thé*) to brew; (*tisane*) to infuse; **infusion** *nf* (*tisane*) herb tea

ingénier [ɛ̃ʒenje]: **s'~** vi: **s'~ à faire to** strive to do

ingénierie [ɛ̃ʒeniʁi] nf engineering; **~ génétique** genetic engineering

ingénieur [ɛ̃ʒenjœʁ] nm engineer; **~ génieur du son** sound engineer

ingénieux, -euse [ɛ̃ʒenjø, jøz] adj ingenious, clever

ingénu, e [ɛ̃ʒeny] adj ingenuous, artless

ingérer [ɛ̃ʒeʁe] vb: **s'~ dans** to interfere in

ingrat, e [ɛ̃ɡʁa, at] adj (personne) ungrateful; (travail, sujet) thankless; (visage) unprepossessing

ingrédient [ɛ̃ɡʁedjɑ̃] nm ingredient

ingurgiter [ɛ̃ɡyʁʒite] vt to swallow

inhabitable [inabitabl] adj uninhabitable

inhabité, e [inabite] adj uninhabited

inhabituel, le [inabityɛl] adj unusual

inhibition [inibisjɔ̃] nf inhibition

inhumain, e [inymɛ̃, ɛn] adj inhuman

inhumation [inymasjɔ̃] nf burial

inhumer [inyme] vt to inter, bury

inimaginable [inimaʒinabl] adj unimaginable

ininterrompu, e [inɛ̃teʁɔ̃py] adj (file, série) unbroken; (flot, vacarme) uninterrupted, non-stop; (effort) unremitting, continuous; (suite, ligne) unbroken

initial, e, -aux [inisjal, jo] adj initial; **initiale** nf initial; **initialiser** vt to initialize

initiation [inisjasjɔ̃] nf: **~ à** introduction to

initiative [inisjativ] nf initiative

initier [inisje] vt: **~ qn à** to initiate sb into; (faire découvrir: art, jeu) to introduce sb to

injecté, e [ɛ̃ʒɛkte] adj: **yeux ~s de sang** bloodshot eyes

injecter [ɛ̃ʒɛkte] vt to inject; **injection** nf injection; **à injection** (AUTO) fuel injection cpd

injure [ɛ̃ʒyʁ] nf insult, abuse no pl; **inju-**

rier vt to insult, abuse; **injurieux, -euse** adj abusive, insulting

injuste [ɛ̃ʒyst] adj unjust, unfair; **injustice** nf injustice

inlassable [ɛ̃lɑsabl] adj tireless

inné, e [ine] adj innate, inborn

innocent, e [inɔsɑ̃, ɑ̃t] adj innocent; **innocenter** vt to clear, prove innocent

innombrable [i(n)nɔ̃bʁabl] adj innumerable

innommable [i(n)nɔmabl] adj unspeakable

innover [inɔve] vi to break new ground

inoccupé, e [inɔkype] adj unoccupied

inodore [inɔdɔʁ] adj (gaz) odourless; (fleur) scentless

inoffensif, -ive [inɔfɑ̃sif, iv] adj harmless, innocuous

inondation [inɔ̃dasjɔ̃] nf flood

inonder [inɔ̃de] vt to flood; **~ de** to flood with

inopiné, e [inɔpine] adj unexpected; (mort) sudden

inopportun, e [inɔpɔʁtœ̃, yn] adj illtimed, untimely

inoubliable [inublijabl] adj unforgettable

inouï, e [inwi] adj unheard-of, extraordinary

inox [inɔks] nm stainless steel

inqualifiable [ɛ̃kalifjabl] adj unspeakable

inquiet, -ète [ɛ̃kjɛ, ɛkjɛt] adj anxious; **inquiétant, e** adj worrying, disturbing; **inquiéter** vt to worry; **s'inquiéter** to worry; **s'inquiéter de** to worry about; (s'enquérir de) to inquire about; **inquiétude** nf anxiety

insaisissable [ɛ̃sezisabl] adj (fugitif, ennemi) elusive; (différence, nuance) imperceptible

insalubre [ɛ̃salybʁ] adj insalubrious

insatisfaisant, e [ɛ̃satisfəzɑ̃, ɑ̃t] adj unsatisfactory

insatisfait, e [ɛ̃satisfɛ, ɛt] adj (non comblé) unsatisfied; (mécontent) dissatisfied

inscription [ɛ̃skʀipsjɔ̃] *nf* inscription; (*immatriculation*) enrolment

inscrire [ɛ̃skʀiʀ] *vt* (*marquer: sur son calepin etc*) to note *ou* write down; (*: sur un mur, une affiche etc*) to write; (*: dans la pierre, le métal*) to inscribe; (*mettre: sur une liste, un budget etc*) to put down; **s'~** (*pour une excursion etc*) to put one's name down; **s'~ à** (*club, parti*) to join; (*université*) to register *ou* enrol (at); (*examen, concours*) to register (for); **~ qn à** (*club, parti*) to enrol sb at

insecte [ɛ̃sɛkt] *nm* insect; **insecticide** [ɛ̃sɛktisid] *nm* insecticide

insensé, e [ɛ̃sɑ̃se] *adj* mad

insensibiliser [ɛ̃sɑ̃sibilize] *vt* to anaesthetize

insensible [ɛ̃sɑ̃sibl] *adj* (*nerf, membre*) numb; (*dur, indifférent*) insensitive

inséparable [ɛ̃sepaʀabl] *adj* inseparable ♦ *nm*: **~s** (*oiseaux*) lovebirds

insigne [ɛ̃siɲ] *nm* (*d'un club, parti*) badge; (*d'une fonction*) insignia ♦ *adj* distinguished

insignifiant, e [ɛ̃siɲifjɑ̃, jɑ̃t] *adj* insignificant; trivial

insinuer [ɛ̃sinɥe] *vt* to insinuate; **s'~ dans** (*fig*) to worm one's way into

insipide [ɛ̃sipid] *adj* insipid

insister [ɛ̃siste] *vi* to insist; (*continuer à sonner*) to keep on trying; **~ sur** (*détail, sujet*) to lay stress on

insolation [ɛ̃sɔlasjɔ̃] *nf* (*MÉD*) sunstroke *no pl*

insolent, e [ɛ̃sɔlɑ̃, ɑ̃t] *adj* insolent

insolite [ɛ̃sɔlit] *adj* strange, unusual

insomnie [ɛ̃sɔmni] *nf* insomnia *no pl*

insonoriser [ɛ̃sɔnɔʀize] *vt* to soundproof

insouciant, e [ɛ̃susjɑ̃, jɑ̃t] *adj* carefree; **~ du danger** heedless of (the) danger

insoumis, e [ɛ̃sumi, iz] *adj* (*caractère, enfant*) rebellious, refractory; (*contrée, tribu*) unsubdued

insoupçonnable [ɛ̃supsɔnabl] *adj* un-

suspected; (*personne*) above suspicion

insoupçonné, e [ɛ̃supsɔne] *adj* unsuspected

insoutenable [ɛ̃sut(ə)nabl] *adj* (*argument*) untenable; (*chaleur*) unbearable

inspecter [ɛ̃spɛkte] *vt* to inspect; **inspecteur, -trice** *nm/f* inspector; **inspecteur d'Académie** (regional) director of education; **inspecteur des finances** ≈ tax inspector (*BRIT*), ≈ Internal Revenue Service agent (*US*); **inspection** *nf* inspection

inspirer [ɛ̃spiʀe] *vt* (*gén*) to inspire ♦ *vi* (*aspirer*) to breathe in; **s'~ de** (*suj: artiste*) to draw one's inspiration from

instable [ɛ̃stabl] *adj* unstable; (*meuble, équilibre*) unsteady; (*temps*) unsettled

installation [ɛ̃stalasjɔ̃] *nf* installation; **~s** *nfpl* facilities

installer [ɛ̃stale] *vt* (*loger, placer*) to put; (*meuble, gaz, électricité*) to put in; (*rideau, étagère, tente*) to put up; (*appartement*) to fit out; **s'~** (*s'établir: artisan, dentiste etc*) to set o.s. up; (*se loger*) to settle; (*emménager*) to settle in; (*sur un siège, à un emplacement*) to settle (down); (*fig: maladie, grève*) to take a firm hold

instance [ɛ̃stɑ̃s] *nf* (*ADMIN: autorité*) authority; **affaire en ~** matter pending; **être en ~ de divorce** to be awaiting a divorce

instant [ɛ̃stɑ̃] *nm* moment, instant; **dans un ~** in a moment; **à l'~** this instant; **pour l'~** for the moment, for the time being

instantané, e [ɛ̃stɑ̃tane] *adj* (*lait, café*) instant; (*explosion, mort*) instantaneous ♦ *nm* snapshot

instar [ɛ̃staʀ]: **à l'~ de** *prép* following the example of, like

instaurer [ɛ̃stɔʀe] *vt* to institute; (*couvre-feu*) to impose

instinct [ɛ̃stɛ̃] *nm* instinct; **instinctivement** *adv* instinctively

instit [ɛ̃stit] (*fam*) *nm/f* (primary school) teacher

instituer [ɛstitɥe] *vt* to establish

institut [ɛstity] *nm* institute; **~ de beauté** beauty salon; **Institut universitaire de technologie** ≃ polytechnic

instituteur, -trice [ɛstitytœr, tris] *nm/f* (primary school) teacher

institution [ɛstitysjɔ̃] *nf* institution; (*collège*) private school

instructif, -ive [ɛstryktif, iv] *adj* instructive

instruction [ɛstryksjɔ̃] *nf* (*enseignement, savoir*) education; (*JUR: préliminaire*) investigation and hearing; **~s** *nfpl* (*ordres, mode d'emploi*) instructions; **~ civique** civics *sg*

instruire [ɛstrɥir] *vt* (*élèves*) to teach; (*recrues*) to train; (*JUR: affaire*) to conduct the investigation for; **s'~** to educate o.s.; **instruit, e** *adj* educated

instrument [ɛstrymɑ̃] *nm* instrument; **~ à cordes/vent** stringed/wind instrument; **~ de mesure** measuring instrument; **~ de musique** musical instrument; **~ de travail** (working) tool

insu [ɛsy] *nm*: **à l'~ de qn** without sb knowing (it)

insubmersible [ɛsybmersibl] *adj* unsinkable

insuffisant, e [ɛsyfizɑ̃, ɑ̃t] *adj* (*en quantité*) insufficient; (*en qualité*) inadequate; (*sur une copie*) poor

insulaire [ɛsyler] *adj* island *cpd*; (*attitude*) insular

insuline [ɛsylin] *nf* insulin

insulte [ɛsylt] *nf* insult; **insulter** *vt* to insult

insupportable [ɛsyportabl] *adj* unbearable

insurger [ɛsyrʒe] *vb*: **s'~ (contre)** to rise up ou rebel (against)

insurmontable [ɛsyrmɔ̃tabl] *adj* (*difficulté*) insuperable; (*aversion*) unconquerable

insurrection [ɛsyreksjɔ̃] *nf* insurrection

intact, e [ɛtakt] *adj* intact

intangible [ɛtɑ̃ʒibl] *adj* intangible; (*principe*) inviolable

intarissable [ɛtarisabl] *adj* inexhaustible

intégral, e, -aux [ɛtegral, o] *adj* complete; **texte ~** unabridged version; **bronzage ~** all-over suntan; **intégralement** *adv* in full; **intégralité** *nf* whole; **dans son intégralité** in full; **intégrant, e** *adj*: **faire partie intégrante de** to be an integral part of

intègre [ɛtegr] *adj* upright

intégrer [ɛtegre] *vt*: **bien s'~** to integrate well

intégrisme [ɛtegrism] *nm* fundamentalism

intellectuel, le [ɛtelektɥel] *adj* intellectual ♦ *nm/f* intellectual; (*péj*) highbrow

intelligence [ɛteliʒɑ̃s] *nf* intelligence; (*compréhension*): **l'~ de** the understanding of; (*complicité*): **regard d'~** glance of complicity; (*accord*): **vivre en bonne ~ avec qn** to be on good terms with sb

intelligent, e [ɛteliʒɑ̃, ɑ̃t] *adj* intelligent

intelligible [ɛteliʒibl] *adj* intelligible

intempéries [ɛtɑ̃peri] *nfpl* bad weather *sg*

intempestif, -ive [ɛtɑ̃pestif, iv] *adj* untimely

intenable [ɛt(ə)nabl] *adj* (*chaleur*) unbearable

intendant, e [ɛtɑ̃dɑ̃] *nm/f* (*MIL*) quartermaster; (*SCOL*) bursar

intense [ɛtɑ̃s] *adj* intense; **intensif, -ive** *adj* intensive; **un cours intensif** a crash course

intenter [ɛtɑ̃te] *vt*: **~ un procès contre** ou **à** to start proceedings against

intention [ɛtɑ̃sjɔ̃] *nf* intention; (*JUR*) intent; **avoir l'~ de faire** to intend to do; **à l'~ de** for; (*renseignement*) for the benefit of; (*film, ouvrage*) aimed at; **à cette ~** with this aim in view; **intentionné, e** *adj*: **bien intentionné** well-meaning ou -intentioned; **mal inten-**

tionné ill-intentioned

interactif, -ive [ɛ̃tɛʀaktif, iv] *adj* (COM-PUT) interactive

intercalaire [ɛ̃tɛʀkalɛʀ] *nm* divider

intercaler [ɛ̃tɛʀkale] *vt* to insert

intercepter [ɛ̃tɛʀsɛpte] *vt* to intercept; (*lumière, chaleur*) to cut off

interchangeable [ɛ̃tɛʀʃɑ̃ʒabl] *adj* interchangeable

interclasse [ɛ̃tɛʀklɑs] *nm* (SCOL) break (between classes)

interdiction [ɛ̃tɛʀdiksjɔ̃] *nf* ban; ~ de **stationner** no parking; ~ **de fumer** no smoking

interdire [ɛ̃tɛʀdiʀ] *vt* to forbid; (ADMIN) to ban, prohibit; (: *journal, livre*) to ban; ~ **à qn de faire** to forbid sb to do; (*suj: empêchement*) to prevent sb from doing

interdit, e [ɛ̃tɛʀdi, it] *adj* (*stupéfait*) taken aback

intéressant, e [ɛ̃teʀesɑ̃, ɑ̃t] *adj* interesting; (*avantageux*) attractive

intéressé, e [ɛ̃teʀese] *adj* (*parties*) involved, concerned; (*amitié, motifs*) self-interested

intéresser [ɛ̃teʀese] *vt* (*captiver*) to interest; (*toucher*) to be of interest to; (ADMIN: *concerner*) to affect, concern; **s'~ à** to be interested in

intérêt [ɛ̃teʀɛ] *nm* interest; (*égoïsme*) self-interest; **tu as ~ à accepter** it's in your interest to accept; **tu as ~ à te dépêcher** you'd better hurry

intérieur, e [ɛ̃teʀjœʀ] *adj* (*mur, escalier, poche*) inside; (*commerce, politique*) domestic; (*cour, calme, vie*) inner; (*navigation*) inland ♦ *nm* (*d'une maison, d'un récipient etc*) inside; (*d'un pays, aussi décor, mobilier*) interior; **à l'~ (de)** inside; **intérieurement** *adv* inwardly

intérim [ɛ̃teʀim] *nm* interim period; **faire de l'~** to temp; **assurer l'~ (de)** to deputize (for); **par ~** interim

intérimaire [ɛ̃teʀimɛʀ] *adj* (*directeur, ministre*) acting; (*secrétaire, personnel*) temporary ♦ *nm/f* (*secrétaire*) temporary

secretary, temp (BRIT)

interlocuteur, -trice [ɛ̃tɛʀlɔkytœʀ, tʀis] *nm/f* speaker; **son ~** the person he was speaking to

interloquer [ɛ̃tɛʀlɔke] *vt* to take aback

intermède [ɛ̃tɛʀmɛd] *nm* interlude

intermédiaire [ɛ̃tɛʀmedjɛʀ] *adj* intermediate; (*solution*) temporary ♦ *nm/f* intermediary; (COMM) middleman; **sans ~** directly; **par l'~ de** through

interminable [ɛ̃tɛʀminabl] *adj* endless

intermittence [ɛ̃tɛʀmitɑ̃s] *nf*: **par ~** sporadically, intermittently

internat [ɛ̃tɛʀna] *nm* boarding school

international, e, -aux [ɛ̃tɛʀnasjɔnal, o] *adj*, *nm/f* international

interne [ɛ̃tɛʀn] *adj* internal ♦ *nm/f* (SCOL) boarder; (MÉD) houseman

interner [ɛ̃tɛʀne] *vt* (POL) to intern; (MÉD) to confine to a mental institution

Internet [ɛ̃tɛʀnɛt] *nm*: **l'~** the Internet

interpeller [ɛ̃tɛʀpəle] *vt* (*appeler*) to call out to; (*apostropher*) to shout at; (POLICE, POL) to question; (*concerner*) to concern

interphone [ɛ̃tɛʀfɔn] *nm* intercom; (*d'immeuble*) entry phone

interposer [ɛ̃tɛʀpoze] *vt*: **s'~** to intervene; **par personnes interposées** through a third party

interprétation [ɛ̃tɛʀpʀetasjɔ̃] *nf* interpretation

interprète [ɛ̃tɛʀpʀɛt] *nm/f* interpreter; (*porte-parole*) spokesperson

interpréter [ɛ̃tɛʀpʀete] *vt* to interpret; (*jouer*) to play; (*chanter*) to sing

interrogateur, -trice [ɛ̃teʀɔgatœʀ, tʀis] *adj* questioning, inquiring

interrogatif, -ive [ɛ̃teʀɔgatif, iv] *adj* (LING) interrogative

interrogation [ɛ̃teʀɔgasjɔ̃] *nf* question; (*action*) questioning; (SCOL) (written *ou* oral) test

interrogatoire [ɛ̃teʀɔgatwaʀ] *nm* (POLICE) questioning no pl; (JUR, aussi fig) cross-examination

interroger [ɛ̃teʀɔʒe] *vt* to question; (IN-

FORM) to consult; (SCOL) to test

interrompre [ɛ̃teʀɔ̃pʀ] vt (_gén_) to interrupt; (_négociations_) to break off; (_match_) to stop; **s'~** to break off; **interrupteur** nm switch; **interruption** nf interruption; (_pause_) break; **sans interruption** without stopping

intersection [ɛ̃tɛʀsɛksjɔ̃] nf intersection

interstice [ɛ̃tɛʀstis] nm crack; (_de volet_) slit

interurbain, e [ɛ̃teʀyʀbɛ̃, ɛn] adj (TÉL) long-distance

intervalle [ɛ̃tɛʀval] nm (_espace_) space; (_de temps_) interval; **à deux jours d'~** two days apart

intervenir [ɛ̃tɛʀvəniʀ] vi (_gén_) to intervene; **~ auprès de qn** to intervene with sb

intervention [ɛ̃tɛʀvɑ̃sjɔ̃] nf intervention; (_discours_) speech; **intervention chirurgicale** (surgical) operation

intervertir [ɛ̃tɛʀvɛʀtiʀ] vt to invert (the order of), reverse

interview [ɛ̃tɛʀvju] nf interview

intestin [ɛ̃tɛstɛ̃, in] nm intestine

intime [ɛ̃tim] adj intimate; (_vie_) private; (_conviction_) inmost; (_dîner, cérémonie_) quiet ♦ nm/f close friend; **un journal ~** a diary

intimider [ɛ̃timide] vt to intimidate

intimité [ɛ̃timite] nf: **dans l'~** in private; (_sans formalités_) with only a few friends, quietly

intitulé, e [ɛ̃tityle] adj entitled

intolérable [ɛ̃tɔleʀabl] adj intolerable

intox [ɛ̃tɔks] (_fam_) nf brainwashing

intoxication [ɛ̃tɔksikasjɔ̃] nf: **~ alimentaire** food poisoning

intoxiquer [ɛ̃tɔksike] vt to poison; (_fig_) to brainwash

intraduisible [ɛ̃tʀadɥizibl] adj untranslatable; (_fig_) inexpressible

intraitable [ɛ̃tʀɛtabl] adj inflexible, uncompromising

intranet [ɛ̃tʀanɛt] nm intranet

intransigeant, e [ɛ̃tʀɑ̃ziʒɑ̃, ɑ̃t] adj intransigent

intransitif, -ive [ɛ̃tʀɑ̃zitif, iv] adj (LING) intransitive

intrépide [ɛ̃tʀepid] adj dauntless

intrigue [ɛ̃tʀig] nf (_scénario_) plot; **intriguer** vt to puzzle, intrigue

intrinsèque [ɛ̃tʀɛ̃sɛk] adj intrinsic

introduction [ɛ̃tʀɔdyksjɔ̃] nf introduction

introduire [ɛ̃tʀɔdɥiʀ] vt to introduce; (_visiteur_) to show in; (_aiguille, clef_): **~ qch dans** to insert ou introduce sth into; **s'~ (dans)** to get in(to); (_dans un groupe_) to get o.s. accepted (into)

introuvable [ɛ̃tʀuvabl] adj which cannot be found; (COMM) unobtainable

introverti, e [ɛ̃tʀɔvɛʀti] nm/f introvert

intrus, e [ɛ̃tʀy, yz] nm/f intruder

intrusion [ɛ̃tʀyzjɔ̃] nf intrusion

intuition [ɛ̃tɥisjɔ̃] nf intuition

inusable [inyzabl] adj hard-wearing

inusité, e [inyzite] adj rarely used

inutile [inytil] adj useless; (_superflu_) unnecessary; **inutilement** adv unnecessarily; **inutilisable** adj unusable

invalide [ɛ̃valid] adj disabled ♦ nm: **~ de guerre** disabled ex-serviceman

invariable [ɛ̃vaʀjabl] adj invariable

invasion [ɛ̃vazjɔ̃] nf invasion

invectiver [ɛ̃vɛktive] vt to hurl abuse at

invendable [ɛ̃vɑ̃dabl] adj unsaleable; (COMM) unmarketable; **invendus** nmpl unsold goods

inventaire [ɛ̃vɑ̃tɛʀ] nm inventory; (COMM: _liste_) stocklist; (: _opération_) stocktaking no pl

inventer [ɛ̃vɑ̃te] vt to invent; (_subterfuge_) to devise, invent; (_histoire, excuse_) to make up, invent; **inventeur** nm inventor; **inventif, -ive** adj inventive; **invention** nf invention

inverse [ɛ̃vɛʀs] adj opposite ♦ nm opposite; **dans l'ordre ~** in the reverse order; **en sens ~** in (ou from) the opposite direction; **dans le sens ~ des aiguilles d'une montre** anticlockwise;

tu t'es trompé, c'est l'~ you've got it wrong, it's the other way round; **inversement** adv conversely; **inverser** vt to invert, reverse; (ÉLEC) to reverse

investigation [ɛ̃vestigasjɔ̃] nf investigation

investir [ɛ̃vestir] vt to invest; **investissement** nm investment; **investiture** nf nomination

invétéré, e [ɛ̃vetere] adj inveterate

invisible [ɛ̃vizibl] adj invisible

invitation [ɛ̃vitasjɔ̃] nf invitation

invité, e [ɛ̃vite] nm/f guest

inviter [ɛ̃vite] vt to invite

invivable [ɛ̃vivabl] adj unbearable

involontaire [ɛ̃vɔlɔ̃tɛr] adj (mouvement) involuntary; (insulte) unintentional; (complice) unwitting

invoquer [ɛ̃vɔke] vt (Dieu, muse) to call upon, invoke; (prétexte) to put forward (as an excuse); (loi, texte) to refer to

invraisemblable [ɛ̃vrɛsɑ̃blabl] adj (fait, nouvelle) unlikely, improbable; (insolence, habit) incredible

iode [jɔd] nm iodine

irai etc [ire] vb voir aller

Irak [irak] nm Iraq; **irakien, ne** Iraqi ♦ nm/f: **Irakien, ne** Iraqi

Iran [irɑ̃] nm Iran; **iranien, ne** Iranian ♦ nm/f: **Iranien, ne** Iranian

irascible [irasibl] adj short-tempered

irions etc [irjɔ̃] vb voir aller

iris [iris] nm iris

irlandais, e [irlɑ̃dɛ, ɛz] adj Irish ♦ nm/f: **Irlandais, e** Irishman(-woman); **les Irlandais** the Irish

Irlande [irlɑ̃d] nf Ireland; **~ du Nord** Northern Ireland; **la République d'~** the Irish Republic

ironie [irɔni] nf irony; **ironique** adj ironical; **ironiser** vi to be ironical

irons etc [irɔ̃] vb voir aller

irradier [iradje] vt to irradiate

irraisonné, e [irezɔne] adj irrational

irrationnel, le [irasjɔnɛl] adj irrational

irréalisable [irealizabl] adj unrealizable; (projet) impracticable

irrécupérable [irekyperabl] adj beyond repair; (personne) beyond redemption

irréductible [iredyktibl] adj (volonté) indomitable; (ennemi) implacable

irréel, le [ireɛl] adj unreal

irréfléchi, e [irefleʃi] adj thoughtless

irrégularité [iregylarite] nf irregularity; (de travail, d'effort, de qualité) unevenness no pl

irrégulier, -ière [iregylje, jɛr] adj irregular; (travail, effort, qualité) uneven; (élève, athlète) erratic

irrémédiable [iremedjabl] adj irreparable

irremplaçable [irɑ̃plasabl] adj irreplaceable

irréparable [ireparabl] adj (objet) beyond repair; (dommage zéro) irreparable

irréprochable [ireproʃabl] adj irreproachable, beyond reproach; (tenue) impeccable

irrésistible [irezistibl] adj irresistible; (besoin, désir, preuve, logique) compelling; (amusant) hilarious

irrésolu, e [irezɔly] adj (personne) irresolute; (problème) unresolved

irrespectueux, -euse [irespektyø, øz] adj disrespectful

irrespirable [irespirabl] adj unbreathable; (fig) oppressive

irresponsable [irespɔ̃sabl] adj irresponsible

irriguer [irige] vt to irrigate

irritable [iritabl] adj irritable

irriter [irite] vt to irritate

irruption [irypsjɔ̃] nf: **faire ~ (chez qn)** to burst in (on sb)

Islam [islam] nm Islam; **islamique** adj Islamic; **islamiste** adj (militant) Islamic; (mouvement) Islamic fundamentalist ♦ nm/f Islamic fundamentalist

Islande [islɑ̃d] nf Iceland

isolant, e [izɔlɑ̃, ɑ̃t] adj insulating; (insonorisant) soundproofing

isolation [izɔlasjɔ̃] nf insulation

isolé, e [izɔle] adj isolated; (contre le

froid) insulated

isoler [izɔle] *vt* to isolate; *(prisonnier)* to put in solitary confinement; *(ville)* to cut off, isolate; *(contre le froid)* to insulate; **s'~** *vi* to isolate o.s.; **isoloir** [izɔlwaʀ] *nm* polling booth

Israël [israɛl] *nm* Israel; **israélien, ne** *adj* Israeli ♦ *nm/f:* **Israélien, ne** Israeli; **israélite** *adj* Jewish ♦ *nm/f:* **Israélite** Jew (Jewess)

issu, e [isy] *adj:* **~ de** *(né de)* descended from; *(résultant de)* stemming from; **issue** *nf (ouverture, sortie)* exit; *(solution)* way out, solution; *(dénouement)* outcome; **à l'issue de** at the conclusion *ou* close of; **voie sans issue** dead end; **issue de secours** emergency exit

Italie [itali] *nf* Italy; **italien, ne** *adj* Italian ♦ *nm/f:* **Italien, ne** Italian ♦ *nm (LING)* Italian

italique [italik] *nm:* **en ~** in italics

itinéraire [itineʀɛʀ] *nm* itinerary, route; **~ bis** diversion

IUT *sigle m* **= Institut universitaire de technologie**

IVG *sigle f* (= **interruption volontaire de grossesse**) abortion

ivoire [ivwaʀ] *nm* ivory

ivre [ivʀ] *adj* drunk; **~ de** *(colère, bonheur)* wild with; **ivresse** *nf* drunkenness; **ivrogne** *nm/f* drunkard

J, j

j' [ʒ] *pron voir* **je**

jacasser [ʒakase] *vi* to chatter

jacinthe [ʒasɛ̃t] *nf* hyacinth

jadis [ʒadis] *adv* long ago

jaillir [ʒajiʀ] *vi (liquide)* to spurt out; *(cris, responses)* to burst forth

jais [ʒɛ] *nm* jet; **(d'un noir) de ~** jet-black

jalousie [ʒaluzi] *nf* jealousy; *(store)* slatted blind

jaloux, -ouse [ʒalu, uz] *adj* jealous

jamais [ʒamɛ] *adv* never; *(sans négation)* ever; **ne ... ~** never; **à ~** for ever

jambe [ʒɑ̃b] *nf* leg

jambon [ʒɑ̃bɔ̃] *nm* ham; **~ blanc** boiled *ou* cooked ham; **jambonneau, x** *nm* knuckle of ham

jante [ʒɑ̃t] *nf (wheel)* rim

janvier [ʒɑ̃vje] *nm* January

Japon [ʒapɔ̃] *nm* Japan; **japonais, e** *adj* Japanese ♦ *nm/f:* **Japonais, e** Japanese ♦ *nm (LING)* Japanese

japper [ʒape] *vi* to yap, yelp

jaquette [ʒakɛt] *nf (de cérémonie)* morning coat

jardin [ʒaʀdɛ̃] *nm* garden; **~ d'enfants** nursery school; **jardinage** *nm* gardening; **jardiner** [ʒaʀdine] *vi* to do some gardening; **jardinier, -ière** *nm/f* gardener; **jardinière** *nf* planter; *(de fenêtre)* window box; **jardinière de légumes** mixed vegetables

jargon [ʒaʀgɔ̃] *nm (baragouin)* gibberish; *(langue professionnelle)* jargon

jarret [ʒaʀɛ] *nm* back of knee; *(CULIN)* knuckle, shin

jarretelle [ʒaʀtɛl] *nf* suspender *(BRIT)*, garter *(US)*

jarretière [ʒaʀtjɛʀ] *nf* garter

jaser [ʒaze] *vi (médire)* to gossip

jatte [ʒat] *nf* basin, bowl

jauge [ʒoʒ] *nf (instrument)* gauge; **~ d'essence** petrol gauge; **~ d'huile** (oil) dipstick

jaune [ʒon] *adj, nm* yellow ♦ *adv (fam):* **rire ~** to laugh on the other side of one's face; **~ d'œuf** (egg) yolk; **jaunir** *vi, vt* to turn yellow; **jaunisse** *nf* jaundice

Javel [ʒavɛl] *nf voir* **eau**

javelot [ʒavlo] *nm* javelin

J.-C. *abr = Jésus-Christ*

je, j' [ʒə] *pron* I

jean [dʒin] *nm* jeans *pl*

Jésus-Christ [ʒezykʀi(st)] *n* Jesus Christ; **600 avant/après ~-~** *ou* **J.-C.** 600 B.C./A.D.

jet¹ [ʒɛ] *nm (lancer: action)* throwing *no*

pl; (: *résultat*) throw; (*jaillissement:
d'eaux*) jet; (: *de sang*) spurt; **~ d'eau**
spray

jet² [dʒɛt] *nm* (*avion*) jet

jetable [ʒ(ə)tabl] *adj* disposable

jetée [ʒəte] *nf* jetty; (*grande*) pier

jeter [ʒ(ə)te] *vt* (*gén*) to throw; (*se défaire de*) to throw away ou out; **se ~
dans** to flow into; **~ qch à qn** to
throw sth to sb; (*de façon agressive*) to
throw sth at sb; **~ un coup d'œil (à)**
to take a look (at); **~ un sort à qn** to
cast a spell on sb; **se ~ sur qn** to rush
at sb

jeton [ʒətɔ̃] *nm* (*au jeu*) counter

jette *etc* [ʒɛt] *vb voir* **jeter**

jeu, x [ʒø] *nm* (*divertissement, TECH:
d'une pièce*) play; (*TENNIS: partie, FOOT-
BALL etc: façon de jouer*) game; (*THÉÂTRE
etc*) acting; (*série d'objets, jouet*) set;
(*CARTES*) hand; (*au casino*): **le ~** gambling; **être en ~** to be at stake;
entrer/mettre en ~ to come/bring
into play; **~ de cartes** pack of cards; **~
d'échecs** chess set; **~ de hasard** game
of chance; **~ de mots** pun; **~ de société** parlour game; **~ télévisé** television quiz; **~ vidéo** video game

jeudi [ʒødi] *nm* Thursday

jeun [ʒœ̃]: **à ~** *adv* on an empty stomach; **être à ~** to have eaten nothing;
rester à ~ not to eat anything

jeune [ʒœn] *adj* young; **les ~s** young
people; **~ fille** girl; **~ homme** young
man; **~s mariés** newly-weds

jeûne [ʒøn] *nm* fast

jeunesse [ʒœnɛs] *nf* youth; (*aspect*)
youthfulness

joaillerie [ʒɔajʀi] *nf* jewellery; (*magasin*) jeweller's; **joaillier, -ière** *nm/f*
jeweller

jogging [dʒɔgin] *nm* jogging; (*survêtement*) tracksuit; **faire du ~** to go
jogging

joie [ʒwa] *nf* joy

joindre [ʒwɛ̃dʀ] *vt* to join; (*à une
lettre*): **~ qch à** to enclose sth with;

(*contacter*) to contact, get in touch
with; **se ~ à** to join; **~ les mains** to
put one's hands together

joint, e [ʒwɛ̃, ɛ̃t] *adj*: **pièce ~e** enclosure ♦ *nm* joint; (*ligne*) join; **~ de
culasse** cylinder head gasket; **~ de robinet** washer

joker [(d)ʒɔkɛʀ] *nm* (*INFORM*: **caractère** *m*) ~ wildcard

joli, e [ʒɔli] *adj* pretty, attractive; **c'est
du ~!** (*ironique*) that's very nice!; **c'est
bien ~, mais ...** that's all very well but
...

jonc [ʒɔ̃] *nm* (bul)rush

jonction [ʒɔ̃ksjɔ̃] *nf* junction

jongleur, -euse [ʒɔ̃glœʀ, øz] *nm/f* jug-
gler

jonquille [ʒɔ̃kij] *nf* daffodil

Jordanie [ʒɔʀdani] *nf*: **la ~** Jordan

joue [ʒu] *nf* cheek

jouer [ʒwe] *vt* to play; (*somme d'argent,
réputation*) to stake, wager; (*simuler:
sentiment*) to affect, feign ♦ *vi* to play;
(*THÉÂTRE, CINÉMA*) to act; (*au casino*) to
gamble; (*bois, porte: se voiler*) to warp;
(*clef, pièce: avoir du jeu*) to be loose; **~
sur** (*miser*) to gamble on; **~ de** (*MUS*)
to play; **~ à** (*jeu, sport, roulette*) to
play; **~ un tour à qn** to play a trick on
sb; **~ serré** to play a close game; **~ la
comédie** to put on an act; **bien joué!**
well done!; **on joue Hamlet au
théâtre X** Hamlet is on at the X
theatre

jouet [ʒwɛ] *nm* toy; **être le ~ de** (*illusion etc*) to be the victim of

joueur, -euse [ʒwœʀ, øz] *nm/f* player;
être beau ~ to be a good loser

joufflu, e [ʒufly] *adj* chubby-cheeked

joug [ʒu] *nm* yoke

jouir [ʒwiʀ] *vi* (*sexe: fam*) to come ♦ *vt*:
~ de to enjoy; **jouissance** *nf* pleasure;
(*JUR*) use

joujou [ʒuʒu] (*fam*) *nm* toy

jour [ʒuʀ] *nm* day; (*opposé à la nuit*)
day, daytime; (*clarté*) daylight; (*fig:
aspect*) light; (*ouverture*) gap; **au ~ le**

from day to day; **de nos ~s** these days; **du ~ au lendemain** overnight; **il fait ~** it's daylight; **au grand ~** (fig) in the open; **mettre au ~** to disclose; **mettre à ~** to update; **donner le ~ à** to give birth to; **voir le ~** to be born; **~ férié** public holiday; **~ de fête** holiday; **~ ouvrable** working day

journal, -aux [ʒuʀnal, o] nm (news)paper; (spécialisé) journal; (intime) diary; **~ de bord** log; **~ télévisé** television news sg

journalier, -ière [ʒuʀnalje, jɛʀ] adj daily; (banal) everyday

journalisme [ʒuʀnalism] nm journalism; **journaliste** nm/f journalist

journée [ʒuʀne] nf day; **faire la ~ continue** to work over lunch

journellement [ʒuʀnɛlmɑ] adv daily

joyau, x [ʒwajo] nm gem, jewel

joyeux, -euse [ʒwajø, øz] adj joyful, merry; **~ Noël!** merry Christmas!; **~ anniversaire!** happy birthday!

jubiler [ʒybile] vi to be jubilant, exult

jucher [ʒyʃe] vt, vi to perch

judas [ʒyda] nm (trou) spy-hole

judiciaire [ʒydisjɛʀ] adj judicial

judicieux, -euse [ʒydisjø, jøz] adj judicious

judo [ʒydo] nm judo

juge [ʒyʒ] nm judge; **~ d'instruction** examining (BRIT) ou committing (US) magistrate; **~ de paix** justice of the peace; **~ de touche** linesman

jugé [ʒyʒe] : **au ~** adv by guesswork

jugement [ʒyʒmɑ] nm judgment; (JUR: au pénal) sentence; (: au civil) decision

jugeote [ʒyʒɔt] (fam) nf commonsense

juger [ʒyʒe] vt to judge; (estimer) to consider; **~ qn/qch satisfaisant** to consider sb/sth (to be) satisfactory; **~ bon de faire** to see fit to do; **~ de** to appreciate

juif, -ive [ʒɥif, ʒɥiv] adj Jewish ♦ nm/f: **J~, ive** Jew (Jewess)

juillet [ʒɥijɛ] nm July

---

14 juillet

In France, **le 14 juillet** is a national holiday commemorating the storming of the Bastille during the French Revolution, celebrated by parades, music, dancing and firework displays. In Paris, there is a military parade along the Champs-Élysées, attended by the President.

---

juin [ʒɥɛ] nm June

jumeau, -elle, x [ʒymo, ɛl] adj, nm/f twin

jumeler [ʒym(ə)le] vt to twin

jumelle [ʒymɛl] adj, nf voir **jumeau**; **~s** nfpl (appareil) binoculars

jument [ʒymɑ] nf mare

jungle [ʒœgl] nf jungle

jupe [ʒyp] nf skirt

jupon [ʒypɔ] nm waist slip

juré, e [ʒyʀe] nm/f juror

jurer [ʒyʀe] vt (obéissance etc) to swear, vow ♦ vi (dire des jurons) to swear, curse; (dissoner): **(avec)** to clash (with); **~ de faire/que** to swear to do/ that; **~ de qch** (s'en porter garant) to swear to sth

juridique [ʒyʀidik] adj legal

juron [ʒyʀɔ] nm curse, swearword

jury [ʒyʀi] nm jury; (ART, SPORT) panel of judges; (SCOL) board of examiners

jus [ʒy] nm juice; (de viande) gravy, (meat) juice; **~ de fruit** fruit juice

jusque [ʒysk]: **jusqu'à** prép (endroit) as far as, (up) to; (moment) until, till; (limite) up to; **~ sur/dans** up to; (y compris) even on/in; **jusqu'à ce que** until, **jusqu'à présent** so far; **jusqu'où?** how far?

justaucorps [ʒystokɔʀ] nm leotard

juste [ʒyst] adj (équitable) just, fair; (légitime) just; (exact) right; (pertinent) apt; (étroit) tight; (insuffisant) on the short side ♦ adv rightly, correctly; (chanter) in tune; (exactement, seulement) just; **~ assez/au-dessus** just enough/above; **au ~** exactly; **le ~ milieu** the happy medium; **c'était ~** it was a close thing; **justement** adv justly; (*précisément*) just, precisely; **justesse** nf (*précision*) accuracy; (*d'une remarque*) aptness; (*d'une opinion*) soundness; **de justesse** only just

justice [ʒystis] nf (*équité*) fairness, justice; (ADMIN) justice; **rendre ~ à qn** to do sb justice; **justicier, -ière** nm/f righter of wrongs

justificatif, -ive [ʒystifikatif, iv] adj (*document*) supporting; **pièce justificative** written proof

justifier [ʒystifje] vt to justify; **~ de** to prove

juteux, -euse [ʒytø, øz] adj juicy

juvénile [ʒyvenil] adj youthful

K, k

K [kɑ] nm (INFORM) K

kaki [kaki] adj inv khaki

kangourou [kãguʀu] nm kangaroo

karaté [kaʀate] nm karate

karting [kaʀtiŋ] nm go-carting, karting

kascher [kaʃɛʀ] adj kosher

kayak [kajak] nm canoe, kayak; **faire du ~** to go canoeing

kermesse [kɛʀmɛs] nf (*fête de charité*) bazaar, (charity) fête

kidnapper [kidnape] vt to kidnap

kilo [kilo] nm = **kilogramme**

kilo...: kilobit [kilobit] nm kilobit; **kilogramme** nm kilogramme; **kilométrage** nm number of kilometres travelled, ≃ mileage; **kilomètre** nm kilometre; **kilométrique** adj (*distance*) in kilometres

kinésithérapeute [kineziteʀapøt] nm/f physiotherapist

kiosque [kjɔsk] nm kiosk, stall; **~ à musique** bandstand

kir [kiʀ] nm kir (*white wine with blackcurrant liqueur*)

kit [kit] nm: **en ~** in kit form

klaxon [klaksɔn] nm horn; **klaxonner** vi, vt to hoot (BRIT), honk (US)

km abr = **kilomètre**

km/h abr (= *kilomètres/heure*) ≃ mph

K.-O. (fam) adj inv shattered, knackered

Kosovo [kɔsɔvo] nm Kosovo

k-way ® [kawe] nm (*lightweight nylon*) cagoule

kyste [kist] nm cyst

L, l

l' [l] art déf voir **le**

la [la] art déf voir **le** ♦ nm (MUS) A; (*en chantant la gamme*) la

là [la] adv there; (*ici*) here; (*dans le temps*) then; **elle n'est pas ~** she isn't here; **c'est ~ que** this is where; **~ où** where; **de ~** (*fig*) hence; **par ~** (*fig*) by that; voir aussi **-ci**; **ce**; **celui**; **là-bas** adv there

label [label] nm stamp, seal

labeur [labœʀ] nm toil no pl, toiling no pl

labo [labo] (fam) nm (= *laboratoire*) lab

laboratoire [labɔʀatwaʀ] nm laboratory; **~ de langues** language laboratory

laborieux, -euse [labɔʀjø, jøz] adj (*tâche*) laborious

labour [labuʀ] nm ploughing no pl; **~s** nmpl (*champs*) ploughed fields; **cheval de ~** plough- ou cart-horse; **labourer** vt to plough

labyrinthe [labiʀɛ̃t] nm labyrinth, maze

lac [lak] nm lake

lacer [lase] vt to lace ou do up

lacérer [laseʀe] vt to tear to shreds

lacet [lasɛ] nm (*de chaussure*) lace; (*de route*) sharp bend; (*piège*) snare

lâche [laʃ] adj (*poltron*) cowardly; (*desserré*) loose, slack ♦ nm/f coward

lâcher [laʃe] vt to let go of; (*ce qui tombe, abandonne*) to drop; (*oiseau, animal: libérer*) to release, set free; (*fig: mot, remarque*) to let slip, come out with ♦ *vi* (*freins*) to fail; ~ **les amarres** (*NAVIG*) to cast off (the moorings); ~ **prise** to let go

lâcheté [lɑʃte] *nf* cowardice

lacrymogène [lakʀimɔʒɛn] *adj*: **gaz** ~ teargas

lacté, e [lakte] *adj* (*produit, régime*) milk *cpd*

lacune [lakyn] *nf* gap

là-dedans [ladədɑ̃] *adv* inside (there), in it; (*fig*) in that

là-dessous [ladsu] *adv* underneath, under there; (*fig*) behind that

là-dessus [ladsy] *adv* on there; (*fig*: *sur ces mots*) at that point; (: *à ce sujet*) about that

ladite [ladit] *dét voir* **ledit**

lagune [lagyn] *nf* lagoon

là-haut [lao] *adv* up there

laïc [laik] *adj, nm/f* = **laïque**

laid, e [lɛ, lɛd] *adj* ugly; **laideur** *nf* ugliness *no pl*

lainage [lɛnaʒ] *nm* (*vêtement*) woollen garment; (*étoffe*) woollen material

laine [lɛn] *nf* wool

laïque [laik] *adj* lay, civil; (*SCOL*) state *cpd* ♦ *nm/f* layman(-woman)

laisse [lɛs] *nf* (*de chien*) lead, leash; **tenir en** ~ to keep on a lead *ou* leash

laisser [lese] *vt* to leave ♦ *vb aux*: ~ **qn faire** to let sb do; **se** ~ **aller** to let o.s. go; **laisse-toi faire** let me (*ou* him *etc*) do it; **laisser-aller** *nm* carelessness, slovenliness; **laissez-passer** *nm inv* pass

lait [lɛ] *nm* milk; **frère/sœur de** ~ foster brother/sister; ~ **condensé/ concentré** evaporated/condensed milk; ~ **démaquillant** cleansing milk; **laitage** *nm* (*ANAT*) milk product; **laiterie** *nf* dairy; **laitier, -ière** *adj* dairy *cpd* ♦ *nm/f* milkman (dairywoman)

laiton [lɛtɔ̃] *nm* brass

laitue [lety] *nf* lettuce

laïus [lajys] *nm* (*péj*) spiel

lambeau, x [lɑ̃bo] *nm* scrap; **en** ~**x** in tatters, tattered

lambris [lɑ̃bʀi] *nm* panelling *no pl*

lame [lam] *nf* blade; (*vague*) wave; (~*lle*) strip; ~ **de fond** ground swell *no pl*; ~ **de rasoir** razor blade; **lamelle** *nf* thin strip *ou* blade

lamentable [lamɑ̃tabl] *adj* appalling

lamenter [lamɑ̃te] *vb*: **se** ~ (**sur**) to moan (over)

lampadaire [lɑ̃padɛʀ] *nm* (*de salon*) standard lamp; (*dans la rue*) street lamp

lampe [lɑ̃p] *nf* lamp; (*TECH*) valve; ~ **à souder** blowlamp; ~ **de chevet** bedside lamp; ~ **de poche** torch (*BRIT*), flashlight (*US*)

lampion [lɑ̃pjɔ̃] *nm* Chinese lantern

lance [lɑ̃s] *nf* spear; ~ **d'incendie** fire hose

lancée [lɑ̃se] *nf*: **être/continuer sur sa** ~ to be under way/keep going

lancement [lɑ̃smɑ̃] *nm* launching

lance-pierres [lɑ̃spjɛʀ] *nm inv* catapult

lancer [lɑ̃se] *nm* (*SPORT*) throwing *no pl*, throw ♦ *vt* to throw; (*émettre, projeter*) to throw out, send out; (*produit, fusée, bateau, artiste*) to launch; (*injure*) to hurl, fling; **se** ~ *vi* (*prendre de l'élan*) to build up speed; (*se précipiter*): **se** ~ **sur** *ou* **contre** to rush at; **se** ~ **dans** (*discussion*) to launch into; (*aventure*) to embark on; (*se lancer qch à qn* to throw sth to sb); (*de façon agressive*) to throw sth at; ~ **du poids** putting the shot

lancinant, e [lɑ̃sinɑ̃, ɑ̃t] *adj* (*douleur*) shooting

landau [lɑ̃do] *nm* pram (*BRIT*), baby carriage (*US*)

lande [lɑ̃d] *nf* moor

langage [lɑ̃gaʒ] *nm* language

langouste [lɑ̃gust] *nf* crayfish *inv*; **langoustine** *nf* Dublin Bay prawn

langue [lɑ̃g] *nf* (*ANAT, CULIN*) tongue; (*LING*) language; **tirer la** ~ (**à**) to stick out one's tongue (at); **de** ~ **française** French-speaking; ~ **maternelle** native language, mother tongue; ~ **vivante/ étrangère** modern/foreign language

langueur [lɑ̃gœʀ] nf languidness

languir [lɑ̃giʀ] vi to languish; (conversation) to flag; **faire ~ qn** to keep sb waiting

lanière [lanjɛʀ] nf (de fouet) lash; (de sac, bretelle) strap

lanterne [lɑ̃tɛʀn] nf (portable) lantern; (électrique) light, lamp; (de voiture) (side)light

laper [lape] vt to lap up

lapidaire [lapidɛʀ] adj (fig) terse

lapin [lapɛ̃] nm rabbit; (peau) rabbitskin; (fourrure) cony; **poser un ~ à qn** (fam) to stand sb up

Laponie [laponi] nf Lapland

laps [laps] nm: **~ de temps** space of time, time no pl

laque [lak] nf (vernis) lacquer; (pour cheveux) hair spray

laquelle [lakɛl] pron voir **lequel**

larcin [laʀsɛ̃] nm theft

lard [laʀ] nm (bacon) (streaky) bacon; (graisse) fat

lardon [laʀdɔ̃] nm: **~s** chopped bacon

large [laʀʒ] adj wide, broad; (fig) generous ♦ adv: **calculer/voir ~** to allow extra/think big ♦ nm (largeur): **5 m de ~** 5 m wide ou in width; (mer): **le ~** the open sea; **au ~ de** off; **~ d'esprit** broad-minded; **largement** adv widely; (de loin) greatly; (au moins) easily; (généreusement) generously; **c'est largement suffisant** that's ample; **largesse** nf generosity; **largesses** nfpl (dons) liberalities; **largeur** nf (qu'on mesure) width; (impression visuelle) wideness, width; (d'esprit) broadness

larguer [laʀge] vt to drop; **~ les amarres** to cast off (the moorings)

larme [laʀm] nf tear; (fam: goutte) drop; **en ~s** in tears; **larmoyer** vi (yeux) to water; (se plaindre) to whimper

larvé, e [laʀve] adj (fig) latent

laryngite [laʀɛ̃ʒit] nf laryngitis

las, lasse [lɑ, lɑs] adj weary

laser [lazɛʀ] nm: **(rayon) ~** laser

(beam); **chaîne ~** compact disc (player); **disque ~** compact disc

lasso [laso] nm voir **las**

lasser [lɑse] vt to weary, tire; **se ~ de** to grow weary ou tired of

latéral, e, -aux [lateʀal, o] adj side cpd, lateral

latin, e [latɛ̃, in] adj Latin ♦ nm/f: **L~, e** Latin ♦ nm (LING) Latin

latitude [latityd] nf latitude

latte [lat] nf lath, slat; (de plancher) board

lauréat, e [lɔʀea, at] nm/f winner

laurier [lɔʀje] nm (BOT) laurel; (CULIN) bay leaves pl

lavable [lavabl] adj washable

lavabo [lavabo] nm washbasin; **~s** nmpl (toilettes) toilet sg

lavage [lavaʒ] nm washing no pl, wash; **~ de cerveau** brainwashing no pl

lavande [lavɑ̃d] nf lavender

lave [lav] nf lava no pl

lave-linge [lavlɛ̃ʒ] nm inv washing machine

laver [lave] vt to wash; (tache) to wash off; **se ~** vi to have a wash, wash; **se ~ les mains/dents** to wash one's hands/clean one's teeth; **~ qn de** (accusation) to clear sb of; **laverie** nf: **laverie (automatique)** launderette; **lavette** nf dish cloth; (fam) drip; **laveur, -euse** nm/f cleaner; **lave-vaisselle** nm inv dishwasher; **lavoir** nm wash house; (évier) sink

laxatif, -ive [laksatif, iv] adj, nm laxative

layette [lɛjɛt] nf baby clothes

MOT-CLÉ

le [lə], **la, l'** (pl **les**) art déf **1** the; **le livre/la pomme/l'arbre** the book/the apple/the tree; **les étudiants** the students

2 (noms abstraits): **le courage/l'amour/la jeunesse** courage/love/youth

3 (indiquant la possession): **se casser la**

jambe etc to break one's leg etc; **levez la main** put your hand up; **avoir les yeux gris/le nez rouge** to have grey eyes/a red nose

4 (temps): **le matin/soir** in the morning/evening; **mornings/evenings**; **le jeudi** etc (d'habitude) on Thursdays etc; (ce jeudi-là etc) on (the) Thursday

5 (distribution, évaluation), a, an; **10 F le mètre/kilo** 10F a ou per metre/kilo; **le tiers/quart de** a third/quarter of

♦ pron 1 (personne: mâle) him; (personne: femelle) her; (: pluriel) them; **je le/la/les vois** I can see him/her/them

2 (animal, chose: singulier) it; (: pluriel) them; **je le (ou la) vois** I can see it; **je les vois** I can see them

3 (remplaçant une phrase): **je ne le savais pas** I didn't know (about it); **il était riche et ne l'est plus** he was once rich but no longer is

lécher [leʃe] vt to lick; (laper: lait, eau) to lick ou lap up; **lèche-vitrines** nm: **faire du lèche-vitrines** to go window-shopping

leçon [l(ə)sɔ̃] nf lesson; **faire la ~ à** (fig) to give a lecture to; **~s de conduite** driving lessons

lecteur, -trice [lektœr, tris] nm/f reader; (d'université) foreign language assistant ♦ nm (TECH): **~ de cassettes/CD** cassette/CD player; **~ de disquette** disk drive

lecture [lektyr] nf reading

ledit [lədi], **ladite** (mpl **lesdits**, fpl **lesdites**) dét the aforesaid

légal, e, -aux [legal, o] adj legal; **légaliser** vt to legalize; **légalité** nf law

légendaire [leʒɑ̃dɛr] adj legendary

légende [leʒɑ̃d] nf (mythe) legend; (de carte, plan) key; (de dessin) caption

léger, -ère [leʒe, ɛr] adj light; (bruit, retard) slight; (personne: superficiel) thoughtless; (: volage) free and easy; **à la légère** (parler, agir) rashly, thoughtlessly; **légèrement** adv (s'habiller, bou-

ger) lightly; (un peu) slightly; **manger légèrement** to eat a light meal; **légèreté** nf lightness; (d'une remarque) flippancy

législatif, -ive [leʒislatif, iv] adj legislative; **législatives** nfpl general election sg

légitime [leʒitim] adj (JUR) lawful, legitimate; (fig) rightful, legitimate; **en état de ~ défense** in self-defence

legs [lɛg] nm legacy

léguer [lege] vt: **~ qch à qn** (JUR) to bequeath sth to sb

légume [legym] nm vegetable

lendemain [lɑ̃dmɛ̃] nm: **le ~** the next ou following day; **le ~ matin/soir** the next ou following morning/evening; **le ~ de** the day after

lent, e [lɑ̃, lɑ̃t] adj slow; **lentement** adv slowly; **lenteur** nf slowness no pl

lentille [lɑ̃tij] nf (OPTIQUE) lens sg; (CULIN) lentil

léopard [leɔpar] nm leopard

lèpre [lɛpr] nf leprosy

MOT-CLÉ

lequel, laquelle [ləkɛl, lakɛl] (mpl **lesquels**, fpl **lesquelles**) (à + lequel = **auquel**, de + lequel = **duquel** etc) pron 1 (interrogatif) which, which one

2 (relatif: personne: sujet) who; (: objet, après préposition) whom; (: chose) which

♦ adj: **auquel cas** in which case

les [le] dét voir **le**

lesbienne [lɛsbjɛn] nf lesbian

lesdites [ledit], **lesdits** [ledi] dét pl

voir **ledit**

léser [leze] *vt* to wrong

lésiner [lezine] *vi*: **ne pas ~ sur les moyens** (*pour mariage etc*) to push the boat out

lésion [lezjɔ̃] *nf* lesion, damage *no pl*

lesquelles, lesquels [lekɛl] *pron pl voir* **lequel**

lessive [lesiv] *nf* (*poudre*) washing powder; (*linge*) washing *no pl*, wash; **lessiver** *vt* to wash; (*fam: fatiguer*) to tire out, exhaust

lest [lɛst] *nm* ballast

leste [lɛst] *adj* sprightly, nimble

lettre [lɛtr] *nf* letter; ~**s** *nfpl* (*littérature*) literature *sg*; (*SCOL*) arts (subjects); **à la ~** literally; **en toutes ~s** in full

leucémie [løsemi] *nf* leukaemia

MOT-CLÉ

---

leur [lœr] *adj possessif* their; **leur maison** their house; **leurs amis** their friends

♦ *pron* **1** (*objet indirect*) (to) them; **je leur ai dit la vérité** I told them the truth; **je le leur ai donné** I gave it to them, I gave them it

2 (*possessif*): **le(la) leur, les leurs** theirs

---

leurre [lœr] *nm* (*fig: illusion*) delusion; (*: duperie*) deception; **leurrer** *vt* to delude, deceive

leurs [lœr] *adj voir* **leur**

levain [ləvɛ̃] *nm* leaven

levé, e [ləve] *adj*: **être ~** to be up; **levée** *nf* (*POSTES*) collection

lever [ləve] *vt* (*vitre, bras etc*) to raise; (*soulever de terre, supprimer: interdiction, siège*) to lift; (*impôts, armée*) to levy ♦ *vi* to rise ♦ *nm*: **au ~** on getting up; **se ~** *vi* to get up; (*soleil*) to rise; (*jour*) to break; (*brouillard*) to lift; ~ **du soleil** sunrise; ~ **du jour** daybreak

levier [ləvje] *nm* lever

lèvre [lɛvr] *nf* lip

lévrier [levrije] *nm* greyhound

levure [l(ə)vyr] *nf* yeast; ~ **chimique** baking powder

lexique [lɛksik] *nm* vocabulary; (*glossaire*) lexicon

lézard [lezar] *nm* lizard

lézarde [lezard] *nf* crack

liaison [ljɛzɔ̃] *nf* (*rapport*) connection; (*transport*) link; (*amoureuse*) affair; (*PHONÉTIQUE*) liaison; **entrer/être en ~ avec** to get/be in contact with

liane [ljan] *nf* creeper

liant, e [ljɑ̃, ljɑ̃t] *adj* sociable

liasse [ljas] *nf* wad, bundle

Liban [libɑ̃] *nm*: **le ~** (the) Lebanon; **libanais, e** *adj* Lebanese ♦ *nm/f*: **Libanais, e** Lebanese

libeller [libele] *vt* (*chèque, mandat*): **(au nom de)** to make out (to); (*lettre*) to word

libellule [libelyl] *nf* dragonfly

libéral, e, -aux [liberal, o] *adj, nm/f* liberal; **profession ~e** (liberal) profession

libérer [libere] *vt* (*délivrer*) to free, liberate; (*relâcher: prisonnier*) to discharge, release; (*: d'inhibitions*) to liberate; (*gaz*) to release; **se ~** *vi* (*de rendez-vous*) to get out of previous engagements

liberté [libɛrte] *nf* freedom; (*loisir*) free time; ~**s** *nfpl* (*privautés*) liberties; **mettre/être en ~** to set/be free; **en ~ provisoire/surveillée/conditionnelle** on bail/probation/parole

libraire [librɛr] *nm/f* bookseller

librairie [libreri] *nf* bookshop

libre [libr] *adj* free; (*route, voie*) clear; (*place, salle*) free; (*ligne*) not engaged; (*SCOL*) non-state; ~ **de qch/de faire** free from sth/to do; ~ **arbitre** free will; **libre-échange** *nm* free trade; **libre-service** *nm* self-service store

Libye [libi] *nf* Libya

licence [lisɑ̃s] *nf* (*permis*) permit; (*diplôme*) degree; (*liberté*) liberty; **licencié, e** *nm/f* (*SCOL*) licencié **ès lettres/ en droit** ≈ Bachelor of Arts/Law

licenciement [lisɑ̃simɑ̃] nm redundancy

licencier [lisɑ̃sje] vt (débaucher) to make redundant; (renvoyer) to dismiss

licite [lisit] adj lawful

lie [li] nf dregs pl, sediment

lié, e [lje] adj: **très ~ avec** very friendly with ou close to

liège [ljɛʒ] nm cork

lien [ljɛ̃] nm (corde, fig: affectif) bond; (rapport) link, connection; **~ de parenté** family tie

lier [lje] vt (attacher) to tie up; (joindre) to link up; (fig: unir, engager) to bind; **se ~ avec** to make friends with; **~ qch à** to tie ou link sth to; **~ conversation avec** to strike up a conversation with

lierre [ljɛr] nm ivy

liesse [ljɛs] nf: **être en ~** to be celebrating ou jubilant

lieu, x [ljø] nm place; **~x** nmpl (locaux) premises; (endroit: d'un accident etc) scene sg; **en ~ sûr** in a safe place; **en premier ~** in the first place; **en dernier ~** lastly; **avoir ~** to take place; **tenir ~ de** to serve as; **donner ~ à** to give rise to; **au ~ de** instead of; **lieu-dit** (pl lieux-dits) nm locality

lieutenant [ljøt(ə)nɑ̃] nm lieutenant

lièvre [ljɛvr] nm hare

ligament [ligamɑ̃] nm ligament

ligne [liɲ] nf (gén) line; (TRANSPORTS: liaison) service; (: trajet) route; (silhouette) figure; **entrer en ~ de compte** to come into it; **en ~** (INFORM) online; **~ fixe** (TEL) fixed line (phone)

lignée [liɲe] nf line, lineage

ligoter [ligɔte] vt to tie up

ligue [lig] nf league; **liguer vt: se liguer contre** (fig) to combine against

lilas [lila] nm lilac

limace [limas] nf slug

limande [limɑ̃d] nf dab

lime [lim] nf lime; **~ à ongles** nail file; **limer** vt to file

limier [limje] nm bloodhound; (détec-

tive) sleuth

limitation [limitasjɔ̃] nf: **~ de vitesse** speed limit

limite [limit] nf (de terrain) boundary; (partie ou point extrême) limit; **vitesse/charge ~** maximum speed/load; **cas ~** borderline case; **date ~** deadline; **limiter** vt (restreindre) to limit, restrict; (délimiter) to border; **limitrophe** adj border cpd

limoger [limɔʒe] vt to dismiss

limon [limɔ̃] nm silt

limonade [limɔnad] nf lemonade

lin [lɛ̃] nm (tissu) linen

linceul [lɛ̃sœl] nm shroud

linge [lɛ̃ʒ] nm (serviettes etc) linen; (lessive) washing; (aussi: **~ de corps**) underwear; **lingerie** nf lingerie, underwear

lingot [lɛ̃go] nm ingot

linguistique [lɛ̃gɥistik] adj linguistic ♦ nf linguistics sg

lion, ne [ljɔ̃, ljɔn] nm/f lion (lioness); (signe): **le L~** Leo; **lionceau, x** nm lion cub

liqueur [likœr] nf liqueur

liquidation [likidasjɔ̃] nf (vente) sale

liquide [likid] adj liquid ♦ nm liquid; (COMM): **en ~** in ready money ou cash; **liquider** vt to liquidate; (COMM: articles) to clear, sell off; **liquidités** nfpl (COMM) liquid assets

lire [lir] nf (monnaie) lira ♦ vt, vi to read

lis [lis] nm = **lys**

lisible [lizibl] adj legible

lisière [lizjɛr] nf (de forêt) edge

lisons [lizɔ̃] vb voir **lire**

lisse [lis] adj smooth

liste [list] nf list; **faire la ~ de** to list; **~ électorale** electoral roll; **listing** nm (IN-FORM) printout

lit [li] nm bed; **petit ~, lit à une place** single bed; **grand ~, lit à deux places** double bed; **faire son ~** to make one's bed; **aller/se mettre au ~** to go to/get into bed; **~ de camp** campbed; **~ d'enfant** cot (BRIT), crib (US)

literie [litʀi] nf bedding, bedclothes pl

litière [litjɛʀ] nf litter

litige [litiʒ] nm dispute

litre [litʀ] nm litre

littéraire [liteʀɛʀ] adj literary ♦ nm/f arts student; **elle est très ~** (she's very literary)

littéral, e, -aux [liteʀal, o] adj literal

littérature [liteʀatyʀ] nf literature

littoral, -aux [litɔʀal, o] nm coast

liturgie [lityʀʒi] nf liturgy

livraison [livʀɛzɔ̃] nf delivery

livre [livʀ] nm book ♦ nf (poids, monnaie) pound; **~ de bord** logbook; **~ de poche** paperback

livré, e [livʀe] adj: **à soi-même** left to o.s. ou one's own devices; **livrée** nf livery

livrer [livʀe] vt (COMM) to deliver; (otage, coupable) to hand over; (secret, information) to give away; **se ~ à** (se confier) to confide in; (se rendre, s'abandonner) to give o.s. up to; (faire: pratiques, actes) to indulge in; (enquête) to carry out

livret [livʀɛ] nm booklet; (d'opéra) libretto; **~ de caisse d'épargne** (savings) bank-book; **~ de famille** (official) family record book; **~ scolaire** (school) report book

livreur, -euse [livʀœʀ, øz] nm/f delivery boy ou man/girl ou woman

local, e, -aux [lɔkal] adj local ♦ nm (salle) premises pl; voir aussi **locaux**; **localiser** vt (repérer) to locate, place; (limiter) to confine; **localité** nf locality

locataire [lɔkatɛʀ] nm/f tenant; (de chambre) lodger

location [lɔkasjɔ̃] nf (par le locataire, le loueur) renting; (par le propriétaire) renting out, letting; (THÉÂTRE) booking office; **"~ de voitures"** "car rental"; **habiter en ~** to live in rented accommodation; **prendre une ~** (pour les vacances) to rent a house etc (for the holidays)

locaux [lɔko] nmpl premises

locomotive [lɔkɔmɔtiv] nf locomotive, engine

locution [lɔkysjɔ̃] nf phrase

loge [lɔʒ] nf (THÉÂTRE: d'artiste) dressing room; (: de spectateurs) box; (de concierge, franc-maçon) lodge

logement [lɔʒmɑ̃] nm accommodation no pl (BRIT), accommodations pl (US); (appartement) flat (BRIT), apartment (US); (hébergement) housing no pl

loger [lɔʒe] vt to accommodate ♦ vi to live; **se ~ dans** (suj: balle, flèche) to lodge itself in; **trouver à se ~** to find accommodation; **logeur, -euse** nm/f landlord(-lady)

logiciel [lɔʒisjɛl] nm software

logique [lɔʒik] adj logical ♦ nf logic

logis [lɔʒi] nm abode, dwelling

logo [lɔgo] nm logo

loi [lwa] nf law; **faire la ~** to lay down the law

loin [lwɛ̃] adv far; (dans le temps: futur) a long way off; (: passé) a long time ago; **plus ~** further; **~ de** far from; **au ~** far off; **de ~** from a distance; (fig: de beaucoup) by far

lointain, e [lwɛ̃tɛ̃, ɛn] adj faraway, distant; (dans le futur, passé) distant; (cause, parent) remote, distant ♦ nm: **dans le ~** in the distance

loir [lwaʀ] nm dormouse

loisir [lwaziʀ] nm: **heures de ~** spare time; **~s** nmpl (temps libre) leisure sg; (activités) leisure activities; **avoir le ~ de faire** to have the time ou opportunity to do; **à ~** at leisure

londonien, ne [lɔ̃dɔnjɛ̃, jɛn] adj London, of London cpd, of London ♦ nm/f: **L~, ne** Londoner

Londres [lɔ̃dʀ] n London

long, longue [lɔ̃, lɔ̃g] adj long ♦ adv: **en savoir** ~ to know a great deal ♦ nm: **de 3 m de** ~ 3 m long, 3 m in length; **ne pas faire ~ feu** not to last long; **(tout) le ~ de** (all) along; **tout au ~ de** (année, vie) throughout; **de ~**

en large (*marcher*) to and fro, up and down; *voir aussi* **longue**

longer [lɔ̃ʒe] *vt* to go (*ou* walk *ou* drive) along(side); (*suj: mur, route*) to border

longiligne [lɔ̃ʒiliɲ] *adj* long-limbed

longitude [lɔ̃ʒityd] *nf* longitude

longtemps [lɔ̃tɑ̃] *adv* (for) a long time, (for) long; **avant ~** before long; **pour** *ou* **pendant ~** for a long time; **mettre ~ à faire** to take a long time to

longue [lɔ̃g] *adj voir* **long ♦** *nf*: **à la ~** in the end; **longuement** *adv* (*longtemps*) for a long time; (*en détail*) at length

longueur [lɔ̃gœʀ] *nf* length; **~s** *nfpl* (*fig: d'un film etc*) tedious parts; **en ~** lengthwise; **tirer en ~** to drag on; **à ~ de journée** all day long; **~ d'onde** wavelength

longue-vue [lɔ̃gvy] *nf* telescope

look [luk] (*fam*) *nm* look, image

lopin [lɔpɛ̃] *nm*: **~ de terre** patch of land

loque [lɔk] *nf* (*personne*) wreck; **~s** *nfpl* (*habits*) rags

loquet [lɔkɛ] *nm* latch

lorgner [lɔʀɲe] *vt* to eye; (*fig*) to have one's eye on

lors [lɔʀ]: **~ de** *prép* at the time of; during

lorsque [lɔʀskə] *conj* when, as

losange [lɔzɑ̃ʒ] *nm* diamond

lot [lo] *nm* (*part*) share; (*de ~erie*) prize; (*fig: destin*) fate, lot; (*COMM, INFORM*) batch; **le gros ~** the jackpot

loterie [lɔtʀi] *nf* lottery

loti, e [lɔti] *adj*: **bien/mal ~** well-/badly off

lotion [losjɔ̃] *nf* lotion

lotissement [lɔtismɑ̃] *nm* housing development; (*parcelle*) plot, lot

loto [lɔto] *nm* lotto

Loto

Le Loto *is a state-run national lottery with large cash prizes. Participants select 7 numbers out of 49. The* more correct numbers, the greater the prize. The draw is televised twice weekly.

---

lotte [lɔt] *nf* monkfish

louable [lwabl] *adj* commendable

louanges [lwɑ̃ʒ] *nfpl* praise *sg*

loubard [lubaʀ] *nm* lout

louche [luʃ] *adj* shady, fishy, dubious **♦** *nf* ladle; **loucher** *vi* to squint

louer [lwe] *vt* (*maison: suj: propriétaire*) to let, rent (out); (: *locataire*) to rent; (*voiture etc: entreprise*) to hire out (*BRIT*), rent (out); (: *locataire*) to hire, rent; (*réserver*) to book; (*faire l'éloge de*) to praise; **"à ~"** "to let" (*BRIT*), "for rent" (*US*)

loup [lu] *nm* wolf

loupe [lup] *nf* magnifying glass

louper [lupe] (*fam*) *vt* (*manquer*) to miss; (*examen*) to flunk

lourd, e [luʀ, luʀd] *adj, adv* heavy; **~ de** (*conséquences, menaces*) charged with; **il fait ~** the weather is close, it's sultry; **lourdaud, e** (*péj*) *adj* clumsy; **lourdement** *adv* heavily; **lourdeur** *nf* weight; **lourdeurs d'estomac** indigestion

loutre [lutʀ] *nf* otter

louveteau, x [luv(ə)to] *nm* wolf-cub; (*scout*) cub (scout)

louvoyer [luvwaje] *vi* (*fig*) to hedge, evade the issue

loyal, e, -aux [lwajal, o] *adj* (*fidèle*) loyal, faithful; (*fair-play*) fair; **loyauté** *nf* loyalty, faithfulness; fairness

loyer [lwaje] *nm* rent

lu, e [ly] *pp de* **lire**

lubie [lybi] *nf* whim, craze

lubrifiant [lybʀifjɑ̃, jɑ̃t] *nm* lubricant

lubrifier [lybʀifje] *vt* to lubricate

lubrique [lybʀik] *adj* lecherous

lucarne [lykaʀn] *nf* skylight

lucide [lysid] *adj* lucid; (*accidenté*) conscious

lucratif, -ive [lykʀatif, iv] *adj* lucrative, profitable; **à but non ~** non profit-making

lueur [lɥœʀ] *nf* (*pâle*) (faint) light; (*chatoyante*) glimmer *no pl*; (*fig*) glimmer; gleam

luge [lyʒ] *nf* sledge (*BRIT*), sled (*US*)

lugubre [lygybʀ] *adj* gloomy, dismal

MOT-CLÉ

---

lui [lɥi] *pron* **1** (*objet indirect: mâle*) (to) him; (: *femelle*) (to) her; (: *chose, animal*) (to) it; **je lui ai parlé** I have spoken to him (*ou* to her); **il lui a offert un cadeau** he gave him (*ou* her) a present

2 (*après préposition, comparatif: personne*) him; (: *chose, animal*) it; **elle est contente de lui** she is pleased with him; **je le connais mieux que lui** I know him better than he does; I know her better than him

3 (*sujet, forme emphatique*) he; **lui, il est à Paris** HE is in Paris

4: **lui-même** himself; itself

---

luire [lɥiʀ] *vi* to shine; (*en rougeoyant*) to glow

lumière [lymjɛʀ] *nf* light; **mettre en ~** (*fig*) to highlight; **~ du jour** daylight

luminaire [lyminɛʀ] *nm* lamp, light

lumineux, -euse [lyminø, øz] *adj* luminous; (*éclairé*) illuminated; (*ciel, couleur*) bright; (*rayon*) of light, light *cpd*; (*fig: regard*) radiant

lunatique [lynatik] *adj* whimsical, temperamental

lundi [lœdi] *nm* Monday; **~ de Pâques** Easter Monday

lune [lyn] *nf* moon; **~ de miel** honeymoon

lunette [lynɛt] *nf*: **~s** ♦ *nfpl* glasses, spectacles; (*protectrices*) goggles; **~ arrière** (*AUTO*) rear window; **~s de soleil** sunglasses

lus *etc* [ly] *vb voir* **lire**

lustre [lystʀ] *nm* (*de plafond*) chandelier; (*fig: éclat*) lustre; **lustrer** *vt* to shine

lut [ly] *vb voir* **lire**

luth [lyt] *nm* lute

lutin [lytɛ̃] *nm* imp, goblin

lutte [lyt] *nf* (*conflit*) struggle; (*sport*) wrestling; **lutter** *vi* to fight, struggle

luxe [lyks] *nm* luxury; **de ~** luxury *cpd*

Luxembourg [lyksɑ̃buʀ] *nm*: **le ~** Luxembourg

luxer [lykse] *vt*: **se ~ l'épaule** to dislocate one's shoulder

luxueux, -euse [lyksɥø, øz] *adj* luxurious

luxure [lyksyʀ] *nf* lust

luxuriant, e [lyksyʀjɑ̃, jɑ̃t] *adj* luxuriant

lycée [lise] *nm* secondary school; **lycéen, ne** *nm/f* secondary school pupil

lyophilisé, e [ljɔfilize] *adj* (*café*) freeze-dried

lyrique [liʀik] *adj* lyrical; (*OPÉRA*) lyric; **artiste ~** opera singer

lys [lis] *nm* lily

M, m

M *abr* = **Monsieur**

m' [m] *pron voir* **me**

ma [ma] *adj voir* **mon**

macaron [makaʀɔ̃] *nm* (*gâteau*) macaroon; (*insigne*) (round) badge

macaronis [makaʀɔni] *nmpl* macaroni *sg*

macédoine [masedwan] *nf*: **~ de fruits** fruit salad; **~ de légumes** mixed vegetables

macérer [maseʀe] *vi, vt* to macerate; (*dans du vinaigre*) to pickle

mâcher [mɑʃe] *vt* to chew; **ne pas ~ ses mots** not to mince one's words

machin [maʃɛ̃] (*fam*) *nm* thing(umajig)

machinal, e, -aux [maʃinal, o] *adj* mechanical, automatic; **machinalement** *adv* mechanically, automatically

machination [maʃinasjɔ̃] *nf* frame-up

machine [maʃin] *nf* machine; (*locomotive*) engine; **~ à écrire** typewriter; **~ à laver/coudre** washing/sewing machine; ~ **à sous** fruit machine

macho [matʃo] (fam) nm male chauvinist

mâchoire [mɑʃwaʀ] nf jaw

mâchonner [mɑʃɔne] vt to chew (at)

maçon [masɔ̃] nm builder; (poseur de briques) bricklayer; **maçonnerie** nf (murs) brickwork; (pierres) masonry, stonework

maculer [makyle] vt to stain

Madame [madam] (pl **Mesdames**) nf: ~ **X** Mrs X; **occupez-vous de** ~/ **Monsieur/Mademoiselle** please serve this lady/gentleman/(young) lady; **bonjour** ~/**Monsieur/Mademoiselle** good morning; (ton déférent) good morning Madam/Sir/Madam; (le nom est connu) good morning Mrs/Mr/Miss X; **Monsieur/Mademoiselle!** (pour appeler) Madam/Sir/Miss!; ~/**Monsieur/ Mademoiselle** (sur lettre) Dear Madam/Sir/Madam; **chère** ~/**cher Monsieur/chère Mademoiselle** Dear Mrs/Mr/Miss X; **Mesdames** Ladies

madeleine [madlɛn] nf madeleine, small sponge cake

Mademoiselle [madmwazɛl] (pl **Mesdemoiselles**) nf Miss; voir aussi **Madame**

madère [madɛʀ] nm Madeira (wine)

magasin [magazɛ̃] nm (boutique) shop; (entrepôt) warehouse; **en** ~ (COMM) in stock

magazine [magazin] nm magazine

Maghreb [magʀɛb] nm: **le** ~ North Africa; **maghrébin, e** adj North African ♦ nm/f: **Maghrébin, e** North African

magicien, ne [maʒisjɛ̃, jɛn] nm/f magician

magie [maʒi] nf magic; **magique** adj magic; (enchanteur) magical

magistral, e, -aux [maʒistʀal, o] adj (œuvre, adresse) masterly; (ton) authoritative; **cours** ~ lecture

magistrat [maʒistʀa] nm magistrate

magnat [magna] nm tycoon

magnétique [maɲetik] adj magnetic

magnétiser [maɲetize] vt to magnetize; (fig) to mesmerize, hypnotize

magnétophone [maɲetɔfɔn] nm tape recorder; ~ **à cassettes** cassette recorder

magnétoscope [maɲetɔskɔp] nm video-tape recorder

magnifique [maɲifik] adj magnificent

magot [mago] (fam) nm (argent) pile (of money); (économies) nest egg

magouille [maguj] (fam) nf scheming; **magouiller** (fam) vi to scheme

magret [magʀɛ] nm: ~ **de canard** duck steaklet

mai [mɛ] nm May

Le premier mai is a public holiday in France marking union demonstrations in the United States in 1886 to secure the eight-hour working day. It is traditional to exchange and wear sprigs of lily of the valley. Le 8 mai is a public holiday in France commemorating the surrender of the German army to Eisenhower on May 7, 1945. There are parades of ex-servicemen in most towns. The social upheavals of May and June 1968, marked by student demonstrations, strikes and rioting, are generally referred to as "les événements de mai 68". De Gaulle's government survived, but reforms in education and a move towards decentralization ensued.

maigre [mɛgʀ] adj (très) thin, skinny; (viande) lean; (fromage) low-fat; (végétation) thin, sparse; (fig) poor, meagre, skimpy; **jours** ~s days of abstinence, fish days; **maigreur** nf thinness; **maigrir** vi to get thinner, lose weight; **maigrir de 2 kilos** to lose 2 kilos

maille [maj] nf stitch; **avoir** ~ **à partir avec qn** to have a brush with sb; ~ **à l'endroit/à l'envers** plain/purl stitch

maillet [majɛ] *nm* mallet

maillon [majɔ̃] *nm* link

maillot [majo] *nm* (*aussi*: ~ **de corps**) vest; (*de sportif*) jersey; ~ **de bain** swimsuit; (*d'homme*) bathing trunks *pl*

main, **e** [mɛ̃] *nf* hand; **à la** ~ in one's hand; **se donner la** ~ à **qn** to hold hands; **donner** *ou* **tendre la** ~ à **qn** to hold out one's hand to sb; **serrer la** ~ à **qn** to shake hands with sb; **sous la** ~ *ou* **à la** ~ at hand; **à remettre en** ~s **propres** to be delivered personally; **mettre la dernière** ~ à to put the finishing touches to; **se faire/perdre la** ~ to get one's hand in/lose one's touch; **avoir qch bien en** ~ to have (got) the hang of sth; **main-d'œuvre** *nf* manpower, labour; **main-forte** *nf*: **prêter main-forte à qn** to come to sb's assistance; **mainmise** *nf* (*fig*): **mainmise sur** complete hold on

maint, **e** [mɛ̃, mɛ̃t] *adj* many a; ~s many; **à** ~**es reprises** time and (time) again

maintenant [mɛ̃t(ə)nɑ̃] *adv* now; (*actuellement*) nowadays

maintenir [mɛ̃t(ə)niʀ] *vt* (*retenir, soutenir*) to support; (*contenir: foule etc*) to hold back; (*conserver, affirmer*) to maintain; **se** ~ *vi* (*prix*) to keep steady; (*amélioration*) to persist

maintien [mɛ̃tjɛ̃] *nm* (*sauvegarde*) maintenance; (*attitude*) bearing

maire [mɛʀ] *nm* mayor; **mairie** *nf* (*bâtiment*) town hall; (*administration*) town council

mais [mɛ] *conj* but; ~ **non!** of course not!; ~ **enfin** but after all; (*indignation*) look here!

maïs [mais] *nm* maize (BRIT), corn (US)

maison [mɛzɔ̃] *nf* house; (*chez-soi*) home; (COMM) firm ♦ *adj inv* (CULIN) home-made; (*fig*) in-house, own; **à la** ~ at home; (*direction*) home; ~ **close** *ou* **de passe** brothel; ~ **de repos** convalescent home; ~ **de retraite** old people's home; ~ **de santé** mental

home; ~ **des jeunes** ≈ youth club; ~ **mère** parent company; **maisonnée** *nf* household, family; **maisonnette** *nf* small house, cottage

maître, **-esse** [mɛtʀ, mɛtʀɛs] *nm/f* master (mistress); (SCOL) teacher, schoolmaster/-mistress ♦ *nm* (*peintre etc*) master; (*titre*): **M**~ Maître, term of address *gen for a barrister* ♦ *adj* (*principal, essentiel*) main; **être** ~ **de** (*soi, situation*) to be in control of; **une maîtresse femme** a managing woman; ~ **chanteur** blackmailer; ~ **d'éco-le** schoolmaster; ~ **d'hôtel** (*domestique*) butler; (*d'hôtel*) head waiter; ~ **nageur** lifeguard; **maîtresse** (*amante*) mistress; **maîtresse** (**d'école**) (*school*)mistress; **maîtresse de maison** hostess; (*ménagère*) housewife

maîtrise [mɛtʀiz] *nf* (*aussi*: ~ **de soi**) self-control, self-possession; (*habileté*) skill, mastery; (*suprématie*) mastery, command; (*diplôme*) ≈ master's degree; **maîtriser** *vt* (*cheval, incendie*) to (bring under) control; (*sujet*) to master; (*émotion*) to control, master; **se maîtriser** to control o.s.

maïzena ® [maizena] *nf* cornflour

majestueux, **-euse** [maʒɛstɥø, øz] *adj* majestic

majeur, **e** [maʒœʀ] *adj* (*important*) major; (JUR) of age ♦ *nm* (*doigt*) middle finger; **en** ~**e partie** for the most part; **la** ~**e partie de** most of

majoration [maʒɔʀasjɔ̃] *nf* rise, increase

majorer [maʒɔʀe] *vt* to increase

majoritaire [maʒɔʀitɛʀ] *adj* majority

majorité [maʒɔʀite] nf (gén) majority; (parti) party in power; **en ~** mainly

majuscule [maʒyskyl] adj, nf: (lettre) **~** capital (letter)

mal [mal, mo] (pl maux) nm (opposé au bien) evil; (tort, dommage) harm; (douleur physique) pain, ache; (~adie) illness, sickness no pl ♦ adv badly ♦ adj bad, wrong; **être ~ à l'aise** to be uncomfortable; **être ~ avec qn** to be on bad terms with sb; **il a ~ compris** he misunderstood; **dire/penser du ~ de** to speak/think ill of; **ne voir aucun ~ à** to see no harm in, see nothing wrong in; **faire ~ à qn** to hurt sb; **se faire ~** to hurt o.s.; **se donner du ~ pour faire qch** to go to a lot of trouble to do sth; **ça fait ~** it hurts; **j'ai ~ au dos** my back hurts; **avoir ~ à la tête/à la gorge/aux dents** to have a headache/a sore throat/toothache; **avoir le ~ du pays** to be homesick; voir aussi **cœur; maux; ~ de mer** seasickness; **~ en point** in a bad state

malade [malad] adj ill, sick; (poitrine, jambe) bad; (plante) diseased ♦ nm/f invalid, sick person; (à l'hôpital etc) patient; **tomber ~** to fall ill; **être ~ du cœur** to have heart trouble ou a bad heart; **~ mental** mentally sick ou ill person; **maladie** nf (spécifique) disease, illness; (mauvaise santé) illness, sickness; **maladif, -ive** adj sickly; (curiosité, besoin) pathological

maladresse [maladʀɛs] nf clumsiness no pl; (gaffe) blunder

maladroit, e [maladʀwa, wat] adj clumsy

malaise [malɛz] nm (MÉD) feeling of faintness; (fig) uneasiness, malaise; **avoir un ~** to feel faint

malaisé, e [maleze] adj difficult

malaxer [malakse] vt (pétrir) to knead; (mélanger) to mix

malbouffe [malbuf] (fam) nf: **la ~** junk food

malchance [malʃɑ̃s] nf misfortune, ill luck no pl; **par ~** unfortunately; **malchanceux, -euse** adj unlucky

mâle [mɑl] adj (aussi ÉLEC, TECH) male; (viril: voix, traits) manly ♦ nm male

malédiction [malediksjɔ̃] nf curse

mal...: malencontreux, -euse adj unfortunate, untoward; **mal-en-point** adj inv in a sorry state; **malentendant, e** nm/f: **les malentendants** the hard of hearing; **malentendu** nm misunderstanding; **malfaçon** nf fault; **malfaisant, e** adj evil, harmful; **malfaiteur** nm lawbreaker, criminal; (voleur) burglar, thief; **malfamé, e** adj disreputable

malgache [malgaʃ] adj Madagascan, Malagasy ♦ nm/f: **M~** Madagascan, Malagasy ♦ nm (LING) Malagasy

malgré [malgʀe] prép in spite of, despite; **~ tout** all the same

malhabile [malabil] adj clumsy, awkward

malheur [malœʀ] nm (situation) adversity, misfortune; (événement) misfortune; (: très grave) disaster, tragedy; **faire un ~** to be a smash hit; **malheureusement** adv unfortunately; **malheureux, -euse** adj (triste) unhappy, miserable; (infortuné, regrettable) unfortunate; (malchanceux) unlucky; (insignifiant) wretched ♦ nm/f poor soul; **les malheureux** the destitute

malhonnête [malɔnɛt] adj dishonest; **malhonnêteté** nf dishonesty

malice [malis] nf mischievousness; (méchanceté): **par ~** out of malice ou spite; **sans ~** guileless; **malicieux, -euse** adj mischievous

malin, -igne [malɛ̃, malin] adj (futé: f gén: ~e) smart, shrewd; (MÉD) malignant

malingre [malɛ̃gʀ] adj puny

malle [mal] nf trunk; **mallette** nf (small) suitcase; (porte-documents) attaché case

malmener [malməne] vt to manhandle; (fig) to give a rough handling to

malodorant, e [malɔdɔʀɑ̃, ɑ̃t] *adj* foul- *ou* ill-smelling

malotru [malɔtʀy] *nm* lout, boor

malpoli, e [malpɔli] *adj* impolite

malpropre [malpʀɔpʀ] *adj* dirty

malsain, e [malsɛ̃, ɛn] *adj* unhealthy

malt [malt] *nm* malt

Malte [malt] *nf* Malta

maltraiter [maltʀete] *vt* to manhandle, ill-treat

malveillance [malvejɑ̃s] *nf* (*animosité*) ill will; (*intention de nuire*) malevolence

malversation [malvɛʀsasjɔ̃] *nf* embezzlement

maman [mamɑ̃] *nf* mum(my), mother

mamelle [mamɛl] *nf* teat

mamelon [mam(ə)lɔ̃] *nm* (ANAT) nipple

mamie [mami] *nf* (*fam*) granny

mammifère [mamifɛʀ] *nm* mammal

mammouth [mamut] *nm* mammoth

manche [mɑ̃ʃ] *nf* (*de vêtement*) sleeve; (*d'un jeu, tournoi*) round; (GÉO): **la M-** **Channel ♦** *nm* (*d'outil, casserole*) handle; (*de pelle, pioche etc*) shaft; **à ~** **courtes/longues** short-/long-sleeved

manchette [mɑ̃ʃɛt] *nf* (*de chemise*) cuff; (*coup*) forearm blow; (*titre*) headline

manchot [mɑ̃ʃo, ɔt] *nm* one-armed man; armless man; (ZOOL) penguin

mandarine [mɑ̃daʀin] *nf* mandarin (orange), tangerine

mandat [mɑ̃da] *nm* (*postal*) postal *ou* money order; (*d'un député etc*) mandate; (*procuration*) power of attorney, proxy; (POLICE) warrant; **~ d'arrêt** warrant for arrest; **mandataire** *nm/f* (*représentant*) representative; (JUR) proxy

manège [manɛʒ] *nm* riding school; (*à la foire*) roundabout, merry-go-round; (*fig*) game, ploy

manette [manɛt] *nf* lever, tap; **~ de** **jeu** joystick

mangeable [mɑ̃ʒabl] *adj* edible, eatable

mangeoire [mɑ̃ʒwaʀ] *nf* trough, manger

manger [mɑ̃ʒe] *vt* to eat; (*ronger: suj:* *rouille etc*) to eat into *ou* away ♦ *vi* to eat; **donner à ~ à** (*enfant*) to feed; **mangeur, -euse** *nm/f* eater; **gros** **mangeur** big eater

mangue [mɑ̃ɡ] *nf* mango

maniable [manjabl] *adj* (*outil*) handy; (*voiture, voilier*) easy to handle

maniaque [manjak] *adj* finicky, fussy ♦ *nm/f* (*méticuleux*) fusspot; (*fou*) maniac

manie [mani] *nf* (*tic*) odd habit; (*obsession*) mania; **avoir la ~ de** to be obsessive about

manier [manje] *vt* to handle

manière [manjɛʀ] *nf* (*façon*) way, manner; **~s** *nfpl* (*attitude*) manners; (*chichis*) fuss *sg*; **de ~ à** so as to; **de cette ~** in this way *ou* manner; **d'une certaine ~** in a way; **de toute ~** in any case

maniéré, e [manjeʀe] *adj* affected

manif [manif] (*fam*) *nm* demo

manifestant, e [manifɛstɑ̃, ɑ̃t] *nm/f* demonstrator

manifestation [manifɛstasjɔ̃] *nf* (*de* *joie, mécontentement*) expression, demonstration; (*symptôme*) outward sign; (*culturelle etc*) event; (POL) demonstration

manifeste [manifɛst] *adj* obvious, evident ♦ *nm* manifesto; **manifester** (*volonté, intentions*) to show, indicate; (*joie, peur*) to express, show ♦ *vi* to demonstrate; **se manifester** *vi* (*émotion*) to show *ou* express itself; (*difficultés*) to arise; (*symptômes*) to appear

manigance [maniɡɑ̃s] *nf* scheme; **ma-** **nigancer** *vt* to plot

manipulation [manipylasjɔ̃] *nf* handling; (POL, génétique) manipulation

manipuler [manipyle] *vt* to handle; (*fig*) to manipulate

manivelle [manivɛl] *nf* crank

mannequin [mankɛ̃] *nm* (COUTURE) dummy; (MODE) model

manœuvre [manœvʀ] *nf* (*gén*) manoeuvre (BRIT), maneuver (US) ♦ *nm* labourer; **manœuvrer** *vt* to manoeuvre

manoir (BRIT), maneuver (US); (levier, machine) to operate ♦ vi to manoeuvre

manoir [manwar] nm manor ou country house

manque [mɑ̃k] nm (insuffisance): ~ de lack of; (vide) emptiness, gap; (MÉD) withdrawal; être en état de ~ to suffer withdrawal symptoms

manqué, e [mɑ̃ke] adj failed; garçon ~ tomboy

manquer [mɑ̃ke] vi (faire défaut) to be lacking; (être absent) to be missing; (échouer) to fail ♦ vt to miss ♦ vb impers: il (nous) manque encore 100 F we are still 100 F short; il manque des pages (au livre) there are some pages missing (from the book); il/cela me manque I miss him/this; ~ à (règles etc) to be in breach of, fail to observe; ~ de to lack; je ne vais pas de le lui dire I'll be sure to tell him; il a manqué (de) se tuer he very nearly got killed

mansarde [mɑ̃sard] nf attic; **mansardé, e** adj: chambre mansardée attic room

manteau, x [mɑ̃to] nm coat

manucure [manykyr] nf manicurist

manuel, le [manɥɛl] adj manual ♦ nm (ouvrage) manual, handbook

manufacture [manyfaktyr] nf factory; **manufacturé, e** adj manufactured

manuscrit, e [manyskri, it] adj handwritten ♦ nm manuscript

manutention [manytɑ̃sjɔ̃] nf (COMM) handling

mappemonde [mapmɔ̃d] nf (plane) map of the world; (sphère) globe

maquereau, x [makro] nm (ZOOL) mackerel inv; (fam) pimp

maquette [makɛt] nf (à échelle réduite) (scale) model; (d'une page illustrée) paste-up

maquillage [makijaʒ] nm making up; (crème etc) make-up

maquiller [makije] vt (personne, visage) to make up; (truquer: passeport, statisti-

que) to fake; (: voiture volée) to do over (respray etc); se ~ vi to make up (one's face)

maquis [maki] nm (GÉO) scrub; (MIL) maquis, underground fighting no pl

maraîcher, ère [mareʃe, ɛr] adj: cultures maraîchères market gardening sg ♦ nm/f market gardener

marais [marɛ] nm marsh, swamp

marasme [marasm] nm stagnation, slump

marathon [maratɔ̃] nm marathon

maraudeur [marodœr, øz] nm prowler

marbre [marbr] nm marble

marc [mar] nm (de raisin, pommes) marc; ~ de café coffee grounds pl ou dregs pl

marchand, e [marʃɑ̃, ɑ̃d] nm/f shopkeeper, tradesman(-woman); (au marché) stallholder; (de vins, charbon) merchant ♦ adj: prix/valeur ~(e) market price/value; ~(e) de fruits fruiterer (BRIT), fruit seller (US); ~(e) de journaux newsagent; ~(e) de légumes greengrocer (BRIT), produce dealer (US); ~(e) de poissons fishmonger; **marchander** vi to bargain, haggle; **marchandise** nf goods pl, merchandise no pl

marche [marʃ] nf (d'escalier) step; (activité) walking; (promenade, trajet, allure) walk; (démarche) walk, gait; (MIL etc) march; (fonctionnement) running; (des événements) course; dans le sens de la ~ (RAIL) facing the engine; en ~ (monter etc) while the vehicle is moving ou in motion; mettre en ~ to start; se mettre en ~ (personne) to get moving; (machine) to start; être en état de ~ to be in working order; ~ à suivre (correct) procedure; ~ arrière reverse (gear); faire ~ arrière to reverse; (fig) to backtrack, back-pedal

marché [marʃe] nm market; (transaction) bargain, deal; faire du ~ noir to buy and sell on the black market; ~ aux puces flea market; M~ commun

Common Market

marchepied [marʃəpje] nm (RAIL) step

marcher [marʃe] vi to walk; (MIL) to march; (aller: voiture, train, affaires) to go; (prospérer) to go well; (fonctionner) to work, run; (fam: consentir) to go along, agree; (: croire naïvement) to be taken in; **faire ~ qn** (taquiner) to pull sb's leg; (tromper) to lead sb up the garden path; **marcheur, -euse** nm/f walker

mardi [mardi] nm Tuesday; **M~ gras** Shrove Tuesday

mare [mar] nf pond; (flaque) pool

marécage [mareka3] nm marsh, swamp; **marécageux, -euse** adj marshy

maréchal, -aux [mareʃal, o] nm marshal; **maréchal-ferrant** [mareʃalferɑ̃, mareʃo-] (pl **maréchaux-ferrants**) nm blacksmith, farrier

marée [mare] nf tide; (poissons) fresh (sea) fish; **~ haute/basse** high/low tide; **~ montante/descendante** rising/ebb tide; **~ noire** oil slick

marelle [marɛl] nf hopscotch

margarine [margarin] nf margarine

marge [mar3] nf margin; **en ~ de** (fig) on the fringe of; **~ bénéficiaire** profit margin

marginal, e, -aux [marʒinal, o] nm/f (original) eccentric; (déshérité) dropout

marguerite [margərit] nf marguerite, (oxeye) daisy; (d'imprimante) daisywheel

mari [mari] nm husband

mariage [marja3] nm marriage; (noce) wedding; (fig) civil/religious registry office (BRIT) ou civil/church wedding

marié, e [marje] adj married ♦ nm (bride)groom; **les ~s** the bride and groom; **les (jeunes) ~s** the newlyweds; **mariée** nf bride

marier [marje] vt to marry; (fig) to blend; **se ~** vr to get married; **se ~ (avec)** to marry

marin, e [marɛ̃, in] adj sea cpd, marine

♦ nm sailor

marine [marin] adj voir marin ♦ adj inv navy (blue) ♦ nm (MIL) marine ♦ nf navy; **~ de guerre** navy; **~ marchande** merchant navy

mariner [marine] vt: **faire ~** to marinade

marionnette [marjɔnɛt] nf puppet

maritalement [maritalmɑ̃] adv: **vivre ~** to live as husband and wife

maritime [maritim] adj sea cpd, maritime

mark [mark] nm mark

marmelade [marməlad] nf stewed fruit, compote; **~ d'oranges** marmalade

marmite [marmit] nf (cooking-)pot

marmonner [marmɔne] vt, vi to mumble, mutter

marmot [marmo] (fam) nm kid

marmotter [marmɔte] vt to mumble

Maroc [marɔk] nm: **le ~** Morocco; **marocain, e** [marɔkɛ̃, ɛn] adj Moroccan ♦ nm/f: **M~/caine, e** Moroccan

maroquinerie [marɔkinri] nf (articles) fine leather goods pl; (boutique) shop selling fine leather goods

marquant, e [markɑ̃, ɑ̃t] adj outstanding

marque [mark] nf mark; (COMM: de nourriture) brand; (: de voiture, produits manufacturés) make; (: de disques) label; **de ~** (produits) high-class; (visiteur etc) distinguished, well-known; **une grande ~ de vin** a well-known brand of wine; **~ de fabrique** trademark; **~ déposée** registered trademark

marquer [marke] vt to mark; (inscrire) to write down; (bétail) to brand; (SPORT: but etc) to score; (: joueur) to mark; (accentuer: taille etc) to emphasize; (manifester: refus, intérêt) to show ♦ vi (événement) to stand out, be outstanding; (SPORT) to score

marqueterie [markɛtri] nf inlaid work, marquetry

marquis [marki] nm marquis, marquess; **marquise** nf marchioness; (auvent) glass canopy ou awning

marraine [maʀɛn] nf godmother

marrant, e [maʀɑ̃, ɑ̃t] (fam) adj funny

marre [maʀ] (fam) adv: **en avoir ~** de to be fed up with

marrer [maʀe]: **se ~** (fam) vi to have a (good) laugh

marron [maʀɔ̃] nm (fruit) chestnut ♦ adj inv brown; **~s glacés** candied chestnuts; **marronnier** nm chestnut (tree)

mars [maʀs] nm March

Marseille [maʀsɛj] n Marseilles

| Marseillaise |

La Marseillaise has been France's national anthem since 1879. The words of the "Chant de guerre de l'armée du Rhin", as the song was originally called, were written to an anonymous tune by the army captain Rouget de Lisle in 1792. Adopted as a marching song by the battalion of Marseilles, it was finally popularized as the Marseillaise.

marsouin [maʀswɛ̃] nm porpoise

marteau, x [maʀto] nm hammer; **être ~** (fam) to be nuts; **marteau-piqueur** nm pneumatic drill

marteler [maʀtəle] vt to hammer

martien, ne [maʀsjɛ̃, jɛn] adj Martian, of ou from Mars

martyr, e [maʀtiʀ] nm/f martyr; **martyre** nm martyrdom; (fig: sens affaibli) agony, torture; **martyriser** vt (REL) to martyr; (fig) to bully; (enfant) to batter, beat

marxiste [maʀksist] adj, nm/f Marxist

mascara [maskaʀa] nm mascara

masculin, e [maskylɛ̃, in] adj masculine; (sexe, population) male; (équipe, vêtements) men's; (viril) manly ♦ nm masculine; **masculinité** nf masculinity

masochiste [mazɔʃist] adj masochistic

masque [mask] nm mask; **masquer** vt (cacher: paysage, porte) to hide, conceal; (dissimuler: vérité, projet) to mask, obscure

massacre [masakʀ] nm massacre, slaughter; **massacrer** vt to massacre, slaughter; (fam: texte etc) to murder

massage [masaʒ] nm massage

masse [mas] nf mass; (ÉLEC) earth; (maillet) sledgehammer; (péj): **la ~** the masses pl; **une ~ de** (fam) masses ou loads of; **en ~** ♦ adv (acheter) in bulk; (en foule) en masse ♦ adj (exécutions, production) mass cpd

masser [mase] vt (assembler: gens) to gather; (pétrir) to massage; **se ~** vi (foule) to gather; **masseur, -euse** nm/f masseur(-euse)

massif, -ive [masif, iv] adj (porte) solid, massive; (visage) heavy, large; (bois, or) solid; (dose) massive; (déportations etc) mass cpd ♦ nm (montagneux) massif; (de fleurs) clump, bank

massue [masy] nf club, bludgeon

mastic [mastik] nm (pour vitres) putty; (pour fentes) filler

mastiquer [mastike] vt (aliment) to chew, masticate

mat, e [mat] adj (couleur, métal) mat(t); (bruit, son) dull ♦ adj inv (ÉCHECS): **être ~** to be checkmate

mât [mɑ] nm (NAVIG) mast; (poteau) pole, post

match [matʃ] nm match; **faire ~ nul** to draw; **~ aller** first leg; **~ retour** second leg, return match

matelas [mat(ə)la] nm mattress; **~ pneumatique** air bed ou mattress; **matelassé, e** adj (vêtement) padded; (tissu) quilted

matelot [mat(ə)lo] nm sailor, seaman

mater [mate] vt (personne) to bring to heel, subdue; (révolte) to put down

matérialiser [mateʀjalize]: **se ~** vi to materialize

matérialiste [mateʀjalist] adj materialistic

matériaux [mateʀjo] nmpl material(s)

matériel, le [mateʀjɛl] *adj* material
♦ *nm* equipment *no pl*; (*de camping etc*)
gear *no pl*; (INFORM) hardware

maternel, le [matɛʀnɛl] *adj* (*amour,
geste*) motherly, maternal; (*grand-père,
oncle*) maternal; **maternelle** *nf* (*aussi:*
école maternelle) (state) nursery
school

maternité [matɛʀnite] *nf* (*établissement*) maternity hospital; (*état de mère*)
motherhood, maternity; (*grossesse*)
pregnancy; **congé de ~** maternity
leave

mathématique [matematik] *adj*
mathematical; **mathématiques** *nfpl*
(*science*) mathematics *sg*

maths [mat] (*fam*) *nfpl* maths

matière [matjɛʀ] *nf* matter; (COMM,
TECH) material, matter *no pl*; (*fig: d'un
livre etc*) subject matter, material; (SCOL)
subject; **en ~ de** as regards; **~s gras-
ses** fat content *sg*; **~s premières** raw
materials

---

hôtel Matignon

L'hôtel Matignon *is the Paris office
and residence of the French Prime
Minister. By extension, the term "Matignon" is often used to refer to the
Prime Minister or his staff.*

---

matin [matɛ̃] *nm, adv* morning; **du ~
au soir** from morning till night; **de
bon ou grand ~** early in the morning;
matinal, e, -aux *adj* (*toilette, gymnastique*) morning *cpd*; **être matinal**
(*personne*) to be up early; to be an early riser; **matinée** *nf* morning; (*spectacle*) matinée

matou [matu] *nm* tom(cat)

matraque [matʀak] *nf* (*de policier*)
truncheon (BRIT), billy (US)

matricule [matʀikyl] *nm* (MIL) regi-
mental number; (ADMIN) reference
number

matrimonial, e, -aux [matʀimɔnjal,
jo] *adj* marital, marriage *cpd*

maudire [modiʀ] *vt* to curse; **maudit,
e** (*fam*) *adj* (*satané*) blasted, confounded

maugréer [mogʀee] *vi* to grumble

maussade [mosad] *adj* sullen; (*temps*)
gloomy

mauvais, e [mɔvɛ, ɛz] *adj* bad; (*faux*):
le ~ numéro/moment the wrong
number/moment; (*méchant, malveil-
lant*) malicious, spiteful; **il fait ~** the
weather is bad; **la mer est ~** the sea
is rough; **~ plaisant** hoaxer; **~e herbe**
weed; **~e langue** gossip, scandal-
monger (BRIT); **~e passe** bad patch

mauve [mov] *adj* mauve

maux [mo] *nmpl de* **mal**; **~ de ventre**
stomachache *sg*

maximum [maksimɔm] *adj, nm* maximum; **au ~** (*le plus possible*) as much
as one can; (*tout au plus*) at the (very)
most *ou* maximum; **faire le ~** to do
one's level best

mayonnaise [majɔnɛz] *nf* mayonnaise

mazout [mazut] *nm* (fuel) oil

Me *abr* = **Maître**

me, m' [m(ə)] *pron* (direct: *téléphoner,
attendre etc*) me; (indirect: *parler, donner etc*) (to) me; (*réfléchi*) myself

mec [mɛk] (*fam*) *nm* bloke, guy

mécanicien, ne [mekanisjɛ̃, jɛn] *nm/f*
mechanic; (RAIL) (train *ou* engine) driver

mécanique [mekanik] *adj* mechanical
♦ *nf* (*science*) mechanics *sg*; (*mécanisme*) mechanism; **ennui ~** engine
trouble *no pl*

mécanisme [mekanism] *nm* mechanism

méchamment [meʃamɑ̃] *adv* nastily,
maliciously, spitefully

méchanceté [meʃɑ̃ste] *nf* nastiness,
maliciousness; **dire des ~s à qn** to say
spiteful things to sb

méchant, e [meʃɑ̃, ɑ̃t] *adj* nasty, malicious, spiteful; (*enfant: pas sage*)
naughty; (*animal*) vicious

mèche [mɛʃ] *nf* (*de cheveux*) lock; (*de
lampe, bougie*) wick; (*d'un explosif*) fuse;

de ~ avec in league with

méchoui [meʃwi] nm barbecue of a whole roast sheep

méconnaissable [mekɔnɛsabl] adj unrecognizable

méconnaître [mekɔnɛtʀ] vt (ignorer) to be unaware of; (mésestimer) to misjudge

mécontent, e [mekɔ̃tɑ̃, ɑ̃t] adj: ~ (de) discontented ou dissatisfied ou displeased (with); (contrarié) annoyed (at); **mécontentement** nm dissatisfaction, discontent, displeasure; (irritation) annoyance

médaille [medaj] nf medal

médaillon [medajɔ̃] nm (bijou) locket

médecin [med(ə)sɛ̃] nm doctor; **légiste** forensic surgeon

médecine [med(ə)sin] nf medicine

média [medja] nmpl: **les ~** the media; **médiatique** [medjatik] adj media cpd; **médiatisé, e** adj reported in the media; **ce procès a été très médiatisé** (péj) this trial was turned into a media event

médical, e, -aux [medikal, o] adj medical; **passer une visite ~e** to have a medical

médicament [medikamɑ̃] nm medicine, drug

médiéval, e, -aux [medjeval, o] adj medieval

médiocre [medjɔkʀ] adj mediocre, poor

médire [mediʀ] vi: ~ de to speak ill of; **médisance** nf scandalmongering (BRIT)

méditer [medite] vt/vi to meditate

Méditerranée [mediteʀane] nf: **la (mer) ~** the Mediterranean (Sea); **méditerranéen, ne** adj Mediterranean ♦ nm/f: **Méditerranéen, ne** native ou inhabitant of a Mediterranean country

méduse [medyz] nf jellyfish

meeting [mitiŋ] nm (POL, SPORT) rally

méfait [mefɛ] nm (faute) misdemeanour, wrongdoing; **~s** nmpl (ravages) ravages, damage sg

méfiance [mefjɑ̃s] nf mistrust, distrust

méfiant, e [mefjɑ̃, jɑ̃t] adj mistrustful, distrustful

méfier [mefje]: **se ~** vi to be wary; to be careful; **se ~ de** to mistrust, distrust, be wary of

mégarde [megaʀd] nf: **par ~** (accidentellement) accidentally; (par erreur) by mistake

mégère [meʒɛʀ] nf shrew

mégot [mego] (fam) nm cigarette end

meilleur, e [mɛjœʀ] adj, adv better ♦ nm: **le ~** the best; **le ~ des deux** the better of the two; **~ marché** (inv) cheaper; **meilleure** **(e)** the best (one)

mélancolie [melɑ̃kɔli] nf melancholy, gloom; **mélancolique** adj melancholic, melancholy

mélange [melɑ̃ʒ] nm mixture; **mélanger** vt to mix; (vins, couleurs) to blend; (mettre en désordre) to mix up, muddle (up)

mélasse [melas] nf treacle, molasses sg

mêlée [mele] nf mêlée, scramble; (RUGBY) scrum(mage)

mêler [mele] vt (unir) to mix; (embrouiller) to muddle (up), mix up; **se ~** vi to mix, mingle; **se ~ à** (personne: se joindre) to join; (: s'associer à) to mix with; **se ~ de** (suj: personne) to meddle with, interfere in; **mêle-toi de ce qui te regarde!** mind your own business!

mélodie [melɔdi] nf melody; **mélodieux, -euse** adj melodious

melon [m(ə)lɔ̃] nm (BOT) (honeydew) melon; (aussi: **chapeau ~**) bowler (hat)

membre [mɑ̃bʀ] nm (ANAT) limb; (personne, pays, élément) member ♦ adj member cpd

mémé [meme] (fam) nf granny

<u>MOT-CLÉ</u>

même [mɛm] adj 1 (avant le nom) same; **en même temps** at the same time

2 (après le nom: renforcement): **il est la loyauté même** he is loyalty itself; **ce**

sont ses paroles/celles-là mêmes they are his very words/the very ones ♦ pron: **le(la) même** the same one ♦ adv **1** (renforcement): **il n'a même pas pleuré** he didn't even cry; **même lui l'a dit** even HE said it; **ici même** at this very place
2: **à même**: **à même la bouteille** straight from the bottle; **à même la peau** next to the skin; **être à même de faire** to be in a position to do, be able to do
3: **de même**: **faire de même** to do likewise; **lui de même** so does (ou did ou is) he; **de même que** just as; **il en va de même pour** the same goes for

mémo [memo] (fam) nm memo
mémoire [memwaʀ] nf memory ♦ nm (SCOL) dissertation, paper; **~s** nmpl (souvenirs) memoirs; **à ~ de** to the ou in memory of; **de ~** from memory; **~ morte/vive** (INFORM) ROM/RAM
mémorable [memɔʀabl] adj memorable, unforgettable

menace [mənas] nf threat; **menacer** vt to threaten
ménage [menaʒ] nm (travail) housework; (couple) (married) couple; (famille, ADMIN) household; **faire le ~** to do the housework; **ménagement** nm care and attention; **ménager, -ère** adj household cpd, domestic ♦ vt (traiter: personne) to handle with tact; (utiliser) to use sparingly; (prendre soin de) to take (great) care of, look after; (organiser) to arrange; **ménager qch à qn** (réserver) to have sth in store for sb; **ménagère** nf housewife
mendiant, e [mãdjã, jãt] nm/f beggar
mendier [mãdje] vi to beg ♦ vt to beg (for)
mener [m(ə)ne] vt to lead; (enquête) to conduct; (affaires) to manage ♦ vi: **~ à/dans** (emmener) to take to/into; **~ qch à bien** to see sth through (to a successful conclusion), complete sth

successfully
meneur, -euse [mənœʀ, øz] nm/f leader; (péj) agitator
méningite [menɛ̃ʒit] nf meningitis no pl
ménopause [menopoz] nf menopause
menottes [mənɔt] nfpl handcuffs
mensonge [mãsɔ̃ʒ] nm lie; (action) lying no pl; **mensonger, -ère** adj false
mensualité [mãsyalite] nf (traite) monthly payment
mensuel, le [mãsyɛl] adj monthly
mensurations [mãsyʀasjɔ̃] nfpl measurements
mental, e, -aux [mãtal, o] adj mental; **mentalité** nf mentality
menteur, -euse [mãtœʀ, øz] nm/f liar
menthe [mãt] nf mint
mention [mãsjɔ̃] nf (annotation) note, comment; (SCOL) grade; **~ bien** ≈ grade B etc (ou upper 2nd class etc) pass (BRIT), ≈ pass with (high) honors (US); (ADMIN): **"rayer les ~s inutiles"** "delete as appropriate"; **mentionner** vt to mention
mentir [mãtiʀ] vi to lie
menton [mãtɔ̃] nm chin
menu, e [məny] adj (personne) slim, slight; (frais, difficulté) minor ♦ adv (couper, hacher) very fine ♦ nm menu; **~ touristique/gastronomique** economy/gourmet's menu
menuiserie [mənɥizʀi] nf (métier) joinery, carpentry; (passe-temps) woodwork; **menuisier** nm joiner, carpenter
méprendre [mepʀɑ̃dʀ]: **se ~** vi: **se ~ sur** to be mistaken (about)
mépris [mepʀi] nm (dédain) contempt, scorn; **au ~ de** regardless of, in defiance of; **méprisable** adj contemptible, despicable; **méprisant, e** adj scornful; **méprise** nf mistake, error; **mépriser** vt to scorn, despise; (gloire, danger) to scorn, spurn
mer [mɛʀ] nf sea; (marée) tide; **en ~** at sea; **en haute** ou **pleine ~** off shore, on the open sea; **la ~ du Nord/Rouge**

the North/Red Sea

mercenaire [mɛʀsənɛʀ] *nm* mercenary, hired soldier

mercerie [mɛʀsəʀi] *nf* (*boutique*) haberdasher's shop (*BRIT*), notions store (*US*)

merci [mɛʀsi] *excl* thank you ♦ *nf*: **à la ~ de qn/qch** at sb's mercy/the mercy of sth; **~ beaucoup** thank you very much; **~ de** thank you for; **sans ~** merciless(ly)

mercredi [mɛʀkʀədi] *nm* Wednesday

mercure [mɛʀkyʀ] *nm* mercury

merde [mɛʀd] (*fam!*) *nf* ♦ *excl* shit (*!*) ♦ *excl* (bloody) hell (*!*)

mère [mɛʀ] *nf* mother; **~ célibataire** unmarried mother

merguez [mɛʀgɛz] *nf* merguez sausage (*type of spicy sausage from N Africa*)

méridional, e, -aux [meʀidjɔnal, o] *adj* southern ♦ *nm/f* Southerner

meringue [məʀɛ̃g] *nf* meringue

mérite [meʀit] *nm* merit; **avoir du ~** (**à faire qch**) to deserve credit (for doing sth); **mériter** *vt* to deserve

merlan [mɛʀlɑ̃] *nm* whiting

merle [mɛʀl] *nm* blackbird

merveille [mɛʀvɛj] *nf* marvel, wonder; **faire ~** to work wonders; **à ~** perfectly, wonderfully; **merveilleux, -euse** *adj* marvellous, wonderful

mes [me] *adj voir* **mon**

mésange [mezɑ̃ʒ] *nf* tit(mouse)

mésaventure [mezavɑ̃tyʀ] *nf* misadventure, misfortune

Mesdames [medam] *nfpl de* **Madame**

Mesdemoiselles [medmwazɛl] *nfpl de* **Mademoiselle**

mesquin, e [mɛskɛ̃, in] *adj* mean, petty; **mesquinerie** *nf* meanness; (*procédé*) mean trick

message [mesaʒ] *nm* message; **messager, -ère** [-aʒe, ɛʀ] *nm/f* messenger; **messagerie** *nf* (*INTERNET*) **messagerie électronique** bulletin board

messe [mɛs] *nf* mass

Messieurs [mesjø] *nmpl de* **Monsieur**

mesure [m(ə)zyʀ] *nf* (*évaluation, dimension*) measurement; (*récipient*) measure; (*MUS: cadence*) time, tempo; (: *division*) bar; (*retenue*) moderation; (*disposition*) measure, step; **sur ~** (*costume*) made-to-measure; **dans la ~ où** insofar as, inasmuch as; **à ~ que** as; **être en ~ de** to be in a position to; **dans une certaine ~** to a certain extent

mesurer [məzyʀe] *vt* to measure; (*juger*) to weigh up, assess; (*modérer: ses paroles etc*) to moderate; **se ~ avec** to have a confrontation with; **il mesure 1 m 80** he's 1 m 80 tall

met [mɛ] *vb voir* **mettre**

métal, -aux [metal, o] *nm* metal; **métallique** *adj* metallic

météo [meteo] *nf* (*bulletin*) weather report

météorologie [meteɔʀɔlɔʒi] *nf* meteorology

méthode [metɔd] *nf* method; (*livre, ouvrage*) manual, tutor

méticuleux, -euse [metikylø, øz] *adj* meticulous

métier [metje] *nm* (*profession: gén*) job; (: *manuel*) trade; (*artisanal*) craft; (*technique, expérience*) (acquired) skill *ou* technique; (*aussi*: **à tisser**) (weaving) loom; **avoir du ~** to have practical experience

métis, se [metis] *adj, nm/f* half-caste, half-breed

métrage [metʀaʒ] *nm*: **long/moyen/court ~** full-length/medium-length/short film

mètre [mɛtʀ] *nm* metre; (*règle, ruban*) rule; (*ruban*) tape measure; **métrique** *adj* metric

métro [metʀo] *nm* underground (*BRIT*), subway

métropole [metʀɔpɔl] *nf* (*capitale*) metropolis; (*pays*) home country

mets [mɛ] *nm* dish

metteur [metœʀ] *nm*: **~ en scène** (*THÉÂTRE*) producer; (*CINÉMA*) director

MOT-CLÉ

mettre [mɛtʀ] vt 1 (placer): to put; **mettre en bouteille/en sac** to bottle/put in bags ou sacks; **mettre en charge (pour)** to charge (with), indict (for)

2 (vêtements: revêtir) to put on; (: porter) to wear; **mets ton gilet** put your cardigan on; **je ne mets plus mon manteau** I no longer wear my coat

3 (faire fonctionner: chauffage, électricité) to put on; (: réveil, minuteur) to set; (installer: gaz, eau) to lay on; **mettre en marche** to start up

4 (consacrer): **mettre du temps à faire qch** to take time to do sth ou over sth

5 (noter, écrire): to say, put (down); **qu'est-ce qu'il a mis sur la carte?** what did he say ou write on the card?; **mettez au pluriel** put ... into the plural

6 (supposer): **mettons que ...** let's suppose ou say that ...

7: **y mettre du sien** to pull one's weight

se mettre vi 1 (se placer): **vous pouvez vous mettre là** you can sit (ou stand) there; **où ça se met?** where does it go?; **se mettre au lit** to get into bed; **se mettre au piano** to sit down at the piano; **se mettre de l'encre sur les doigts** to get ink on one's fingers

2 (s'habiller): **se mettre en maillot de bain** to get into ou put on a swimsuit; **n'avoir rien à se mettre** to have nothing to wear

3: **se mettre à** to begin, start; **se mettre à faire** to begin ou start doing ou to do; **se mettre au piano** to start learning the piano; **se mettre au travail/à l'étude** to get down to work/one's studies

meuble [mœbl] nm piece of furniture; **des ~s** furniture; **meublé** nm furnished

flatlet (BRIT) ou room; **meubler** vt to furnish

meugler [møgle] vi to low, moo

meule [møl] nf (de foin, blé) stack; (de fromage) round; (à broyer) millstone

meunier, -ière [mønje, jɛʀ] nm miller; **meunière** nf miller's wife

meure etc [mœʀ] vb voir **mourir**

meurtre [mœʀtʀ] nm murder; **meurtrier, -ière** adj (arme etc) deadly; (fureur, instincts) murderous ♦ nm/f murderer(-eress)

meurtrir [mœʀtʀiʀ] vt to bruise; (fig) to wound; **meurtrissure** nf bruise

meus etc [mø] vb voir **mouvoir**

meute [møt] nf pack

mexicain, e [mɛksikɛ̃, ɛn] adj Mexican ♦ nm/f: **M~, e** Mexican

Mexico [mɛksiko] n Mexico City

Mexique [mɛksik] nm: **le ~** Mexico

Mgr abr = **Monseigneur**

mi [mi] nm (MUS) E; (en chantant la gamme) mi ♦ préfixe: **~... half(-); mid-**; **à la ~-janvier** in mid-January; **à ~-hauteur** halfway up; **mi-bas** nm inv knee sock

miauler [mjole] vi to mew

miche [miʃ] nf round ou cob loaf

mi-chemin [miʃmɛ̃]: **à ~-~** adv halfway, midway

mi-clos, e [miklo, kloz] adj half-closed

micro [mikʀo] nm mike, microphone; (INFORM) micro

microbe [mikʀɔb] nm germ, microbe

micro...: **micro-onde** nf: **four à micro-ondes** microwave oven; **micro-ordinateur** nm microcomputer; **microscope** nm microscope; **microscopique** adj microscopic

midi [midi] nm midday, noon; (moment du déjeuner) lunchtime; (sud) south; **à ~** at 12 (o'clock) ou midday ou noon; **le M~** the South (of France), the Midi

mie [mi] nf crumb (of the loaf)

miel [mjɛl] nm honey; **mielleux, -euse** (personne) unctuous, syrupy

mien, ne [mjɛ̃, mjɛn] pron: **le(la)**

miette 181 **mine**

~(ne), les ~(ne)s mine; les ~s my family

miette [mjɛt] *nf* (*de pain, gâteau*) crumb; (*fig: de la conversation etc*) scrap; **en ~s** in pieces *ou* bits

MOT-CLÉ

mieux [mjø] *adv* **1** (*d'une meilleure façon*): **mieux (que)** better (than); **elle travaille/mange mieux** she works/eats better; **elle va mieux** she is better **2** (*de la meilleure façon*) best; **ce que je sais le mieux** what I know best; **les livres les mieux faits** the best made books
3: **de mieux en mieux** better and better
♦ *adj* **1** (*plus à l'aise, en meilleure forme*) better; **se sentir mieux** to feel better **2** (*plus satisfaisant*) better; **c'est mieux ainsi** it's better like this; **c'est le mieux des deux** it's the better of the two; **le(la) mieux, les mieux** the best; **demandez-lui, c'est le mieux** ask him, it's the best thing
3 (*plus joli*) better-looking
4: **au mieux** at best; **au mieux avec** on the best of terms with; **pour le mieux** for the best
♦ *nm* **1** (*progrès*) improvement
2: **de mon/ton mieux** as best I/you can (*ou* could); **faire de son mieux** to do one's best

mièvre [mjɛvʀ] *adj* mawkish (*BRIT*), sickly sentimental

mignon, ne [miɲɔ̃, ɔn] *adj* sweet, cute

migraine [migʀɛn] *nf* headache; (*MÉD*) migraine

mijoter [miʒɔte] *vt* to simmer; (*préparer avec soin*) to cook lovingly; (*fam: tramer*) to plot, cook up ♦ *vi* to simmer

mil [mil] *num* = **mille**

milieu, x [miljø] *nm* (*centre*) middle; (*BIO, GÉO*) environment; (*entourage social*) milieu; (*provenance*) background; (*pègre*): **le ~** the underworld; **au ~ de**
in the middle of; **au beau** *ou* **en plein ~ (de)** right in the middle (of); **un juste ~** a happy medium

militaire [militɛʀ] *adj* military, army *cpd* ♦ *nm* serviceman

militant, e [militɑ̃, ɑ̃t] *adj, nm/f* militant

militer [milite] *vi* to be a militant

mille [mil] *num* a *ou* one thousand
♦ *nm* (*mesure*): **~ (marin)** nautical mile; **mettre dans le ~** (*fig*) to be bang on target; **millefeuille** *nm* cream *ou* vanilla slice; **millénaire** *nm* millennium
♦ *adj* thousand-year-old; (*fig*) ancient; **mille-pattes** *nm inv* centipede

millésimé, e [milezime] *adj* vintage *cpd*

millet [mijɛ] *nm* millet

milliard [miljaʀ] *nm* milliard, thousand million (*BRIT*), billion (*US*); **milliardaire** *nm/f* multimillionaire (*BRIT*), billionaire (*US*)

millier [milje] *nm* thousand; **un ~ (de)** a thousand or so, about a thousand; **par ~s** in (their) thousands, by the thousand

milligramme [miligʀam] *nm* milligramme

millimètre [milimɛtʀ] *nm* millimetre

million [miljɔ̃] *nm* million; **deux ~s de** two million; **millionnaire** *nm/f* millionaire

mime [mim] *nm/f* (*acteur*) mime(r) ♦ *nm* (*art*) mime, miming; **mimer** *vt* to mime; (*singer*) to mimic, take off

mimique [mimik] *nf* (*grimace*) funny face; (*signes*) gesticulations *pl*, sign language *no pl*

minable [minabl] *adj* (*décrépit*) shabby(-looking); (*médiocre*) pathetic

mince [mɛ̃s] *adj* thin; (*personne, taille*) slim, slender; (*fig: profit, connaissances*) slight, small, weak ♦ *excl*: **~ alors!** that it, darn it! (*US*); **minceur** *nf* thinness; (*d'une personne*) slimness, slenderness; **mincir** *vi* to get slimmer

mine [min] *nf* (*physionomie*) expression,

look; (allure) exterior, appearance; (de
crayon) lead; (gisement, explosif, fig:
source) mine; **avoir bonne ~** (personne) to look well; (ironique) to look
an utter idiot; **avoir mauvaise ~** to
look unwell ou poorly; **faire ~ de faire**
to make a pretence of doing; **~ de rien**
although you wouldn't think so

miner [mine] vt (saper) to undermine,
erode; (MIL) to mine

minerai [minʀɛ] nm ore

minéral, e, -aux [mineʀal, o] adj, nm
mineral

minéralogique [mineʀalɔʒik] adj: **numéro ~** registration number

minet, te [minɛ, ɛt] nm/f (chat) pussy-
cat; (péj) trendy young thing

mineur, e [minœʀ] adj minor ♦ nm/f
(JUR) minor, person under age ♦ nm
(travailleur) miner

miniature [minjatyʀ] adj, nf miniature

minibus [minibys] nm minibus

mini-cassette [minikasɛt] nf cassette
(recorder)

minier, -ière [minje, jɛʀ] adj mining

mini-jupe [miniʒyp] nf mini-skirt

minime [minim] adj minor, minimal

minimiser [minimize] vt to minimize;
(fig) to play down

minimum [minimɔm] adj, nm minimum; **au ~** (au moins) at the very
least

ministère [ministɛʀ] nm (aussi REL)
ministry; (cabinet) government

ministre [ministʀ] nm (aussi REL) minister

Minitel ® [minitel] nm videotext terminal and service

stock market and situations vacant.
Services are accessed by phoning the
relevant number and charged to the
subscriber's phone bill.

---

minoritaire [minɔʀitɛʀ] adj minority

minorité [minɔʀite] nf minority; **être
en ~** to be in the ou a minority

minuit [minɥi] nm midnight

minuscule [minyskyl] adj minute, tiny
♦ nf: **(lettre) ~** small letter

minute [minyt] nf minute; **à la ~**
(just) this instant; (faire) there and
then; **minuter** vt to time; **minuterie**
nf time switch

minutieux, -euse [minysjø, jøz] adj
(personne) meticulous; (travail) mi-
nutely detailed

mirabelle [miʀabɛl] nf (cherry) plum

miracle [miʀakl] nm miracle

mirage [miʀaʒ] nm mirage

mire [miʀ] nf: **point de ~** (fig) focal
point

miroir [miʀwaʀ] nm mirror

miroiter [miʀwate] vi to sparkle, shimmer; **faire ~ qch à qn** to paint sth in
glowing colours for sb, dangle sth in
front of sb's eyes

mis, e [mi, miz] pp de **mettre** ♦ adj:
bien ~ well-dressed

mise [miz] nf (argent: au jeu) stake; (tenue) clothing, attire; **être de ~** to be
acceptable ou in season; **~ au point**
(fig) clarification; **~ de fonds** capital
outlay; **~ en examen** charging, indictment; **~ en plis** set; **~ en scène** production

miser [mize] vt (enjeu) to stake, bet; **~
sur** (cheval, numéro) to bet on; (fig) to
bank ou count on

misérable [mizeʀabl] adj (lamentable,
malheureux) pitiful, wretched; (pauvre)
poverty-stricken; (insignifiant, mesquin)
miserable ♦ nm/f wretch

misère [mizɛʀ] nf (extreme) poverty,
destitution; **~s** nfpl (malheurs) woes,
miseries; (ennuis) little troubles; **salaire**

de ~ starvation wage

missile [misil] *nm* missile

mission [misjɔ] *nf* mission; **partir en ~** (*ADMIN, POL*) to go on an assignment;

missionnaire *nm/f* missionary

mit [mi] *vb voir* **mettre**

mité, e [mite] *adj* moth-eaten

mi-temps [mitɑ̃] *nf inv* (*SPORT: période*) half; (*: pause*) half-time; **à ~~** part-time

miteux, -euse [mitø, øz] *adj* (*lieu*) seedy

mitigé, e [mitiʒe] *adj*: **sentiments ~s** mixed feelings

mitonner [mitɔne] *vt* to cook with loving care; (*fig*) to cook up quietly

mitoyen, ne [mitwajɛ̃, jɛn] *adj* (*mur*) common, party *cpd*

mitrailler [mitraje] *vt* to machine-gun; (*fig*) to pelt, bombard; (*: photographier*) to take shot after shot of; **mitraillette** *nf* submachine gun; **mitrailleuse** *nf* machine gun

mi-voix [mivwa]: **à ~~** *adv* in a low *ou* hushed voice

mixage [miksaʒ] *nm* (*CINÉMA*) (sound) mixing

mixer [miksœʀ] *nm* (food) mixer

mixte [mikst] *adj* (*gén*) mixed; (*SCOL*) mixed, coeducational

mixture [mikstyʀ] *nf* mixture; (*fig*) concoction

Mlle (*pl* **Mlles**) *abr* = **Mademoiselle**

MM *abr* = **Messieurs**

Mme (*pl* **Mmes**) *abr* = **Madame**

mobile [mɔbil] *adj* mobile; (*pièce de machine*) moving ♦ *nm* (*motif*) motive; (*œuvre d'art*) mobile

mobilier, -ière [mɔbilje, jɛʀ] *nm* furniture

mobiliser [mɔbilize] *vt* to mobilize

mocassin [mɔkasɛ̃] *nm* moccasin

moche [mɔʃ] (*fam*) *adj* (*laid*) ugly; (*mauvais*) rotten

modalité [mɔdalite] *nf* form, mode; **~s de paiement** methods of payment

mode [mɔd] *nf* fashion ♦ *nm* (*manière*) form, mode; **à la ~** fashionable, in fashion; **~ d'emploi** directions *pl* (for use)

modèle [mɔdɛl] *adj, nm* model; (*qui pose: de peintre*) sitter; **~ déposé** registered design; **~ réduit** small-scale model; **modeler** *vt* to model

modem [mɔdɛm] *nm* modem

modéré, e [mɔdeʀe] *adj, nm/f* moderate

modérer [mɔdeʀe] *vt* to moderate; **se ~** *vi* to restrain o.s.

moderne [mɔdɛʀn] *adj* modern ♦ *nm* (*style*) modern style; (*meubles*) modern furniture; **moderniser** *vt* to modernize

modeste [mɔdɛst] *adj* modest; **modestie** *nf* modesty

modifier [mɔdifje] *vt* to modify, alter; **se ~** *vi* to alter

modique [mɔdik] *adj* modest

modiste [mɔdist] *nf* milliner

module [mɔdyl] *nm* module

moelle [mwal] *nf* marrow; **~ épinière** spinal cord

moelleux, -euse [mwalø, øz] *adj* soft; (*gâteau*) light and moist

mœurs [mœʀ] *nfpl* (*conduite*) morals; (*manières*) manners; (*pratiques sociales, mode de vie*) habits

mohair [mɔɛʀ] *nm* mohair

moi [mwa] *pron me*; (*emphatique*): **~, je** ... for my part, I ...; I, I myself ...; **à ~** mine; **moi-même** *pron* myself; (*emphatique*) myself

moindre [mwɛ̃dʀ] *adj* lesser; lower; **le(la) ~, les ~s** the least, the slightest; **merci – c'est la ~ des choses!** thank you – it's a pleasure!

moine [mwan] *nm* monk, friar

moineau, x [mwano] *nm* sparrow

MOT-CLÉ

moins [mwɛ̃] *adv* **1** (*comparatif*): **moins (que)** less (than); **moins grand que** less tall than, not as tall as; **moins je travaille, mieux je me porte** the less I work, the better I feel

2 (superlatif): **le moins** (the) least; **c'est ce que j'aime le moins** it's what I like (the) least; **le(la) moins doué(e)** the least gifted; **au moins, du moins** at least; **pour le moins** at the very least

3: **moins de** (quantité) less (than); (nombre) fewer (than); **moins de sable/d'eau** less sand/water; **moins de livres/gens** fewer books/people; **moins de 2 ans** less than 2 years; **moins de midi** not yet midday

4: **de moins, en moins**: **100 F/3 jours de moins** 100F/3 days less; **3 livres en moins** 3 books fewer; **3 books too few**; **de l'argent en moins** less money; **le soleil en moins** but for the sun, minus the sun; **de moins en moins** less and less

5: **à moins de, à moins que** unless; **à moins de faire** unless we do (ou he does etc); **à moins que tu ne fasses** unless you do; **à moins d'un accident** barring any accident

♦ prép: **4 moins 2** 4 minus 2; **il est moins 5** it's 5 to; **il fait moins 5** it's 5 (degrees) below (freezing), it's minus 5

mois [mwa] *nm* month

moisi [mwazi] *nm* mould, mildew; **odeur de ~** musty smell; **moisir** *vi* to go mouldy; **moisissure** *nf* mould *no pl*

moisson [mwasɔ̃] *nf* harvest; **moissonner** *vt* to harvest, reap; **moissonneuse** *nf* (machine) harvester

moite [mwat] *adj* sweaty, sticky

moitié [mwatje] *nf* half; **la ~** half; **la ~ de** half (of); **la du temps** half the time; **à la ~ de** halfway through; **à ~** (avant le verbe) half; (avant l'adjectif) half-; **à ~ prix** (at) half-price; **~ moitié** half-and-half

moka [mɔka] *nm* coffee gateau

mol [mɔl] *adj voir* **mou**

molaire [mɔlɛʀ] *nf* molar

molester [mɔlɛste] *vt* to manhandle, maul (about)

molle [mɔl] *adj voir* **mou; mollement** *adv* (péj: travailler) sluggishly; (protester) feebly

mollet [mɔlɛ] *nm* calf ♦ *adj m*: **œuf ~** soft-boiled egg

molletonné, e [mɔltɔne] *adj* fleece-lined

mollir [mɔliʀ] *vi* (fléchir) to relent; (substance) to go soft

mollusque [mɔlysk] *nm* mollusc

môme [mom] (fam) *nm/f* (enfant) brat

moment [mɔmɑ̃] *nm* moment; **ce n'est pas le ~** this is not the (right) time; **pour un bon ~** for a good while; **pour le ~** for the moment, for the time being; **au ~ de** at the time of; **au ~ où** just as; **à tout ~** (peut arriver etc) at any time ou moment; (constamment) constantly, continually; **en ce ~** at the moment; at present; **sur le ~** at the time; **par ~s** now and then, at times; **du ~ où** ou que seeing that, since; **momentané, e** *adj* temporary, momentary; **momentanément** *adv* (court instant) for a short while

momie [mɔmi] *nf* mummy

mon, ma [mɔ̃, ma] (*pl* **mes**) *adj* my

Monaco [mɔnako] *nm* Monaco

monarchie [mɔnaʀʃi] *nf* monarchy

monastère [mɔnastɛʀ] *nm* monastery

monceau, x [mɔ̃so] *nm* heap

mondain, e [mɔ̃dɛ̃, ɛn] *adj* (vie) society *cpd*

monde [mɔ̃d] *nm* world; (haute société): **le ~** (high) society; **il y a du ~** (beaucoup de gens) there are a lot of people; (quelques personnes) there are some people; **beaucoup/peu de ~** many/few people; **mettre au ~** to bring into the world; **pas le moins du ~** not in the least; **se faire un ~ de qch** to make a great deal of fuss about sth; **mondial, e, -aux** *adj* (population) world *cpd*; (influence) world-wide; **mondialement** *adv* throughout the world

monégasque [mɔnegask] *adj* Monegasque, of *ou* from Monaco

monétaire [mɔnetɛʀ] *adj* monetary

moniteur, -trice [mɔnitœʀ, tʀis] *nm/f* (SPORT) instructor(-tress); (*de colonie de vacances*) supervisor ♦ *nm* (*écran*) monitor

monnaie [mɔnɛ] *nf* (ÉCON. *gén: moyen d'échange*) currency; (*petites pièces*) ~ to have (some) change; **une pièce de ~** a coin; **faire de la ~** to get (some) change; **avoir/faire de la de 20 F** to have change of/get change for 20 F; **rendre à qn la ~ (sur 20 F)** to give sb the change (out of *ou* from 20 F); **monnayer** *vt* to convert into cash; (*talent*) to capitalize on

monologue [mɔnɔlɔɡ] *nm* monologue, soliloquy; **monologuer** *vi* to soliloquize

monopole [mɔnɔpɔl] *nm* monopoly

monotone [mɔnɔtɔn] *adj* monotonous

Monsieur [məsjø] (*pl* **Messieurs**) *titre* Mr ♦ *nm* (*homme quelconque*): **un/le m~`** a/the gentleman; **~, ...** (*en tête de lettre*) Dear Sir, ...; *voir aussi* **Madame**

monstre [mɔstʀ] *nm* monster ♦ *adj* (*fam: colossal*) monstrous; **un travail ~** a fantastic amount of work; **monstrueux, -euse** *adj* monstrous

mont [mɔ̃] *nm:* **par ~s et par vaux** up hill and down dale; **le M~ Blanc** Mont Blanc

montage [mɔ̃taʒ] *nm* (*assemblage: d'appareil*) assembly; (PHOTO) photo-montage; (CINÉMA) editing

montagnard, e [mɔ̃taɲaʀ, aʀd] *adj* mountain *cpd* ♦ *nm/f* mountain-dweller

montagne [mɔ̃taɲ] *nf* (*cime*) mountain; (*région*): **la ~** the mountains *pl*; **~s russes** big dipper *sg*, switchback *sg*; **montagneux, -euse** *adj* mountainous; (*basse montagne*) hilly

montant, e [mɔ̃tɑ̃, ɑ̃t] *adj* rising; **pull à col ~** high-necked jumper ♦ *nm* (*somme, total*) (sum) total, (total) amount; (*de fenêtre*) upright; (*de lit*) post

monte-charge [mɔ̃tʃaʀʒ] *nm inv* goods lift, hoist

montée [mɔ̃te] *nf* (*des prix, hostilités*) rise; (*escalade*) climb; (*côte*) hill; **au milieu de la ~** halfway up

monter [mɔ̃te] *vt* (*escalier, côte*) to go (*ou* come) up; (*valise, paquet*) to take (*ou* bring) up; (*étagère*) to raise; (*tente, échafaudage*) to put up; (*machine*) to assemble; (CINÉMA) to edit; (THÉÂTRE) to put on, stage; (*société etc*) to set up ♦ *vi* to go (*ou* come) up; (*prix, niveau, température*) to go up, rise; (*passager*) to get on; **se ~ à** (*frais etc*) to add up to, come to; **~ à pied** to walk up, go up on foot; **~ dans le train/l'avion** to get into the train/plane, board the train/plane; **~ sur** to climb up onto; **~ à cheval** (*faire du cheval*) to ride, go riding

montre [mɔ̃tʀ] *nf* watch; **contre la ~** (SPORT) against the clock; **montre-bracelet** *nf* wristwatch

montrer [mɔ̃tʀe] *vt* to show; **~ qch à qn** to show sb sth

monture [mɔ̃tyʀ] *nf* (*cheval*) mount; (*de lunettes*) frame; (*d'une bague*) setting

monument [mɔnymɑ̃] *nm* monument; **~ aux morts** war memorial

moquer [mɔke]: **se ~ de** *vt* to make fun of, laugh at; (*fam: se désintéresser de*) not to care about; (*tromper*): **se ~ de qn** to take sb for a ride; **moquerie** *nf* mockery

moquette [mɔkɛt] *nf* fitted carpet

moqueur, -euse [mɔkœʀ, øz] *adj* mocking

moral, e, -aux [mɔʀal, o] *adj* moral ♦ *nm* morale; **avoir le ~** (*fam*) to be in good spirits; **avoir le ~ à zéro** (*fam*) to be really down; **morale** *nf* (*de mœurs*) morals *pl*; (*valeurs*) moral standards *pl*, morality; (*d'une fable etc*) moral; **faire la morale à** to lecture, preach at; **moralité** *nf* morality; (*conduite*) moral

morceau, x [mɔʀso] *nm* piece, bit;

morceler

(d'une œuvre) passage, extract; (MUS) piece; (CULIN: de viande) cut; (de sucre) lump; **mettre en ~x** to pull to pieces ou bits; **manger un ~** to have a bite (to eat)

morceler [mɔrsəle] vt to break up, divide up

mordant, e [mɔrdɑ̃, ɑ̃t] adj (ton, remarque) scathing, cutting; (ironie, froid) biting ♦ nm (style) bite, punch

mordiller [mɔrdije] vt to nibble at, chew at

mordre [mɔrdr] vt to bite ♦ vi (poisson) to bite; **~ sur** (fig) to go over into, overlap into; **~ à l'hameçon** to bite, rise to the bait

mordu, e [mɔrdy] (fam) nm/f enthusiast; **un ~ de jazz** a jazz fanatic

morfondre [mɔrfɔ̃dr]: **se ~** vi to mope

morgue [mɔrg] nf (arrogance) haughtiness; (lieu: de la police) morgue; (: à l'hôpital) mortuary

morne [mɔrn] adj dismal, dreary

morose [mɔroz] adj sullen, morose

mors [mɔr] nm bit

morse [mɔrs] nm (ZOOL) walrus; (TÉL) Morse (code)

morsure [mɔrsyr] nf bite

mort[1] [mɔr] nf death

mort[2]**, e** [mɔr, mɔrt] pp de **mourir** ♦ adj dead ♦ nm/f (défunt) dead man/woman; (victime): **il y a eu plusieurs ~s** several people were killed, there were several killed; **~ de peur/fatigue** frightened to death/dead tired

mortalité [mɔrtalite] nf mortality, death rate

mortel, le [mɔrtɛl] adj (poison etc) deadly, lethal; (accident, blessure) fatal; (silence, ennemi) deadly; (péché) mortal; (fam: ennuyeux) deadly boring

mortier [mɔrtje] nm (gén) mortar

mort-né, e [mɔrne] adj (enfant) stillborn

mortuaire [mɔrtyer] adj: **avis ~** death announcement

morue [mɔry] nf (ZOOL) cod fish

mosaïque [mɔzaik] nf mosaic

Moscou [mɔsku] n Moscow

mosquée [mɔske] nf mosque

mot [mo] nm word; (message) line, note; **~ à ~** word for word; **~ d'ordre** watchword; **~ de passe** password; **~s croisés** crossword (puzzle) sg

motard [mɔtar, ard] nm biker; (policier) motorcycle cop

motel [mɔtɛl] nm motel

moteur, -trice [mɔtœr, tris] adj (ANAT, PHYSIOL) motor; (TECH) driving; (AUTO): **à 4 roues motrices** 4-wheel drive ♦ nm engine, motor; **à ~** power-driven, motor cpd

motif [mɔtif] nm (cause) motive; (décoratif) design, pattern, motif; **sans ~** groundless

motivation [mɔtivasjɔ̃] nf motivation

motiver [mɔtive] vt to motivate; (justifier) to justify, account for

moto [mɔto] nf (motor)bike; **motocycliste** nm/f motorcyclist

motorisé, e [mɔtɔrize] adj (personne) having transport ou a car

motrice [mɔtris] adj voir **moteur**

motte [mɔt] nf: **~ de terre** lump of earth, clod of earth; **~ de beurre** lump of butter

mou (mol), molle [mu, mɔl] adj soft; (personne) lethargic; (protestations) weak ♦ nm: **avoir du mou** to be slack

moucharder [muʃarde] (fam) vt (SCOL) to sneak on; (POLICE) to grass on

mouche [muʃ] nf fly

moucher [muʃe]: **se ~** vi to blow one's nose

moucheron [muʃrɔ̃] nm midge

mouchoir [muʃwar] nm handkerchief, hanky; **~ en papier** tissue, paper hanky

moudre [mudr] vt to grind

moue [mu] nf pout; **faire la ~** to pout; (fig) to pull a face

mouette [mwet] nf (sea)gull

moufle [mufl] nf (gant) mitt(en)

mouillé, e [muje] adj wet

mouiller [muje] vt (humecter) to wet, moisten; (tremper): to make sb/sth wet ♦ vi (NAVIG) to lie ou be at anchor; **se ~** to get wet; (fam: prendre des risques) to commit o.s.

moulant, e [mulɑ̃, ɑ̃t] adj figure-hugging

moule [mul] nf mussel ♦ nm (CULIN) mould; **~ à gâteaux** cake tin (BRIT) ou pan (US)

moulent [mul] voir **moudre; mouler**

mouler [mule] vt (suj: vêtement) to hug, fit closely round

moulin [mulɛ̃] nm mill; **~ à café/à poivre** coffee/pepper mill; **~ à légumes** (vegetable) shredder; **~ à paroles** (fig) chatterbox; **~ à vent** windmill

moulinet [muline] nm (de canne à pêche) reel; (mouvement): **faire des ~s avec qch** to whirl sth around

moulinette ® [mulinɛt] nf (vegetable) shredder

moulu, e [muly] pp de **moudre**

mourant, e [murɑ̃, ɑ̃t] adj dying

mourir [murir] vi to die; **~ de froid/faim** to die of exposure/hunger; **~ de faim/d'ennui** (fig) to be starving/be bored to death; **~ d'envie de faire** to be dying to do

mousse [mus] nf (BOT) moss; (de savon) lather; (écume: sur eau, bière) froth, foam; (CULIN) mousse ♦ nm (NAVIG) ship's boy; **~ à raser** shaving foam

mousseline [muslin] nf muslin; **pommes ~** mashed potatoes

mousser [muse] vi (bière, détergent) to foam; (savon) to lather; **mousseux, -euse** adj frothy ♦ nm: **(vin) mousseux** sparkling wine

mousson [musɔ̃] nf monsoon

moustache [mustaʃ] nf moustache; **~s** nfpl (du chat) whiskers pl; **moustachu, e** adj with a moustache

moustiquaire [mustikɛr] nf mosquito net

moustique [mustik] nm mosquito

moutarde [mutard] nf mustard

mouton [mutɔ̃] nm sheep inv; (peau) sheepskin; (CULIN) mutton

mouvement [muvmɑ̃] nm movement; (fig: impulsion) gesture; **avoir un bon ~** to make a nice gesture; **en ~** in motion; on the move; **mouvementé, e** adj (vie, poursuite) eventful; (réunion) turbulent

mouvoir [muvwar]: **se ~** vi to move

moyen, ne [mwajɛ̃, jɛn] adj average; (tailles, prix) medium; (de grandeur moyenne) medium-sized ♦ nm (façon) means sg, way; **~s** nmpl (capacités) means; **très ~** (résultats) pretty poor; **je n'en ai pas les ~s** I can't afford it; **au ~ de** by means of; **par tous les ~s** by every possible means, every possible way; **par ses propres ~s** all by oneself; **~ âge** Middle Ages; **~ de transport** means of transport

moyennant [mwajɛnɑ̃] prép (somme) for; (service, conditions) in return for; (travail, effort) with

moyenne [mwajɛn] nf average; (MATH) mean; (SCOL) pass mark; **en ~** on (an) average; **~ d'âge** average age

Moyen-Orient [mwajɛnɔrjɑ̃] nm: **le ~~** the Middle East

moyeu, x [mwajø] nm hub

MST sigle f = **maladie sexuellement transmissible** STD

MTC sigle m = **mécanisme du taux de change** ERM

mû, mue [my] pp de **mouvoir**

muer [mɥe] vi (oiseau, mammifère) to moult; (serpent) to slough; (jeune garçon): **il mue** his voice is breaking; **se ~ en** to transform into

muet, te [mɥɛ, mɥɛt] adj dumb; (fig): **~ d'admiration** etc speechless with admiration etc; (CINÉMA) silent ♦ nm/f mute

mufle [myfl] nm muzzle; (fam: goujat) boor

mugir [myʒir] vi (taureau) to bellow; (vache) to low; (fig) to howl

muguet [mygɛ] nm lily of the valley

mule [myl] nf (ZOOL) (she-)mule

mulet [myle] *nm* (ZOOL) (he-)mule

multinationale [myltinasjɔnal] *nf* multinational

multiple [myltipl] *adj* multiple, numerous; (*varié*) many, manifold; **multiplication** *nf* multiplication; **multiplier** *vt* to multiply; **se multiplier** *vi* to multiply

municipal, e, -aux [mynisipal, o] *adj* (*élections, stade*) municipal; (*conseil*) town *cpd*; **piscine/bibliothèque ~e** public swimming pool/library; **municipalité** *nf* (*ville*) municipality; (*conseil*) town council

munir [mynir] *vt*: **~ qch de** to equip sth with; **se ~ de** to arm o.s. with

munitions [mynisjɔ̃] *nfpl* ammunition *sg*

mur [myr] *nm* wall; **~ du son** sound barrier

mûr, e [myr] *adj* ripe; (*personne*) mature

muraille [myraj] *nf* (high) wall

mural, e, -aux [myral, o] *adj* wall *cpd*; (*art*) mural

mûre [myr] *nf* blackberry

muret [myrε] *nm* low wall

mûrir [myrir] *vi* (*fruit, blé*) to ripen; (*abcès*) to come to a head; (*fig: idée, personne*) to mature ♦ *vt* (*projet*) to nurture; (*personne*) to (make) mature

murmure [myrmyr] *nm* murmur; **murmurer** *vi* to murmur

muscade [myskad] *nf* (*aussi:* **noix (de) ~**) nutmeg

muscat [myska] *nm* (*raisins*) muscat grape; (*vin*) muscatel (wine)

muscle [myskl] *nm* muscle; **musclé, e** *adj* muscular; (*fig*) strong-arm

museau, x [myzo] *nm* muzzle; (CULIN) brawn

musée [myze] *nm* museum; (*de peinture*) art gallery

museler [myz(ə)le] *vt* to muzzle; **muselière** *nf* muzzle

musette [myzεt] *nf* (*sac*) lunchbag

musical, e, -aux [myzikal, o] *adj* musical

music-hall [myzikol] *nm* (*salle*) variety theatre; (*genre*) variety

musicien, ne [myzisjε̃, jεn] *adj* musical ♦ *nm/f* musician

musique [myzik] *nf* music; **~ d'ambiance** background music

musulman, e [myzylmɑ̃, an] *adj, nm/f* Moslem, Muslim

mutation [mytasjɔ̃] *nf* (ADMIN) transfer

muter [myte] *vt* to transfer, move

mutilé, e [mytile] *nm/f* disabled person (*through loss of limbs*)

mutiler [mytile] *vt* to mutilate, maim

mutin, e [mytε̃, in] *adj* (*air, ton*) mischievous, impish ♦ *nm/f* (MIL, NAVIG) mutineer; **mutinerie** *nf* mutiny

mutisme [mytism] *nm* silence

mutuel, le [mytɥεl] *adj* mutual; **mutuelle** *nf* voluntary insurance premiums for back-up health cover

myope [mjɔp] *adj* short-sighted

myosotis [mjɔzɔtis] *nm* forget-me-not

myrtille [mirtij] *nf* bilberry

mystère [mistεr] *nm* mystery; **mystérieux, -euse** *adj* mysterious

mystifier [mistifje] *vt* to fool

mythe [mit] *nm* myth

mythologie [mitɔlɔʒi] *nf* mythology

N, n

n' [n] *adv voir* **ne**

nacre [nakr] *nf* mother of pearl

nage [naʒ] *nf* swimming; (*manière*) style of swimming, stroke; **traverser/s'éloigner à la ~** to swim across/away; **en ~** bathed in sweat; **nageoire** *nf* fin; **nager** *vi* to swim; **nageur, -euse** *nm/f* swimmer

naguère [nagεr] *adv* formerly

naïf, -ïve [naif, naiv] *adj* naïve

nain, e [nε̃, nεn] *nm/f* dwarf

naissance [nεsɑ̃s] *nf* birth; **donner ~ à** to give birth to; (*fig*) to give rise to

naître [nεtr] *vi* to be born; (*fig*): **~ de** to arise from, be born out of; **il est né**

en 1960 he was born in 1960; **faire ~** (fig) to give rise to, arouse

naïve [naiv] adj voir **naïf**

naïveté [naivte] nf naivety

nana [nana] (fam) nf (fille) chick, bird (BRIT)

nantir [nɑ̃tiʀ] vt: **~ qn de** to provide sb with; **les nantis** (péj) the well-to-do

nappe [nap] nf tablecloth; (de pétrole, gaz) layer; **~ phréatique** ground water; **napperon** nm table-mat

naquit etc [naki] vb voir **naître**

narcodollars [naʀkodɔlaʀ] nmpl drug money §§

narguer [naʀge] vt to taunt

narine [naʀin] nf nostril

narquois, e [naʀkwa, waz] adj mocking

natal, e [natal] adj native; **natalité** nf birth rate

natation [natasjɔ̃] nf swimming

natif, -ive [natif, iv] adj native

nation [nasjɔ̃] nf nation; **national, e, -aux** [nasjɔnal, o] adj national; **nationale** nf: (route) **nationale** ≈ A road (BRIT), ≈ state highway (US); **nationaliser** vt to nationalize; **nationalisme** nm nationalism; **nationalité** nf nationality

natte [nat] nf (cheveux) plait; (tapis) mat

naturaliser [natyʀalize] vt to naturalize

nature [natyʀ] nf nature ♦ adj, adv (CULIN) plain, without seasoning or sweetening; (café, thé) black, without sugar; (yaourt) natural; **payer en ~** to pay in kind; **~ morte** still-life; **naturel, le** [natyʀɛl] adj (gén, aussi enfant) natural ♦ nm (absence d'affectation) naturalness; (caractère) disposition, nature; **naturellement** adv naturally; (bien sûr) of course

naufrage [nofʀaʒ] nm (ship)wreck; **faire ~** to be shipwrecked

nauséabond, e [nozeabɔ̃, ɔ̃d] adj foul

nausée [noze] nf nausea

nautique [notik] adj nautical, water cpd; **sports ~s** water sports

naval, e [naval] adj naval; (industrie) shipbuilding

navet [navɛ] nm turnip; (péj: film) rubbishy film

navette [navɛt] nf shuttle; **faire la ~ (entre)** to go to and fro ou shuttle (between)

navigateur [navigatœʀ, tʀis] nm (NAVIG) seafarer; (INFORM) browser

navigation [navigasjɔ̃] nf navigation, sailing

naviguer [navige] vi to navigate, sail; **~ sur Internet** to browse the Internet

navire [naviʀ] nm ship

navrer [navʀe] vt to upset, distress; **je suis navré** I'm so sorry

ne, n' [n(ə)] adv voir **pas**; **plus**; **jamais** etc; (sans valeur négative: non traduit): **c'est plus loin que je ~ le croyais** it's further than I thought

né, e [ne] pp (voir **naître**): **~ en 1960** born in 1960; **~e Scott** née Scott

néanmoins [neɑ̃mwɛ̃] adv nevertheless

néant [neɑ̃] nm nothingness; **réduire à ~** to bring to nought; (espoir) to dash

nécessaire [neseseʀ] adj necessary ♦ nm necessary; (sac) kit; **je vais faire le ~** I'll see to it; **~ de couture** sewing kit; **nécessité** nf necessity; **nécessiter** vt to require

nécrologique [nekʀɔlɔʒik] adj: rubrique **~** obituary column

néerlandais, e [neɛʀlɑ̃dɛ, ɛz] adj Dutch

nef [nɛf] nf (d'église) nave

néfaste [nefast] adj (nuisible) harmful; (funeste) ill-fated

négatif, -ive [negatif, iv] adj negative ♦ nm (PHOTO) negative

négligé, e [negliʒe] adj (en désordre) slovenly ♦ nm (tenue) negligee

négligeable [negliʒabl] adj negligible

négligent, e [negliʒɑ̃, ɑ̃t] adj careless, negligent

négliger [negliʒe] vt (tenue) to be careless about; (avis, précautions) to disregard; (épouse, jardin) to neglect; **~**

faire to fail to do, not bother to do

négoce [negɔs] *nm* trade

négociant [negɔsjɑ̃, jɑ̃t] *nm* merchant

négociation [negɔsjasjɔ̃] *nf* negotiation; **négocier** *vi, vt* to negotiate

nègre [nɛgr] (*péj*) *nm* (*écrivain*) ghost (writer)

neige [nɛʒ] *nf* snow; **neiger** *vi* to snow

nénuphar [nenyfar] *nm* water-lily

néon [neɔ̃] *nm* neon

néo-zélandais, e [neozelɑ̃dɛ, ɛz] *adj* New Zealand *cpd* ♦ *nm/f*: **N~~Z~, e** New Zealander

nerf [nɛr] *nm* nerve; **être sur les ~s** to be all keyed up; **allons, du ~!** come on, buck up!; **nerveux, -euse** *adj* nervous; (*irritable*) touchy, nervy; (*voiture*) nippy, responsive; **nervosité** *nf* excitability, tenseness; (*irritabilité passagère*) irritability, tenseness

nervure [nɛrvyr] *nf* vein

n'est-ce pas [nɛspa] *adv* isn't it?, won't you? *etc, selon le verbe qui précède*

Net [nɛt] *nm* (*Internet*): **le ~** the Net

net, nette [nɛt] *adj* (*sans équivoque, distinct*) clear; (*évident: amélioration, différence*) marked, distinct; (*propre*) neat, clean; (*COMM: prix, salaire*) net ♦ *adv* (*refuser*) flatly ♦ *nm*: **mettre au ~** to copy out; **s'arrêter ~** to stop dead; **nettement** *adv* clearly, distinctly; (*incontestablement*) decidedly, distinctly; **netteté** *nf* clearness

nettoyage [netwajaʒ] *nm* cleaning; **~ à sec** dry cleaning

nettoyer [netwaje] *vt* to clean

neuf¹ [nœf] *num* nine

neuf², neuve [nœf, nœv] *adj* new ♦ *nm*: **remettre à ~** to do up (as good as new), refurbish; **quoi de ~?** what's new?

neutre [nøtr] *adj* neutral; (*LING*) neuter

neuve [nœv] *adj voir* **neuf²**

neuvième [nœvjɛm] *num* ninth

neveu, x [n(ə)vø] *nm* nephew

névrosé, e [nevroze] *adj, nm/f* neurotic

nez [ne] *nm* nose; **~ à ~ avec** face to face with; **avoir du ~** to have flair

ni [ni] *conj*: **~ ... ~** neither ... nor; **je n'aime ~ les lentilles ~ les épinards** I like neither lentils nor spinach; **il n'a dit ~ oui ~ non** he didn't say either yes or no; **elles ne sont venues ~ l'une ~ l'autre** neither of them came

niais, e [njɛ, njɛz] *adj* silly, thick

niche [niʃ] *nf* (*du chien*) kennel; (*de mur*) recess, niche; **nicher** *vi* to nest

nid [ni] *nm* nest; **~ de poule** pothole

nièce [njɛs] *nf* niece

nier [nje] *vt* to deny

nigaud, e [nigo, od] *nm/f* booby, fool

Nil [nil] *nm*: **le ~** the Nile

n'importe [nɛ̃pɔrt] *adv*: **~ qui/quoi/où** anybody/anything/anywhere; **~ quand** any time; **~ quel/quelle** any; **~ lequel/laquelle** any (one); **~ comment** (*sans soin*) carelessly

niveau, x [nivo] *nm* level; (*des élèves, études*) standard; **~ de vie** standard of living

niveler [niv(ə)le] *vt* to level

NN *abr* (= *nouvelle norme*) revised standard of hotel classification

noble [nɔbl] *adj* noble; **noblesse** *nf* nobility; (*d'une action etc*) nobleness

noce [nɔs] *nf* wedding; (*gens*) wedding party (*ou* guests *pl*); **faire la ~** (*fam*) to go on a binge

nocif, -ive [nɔsif, iv] *adj* harmful

nocturne [nɔktyrn] *adj* nocturnal ♦ *nf* late-night opening

Noël [nɔɛl] *nm* Christmas

nœud [nø] *nm* knot; (*ruban*) bow; **~ papillon** bow tie

noir, e [nwar] *adj* black; (*obscur, sombre*) dark ♦ *nm/f* black man/woman ♦ *nm*: **dans le ~** in the dark; **travail au ~** moonlighting; **travailler au ~** to work on the side; **noircir** *vt, vi* to blacken; **noire** *nf* (*MUS*) crotchet (*BRIT*), quarter note (*US*)

noisette [nwazɛt] *nf* hazelnut

noix [nwa] *nf* walnut; (*CULIN*): **une ~ de**

beurre a knob of butter; **~ de cajou** cashew nut; **~ de coco** coconut; **à la ~** (fam) worthless

nom [nɔ̃] nm name; (LING) noun; **~ de famille** surname; **~ de jeune fille** maiden name; **~ déposé** trade name; **~ propre** proper noun

nomade [nɔmad] nm/f nomad

nombre [nɔ̃bʀ] nm number; **venir en ~** to come in large numbers; **depuis ~ d'années** for many years; **au ~ de mes amis** among my friends; **nombreux, -euse** adj many, numerous; (avec nom sg: foule etc) large; **peu nombreux** few

nombril [nɔ̃bʀi(l)] nm navel

nommer [nɔme] vt to name; (élire): to appoint, nominate; **se ~: il se nomme Pascal** his name's Pascal, he's called Pascal

non [nɔ̃] adv (réponse) no; (avec loin, sans, seulement) not; **~ (pas) que** not that; **moi ~ plus** neither do I, I don't either; **c'est bon ~?** (exprimant le doute) it's good, isn't it?

non-alcoolisé, e [nɔ̃alkɔlize] adj non alcoholic

nonante [nɔnɑ̃t] (BELGIQUE, SUISSE) num ninety

non-fumeur [nɔ̃fymœʀ, øz] nm non-smoker

non-sens [nɔ̃sɑ̃s] nm absurdity

nonchalant, e [nɔ̃ʃalɑ̃, ɑ̃t] adj nonchalant

nord [nɔʀ] nm North ♦ adj northern; north; **au ~** (situation) in the north; (direction) to the north; **au ~ de** (to the north of); **nord-est** nm North-East; **nord-ouest** nm North-West

normal, e, -aux [nɔʀmal, o] adj normal; **c'est tout à fait ~** it's perfectly natural; **vous trouvez ça ~?** does it seem right to you?; **normale** nf: **la normale** the norm, the average; **normalement** adv (en général) normally

normand, e [nɔʀmɑ̃, ɑ̃d] adj of Normandy

Normandie [nɔʀmɑ̃di] nf Normandy

norme [nɔʀm] nf norm; (TECH) standard

Norvège [nɔʀvɛʒ] nf Norway; **norvégien, ne** adj nm/f: **Norvégien, ne** Norwegian ♦ nm (LING) Norwegian

nos [no] adj voir **notre**

nostalgie [nɔstalʒi] nf nostalgia; **nostalgique** adj nostalgic

notable [nɔtabl] adj (fait) notable, noteworthy; (marqué) noticeable, marked ♦ nm prominent citizen

notaire [nɔtɛʀ] nm solicitor

notamment [nɔtamɑ̃] adv in particular, among others

note [nɔt] nf (écrite, MUS) note; (SCOL) mark (BRIT), grade; (facture) bill; **~ de service** memorandum

noté, e [nɔte] adj: **être bien/mal ~** (employé etc) to have a good/bad record

noter [nɔte] vt (écrire) to write down; (remarquer) to note, notice; (devoir) to mark, grade

notice [nɔtis] nf summary, short article; (brochure) leaflet, instruction book

notifier [nɔtifje] vt: **~ qch à qn** to notify sb of sth, notify sth to sb

notion [nɔsjɔ̃] nf notion, idea

notoire [nɔtwaʀ] adj widely known; (en mal) notorious

notre [nɔtʀ] (pl **nos**) adj our

nôtre [nɔtʀ] pron: **le ~, la ~, les ~s** ours ♦ adj ours; **les ~s** ours; (alliés etc) our own people; **soyez des ~s** join us

nouer [nwe] vt to tie, knot; (fig: alliance etc) to strike up

noueux, -euse [nwø, øz] adj gnarled

nouilles [nuj] nfpl noodles

nourrice [nuʀis] nf (gardienne) childminder

nourrir [nuʀiʀ] vt to feed; (fig: espoir) to harbour, nurse; **se ~: se ~ de** to feed (o.s.) on; **nourrissant, e** adj nourishing, nutritious; **nourrisson** nm (unweaned) infant; **nourriture** nf food

nous [nu] *pron* (*sujet*) we; (*objet*) us; **nous-mêmes** *pron* ourselves

nouveau (**nouvel**), **-elle**, **x** [nuvo, nuvɛl] *adj* new ♦ *nm*: **y a-t-il du ~?** is there anything new on this? ♦ *nm/f* new pupil (*ou* employee); **de ~**, **à ~** again; **~ venu**, **nouvelle venue** newcomer; **~x mariés** newly-weds; **nouveau-né**, **x** *nm/f* newborn baby; **nouveauté** *nf* novelty; (*objet*) new thing *ou* article

nouvel [nuvɛl] *adj voir* **nouveau**; **N~ An** New Year

nouvelle [nuvɛl] *adj voir* **nouveau** ♦ *nf* (*piece*) *of news* sg; (*LITTÉRATURE*) short story; **les ~s** the news; **je suis sans ~s de lui** I haven't heard from him; **Nouvelle-Calédonie** *nf* New Caledonia; **nouvellement** *adv* recently, newly; **Nouvelle-Zélande** *nf* New Zealand

novembre [nɔvɑ̃bʁ] *nm* November

novice [nɔvis] *adj* inexperienced

noyade [nwajad] *nf* drowning *no pl*

noyau, **x** [nwajo] *nm* (*de fruit*) stone; (*BIO*, *PHYSIQUE*) nucleus; (*fig*: *centre*) core; **noyauter** *vt* (*POL*) to infiltrate

noyer [nwaje] *nm* walnut (tree); (*bois*) walnut ♦ *vt* to drown; (*moteur*) to flood; **se ~** *vi* to be drowned, drown; (*suicide*) to drown o.s.

nu, **e** [ny] *adj* naked; (*membres*) naked, bare; (*pieds*, *mains*, *chambre*, *fil électrique*) bare ♦ *nm* (*ART*) nude; **tout ~** stark naked; **se mettre ~** to strip; **mettre à ~** to bare

nuage [nɥaʒ] *nm* cloud; **nuageux**, **-euse** *adj* cloudy

nuance [nɥɑ̃s] *nf* (*de couleur*, *sens*) shade; **il y a une ~** (**entre**) there's a slight difference (between); **nuancer** *vt* (*opinion*) to bring some reservations *ou* qualifications to

nucléaire [nyklecʁ] *adj* nuclear ♦ *nm*: **le ~** nuclear energy

nudiste [nydist] *nm/f* nudist

nuée [nɥe] *nf*: **une ~ de** a cloud *ou* host *ou* swarm of

nues [ny] *nfpl*: **tomber des ~** to be taken aback; **porter qn aux ~** to praise sb to the skies

nuire [nɥiʁ] *vi* to be harmful; **~ à** to harm, do damage to; **nuisible** *adj* harmful; **animal nuisible** pest

nuit [nɥi] *nf* night; **il fait ~** it's dark; **cette ~** (*hier*) last night; (*aujourd'hui*) tonight; **~ blanche** sleepless night

nul, **nulle** [nyl] *adj* (*aucun*) no; (*minime*) nil, non-existent; (*non valable*) null; (*péj*) useless, hopeless ♦ *pron* none, no one; **match** *ou* **résultat ~** draw; **~le part** nowhere; **nullement** *adv* by no means; **nullité** *nf* (*personne*) nonentity

numérique [nymeʁik] *adj* numerical; (*affichage*) digital

numéro [nymeʁo] *nm* number; (*spectacle*) act, turn; (*PRESSE*) issue, number; **~ de téléphone** (tele)phone number; **~ vert** ≃ freefone ® number (*BRIT*), ≃ toll-free number (*US*); **numéroter** *vt* to number

nu-pieds [nypje] *adj inv*, *adv* barefoot

nuque [nyk] *nf* nape of the neck

nu-tête [nytɛt] *adj inv*, *adv* bareheaded

nutritif, **-ive** [nytʁitif, iv] *adj* (*besoins*, *valeur*) nutritional; (*nourrissant*) nutritious

nylon [nilɔ̃] *nm* nylon

O, o

oasis [ɔazis] *nf* oasis

obéir [ɔbeiʁ] *vi* to obey; **~ à** to obey; **obéissance** *nf* obedience; **obéissant**, **e** *adj* obedient

obèse [ɔbɛz] *adj* obese; **obésité** *nf* obesity

objecter [ɔbʒɛkte] *vt* (*prétexter*) to plead, put forward as an excuse; **~ (à qn)** to object (to sb) that; **objecteur** *nm*: **objecteur de conscience** conscientious objector

objectif, **-ive** [ɔbʒɛktif, iv] *adj* objective ♦ *nm* objective; (*PHOTO*) lens sg, objective; **objectivité** nf objectivity

objection [ɔbʒɛksjɔ̃] nf objection

objet [ɔbʒɛ] nm object; (d'une discussion, recherche) subject; **être ou faire l'~ de** (discussion) to be the subject of; (soins) to be given ou shown; **sans ~** purposeless; groundless; **~ d'art** object d'art; **~s trouvés** lost property sg (BRIT), lost-and-found sg (US); **~s de valeur** valuables

obligation [ɔbligasjɔ̃] nf obligation; (COMM) bond, debenture; **obligatoire** adj compulsory, obligatory; **obligatoirement** adv necessarily; (fam: sans aucun doute) inevitably

obligé, e [ɔbliʒe] adj (redevable): **être très ~ à qn** to be most obliged to sb

obligeance [ɔbliʒɑ̃s] nf: **avoir l'~ de ...** to be kind ou good enough to ...; **obligeant, e** adj (personne) obliging, kind

obliger [ɔbliʒe] vt (contraindre): **~ qn à faire** to force ou oblige sb to do; **je suis bien obligé** I have to

oblique [ɔblik] adj oblique; **en ~** diagonally; **obliquer** vi: **obliquer vers** to turn off towards

oblitérer [ɔblitere] vt (timbre-poste) to cancel

obnubiler [ɔbnybile] vt to obsess

obscène [ɔpsɛn] adj obscene

obscur, e [ɔpskyr] adj dark; (méconnu) obscure; **obscurcir** vt to darken; (fig) to obscure; **s'obscurcir** vi to grow dark; **obscurité** nf darkness; **dans l'obscurité** in the dark, in darkness

obsédé, e [ɔpsede] nm/f: **un ~ (sexuel)** a sex maniac

obséder [ɔpsede] vt to obsess, haunt

obsèques [ɔpsɛk] nfpl funeral sg

observateur, -trice [ɔpsɛrvatœr, tris] adj observant, perceptive ♦ nm/f observer

observation [ɔpsɛrvasjɔ̃] nf observation; (d'un règlement etc) observance; (reproche) reproof; **être en ~** (MÉD) to be under observation

observatoire [ɔpsɛrvatwar] nm observatory

observer [ɔpsɛrve] vt (regarder) to observe, watch; (scientifiquement: aussi règlement etc) to observe; (surveiller) to watch; (remarquer) to observe, notice; **faire ~ qch à qn** (dire) to point out sth to sb

obsession [ɔpsesjɔ̃] nf obsession

obstacle [ɔpstakl] nm obstacle; (ÉQUITATION) jump, hurdle; **faire ~ à** (projet) to hinder, put obstacles in the path of

obstiné, e [ɔpstine] adj obstinate

obstiner [ɔpstine]: **s'~** vi to insist, dig one's heels in; **s'~ à faire** to persist (obstinately) in doing

obstruer [ɔpstrye] vt to block, obstruct

obtenir [ɔptanir] vt to obtain, get; (résultat) to achieve, obtain; **~ de pouvoir faire** to obtain permission to do

obturateur [ɔptyratœr, tris] nm (PHOTO) shutter

obus [ɔby] nm shell

occasion [ɔkazjɔ̃] nf (aubaine, possibilité) opportunity; (circonstance) occasion; (COMM: article non neuf) secondhand buy; (: acquisition avantageuse) bargain; **à plusieurs ~s** on several occasions; **à l'~** sometimes, on occasions; **d'~** secondhand; **occasionnel, le** adj (non régulier) occasional; **occasionnellement** adv occasionally, from time to time

occasionner [ɔkazjɔne] vt to cause

occident [ɔksidɑ̃] nm: **l'O~** the West; **occidental, e, -aux** adj western; (POL) Western ♦ nm/f Westerner

occupation [ɔkypasjɔ̃] nf occupation

occupé, e [ɔkype] adj (personne) busy; (place, sièges) taken; (toilettes) engaged; (ligne) engaged (BRIT), busy (US); (MIL, POL) occupied

occuper [ɔkype] vt to occupy; (poste) to hold; **s'~ de** (être responsable de) to be in charge of; (se charger de: affaire) to take charge of, deal with; (: clients *etc*) to attend to; **s'~ (à qch)** to occupy o.s. *ou* keep o.s. busy (with sth)

occurrence [ɔkyʀɑ̃s] *nf*: **en l'~** in this case

océan [ɔseɑ̃] *nm* ocean

octante [ɔktɑ̃t] *adj (regional)* eighty

octet [ɔktɛ] *nm* byte

octobre [ɔktɔbʀ] *nm* October

octroyer [ɔktʀwaje]: **s'~** *vt (vacances etc)* to treat o.s. to

oculiste [ɔkylist] *nm/f* eye specialist

odeur [ɔdœʀ] *nf* smell

odieux, -euse [ɔdjø, jøz] *adj* hateful

odorant, e [ɔdɔʀɑ̃, ɑ̃t] *adj* sweet-smelling, fragrant

odorat [ɔdɔʀa] *nm* (sense of) smell

œil [œj] *(pl* **yeux)** *nm* eye; **à l'~** *(fam)* for free; **à l'~ nu** with the naked eye; **tenir qn à l'œil** to keep an eye *ou* a watch on; **avoir l'œil à** to keep an eye on; **fermer les yeux (sur)** *(fig)* to turn a blind eye (to); **voir qch d'un bon/mauvais œil** to look on sth favourably/unfavourably

œillères [œjɛʀ] *nfpl* blinkers *(BRIT)*, blinders *(US)*

œillet [œjɛ] *nm (BOT)* carnation

œuf [œf, *pl* ø] *nm* egg; **œuf à la coque/sur le plat/dur** boiled/fried/hard-boiled egg; **œuf de Pâques** Easter egg; **œufs brouillés** scrambled eggs

œuvre [œvʀ] *nf (tâche)* task, undertaking; *(livre, tableau etc)* work; *(ensemble de la production artistique)* works *pl ♦ nm (CONSTR)*: **le gros œuvre** the shell; **œuvre (de bienfaisance)** charity; **mettre en œuvre** *(moyens)* to make use of; **œuvre d'art** work of art

offense [ɔfɑ̃s] *nf* insult; **offenser** *vt* to offend, hurt

offert, e [ɔfɛʀ, ɛʀt] *pp de* **offrir**

office [ɔfis] *nm (agence)* bureau, agency; *(REL)* service *♦ nm ou f (pièce)* pantry; **faire ~ de** to act as; **d'~** automatically; **~ du tourisme** tourist bureau

officiel, le [ɔfisjɛl] *adj, nm/f* official

officier [ɔfisje] *nm* officer

officieux, -euse [ɔfisjø, jøz] *adj* unofficial

offrande [ɔfʀɑ̃d] *nf* offering

offre [ɔfʀ] *nf* offer; *(aux enchères)* bid; *(ADMIN: soumission)* tender; *(ÉCON)*: **l'~ et la demande** supply and demand; **"~s d'emploi"** "situations vacant"; **~ d'emploi** job advertised

offrir [ɔfʀiʀ] *vt*: **~ (à qn)** to offer (to sb); *(faire cadeau de)* to give (to sb); **s'~** *vt (vacances, voiture)* to treat o.s. to; **~ (à qn) de faire qch** to offer to do sth (for sb); **~ à boire à qn** *(chez soi)* to offer sb a drink

offusquer [ɔfyske] *vt* to offend

OGM *sigle m (= organisme génétiquement modifié)* GMO

oie [wa] *nf (ZOOL)* goose

oignon [ɔɲɔ̃] *nm* onion; *(de tulipe etc)* bulb

oiseau, x [wazo] *nm* bird; **~ de proie** bird of prey

oisif, -ive [wazif, iv] *adj* idle

oléoduc [ɔleɔdyk] *nm* (oil) pipeline

olive [ɔliv] *nf (BOT)* olive; **olivier** *nm* olive (tree)

OLP *sigle f (= Organisation de libération de la Palestine)* PLO

olympique [ɔlɛ̃pik] *adj* Olympic

ombragé, e [ɔ̃bʀaʒe] *adj* shaded, shady; **ombrageux, -euse** *adj (personne)* touchy, easily offended

ombre [ɔ̃bʀ] *nf (espace non ensoleillé)* shade; *(~ portée, tache)* shadow; **à l'~** in the shade; **dans l'~** *(fig)* in the dark; **~ à paupières** eyeshadow; **ombrelle** *nf* parasol, sunshade

omelette [ɔmlɛt] *nf* omelette; **~ norvégienne** baked Alaska

omettre [ɔmɛtʀ] *vt* to omit, leave out

omnibus [ɔmnibys] *nm* slow *ou* stopping train

omoplate [ɔmɔplat] *nf* shoulder blade

MOT-CLÉ

on [ɔ̃] *pron* **1** *(indéterminé)* you, one; **on peut le faire ainsi** you *ou* one can do it like this, it can be done like this

2 (*quelqu'un*): **on les a attaqués** they were attacked; **on vous demande au téléphone** there's a phone call for you, you're wanted on the phone

3 (*nous*) we; **on va y aller demain** we're going tomorrow

4 (*les gens*) they; **autrefois, on croyait ...** they used to believe ...

5: on ne peut plus

♦ *adv*: **on ne peut plus stupide** as stupid as can be

oncle [ɔ̃kl] *nm* uncle

onctueux, -euse [ɔ̃ktɥø, øz] *adj* creamy, smooth

onde [ɔ̃d] *nf* wave; **sur les ~s** on the radio; **sur ~s courtes** on short wave *sg*; **moyennes/longues ~s** medium/long wave *sg*

ondée [ɔ̃de] *nf* shower

on-dit [ɔ̃di] *nm inv* rumour

onduler [ɔ̃dyle] *vi* to undulate; (*cheveux*) to wave

onéreux, -euse [ɔnerø, øz] *adj* costly

ongle [ɔ̃gl] *nm* nail

ont [ɔ̃] *vb voir* **avoir**

ONU *sigle f* (= Organisation des Nations Unies) UN

onze [ɔ̃z] *num* eleven; **onzième** *num* eleventh

OPA *sigle f* = **offre publique d'achat**

opaque [ɔpak] *adj* opaque

opéra [ɔpera] *nm* opera; (*édifice*) opera house

opérateur, -trice [ɔperatœr, tris] *nm/f* operator; **~ (de prise de vues)** cameraman

opération [ɔperasjɔ̃] *nf* operation; (COMM) dealing

opératoire [ɔperatwar] *adj* (*choc etc*) post-operative

opérer [ɔpere] *vt* (*personne*) to operate on; (*faire, exécuter*) to carry out, make ♦ *vi* (*remède: faire effet*) to act, work; (MÉD) to operate; **s'~** *vi* (*avoir lieu*) to occur, take place; **se faire ~** to have

an operation

opérette [ɔperet] *nf* operetta, light opera

ophtalmologiste [ɔftalmɔlɔʒist] *nm/f* ophthalmologist, optician

opiner [ɔpine] *vi*: **~ de la tête** to nod assent

opinion [ɔpinjɔ̃] *nf* opinion; **l'~ (publique)** public opinion

opportun, e [ɔpɔrtœ̃, yn] *adj* timely, opportune; **opportuniste** *nm/f* opportunist

opposant, e [ɔpozɑ̃, ɑ̃t] *nm/f* opponent

opposé, e [ɔpoze] *adj* (*direction*) opposite; (*faction*) opposing; (*opinions, intérêts*) conflicting; (*contre*): **~ à** opposed to, against ♦ *nm*: **l'~** the other *ou* opposite side (*ou* direction); (*contraire*) the opposite; **à l'~** (*fig*) on the other hand; **à l'~ de** (*fig*) contrary to, unlike

opposer [ɔpoze] *vt* (*personnes, équipes*) to oppose; (*couleurs*) to contrast; **s'~** *vi* (*équipes*) to confront each other; (*opinions*) to conflict; (*couleurs, styles*) to contrast; **s'~ à** (*interdire*) to oppose; **~ qch** (*comme obstacle, défense*) to set sth against; (*comme objection*) to put sth forward against

opposition [ɔpozisjɔ̃] *nf* opposition; **par ~ à** as opposed to, **entrer en ~ avec** to come into conflict with; **faire ~ à un chèque** to stop a cheque

oppressant, e [ɔpresɑ̃, ɑ̃t] *adj* oppressive

oppresser [ɔprese] *vt* to oppress; **oppression** *nf* oppression

opprimer [ɔprime] *vt* to oppress

opter [ɔpte] *vi*: **~ pour** to opt for

opticien, ne [ɔptisjɛ̃, jɛn] *nm/f* optician

optimisme [ɔptimism] *nm* optimism; **optimiste** *nm/f* optimist ♦ *adj* optimistic

option [ɔpsjɔ̃] *nf* option; **matière à ~** (SCOL) optional subject

optique [ɔptik] *adj* (*nerf*) optic; (*verres*) optical ♦ *nf* (*fig: manière de voir*) perspective

opulent, e [ɔpylɑ̃, ɑ̃t] *adj* wealthy, opulent; (*formes, poitrine*) ample, generous

or [ɔR] *nm* gold ♦ *conj* now, but; **en ~** (*objet*) gold *cpd*; **une affaire en ~** a real bargain; **il croyait gagner ~ il a perdu** he was sure he would win and yet he lost

orage [ɔRaʒ] *nm* (thunder)storm; **orageux, -euse** *adj* stormy

oral, e, -aux [ɔRal, o] *adj, nm* oral; **par voie ~e** (*MÉD*) orally

orange [ɔRɑ̃ʒ] *nf* orange ♦ *adj inv* orange; **orangeade** *nf* orangeade; **orangé, e** *adj* orangey, orange-coloured; **oranger** *nm* orange tree

orateur [ɔRatœR, tRis] *nm* speaker

orbite [ɔRbit] *nf* (*ANAT*) (eye-)socket; (*PHYSIQUE*) orbit

orchestre [ɔRkɛstR] *nm* orchestra; (*de jazz*) band; (*places*) stalls *pl* (*BRIT*), orchestra (*US*); **orchestrer** *vt* to orchestrate

orchidée [ɔRkide] *nf* orchid

ordinaire [ɔRdinɛR] *adj* ordinary; (*qualité*) standard; (*péj: commun*) common ♦ *nm* ordinary; (*menus*) everyday fare ♦ *nf* (*essence*) ≈ two-star (petrol) (*BRIT*), ≈ regular gas (*US*); **d'~** usually, normally; **comme à l'~** as usual

ordinateur [ɔRdinatœR] *nm* computer

ordonnance [ɔRdɔnɑ̃s] *nf* (*MÉD*) prescription; (*MIL*) orderly, batman (*BRIT*)

ordonné, e [ɔRdɔne] *adj* tidy, orderly

ordonner [ɔRdɔne] *vt* (*agencer*) to organize, arrange; (*donner un ordre*): **~ à qn de faire** to order sb to do; (*REL*) to ordain; (*MÉD*) to prescribe

ordre [ɔRdR] *nm* order; (*propreté et soin*) orderliness, tidiness; (*nature*): **d'~ pratique** of a practical nature; **~s** *nmpl* (*REL*) holy orders; **mettre en ~** to tidy (up), put in order; **à l'~ de qn** payable to sb; **être aux ~s de qn/sous les ~s de qn** to be at sb's disposal/under sb's command; **jusqu'à nouvel ~** until

further notice; **de premier ~** first-rate; **~ du jour** (*d'une réunion*) agenda; **à l'~ du jour** (*fig*) topical

ordure [ɔRdyR] *nf* filth *no pl*; **~s** *nfpl* (*balayures, déchets*) rubbish *sg*, refuse *sg*; **~s ménagères** household refuse

oreille [ɔRɛj] *nf* ear; **avoir de l'~** to have a good ear (for music)

oreiller [ɔReje] *nm* pillow

oreillons [ɔRɛjɔ̃] *nmpl* mumps *sg*

ores [ɔR]: **d'~ et déjà** *adv* already

orfèvrerie [ɔRfɛvRəRi] *nf* goldsmith's (*ou* silversmith's) trade; (*ouvrage*) gold (*ou* silver) plate

organe [ɔRgan] *nm* organ; (*porte-parole*) representative, mouthpiece

organigramme [ɔRganigRam] *nm* (*tableau hiérarchique*) organization chart; (*schéma*) flow chart

organique [ɔRganik] *adj* organic

organisateur, -trice [ɔRganizatœR, tRis] *nm/f* organizer

organisation [ɔRganizasjɔ̃] *nf* organization

organiser [ɔRganize] *vt* to organize; (*mettre sur pied: service etc*) to set up; **s'~** to get organized

organisme [ɔRganism] *nm* (*BIO*) organism; (*corps, ADMIN*) body

organiste [ɔRganist] *nm/f* organist

orgasme [ɔRgasm] *nm* orgasm, climax

orge [ɔRʒ] *nf* barley

orgue [ɔRg] *nm* organ; **~s** *nfpl* (*MUS*) organ *sg*

orgueil [ɔRgœj] *nm* pride; **orgueilleux, -euse** *adj* proud

Orient [ɔRjɑ̃] *nm*: **l'~** the East, the Orient; **oriental, e, -aux** *adj* (*langue, produit*) oriental; (*frontière*) eastern

orientation [ɔRjɑ̃tasjɔ̃] *nf* (*de recherches*) orientation; (*d'une maison etc*) aspect; (*d'un journal*) leanings *pl*; **avoir le sens de l'~** to have a (good) sense of direction; **~ professionnelle** careers advisory service

orienté, e [ɔRjɑ̃te] *adj* (*fig: article, journal*) slanted; **bien/mal ~** (*apparte-*

ment) well/badly positioned; **~ au sud**
facing south, with a southern aspect

orienter [ɔʀjɑ̃te] *vt (tourner: antenne)*
to direct, turn; *(personne, recherches)*
to direct; *(fig: élève)* to orientate; **s'~** *(se
repérer)* to find one's bearings; **s'~ vers**
(fig) to turn towards

origan [ɔʀigɑ̃] *nm* oregano

originaire [ɔʀiʒinɛʀ] *adj*: **être ~ de** to
be a native of

original, e, -aux [ɔʀiʒinal, o] *adj*
original; *(bizarre)* eccentric ♦ *nm/f* eccentric ♦ *nm (document etc, ART)* original

origine [ɔʀiʒin] *nf* origin; **dès l'~** at
from the outset; **à l'~** originally; **origi-
nel, le** *adj* original

orme [ɔʀm] *nm* elm

ornement [ɔʀnamɑ̃] *nm* ornament

orner [ɔʀne] *vt* to decorate, adorn

ornière [ɔʀnjɛʀ] *nf* rut

orphelin, e [ɔʀfalɛ̃, in] *adj* orphan(ed)
♦ *nm/f* orphan; **~ de père/mère**
fatherless/motherless; **orphelinat** *nm*
orphanage

orteil [ɔʀtɛj] *nm* toe; **gros ~** big toe

orthographe [ɔʀtɔgʀaf] *nf* spelling

ortie [ɔʀti] *nf* (stinging) nettle

os [ɔs] *nm* bone; **tomber sur un ~**
(fam) to hit a snag

osciller [ɔsile] *vi (au vent etc)* to rock;
(fig): **~ entre** to waver *ou* fluctuate between

osé, e [oze] *adj* daring, bold

oseille [ozɛj] *nf* sorrel

oser [oze] *vi, vt* to dare; **~ faire** to dare
(to) do

osier [ozje] *nm* willow; **d'~, en ~** wick-
er(work)

ossature [ɔsatyʀ] *nf (ANAT)* frame, skel-
etal structure; *(fig)* framework

osseux, -euse [ɔsø, øz] *adj* bony; *(tissu, maladie, greffe)* bone *cpd*

ostensible [ɔstɑ̃sibl] *adj* conspicuous

otage [ɔtaʒ] *nm* hostage; **prendre qn
comme ~** to take sb hostage

OTAN *sigle f (= Organisation du traité de
l'Atlantique Nord)* NATO

otarie [ɔtaʀi] *nf* sea-lion

ôter [ote] *vt* to remove; *(soustraire)* to
take away; **~ qch à qn** to take sth
(away) from sb; **~ qch de** to remove
sth from

otite [ɔtit] *nf* ear infection

ou [u] *conj* or; **~ ... ~** either ... or; **~
bien** or (else)

┌─── MOT-CLÉ ──────────────┐

où [u] *pron relatif* **1** *(position, situation)*
where, that *(souvent omis)*; **la chambre
où il était** the room (that) he was in,
the room where he was; **la ville où je
l'ai rencontré** the town where I met
him; **la pièce d'où il est sorti** the
room he came out of; **le village d'où
je viens** the village I come from; **les
villes par où il est passé** the towns
he went through

2 *(temps, état)* that *(souvent omis)*; **le
jour où il est parti** the day (that) he
left; **au prix où c'est** at the price it is
♦ *adv* **1** *(interrogation)* where; **où est-
il/va-t-il?** where is he/is he going?; **par
où?** which way?; **d'où vient que ...?**
how come .. ?

2 *(position)* where; **je sais où il est** I
know where he is; **où que l'on aille**
wherever you go

└──────────────────────────┘

ouate ['wat] *nf* cotton wool *(BRIT)*, cotton *(US)*

oubli [ubli] *nm (acte)*: **l'~ de** forgetting;
(trou de mémoire) lapse of memory;
(négligence) omission, oversight; **tomber dans l'~** to sink into oblivion

oublier [ublije] *vt* to forget; *(laisser
quelque part: chapeau etc)* to leave behind; *(ne pas voir: erreurs etc)* to miss

oubliettes [ublijɛt] *nfpl* dungeon *sg*

ouest [wɛst] *nm* west ♦ *adj inv* west; *(région)* western; **à l'~** in the west; *(direction)* (to the) west, westwards; **à l'~ de**
(to the) west of

ouf ['uf] *excl* phew!

oui ['wi] *adv* yes

ouï-dire ['widir]: **par ~-~** adv by hear-say

ouïe [wi] nf hearing; **~s** nfpl (de poisson) gills

ouille ['uj] excl ouch!

ouragan [uʀagɑ̃] nm hurricane

ourlet [uʀlɛ] nm hem

ours [uʀs] nm bear; **~ brun/blanc** brown/polar bear; **~ (en peluche)** teddy (bear)

oursin [uʀsɛ̃] nm sea urchin

ourson [uʀsɔ̃] nm (bear-)cub

ouste [ust] excl hop it!

outil [uti] nm tool; **outiller** vt to equip

outrage [utʀaʒ] nm insult; **~ à la pudeur** indecent conduct no pl; **outrager** vt to offend gravely

outrance [utʀɑ̃s]: **à ~** adv excessively, to excess

outre [utʀ] prép besides ♦ adv: **passer ~ à** to disregard, take no notice of; **en ~** besides, moreover; **~ mesure** to excess; (manger, boire) immoderately; **outre-Atlantique** adv across the Atlantic; **outre-Manche** adv across the Channel; **outre-mer** adv overseas; **outrepasser** vt to go beyond, exceed

ouvert, e [uvɛʀ, ɛʀt] pp de **ouvrir** ♦ adj open; (robinet, gaz etc) on; **ouvertement** adv openly; **ouverture** nf opening; (MUS) overture; **ouverture d'esprit** open-mindedness

ouvrable [uvʀabl] adj: **jour ~** working day, weekday

ouvrage [uvʀaʒ] nm (tâche, de tricot etc) work no pl; (texte, livre) work; **ouvragé, e** adj finely embroidered (ou worked ou carved)

ouvre-boîte(s) [uvʀəbwat] nm inv tin (BRIT) ou can opener

ouvre-bouteille(s) [uvʀəbutɛj] nm inv bottle-opener

ouvreuse [uvʀøz] nf usherette

ouvrier, -ière [uvʀije, ijɛʀ] nm/f worker ♦ adj working-class; (conflit) industrial; (mouvement) labour cpd; **classe ouvrière** working class

ouvrir [uvʀiʀ] vt (gén) to open; (brèche, passage, MÉD: abcès) to open up; (commencer l'exploitation de, créer) to open (up); (eau, électricité, chauffage, robinet) to turn on ♦ vi to open; to open up; **s'~** vi to open; **s'~ à qn** to open one's heart to sb; **~ l'appétit à qn** to whet sb's appetite

ovaire [ɔvɛʀ] nm ovary

ovale [ɔval] adj oval

ovni [ɔvni] sigle m (= objet volant non identifié) UFO

oxyder [ɔkside]: **s'~** vi to become oxidized

oxygène [ɔksiʒɛn] nm oxygen

oxygéné, e [ɔksiʒene] adj: **eau ~e** hydrogen peroxide

oxygéner [ɔksiʒene]: **s'~** (fam) vi to get some fresh air

ozone [ozon] nf ozone; **la couche d'~** the ozone layer

P, p

pacifique [pasifik] adj peaceful ♦ nm: **le P~, l'océan P~** the Pacific (Ocean)

pacotille [pakɔtij] nf cheap junk

pack [pak] nm pack

pacte [pakt] nm pact, treaty

pagaie [pagɛ] nf paddle

pagaille [pagaj] nf mess, shambles sg

pagayer vi to paddle

page [paʒ] nf page ♦ nm page (boy); **à la ~** (fig) up-to-date; **~ d'accueil** (INFORM) home page

paiement [pɛmɑ̃] nm payment

païen, ne [pajɛ̃, pajɛn] adj, nm/f pagan, heathen

paillasson [pajasɔ̃] nm doormat

paille [paj] nf straw

paillettes [pajɛt] nfpl (décoratives) sequins, spangles

pain [pɛ̃] nm (substance) bread; (unité) loaf (of bread); (morceau): **~ de savon** etc bar of soap etc; **~ au chocolat** chocolate-filled pastry; **~ aux raisins**

currant bun; **~ bis/complet** brown/wholemeal ou wholewheat (US) bread; **~ d'épice** gingerbread; **~ de mie** sandwich loaf; **~ grillé** toast

pair, e [pɛʀ] adj (nombre) even ♦ nm peer; **aller de ~** to go hand in hand ou together; **jeune fille au ~** au pair; **paire** nf pair

paisible [pezibl] adj peaceful, quiet

paître [pɛtʀ] vi to graze

paix [pɛ] nf peace; **faire/avoir la ~** to make/have peace; **fiche-lui la ~!** (fam) leave him alone!

Pakistan [pakistã] nm: **le ~** Pakistan

palace [palas] nm luxury hotel

palais [palɛ] nm palace; (ANAT) palate

pâle [pɑl] adj pale; **bleu ~** pale blue

Palestine [palɛstin] nf: **la ~** Palestine

palet [palɛ] nm disc; (HOCKEY) puck

paletot [palto] nm (thick) cardigan

palette [palɛt] nf (de peintre) palette; (produits) range

pâleur [pɑlœʀ] nf paleness

palier [palje] nm (d'escalier) landing; (fig) level, plateau; **par ~s** in stages

pâlir [paliʀ] vi to turn ou go pale; (couleur) to fade

palissade [palisad] nf fence

pallier [palje]: vt to offset, make up for

palmarès [palmaʀɛs] nm record (of achievements); (SPORT) list of winners

palme [palm] nf (de plongeur) flipper; **palmé, e** adj (pattes) webbed

palmier [palmje] nm palm tree; (gâteau) heart-shaped biscuit made of flaky pastry

pâlot, te [pɑlo, ɔt] adj pale, peaky

palourde [paluʀd] nf clam

palper [palpe] vt to feel, finger

palpitant, e [palpitã, ɑt] adj thrilling

palpiter [palpite] vi (cœur, pouls) to beat; (: plus fort) to pound, throb

paludisme [palydism] nm malaria

pamphlet [pãflɛ] nm lampoon, satirical tract

pamplemousse [pãpləmus] nm grapefruit

pan [pã] nm section, piece ♦ excl bang!

panache [panaʃ] nm plume; (fig) spirit, panache

panaché, e [panaʃe] adj: **glace ~e** mixed-flavour ice cream ♦ nm (bière) shandy

pancarte [pãkaʀt] nf sign, notice

pancréas [pãkʀeas] nm pancreas

pané, e [pane] adj fried in breadcrumbs

panier [panje] nm basket; **mettre au ~** to chuck away; **~ à provisions** shopping basket; **panier-repas** nm packed lunch

panique [panik] nf, adj panic; **paniquer** vi to panic

panne [pan] nf breakdown; **être/tomber en ~** to have broken down/break down; **être en ~ d'essence** ou **sèche** to have run out of petrol (BRIT) ou gas (US); **~ d'électricité** ou **de courant** power ou electrical failure

panneau, x [pano] nm (écriteau) sign, notice; **~ d'affichage** notice board; **~ de signalisation** roadsign

panoplie [panɔpli] nf (jouet) outfit; (fig) array

panorama [panɔʀama] nm panorama

panse [pãs] nf paunch

pansement [pãsmã] nm dressing, bandage; **~ adhésif** sticking plaster

panser [pãse] vt (plaie) to dress, bandage; (bras) to put a dressing on, bandage; (cheval) to groom

pantalon [pãtalɔ̃] nm trousers pl, pair of trousers; **~ de ski** ski pants pl

panthère [pãtɛʀ] nf panther

pantin [pãtɛ̃] nm puppet

pantois [pãtwa] adj m: **rester ~** to be flabbergasted

pantoufle [pãtufl] nf slipper

paon [pã] nm peacock

papa [papa] nm dad(dy)

pape [pap] nm pope

paperasse [papʀas] (péj) nf bumf no pl, papers pl; **paperasserie** (péj) nf paperwork no pl; (tracasserie) red tape no pl

papeterie [papetri] *nf* (*magasin*) stationer's (shop)

papi *nm* (*fam*) granddad

papier [papje] *nm* paper; (*article*) article; **~s** *nmpl* (*aussi:* **~s d'identité**) (identity) papers; **~ à lettres** writing paper, notepaper; **~ carbone** carbon paper; **~ (d')aluminium** aluminium (BRIT) *ou* aluminum (US) foil, tinfoil; **~ de verre** sandpaper; **~ hygiénique** *ou* **de toilette** toilet paper; **~ journal** newspaper; **~ peint** wallpaper

papillon [papijɔ̃] *nm* butterfly; (*fam: contravention*) (parking) ticket; **~ de nuit** moth

papillote [papijɔt] *nf*: **en ~** cooked in tinfoil

papoter [papɔte] *vi* to chatter

paquebot [pak(ə)bo] *nm* liner

pâquerette [pakrɛt] *nf* daisy

Pâques [pak] *nm, nfpl* Easter

paquet [pakɛ] *nm* packet; (*colis*) parcel; (*fig: tas*): **~ de** pile *ou* heap of; **paquet-cadeau** *nm*: **faites-moi un paquet-cadeau** gift-wrap it for me

par [par] *prép* by; **finir** *etc* **~** to end *etc* with; **~ amour** out of love; **passer ~ Lyon/la côte** to go via *ou* through Lyons/along by the coast; **~ la fenêtre** (*jeter, regarder*) out of the window; **3 ~ jour/personne** 3 a *ou* per day/head; **2 ~ 2** in twos; **~ ici** this way; (*dans le coin*) round here; **~-ci, ~-là** here and there; **~ temps de pluie** in wet weather

parabolique [parabɔlik] *adj*: **antenne ~** parabolic *ou* dish aerial

parachever [paraʃ(ə)ve] *vt* to perfect

parachute [paraʃyt] *nm* parachute; **parachutiste** *nm/f* parachutist; (MIL) paratrooper

parade [parad] *nf* (*spectacle, défilé*) parade; (ESCRIME, BOXE) parry

paradis [paradi] *nm* heaven, paradise

paradoxe [paradɔks] *nm* paradox

paraffine [parafin] *nf* paraffin

parages [paraʒ] *nmpl*: **dans les ~ (de)** in the area *ou* vicinity (of)

paragraphe [paragraf] *nm* paragraph

paraître [parɛtr] *vb +attrib* to seem, look, appear ♦ *vi* to appear; (*être visible*) to show; (PRESSE, ÉDITION) to be published, come out, appear ♦ *vb impers*: **il paraît que** it seems *ou* appears that, they say that; **chercher à ~** to show off

parallèle [paralɛl] *adj* parallel; (*non officiel*) unofficial ♦ *nm* (*comparaison*): **faire un ~ entre** to draw a parallel between ♦ *nf* parallel (line)

paralyser [paralize] *vt* to paralyse

paramédical, e, -aux [paramedikal, o] *adj*: **personnel ~** paramedics *pl*, paramedical workers *pl*

paraphrase [parafraz] *nf* paraphrase

parapluie [paraplɥi] *nm* umbrella

parasite [parazit] *nm* parasite; **~s** (TÉL) interference *sg*

parasol [parasɔl] *nm* parasol, sunshade

paratonnerre [paratɔnɛr] *nm* lightning conductor

paravent [paravɑ̃] *nm* folding screen

parc [park] *nm* (*public*) park, gardens *pl*; (*de château etc*) grounds *pl*; (*d'enfant*) playpen; (*ensemble d'unités*) stock; (*de voitures etc*) fleet; **~ d'attractions** theme park; **~ de stationnement** car park

parcelle [parsɛl] *nf* fragment, scrap; (*de terrain*) plot, parcel

parce que [parsk(ə)] *conj* because

parchemin [parʃəmɛ̃] *nm* parchment

parcmètre [parkmɛtr] *nm* parking meter

parcourir [parkurir] *vt* (*trajet, distance*) to cover; (*article, livre*) to skim *ou* glance through; (*lieu*) to go all over, travel up and down; (*suj: frisson*) to run through

parcours [parkur] *nm* (*trajet*) journey; (*itinéraire*) route

par-derrière [parderjɛr] *adv* round the back; **dire du mal de qn ~~** to speak ill of sb behind his back

par-dessous [pard(ə)su] *prép, adv* under(neath)

pardessus [pardəsy] *nm* overcoat

par-dessus [pard(ə)sy] *prép* over (the top of) ♦ *adv* over (the top); **~~ le marché** on top of all that; **~~ tout** above all; **en avoir ~~ la tête** to have had enough

par-devant [pard(ə)vã] *adv* (*passer*) round the front

pardon [pardɔ̃] *nm* forgiveness *no pl* ♦ *excl* sorry!; (*pour interpeller etc*) excuse me!; **demander ~ à qn (de)** to apologize to sb (for); **je vous demande ~** I'm sorry; (*pour interpeller*) excuse me!

pardonner [pardɔne] *vt* to forgive; **pardonner qch à qn** to forgive sb for sth

pare...: **pare-balles** *inv* bulletproof; **pare-brise** *nm inv* windscreen (*BRIT*), windshield (*US*); **pare-chocs** *nm inv* bumper

paré, e [pare] *adj* ready, all set

pareil, le [parɛj] *adj* (*identique*) the same, alike; (*similaire*) similar; (*tel*): **un courage/livre ~** such courage/a book, courage/a book like this; **de ~s livres** such books; **ne pas avoir son(sa) ~(le)** to be second to none; **à la** same as; (*similaire*) similar to; **sans ~** unparalleled, unequalled

parent, e [parã, ãt] *nm/f*: **un(e) ~(e)** a relative *ou* relation; **~s** *nmpl* (*père et mère*) parents; **parenté** *nf* (*lien*) relationship

parenthèse [parãtez] *nf* (*ponctuation*) bracket, parenthesis; (*digression*) parenthesis, digression; **entre ~s** in brackets; (*fig*) incidentally

parer [pare] *vt* to adorn; (*éviter*) to ward off; **~ au plus pressé** to attend to the most urgent things first

paresse [parɛs] *nf* laziness; **paresseux, -euse** *adj* lazy

parfaire [parfɛr] *vt* to perfect

parfait, e [parfɛ, ɛt] *adj* perfect ♦ *nm* (*LING*) perfect (tense); **parfaitement** *adv* perfectly ♦ *excl* (most) certainly

parfois [parfwa] *adv* sometimes

parfum [parfœ̃] *nm* (*produit*) perfume, scent; (*odeur: de fleur*) scent, fragrance; (*goût*) flavour; **parfumé, e** *adj* (*fleur, fruit*) fragrant; (*femme*) perfumed; **parfumé au café** coffee-flavoured; **parfumer** *vt* (*suj: odeur, bouquet*) to perfume; (*crème, gâteau*) to flavour; **parfumerie** *nf* (*produits*) perfumes *pl*; (*boutique*) perfume shop

pari [pari] *nm* bet; **parier** *vt* to bet

Paris [pari] *n* Paris; **parisien, ne** *adj* Parisian; (*GÉO, ADMIN*) Paris *cpd* ♦ *nm/f*: **Parisien, ne** Parisian

parjure [parʒyr] *nm* perjury

parking [parkiŋ] *nm* (*lieu*) car park

parlant, e [parlã, ãt] *adj* (*regard*) eloquent; (*CINÉMA*) talking; **les chiffres sont ~s** the figures speak for themselves

parlement [parləmã] *nm* parliament; **parlementaire** *adj* parliamentary ♦ *nm/f* member of parliament; **parlementer** *vi* to negotiate, parley

parler [parle] *vi* to speak, talk; (*avouer*) to talk; **~ (à qn) de** to talk *ou* speak (to sb) about; **~ le/en français** to speak French/in French; **~ affaires** to talk business; **sans ~ de** (*fig*) not to mention, to say nothing of; **tu parles!** (*fam: bien sûr*) you bet!

parloir [parlwar] *nm* (*de prison, d'hôpital*) visiting room

parmi [parmi] *prép* among(st)

paroi [parwa] *nf* wall; (*cloison*) partition; **~ rocheuse** rock face

paroisse [parwas] *nf* parish

parole [parɔl] *nf* (*faculté*): **la ~** speech; (*mot, promesse*) word; **~s** *nfpl* (*MUS*) words, lyrics; **tenir ~** to keep one's word; **prendre la ~** to speak; **demander la ~** to ask for permission to speak; **je te crois sur ~** I'll take your word for it

parquer [parke] *vt* (*voiture, matériel*) to park; (*bestiaux*) to pen (in *ou* up)

parquet [parke] *nm* (*plancher*) floor;

(JUR): **le ~** the Public Prosecutor's department

parrain [paʀɛ̃] nm godfather; **parrainer** vt (suj: entreprise) to sponsor

pars [paʀ] vb voir **partir**

parsemer [paʀsəme] vt (suj: feuilles, papiers) to be scattered over; **~ qch de** to scatter sth with

part [paʀ] nf (qui revient à qn) share; (fraction, -ie) part; **prendre ~ à** (débat etc) to take part in; (soucis, douleur de qn) to share in; **faire ~ de qch à qn** to announce sth to sb, inform sb of sth; **pour ma ~** as for me, as far as I'm concerned; **à ~ entière** full; **de la ~ de** (au nom de) on behalf of; (donné par) from; **de toute(s) ~s** from all sides ou quarters; **de ~ et d'autre** on both sides, on either side; **d'une ~ ... d'autre ~** on the one hand ... on the other hand; **d'autre ~** (de plus) moreover; **à ~** (séparément) separately; (de côté) aside ♦ prép apart from, except for; **faire la ~ des choses** to make allowances

partage [paʀtaʒ] nm (fractionnement) dividing up; (répartition) sharing (out) no pl, share-out

partager [paʀtaʒe] vt to share; (distribuer, répartir) to share (out); (morceler, diviser) to divide (up); **se ~** vt (héritage etc) to share between themselves (ou ourselves)

partance [paʀtɑ̃s]: **en ~** adv: **en ~ pour** (bound) for

partenaire [paʀtənɛʀ] nm/f partner

parterre [paʀtɛʀ] nm (de fleurs) (flower) bed; (THÉÂTRE) stalls pl

parti [paʀti] nm (POL) party; (décision) course of action; (personne à marier) match; **tirer ~ de** to take advantage of, turn to good account; **prendre ~ (pour/contre)** to take sides ou a stand (for/against); **~ pris** bias

partial, e, -aux [paʀsjal, jo] adj biased, partial

participant, e [paʀtisipɑ̃, ɑ̃t] nm/f participant; (à un concours) entrant

participation [paʀtisipasjɔ̃] nf participation; (financière) contribution

participer [paʀtisipe]: **~ à** vt (course, réunion) to take part in; (frais etc) to contribute to; (chagrin, succès de qn) to share (in)

particularité [paʀtikylaʀite] nf (distinctive) characteristic

particulier, -ière [paʀtikylje, jɛʀ] adj (spécifique) particular; (spécial) special, particular; (personnel, privé) private; (étrange) peculiar, odd ♦ nm (individu: ADMIN) private individual; **~ à** peculiar to; **en ~** (surtout) in particular, particularly; (en privé) in private; **particulièrement** adv particularly

partie [paʀti] nf (gén) part; (JUR etc: protagonistes) party; (de cartes, tennis etc) game; **une ~ de pêche** a fishing party ou trip; **en ~** partly, in part; **faire ~ de** (suj: chose) to be part of; **prendre qn à ~** to take sb to task; **en grande ~** largely, in the main; **~ civile** (JUR) party claiming damages in a criminal case

partiel, le [paʀsjɛl] adj partial ♦ nm (SCOL) class exam

partir [paʀtiʀ] vi (gén) to go; (quitter) to go, leave; (tache) to go, come out; **~ de** (lieu: quitter) to leave; (: commencer à) to start from; **à ~ de** from

partisan, e [paʀtizɑ̃, an] nm/f partisan ♦ adj: **être ~ de qch/de faire** to be in favour of sth/doing

partition [paʀtisjɔ̃] nf (MUS) score

partout [paʀtu] adv everywhere; **~ où** **il allait** everywhere ou wherever he went

paru [paʀy] pp de **paraître**

parure [paʀyʀ] nf (bijoux etc) finery no pl; (assortiment) set

parution [paʀysjɔ̃] nf publication

parvenir [paʀvəniʀ]: **~ à** vt (atteindre) to reach; (réussir): **~ à faire** to manage to do, succeed in doing; **~ à ses fins** to achieve one's ends

pas¹ [pɑ] nm (enjambée, DANSE) step;

(allure, mesure) pace; *(bruit)* (foot)step; *(trace)* footprint; **~ à ~** step by step; **au ~** at walking pace; **faire les cent ~** to pace up and down; **faire les premiers ~** to make the first move; **sur le ~ de la porte** on the doorstep

MOT-CLÉ

pas² [pɑ] *adv* **1** *(en corrélation avec ne, non etc)* not; **il ne pleure pas** he does not *ou* doesn't cry; **he's not *ou* isn't crying; **il n'a pas pleuré/ne pleurera pas** he did not *ou* didn't/will not *ou* won't cry; **ils n'ont pas de voiture/d'enfants** they haven't got a car/any children, they have no car/children; **il m'a dit de ne pas le faire** he told me not to do it; **non pas que ... not that ...

2 *(employé sans ne etc)*: **pas moi** not me; not I, I don't *ou* can't etc); **une pomme pas mûre** an apple which isn't ripe; **pas plus tard qu'hier** only yesterday; **pas du tout** not at all
3: pas mal not bad; not badly; **pas mal de** quite a lot of

passage [pɑsaʒ] *nm (fait de passer)* voir **passer**; *(lieu, prix de la traversée)* passage; *(chemin)* way; **de ~** *(touristes)* passing through; **~ à niveau** level crossing; **"~ clouté** pedestrian crossing; **"~ interdit"** "no entry"; **~ souterrain** subway *(BRIT)*, underpass

passager, -ère [pɑsaʒe, ɛʀ] *adj* passing ♦ *nm/f* passenger; **~ clandestin** stowaway

passant, e [pɑsɑ̃, ɑ̃t] *adj (rue, endroit)* busy ♦ *nm/f* passer-by; **en ~** in passing

passe¹ [pɑs] *nf (SPORT, NAVIG)* pass; **être en ~ de faire** to be on the way to doing; **être dans une mauvaise ~** to be going through a rough patch

passe² [pɑs] *nm (~-partout)* master *ou* skeleton key

passé, e [pɑse] *adj (révolu)* past; *(dernier: semaine etc)* last; *(couleur)* faded ♦

prép after ♦ *nm* past; *(LING)* past (tense); **~ de mode** out of fashion; **~ composé** perfect (tense); **~ simple** past historic

passe-partout [pɑspaʀtu] *nm inv* master *ou* skeleton key ♦ *adj inv* all-purpose

passeport [pɑspɔʀ] *nm* passport

passer [pɑse] *vi (aller)* to go; *(voiture, piétons)* défiler) to pass (by), go by; *(facteur, laitier etc)* to come, call; *(pour rendre visite)* to call *ou* drop in; *(film, émission)* to be on; *(temps, jours)* to pass, go by; *(couleur)* to fade; *(mode)* to die out; *(douleur)* to pass, go away; *(SCOL)* to go up (to the next class) ♦ *vt (frontière, rivière etc)* to cross; *(douane)* to go through; *(examen)* to sit, take; *(visite médicale etc)* to have; *(journée, temps)* to spend; *(enfiler: vêtement)* to slip on; *(film, pièce)* to show, put on; *(disque)* to play, put on; *(marché, accord)* to agree on; **se ~** *vi (avoir lieu: scène, action)* to take place; *(se dérouler: entretien etc)* to pass, go by; *(s'écouler: semaine etc)* to pass, go by; *(arriver)*: **que s'est-il passé?** what happened?; **~ qch à qn** *(sel etc)* to pass sth to sb; *(prêter)* to lend sb sth; *(lettre, message)* to pass sth on to sb; *(tolérer)* to let sb get away with sth; **~ par** to go through; **~ avant qch/qn** *(fig)* to come before sth/sb; **~ un coup de fil à qn** *(fam)* to give sb a ring; **laisser ~** *(air, lumière, personne)* to let through; *(occasion)* to let slip, miss; *(erreur)* to overlook; **~ la seconde** *(AUTO)* to change into second; **~ le balai/l'aspirateur** to sweep up/hoover; **je vous passe M. X** *(je vous mets en communication avec lui)* I'm putting you through to Mr X; *(je lui passe l'appareil)* here is Mr X, I'll hand you over to Mr X; **se ~ de** to go *ou* do without

passerelle [pɑsʀɛl] *nf* footbridge; *(de navire, avion)* gangway

passe-temps [pɑstɑ̃] *nm inv* pastime

passible [pɑsibl] *adj*: **~ de** liable to

passif, -ive [pɑsif, iv] *adj* passive

passion [pasjɔ̃] nf passion; **passionnant, e** adj fascinating; **passionné, e** adj (personne) passionate; (récit) impassioned; **être passionné de** to have a passion for; **passionner** vt (personne) to fascinate, grip; **se passionner pour** (sport) to have a passion for

passoire [paswaʀ] nf sieve; (à légumes) colander; (à thé) strainer

pastèque [pastɛk] nf watermelon

pasteur [pastœʀ] nm (protestant) minister, pastor

pasteurisé, e [pastœʀize] adj pasteurized

pastille [pastij] nf (à sucer) lozenge, pastille

patate [patat] nf (fam: pomme de terre) spud; **~ douce** sweet potato

patauger [patoʒe] vi to splash about

pâte [pat] nf (à tarte) pastry; (à pain) dough; (à frire) batter; **~s** nfpl (macaroni etc) pasta sg; **~ à modeler** modelling clay, Plasticine ® (BRIT); **~ brisée** shortcrust pastry; **~ d'amandes** almond paste; **~ de fruits** crystallized fruit no pl; **~ feuilletée** puff ou flaky pastry

pâté [pate] nm (charcuterie) pâté; (tache) ink blot; (de sable) sandpie; **~ de maisons** block (of houses); **~ en croûte** ≈ pork pie

pâtée [pate] nf mash, feed

patente [patãt] nf (COMM) trading licence

paternel, le [patɛʀnɛl] adj (amour, soins) fatherly; (ligne, autorité) paternal

pâteux, -euse [patø, øz] adj pasty; (langue) coated

pathétique [patetik] adj moving

patience [pasjãs] nf patience

patient, e [pasjã, ãt] adj, nm/f patient; **patienter** vi to wait

patin [patɛ̃] nm (sport) skating; **~s (à glace)** (ice) skates; **~s à roulettes** roller skates

patinage [patinaʒ] nm skating

patiner [patine] vi to skate; (roue, voiture) to spin; **se ~** vi (meuble, cuir) to acquire a sheen; **patineur, -euse** nm/f skater; **patinoire** nf skating rink, (ice) rink

pâtir [patiʀ]: **~ de** vt to suffer because of

pâtisserie [patisʀi] nf (boutique) cake shop; (gâteau) cake, pastry; (à la maison) pastry- ou cake-making, baking; **pâtissier, -ière** nm/f pastrycook

patois [patwa, waz] nm dialect, patois

patraque [patʀak] (fam) adj peaky, off-colour

patrie [patʀi] nf homeland

patrimoine [patʀimwan] nm (culture) heritage

patriotique [patʀijɔtik] adj patriotic

patron, ne [patʀɔ̃, ɔn] nm/f boss; (REL) patron saint ♦ nm (COUTURE) pattern; **patronat** nm employers pl; **patronner** vt to sponsor, support

patrouille [patʀuj] nf patrol

patte [pat] nf (jambe) leg; (pied: de chien, chat) paw; (: d'oiseau) foot

pâturage [patyʀaʒ] nm pasture

paume [pom] nf palm

paumé, e [pome] (fam) adj drop-out

paumer [pome] (fam) vt to lose

paupière [popjɛʀ] nf eyelid

pause [poz] nf (arrêt) break; (en parlant, MUS) pause

pauvre [povʀ] adj poor; **pauvreté** nf (état) poverty

pavaner [pavane]: **se ~** vi to strut about

pavé, e [pave] adj (cour) paved; (chaussée) cobbled ♦ nm (bloc) paving stone; cobblestone

pavillon [pavijɔ̃] nm (de banlieue) small (detached) house; pavilion; (drapeau) flag

pavoiser [pavwaze] vi (fig) to rejoice, exult

pavot [pavo] nm poppy

payant, e [pejã, ãt] adj (spectateurs etc) paying; (fig: entreprise) profitable; (effort) which pays off; **c'est ~** you have

to pay, there is a charge
paye [pɛj] nf pay, wages pl
payer [peje] vt (créancier, employé, loyer) to pay; (achat, réparations, fig: faute) to pay for ♦ vi to pay; (métier) to be well-paid; (tactique etc) to pay off; **il me l'a fait ~ 10 F** he charged me 10 F for it; **~ qch à qn** to buy sth for sb, buy sb sth; **se ~ la tête de qn** (fam) to take the mickey out of sb
pays [pei] nm country; (région) region; **du ~** local
paysage [peizaʒ] nm landscape
paysan, ne [peizɑ̃, an] nm/f farmer; (péj) peasant ♦ adj (agricole) farming; (rural) country
Pays-Bas [peiba] nmpl: **les ~-~** the Netherlands
PC nm (INFORM) PC ♦ sigle m = **parti communiste**
P.D.G. sigle m = **président directeur général**
péage [peaʒ] nm toll; (endroit) tollgate
peau, x [po] nf skin; **gants de ~** fine leather gloves; **être bien/mal dans sa ~** to be quite at ease/ill-at-ease; **~ de chamois** (chiffon) chamois leather, shammy; **Peau-Rouge** nm/f Red Indian, redskin
pêche [pɛʃ] nf (sport, activité) fishing; (poissons pêchés) catch; (fruit) peach; **~ à la ligne** (en rivière) angling
péché [peʃe] nm sin
pécher [peʃe] vi (REL) to sin
pêcher [peʃe] nm peach tree ♦ vi to go fishing ♦ vt (attraper) to catch; (être pêcheur de) to fish for
pécheur,- eresse [peʃœʀ, peʃʀɛs] nm/f sinner
pêcheur [peʃœʀ] nm fisherman; (à la ligne) angler
pécule [pekyl] nm savings pl, nest egg
pédagogie [pedagɔʒi] nf educational methods pl, pedagogy; **pédagogique** adj educational
pédale [pedal] nf pedal
pédalo [pedalo] nm pedal-boat

pédant, e [pedɑ̃, ɑ̃t] (péj) adj pedantic
pédestre [pedɛstʀ] adj: **randonnée ~** ramble; **sentier ~** pedestrian footpath
pédiatre [pedjatʀ] nm/f paediatrician, child specialist
pédicure [pedikyʀ] nm/f chiropodist
pègre [pɛgʀ] nf underworld
peignais etc [peɲɛ] vb voir **peindre**; **peigner**
peigne [pɛɲ] nm comb; **peigner** vt to comb (the hair of); **se peigner** vi to comb one's hair
peignoir [peɲwaʀ] nm dressing gown; **peignoir de bain** bathrobe
peindre [pɛ̃dʀ] vt to paint; (fig) to portray, depict
peine [pɛn] nf (affliction) sorrow, sadness no pl; (mal, effort) trouble no pl, effort; (difficulté) difficulty; (JUR) sentence; **avoir de la ~** to be sad; **faire de la ~ à qn** to distress ou upset sb; **prendre la ~ de faire** to go to the trouble of doing; **se donner de la ~** to make an effort; **ce n'est pas la ~ de faire** there's no point in doing, it's not worth doing; **à ~** scarcely, hardly, barely; **à ~ ... que** hardly ... than; **~ capitale** ou **de mort** capital punishment, death sentence; **peiner** vi (personne) to work hard; (moteur, voiture) to labour ♦ vt to grieve, sadden
peintre [pɛ̃tʀ] nm painter; **~ en bâtiment** house painter
peinture [pɛ̃tyʀ] nf painting; (matière) paint; (surfaces peintes: aussi: **~s**) paintwork; **" ~ fraîche "** "wet paint"
péjoratif, -ive [peʒɔʀatif, iv] adj pejorative, derogatory
pelage [pəlaʒ] nm coat, fur
pêle-mêle [pɛlmɛl] adv higgledy-piggledy
peler [pəle] vt, vi to peel
pèlerin [pɛlʀɛ̃] nm pilgrim
pèlerinage [pɛlʀinaʒ] nm pilgrimage
pelle [pɛl] nf shovel; (d'enfant, de terrassier) spade
pellicule [pelikyl] nf film; **~s** nfpl (MÉD)

dandruff *sg*

pelote [p(ə)lɔt] *nf* (de fil, laine) ball

peloton [p(ə)lɔtɔ̃] *nm* group, squad; (CYCLISME) pack; ~ **d'exécution** firing squad

pelotonner: **se** ~ *vi* to curl (o.s.) up

pelouse [p(ə)luz] *nf* lawn

peluche [p(ə)lyʃ] *nf*: (**animal en**) ~ fluffy animal, soft toy; **chien/lapin en** ~ fluffy dog/rabbit

pelure [p(ə)lyʀ] *nf* peeling, peel *no pl*

pénal, e, -aux [penal, o] *adj* penal; **pénalité** *nf* penalty

penaud, e [pəno, od] *adj* sheepish, contrite

penchant [pɑ̃ʃɑ̃] *nm* (tendance) tendency, propensity; (faible) liking, fondness

pencher [pɑ̃ʃe] *vi* to tilt, lean over ♦ *vt* to tilt; **se** ~ *vi* to lean over; (se baisser) to bend down; **se** ~ **sur** (fig: problème) to look into; ~ **pour** to be inclined to favour

pendaison [pɑ̃dɛzɔ̃] *nf* hanging

pendant [pɑ̃dɑ̃] *prép* (au cours de) during; (indique la durée) for; ~ **que** while

pendentif [pɑ̃dɑ̃tif] *nm* pendant

penderie [pɑ̃dʀi] *nf* wardrobe

pendre [pɑ̃dʀ] *vt, vi* to hang; **se** ~ (se suicider) to hang o.s.; ~ **la crémaillère** to have a house-warming party

pendule [pɑ̃dyl] *nf* clock ♦ *nm* pendulum

pénétrer [penetʀe] *vi, vt* to penetrate; ~ **dans** to enter

pénible [penibl] *adj* (travail) hard; (sujet) painful; (personne) tiresome; **péniblement** *adv* with difficulty

péniche [peniʃ] *nf* barge

pénicilline [penisilin] *nf* penicillin

péninsule [penɛ̃syl] *nf* peninsula

pénis [penis] *nm* penis

pénitence [penitɑ̃s] *nf* (peine) penance; (repentir) penitence; **pénitencier** *nm* penitentiary

pénombre [penɔ̃bʀ] *nf* (faible clarté)

half-light; (obscurité) darkness

pensée [pɑ̃se] *nf* thought; (démarche, doctrine) thinking *no pl*; (fleur) pansy; **en** ~ in one's mind

penser [pɑ̃se] *vi, vt* to think; ~ **à** (ami, vacances) to think of *ou* about; (réfléchir à: problème, offre) to think about *ou* over; (prévoir) to think of; **faire** ~ **à** to remind one of; ~ **faire qch** to be thinking of doing sth, intend to do sth; **pensif, -ive** *adj* pensive, thoughtful

pension [pɑ̃sjɔ̃] *nf* (allocation) pension; (prix du logement) board and lodgings, bed and board; (école) boarding school; ~ **alimentaire** (de divorcée) maintenance allowance, alimony; ~ **complète** full board; ~ (**de famille**) boarding house, guesthouse; **pensionnaire** *nm/f* (SCOL) boarder; **pensionnat** *nm* boarding school

pente [pɑ̃t] *nf* slope; **en** ~ sloping

Pentecôte [pɑ̃tkot] *nf*: **la** ~ Whitsun (BRIT), Pentecost

pénurie [penyʀi] *nf* shortage

pépé [pepe] (fam) *nm* grandad

pépin [pepɛ̃] *nm* (BOT: graine) pip; (ennui) snag, hitch

pépinière [pepinjɛʀ] *nf* nursery

perçant, e [pɛʀsɑ̃, ɑ̃t] *adj* (cri) piercing, shrill; (regard) piercing

percée [pɛʀse] *nf* (trouée) opening; (MIL, technologique) breakthrough

perce-neige [pɛʀsənɛʒ] *nf inv* snowdrop

percepteur [pɛʀsɛptœʀ, tʀis] *nm* tax collector

perception [pɛʀsɛpsjɔ̃] *nf* perception; (bureau) tax office

percer [pɛʀse] *vt* to pierce; (ouverture etc) to make; (mystère, énigme) to penetrate ♦ *vi* to break through; **perceuse** *nf* drill

percevoir [pɛʀsəvwaʀ] *vt* (distinguer) to perceive, detect; (taxe, impôt) to collect; (revenu, indemnité) to receive

perche [pɛʀʃ] *nf* (bâton) pole

percher [pɛʀʃe] *vt, vi* to perch; **se** ~ ~

to perch; **perchoir** nm perch

perçois etc [pɛʀswa] vb voir **percevoir**

percolateur [pɛʀkɔlatœʀ] nm percolator

perçu, e [pɛʀsy] pp de **percevoir**

percussion [pɛʀkysjɔ̃] nf percussion

percuter [pɛʀkyte] vt to strike; (suj: véhicule) to crash into

perdant, e [pɛʀdɑ̃, ɑ̃t] nm/f loser

perdre [pɛʀdʀ] vt to lose; (gaspiller: temps, argent) to waste; (personne: moralement etc) to ruin ♦ vi to lose; (sur une vente etc) to lose out; **se ~** vi (s'égarer) to get lost, lose one's way; (denrées) to go to waste

perdrix [pɛʀdʀi] nf partridge

perdu, e [pɛʀdy] pp de **perdre** ♦ adj (isolé) out-of-the-way; (COMM: emballage) non-returnable; (malade): **il est ~** there's no hope left for him; **à vos moments ~s** in your spare time

père [pɛʀ] nm father; **~ de famille** father; **le ~ Noël** Father Christmas

perfection [pɛʀfɛksjɔ̃] nf perfection; **à la ~** to perfection; **perfectionné, e** adj sophisticated; **perfectionner** vt to improve, perfect

perforatrice [pɛʀfɔʀatʀis] nf (de bureau) punch

perforer [pɛʀfɔʀe] vt (poinçonner) to punch

performant, e [pɛʀfɔʀmɑ̃, ɑ̃t] adj: **très ~** high-performance cpd

perfusion [pɛʀfyzjɔ̃] nf: **faire une ~ à qn** to put sb on a drip

péricliter [peʀiklite] vi to collapse

péril [peʀil] nm peril

périmé, e [peʀime] adj (ADMIN) out-of-date, expired

périmètre [peʀimɛtʀ] nm perimeter

période [peʀjɔd] nf period; **périodique** adj periodic ♦ nm periodical

péripéties [peʀipesi] nfpl events, episodes

périphérique [peʀifeʀik] adj (quartiers) outlying ♦ nm (AUTO) ring road

périple [peʀipl] nm journey

périr [peʀiʀ] vi to die, perish

périssable [peʀisabl] adj perishable

perle [pɛʀl] nf pearl; (de plastique, métal, sueur) bead

permanence [pɛʀmanɑ̃s] nf permanence; (local) (duty) office; **assurer une ~** (service public, bureaux) to operate ou maintain a basic service; **être de ~** to be on call ou duty; **en ~** continuously

permanent, e [pɛʀmanɑ̃, ɑ̃t] adj permanent; (spectacle) continuous; **permanente** nf perm

perméable [pɛʀmeabl] adj (terrain) permeable; **~ à** (fig) receptive ou open to

permettre [pɛʀmɛtʀ] vt to allow, permit; **~ à qn/qch** to allow sb to do/sth; **se ~ de faire** to take the liberty of doing

permis [pɛʀmi, iz] nm permit, licence; **~ de chasse** hunting permit; **~ (de conduire)** (driving) licence (BRIT), (driver's) license (US); **~ de construire** planning permission (BRIT), building permit (US); **~ de séjour** residence permit; **~ de travail** work permit

permission [pɛʀmisjɔ̃] nf permission; (MIL) leave; **avoir la ~ de faire** to have permission to do; **en ~** on leave

permuter [pɛʀmyte] vt to change around, permutate ♦ vi to change, permutate, swap

Pérou [peʀu] nm Peru

perpétuel, le [pɛʀpetɥɛl] adj perpetual; **perpétuité** nf: **à perpétuité** for life; **être condamné à perpétuité** to receive a life sentence

perplexe [pɛʀplɛks] adj perplexed, puzzled

perquisitionner [pɛʀkizisjɔne] vi to carry out a search

perron [pɛʀɔ̃] nm steps pl (leading to entrance)

perroquet [pɛʀɔkɛ] nm parrot

perruche [pɛʀyʃ] nf budgerigar (BRIT), budgie (BRIT), parakeet (US)

perruque [peʀyk] *nf* wig
persan, e [peʀsɑ̃, an] *adj* Persian
persécuter [peʀsekyte] *vt* to persecute
persévérer [peʀseveʀe] *vi* to persevere
persiennes [peʀsjen] *nfpl* shutters
persil [peʀsi] *nm* parsley
Persique [peʀsik] *adj*: **le golfe ~** the (Persian) Gulf
persistant, e [peʀsistɑ̃, ɑ̃t] *adj* persistent
persister [peʀsiste] *vi* to persist; **~ à faire qch** to persist in doing sth
personnage [peʀsɔnaʒ] *nm* (*individu*) character, individual; (*célébrité*) important person; (*de roman, film*) character; (*PEINTURE*) figure
personnalité [peʀsɔnalite] *nf* personality; (*personnage*) prominent figure
personne [peʀsɔn] *nf* person ♦ *pron* nobody, no one; (*avec négation en anglais*) anybody, anyone; **~s** *nfpl* (*gens*) people *pl*; **il n'y a ~** there's nobody there, there isn't anybody there; **~ âgée** elderly person; **personnel, le** *adj* personal; (*égoïste*) selfish ♦ *nm* staff, personnel; **personnellement** *adv* personally
perspective [peʀspektiv] *nf* (*ART*) perspective; (*vue*) view; (*point de vue*) viewpoint, angle; (*chose envisagée*) prospect; **en ~** in prospect
perspicace [peʀspikas] *adj* clear-sighted, gifted with (*ou* showing) insight; **perspicacité** *nf* clear-sightedness
persuader [peʀsɥade] *vt*: **~ qn (de faire)** to persuade sb (to do); **persuasif, -ive** *adj* persuasive
perte [peʀt] *nf* loss; (*de temps*) waste; (*fig: morale*) ruin; **à ~ de vue** as far as the eye can (*ou* could) see; **~s blanches** (vaginal) discharge *sg*
pertinemment [peʀtinamɑ̃] *adv* (*savoir*) full well
pertinent, e [peʀtinɑ̃, ɑ̃t] *adj* apt, relevant
perturbation [peʀtyʀbasjɔ̃] *nf*: **~ (at-**

mosphérique) atmospheric disturbance
perturber [peʀtyʀbe] *vt* to disrupt; (*PSYCH*) to perturb, disturb
pervers, e [peʀveʀ, eʀs] *adj* perverted
pervertir [peʀveʀtiʀ] *vt* to pervert
pesant, e [pəzɑ̃, ɑ̃t] *adj* heavy; (*fig: présence*) burdensome
pèse-personne [pezpeʀsɔn] *nm* (bathroom) scales *pl*
peser [pəze] *vt* to weigh ♦ *vi* to weigh; (*fig: avoir de l'importance*) to carry weight; **~ lourd** to be heavy
pessimisme [pesimism] *nm* pessimism
pessimiste [pesimist] *adj* pessimistic ♦ *nm/f* pessimist
peste [pest] *nf* plague
pester [peste] *vi*: **~ contre** to curse
pétale [petal] *nm* petal
pétanque [petɑ̃k] *nf* type of bowls

> Pétanque, *which originated in the south of France, is a version of the game of* boules *played on a variety of hard surfaces. Standing with their feet together, players throw steel bowls towards a wooden jack.*

pétarader [petaʀade] *vi* to backfire
pétard [petaʀ] *nm* banger (*BRIT*), firecracker
péter [pete] *vi* (*fam: casser*) to bust; (*fam!*) to fart (*!*)
pétillant, e [petijɑ̃, ɑ̃t] *adj* (*eau etc*) sparkling
pétiller [petije] *vi* (*feu*) to crackle; (*champagne*) to bubble; (*yeux*) to sparkle
petit, e [p(ə)ti, it] *adj* small; (*avec nuance affective*) little; (*voyage*) short, little; (*bruit etc*) faint, slight; **~s** *nmpl* (*d'un animal*) young *pl*; **les tout-~s** the little ones, the tiny tots; **~ à ~** bit by bit, gradually; **~ ami(e)** boyfriend/girlfriend; **~ déjeuner** breakfast; **~ pain** (bread) roll; **les ~es annonces** the

small ads; **~s pois** garden peas;
petite-fille *nf* granddaughter; **petit-fils** *nm* grandson

pétition [petisjɔ̃] *nf* petition

petits-enfants [pətizɑ̃fɑ̃] *nmpl* grandchildren

petit-suisse [pətisɥis] (*pl* **~s-~s**) *nm* small individual pot of cream cheese

pétrin [petʀɛ̃] *nm* (*fig*): **dans le ~** (*fam*) in a jam ou fix

pétrir [petʀiʀ] *vt* to knead

pétrole [petʀɔl] *nm* oil; (*pour lampe, réchaud etc*) paraffin (oil); **pétrolier, -ière** *nm* oil tanker

---

MOT-CLÉ

---

peu [pø] *adv* **1** (*modifiant verbe, adjectif, adverbe*): **il boit peu** he doesn't drink (very) much; **il est peu bavard** he's not very talkative; **peu avant/après** shortly before/afterwards

2 (*modifiant nom*): **peu de**: **peu de gens/d'arbres** few ou not (very) many people/trees; **il a peu d'espoir** he hasn't (got) much hope, he has little hope; **pour peu de temps** for (only) a short while

3: peu à peu little by little; **à peu près** just about, more or less; **à peu près 10 kg/10 F** approximately 10 kg/10F

♦ *nm* **1: le peu de gens qui** the few people who; **le peu de sable qui** what little sand, the little sand which

2: un peu a little; **un petit peu** a little bit; **un peu d'espoir** a little hope

♦ *pron*: **peu le savent** few know (it); **avant** ou **sous peu** shortly, before long; **de peu** (only) just

peuple [pœpl] *nm* people; **peupler** *vt* (*pays, région*) to populate; (*étang*) to stock; (*suj: hommes, poissons*) to inhabit

peuplier [pøplije] *nm* poplar (tree)

peur [pœʀ] *nf* fear; **avoir ~** (**de/de faire/que**) to be frightened ou afraid (of/of doing/that); **faire ~ à** to frighten; **de ~ de/que** for fear of/that; **peu-**

reux, -euse *adj* fearful, timorous

peut [pø] *vb voir* **pouvoir**

peut-être [pøtɛtʀ] *adv* perhaps, maybe; **~-~ que** perhaps, maybe; **~-~ bien qu'il fera/est** he may well do/be

peux [pø] *vb voir* **pouvoir**

phare [faʀ] *nm* (*en mer*) lighthouse; (*de véhicule*) headlight; **~s de recul** reversing lights

pharmacie [faʀmasi] *nf* (*magasin*) chemist's (*BRIT*), pharmacy; (*de salle de bain*) medicine cabinet; **pharmacien, ne** *nm/f* pharmacist, chemist (*BRIT*)

phénomène [fenɔmɛn] *nm* phenomenon

philatélie [filateli] *nf* philately, stamp collecting

philosophe [filɔzɔf] *nm/f* philosopher ♦ *adj* philosophical

philosophie [filɔzɔfi] *nf* philosophy

phobie [fɔbi] *nf* phobia

phonétique [fɔnetik] *nf* phonetics *sg*

phoque [fɔk] *nm* seal

phosphorescent, e [fɔsfɔʀesɑ̃, ɑ̃t] *adj* luminous

photo [fɔto] *nf* photo(graph); **prendre en ~** to take a photo of; **faire de la ~** to take photos; **~ d'identité** passport photograph; **photocopie** *nf* photocopy; **photocopier** *vt* to photocopy; **photocopieuse** *nf* photocopier; **photographe** *nm/f* photographer; **photographie** *nf* (*technique*) photography; (*cliché*) photograph; **photographier** *vt* to photograph

phrase [fʀɑz] *nf* sentence

physicien, ne [fizisjɛ̃, jɛn] *nm/f* physicist

physionomie [fizjɔnɔmi] *nf* face

physique [fizik] *adj* physical ♦ *nm* physique ♦ *nf* physics *sg*; **au ~** physically; **physiquement** *adv* physically

piailler [pjaje] *vi* to squawk

pianiste [pjanist] *nm/f* pianist

piano [pjano] *nm* piano; **pianoter** *vi* to tinkle away (at the piano)

pic [pik] *nm* (*instrument*) pick(axe);

(montagne) peak; (ZOOL) woodpecker; **à ~** vertically; (fig: tomber, arriver) just at the right time

pichet [piʃɛ] nm jug

picorer [pikɔʀe] vt to peck

picoter [pikɔte] vt (suj: oiseau) to peck ♦ vi (irriter) to smart, prickle

pie [pi] nf magpie

pièce [pjɛs] nf (d'un logement): room; (THÉÂTRE) play; (de machine) part; (de monnaie) coin; (document) document; (fragment, de collection) piece; **dix francs ~** ten francs each; **vendre à la ~** to sell separately; **travailler à la ~** to do piecework; **un maillot une ~** a one-piece swimsuit; **un deux-~s cuisine** a two-room(ed) flat (BRIT) ou apartment (US) with kitchen; **à conviction** exhibit; **~ d'identité: avez-vous une ~ d'identité?** have you got any (means of) identification?; **~ montée** tiered cake; **~s détachées** spares, (spare) parts; **~s justificatives** supporting documents

pied [pje] nm foot; (de table) leg; (de lampe) base; **à ~** on foot; **au ~ de la lettre** literally; **avoir ~** to be able to touch the bottom, not to be out of one's depth; **avoir le ~ marin** to be a good sailor; **sur ~** (debout, rétabli) up and about; **mettre sur ~** (entreprise) to set up; **c'est le ~** (fam) it's brilliant; **mettre les ~s dans le plat** (fam) to put one's foot in it; **il se débrouille comme un ~** (fam) he's completely useless; **pied-noir** nm Algerian-born Frenchman

piège [pjɛʒ] nm trap; **prendre au ~** to trap; **piéger** vt (avec une bombe) to booby-trap; **lettre/voiture piégée** letter-/car-bomb

pierre [pjɛʀ] nf stone; **~ précieuse** precious stone, gem; **~ tombale** tombstone; **pierreries** nfpl gems, precious stones

piétiner [pjetine] vi (trépigner) to stamp (one's feet); (fig) to he at a

standstill ♦ vt to trample on

piéton, ne [pjetɔ̃, ɔn] nm/f pedestrian; **piétonnier, -ière** adj: **rue** ou **zone piétonnière** pedestrian precinct

pieu, x [pjø] nm post; (pointu) stake

pieuvre [pjœvʀ] nf octopus

pieux, -euse [pjø, pjøz] adj pious

piffer [pife] (fam) vt: **je ne peux pas le ~** I can't stand him

pigeon [piʒɔ̃] nm pigeon

piger [piʒe] (fam) vt, vi to understand

pigiste [piʒist] nm/f freelance(r)

pignon [piɲɔ̃] nm (de mur) gable

pile [pil] nf (tas) pile; (ÉLEC) battery ♦ adv (fam: s'arrêter etc) dead; **à deux heures ~** at two on the dot; **jouer à ~ ou face** to toss up (for it); **~ ou face?** heads or tails?

piler [pile] vt to crush, pound

pilier [pilje] nm pillar

piller [pije] vt to pillage, plunder, loot

pilote [pilɔt] nm pilot; (de voiture) driver ♦ adj pilot cpd; **~ de course** racing driver; **~ de ligne/d'essai/de chasse** airline/test/fighter pilot; **piloter** vt (avion) to pilot, fly; (voiture) to drive

pilule [pilyl] nf pill; **prendre la ~** to be on the pill

piment [pimɑ̃] nm (aussi: **~ rouge**) chilli; (fig) spice, piquancy; **~ doux** pepper, capsicum; **pimenté, e** adj (plat) hot, spicy

pimpant, e [pɛ̃pɑ̃, ɑ̃t] adj spruce

pin [pɛ̃] nm pine

pinard [pinaʀ] (fam) nm (cheap) wine, plonk (BRIT)

pince [pɛ̃s] nf (outil) pliers pl; (de homard, crabe) pincer, claw; (COUTURE: pli) dart; **~ à épiler** tweezers pl; **~ à linge** clothes peg (BRIT) ou pin (US)

pincé, e [pɛ̃se] adj (air) stiff

pincée [pɛ̃se] nf: **une ~ de** a pinch of

pincer [pɛ̃se] vt to pinch; (fam) to nab

pinède [pined] nf pinewood, pine forest

pingouin [pɛ̃gwɛ̃] nm penguin

ping-pong ® [piŋpɔ̃g] *nm* table tennis

pingre [pɛ̃gʀ] *adj* niggardly

pinson [pɛ̃sɔ̃] *nm* chaffinch

pintade [pɛ̃tad] *nf* guinea-fowl

pioche [pjɔʃ] *nf* pickaxe; **piocher** *vt* to dig up (with a pickaxe); **piocher dans** (*le tas, ses économies*) to dig into

pion [pjɔ̃] *nm* (ÉCHECS) pawn; (DAMES) piece; (SCOL) supervisor

pionnier [pjɔnje] *nm* pioneer

pipe [pip] *nf* pipe; **fumer la ~** to smoke a pipe

pipeau, X [pipo] *nm* (reed-)pipe

piquant, e [pikɑ̃, ɑ̃t] *adj* (*barbe, rosier etc*) prickly; (*saveur, sauce*) hot, pungent; (*détail*) titillating; (*froid*) biting ♦ *nm* (*épine*) thorn, prickle; (*fig*) spiciness, spice

pique [pik] *nf* pike; (*fig*) cutting remark ♦ *nm* (CARTES) spades *pl*

pique-nique [piknik] *nm* picnic; **pique-niquer** *vi* to have a picnic

piquer [pike] *vt* (*suj: guêpe, fumée, orties*) to sting; (: *moustique*) to bite; (: *barbe*) to prick; (: *froid*) to bite; (MÉD) to give a jab to; (*chien, chat*) to put to sleep; (*intérêt*) to arouse; (*fam: voler*) to pinch ♦ *vi* (*avion*) to go into a dive; **se ~** (*avec une aiguille*) to prick o.s.; (*dans les orties*) to get stung; (*suj: toxicomane*) to shoot up; **~ une colère** to fly into a rage

piquet [pikɛ] *nm* (*pieu*) post, stake; (*de tente*) peg; **~ de grève** (strike-)picket

piqûre [pikyʀ] *nf* (*d'épingle*) prick; (*d'ortie*) sting; (*de moustique*) bite; (MÉD) injection, shot (US); **faire une ~ à qn** to give sb an injection

pirate [piʀat] *nm, adj* pirate; **~ de l'air** hijacker

pire [piʀ] *adj* worse; (*superlatif*): **le(la) ~ ... the worst** ♦ *nm*: **le ~** (de) the worst (of); **au ~** at (the very) worst

pis [pi] *nm* (*de vache*) udder; (*pire*): **le ~** the worst ♦ *adj, adv* worse; **de mal en ~** from bad to worse

piscine [pisin] *nf* (swimming) pool; **~ couverte** indoor (swimming) pool

pissenlit [pisɑ̃li] *nm* dandelion

pistache [pistaʃ] *nf* pistachio (nut)

piste [pist] *nf* (*d'un animal, sentier*) track, trail; (*indice*) lead; (*de stade*) track; (*de cirque*) ring; (*de danse*) floor; (*de patinage*) rink; (*de ski*) run; (AVIAT) runway; **~ cyclable** cycle track

pistolet [pistɔlɛ] *nm* (*arme*) pistol, gun; (*à peinture*) spray gun; **pistolet-mitrailleur** *nm* submachine gun

piston [pistɔ̃] *nm* (TECH) piston; **avoir du ~** (*fam*) to have friends in the right places; **pistonner** *vt* (*candidat*) to pull strings for

piteux, -euse [pitø, øz] *adj* pitiful, sorry (*avant le nom*)

pitié [pitje] *nf* pity; **il me fait ~** I feel sorry for him; **avoir ~ de** (*compassion*) to pity, feel sorry for; (*merci*) to have pity on mercy on

pitoyable [pitwajabl] *adj* pitiful

pitre [pitʀ] *nm* clown; **pitrerie** *nf* tomfoolery no *pl*

pittoresque [pitɔʀɛsk] *adj* picturesque

pivot [pivo] *nm* pivot; **pivoter** *vi* to revolve; (*fauteuil*) to swivel

P.J. *sigle f* (= *police judiciaire*) ≃ CID (BRIT), ≃ FBI (US)

placard [plakaʀ] *nm* (*armoire*) cupboard; (*affiche*) poster, notice

place [plas] *nf* (*emplacement, classement*) place; (*de ville, village*) square; (*espace libre*) room, space; (*de parking*) space; (*siège: de train, cinéma, voiture*) seat; (*emploi*) job; **se ~** (*mettre*) in its place; **sur ~** on the spot; **faire ~ à** to give way to; **ça prend de la ~** it takes up a lot of room ou space; **à la ~ de** in place of, instead of; **à ta ~ ...** if I were you ...; **se mettre à la ~ de qn** to put o.s. in sb's place ou in sb's shoes

placé, e [plase] *adj*: **être bien/mal ~** (*spectateur*) to have a good/a poor seat; (*concurrent*) to be in a good/bad position; **il est bien ~ pour le savoir**

he is in a position to know

placement [plasmɑ̃] *nm* (FINANCE) investment; **bureau de ~** employment agency

placer [plase] *vt* to place; (*convive, spectateur*) to seat; (*argent*) to place, invest; **il n'a pas pu ~ un mot** he couldn't get a word in; **se ~ au premier rang** to go and stand (*ou* sit) in the first row

plafond [plafɔ̃] *nm* ceiling

plage [plaʒ] *nf* beach

plagiat [plaʒja] *nm* plagiarism

plaid [plɛd] *nm* (tartan) car rug

plaider [plede] *vi* (*avocat*) to plead ♦ *vt* to plead; **~ pour** (*fig*) to speak for; **plaidoyer** *nm* (JUR) speech for the defence; (*fig*) plea

plaie [plɛ] *nf* wound

plaignant, e [plɛɲɑ̃, ɑ̃t] *nm/f* plaintiff

plaindre [plɛ̃dʀ] *vt* to pity, feel sorry for; **se ~** *vi* (*gémir*) to moan; (*protester*): **se ~ (à qn) (de)** to complain (to sb) (about); (*souffrir*): **se ~ de** to complain of

plaine [plɛn] *nf* plain

plain-pied [plɛ̃pje] *adv*: **de ~~ (avec)** on the same level (as)

plainte [plɛ̃t] *nf* (*gémissement*) moan, groan; (*doléance*) complaint; **porter ~** to lodge a complaint

plaire [plɛʀ] *vi* to be a success, be successful; **ça plaît beaucoup aux jeunes** it's very popular with young people; **~ à: cela me plaît** I like it; **se ~ quelque part** to like being somewhere *ou* like it somewhere; **j'irai si ça me plaît** I'll go if I feel like it; **s'il vous plaît** please

plaisance [plɛzɑ̃s] *nf* (*aussi*: **navigation de ~**) (pleasure) sailing, yachting

plaisant, e [plɛzɑ̃, ɑ̃t] *adj* pleasant; (*histoire, anecdote*) amusing

plaisanter [plɛzɑ̃te] *vi* to joke; **plaisanterie** *nf* joke

plaise *etc* [plɛz] *vb voir* **plaire**

plaisir [plɛziʀ] *nm* pleasure; **faire ~ à qn** (*délibérément*) to be nice to sb, please sb; **ça me fait ~** I like (doing)

it; **j'espère que ça te fera ~** I hope you'll like it; **pour le ~** for pleasure

plaît [plɛ] *vb voir* **plaire**

plan, e [plɑ̃, an] *adj* flat ♦ *nm* plan; (*fig*) level, plane; (CINÉMA) shot; **au premier/second ~** in the foreground/middle distance; **à l'arrière ~** in the background; **rester en ~** (*fam*) to be left stranded; **laisser en ~** (*fam*: *travail*) to drop, abandon; **~ d'eau** lake

planche [plɑ̃ʃ] *nf* (*pièce de bois*) plank, (wooden) board; (*illustration*) plate; **~ à repasser** ironing board; **~ à roulettes** skateboard; **~ à voile** (*sport*) windsurfing

plancher [plɑ̃ʃe] *nm* floor; floorboards *pl* ♦ *vi* (*fam*) to work hard

planer [plane] *vi* to glide; (*fam: rêveur*) to have one's head in the clouds; **~ sur** (*fig: danger*) to hang over

planète [planɛt] *nf* planet

planeur [planœʀ] *nm* glider

planification [planifikasjɔ̃] *nf* (economic) planning

planifier [planifje] *vt* to plan

planning [planiŋ] *nm* programme, schedule

planque [plɑ̃k] *nf* (*fam*) (*emploi peu fatigant*) cushy (BRIT) *ou* easy number; (*cachette*) hiding place

plant [plɑ̃] *nm* seedling, young plant

plante [plɑ̃t] *nf* plant; **~ d'appartement** house *ou* pot plant; **~ des pieds** sole (of the foot)

planter [plɑ̃te] *vt* (*plante*) to plant; (*enfoncer*) to hammer *ou* drive in; (*tente*) to put up, pitch; (*fam*: *personne*) to dump; **se ~** (*fam*: *se tromper*) to get it wrong

plantureux, -euse [plɑ̃tyʀø, øz] *adj* copious, lavish; (*femme*) buxom

plaque [plak] *nf* plate; (*de verglas, d'eczéma*) patch; (*avec inscription*) plaque; **~ chauffante** hotplate; **~ de chocolat** bar of chocolate; **~ (minéralogique *ou* d'immatriculation)** number

(BRIT) ou license (US) plate; **~ tournante** (fig) centre

plaqué, e [plake] adj: **~ or/argent** gold-/silver-plated

plaquer [plake] vt (aplatir): **~ qch sur** ou **contre** to make sth stick ou cling to; (RUGBY) to bring down; (fam: laisser tomber) to drop

plaquette [plakɛt] nf (de chocolat) bar; (beurre) pack(et); **~ de frein** brake pad

plastique [plastik] adj, nm plastic; **plastiquer** vt to blow up (with a plastic bomb)

plat, e [pla, -at] adj flat; (cheveux) straight; (style) flat, dull ♦ nm (récipient, CULIN) dish; (d'un repas) course; **à ~ ventre** face down; **à ~** (pneu, batterie) flat; (fam: personne) dead beat; **~ cuisiné** pre-cooked meal; **~ de résistance** main course; **~ du jour** dish of the day

platane [platan] nm plane tree

plateau, x [plato] nm (support) tray; (GÉO) plateau; (CINÉMA) set; **~ de fromages** cheeseboard

plate-bande [platbãd] nf flower bed

plate-forme [platfɔrm] nf platform; **~~ de forage/pétrolière** drilling/oil rig

platine [platin] nm platinum ♦ nf (d'un tourne-disque) turntable

plâtre [plɑtr] nm (matériau) plaster; (statue) plaster statue; (MÉD) plaster cast; **avoir un bras dans le ~** to have an arm in plaster

plein, e [plɛ̃, plɛn] adj full ♦ nm: **faire le ~ (d'essence)** to fill up (with petrol); **à ~es mains** (ramasser) in handfuls; **à ~ temps** full-time; **en ~ air** in the open air; **en ~ soleil** in direct sunlight; **en ~e nuit/rue** in the middle of the night/street; **en ~ jour** in broad daylight

pleurer [plœre] vi to cry; (yeux) to water ♦ vt to mourn (for); **~ sur** to lament (over), to bemoan

pleurnicher [plœrniʃe] vi to snivel, whine

pleurs [plœr] nmpl: **en ~** in tears

pleut [plø] vb voir **pleuvoir**

pleuvoir [pløvwar] vb impers to rain ♦ vi (coups) to rain down; (critiques, invitations) to shower down; **il pleut** it's raining

pli [pli] nm fold; (de jupe) pleat; (de pantalon) crease; **prendre le ~ de faire** to get into the habit of doing; **un mauvais ~** a bad habit

pliant, e [plijã, plijãt] adj folding

plier [plije] vt to fold; (pour ranger) to fold up; (genou, bras) to bend ♦ vi to bend; (fig) to yield; **se ~** vi to fold; **~ à** to submit to

plinthe [plɛ̃t] nf skirting board

plisser [plise] vt (jupe) to put pleats in; (yeux) to screw up; (front) to crease

plomb [plɔ̃] nm (métal) lead; (d'une cartouche) (lead) shot; (PÊCHE) sinker; (ÉLEC) fuse; **sans ~** (essence etc) unleaded

plombage [plɔ̃baʒ] nm (de dent) filling

plomberie [plɔ̃bri] nf plumbing

plombier [plɔ̃bje] nm plumber

plonge [plɔ̃ʒ] nf washing-up

plongeant, e [plɔ̃ʒã, ãt] adj (vue) from above; (décolleté) plunging

plongée [plɔ̃ʒe] nf (SPORT) diving no pl; (sans scaphandre) skin diving; **~ sous-marine** diving

plongeoir [plɔ̃ʒwar] nm diving board

plongeon [plɔ̃ʒɔ̃] nm dive

plonger [plɔ̃ʒe] vi to dive ♦ vt: **~ qch dans** to plunge sth into; **se ~ dans** (études, lecture) to bury ou immerse o.s. in; plonger vi dive

ployer [plwaje] vt, vi to bend

plu [ply] pp de **plaire**; **pleuvoir**

pluie [plɥi] nf rain

plume [plym] nf feather; (pour écrire) (pen) nib; (fig) pen

plupart [plypar]: **la ~** pron the majority, most (of them); **la ~ des** the majority of, the most of; **la ~ du temps/d'entre nous** most of the time/of us; **pour la ~** for the most part, mostly

pluriel [plyrjɛl] nm plural

plus[1] [ply] *vb voir* **plaire**

---MOT-CLÉ---

plus[2] [ply] *adv* **1** (*forme négative*): **ne ... plus** no more, no longer; **je n'ai plus d'argent** I've got no more money *ou* no money left; **il ne travaille plus** he's no longer working, he doesn't work any more

2 (*comparatif*) more, ...+er; (*superlatif*): **le plus** the most, the ...+est; **plus grand/intelligent (que)** bigger/more intelligent (than); **le plus grand/intelligent** the biggest/most intelligent; **tout au plus** at the very most

3 (*davantage*) more; **il travaille plus (que)** he works more (than); **plus il travaille, plus il est heureux** the more he works, the happier he is; **plus de pain** more bread; **plus de 10 personnes** more than 10 people, over 10 people; **3 heures de plus que** 3 hours more than; **de plus** what's more, moreover; **3 kilos en plus** 3 kilos more; **en plus de** in addition to; **de plus en plus** more and more; **plus ou moins** more or less; **ni plus ni moins** no more, no less

♦ *prép*: **4 plus 2** 4 plus 2

plusieurs [plyzjœR] *dét, pron* several; **ils sont ~** there are several of them

plus-value [plyvaly] *nf* (*bénéfice*) surplus

plut [ply] *vb voir* **plaire**

plutôt [plyto] *adv* rather; **je préfère ~ celui-ci** I'd rather have this one; **~ que (de) faire** rather than *ou* instead of doing

pluvieux, -euse [plyvjø, jøz] *adj* rainy, wet

PME *sigle f* (= petite(s) et moyenne(s) entreprise(s)) small business(es)

PMU *sigle m* (= Pari mutuel urbain) system of betting on horses; (*café*) betting agency

PNB *sigle m* (= produit national brut)

GNP

pneu [pnø] *nm* tyre (BRIT), tire (US)

pneumonie [pnømɔni] *nf* pneumonia

poche [pɔʃ] *nf* pocket; (*sous les yeux*) bag, pouch; **argent de ~** pocket money

pocher [pɔʃe] *vt* (CULIN) to poach

pochette [pɔʃɛt] *nf* (*d'aiguilles etc*) case; (*mouchoir*) breast pocket handkerchief; (*sac à main*) clutch bag; **~ de disque** record sleeve

poêle [pwal] *nm* stove ♦ *nf*: **~ (à frire)** frying pan

poème [pɔɛm] *nm* poem

poésie [pɔezi] *nf* (*poème*) poem; (*art*): **la ~** poetry

poète [pɔɛt] *nm* poet

poids [pwa] *nm* weight; (SPORT) shot; **vendre au ~** to sell by weight; **prendre du ~** to put on weight; **~ lourd** (*camion*) lorry (BRIT), truck (US)

poignant, e [pwaɲɑ̃, ɑ̃t] *adj* poignant

poignard [pwaɲaR] *nm* dagger; **poignarder** *vt* to stab, knife

poigne [pwaɲ] *nf* grip; **avoir de la ~** (*fig*) to rule with a firm hand

poignée [pwaɲe] *nf* (*de sel etc, fig*) handful; (*de couvercle, porte*) handle; **~ de main** handshake

poignet [pwaɲɛ] *nm* (ANAT) wrist; (*de chemise*) cuff

poil [pwal] *nm* (ANAT) hair; (*de pinceau, brosse*) bristle; (*de tapis*) strand; (*pelage*) coat; **à ~** (*fam*) starkers; **au ~** (*fam*) hunky-dory; **poilu, e** *adj* hairy

poinçon [pwɛ̃sɔ̃] *nm* (*marque*) hallmark; **poinçonner** [pwɛ̃sɔne] *vt* (*bijou*) to hallmark; (*billet*) to punch

poing [pwɛ̃] *nm* fist; **coup de ~** punch

point [pwɛ̃] *nm* point; (*endroit*) spot; (*marque, signe*) dot; (: *de ponctuation*) full stop, period (US); (COUTURE, TRICOT) stitch ♦ *adv* = **pas**[2]; **faire le ~** (*fig*) to take stock (of the situation); **sur le ~ de faire** (just) about to do; **à tel ~ que** so much so that; **mettre au ~** (*procédé*) tu develop; (*affaire*) to settle; **à ~**

(CULIN: viande) medium; **à ~ (nommé)** just at the right time; **deux ~s** colon; **~ (de côté)** stitch (pain); **~ d'exclamation/d'interrogation** exclamation/question mark; **~ de repère** landmark; (dans le temps) point of reference; **~ de suture** (MÉD) stitch; **~ de vente** retail outlet; **~ de vue** viewpoint; (fig: opinion) point of view; **~ d'honneur: mettre un ~ d'honneur à faire qch** to make it a point of honour to do sth; **~ faible/fort** weak/strong point; **~ noir** blackhead; **~s de suspension** suspension points

pointe [pwɛ̃t] nf point; (clou) tack; (fig): **une ~ de** a hint of; **être à la ~ de** (fig) to be in the forefront of; **sur la ~ des pieds** on tiptoe; **en ~** pointed, tapered; **de ~** (technique etc) leading; **heures de ~** peak hours

pointer [pwɛ̃te] vt (diriger: canon, doigt): **~ sur qch** to point at sth ♦ vi (employé) to clock in

pointillé [pwɛ̃tije] nm (trait) dotted line

pointilleux, -euse [pwɛ̃tijø, øz] adj particular, pernickety

pointu, e [pwɛ̃ty] adj pointed; (voix) shrill; (analyse) precise

pointure [pwɛ̃tyʀ] nf size

point-virgule [pwɛ̃viʀgyl] nm semicolon

poire [pwaʀ] nf pear; (fam: péj) mug

poireau, x [pwaʀo] nm leek

poireauter [pwaʀote] vi (fam) to be left kicking one's heels

poirier [pwaʀje] nm pear tree

pois [pwa] nm (BOT) pea, (sur une étoffe) dot, spot; **~ chiche** chickpea; **à ~** (cravate etc) spotted, polka-dot cpd

poison [pwazɔ̃] nm poison

poisse [pwas] (fam) nf rotten luck

poisseux, -euse [pwasø, øz] adj sticky

poisson [pwasɔ̃] nm fish gén inv; **les P~s** (signe) Pisces; **~ d'avril!** April fool!; **~ rouge** goldfish; **poissonnerie** nf fish-shop; **poissonnier, -ière** nm/f

fishmonger (BRIT), fish merchant (US)

poitrine [pwatʀin] nf chest; (seins) bust, bosom; (CULIN) breast

poivre [pwavʀ] nm pepper

poivron [pwavʀɔ̃] nm pepper, capsicum

polaire [pɔlɛʀ] adj polar

polar [pɔlaʀ] (fam) nm detective novel

pôle [pol] nm (GÉO, ÉLEC) pole

poli, e [pɔli] adj polite; (lisse) smooth

police [pɔlis] nf police; **~ d'assurance** insurance policy; **~ judiciaire** ≃ Criminal Investigation Department (BRIT), ≃ Federal Bureau of Investigation (US); **~ secours** ≃ emergency services pl (BRIT), ≃ paramedics pl (US); **policier, -ière** adj police cpd ♦ nm policeman; (aussi: **roman policier**) detective novel

polir [pɔliʀ] vt to polish

polisson, ne [pɔlisɔ̃, ɔn] nm/f (enfant) (little) rascal

politesse [pɔlitɛs] nf politeness

politicien, ne [pɔlitisjɛ̃, jɛn] (péj) nm/f politician

politique [pɔlitik] adj political ♦ nf politics sg; (mesures, méthode) policies pl

pollen [pɔlɛn] nm pollen

polluant, e [pɔlɥɑ̃, ɑ̃t] adj polluting ♦ nm: **(produit) ~** pollutant; **non ~** non-polluting

polluer [pɔlɥe] vt to pollute; **pollution** nf pollution

polo [pɔlo] nm (chemise) polo shirt

Pologne [pɔlɔɲ] nf: **la ~** Poland; **polonais, e** adj Polish ♦ nm/f: **Polonais, e** Pole ♦ nm (LING) Polish

poltron, ne [pɔltʀɔ̃, ɔn] adj cowardly

polycopier [pɔlikɔpje] vt to duplicate

Polynésie [pɔlinezi] nf: **la ~** Polynesia

polyvalent, e [pɔlivalɑ̃, ɑ̃t] adj (rôle) varied; (salle) multi-purpose

pommade [pɔmad] nf ointment, cream

pomme [pɔm] nf apple; **tomber dans les ~s** (fam) to pass out; **~ d'Adam** Adam's apple; **~ de pin** pine ou fir cone; **~ de terre** potato

pommeau 216 **porter**

pommeau, x [pɔmo] nm (boule) knob; (de selle) pommel

pommette [pɔmɛt] nf cheekbone

pommier [pɔmje] nm apple tree

pompe [pɔ̃p] nf pump; (faste) pomp (and ceremony); **~ à essence** petrol pump; **~s funèbres** funeral parlour sg, undertaker's sg; **pomper** vt to pump; (aspirer) to pump up; (absorber) to soak up

pompeux, -euse [pɔ̃pø, øz] adj pompous

pompier [pɔ̃pje] nm fireman

pompiste [pɔ̃pist] nm/f petrol (BRIT) ou gas (US) pump attendant

poncer [pɔ̃se] vt to sand (down)

ponctuation [pɔ̃ktɥasjɔ̃] nf punctuation

ponctuel, le [pɔ̃ktɥɛl] adj punctual

pondéré, e [pɔ̃dere] adj level-headed, composed

pondre [pɔ̃dʀ] vt to lay

poney [pɔnɛ] nm pony

pont [pɔ̃] nm bridge; (NAVIG) deck; **faire le ~** to take the extra day off; **~ suspendu** suspension bridge; **pont-levis** nm drawbridge

faire le pont

The expression "faire le pont" refers to the practice of taking a Monday or Friday off to make a long weekend if a public holiday falls on a Tuesday or Thursday. The French often do this at l'Ascension, l'Assomption and le 14 juillet.

pop [pɔp] adj inv pop

populace [pɔpylas] (péj) nf rabble

populaire [pɔpylɛʀ] adj popular; (manifestation) mass cpd; (milieux, quartier) working-class; (expression) vernacular

popularité [pɔpylaʀite] nf popularity

population [pɔpylasjɔ̃] nf population; **~ active** working population

populeux, -euse [pɔpylø, øz] adj densely populated

porc [pɔʀ] nm pig; (CULIN) pork

porcelaine [pɔʀsəlɛn] nf porcelain, china; piece of china(ware)

porc-épic [pɔʀkepik] nm porcupine

porche [pɔʀʃ] nm porch

porcherie [pɔʀʃəʀi] nf pigsty

pore [pɔʀ] nm pore

porno [pɔʀno] adj porno ♦ nm porn

port [pɔʀ] nm harbour, port; (ville); (de l'uniforme etc) wearing; (pour lettre) postage; (pour colis, aussi: posture) carriage; **~ de pêche/de plaisance** fishing/sailing harbour

portable [pɔʀtabl] nm (COMPUT) laptop (computer)

portail [pɔʀtaj] nm gate

portant, e [pɔʀtɑ̃, ɑ̃t] adj: **bien/mal ~** in good/poor health

portatif, -ive [pɔʀtatif, iv] adj portable

porte [pɔʀt] nf door; (de ville, jardin) gate; **mettre à la ~** to throw out; **~ à ~** nm door-to-door selling; **~ d'entrée** front door; **~-avions** nm inv aircraft carrier; **porte-bagages** nm inv luggage rack; **porte-bonheur** nm inv lucky charm; **porte-clefs** nm inv key ring; **porte-documents** nm inv attaché ou document case

porté, e [pɔʀte] adj: **être ~ à faire** to be inclined to do; **être ~ sur qch** to be keen on sth; **portée** nf (d'une arme) range; (fig: effet) impact, import; (capacité) scope, capability; (de chatte etc) litter; (MUS) stave, staff; **à/hors de portée (de)** within/out of reach (of); **à portée de (la) main** within (arm's) reach; **à la portée de qn** (fig) at sb's level, within sb's capabilities

porte...: porte-fenêtre nf French window; **portefeuille** nm wallet; **porte-manteau, x** nm (cintre) coat hanger; (au mur) coat rack; **porte-monnaie** nm inv purse; **porte-parole** nm inv spokesman

porter [pɔʀte] vt to carry; (sur soi: vêtement, barbe, bague) to wear; (fig: responsabilité etc) to bear, carry; (inscription, nom, fruits) to bear; (coup) to deal; (attention) to turn; (apporter): ~ **qch à qn** to take sth to sb ♦ vi (voix) to carry; (coup, argument) to hit home; **se** ~ vi (se sentir): **se** ~ **bien/mal** to be well/unwell; ~ **sur** (recherches) to be concerned with; **se faire** ~ **malade** to report sick

porteur [pɔʀtœʀ, øz] nm (de bagages) porter; (de chèque) bearer

porte-voix [pɔʀtəvwa] nm inv megaphone

portier [pɔʀtje] nm doorman

portière [pɔʀtjeʀ] nf door

portillon [pɔʀtijɔ̃] nm gate

portion [pɔʀsjɔ̃] nf (part) portion, share; (partie) portion, section

porto [pɔʀto] nm port (wine)

portrait [pɔʀtʀɛ] nm (peinture) portrait; (photo) photograph; **portrait-robot** nm Identikit ® ou photo-fit ® picture

portuaire [pɔʀtɥeʀ] adj port cpd, harbour cpd

portugais, e [pɔʀtygɛ, ɛz] adj Portuguese ♦ nm/f: **P~, e** Portuguese ♦ nm (LING) Portuguese

Portugal [pɔʀtygal] nm: **le** ~ Portugal

pose [poz] nf (de moquette) laying; (attitude, d'un modèle) pose; (PHOTO) exposure

posé, e [poze] adj serious

poser [poze] vt to put; (installer: moquette, carrelage) to lay; (rideaux, papier peint) to hang; (question) to ask; (principe, conditions) to lay ou set down; (problème) to formulate; (difficulté) to pose ♦ vi (modèle) to pose; **se** ~ vi (oiseau, avion) to land; (question) to arise: ~ **qch (sur)** (déposer) to put sth down (on); ~ **qch sur/quelque part** (placer) to put sth on/somewhere; ~ **sa candidature à un poste** to apply for a post

positif, -ive [pozitif, iv] adj positive

position [pozisjɔ̃] nf position; **prendre** ~ (fig) to take a stand

posologie [pozɔlɔʒi] nf dosage

posséder [pɔsede] vt to own, possess; (qualité, talent) to have, possess; (sexuellement) to possess; **possession** nf ownership ou pl, possession

possibilité [pɔsibilite] nf possibility; **~s** nfpl (potentiel) potential sg

possible [pɔsibl] adj possible; (projet, entreprise) feasible ♦ nm: **faire son** ~ to do all one can, do one's utmost; **le plus/moins de livres** ~ as many/few books as possible; **le plus vite** ~ as quickly as possible; **dès que** ~ as soon as possible

postal, e, -aux [pɔstal, o] adj postal

poste [pɔst] nf (service) post, postal service; (administration, bureau) post office ♦ nm (fonction, MIL) post; (TÉL) extension; (de radio etc) set: **mettre à la** ~ to post; ~ **(de police)** nm police station; ~ **de secours** nm first-aid post; ~ **restante** nm poste restante (BRIT), general delivery (US)

poster¹ [pɔste] vt to post

poster² [pɔsteʀ] nm poster

postérieur, e [pɔsteʀjœʀ] adj (date) later; (partie) back ♦ nm (fam) behind

posthume [pɔstym] adj posthumous

postulant, e [pɔstylɑ̃, ɑ̃t] nm/f applicant

postuler [pɔstyle] vi: ~ **à ou pour un emploi** to apply for a job

posture [pɔstyʀ] nf position

pot [po] nm (en verre) jar; (en terre) pot; (en plastique, carton) carton; (fam: chance) luck; **avoir du** ~ (fam) to be lucky; **boire ou prendre un** ~ (fam) to have a drink; **petit** ~ **(pour bébé)** (jar of) baby food; ~ **catalytique** catalytic converter; ~ **d'échappement** exhaust pipe; ~ **de fleurs** plant pot, flowerpot; (plante) pot plant

potable [pɔtabl] adj: **eau (non)** ~ (non-)drinking water

potage [pɔtaʒ] nm soup; **potager, -ère** adj: **(jardin) potager** kitchen ou vegetable garden

pot-au-feu [pɔtofø] nm inv (beef) stew

pot-de-vin [pɔdvɛ̃] nm bribe

pote [pɔt] (fam) nm pal

poteau, x [pɔto] nm post; **~ indicateur** signpost

potelé, e [pɔt(ə)le] adj plump, chubby

potence [pɔtɑ̃s] nf gallows sg

potentiel, le [pɔtɑ̃sjɛl] adj, nm potential

poterie [pɔtri] nf pottery; (objet) piece of pottery

potier [pɔtje, jɛʀ] nm potter

potins [pɔtɛ̃] (fam) nmpl gossip sg

potiron [pɔtiʀɔ̃] nm pumpkin

pou, x [pu] nm louse

poubelle [pubɛl] nf (dust)bin

pouce [pus] nm thumb

poudre [pudʀ] nf powder; (fard) (face) powder; (explosif) gunpowder; **en ~: café en ~** instant coffee; **lait en ~** dried ou powdered milk; **poudreuse** nf powder snow; **poudrier** nm (powder) compact

pouffer [pufe] vi: **~ (de rire)** to burst out laughing

poulailler [pulaje] nm henhouse

poulain [pulɛ̃] nm foal; (fig) protégé

poule [pul] nf hen; (CULIN) (boiling) fowl

poulet [pulɛ] nm chicken; (fam) cop

poulie [puli] nf pulley

pouls [pu] nm pulse; **prendre le ~ de qn** to feel sb's pulse

poumon [pumɔ̃] nm lung

poupe [pup] nf stern; **en ~** astern

poupée [pupe] nf doll

pouponnière [pupɔnjɛʀ] nf crèche, day nursery

pour [puʀ] prép for ♦ nm: **le ~ et le contre** the pros and cons; **~ faire** (so as) to do, in order to do; **~ avoir fait** for having done; **~ que** so that, in order that; **~ 100 francs d'essence** 100 francs' worth of petrol; **~ cent** per cent; **~ ce qui est de** as for

pourboire [puʀbwaʀ] nm tip

pourcentage [puʀsɑ̃taʒ] nm percentage

pourchasser [puʀʃase] vt to pursue

pourparlers [puʀpaʀle] nmpl talks, negotiations

pourpre [puʀpʀ] adj crimson

pourquoi [puʀkwa] adv, conj why ♦ nm inv: **le ~ (de)** the reason (for)

pourrai etc [puʀe] vb voir **pouvoir**

pourri, e [puʀi] adj rotten

pourrir [puʀiʀ] vi to rot; (fruit) to go rotten ou bad ♦ vt to rot; (fig) to spoil thoroughly; **pourriture** nf rot

pourrons etc [puʀɔ̃] vb voir **pouvoir**

poursuite [puʀsɥit] nf pursuit, chase; **~s** nfpl (JUR) legal proceedings

poursuivre [puʀsɥivʀ] vt: **qch/qn** to pursue, chase (after); (obséder) to haunt; (JUR) to bring proceedings against, prosecute; (: au civil) to sue; (but) to strive towards; (continuer: études etc) to carry on with, continue; **se ~** vi to go on, continue

pourtant [puʀtɑ̃] adv yet; **c'est ~ facile** (and) yet it's easy

pourtour [puʀtuʀ] nm perimeter

pourvoir [puʀvwaʀ] vt: **qch/qn** to equip sth/sb with ♦ vi: **~ à** to provide for; **pourvoyeur** nm supplier; **pourvu, e** adj: **pourvu de** equipped with; **pourvu que** (si) provided that, so long as; (espérons que) let's hope (that)

pousse [pus] nf growth; (bourgeon) shoot

poussé, e [puse] adj (enquête) exhaustive; (études) advanced; **poussée** nf thrust; (d'acné) eruption; (fig: prix) upsurge

pousser [puse] vt to push; (émettre: cri, soupir) to give; (stimuler: élève) to urge on; (poursuivre: études, discussion) to carry on (further) ♦ vi to push; (croître) to grow; **se ~** vi to move over; **~ qn à** (inciter) to urge ou press sb to; (accabler) to drive sb to; **faire ~** (plante) to grow

poussette [pusɛt] nf push chair (BRIT), stroller (US)

poussière [pusjɛʀ] nf dust; **poussié-**

poussin reux, -euse *adj* dusty
poussin [pusɛ̃] *nm* chick
poutre [putʀ] *nf* beam

MOT-CLÉ

pouvoir [puvwaʀ] *nm* power; (POL: *dirigeants*): **le pouvoir** those in power; **les pouvoirs publics** the authorities; **pouvoir d'achat** purchasing power

♦ *vb semi-aux* **1** (*être en état de*) can, be able to; **je ne peux pas le réparer** I can't *ou* I am not able to repair it; **déçu de ne pas pouvoir le faire** disappointed not to be able to do it

2 (*avoir la permission*) can, may, be allowed to; **vous pouvez aller au cinéma** you can *ou* may go to the pictures

3 (*probabilité, hypothèse*) may, might, could; **il a pu avoir un accident** he may *ou* might *ou* could have had an accident; **il aurait pu le dire!** he might *ou* could have said (so)!

♦ *vb impers* may, might, could; **il peut arriver que** it may *ou* might *ou* could happen that

♦ *vt* can, be able to; **j'ai fait tout ce que j'ai pu** I did all I could; **je n'en peux plus** (*épuisé*) I'm exhausted; (*à bout*) I can't take any more; **se pouvoir** *vi*: **il se peut que** it may *ou* might he that; **cela se pourrait** that's quite possible

prairie [pʀeʀi] *nf* meadow
praline [pʀalin] *nf* sugared almond
praticable [pʀatikabl] *adj* passable, practicable
pratiquant, e [pʀatikɑ̃, ɑ̃t] *nm/f* (regular) churchgoer
pratique [pʀatik] *nf* practice ♦ *adj* practical; **pratiquement** *adv* (*pour ainsi dire*) practically, virtually; **pratiquer** *vt* to practise; (*l'équitation, la pêche*) to go in for; (*le golf, football*) to play; (*intervention, opération*) to carry out
pré [pʀe] *nm* meadow
préados [pʀeado] *nmpl* preteens

préalable [pʀealabl] *adj* preliminary; **au ~** beforehand
préambule [pʀeɑ̃byl] *nm* preamble; (*fig*) prelude; **sans ~** straight away
préau [pʀeo] *nm* (SCOL) covered playground
préavis [pʀeavi] *nm* notice
précaution [pʀekosjɔ̃] *nf* precaution; **avec ~** cautiously; **par ~** as a precaution
précédemment [pʀesedamɑ̃] *adv* before, previously
précédent, e [pʀesedɑ̃, ɑ̃t] *adj* previous ♦ *nm* precedent
précéder [pʀesede] *vt* to precede
précepteur, -trice [pʀeseptœʀ, tʀis] *nm/f* (private) tutor
prêcher [pʀeʃe] *vt* to preach
précieux, -euse [pʀesjø, jøz] *adj* precious; (*aide, conseil*) invaluable
précipice [pʀesipis] *nm* drop, chasm
précipitamment [pʀesipitamɑ̃] *adv* hurriedly, hastily
précipitation [pʀesipitasjɔ̃] *nf* (*hâte*) haste; **~s** *nfpl* (*pluie*) rain *sg*
précipité, e [pʀesipite] *adj* hasty
précipiter [pʀesipite] *vt* (*hâter: départ*) to hasten; (*faire tomber*): **~ qn/qch du haut de** to throw *ou* hurl sb/sth off *ou* from; **se ~** *vi* to speed up; **se ~ sur/vers** to rush at/towards
précis, e [pʀesi, iz] *adj* precise; (*mesures*) accurate, precise; **à 4 heures ~es** at 4 o'clock sharp; **précisément** *adv* precisely; **préciser** *vt* (*expliquer*) to be more specific about, clarify; (*spécifier*) to state, specify; **se préciser** *vi* to become clear(er); **précision** *nf* precision; (*détail*) point *ou* detail; **demander des précisions** to ask for further explanation
précoce [pʀekɔs] *adj* early; (*enfant*) precocious
préconçu, e [pʀekɔ̃sy] *adj* preconceived
préconiser [pʀekɔnize] *vt* to advocate
prédécesseur [pʀedesesœʀ] *nm* pre-

decessor

prédilection [predilɛksjɔ̃] *nf*: **avoir une ~ pour** to be partial to

prédire [predir] *vt* to predict

prédominer [predɔmine] *vi* to predominate

préface [prefas] *nf* preface

préfecture [prefɛktyr] *nf* prefecture; **~ de police** police headquarters *pl*

préférable [preferabl] *adj* preferable

préféré, e [prefere] *adj*, *nm/f* favourite

préférence [preferɑ̃s] *nf* preference; **de ~** preferably

préférer [prefere] *vt*: **~ qn/qch (à)** to prefer sb/sth '(to), like sb/sth better (than); **~ faire** to prefer to do; **je ~ais du thé** I would rather have tea, I'd prefer tea

préfet [prefe] *nm* prefect

préhistorique [preistɔrik] *adj* prehistoric

préjudice [preʒydis] *nm* (*matériel*) loss; (*moral*) harm *no pl*; **porter ~ à** to harm, be detrimental to; **au ~ de** at the expense of

préjugé [preʒyʒe] *nm* prejudice; **avoir un ~ contre** to be prejudiced *ou* biased against

préjuger [preʒyʒe]: **~ de** *vt* to prejudge

prélasser [prelase]: **se ~** *vi* to lounge

prélèvement [prelɛvmɑ̃] *nm* (*montant*) deduction; **faire un ~ de sang** to take a blood sample

prélever [prel(ə)ve] *vt* (*échantillon*) to take; **~ (sur)** (*montant*) to deduct (from); (*argent: sur son compte*) to withdraw (from)

prématuré, e [prematyre] *adj* premature ♦ *nm* premature baby

premier, -ière [prəmje, jɛr] *adj* first; (*rang*) front; (*fig: objectif*) basic; **le ~ venu** the first person to come along; **de ~ ordre** first-rate; **P~ Ministre** Prime Minister; **première** (*SCOL*) lower sixth form; (*THÉÂTRE*) first night; (*AUTO*) first (gear); (*AVIAT, RAIL etc*) first

class; (*CINÉMA*) première; (*exploit*) first;

premièrement *adv* firstly

prémonition [premɔnisjɔ̃] *nf* premonition

prémunir [premynir]: **se ~ vi**: **se ~ contre** to guard against

prenant, e [prənɑ̃, ɑ̃t] *adj* absorbing, engrossing

prénatal, e [prenatal] *adj* (*MÉD*) antenatal

prendre [prɑ̃dr] *vt* to take; (*repas*) to have; (*se procurer*) to get; (*malfaiteur, poisson*) to catch; (*passager*) to pick up; (*personnel*) to take on; (*traiter: personne*) to handle; (*voix, ton*) to put on; (*ôter*): **~ qch à** to take sth from; (*coincer*): **se ~ les doigts dans** to get one's fingers caught in ♦ *vi* (*liquide, ciment*) to set; (*greffe, vaccin*) to take; (*feu: foyer*) to go; (*se diriger*): **à gauche** to turn (to the) left; **~ froid** to catch cold; **se ~ pour** to think one is; **s'en ~ à** to attack; **se ~ d'amitié pour** to befriend; **s'y ~** (*procéder*) to set about it

preneur [prənœr, øz] *nm*: **être/trouver ~** to be willing to buy/find a buyer

preniez [prənje] *vb voir* **prendre**

prenne *etc* [prɛn] *vb voir* **prendre**

prénom [prenɔ̃] *nm* first *ou* Christian name

préoccupation [preɔkypasjɔ̃] *nf* (*souci*) concern; (*idée fixe*) preoccupation

préoccuper [preɔkype] *vt* (*inquiéter*) to worry; (*absorber*) to preoccupy; **se ~ de** to be concerned with

préparatifs [preparatif] *nmpl* preparations

préparation [preparasjɔ̃] *nf* preparation

préparer [prepare] *vt* to prepare; (*café, thé*) to make; (*examen*) to prepare for; (*voyage, entreprise*) to plan; **se ~** *vi* (*orage, tragédie*) to brew, be in the air; **~ qch à qn** (*surprise etc*) to have sth in store for sb; **se ~ (à qch/faire)** to prepare (o.s.) *ou* get ready (for sth/to do)

prépondérant, e [prepɔ̃derɑ̃, ɑ̃t] *adj* major, dominating

préposé, e [prepoze] *nm/f* employee; *(facteur)* postman

préposition [prepozisjɔ̃] *nf* preposition

près [prɛ] *adv* near, close; **~ de** near (to), close to; *(environ)* nearly, almost; **de ~** closely; **à 5 kg ~** to within about 5 kg; **à cela ~ que** apart from the fact that; **il n'est pas à 10 minutes ~** he can spare 10 minutes

présage [preʒaʒ] *nm* omen; **présager** *vt* to foresee

presbyte [prɛsbit] *adj* long-sighted

presbytère [prɛsbitɛr] *nm* presbytery

prescription [prɛskripsjɔ̃] *nf* prescription

prescrire [prɛskrir] *vt* to prescribe

présence [prezɑ̃s] *nf* presence; *(au bureau, à l'école)* attendance

présent, e [prezɑ̃, ɑ̃t] *adj, nm* present; **à ~ (que)** now (that)

présentation [prezɑ̃tasjɔ̃] *nf* presentation; *(de nouveau venu)* introduction; *(allure)* appearance; **faire les ~s** to do the introductions

présenter [prezɑ̃te] *vt* to present; *(excuses, condoléances)* to offer; *(invité, conférencier)*: **~ qn (à)** to introduce sb (to) ♦ *vi*: **~ bien** to have a pleasing appearance; **se ~** *vi (occasion)* to arise; **se ~ à** *(examen)* to sit; *(élection)* to stand, run for

préservatif [prezervatif, iv] *nm* sheath, condom

préserver [prezɛrve] *vt*: **~ de** *(protéger)* to protect from

président [prezidɑ̃] *nm* (POL) president; *(d'une assemblée, COMM)* chairman; **~ directeur général** chairman and managing director; **présidentielles** *nfpl* presidential elections

présider [prezide] *vt* to preside over; *(dîner)* to be the guest of honour at

présomptueux, -euse [prezɔ̃ptyø,

øz] *adj* presumptuous

presque [prɛsk] *adv* almost, nearly; **~ personne** hardly anyone; **~ rien** hardly anything; **~ pas** hardly (at all); **~ pas (de)** hardly any

presqu'île [prɛskil] *nf* peninsula

pressant, e [prɛsɑ̃, ɑ̃t] *adj* urgent

presse [prɛs] *nf* press; *(affluence)*: **heures de ~** busy times

pressé, e [prese] *adj* in a hurry; *(travail)* urgent; **orange ~e** freshly-squeezed orange juice

pressentiment [prɛsɑ̃timɑ̃] *nm* foreboding, premonition

pressentir [prɛsɑ̃tir] *vt* to sense

presse-papiers [prɛspapje] *nm inv* paperweight

presser [prese] *vt (fruit, éponge)* to squeeze; *(bouton)* to press; *(allure)* to speed up; *(inciter)*: **~ qn de faire** to urge ou press sb to do ♦ *vi* to be urgent; **se ~** *vi (se hâter)* to hurry (up); **se ~ contre qn** to squeeze up against sb; **rien ne presse** there's no hurry

pressing [prɛsiŋ] *nm (magasin)* dry-cleaner's

pression [prɛsjɔ̃] *nf* pressure; *(bouton)* press stud; *(fam: bière)* draught beer; **faire ~ sur** to put pressure on; **~ artérielle** blood pressure

prestance [prɛstɑ̃s] *nf* presence, imposing bearing

prestataire [prɛstatɛr] *nm/f* supplier

prestation [prɛstasjɔ̃] *nf (allocation)* benefit; *(d'une entreprise)* service provided; *(d'un artiste)* performance

prestidigitateur, -trice [prɛstidiʒitatœr, tris] *nm/f* conjurer

prestige [prɛstiʒ] *nm* prestige; **prestigieux, -euse** *adj* prestigious

présumer [prezyme] *vt*: **~ que** to presume ou assume that

prêt, e [prɛ, prɛt] *adj* ready ♦ *nm (somme)* loan; **prêt-à-porter** *nm* ready-to-wear ou off-the-peg (BRIT) clothes *pl*

prétendre [pretɑ̃dr] *vt (affirmer)*: **~**

que to claim that; (*avoir l'intention de*): **~ faire qch** to mean *ou* intend to do sth; **prétendu, e** *adj* (*supposé*) socalled

prétentieux, -euse [pretɑ̃sjø, jøz] *adj* pretentious

prétention [pretɑ̃sjɔ̃] *nf* claim; (*vanité*) pretentiousness; **~s** *nfpl* (*salaire*) expected salary

prêter [prete] *vt* (*livres, argent*): **~ qch (à)** to lend sth (to); (*supposer*): **~ qch** (*caractère, propos*) to attribute to sb; **se ~ à** to lend o.s. (*ou* itself) to; (*manigances etc*) to go along with; **~ à** (*critique, commentaires etc*) to be open to, give rise to; **~ attention à** to pay attention to; **~ serment** to take the oath

prétexte [pretεkst] *nm* pretext, excuse; **sous aucun ~** on no account; **prétexter** *vt* to give as a pretext *ou* an excuse

prêtre [pretʀ] *nm* priest

preuve [pʀœv] *nf* (*indice*) proof, evidence *no pl*; **faire ~ de** to show; **faire ses ~s** to prove o.s. (*ou* itself)

prévaloir [pʀevalwaʀ] *vi* to prevail

prévenant, e [pʀev(ə)nɑ̃, ɑ̃t] *adj* thoughtful, kind

prévenir [pʀev(ə)niʀ] *vt* (*éviter: catastrophe etc*) to avoid, prevent; (*anticiper: désirs, besoins*) to anticipate; **~ qn (de)** (*avertir*) to warn sb (about); (*informer*) to tell *ou* inform sb (about)

préventif, -ive [pʀevɑ̃tif, iv] *adj* preventive

prévention [pʀevɑ̃sjɔ̃] *nf* prevention; **~ routière** road safety

prévenu, e [pʀev(ə)ny] *nm/f* (*JUR*) defendant, accused

prévision [pʀevizjɔ̃] *nf*: **~s** predictions; (*ÉCON*) forecast *sg*; **en ~ de** in anticipation of; **~s météorologiques** weather forecast *sg*

prévoir [pʀevwaʀ] *vt* (*anticiper*) to foresee; (*s'attendre à*) to expect, reckon on; (*organiser: voyage etc*) to plan; (*envisager*) to plan; **comme prévu** as

planned; **prévoyant, e** *adj* gifted with (*ou* showing) foresight; **prévu, e** *pp de* **prévoir**

prier [pʀije] *vi* to pray ♦ *vt* (*Dieu*) to pray to; (*implorer*) to beg; (*demander*): **~ qn de faire** to ask sb to do; **se faire ~** to need coaxing *ou* persuading; **je vous en prie** (*allez-y*) please do; (*de rien*) don't mention it; **prière** *nf* prayer; **"prière de ..."** "please ..."

primaire [pʀimεʀ] *adj* primary ♦ *nm* (*SCOL*) primary education

prime [pʀim] *nf* (*bonus*) bonus; (*subvention*) premium; (*COMM: cadeau*) free gift; (*ASSURANCES, BOURSE*) premium ♦ *adj*: **de ~ abord** at first glance; **primer** *vt* (*récompenser*) to award a prize to ♦ *vi* to dominate; to be most important

primeurs [pʀimœʀ] *nfpl* early fruits and vegetables

primevère [pʀimvεʀ] *nf* primrose

primitif, -ive [pʀimitif, iv] *adj* primitive; (*original*) original

primordial, e, -iaux [pʀimɔʀdjal, jo] *adj* essential

prince [pʀε̃s] *nm* prince; **princesse** *nf* princess

principal, e, -aux [pʀε̃sipal, o] *adj* principal, main ♦ *nm* (*SCOL*) principal, head(master); (*essentiel*) main thing

principe [pʀε̃sip] *nm* principle; **par ~** on principle; **en ~** (*habituellement*) as a rule; (*théoriquement*) in principle

printemps [pʀε̃tɑ̃] *nm* spring

priorité [pʀijɔʀite] *nf* priority; (*AUTO*) right of way; **~ à droite** right of way to vehicles coming from the right

pris, e [pʀi, pʀiz] *pp de* **prendre** ♦ *adj* (*place*) taken; (*mains*) full; (*personne*) busy; **avoir le nez/la gorge ~(e)** to have a stuffy nose/a hoarse throat; **être ~ de panique** to be panic-stricken

prise [pʀiz] *nf* (*d'une ville*) capture; (*PÊCHE, CHASSE*) catch; (*point d'appui ou pour empoigner*) hold; (*ÉLEC: fiche*) plug; (*: femelle*) socket; **être aux ~s avec** to be grappling with; **~ de conscience**

awareness, realization; ~ **de contact** (rencontre) initial meeting, first contact; ~ **de courant** power point; ~ **sang** blood test; ~ **de vue** (photo) shot; ~ **multiple** adaptor

priser [prize] vt (estimer) to prize, value

prison [prizõ] nf prison; **aller/être en** ~ to go to/be in prison ou jail; **prisonnier, -ière** nm/f prisoner ♦ adj captive

prit [pri] vb voir **prendre**

privé, e [prive] adj private ♦ nm (COMM) private sector; **en** ~ in private

priver [prive] vt: ~ **qn de** to deprive sb of; **se** ~ **de** to go ou do without

privilège [privilɛʒ] nm privilege

prix [pri] nm price; (récompense, SCOL) prize; **hors de** ~ exorbitantly priced; **à aucun** ~ not at any price; **à tout** ~ at all costs; ~ **d'achat/de vente/de revient** purchasing/selling/cost price

probable [prɔbabl] adj likely, probable; **probablement** adv probably

probant, e [prɔbã, ãt] adj convincing

problème [prɔblɛm] nm problem

procédé [prɔsede] nm (méthode) process; (comportement) behaviour no pl

procéder [prɔsede] vi to proceed; (moralement) to behave; ~ **à** to carry out

procès [prɔsɛ] nm trial; (poursuites) proceedings pl; **être en** ~ **avec** to be involved in a lawsuit with

processus [prɔsesys] nm process

procès-verbal, -aux [prɔsɛverbal, o] nm (de réunion) minutes pl; (aussi: **P.V.**) parking ticket

prochain, e [prɔʃɛ̃, ɛn] adj next; (proche: départ, arrivée) impending ♦ nm fellow man; **la** ~**e fois/semaine** ~**e** next time/week; **prochainement** adv soon, shortly

proche [prɔʃ] adj nearby; (dans le temps) imminent; (parent, ami) close; ~**s** nmpl (parents) close relatives; **être** ~ **(de)** to be near, be close (to); **le P-Orient** the Middle East

proclamer [prɔklame] vt to proclaim

procuration [prɔkyrasjõ] nf proxy

procurer [prɔkyre] vt: ~ **qch à qn** (fournir) to obtain sth for sb; (causer: plaisir etc) to bring sb sth; **se** ~ vt to get; **procureur** nm public prosecutor

prodige [prɔdiʒ] nm marvel, wonder; (personne) prodigy; **prodiguer** vt (soins, attentions): **prodiguer qch à qn** to give sb sth

producteur, -trice [prɔdyktœr, tris] nm/f producer

productif, -ive [prɔdyktif, iv] adj productive

production [prɔdyksjõ] nf production; (rendement) output

productivité [prɔdyktivite] nf productivity

produire [prɔdɥir] vt to produce; **se** ~ vi (événement) to happen, occur; (acteur) to perform, appear

produit [prɔdɥi] nm product; ~ **chimique** chemical; ~ **d'entretien** cleaning product; ~ **national brut** gross national product; ~**s alimentaires** foodstuffs

prof [prɔf] (fam) nm teacher

profane [prɔfan] adj (REL) secular ♦ nm/f layman(-woman)

proférer [prɔfere] vt to utter

professeur, e [prɔfesœr] nm/f teacher; (de faculté) (university) lecturer; (: titulaire d'une chaire) professor

profession [prɔfesjõ] nf occupation; ~ **libérale** (liberal) profession; **sans** ~ unemployed; **professionnel, le** adj professional

profil [prɔfil] nm profile; **de** ~ in profile

profit [prɔfi] nm (avantage) benefit, advantage; (COMM, FINANCE) profit; **au** ~ **de** in aid of; **tirer** ~ **de** to profit from; **profitable** adj (utile) beneficial; (lucratif) profitable; **profiter** vi: **profiter de** (situation, occasion) to take advantage of; (vacances, jeunesse etc) to make the most of

profond, e [prɔfõ, õd] adj deep; (sentiment, intérêt) profound; **profondément** adv deeply; **il dort profondément** he is sound asleep; **profondeur** nf depth

progéniture [prɔʒenityr] nf offspring inv

programme [prɔgram] nm programme; (SCOL) syllabus, curriculum; (INFORM) program; **programmer** vt (émission) to schedule; (INFORM) to program; **programmeur, -euse** nm/f programmer

progrès [prɔgrɛ] nm progress no pl; **faire des ~** to make progress; **progresser** vi to progress; **progressif, -ive** adj progressive

prohiber [prɔibe] vt to prohibit, ban

proie [prwa] nf prey no pl

projecteur [prɔʒɛktœr] nm (pour film) projector; (de théâtre, cirque) spotlight

projectile [prɔʒɛktil] nm missile

projection [prɔʒɛksjɔ̃] nf projection; (séance) showing

projet [prɔʒɛ] nm plan; (ébauche) draft; **~ de loi** bill; **projeter** vt (envisager) to plan; (film, photos) to project; (ombre, lueur) to throw, cast; (jeter) to throw up (ou off ou out)

prolétaire [prɔleter] adj, nmf proletarian

prolongement [prɔlɔ̃ʒmɑ̃] nm extension; **dans le ~ de** running on from

prolonger [prɔlɔ̃ʒe] vt (débat, séjour) to prolong; (délai, billet, rue) to extend; **se ~** vi to go on

promenade [prɔm(ə)nad] nf walk (ou drive ou ride); **faire une ~** to go for a walk; **une ~ en voiture/à vélo** a drive/(bicycle) ride

promener [prɔm(ə)ne] vt (chien) to take out for a walk; (doigts, regard): **~ qch sur** to run sth over; **se ~** vi to go for (ou be out for) a walk

promesse [prɔmɛs] nf promise

promettre [prɔmɛtr] vt to promise ♦ vi to be ou look promising; **~ à qn de faire** to promise sb that one will do

promiscuité [prɔmiskɥite] nf (chambre) lack of privacy

promontoire [prɔmɔ̃twar] nm headland

promoteur, -trice [prɔmɔtœr, tris] nm/f: **~ (immobilier)** property developer (BRIT), real estate promoter (US)

promotion [prɔmɔsjɔ̃] nf promotion; **en ~** on special offer

promouvoir [prɔmuvwar] vt to promote

prompt, e [prɔ̃(pt), prɔ̃(p)t] adj swift, rapid

prôner [prone] vt (préconiser) to advocate

pronom [prɔnɔ̃] nm pronoun

prononcer [prɔnɔ̃se] vt to pronounce; (dire) to utter; (discours) to deliver; **se ~** vi to be pronounced; **se ~ (sur)** (se décider) to reach a decision (ou about), give a verdict (on); **prononciation** nf pronunciation

pronostic [prɔnɔstik] nm (MÉD) prognosis; (fig: aussi: **~s**) forecast

propagande [prɔpagɑ̃d] nf propaganda

propager [prɔpaʒe] vt to spread; **se ~** vi to spread

prophète [prɔfɛt] nm prophet

prophétie [prɔfesi] nf prophecy

propice [prɔpis] adj favourable

proportion [prɔpɔrsjɔ̃] nf proportion; **toute(s) ~(s) gardée(s)** making due allowance(s)

propos [prɔpo] nm (intention) intention, aim; (sujet): **à quel ~?** what about? ♦ nmpl (paroles) talk no pl, remarks; **à ~ de** about, regarding; **à tout ~** for the slightest thing ou reason; **à ~** by the way; (opportunément) at the right moment

proposer [prɔpoze] vt to propose; **~ qch (à qn)** (suggérer) to suggest sth (to sb), propose sth (to sb); (offrir) to offer (sb) sth; **se ~** to offer one's services; **se ~ de faire** to intend ou propose to do; **proposition** (suggestion) nf propo sal, suggestion; (LING) clause

propre [prɔpr] adj clean; (net) neat, tidy; (possessif) own; (sens) literal; (particulier): ~ à peculiar to; (approprié): ~ à suitable for ♦ nm: **recopier au ~** to make a fair copy of; **proprement** adv (avec propreté) cleanly; **le village proprement dit** the village itself; **à proprement parler** strictly speaking; **propreté** nf cleanliness

propriétaire [prɔprijetɛr] nm/f owner; (pour le locataire) landlord(-lady)

propriété [prɔprijete] nf property; (droit) ownership

propulser [prɔpylse] vt to propel

proroger [prɔrɔʒe] vt (prolonger) to extend

proscrire [prɔskrir] vt (interdire) to ban, prohibit

prose [proz] nf (style) prose

prospecter [prɔspekte] vt to prospect; (COMM) to canvass

prospectus [prɔspektys] nm leaflet

prospère [prɔspɛr] adj prosperous; **prospérer** vi to prosper

prosterner [prɔstɛrne]: **se ~** vi to bow low, prostrate o.s.

prostituée [prɔstitɥe] nf prostitute

prostitution [prɔstitysjɔ̃] nf prostitution

protecteur, -trice [prɔtɛktœr, tris] adj protective; (air, ton: péj) patronizing ♦ nm/f protector

protection [prɔtɛksjɔ̃] nf protection; (d'un personnage influent: aide) patronage

protéger [prɔteʒe] vt to protect; **se ~ de ou contre** to protect o.s. from

protéine [prɔtein] nf protein

protestant, e [prɔtɛstɑ̃, ɑ̃t] adj, nm/f Protestant

protestation [prɔtɛstasjɔ̃] nf (plainte) protest

protester [prɔtɛste] vi: ~ (contre) to protest (against ou about); ~ **de** (son innocence) to protest

prothèse [prɔtɛz] nf: ~ **dentaire** denture

protocole [prɔtɔkɔl] nm (fig) etiquette

proue [pru] nf bow(s pl), prow

prouesse [prues] nf feat

prouver [pruve] vt to prove

provenance [prɔvnɑ̃s] nf origin; **avion en ~ de** plane (arriving) from

provenir [prɔv(ə)nir]: ~ **de** vt to come from

proverbe [prɔvɛrb] nm proverb

province [prɔvɛ̃s] nf province

proviseur [prɔvizœr] nm ≃ head(teacher) (BRIT), ≃ principal (US)

provision [prɔvizjɔ̃] nf (réserve) stock, supply; ~**s** nfpl (vivres) provisions, food no pl

provisoire [prɔvizwar] adj temporary; **provisoirement** adv temporarily

provocant, e [prɔvɔkɑ̃, ɑ̃t] adj provocative

provoquer [prɔvɔke] vt (défier) to provoke; (causer) to cause, bring about; (inciter): ~ **qn à** to incite sb to

proxénète [prɔksenɛt] nm procurer

proximité [prɔksimite] nf nearness, closeness; (dans le temps) imminence, closeness; **à ~** near ou close by; **à ~ de** near (to), close to

prudemment [prydamɑ̃] adv carefully; wisely, sensibly

prudence [prydɑ̃s] nf carefulness; **avec ~** carefully; **par ~** as a precaution

prudent, e [prydɑ̃, ɑ̃t] adj (pas téméraire) careful; (: en général) safety-conscious; (sage, conseillé) wise, sensible; **c'est plus ~** it's wiser

prune [pryn] nf plum

pruneau, x [pryno] nm prune

prunelle [prynɛl] nf (BOT) sloe; **il y tient comme à la ~ de ses yeux** he treasures ou cherishes it

prunier [prynje] nm plum tree

PS sigle m = **parti socialiste**

psaume [psom] nm psalm

pseudonyme [psødɔnim] nm (gén) fictitious name; (d'écrivain) pseudonym,

pen name
psychanalyse [psikanaliz] *nf* psycho-analysis
psychiatre [psikjatʀ] *nm/f* psychiatrist; **psychiatrique** *adj* psychiatric
psychique [psiʃik] *adj* psychological
psychologie [psikɔlɔʒi] *nf* psychology; **psychologique** *adj* psychological; **psychologue** *nm/f* psychologist
P.T.T. *sigle fpl* = Postes, Télécommunications et Télédiffusion
pu [py] *pp de* pouvoir
puanteur [pɥɑ̃tœʀ] *nf* stink, stench
pub [pyb] *nf* (*fam: annonce*) ad, advert; (*pratique*) advertising
public, -ique [pyblik] *adj* public; (*école, instruction*) state *cpd* ♦ *nm* public; (*assistance*) audience; **en ~** in public
publicitaire [pyblisitɛʀ] *adj* advertising *cpd*; (*film*) publicity *cpd*
publicité [pyblisite] *nf* (*méthode, profession*) advertising; (*annonce*) advertisement; (*révélations*) publicity
publier [pyblije] *vt* to publish
publique [pyblik] *adj voir* public
puce [pys] *nf* flea; (*INFORM*) chip; **carte à ~** smart card; **~s** *nfpl* (*marché*) flea market *sg*
pudeur [pydœʀ] *nf* modesty; **pudique** *adj* (*chaste*) modest; (*discret*) discreet
puer [pɥe] (*péj*) *vi* to stink
puéricultrice [pɥeʀikyltʀis] *nf* p(a)ediatric nurse
puéril, e [pɥeʀil] *adj* childish
puis [pɥi] *vb voir* pouvoir ♦ *adv* then
puiser [pɥize] *vt* ~ (**dans**) to draw (from)
puisque [pɥisk] *conj* since
puissance [pɥisɑ̃s] *nf* power; **en ~** ♦ *adj* potential
puissant, e [pɥisɑ̃, ɑ̃t] *adj* powerful
puisse *etc* [pɥis] *vb voir* pouvoir
puits [pɥi] *nm* well
pull(-over) [pyl(ɔvɛʀ)] *nm* sweater
pulluler [pylyle] *vi* to swarm
pulvérisateur [pylveʀizatœʀ] *nm* spray

pulvériser [pylveʀize] *vt* to pulverize; (*liquide*) to spray
punaise [pynɛz] *nf* (*ZOOL*) bug; (*clou*) drawing pin (*BRIT*), thumbtack (*US*)
punch¹ [pɔ̃ʃ] *nm* (*boisson*) punch
punch² [pœnʃ] *nm* (*BOXE, fig*) punch
punir [pyniʀ] *vt* to punish; **punition** *nf* punishment
pupille [pypij] *nf* (*ANAT*) pupil ♦ *nm/f* (*enfant*) ward
pupitre [pypitʀ] *nm* (*SCOL*) desk
pur, e [pyʀ] *adj* pure; (*vin*) undiluted; (*whisky*) neat; **en ~e perte** to no avail; **c'est de la folie ~e** it's sheer madness; **purement** *adv* purely
purée [pyʀe] *nf:* ~ (**de pommes de terre**) mashed potatoes *pl*; ~ **de marrons** chestnut purée
purgatoire [pyʀɡatwaʀ] *nm* purgatory
purger [pyʀʒe] *vt* (*MÉD, POL*) to purge; (*JUR: peine*) to serve
purin [pyʀɛ̃] *nm* liquid manure
pur-sang [pyʀsɑ̃] *nm inv* thoroughbred
putain [pytɛ̃] (*fam!*) *nf* whore (*!*)
puzzle [pœzl] *nm* jigsaw (puzzle)
P.-V. *sigle m* = procès-verbal
pyjama [piʒama] *nm* pyjamas *pl* (*BRIT*), pajamas *pl* (*US*)
Pyrénées [piʀene] *nfpl:* **les ~** the Pyrenees

Q, q

QI *sigle m* (= quotient intellectuel) IQ
quadra [k(w)adʀa] *nm/f* man/woman in his/her forties; **les ~s** forty somethings (*fam*)
quadragénaire [k(w)adʀaʒenɛʀ] *nm/f* man/woman in his/her forties
quadriller [kadʀije] *vt* (*POLICE*) to keep under tight control
quadruple [k(w)adʀypl] *nm:* **le ~ de** four times as much as; **quadruplés, -ées** *nm/fpl* quadruplets, quads
quai [ke] *nm* (*de port*) quay; (*de gare*) platform; **être à ~** (*navire*) to be

alongside

qualification [kalifikasjɔ̃] *nf* (*aptitude*) qualification

qualifié, e [kalifje] *adj* qualified; (*main d'œuvre*) skilled

qualifier [kalifje] *vt* to qualify; **se ~** *vi* to qualify; **~ qch/qn de** to describe sth/sb as

qualité [kalite] *nf* quality

quand [kɑ̃] *conj, adv* when; **je serai riche** when I'm rich; **~ même** all the same; **~ même, il exagère!** really, he overdoes it!; **~ bien même** even though

quant [kɑ̃]: **à ~** *prép* (*pour ce qui est de*) as for, as to; (*au sujet de*) regarding; **quant-à-soi** *nm*: **rester sur son quant-à-soi** to remain aloof

quantité [kɑ̃tite] *nf* quantity, amount; (*grand nombre*): **une** *ou* **des ~(s) de** a great deal of

quarantaine [karɑ̃tɛn] *nf* (*MÉD*) quarantine; **avoir la ~** (*âge*) to be around forty; **une ~ (de)** forty or so, about forty

quarante [karɑ̃t] *num* forty

quart [kar] *nm* (*fraction*) quarter; (*surveillance*) watch; **un ~ de vin** a quarter litre of wine; **le ~ de qch** a quarter of; **~ d'heure** quarter of an hour; **~s de finale** quarter finals

quartier [kartje] *nm* (*de ville*) district, area; (*de bœuf*) quarter; (*de fruit*) piece; **cinéma ~** local cinema; **avoir ~ libre** (*fig*) to be free; **~ général** headquarters *pl*

quartz [kwarts] *nm* quartz

quasi [kazi] *adv* almost, nearly; **quasiment** *adv* almost, nearly; **quasiment jamais** hardly ever

quatorze [katɔrz] *num* fourteen

quatre [katr] *num* four; **à ~ pattes** on all fours; **se mettre en ~ pour qn** to go out of one's way for sb; **à ~ à ~** (*monter, descendre*) four at a time; **quatre-quarts** *nm inv* pound cake; **quatre-vingt-dix** *num* ninety;

quatre-vingts *num* eighty; **quatre-vingt-un** *num* eighty-one; **quatrième** *num* fourth ♦ *nf* (*SCOL*) third form *ou* year

quatuor [kwatɥɔr] *nm* quartet(te)

MOT-CLÉ

---

que [kə] *conj* **1** (*introduisant complétive*) that; **il sait que tu es là** he knows (that) you're here; **je veux que tu acceptes** I want you to accept; **il a dit que oui** he said he would (*ou* it was *etc*)

2 (*reprise d'autres conjonctions*): **quand il rentrera et qu'il aura mangé** when he gets back and (when) he has eaten; **si vous y allez ou que vous ...** if you go there or if you ...

3 (*en tête de phrase: hypothèse, souhait etc*): **qu'il le veuille ou non** whether he likes it or not; **qu'il fasse ce qu'il voudra!** let him do as he pleases!

4 (*après comparatif*) than, as; *voir aussi* **plus; aussi; autant** *etc*

5 (*seulement*): **ne ... que** only; **il ne boit que de l'eau** he only drinks water

♦ *adv* (*exclamation*): **qu'il** *ou* **qu'est-ce qu'il est bête/court vite!** he's so silly!/he runs so fast!; **que de livres!** what a lot of books!

♦ *pron* **1** (*relatif: personne*) whom; (: *chose*) that, which; **l'homme que je vois** the man (whom) I see; **le livre que tu vois** the book (that *ou* which) you see; **un jour que j'étais ...** a day when I was ...

2 (*interrogatif*) what; **que fais-tu?, qu'est-ce que tu fais?** what are you doing?; **qu'est-ce que c'est?** what is it?, what's that?; **que faire?** what can one do?

Québec [kebek] *n*: **le ~** Quebec; **québecois, e** *adj* Quebec ♦ *nm/f*: **Québecois, e** a Quebecker ♦ *nm* (*LING*) Quebec French

---

MOT-CLÉ

---

quel, quelle [kɛl] adj 1 (interrogatif: personne) who; (: chose) what; which; **quel est cet homme?** who is this man?; **quel est ce livre?** what is this book?; **quel livre/homme?** what book/man?; (parmi un certain choix) which book/man?; **quels acteurs préférez-vous?** which actors do you prefer?; **dans quels pays êtes-vous allé?** which ou what countries did you go to?
2 (exclamatif): **quelle surprise!** what a surprise!
3: **quel que soit le coupable** whoever is guilty; **quel que soit votre avis** whatever your opinion

quelconque [kɛlkɔ̃k] adj (indéfini): **un ami/prétexte ~** some friend/pretext or other; (médiocre: repas) indifferent, poor; (laid: personne) plain-looking

---

MOT-CLÉ

---

quelque [kɛlk] adj 1 some; a few; (tournure interrogative) any; **quelque espoir** some hope; **il a quelques amis** he has a few ou some friends; **a-t-il quelques amis?** has he any friends?; **les quelques livres qui** the few books which; **20 kg et quelque(s)** a bit over 20 kg
2: **quelque ... que: quelque livre qu'il choisisse** whatever (ou whichever) book he chooses
3: **quelque chose** something; (tournure interrogative) anything; **quelque chose d'autre** something else; anything else; **quelque part** somewhere; anywhere; **en quelque sorte** as it were
♦ adv 1 (environ): **quelque 100 mètres** some 100 metres
2: **quelque peu** rather, somewhat

quelquefois [kɛlkəfwa] adv sometimes
quelques-uns, -unes [kɛlkəzœ̃, yn]

pron a few, some

quelqu'un [kɛlkœ̃] pron someone, somebody; (+tournure interrogative) anyone, anybody; **~ d'autre** someone ou somebody else; (+ tournure interrogative) anybody else

quémander [kemɑ̃de] vt to beg for
qu'en dira-t-on [kɑ̃diʀatɔ̃] nm inv: **le ~** ~~~ gossip, what people say

querelle [kəʀɛl] nf quarrel; **quereller: se quereller** vi to quarrel

qu'est-ce que [kɛskə] voir **que**
qu'est-ce qui [kɛski] voir **que**

question [kɛstjɔ̃] nf question; (fig) matter, issue; **il a été ~ de** we (ou they) spoke about; **de quoi est-il ~?** what is it about?; **il n'en est pas ~** there's no question of it; **hors de ~** out of the question; **remettre en ~** to question; **questionnaire** nm questionnaire; **questionner** vt to question

quête [kɛt] nf collection; (recherche) quest, search; **faire la ~** (à l'église) to take the collection; (artiste) to pass the hat round

quetsche [kwɛtʃ] nf kind of dark-red plum

queue [kø] nf tail; (fig: du classement) bottom; (: de poêle) handle; (: de fruit, feuille) stalk; (: de train, colonne, file) rear; **faire la ~** to queue (up) (BRIT), line up (US); **~ de cheval** ponytail; **~ de poisson** (AUT): **faire une ~ de poisson à qn** to cut in front of sb

qui [ki] pron (personne) who; (+prép) whom; (chose, animal) which, that; **qu'est-ce ~ est sur la table?** what is on the table?; **~ est-ce ~?** who?; **~ est-ce que?** who?; **à ~ est ce sac?** whose bag is this?; **à ~ parlais-tu?** who were you talking to?, to whom were you talking?; **amenez ~ vous voulez** bring who you like, bring who you like; **~ que ce soit** whoever it may be

quiconque [kikɔ̃k] pron (celui qui) whoever, anyone who; (n'importe qui) anyone, anybody

quiétude [kjetyd] *nf*: **en toute ~** in complete peace

quille [kij] *nf*: **(jeu de) ~s** skittles *sg* (*BRIT*), bowling (*US*)

quincaillerie [kɛ̃kajʀi] *nf* (*ustensiles*) hardware; (*magasin*) hardware shop; **quincaillier, -ière** *nm/f* hardware dealer

quinquagénaire [kɛ̃kaʒenɛʀ] *nm/f* man/woman in his/her fifties

quintal, -aux [kɛ̃tal, o] *nm* quintal (*100 kg*)

quinte [kɛ̃t] *nf*: **~ (de toux)** coughing fit

quintuple [kɛ̃typl] *nm*: **le ~ de** five times as much as; **quintuplés, -ées** *nm/fpl* quintuplets, quins

quinzaine [kɛ̃zɛn] *nf*: **une ~ (de)** about fifteen, fifteen or so; **une ~ (de jours)** a fortnight, two weeks

quinze [kɛ̃z] *num* fifteen; **dans ~ jours** in a fortnight('s time), in two weeks('' time)

quiproquo [kipʀɔko] *nm* misunderstanding

quittance [kitɑ̃s] *nf* (*reçu*) receipt

quitte [kit] *adj*: **être ~ envers qn** to be no longer in sb's debt; (*fig*) to be quits with sb; **~ à faire** even if it means doing

quitter [kite] *vt* to leave; (*vêtement*) to take off; **se ~** *vi* (*couples, interlocuteurs*) to part; **ne quittez pas** (*au téléphone*) hold the line

qui-vive [kiviv] *nm*: **être sur le ~~** to be on the alert

quoi [kwa] *pron* (*interrogatif*) what; **~ de neuf?** what's the news?; **as-tu de ~ écrire** have you anything to write with?; **~ qu'il arrive** whatever happens; **~ qu'il en soit** be that as it may; **~ que ce soit** anything at all; **"il n'y a pas de ~"** "(please) don't mention it"; **il n'y a pas de ~ rire** there's nothing to laugh about; **à ~ bon?** what's the use?; **en ~ puis-je vous aider?** how can I help you?

quoique [kwak] *conj* (al)though

quote-part [kɔtpaʀ] *nf* share

quotidien, ne [kɔtidjɛ̃, jɛn] *adj* daily; (*banal*) everyday ♦ *nm* (*journal*) daily (paper); **quotidiennement** *adv* daily

R, r

r. *abr* = **route; rue**

rab [ʀab] (*fam*) *nm* (*nourriture*) extra; **est-ce qu'il y a du ~?** is there any extra (left)?

rabâcher [ʀabɑʃe] *vt* to keep on repeating

rabais [ʀabɛ] *nm* reduction, discount; **rabaisser** *vt* (*dénigrer*) to belittle; (*rabattre: prix*) to reduce

rabat-joie [ʀabaʒwa] *nm inv* killjoy

rabattre [ʀabatʀ] *vt* (*couvercle, siège*) to pull down; (*déduire*) to reduce; **se ~** *vi* (*se refermer: couvercle*) to fall shut; (*véhicule, coureur*) to cut in; **se ~ sur** to fall back on

rabbin [ʀabɛ̃] *nm* rabbi

râblé, e [ʀɑble] *adj* stocky

rabot [ʀabo] *nm* plane

rabougri, e [ʀabugʀi] *adj* stunted

rabrouer [ʀabʀue] *vt* to snub

racaille [ʀakaj] (*péj*) *nf* rabble, riffraff

raccommoder [ʀakɔmɔde] *vt* to mend, repair; **se ~** *vi* (*fam*) to make it up

raccompagner [ʀakɔ̃paɲe] *vt* to take *ou* see back

raccord [ʀakɔʀ] *nm* link; (*retouche*) touch up; **raccorder** *vt* to join (up), link up; (*suj: pont etc*) to connect, link

raccourci [ʀakuʀsi] *nm* short cut

raccourcir [ʀakuʀsiʀ] *vt* to shorten ♦ *vi* (*jours*) to grow shorter, draw in

raccrocher [ʀakʀɔʃe] *vt* (*tableau*) to hang back up; (*récepteur*) to put down ♦ *vi* (*TÉL*) to hang up, ring off; **se ~** *vi*: **se ~ à** to cling to, hang on to

race [ʀas] *nf* race; (*d'animaux, fig*) breed; **de ~** purebred, pedigree

rachat [Raʃa] nm buying; (du même objet) buying back

racheter [Raʃ(ə)te] vt (article perdu) to buy another; (après avoir vendu) to buy back; (d'occasion) to buy; (COMM: part, firme) to buy up; (davantage): ~ du lait/3 œufs to buy more milk/another 3 eggs ou 3 more eggs; se ~ vi (fig) to make amends

racial, e, -aux [Rasjal, jo] adj racial

racine [Rasin] nf root; ~ carrée/cubique square/cube root

raciste [Rasist] adj, nm/f raci(al)ist

racket [Raket] nm racketeering no pl

raclée [Rakle] (fam) nf hiding, thrashing

racler [Rakle] vt (surface) to scrape; se ~ la gorge to clear one's throat

racoler [Rakɔle] vt (suj: prostituée) to solicit; (: parti, marchand) to tout for

racontars [Rakɔ̃tar] nmpl story, lie

raconter [Rakɔ̃te] vt: ~ (à qn) (décrire) to relate to sb, tell (sb) about; (dire de mauvaise foi) to tell (sb); ~ une histoire to tell a story

racorni, e [Rakɔʀni] adj hard(ened)

radar [Radar] nm radar

rade [Rad] nf (natural) harbour; rester en ~ (fig) to be left stranded

radeau, x [Rado] nm raft

radiateur [Radjatœr] nm radiator, heater; (AUTO) radiator; ~ électrique/à gaz electric/gas heater ou fire

radiation [Radjasjɔ̃] nf (PHYSIQUE) radiation

radical, e, -aux [Radikal, o] adj radical

radier [Radje] vt to strike off

radieux, -euse [Radjø, jøz] adj radiant

radin, e [Radɛ̃, in] (fam) adj stingy

radio [Radjo] nf radio; (MÉD) X-ray ♦ nm radio operator; à la ~ on the radio; **radioactif, -ive** adj radioactive; **radio-cassette** nf cassette radio, radio cassette player; **radiodiffuser** vt to broadcast; **radiographie** nf radiography; (photo) X-ray photograph; **radiophonique** adj radio cpd; **radio-réveil** (pl

radios-réveils) nm radio alarm clock

radis [Radi] nm radish

radoter [Radɔte] vi to ramble on

radoucir [Radusir]: se ~ vi (temps) to become milder; (se calmer) to calm down

rafale [Rafal] nf (vent) gust of wind; (tir) burst of gunfire

raffermir [Rafɛrmir] vt to firm up; se ~ vi (fig: autorité, prix) to strengthen

raffiner [Rafine] vt to refine; **raffinerie** nf refinery

raffoler [Rafɔle]: ~ de vt to be very keen on

rafistoler [Rafistɔle] (fam) vt to patch up

rafle [Rafl] nf (de police) raid; **rafler** (fam) vt to swipe, nick

rafraîchir [Rafreʃir] vt (atmosphère, température) to cool (down); (aussi: mettre à ~) to chill; (: fig: rénover) to brighten up; se ~ vi (temps) to grow cooler; (en se lavant) to freshen up; (en buvant) to refresh o.s.; **rafraîchissant, e** adj refreshing; **rafraîchissement** nm (boisson) cool drink; **rafraîchissements** nmpl (boissons, fruits etc) refreshments

rage [Raʒ] nf (MÉD): la ~ rabies; (fureur) rage, fury; faire ~ to rage; ~ de dents (raging) toothache

ragot [Rago] (fam) nm malicious gossip no pl

ragoût [Ragu] nm stew

raide [Red] adj stiff; (câble) taut, tight; (escarpé) steep; (droit: cheveux) straight; (fam: sans argent) flat broke; (osé: ladin, bold ♦ adv (en pente) steeply; ~ mort stone dead; **raidir** vt (muscles) to stiffen; **se raidir** vi (tissu) to stiffen; (personne) to tense up; (: se préparer moralement) to brace o.s.; (: fig: position) to harden; **raideur** nf (rigidité) stiffness; **avec raideur** (répondre) stiffly, abruptly

raie [Re] nf (ZOOL) skate, ray; (rayure) stripe; (des cheveux) parting

raifort [Refɔr] nm horseradish

rail [ʀɑj] nm rail; (chemins de fer) railways pl; **par ~** by rail

railler [ʀɑje] vt to scoff at, jeer at

rainure [ʀenyʀ] nf groove

raisin [ʀezɛ̃] nm (aussi: **~s**) grapes pl; **~s secs** raisins

raison [ʀezɔ̃] nf reason; **avoir ~** to be right; **donner ~ à qn** to agree with sb; (événement) to prove sb right; **perdre la ~** to become insane; **~ de plus** all the more reason; **à plus forte ~** all the more so; **en ~ de** because of; **à ~ de** at the rate of; **sans ~** for no reason; **raisonnable** adj reasonable, sensible

raisonnement [ʀezɔnmɑ̃] nm (façon de réfléchir) reasoning; (argumentation) argument

raisonner [ʀezɔne] vi (penser) to reason; (argumenter, discuter) to argue ♦ vt (personne) to reason with

rajeunir [ʀaʒœniʀ] vt (suj: coiffure, robe): **~ qn** to make sb look younger; (fig: personnel) to inject new blood into ♦ vi to become (ou look) younger

rajouter [ʀaʒute] vt to add

rajuster [ʀaʒyste] vt (vêtement) to straighten, tidy; (salaires) to adjust

ralenti [ʀalɑ̃ti] nm: **au ~** (fig) at a slower pace; **tourner au ~** (AUTO) to tick over, idle

ralentir [ʀalɑ̃tiʀ] vt to slow down

râler [ʀale] vi to groan; (fam) to grouse, moan (and groan)

rallier [ʀalje] vt (rejoindre) to rejoin; (gagner à sa cause) to win over; **se ~ à** (avis) to come over ou round to

rallonge [ʀalɔ̃ʒ] nf (de table) (extra) leaf

rallonger [ʀalɔ̃ʒe] vt to lengthen

rallye [ʀali] nm rally; (POL) march

ramassage [ʀamasaʒ] nm: **~ scolaire** school bus service

ramassé, e [ʀamase] adj (trapu) squat

ramasser [ʀamase] vt (objet tombé ou par terre, fam) to pick up; (recueillir: copies, ordures) to collect; (récolter) to gather; **se ~** vi (sur soi-même) to huddle up; **ramassis** (péj) nm (de voyous) bunch; (d'objets) jumble

rambarde [ʀɑ̃baʀd] nf guardrail

rame [ʀam] nf (aviron) oar; (de métro) train; (de papier) ream

rameau, x [ʀamo] nm (small) branch; **les R~x** (REL) Palm Sunday sg

ramener [ʀam(ə)ne] vt to bring back; (reconduire) to take back; **~ qch à** (réduire à) to reduce sth to

ramer [ʀame] vi to row

ramollir [ʀamɔliʀ] vt to soften; **se ~** vi to go soft

ramoner [ʀamɔne] vt to sweep

rampe [ʀɑ̃p] nf (d'escalier) banister(s pl); (dans un garage) ramp; (THÉÂTRE): **la ~** the footlights pl; **~ de lancement** launching pad

ramper [ʀɑ̃pe] vi to crawl

rancard [ʀɑ̃kaʀ] (fam) nm (rendez-vous) date

rancart [ʀɑ̃kaʀ] nm: **mettre au ~** (fam) to scrap

rance [ʀɑ̃s] adj rancid

rancœur [ʀɑ̃kœʀ] nf rancour

rançon [ʀɑ̃sɔ̃] nf ransom

rancune [ʀɑ̃kyn] nf grudge, rancour; **garder ~ à qn (de qch)** to bear sb a grudge (for sth); **sans ~!** no hard feelings!; **rancunier, -ière** adj vindictive, spiteful

randonnée [ʀɑ̃dɔne] nf ride; (à pied) walk, ramble; (: en montagne) hike, hiking no pl

rang [ʀɑ̃] nm (rangée) row; (grade, classement) rank; **~s** nmpl (MIL) ranks; **se mettre en ~s** to get into ou form rows; **au premier ~** in the first row; (fig) ranking first

rangé, e [ʀɑ̃ʒe] adj (vie) well-ordered; (personne) steady

rangée [ʀɑ̃ʒe] nf row

ranger [ʀɑ̃ʒe] vt (mettre de l'ordre dans) to tidy up; (classer, grouper) to order, arrange; (mettre à sa place) to put away; (fig: classer): **~ qn/qch parmi** to rank sb/sth among; **se ~** vi (véhicule, conducteur) to pull over ou in; (piéton) to step aside; (s'assagir) to settle down; **se ~ à** (avis) to come round to

ranimer [ranime] vt (personne) to bring round; (douleur, souvenir) to revive; (feu) to rekindle

rap [rap] nm rap (music)

rapace [rapas] nm bird of prey

râpe [rɑp] nf (CULIN) grater; **râper** vt (CULIN) to grate

rapetisser [rap(ə)tise] vt to shorten

rapide [rapid] adj (pas; (prompt: coup d'œil, mouvement) quick ♦ nm express (train); (de cours d'eau) rapid; **rapidement** adv fast; quickly

rapiécer [rapjese] vt to patch

rappel [rapɛl] nm (THÉÂTRE) curtain call; (MÉD: vaccination) booster; (deuxième avis) reminder; **rappeler** vt to call back; (ambassadeur, MIL) to recall; (faire se souvenir): **rappeler qch à qn** to remind sb of sth; **se rappeler** vt (se souvenir de) to remember, recall

rapport [rapɔr] nm (lien, analogie) connection; (compte rendu) report; (profit) yield, return; **~s** nmpl (entre personnes, pays) relations; **avoir ~ à** to have something to do with; **être/se mettre en ~ avec qn** to be/get in touch with sb; **par ~ à** in relation to; **~s (sexuels)** (sexual) intercourse sg

rapporter [rapɔrte] vt (rendre, ramener) to bring back; (bénéfice) to yield, bring in; (mentionner, répéter) to report ♦ vi (investissement) to give a good return ou yield; (: activité) to be very profitable; **se ~ à** (correspondre à) to relate to; **rapporteur, -euse** nm/f (péj) telltale ♦ nm (GÉOM) protractor

rapprochement [raprɔʃmɑ̃] nm (de nations) reconciliation; (rapport) parallel

rapprocher [raprɔʃe] vt (deux objets) to bring closer together; (fig: ennemis, partis etc) to bring together; (comparer) to establish a parallel between; (chaise d'une table): **~ qch (de)** to bring sth

closer (to); **se ~** vi to draw closer ou nearer; **se ~ de** to come closer to; (présenter une analogie avec) to be close to

rapt [rapt] nm abduction

raquette [rakɛt] nf (de tennis) racket; (de ping-pong) bat

rare [rɑr] adj rare; **se faire ~** to become scarce; **rarement** adv rarely, seldom

ras, e [rɑ, rɑz] adj (poil, herbe) short; (tête) close-cropped ♦ adv short; **en ~e campagne** in open country; **à ~ bords** to the brim; **en avoir ~ le bol** (fam) to be fed up; **~ du cou** ♦ adj (pull, robe) crew-neck

rasade [razad] nf glassful

raser [rɑze] vt (barbe, cheveux) to shave off; (menton, personne) to shave; (fam: ennuyer) to bore; (démolir) to raze (to the ground); (frôler) to graze, skim; **se ~** vi to shave; (fam) to be bored (to tears); **rasoir** nm razor

rassasier [rasazje] vt: **être rassasié** to have eaten one's fill

rassemblement [rasɑ̃bləmɑ̃] nm (groupe) gathering; (POL) union

rassembler [rasɑ̃ble] vt (réunir) to assemble, gather; (documents, notes) to gather together, collect; **se ~** vi to gather

rassis, e [rasi, iz] adj (pain) stale

rassurer [rasyre] vt to reassure; **se ~** vi to reassure o.s.; **rassure-toi** don't worry

rat [ra] nm rat

rate [rat] nf spleen

raté, e [rate] adj (tentative) unsuccessful, failed ♦ nm/f (fam: personne) failure

râteau, x [rɑto] nm rake

rater [rate] vi (affaire, projet etc) to go wrong, fail ♦ vt (cible, train, occasion) to miss; (plat) to spoil; (fam: examen) to fail

ration [rasjɔ̃] nf ration

ratisser [ratise] vt (allée) to rake; (feuilles) to rake up; (suj: armée, police) to comb

RATP sigle f (= Régie autonome des transports parisiens) Paris transport authority

rattacher [Rataʃe] vt (animal, cheveux) to tie up again; (fig: relier): ~ qch à to link sth with

rattrapage [RatRapaʒ] nm: cours de ~ remedial class

rattraper [RatRape] vt (fugitif) to recapture; (empêcher de tomber) to catch (hold of); (atteindre, rejoindre) to catch up with; (réparer: erreur) to make up for; se ~ vi to make up for it; se ~ (à) (se raccrocher) to stop o.s. falling (by catching hold of)

rature [RatyR] nf deletion, erasure

rauque [Rok] adj (voix) hoarse

ravages [Ravaʒ] nmpl: faire des ~ to wreak havoc

ravaler [Ravale] vt (mur, façade) to restore; (déprécier) to lower

ravi, e [Ravi] adj: être ~ de/que to be delighted with/that

ravigoter [Ravigɔte] (fam) vt to buck up

ravin [Ravɛ̃] nm gully, ravine

ravir [RaviR] vt (enchanter) to delight; à ~ adv beautifully

raviser [Ravize]: se ~ vi to change one's mind

ravissant, e [Ravisɑ̃, ɑ̃t] adj delightful

ravisseur, -euse [RavisœR, øz] nm/f abductor, kidnapper

ravitaillement [Ravitajmɑ̃] nm (réserves) supplies pl

ravitailler [Ravitaje] vt (en vivres, munitions) to provide with fresh supplies; (avion) to refuel; se ~ vi to get fresh supplies; (avion) to refuel

raviver [Ravive] vt (feu, douleur) to revive; (couleurs) to brighten up

rayé, e [Reje] adj (à rayures) striped

rayer [Reje] vt (érafler) to scratch; (barrer) to cross out; (d'une liste) to cross off

rayon [Rejɔ̃] nm (de soleil etc) ray; (GÉOM) radius; (de roue) spoke; (étagère)

shelf; (de grand magasin) department; **dans un ~ de** within a radius of; **~ de soleil** sunbeam; **~s X** X-rays

rayonnement [Rejɔnmɑ̃] nm (fig: d'une culture) influence

rayonner [Rejɔne] vi (fig) to shine forth; (personne: de joie, de beauté) to be radiant; (touriste) to go touring (from one base)

rayure [RejyR] nf (motif) stripe; (éraflure) scratch; à ~s striped

raz-de-marée [Radmare] nm inv tidal wave

ré [Re] nm (MUS) D; (en chantant la gamme) re

réacteur [ReaktœR] nm (d'avion) jet engine; (nucléaire) reactor

réaction [Reaksjɔ̃] nf reaction

réadapter [Readapte]: se ~ (à) vi to re-adjust (to)

réagir [ReaʒiR] vi to react

réalisateur, -trice [RealizatœR, tRis] nm/f (TV, CINÉMA) director

réalisation [Realizasjɔ̃] nf realization; (cinéma) production; **en cours de ~** under way

réaliser [Realize] vt (projet, opération) to carry out, realize; (rêve, souhait) to realize, fulfil; (exploit) to achieve; (film) to produce; (se rendre compte de) to realize; **se ~** to be realized

réaliste [Realist] adj realistic

réalité [Realite] nf reality; **en ~** in (actual) fact; **dans la ~** in reality

réanimation [Reanimasjɔ̃] nf resuscitation; **service de ~** intensive care unit

rébarbatif, -ive [RebaRbatif, iv] adj forbidding

rebattu, e [R(ə)baty] adj hackneyed

rebelle [Rəbɛl] nm/f rebel ♦ adj (troupes) rebel; (enfant) rebellious; (mèche etc) unruly

rebeller [R(ə)bele]: se ~ vi to rebel

rebondi, e [R(ə)bɔ̃di] adj (joues) chubby

rebondir [R(ə)bɔ̃diR] vi (ballon: au sol) to bounce; (: contre un mur) to rebound; *(fig)* to get moving again; **re-bondissement** *nm* new development

rebord [R(ə)bɔR] *nm* edge; **le ~ de la fenêtre** the windowsill

rebours [R(ə)buR]: **à ~** *adv* the wrong way

rebrousser [R(ə)bRuse] *vt*: **~ chemin** to turn back

rebut [Rəby] *nm*: **mettre au ~** to scrap; **rebutant, e** *adj* off-putting; **rebuter** *vt* to put off

récalcitrant, e [Rekalsitʀɑ̃, ɑ̃t] *adj* refractory

recaler [R(ə)kale] *vt (SCOL)* to fail; **se faire ~** to fail

récapituler [Rekapityle] *vt* to recapitulate, sum up

receler [R(ə)səle] *vt (produit d'un vol)* to receive; *(fig)* to conceal; **receleur, -euse** *nm/f* receiver

récemment [Resamã] *adv* recently

recensement [R(ə)sãsmã] *nm (population) census*

recenser [R(ə)sãse] *vt (population)* to take a census of; *(inventorier)* to list

récent, e [Resã, ãt] *adj* recent

récépissé [Resepise] *nm* receipt

récepteur [Reseptœʀ, tʀis] *nm* receiver

réception [Resepsjɔ̃] *nf* receiving *no pl*; *(accueil)* reception, welcome; *(bureau)* reception desk; *(réunion mondaine)* reception, party; **réceptionniste** *nm/f* receptionist

recette [R(ə)set] *nf* recipe; *(COMM)* takings *pl*; **~s** *nfpl (COMM: rentrées)* receipts

receveur, -euse [R(ə)səvœʀ, øz] *nm/f (des contributions)* tax collector; *(des postes)* postmaster(-mistress)

recevoir [R(ə)səvwaʀ] *vt* to receive; *(client, patient)* to see; **être reçu** *(à un examen)* to pass

rechange [R(ə)ʃɑ̃ʒ]: **de ~** *adj (pièces)* spare; *(fig: solution)* alternative; **des vêtements de ~** a change of clothes

réchapper [Reʃape]: **~ de** ou **à** *vt (accident, maladie)* to come through

recharge [R(ə)ʃaʀʒ] *nf* refill; **rechar-**

geable *adj (stylo etc)* refillable; **recharger** *vt (stylo)* to refill; *(batterie)* to recharge

réchaud [Reʃo] *nm (portable)* stove

réchauffement [Reʃofmã] *nm*: **le ~ climatique** global warming

réchauffer [Reʃofe] *vt (plat)* to reheat; *(mains, personne)* to warm; **se ~** *vi (température)* to get warmer; *(personne)* to warm o.s. (up)

rêche [Rɛʃ] *adj* rough

recherche [R(ə)ʃɛʀʃ] *nf (action)* search; *(raffinement)* studied elegance; *(scientifique etc)*: **la ~** research; **~s** *nfpl (de la police)* investigations; *(scientifiques)* research *sg*; **la ~ de** the search for; **être à la ~ de qch** to be looking for sth

recherché, e [R(ə)ʃɛʀʃe] *adj (rare, demandé)* much sought-after; *(raffiné: style)* mannered; *(: tenue)* elegant

rechercher [R(ə)ʃɛʀʃe] *vt (objet égaré, personne)* to look for; *(causes, nouveau procédé)* to try to find; *(bonheur, compliments)* to seek

rechigner [R(ə)ʃiɲe] *vi*: **~ à faire qch** to balk ou jib at doing sth

rechute [R(ə)ʃyt] *nf (MÉD)* relapse

récidiver [Residive] *vi* to commit a subsequent offence; *(fig)* to do it again

récif [Resif] *nm* reef

récipient [Resipjã] *nm* container

récit [Resi] *nm* story; **récital** *nm* recital; **réciter** *vt* to recite

réclamation [Reklamasjɔ̃] *nf* complaint; **~s** *nfpl (bureau)* complaints department *sg*

réclame [Reklam] *nf* ad, advert(isement); **en ~** on special offer; **réclamer** *vt* to ask for; *(revendiquer)* to claim, demand ♦ *vi* to complain

réclusion [Reklyzjɔ̃] *nf* imprisonment

recoin [Rəkwɛ̃] *nm* nook, corner

reçois *etc* [Rəswa] *vb voir* **recevoir**

récolte [Rekɔlt] *nf* harvesting, gathering; *(produits)* harvest, crop; **récolter** *vt* to harvest, gather (in); *(fig)* to collect

recommandé [R(ə)kɔmãde] *nm*

(POSTES): **en ~** by registered mail

recommander [R(ə)kɔmɑ̃de] *vt* to recommend; *(POSTES)* to register

recommencer [R(ə)kɔmɑ̃se] *vt (reprendre: lutte, séance)* to resume, start again; *(refaire: travail, explications)* to start afresh, start (over) ♦ *vi* to start again; *(récidiver)* to do it again

récompense [Rekɔ̃pɑ̃s] *nf* reward; *(prix)* award; **récompenser** *vt*: **récompenser** (**de** *ou* **pour**) to reward sb (for)

réconcilier [Rekɔ̃silje] *vt* to reconcile; **se ~ (avec)** to be reconciled (with)

reconduire [R(ə)kɔ̃dɥiR] *vt (raccompagner)* to take *ou* see back; *(renouveler)* to renew

réconfort [Rekɔ̃fɔR] *nm* comfort; **réconforter** *vt (consoler)* to comfort

reconnaissance [R(ə)kɔnɛsɑ̃s] *nf (gratitude)* gratitude, gratefulness; *(action de reconnaître)* recognition; *(MIL)* reconnaissance, recce; **reconnaissant, e** *adj* grateful

reconnaître [R(ə)kɔnɛtR] *vt* to recognize; *(MIL: lieu)* to reconnoitre; *(enfant, torts)* to acknowledge; **~ que** to admit *ou* acknowledge that; **reconnu, e** *adj (indiscuté, connu)* recognized

reconstituant, e [R(ə)kɔ̃stitɥɑ̃, ɑ̃t] *adj (aliment, régime)* strength-building

reconstituer [R(ə)kɔ̃stitɥe] *vt (événement, accident)* to reconstruct; *(fresque, vase brisé)* to piece together, reconstitute

reconstruction [R(ə)kɔ̃stryksjɔ̃] *nf* rebuilding

reconstruire [R(ə)kɔ̃stRɥiR] *vt* to rebuild

reconvertir [R(ə)kɔ̃vɛRtiR]: **se ~ dans** *vt (un métier, une branche)* to go into

record [R(ə)kɔR] *nm, adj inv*: **par ~** by cross-checking

recoupement [R(ə)kupmɑ̃] *nm*: **par ~** by cross-checking

recouper [R(ə)kupe]: **se ~** *vi (témoignages)* to tie *ou* match up

recourber [R(ə)kuRbe]: **se ~** *vi* to

curve (up), bend (up)

recourir [R(ə)kuRiR]: **~ à** *vt (ami, agence)* to turn *ou* appeal to; *(force, ruse, emprunt)* to resort to

recours [R(ə)kuR] *nm*: **avoir ~ à** = **recourir à**; **en dernier ~** as a last resort

recouvrer [R(ə)kuvRe] *vt (vue, santé etc)* to recover, regain

recouvrir [R(ə)kuvRiR] *vt (couvrir à nouveau)* to re-cover; *(couvrir entièrement, aussi fig)* to cover

récréation [RekReasjɔ̃] *nf (SCOL)* break

récrier [RekRije]: **se ~** *vi* to exclaim

récriminations [RekRiminasjɔ̃] *nfpl* remonstrations, complaints

recroqueviller [R(ə)kRɔk(ə)vije]: **se ~** *vi (personne)* to huddle up

recrudescence [R(ə)kRydesɑ̃s] *nf* fresh outbreak

recrue [RəkRy] *nf* recruit

recruter [R(ə)kRyte] *vt* to recruit

rectangle [Rektɑ̃gl] *nm* rectangle; **rectangulaire** *adj* rectangular

rectificatif [Rektifikatif, iv] *nm* correction

rectifier [Rektifje] *vt (calcul, adresse, paroles)* to correct; *(erreur)* to rectify

rectiligne [Rektiliɲ] *adj* straight

recto [Rekto] *nm* front (of a page); **~ verso** on both sides (of the page)

reçu, e [R(ə)sy] *pp de* **recevoir** ♦ *adj (candidat)* successful; *(admis, consacré)* accepted ♦ *nm (COMM)* receipt

recueil [Rakœj] *nm* collection; **recueillir** *vt* to collect; *(voix, suffrages)* to win; *(accueillir: réfugiés, chat)* to take in; **se recueillir** *vi* to gather one's thoughts, meditate

recul [R(ə)kyl] *nm (éloignement)* distance; *(déclin)* decline; **être en ~** to be on the decline; **avec du ~** with hindsight; **avoir un mouvement de ~** to recoil; **prendre du ~** to stand back; **reculé, e** *adj* remote; **reculer** *vi* to move back, back away; *(AUTO)* to reverse, back (up); *(fig)* to (be on the) decline ♦ *vt* to move back; *(véhicule)* to reverse, back (up); (date, décision) to postpone; **reculons**: **à reculons** adv backwards

récupérer [ʀekypeʀe] vt to recover, get back; (heures de travail) to make up; (déchets) to salvage ♦ vi to recover

récurer [ʀekyʀe] vt to scour

récuser [ʀekyze] vt to challenge; **se ~** vi to decline to give an opinion

reçut [ʀəsy] vb voir **recevoir**

recycler [ʀ(ə)sikle] vt (TECH) to recycle; **se ~** vi to retrain

rédacteur, -trice [ʀedaktœʀ, tʀis] nm/f (journaliste) writer; subeditor; (d'ouvrage de référence) editor, compiler; **~ en chef** chief editor

rédaction [ʀedaksjɔ̃] nf writing; (rédacteurs) editorial staff; (SCOL: devoir) essay, composition

redemander [ʀədmɑ̃de] vt (une nouvelle fois) to ask again for; (davantage) to ask for more of

redescendre [ʀ(ə)desɑ̃dʀ] vi to go back down ♦ vt (pente) etc) to go down

redevance [ʀ(ə)dəvɑ̃s] nf (TÉL) rental charge; (TV) licence fee

rédiger [ʀediʒe] vt to write; (contrat) to draw up

redire [ʀ(ə)diʀ] vt to repeat; **trouver à ~ à** to find fault with

redonner [ʀ(ə)dɔne] vt (rendre) to give back; (resservir: nourriture) to give more

redoubler [ʀ(ə)duble] vi (tempête, violence) to intensify; (SCOL) to repeat a year; **~ de patience/prudence** to be doubly patient/careful

redoutable [ʀ(ə)dutabl] adj formidable, fearsome

redouter [ʀ(ə)dute] vt to dread

redressement [ʀ(ə)dʀɛsmɑ̃] nm (économique) recovery

redresser [ʀ(ə)dʀɛse] vt (relever) to set upright; (pièce tordue) to straighten out; (situation, économie) to put right; **se ~** vi (personne) to sit (ou stand) up (straight); (économie) to recover

réduction [ʀedyksjɔ̃] nf reduction

réduire [ʀedɥiʀ] vt to reduce; (prix, dépenses) to cut, reduce; **se ~ à** (revenir à) to boil down to; **réduit** nm (pièce) tiny room

rééducation [ʀeedykasjɔ̃] nf (d'un membre) re-education; (de délinquants, d'un blessé) rehabilitation

réel, le [ʀeɛl] adj real; **réellement** adv really

réexpédier [ʀeɛkspedje] vt (à l'envoyeur) to return, send back; (au destinataire) to send on, forward

refaire [ʀ(ə)fɛʀ] vt to do again; (faire de nouveau: sport) to take up again; (réparer, restaurer) to do up

réfection [ʀefɛksjɔ̃] nf repair

réfectoire [ʀefɛktwaʀ] nm refectory

référence [ʀefeʀɑ̃s] nf reference; **~s** nfpl (recommandations) reference sg

référer [ʀefeʀe]: **se ~ à** vt to refer to

refermer [ʀ(ə)fɛʀme] vt to close ou shut again; **se ~** vi (porte) to close ou shut (again)

refiler [ʀ(ə)file] vt (fam) to palm off

réfléchi, e [ʀefleʃi] adj (caractère) thoughtful; (action) well-thought-out; (LING) reflexive; **c'est tout ~** my mind's made up

réfléchir [ʀefleʃiʀ] vt to reflect ♦ vi to think; **~ à** to think about

reflet [ʀəflɛ] nm reflection; (sur l'eau etc) sheen no pl, glint; **refléter** vt to reflect; **se refléter** vi to be reflected

réflexe [ʀeflɛks] nm, adj reflex

réflexion [ʀeflɛksjɔ̃] nf (de la lumière etc) reflection; (fait de penser) thought; (remarque) remark; **~ faite, à la ~** on reflection

refluer [ʀ(ə)flye] vi to flow back; (foule) to surge back

reflux [ʀafly] nm (de la mer) ebb

réforme [ʀefɔʀm] nf reform; (REL): **la R~** the Reformation; **réformer** vt to reform; (MIL) to declare unfit for service

refouler [ʀ(ə)fule] vt (envahisseurs) to drive back; (larmes) to force back; (désir, colère) to repress

refrain [R(ə)frɛ̃] *nm* refrain, chorus

refréner [Rəfʀene] *vt*, **réfréner** [ʀefʀene] *vt* to curb, check

réfrigérateur [ʀefʀiʒeʀatœʀ] *nm* refrigerator, fridge

refroidir [R(ə)fʀwadiʀ] *vt* to cool; (*fig: personne*) to put off ♦ *vi* to cool (down); **se ~** *vi* (*temps*) to get cooler *ou* colder; (*fig: ardeur*) to cool (off); **refroidissement** [R(ə)fʀwadismɑ̃] *nm* (*grippe etc*) chill

refuge [R(ə)fyʒ] *nm* refuge; **réfugié, e** *adj, nm/f* refugee; **réfugier**: **se réfugier** *vi* to take refuge

refus [R(ə)fy] *nm* refusal; **ce n'est pas de ~** I won't say no, it's welcome; **refuser** *vt* to refuse; (*SCOL: candidat*) to fail; **refuser qch à qn** to refuse sb sth; **se refuser à faire** to refuse to do

réfuter [ʀefyte] *vt* to refute

regagner [R(ə)gaɲe] *vt* (*faveur*) to win back; (*lieu*) to get back to

regain [R(ə)gɛ̃] *nm* (*renouveau*): **un ~ de** renewed +*nom*

régal [ʀegal] *nm* treat; **régaler**: **se régaler** *vi* to have a delicious meal; (*fig*) to enjoy o.s.

regard [R(ə)gaʀ] *nm* (*coup d'œil*) look, glance; (*expression*) look (in one's eye); **au ~ de** (*loi, morale*) from the point of view of; **en ~ de** in comparison with

regardant, e [R(ə)gaʀdɑ̃, ɑ̃t] *adj* (*économe*) tight-fisted; **peu ~ (sur)** quite free (about)

regarder [R(ə)gaʀde] *vt* to look at; (*film, télévision, match*) to watch; (*concerner*) to concern ♦ *vi* to look; **ne pas ~ à la dépense** to spare no expense; **~ qn/qch comme** to regard sb/sth as

régie [ʀeʒi] *nf* (*COMM, INDUSTRIE*) state-owned company; (*THÉÂTRE, CINÉMA*) production; (*RADIO, TV*) control room

regimber [R(ə)ʒɛ̃be] *vi* to balk, jib

régime [ʀeʒim] *nm* (*POL*) regime; (*MÉD*) diet; (*ADMIN: carcéral, fiscal etc*) system; (*de bananes, dattes*) bunch; **se mettre un ~/suivre un ~** to go on/be on a diet

régiment [ʀeʒimɑ̃] *nm* regiment

région [ʀeʒjɔ̃] *nf* region; **régional, e, -aux** *adj* regional

régir [ʀeʒiʀ] *vt* to govern

régisseur [ʀeʒisœʀ] *nm* (*d'un domaine*) steward; (*CINÉMA, TV*) assistant director; (*THÉÂTRE*) stage manager

registre [ʀəʒistʀ] *nm* register

réglage [ʀeglaʒ] *nm* adjustment

règle [ʀɛgl] *nf* (*instrument*) ruler; (*loi*) rule; **~s** *nfpl* (*menstruation*) period *sg*; **en ~** (*papiers d'identité*) in order; **en ~ générale** as a (general) rule

réglé, e [ʀegle] *adj* (*vie*) well-ordered; (*arrangé*) settled

règlement [ʀegləmɑ̃] *nm* (*paiement*) settlement; (*arrêté*) regulation; (*règles, statuts*) regulations *pl*, rules *pl*; **~ de compte(s)** settling of old scores; **réglementaire** *adj* conforming to the regulations; (*tenue*) regulation *cpd*; **réglementation** *nf* (*règles*) regulations; **réglementer** *vt* to regulate

régler [ʀegle] *vt* (*conflit, facture*) to settle; (*personne*) to settle up with; (*mécanisme, machine*) to regulate, adjust; (*thermostat etc*) to set, adjust

réglisse [ʀeglis] *nf* liquorice

règne [ʀɛɲ] *nm* (*d'un roi etc, fig*) reign; **régner** *vi* (*roi*) to rule, reign; (*fig*) to reign

regorger [R(ə)gɔʀʒe] *vi*: **~ de** to overflow with, be bursting with

regret [R(ə)gʀɛ] *nm* regret; **à ~** with regret; **sans ~** with no regrets; **regrettable** *adj* regrettable; **regretter** *vt* to regret; (*personne*) to miss; **je regrette mais ...** I'm sorry but ...

regrouper [R(ə)gʀupe] *vt* (*grouper*) to group together; (*contenir*) to include, comprise; **se ~** *vi* to gather (together)

régulier, -ière [ʀegylje, jɛʀ] *adj* (*gén*) regular; (*vitesse, qualité*) steady; (*égal: couche, ligne*) even, (*TRANSPORTS: ligne, service*) scheduled, regular; (*légal*) lawful, in order; (*honnête*) straight, on the level; **régulièrement** *adv* regularly; (*uniformément*) evenly

rehausser [ʀaose] *vt* (*relever*) to heighten, raise; (*fig: souligner*) to set off, enhance

rein [ʀɛ̃] *nm* kidney; **~s** *nmpl* (*dos*) back *sg*

reine [ʀɛn] *nf* queen

reine-claude [ʀɛnklod] *nf* greengage

réinsertion [ʀeɛ̃sɛʀsjɔ̃] *nf* (*de délinquant*) reintegration, rehabilitation

réintégrer [ʀeɛ̃tegʀe] *vt* (*lieu*) to return to; (*fonctionnaire*) to reinstate

rejaillir [ʀ(ə)ʒajiʀ] *vi* to splash up; **~ sur** (*fig: scandale*) to rebound on; (*: gloire*) to be reflected on

rejet [ʀəʒɛ] *nm* rejection; **rejeter** *vt* (*relancer*) to throw back; (*écarter*) to reject; (*déverser*) to throw out, discharge; (*vomir*) to bring ou throw up; **rejeter la responsabilité de qch sur qn** to lay the responsibility for sth at sb's door

rejoindre [ʀ(ə)ʒwɛ̃dʀ] *vt* (*famille, régiment*) to rejoin, return to; (*lieu*) to get (back) to; (*suj: route etc*) to meet, join; (*rattraper*) to catch up (with); **se ~** *vi* to meet; **je te rejoins à la gare** I'll see ou meet you at the station

réjouir [ʀeʒwiʀ] *vt* to delight; **se ~ (de)** *vi* to be delighted (about); **réjouissances** [ʀeʒwisɑ̃s] *nfpl* (*fête*) festivities

relâche [ʀəlɑʃ] *nm ou nf*: **sans ~** without respite ou a break; **relâché, e** *adj* loose, lax; **relâcher** *vt* (*libérer*) to release; (*desserrer*) to loosen; **se relâcher** *vi* (*discipline*) to become slack ou lax; (*élève etc*) to slacken off

relais [ʀ(ə)lɛ] *nm* (*SPORT*: **course de**) relay (race); **prendre le ~ (de)** to take over (from); **~ routier** ≃ transport café (*BRIT*), ≃ truck stop (*US*)

relancer [ʀ(ə)lɑ̃se] *vt* (*balle*) to throw back; (*moteur*) to restart; (*fig*) to boost, revive; (*harceler*): **~ qn** to pester sb

relatif, -ive [ʀ(ə)latif, iv] *adj* relative

relation [ʀ(ə)lasjɔ̃] *nf* (*rapport*) relation(ship); (*connaissance*) acquaintance; **~s** *nfpl* (*rapports*) relations; (*connaissances*) connections; **être/entrer en**

~(s) avec to be/get in contact with

relaxe [ʀəlaks] (*fam*) *adj* (*tenue*) informal; (*personne*) relaxed; **relaxer: se relaxer** *vi* to relax

relayer [ʀ(ə)leje] *vt* (*collaborateur, coureur etc*) to relieve; **se ~** *vi* (*dans une activité*) to take it in turns

reléguer [ʀ(ə)lege] *vt* to relegate

relent(s) [ʀəlɑ̃] *nm(pl)* (*foul*) smell

relevé, e [ʀəl(ə)ve] *adj* (*manches*) rolled-up; (*sauce*) highly-seasoned ♦ *nm* (*de compteur*) reading; (*bancaire*) statement

relève [ʀəlɛv] *nf* (*personne*) relief; **prendre la ~** to take over

relever [ʀəl(ə)ve] *vt* (*meuble*) to stand up again; (*personne tombée*) to help up; (*vitre, niveau de vie*) to raise; (*col*) to turn up; (*style*) to elevate; (*plat, sauce*) to season; (*sentinelle, équipe*) to relieve; (*fautes*) to pick out; (*défi*) to accept, take up; (*noter: adresse etc*) to take down, note; (*: plan*) to sketch; (*compteur*) to read; (*ramasser: cahiers*) to collect, take in; **se ~** (*se remettre debout*) to get up; **~ de** (*maladie*) to be recovering from; (*être du ressort de*) to be a matter for; (*fig*) to pertain to; **~ qn de** (*fonctions*) to relieve sb of

relief [ʀəljɛf] *nm* relief; **mettre en ~** (*fig*) to bring out, highlight

relier [ʀəlje] *vt* to link up; (*livre*) to bind; **~ qch à** to link sth to

religieuse [ʀ(ə)liʒjøz] *nf* nun; (*gâteau*) cream bun

religieux, -euse [ʀ(ə)liʒjø, jøz] *adj* religious ♦ *nm* monk

religion [ʀ(ə)liʒjɔ̃] *nf* religion

relire [ʀ(ə)liʀ] *vt* (*à nouveau*) to reread, read again; (*vérifier*) to read over

reliure [ʀəljyʀ] *nf* binding

reluire [ʀ(ə)lɥiʀ] *vi* to gleam

remanier [ʀ(ə)manje] *vt* to reshape, recast; (*POL*) to reshuffle

remarquable [ʀ(ə)maʀkabl] *adj* remarkable

remarque [ʀ(ə)maʀk] *nf* remark;

(écrite) note

remarquer [R(ə)maRke] vt (voir) to notice; **se ~** vi to be noticeable; **faire ~ (à qn) que** to point out (to sb) that; **faire ~ qch (à qn)** to point sth out (to sb); **remarquez,** ... mind you ...; **se faire ~** to draw attention to o.s.

rembourrer [Rãbure] vt to stuff

remboursement [Rãbursəmã] nm (de dette, d'emprunt) repayment; (de frais) refund; **rembourser** vt to pay back, repay; (frais, billet etc) to refund; **se faire rembourser** to get a refund

remède [R(ə)med] nm (médicament) medicine; (traitement, fig) remedy, cure

remémorer [R(ə)memɔre]: **se ~** vt to recall, recollect

remerciements [RəmɛRsimã] nmpl thanks

remercier [R(ə)mɛRsje] vt to thank; (congédier) to dismiss; **~ qn de/d'avoir fait** to thank sb for/for having done

remettre [R(ə)mɛtR] vt (replacer) to put back; (vêtement) to put back on; (ajouter) to add; (ajourner): **~ qch (à)** to postpone sth (until); **se ~** vi: **se ~ (de)** to recover (from); **~ qch à qn** (donner: lettre, clé etc) to hand over sth to sb; (: prix, décoration) to present sb with sth; **se ~ à faire qch** to start doing sth again

remise [R(ə)miz] nf (rabais) discount; (local) shed; **~ de peine** reduction of sentence; **~ en jeu** (FOOTBALL) throw-in

remontant [R(ə)mõtã] nm tonic, pick-me-up

remonte-pente [R(ə)mõtpãt] nm ski-lift

remonter [R(ə)mõte] vi to go back up; (prix, température) to go up again ♦ vt (pente) to go up; (fleuve) to sail (ou swim etc) up; (manches, pantalon) to roll up; (col) to turn up; (niveau, limite) to raise; (fig: personne) to buck up; (qch de démonté) to put back together, reassemble; (montre) to wind up; **~ le moral à qn** to raise sb's spirits; **~ à** (dater de) to date ou go back to

remontrance [R(ə)mõtRãs] nf reproof, reprimand

remontrer [R(ə)mõtRe] vt (fig): **en ~ à** to prove one's superiority over

remords [R(ə)mɔR] nm remorse no pl; **avoir des ~** to feel remorse

remorque [R(ə)mɔRk] nf trailer; **remorquer** vt to tow; **remorqueur** nm tug(boat)

remous [Rəmu] nm (d'un navire) (back)wash no pl; (de rivière) swirl, eddy ♦ nmpl (fig) stir sg

remparts [Rãpar] nmpl walls, ramparts

remplaçant, e [Rãplasã, ãt] nm/f replacement, stand-in; (SCOL) supply teacher

remplacement [Rãplasmã] nm replacement; **faire des ~s** (professeur) to do supply teaching; (secrétaire) to temp

remplacer [Rãplase] vt to replace; **qch/qn par** to replace sth/sb with

rempli, e [Rãpli] adj (emploi du temps) full, busy; **~ de** full of, filled with

remplir [Rãplir] vt to fill (up); (questionnaire) to fill out ou up; (obligations, fonction, condition) to fulfil; **se ~** vi to fill up

remporter [Rãpɔrte] vt (marchandise) to take away; (fig) to win, achieve

remuant, e [Rəmɥã, ãt] adj restless

remue-ménage [R(ə)mymenaʒ] nm inv commotion

remuer [Rəmɥe] vt to move; (café, sauce) to stir ♦ vi to move; **se ~** vi to move; (fam: s'activer) to get a move on

rémunérer [Remynere] vt to remunerate

renard [R(ə)naR] nm fox

renchérir [RãʃeRiR] vi (fig): **~ (sur)** (en paroles) to add something (to)

rencontre [Rãkõtr] nf meeting; (imprévue) encounter; **aller à la ~ de qn** to go and meet sb; **rencontrer** vt to meet; (mot, expression) to come across; (difficultés) to meet with; **se rencontrer** vi to meet

rendement [Rɑ̃dmɑ̃] nm (d'un travailleur, d'une machine) output; (d'un champ) yield

rendez-vous [Rɑ̃devu] nm appointment; (d'amoureux) date; (lieu) meeting place; **donner ~~ à qn** to arrange to meet sb; **avoir/prendre ~~ (avec)** to have/make an appointment (with)

rendre [Rɑ̃dR] vt (restituer) to give back, return; (invitation) to return, repay; (vomir) to bring up; (exprimer, traduire) to render; (faire devenir): ~ **qn célèbre/qch possible** to make sb famous/sth possible; **se ~** vi (capituler) to surrender, give o.s. up; (aller): **se ~ quelque part** to go somewhere; ~ **la monnaie à qn** to give sb his change; **se ~ compte de qch** to realize sth

rênes [Rɛn] nfpl reins

renfermé, e [Rɑ̃fɛRme] adj (fig) withdrawn ♦ nm: **sentir le ~** to smell stuffy

renfermer [Rɑ̃fɛRme] vt to contain

renflouer [Rɑ̃flue] vt to refloat; (fig) to set back on its (ou his/her etc) feet

renfoncement [Rɑ̃fɔ̃smɑ̃] nm recess

renforcer [Rɑ̃fɔRse] vt to reinforce; **renfort: renforts** nmpl reinforcements; **à grand renfort de** with a great deal of

renfrogné, e [Rɑ̃fRɔɲe] adj sullen

rengaine [Rɑ̃gɛn] (péj) nf old tune

renier [Rənje] vt (personne) to disown, repudiate; (foi) to renounce

renifler [R(ə)nifle] vi, vt to sniff

renne [Rɛn] nm reindeer inv

renom [Rənɔ̃] nm reputation; (célébrité) renown; **renommé, e** adj celebrated, renowned; **renommée** nf fame

renoncer [Rənɔ̃se]: ~ **à** vt to give up; ~ **à faire** to give up the idea of doing

renouer [Rənwe] vt: ~ **avec** (habitude) to take up again

renouvelable [R(ə)nuv(ə)labl] adj (énergie etc) renewable

renouveler [R(ə)nuv(ə)le] vt to renew; (exploit, méfait) to repeat; **se ~** vi (incident) to recur, happen again; **renouvellement** nm (remplacement) renewal

rénover [Renɔve] vt (immeuble) to renovate, do up; (quartier) to redevelop

renseignement [Rɑ̃sɛɲmɑ̃] nm information ou pl, piece of information; **(bureau des) ~s** information office

renseigner [Rɑ̃sɛɲe]: ~ **qn (sur)** to give information to sb (about); **se ~** vi to ask for information, make inquiries

rentabilité [Rɑ̃tabilite] nf profitability

rentable [Rɑ̃tabl] adj profitable

rente [Rɑ̃t] nf private income; (pension) pension

rentrée [Rɑ̃tre] nf: **(d'argent)** cash no pl coming in; **la ~ (des classes)** the start of the new school year

---

rentrée (des classes)

La rentrée (des classes) in September marks an important point in the French year. Children and teachers return to school, and political and social life begin again after the long summer break.

---

rentrer [Rɑ̃tre] vi (revenir chez soi) to go (ou come) back home; (entrer de nouveau) to go (ou come) back in; (entrer) to go (ou come) in; (air, clou: pénétrer) to go in; (revenu) to come in ♦ vt to bring in; (véhicule) to put away; (chemise dans pantalon etc) to tuck in; (griffes) to draw in; ~ **le ventre** to pull in one's stomach; ~ **dans** (heurter) to crash into; ~ **dans l'ordre** to be back to normal; ~ **dans ses frais** to recover one's expenses

renverse [Rɑ̃vɛRs]: **à la ~** adv backwards

renverser [Rɑ̃vɛRse] vt (faire tomber) chaise, verre) to knock over, overturn; (liquide, contenu) to spill, upset; (piéton) to knock down; (retourner) to turn upside down; (: ordre des mots etc) to reverse; (fig: gouvernement etc) to overthrow; (fam: stupéfier) to bowl over; **se ~** vi (verre, vase) to fall over; (contenu) to spill

(COMM) comptabilité f, comptes; **of no ~** sans importance; **on ~** en acompte; **on no ~** en aucun cas; **on ~ of** à cause de; **to take into ~, take ~ of** tenir compte de; **~ for** vt fus expliquer, rendre compte de; **~able** adj: **~able (to)** responsable (devant); **~ancy** n comptabilité f; **~ant** n comptable m/f; **~ number** n (at bank etc) numéro m de compte

accrued interest [ə'kru:d-] n intérêt m cumulé

accumulate [ə'kju:mjuleɪt] vt accumuler, amasser ♦ vi s'accumuler, s'amasser

accuracy ['ækjurəsɪ] n exactitude f, précision f

accurate ['ækjurɪt] adj exact(e), précis(e); **~ly** adv avec précision

accusation [ækju'zeɪʃən] n accusation f

accuse [ə'kju:z] vt: **to ~ sb (of sth)** accuser qn (de qch); **the ~d** l'accusé(e)

accustom [ə'kʌstəm] vt accoutumer, habituer; **~ed** adj (usual) habituel(le); (in the habit): **~ed to** habitué(e) or accoutumé(e) à

ace [eɪs] n as m

ache [eɪk] n mal m, douleur f ♦ vi (yearn): **to ~ to do sth** mourir d'envie de faire qch; **my head ~s** j'ai mal à la tête

achieve [ə'tʃi:v] vt (aim) atteindre; (victory, success) remporter, obtenir; **~ment** n exploit m, réussite f

acid ['æsɪd] adj acide ♦ n acide m; **~ rain** n pluies fpl acides

acknowledge [ək'nɒlɪdʒ] vt (letter: also: **~ receipt of**) accuser réception de; (fact) reconnaître; **~ment** n (of letter) accusé m de réception

acne ['æknɪ] n acné m

acorn ['eɪkɔ:n] n gland m

acoustic [ə'ku:stɪk] adj acoustique; **~s** n, npl acoustique f

acquaint [ə'kweɪnt] vt: **to ~ sb with sth** mettre qn au courant de qch; **to be ~ed with** connaître; **~ance** n

connaissance f

acquire [ə'kwaɪə^r] vt acquérir

acquit [ə'kwɪt] vt acquitter; **to ~ o.s. well** bien se comporter, s'en tirer très honorablement

acre ['eɪkə^r] n acre f (= 4047 m²)

acrid ['ækrɪd] adj âcre

acrobat ['ækrəbæt] n acrobate m/f

across [ə'krɒs] prep (on the other side) de l'autre côté de; (crosswise) en travers de ♦ adv de l'autre côté; en travers; **to run/swim ~** traverser en courant/à la nage; **~ from** en face de

acrylic [ə'krɪlɪk] adj acrylique

act [ækt] n acte m, action f; (of play) acte; (in music-hall etc) numéro m; (LAW) loi f ♦ vi agir; (THEATRE) jouer; (pretend) jouer la comédie ♦ vt (part) jouer, tenir; **in the ~ of** en train de; **to ~ as** servir de; **~ing** adj suppléant(e), par intérim ♦ n (activity): **to do some ~ing** faire du théâtre (or du cinéma)

action ['ækʃən] n action f; (MIL) combat(s) m(pl); **out of ~** hors de combat; (machine) hors d'usage; **to take ~** agir, prendre des mesures; **~ replay** n (TV) ralenti m

activate ['æktɪveɪt] vt (mechanism) actionner, faire fonctionner

active ['æktɪv] adj actif(-ive); (volcano) en activité; **~ly** adv activement; **activity** [æk'tɪvɪtɪ] n activité f; **activity holiday** n vacances actives

actor ['æktə^r] n acteur m

actress ['æktrɪs] n actrice f

actual ['æktjuəl] adj réel(le), véritable; **~ly** adv (really) réellement, véritablement; (in fact) en fait

acute [ə'kju:t] adj aigu(ë); (mind, observer) pénétrant(e), perspicace

ad [æd] n abbr = **advertisement**

A.D. adv abbr (= anno Domini) ap. J.-C.

adamant ['ædəmənt] adj inflexible

adapt [ə'dæpt] vt adapter ♦ vi: **to ~ (to)** s'adapter (à); **~able** adj (device) adaptable; (person) qui s'adapte facilement; **~er**, **~or** n (ELEC) adaptateur m

add [æd] vt ajouter; (figures: also: **to ~ up**) additionner ♦ vi: **to ~** (increase) ajouter, accroître

adder [ˈædər] n vipère f

addict [ˈædɪkt] n intoxiqué(e); (fig) fanatique m/f; **~ed** [əˈdɪktɪd] adj: **to be ~ed to** (drugs, drink etc) être adonné(e) à; (fig: football etc) être un(e) fanatique de; **~ion** n (MED) dépendance f; **~ive** adj qui crée une dépendance

addition [əˈdɪʃən] n addition f; (thing added) ajout m; **in ~** de plus; de surcroît; **in ~ to** en plus de; **~al** adj supplémentaire

additive [ˈædɪtɪv] n additif m

address [əˈdres] n adresse f; (talk) discours m, allocution f ♦ vt adresser; (speak to) s'adresser à; **to ~ (o.s. to) a problem** s'attaquer à un problème

adept [ˈædept] adj: **~ at** expert(e) à or en

adequate [ˈædɪkwɪt] adj adéquat(e); suffisant(e)

adhere [ədˈhɪər] vi: **to ~ to** adhérer à; (fig: rule, decision) se tenir à

adhesive [ədˈhiːzɪv] n adhésif m; **~ tape** n (BRIT) ruban adhésif; (US: MED) sparadrap m

ad hoc [ˌædˈhɔk] adj improvisé(e), ad hoc

adjacent [əˈdʒeɪsənt] adj: **~ (to)** adjacent (à)

adjective [ˈædʒektɪv] n adjectif m

adjoining [əˈdʒɔɪnɪŋ] adj voisin(e), adjacent(e), attenant(e)

adjourn [əˈdʒɜːn] vt ajourner ♦ vi suspendre la séance; clore la séance

adjust [əˈdʒʌst] vt (machine) ajuster, régler; (prices, wages) rajuster ♦ vi: **to ~ (to)** s'adapter (à); **~able** adj réglable; **~ment** n (PSYCH) adaptation f; (to machine) ajustage m, réglage m; (of prices, wages) rajustement m

ad-lib [ædˈlɪb] vt, vi improviser; **ad lib** adv à volonté, à loisir

administer [ədˈmɪnɪstər] vt adminis-

trer; (justice) rendre; **administration** [ədˌmɪnɪsˈtreɪʃən] n administration f; **administrative** [ədˈmɪnɪstrətɪv] adj administratif(-ive)

admiral [ˈædmərəl] n amiral m; **A~ty** [ˈædmərəltɪ] (BRIT) n: **the A~ty** ministère m de la Marine

admire [ədˈmaɪər] vt admirer

admission [ədˈmɪʃən] n admission f; (to exhibition, night club etc) entrée f; (confession) aveu m; **~ charge** n droits mpl d'admission

admit [ədˈmɪt] vt laisser entrer; admettre; (agree) reconnaître, admettre; **~ to** vt fus reconnaître, avouer; **~tance** n admission f, (droit m d')entrée f; **~tedly** adv il faut en convenir

ado [əˈduː] n: **without (any) more ~** sans plus de cérémonies

adolescence [ˌædəʊˈlesns] n adolescence f; **adolescent** adj, n adolescent(e)

adopt [əˈdɔpt] vt adopter; **~ed** adj adoptif(-ive), adoptée(e); **~ion** n adoption f

adore [əˈdɔːr] vt adorer

adorn [əˈdɔːn] vt orner

Adriatic (Sea) [ˌeɪdrɪˈætɪk-] n Adriatique f

adrift [əˈdrɪft] adv à la dérive

adult [ˈædʌlt] n adulte m/f ♦ adj adulte; (literature, education) pour adultes

adultery [əˈdʌltərɪ] n adultère m

advance [ədˈvɑːns] n avance f ♦ adj: **~ booking** réservation f ♦ vt avancer ♦ vi avancer, s'avancer; **~ notice** avertissement m; **to make ~s (to sb)** faire des propositions (à qn); (amorously) faire des avances (à qn); **in ~** à l'avance, d'avance; **~d** adj avancé(e); (SCOL: studies) supérieur(e)

advantage [ədˈvɑːntɪdʒ] n (also TENNIS) avantage m; **to take ~ of** (person) exploiter

advent [ˈædvənt] n avènement m, venue f; **A~** Avent m

adventure [ədˈventʃər] n aventure f

adverb [ˈædvɜːb] n adverbe m

adverse ['ædvə:s] adj défavorable, contraire

advert ['ædvə:t] (BRIT) n abbr = **advertisement**

advertise ['ædvətaɪz] vi, vt faire de la publicité (pour); (in classified ads etc) mettre une annonce (pour vendre); **to ~ for** (staff, accommodation) faire paraître une annonce pour trouver; **~ment** [əd'və:tɪsmənt] (n COMM) réclame f, publicité f; (in classified ads) annonce f; **advertising** n publicité f

advice [əd'vaɪs] n conseils mpl; (notification) avis m; **piece of ~** conseil; **to take legal ~** consulter un avocat

advisable [əd'vaɪzəbl] adj conseillé(e), indiqué(e)

advise [əd'vaɪz] vt conseiller; **to ~ sb of sth** aviser or informer qn de qch; **to ~ against sth/doing sth** déconseiller qch/conseiller de ne pas faire qch; **~r**, **advisor** n conseiller(-ère); **advisory** adj consultatif(-ive)

advocate [n 'ædvəkɪt, vb 'ædvəkeɪt] n (upholder) défenseur m, avocat(e); (LAW) avocat(e) ♦ vt recommander, prôner

Aegean (Sea) [i:'dʒi:ən-] n (mer f) Égée f

aerial ['ɛərɪəl] n antenne f ♦ adj aérien(ne)

aerobics [ɛə'rəubɪks] n aérobic f

aeroplane ['ɛərəpleɪn] (BRIT) n avion m

aerosol ['ɛərəsɔl] n aérosol m

aesthetic [i:s'θɛtɪk] adj esthétique

afar [ə'fɑ:] adv: **from ~** de loin

affair [ə'fɛə] n affaire f; (also: **love ~**) liaison f; aventure f

affect [ə'fɛkt] vt affecter; (disease) atteindre; **~ed** adj affecté(e); **~ion** n affection f; **~ionate** adj affectueux(-euse)

affinity [ə'fɪnɪtɪ] n (bond, rapport): **to have an ~ with/for** avoir une affinité avec/pour

afflict [ə'flɪkt] vt affliger

affluence ['æfluəns] n abondance f, opulence f

affluent ['æfluənt] adj (person, family, surroundings) aisé(e), riche; **the ~ society** la société d'abondance

afford [ə'fɔ:d] vt se permettre; (provide) fournir, procurer

afloat [ə'fləut] adj, adv à flot; **to stay ~** surnager

afoot [ə'fut] adv: **there is something ~** il se prépare quelque chose

afraid [ə'freɪd] adj effrayé(e); **to be ~ of** or **to** avoir peur de; **I am ~ that ...** je suis désolé(e), mais ...; **I am ~ so/ not** hélas oui/non

Africa ['æfrɪkə] n Afrique f; **~n** adj africain(e) ♦ n Africain(e)

after ['ɑ:ftə] prep, adv après ♦ conj après que, après avoir or être +pp; **what/who are you ~?** que/qui cherchez-vous?; **he left/having done** après qu'il fut parti/après avoir fait; **ask ~ him** demandez de ses nouvelles; **to name sb ~ sb** donner à qn le nom de qn; **twenty ~ eight** (US) huit heures vingt; **~ all** après tout; **~ you!** après vous, Monsieur (or Madame etc); **~effects** npl (of disaster, radiation, drink etc) répercussions fpl; (of illness) séquelles fpl, suites fpl; **~math** n conséquences fpl, suites fpl; **~noon** n après-midi m or f; **~s** (inf) n (dessert) dessert m; **~sales service** (BRIT) n (for car, washing machine etc) service m après-vente; **~shave (lotion)** n after-shave m; **~sun** n après-soleil m inv; **~thought** n: **I had an ~thought** il m'est venu une idée après coup; **~wards** (US **afterward**) adv après

again [ə'gɛn] adv de nouveau; encore (une fois); **to do sth ~** refaire qch; **not ... ~** ne ... plus; **~ and ~** à plusieurs reprises

against [ə'gɛnst] prep contre; (compared to) par rapport à

age [eɪdʒ] n âge m ♦ vt, vi vieillir; **it's been ~s since** ça fait une éternité que ... ne; **he is 20 years of ~** il a 20 ans; **to come of ~** atteindre sa majorité; **~d** [adj eɪdʒd, npl 'eɪdʒɪd] adj: **~d 10**

âgé(e) de 10 ans ♦ *npl:* **the ~d** les personnes âgées; **~ group** *n* tranche *f* d'âge; **~ limit** *n* limite *f* d'âge

agency ['eidʒənsi] *n* agence *f;* (*government body*) organisme *m,* office *m*

agenda [ə'dʒendə] *n* ordre du jour

agent ['eidʒənt] *n* agent *m,* représentant *m;* (*firm*) concessionnaire *m*

aggravate ['ægrəveit] *vt* aggraver; (*annoy*) exaspérer

aggressive [ə'gresiv] *adj* agressif(-ive)

agitate ['ædʒiteit] *vt* agiter, émouvoir, troubler ♦ *vi:* **to ~ for/ against** faire campagne pour/contre

AGM *n abbr* (= *annual general meeting*) AG *f*

ago [ə'gəu] *adv:* **2 days ~** il y a deux jours; **not long ~** il n'y a pas longtemps; **how long ~?** il y a combien de temps de cela?

agony ['ægəni] *n* (*pain*) douleur *f* atroce; **to be in ~** souffrir le martyre

agree [ə'gri:] *vt* (*price*) convenir de ♦ *vi:* **to ~ with** (*person*) être d'accord avec; (*statements etc*) concorder avec; (*LING*) s'accorder avec; **to ~ to do** accepter de *ou* consentir à faire; **to ~ to sth** consentir à qch; **to ~ that** (*admit*) convenir *ou* reconnaître que; **garlic doesn't ~ with me** je ne supporte pas l'ail; **~able** *adj* agréable; (*willing*) consentant(e), d'accord; **~d** *adj* (*time, place*) convenu(e); **~ment** *n* accord *m;* **in ~ment** d'accord

agricultural [ægri'kʌltʃərəl] *adj* agricole

agriculture ['ægrikʌltʃə*r*] *n* agriculture *f*

aground [ə'graund] *adv:* **to run ~** échouer, s'échouer

ahead [ə'hed] *adv* (*in front: of position, place*) devant; (*: at the head*) en avant; (*look, plan, think*) en avant; **~ of** devant; (*fig: schedule etc*) en avance sur; **~ of time** en avance; **go right** *or* **straight ~** allez tout droit; **go ~!** (*fig: permission*) allez-y!

aid [eid] *n* aide *f;* (*device*) appareil *m* ♦ *vt* aider; **in ~ of** en faveur de; *see also* **hearing**

aide [eid] *n* (*person*) aide *mf,* assistant(e)

AIDS [eidz] *n abbr* (= *acquired immune deficiency syndrome*) SIDA *m;* **AIDS-related** *adj* associé(e) au sida

aim [eim] *vt:* **to ~ sth (at)** (*gun, camera*) braquer *ou* pointer qch (sur); (*missile*) lancer qch (à *ou* contre *ou* en direction de); (*blow*) allonger qch (à); (*remark*) destiner *ou* adresser qch (à) ♦ *vi* (*also:* **to take ~**) viser ♦ *n* but *m;* (*skill*): **his ~ is bad** il vise mal; (*fig*) viser (à); **to ~ to do** avoir l'intention de faire; **~less** *adj* sans but

ain't [eint] (*inf*) = **am not; aren't; isn't**

air [eə*r*] *n* air *m* ♦ *vt* (*room, bed, clothes*) aérer; (*grievances, views, ideas*) exposer, faire connaître ♦ *cpd* (*currents, attack etc*) aérien(ne); **to throw sth into the ~** jeter qch en l'air; **by ~** (*travel*) par avion; **to be on the ~** (*RADIO, TV: programme*) être diffusé(e); (*: station*) diffuser; **~bed** *n* matelas *m* pneumatique; **~-conditioned** *adj* climatisé(e); **~-conditioning** *n* climatisation *f;* **~craft** *n inv* avion *m;* **~craft carrier** *n* porte-avions *m* inv; **~field** *n* terrain *m* d'aviation; **A~ Force** *n* armée *f* de l'air; **~ freshener** *n* désodorisant *m;* **~gun** *n* fusil *m* à air comprimé; **~ hostess** *n* (*BRIT*) hôtesse *f* de l'air; **~ letter** *n* aérogramme *m;* **~lift** *n* pont aérien; **~line** *n* ligne aérienne, compagnie *f* d'aviation; **~liner** *n* avion *m* de ligne; **~mail** *n:* **by ~mail** par avion; **~ mile** *n* air mile *m;* **~plane** *n* (*US*) avion *m;* **~port** *n* aéroport *m;* **~ raid** *n* attaque *ou* raid aérien(ne); **~sick** *adj:* **to be ~sick** avoir le mal de l'air; **~tight** *adj* hermétique; **~-traffic controller** *n* aiguilleur *m* du ciel; **~y** *adj* bien aéré(e); (*manners*) dégagé(e)

aisle [ail] *n* (*of church*) allée centrale; nef latérale; (*of theatre etc*) couloir *m,* passage *m*, allée; **~ seat** *n* place *f* côté couloir

ajar [ə'dʒɑ:ʳ] *adj* entrouvert(e)

akin [ə'kɪn] *adj*: **~ to** (similar) qui tient de *or* ressemble à

alarm [ə'lɑ:m] *n* alarme *f* ♦ *vt* alarmer; **~ call** *n* coup de fil *m* pour réveiller; **~ clock** *n* réveille-matin *m inv*, réveil *m*

alas [ə'læs] *excl* hélas!

album ['ælbəm] *n* album *m*

alcohol ['ælkəhɔl] *n* alcool *m*; **~-free** *adj* sans alcool; **~ic** [ælkə'hɔlɪk] *adj* alcoolique ♦ *n* alcoolique *m/f*; **A~s Anonymous** Alcooliques anonymes

ale [eɪl] *n* bière *f*

alert [ə'lə:t] *adj* alerte, vif (vive); vigilant(e) ♦ *n* alerte *f* ♦ *vt* alerter; **on the ~** sur le qui-vive; (MIL) en état d'alerte

algebra ['ældʒɪbrə] *n* algèbre *m*

Algeria [æl'dʒɪərɪə] *n* Algérie *f*

alias ['eɪlɪəs] *adv* alias ♦ *n* faux nom, nom d'emprunt; (writer) pseudonyme *m*

alibi ['ælɪbaɪ] *n* alibi *m*

alien ['eɪlɪən] *n* étranger(-ère); (from outer space) extraterrestre *mf* ♦ *adj*: **~ (to)** étranger(-ère) (à)

alight [ə'laɪt] *adj, adv* en feu ♦ *vi* mettre pied à terre; (passenger) descendre

alike [ə'laɪk] *adj* semblable, pareil(le) ♦ *adv* de même; **to look ~** se ressembler

alimony ['ælɪmənɪ] *n* (payment) pension *f* alimentaire

alive [ə'laɪv] *adj* vivant(e); (lively) plein(e) de vie

KEYWORD

all [ɔ:l] *adj* (singular) tout(e); (plural) tous (toutes); **all day** toute la journée; **all night** toute la nuit; **all men** tous les hommes; **all five** tous les cinq; **all the food** toute la nourriture; **all the books** tous les livres; **all the time** tout le temps; **all his life** toute sa vie

♦ *pron* 1 tout(e); **I ate it all, I ate all of it** j'ai tout mangé; **all of us went** nous sommes tous allés; **all of the boys**

went tous les garçons y sont allés

2 (in phrases): **above all** surtout, pardessus tout; **after all** après tout; **not at all** (in answer to question) pas du tout; (in answer to thanks) je vous en prie!; **I'm not at all tired** je ne suis pas du tout fatigué(e); **anything at all will do** n'importe quoi fera l'affaire; **all in all** tout bien considéré, en fin de compte

♦ *adv*: **all alone** tout(e) seul(e); **it's not as hard as all that** ce n'est pas si difficile que ça; **all the more/the better** d'autant plus/mieux; **all but** presque, pratiquement; **the score is 2 all** le score est de 2 partout

allege [ə'ledʒ] *vt* alléguer, prétendre; **~dly** [ə'ledʒɪdlɪ] *adv* à ce que l'on prétend, paraît-il

allegiance [ə'li:dʒəns] *n* allégeance *f*, fidélité *f*, obéissance *f*

allergic [ə'lə:dʒɪk] *adj*: **~ to** allergique à

allergy ['ælədʒɪ] *n* allergie *f*

alleviate [ə'li:vɪeɪt] *vt* soulager, adoucir

alley ['ælɪ] *n* ruelle *f*

alliance [ə'laɪəns] *n* alliance *f*

allied ['ælaɪd] *adj* allié(e)

all-in ['ɔ:lɪn] (BRIT) *adj* (also: adv: charge) tout compris

all-night ['ɔ:l'naɪt] *adj* ouvert(e) *or* qui dure toute la nuit

allocate ['æləkeɪt] *vt* (share out) répartir, distribuer; **to ~ sth to** (duties) assigner *or* attribuer qch à; (sum, time) allouer qch à

allot [ə'lɔt] *vt*: **to ~ (to)** (money) répartir (entre), distribuer (à); (time) allouer (à); **~ment** *n* (share) part *f*; (garden) lopin *m* de terre (loué à la municipalité)

all-out ['ɔ:laut] *adj* (effort etc) total(e) ♦ *adv*: **all out** à fond

allow [ə'lau] *vt* (practice, behaviour) permettre, autoriser; (sum to spend etc) accorder; allouer; (sum, time estimated) compter, prévoir; (claim, goal) admettre; (concede): **to ~ that** convenir que; **to ~ sb to do** permettre à qn de faire, autoriser qn à faire; **he is ~ed to ...** on lui permet de ...; **~ for** vt fus tenir compte de; **~ance** [ə'lauəns] n (money received) allocation f, subside m; indemnité f; (TAX) somme f déductible du revenu imposable, abattement m; **to make ~ances for** tenir compte de

alloy ['ælɔɪ] n alliage m

all: ~ right adv (feel, work) bien; (as answer) d'accord; **~-rounder** n: **to be a good ~-rounder** être doué(e) en tout; **~-time** adj (record) sans précédent, absolu(e)

ally [n 'ælaɪ, vb ə'laɪ] n allié m ♦ vt: **to ~ o.s. with** s'allier avec

almighty [ɔ:l'maɪtɪ] adj tout-puissant; (tremendous) énorme

almond ['ɑ:mənd] n amande f

almost ['ɔ:lməʊst] adv presque

alone [ə'ləʊn] adj, adv seul(e); **to leave sb ~** laisser qn tranquille; **to leave sth ~** ne pas toucher à qch; **let ~ ...** sans parler de ...; encore moins ...

along [ə'lɔŋ] prep le long de ♦ adv: **is he coming ~ with us?** vient-il avec nous?; **he was hopping/limping ~** il avançait en sautillant/boitant; **~ with** (together with: person) en compagnie de; (: thing) avec, en plus de; **all ~** (all the time) depuis le début; **~side** prep le long de; à côté de ♦ adv bord à bord

aloof [ə'lu:f] adj distant(e) ♦ adv: **to stand ~** se tenir à distance ou à l'écart

aloud [ə'laʊd] adv à haute voix

alphabet ['ælfəbɛt] n alphabet m; **~ical** [ælfə'bɛtɪkl] adj alphabétique

alpine ['ælpaɪn] adj alpin(e), alpestre

Alps [ælps] npl: **the ~** les Alpes fpl

already [ɔ:l'rɛdɪ] adv déjà

alright ['ɔ:l'raɪt] (BRIT) adv = **all right**

Alsatian [æl'seɪʃən] (BRIT) n (dog) berger allemand

also ['ɔ:lsəʊ] adv aussi

altar ['ɔltər] n autel m

alter ['ɔltər] vt, vi changer

alternate [adj ɔl'tɜ:nɪt, vb 'ɔltɜ:neɪt] adj alterné(e), alternant(e), alternatif(-ive) ♦ vi alterner; **on ~ days** un jour sur deux, tous les deux jours; **alternating current** n courant alternatif

alternative [ɔl'tɜ:nətɪv] adj (solutions) possible, au choix; (plan) autre, de rechange; (lifestyle etc) parallèle ♦ n (choice) alternative f, (other possibility) solution f de remplacement ou de rechange, autre possibilité f; **~ medicine** médicines fpl parallèles ou douces; **~ly** adv: **~ly one could** une autre ou l'autre solution serait de, on pourrait aussi

alternator ['ɔltɜ:neɪtər] n (AUT) alternateur m

although [ɔ:l'ðəʊ] conj bien que +sub

altitude ['æltɪtju:d] n altitude f

alto ['æltəʊ] n (female) contralto m; (male) haute-contre f

altogether [ɔ:ltə'gɛðər] adv entièrement, tout à fait; (on the whole) tout compte fait; (in all) en tout

aluminium [ælju'mɪnɪəm] (BRIT), **aluminum** [ə'lu:mɪnəm] (US) n aluminium m

always ['ɔ:lweɪz] adv toujours

Alzheimer's (disease) ['æltshaɪməz-] n maladie f d'Alzheimer

AM n abbr (= Assembly Member) député m au Parlement gallois

am [æm] vb see **be**

a.m. adv abbr (= ante meridiem) du matin

amalgamate [ə'mælgəmeɪt] vt, vi fusionner

amateur ['æmətər] n amateur m; **~ish** (pej) adj d'amateur

amaze [ə'meɪz] vt stupéfier; **to be ~d (at)** être stupéfait(e) (de); **~ment** n stupéfaction f, stupeur f; **amazing** adj étonnant(e); exceptionnel(le)

ambassador [æm'bæsədər] n ambassadeur m

amber ['æmbər] n ambre m; **at ~** (AUT) à l'orange

ambiguous [æm'bɪgjuəs] adj ambigu(ë)

ambition [æm'bɪʃən] n ambition f;

ambitious *adj* ambitieux(-euse)

ambulance [ˈæmbjuləns] *n* ambulance *f*

ambush [ˈæmbuʃ] *n* embuscade *f* ♦ *vt* tendre une embuscade à

amenable [əˈmiːnəbl] *adj*: ~ **to** (*advice etc*) disposé(e) à écouter

amend [əˈmɛnd] *vt* (*law*) amender; (*text*) corriger; **to make ~s** réparer ses torts, faire amende honorable

amenities [əˈmiːnɪtɪz] *npl* aménagements *mpl*, équipements *mpl*

America [əˈmɛrɪkə] *n* Amérique *f*; **~n** *adj* américain(e) ♦ *n* Américain(e)

amiable [ˈeɪmɪəbl] *adj* aimable, affable

amicable [ˈæmɪkəbl] *adj* amical(e); (*LAW*) à l'amiable

amid(st) [əˈmɪd(st)] *prep* parmi, au milieu de

amiss [əˈmɪs] *adj*, *adv*: **there's something ~** il y a quelque chose qui ne va pas *or* qui cloche; **to take sth ~** prendre qch mal *or* de travers

ammonia [əˈməʊnɪə] *n* (*gas*) ammoniac *m*; (*liquid*) ammoniaque *f*

ammunition [æmjuˈnɪʃən] *n* munitions *fpl*

amok [əˈmɔk] *adv*: **to run ~** être pris(e) d'un accès de folie furieuse

among(st) [əˈmʌŋ(st)] *prep* parmi, entre

amorous [ˈæmərəs] *adj* amoureux(-euse)

amount [əˈmaʊnt] *n* (*sum*) somme *f*, montant *m*; (*quantity*) quantité *f*, nombre *m* ♦ *vi*: **to ~ to** (*total*) s'élever à; (*be same as*) équivaloir à, revenir à

amp(ere) [ˈæmp(ɛəʳ)] *n* ampère *m*

ample [ˈæmpl] *adj* ample, spacieux(-euse); (*enough*): **this is ~** c'est largement suffisant; **to have ~ time/room** avoir bien assez de temps/place

amplifier [ˈæmplɪfaɪəʳ] *n* amplificateur *m*

amuse [əˈmjuːz] *vt* amuser, divertir; **~ment** *n* amusement *m*; **~ment arcade** *n* salle *f* de jeu; **~ment park** *n*

parc *m* d'attractions

an [æn, ən] *indef art see* **a**

anaemic [əˈniːmɪk] (*US* **anemic**) *adj* anémique

anaesthetic [ænɪsˈθetɪk] (*US* **anesthetic**) *n* anesthésique *m*

analog(ue) [ˈænəlɔg] *adj* (*watch, computer*) analogique

analyse [ˈænəlaɪz] (*US* **analyze**) *vt* analyser; **analysis** [əˈnæləsɪs] (*pl* **analyses**) *n* analyse *f*; **analyst** [ˈænəlɪst] *n* (*POL etc*) spécialiste *m/f*; (*US*) psychanalyste *m/f*

analyze [ˈænəlaɪz] (*US*) *vt* = **analyse**

anarchist [ˈænəkɪst] *n* anarchiste *m/f*

anarchy [ˈænəkɪ] *n* anarchie *f*

anatomy [əˈnætəmɪ] *n* anatomie *f*

ancestor [ˈænsɪstəʳ] *n* ancêtre *m*

anchor [ˈæŋkəʳ] *n* ancre *f* ♦ *vi* (*also*: **to drop ~**) jeter l'ancre, mouiller ♦ *vt* mettre à l'ancre; (*fig*): **to ~ sth** fixer qch à

anchovy [ˈæntʃəvɪ] *n* anchois *m*

ancient [ˈeɪnʃənt] *adj* ancien(ne), antique; (*person*) d'un âge vénérable; (*car*) antédiluvien(ne)

ancillary [ænˈsɪlərɪ] *adj* auxiliaire

and [ænd] *conj* et; **~ so on** et ainsi de suite; **try ~ come** tâchez de venir; **he talked ~ talked** il n'a pas arrêté de parler; **better ~ better** de mieux en mieux

anew [əˈnjuː] *adv* à nouveau

angel [ˈeɪndʒəl] *n* ange *m*

anger [ˈæŋgəʳ] *n* colère *f*

angina [ænˈdʒaɪnə] *n* angine *f* de poitrine

angle [ˈæŋgl] *n* angle *m*; **from their ~** de leur point de vue

angler [ˈæŋgləʳ] *n* pêcheur(-euse) à la ligne

Anglican [ˈæŋglɪkən] *adj, n* anglican(e)

angling [ˈæŋglɪŋ] *n* pêche *f* à la ligne

Anglo- [ˈæŋgləʊ] *prefix* anglo(-)

angrily [ˈæŋgrɪlɪ] *adv* avec colère

angry [ˈæŋgrɪ] *adj* en colère, furieux(-euse); (*wound*) enflammé(e); **to be ~**

with sb/at sth être furieux contre qn/
de qch; **to get ~** se fâcher, se mettre
en colère

anguish ['æŋgwɪʃ] n (mental) angoisse
f

animal ['ænɪməl] n animal m ♦ adj ani-
mal(e)

animate [vb 'ænɪmeɪt, adj 'ænɪmɪt] vt
animer ♦ adj animé(e), vivant(e); **~d** adj
animé(e)

aniseed ['ænɪsiːd] n anis m

ankle ['æŋkl] n cheville f; **~ sock** n socquette f

annex ['æneks] n (BRIT: ~e) annexe f

anniversary [ænɪ'vəːsərɪ] n anniversaire m

announce [ə'nauns] vt annoncer;
(birth, death) faire part de; **~ment** n
annonce f; (for births etc: in newspaper)
avis m de faire-part; (: letter, card)
faire-part m; **~r** n (RADIO, TV: between
programmes) speaker(ine)

annoy [ə'nɔɪ] vt agacer, ennuyer,
contrarier; **don't get ~ed!** ne vous
fâchez pas!; **~ance** n mécontentement
m, contrariété f; **~ing** adj agaçant(e),
contrariant(e)

annual ['ænjuəl] adj annuel(le) ♦ n
(BOT) plante annuelle; (children's book)
album m

annul [ə'nʌl] vt annuler

annum ['ænəm] n see per

anonymous [ə'nɔnɪməs] adj anonyme

anorak ['ænəræk] n anorak m

anorexia [ænə'reksɪə] n anorexie f

another [ə'nʌðə*] adj: **~ book** (one
more) un autre livre, encore un livre, un
livre de plus; (a different one) un autre
livre ♦ pron un(e) autre, encore un(e),
un(e) de plus; see also one

answer ['ɑːnsə*] n réponse f; (to problem) solution f ♦ vi répondre ♦ vt (reply to) répondre à; (problem) résoudre;
(prayer) exaucer; **in ~ to your letter**
en réponse à votre lettre; **to ~ the
phone** répondre (au téléphone); **to ~
the bell** or **the door** aller or venir

ouvrir (la porte); **~ back** vi répondre,
répliquer; **~ for** vt fus (person) répondre
de, se porter garant de; (crime, one's
actions) être responsable de; **~ to** vt fus
(description) répondre or correspondre
à; **~able** adj: **~able (to sb/for sth)**
responsable (devant qn/de qch); **~ing
machine** n répondeur m automatique

ant [ænt] n fourmi f

antagonism [æn'tægənɪzəm] n antago-
nisme m

antagonize [æn'tægənaɪz] vt éveiller
l'hostilité de, contrarier

Antarctic [ænt'ɑːktɪk] n: **the ~** l'Antarctique m

antenatal ['æntɪ'neɪtl] adj prénatal(e);
~ clinic n service m de consultation
prénatale

anthem ['ænθəm] n: **national ~** hymne national

anti: **~aircraft** adj (missile) anti-
aérien(ne); **~biotic** ['æntɪbaɪ'ɔtɪk] n
antibiotique m; **~body** n anticorps m

anticipate [æn'tɪsɪpeɪt] vt s'attendre à,
prévoir; (wishes, request) aller au devant
de, devancer

anticipation [æntɪsɪ'peɪʃən] n attente
f; **in ~** par anticipation, à l'avance

anticlimax ['æntɪ'klaɪmæks] n déception f, douche froide (fam)

anticlockwise ['æntɪ'klɔkwaɪz] adj, adv
dans le sens inverse des aiguilles d'une
montre

antics ['æntɪks] npl singeries fpl

antidepressant ['æntɪdɪ'prɛsənt] n
antidépresseur m

antifreeze ['æntɪfriːz] n antigel m

antihistamine ['æntɪ'hɪstəmɪn] n antihistaminique m

antiquated ['æntɪkweɪtɪd] adj vieilli(e),
suranné(e), vieillot(te)

antique [æn'tiːk] n objet m d'art ancien, meuble ancien or d'époque, antiquité f ♦ adj ancien(ne); **~ dealer** n
antiquaire m; **~ shop** n magasin m
d'antiquités

anti: **~Semitism** ['æntɪ'semɪtɪzəm]

antisémitisme m; **~septic** [æntɪ'sɛptɪk] n antiseptique m; **~social** [æntɪ'səʊʃəl] adj peu liant(e), sauvage, insociable; (against society) antisocial(e)

antlers ['æntləz] npl bois mpl, ramure f

anvil ['ænvɪl] n enclume f

anxiety [æŋ'zaɪətɪ] n anxiété f; (keenness): **~ to do** grand désir or impatience f de faire

anxious ['æŋkʃəs] adj anxieux(-euse), angoissé(e); (worrying: time, situation) inquiétant(e); (keen): **~ to do/that** qui tient beaucoup à faire/à ce que; impatient(e) de faire/que

KEYWORD

any ['ɛnɪ] adj 1 (in questions etc: singular) du, de l', de la, (: plural) des; **have you any butter/children/ink?** avez-vous du beurre/des enfants/de l'encre?
2 (with negative) de, d'; **I haven't any money/books** je n'ai pas d'argent/de livres
3 (no matter which) n'importe quel(le); **choose any book you like** vous pouvez choisir n'importe quel livre
4 (in phrases): **in any case** de toute façon; **any day now** d'un jour à l'autre; **at any moment** à tout moment, d'un instant à l'autre; **at any rate** en tout cas

♦ pron 1 (in questions etc) en; **have you got any?** est-ce que vous en avez?; **can any of you sing?** est-ce que parmi vous il y en a qui savent chanter?
2 (with negative) en; **I haven't any (of them)** je n'en ai pas, je n'en ai aucun
3 (no matter which one(s)) n'importe lequel (or laquelle); **take any of those books (you like)** vous pouvez prendre n'importe lequel de ces livres

♦ adv 1 (in questions etc): **do you want any more soup/sandwiches?** voulez-vous encore de la soupe/des sandwichs?; **are you feeling any better?** est-ce que vous vous sentez mieux?

2 (with negative): **I can't hear him any more** je ne l'entends plus; **don't wait any longer** n'attendez pas plus longtemps

any: ~body pron n'importe qui; (in interrogative sentences) quelqu'un; (in negative sentences) **I don't see ~body** je ne vois personne; **~how** adv (at any rate) de toute façon, quand même; (haphazard) n'importe comment; **~one** pron = anybody; **~thing** pron n'importe quoi, quelque chose, ne ... rien; **~way** adv de toute façon; **~where** adv n'importe où, quelque part; **I don't see him ~where** je ne le vois nulle part

apart [ə'pɑːt] adv (to one side) à part; de côté; à l'écart; (separately) séparé(e); **10 miles ~** à 10 miles l'un de l'autre; **to take ~** démonter; **~ from** part, excepté

apartheid [ə'pɑːteɪt] n apartheid m

apartment [ə'pɑːtmənt] n (US) appartement m, logement m; (room) chambre f; **~ building** (US) n immeuble m, (divided house) maison divisée en appartements

ape [eɪp] n (grand) singe ♦ vt singer

apéritif [ə'pɛrɪtiːf] n apéritif m

aperture ['æpətʃʊəʳ] n orifice m, ouverture f; (PHOT) ouverture (du diaphragme)

APEX ['eɪpɛks] n abbr (AVIAT) (= advance purchase excursion) APEX m

apologetic [əpɔlə'dʒɛtɪk] adj (tone, letter) d'excuse; (person): **to be ~** s'excuser

apologize [ə'pɔlədʒaɪz] vi: **to ~ (for sth to sb)** s'excuser (de qch auprès de qn), présenter ses excuses (à qn pour qch)

apology [ə'pɔlədʒɪ] n excuses fpl

apostle [ə'pɔsl] n apôtre m

apostrophe [ə'pɔstrəfɪ] n apostrophe f

appalling [ə'pɔːlɪŋ] adj épouvantable; (stupidity) consternant(e)

apparatus [æpə'reɪtəs] n appareil m, dispositif m; (in gymnasium) agrès mpl; (of government) dispositif m

apparel [ə'pærəl] (US) n habillement m

apparent [ə'pærənt] adj apparent(e); **~ly** adv apparemment

appeal [ə'piːl] vi (LAW) faire or interjeter appel ♦ n appel m; (request) prière f; appel m; (charm) attrait m, charme m; **to ~ for** lancer un appel pour; **to ~ to** (beg) faire appel à; (be attractive) plaire à; **it doesn't ~ to me** cela ne m'attire pas; **~ing** adj (attractive) attrayant(e)

appear [ə'pɪə'] vi apparaître, se montrer; (LAW) comparaître; (publication) paraître, sortir, être publié(e); (seem) paraître, sembler; **it would ~ that** il semble que; **to ~ in Hamlet** jouer dans Hamlet; **to ~ on TV** passer à la télé; **~ance** n apparition f; parution f; (look, aspect) apparence f, aspect m

appease [ə'piːz] vt apaiser, calmer

appendicitis [əpendɪ'saɪtɪs] n appendicite f

appendix [ə'pendɪks] (pl appendices) n appendice m

appetite ['æpɪtaɪt] n appétit m; **appetizer** n amuse-gueule m; (drink) apéritif m

applaud [ə'plɔːd] vt, vi applaudir

applause [ə'plɔːz] n applaudissements mpl

apple ['æpl] n pomme f; **~ tree** n pommier m

appliance [ə'plaɪəns] n appareil m

applicable [ə'plɪkəbl] adj (relevant): **to be ~** valoir pour

applicant ['æplɪkənt] n: **~ (for)** candidat(e) (à)

application [æplɪ'keɪʃən] n application f; (for a job, a grant etc) demande f; candidature f; **~ form** n formulaire m de demande

applied [ə'plaɪd] adj appliqué(e)

apply [ə'plaɪ] vt: **to ~ (to)** (paint, ointment) appliquer (sur); (law etc) appli-

quer (à) ♦ vi: **to ~ to** (be suitable for, relevant to) s'appliquer à; (ask) s'adresser à; **to ~ for** (permit, grant) faire une demande (en vue d'obtenir); (job) poser sa candidature f, faire une demande d'emploi (concernant); **to ~ o.s. to** s'appliquer à

appoint [ə'pɔɪnt] vt nommer, engager; **~ed** adj: **at the ~ed time** à l'heure dite; **~ment** n nomination f; (meeting) rendez-vous m; **to make an ~ment (with)** prendre rendez-vous (avec)

appraisal [ə'preɪzl] n évaluation f

appreciate [ə'priːʃɪeɪt] vt (like) apprécier; (be grateful for) être reconnaissant(e) de; (understand) comprendre; se rendre compte de ♦ vi (FINANCE) prendre de la valeur

appreciation [əpriːʃɪ'eɪʃən] n appréciation f; (gratitude) reconnaissance f; (COMM) hausse f, valorisation f

appreciative [ə'priːʃɪətɪv] adj (person) sensible; (comment) élogieux(-euse)

apprehensive [æprɪ'hensɪv] adj inquiet(-ète), appréhensif(-ive)

apprentice [ə'prentɪs] n apprenti m; **~ship** n apprentissage m

approach [ə'prəʊtʃ] vi approcher ♦ vt (come near) approcher de; (ask, apply to) s'adresser à; (situation, problem) aborder ♦ n approche f; (access) accès m; **~able** adj accessible

appropriate [adj ə'prəʊprɪɪt, vb ə'prəʊprɪeɪt] adj (moment, remark) opportun(e); (tool etc) approprié(e) ♦ vt (take) s'approprier

approval [ə'pruːvəl] n approbation f; **on ~** (COMM) à l'examen

approve [ə'pruːv] vt approuver; **~ of** vt fus approuver

approximate [adj ə'prɒksɪmɪt, vb ə'prɒksɪmeɪt] adj approximatif(-ive) ♦ vt se rapprocher de, être proche de; **~ly** adv approximativement

apricot ['eɪprɪkɒt] n abricot m

April ['eɪprəl] n avril m; **~ Fool's Day** le premier avril

apron ['eɪprən] n tablier m

apt [æpt] adj (suitable) approprié(e);
(likely): ~ **to do** susceptible de faire; qui
a tendance à faire

Aquarius [ə'kwɛərɪəs] n le Verseau

Arab ['ærəb] adj arabe ♦ n Arabe m/f;
~ian [ə'reɪbɪən] adj arabe; **~ic** adj arabe ♦ n arabe m

arbitrary ['ɑːbɪtrərɪ] adj arbitraire

arbitration [ɑːbɪ'treɪʃən] n arbitrage m

arcade [ɑː'keɪd] n arcade f; (passage
with shops) passage m, galerie marchande; (with video games) salle f de
jeu

arch [ɑːtʃ] n arc m; (of foot) cambrure f,
voûte f plantaire ♦ vt arquer, cambrer

archaeologist [ɑːkɪ'ɔlədʒɪst] n archéologue m/f

archaeology [ɑːkɪ'ɔlədʒɪ] n archéologie f

archbishop [ɑːtʃ'bɪʃəp] n archevêque
m

archeology etc (US) [ɑːkɪ'ɔlədʒɪ] = **archaeology** etc

archery ['ɑːtʃərɪ] n tir m à l'arc

architect ['ɑːkɪtɛkt] n architecte m;
~ure n architecture f

archives ['ɑːkaɪvz] npl archives fpl

Arctic ['ɑːktɪk] adj arctique ♦ n Arctique
m

ardent ['ɑːdənt] adj fervent(e)

are [ɑːʳ] vb see **be**

area ['ɛərɪə] n (GEOM) superficie f; (zone)
région f; (: smaller) secteur m, partie f;

(in room) coin m; (knowledge, research)
domaine m; ~ **code** (US) n (TEL) indicatif m téléphonique

aren't [ɑːnt] = **are not**

Argentina [ɑːdʒən'tiːnə] n Argentine f;
Argentinian [ɑːdʒən'tɪnɪən] adj ar-
gentin(e) ♦ n Argentin(e)

arguably [ɑː'gjuːəblɪ] adv: **it is ~** ... on
peut soutenir que c'est ...

argue ['ɑːgjuː] vi (quarrel) se disputer;
(reason) argumenter; **to ~ that** objecter ou alléguer que

argument ['ɑːgjumənt] n (reasons) argument m; (quarrel) dispute f; **~ative**
[ɑːgjuˈmɛntətɪv] adj ergoteur(-euse),
raisonneur(-euse)

Aries ['ɛərɪz] n le Bélier

arise [ə'raɪz] (pt **arose**, pp **arisen**) vi
survenir, se présenter

aristocrat ['ærɪstəkræt] n aristocrate
m/f

arithmetic [ə'rɪθmətɪk] n arithmétique
f

ark [ɑːk] n: **Noah's A~** l'Arche f de
Noé

arm [ɑːm] n bras m ♦ vt armer; **~s** npl
(weapons, HERALDRY) armes fpl; **~ in ~**
bras dessus bras dessous

armaments ['ɑːməmənts] npl armement m

armchair ['ɑːmtʃɛəʳ] n fauteuil m

armed [ɑːmd] adj armé(e); ~ **robbery**
n vol m à main armée

armour ['ɑːməʳ] (US **armor**) n armure f;
(MIL: tanks) blindés mpl; **~ed car** n véhicule blindé

armpit ['ɑːmpɪt] n aisselle f

armrest ['ɑːmrɛst] n accoudoir m

army ['ɑːmɪ] n armée f

A road (BRIT) n (AUT) route nationale

aroma [ə'rəumə] n arôme m; **~thera-
py** n aromathérapie f

arose [ə'rəuz] pt of **arise**

around [ə'raund] adv autour; (nearby)
dans les parages ♦ prep autour de;
(near) près de; (fig: about) environ; (:
date, time) vers

arouse [ə'rauz] vt (sleeper) éveiller; (curiosity, passions) éveiller, susciter; (anger) exciter

arrange [ə'reɪndʒ] vt arranger; **to ~ to do sth** prévoir de faire qch; **~ment** n arrangement m; **~ments** npl (plans etc) arrangements mpl, dispositions fpl

array [ə'reɪ] n: **~ of** déploiement m or étalage m de

arrears [ə'rɪəz] npl arriéré m; **to be in ~ with one's rent** devoir un arriéré de loyer

arrest [ə'rest] vt arrêter; (sb's attention) retenir, attirer ♦ n arrestation f; **under ~** en état d'arrestation

arrival [ə'raɪvl] n arrivée f; **new ~** nouveau venu, nouvelle venue; (baby) nouveau-né(e)

arrive [ə'raɪv] vi arriver

arrogant ['ærəgənt] adj arrogant(e)

arrow ['ærəu] n flèche f

arse [ɑːs] (BRIT: inf!) n cul m (!)

arson ['ɑːsn] n incendie criminel

art [ɑːt] n art m; **A~s** npl (SCOL) les lettres fpl

artery ['ɑːtərɪ] n artère f

art gallery n musée m d'art; (small and private) galerie f de peinture

arthritis [ɑː'θraɪtɪs] n arthrite f

artichoke ['ɑːtɪtʃəuk] n (also: **globe ~**) artichaut m; (also: **Jerusalem ~**) topinambour m

article ['ɑːtɪkl] n article m; **~s** npl (BRIT: LAW: training) ≃ stage m; **~ of clothing** vêtement m

articulate [adj ɑː'tɪkjulɪt, vb ɑː'tɪkjuleɪt] adj (person) qui s'exprime bien; (speech) bien articulé(e), prononcé(e) clairement ♦ vt exprimer; **~d lorry** (BRIT) n (camion m) semi-remorque m

artificial [ɑːtɪ'fɪʃəl] adj artificiel(le); **~ respiration** n respiration artificielle

artist ['ɑːtɪst] n artiste m/f; **~ic** [ɑː'tɪstɪk] adj artistique; **~ry** n art m, talent m

art school n ≃ école f des beaux-arts

KEYWORD

as [æz, əz] conj **1** (referring to time) comme, alors que; à mesure que; **he came in as I was leaving** il est arrivé comme je partais; **as the years went by** à mesure que les années passaient; **as from tomorrow** à partir de demain

2 (in comparisons): **as big as** aussi grand que; **twice as big as** deux fois plus grand que; **as much** or **many as** autant que; **as much money/many books** autant d'argent/de livres que; **as soon as** dès que

3 (since, because) comme, puisque; **as he had to be home by 10 ...** comme il or puisqu'il devait être de retour avant 10 h ...

4 (referring to manner, way) comme; **do as you wish** faites comme vous voudrez

5 (concerning): **as for** or **to that** quant à cela, pour ce qui est de cela

6: **as if** or **though** comme si; **he looked as if he was ill** il avait l'air d'être malade; see also **long**; **such**; **well**

♦ prep: **he works as a driver** il travaille comme chauffeur; **as chairman of the company, he ...** en tant que président de la société, il ...; **dressed up as a cowboy** déguisé en cowboy; **he gave me it as a present** il me l'a offert, il m'en a fait cadeau

a.s.a.p. abbr (= as soon as possible) dès que possible

asbestos [æz'bestəs] n amiante f

ascend [ə'send] vt gravir; (throne) monter sur

ascertain [æsə'teɪn] vt vérifier

ash [æʃ] n (dust) cendre f; (also: **~ tree**) frêne m

ashamed [ə'ʃeɪmd] adj honteux(-euse), confus(e); **to be ~ of** avoir honte de

ashore [ə'ʃɔː] adv à terre

ashtray ['æʃtreɪ] n cendrier m

Ash Wednesday n mercredi m des cendres

Asia ['eɪʃə] n Asie f; **~n** n Asiatique m/f ♦ adj asiatique

aside [ə'saɪd] adv de côté; à l'écart ♦ n aparté m

ask [ɑːsk] vt demander; (invite) inviter; **to ~ sb sth/to do sth** demander à qn à qn de faire qch; **to ~ sb about sth** questionner qn sur qch; se renseigner auprès de qn sur qch; **to ~ (sb) a question** poser une question (à qn); **to ~ sb out to dinner** inviter qn au restaurant; **~ after** vt fus demander des nouvelles de; **~ for** vt fus demander; (trouble) chercher

asking price ['ɑːskɪŋ-] n: **the ~** le prix de départ

asleep [ə'sliːp] adj endormi(e); **to fall ~** s'endormir

asparagus [əs'pærəgəs] n asperges fpl

aspect ['æspekt] n aspect m; (direction in which a building etc faces) orientation f, exposition f

aspire [əs'paɪə'] vi: **to ~ to** aspirer à

aspirin ['æsprɪn] n aspirine f

ass [æs] n âne m; (inf) imbécile m/f; (US: inf!) cul m (!)

assailant [ə'seɪlənt] n agresseur m, assaillant m

assassinate [ə'sæsɪneɪt] vt assassiner; **assassination** [əsæsɪ'neɪʃən] n assassinat m

assault [ə'sɔːlt] n (MIL) assaut m; (gen: attack) agression f ♦ vt attaquer; (sexually) violenter

assemble [ə'sembl] vt assembler ♦ vi s'assembler, se rassembler; **assembly** n assemblée f, réunion f; (institution) assemblée; (construction) assemblage m; **assembly line** n chaîne f de montage

assent [ə'sent] n assentiment m, consentement m

assert [ə'səːt] vt affirmer, déclarer; (one's authority) faire valoir; (one's innocence) protester de

assess [ə'ses] vt évaluer; (tax, payment) établir or fixer le montant de; (property etc: for tax) calculer la valeur imposable de; (person) juger la valeur de; **~ment** n évaluation f, fixation f, calcul m de la valeur imposable de, jugement m; **~or** n expert m (impôt et assurance)

asset ['æset] n avantage m, atout m; **~s** npl (FINANCE) capital m; avoir(s) m(pl); actif m

assign [ə'saɪn] vt (date) fixer; (task) assigner à; (resources) affecter à; **~ment** n tâche f, mission f

assist [ə'sɪst] vt aider, assister; **~ance** n aide f, assistance f; **~ant** n assistant(e), adjoint(e); (BRIT: also: **shop ~ant**) vendeur(-euse)

associate [n, adj ə'səuʃɪt, vb ə'səuʃɪeɪt] adj, n associé(e) ♦ vt associer ♦ vi: **to ~ with sb** fréquenter qn; **association** [əsəuʃɪ'eɪʃən] n association f

assorted [ə'sɔːtɪd] adj assorti(e)

assortment [ə'sɔːtmənt] n assortiment m

assume [ə'sjuːm] vt supposer; (responsibilities etc) assumer; (attitude, name) prendre, adopter; **assumption** [ə'sʌmpʃən] n supposition f, hypothèse f; (of power) assomption f, prise f

assurance [ə'ʃuərəns] n assurance f

assure [ə'ʃuə'] vt assurer

asthma ['æsmə] n asthme m

astonish [ə'stɒnɪʃ] vt étonner, stupéfier; **~ment** n étonnement m

astound [ə'staund] vt stupéfier, sidérer

astray [ə'streɪ] adv: **to go ~** s'égarer; (fig) quitter le droit chemin; **to lead ~** détourner du droit chemin

astride [ə'straɪd] prep à cheval sur

astrology [əs'trɒlədʒɪ] n astrologie f

astronaut ['æstrənɔːt] n astronaute m/f

astronomy [əs'trɒnəmɪ] n astronomie f

asylum [ə'saɪləm] n asile m

KEYWORD

at [æt] prep **1** (referring to position, direction) à; **at the top** au sommet; **at home/school** à la maison or chez soi/à

l'école; **at the baker's** à la boulangerie, chez le boulanger; **to look at sth** regarder qch
2 (*referring to time*): **at 4 o'clock** à 4 heures; **at Christmas** à Noël; **at night** la nuit; **at times** par moments, parfois
3 (*referring to rates, speed etc*) à; **at a kilo** a une livre le kilo; **two at a time** deux à la fois; **at 50 km/h** à 50 km/h
4 (*referring to manner*): **at a stroke** d'un seul coup; **at peace** en paix
5 (*referring to activity*): **to be at work** être au travail, travailler; **to play at cowboys** jouer aux cowboys; **to be good at sth** être bon en qch
6 (*referring to cause*): **shocked/ surprised/annoyed at sth** choqué par/étonné de/agacé par qch; **I went at his suggestion** j'y suis allé sur son conseil

ate [eɪt] *pt of* **eat**

atheist ['eɪθɪɪst] *n* athée *m/f*

Athens ['æθɪnz] *n* Athènes

athlete ['æθliːt] *n* athlète *m/f*; **athletic** [æθ'letɪk] *adj* athlétique; **athletics** *n* athlétisme *m*

Atlantic [ət'læntɪk] *adj* atlantique ♦ *n*: **the ~ (Ocean)** l'océan *m* Atlantique *m*

atlas ['ætləs] *n* atlas *m*

ATM *n abbr* (= *automated telling machine*) guichet *m* automatique

atmosphere ['ætməsfɪə'] *n* atmosphère *f*

atom ['ætəm] *n* atome *m*; **~ic** [ə'tɒmɪk] *adj* atomique; **~(ic) bomb** *n* bombe *f* atomique; **~izer** *n* atomiseur *m*

atone [ə'təun] *vi*: **to ~ for** expier, racheter

atrocious [ə'trəuʃəs] *adj* (*very bad*) atroce, exécrable

attach [ə'tætʃ] *vt* attacher; (*document, letter*) joindre; **to be ~ed to sb/sth** être attaché à qn/qch

attaché case [ə'tæʃeɪ] *n* mallette *f*, attaché-case *m*

attachment [ə'tætʃmənt] *n* (*tool*) accessoire *m*; (*love*): **~ (to)** affection *f* (pour), attachement *m* (à)

attack [ə'tæk] *vt* attaquer; (*task etc*) s'attaquer à ♦ *n* attaque *f*; (*also*: **heart ~**) crise *f* cardiaque

attain [ə'teɪn] *vt* (*also*: **to ~ to**) parvenir à, atteindre; (: *knowledge*) acquérir

attempt [ə'tempt] *n* tentative *f* ♦ *vt* essayer, tenter; **to make an ~ on sb's life** attenter à la vie de qn; **~ed** *adj*: **~ed murder/suicide** tentative *f* de meurtre/suicide

attend [ə'tend] *vt* (*course*) suivre; (*meeting, talk*) assister à; (*school, church*) aller à, fréquenter; (*patient*) soigner, s'occuper de; **~ to** *vt fus* (*needs, affairs etc*) s'occuper de; (*customer, patient*) s'occuper de; **~ance** *n* (*being present*) présence *f*; (*people present*) assistance *f*; **~ant** *n* employé(e) ♦ *adj* (*dangers*) inhérent(e), concomitant(e)

attention [ə'tenʃən] *n* attention *f*; **~!** (*MIL*) garde-à-vous!; **for the ~ of** (*ADMIN*) à l'attention de

attentive [ə'tentɪv] *adj* attentif(-ive); (*kind*) prévenant(e)

attest [ə'test] *vi*: **to ~ to** (*demonstrate*) démontrer; (*confirm*) témoigner

attic ['ætɪk] *n* grenier *m*

attitude ['ætɪtjuːd] *n* attitude *f*; pose *f*, maintien *m*

attorney [ə'tɜːnɪ] *n* (*US*: *lawyer*) avoué *m*; **A~ General** *n* (*BRIT*) ≈ procureur général; (*US*) ≈ garde *m* des Sceaux, ministre *m* de la Justice

attract [ə'trækt] *vt* attirer; **~ion** (*gen pl*: *pleasant things*) attraction *f*, attrait *m*; (*PHYSICS*) attraction *f*; (*fig*: *towards sb or sth*) attirance *f*; **~ive** *adj* attrayant(e); (*person*) séduisant(e)

attribute [*n* 'ætrɪbjuːt, *vb* ə'trɪbjuːt] *n* attribut *m* ♦ *vt*: **to ~ sth to** attribuer qch à

attrition [ə'trɪʃən] *n*: **war of ~** guerre *f* d'usure

aubergine ['əubəʒiːn] *n* aubergine *f*

auction ['ɔːkʃən] *n (also:* **sale by ~)** vente *f* aux enchères; ♦ *vt (also:* **sell by ~)** vendre aux enchères; (*BRIT:* **put up for ~**) mettre aux enchères; **~eer** [ɔːkʃə'nɪə⁺] *n* commissaire-priseur *m*

audience ['ɔːdɪəns] *n (people)* assistance *f*; public *m*; spectateurs *mpl*; (*interview*) audience *f*

audiovisual ['ɔːdɪəʊ'vɪzjuəl] *adj* audiovisuel(le); ♦ **aids** *npl* supports *or* moyens audiovisuels

audit ['ɔːdɪt] *vt* vérifier

audition [ɔː'dɪʃən] *n* audition *f*

auditor ['ɔːdɪtə⁺] *n* vérificateur *m* des comptes

augur ['ɔːgə⁺] *vi:* **it ~s well** c'est bon signe *or* de bon augure

August ['ɔːgəst] *n* août *m*

aunt [ɑːnt] *n* tante *f*; **~ie, ~y** ['ɑːntɪ] *n dimin* of **aunt**

au pair ['əʊ'pɛə⁺] *n (also:* **~ girl**) jeune fille *f* au pair

auspicious [ɔːs'pɪʃəs] *adj* de bon augure, propice

Australia [ɔs'treɪlɪə] *n* Australie *f*; **~n** *adj* australien(ne) ♦ *n* Australien(ne)

Austria ['ɔstrɪə] *n* Autriche *f*; **~n** *adj* autrichien(ne) ♦ *n* Autrichien(ne)

authentic [ɔː'θɛntɪk] *adj* authentique

author ['ɔːθə⁺] *n* auteur *m*

authoritarian [ɔːθɔrɪ'tɛərɪən] *adj* autoritaire

authoritative [ɔː'θɔrɪtətɪv] *adj (account)* digne de foi; (*study, treatise*) qui fait autorité; (*person, manner*) autoritaire

authority [ɔː'θɔrɪtɪ] *n* autorité *f*; (*permission*) autorisation *f* (formelle); **the authorities** *npl (ruling body)* les autorités *fpl*, l'administration *f*

authorize ['ɔːθəraɪz] *vt* autoriser

auto ['ɔːtəʊ] (*US*) *n* auto *f*, voiture *f*

auto: **~biography** [ɔːtəbaɪ'ɔgrəfɪ] *n* autobiographie *f*; **~graph** ['ɔːtəgrɑːf] *n* autographe *m* ♦ *vt* signer, dédicacer; **~mated** ['ɔːtəmeɪtɪd] *adj* automatisé(e), automatique; **~matic** [ɔːtə'mæt-

-ɪk] *adj* automatique ♦ *n (gun)* automatique *m*; (*washing machine*) machine *f* à laver automatique; (*BRIT:* AUT) voiture *f* à transmission automatique; **~matically** *adv* automatiquement; **~mation** [ɔːtə'meɪʃən] *n* automatisation *f* (électronique); **~mobile** [ɔːtəmə'biːl] (*US*) *n* automobile *f*; **~nomy** [ɔː'tɔnəmɪ] *n* autonomie *f*

autumn [ɔːtəm] *n* automne *m*; **in ~** en automne

auxiliary [ɔːg'zɪlɪərɪ] *adj* auxiliaire ♦ *n* auxiliaire *m/f*

avail [ə'veɪl] *vt:* **to ~ o.s. of** profiter de ♦ *n:* **to no ~** sans résultat, en vain, en pure perte

availability [əveɪlə'bɪlɪtɪ] *n* disponibilité *f*

available [ə'veɪləbl] *adj* disponible

avalanche ['ævəlɑːnʃ] *n* avalanche *f*

Ave *abbr* = **avenue**

avenge [ə'vɛndʒ] *vt* venger

avenue ['ævənjuː] *n* avenue *f*; (*fig*) moyen *m*

average ['ævərɪdʒ] *n* moyenne *f*; (*fig*) moyen *m* ♦ *adj* moyen(ne) ♦ *vt (a certain figure)* atteindre *or* faire *etc* en moyenne; **on ~** en moyenne; **~ out** *vi:* **to ~ out at** représenter en moyenne, donner une moyenne de

averse [ə'vɜːs] *adj:* **to be ~ to sth/doing sth** éprouver une forte répugnance envers qch/à faire qch

avert [ə'vɜːt] *vt (danger)* prévenir, écarter; (*one's eyes*) détourner

aviary ['eɪvɪərɪ] *n* volière *f*

avocado [ævə'kɑːdəʊ] *n (BRIT: ~ pear)* avocat *m*

avoid [ə'vɔɪd] *vt* éviter

await [ə'weɪt] *vt* attendre

awake [ə'weɪk] (*pt* **awoke**, *pp* **awoken**) *adj* éveillé(e) ♦ *vt* éveiller ♦ *vi* s'éveiller; **~ to** (*dangers, possibilities*) conscient(e) de; **to be ~** être réveillé(e); **he was still ~** il ne dormait pas encore; **~ning** *n* réveil *m*

award [ə'wɔːd] *n* récompense *f*, prix *m*;

(LAW: damages) dommages-intérêts mpl
♦ vt (prize) décerner; (LAW: damages)
accorder

aware [əˈwɛəʳ] adj: ~ (of) (conscious)
conscient(e) (de); (informed) au courant
(de); **to become ~ of/that** prendre
conscience de/que; se rendre compte
de/que; **~ness** n conscience f, connaissance f

away [əˈweɪ] adj, adv (au) loin; ab-
sent(e); **two kilometres ~** à (une distance de) deux kilomètres, à deux kilomètres de distance; **two hours ~ by
car** à deux heures de voiture or de route;
the holiday was two weeks ~ il
restait deux semaines jusqu'aux vacances; **~ from loin de; he's ~ for a week**
il est parti (pour) une semaine; **to
pedal/work/laugh ~** être en train de
pédaler/travailler/rire; **to fade ~**
(sound) s'affaiblir; (colour) s'estomper;
to wither ~ (plant) se dessécher; **to
take ~** (subtract) enlever; **~
game** n (SPORT) match m à l'extérieur

awe [ɔː] n respect mêlé de crainte; **~-
inspiring** [ˈɔːɪnspaɪərɪŋ] adj impres-
sionnant(e)

awful [ˈɔːfəl] adj affreux(-euse); **an ~
lot (of)** un nombre incroyable (de); **~ly**
adv (very) terriblement, vraiment

awkward [ˈɔːkwəd] adj (clumsy) gauche, maladroit(e); (inconvenient) peu
pratique; (embarrassing) gênant(e), dé-
licat(e)

awning [ˈɔːnɪŋ] n (of tent) auvent m;
(of shop) store m; (of hotel etc) marquise f

awoke [əˈwəuk] pt of **awake**; **~n**
[əˈwəukən] pp of **awake**

axe [æks] (US **ax**) n hache f ♦ vt (project
etc) abandonner; (jobs) supprimer

axes¹ [ˈæksɪz] npl of **axe**

axes² [ˈæksiːz] npl of **axis**

axis [ˈæksɪs] (pl **axes**) n axe m

axle [ˈæksl] n (also: **~-tree**: AUT) essieu m

ay(e) [aɪ] excl (yes) oui

B, b

B [biː] n (MUS) si m; **~ road** (BRIT) route
départementale

B.A. abbr = **Bachelor of Arts**

babble [ˈbæbl] vi bredouiller; (baby,
stream) gazouiller

baby [ˈbeɪbɪ] n bébé m; (US: inf: darling): **come on, ~!** viens ma belle/mon
gars!; **~ carriage** (US) n voiture f d'enfant; **~ food** n aliments mpl pour bé-
bé(s); **~-sit** vi garder les enfants; **~-
sitter** n baby-sitter m/f; **~ wipe** n lin-
gette f (pour bébé)

bachelor [ˈbætʃələʳ] n célibataire m; **B~
of Arts/Science** n licencié(e) ès or en
lettres/sciences

back [bæk] n (of person, horse, book)
dos m; (of hand) dos, revers m; (of
house) derrière m; (of car, train) arrière
m; (of chair) dossier m; (of page) verso
m; (of room, audience) fond m; (SPORT)
arrière m ♦ vt (candidate: also: ~ up)
soutenir, appuyer; (horse: at races) parier or miser sur; (car) (faire) reculer ♦ vi
(also: ~ up: car etc) faire marche arrière
♦ adj (in compounds) de derrière, à
l'arrière ♦ adv (not for-
ward) en arrière; (returned): **he's ~** il
est rentré, il est de retour; (restitution):
throw the ball ~ renvoie la balle;
(again): **he called ~** il a rappelé; **~
seat/wheel** (AUT) siège m/roue f arrière
inv; **~ payments/rent** arriéré m de
paiements/loyer; **he ran ~** il est revenu en courant; **~ down** vi rabattre de
ses prétentions; **~ out** vi (of promise) se
dédire; **~ up** vt (candidate etc) soutenir,
appuyer; (COMPUT) sauvegarder; **~ache**
n mal m de dos; **~bencher** (BRIT) n
membre du parlement sans portefeuille;
~bone n colonne vertébrale, épine
dorsale; **~date** vt (letter) antidater;
~dated pay rise augmentation f avec
effet rétroactif; **~fire** vi (AUT) pétarder;

(*plans*) mal tourner; **~ground** *n* arrière-plan *m*; (*of events*) situation *f*, conjoncture *f*; (*basic knowledge*) éléments *mpl* de base; (*experience*) formation *f*; **family ~ground** milieu familial; **~hand** *n* (TENNIS: *also:* **~hand stroke**) revers *m*; **~hander** (BRIT) *n* (*bribe*) pot-de-vin *m*; **~ing** *n* (*fig*) soutien *m*, appui *m*; **~lash** *n* contre-coup *m*, répercussion *f*; **~log** *n*: **~log of work** travail *m* en retard; **~ number** *n* (*of magazine etc*) vieux numéro; **~pack** *n* sac *m* à dos; **~packer** *n* randonneur(-euse); **~pain** *n* mal *m* de dos; **~ pay** *n* rappel *m* de salaire; **~side** (*inf*) *n* derrière *m*, postérieur *m*; **~stage** *adv* ♦ *n* derrière la scène, dans la coulisse; **~stroke** *n* dos crawlé; **~up** *adj* (*train, plane*) supplémentaire, de réserve; (COMPUT) de sauvegarde ♦ *n* (*support*) appui *m*, soutien *m*; (*also:* **~up disk/file**) sauvegarde *f*; **~ward** *adj* (*movement*) en arrière; (*person, country*) arriéré(e); attardé(e); **~wards** *adv* (*move, go*) en arrière; (*read a list*) à l'envers, à rebours; (*fall*) à la renverse; (*walk*) à reculons; **~water** *n* (*fig*) coin reculé; bled perdu (*péj*); **~yard** *n* arrière-cour *f*

bacon ['beɪkən] *n* bacon *m*, lard *m*

bacteria [bæk'tɪərɪə] *npl* bactéries *fpl*

bad [bæd] *adj* mauvais(e); (*child*) vilain(e); (*mistake, accident etc*) grave; (*meat, food*) gâté(e), avarié(e); **his ~ leg** sa jambe malade; **to go ~** (*meat, food*) se gâter

badge [bædʒ] *n* insigne *m*; (*of policeman*) plaque *f*

badger ['bædʒə'] *n* blaireau *m*

badly ['bædlɪ] *adv* (*work, dress etc*) mal; **~ wounded** grièvement blessé; **he needs it ~** il en a absolument besoin; **~ off** *adv* dans la gêne

badminton ['bædmɪntən] *n* badminton *m*

bad-tempered ['bæd'tempəd] *adj* (*person: by nature*) ayant mauvais caractère; (: *on one occasion*) de mauvaise

humeur

baffle ['bæfl] *vt* (*puzzle*) déconcerter

bag [bæg] *n* sac *m* ♦ *vt* (*inf: take*) empocher; s'approprier; **~s of** (*inf: lots of*) des masses de; **~gage** *n* bagages *mpl*; **~gage allowance** *n* franchise *f* de bagages; **~gage reclaim** *n* livraison *f* de bagages; **~gy** *adj* avachi(e), qui fait des poches; **~pipes** *npl* cornemuse *f*

bail [beɪl] *n* (*payment*) caution *f*; (*release*) mise *f* en liberté sous caution ♦ *vt* (*prisoner: also:* **grant ~ to**) mettre en liberté sous caution; (*boat: also:* **~ out**) écoper; **on ~** (*prisoner*) sous caution; *see also* **bale**; **~ out** *vt* (*prisoner*) payer la caution de

bailiff ['beɪlɪf] *n* (BRIT) ≈ huissier *m*; (US) ≈ huissier-audiencier *m*

bait [beɪt] *n* appât *m* ♦ *vt* appâter; (*fig: tease*) tourmenter

bake [beɪk] *vt* (*faire*) cuire au four ♦ *vi* (*bread etc*) cuire (au four); (*make cakes etc*) faire de la pâtisserie; **~d beans** *npl* haricots blancs à la sauce tomate; **~d potato** *n* pomme *f* de terre en robe des champs; **~r** *n* boulanger *m*; **~ry** *n* boulangerie *f*; boulangerie industrielle; **baking** *n* cuisson *f*; **baking powder** *n* levure *f* (chimique)

balance ['bæləns] *n* équilibre *m*; (COMM: *sum*) solde *m*; (*remainder*) reste *m*; (*scales*) balance *f* ♦ *vt* mettre ou faire tenir en équilibre; (*pros and cons*) peser; (*budget*) équilibrer; (*account*) balancer; **~ of trade/payments** balance commerciale/des comptes ou paiements; **~d** *adj* (*personality, diet*) équilibré(e); (*report*) objectif(-ive); **~ sheet** *n* bilan *m*

balcony ['bælkənɪ] *n* balcon *m*; (*in theatre*) deuxième balcon

bald [bɔːld] *adj* chauve; (*tyre*) lisse

bale [beɪl] *n* balle *f*, ballot *m*; **~ out** *vi* (*of a plane*) sauter en parachute

ball [bɔːl] *n* boule *f*; (*football*) ballon *m*; (*for tennis, golf*) balle *f*; (*of wool*) pelote *f*; (*of string*) bobine *f*; (*dance*) bal *m*; **to**

play ~ (with sb) (fig) coopérer (avec qn)

ballast ['bæləst] n lest m

ball bearings npl roulement m à billes

ballerina [bælə'ri:nə] n ballerine f

ballet ['bæleɪ] n ballet m; (art) danse f (classique); ~ **dancer** n danceur(-euse) m/f de ballet; ~ **shoe** n chausson m de danse

balloon [bə'lu:n] n ballon m; (in comic strip) bulle f

ballot ['bælət] n scrutin m; ~ **paper** n bulletin m de vote

ballpoint (pen) ['bɔ:lpɔɪnt(-)] n stylo m à bille

ballroom ['bɔ:lrum] n salle f de bal

ban [bæn] n interdiction f ♦ vt interdire

banana [bə'nɑ:nə] n banane f

band [bænd] n bande f; (at a dance) orchestre m; (MIL) musique f, fanfare f; ~ **together** vi se liguer

bandage ['bændɪdʒ] n bandage m, pansement m ♦ vt bander

Bandaid ® ['bændeɪd] n (US) n pansement adhésif

bandit ['bændɪt] n bandit m

bandy-legged ['bændɪ'legɪd] adj aux jambes arquées

bang [bæŋ] n détonation f; (of door) claquement m; (blow) coup (violent) ♦ vt frapper (violemment); (door) claquer ♦ vi détoner; claquer ♦ excl pan!; ~**s** (US) npl (fringe) frange f

banish ['bænɪʃ] vt bannir

banister(s) ['bænɪstə(z)] n(pl) rampe f (d'escalier)

bank [bæŋk] n banque f; (of river, lake) bord m, rive f; (of earth) talus m, remblai m ♦ vi (AVIAT) virer sur l'aile; ~ **on** vt fus miser or tabler sur; ~ **account** n compte m en banque; ~ **card** n carte f d'identité bancaire; ~**er** n banquier m; ~**er's card** (BRIT) n = **bank card**; ~ **holiday** (BRIT) n jour férié (les banques sont fermées); ~**ing** n opérations fpl bancaires; profession f de banquier; ~**note** n billet m de banque; ~ **rate** n

taux m de l'escompte

Un **bank holiday** *en Grande-Bretagne est un lundi férié et donc l'occasion d'un week-end prolongé. La circulation sur les routes et le trafic dans les gares et les aéroports augmentent considérablement à ces périodes. Les principaux* **bank holidays**, *à part Pâques et Noël, ont lieu au mois de mai et fin août.*

bankrupt ['bæŋkrʌpt] adj en faillite; **to go** ~ faire faillite; ~**cy** n faillite f

bank statement n relevé m de compte

banner ['bænə^r] n bannière f

bannister(s) ['bænɪstə(z)] n(pl) = **ban-nister(s)**

baptism ['bæptɪzəm] n baptême m

bar [bɑ:^r] n (pub) bar m; (counter: in pub) comptoir m, bar; (rod: of metal etc) barre f; (on window etc) barreau m; (of chocolate) tablette f, plaque f; (fig) obstacle m; (prohibition) mesure f d'exclusion; (MUS) mesure f ♦ vt (road) barrer; (window) munir de barreaux; (person) exclure; (activity) interdire; ~ **of soap** savonnette f; **the B~** (LAW) le barreau; **behind ~s** (prisoner) sous les verrous; ~ **none** sans exception

barbaric [bɑ:'bærɪk] adj barbare

barbecue ['bɑ:bɪkju:] n barbecue m

barbed wire ['bɑ:bd-] n fil m de fer barbelé

barber ['bɑ:bə^r] n coiffeur m (pour hommes)

bar code n (on goods) code m à barres

bare [bɛə^r] adj nu(e) ♦ vt mettre à nu, dénuder; (teeth) montrer; **the ~ neces-sities** le strict nécessaire; ~**back** adv à cru, sans selle; ~**faced** adj impudent(e), effronté(e); ~**foot** adj, adv nu-pieds, (les) pieds nus; ~**ly** adv à peine

bargain ['bɑ:gɪn] n (transaction) mar-ché m; (good buy) affaire f, occasion f ♦

vi (*haggle*) marchander; (*negotiate*): **to ~ (with sb)** négocier (avec qn), traiter (avec qn); **into the ~** par-dessus le marché; **~ for** *vt fus*: **he got more than he ~ed for** il ne s'attendait pas à un coup pareil

barge [bɑːdʒ] *n* péniche *f*; **~ in** *vi* (*walk in*) faire irruption; (*interrupt talk*) intervenir mal à propos

bark [bɑːk] *n* (*of tree*) écorce *f*; (*of dog*) aboiement *m* ♦ *vi* aboyer

barley [bɑːlɪ] *n* orge *f*; **~ sugar** *n* sucre *m* d'orge

bar: ~maid *n* serveuse *f* de bar, barmaid *f*; **~man** (*irreg*) *n* barman *m*; **~ meal** *n* repas *m* de bistrot; **to go for a ~ meal** aller manger au bistrot

barn [bɑːn] *n* grange *f*

barometer [bəˈrɒmɪtə*] *n* baromètre *m*

baron [ˈbærən] *n* baron *m*; **~ess** [ˈbærənɪs] *n* baronne *f*

barracks [ˈbærəks] *npl* caserne *f*

barrage [ˈbærɑːʒ] *n* (*MIL*) tir *m* de barrage; (*dam*) barrage *m*; (*fig*) pluie *f*

barrel [ˈbærəl] *n* tonneau *m*; (*of oil*) baril *m*; (*of gun*) canon *m*

barren [ˈbærən] *adj* stérile

barricade [ˌbærɪˈkeɪd] *n* barricade *f*

barrier [ˈbærɪə*] *n* barrière *f*; (*fig: to progress etc*) obstacle *m*

barring [ˈbɑːrɪŋ] *prep* sauf

barrister [ˈbærɪstə*] (*BRIT*) *n* avocat (plaidant)

barrow [ˈbærəu] *n* (*wheelbarrow*) charrette *f* à bras

bartender [ˈbɑːtɛndə*] (*US*) *n* barman *m*

barter [ˈbɑːtə*] *vt*: **to ~ sth for** échanger qch contre

base [beɪs] *n* base *f*; (*of tree, post*) pied *m* ♦ *vt*: **to ~ sth on** baser *or* fonder qch sur ♦ *adj* vil(e), bas(se)

baseball [ˈbeɪsbɔːl] *n* base-ball *m*

basement [ˈbeɪsmənt] *n* sous-sol *m*

bases¹ [ˈbeɪsɪz] *npl of* **base**

bases² [ˈbeɪsiːz] *npl of* **basis**

bash [bæʃ] (*inf*) *vt* frapper, cogner

bashful [ˈbæʃful] *adj* timide; modeste

basic [ˈbeɪsɪk] *adj* fondamental(e), de base; (*minimal*) rudimentaire; **~ally** *adv* fondamentalement, à la base; (*in fact*) en fait, au fond; **~s** *npl*: **the ~s** l'essentiel *m*

basil [ˈbæzl] *n* basilic *m*

basin [ˈbeɪsn] *n* (*vessel, also GEO*) cuvette *f*, bassin *m*; (*also:* **washbasin**) lavabo *m*

basis [ˈbeɪsɪs] (*pl* **bases**) *n* base *f*; **on a trial ~** à titre d'essai; **on a part-time ~** à temps partiel

bask [bɑːsk] *vi*: **to ~ in the sun** se chauffer au soleil

basket [ˈbɑːskɪt] *n* corbeille *f*; (*with handle*) panier *m*; **~ball** *n* basket-ball *m*

bass [beɪs] *n* (*MUS*) basse *f*; **~ drum** *n* grosse caisse *f*

bassoon [bəˈsuːn] *n* (*MUS*) basson *m*

bastard [ˈbɑːstəd] *n* enfant naturel(le), bâtard(e); (*inf!*) salaud *m* (!)

bat [bæt] *n* chauve-souris *f*; (*for baseball etc*) batte *f*; (*BRIT: for table tennis*) raquette *f* ♦ *vt*: **he didn't ~ an eyelid** il n'a pas sourcillé *or* bronché

batch [bætʃ] *n* (*of bread*) fournée *f*; (*of papers*) liasse *f*

bated [ˈbeɪtɪd] *adj*: **with ~ breath** en retenant son souffle

bath [bɑːθ] *n* bain *m*; (*~tub*) baignoire *f* ♦ *vt* baigner, donner un bain à; **to have a ~** prendre un bain; *see also* **baths**

bathe [beɪð] *vi* se baigner ♦ *vt* (*wound*) laver; **bathing** *n* baignade *f*; **bathing costume, bathing suit** (*US*) *n* maillot *m* (de bain)

bath: ~robe *n* peignoir *m* de bain; **~room** *n* salle *f* de bains; **~s** *npl* (*also:* **swimming ~s**) piscine *f*; **~ towel** *n* serviette *f* de bain

baton [ˈbætən] *n* bâton *m*; (*MUS*) baguette *f*; (*club*) matraque *f*

batter [ˈbætə*] *vt* battre ♦ *n* pâte *f* à frire; **~ed** [ˈbætəd] *adj* (*hat, pan*) cabossé(e)

battery ['bætərɪ] *n* batterie *f*; (*of torch*) pile *f*; **~ farming** *n* élevage *f* en batterie

battle ['bætl] *n* bataille *f*, combat *m* ♦ *vi* se battre, lutter; **~field** *n* champ *m* de bataille; **~ship** *n* cuirassé *m*

Bavaria [bə'vɛərɪə] *n* Bavière *f*

bawl [bɔːl] *vi* hurler; (*child*) brailler

bay [beɪ] *n* (*of sea*) baie *f*; **to hold sb at ~** tenir qn à distance *or* en échec; **~ leaf** *n* laurier *m*; **~ window** *n* baie vitrée

bazaar [bə'zɑːr] *n* bazar *m*; vente *f* de charité

B & B *n abbr* = **bed and breakfast**

BBC *n abbr* (= *British Broadcasting Corporation*) la BBC

B.C. *adv abbr* (= *before Christ*) av. J.-C.

<hr>

KEYWORD

be [biː] (*pt* **was, were,** *pp* **been**) *aux vb*
1 (*with present participle: forming continuous tenses*): **what are you doing?** que faites-vous?; **they're coming tomorrow** ils viennent demain; **I've been waiting for you for 2 hours** je t'attends depuis 2 heures

2 (*with passive: forming passives*) être; **to be killed** être tué(e); **he was nowhere to be seen** on ne le voyait nulle part

3 (*in tag questions*): **it was fun, wasn't it?** c'était drôle, n'est-ce pas?; **she's back, is she?** elle est rentrée, n'est-ce pas *or* alors?

4 (*+to +infinitive*): **the house is to be sold** la maison doit être vendue; **he's not to open it** il ne doit pas l'ouvrir

♦ *vb + complement* **1** (*gen*) être; **I'm English** je suis anglais(e); **I'm tired** je suis fatigué(e); **I'm hot/cold** j'ai chaud/froid; **he's a doctor** il est médecin; **2 and 2 are 4** 2 et 2 font 4

2 (*of health*): **how are you?** comment allez-vous?; **he's fine now** il va bien maintenant; **he's very ill** il est très malade

3 (*of age*) avoir; **how old are you?** quel âge avez-vous?; **I'm sixteen (years old)** j'ai seize ans

4 (*cost*) coûter; **how much was the meal?** combien a coûté le repas?; **that'll be £5, please** ça fera 5 livres, s'il vous plaît

♦ *vi* **1** (*exist, occur etc*) être, exister; **the prettiest girl that ever was** la fille la plus jolie qui ait jamais existé; **be that as it may** quoi qu'il en soit; **so be it** soit

2 (*referring to place*) être, se trouver; **I won't be here tomorrow** je ne serai pas là demain; **Edinburgh is in Scotland** Édimbourg est *or* se trouve en Écosse

3 (*referring to movement*) aller; **where have you been?** où êtes-vous allé(s)?

♦ *impers vb* **1** (*referring to time, distance*) être; **it's 5 o'clock** il est 5 heures; **it's the 28th of April** c'est le 28 avril; **it's 10 km to the village** le village est à 10 km

2 (*referring to the weather*) faire; **it's too hot/cold** il fait trop chaud/froid; **it's windy** il y a du vent

3 (*emphatic*): **it's me/the postman** c'est moi/le facteur

<hr>

beach [biːtʃ] *n* plage *f* ♦ *vt* échouer; **~ towel** *n* serviette *f* de plage

beacon ['biːkən] *n* (*lighthouse*) fanal *m*; (*marker*) balise *f*

bead [biːd] *n* perle *f*

beak [biːk] *n* bec *m*

beaker ['biːkər] *n* gobelet *m*

beam [biːm] *n* poutre *f*; (*of light*) rayon *m* ♦ *vi* rayonner

bean [biːn] *n* haricot *m*; (*of coffee*) grain *m*; **runner ~** haricot *m* à rames; **broad ~** fève *f*; **~sprouts** *npl* germes *mpl* de soja

bear [bɛər] (*pt* **bore,** *pp* **borne**) *n* ours *m* ♦ *vt* porter; (*endure*) supporter ♦ *vi*: **to ~ right/left** obliquer à droite/gauche, se diriger vers la droite/gauche; ~ **out** vt corroborer, confirmer; ~ **up** vi (person) tenir le coup

beard [bɪəd] n barbe f; ~**ed** adj barbu(e)

bearer ['bɛərəʳ] n porteur m; (of passport) titulaire m/f

bearing ['bɛərɪŋ] n maintien m, allure f; (connection) rapport m; ~**s** npl (also: **ball** ~**s**) roulement m (à billes); **to take a** ~ faire le point

beast [bi:st] n bête f; (inf: person) brute f; ~**ly** adj infect(e)

beat [bi:t] (pt **beat**, pp **beaten**) n battement m; (MUS) temps m, mesure f; (of policeman) ronde f ♦ vt, vi battre; **off the** ~ **en track** hors des chemins or sentiers battus; ~ **it!** (inf) fiche(-moi) le camp!; ~ **off** vt repousser; ~ **up** vt (inf: person) tabasser; (eggs) battre; ~**ing** n raclée f

beautiful ['bju:tɪful] adj beau (belle); ~**ly** adv admirablement

beauty ['bju:tɪ] n beauté f; ~ **parlour** n institut m de beauté; ~ **salon** n, ~ **shop** n = ~ **parlour**; ~ **spot** (BRIT) n (TOURISM) site naturel (d'une grande beauté)

beaver ['bi:vəʳ] n castor m

because [bɪ'kɔz] conj parce que; ~ **of** prep à cause de

beck [bɛk] n: **to be at sb's** ~ **and call** être à l'entière disposition de qn

beckon ['bɛkən] vt (also: ~ **to**) faire signe (de venir) à

become [bɪ'kʌm] (irreg: like **come**) vi devenir; **to** ~ **fat/thin** grossir/maigrir; **becoming** adj (behaviour) convenable, bienséant(e); (clothes) seyant(e)

bed [bɛd] n lit m; (of flowers) parterre m; (of coal, clay) couche f; (of sea) fond m; **to go to** ~ aller se coucher; ~ **and breakfast** n (terms) chambre et petit déjeuner; (place) voir encadré; ~**clothes** npl couvertures fpl et draps mpl; ~**ding** n literie f; ~ **linen** n draps mpl de lit (et taies fpl d'oreillers), literie f

---

| **bed and breakfast** |

Un **bed and breakfast** est une petite pension dans une maison particulière ou une ferme où l'on peut louer une chambre avec petit déjeuner compris pour un prix modique par rapport à ce que l'on paierait dans un hôtel. Ces établissements sont communément appelés B & B, et sont signalés par une pancarte dans le jardin ou au-dessus de la porte.

---

bedraggled [bɪ'drægld] adj (person, clothes) débraillé(e); (hair: wet) trempé(e)

bed: ~**ridden** adj cloué(e) au lit; ~**room** n chambre f (à coucher); ~**side** n: **at sb's** ~**side** au chevet de qn; ~**sit(ter)** (BRIT) n chambre meublée, studio m; ~**spread** n couvre-lit m, dessus-de-lit m inv; ~**time** n heure f du coucher

bee [bi:] n abeille f

beech [bi:tʃ] n hêtre m

beef [bi:f] n bœuf m; **roast** ~ rosbif m; ~**burger** n hamburger m; ~**eater** n hallebardier m de la Tour de Londres

bee: ~**hive** n ruche f; ~**line** n: **to make a** ~**line for** se diriger tout droit vers

been [bi:n] pp of **be**

beer [bɪəʳ] n bière f

beet [bi:t] n (vegetable) betterave f; (US: also: **red** ~) betterave (potagère)

beetle ['bi:tl] n scarabée m

beetroot ['bi:tru:t] (BRIT) n betterave f

before [bɪ'fɔːʳ] prep (in time) avant; (in space) devant ♦ conj avant que +sub; avant de ♦ adv avant; devant; ~ **going** avant de partir; ~ **she goes** avant qu'elle ne parte; **the week** ~ la semaine précédente or d'avant; **I've seen it** ~ je l'ai déjà vu; ~**hand** adv au préalable, à l'avance

beg [bɛg] vi mendier ♦ vt mendier; (forgiveness, mercy etc) demander; (entreat) supplier; see also **pardon**

began [bɪ'gæn] *pt of* **begin**

beggar ['begə^r] *n* mendiant(e)

begin [bɪ'gɪn] (*pt* **began**, *pp* **begun**) *vt, vi* commencer; **to ~ doing** *or* **to do sth** commencer à *or* de faire qch; **~ner** *n* débutant(e); **~ning** *n* commencement *m*, début *m*

behalf [bɪ'hɑːf] *n*: **on ~ of**, (*US*) **in ~ of** (*representing*) de la part de; (*for benefit of*) pour le compte de; **on my/his ~** pour moi/lui

behave [bɪ'heɪv] *vi* se conduire, se comporter; (*well*: *also*: **~ o.s.**) se conduire bien *or* comme il faut; **behaviour** (*US* **behavior**) [bɪ'heɪvjə^r] *n* comportement *m*, conduite *f*

behead [bɪ'hed] *vt* décapiter

behind [bɪ'haɪnd] *prep* derrière; (*time, progress*) en retard sur; (*work, studies*) en retard dans ♦ *adv* derrière ♦ *n* derrière *m*; **to be ~** (*schedule*) avoir du retard; **~ the scenes** dans les coulisses

behold [bɪ'həʊld] (*irreg*: *like* **hold**) *vt* apercevoir, voir

beige [beɪʒ] *adj* beige

Beijing ['beɪ'dʒɪŋ] *n* Bei-jing, Pékin

being ['biːɪŋ] *n* être *m*

Beirut [beɪ'ruːt] *n* Beyrouth

Belarus [belə'ruːs] *n* Bélarus *f*

belated [bɪ'leɪtɪd] *adj* tardif(-ive)

belch [beltʃ] *vi* avoir un renvoi, roter ♦ *vt* (*also*: **~ out**: *smoke etc*) vomir, cracher

Belgian ['beldʒən] *adj* belge, de Belgique ♦ *n* Belge *m/f*

Belgium ['beldʒəm] *n* Belgique *f*

belie [bɪ'laɪ] *vt* démentir

belief [bɪ'liːf] *n* (*opinion*) conviction *f*; (*trust, faith*) foi *f*

believe [bɪ'liːv] *vt, vi* croire; **to ~ in** (*God*) croire en; (*method, ghosts*) croire à; **~r** *n* (*in idea, activity*): **~r in** partisan(e) de; (*REL*) croyant(e)

belittle [bɪ'lɪtl] *vt* déprécier, rabaisser

bell [bel] *n* cloche *f*; (*small*) clochette *f*, grelot *m*; (*on door*) sonnette *f*; (*electric*) sonnerie *f*

belligerent [bɪ'lɪdʒərənt] *adj* (*person, attitude*) agressif(-ive)

bellow ['beləʊ] *vi* (*bull*) meugler; (*person*) brailler

belly ['belɪ] *n* ventre *m*

belong [bɪ'lɒŋ] *vi*: **to ~ to** appartenir à; (*club etc*) faire partie de; **this book ~s here** ce livre va ici; **~ings** *npl* affaires *fpl*, possessions *fpl*

beloved [bɪ'lʌvɪd] *adj* (bien-)aimé(e)

below [bɪ'ləʊ] *prep* sous, au-dessous de ♦ *adv* en dessous; **see ~** voir plus bas *or* plus loin *or* ci-dessous

belt [belt] *n* ceinture *f*; (*of land*) région *f*; (*TECH*) courroie *f* ♦ *vt* (*thrash*) donner une raclée à; **~way** (*US*) *n* (*AUT*) route *f* de ceinture; (: *motorway*) périphérique *m*

bemused [bɪ'mjuːzd] *adj* stupéfié(e)

bench [bentʃ] *n* (*gen, also BRIT: POL*) banc *m*; (*in workshop*) établi *m*; **the B~** (*LAW: judge*) le juge; (: *judges collectively*) la magistrature, la Cour

bend [bend] (*pt, pp* **bent**) *vt* courber; (*leg, arm*) plier ♦ *vi* se courber ♦ *n* (*BRIT: in road*) virage *m*, tournant *m*; (*in pipe, river*) coude *m*; **~ down** *vi* se baisser; **~ over** *vi* se pencher

beneath [bɪ'niːθ] *prep* sous, au-dessous de; (*unworthy of*) indigne de ♦ *adv* dessous, au-dessous, en bas

benefactor ['benɪfæktə^r] *n* bienfaiteur *m*

beneficial [benɪ'fɪʃl] *adj* salutaire; avantageux(-euse); **~ to the health** bon(ne) pour la santé

benefit ['benɪfɪt] *n* avantage *m*, profit *m*; (*allowance of money*) allocation *f* ♦ *vt* faire du bien à, profiter à ♦ *vi*: **he'll ~ from it** cela lui fera du bien, il y gagnera *or* s'en trouvera bien

Benelux ['benɪlʌks] *n* Bénélux *m*

benevolent [bɪ'nevələnt] *adj* bienveillant(e); (*organization*) bénévole

benign [bɪ'naɪn] *adj* (*person, smile*) bienveillant(e), affable; (*MED*) bénin(-igne)

bent [bɛnt] *pt, pp of* **bend** ♦ *n* inclination *f*, penchant *m*; **to be ~ on** être résolu(e) à

bequest [bɪ'kwɛst] *n* legs *m*

bereaved [bɪ'riːvd] *n*: **the ~** la famille du disparu

beret ['bɛreɪ] *n* béret *m*

Berlin [bəː'lɪn] *n* Berlin

berm [bəːm] (*US*) *n* (*AUT*) accotement *m*

Bermuda [bəː'mjuːdə] *n* Bermudes *fpl*

berry ['bɛrɪ] *n* baie *f*

berserk [bə'səːk] *adj*: **to go ~** (*madman, crowd*) se déchaîner

berth [bəːθ] *n* (*bed*) couchette *f*, (*for ship*) poste *m* d'amarrage, mouillage *m* ♦ *vi* (*in harbour*) venir à quai; (*at anchor*) mouiller

beseech [bɪ'siːtʃ] (*pt, pp* **besought**) *vt* implorer, supplier

beset [bɪ'sɛt] (*pt, pp* **beset**) *vt* assaillir

beside [bɪ'saɪd] *prep* à côté de; **to be ~ o.s. (with anger)** être hors de soi; **that's ~ the point** cela n'a rien à voir; **~s** *adv* en outre, de plus; (*in any case*) d'ailleurs ♦ *prep* (*as well as*) en plus de

besiege [bɪ'siːdʒ] *vt* (*town*) assiéger; (*fig*) assaillir

best [bɛst] *adj* meilleur(e) ♦ *adv* le mieux; **the ~ part of** (*quantity*) le plus clair de, la plus grande partie de; **at ~** au mieux; **to make the ~ of sth** s'accommoder de qch (du mieux que l'on peut); **to do one's ~** faire de son mieux; **to the ~ of my knowledge** pour autant que je sache; **to the ~ of my ability** du mieux que je pourrai; **~ before date** *n* date *f* de limite d'utilisation *or* de consommation; **~ man** *n* garçon *m* d'honneur

bestow [bɪ'stəu] *vt*: **to ~ sth on sb** accorder qch à qn; (*title*) conférer qch à qn

bet [bɛt] (*pt, pp* **bet** *or* **betted**) *n* pari *m* ♦ *vt, vi* parier

betray [bɪ'treɪ] *vt* trahir

better ['bɛtə'] *adj* meilleur(e) ♦ *adv* mieux ♦ *vt* améliorer ♦ *n*: **to get the ~**

of triompher de, l'emporter sur; **you had ~ do it** vous feriez mieux de le faire; **he thought ~ of it** il s'est ravisé; **to get ~** aller mieux; s'améliorer; **~ off** *adj* plus à l'aise financièrement; (*fig*): **you'd be ~ off this way** vous vous en trouveriez mieux ainsi

betting ['bɛtɪŋ] *n* paris *mpl*; **~ shop** (*BRIT*) *n* bureau *m* de paris

between [bɪ'twiːn] *prep* entre ♦ *adv*: **(in) ~** au milieu; dans l'intervalle; (*in time*) dans l'intervalle

beverage ['bɛvərɪdʒ] *n* boisson *f* (*gén sans alcool*)

beware [bɪ'wɛə'] *vi*: **to ~ (of)** prendre garde (à); **"~ of the dog"** "(attention) chien méchant"

bewildered [bɪ'wɪldəd] *adj* dérouté(e), ahuri(e)

beyond [bɪ'jɔnd] *prep* (*in space, time*) au-delà de; (*exceeding*) au-dessus de ♦ *adv* au-delà; **~ doubt** hors de doute; **~ repair** irréparable

bias ['baɪəs] *n* (*prejudice*) préjugé *m*, parti pris; **~(s)ed** *adj* partial(e), montrant un parti pris

bib [bɪb] *n* bavoir *m*, bavette *f*

Bible ['baɪbl] *n* Bible *f*

bicarbonate of soda [baɪ'kɑːbənɪt-] *n* bicarbonate *m* de soude

bicker ['bɪkə'] *vi* se chamailler

bicycle ['baɪsɪkl] *n* bicyclette *f*

bid [bɪd] (*pt* **bad** *or* **bade**, *pp* **bid(den)**) *n* offre *f*; (*at auction*) enchère *f*; (*attempt*) tentative *f* ♦ *vi* faire une enchère *or* offre ♦ *vt* faire une enchère *or* offre de; **to ~ sb good day** souhaiter le bonjour à qn; **~der** *n*: **the highest ~der** le plus offrant; **~ding** *n* enchères *fpl*

bide [baɪd] *vt*: **to ~ one's time** attendre son heure

bifocals [baɪ'fəuklz] *npl* verres *mpl* à double foyer, lunettes bifocales

big [bɪg] *adj* grand(e); gros(se); **~headed** *adj* prétentieux(-euse)

bigot ['bɪgət] *n* fanatique *m/f*, sectaire *m/f*; **~ed** *adj* fanatique, sectaire; **~ry** *n* fanatisme *m*, sectarisme *m*

big top *n* grand chapiteau

bike [baɪk] *n* vélo *m*, bécane *f*

bikini [bɪ'ki:nɪ] *n* bikini *m*

bilingual [baɪ'lɪŋgwəl] *adj* bilingue

bill [bɪl] *n* note *f*, facture *f*; (POL) projet *m* de loi; (US: banknote) billet *m* (de banque); (of bird) bec *m*; (THEATRE): **on the ~** à l'affiche; **"post no ~s"** "défense d'afficher"; **to fit** or **fill the ~** (fig) faire l'affaire; **~board** *n* panneau *m* d'affichage

billet [bɪlɪt] *n* cantonnement *m* (chez l'habitant)

billfold ['bɪlfəuld] (US) *n* portefeuille *m*

billiards ['bɪljədz] *n* (jeu *m* de) billard *m*

billion ['bɪljən] *n* (BRIT) billion *m* (million de millions); (US) milliard *m*

bimbo ['bɪmbəu] (inf) *n* ravissante idiote *f*, potiche *f*

bin [bɪn] *n* boîte *f*; (also: **dustbin**) poubelle *f*; (for coal) coffre *m*

bind [baɪnd] (pt, pp **bound**) *vt* attacher; (book) relier; (oblige) obliger, contraindre ♦ *n* (inf: nuisance) scie *f*; **~ing** (of contract) constituant une obligation

binge [bɪndʒ] (inf) *n*: **to go on a/the ~** aller faire la bringue

bingo ['bɪŋgəu] *n* jeu de loto pratiqué dans des établissements publics

binoculars [bɪ'nɔkjuləz] *npl* jumelles *fpl*

bio prefix: **~chemistry** *n* biochimie *f*; **~degradable** *adj* biodégradable; **~graphy** *n* biographie *f*; **~logical** *adj* biologique; **~logy** *n* biologie *f*

birch [bɜ:tʃ] *n* bouleau *m*

bird [bɜ:d] *n* oiseau *m*; (BRIT: inf: girl) nana *f*; **~'s-eye view** *n* vue *f* à vol d'oiseau; (fig) vue d'ensemble or générale; **~-watcher** *n* ornithologue *m/f* amateur

Biro ['baɪərəu] ® *n* stylo *m* à bille

birth [bɜ:θ] *n* naissance *f*; **to give ~ to** (subj: woman) donner naissance à; (: animal) mettre bas; **~ certificate** *n*

acte *m* de naissance; **~ control** *n* (policy) limitation *f* des naissances; (method) méthode(s) contraceptive(s); (BRIT) **~day** *n* anniversaire *m* ♦ *cpd* d'anniversaire; **~place** *n* lieu *m* de naissance; (fig) berceau *m*; **~ rate** *n* (taux *m* de) natalité *f*

biscuit ['bɪskɪt] *n* (BRIT) biscuit *m*; (US) petit pain au lait

bisect [baɪ'sɛkt] *vt* couper or diviser en deux

bishop ['bɪʃəp] *n* évêque *m*; (CHESS) fou *m*

bit [bɪt] pt of **bite** ♦ *n* morceau *m*; (of tool) mèche *f*; (of horse) mors *m*; (COMPUT) élément *m* binaire, bit *m*; **a ~ of** un peu de; **a ~ mad** un peu fou; **~ by ~** petit à petit

bitch [bɪtʃ] *n* (dog) chienne *f*; (inf!) salope *f* (!), garce *f*

bite [baɪt] (pt **bit**, pp **bitten**) *vt*, *vi* mordre; (insect) piquer ♦ *n* (insect ~) piqûre *f*; (mouthful) bouchée *f*; **let's have a ~ (to eat)** (inf) mangeons un morceau; **to ~ one's nails** se ronger les ongles

bitter ['bɪtər] *adj* amer(-ère); (weather, wind) glacial(e); (criticism) cinglant(e); (struggle) acharné(e) ♦ *n* (BRIT: beer) bière *f* (forte); **~ness** *n* amertume *f*; (taste) goût amer

black [blæk] *adj* noir(e); (colour) noir *m*; (person): B~ noir(e) ♦ *vt* (BRIT: INDUSTRY) boycotter; **to give sb a ~ eye** pocher l'œil à qn, faire un œil au beurre noir à qn; **~ and blue** couvert(e) de bleus; **to be in the ~** (in credit) être créditeur(-trice); **~berry** *n* mûre *f*; **~bird** *n* merle *m*; **~board** *n* tableau noir; **~ coffee** *n* café noir; **~currant** *n* cassis *m*; **~en** *vt* noircir; **~ ice** *n* verglas *m*; **~leg** (BRIT) *n* briseur de grève, jaune *m*; **~list** *n* liste noire; **~mail** *n* chantage *m* ♦ *vt* faire chanter, soumettre au chantage; **~ market** *n* marché noir; **~out** *n* panne *f* d'électricité, (TV etc) interruption *f* d'émission; (fainting) syncope *f*; **~ pudding** *n* boudin (noir); B~ **Sea**: **the B~ Sea** la mer Noire; **~**

sheep n brebis galeuse; **~smith** n forgeron m ♦ **~ spot** (AUT) n point noir

bladder ['blædə^r] n vessie f

blade [bleɪd] n lame f; (of propeller) pale f; **~ of grass** brin m d'herbe

blame [bleɪm] n faute f, blâme m ♦ vt: **to ~ sb/sth for sth** attribuer à qn/qch la responsabilité de qch; reprocher qch à qn/qch; **who's to ~?** qui est le fautif or coupable or responsable?

bland [blænd] adj (taste, food) doux (douce), fade

blank [blæŋk] adj blanc (blanche); (look) sans expression, dénué(e) d'expression ♦ n espace m vide, blanc m; (cartridge) cartouche f à blanc; **his mind was a ~** il avait la tête vide; **~ cheque** chèque m en blanc

blanket ['blæŋkɪt] n couverture f; (of snow, cloud) couche f

blare [blɛə^r] vi beugler

blast [blɑːst] n souffle m; (of explosive) explosion f ♦ vt faire sauter or exploser; **~-off** n (SPACE) lancement m

blatant ['bleɪtənt] adj flagrant(e), criant(e)

blaze [bleɪz] n (fire) incendie m; (fig) flamboiement m ♦ vi (fire) flamber; (fig: eyes) flamboyer; (: guns) crépiter ♦ vt: **to ~ a trail** (fig) montrer la voie

blazer ['bleɪzə^r] n blazer m

bleach [bliːtʃ] n (also: **household ~**) eau f de Javel ♦ vt (linen etc) blanchir; **~ed** adj (hair) oxygéné(e), décoloré(e)

bleak [bliːk] adj morne; (countryside) désolé(e)

bleat [bliːt] vi bêler

bleed [bliːd] (pt, pp bled) vt, vi saigner; **my nose is ~ing** je saigne du nez

bleeper ['bliːpə^r] n (device) bip m

blemish ['blemɪʃ] n défaut m; (on fruit, reputation) tache f

blend [blend] n mélange m ♦ vt mélanger ♦ vi (colours etc: also: **~ in**) se mélanger, se fondre; **~er** n mixeur m

bless [bles] (pt, pp blessed or blest) vt bénir; **~ you!** (after sneeze) à vos sou-

haits!; **~ing** n bénédiction f; (godsend) bienfait m

blew [bluː] pt of **blow**

blight [blaɪt] vt (hopes etc) anéantir; (life) briser

blimey ['blaɪmɪ] (BRIT: inf) excl mince alors!

blind [blaɪnd] adj aveugle ♦ n (for window) store m ♦ vt aveugler; **~ alley** n impasse f; **~ corner** (BRIT) n virage m sans visibilité; **~fold** n bandeau m ♦ adj, adv les yeux bandés ♦ vt bander les yeux à; **~ly** adv aveuglément; **~ness** n cécité f; **~ spot** n (AUT etc) angle mort; **that is her ~ spot** (fig) elle refuse de voir clair sur ce point

blink [blɪŋk] vi cligner des yeux; (light) clignoter; **~ers** npl œillères fpl

bliss [blɪs] n félicité f, bonheur m sans mélange

blister ['blɪstə^r] n (on skin) ampoule f, cloque f; (on paintwork, rubber) boursouflure f ♦ vi (paint) se boursoufler, se cloquer

blizzard ['blɪzəd] n blizzard m, tempête f de neige

bloated ['bləʊtɪd] n (face) bouffi(e); (stomach, person) gonflé(e)

blob [blɒb] n (drop) goutte f; (stain, spot) tache f

block [blɒk] n bloc m; (in pipes) obstruction f; (toy) cube m; (of buildings) pâté m (de maisons) ♦ vt bloquer; (fig) faire obstacle à; **~ of flats** (BRIT) immeuble (locatif); **mental ~** trou m de mémoire; **~ade** [blɒ'keɪd] n blocus m; **~age** n obstruction f; **~buster** n (film, book) grand succès; **~ letters** npl majuscules fpl

bloke [bləʊk] (BRIT: inf) n type m

blond(e) [blɒnd] adj, n blond(e) f

blood [blʌd] n sang m; **~ donor** n donneur(-euse) de sang; **~ group** n groupe sanguin; **~hound** n limier m; **~ poisoning** n empoisonnement m du sang; **~ pressure** n tension f (artérielle); **~shed** n effusion f de sang, carna-

bloom   330   **body**

ge m; ~ **sports** npl sports mpl sanguinaires; ~**shot** adj: ~**shot eyes** yeux injectés de sang; ~**stream** n sang m, système sanguin; ~ **test** n prise f de sang; ~**thirsty** adj sanguinaire; ~ **vessel** n vaisseau sanguin; ~**y** adj sanglant(e); (nose) en sang; (BRIT: inf!): **this ~y ...** ce foutu ... (!), ce putain de ... (!); ~**y strong/good** vachement or sacrément fort/bon; ~**y-minded** (BRIT: inf) adj contrariant(e), obstiné(e)

bloom [blu:m] n fleur f ♦ vi être en fleur

blossom ['blɔsəm] n fleur(s) f(pl) ♦ vi être en fleurs; (fig) s'épanouir; **to ~ into** devenir

blot [blɔt] n tache f ♦ vt tacher; ~ **out** vt (memories) effacer; (view) cacher, masquer

blotchy ['blɔtʃɪ] adj (complexion) couvert(e) de marbrures

blotting paper ['blɔtɪŋ-] n buvard m

blouse [blauz] n chemisier m, corsage m

blow [bləu] n (pt **blew**, pp **blown**) n coup m ♦ vi souffler ♦ vt souffler; (fuse) faire sauter; (instrument) jouer de; **to ~ one's nose** se moucher; **to ~ a whistle** siffler; ~ **away** vt chasser, faire s'envoler; ~ **down** vt faire tomber, renverser; ~ **off** vt emporter; ~ **out** vt (fire, flame) s'éteindre; ~ **over** vi s'apaiser; ~ **up** vt faire sauter; (tyre) gonfler; (PHOT) agrandir ♦ vi exploser, sauter; ~**-dry** n brushing m; ~**lamp** (BRIT) n chalumeau m; ~**-out** n (of tyre) éclatement m; ~**torch** n = **blowlamp**

blue [blu:] adj bleu(e); (fig) triste; ~**s** n (MUS): **the ~s** le blues; ~ **film/joke** n film/histoire f pornographique; **to come out of the ~** (fig) être complètement inattendu; ~**bell** n jacinthe f des bois; ~**bottle** n mouche f à viande; ~**print** n (fig) projet m, plan directeur

bluff [blʌf] vi bluffer ♦ n bluff m; **to call sb's ~** mettre qn au défi d'exécuter ses menaces

blunder ['blʌndə⁽ʳ⁾] n gaffe f, bévue f ♦ vi faire une gaffe or une bévue

blunt [blʌnt] adj (person) brusque, ne mâchant pas ses mots; (knife) émoussé(e), peu tranchant(e); (pencil) mal taillé

blur [blə:⁽ʳ⁾] n tache or masse floue or confuse ♦ vt brouiller

blush [blʌʃ] vi rougir ♦ n rougeur f

blustery ['blʌstərɪ] adj (weather) à bourrasques

boar [bɔ:⁽ʳ⁾] n sanglier m

board [bɔ:d] n planche f; (on wall) panneau m; (for chess) échiquier m; (cardboard) carton m; (committee) conseil m, comité m; (in firm) conseil d'administration; (NAUT, AVIAT): **on ~** à bord ♦ vt (ship) monter à bord de; (train) monter dans; **full ~** (BRIT) pension complète; **half ~** demi-pension f; ~ **and lodging** chambre f avec pension; **which goes by the ~** (fig) qu'on laisse tomber, qu'on abandonne; ~ **up** vt (door, window) boucher; ~**er** n (SCOL) interne m/f, pensionnaire; ~ **game** n jeu m de société; ~**ing card** n = **boarding pass**; ~**ing house** n pension f; ~**ing pass** (AVIAT, NAUT) carte f d'embarquement; ~**ing school** n internat m, pensionnat m; ~ **room** n salle f du conseil d'administration

boast [bəust] vi: **to ~ (about or of)** se vanter de

boat [bəut] n bateau m; (small) canot m; barque f; ~ **train** n train m (qui assure correspondance avec le ferry)

bob [bɔb] vi (boat, cork on water: also: ~ **up and down**) danser, se balancer

bobby ['bɔbɪ] (BRIT: inf) n ≃ agent m (de police)

bobsleigh ['bɔbsleɪ] n bob m

bode [bəud] vi: **to ~ well/ill (for)** être de bon/mauvais augure (pour)

bodily ['bɔdɪlɪ] adj corporel(le) ♦ adv dans ses bras

body ['bɔdɪ] n corps m; (of car) carrosserie f; (of plane) fuselage m; (fig: soci ety) organe m, organisme m; (: quantity) ensemble m, masse f; (of wine) corps; **~-building** n culturisme m; **~guard** n garde m du corps; **~work** n carrosserie f

bog [bɔg] n tourbière f ♦ vt: **to get ~ged down** (fig) s'enliser

bog-standard (inf) adj tout à fait ordinaire

bogus ['bəugəs] adj bidon inv; fantôme

boil [bɔɪl] vt (faire) bouillir ♦ vi bouillir ♦ n (MED) furoncle m; **to come to the (BRIT) ~ or a (US) ~** bouillir; **~ down to** vt fus (fig) se réduire or ramener à; **~ over** vi déborder; **~ed egg** n œuf m à la coque; **~ed potatoes** npl pommes fpl à l'anglaise or à l'eau; **~er** n chaudière f; **~ing point** n point m d'ébullition

boisterous ['bɔɪstərəs] adj bruyant(e), tapageur(-euse)

bold [bəuld] adj hardi(e), audacieux(-euse); (pej) effronté(e); (outline, colour) franc (franche), tranché(e), marqué(e); (pattern) grand(e)

bollard ['bɔləd] (BRIT) n (AUT) borne f lumineuse or de signalisation

bolt [bəult] n (lock) verrou m; (with nut) boulon m ♦ adv: **~ upright** droit(e) comme un piquet ♦ vt verrouiller; (TECH: also: **~ on, ~ together**) boulonner; (food) engloutir ♦ vi (horse) s'emballer

bomb [bɔm] n bombe f ♦ vt bombarder; **~ing** n (by terrorist) attentat m à la bombe; **~ disposal unit** n section f de déminage; **~er** n (AVIAT) bombardier m; **~shell** n (fig) bombe f

bond [bɔnd] n lien m; (binding promise) engagement m, obligation f; (COMM) obligation f; **in ~** (of goods) en douane

bondage ['bɔndɪdʒ] n esclavage m

bone [bəun] n os m; (of fish) arête f ♦ vt désosser; ôter les arêtes de; **~ dry** adj complètement sec (sèche); **~ idle** adj fainéant(e); **~ marrow** n moelle f osseuse

bonfire ['bɔnfaɪə*] n feu m (de joie);

(for rubbish) feu

bonnet ['bɔnɪt] n bonnet m; (BRIT: of car) capot m

bonus ['bəunəs] n prime f, gratification f

bony ['bəunɪ] adj (arm, face, MED: tissue) osseux(-euse); (meat) plein(e) d'os; (fish) plein d'arêtes

boo [bu:] excl hou!, peuh! ♦ vt huer

booby trap ['bu:bɪ-] n engin piégé

book [buk] n livre m; (of stamps, tickets) carnet m ♦ vt (ticket) prendre; (seat, room) réserver; (driver) dresser un procès-verbal à; (football player) prendre le nom de; **~s** npl (accounts) comptes mpl, comptabilité f; **~case** n bibliothèque f (meuble); **~ing office** (BRIT) n bureau m de location; **~-keeping** n comptabilité f; **~let** n brochure f; **~maker** n bookmaker m; **~seller** n libraire m/f; **~shelf** n (single) étagère f (à livres); **~shop** n librairie f; **~store** n librairie f

boom [bu:m] n (noise) grondement m; (in prices, population) forte augmentation f ♦ vi gronder; prospérer

boon [bu:n] n bénédiction f, grand avantage

boost [bu:st] n stimulant m, remontant m ♦ vt stimuler; **~er** n (MED) rappel m

boot [bu:t] n botte f; (for hiking) chaussure f (de marche); (for football etc) soulier m; (BRIT: of car) coffre m ♦ vt (COMPUT) amorcer, initialiser; **to ~** (in addition) par-dessus le marché

booth [bu:ð] n (at fair) baraque (foraine); (telephone etc) cabine f; (also: **voting ~**) isoloir m

booze [bu:z] (inf) n boissons fpl alcooliques, alcool m

border ['bɔ:də*] n bordure f; bord m; (of a country) frontière f; (also: **~ on**: country) être limitrophe de; **B~s** (GEO): **the B~s** la région frontière entre l'Écosse et l'Angleterre; **~ on** vt fus être voisin(e) de, toucher à; **~line** n (fig) ligne f de démarcation; **~line case**

cas *m* limite

bore [bɔːʳ] *pt of* **bear** ♦ *vt* (*hole*) percer; (*oil well, tunnel*) creuser; (*person*) ennuyer, raser ♦ *n* raseur(-euse); (*of gun*) calibre *m*; **to be ~d** s'ennuyer; **~dom** *n* ennui *m*; **boring** *adj* ennuyeux(-euse)

born [bɔːn] *adj*: **to be ~** naître; **I was ~ in 1960** je suis né en 1960

borne [bɔːn] *pp of* **bear**

borough ['bʌrə] *n* municipalité *f*

borrow ['bɔrəu] *vt*: **to ~ sth (from sb)** emprunter qch (à qn)

Bosnia (and) Herzegovina ['bɔznɪə(ənd)hɜːtsəgəuˈviːnə] *n* Bosnie-Herzégovine *f*; **Bosnian** *adj* bosniaque, bosnien(ne) ♦ *n* Bosniaque *m/f*

bosom ['buzəm] *n* poitrine *f*, (*fig*) sein *m*

boss [bɔs] *n* patron(ne) ♦ *vt* (*also*: **~ around/about**) mener à la baguette; **~y** *adj* autoritaire

bosun ['bəusn] *n* maître *m* d'équipage

botany ['bɔtənɪ] *n* botanique *f*

botch [bɔtʃ] *vt* (*also*: **~ up**) saboter, bâcler

both [bəuθ] *adj* les deux, l'un(e) et l'autre ♦ *pron*: **~ (of them)** les deux, tous (toutes) les deux, l'un(e) et l'autre; **they sell ~ the fabric and the finished curtains** ils vendent (et) le tissu et les rideaux (finis), ils vendent à la fois le tissu et les rideaux (finis); **~ of us went, we ~ went** nous y sommes allés (tous les deux)

bother ['bɔðəʳ] *vt* (*worry*) tracasser; (*disturb*) déranger ♦ *vi* (*also*: **~ o.s.**) se tracasser, se faire du souci ♦ *n*: **it is a ~ to have to do** c'est vraiment ennuyeux d'avoir à faire; **it's no ~** aucun problème; **to ~ doing** prendre la peine de faire

bottle ['bɔtl] *n* bouteille *f*; (*baby's*) biberon *m* ♦ *vt* mettre en bouteille(s); **~d beer** bière *f* en canette; **~d water** eau minérale; **~ up** *vt* refouler, contenir; **~ bank** *n* conteneur *m* à verre; **~neck** *n* étranglement *m*; **~-opener** *n* ouvre-

bouteille *m*

bottom ['bɔtəm] *n* (*of container, sea etc*) fond *m*; (*buttocks*) derrière *m*; (*of page, list*) bas *m* ♦ *adj* du fond; du bas; **the ~ of the class** le dernier de la classe

bough [bau] *n* branche *f*, rameau *m*

bought [bɔːt] *pt, pp of* **buy**

boulder ['bəuldəʳ] *n* gros rocher

bounce [bauns] *vi* (*ball*) rebondir; (*cheque*) être refusé(e) (*étant sans provision*) ♦ *vt* faire rebondir ♦ *n* (*rebound*) rebond *m*; **~r** (*inf*) *n* (*at dance, club*) videur *m*

bound [baund] *pt, pp of* **bind** ♦ *n* (*gen pl*) limite *f*; (*leap*) bond *m* ♦ *vi* (*leap*) bondir ♦ *vt* (*limit*) borner ♦ *adj*: **to be ~ to do sth** (*obliged*) être obligé(e) *or* avoir obligation de faire qch; **he's ~ to fail** (*likely*) il est sûr d'échouer, son échec est inévitable *or* assuré; **~ by** (*law, regulation*) engagé(e) par; **~ for** à destination de; **out of ~s** dont l'accès est interdit

boundary ['baundrɪ] *n* frontière *f*

bout [baut] *n* période *f*; (*of malaria etc*) accès *m*, crise *f*, attaque *f*; (*BOXING etc*) combat *m*, match *m*

bow¹ [bəu] *n* nœud *m*; (*weapon*) arc *m*; (*MUS*) archet *m*

bow² [bau] *n* (*with body*) révérence *f*, inclination *f* (*du buste or corps*); (*NAUT: also*: **~s**) proue *f* ♦ *vi* faire une révérence, s'incliner; (*yield*): **to ~ to** *or* **before** s'incliner devant, se soumettre à

bowels [bauəlz] *npl* intestins *mpl*; (*fig*) entrailles *fpl*

bowl [bəul] *n* (*for eating*) bol *m*; (*ball*) boule *f* ♦ *vi* (*CRICKET, BASEBALL*) lancer (la balle)

bow-legged ['bəuˈlegɪd] *adj* aux jambes arquées

bowler ['bəuləʳ] *n* (*CRICKET, BASEBALL*) lanceur *m* (de la balle); (*BRIT: also*: **~ hat**) (chapeau *m*) melon *m*

bowling ['bəulɪŋ] *n* (*game*) jeu *m* de boules; jeu *m* de quilles; **~ alley** *n* bowling m; **~ green** n terrain m de boules (gazonné et carré)

bowls [bəulz] n (game) (jeu m de) boules fpl

bow tie [bəu-] n nœud m papillon

box [bɔks] n boîte f; (also: **cardboard ~**) carton m; (THEATRE) loge f ♦ vt mettre en boîte; (SPORT) boxer avec ♦ vi boxer, faire de la boxe; **~er** n (person) boxeur m; **~er shorts** npl caleçon msg; **~ing** n (SPORT) boxe f; **B~ing Day** (BRIT) le lendemain de Noël; **~ing gloves** npl gants mpl de boxe; **~ing ring** n ring m; **~ office** n bureau m de location; **~room** n débarras m; chambrette f

---

Boxing Day

Boxing Day est le lendemain de Noël, férié en Grande-Bretagne. Si Noël tombe un samedi, le jour férié est reculé jusqu'au lundi suivant. Ce nom vient d'une coutume du XIXe siècle qui consistait à donner des cadeaux de Noël (dans des boîtes) à ses employés etc le 26 décembre.

---

boy [bɔɪ] n garçon m

boycott [ˈbɔɪkɔt] n boycottage m ♦ vt boycotter

boyfriend [ˈbɔɪfrɛnd] n (petit) ami

boyish [ˈbɔɪʃ] adj (behaviour) de garçon; (girl) garçonnier(-ière)

BR n abbr = **British Rail**

bra [brɑː] n soutien-gorge m

brace [breɪs] n (on teeth) appareil m (dentaire); (tool) vilbrequin m ♦ vt (knees, shoulders) appuyer; **~s** npl (BRIT: for trousers) bretelles fpl; **to ~ o.s.** (lit) s'arc-bouter; (fig) se préparer mentalement

bracelet [ˈbreɪslɪt] n bracelet m

bracing [ˈbreɪsɪŋ] adj tonifiant(e), tonique

bracket [ˈbrækɪt] n (TECH) tasseau m, support m; (group) classe f, tranche f (also: **brace ~**) accolade f; (also: **round ~**) parenthèse f; (also: **square ~**) cro-

chet m ♦ vt mettre entre parenthèse(s); (fig: also: **~ together**) regrouper

brag [bræg] vi se vanter

braid [breɪd] n (trimming) galon m; (of hair) tresse f

brain [breɪn] n cerveau m; **~s** npl (intellect, CULIN) cervelle f; **he's got ~s** il est intelligent; **~wash** vt faire subir un lavage de cerveau à; **~wave** n idée géniale; **~y** adj intelligent(e), doué(e)

braise [breɪz] vt braiser

brake [breɪk] n (on vehicle, also fig) frein m ♦ vi freiner; **~ light** n feu m de stop

bran [bræn] n son m

branch [brɑːntʃ] n branche f; (COMM) succursale f ♦ vi bifurquer; **~ out** vi (fig): **to ~ out into** étendre ses activités à

brand [brænd] n marque (commerciale) ♦ vt (cattle) marquer (au fer rouge); **~new** adj tout(e) neuf (neuve), flambant neuf (neuve)

brandy [ˈbrændɪ] n cognac m, fine f

brash [bræʃ] adj effronté(e)

brass [brɑːs] n cuivre m (jaune), laiton m; **the ~** (MUS) les cuivres; **~ band** n fanfare f

brat [bræt] n (pej) mioche m/f, môme m/f

brave [breɪv] adj courageux(-euse), brave ♦ n guerrier indien ♦ vt braver, affronter; **~ry** n bravoure f, courage m

brawl [brɔːl] n rixe f, bagarre f

brazen [ˈbreɪzn] adj impudent(e), effronté(e) ♦ vt: **to ~ it out** payer d'effronterie, crâner

brazier [ˈbreɪzɪəʳ] n brasero m

Brazil [brəˈzɪl] n Brésil m

breach [briːtʃ] vt ouvrir une brèche dans ♦ n (gap) brèche f; (breaking): **~ of contract** rupture f de contrat; **~ of the peace** attentat m à l'ordre public

bread [brɛd] n pain m; **~ and butter** n tartines (beurrées); (fig) subsistance f; **~bin** (BRIT) n boîte f à pain; (bigger) huche f à pain; **~crumbs** npl miettes fpl

de pain; (CULIN) chapelure f, panure f;
~line n: **to be on the ~line** être sans
le sou or dans l'indigence
breadth [brεtθ] n largeur f, (fig) ampleur f
breadwinner ['brεdwɪnər] n soutien m
de famille
break [breɪk] (pt **broke**, pp **broken**) vt
casser, briser; (promise) rompre; (law)
violer ♦ vi (se) casser, se briser; (weather) tourner; (story, news) se répandre;
(day) se lever ♦ n (gap) brèche f, (fracture) cassure f; (pause, interval) interruption f, arrêt m; (: short) pause f; (: at
school) récréation f; (chance) chance f,
occasion f favorable; **to ~ one's leg** etc
se casser la jambe etc; **to ~ a record**
battre un record; **to ~ the news to sb**
annoncer la nouvelle à qn; **~ even** rentrer dans ses frais; **~ free** or **loose** se
dégager, s'échapper; **~ open** (door etc)
forcer, fracturer; **~ down** (figures,
data) décomposer, analyser ♦ vi s'effondrer; (MED) faire une dépression (nerveuse); (AUT) tomber en panne; **~ in**
(horse etc) dresser ♦ vi (burglar) entrer
par effraction; (interrupt) interrompre; **~
into** vt fus (house) s'introduire or pénétrer par effraction dans; **~ off** vi (speaker) s'interrompre; (branch) se rompre; **~
out** vi éclater, se déclarer; (prisoner)
s'évader; **to ~ out in spots** or **a rash**
avoir une éruption de boutons; **~ up** vi
(ship) se disloquer; (crowd, meeting) se
disperser, se séparer; (marriage) se briser; (SCOL) entrer en vacances ♦ vt casser; (fight etc) interrompre, faire cesser;
~age n casse f; **~down** n (AUT) panne
f; (in communications, marriage) rupture
f; (MED: also: **nervous ~down**) dépression (nerveuse); (of statistics) ventilation
f; **~down van** (BRIT) n dépanneuse f;
~er n brisant m
breakfast ['brεkfəst] n petit déjeuner
break: ~in n cambriolage m; **~ing
and entering** n (LAW) effraction f;
~through n percée f; **~water** n brise-

lames m inv, digue f
breast [brεst] n (of woman) sein m;
(chest, of meat) poitrine f; **~feed** (irreg:
like **feed**) vt, vi allaiter; **~stroke** n brasse f
breath [brεθ] n haleine f; **out of ~** à
bout de souffle, essoufflé(e); **B~alyser**
® ['brεθəlaɪzər] n Alcootest ® m
breathe [bri:ð] vt, vi respirer; **~ in** vt, vi
aspirer, inspirer; **~ out** vt, vi expirer; **~r**
n moment m de repos or de répit;
breathing n respiration f
breathless ['brεθlɪs] adj essoufflé(e),
haletant(e)
breathtaking ['brεθteɪkɪŋ] adj stupéfiant(e)
breed [bri:d] (pt,pp **bred**) vt élever, faire
l'élevage de ♦ vi se reproduire ♦ n race
f, variété f; **~ing** n (upbringing) éducation f
breeze [bri:z] n brise f; **breezy** adj
(fraîche), aéré(e); (manner etc) désinvolte, jovial(e)
brevity ['brεvɪtɪ] n brièveté f
brew [bru:] vt (tea) faire infuser; (beer)
brasser ♦ vi (fig) se préparer, couver;
~ery n brasserie f (fabrique)
bribe [braɪb] n pot-de-vin m ♦ vt acheter; soudoyer; **~ry** n corruption f
brick [brɪk] n brique f; **~layer** n maçon
m
bridal ['braɪdl] adj nuptial(e)
bride [braɪd] n mariée f, épouse f;
~groom n marié m, époux m; **~smaid**
n demoiselle f d'honneur
bridge [brɪdʒ] n pont m; (NAUT) passerelle f (de commandement); (of nose)
arête f; (CARDS, DENTISTRY) bridge m ♦ vt
(fig: gap, gulf) combler
bridle ['braɪdl] n bride f; **~ path** n piste
or allée cavalière
brief [bri:f] adj bref (brève) ♦ n (LAW)
dossier m, cause f; (gen) tâche f ♦ vt
mettre au courant; **~s** npl (undergarment) slip m; **~case** n serviette f,
porte-documents m inv; **~ly** adv
brièvement

bright [braɪt] *adj* brillant(e); (*room, weather*) clair(e); (*clever: person, idea*) intelligent(e); (*cheerful: colour, person*) vif (vive)

brighten ['braɪtn] (*also:* ~ **up**) *vt* (*room*) éclaircir, égayer; (*event*) égayer ♦ *vi* s'éclaircir; (*person*) retrouver un peu de sa gaieté; (*face*) s'éclairer; (*prospects*) s'améliorer

brilliance ['brɪljəns] *n* éclat *m*

brilliant ['brɪljənt] *adj* brillant(e); (*sunshine, light*) éclatant(e); (*inf: holiday etc*) super

brim [brɪm] *n* bord *m*

brine [braɪn] *n* (CULIN) saumure *f*

bring [brɪŋ] (*pt, pp* **brought**) *vt* apporter; (*person*) amener; ~ **about** *vt* provoquer, entraîner; ~ **back** *vt* rapporter; ramener; (*restore*) réinstaurer; ~ **down** *vt* (*price*) faire baisser; (*enemy plane*) descendre; (*government*) faire tomber; ~ **forward** *vt* avancer; ~ **off** *vt* (*task, plan*) réussir, mener à bien; ~ **out** *vt* (*meaning*) faire ressortir; (*book*) publier; (*object*) sortir; ~ **round** *vt* (*unconscious person*) ranimer; ~ **up** *vt* (*child*) élever; (*carry up*) monter; (*question*) soulever; (*food: vomit*) vomir, rendre

brink [brɪŋk] *n* bord *m*

brisk [brɪsk] *adj* vif (vive)

bristle ['brɪsl] *n* poil *m* ♦ *vi* se hérisser

Britain ['brɪtən] *n* (*also:* **Great ~**) Grande-Bretagne *f*

British ['brɪtɪʃ] *adj* britannique ♦ *npl*: **the ~** les Britanniques *mpl*; ~ **Isles** *npl*: **the ~ Isles** les Îles *fpl* Britanniques; ~ **Rail** *n compagnie ferroviaire britannique*

Briton ['brɪtən] *n* Britannique *m/f*

Brittany ['brɪtənɪ] *n* Bretagne *f*

brittle ['brɪtl] *adj* cassant(e), fragile

broach [brəʊtʃ] *vt* (*subject*) aborder

broad [brɔːd] *adj* large; (*general: outlines*) grand(e); (: *distinction*) général(e); (*accent*) prononcé(e); **in ~ daylight** en plein jour; **~cast** (*pt, pp* **broadcast**) *n* émission *f* ♦ *vt* radiodiffuser; téléviser ♦

vi émettre; **~en** *vt* élargir ♦ *vi* s'élargir; **to ~en one's mind** élargir ses horizons; **~ly** *adv* en gros, généralement; **~-minded** *adj* large d'esprit

broccoli ['brɒkəlɪ] *n* brocoli *m*

brochure ['brəʊʃjʊər] *n* prospectus *m*, dépliant *m*

broil [brɔɪl] *vt* griller

broke [brəʊk] *pt of* **break** ♦ *adj* (*inf*) fauché(e)

broken ['brəʊkn] *pp of* **break** ♦ *adj* cassé(e); (*machine: also:* ~ **down**) fichu(e); **in ~ English/French** dans un anglais/français approximatif or hésitant; ~ **leg** *etc* jambe *etc* cassée; **~-hearted** *adj* (ayant) le cœur brisé

broker ['brəʊkər] *n* courtier *m*

brolly ['brɒlɪ] *n* (BRIT: *inf*) pépin *m*, parapluie *m*

bronchitis [brɒŋ'kaɪtɪs] *n* bronchite *f*

bronze [brɒnz] *n* bronze *m*

brooch [brəʊtʃ] *n* broche *f*

brood [bruːd] *n* couvée *f* ♦ *vi* (*person*) méditer (sombrement), ruminer

broom [brum] *n* balai *m*; (BOT) genêt *m*; **~stick** *n* manche *m* à balai

Bros. *abbr* = **Brothers**

broth [brɒθ] *n* bouillon *m* de viande et de légumes

brothel ['brɒθl] *n* maison close *f*

brother ['brʌðər] *n* frère *m*; **~-in-law** *n* beau-frère *m*

brought [brɔːt] *pt, pp of* **bring**

brow [brau] *n* front *m*; (*eyebrow*) sourcil *m*; (*of hill*) sommet *m*

brown [braun] *adj* brun(e), marron *inv*; (*hair*) châtain *inv*, brun; (*eyes*) marron *inv*; (*tanned*) bronzé(e) ♦ *n* (*colour*) brun *m* ♦ *vt* (CULIN) faire dorer; **~ bread** *n* pain *m* bis; **B~ie** *n* (*also:* **B~ie Guide**) jeannette *f*, éclaireuse (cadette); **~ie** (*US*) *n* (*cake*) gâteau *m* au chocolat et aux noix; **~ paper** *n* papier *m* d'emballage; **~ sugar** *n* cassonade *f*

browse [brauz] *vi* (*among books*) bouquiner, feuilleter les livres; (COMPUT) surfer ou naviguer sur le Net; **to ~**

through a book feuilleter un livre

browser ['brauzə'] n (COMPUT) navigateur m

bruise [bru:z] n bleu m, contusion f ♦ vt
contusionner, meurtrir

brunette [bru:'net] n (femme) brune

brunt [brʌnt] n: **the ~ of** (attack, criticism etc) le plus gros de

brush [brʌʃ] n brosse f; (painting) pinceau m; (shaving) blaireau m; (quarrel)
accrochage m, prise f de bec ♦ vt brosser; (also: **~ against**) effleurer, frôler; **~
aside** vt écarter, balayer; **~ up**
(knowledge) rafraîchir, réviser; **~wood**
n broussailles fpl, taillis m

Brussels ['brʌslz] n Bruxelles; **~
sprout** n chou m de Bruxelles

brutal ['bru:tl] adj brutal(e)

brute [bru:t] n brute f ♦ adj: **by ~ force**
par la force

BSc abbr = **Bachelor of Science**

BSE n abbr (= bovine spongiform encepha-
lopathy) ESB f, BSE f

bubble ['bʌbl] n bulle f ♦ vi bouillonner, faire des bulles; (sparkle) pétiller; **~
bath** n bain moussant; **~ gum** n bub-
blegum m

buck [bʌk] n mâle m (d'un lapin, daim
etc); (US: inf) dollar m ♦ vi ruer, lancer
une ruade; **to pass the ~ (to sb)** se
décharger de la responsabilité (sur qn);
~ up vi (cheer up) reprendre du poil de
la bête, se remonter

bucket ['bʌkɪt] n seau m

Buckingham Palace

*Buckingham Palace est la résidence
officielle londonienne du souverain
britannique depuis 1762. Construit en
1703, il fut à l'origine le palais du
duc de Buckingham. Il a été partiellement reconstruit au début du siècle.*

---

buckle ['bʌkl] n boucle f ♦ vt (belt etc)
boucler, attacher ♦ vi (warp) tordre,
gauchir; (: wheel) se voiler; se déformer

bud [bʌd] n bourgeon m; (of flower)

bouton m ♦ vi bourgeonner; (flower)
éclore

Buddhism ['budɪzəm] n bouddhisme m

Buddhist adj bouddhiste ♦ n Bouddhiste m/f

budding ['bʌdɪŋ] adj (poet etc) en herbe; (passion etc) naissant(e)

buddy ['bʌdɪ] n (US) n copain m

budge [bʌdʒ] vt faire bouger; (fig: person) faire changer d'avis ♦ vi bouger;
changer d'avis

budgerigar ['bʌdʒərɪɡɑ:'] n (BRIT) perruche f

budget ['bʌdʒɪt] n budget m ♦ vi: **to ~
for sth** inscrire qch au budget

budgie ['bʌdʒɪ] n (BRIT) n = **budgerigar**

buff [bʌf] n (colour f) chamois m ♦ n
(inf: enthusiast) mordu(e); **he's a ... ~**
c'est un mordu de ...

buffalo ['bʌfələu] n (pl ~ or ~es) n buffle
m; (US) bison m

buffer ['bʌfə'] n tampon m; (COMPUT)
mémoire f tampon

buffet¹ ['bʌfɪt] vt secouer, ébranler

buffet² ['bufeɪ] n (food, BRIT: bar) buffet
m; **~ car** (BRIT) n (RAIL) voiture-buffet f

bug [bʌɡ] n (insect) punaise f; (: gen) insecte m, bestiole f; (fig: germ) virus m,
microbe m; (COMPUT) erreur f; (fig: spy
device) dispositif m d'écoute (électronique) ♦ vt garnir de dispositifs d'écoute;
(inf: annoy) embêter; **~ged** adj sur
écoute

bugle ['bju:ɡl] n clairon m

build [bɪld] (pt, pp **built**) n (of person)
carrure f, charpente f ♦ vt construire,
bâtir; **~ up** vt accumuler, amasser; accroître; **~er** n (trade) construction f;
(house, structure) bâtiment m, construction
f; (offices, flats) immeuble m; **~ing society**
(BRIT) n so-
ciété f de crédit immobilier

---

building society

*Une building society est une mu-
tuelle dont les épargnants et emprun-
teurs sont les propriétaires. Ces mu-*

tuelles offrent deux services principaux: on peut y avoir un compte d'épargne duquel on peut retirer son argent sur demande ou moyennant un court préavis; et on peut également y faire des emprunts à long terme, par exemple pour acheter une maison.

built [bɪlt] *pt, pp of* **build**

built-in [bɪlt'ɪn] *adj* (*cupboard, device*) encastré(e); (*device*) incorporé(e); intégré(e); **~-up area** [bɪltʌp-] *n* zone urbanisée

bulb [bʌlb] *n* (*BOT*) bulbe *m*, oignon *m*; (*ELEC*) ampoule *f*

Bulgaria [bʌl'gɛərɪə] *n* Bulgarie *f*

bulge [bʌldʒ] *n* renflement *m*, gonflement *m* ♦ *vi* (*pocket, file etc*) être plein(e) à craquer; (*cheeks*) être gonflé(e)

bulk [bʌlk] *n* masse *f*, volume *m*; (*of person*) corpulence *f*; **in ~** (*COMM*) en vrac; **the ~ of** la plus grande ou grosse partie de; **~y** *adj* volumineux(-euse), encombrant(e)

bull [bul] *n* taureau *m*; (*male elephant/whale*) mâle *m*; **~dog** *n* bouledogue *m*

bulldozer [bul'dəʊzəʳ] *n* bulldozer *m*

bullet [bulɪt] *n* balle *f* (*de fusil etc*)

bulletin [bulɪtɪn] *n* bulletin *m*, communiqué *m*; (*news* ~) (bulletin d')informations *fpl*; **~ board** *n* (*INTERNET*) messagerie *f* électronique

bulletproof [bulɪtpruːf] *adj* (*car*) blindé(e); (*vest etc*) pare-balles *inv*

bullfight [bulfaɪt] *n* corrida *f*, course *f* de taureaux; **~er** *n* torero *m*; **~ing** *n* tauromachie *f*

bullion [buljən] *n* or *m* ou argent *m* en lingots

bullock [bulək] *n* bœuf *m*

bullring [bulrɪŋ] *n* arènes *fpl*

bull's-eye [bulzaɪ] *n* centre *m* (*de la cible*)

bully [bulɪ] *n* brute *f*, tyran *m* ♦ *vt* tyranniser, rudoyer

bum [bʌm] *n* (*inf: backside*) derrière *m*; (*esp US: tramp*) vagabond(e), traîne-

savates *m/f inv*

bumblebee [bʌmblbiː] *n* bourdon *m*

bump [bʌmp] *n* (*in car: minor accident*) accrochage *m*; (*jolt*) cahot *m*; (*on road etc: swelling*) bosse *f* ♦ *vt* heurter, cogner; **~ into** *vt fus* rentrer dans, tamponner; (*meet*) tomber sur; **~er** *n* pare-chocs *m inv* ♦ *adj*: **~er crop/harvest** récolte/moisson exceptionnelle; **~er cars** (*US*) *npl* autos tamponneuses; **~y** *adj* cahoteux(-euse)

bun [bʌn] *n* petit pain au lait; (*of hair*) chignon *m*

bunch [bʌntʃ] *n* (*of flowers*) bouquet *m*; (*of keys*) trousseau *m*; (*of bananas*) régime *m*; (*of people*) groupe *m*; **~es** *npl* (*in hair*) couettes *fpl*; **~ of grapes** grappe *f* de raisin

bundle [bʌndl] *n* paquet *m* ♦ *vt* (*also*: **~ up**) faire un paquet de; (*put*): **to ~ sth/sb into** fourrer ou enfourner qch/qn dans

bungalow [bʌŋgələʊ] *n* bungalow *m*

bungle [bʌŋgl] *vt* bâcler, gâcher

bunion [bʌnjən] *n* oignon *m* (*au pied*)

bunk [bʌŋk] *n* couchette *f*; **~ beds** *npl* lits superposés

bunker [bʌŋkəʳ] *n* (*coal store*) soute *f* à charbon; (*MIL, GOLF*) bunker *m*

bunting [bʌntɪŋ] *n* pavoisement *m*, drapeaux *mpl*

buoy [bɔɪ] *n* bouée *f*; **~ up** *vt* faire flotter; (*fig*) soutenir, épauler; **~ant** *adj* capable de flotter; (*carefree*) gai(e), plein(e) d'entrain; (*economy*) ferme, actif

burden [bəːdn] *n* fardeau *m* ♦ *vt* (*trouble*) accabler, surcharger

bureau [bjʊərəʊ] (*pl* **~x**) *n* (*BRIT: writing desk*) bureau *m*, secrétaire *m*; (*US: chest of drawers*) commode *f*; (*office*) bureau, office *m*; **~cracy** [bjuəˈrɔkrəsɪ] *n* bureaucratie *f*

burglar [bəːgləʳ] *n* cambrioleur *m*; **~ alarm** *n* sonnerie *f* d'alarme

Burgundy [bəːgəndɪ] *n* Bourgogne *f*

burial [berɪəl] *n* enterrement *m*

burly ['bə:lɪ] adj de forte carrure, costaud(e)

Burma ['bə:mə] n Birmanie f

burn [bə:n] (pt, pp **burned** or **burnt**) vt, vi brûler ♦ n brûlure f; ~ **down** vt incendier, détruire par le feu; **~er** n brûleur m; **~ing** adj brûlant(e); (house) en flammes; (ambition) dévorant(e)

burrow ['bʌrəu] n terrier m ♦ vt creuser

bursary ['bə:sərɪ] (BRIT) n bourse f (d'études)

burst [bə:st] (pt,pp **burst**) vt crever; faire éclater; (subj: river: banks etc) rompre ♦ vi éclater; (tyre) crever ♦ n (of gunfire) rafale f (de tir); (also: ~ **pipe**) rupture f, fuite f; **a ~ of enthusiasm/energy** un accès d'enthousiasme/d'énergie; **to ~ into flames** s'enflammer soudainement; **to ~ out laughing** éclater de rire; **to ~ into tears** fondre en larmes; **to be ~ing with** être plein (à craquer) de; (fig) être débordant(e) de; **~ into** vt fus (room etc) faire irruption dans

bury ['berɪ] vt enterrer

bus [bʌs] (pl **~es**) n autobus m

bush [buʃ] n buisson m; (scrubland) brousse f; **to beat about the ~** tourner autour du pot; **~y** adj broussailleux(-euse), touffu(e)

busily ['bɪzɪlɪ] adv activement

business ['bɪznɪs] n (matter, firm) affaire f; (trading) affaires fpl; (job, duty) travail m; **to be away on ~** être en déplacement d'affaires; **it's none of my ~** cela ne me regarde pas, ce ne sont pas mes affaires; **he means ~** il ne plaisante pas, il est sérieux; **~like** adj (firm) sérieux(-euse); (method) efficace; **~man** (irreg) n homme m d'affaires; **~ trip** n voyage m d'affaires; **~woman** (irreg) n femme f d'affaires

busker ['bʌskə] (BRIT) n musicien m ambulant

bus: ~ shelter n abribus m; **~ station** n gare routière; **~ stop** n arrêt m d'autobus

bust [bʌst] n buste m; (measurement)

tour m de poitrine ♦ adj (inf: broken) fichu(e), fini(e); **to go ~** faire faillite

bustle ['bʌsl] n remue-ménage m, affairement m ♦ vi s'affairer, se démener; **bustling** adj (town) bruyant(e), affairé(e)

busy ['bɪzɪ] adj (shop, street) très fréquenté(e) ♦ vt: **to ~ o.s.** s'occuper; **~body** n mouche f du coche, âme f charitable; **~ signal** (US) n (TEL) tonalité f occupé inv

---

KEYWORD

but [bʌt] conj mais; **I'd love to come, but I'm busy** j'aimerais venir mais je suis occupé
♦ prep (apart from, except) sauf, excepté; **we've had nothing but trouble** nous n'avons eu que des ennuis; **no-one but him can do it** lui seul peut le faire; **but for you/your help** sans toi/ton aide; **anything but that** tout sauf or excepté ça, tout mais pas ça
♦ adv (just, only) ne ... que; **she's but a child** elle n'est qu'une enfant; **had I but known** si seulement j'avais su; **all but finished** pratiquement terminé

---

butcher ['butʃə] n boucher m ♦ vt massacrer; (cattle etc for meat) tuer; **~'s (shop)** n boucherie f

butler ['bʌtlə] n maître m d'hôtel

butt [bʌt] n (large barrel) gros tonneau; (of gun) crosse f; (of cigarette) mégot m; (BRIT: fig: target) cible f ♦ vt donner un coup de tête à; **~ in** vi (interrupt) s'immiscer dans la conversation

butter ['bʌtə] n beurre m ♦ vt beurrer; **~cup** n bouton m d'or

butterfly ['bʌtəflaɪ] n papillon m; (SWIMMING: also: ~ **stroke**) brasse f papillon

buttocks ['bʌtəks] npl fesses fpl

button ['bʌtn] n bouton m; (US: badge) pin m ♦ vt (also: ~ **up**) boutonner ♦ vi se boutonner

buttress ['bʌtrɪs] n contrefort m

buy [baɪ] (pt, pp **bought**) vt acheter ♦ n achat m; **to ~ sb sth/sth from sb** acheter qch à qn; **to ~ sb a drink** offrir un verre or à boire à qn; **~er** n acheteur(-euse)

buzz [bʌz] n bourdonnement m; (inf: phone call): **to give sb a ~** passer un coup de fil à qn ♦ vi bourdonner; **~er** n timbre m électrique; **~ word** n (inf) mot m à la mode

KEYWORD

by [baɪ] prep 1 (referring to cause, agent) par, de; **killed by lightning** tué par la foudre; **surrounded by a fence** entouré d'une barrière; **a painting by Picasso** un tableau de Picasso

2 (referring to method, manner, means): **by bus/car** en autobus/voiture; **by train** par le or en train; **to pay by cheque** payer par chèque; **by saving hard, he ...** à force d'économiser, il ...

3 (via, through) par; **we came by Dover** nous sommes venus par Douvres

4 (close to, past) à côté de; **the house by the school** la maison à côté de l'école; **a holiday by the sea** des vacances au bord de la mer; **she sat by his bed** elle était assise à son chevet; **she went by me** elle est passée à côté de moi; **I go by the post office every day** je passe devant la poste tous les jours

5 (with time: not later than) avant; (: during): **by daylight** à la lumière du jour; **by night** la nuit, de nuit; **by 4 o'clock** avant 4 heures; **by this time tomorrow** d'ici demain à la même heure; **by the time I got here it was too late** lorsque je suis arrivé il était déjà trop tard

6 (amount) à; **by the kilo/metre** au kilo/au mètre; **paid by the hour** payé à l'heure

7 (MATH, measure): **to divide/multiply by 3** diviser/multiplier par 3; **a room 3**

metres by 4 une pièce de 3 mètres sur 4; **it's broader by a metre** c'est plus large d'un mètre; **one by one** un à un; **little by little** petit à petit, peu à peu

8 (according to) d'après, selon; **it's 3 o'clock by my watch** il est 3 heures à ma montre; **it's all right by me** je n'ai rien contre

9: **(all) by oneself** etc tout(e) seul(e)

10: **by the way** au fait, à propos
♦ adv 1 see go; pass etc

2: **by and by** un peu plus tard, bientôt; **by and large** dans l'ensemble

bye(-bye) ['baɪ'baɪ] excl au revoir!, salut!

by(e)-law ['baɪlɔ:] n arrêté municipal

by-: **~election** (BRIT) n élection (législative) partielle; **~gone** adj passé(e) ♦ n: **let ~gones be ~gones** passons l'éponge, oublions le passé; **~pass** n (route f de) contournement m; (MED) pontage m ♦ vt éviter; **~-product** n sous-produit m, dérivé m; (fig) conséquence f secondaire, retombée f; **~stander** n spectateur(-trice), badaud(e)

byte [baɪt] n (COMPUT) octet m

byword ['baɪwə:d] n: **to be a ~ for** être synonyme de (fig)

C, c

C [si:] n (MUS) do m

CA abbr = **chartered accountant**

cab [kæb] n taxi m; (of train, truck) cabine f

cabaret ['kæbəreɪ] n (show) spectacle m de cabaret

cabbage ['kæbɪdʒ] n chou m

cabin ['kæbɪn] n (house) cabane f, hutte f; (on ship) cabine f; (on plane) compartiment m; **~ crew** n (AVIAT) équipage m; **~ cruiser** n cruiser m

cabinet ['kæbɪnɪt] n (POL) cabinet m; (furniture) petit meuble à tiroirs et rayons; (also: display ~) vitrine f, petite armoire vitrée

cable ['keɪbl] n câble m ♦ vt câbler, télégraphier; **~-car** n téléphérique m; **~ television** n télévision f par câble

cache [kæʃ] n stock m

cackle ['kækl] vi caqueter

cactus ['kæktəs] (pl **cacti**) n cactus m

cadet [kə'dɛt] n (MIL) élève m officier

cadge [kædʒ] (inf) vt: **to ~ (from** or **off)** se faire donner (par)

Caesarian [sɪ'zɛərɪən] n (also: **~ section**) césarienne f

café ['kæfeɪ] n ≈ café(-restaurant) m (sans alcool)

cage [keɪdʒ] n cage f

cagey ['keɪdʒɪ] (inf) adj réticent(e); méfiant(e)

cagoule [kə'gu:l] n K-way ® m

Cairo ['kaɪərəu] n le Caire

cajole [kə'dʒəul] vt couvrir de flatteries or de gentillesses

cake [keɪk] n gâteau m; (of soap) morceau m; **~d** adj: **~d with** raidi(e) par, couvert(e) d'une croûte de

calculate ['kælkjuleɪt] vt calculer; (estimate: chances, effect) évaluer; **calculation** n calcul m; **calculator** n machine f à calculer, calculatrice f; (pocket) calculette f

calendar ['kæləndər] n calendrier m; **~ year** n année civile

calf [kɑ:f] (pl **calves**) n (of cow) veau m; (of other animals) petit m; (also: **~skin**) veau m, vachette f; (ANAT) mollet m

calibre ['kælɪbər] (US **caliber**) n calibre m

call [kɔ:l] vt appeler; to ~ appeler or appeler; (meeting) convoquer ♦ vi appeler; (visit: also: **~ in**, **~ round**) passer ♦ n (shout) appel m, cri m; (also: **telephone** ~) coup m de téléphone; (visit) visite f; **she's ~ed Suzanne** elle s'appelle Suzanne; **to be on ~** être de permanence; **~ back** vi (return) repasser; (TEL) rappeler; **~ for** vt fus (demand) demander; (fetch) passer prendre; **~ off** vt annuler; **~ on** vt fus (visit) rendre visite à, passer voir; (re-

quest): **to ~ on sb to do** inviter qn à faire; **~ out** vi pousser un cri or des cris; **~ up** vt (MIL) appeler, mobiliser; (TEL) appeler; **~box** (BRIT) n (TEL) cabine f téléphonique; **~ centre** n centre m d'appels; **~er** n (TEL) personne f qui appelle; (visitor) visiteur m; **~ girl** n call-girl f; **~-in** (US) n (RADIO, TV: phone-in) programme m à ligne ouverte; **~ing** n vocation f; (trade, occupation) état m; **~ing card** (US) n carte f de visite

callous ['kæləs] adj dur(e), insensible

calm [kɑ:m] adj calme ♦ n calme m ♦ vt calmer, apaiser; **~ down** vi se calmer ♦ vt calmer, apaiser

Calor gas ® ['kælər-] n butane m, butagaz m ®

calorie ['kælərɪ] n calorie f

calves [kɑ:vz] npl of **calf**

camber ['kæmbər] n (of road) bombement m

Cambodia [kæm'bəudɪə] n Cambodge m

camcorder ['kæmkɔ:dər] n caméscope m

came [keɪm] pt of **come**

camel ['kæməl] n chameau m

camera ['kæmərə] n (PHOT) appareil-photo m; (also: **cine-~**, **movie ~**) caméra f; **in ~** à huis clos; **~man** (irreg) n caméraman m

camouflage ['kæməflɑ:ʒ] n camouflage m ♦ vt camoufler

camp [kæmp] n camp m ♦ vi camper ♦ adj (man) efféminé(e)

campaign [kæm'peɪn] n (MIL, POL etc) campagne f ♦ vi faire campagne

camp: **~bed** (BRIT) n lit m de camp; **~er** n campeur(-euse); (vehicle) camping-car m; **~ing** n camping m; **to go ~ing** faire du camping; **~ing gas** ® n butane m; **~site** n campement m, (terrain m de) camping m

campus ['kæmpəs] n campus m

can¹ [kæn] n (of milk, oil, water) bidon m; (tin) boîte f de conserve ♦ vt mettre en conserve

can² [kæn] (*negative* **cannot, can't,** *conditional and pt* **could**) *aux vb* **1** (*be able to*) pouvoir; **you can do it if you try** vous pouvez le faire si vous essayez; **I can't hear you** je ne t'entends pas **2** (*know how to*) savoir; **I can swim/ play tennis/drive** je sais nager/jouer au tennis/conduire; **can you speak French?** parlez-vous français? **3** (*may*) pouvoir; **can I use your phone?** puis-je me servir de votre téléphone? **4** (*expressing disbelief, puzzlement etc*): **it can't be true!** ce n'est pas possible!; **what CAN he want?** qu'est-ce qu'il peut bien vouloir? **5** (*expressing possibility, suggestion etc*): **he could be in the library** il est peut-être dans la bibliothèque; **she could have been delayed** il se peut qu'elle ait été retardée

Canada ['kænədə] *n* Canada *m*; **Canadian** [kə'neɪdɪən] *adj* canadien(ne) ♦ *n* Canadien(ne)

canal [kə'næl] *n* canal *m*

canapé ['kænəpeɪ] *n* canapé *m*

canary [kə'nɛərɪ] *n* canari *m*, serin *m*

cancel ['kænsəl] *vt* annuler; (*train*) supprimer; (*party, appointment*) décommander; (*cross out*) barrer, rayer; **~lation** [kænsə'leɪʃən] *n* annulation *f*; suppression *f*

cancer ['kænsər] *n* (*MED*) cancer *m*; **C~** (*ASTROLOGY*) le Cancer

candid ['kændɪd] *adj* (très) franc (franche), sincère

candidate ['kændɪdeɪt] *n* candidat(e)

candle ['kændl] *n* bougie *f*; (*of tallow*) chandelle *f*; (*in church*) cierge *m*; **~light** *n*: **by ~light** à la lumière d'une bougie; (*dinner*) aux chandelles; **~stick** *n* (*also*: **~ holder**) bougeoir *m*; (*bigger, ornate*) chandelier *m*

candour ['kændər] (*US* **candor**) *n*

(grande) franchise *or* sincérité

candy ['kændɪ] *n* sucre candi; (*US*) bonbon *m*; **~-floss** (*BRIT*) *n* barbe *f* à papa

cane [keɪn] *n* canne *f*; (*for furniture, baskets etc*) rotin *m* ♦ *vt* (*BRIT*: *SCOL*) administrer des coups de bâton à

canister ['kænɪstər] *n* boîte *f*; (*of gas, pressurized substance*) bombe *f*

cannabis ['kænəbɪs] *n* (*drug*) cannabis *m*

canned [kænd] *adj* (*food*) en boîte, en conserve

cannon ['kænən] (*pl* ~ *or* ~**s**) *n* (*gun*) canon *m*

cannot ['kænɔt] = **can not**

canoe [kə'nuː] *n* pirogue *f*; (*SPORT*) canoë *m*; **~ing** *n*: **to go ~ing** faire du canoë

canon ['kænən] *n* (*clergyman*) chanoine *m*; (*standard*) canon *m*

can-opener ['kænəupnər] *n* ouvre-boîte *m*

canopy ['kænəpɪ] *n* baldaquin *m*; dais *m*

can't [kænt] = **cannot**

canteen [kæn'tiːn] *n* cantine *f*; (*BRIT*: *of cutlery*) ménagère *f*

canter ['kæntər] *vi* (*horse*) aller au petit galop

canvas ['kænvəs] *n* toile *f*

canvass ['kænvəs] *vi* (*POL*): **to ~ for** faire campagne pour ♦ *vt* (*investigate: opinions etc*) sonder

canyon ['kænjən] *n* cañon *m*, gorge *f* (profonde)

cap [kæp] *n* casquette *f*; (*of pen*) capuchon *m*; (*of bottle*) capsule *f*; (*contraceptive: also*: **Dutch ~**) diaphragme *m*; (*for toy gun*) amorce *f* ♦ *vt* (*outdo*) surpasser; (*put limit on*) plafonner

capability [keɪpə'bɪlɪtɪ] *n* aptitude *f*, capacité *f*

capable ['keɪpəbl] *adj* capable

capacity [kə'pæsɪtɪ] *n* capacité *f*; (*capability*) aptitude *f*; (*of factory*) rendement *m*

cape [keɪp] *n* (*garment*) cape *f*; (*GEO*)

cap m

caper ['keɪpə'] n (CULIN: gen pl) câpre f; (prank) farce f

capital ['kæpɪtl] n (also: ~ city) capitale f; (money) capital m; (also: ~ letter) majuscule f; ~ **gains tax** n (COMM) impôt m sur les plus-values; **~ism** n capitalisme m; **~ist** n capitaliste ♦ n capitaliste m/f; **~ize** ['kæpɪtəlaɪz] vi: to **~ize on** tirer parti de; **~ punishment** n peine capitale

Capricorn ['kæprɪkɔːn] n le Capricorne

capsize [kæp'saɪz] vt faire chavirer ♦ vi chavirer

capsule ['kæpsjuːl] n capsule f

captain ['kæptɪn] n capitaine m

caption ['kæpʃən] n légende f

captive ['kæptɪv] adj, n captif(-ive)

capture ['kæptʃə'] vt capturer, prendre; (attention) capter; (COMPUT) saisir ♦ n capture f; (data ~) saisie f de données

car [kaː'] n voiture f, auto f; (RAIL) wagon m, voiture

caramel ['kærəməl] n caramel m

caravan ['kærəvæn] n caravane f; **~ning** n: to go **~ning** faire du caravaning; **~ site** (BRIT) n camping m pour caravanes

carbohydrate [kaːbəu'haɪdreɪt] n hydrate m de carbone; (food) féculent m

carbon ['kaːbən] n carbone m; **~ dioxide** n gaz m carbonique; **~ monoxide** n oxyde m de carbone; **~ paper** n papier m carbone

car boot sale n marché aux puces où les particuliers vendent des objets entreposés dans le coffre de leur voiture

carburettor [kaːbju'retə'] (US **carburetor**) n carburateur m

card [kaːd] n carte f; (material) carton m; **~board** n carton m; **~ game** n jeu

m de cartes

cardiac ['kaːdɪæk] adj cardiaque

cardigan ['kaːdɪgən] n cardigan m

cardinal ['kaːdɪnl] adj cardinal(e) ♦ n cardinal m

card index n fichier m

cardphone n téléphone m à carte

care [keə'] n soin m, attention f; (worry) souci m; (charge) charge f, garde f ♦ vi: to **~ about** se soucier de, s'intéresser à; (person) être attaché(e) à; **~ of** chez, aux bons soins de; **in sb's ~** à la garde de qn, confié(e) à qn; **to take ~ (to do)** faire attention (à faire); **to take ~ of** s'occuper de; **I don't ~** ça m'est bien égal; **I couldn't ~ less** je m'en fiche complètement (inf); **~ for** vt fus s'occuper de; (like) aimer

career [kə'rɪə'] n carrière f ♦ vi (also: ~ **along**) aller à toute allure; **~ woman** (irreg) n femme ambitieuse

care: ~free adj sans souci, insouciant(e); **~ful** adj (thorough) soigneux(-euse); (cautious) prudent(e); **(be) ~ful!** (fais) attention!; **~fully** adv avec soin, soigneusement; prudemment; **~less** adj négligent(e); (heedless) insouciant(e); **~r** n (MED) aide m

caress [kə'res] n caresse f ♦ vt caresser

caretaker ['keəteɪkə'] n gardien(ne), concierge m/f

car-ferry ['kaːferɪ] n (on sea) ferry(-boat) m

cargo ['kaːgəu] (pl **~es**) n cargaison f, chargement m

car hire n location f de voitures

Caribbean [kærɪ'biːən] adj: **the ~ (Sea)** la mer des Antilles ou Caraïbes

caring ['keərɪŋ] adj (person) bienveillant(e); (society, organization) humanitaire

carnation [kaː'neɪʃən] n œillet m

carnival ['kaːnɪvl] n (public celebration) carnaval m; (US: funfair) fête foraine

carol ['kærəl] n: **(Christmas) ~** chant m de Noël

carp [kaːp] n (fish) carpe f

car park (BRIT) n parking m, parc m de stationnement

carpenter ['kɑːpɪntə^r] n charpentier m; **carpentry** n menuiserie f

carpet ['kɑːpɪt] n tapis m ♦ vt recouvrir d'un tapis; **~ sweeper** n balai m mécanique

car phone n (TEL) téléphone m de voiture

car rental n location f de voitures

carriage ['kærɪdʒ] n voiture f; (of goods) transport m; (: cost) port m; **~way** (BRIT) n (part of road) chaussée f

carrier ['kærɪə^r] n transporteur m, camionneur m; (company) entreprise f de transport; (MED) porteur(-euse); **~ bag** (BRIT) n sac m (en papier ou en plastique)

carrot ['kærət] n carotte f

carry ['kærɪ] vt (subj: person) porter; (: vehicle) transporter; (involve: responsibilities etc) comporter, impliquer ♦ vi (sound) porter; **to get carried away** (fig) s'emballer, s'enthousiasmer; **~ on** vi: **to ~ on with sth/doing** continuer qch/de faire ♦ vt poursuivre; **~ out** vt (orders) exécuter; (investigation) mener; **~cot** (BRIT) n porte-bébé m; **~on** (inf) n fuss) histoires fpl

cart [kɑːt] n charrette f ♦ vt (inf) transporter, trimballer (inf)

carton ['kɑːtən] n (box) carton m; (of yogurt) pot m; (of cigarettes) cartouche f

cartoon [kɑːˈtuːn] n (PRESS) dessin m (humoristique), caricature f; (BRIT: comic strip) bande dessinée; (CINEMA) dessin animé

cartridge ['kɑːtrɪdʒ] n cartouche f

carve [kɑːv] vt (meat) découper; (wood, stone) tailler, sculpter; **~ up** vt découper; (fig: country) morceler; **carving** n sculpture f; **carving knife** n couteau m à découper

car wash n station f de lavage (de voitures)

case [keɪs] n cas m; (LAW) affaire f, procès m; (box) caisse f, boîte f, étui m; (BRIT: also: **suitcase**) valise f; **in ~** en cas de; **in ~ he ... au** cas où il ...; **just in ~** à tout hasard; **in any ~** en tout cas, de toute façon

cash [kæʃ] n argent m; (COMM) argent liquide, espèces fpl ♦ vt encaisser; **to pay (in) ~** payer comptant; **~ on delivery** payable ou paiement à la livraison; **~ book** n livre m de caisse; **~ card** (BRIT) n carte f de retrait; **~ desk** (BRIT) n caisse f; **~ dispenser** (BRIT) n distributeur m automatique de billets, billetterie f

cashew [kæˈʃuː] n (also: **~ nut**) noix f de cajou

cashier [kæˈʃɪə^r] n caissier(-ère)

cashmere ['kæʃmɪə^r] n cachemire m

cash register n caisse (enregistreuse)

casing ['keɪsɪŋ] n revêtement (protecteur), enveloppe (protectrice)

casino [kəˈsiːnəu] n casino m

casket ['kɑːskɪt] n coffret m; (US: coffin) cercueil m

casserole ['kæsərəul] n (container) cocotte f; (food) ragoût m en cocotte)

cassette [kæˈset] n cassette f, musicassette f; **~ player** n lecteur m de cassettes; **~ recorder** n magnétophone m à cassettes

cast [kɑːst] (pt, pp **cast**) vt (throw) jeter; (shed) perdre; se dépouiller de; (statue) mouler; (THEATRE): **to ~ sb as Hamlet** attribuer à qn le rôle de Hamlet ♦ n (THEATRE) distribution f; (also: **plaster ~**) plâtre m; **to ~ one's vote** voter; **~ off** vi (NAUT) larguer les amarres; (KNITTING) arrêter les mailles; **~ on** vi (KNITTING) monter les mailles

castaway ['kɑːstəweɪ] n naufragé(e)

caster sugar ['kɑːstə-] (BRIT) n sucre m semoule

casting vote (BRIT) n voix prépondérante (pour départager)

cast iron n fonte f

castle ['kɑːsl] n château (fort); (CHESS) tour f

castor ['kɑːstə^r] n (wheel) roulette f; **~**

oil *n* huile *f* de ricin

castrate [kæs'treɪt] *vt* châtrer

casual ['kæʒjul] *adj (by chance)* de hasard, fait(e) au hasard, fortuit(e); *(irregular: work etc)* temporaire; *(unconcerned)* désinvolte; **~ly** *adv* avec désinvolture, négligemment; *(dress)* de façon décontractée

casualty ['kæʒjultɪ] *n* accidenté(e), blessé(e); *(dead)* victime *f*, mort(e); *(MED: department)* urgences *fpl*

casual wear *n* vêtements *mpl* décontractés

cat [kæt] *n* chat *m*

catalogue ['kætəlɔg] *(US* catalog) *n* catalogue *m* ♦ *vt* cataloguer

catalyst ['kætəlɪst] *n* catalyseur *m*

catalytic converter [kætə'lɪtɪk kən'vɜːtəʳ] *n* pot *m* catalytique

catapult ['kætəpʌlt] *(BRIT)* *n (sling)* lance-pierres *m inv*, fronde *f*

catarrh [kə'tɑːʳ] *n* rhume *m* chronique, catarrhe *m*

catastrophe [kə'tæstrəfɪ] *n* catastrophe *f*

catch [kætʃ] *(pt, pp* caught) *vt* attraper; *(person: by surprise)* prendre, surprendre; *(understand, hear)* saisir ♦ *vi (fire)* prendre; *(become trapped)* se prendre, s'accrocher ♦ *n* prise *f*; *(trick)* attrape *f*; *(of lock)* loquet *m*; **to ~ sb's attention** or **eye** attirer l'attention de qn; **to ~ one's breath** retenir son souffle; **to ~ fire** prendre feu; **to ~ sight of** apercevoir; **~ on** *vi* saisir; *(grow popular)* prendre; **~ up** *vi* se rattraper, combler son retard ♦ *vt (also:* **~ up with**) rattraper; **~ing** *adj (MED)* contagieux(-euse); **~ment area** ['kætʃmənt-] *(BRIT)* *n (SCOL)* secteur *m* de recrutement; **~ phrase** *n* slogan *m*; expression *f* (à la mode); **~y** *adj (tune)* facile à retenir

category ['kætɪgərɪ] *n* catégorie *f*

cater ['keɪtəʳ] *vi (provide food):* **to ~ (for)** préparer des repas (pour), se charger de la restauration (pour); **~ for** *(BRIT)* *vt fus (needs)* satisfaire, pourvoir à;

(readers, consumers) s'adresser à, pourvoir aux besoins de; **~er** *n* traiteur *m*; fournisseur *m*; **~ing** *n* restauration *f*; approvisionnement *m*, ravitaillement *m*

caterpillar ['kætəpɪləʳ] *n* chenille *f*

cathedral [kə'θiːdrəl] *n* cathédrale *f*

catholic ['kæθəlɪk] *adj (tastes)* éclectique, varié(e); **C~** *adj* catholique ♦ *n* catholique *m/f*

Catseye ® ['kæts'aɪ] *(BRIT)* *n (AUT)* catadioptre *m*

cattle ['kætl] *npl* bétail *m*

catty ['kætɪ] *adj* méchant(e)

caucus ['kɔːkəs] *n (POL: group)* comité local d'un parti politique; *(US: POL)* comité électoral *(pour désigner des candidats)*

caught [kɔːt] *pt, pp of* **catch**

cauliflower ['kɔlɪflauəʳ] *n* chou-fleur *m*

cause [kɔːz] *n* cause *f* ♦ *vt* causer

caution ['kɔːʃən] *n* prudence *f*; *(warning)* avertissement *m* ♦ *vt* avertir, donner un avertissement à; **cautious** *adj* prudent(e)

cavalry ['kævəlrɪ] *n* cavalerie *f*

cave [keɪv] *n* caverne *f*, grotte *f*; **~ in** *vi (roof etc)* s'effondrer; **~man** *(irreg)* *n* homme *m* des cavernes

caviar(e) ['kævɪɑːʳ] *n* caviar *m*

CB *n abbr (= Citizens' Band (Radio))* CB *f*

CBI *n abbr (= Confederation of British Industries)* groupement *du* patronat

cc *abbr = carbon copy; cubic centimetres*

CD *n abbr (= compact disc (player))* CD *m*; **CDI** *n abbr (= Compact Disk Interactive)* CDI *m*; **CD player** *n* platine *f* laser; **CD-ROM** [siːdiː'rɔm] *n abbr (= compact disc read-only memory)* CD-Rom *m*

CDT *BRIT abbr SCOL (= Craft, Design and Technology)* EMT *f*

cease [siːs] *vi, vi* cesser; **~fire** *n* cessez-le-feu *m*; **~less** *adj* incessant(e), continuel(le)

cedar ['siːdəʳ] *n* cèdre *m*

ceiling ['siːlɪŋ] *n* plafond *m*

celebrate ['sɛlɪbreɪt] *vt, vi* célébrer; **~d** *adj* célèbre; **celebration** [sɛlɪ'breɪʃən] *n* célébration *f*; **celebrity** [sɪ'lɛbrɪtɪ] *n* célébrité *f*

celery ['sɛlərɪ] *n* céleri *m* (à côtes)

cell [sɛl] *n* cellule *f*; (ELEC) élément *m* (de pile)

cellar ['sɛlər] *n* cave *f*

cello ['tʃɛləu] *n* violoncelle *m*

cellphone ['sɛlfəun] *n* téléphone *m* cellulaire

Celt [kɛlt, sɛlt] *n* Celte *m/f*; **~ic** *adj* celte

cement [sə'mɛnt] *n* ciment *m*; **~ mixer** *n* bétonnière *f*

cemetery ['sɛmɪtrɪ] *n* cimetière *m*

censor ['sɛnsər] *n* censeur *m* ♦ *vt* censurer; **~ship** *n* censure *f*

censure ['sɛnʃər] *vt* blâmer, critiquer

census ['sɛnsəs] *n* recensement *m*

cent [sɛnt] *n* (US, euro etc: coin) cent *m* (= un centième du dollar, de l'euro etc); *see also* **per**

centenary [sɛn'tiːnərɪ] *n* centenaire *m*

center ['sɛntər] (US) *n* = **centre**

centigrade ['sɛntɪgreɪd] *adj* centigrade

centimetre ['sɛntɪmiːtər] (US **centimeter**) *n* centimètre *m*

centipede ['sɛntɪpiːd] *n* mille-pattes *m inv*

central ['sɛntrəl] *adj* central(e); **C~ America** *n* Amérique centrale; **~ heating** *n* chauffage central; **~ reservation** (BRIT) (AUT) terre-plein central

centre ['sɛntər] (US **center**) *n* centre *m* ♦ *vt* centrer; **~-forward** *n* (SPORT) avant-centre *m*; **~-half** *n* (SPORT) demi-centre *m*

century ['sɛntjurɪ] *n* siècle *m*; **20th ~** XXe siècle

ceramic [sɪ'ræmɪk] *adj* céramique

cereal ['siːrɪəl] *n* céréale *f*

ceremony ['sɛrɪmənɪ] *n* cérémonie *f*; **to stand on ~** faire des façons

certain ['sɜːtən] *adj* certain(e); **for ~** certainement, sûrement; **~ly** *adv* certainement; **~ty** *n* certitude *f*

certificate [sə'tɪfɪkɪt] *n* certificat *m*

certified ['sɜːtɪfaɪd] *adj*: **by ~ mail** (US) en recommandé, avec avis de réception; **~ public accountant** (US) expert-comptable *m*

certify ['sɜːtɪfaɪ] *vt* certifier; *(award diploma to)* conférer un diplôme *etc* à; *(declare insane)* déclarer malade mental(e)

cervical ['sɜːvɪkl] *adj*: **~ cancer** cancer *m* du col de l'utérus; **~ smear** frottis vaginal

cervix ['sɜːvɪks] *n* col *m* de l'utérus

cf. *abbr* (= *compare*) cf., voir

CFC *n abbr* (= *chlorofluorocarbon*) CFC *m* (*gen pl*)

ch. *abbr* (= *chapter*) chap.

chafe [tʃeɪf] *vt* irriter, frotter contre

chain [tʃeɪn] *n* chaîne *f* ♦ *vt* (*also*: **~ up**) enchaîner, attacher (avec une chaîne); **~ reaction** *n* réaction *f* en chaîne; **~-smoke** *vi* fumer cigarette sur cigarette; **~ store** *n* magasin *m* à succursales multiples

chair [tʃeər] *n* chaise *f*; (*armchair*) fauteuil *m*; (*of university*) chaire *f*; (*of meeting, committee*) présidence *f* ♦ *vt* (*meeting*) présider; **~lift** *n* télésiège *m*; **~man** (*irreg*) *n* président *m*

chalet ['ʃæleɪ] *n* chalet *m*

chalk [tʃɔːk] *n* craie *f*

challenge ['tʃælɪndʒ] *n* défi *m* ♦ *vt* défier; (*statement, right*) mettre en question, contester; **to ~ sb to do** mettre qn au défi de faire; **challenging** *adj* (*tone, look*) de défi, provocateur(-trice); (*task, career*) qui représente un défi or une gageure

chamber ['tʃeɪmbər] *n* chambre *f*; **~ of commerce** chambre de commerce; **~maid** *n* femme de chambre; **~ music** *n* musique *f* de chambre

champagne [ʃæm'peɪn] *n* champagne *m*

champion ['tʃæmpɪən] *n* champion(ne); **~ship** *n* championnat *m*

chance [tʃɑːns] *n* (*opportunity*) occasion *f*, possibilité *f*; (*hope, likelihood*) chance *f*; (*risk*) risque *m* ♦ *vt*: **to ~ it** risquer (le coup), essayer ♦ *adj* fortuit(e), de hasard; **to take a ~** prendre un risque; **by ~** par hasard

chancellor ['tʃɑːnsələ'] *n* chancelier *m*; **C~ of the Exchequer** (BRIT) *n* chancelier *m* de l'Échiquier; ≈ ministre *m* des Finances

chandelier [ʃændə'lɪə'] *n* lustre *m*

change [tʃeɪndʒ] *vt* (alter, replace, COMM: money) changer; (hands, trains, clothes, one's name) changer de; (transform): **to ~ sb into** changer or transformer qn en ♦ *vi* (gen) changer; (one's clothes) se changer; (be transformed): **to ~ into** se changer or transformer en ♦ *n* changement *m*; (money) monnaie *f*; **to ~ gear** (AUT) changer de vitesse; **to ~ one's mind** changer d'avis; **a ~ of clothes** des vêtements de rechange; **for a ~** pour changer; **~able** *adj* (weather) variable; **~ machine** *n* distributeur *m* de monnaie; **~over** *n* (to new system) changement *m*, passage *m*; **changing** *adj* changeant(e); **changing room** (BRIT) *n* (in shop) salon *m* d'essayage; (SPORT) vestiaire *m*

channel ['tʃænl] *n* (TV) chaîne *f*; (navigable passage) chenal *m*; (irrigation) canal *m* ♦ *vt* canaliser; **the (English) C~** la Manche, **the C~ Islands** les îles de la Manche, les îles Anglo-Normandes; **the C~ Tunnel** le tunnel sous la Manche; **~-hopping** *n* (TV) zapping *m*

chant [tʃɑːnt] *n* chant *m*; (REL) psalmodie *f* ♦ *vt* chanter, scander

chaos ['keɪɔs] *n* chaos *m*

chap [tʃæp] (BRIT: inf) *n* (man) type *m*

chapel ['tʃæpl] *n* chapelle *f*; (BRIT: nonconformist's) église *f*

chaplain ['tʃæplɪn] *n* aumônier *m*

chapped [tʃæpt] *adj* (skin, lips) gercé(e)

chapter ['tʃæptə'] *n* chapitre *m*

char [tʃɑː'] *vt* (burn) carboniser

character ['kærɪktə'] *n* caractère *m*; (in novel, film) personnage *m*; (eccentric) numéro *m*, phénomène *m*; **~istic** [kærɪktə'rɪstɪk] *adj* caractéristique ♦ *n*

caractéristique *f*

charcoal ['tʃɑːkəul] *n* charbon *m* de bois; (for drawing) charbon *m*

charge [tʃɑːdʒ] *n* (cost) prix (demandé); (accusation) accusation *f*, inculpation *f* ♦ *vt*: **to ~ sb (with)** inculper qn (de); (battery, enemy) charger; (customer, sum) faire payer ♦ *vi* foncer; **~s** *npl* (costs) frais *mpl*; **to reverse the ~s** (TEL) téléphoner en P.C.V.; **to take ~ of** se charger de; **to be in ~ of** être responsable de, s'occuper de; **how much do you ~?** combien prenez-vous?; **to ~ an expense (up) to sb** mettre une dépense sur le compte de qn; **~ card** *n* carte *f* de client

charity ['tʃærɪtɪ] *n* charité *f*; (organization) institution *f* charitable or de bienfaisance, œuvre *f* (de charité)

charm [tʃɑːm] *n* charme *m*; (on bracelet) breloque *f* ♦ *vt* charmer, enchanter; **~ing** *adj* charmant(e)

chart [tʃɑːt] *n* tableau *m*, diagramme *m*; graphique *m*; (map) carte marine ♦ *vt* dresser or établir la carte de; **~s** *npl* (hit parade) hit-parade *m*

charter ['tʃɑːtə'] *vt* (plane) affréter ♦ *n* (document) charte *f*; **~ed accountant** (BRIT) *n* expert-comptable *m*; **~ flight** *n* charter *m*

chase [tʃeɪs] *vt* poursuivre, pourchasser; (also: **~ away**) chasser ♦ *n* poursuite *f*, chasse *f*

chasm ['kæzəm] *n* gouffre *m*, abîme *m*

chat [tʃæt] *vi* (also: **have a ~**) bavarder, causer ♦ *n* conversation *f*; **~ show** (BRIT) *n* causerie télévisée

chatter ['tʃætə'] *vi* (person) bavarder; (animal) jacasser ♦ *n* bavardage *m*; **my teeth are ~ing** je claque des dents; **~box** (inf) *n* moulin *m* à paroles

chatty ['tʃætɪ] *adj* (style) familier(-ère); (person) bavard(e)

chauffeur ['ʃəufə'] *n* chauffeur *m* (de maître)

chauvinist ['ʃəuvɪnɪst] *n* (male ~) phallocrate m; (nationalist) chauvin(e)

cheap [tʃiːp] adj bon marché inv, pas cher (chère); (joke) facile, d'un goût douteux; (poor quality) à bon marché, de qualité médiocre ♦ adv à bon marché, pour pas cher; ~ **day return** billet m d'aller et retour réduit (valable pour la journée); ~**er** adj moins cher (chère); ~**ly** adv à bon marché, à bon compte

cheat [tʃiːt] vi tricher, duper; (rob): **to ~ sb out of sth** escroquer qch à qn ♦ n tricheur(-euse); escroc m

check [tʃɛk] vt vérifier; (passport, ticket) contrôler; (halt) arrêter; (restrain) maîtriser ♦ n vérification f; contrôle m; (curb) frein m; (US: bill) addition f; (pattern: gen pl) carreaux mpl; (US = **cheque**) ♦ adj (pattern, cloth) à carreaux; ~ **in** vi (in hotel) remplir sa fiche (d'hôtel); (at airport) se présenter à l'enregistrement ♦ vt (luggage) (faire) enregistrer; ~ **out** vi (in hotel) régler sa note; ~ **up** vi: **to ~ up (on sth)** vérifier (qch); **to ~ up on sb** se renseigner sur le compte de qn; ~**ered** (US) adj = **chequered**; ~**ers** (US) npl jeu m de dames; ~**-in (desk)** n enregistrement m; ~**ing account** (US) n (current account) compte courant; ~**mate** n échec et mat m; ~**out** n (in shop) caisse f; ~**point** n contrôle m; ~**room** (US) n (left-luggage office) consigne f; ~**up** n (MED) examen médical, check-up m

cheek [tʃiːk] n joue f; (impudence) toupet m, culot m; ~**bone** n pommette f; ~**y** adj effronté(e), culotté(e)

cheep [tʃiːp] vi piauler

cheer [tʃɪəʳ] vt acclamer, applaudir; (gladden) réjouir, réconforter ♦ vi applaudir ♦ n (gen pl) acclamations fpl, applaudissements mpl; bravos mpl, hourras mpl; ~**s!** à la vôtre!; ~ **up** vi se dérider, reprendre courage ♦ vt remonter le moral à qn, dérider; ~**ful** adj gai(e), joyeux(-euse)

cheerio [tʃɪərɪ'əʊ] (BRIT) excl salut!, au revoir!

cheese [tʃiːz] n fromage m; ~**board** n plateau m de fromages

cheetah ['tʃiːtə] n guépard m

chef [ʃɛf] n chef (cuisinier)

chemical ['kɛmɪkl] adj chimique ♦ n produit m chimique

chemist ['kɛmɪst] n (BRIT: pharmacist) pharmacien(ne); (scientist) chimiste m/f; ~**ry** n chimie f; ~**'s (shop)** (BRIT) n pharmacie f

cheque [tʃɛk] (BRIT) n chèque m; ~**book** n chéquier m, carnet m de chèques; ~ **card** n carte f (d'identité) bancaire

chequered ['tʃɛkəd] (US **checkered**) adj (fig) varié(e)

cherish ['tʃɛrɪʃ] vt chérir

cherry ['tʃɛrɪ] n cerise f; (also: ~ **tree**) cerisier m

chess [tʃɛs] n échecs mpl; ~**board** n échiquier m

chest [tʃɛst] n poitrine f; (box) coffre m, caisse f; ~ **of drawers** n commode f

chestnut ['tʃɛsnʌt] n châtaigne f; (also: ~ **tree**) châtaignier m

chew [tʃuː] vt mâcher; ~**ing gum** n chewing-gum m

chic [ʃiːk] adj chic inv, élégant(e)

chick [tʃɪk] n poussin m; (inf) nana f

chicken ['tʃɪkɪn] n poulet m; (inf: coward) poule mouillée; ~ **out** (inf) vi se dégonfler; ~**pox** n varicelle f

chicory ['tʃɪkərɪ] n (for coffee) chicorée f; (salad) endive f

chief [tʃiːf] n chef ♦ adj principal(e); ~ **executive** (US **chief executive officer**) n directeur(-trice) général(e); ~**ly** adv principalement, surtout

chiffon ['ʃɪfɔn] n mousseline f de soie

chilblain ['tʃɪlbleɪn] n engelure f

child [tʃaɪld] (pl ~**ren**) n enfant m/f; ~**birth** n accouchement m; ~**hood** n enfance f; ~**ish** adj puéril(e), enfantin(e); ~**like** adj d'enfant, innocent(e), ~ **minder** (BRIT) n garde f d'enfants; ~**ren** ['tʃɪldrən] npl of **child**

Chile ['tʃɪlɪ] n Chili m

Chill [tʃɪl] n (of water) froid m; (of air) fraîcheur f; (MED) refroidissement m, coup m de froid ♦ vt (person) faire frissonner; (CULIN) mettre au frais, rafraîchir

chil(l)i ['tʃɪlɪ] n piment m (rouge)

chilly ['tʃɪlɪ] adj froid(e), glacé(e); (sensitive to cold) frileux(-euse); **to feel ~** avoir froid

chime [tʃaɪm] n carillon m ♦ vi carillonner, sonner

chimney ['tʃɪmnɪ] n cheminée f; **~ sweep** n ramoneur m

chimpanzee [tʃɪmpæn'ziː] n chimpanzé m

chin [tʃɪn] n menton m

China ['tʃaɪnə] n Chine f

china ['tʃaɪnə] n porcelaine f; (crockery) (vaisselle f en) porcelaine

Chinese [tʃaɪ'niːz] adj chinois(e) ♦ n inv (person) Chinois(e); (LING) chinois m

chink [tʃɪŋk] n (opening) fente f, fissure f; (noise) tintement m

chip [tʃɪp] n (gen pl: CULIN: BRIT) frite f; (: US: potato ~) chip m; (of wood) copeau m; (of glass, stone) éclat m; (also: **microchip**) puce f ♦ vt (cup, plate) ébrécher

```
chip shop
```

Un chip shop, que l'on appelle également un "fish-and-chip shop", est un magasin où l'on vend des plats à emporter. Les chip shops sont d'ailleurs à l'origine des takeaways. On y achète en particulier du poisson frit et des frites, mais on y trouve également des plats traditionnels britanniques (steak pies, saucisses, etc). Tous les plats étaient à l'origine emballés dans du papier journal. Dans certains de ces magasins, on peut s'asseoir pour consommer sur place.

chiropodist [kɪ'rɔpədɪst] (BRIT) n pédicure m/f

chirp [tʃəːp] vi pépier, gazouiller

chisel ['tʃɪzl] n ciseau m

chit [tʃɪt] n mot m, note f

chitchat ['tʃɪttʃæt] n bavardage m

chivalry ['ʃɪvəlrɪ] n esprit m chevaleresque, galanterie f

chives [tʃaɪvz] npl ciboulette f, civette f

chock-a-block ['tʃɔkə'blɔk], **chock-full** [tʃɔk'ful] adj plein(e) à craquer

chocolate ['tʃɔklɪt] n chocolat m

choice [tʃɔɪs] n choix m ♦ adj de choix

choir ['kwaɪə*] n chœur m, chorale f; **~boy** n jeune choriste m

choke [tʃəuk] vi étouffer ♦ vt étrangler; étouffer ♦ n (AUT) starter m; **street ~d with traffic** rue engorgée ou embouteillée

cholesterol [kə'lestərɔl] n cholestérol m

choose [tʃuːz] (pt **chose**, pp **chosen**) vt choisir; **to ~ to do** décider de faire, juger bon de faire; **choosy** adj: **(to be) choosy** (faire le/la) difficile

chop [tʃɔp] vt (wood) couper (à la hache); (CULIN: also: **~ up**) couper (fin), émincer, hacher (en morceaux) ♦ n (CULIN) côtelette f; **~s** npl (jaws) mâchoires fpl

chopper ['tʃɔpə*] n (helicopter) hélicoptère m, hélico m

choppy ['tʃɔpɪ] adj (sea) un peu agité(e)

chopsticks ['tʃɔpstɪks] npl baguettes fpl

chord [kɔːd] n (MUS) accord m

chore [tʃɔː*] n travail m de routine; **household ~s** travaux mpl du ménage

chortle ['tʃɔːtl] vi glousser

chorus ['kɔːrəs] n chœur m; (repeated part of song: also fig) refrain m

chose [tʃəuz] pt of **choose**; **~n** pp of **choose**

chowder ['tʃaudə*] n soupe f de poisson

Christ [kraɪst] n Christ m

christen ['krɪsn] vt baptiser

christening n baptême m

Christian ['krɪstɪən] adj, n chrétien(ne); **~ity** [krɪstɪ'ænɪtɪ] n christianisme m; **~**

name n prénom m

Christmas ['krɪsməs] n Noël m or f;
Happy or **Merry ~!** joyeux Noël!; **~
card** n carte f de Noël; **~ Day** n le jour
de Noël; **~ Eve** n la veille de Noël, la
nuit de Noël; **~ tree** n arbre m de Noël

chrome [krəʊm] n chrome m

chromium ['krəʊmɪəm] n chrome m

chronic ['krɒnɪk] adj chronique

chronicle ['krɒnɪkl] n chronique f

chronological [krɒnə'lɒdʒɪkl] adj chronologique

chrysanthemum [krɪ'sænθəməm] n
chrysanthème m

chubby ['tʃʌbɪ] adj potelé(e), ronde-
let(te)

chuck [tʃʌk] (inf) vt (throw) lancer, jeter; (BRIT: person) plaquer; (: also: **~ up**:
job) lâcher; **~ out** vt flanquer dehors or
à la porte; (rubbish) jeter

chuckle ['tʃʌkl] vi glousser

chug [tʃʌg] vi faire teuf-teuf; (also: **~
along**) avancer en faisant teuf-teuf

chum [tʃʌm] n copain (copine)

chunk [tʃʌŋk] n gros morceau

church [tʃəːtʃ] n église f; **~yard** n cimetière m

churn [tʃəːn] n (for butter) baratte f;
(also: **milk ~**) (grand) bidon à lait; **~
out** vt débiter

chute [ʃuːt] n glissoire f; (also: rubbish
~) vide-ordures m inv

chutney ['tʃʌtnɪ] n condiment m à base
de fruits au vinaigre

CIA n abbr (= Central Intelligence Agency)
CIA f

CID (BRIT) n abbr (= Criminal Investigation
Department) P.J. f

cider ['saɪdə*] n cidre m

cigar [sɪ'gɑː*] n cigare m

cigarette [sɪgə'ret] n cigarette f; **~
case** n étui m à cigarettes; **~ end** n
mégot m

Cinderella [sɪndə'relə] n Cendrillon

cinders ['sɪndəz] npl cendres fpl

cine-camera ['sɪnɪ'kæmərə] (BRIT) n caméra f

cinema ['sɪnəmə] n cinéma m

cinnamon ['sɪnəmən] n cannelle f

circle ['səːkl] n cercle m; (in cinema,
theatre) balcon m ♦ vi faire or décrire
des cercles ♦ vt (move round) faire le
tour de, tourner autour de; (surround)
entourer, encercler

circuit ['səːkɪt] n circuit m; **~ous**
[səː'kjuːɪtəs] adj indirect(e), qui fait un
détour

circular ['səːkjulə*] adj circulaire ♦ n circulaire f

circulate ['səːkjuleɪt] vi circuler ♦ vt faire circuler; **circulation** [səːkju'leɪʃən]
n circulation f; (of newspaper) tirage m

circumflex ['səːkəmfleks] n (also: **~ accent**) accent m circonflexe

circumstances ['səːkəmstənsɪz] npl
circonstances fpl; (financial condition)
moyens mpl, situation financière

circus ['səːkəs] n cirque m

CIS n abbr (= Commonwealth of Independent States) CEI f

cistern ['sɪstən] n réservoir m (d'eau);
(in toilet) réservoir de la chasse d'eau

citizen ['sɪtɪzn] n citoyen(ne); (resident):
the ~s of this town les habitants de
cette ville; **~ship** n citoyenneté f

citrus fruit ['sɪtrəs-] n agrume m

city ['sɪtɪ] n ville f, cité f; **the C~** la Cité
de Londres (centre des affaires); **~ technology college** n établissement m
d'enseignement technologique

civic ['sɪvɪk] adj civique; (authorities)
municipal(e); **~ centre** (BRIT) n centre
administratif (municipal)

civil ['sɪvɪl] adj civil(e); (polite) poli(e),
courtois(e); (disobedience, defence)
passif(-ive); **~ engineer** n ingénieur m
des travaux publics; **~ian** [sɪ'vɪlɪən] adj,
n civil(e)

civilization [sɪvɪlaɪ'zeɪʃən] n civilisation
f

civilized ['sɪvɪlaɪzd] adj civilisé(e); (fig)
où règnent les bonnes manières

civil: ~ law n code civil; (study) droit civil; **~ servant** n fonctionnaire m/f; **~**

Service n fonction publique, administration f; ~ **war** n guerre civile

clad [klæd] adj: ~ **(in)** habillé(e) (de)

claim [kleɪm] vt revendiquer; (rights, inheritance) demander, prétendre à; (assert) déclarer, prétendre ♦ vi (for insurance) faire une déclaration de sinistre ♦ n revendication f; demande f; prétention f, déclaration f; (right) droit m, titre m; ~**ant** n (ADMIN, LAW) requérant(e)

clairvoyant [klɛə'vɔɪənt] n voyant(e)

clam [klæm] n palourde f

clamber ['klæmbə'] vi grimper, se hisser

clammy ['klæmɪ] adj humide (et froid(e)), moite

clamour ['klæmə'] (US **clamor**) vi: to ~ **for** réclamer à grands cris

clamp [klæmp] n agrafe f, crampon m ♦ vt serrer; (sth to sth) fixer; (wheel) mettre un sabot à; ~ **down on** vt fus sévir or prendre des mesures draconiennes contre

clan [klæn] n clan m

clang [klæŋ] vi émettre un bruit or fracas métallique

clap [klæp] vi applaudir; ~**ping** n applaudissements mpl

claret ['klærət] n (vin m de) bordeaux m (rouge)

clarinet [klærɪ'nɛt] n clarinette f

clarity ['klærɪtɪ] n clarté f

clash [klæʃ] n choc m, (fig) conflit m ♦ vi se heurter; être or entrer en conflit; (colours) jurer; (two events) tomber en même temps

clasp [klɑːsp] n (of necklace, bag) fermoir m; (hold, embrace) étreinte f ♦ vt serrer, étreindre

class [klɑːs] n classe f ♦ vt classer, classifier

classic ['klæsɪk] adj classique ♦ n (author, work) classique m; ~**al** adj classique

classified ['klæsɪfaɪd] adj (information) secret(-ète); ~ **advertisement** n petite annonce

classmate ['klɑːsmeɪt] n camarade m/f de classe

classroom ['klɑːsrum] n (salle f de) classe f; ~ **assistant** n aide-éducateur(-trice)

clatter ['klætə'] n cliquetis m ♦ vi cliqueter

clause [klɔːz] n clause f; (LING) proposition f

claw [klɔː] n griffe f; (of bird of prey) serre f; (of lobster) pince f

clay [kleɪ] n argile f

clean [kliːn] adj propre; (clear, smooth) net(te); (record, reputation) sans tache; (joke, story) correct(e) ♦ vt nettoyer; ~ **out** vt nettoyer (à fond); ~ **up** vt nettoyer; (fig) remettre de l'ordre dans; ~-**cut** adj (person) net(te), soigné(e); ~**er** n (person) nettoyeur(-euse), femme f de ménage; (product) détachant m; ~**er's** n (also: **dry** ~**er's**) teinturier m; ~**ing** n nettoyage m; ~**liness** ['klɛnlɪnɪs] n propreté f

cleanse [klɛnz] vt nettoyer; (purify) purifier; ~**r** n (for face) démaquillant m

clean-shaven ['kliːn'ʃeɪvn] adj rasé(e) de près

cleansing department ['klɛnzɪŋ-] (BRIT) n service m de voirie

clear [klɪə'] adj clair(e); (glass, plastic) transparent(e); (road, way) libre, dégagé(e); (conscience) net(te) ♦ vt (room) débarrasser; (of people) faire évacuer; (cheque) compenser; (LAW: suspect) innocenter; (obstacle) franchir or sauter sans heurter ♦ vi (weather) s'éclaircir; (fog) se dissiper ♦ adv: ~ **of** à distance de, à l'écart de; **to ~ the table** débarrasser la table, desservir; ~ **up** vt ranger, mettre en ordre; (mystery) éclaircir, résoudre; ~**ance** n (removal) déblaiement m; (permission) autorisation f; ~-**cut** adj clair(e), nettement défini(e); ~**ing** n (in forest) clairière f; ~**ing bank** (BRIT) n banque qui appartient à une chambre de compensation; ~**ly** adv clairement; (evidently) de toute évidence;

~way (BRIT) n route f à stationnement interdit

clef [klɛf] n (MUS) clé f

cleft [klɛft] n (in rock) crevasse f, fissure f

clementine ['klemǝntaɪn] n clémentine f

clench [klɛntʃ] vt serrer

clergy ['klɜːdʒɪ] n clergé m; **~man** (irreg) n ecclésiastique m

clerical ['klerɪkl] adj de bureau, d'employé de bureau; (REL) clérical(e), du clergé

clerk [klɑːk, (US) klɜːrk] n employé(e) de bureau; (US: salesperson) vendeur (-euse)

clever ['klevǝr] adj (mentally) intelligent(e); (deft, crafty) habile, adroit(e); (device, arrangement) ingénieux(-euse), astucieux(-euse)

click [klɪk] vi faire un bruit sec or un déclic

client ['klaɪǝnt] n client(e)

cliff [klɪf] n falaise f

climate ['klaɪmɪt] n climat m

climax ['klaɪmæks] n apogée m, point culminant; (sexual) orgasme m

climb [klaɪm] vi grimper, monter ♦ vt gravir, escalader, monter sur ♦ n montée f, escalade f; **~down** vi reculade f; **~er** n (mountaineer) grimpeur(-euse), varappeur(-euse); (plant) plante grimpante; **~ing** n (mountaineering) escalade f, varappe f

clinch [klɪntʃ] vt (deal) conclure, sceller

cling [klɪŋ] (pt, pp **clung**) vi: **to ~ (to)** se cramponner (à), s'accrocher (à); (of clothes) coller (à)

clinic ['klɪnɪk] n centre médical; **~al** adj clinique; (attitude) froid(e), détaché(e)

clink [klɪŋk] vi tinter, cliqueter

clip [klɪp] n (for hair) barrette f; (also: **paper ~**) trombone m ♦ vt (fasten) attacher; (hair, nails) couper; (hedge) tailler; **~pers** npl (for hedge) sécateur m; (also: **nail ~pers**) coupe-ongles m inv; **~ping** n (from newspaper) coupure f de journal

cloak [klǝuk] n grande cape ♦ vt (fig) masquer, cacher; **~room** n (for coats etc) vestiaire m; (BRIT: WC) toilettes fpl

clock [klɔk] n (large) horloge f; (small) pendule f; **~ in** (BRIT) vi pointer (en arrivant); **~ off** (BRIT) vi pointer (en partant); **~ on** (BRIT) vi = **clock in**; **~ out** (BRIT) vi = **clock off**; **~wise** adv dans le sens des aiguilles d'une montre; **~work** n rouages mpl, mécanisme m; (of clock) mouvement m (d'horlogerie) ♦ adj mécanique

clog [klɔg] n sabot m ♦ vt boucher ♦ vi (also: **~ up**) se boucher

cloister ['klɔɪstǝr] n cloître m

close¹ [klǝus] adj (near) près, proche; (contact, link) étroit(e); (contest) très serré(e); (watch) étroit(e), strict(e); (examination) attentif(-ive), minutieux (-euse); (weather) lourd(e), étouffant(e) ♦ adv près, à proximité; **~ to** près de, proche de; **~ by** adj proche ♦ adv tout(e) près; **~ at hand** = **close by**; **a ~ friend** un ami intime; **to have a ~ shave** (fig) l'échapper belle

close² [klǝuz] vt fermer ♦ vi (shop etc) fermer; (lid, door etc) se fermer; (end) se terminer, se conclure ♦ n (end) conclusion f, fin f; **~ down** vt, vi fermer (définitivement); **~d** adj fermé(e); **~d shop** n organisation f qui n'admet que des travailleurs syndiqués

close-knit ['klǝus'nɪt] adj (family, community) très uni(e)

closely ['klǝuslɪ] adv (examine, watch) de près

closet ['klɔzɪt] n (cupboard) placard m, réduit m

close-up ['klǝusʌp] n gros plan

closure ['klǝuʒǝr] n fermeture f

clot [klɔt] n (gen: blood ~) caillot m; (inf: person) ballot m ♦ vi (blood) se coaguler; **~ted cream** crème fraîche très épaisse

cloth [klɔθ] n (material) tissu m, étoffe f; (also: **teacloth**) torchon m; lavette f

clothe [klǝuð] vt habiller, vêtir; **~s** npl

vêtements *mpl*, habits *mpl*; **~s brush** *n* brosse *f* à habits; **~s line** *n* corde *f* (à linge); **~s peg** (*US* **clothes pin**) *n* pince *f* à linge; **clothing** *n* = clothes

cloud [klaud] *n* nuage *m*; **~burst** *n* grosse averse; **~y** *adj* nuageux(-euse), couvert(e); (*liquid*) trouble

clout [klaut] *vt* flanquer une taloche à

clove [kləuv] *n* (*CULIN: spice*) clou *m* de girofle; **~ of garlic** gousse *f* d'ail

clover ['kləuvər] *n* trèfle *m*

clown [klaun] *n* clown *m* ♦ *vi* (*also:* **~ about, ~ around**) faire le clown

cloying ['klɔɪɪŋ] *adj* (*taste, smell*) écœurant(e)

club [klʌb] *n* (*society, place: also: golf ~*) club *m*; (*weapon*) massue *f*, matraque *f* ♦ *vt* matraquer ♦ *vi*: **to ~ together** s'associer; **~s** *npl* (*CARDS*) trèfle *m*; **~ class** *n* (*AVIAT*) classe *f* club; **~house** *n* club *m*

cluck [klʌk] *vi* glousser

clue [klu:] *n* indice *m*; (*in crosswords*) définition *f*; **I haven't a ~** je n'en ai pas la moindre idée

clump [klʌmp] *n*: **~ of trees** bouquet *m* d'arbres

clumsy ['klʌmzɪ] *adj* gauche, maladroit(e)

clung [klʌŋ] *pt, pp of* **cling**

cluster ['klʌstər] *n* (*of people*) (petit) groupe; (*of flowers*) grappe *f*; (*of stars*) amas *m* ♦ *vi* se rassembler

clutch [klʌtʃ] *n* (*grip, grasp*) étreinte *f*, prise *f*; (*AUT*) embrayage *m* ♦ *vt* (*grasp*) agripper; (*hold tightly*) serrer fort; (*hold on to*) se cramponner à

clutter ['klʌtər] *vt* (*also:* **~ up**) encombrer

CND *n abbr* (= *Campaign for Nuclear Disarmament*) mouvement pour le désarmement nucléaire

Co. *abbr* = **county; company**

c/o *abbr* (= *care of*) aux bons soins de

coach [kəutʃ] *n* (*bus*) autocar *m*; (*horse-drawn*) diligence *f*; (*of train*) voiture *f*, wagon *m*; (*SPORT: trainer*)

entraîneur(-euse); (*SCOL: tutor*) répétiteur(-trice) ♦ *vt* entraîner; (*student*) faire travailler; **~ trip** *n* excursion *f* en car

coal [kəul] *n* charbon *m*; **~ face** *n* front *m* de taille; **~field** *n* bassin houiller

coalition [kəuə'lɪʃən] *n* coalition *f*

coalman (*irreg*) *n* charbonnier *m*, marchand *m* de charbon

coalmine *n* mine *f* de charbon

coarse [kɔ:s] *adj* grossier(-ère), rude

coast [kəust] *n* côte *f* ♦ *vi* (*car, cycle etc*) descendre en roue libre; **~al** *adj* côtier(-ère); **~guard** *n* garde-côte *m*; (*service*) gendarmerie *f* maritime; **~line** *n* côte *f*, littoral *m*

coat [kəut] *n* manteau *m*; (*of animal*) pelage *m*, poil *m*; (*of paint*) couche *f* ♦ *vt* couvrir; **~ hanger** *n* cintre *m*; **~ing** *n* couche *f*, revêtement *m*; **~ of arms** *n* blason *m*, armoiries *fpl*

coax [kəuks] *vt* persuader par des cajoleries

cobbler ['kɔblər] *n* cordonnier *m*

cobbles ['kɔblz] (*also:* **~tones**) *npl* pavés (ronds)

cobweb ['kɔbwɛb] *n* toile *f* d'araignée

cocaine [kə'keɪn] *n* cocaïne *f*

cock [kɔk] *n* (*rooster*) coq *m*; (*male bird*) mâle *m* ♦ *vt* (*gun*) armer; **~erel** *n* jeune coq *m*

cockle ['kɔkl] *n* coque *f*

cockney ['kɔknɪ] *n* cockney *m*, habitant des quartiers populaires de l'East End de Londres; ≈ faubourien(ne)

cockpit ['kɔkpɪt] *n* (*in aircraft*) poste *m* de pilotage, cockpit *m*

cockroach ['kɔkrəutʃ] *n* cafard *m*

cocktail ['kɔkteɪl] *n* cocktail *m*; (*fruit etc*) salade *f*; **~ cabinet** *n* (*meuble-*)bar *m*; **~ party** *n* cocktail *m*

cocoa ['kəukəu] *n* cacao *m*

coconut ['kəukənʌt] *n* noix *f* de coco

COD *abbr* = **cash on delivery**

cod [kɔd] *n* morue fraîche, cabillaud *m*

code [kəud] *n* code *m*; (*TEL: area code*) indicatif *m*

cod-liver oil n huile f de foie de morue

coercion [kəu'ə:ʃən] n contrainte f

coffee ['kɔfɪ] n café m; ~ **bar** (BRIT) n café m; ~ **bean** n grain m de café; ~ **break** n pause-café f; ~**pot** n cafetière f; ~ **table** n (petite) table basse

coffin ['kɔfɪn] n cercueil m

cog [kɔg] n dent f (d'engrenage); (wheel) roue dentée

cogent ['kəudʒənt] adj puissant(e), convaincant(e)

coil [kɔɪl] n rouleau m, bobine f; (contraceptive) stérilet m ♦ vt enrouler

coin [kɔɪn] n pièce f de monnaie ♦ vt (word) inventer; ~**age** n monnaie f, système m monétaire; ~ **box** (BRIT) n cabine f téléphonique

coincide [kəuɪn'saɪd] vi coïncider; ~**nce** [kəu'ɪnsɪdəns] n coïncidence f

Coke [kəuk] ® n coca m

coke [kəuk] n coke m

colander ['kɔləndə*] n passoire f

cold [kəuld] adj froid(e) ♦ n froid m; (MED) rhume m; **it's** ~ il fait froid; **to be** or **feel** ~ (person) avoir froid; **to catch** ~ prendre or attraper froid; **to catch a** ~ attraper un rhume; **in** ~ **blood** de sang-froid; ~**shoulder** vt se montrer froid(e) envers, snober; ~ **sore** n bouton m de fièvre

coleslaw ['kəulslɔ:] n sorte de salade de chou cru

colic ['kɔlɪk] n colique(s) f(pl)

collapse [kə'læps] vi s'effondrer, s'écrouler ♦ n effondrement m, écroulement m; **collapsible** adj pliant(e); télescopique

collar ['kɔlə*] n (of coat, shirt) col m; (for animal) collier m; ~**bone** n clavicule f

collateral [kə'lætərl] n nantissement m

colleague ['kɔli:g] n collègue m/f

collect [kə'lɛkt] vt rassembler; ramasser; (as a hobby) collectionner; (BRIT: call and pick up) (passer) prendre; (mail) faire la levée de, ramasser; (money owed) encaisser; (donations, subscriptions) re-

cueillir ♦ vi (people) se rassembler; (things) s'amasser; **to call** ~ (US: TEL) téléphoner en P.C.V.; ~**ion** n collection f; (of mail) levée f; (for money) collecte f, quête f; ~**or** n collectionneur m

college ['kɔlɪdʒ] n collège m

collide [kə'laɪd] vi entrer en collision

colliery ['kɔlɪərɪ] (BRIT) n mine f de charbon, houillère f

collision [kə'lɪʒən] n collision f

colloquial [kə'ləukwɪəl] adj familier(-ère)

colon ['kəulən] n (sign) deux-points m inv; (MED) côlon m

colonel ['kə:nl] n colonel m

colony ['kɔlənɪ] n colonie f

colour ['kʌlə*] (US **color**) n couleur f ♦ vt (paint) peindre; (dye) teindre; (news) fausser, exagérer ♦ vi (blush) rougir; ~**s** npl (of party, club) couleurs fpl; ~ **in** vt colorier; ~ **bar** n discrimination raciale (dans un établissement); ~**blind** adj daltonien(ne); ~**ed** adj (person) de couleur; (illustration) en couleur; ~ **film** n (for camera) pellicule f (en) couleur; ~**ful** adj coloré(e), vif(-vive); (personality) pittoresque, haut(e) en couleurs; ~**ing** n colorant m; (complexion) teint m; ~ **scheme** n combinaison f de(s) couleurs; ~ **television** n télévision f (en) couleur

colt [kəult] n poulain m

column ['kɔləm] n colonne f; ~**ist** ['kɔləmnɪst] n chroniqueur(-euse)

coma ['kəumə] n coma m

comb [kəum] n peigne m ♦ vt (hair) peigner; (area) ratisser, passer au peigne fin

combat ['kɔmbæt] n combat m ♦ vt combattre, lutter contre

combination [kɔmbɪ'neɪʃən] n combinaison f

combine [vb kəm'baɪn, n 'kɔmbaɪn] vt: **to** ~ **sth with sth** combiner qch avec qch; (one quality with another) joindre or allier qch à qch ♦ vi s'associer; (CHEM) se combiner ♦ n (ECON) trust m; ~ **(har-**

vester) n moissonneuse-batteuse(-lieuse) f

come [kʌm] (pt **came**, pp **come**) vi venir, arriver; **to ~ to** (decision etc) parvenir or arriver à; **to ~ undone/loose** se défaire/desserrer; **~ about** vi se produire, arriver; **~ across** vt fus rencontrer par hasard, tomber sur; **~ along** vi = **come on**; **~ away** vi partir, s'en aller, se détacher; **~ back** vi revenir; **~ by** vt fus (acquire) obtenir, se procurer; **~ down** vi descendre; (prices) baisser; (buildings) s'écrouler, être démoli(e); **~ forward** vi s'avancer, se présenter, s'annoncer; **~ from** vt fus être originaire de, venir de; **~ in** vi entrer; **~ in for** vt fus (criticism etc) être l'objet de; **~ into** vt fus (money) hériter de; **~ off** vi (button) se détacher; (stain) s'enlever; (attempt) réussir; **~ on** vi (pupil, work, project) faire des progrès, s'avancer; (lights, electricity) s'allumer; (central heating) se mettre en marche; **~ on!** viens!, allons!, allez!; **~ out** vi sortir; (book) paraître; (strike) cesser le travail, se mettre en grève; **~ round** vi (after faint, operation) revenir à soi, reprendre connaissance; **~ to** vi revenir à soi; **~ up** vi monter; **~ up against** vt fus (resistance, difficulties) rencontrer; **~ up with** vt fus: **he came up with an idea** il a eu une idée, il a proposé quelque chose; **~ upon** vt fus tomber sur; **~back** n (THEATRE etc) rentrée f

comedian [kə'miːdɪən] n (in music hall etc) comique m; (THEATRE) comédien m

comedy ['kɒmɪdɪ] n comédie f

comeuppance [kʌm'ʌpəns] n: **to get one's ~** recevoir ce qu'on mérite

comfort ['kʌmfət] n confort m, bien-être m; (relief) soulagement m, réconfort m ♦ vt consoler, réconforter; **the ~s of home** les commodités fpl de la maison; **~able** adj confortable; (person) à l'aise; (patient) dont l'état est stationnaire; (walk etc) facile; **~ably** adv (sit) confortablement; (live) à l'aise;

station (US) n toilettes fpl

comic ['kɒmɪk] adj (also: **~al**) comique ♦ n comique m; (BRIT: magazine) illustré m; **~ strip** n bande dessinée

coming ['kʌmɪŋ] n arrivée f ♦ adj prochain(e), à venir; **~(s) and going(s)** n(pl) va-et-vient m inv

comma ['kɒmə] n virgule f

command [kə'mɑːnd] n ordre m, commandement m; (MIL: authority) commandement m; (mastery) maîtrise f ♦ vt (troops) commander; **to ~ sb to do** ordonner à qn de faire; **~eer** [kɒmən'dɪə] vt réquisitionner; **~er** n (MIL) commandant m

commando [kə'mɑːndəu] n commando m; membre m d'un commando

commemorate [kə'meməreɪt] vt commémorer

commence [kə'mens] vt, vi commencer

commend [kə'mend] vt louer; (recommend) recommander

commensurate [kə'menʃərɪt] adj: **~ with** or **to** en proportion de, proportionné(e) à

comment ['kɒment] n commentaire m ♦ vi: **to ~ (on)** faire des remarques (sur); **"no ~"** "je n'ai rien à dire"; **~ary** ['kɒməntərɪ] n commentaire m; (SPORT) reportage m (en direct); **~ator** ['kɒmənteɪtə] n commentateur m; reporter m

commerce ['kɒməːs] n commerce m

commercial [kə'məːʃəl] adj commercial(e) ♦ n (TV, RADIO) annonce f publicitaire, spot m (publicitaire)

commiserate [kə'mɪzəreɪt] vi: **to ~ with sb** témoigner de la sympathie pour qn

commission [kə'mɪʃən] n (order for work) commande f; (committee, fee) commission f ♦ vt (work of art) commander, charger un artiste de l'exécution de; **out of ~** (not working) hors service; **~aire** [kəmɪʃə'nɛə] (BRIT) n (at shop, cinema etc) portier m (en uniforme); **~er** n (POLICE) préfet m (de police)

commit [kə'mɪt] vt (act) commettre; (resources) consacrer; (to sb's care) confier (à); **to ~ o.s. (to do)** s'engager (à faire); **to ~ suicide** se suicider; **~ment** n engagement m; (obligation) responsabilité f(pl)

committee [kə'mɪtɪ] n comité m

commodity [kə'mɔdɪtɪ] n produit m, marchandise f, article m

common ['kɔmən] adj commun(e); (usual) courant(e) ♦ n terrain communal; **the C~s** (BRIT) npl la chambre des Communes; **in ~** en commun; **~er** n roturier(-ière); **~ law** droit coutumier; **~ly** adv communément, généralement; couramment; **C~ Market** n Marché commun; **~place** adj banal(e), ordinaire; **~ room** n salle commune; **~ sense** n bon sens; **C~wealth** (BRIT) n Commonwealth m

commotion [kə'məuʃən] n désordre m, tumulte m

communal ['kɔmjuːnl] adj (life) communautaire; (for common use) commun(e)

commune [n 'kɔmjuːn, vb kə'mjuːn] n (group) communauté f ♦ vi: **to ~ with** communier avec

communicate [kə'mjuːnɪkeɪt] vt, vi communiquer; **communication** [kəmjuːnɪ'keɪʃən] n communication f; **communication cord** (BRIT) n sonnette f d'alarme

communion [kə'mjuːnɪən] n (also: **Holy C~**) communion f

communism ['kɔmjunɪzəm] n communisme m; **communist** adj communiste ♦ n communiste m/f

community [kə'mjuːnɪtɪ] n communauté f; **~ centre** n centre m de loisirs; **~ chest** (US) n fonds commun

commutation ticket [kɔmju'teɪʃən-] (US) n carte f d'abonnement

commute [kə'mjuːt] vi faire un trajet journalier pour se rendre à son travail ♦

vt (LAW) commuer; **~r** n banlieusard(e) (qui fait un trajet journalier pour se rendre à son travail)

compact [adj kəm'pækt, n 'kɔmpækt] adj compact(e) ♦ n (also: **powder ~**) poudrier m; **~ disc** n disque compact; **~ disc player** n lecteur m de disque compact

companion [kəm'pænjən] n compagnon (compagne); **~ship** n camaraderie f

company ['kʌmpənɪ] n compagnie f; **to keep sb ~** tenir compagnie à qn; **~ secretary** (BRIT) n (COMM) secrétaire général (d'une société)

comparative [kəm'pærətɪv] adj (study) comparatif(-ive); (relative) relatif(-ive); **~ly** adv (relatively) relativement

compare [kəm'pɛər] vt: **to ~ sth/sb with/to** comparer qch/qn avec or et/à ♦ vi: **to ~ (with)** se comparer (à); être comparable (à); **comparison** [kəm'pærɪsn] n comparaison f

compartment [kəm'pɑːtmənt] n compartiment m

compass ['kʌmpəs] n boussole f; **~es** npl (GEOM: also: **pair of ~es**) compas m

compassion [kəm'pæʃən] n compassion f; **~ate** adj compatissant(e)

compatible [kəm'pætɪbl] adj compatible

compel [kəm'pɛl] vt contraindre, obliger

compensate ['kɔmpənseɪt] vt indemniser, dédommager ♦ vi: **to ~ for** compenser; **compensation** [kɔmpən'seɪʃən] n compensation f, (money) dédommagement m, indemnité f

compère ['kɔmpɛər] n (TV) animateur(-trice)

compete [kəm'piːt] vi: **to ~ (with)** rivaliser (avec), faire concurrence (à)

competent ['kɔmpɪtənt] adj compétent(e), capable

competition [kɔmpɪ'tɪʃən] n (contest) compétition f, concours m; (ECON.

concurrence f

competitive [kəmˈpetɪtɪv] *adj* (ECON) concurrentiel(le); (*sport*) de compétition; (*person*) qui a l'esprit de compétition; **competitor** *n* concurrent(e)

complacency [kəmˈpleɪsnsɪ] *n* suffisance f, vaine complaisance

complain [kəmˈpleɪn] *vi*: to ~ (about) se plaindre (de); (*in shop etc*) réclamer (au sujet de); to ~ of (*pain*) se plaindre de; ~t *n* plainte f; réclamation f; (MED) affection f

complement [*n* ˈkɒmplɪmənt, *vb* ˈkɒmplɪment] *n* complément *m*; (*especially of ship's crew etc*) effectif complet ♦ *vt* (*enhance*) compléter; **~ary** [kɒmplɪˈmentərɪ] *adj* complémentaire

complete [kəmˈpliːt] *adj* complet(-ète) ♦ *vt* achever, parachever; (*set, group*) compléter; (*a form*) remplir; **~ly** *adv* complètement; **completion** *n* achèvement *m*; (*of contract*) exécution f

complex [ˈkɒmpleks] *adj* complexe ♦ *n* complexe *m*

complexion [kəmˈplekʃən] *n* (*of face*) teint *m*

compliance [kəmˈplaɪəns] *n* (*submission*) docilité f; (*agreement*): ~ **with** le fait de se conformer à; **in** ~ **with** en accord avec

complicate [ˈkɒmplɪkeɪt] *vt* compliquer; **~d** *adj* compliqué(e); **complication** [kɒmplɪˈkeɪʃən] *n* complication f

compliment [*n* ˈkɒmplɪmənt, *vb* ˈkɒmplɪment] *n* compliment *m* ♦ *vt* complimenter; **~s** *npl* (*respects*) compliments *mpl*, hommages *mpl*; **to pay sb a** ~ faire *or* adresser un compliment à qn; **~ary** [kɒmplɪˈmentərɪ] *adj* flatteur(-euse); (*free*) (offert(e)) à titre gracieux; **~ary ticket** *n* billet *m* de faveur

comply [kəmˈplaɪ] *vi*: to ~ **with** se soumettre à, se conformer à

component [kəmˈpəʊnənt] *n* composant *m*, élément *m*

compose [kəmˈpəʊz] *vt* composer;

(*form*): **to be ~d of** se composer de; **to** ~ **o.s.** se calmer, se maîtriser; prendre une contenance; **~d** *adj* calme, maître de soi; **~r** *n* (MUS) compositeur *m*; **composition** [kɒmpəˈzɪʃən] *n* composition f; **composure** [kəmˈpəʊʒəʳ] *n* calme *m*, maîtrise f de soi

compound [ˈkɒmpaʊnd] *n* composé *m*; (*enclosure*) enclos *m*, enceinte f; ~ **fracture** *n* fracture compliquée; ~ **interest** *n* intérêt composé

comprehend [kɒmprɪˈhend] *vt* comprendre; **comprehension** *n* compréhension f

comprehensive [kɒmprɪˈhensɪv] *adj* (très) complet(-ète); ~ **policy** *n* (INSURANCE) assurance f tous risques; ~ **(school)** (BRIT) *n* école secondaire polyvalente; = C.E.S. *m*

compress [*vb* kəmˈpres, *n* ˈkɒmpres] *vt* comprimer; (*text, information*) condenser ♦ *n* (MED) compresse f

comprise [kəmˈpraɪz] *vt* (*also*: **be ~d of**) comprendre; (*constitute*) constituer, représenter

compromise [ˈkɒmprəmaɪz] *n* compromis *m* ♦ *vt* compromettre ♦ *vi* transiger, accepter un compromis

compulsion [kəmˈpʌlʃən] *n* contrainte f, force f

compulsive [kəmˈpʌlsɪv] *adj* (PSYCH) compulsif(-ive); (*book, film etc*) captivant(e)

compulsory [kəmˈpʌlsərɪ] *adj* obligatoire

computer [kəmˈpjuːtəʳ] *n* ordinateur *m*; ~ **game** *n* jeu *m* vidéo; **~-generated** *adj* de synthèse; **~ize** *vt* informatiser; ~ **programmer** *n* programmeur(-euse); ~ **programming** *n* programmation f; ~ **science** *n* informatique f; **computing** *n* = **computer science**

comrade [ˈkɒmrɪd] *n* camarade *m/f*

con [kɒn] *vt* duper; (*cheat*) escroquer ♦ *n* escroquerie f

conceal [kənˈsiːl] *vt* cacher, dissimuler

conceit [kən'si:t] n vanité f, suffisance f, prétention f; **~ed** adj vaniteux(-euse), suffisant(e)

conceive [kən'si:v] vt, vi concevoir

concentrate ['kɔnsəntreit] vi se concentrer ♦ vt concentrer; **concentration** n concentration f; **concentration camp** n camp m de concentration

concept ['kɔnsept] n concept m

concern [kən'sə:n] n affaire f, (COMM) entreprise f, firme f; (anxiety) inquiétude f, souci m ♦ vt concerner; **to be ~ed (about)** s'inquiéter (de), être inquiet(-ète) (au sujet de); **~ing** prep en ce qui concerne, à propos de

concert ['kɔnsət] n concert m; **~ed** [kən'sə:tid] adj concerté(e); **~ hall** n salle f de concert

concerto [kən'tʃə:təu] n concerto m

concession [kən'sɛʃən] n concession f; **tax ~** dégrèvement fiscal

conclude [kən'klu:d] vt conclure; **conclusion** [kən'klu:ʒən] n conclusion f; **conclusive** [kən'klu:sɪv] adj concluant(e), définitif(-ive)

concoct [kən'kɔkt] vt confectionner, composer; (fig) inventer; **~ion** n mélange m

concourse ['kɔŋkɔ:s] n (hall) hall m, salle f des pas perdus

concrete ['kɔŋkri:t] n béton m ♦ adj concret(-ète); (floor etc) en béton

concur [kən'kə:r] vi (agree) être d'accord

concurrently [kən'kʌrntlɪ] adv simultanément

concussion [kən'kʌʃən] n (MED) commotion (cérébrale)

condemn [kən'dɛm] vt condamner

condensation [kɔndɛn'seɪʃən] n condensation f

condense [kən'dɛns] vi se condenser ♦ vt condenser; **~d milk** n lait concentré (sucré)

condition [kən'dɪʃən] n condition f; (MED) état m ♦ vt déterminer, condition-

ner; **on ~ that** à condition que +sub, à condition de; **~al** adj conditionnel(le); **~er** n (for hair) baume après-shampooing m; (for fabrics) assouplissant m

condolences [kən'dəulənsɪz] npl condoléances fpl

condom ['kɔndəm] n préservatif m

condominium [kɔndə'mɪnɪəm] (US) n (building) immeuble m (en copropriété)

condone [kən'dəun] vt fermer les yeux sur, approuver (tacitement)

conducive [kən'dju:sɪv] adj: **~ to** favorable à, qui contribue à

conduct [n 'kɔndʌkt, vb kən'dʌkt] n conduite f ♦ vt conduire; (MUS) diriger; **to ~ o.s.** se conduire, se comporter; **~ed tour** n voyage organisé; (of building) visite guidée; **~or** n (of orchestra) chef m d'orchestre; (on bus) receveur m; (US: on train) chef m de train; (ELEC) conducteur m; **~ress** n (on bus) receveuse f

cone [kəun] n cône m; (for ice-cream) cornet m; (BOT) pomme f de pin, cône

confectioner [kən'fɛkʃənər] n confiseur(-euse); **~'s (shop)** n confiserie f; **~y** n confiserie f

confer [kən'fə:r] vt: **to ~ sth on** conférer qch à ♦ vi conférer, s'entretenir

conference ['kɔnfərəns] n conférence f

confess [kən'fɛs] vt confesser, avouer ♦ vi se confesser; **~ion** n confession f

confetti [kən'fɛtɪ] n confettis mpl

confide [kən'faɪd] vi: **to ~ in** se confier à

confidence ['kɔnfɪdns] n confiance f; (also: **self-~**) assurance f, confiance en soi; (secret) confidence f; **in ~** (speak, write) en confidence, confidentiellement; **~ trick** n escroquerie f; **confident** adj sûr(e), assuré(e); **confidential** [kɔnfɪ'dɛnʃəl] adj confidentiel(le)

confine [kən'faɪn] vt limiter, borner; (shut up) confiner, enfermer; **~d** adj (space) restreint(e), réduit(e); **~ment** n emprisonnement m, détention f; **~s**

confirm 358 consider

['kɒnfaɪnz] npl confins mpl, bornes fpl
confirm [kən'fɜːm] vt confirmer; (appointment) ratifier; **~ation** [kɒnfə'meɪʃən] n confirmation f; **~ed** adj invétéré(e), incorrigible
confiscate ['kɒnfɪskeɪt] vt confisquer
conflict [n 'kɒnflɪkt, vb kən'flɪkt] n conflit m, lutte f ♦ vi être or entrer en conflit; (opinions) s'opposer, se heurter; **~ing** [kən'flɪktɪŋ] adj contradictoire
conform [kən'fɔːm] vi: **to ~ (to)** se conformer (à)
confound [kən'faund] vt confondre
confront [kən'frʌnt] vt confronter, mettre en présence; (enemy, danger) affronter, faire face à; **~ation** [kɒnfrən'teɪʃən] n confrontation f
confuse [kən'fjuːz] vt (person) troubler; (situation) embrouiller; (one thing with another) confondre; **~d** adj (person) dérouté(e), désorienté(e); **confusing** adj peu clair(e), déroutant(e); **confusion** [kən'fjuːʒən] n confusion f
congeal [kən'dʒiːl] vi (blood) se coaguler; (oil etc) se figer
congenial [kən'dʒiːnɪəl] adj sympathique, agréable
congested [kən'dʒestɪd] adj (MED) congestionné(e); (area) surpeuplé(e); (road) bloqué(e); **congestion** n congestion f; (fig) encombrement m
congratulate [kən'grætjuleɪt] vt: **to ~ sb (on)** féliciter qn (de); **congratulations** [kəngrætju'leɪʃənz] npl félicitations fpl
congregate ['kɒngrɪgeɪt] vi se rassembler, se réunir; **congregation** [kɒngrɪ'geɪʃən] n assemblée f (des fidèles)
congress ['kɒngres] n congrès m; **~man** (irreg) (US) n membre m du Congrès
conjunction [kən'dʒʌŋkʃən] n (LING) conjonction f
conjunctivitis [kəndʒʌŋktɪ'vaɪtɪs] n conjonctivite f
conjure ['kʌndʒər] vi faire des tours de

passe-passe; **~ up** vt (ghost, spirit) faire apparaître; (memories) évoquer; **~r** n prestidigitateur m, illusionniste m/f
con man (irreg) n escroc m
connect [kə'nekt] vt joindre, relier; (ELEC) connecter; (TEL: caller) mettre en connection (with avec); (: new subscriber) brancher; (fig) établir un rapport entre, faire un rapprochement entre ♦ vi (train): **to ~ with** assurer la correspondance avec; **to be ~ed with** (fig) avoir un rapport avec, avoir des rapports avec, être en relation avec; **~ion** n relation f, lien m; (ELEC) connexion f; (train, plane etc) correspondance f; (TEL) branchement m, communication f
connive [kə'naɪv] vi: **to ~ at** se faire le complice de
conquer ['kɒŋkər] vt conquérir; (feelings) vaincre, surmonter; **conquest** ['kɒŋkwest] n conquête f
cons [kɒnz] npl **see convenience; pro**
conscience ['kɒnʃəns] n conscience f; **conscientious** [kɒnʃɪ'enʃəs] adj consciencieux(-euse)
conscious ['kɒnʃəs] adj conscient(e); **~ness** n conscience f; (MED) connaissance f
conscript ['kɒnskrɪpt] n conscrit m
consent [kən'sent] n consentement m ♦ vi: **to ~ (to)** consentir (à)
consequence ['kɒnsɪkwəns] n conséquence f, suites fpl; (significance) importance f; **consequently** adv par conséquent, donc
conservation [kɒnsə'veɪʃən] n préservation f, protection f
conservative [kən'sɜːvətɪv] adj conservateur(-trice); **at a ~ estimate** au bas mot; **C~** (BRIT) adj, n (POL) conservateur(-trice)
conservatory [kən'sɜːvətri] n (greenhouse) serre f
conserve [kən'sɜːv] vt conserver, préserver; (supplies, energy) économiser ♦ n confiture f
consider [kən'sɪdər] vt (study) considé-

rer, réfléchir à; (*take into account*) penser à, prendre en considération; (*regard, judge*) considérer, estimer; **to ~ doing sth** envisager de faire qch; **~able** *adj* considérable; **~ably** *adv* nettement; **~ate** *adj* prévenant(e), plein(e) d'égards; **~ation** [kənsɪdə'reɪʃən] *n* considération *f*; **~ing** *prep* étant donné

consign [kən'saɪn] *vt* expédier; (*to sb's care*) confier; (*fig*) livrer; **~ment** *n* arrivage *m*, envoi *m*

consist [kən'sɪst] *vi:* **to ~ of** consister en, se composer de

consistency [kən'sɪstənsɪ] *n* consistance *f*; (*fig*) cohérence *f*

consistent [kən'sɪstənt] *adj* logique, cohérent(e)

consolation [kɒnsə'leɪʃən] *n* consolation *f*

console¹ [kən'səul] *vt* consoler

console² ['kɒnsəul] *n* (COMPUT) console *f*

consonant ['kɒnsənənt] *n* consonne *f*

conspicuous [kən'spɪkjuəs] *adj* voyant(e), qui attire l'attention

conspiracy [kən'spɪrəsɪ] *n* conspiration *f*, complot *m*

constable ['kʌnstəbl] (BRIT) *n* ≈ agent *m* de police, gendarme *m*; **chief ~** ≈ préfet *m* de police; **constabulary** [kən'stæbjulərɪ] (BRIT) *n* ≈ police *f*, gendarmerie *f*

constant ['kɒnstənt] *adj* constant(e); incessant(e); **~ly** *adv* constamment, sans cesse

constipated ['kɒnstɪpeɪtɪd] *adj* constipé(e); **constipation** [kɒnstɪ'peɪʃən] *n* constipation *f*

constituency [kən'stɪtjuənsɪ] *n* circonscription électorale

constituent [kən'stɪtjuənt] *n* (POL) électeur(-trice); (*part*) élément constitutif, composant *m*

constitution [kɒnstɪ'tju:ʃən] *n* constitution *f*; **~al** *adj* constitutionnel(le)

constraint [kən'streɪnt] *n* contrainte *f*

construct [kən'strʌkt] *vt* construire;

~ion *n* construction *f*; **~ive** *adj* constructif(-ive); **~ive dismissal** démission forcée

consul ['kɒnsl] *n* consul *m*; **~ate** ['kɒnsjulɪt] *n* consulat *m*

consult [kən'sʌlt] *vt* consulter; **~ant** *n* (MED) médecin consultant; (*other specialist*) consultant *m*, (*expert-*)conseil *m*; **~ing room** (BRIT) *n* cabinet *m* de consultation

consume [kən'sju:m] *vt* consommer; **~r** *n* consommateur(-trice); **~r goods** *npl* biens *mpl* de consommation; **~r society** *n* société *f* de consommation

consummate ['kɒnsʌmeɪt] *vt* consommer

consumption [kən'sʌmpʃən] *n* consommation *f*

cont. *abbr* (= *continued*) suite

contact ['kɒntækt] *n* contact *m*; (*person*) connaissance *f*, relation *f* ♦ *vt* contacter, se mettre en contact or en rapport avec; **~ lenses** *npl* verres *mpl* de contact, lentilles *fpl*

contagious [kən'teɪdʒəs] *adj* contagieux(-euse)

contain [kən'teɪn] *vt* contenir; **to ~ o.s.** se contenir, se maîtriser; **~er** *n* récipient *m*; (*for shipping etc*) container *m*

contaminate [kən'tæmɪneɪt] *vt* contaminer

cont'd *abbr* (= *continued*) suite

contemplate ['kɒntəmpleɪt] *vt* contempler; (*consider*) envisager

contemporary [kən'tempərərɪ] *adj* contemporain(e); (*design, wallpaper*) moderne ♦ *n* contemporain(e)

contempt [kən'tempt] *n* mépris *m*, dédain *m*; **~ of court** (LAW) outrage *m* à l'autorité de la justice; **~uous** [kən'temptjuəs] *adj* dédaigneux(-euse), méprisant(e)

contend [kən'tend] *vt:* **to ~ that** soutenir or prétendre que ♦ *vi:* **to ~ with** (*compete*) rivaliser avec; (*struggle*) lutter avec; **~er** *n* concurrent(e); (POL) candidat(e)

content [adj, vb kən'tɛnt, n 'kɒntɛnt] adj content(e), satisfait(e) ♦ vt contenter, satisfaire ♦ n contenu m; (of fat, moisture) teneur f; ~s npl (of container etc) contenu m; (table of) ~s table f des matières; ~ed adj content(e), satisfait(e)

contention [kən'tɛnʃən] n dispute f, contestation f; (argument) assertion f, affirmation f

contest [n 'kɒntɛst, vb kən'tɛst] n combat m, lutte f; (competition) concours m ♦ vt (decision, statement) contester, discuter; (compete for) disputer; ~ant [kən'tɛstənt] n concurrent(e) m/f; (in fight) adversaire m/f

context ['kɒntɛkst] n contexte m

continent ['kɒntɪnənt] n continent m; **the C~** (BRIT) l'Europe continentale; ~al [kɒntɪ'nɛntl] adj continental(e); ~al breakfast n petit déjeuner m à la française; ~al quilt (BRIT) n couette f

contingency [kən'tɪndʒənsɪ] n éventualité f, événement imprévu

continual [kən'tɪnjuəl] adj continuel(le)

continuation [kəntɪnju'eɪʃən] n continuation f; (after interruption) reprise f, (of story) suite f

continue [kən'tɪnju:] vi, vt continuer; (after interruption) reprendre, poursuivre; **continuity** [kɒntɪ'njuːɪtɪ] n continuité f; (TV etc) enchaînement m; **continuous** [kən'tɪnjuəs] adj continu(e); (LING) progressif(-ive)

contort [kən'tɔ:t] vt tordre, crisper

contour ['kɒntuə'] n contour m, profil m; (on map: also: ~ line) courbe f de niveau

contraband ['kɒntrəbænd] n contrebande f

contraceptive [kɒntrə'sɛptɪv] adj contraceptif(-ive), anticonceptionnel(le) ♦ n contraceptif m

contract [n 'kɒntrækt, vb kən'trækt] n contrat m ♦ vi (become smaller) se contracter, se resserrer; (COMM): **to ~ to do sth** s'engager (par contrat) à faire qch; ~ion [kən'trækʃən] n contraction f; ~or [kən'træktə'] n entrepreneur m

contradict [kɒntrə'dɪkt] vt contredire

contraflow ['kɒntrəfləu] n (AUT): ~ **lane** voie f à contresens; **there's a ~ system in operation on ...** une voie a été mise en sens inverse sur ...

contraption [kən'træpʃən] (pej) n machin m, truc m

contrary¹ ['kɒntrərɪ] adj contraire, opposé(e) ♦ n contraire m; **on the ~** au contraire; **unless you hear to the ~** sauf avis contraire

contrary² [kən'trɛərɪ] adj (perverse) contrariant(e), entêté(e)

contrast [n 'kɒntrɑːst, vb kən'trɑːst] n contraste m ♦ vt mettre en contraste, contraster; **in ~ to** en contraste avec

contravene [kɒntrə'viːn] vt enfreindre, violer, contrevenir à

contribute [kən'trɪbjuːt] vi contribuer ♦ vt: **to ~ £10/an article to** donner 10 livres/un article à; **to ~** contribuer à; (newspaper) collaborer à; **contribution** [kɒntrɪ'bjuːʃən] n contribution f; **contributor** [kən'trɪbjutə'] n (to newspaper) collaborateur(-trice)

contrive [kən'traɪv] vt: **to ~ to do** s'arranger pour faire, trouver le moyen de faire

control [kən'trəul] vt maîtriser, commander; (check) contrôler ♦ n contrôle m, autorité f; maîtrise f; ~s npl (of machine etc) commandes fpl; (on radio, TV) boutons mpl de réglage; ~led **substance** narcotique m; **everything is under ~** tout va bien, j'ai (or il a etc) la situation en main; **to be in ~ of** être maître de, maîtriser; **the car went out of ~** j'ai (or il a etc) perdu le contrôle du véhicule; ~ **panel** n tableau m de commande; ~ **room** n salle f des commandes; ~ **tower** n (AVIAT) tour f de contrôle

controversial [kɒntrə'vəːʃl] adj (topic)

discutable, controversé(e); *(person)* qui fait beaucoup parler de lui; **controversy** ['kɔntrəvə:sɪ] *n* controverse *f*, polémique *f*

convalesce [kɔnvə'les] *vi* relever de maladie, se remettre (d'une maladie)

convector [kən'vektər] *n (heater)* radiateur *m* (à convexion)

convene [kən'vi:n] *vt* convoquer, assembler ♦ *vi* se réunir, s'assembler

convenience [kən'vi:nɪəns] *n* commodité *f*; **at your ~** quand *or* comme cela vous convient; **all modern ~s, (BRIT) all mod cons** avec tout le confort moderne, tout confort

convenient [kən'vi:nɪənt] *adj* commode

convent ['kɔnvənt] *n* couvent *m*; **~ school** *n* couvent *m*

convention [kən'venʃən] *n* convention *f*; **~al** *adj* conventionnel(le)

conversant [kən'və:sənt] *adj*: **to be ~ with** s'y connaître en; être au courant de

conversation [kɔnvə'seɪʃən] *n* conversation *f*

converse [*n* 'kɔnvə:s, *vb* kən'və:s] *n* contraire *m*, inverse *m* ♦ *vi* s'entretenir; **~ly** [kɔn'və:slɪ] *adv* inversement, réciproquement

convert [*vb* kən'və:t, *n* 'kɔnvə:t] *vt (REL, COMM)* convertir; *(alter)* transformer; *(house)* aménager ♦ *n* converti(e); **~ible** [kən'və:təbl] *n (voiture f)* décapotable *f*

convey [kən'veɪ] *vt* transporter; *(thanks)* transmettre; *(idea)* communiquer; **~or belt** *n* convoyeur *m*, tapis roulant

convict [*vb* kən'vɪkt, *n* 'kɔnvɪkt] *vt* déclarer *(or* reconnaître) coupable ♦ *n* forçat *m*, détenu *m*; **~ion** [-ʃən] *n (LAW)* condamnation *f*; *(belief)* conviction *f*

convince [kən'vɪns] *vt* convaincre, persuader; **convincing** *adj* persuasif(-ive), convaincant(e)

convoluted ['kɔnvəlu:tɪd] *adj (argu-*

ment) compliqué(e)

convulse [kən'vʌls] *vt*: **to be ~d with laughter/pain** se tordre de rire/douleur

cook [kuk] *vt* (faire) cuire ♦ *vi* cuire; *(person)* faire la cuisine ♦ *n* cuisinier (-ière); **~book** *n* livre *m* de cuisine; **~er** *n* cuisinière *f*; **~ery** *n* cuisine *f*; **~ery book** *(BRIT) n* = cookbook; **~ie** *(US) n* biscuit *m*, petit gâteau sec; **~ing** *n* cuisine *f*

cool [ku:l] *adj* frais (fraîche); *(calm, unemotional)* calme; *(unfriendly)* froid(e) ♦ *vt, vi* rafraîchir, refroidir

coop [ku:p] *n* poulailler *m*; *(for rabbits)* clapier *m* ♦ *vt*: **to ~ up** *(fig)* cloîtrer, enfermer

cooperate [kəu'ɔpəreɪt] *vi* coopérer, collaborer; **cooperation** [kəuɔpə'reɪʃən] *n* coopération *f*, collaboration *f*; **cooperative** [kəu'ɔpərətɪv] *adj* coopératif(-ive) ♦ *n* coopérative *f*

coordinate [*vb* kəu'ɔ:dɪneɪt, *n* kəu'ɔ:dɪnət] *vt* coordonner ♦ *n (MATH)* coordonnée *f*; **~s** *npl (clothes)* ensemble *m*, coordonnés *mpl*

co-ownership [kəu'əunəʃɪp] *n* copropriété *f*

cop [kɔp] *(inf) n* flic *m*

cope [kəup] *vi*: **to ~ with** faire face à; *(solve)* venir à bout de

copper ['kɔpər] *n* cuivre *m*; *(BRIT: inf: policeman)* flic *m*; **~s** *npl (coins)* petite monnaie

copy ['kɔpɪ] *n* copie *f*; *(of book etc)* exemplaire *m* ♦ *vt* copier; **~right** *n* droit *m* d'auteur, copyright *m*

coral ['kɔrəl] *n* corail *m*

cord [kɔ:d] *n* corde *f*; *(fabric)* velours côtelé; *(ELEC)* cordon *m*, fil *m*

cordial ['kɔ:dɪəl] *adj* cordial(e), chaleureux(-euse) ♦ *n* cordial *m*

cordon ['kɔ:dən] *n* cordon *m*; **~ off** *vt* boucler *(par cordon de police)*

corduroy ['kɔ:dərɔɪ] *n* velours côtelé

core [kɔ:r] *n* noyau *m*; *(of fruit)* trognon *m*, cœur *m*; *(of building, problem)* cœur

◆ *vt* enlever le trognon *or* le cœur de

cork [kɔːk] *n* liège *m*; (*of bottle*) bouchon *m*; **~screw** *n* tire-bouchon *m*

corn [kɔːn] *n* (*BRIT: wheat*) blé *m*; (*US: maize*) maïs *m*; (*on foot*) cor *m*; **on the cob** (*CULIN*) épi de maïs; **~ed beef** *n* corned-beef *m*

corner ['kɔːnə*ʳ*] *n* coin *m*, (*AUT*) tournant *m*, virage *m*; (*FOOTBALL: also:* **~ kick**) corner *m* ◆ *vt* acculer, mettre au pied du mur; coincer; (*COMM: market*) accaparer ◆ *vi* prendre un virage; **~stone** *n* pierre *f* angulaire

cornet ['kɔːnɪt] *n* (*MUS*) cornet *m* à pistons; (*BRIT: of ice-cream*) cornet (de glace)

cornflakes ['kɔːnfleɪks] *npl* corn-flakes *mpl*

cornflour ['kɔːnflauə*ʳ*] (*BRIT*), **cornstarch** ['kɔːnstɑːtʃ] (*US*) *n* farine *f* de maïs, maïzena *f* ®

Cornwall ['kɔːnwəl] *n* Cornouailles *f*

corny ['kɔːnɪ] (*inf*) *adj* rebattu(e)

coronary ['kɔrənərɪ] *n* (*also:* **~ thrombosis**) infarctus *m* (du myocarde), thrombose *f* coronarienne

coronation [kɔrə'neɪʃən] *n* couronnement *m*

coroner ['kɔrənə*ʳ*] *n* officiel chargé de déterminer les causes d'un décès

corporal ['kɔːpərl] *n* caporal *m*, brigadier *m* ◆ *adj*: **~ punishment** châtiment corporel

corporate ['kɔːpərɪt] *adj* en commun, collectif(-ive); (*COMM*) de l'entreprise

corporation [kɔːpə'reɪʃən] *n* (*of town*) municipalité *f*, conseil municipal; (*COMM*) société *f*

corps [kɔː*ʳ*] (*pl* **~**) *n* corps *m*

corpse [kɔːps] *n* cadavre *m*

correct [kə'rɛkt] *adj* (*accurate*) correct(e), exact(e); (*proper*) correct(e), convenable ◆ *vt* corriger; **~ion** *n* correction *f*

correspond [kɔrɪs'pɔnd] *vi* correspondre; **~ence** *n* correspondance *f*; **~ence course** *n* cours *m* par correspondance;

~ent *n* correspondant(e)

corridor ['kɔrɪdɔː*ʳ*] *n* couloir *m*, corridor *m*

corrode [kə'rəud] *vt* corroder, ronger ◆ *vi* se corroder

corrugated ['kɔrəgeɪtɪd] *adj* plissé(e); ondulé(e); **~ iron** *n* tôle ondulée

corrupt [kə'rʌpt] *adj* corrompu(e) ◆ *vt* corrompre; **~ion** *n* corruption *f*

Corsica ['kɔːsɪkə] *n* Corse *f*

cosmetic [kɔz'mɛtɪk] *n* produit *m* de beauté, cosmétique *m*

cost [kɔst] (*pt, pp* **cost**) *n* coût *m* ◆ *vi* coûter ◆ *vt* établir *or* calculer le prix de revient ◆ **~s** *npl* (*COMM*) frais *mpl*; (*LAW*) dépens *mpl*; **it ~s £5/too much** cela coûte cinq livres/c'est trop cher; **at all ~s** coûte que coûte, à tout prix

co-star ['kəustɑː*ʳ*] *n* partenaire *m/f*

cost: **~-effective** *adj* rentable; **~ly** *adj* coûteux(-euse); **~-of-living** *adj*: **~-of-living allowance** indemnité *f* de vie chère; **~-of-living index** index *m* du coût de la vie; **~ price** (*BRIT*) *n* prix coûtant *or* de revient

costume ['kɔstjuːm] *n* costume *m*; (*lady's suit*) tailleur *m*; (*BRIT: also:* **swimming ~**) maillot *m* (de bain); **~ jewellery** *n* bijoux *mpl* fantaisie

cosy ['kəuzɪ] (*US* **cozy**) *adj* douillet(te); (*person*) à l'aise, au chaud

cot [kɔt] *n* (*BRIT: child's*) lit *m* d'enfant, petit lit; (*US: campbed*) lit de camp

cottage ['kɔtɪdʒ] *n* petite maison (à la campagne), cottage *m*; **~ cheese** *n* fromage blanc (*maigre*)

cotton ['kɔtn] *n* coton *m*; **~ on** (*inf*) *vi*: **to ~ on to** piger; **~ candy** (*US*) *n* barbe *f* à papa; **~ wool** (*BRIT*) *n* ouate *f*, coton *m* hydrophile

couch [kautʃ] *n* canapé *m*; divan *m*

couchette [kuː'ʃɛt] *n* couchette *f*

cough [kɔf] *vi* tousser ◆ *n* toux *f*; **~ sweet** *n* pastille *f* pour *or* contre la toux

could [kud] *pt* of **can**[2]; **~n't** = **could not**

council ['kaunsl] n conseil m; **city** or **town ~** conseil municipal; **~ estate** (BRIT) n (zone f de) logements loués par/par la municipalité; **~ house** (BRIT) n maison f (à loyer modéré louée par la municipalité; **~lor** n conseiller(-ère)

counsel ['kaunsl] n (lawyer) avocat(e); (advice) conseil m, consultation f; **~lor** n conseiller(-ère); (US: lawyer) avocat(e)

count [kaunt] vt, vi compter ♦ n compte m; (nobleman) comte m; **~ on** vt fus compter sur; **~down** n compte m à rebours

countenance ['kauntinans] n expression f ♦ vt approuver

counter ['kauntar] n comptoir m; (in post office, bank) guichet m; (in game) jeton m ♦ vt aller à l'encontre de, opposer ♦ adv: **~ to** contrairement à; **~act** vt neutraliser, contrebalancer; **~feit** n faux m, contrefaçon f ♦ vt contrefaire ♦ adj faux (fausse); **~foil** n talon m, souche f; **~part** n (of person etc) homologue m/f

countess ['kauntis] n comtesse f

countless ['kauntlis] adj innombrable

country ['kʌntri] n pays m; (native land) patrie f; (as opposed to town) campagne f; (region) région f, pays; **~ dancing** (BRIT) n danse f folklorique; **~ house** n manoir m, (petit) château; **~man** (irreg) n (compatriot) compatriote m; (country dweller) habitant m de la campagne, campagnard m; **~side** n campagne f

county ['kaunti] n comté m

coup [ku:] (pl **~s**) n beau coup m; (also: **~ d'état**) coup d'État

couple ['kʌpl] n couple m; **a ~ of** deux; (a few) quelques

coupon ['ku:pɔn] n coupon m, bon-prime m, bon-réclame m; (COMM) coupon

courage ['kʌrɪdʒ] n courage m

courier ['kurɪər] n messager m, courrier m; (for tourists) accompagnateur(-trice), guide m/f

course [kɔ:s] n cours m; (of ship) route

f; (for golf) terrain m; (part of meal) plat m; **first ~** entrée f; **of ~** bien sûr; **~ of action** parti m, ligne f de conduite; **~ of treatment** (MED) traitement m

court [kɔ:t] n cour f; (LAW) cour, tribunal m; (TENNIS) court m ♦ vt (woman) courtiser, faire la cour à; **to take to ~** actionner or poursuivre en justice

courteous ['kə:tɪəs] adj courtois(e), poli(e); **courtesy** ['kə:təsɪ] n courtoisie f, politesse f; **(by) courtesy of** avec l'aimable autorisation de; **courtesy bus** or **coach** navette gratuite

court: ~-house (US) n palais m de justice; **~ier** n courtisan m, dame f de la cour; **~ martial** (pl **courts martial**) n cour martiale, conseil m de guerre; **~room** n salle f de tribunal; **~yard** n cour f

cousin ['kʌzn] n cousin(e); **first ~** cousin(e) germain(e)

cove [kəuv] n petite baie, anse f

covenant ['kʌvənənt] n engagement m

cover ['kʌvər] vt couvrir ♦ n couverture f; (of pan) couvercle m; (over furniture) housse f; (shelter) abri m; **to take ~** se mettre à l'abri; **under ~** à l'abri; **under ~ of darkness** à la faveur de la nuit; **under separate ~** (COMM) sous pli séparé; **to ~ up for sb** couvrir qn; **~age** n (TV, PRESS) reportage m; **~charge** n (supplément de payer); **~ing** n couche f; **~ing letter** (US **cover letter**) n lettre explicative; **~ note** n (INSURANCE) police f provisoire

covert ['kʌvət] adj (threat) voilé(e), caché(e); (glance) furtif(-ive)

cover-up ['kʌvərʌp] n tentative f pour étouffer une affaire

covet ['kʌvɪt] vt convoiter

cow [kau] n vache f ♦ vt effrayer, intimider

coward ['kauəd] n lâche m/f; **~ice** n lâcheté f; **~ly** adj lâche

cowboy ['kaubɔɪ] n cow-boy m

cower ['kauər] vi se recroqueviller

coy [kɔɪ] *adj* faussement effarouché(e) *or* timide

cozy ['kəʊzɪ] *(US) adj* = **cosy**

CPA *(US) n abbr* = **certified public accountant**

crab [kræb] *n* crabe *m*; **~ apple** *n* pomme *f* sauvage

crack [kræk] *n (split)* fente *f*, fissure *f*; *(in cup, bone etc)* fêlure *f*; *(in wall)* lézarde *f*; *(noise)* craquement *m*, coup (sec); *(drug)* crack ♦ *vt* fendre, fissurer; fêler; lézarder; *(nut)* casser; *(code)* déchiffrer; *(problem)* résoudre ♦ *adj (athlete)* de première classe, d'élite; **~ down on** *vt fus* mettre un frein à; **~ up** *vi* être au bout du rouleau, s'effondrer; **~ed** *adj (cup, bone)* fêlé(e); *(broken)* cassé(e); *(wall)* lézardé(e); *(surface)* craquelé(e); *(inf: mad)* cinglé(e); **~er** *n (Christmas cracker)* pétard *m*; *(biscuit)* biscuit (salé)

crackle ['krækl] *vi* crépiter, grésiller

cradle ['kreɪdl] *n* berceau *m*

craft [krɑːft] *n* métier (artisanal); *(pl inv: boat)* embarcation *f*, barque *f*; *(: plane)* appareil *m*; **~sman** *(irreg) n* artisan *m*, ouvrier (qualifié); **~smanship** *n* travail *m*; **~y** *adj* rusé(e), malin(-igne)

crag [kræg] *n* rocher escarpé

cram [kræm] *vt (fill):* **to ~ sth with** bourrer qch de; *(put):* **to ~ sth into** fourrer qch dans ♦ *vi (for exams)* bachoter

cramp [kræmp] *n* crampe *f* ♦ *vt* gêner, entraver; **~ed** *adj* à l'étroit, très serré(e)

cranberry ['krænbərɪ] *n* canneberge *f*

crane [kreɪn] *n* grue *f*

crank [kræŋk] *n* manivelle *f*; *(person)* excentrique *m/f*

cranny ['krænɪ] *n see* **nook**

crash [kræʃ] *n* fracas *m*; *(of car)* collision *f*; *(of plane)* accident *m* ♦ *vt* avoir un accident avec ♦ *vi (plane)* s'écraser; *(two cars)* se percuter, s'emboutir; *(COMM)* s'effondrer; **to ~ into** se jeter *or* se fracasser contre; **~ course** *n* cours intensif; **~ helmet** *n* casque (protecteur); **~**

landing *n* atterrissage forcé *or* en catastrophe

crate [kreɪt] *n* cageot *m*; *(for bottles)* caisse *f*

cravat(e) [krə'væt] *n* foulard (noué autour du cou)

crave [kreɪv] *vt, vi:* **to ~ (for)** avoir une envie irrésistible de

crawl [krɔːl] *vi* ramper; *(vehicle)* avancer au pas ♦ *n (SWIMMING)* crawl *m*

crayfish ['kreɪfɪʃ] *n inv (freshwater)* écrevisse *f*; *(saltwater)* langoustine *f*

crayon ['kreɪən] *n* crayon *m* (de couleur)

craze [kreɪz] *n* engouement *m*

crazy ['kreɪzɪ] *adj* fou (folle)

creak [kriːk] *vi* grincer; craquer

cream [kriːm] *n* crème *f* ♦ *adj (colour)* crème *inv*; **~ cake** *n (petit)* gâteau *m* à la crème; **~ cheese** *n* fromage *m* à la crème, fromage blanc; **~y** *adj* crémeux(-euse)

crease [kriːs] *n* pli *m* ♦ *vt* froisser, chiffonner ♦ *vi* se froisser, se chiffonner

create [kriː'eɪt] *vt* créer; **creation** *n* création *f*; **creative** *adj (artistic)* créatif(-ive); *(ingenious)* ingénieux (-euse)

creature ['kriːtʃə] *n* créature *f*

crèche [krɛʃ] *n* garderie *f*, crèche *f*

credence ['kriːdns] *n:* **to lend** *or* **give ~ to** ajouter foi à

credentials [krɪ'dɛnʃlz] *npl (references)* références *fpl*; *(papers of identity)* pièce *f* d'identité

credit ['krɛdɪt] *n* crédit *m*; *(recognition)* honneur *m* ♦ *vt (COMM)* créditer; *(believe: also:* **give ~ to**) ajouter foi à, croire; **~s** *npl (CINEMA, TV)* générique *m*; **to be in ~** *(person, bank account)* être créditeur(-trice); **to ~ sb with** *(fig)* prêter *or* attribuer à qn; **~ card** *n* carte *f* de crédit; **~or** *n* créancier(-ière)

creed [kriːd] *n* croyance *f*; credo *m*

creek [kriːk] *n* crique *f*, anse *f*; *(US: stream)* ruisseau *m*, petit cours d'eau

creep [kriːp] *(pt, pp* **crept***) vi* ramper;

~er n plante grimpante; **~y** adj (frightening) qui fait frissonner, qui donne la chair de poule

cremate [krɪ'meɪt] vt incinérer; **crematorium** [kremə'tɔ:rɪəm] (pl **crematoria**) n four m crématoire

crêpe [kreɪp] n crêpe m; **~ bandage** (BRIT) n bande f Velpeau ®

crept [krept] pt, pp of **creep**

crescent ['kresnt] n croissant m; (street) rue f (en arc de cercle)

cress [kres] n cresson m

crest [krest] n crête f; **~fallen** adj déconfit(e), découragé(e)

Crete [kri:t] n Crète f

crevice ['krevɪs] n fissure f, lézarde f, fente f

crew [kru:] n équipage m; (CINEMA) équipe f; **~-cut** n: **to have a ~-cut** avoir les cheveux en brosse; **~-neck** n col ras du cou

crib [krɪb] n lit m d'enfant; (for baby) berceau m ♦ vt (inf) copier

crick [krɪk] n: **~ in the neck** torticolis m; **~ in the back** tour m de reins

cricket ['krɪkɪt] n (insect) grillon m, cricri m inv; (game) cricket m

crime [kraɪm] n crime m; **criminal** ['krɪmɪnl] adj, n criminel(le)

crimson ['krɪmzn] adj cramoisi(e)

cringe [krɪndʒ] vi avoir un mouvement de recul

crinkle ['krɪŋkl] vt froisser, chiffonner

cripple ['krɪpl] n boiteux(-euse), infirme m/f ♦ vt estropier

crisis ['kraɪsɪs] (pl **crises**) n crise f

crisp [krɪsp] adj croquant(e), croustillant(e); (weather) vif (vive); (manner etc) brusque; **~s** (BRIT) npl (pommes) chips fpl

crisscross ['krɪskrɔs] adj entrecroisé(e)

criterion [kraɪ'tɪərɪən] (pl **criteria**) n critère m

critic ['krɪtɪk] n critique m; **~al** adj critique; **~ally** adv (examine) d'un œil critique; (speak etc) sévèrement; **~ally ill** gravement malade; **~ism** ['krɪtɪsɪzəm] n critique f; **~ize** ['krɪtɪsaɪz] vt critiquer

croak [krəuk] vi (frog) coasser; (raven) croasser; (person) parler d'une voix rauque

Croatia [krəu'eɪʃə] n Croatie f

crochet ['krəuʃeɪ] n travail m au crochet

crockery ['krɔkərɪ] n vaisselle f

crocodile ['krɔkədaɪl] n crocodile m

crocus ['krəukəs] n crocus m

croft [krɔft] (BRIT) n petite ferme

crony ['krəunɪ] (inf: pej) n copain (copine)

crook [kruk] n escroc m; (of shepherd) houlette f; **~ed** ['krukɪd] adj courbé(e), tordu(e); (action) malhonnête

crop [krɔp] n (produce) culture f; (amount produced) récolte f; (riding ~) cravache f ♦ vt (hair) tondre; **~ up** vi surgir, se présenter, survenir

cross [krɔs] n croix f; (BIO etc) croisement m ♦ vt (street etc) traverser; (arms, legs, BIO) croiser; (cheque) barrer ♦ adj en colère, fâché(e); **~ out** vt barrer, biffer; **~ over** vi traverser; **~bar** n barre (transversale); **~-country (race)** n cross(-country) m; **~-examine** vt (LAW) faire subir un examen contradictoire à; **~-eyed** adj qui louche; **~fire** n feux croisés; **~ing** n (sea passage) traversée f; (also: **pedestrian ~ing**) passage clouté; **~ing guard** (US) n contractuel qui fait traverser la rue aux enfants; **~ purposes** npl: **to be at ~ purposes with sb** comprendre qn de travers; **~ reference** n renvoi m, référence f; **~roads** n carrefour m; **~ section** n (of object) coupe transversale; (in population) échantillon m; **~walk** (US) n passage clouté; **~wind** n vent m de travers; **~word** n mots mpl croisés

crotch [krɔtʃ] n (ANAT, of garment) entre-jambes m inv

crouch [krautʃ] vi s'accroupir; se tapir

crow [krəu] n (bird) corneille f; (of cock) chant m du coq, cocorico m ♦ vi (cock) chanter

crowbar ['krəuba:r] n levier m

crowd [kraud] n foule f ♦ vt remplir ♦ vi affluer, s'attrouper, s'entasser; **to ~ in** entrer en foule; **~ed** adj bondé(e), plein(e)

crown [kraun] n couronne f; (of head) sommet m de la tête; (of hill) sommet ♦ vt couronner; **~ jewels** npl joyaux mpl de la Couronne

crow's-feet ['krəuzfiːt] npl pattes fpl d'oie

crucial ['kruːʃl] adj crucial(e), décisif (-ive)

crucifix ['kruːsɪfɪks] n (REL) crucifix m; **~ion** [kruːsɪ'fɪkʃən] n (REL) crucifixion f

crude [kruːd] adj (materials) brut(e); non raffiné(e); (fig: basic) rudimentaire, sommaire, (: vulgar) cru(e), grossier (-ère); **~ (oil)** n (pétrole) brut m

cruel ['kruəl] adj cruel(le); **~ty** n cruauté f

cruise [kruːz] n croisière f ♦ vi (ship) croiser; (car) rouler; **~r** n croiseur m; (motorboat) yacht m de croisière

crumb [krʌm] n miette f

crumble ['krʌmbl] vt émietter ♦ vi (plaster etc) s'effriter; (land, earth) s'ébouler; (building) s'écrouler, crouler; (fig) s'effondrer; **crumbly** adj friable

crumpet ['krʌmpɪt] n petite crêpe (épaisse)

crumple ['krʌmpl] vt froisser, friper

crunch [krʌntʃ] vt croquer; (underfoot) faire craquer or crisser, écraser ♦ n (fig) instant m or moment m critique, moment de vérité; **~y** adj croquant(e), croustillant(e)

crusade [kruː'seɪd] n croisade f

crush [krʌʃ] n foule f, cohue f; (love): **to have a ~ on sb** avoir le béguin pour qn (inf); (drink): **lemon ~** citron pressé ♦ vt écraser; (crumple) froisser; (fig: hopes) anéantir

crust [krʌst] n croûte f

crutch [krʌtʃ] n béquille f

crux [krʌks] n point crucial

cry [kraɪ] vi pleurer; (shout: also: ~ **out**) crier ♦ n cri m; **~ off** (inf) vi se dédire;

se décommander

cryptic ['krɪptɪk] adj énigmatique

crystal ['krɪstl] n cristal m; **~-clear** adj clair(e) comme de l'eau de roche

CSA n abbr (= Child Support Agency) organisme pour la protection des enfants de parents séparés, qui contrôle le versement des pensions alimentaires

CTC n abbr = **city technology college**

cub [kʌb] n petit m (d'un animal); (also: **C~ scout**) louveteau m

Cuba ['kjuːbə] n Cuba m

cube [kjuːb] n cube m ♦ vt (MATH) élever au cube; **cubic** adj cubique; **cubic metre** etc mètre m etc cube; **cubic capacity** n cylindrée f

cubicle ['kjuːbɪkl] n (in hospital) box m; (at pool) cabine f

cuckoo ['kuku:] n coucou m; **~ clock** n (pendule f à) coucou m

cucumber ['kjuːkʌmbər] n concombre m

cuddle ['kʌdl] vt câliner, caresser ♦ vi se blottir l'un contre l'autre

cue [kjuː] n (snooker ~) queue f de billard; (THEATRE etc) signal m

cuff [kʌf] n (BRIT: of shirt, coat etc) poignet m, manchette f; (US: of trousers) revers m; (blow) tape f; **off the ~** à l'improviste; **~ links** npl boutons mpl de manchette

cul-de-sac ['kʌldəsæk] n cul-de-sac m, impasse f

culinary ['kʌlɪnərɪ] adj culinaire

cull [kʌl] vt sélectionner ♦ n (of animals) massacre m

culminate ['kʌlmɪneɪt] vi: **to ~ in** finir or se terminer par; (end in) mener à; **culmination** [kʌlmɪ'neɪʃən] n point culminant

culottes [kjuː'lɒts] npl jupe-culotte f

culprit ['kʌlprɪt] n coupable m/f

cult [kʌlt] n culte m

cultivate ['kʌltɪveɪt] vt cultiver; **cultivation** [kʌltɪ'veɪʃən] n culture f

cultural ['kʌltʃərəl] adj culturel(le)

culture ['kʌltʃər] n culture f; **~d** adj (person) cultivé(e)

cumbersome ['kʌmbəsəm] adj encombrant(e), embarrassant(e)

cunning ['kʌnɪŋ] n ruse f, astuce f ♦ adj rusé(e), malin(-igne); (device, idea) astucieux(-euse)

cup [kʌp] n tasse f; (as prize) coupe f; (of bra) bonnet m

cupboard ['kʌbəd] n armoire f; (built-in) placard m

cup tie (BRIT) n match m de coupe

curate ['kjuərɪt] n vicaire m

curator [kjuə'reɪtə*] n conservateur m (d'un musée etc)

curb [kɜːb] vt refréner, mettre un frein à ♦ n (fig) frein m, restriction f; (US: kerb) bord m du trottoir

curdle ['kɜːdl] vi se cailler

cure [kjuə*] vt guérir; (CULIN: salt) saler; (: smoke) fumer; (: dry) sécher ♦ n remède m

curfew ['kɜːfjuː] n couvre-feu m

curiosity [kjuərɪ'ɔsɪtɪ] n curiosité f

curious ['kjuərɪəs] adj curieux(-euse)

curl [kɜːl] n boucle f (de cheveux) ♦ vt, vi boucler; (tightly) friser; ~ **up** vi s'enrouler; se pelotonner; **~er** n bigoudi m, rouleau m; **~y** adj bouclé(e); frisé(e)

currant ['kʌrnt] n (dried) raisin m de Corinthe, raisin sec; (bush) groseiller m; (fruit) groseille f

currency ['kʌrnsɪ] n monnaie f; **to gain** ~ (fig) s'accréditer

current ['kʌrnt] n courant m ♦ adj courant(e); ~ **account** (BRIT) n compte courant; ~ **affairs** npl (questions fpl d'actualité f); **~ly** adv actuellement

curriculum [kə'rɪkjuləm] (pl **~s** or **curricula**) n programme m d'études; ~ **vitae** [-'viːtaɪ] n curriculum vitae m

curry ['kʌrɪ] n curry m ♦ vt: **to ~ favour with** chercher à s'attirer les bonnes grâces de

curse [kɜːs] vi jurer, blasphémer ♦ vt maudire ♦ n (spell) malédiction f; (problem, scourge) fléau m; (swearword) juron m

cursor ['kɜːsə*] n (COMPUT) curseur m

cursory ['kɜːsərɪ] adj superficiel(le), hâtif(-ive)

curt [kɜːt] adj brusque, sec (sèche)

curtail [kɜː'teɪl] vt (visit etc) écourter; (expenses, freedom etc) réduire

curtain ['kɜːtn] n rideau m

curts(e)y ['kɜːtsɪ] vi faire une révérence

curve [kɜːv] n courbe f; (in the road) tournant m, virage m ♦ vi se courber; (road) faire une courbe

cushion ['kuʃən] n coussin m ♦ vt (fall, shock) amortir

custard ['kʌstəd] n (for pouring) crème anglaise

custody ['kʌstədɪ] n (of child) garde f; **to take sb into** ~ (suspect) placer en détention préventive

custom ['kʌstəm] n coutume f, usage m; (COMM) clientèle f; **~ary** adj habituel(le)

customer ['kʌstəmə*] n client(e)

customized ['kʌstəmaɪzd] adj (car etc) construit(e) sur commande

custom-made ['kʌstəm'meɪd] adj (clothes) fait(e) sur mesure; (other goods) hors série, fait(e) sur commande

customs ['kʌstəmz] npl douane f; ~ **officer** n douanier(-ière)

cut [kʌt] (pt, pp **cut**) vt couper; (meat) découper; (reduce) réduire ♦ vi couper ♦ n coupure f; (of clothes) coupe f; (in salary etc) réduction f; (of meat) morceau m; **to** ~ **one's hand** se couper la main; **to** ~ **a tooth** percer une dent; ~ **down** vt fus (tree etc) couper, abattre; (consumption) réduire; ~ **off** vt couper; (fig) isoler; ~ **out** vt découper; (stop) arrêter; (remove) ôter; ~ **up** vt (paper, meat) découper; **~back** n réduction f

cute [kjuːt] adj mignon(ne), adorable

cutlery ['kʌtlərɪ] n couverts mpl

cutlet ['kʌtlɪt] n côtelette f

cut: **~out** n (switch) coupe-circuit m inv; (cardboard cutout) découpage m; **~-price** (US **cut-rate**) adj au rabais, à prix réduit; **~-throat** n assassin m ♦ adj acharné(e); **~ting** adj tranchant(e) coupant(e); (fig) cinglant(e), mordant(e) ♦ n (BRIT: from newspaper) coupure f (de journal); (from plant) bouture f

CV n abbr = **curriculum vitae**

cwt abbr = **hundredweight(s)**

cyanide ['saɪənaɪd] n cyanure m

cybercafé ['saɪbəkæfeɪ] n cybercafé m

cyberspace ['saɪbəspeɪs] n cyberspace m

cycle ['saɪkl] n cycle m; (bicycle) bicyclette f, vélo m ♦ vi faire de la bicyclette; ~ **hire** n location f de vélos; ~ **lane** or **path** n piste f cyclable; **cycling** n cyclisme m; **cyclist** ['saɪklɪst] n cycliste m/f

cygnet ['sɪgnɪt] n jeune cygne m

cylinder ['sɪlɪndə'] n cylindre m; ~ **head gasket** n joint m de culasse

cymbals ['sɪmblz] npl cymbales fpl

cynic ['sɪnɪk] n cynique m/f; ~**al** adj cynique; ~**ism** ['sɪnɪsɪzəm] n cynisme m

Cypriot ['sɪprɪət] adj cypriote, chypriote ♦ n Cypriote m/f, Chypriote m/f

Cyprus ['saɪprəs] n Chypre f

cyst [sɪst] n kyste m

cystitis [sɪs'taɪtɪs] n cystite f

czar [zɑ:'] n tsar m

Czech [tʃɛk] adj tchèque ♦ n Tchèque m/f; (LING) tchèque m

Czechoslovak [tʃɛkə'sləuvæk] adj tchécoslovaque ♦ n Tchécoslovaque m/f

Czechoslovakia [tʃɛkəslə'vækɪə] n Tchécoslovaquie f

D, d

D [di:] n (MUS) ré m

dab [dæb] vt (eyes, wound) tamponner; (paint, cream) appliquer (par petites touches or rapidement)

dabble ['dæbl] vi: **to ~ in** faire or se mêler or s'occuper un peu de

dad [dæd] n, **daddy** ['dædɪ] n papa m

daffodil ['dæfədɪl] n jonquille f

daft [dɑ:ft] adj idiot(e), stupide

dagger ['dægə'] n poignard m

daily ['deɪlɪ] adj quotidien(ne), journalier(-ère) ♦ n quotidien m ♦ adv tous les jours

dainty ['deɪntɪ] adj délicat(e), mignon(ne)

dairy ['dɛərɪ] n (BRIT: shop) crémerie f, laiterie f; (on farm) laiterie; ~ **products** npl produits laitiers; ~ **store** (US) n crémerie f, laiterie f

daisy ['deɪzɪ] n pâquerette f

dale [deɪl] n vallon m

dam [dæm] n barrage m ♦ vt endiguer

damage ['dæmɪdʒ] n dégâts mpl, dommages mpl; (fig) tort m ♦ vt endommager, abîmer; (fig) faire du tort à; ~**s** npl (LAW) dommages-intérêts mpl

damn [dæm] vt condamner; (curse) maudire ♦ n (inf): **I don't give a ~** je m'en fous ♦ adj (inf: also: ~**ed**): **this ~** ... ce sacré or foutu ...; ~ **(it)!** zut!; ~**ing** adj accablant(e)

damp [dæmp] adj humide ♦ n humidité f ♦ vt (also: ~**en**: cloth, rag) humecter; (: enthusiasm) refroidir

damson ['dæmzən] n prune f de Damas

dance [dɑ:ns] n danse f; (social event) bal m ♦ vi danser; ~ **hall** n salle f de bal, dancing m; ~**r** n danseur(-euse)

dancing n danse f

dandelion ['dændɪlaɪən] n pissenlit m

dandruff ['dændrəf] n pellicules fpl

Dane [deɪn] n Danois(e)

danger ['deɪndʒə'] n danger m; **there is a ~ of fire** il y a (un) risque d'incendie; **in ~** en danger; **he was in ~ of falling** il risquait de tomber; ~**ous** adj dangereux(-euse)

dangle ['dæŋgl] vt balancer ♦ vi pendre

Danish ['deɪnɪʃ] adj danois(e) ♦ n (LING) danois m

dare [dɛə'] vt: **to ~ sb to do** défier qn de faire ♦ vi: **to ~ (to) do sth** oser faire qch; **I ~ say** (I suppose) il est probable (que); **daring** adj hardi(e), audacieux (-euse); (dress) osé(e) ♦ n audace f, har-

renvoi [ʀɑ̃vwa] *nm* (*d'employé*) dismissal; (*d'élève*) expulsion; (*référence*) cross-reference; (*éructation*) belch; **renvoyer** *vt* to send back; (*congédier*) to dismiss; (*élève: définitivement*) to expel; (*lumière*) to reflect; (*ajourner*): **renvoyer qch (à)** to put sth off *ou* postpone sth (until)

repaire [ʀ(ə)pɛʀ] *nm* den

répandre [ʀepɑ̃dʀ] *vt* (*renverser*) to spill; (*étaler, diffuser*) to spread; (*odeur*) to give off; **se ~** *vi* to spill; (*se propager*) to spread; **répandu, e** *adj* (*opinion, usage*) widespread

réparation [ʀepaʀasjɔ̃] *nf* repair

réparer [ʀepaʀe] *vt* to repair; (*fig: offense*) to make up for, atone for; (: *oubli, erreur*) to put right

repartie [ʀepaʀti] *nf* retort; **avoir de la ~** to be quick at repartee

repartir [ʀ(ə)paʀtiʀ] *vi* to leave again; (*voyageur*) to set off again; (*fig*) to get going again; **~ à zéro** to start from scratch (again)

répartir [ʀepaʀtiʀ] *vt* (*pour attribuer*) to share out; (*pour disperser, disposer*) to divide up; (*poids*) to distribute; **se ~** (*travail, rôles*) to share out between themselves; **répartition** *nf* (*des richesses etc*) distribution

repas [ʀ(ə)pɑ] *nm* meal

repassage [ʀ(ə)pɑsaʒ] *nm* ironing

repasser [ʀ(ə)pɑse] *vi* to come (*ou* go) back ♦ *vt* (*vêtement, tissu*) to iron; (*examen*) to retake, resit; (*film*) to show again; (*leçon: revoir*) to go over (again)

repêcher [ʀ(ə)peʃe] *vt* to fish out; (*candidat*) to pass (*by inflating marks*)

repentir [ʀapɑ̃tiʀ] *nm* repentance; **se ~** *vi* to repent; **se ~ d'avoir fait qch** (*regretter*) to regret having done sth

répercussions [ʀepɛʀkysjɔ̃] *nfpl* (*fig*) repercussions

répercuter [ʀepɛʀkyte]: **se ~** *vi* (*bruit*) to reverberate; (*fig*): **se ~ sur** to have repercussions on

repère [ʀ(ə)pɛʀ] *nm* mark; (*monument,

événement) landmark

repérer [ʀ(ə)peʀe] *vt* (*fam: erreur, personne*) to spot; (: *endroit*) to locate; **se ~** *vi* to find one's way about

répertoire [ʀepɛʀtwaʀ] *nm* (*liste*) (alphabetical) list; (*carnet*) index notebook; (*INFORM*) folder, directory; (*d'un artiste*) repertoire

répéter [ʀepete] *vt* to repeat; (*préparer: leçon*) to learn, go over; (*THÉÂTRE*) to rehearse; **se ~** *vi* (*redire*) to repeat o.s.; (*se reproduire*) to be repeated, recur

répétition [ʀepetisjɔ̃] *nf* repetition; (*THÉÂTRE*) rehearsal

répit [ʀepi] *nm* respite

replier [ʀ(ə)plije] *vt* (*rabattre*) to fold down *ou* over; **se ~** *vi* (*troupes, armée*) to withdraw, fall back; (*sur soi-même*) to withdraw into o.s.

réplique [ʀeplik] *nf* (*repartie, fig*) reply; (*THÉÂTRE*) line; (*copie*) replica; **répliquer** *vi* to reply; (*riposter*) to retaliate

répondeur [ʀepɔ̃dœʀ, øz] *nm*: **~ automatique** (*TÉL*) answering machine

répondre [ʀepɔ̃dʀ] *vi* to answer, reply; (*freins*) to respond; **~ à** to reply to, answer; (*affection, salut*) to return; (*provocation*) to respond to; (*correspondre à: besoin*) to answer; (: *conditions*) to meet; (: *description*) to match; (*avec impertinence*): **~ à qn** to answer sb back; **~ de** to answer for

réponse [ʀepɔ̃s] *nf* answer, reply; **en ~ à** in reply to

reportage [ʀ(ə)pɔʀtaʒ] *nm* report; (*fonction*) reporting; (*en direct*) live commentary

reporter¹ [ʀapɔʀtɛʀ] *nm* reporter

reporter² [ʀapɔʀte] *vt* (*ajourner*): **~ qch (à)** to postpone sth (until); (*transférer*): **~ qch sur** to transfer sth to; (*se référer à: époque*) to think back to; (*document*) to refer to

repos [ʀ(ə)po] *nm* rest; (*tranquillité*) peace and quiet; (*MIL*): **~!** stand at ease!; **ce n'est pas de tout ~!** it's no picnic!

reposant, e [ʀ(ə)pozɑ̃, ɑ̃t] *adj* restful

reposer [R(ə)poze] vt (verre, livre) to put down; (délasser) to rest ♦ vi: **laisser ~** (pâte) to leave to stand; **se ~** vi to rest; **se ~ sur qn** to rely on sb; **~ sur** (fig) to rest on

repoussant, e [R(ə)pusɑ̃, ɑ̃t] adj repulsive

repousser [R(ə)puse] vi to grow again ♦ vt to repel, repulse; (offre) to turn down, reject; (personne) to push back; (différer) to put back

reprendre [R(ə)pRɑ̃dR] vt (objet prêté, donné) to take back; (prisonnier, ville) to recapture; (firme, entreprise) to take over; (le travail) to resume; (emprunter. argument, idée) to take up; (refaire: article etc) to go over again; (vêtement) to alter; (réprimander) to tell off; (corriger) to correct; (chercher): **je viendrai te ~ à 4 h** I'll come and fetch you at 4 (se resservir de): **~ du pain/un œuf** to take (ou eat) more bread/another egg ♦ vi (classes, pluie) to start (up) again; (activités, travaux, combats) to resume, start (up) again; (affaires) to pick up; (dire): **reprit-il** he went on; **se ~** vi (se ressaisir) to recover; **~ des forces** to recover one's strength; **~ courage** to take new heart; **~ la route** to set off again; **~ haleine** ou **son souffle** to get one's breath back

représailles [R(ə)pRezaj] nfpl reprisals

représentant, e [R(ə)pRezɑ̃tɑ̃, ɑ̃t] nm/f representative

représentation [R(ə)pRezɑ̃tasjɔ̃] nf (symbole, image) representation; (spectacle) performance

représenter [R(ə)pRezɑ̃te] vt to represent; (donner: pièce, opéra) to perform; **se ~** vt (se figurer) to imagine

répression [RepResjɔ̃] nf repression

réprimer [RepRime] vt (émotions) to suppress; (peuple etc) to repress

repris [R(ə)pRi, iz] nm: **~ de justice** ex-prisoner, ex-convict

reprise [R(ə)pRiz] nf (recommencement) resumption; (économique) recovery; (TV) repeat; (COMM) trade-in, part exchange; (raccommodage) mend; **à plusieurs ~s** on several occasions

repriser [R(ə)pRize] vt (chaussette, lainage) to darn; (tissu) to mend

reproche [R(ə)pRɔʃ] nm (remontrance) reproach; **faire des ~s à qn** to reproach sb; **sans ~(s)** beyond reproach

reprocher vt: **reprocher qch à qn** to reproach ou blame sb for sth; **reprocher qch à** (critiquer) to have sth against

reproduction [R(ə)pRɔdyksjɔ̃] nf reproduction

reproduire [R(ə)pRɔdɥiR] vt to reproduce; **se ~** vi (BIO) to reproduce; (récommencer) to recur, re-occur

réprouver [RepRuve] vt to reprove

reptile [Reptil] nm reptile

repu, e [Rəpy] adj satisfied, sated

république [Repyblik] nf republic

répugnant, e [Repyɲɑ̃, ɑ̃t] adj disgusting

répugner [Repyɲe] vt: **~ à** vt: **~ à qn** to repel ou disgust sb; **~ à faire** to be loath ou reluctant to do

réputation [Repytasjɔ̃] nf reputation; **réputé, e** adj renowned

requérir [RəkeRiR] vt (nécessiter) to require, call for

requête [Rəket] nf request

requin [Rəkɛ̃] nm shark

requis, e [Rəki, iz] adj required

RER sigle m (= réseau express régional) Greater Paris high-speed train service

rescapé, e [Reskape] nm/f survivor

rescousse [Reskus] nf: **aller à la ~ de qn** to go to sb's aid ou rescue

réseau, x [Rezo] nm network

réservation [RezeRvasjɔ̃] nf booking, reservation

réserve [RezeRv] nf (retenue) reserve; (entrepôt) storeroom; (restriction, d'Indiens) reservation; (de pêche, chasse) preserve; **de ~** (provisions etc) in reserve

réservé, e [RezeRve] adj reserved;

chasse/pêche ~e private hunting/ fishing

réserver [REZERVe] *vt* to reserve; (*chambre, billet etc*) to book, reserve; (*fig: destiner*) to have in store; (*garder*): **~ qch pour/à** to keep *ou* save sth for

réservoir [REZERVWAR] *nm* tank

résidence [Rezidɑ̃s] *nf* residence; **~ secondaire** second home; **résidentiel, le** *adj* residential; **résider** *vi*: **résider à/dans/en** to reside in; **résider dans** (*fig*) to lie in

résidu [Rezidy] *nm* residue *no pl*

résigner [Rezine]: **se ~** *vi*: **se ~ (à qch/à faire)** to resign o.s. (to sth/to doing)

résilier [Rezilje] *vt* to terminate

résistance [Rezistɑ̃s] *nf* resistance; (*de réchaud, bouilloire: fil*) element

résistant, e [Rezistɑ̃, ɑ̃t] *adj* (*personne*) robust, tough; (*matériau*) strong, hard-wearing

résister [Reziste] *vi* to resist; **~ à** (*assaut, tentation*) to resist; (*supporter: gel etc*) to withstand; (*désobéir à*) to stand up to, oppose

résolu, e [Rezɔly] *pp de* **résoudre**
♦ *adj*: **être ~ à qch/faire** to be set upon sth/doing

résolution [Rezɔlysjɔ̃] *nf* (*fermeté, décision*) resolution; (*d'un problème*) solution

résolve *etc* [Rezɔlv] *vb voir* **résoudre**

résonner [Rezɔne] *vi* (*cloche, pas*) to reverberate, resound; (*salle*) to be resonant

résorber [Rezɔrbe]: **se ~** *vi* (*fig: chômage*) to be reduced; (: *déficit*) to be absorbed

résoudre [Rezudr] *vt* to solve; **se ~ à faire** to bring o.s. to do

respect [RESpɛ] *nm* respect; **tenir en ~** to keep at bay; **respecter** *vt* to respect; **respectueux, -euse** *adj* respectful

respiration [RESpiRasjɔ̃] *nf* breathing *no pl*

respirer [RESpiRe] *vi* to breathe; (*fig: se détendre*) to get one's breath; (: *se rassurer*) to breathe again ♦ *vt* to breathe (in), inhale; (*manifester: santé, calme etc*) to exude

resplendir [RESplɑ̃diR] *vi* to shine; (*fig*): **~ (de)** to be radiant (with)

responsabilité [RESpɔ̃sabilite] *nf* responsibility; (*légale*) liability

responsable [RESpɔ̃sabl] *adj* responsible ♦ *nm/f* (*coupable*) person responsible; (*personne compétente*) person in charge; (*de parti, syndicat*) official; **~ de** responsible for

resquiller [Reskije] (*fam*) *vi* to get in without paying; (*ne pas faire la queue*) to jump the queue

ressaisir [R(ə)seziR]: **se ~** *vi* to regain one's self-control

ressasser [R(ə)sase] *vt* to keep going over

ressemblance [R(ə)sɑ̃blɑ̃s] *nf* resemblance, similarity, likeness

ressemblant, e [R(ə)sɑ̃blɑ̃, ɑ̃t] *adj* (*portrait*) lifelike, true to life

ressembler [R(ə)sɑ̃ble]: **~ à** *vt* to be like, resemble; (*visuellement*) to look like; **se ~** *vi* to be alike (*ou* look) alike

ressemeler [R(ə)sɑm(ə)le] *vt* to (re)sole

ressentiment [R(ə)sɑ̃timɑ̃] *nm* resentment

ressentir [R(ə)sɑ̃tiR] *vt* to feel

resserrer [R(ə)seRe] *vt* (*nœud, boulon*) to tighten (up); (*fig: liens*) to strengthen

resservir [R(ə)seRviR] *vi* to do *ou* serve again; **se ~** *vi* to help o.s. again

ressort [RəsɔR] *nm* (*pièce*) spring; (*énergie*) spirit; (*recours*): **en dernier ~** as a last resort; (*compétence*): **être du ~ de** to fall within the competence of

ressortir [RəsɔRtiR] *vi* to go (*ou* come) out (again); (*contraster*) to stand out; **~ de** to emerge from; **faire ~** (*fig: souligner*) to bring out

ressortissant, e [R(ə)sɔRtisɑ̃, ɑ̃t] *nm/f*

national

ressources [R(ə)suRs] *nfpl (moyens)* resources

ressusciter [Resysite] *vt (fig)* to revive, bring back ♦ *vi* to rise (from the dead)

restant, e [Rɛstɑ̃, ɑ̃t] *adj* remaining ♦ *nm:* **le ~ (de)** the remainder (of); **un ~ de** *(de trop)* some left-over

restaurant [Rɛstɔrɑ̃] *nm* restaurant

restauration [Rɛstɔrasjɔ̃] *nf* restoration; *(hôtellerie)* catering; **~ rapide** fast food

restaurer [Rɛstɔre] *vt* to restore; **se ~** *vi* to have something to eat

reste [Rɛst] *nm (restant):* **le ~ (de)** the rest (of); *(de trop):* **un ~ (de)** some left-over; **~s** *nmpl (nourriture)* left-overs; *(d'une cité antique, dépouille mortelle)* remains; **du ~, au ~** besides, moreover

rester [Rɛste] *vi* to stay, remain; *(subsister)* to remain, be left; *(durer)* to last, live on ♦ *vb impers:* **il reste du pain/2 œufs** there's some bread/there are 2 eggs left (over); **restons-en là** let's leave it at that; **il me reste assez de temps** I have enough time left; **il ne me reste plus qu'à ...** I've just got to ...

restituer [Rɛstitɥe] *vt (objet, somme):* **~ qch (à qn)** to return sth (to sb)

restreindre [Rɛstrɛ̃dr] *vt* to restrict, limit

restriction [Rɛstriksjɔ̃] *nf* restriction

résultat [Rezylta] *nm* result; *(d'examen, d'élection)* results *pl*

résulter [Rezylte]: **~ de** *vt* to result from, be the result of

résumé [Rezyme] *nm* summary, résumé

résumer [Rezyme] *vt (texte)* to summarize; *(récapituler)* to sum up

résurrection [Rezyrɛksjɔ̃] *nf* resurrection

rétablir [Retablir] *vt* to restore, re-establish; **se ~** *vi (guérir)* to recover; *(silence, calme)* to return, be restored;

rétablissement [Retablismɑ̃] *nm* restoring; *(guéri-*

son) recovery

retaper [R(ə)tape] *(fam) vt (maison, voiture etc)* to do up; *(revigorer)* to buck up

retard [R(ə)taR] *nm (d'une personne attendue)* lateness *no pl; (sur l'horaire, un programme)* delay; *(fig: scolaire, mental etc)* backwardness; **en ~ (de 2 heures)** (2 hours) late; **avoir du ~** to be late; *(sur un programme)* to be behind (schedule); **prendre du ~** *(train, avion)* to be delayed; **sans ~** without delay

retardataire [R(ə)taRdatɛR] *nmf* latecomer

retardement [R(ə)taRdəmɑ̃]: **à ~** *adj* delayed action *cpd;* **bombe à ~** time bomb

retarder [R(ə)taRde] *vt* to delay; *(montre)* to put back ♦ *vi (montre)* to be slow; **~ qn (d'une heure)** to delay sb (by an hour); **~ qch (de 2 jours)** *(départ, date)* to put sth back (2 days)

retenir [Rət(ə)niR] *vt (garder, retarder)* to keep, detain; *(maintenir: objet qui glisse, fig: colère, larmes)* to hold back; *(se rappeler)* to retain; *(réserver)* to reserve; *(accepter: proposition etc)* to accept; *(fig: empêcher d'agir):* **~ qn (de faire)** to hold sb back (from doing); *(prélever):* **~ qch (sur)** to deduct sth (from); **se ~** *(se raccrocher):* **se ~ à** to hold onto; *(se contenir):* **se ~ de faire** to restrain o.s. from doing; **~ son souffle** to hold one's breath

retentir [R(ə)tɑ̃tiR] *vi* to ring out; *(salle):* **~ de** to ring ou resound with; **retentissant, e** *adj* resounding; **retentissement** *nm* repercussion

retenu, e [Rət(ə)ny] *adj (place)* reserved; *(personne: empêché)* held up; **retenue** *nf (prélèvement)* deduction; *(scol)* detention; *(modération)* (self-)restraint

réticence [Retisɑ̃s] *nf* hesitation, reluctance *no pl;* **réticent, e** *adj* hesitant, reluctant

rétine [retin] *nf* retina

retiré, e [R(ə)tiʀe] *adj* (*vie*) secluded; (*lieu*) remote

retirer [R(ə)tiʀe] *vt* (*vêtement, lunettes*) to take off, remove; (*argent, plainte*) to withdraw; (*reprendre: bagages, billets*) to collect, pick up; (*extraire*): ~ **qch** to take sth out of, remove sth from

retombées [ʀətɔ̃be] *nfpl* (*radioactives*) fallout *sg*; (*fig: répercussions*) effects

retomber [ʀ(ə)tɔ̃be] *vi* (*à nouveau*) to fall again; (*atterrir: après un saut etc*) to land; (*échoir*): ~ **sur qn** to fall on sb

rétorquer [Retɔʀke] *vt*: ~ **(à qn) que** to retort (to sb) that

retouche [R(ə)tuʃ] *nf* (*sur vêtement*) alteration; **retoucher** [R(ə)tuʃe] *vt* (*photographie*) to touch up; (*texte, vêtement*) to alter

retour [R(ə)tuʀ] *nm* return; **au** ~ (*en route*) on the way back; **à mon** ~ when I get/got back; **être de** ~ **(de)** to be back (from); **par** ~ **du courrier** by return of post

retourner [R(ə)tuʀne] *vt* (*dans l'autre sens: matelas, crêpe etc*) to turn (over); (*: sac, vêtement*) to turn inside out; (*fam: bouleverser*) to shake; (*renvoyer, restituer*): ~ **qch à qn** to return sth to sb ♦ *vi* (*aller, revenir*): ~ **quelque part/à** to go back or return somewhere/to; **se** ~ *vi* (*tourner la tête*) to turn round; ~ **à** (*état, activité*) to return to, go back to; **se** ~ **contre** (*fig*) to turn against

retrait [R(ə)tʀɛ] *nm* (*d'argent*) withdrawal; **en** ~ set back; ~ **du permis (de conduire)** disqualification from driving (*BRIT*), revocation of driver's license (*US*)

retraite [R(ə)tʀɛt] *nf* (*d'un employé*) retirement; (*revenu*) pension; (*d'une armée, REL*) retreat; **prendre sa** ~ to retire; ~ **anticipée** early retirement; **retraité, e** *adj* retired ♦ *nm/f* pensioner

retrancher [R(ə)tʀɑ̃ʃe] *vt* (*nombre, somme*) to take *ou* deduct; ~ **qch de** to take *ou* deduct sth from; **se** ~ **derrière/dans** to take refuge behind/in

retransmettre [R(ə)tʀɑ̃smɛtʀ] *vt* (*RADIO*) to broadcast; (*TV*) to show

rétrécir [Retʀesiʀ] *vt* (*vêtement*) to take in ♦ *vi* to shrink

rétribution [Retʀibysjɔ̃] *nf* payment

rétro [Retʀo] *adj inv*: **la mode** ~ the nostalgia vogue

rétrograde [Retʀogʀad] *adj* reactionary, backward-looking

rétroprojecteur [Retʀopʀɔʒɛktœʀ] *nm* overhead projector

rétrospective [Retʀɔspɛktiv] *nf* retrospective exhibition/season; **rétrospectivement** *adv* in retrospect

retrousser [R(ə)tʀuse] *vt* to roll up

retrouvailles [R(ə)tʀuvaj] *nfpl* reunion *sg*

retrouver [R(ə)tʀuve] *vt* (*fugitif, objet perdu*) to find; (*calme, santé*) to regain; (*revoir*) to see again; (*rejoindre*) to meet (again), join; **se** ~ *vi* to meet; (*s'orienter*) to find one's way; **se** ~ **quelque part** to find o.s. somewhere; **s'y** ~ (*y voir clair*) to make sense of it; (*rentrer dans ses frais*) to break even

rétroviseur [Retʀovizœʀ] *nm* (rear-view) mirror

réunion [Reynjɔ̃] *nf* (*séance*) meeting

réunir [Reyniʀ] *vt* (*rassembler*) to gather together; (*inviter: amis, famille*) to have round, have in; (*cumuler: qualités etc*) to combine; (*rapprocher: ennemis*) to bring together (again), reunite; (*rattacher: parties*) to join (together); **se** ~ *vi* (*se rencontrer*) to meet

réussi, e [Reysi] *adj* successful

réussir [Reysiʀ] *vi* to succeed, be successful; (*à un examen*) to pass ♦ *vt* to make a success of; ~ **à faire** to succeed in doing; ~ **à qn** (*être bénéfique à*) to agree with sb; **réussite** *nf* success; (*CARTES*) patience

revaloir [R(ə)valwaʀ] *vt*: **je vous revaudrai cela** I'll repay you some day; (*en mal*) I'll pay you back for this

revanche [R(ə)vɑ̃ʃ] *nf* revenge; (*sport*) revenge match; **en** ~ on the other hand

rêve [REV] *nm* dream; **de ~** dream *cpd*; **faire un ~** to have a dream

revêche [Rəvɛʃ] *adj* surly, sour-tempered

réveil [Revɛj] *nm* waking up *no pl*; (*fig*) awakening; (*pendule*) alarm (clock); **au ~** on waking (up); **réveille-matin** *inv* alarm clock; **réveiller** *vt* (*personne*) to wake up; (*fig*) to awaken, revive; **se réveiller** *vi* to wake up

réveillon [Revɛjɔ̃] *nm* Christmas Eve; (*de la Saint-Sylvestre*) New Year's Eve; **réveillonner** *vi* to celebrate Christmas Eve (*ou* New Year's Eve)

révélateur, -trice [Revelatœr, tris] *adj*: **~ (de qch)** revealing (sth)

révéler [Revele] *vt* to reveal; **se ~** *vi* to be revealed, reveal itself ♦ *vb +attrib*: **se ~ difficile/aisé** to prove difficult/easy

revenant, e [Rəvənɑ̃, ɑ̃t] *nm/f* ghost

revendeur, -euse [Rəvɑ̃dœr, øz] *nm/f* (*détaillant*) retailer; (*de drogue*) (drug-)dealer

revendication [Rəvɑ̃dikasjɔ̃] *nf* claim, demand

revendiquer [Rəvɑ̃dike] *vt* to claim, demand; (*responsabilité*) to claim

revendre [Rəvɑ̃dr] *vt* (*d'occasion*) to resell; (*détailler*) to sell; **à ~** (*en abondance*) to spare

revenir [Rəvənir] *vi* to come back; (*coûter*): **~ cher/à 100 F (à qn)** to cost (sb) a lot/100 F; **~ à** (*reprendre: études, projet*) to return to, go back to; (*équivaloir à*) to amount to; **~ à qn** (*part, honneur*) to go to sb, be sb's; (*souvenir, nom*) to come back to sb; **~ sur** (*question, sujet*) to go back over; (*engagement*) to go back on; **~ à soi** to come round; **n'en pas ~: je n'en reviens pas** I can't get over it; **~ sur ses pas** to retrace one's steps; **cela revient à dire que/au même** it amounts to saying that/the same thing; **faire ~** (*CULIN*) to brown

revenu [Rəvəny] *nm* income; **~s** *nmpl*

income *sg*

rêver [Reve] *vi, vt* to dream; **~ de/à** to dream of

réverbère [Reverber] *nm* street lamp *ou* light; **réverbérer** *vt* to reflect

révérence [Reverɑ̃s] *nf* (*salut*) bow; (: *de femme*) curtsey

rêverie [Revri] *nf* daydreaming *no pl*, daydream

revers [Rəver] *nm* (*de feuille, main*) back; (*d'étoffe*) wrong side; (*de pièce, médaille*) back, reverse; (*TENNIS, PINGPONG*) backhand; (*de veste*) lapel; (*fig: échec*) setback

revêtement [Rəvɛtmɑ̃] *nm* (*des sols*) flooring; (*de chaussée*) surface

revêtir [Rəvɛtir] *vt* (*habit*) to don, put on; (*prendre: importance, apparence*) to take on; **~ qch de** to cover sth with

rêveur, -euse [Revœr, øz] *adj* dreamy ♦ *nm/f* dreamer

revient [Rəvjɛ̃] *vb voir* **revenir**

revigorer [Rəvigɔre] *vt* (*air frais*) to invigorate, brace up; (*repas, boisson*) to revive, buck up

revirement [Rəvirmɑ̃] *nm* change of mind; (*d'une situation*) reversal

réviser [Revize] *vt* to revise; (*machine*) to overhaul, service

révision [Revizjɔ̃] *nf* revision; (*de voiture*) servicing *no pl*

revivre [Rəvivr] *vi* (*reprendre des forces*) to come alive again ♦ *vt* (*épreuve, moment*) to relive

revoir [Rəvwar] *vt* to see again; (*réviser*) to revise ♦ *nm*: **au ~** goodbye

révoltant, e [Revɔltɑ̃, ɑ̃t] *adj* revolting, appalling

révolte [Revɔlt] *nf* rebellion, revolt

révolter [Revɔlte] *vt* to revolt; **se ~ (contre)** to rebel (against); **ça me révolte (de voir que ...)** I'm revolted *ou* appalled (to see that ...)

révolu, e [Revɔly] *adj* past; (*ADMIN*): **âgé de 18 ans ~s** over 18 years of age

révolution [Revɔlysjɔ̃] *nf* revolution; **révolutionnaire** *adj, nm/f* revolutionary

revolver [ʀevɔlvɛʀ] nm gun; (à barillet) revolver

révoquer [ʀevɔke] vt (fonctionnaire) to dismiss; (arrêt, contrat) to revoke

revue [ʀ(ə)vy] nf review, magazine; (de music-hall) variety show; **passer en ~** (mentalement) to go through

rez-de-chaussée [ʀed(ə)ʃose] nm inv ground floor

RF sigle f = **République française**

Rhin [ʀɛ̃] nm Rhine

rhinocéros [ʀinɔseʀɔs] nm rhinoceros

Rhône [ʀon] nm Rhone

rhubarbe [ʀybaʀb] nf rhubarb

rhum [ʀɔm] nm rum

rhumatisme [ʀymatism] nm rheumatism no pl

rhume [ʀym] nm cold; **~ de cerveau** head cold; **le ~ des foins** hay fever

ri [ʀi] pp de **rire**

riant, e [ʀ(i)jɑ̃, ʀ(i)jɑ̃t] adj smiling, cheerful

ricaner [ʀikane] vi (avec méchanceté) to snigger; (bêtement) to giggle

riche [ʀiʃ] adj rich; (personne, pays) rich, wealthy; **~ en** rich in; **richesse** nf wealth; (fig: de son, musée etc) richness; **richesses** nfpl (ressources, argent) wealth sg; (fig: trésors) treasures

ricochet [ʀikɔʃɛ] nm: **faire des ~s** to skip stones; **par ~** (fig) as an indirect result

rictus [ʀiktys] nm grin

ride [ʀid] nf wrinkle

rideau, x [ʀido] nm curtain; **~ de fer** (boutique) metal shutter(s)

rider [ʀide] vt to wrinkle; **se ~** vi to become wrinkled

ridicule [ʀidikyl] adj ridiculous ♦ nm: **le ~** ridicule; **ridiculiser; se ridiculiser** vi to make a fool of o.s.

MOT-CLÉ

rien [ʀjɛ̃] pron 1: **(ne) ... rien** nothing; tournure negative + anything; **qu'est-ce**

que vous avez? – **rien** what have you got? – nothing; **il n'a rien dit/fait** he said/did nothing; he hasn't said/done anything; **il n'a rien** (n'est pas blessé) he's all right; **de rien!** not at all!

2 (quelque chose): **a-t-il jamais rien fait pour nous?** has he ever done anything for us?

3: **rien de**: **rien d'intéressant** nothing interesting; **rien d'autre** nothing else; **rien du tout** nothing at all

4: **rien que** just, only; nothing but; **rien que pour lui faire plaisir** only ou just to please him; **rien que la vérité** nothing but the truth; **rien que cela** that alone

♦ nm: **un petit rien** (cadeau) a little something; **des riens** trivia pl; **un rien de** a hint of; **en un rien de temps** in no time at all

rieur, -euse [ʀ(i)jœʀ, ʀ(i)jøz] adj cheerful

rigide [ʀiʒid] adj stiff; (fig) rigid; strict

rigole [ʀiɡɔl] nf (conduit) channel

rigoler [ʀiɡɔle] vi (fam: rire) to laugh; (s'amuser) to have some fun; (plaisanter) to be joking ou kidding; **rigolo, -ote** (fam) adj funny ♦ nm/f comic; (péj) fraud, phoney

rigoureusement [ʀiɡuʀøzmɑ̃] adv (vrai) absolutely; (interdit) strictly

rigoureux, -euse [ʀiɡuʀø, øz] adj rigorous; (hiver) hard, harsh

rigueur [ʀiɡœʀ] nf rigour; **être de ~** to be the rule; **à la ~** at a pinch; **tenir ~ à qn de qch** to hold sth against sb

rillettes [ʀijɛt] nfpl potted meat (made from pork ou goose)

rime [ʀim] nf rhyme

rinçage [ʀɛ̃saʒ] nm rinsing (out); (opération) rinse

rincer [ʀɛ̃se] vt to rinse; (récipient) to rinse out

ring [ʀiŋ] nm (boxing) ring

ringard, e [ʀɛ̃ɡaʀ, aʀd] (fam) adj old-fashioned

rions [ri̯ɔ̃] vb voir **rire**

riposter [ripɔste] vi to retaliate ♦ vt: ~ **que** to retort that

rire [RiR] vi to laugh; (se divertir) to have fun ♦ nm laugh; **le** ~ laughter; ~ **de** to laugh at; **pour** ~ (pas sérieusement) for a joke ou a laugh

risée [Rize] nf: **être la** ~ **de** to be the laughing stock of

risible [Rizibl] adj laughable

risque [Risk] nm risk; **le** ~ danger; **à ses** ~**s et périls** at his own risk; **risqué, e** adj risky; (plaisanterie) risqué, daring; **risquer** vt to risk; (allusion, question) to venture, hazard; **ça ne risque rien** it's quite safe; **risquer de**: **il risque de se tuer** he could get himself killed; **ce qui risque de se produire** what might ou could well happen; **il ne risque pas de recommencer** there's no chance of him doing that again; **se risquer à faire** (tenter) to venture ou dare to do

rissoler [Risɔle] vi, vt: **(faire)** ~ to brown

ristourne [RistuRn] nf discount

rite [Rit] nm rite; (fig) ritual

rivage [Rivaʒ] nm shore

rival, e, -aux [Rival, o] adj, nm/f rival; **rivaliser** vi: **rivaliser avec** (personne) to rival, vie with; **rivalité** nf rivalry

rive [Riv] nf shore; (de fleuve) bank; **riverain, e** nm/f riverside (ou lakeside) resident; (d'une route) local resident

rivet [Rive] nm rivet

rivière [Rivjɛr] nf river

rixe [Riks] nf brawl, scuffle

riz [Ri] nm rice; **rizière** nf paddy-field, ricefield

RMI sigle m (= revenu minimum d'insertion) ≃ income support (BRIT), welfare (US)

RN sigle f = **route nationale**

robe [Rɔb] nf dress; (de juge) robe; (pelage) coat; ~ **de chambre** dressing gown; ~ **de soirée/de mariée** evening/wedding dress

robinet [Rɔbinɛ] nm tap

robot [Rɔbo] nm robot

robuste [Rɔbyst] adj robust, sturdy; **robustesse** nf robustness, sturdiness

roc [Rɔk] nm rock

rocade [Rɔkad] nf bypass

rocaille [Rɔkaj] nf loose stones pl; (jardin) rockery, rock garden

roche [Rɔʃ] nf rock

rocher [Rɔʃe] nm rock

rocheux, -euse [Rɔʃø, øz] adj rocky

rodage [Rɔdaʒ] nm: **en** ~ running in

roder [Rɔde] vt (AUTO) to run in

rôder [Rode] vi to roam about; (de façon suspecte) to lurk about (ou around); **rôdeur, -euse** nm/f prowler

rogne [Rɔɲ] (fam) nf: **être en** ~ to be in a temper

rogner [Rɔɲe] vt to clip; ~ **sur** (fig) to cut down ou back on

rognons [Rɔɲɔ̃] nmpl (CULIN) kidneys

roi [Rwa] nm king; **la fête des R**~**s, les R**~**s** Twelfth Night

---

fête des Rois

La **fête des Rois** is celebrated on January 6. Figurines representing the magi are traditionally added to the Christmas crib and people eat **la galette des Rois**, a plain, flat cake in which a porcelain charm (**la fève**) is hidden. Whoever finds the charm is king or queen for the day and chooses a partner.

---

rôle [Rol] nm role, part

romain, e [Rɔmɛ̃, ɛn] adj Roman ♦ nm/f: **R**~**, e** Roman

roman, e [Rɔmɑ̃, an] adj (ARCHIT) Romanesque ♦ nm novel ou story; ~ **d'espionnage** spy novel ou story; ~ **policier** detective story

romance [Rɔmɑ̃s] nf ballad

romancer [Rɔmɑ̃se] vt (agrémenter) to romanticize; **romancier, -ière** nm/f novelist; **romanesque** adj (amours, aventures) storybook cpd; (sentimental, *personne)* romantic

roman-feuilleton [ʀɔmɑ̃fœjtɔ̃] *nm*
serialized novel

romanichel, le [ʀɔmaniʃɛl] *nm/f* (*péj*)
gipsy

romantique [ʀɔmɑ̃tik] *adj* romantic

romarin [ʀɔmaʀɛ̃] *nm* rosemary

rompre [ʀɔ̃pʀ] *vt* to break; (*entretien,
fiançailles*) to break off ♦ *vi* (*fiancés*) to
break it off; **se ~** *vi* to break; **rompu,
e** *adj* (*fourbu*) exhausted

ronces [ʀɔ̃s] *nfpl* brambles

ronchonner [ʀɔ̃ʃɔne] (*fam*) *vi* to
grouse, grouch

rond, e [ʀɔ̃, ʀɔ̃d] *adj* round; (*joues, mol-
lets*) well-rounded; (*fam: ivre*) tight ♦
nm (*cercle*) ring; (*fam: sou*): **je n'ai plus
un ~** I haven't a penny left; **en ~**
(*s'asseoir, danser*) in a ring; **ronde** *nf*
(*gén: de surveillance*) rounds *pl*, patrol;
(*danse*) round (dance); (*MUS*) semibreve
(*BRIT*), whole note (*US*); **à la ronde**
(*alentour*): **à 10 km à la ronde** for 10
km round; **rondelet, te** *adj* plump

rondelle [ʀɔ̃dɛl] *nf* (*tranche*) slice,
round; (*TECH*) washer

rondement [ʀɔ̃dmɑ̃] *adv* (*efficacement*)
briskly

rondin [ʀɔ̃dɛ̃] *nm* log

rond-point [ʀɔ̃pwɛ̃] *nm* roundabout

ronflant, e [ʀɔ̃flɑ̃, ɑ̃t] (*péj*) *adj* high-
flown, grand

ronflement [ʀɔ̃flamɑ̃] *nm* snore, snor-
ing

ronfler [ʀɔ̃fle] *vi* to snore; (*moteur,
poêle*) to hum

ronger [ʀɔ̃ʒe] *vt* to gnaw (at); (*suj: vers,
rouille*) to eat into; **se ~ les ongles** to
bite one's nails; **se ~ les sangs** to worry o.s. sick; **rongeur** *nm* rodent

ronronner [ʀɔ̃ʀɔne] *vi* to purr

rosace [ʀozas] *nf* (*vitrail*) rose window

rosbif [ʀɔsbif] *nm*: **du ~** roasting beef;
(*cuit*) roast beef

rose [ʀoz] *nf* rose ♦ *adj* pink

rosé, e [ʀoze] *adj* pinkish; (*vin*) **~** rosé

roseau, x [ʀozo] *nm* reed

rosée [ʀoze] *nf* dew

rosette [ʀozɛt] *nf* (*nœud*) bow

rosier [ʀozje] *nm* rosebush, rose tree

rosse [ʀɔs] (*fam*) *adj* nasty, vicious

rossignol [ʀɔsiɲɔl] *nm* (*ZOOL*) night-
ingale

rot [ʀo] *nm* belch; (*de bébé*) burp

rotatif, -ive [ʀɔtatif, iv] *adj* rotary

rotation [ʀɔtasjɔ̃] *nf* rotation

roter [ʀɔte] (*fam*) *vi* to burp, belch

rôti [ʀoti] *nm*: **du ~** roasting meat;
(*cuit*) roast meat; **~ de bœuf/porc**
joint of beef/pork

rotin [ʀɔtɛ̃] *nm* rattan (cane); **fauteuil
en ~** cane (arm)chair

rôtir [ʀotiʀ] *vi, vt* (*aussi*: **faire ~**) to
roast; **rôtisserie** *nf* (*restaurant*) steak-
house; (*traiteur*) roast meat shop;
rôtissoire *nf* (roasting) spit

rotule [ʀɔtyl] *nf* kneecap

roturier, -ière [ʀɔtyʀje, jɛʀ] *nm/f* com-
moner

rouage [ʀwaʒ] *nm* cog(wheel), gear-
wheel; **les ~s de l'État** the wheels of
State

roucouler [ʀukule] *vi* to coo

roue [ʀu] *nf* wheel; **~ de secours** spare
wheel

roué, e [ʀwe] *adj* wily

rouer [ʀwe] *vt*: **~ qn de coups** to give
sb a thrashing

rouge [ʀuʒ] *adj, nm/f* red ♦ *nm* red;
(*vin*) **~** red wine; **sur la liste ~** ex-
directory (*BRIT*), unlisted (*US*); **passer
au ~** (*signal*) to go red; (*automobiliste*)
to go through a red light; **~ (à lèvres)**
lipstick; **rouge-gorge** *nm* robin (red-
breast)

rougeole [ʀuʒɔl] *nf* measles *sg*

rougeoyer [ʀuʒwaje] *vi* to glow red

rouget [ʀuʒɛ] *nm* mullet

rougeur [ʀuʒœʀ] *nf* redness; (*MÉD:
tache*) red blotch

rougir [ʀuʒiʀ] *vi* to turn red; (*de honte,
timidité*) to blush, flush; (*de plaisir, colère*) to flush

rouille [ʀuj] *nf* rust; **rouillé, e** *adj*

rusty; **rouiller** *vt* to rust ♦ *vi* to rust, go rusty; **se rouiller** *vi* to rust

roulant, e [Rulɑ̃, ɑ̃t] *adj* (*meuble*) on wheels; (*tapis etc*) moving; **escalier ~** escalator

rouleau, x [Rulo] *nm* roll; (*à mise en plis, à peinture, vague*) roller; **~ à pâtisserie** rolling pin

roulement [Rulmɑ̃] *nm* (*rotation*) rotation; (*bruit*) rumbling *no pl*, rumble; **travailler par ~** to work on a rota (*BRIT*) *ou* rotation (*US*) basis; **~ (à billes)** ball bearings *pl*; **~ de tambour** drum roll

rouler [Rule] *vt* to roll; (*papier, tapis*) to roll up; (*CULIN: pâte*) to roll out; (*fam: duper*) to do, con ♦ *vi* (*bille, boule*) to roll; (*voiture, train*) to go, run; (*automobiliste*) to drive; (*bateau*) to roll; **se ~ dans** (*boue*) to roll in; (*couverture*) to roll o.s. (up) in

roulette [Rulet] *nf* (*de table, fauteuil*) castor; (*de dentiste*) drill; (*jeu*) roulette; **à ~s** on castors; **ça a marché comme sur des ~s** (*fam*) it went off very smoothly

roulis [Ruli] *nm* roll(ing)

roulotte [Rulɔt] *nf* caravan

roumain, e [Rumɛ̃, ɛn] *adj* Rumanian ♦ *nm/f:* **R~, e** Rumanian

Roumanie [Rumani] *nf* Rumania

rouquin, e [Rukɛ̃, in] (*péj*) *nm/f* redhead

rouspéter [Ruspete] (*fam*) *vi* to moan

rousse [Rus] *adj voir* **roux**

roussir [Rusir] *vt* to scorch ♦ *vi* (*CULIN*): **faire ~** to brown

route [Rut] *nf* road; (*fig: chemin*) way; (*itinéraire, parcours*) route; (*fig: voie*) road, path; **il y a 3h de ~** it's a 3-hour ride *ou* journey; **en ~** on the way; **mettre en ~** to start up; **se mettre en ~** to set off; **~ nationale** ≃ A road (*BRIT*), ≃ state highway (*US*); **routier, -ière** *adj* road *cpd* ♦ *nm* (*camionneur*) (long-distance) lorry (*BRIT*) *ou* truck (*US*) driver; (*restaurant*) ≃ transport café

(*BRIT*) ≃ truck stop (*US*)

routine [Rutin] *nf* routine; **routinier, -ière** (*péj*) *adj* (*activité*) humdrum; (*personne*) addicted to routine

rouvrir [Ruvrir] *vt, vi* to reopen, open again; **se ~** *vi* to reopen, open again

roux, rousse [Ru, Rus] *adj* red; (*personne*) red-haired ♦ *nm/f* redhead

royal, e, -aux [Rwajal, o] *adj* royal; (*cadeau etc*) fit for a king

royaume [Rwajom] *nm* kingdom; (*fig*) realm; **le R~-Uni** the United Kingdom

royauté [Rwajote] *nf* (*régime*) monarchy

RPR *sigle m*: **Rassemblement pour la République** French right-wing political party

ruban [Rybɑ̃] *nm* ribbon; **~ adhésif** adhesive tape

rubéole [Rybeɔl] *nf* German measles *sg*, rubella

rubis [Rybi] *nm* ruby

rubrique [Rybrik] *nf* (*titre, catégorie*) heading; (*PRESSE: article*) column

ruche [Ryʃ] *nf* hive

rude [Ryd] *adj* (*au toucher*) rough; (*métier, tâche*) hard, tough; (*climat*) severe, harsh; (*bourru*) harsh, rough; (*fruste: manières*) rugged, tough; (*fam: fameux*) jolly good; **rudement** (*fam*) *adv* (*très*) terribly

rudimentaire [Rydimɑ̃ter] *adj* rudimentary, basic

rudiments [Rydimɑ̃] *nmpl*: **avoir des ~ d'anglais** to have a smattering of English

rudoyer [Rydwaje] *vt* to treat harshly

rue [Ry] *nf* street

ruée [Rɥe] *nf* rush

ruelle [Rɥel] *nf* alley(-way)

ruer [Rɥe] *vi* (*cheval*) to kick out; **se ~** *vi:* **se ~ sur** to pounce on; **se ~ vers/dans/hors de** to rush *ou* dash towards/into/out of

rugby [Rygbi] *nm* rugby (football)

rugir [Ryʒir] *vi* to roar

rugueux, -euse [Rygø, øz] *adj* rough

ruine [ʀɥin] nf ruin; **ruiner** vt to ruin;
ruineux, -euse adj ruinous

ruisseau, x [ʀɥiso] nm stream, brook

ruisseler [ʀɥis(ə)le] vi to stream

rumeur [ʀymœʀ] nf (nouvelle) rumour;
(bruit confus) rumbling

ruminer [ʀymine] vt (herbe) to ruminate; (fig) to ruminate on ou over,
chew over

rupture [ʀyptyʀ] nf (séparation, désu-
nion) break-up, split; (de négociations
etc) breakdown; (de contrat) breach;
(dans continuité) break

rural, e, -aux [ʀyʀal, o] adj rural,
country cpd

ruse [ʀyz] nf: **la ~** cunning, craftiness;
(pour tromper) trickery; **une ~** a trick, a
ruse; **rusé, e** adj cunning, crafty

russe [ʀys] adj Russian ♦ nm/f: **R~** Russian ♦ nm (LING) Russian

Russie [ʀysi] nf: **la ~** Russia

rustine ® [ʀystin] nf rubber repair
patch (for bicycle tyre)

rustique [ʀystik] adj rustic

rustre [ʀystʀ] nm boor

rutilant, e [ʀytilɑ̃, ɑ̃t] adj gleaming

rythme [ʀitm] nm rhythm; (vitesse)
rate; (: de la vie) pace, tempo; **rythmé,
e** adj rhythmic(al)

S, s

s' [s] pron voir **se**

sa [sa] adj voir **son**[1]

SA sigle (= société anonyme) ≈ Ltd (BRIT),
≈ Inc. (US)

sable [sabl] nm sand; **~s mouvants**
quicksand(s)

sablé [sable] nm shortbread biscuit

sabler [sable] vt (contre le verglas) to
grit; **~ le champagne** to drink champagne

sablier [sablije] nm hourglass; (de cuisine) egg timer

sablonneux, -euse [sablɔnø, øz] adj
sandy

saborder [sabɔʀde] vt (navire) to scuttle; (fig: projet) to put paid to, scupper

sabot [sabo] nm clog; (de cheval) hoof;
~ de frein brake shoe

saboter [sabɔte] vt to sabotage; (bâcler)
to make a mess of, botch

sac [sak] nm bag; (à charbon etc) sack;
~ à dos rucksack; **~ à main** handbag;
~ de couchage sleeping bag; **~ de
voyage** travelling bag; **~ poubelle** bin
liner

saccadé, e [sakade] adj jerky; (respiration) spasmodic

saccager [sakaʒe] vt (piller) to sack;
(dévaster) to create havoc in

saccharine [sakaʀin] nf saccharin

sacerdoce [saseʀdɔs] nm priesthood;
(fig) calling, vocation

sache etc [saʃ] vb voir **savoir**

sachet [saʃɛ] nm (small) bag; (de sucre,
café) sachet; **du potage en ~** packet
soup; **~ de thé** tea bag

sacoche [sakɔʃ] nf (gén) bag; (de bicyclette) saddlebag

sacquer [sake] (fam) vt (employé) to
fire; (détester): **je ne peux pas le ~** I
can't stand him

sacre [sakʀ] nm (roi) coronation

sacré, e [sakʀe] adj sacred; (fam: satané) blasted; (: fameux): **un ~ toupé** a
heck of a cheek

sacrement [sakʀəmɑ̃] nm sacrament

sacrifice [sakʀifis] nm sacrifice; **sacrifier** vt to sacrifice

sacristie [sakʀisti] nf (catholique) sac-
risty; (protestante) vestry

sadique [sadik] adj sadistic

safran [safʀɑ̃] nm saffron

sage [saʒ] adj wise; (enfant) good

sage-femme [saʒfam] nf midwife

sagesse [saʒɛs] nf wisdom

Sagittaire [saʒitɛʀ] nm: **le ~** Sagittarius

Sahara [saaʀa] nm: **le ~** the Sahara
(desert)

saignant, e [sɛɲɑ̃, ɑ̃t] adj (viande) rare

saignée [seɲe] nf (fig) heavy losses pl

saigner [seɲe] vi to bleed ♦ vt to bleed; (animal) to kill (by bleeding); ~ **du nez** to have a nosebleed

saillie [saji] nf (sur un mur etc) projection

saillir [sajiʀ] vi to project, stick out; (veine, muscle) to bulge

sain, e [sɛ̃, sɛn] adj healthy; ~ **d'esprit** sound in mind, sane; ~ **et sauf** safe and sound, unharmed

saindoux [sɛ̃du] nm lard

saint, e [sɛ̃, sɛ̃t] adj holy ♦ nm/f saint; **le S~ Esprit** the Holy Spirit ou Ghost; **la S~e Vierge** the Blessed Virgin; **la S~ Sylvestre** New Year's Eve; **sainteté** nf holiness

sais [sɛ] vb voir **savoir**

saisi, e [sezi] adj: ~ **de panique** panic-stricken; **être** ~ **(par le froid)** to be struck by the sudden cold; **saisie** nf seizure; ~**e (de données)** (data) capture

saisir [seziʀ] vt to take hold of, grab; (fig: occasion) to seize; (comprendre) to grasp; (entendre) to get, catch; (données) to capture; (CULIN) to fry quickly; (JUR: biens, publication) to seize; **se** ~ **de** vt to seize; **saisissant, e** adj startling, striking

saison [sezɔ̃] nf season; **morte** ~ slack season; **saisonnier, -ière** adj seasonal

sait [sɛ] vb voir **savoir**

salade [salad] nf (BOT) lettuce etc; (CULIN) (green) salad; (fam: confusion) tangle, muddle; ~ **composée** mixed salad; ~ **de fruits** fruit salad; **saladier** nm (salad) bowl

salaire [salɛʀ] nm (annuel, mensuel) salary; (hebdomadaire, journalier) pay, wages pl; ~ **minimum interprofessionnel de croissance** index-linked guaranteed minimum wage

salarié, e [salaʀje] nm/f salaried employee; wage-earner

salaud [salo] (fam!) nm sod (!), bastard (!)

sale [sal] adj dirty, filthy; (fam: mauvais)

nasty

salé, e [sale] adj (mer, goût) salty; (CULIN: amandes, beurre etc) salted; (: gâteaux) savoury; (fam: grivois) spicy; (: facture) steep

saler [sale] vt to salt

saleté [salte] nf (état) dirtiness; (crasse) dirt, filth; (tache etc) dirt no pl; (fam: méchanceté) dirty trick; (: camelote) rubbish no pl; (: obscénité) filthy thing (to say)

salière [saljɛʀ] nf saltcellar

salir [saliʀ] vt to (make) dirty; (fig: quelqu'un) to soil the reputation of; **se** ~ vi to get dirty; **salissant, e** adj (tissu) which shows the dirt; (travail) dirty, messy

salle [sal] nf room; (d'hôpital) ward; (de restaurant) dining room; (d'un cinéma) auditorium; (: public) audience; ~ **à manger** dining room; ~ **d'attente** waiting room; ~ **de bain(s)** bathroom; ~ **de classe** classroom; ~ **de concert** concert hall; ~ **d'eau** shower-room; ~ **d'embarquement** (à l'aéroport) departure lounge; ~ **de jeux** (pour enfants) playroom; ~ **d'opération** (d'hôpital) operating theatre; ~ **de séjour** living room; ~ **des ventes** saleroom

salon [salɔ̃] nm lounge, sitting room; (mobilier) lounge suite; (exposition) exhibition, show; ~ **de beauté** beauty salon; ~ **de coiffure** hairdressing salon; ~ **de thé** tearoom

salope [salɔp] (fam!) nf bitch (!); **saloperie** (fam!) nf (action) dirty trick; (chose sans valeur) rubbish no pl

salopette [salɔpɛt] nf dungarees pl; (d'ouvrier) overall(s)

salsifis [salsifi] nm salsify

salubre [salybʀ] adj healthy, salubrious

saluer [salɥe] vt (pour dire bonjour, fig) to greet; (pour dire au revoir) to take one's leave; (MIL) to salute

salut [saly] nm (geste) wave; (parole) greeting; (MIL) salute; (sauvegarde) safety; (REL) salvation ♦ excl (fam: bonjour) hi (there); (: *au revoir*) see you, bye

salutations [salytasjɔ̃] *nfpl* greetings;
**Veuillez agréer, Monsieur, mes ~
distinguées** yours faithfully

samedi [samdi] *nm* Saturday

SAMU [samy] *sigle m* (= *service
d'assistance médicale d'urgence*) ≃ ambulance (service) (*BRIT*), ≃ paramedics
pl (*US*)

sanction [sãksjɔ̃] *nf* sanction; **sanctionner** *vt* (*loi, usage*) to sanction; (*punir*) to punish

sandale [sãdal] *nf* sandal; **~s à lanières**
strappy sandals

sandwich [sãdwi(t)ʃ] *nm* sandwich

sang [sã] *nm* blood; **en ~** covered in
blood; **se faire du mauvais ~** to fret,
get in a state; **sang-froid** *nm* calm,
sangfroid; **de sang-froid** in cold blood;
sanglant, e *adj* bloody

sangle [sãgl] *nf* strap

sanglier [sãglije] *nm* (wild) boar

sanglot [sãglo] *nm* sob; **sangloter** *vi*
to sob

sangsue [sãsy] *nf* leech

sanguin, e [sãgɛ̃, in] *adj* blood *cpd*;
sanguinaire *adj* bloodthirsty

sanitaire [sanitɛʀ] *adj* health *cpd*; **~s**
nmpl (*lieu*) bathroom *sg*

sans [sã] *prép* without; **un pull ~ manches** a sleeveless jumper; **~ faute** without fail; **~ arrêt** without a break; **~ ça**
(*fam*) otherwise; **~ qu'il s'en aperçoive** without him on his noticing;
sans-abri *nmpl* homeless; **sans-emploi** *nm/f inv* unemployed person;
les sans-emploi the unemployed;
sans-gêne *adj inv* inconsiderate

santé [sãte] *nf* health; **en bonne ~** in
good health; **boire à la ~ de qn** to
drink (to) sb's health; **à ta/votre ~!**
cheers!

saoudien, ne [saudjɛ̃, jɛn] *adj* Saudi
Arabian ♦ *nm/f*: **S~, ne** Saudi Arabian

saoul, e [su, sul] *adj* = **soûl**

saper [sape] *vt* to undermine, sap

sapeur-pompier [sapœʀpɔ̃pje] *nm*
fireman

saphir [safiʀ] *nm* sapphire

sapin [sapɛ̃] *nm* fir (tree); (*bois*) fir; **~ de
Noël** Christmas tree

sarcastique [saʀkastik] *adj* sarcastic

sarcler [saʀkle] *vt* to weed

Sardaigne [saʀdɛɲ] *nf*: **la ~** Sardinia

sarrasin [saʀazɛ̃] *nm* buckwheat

SARL *sigle f* (= *société à responsabilité limitée*) ≃ plc (*BRIT*), ≃ Inc. (*US*)

sas [sas] *nm* (*de sous-marin, d'engin spatial*) airlock; (*d'écluse*) lock

satané, e [satane] (*fam*) *adj* confounded

satellite [satelit] *nm* satellite

satin [satɛ̃] *nm* satin

satire [satiʀ] *nf* satire; **satirique** *adj* satirical

satisfaction [satisfaksjɔ̃] *nf* satisfaction

satisfaire [satisfɛʀ] *vt* to satisfy; **~ à**
(*conditions*) to meet; **satisfaisant, e**
adj (*acceptable*) satisfactory; **satisfait,
e** *adj* satisfied; **satisfait de** happy *ou*
satisfied with

saturer [satyʀe] *vt* to saturate

sauce [sos] *nf* sauce; (*avec un rôti*) gravy; **saucière** *nf* sauceboat

saucisse [sosis] *nf* sausage

saucisson [sosisɔ̃] *nm* (slicing) sausage

sauf, sauve [sof, sov] *adj* unharmed,
unhurt; (*fig: honneur*) intact, saved
♦ *prép* except; **laisser la vie sauve à
qn** to spare sb's life; **~ si** (*à moins que*)
unless; **~ erreur** if I'm not mistaken;
~ avis contraire unless you hear to the
contrary

sauge [soʒ] *nf* sage

saugrenu, e [sogʀəny] *adj* preposterous

saule [sol] *nm* willow (tree)

saumon [somɔ̃] *nm* salmon *inv*

saumure [somyʀ] *nf* brine

saupoudrer [sopudʀe] *vt*: **~ qch de** to
sprinkle sth with

saur [soʀ] *adj m*: **hareng ~** smoked *ou*
red herring, kipper

saurai *etc* [soʀe] *vb voir* **savoir**

saut [so] *nm* jump; (*discipline sportive*) jumping; **faire un ~ chez qn** to pop over to sb's (place); **~ à l'élastique** bungee jumping; **~ à la perche** pole vaulting; **~ en hauteur/longueur** high/long jump; **~ périlleux** somersault

saute [sot] *nf:* **~ d'humeur** sudden change of mood

sauter [sote] *vi* to jump, leap; (*exploser*) to blow up, explode; (: *fusibles*) to blow; (*se détacher*) to pop out (*ou* off) ♦ *vt* to jump (over), leap (over); (*fig: omettre*) to skip, miss (out); **faire ~** to blow up; (*CULIN*) to sauté; **~ au cou de qn** to fly into sb's arms; **~ sur une occasion** to jump at an opportunity; **~ aux yeux** to be (quite) obvious

sauterelle [sotʀɛl] *nf* grasshopper

sautiller [sotije] *vi* (*oiseau*) to hop; (*enfant*) to skip

sauvage [sovaʒ] *adj* (*gén*) wild; (*peuplade*) savage; (*farouche: personne*) unsociable; (*barbare*) wild, savage; (*non officiel*) unauthorized, unofficial; **faire du camping ~** to camp in the wild ♦ *nm/f* savage; (*timide*) unsociable type

sauve [sov] *adj f voir* **sauf**

sauvegarde [sovgaʀd] *nf* safeguard; (*INFORM*) backup; **sauvegarder** *vt* to safeguard; (*INFORM: enregistrer*) to save; (: *copier*) to back up

sauve-qui-peut [sovkipø] *excl* run for your life!

sauver [sove] *vt* to save; (*porter secours à*) to rescue; (*récupérer*) to salvage, rescue; **se ~** *vi* (*s'enfuir*) to run away; (*fam: partir*) to be off; **sauvetage** *nm* rescue; **sauveteur** *nm* rescuer; **sauvette**: **à la sauvette** *adv* (*se marier etc*) hastily, hurriedly; **sauveur** *nm* saviour (*BRIT*), savior (*US*)

savais *etc* [save] *vb voir* **savoir**

savamment [savamɑ̃] *adv* (*avec érudition*) learnedly; (*habilement*) skilfully, cleverly

savant, e [savɑ̃, ɑ̃t] *adj* scholarly,

learned ♦ *nm* scientist

saveur [savœʀ] *nf* flavour; (*fig*) savour

savoir [savwaʀ] *vt* to know; (*être capable de*): **il sait nager** he can swim ♦ *nm* knowledge; **se ~** *vi* (*être connu*) to be known; **à ~** that is, namely; **faire ~ qch à qn** to let sb know sth; **pas que je sache** not as far as I know

savon [savɔ̃] *nm* (*produit*) soap; (*morceau*) bar of soap; (*fam*): **passer un ~ à qn** to give sb a good dressing-down; **savonner** *vt* to soap; **savonnette** *nf* bar of soap

savons [savɔ̃] *vb voir* **savoir**

savourer [savuʀe] *vt* to savour; **savoureux, -euse** *adj* tasty; (*fig: anecdote*) spicy, juicy

saxo(phone) [saksɔ(fɔn)] *nm* sax(ophone)

scabreux, -euse [skabʀø, øz] *adj* risky; (*indécent*) improper, shocking

scandale [skɑ̃dal] *nm* scandal; (*tapage*): **faire un ~** to make a scene, create a disturbance; **faire ~** to scandalize people; **scandaleux, -euse** *adj* scandalous, outrageous

scandinave [skɑ̃dinav] *adj* Scandinavian ♦ *nm/f*: **S~** Scandinavian

Scandinavie [skɑ̃dinavi] *nf* Scandinavia

scaphandre [skafɑ̃dʀ] *nm* (*de plongeur*) diving suit

scarabée [skaʀabe] *nm* beetle

scarlatine [skaʀlatin] *nf* scarlet fever

scarole [skaʀɔl] *nf* endive

scélérat, e [seleʀa, at] *nm/f* villain

sceller [sele] *vt* to seal

scénario [senaʀjo] *nm* scenario

scène [sɛn] *nf* (*gén*) scene; (*estrade, fig: théâtre*) stage; **entrer en ~** to come on stage; **mettre en ~** (*THÉÂTRE*) to stage; (*CINÉMA*) to direct; **~ de ménage** domestic scene

sceptique [sɛptik] *adj* sceptical

schéma [ʃema] *nm* (*diagramme*) diagram, sketch; **schématique** *adj* diagrammatical(al), schematic; (*fig*) oversimplified

sciatique [sjatik] *nf* sciatica

scie [si] *nf* saw; **~ à métaux** hacksaw

sciemment [sjamã] *adv* knowingly

science [sjɑ̃s] *nf* science; (*savoir*) knowledge; **~s naturelles** (SCOL) natural science *sg*, biology *sg*; **~s po** political science *ou* studies *pl*; **science-fiction** *nf* science fiction; **scientifique** *adj* scientific ♦ *nm/f* scientist; (*étudiant*) science student

scier [sje] *vt* to saw; (*retrancher*) to saw off; **scierie** *nf* sawmill

scinder [sɛ̃de] *vt* to split up; **se ~** *vi* to split up

scintiller [sɛ̃tije] *vi* to sparkle; (*étoile*) to twinkle

scission [sisjɔ̃] *nf* split

sciure [sjyr] *nf*: **~ (de bois)** sawdust

sclérose [skleroz] *nf*: **~ en plaques** multiple sclerosis

scolaire [skɔler] *adj* school *cpd*; **scolariser** *vt* to provide with schooling *ou* schools; **scolarité** *nf* schooling

scooter [skutœr] *nm* (motor) scooter

score [skɔr] *nm* score

scorpion [skɔrpjɔ̃] *nm* (*signe*): **le S~** Scorpio

Scotch ® [skɔtʃ] *nm* adhesive tape

scout, e [skut] *adj, nm* scout

script [skript] *nm* (*écriture*) printing; (CINÉMA) (shooting) script

scrupule [skrypyl] *nm* scruple

scruter [skryte] *vt* to scrutinize; (*l'obscurité*) to peer into

scrutin [skrytɛ̃] *nm* (*vote*) ballot; (*ensemble des opérations*) poll

sculpter [skylte] *vt* to sculpt; (*bois*) to carve; **sculpteur** *nm* sculptor; **sculpture** *nf* sculpture; **sculpture sur bois** wood carving

SDF *sigle m* (= *sans domicile fixe*) homeless person; **les SDF** the homeless

MOT-CLÉ

se [sə], **s'** *pron* **1** (*emploi réfléchi*) oneself;

(: *masc*) himself; (: *fém*) herself; (: *sujet non humain*) itself; (: *pl*) themselves; **se voir comme l'on est** to see o.s. as one is

2 (*réciproque*) one another, each other; **ils s'aiment** they love one another *ou* each other

3 (*passif*): **cela se répare facilement** it is easily repaired

4 (*possessif*): **se casser la jambe/laver les mains** to break one's leg/wash one's hands

séance [seãs] *nf* (*d'assemblée*) meeting, session; (*de tribunal*) sitting, session; (*musicale*, CINÉMA, THÉÂTRE) performance; **~ tenante** forthwith

seau, x [so] *nm* bucket, pail

sec, sèche [sɛk, sɛʃ] *adj* dry; (*raisins, figues*) dried; (*cœur*: *insensible*) hard, cold ♦ *nm*: **tenir au ~** to keep in a dry place ♦ *adv* hard; **je le bois ~** I drink it straight *ou* neat; **à ~** (*puits*) dried up

sécateur [sekatœr] *nm* secateurs *pl*, (BRIT), shears *pl*

sèche [sɛʃ] *adj f voir* **sec**; **sèche-cheveux** *nm inv* hair-drier; **sèche-linge** *nm inv* tumble dryer; **sèchement** *adv* (*répondre*) drily

sécher [seʃe] *vt* to dry; (*dessécher*: *peau, blé*) to dry (out); (: *étang*) to dry up; (*fam*: *cours*) to skip ♦ *vi* to dry; to dry out; to dry up; (*fam*: *candidat*) to be stumped; **se ~** (*après le bain*) to dry o.s.; **sécheresse** *nf* dryness; (*absence de pluie*) drought; **séchoir** *nm* drier

second, e [s(ə)gɔ̃, ɔ̃d] *adj* second ♦ *nm* (*assistant*) second in command; (NAVIG) first mate; **voyager en ~e** to travel second-class; **secondaire** *adj* secondary; **seconde** *nf* second; **seconder** *vt* to assist

secouer [s(ə)kwe] *vt* to shake; (*passagers*) to rock; (*traumatiser*) to shake (up); **se ~** *vi* (*fam*: *faire un effort*) to shake o.s. up; (: *se dépêcher*) to get a move on

secourir [s(ə)kuʀiʀ] vt (venir en aide à) to assist, aid; **secourisme** nm first aid; **secouriste** nmf first-aid worker

secours [s(ə)kuʀ] nm help, aid, assistance ♦ nmpl aid sg; **au ~!** h'lp!; **appeler au ~** to shout ou call for help; **porter ~ à qn** to give sb assistance, help sb; **les premiers ~** first aid sg

secousse [s(ə)kus] nf jolt, bump; (électrique) shock; (fig: psychologique) jolt, shock; **~ sismique** earth tremor

secret, ète [səkʀɛ, ɛt] adj secret; (fig: renfermé) reticent, reserved ♦ nm secret; (discrétion absolue): **le ~** secrecy

secrétaire [s(ə)kʀetɛʀ] nmf secretary ♦ nm (meuble) writing desk; **~ de direction** private ou personal secretary; **~ d'État** junior minister; **~ général** (COMM) company secretary; **secrétariat** nm (profession) secretarial work; (bureau) office; (: d'organisation internationale) secretariat

secteur [sɛktœʀ] nm sector; (zone) area; (ÉLEC) **branché sur ~** plugged into the mains (supply)

section [sɛksjɔ̃] nf section; (de parcours d'autobus) fare stage; (MIL: unité) platoon; **sectionner** vt to sever

Sécu [seky] abr f = **sécurité sociale**

séculaire [sekylɛʀ] adj (très vieux) age-old

sécuriser [sekyʀize] vt to give a (feeling of) security to

sécurité [sekyʀite] nf (absence de danger) safety; (absence de troubles) security; **système de ~** security system; **être en ~** to be safe; **la ~ routière** road safety; **la ~ sociale** ≈ (the) Social Security (BRIT), ≈ Welfare (US)

sédentaire [sedɑ̃tɛʀ] adj sedentary

séduction [sedyksjɔ̃] nf seduction; (charme, attrait) appeal, charm

séduire [sedɥiʀ] vt to charm; (femme: abuser de) to seduce; **séduisant, e** adj (femme, offre) very attractive; (homme, offre) very attractive

ségrégation [segʀegasjɔ̃] nf segrega-tion

seigle [sɛgl] nm rye

seigneur [sɛɲœʀ] nm lord

sein [sɛ̃] nm breast; (entrailles) womb; **au ~ de** (équipe, institution) within

séisme [seism] nm earthquake

seize [sɛz] num sixteen; **seizième** num sixteenth

séjour [seʒuʀ] nm stay; (pièce) living room; **séjourner** vi to stay

sel [sɛl] nm salt; (fig: piquant) spice

sélection [seleksjɔ̃] nf selection; **sélectionner** vt to select

self-service [sɛlfsɛʀvis] adj, nm self-service

selle [sɛl] nf saddle; **~s** nfpl (MÉD) stools; **seller** vt to saddle

sellette [sɛlɛt] nf: **être sur la ~** to be in the hot seat

selon [s(ə)lɔ̃] prép according to; (en se conformant à) in accordance with; **~ que** according to whether; **~ moi** as I see it

semaine [s(ə)mɛn] nf week; **en ~** during the week, on weekdays

semblable [sɑ̃blabl] adj similar; (de ce genre): **de ~s mésaventures** such mishaps ♦ nm fellow creature ou man; **~ à** similar to, like

semblant [sɑ̃blɑ̃] nm: **un ~ de ...** a semblance of ...; **faire ~ (de faire)** to pretend (to do)

sembler [sɑ̃ble] vb +attrib to seem ♦ vb impers: **il semble (bien) que/inutile de** it (really) seems ou appears that/useless to; **il me semble que** it seems to me that; **comme bon lui semble** as he sees fit

semelle [s(ə)mɛl] nf sole; (intérieure) insole, inner sole

semence [s(ə)mɑ̃s] nf (graine) seed

semer [s(ə)me] vt to sow; (fig: éparpiller) to scatter; (: confusion) to spread; (fam: poursuivants) to lose, shake off; **semé de** (difficultés) riddled with

semestre [s(ə)mɛstʀ] nm half-year; (SCOL) semester

séminaire [seminɛʀ] nm seminar

semi-remorque [səmiʀəmɔʀk] nm articulated lorry (BRIT), semi(trailer) (US)

semoule [s(ə)mul] nf semolina

sempiternel, le [sɑ̃piternɛl] adj eternal, never-ending

sénat [sena] nm senate; **sénateur** [senatœʀ] nm senator

sens [sɑ̃s] nm (PHYSIOL, instinct) sense; (signification) meaning, sense; (direction) direction; **à mon ~** to my mind; **dans le ~ des aiguilles d'une montre** clockwise; **~ dessus dessous** upside down; **~ interdit** one-way street; **~ unique** one-way street

sensation [sɑ̃sasjɔ̃] nf sensation; **à ~** (péj) sensational; **faire ~** to cause ou create a sensation; **sensationnel, le** adj (fam) fantastic, terrific

sensé, e [sɑ̃se] adj sensible

sensibiliser [sɑ̃sibilize] vt: **~ qn à** to make sb sensitive to

sensibilité [sɑ̃sibilite] nf sensitivity

sensible [sɑ̃sibl] adj sensitive; (aux sens) perceptible; (appréciable: différence, progrès) appreciable, noticeable; **sensiblement** (à peu près): **ils sont sensiblement du même âge** they are approximately the same age; **sensiblerie** nf sentimentality

sensuel, le [sɑ̃sɥɛl] adj (personne) sensual; (musique) sensuous

sentence [sɑ̃tɑ̃s] nf (jugement) sentence

sentier [sɑ̃tje] nm path

sentiment [sɑ̃timɑ̃] nm feeling; **sentimental, e, -aux** adj sentimental; (vie, aventure) love cpd

sentinelle [sɑ̃tinɛl] nf sentry

sentir [sɑ̃tiʀ] vt (par l'odorat) to smell; (par le goût) to taste; (au toucher, fig) to feel; (répandre une odeur de) to smell of; (: ressemblance) to smell like ♦ vi to smell; **~ mauvais** to smell bad; **se ~ bien** to feel good; **se ~ mal** (être indisposé) to feel unwell ou ill; **se ~ le courage/la force de faire** to feel

brave/strong enough to do; **il ne peut pas le ~** (fam) he can't stand him

séparation [separasjɔ̃] nf separation; (cloison) division, partition

séparé, e [separe] adj (distinct) separate; (époux) separated; **séparément** adv separately

séparer [separe] vt to separate; (désunir) to drive apart; (détacher): **~ qch de** to pull sth (off) from; **se ~** vi (époux, amis) to separate; (se diviser: route etc) to divide; **se ~ de** (époux) to separate ou part from; (employé, objet personnel) to part with

sept [sɛt] num seven; **septante** (BELGIQUE, SUISSE) adj inv seventy

septembre [sɛptɑ̃bʀ] nm September

septennat [sɛptena] nm seven year term of office (of French President)

septentrional, e, -aux [sɛptɑ̃tʀijɔnal, o] adj northern

septicémie [sɛptisemi] nf blood poisoning, septicaemia

septième [sɛtjɛm] num seventh

septique [sɛptik] adj: **fosse ~** septic tank

sépulture [sepyltyʀ] nf (tombeau) burial place, grave

séquelles [sekel] nfpl after-effects; (fig) aftermath sg

séquestrer [sekɛstʀe] vt (personne) to confine illegally; (biens) to impound

serai etc [səʀe] vb voir **être**

serein, e [səʀɛ̃, ɛn] adj serene

serez [səʀe] vb voir **être**

sergent [sɛʀʒɑ̃] nm sergeant

série [seʀi] nf series inv; (de clés, casseroles, outils) set; (catégorie: SPORT) rank; **en ~** in quick succession; (COMM) mass cpd; **hors ~** (COMM) custom-built

sérieusement [seʀjøzmɑ̃] adv seriously

sérieux, -euse [seʀjø, jøz] adj serious; (élève, employé) reliable, responsible; (client, maison) reliable, dependable; (d'une entreprise etc) reliable ♦ nm seriousness, gravity; **garder son ~** to keep a

straight face; **prendre qch/qn au ~** to
take sth/sb seriously

serin [s(ə)ʀɛ̃] *nm* canary

seringue [s(ə)ʀɛ̃g] *nf* syringe

serions [səʀjɔ̃] *vb voir* **être**

serment [sɛʀmɑ̃] *nm* (*juré*) oath; (*promesse*) pledge, vow

séronégatif, -ive [seʀonegatif, iv] *adj*
(*MÉD*) HIV negative

séropositif, -ive [seʀopozitif, iv] *adj*
(*MÉD*) HIV positive

serpent [sɛʀpɑ̃] *nm* snake; **serpenter**
vi to wind

serpillière [sɛʀpijɛʀ] *nf* floorcloth

serre [sɛʀ] *nf* (*AGR*) greenhouse; **~s** *nfpl*
(*griffes*) claws, talons

serré, e [seʀe] *adj* (*habits*) tight; (*fig:
lutte, match*) tight, close-fought; (*passagers etc*) (tightly) packed; (*réseau*)
dense; **avoir le cœur ~** to have a
heavy heart

serrer [seʀe] *vt* (*tenir*) to grip *ou* hold
tight; (*comprimer, coincer*) to squeeze;
(*poings, mâchoires*) to clench; (*suj:
vêtement*) to be too tight for; (*ceinture,
nœud, vis*) to tighten ♦ *vi:* **à droite**
to keep *ou* get over to the right; **se**
~i (*se rapprocher*) to squeeze up; **se ~**
contre qn to huddle up to sb; **~ la**
main à qn to shake sb's hand; **~ qn**
dans ses bras to hug sb, clasp sb in
one's arms

serrure [seʀyʀ] *nf* lock; **serrurier** *nm*
locksmith

sert *etc* [sɛʀ] *vb voir* **servir**

servante [sɛʀvɑ̃t] *nf* (*maid*)servant

serveur, -euse [sɛʀvœʀ, øz] *nm/f*
waiter (waitress)

serviable [sɛʀvjabl] *adj* obliging, willing to help

service [sɛʀvis] *nm* service; (*assortiment
de vaisselle*) set, service; (*bureau: de la
vente etc*) department, section; (*travail*)
duty; **premier ~** (*série de repas*) first
sitting; **être de ~** to be on duty; **faire**
le ~ to serve; **rendre un ~ à qn** to do
sb a favour; (*objet: s'avérer utile*) to

come in useful *ou* handy for sb; **mettre**
en ~ to put into service *ou* operation;
~ compris/non compris service
included/not included; **hors ~** out of
order; **~ après-vente** after-sales service; **~ d'ordre** police (*ou* stewards) in
charge of maintaining order; **~ militai-**
re military service; **~s secrets** secret
service *sg*

serviette [sɛʀvjɛt] *nf* (*de table*) (table)
napkin, serviette; (*de toilette*) towel;
(*porte-documents*) briefcase; **~ de plage**
beach towel; **~ hygiénique** sanitary towel

servir [sɛʀviʀ] *vt* to serve; (*au restaurant*) to wait on; (*au magasin*) to serve,
attend to ♦ *vi* (*TENNIS*) to serve; (*CARTES*)
to deal; **se ~** *vi* (*prendre d'un plat*) to
help o.s.; **vous êtes servi?** are you
being served?; **~ à qn** (*diplôme, livre*) to
be of use to sb; **~ à qch/faire** (*outil
etc*) to be used for sth/doing; **ça ne**
sert à rien it's no use; **~ (à qn) de** to
serve as (for sb); **se ~ de** (*plat*) to help
o.s. to; (*voiture, outil, relations*) to use

serviteur [sɛʀvitœʀ] *nm* servant

ses [se] *adj voir* **son**[1]

set [sɛt] *nm:* **~ (de table)** tablemat,
place mat

seuil [sœj] *nm* doorstep; (*fig*) threshold

seul, e [sœl] *adj* (*sans compagnie*)
alone; (*unique*): **un ~ livre** only one
book, a single book ♦ *adv* (*vivre*) alone,
on one's own ♦ *nm, pl:* **il en reste**
un(e) ~(e) there's only one left; **le ~ li-**

vre the only book; **parler tout ~** to talk to oneself; **faire qch (tout) ~** to do sth (all) on one's own *ou* (all) by oneself; **à lui (tout) ~** single-handed, on his own; **se sentir ~** to feel lonely; **seulement** *adv* only; **non seulement ... mais aussi** *ou* **encore** not only ... but also

sève [sɛv] *nf* sap

sévère [sevɛʀ] *adj* severe

sévices [sevis] *nmpl* (physical) cruelty *sg*, ill treatment *sg*

sévir [seviʀ] *vi* (*punir*) to use harsh measures, crack down; (*suj: fléau*) to rage, be rampant

sevrer [səvʀe] *vt* (*enfant etc*) to wean

sexe [sɛks] *nm* sex; (*organes génitaux*) genitals, sex organs; **sexuel, le** *adj* sexual

seyant, e [sejɑ̃, ɑ̃t] *adj* becoming

shampooing [ʃɑ̃pwɛ̃] *nm* shampoo

short [ʃɔʀt] *nm* (pair of) shorts *pl*

`MOT-CLÉ`

si [si] *nm* (*MUS*) B; (*en chantant la gamme*) ti

♦ *adv* **1** (*oui*) yes

2 (*tellement*) so; **si gentil/rapidement** so kind/fast; (**tant et**) **si bien que** so much so that; **si rapide qu'il soit** however fast he may be

♦ *conj* if; **si tu veux** if you want; **je me demande si** I wonder if *ou* whether; **si seulement** if only

---

Sicile [sisil] *nf*: **la ~** Sicily

SIDA [sida] *sigle m* (= *syndrome immuno-déficitaire acquis*) AIDS *sg*

sidéré, e [sideʀe] *adj* staggered

sidérurgie [sideʀyʀʒi] *nf* steel industry

siècle [sjɛkl] *nm* century

siège [sjɛʒ] *nm* seat; (*d'entreprise*) head office; (*d'organisation*) headquarters *pl*; (*MIL*) siege; **~ social** registered office; **siéger** *vi* to sit

sien, ne [sjɛ̃, sjɛn] *pron*: **le(la) ~(ne)**, **les ~(ne)s** (*homme*) his; (*femme*) hers;

(*chose, animal*) its; **les ~s** (*sa famille*) one's family; **faire des ~nes** (*fam*) to be up to one's (usual) tricks

sieste [sjɛst] *nf* (afternoon) snooze *ou* nap; **faire la ~** to have a snooze *ou* nap

sifflement [siflamɑ̃] *nm*: **un ~** a whistle

siffler [sifle] *vi* (*gén*) to whistle; (*en respirant*) to wheeze; (*serpent, vapeur*) to hiss ♦ *vt* (*chanson*) to whistle; (*chien etc*) to whistle for; (*fille*) to whistle at; (*pièce, orateur*) to hiss, boo; (*fin du match, départ*) to blow one's whistle for; (*fam: verre*) to guzzle

sifflet [siflɛ] *nm* whistle; **coup de ~** whistle

siffloter [siflɔte] *vi*, *vt* to whistle

sigle [sigl] *nm* acronym

signal, -aux [siɲal, o] *nm* signal; (*indice, écriteau*) sign; **donner le ~ de** to give the signal for; **~ d'alarme** alarm signal; **signaux (lumineux)** (*AUTO*) traffic signals; **signalement** *nm* description, particulars *pl*

signaler [siɲale] *vt* to indicate; (*personne: faire un signe*) to signal; (*vol, perte*) to report; (*faire remarquer*): **~ qch à qn/(à qn) que** to point out sth to sb/(to sb) that; **se ~ (par)** to distinguish o.s. (by)

signature [siɲatyʀ] *nf* signature; (*action*) signing

signe [siɲ] *nm* sign; (*TYPO*) mark; **faire un ~ de la main** to give a sign with one's hand; **faire ~ à qn** (fig: *contacter*) to get in touch with sb; **faire ~ à qn d'entrer** to motion (to) sb to come in; **signer** *vt* to sign; **se signer** *vi* to cross o.s.

significatif, -ive [siɲifikatif, iv] *adj* significant

signification [siɲifikasjɔ̃] *nf* meaning

signifier [siɲifje] *vt* (*vouloir dire*) to mean; (*faire connaître*): **~ qch (à qn)** to make sth known (to sb)

silence [silɑ̃s] *nm* silence; (*MUS*) rest;

garder le ~ to keep silent, say nothing; **silencieux, -euse** adj quiet, silent ♦ nm silencer

silex [silɛks] nm flint

silhouette [silwɛt] nf outline, silhouette; (allure) figure

silicium [silisjɔm] nm silicon

sillage [sijaʒ] nm wake

sillon [sijɔ̃] nm furrow; (de disque) groove; **sillonner** vt to criss-cross

simagrées [simagʀe] nfpl fuss sg

similaire [similɛʀ] adj similar; **similicuir** nm imitation leather; **similitude** nf similarity

simple [sɛ̃pl] adj simple; (non multiple) single; **~ messieurs** (TENNIS) men's singles sg; **~ soldat** private

simplicité [sɛ̃plisite] nf simplicity

simplifier [sɛ̃plifje] vt to simplify

simulacre [simylakʀ] nm (péj): **un ~ de** a pretence of

simuler [simyle] vt to sham, simulate

simultané, e [simyltane] adj simultaneous

sincère [sɛ̃sɛʀ] adj sincere; **sincèrement** adv sincerely; (pour parler franchement) honestly, really; **sincérité** nf sincerity

sine qua non [sinekwanɔn] adj: **condition ~** indispensable condition

singe [sɛ̃ʒ] nm monkey; (de grande taille) ape; **singer** vt to ape, mimic; **singeries** nfpl antics

singulariser [sɛ̃gylaʀize]: **se ~** vi to call attention to o.s.

singularité [sɛ̃gylaʀite] nf peculiarity

singulier, -ière [sɛ̃gylje, jɛʀ] adj remarkable, singular ♦ nm singular

sinistre [sinistʀ] adj sinister ♦ nm (incendie) blaze; (catastrophe) disaster; (ASSURANCES) damage (giving rise to a claim); **sinistré, e** adj disaster-stricken ♦ nm/f disaster victim

sinon [sinɔ̃] conj (autrement, sans quoi) otherwise, or else; (sauf) except, other than; (si ce n'est) if not

sinueux, -euse [sinɥø, øz] adj wind-

ing

sinus [sinys] nm (ANAT) sinus; (GÉOM) sine; **sinusite** nf sinusitis

siphon [sifɔ̃] nm (tube, d'eau gazeuse) siphon; (d'évier etc) U-bend

sirène [siʀɛn] nf siren; **~ d'alarme** fire alarm; (en temps de guerre) air-raid siren

sirop [siʀo] nm (à diluer: de fruit etc) syrup; (pharmaceutique) syrup, mixture; **~ pour la toux** cough mixture

siroter [siʀɔte] vt to sip

sismique [sismik] adj seismic

site [sit] nm (paysage, environnement) setting; (d'une ville etc: emplacement) site; **~ (pittoresque)** beauty spot; **~s touristiques** places of interest; **~ Web** (INFORM) website

sitôt [sito] adv: **~ parti** as soon as he etc had left; **~ que** as soon as; **pas de ~** not for a long time

situation [sitɥasjɔ̃] nf situation; (d'un édifice, d'une ville) position, location; **~ de famille** marital status

situé, e [sitɥe] adj situated

situer [sitɥe] vt to site, situate; (en pensée) to set, place; **se ~** vi to be situated

six [sis] num six; **sixième** num sixth ♦ nf (SCOL) first form

Skaï ® [skaj] nm Leatherette ®

ski [ski] nm (objet) ski; (sport) skiing; **faire du ~** to ski; **~ de fond** cross-country skiing; **~ nautique** water-skiing; **~ de piste** downhill skiing; **~ de randonnée** cross-country skiing; **skier** vi to ski; **skieur, -euse** nm/f skier

slip [slip] nm (sous-vêtement) pants pl, briefs pl; (de bain: d'homme) trunks pl; (: du bikini) (bikini) briefs pl

slogan [slɔgã] nm slogan

SMIC [smik] sigle m = **salaire minimum interprofessionnel de croissance**

SMIC

In France, the **SMIC** is the minimum

legal hourly rate for workers over
eighteen. It is index-linked and is
raised each time the cost of living
rises by 2%.

smicard, e [smikar, ard] (fam) nm/f
minimum wage earner

smoking [smɔkiŋ] nm dinner ou evening suit

SNCF sigle f (= Société nationale des chemins de fer français) French railways

snob [snɔb] adj snobbish ♦ nm/f snob;
snobisme nm snobbery, snobbishness

sobre [sɔbr] adj (personne) temperate,
abstemious; (élégance, style) sober

sobriquet [sɔbrikɛ] nm nickname

social, e, -aux [sɔsjal, jo] adj social

socialisme [sɔsjalism] nm socialism;
socialiste nm/f socialist

société [sɔsjete] nf society; (sportive)
club; (COMM) company; **la ~ de
consommation** the consumer society;
~ anonyme ≈ limited (BRIT) ou incorporated (US) company

sociologie [sɔsjɔlɔʒi] nf sociology

socle [sɔkl] nm (de colonne, statue)
plinth, pedestal; (de lampe) base

socquette [sɔkɛt] nf ankle sock

sœur [sœr] nf sister; (religieuse) nun,
sister

soi [swa] pron oneself; **en ~** (intrin-
sèquement) in itself; **cela va de ~** that
ou it goes without saying; **soi-disant**
adj inv so-called ♦ adv supposedly

soie [swa] nf silk; **soierie** nf (tissu) silk

soif [swaf] nf thirst; **avoir ~** to be thirsty; **donner ~ à qn** to make sb thirsty

soigné, e [swaɲe] adj (tenue) well-
groomed, neat; (travail) careful, meticulous

soigner [swaɲe] vt (malade, maladie:
suj: docteur) to treat; (suj: infirmière,
mère) to nurse, look after; (travail, détails) to take care over; (jardin, invités)
to look after; **soigneux, -euse** adj
(propre) tidy, neat; (appliqué) painstaking, careful

soi-même [swamɛm] pron oneself

soin [swɛ̃] nm (application) care; (propreté, ordre) tidiness, neatness; **~s**
nmpl (à un malade, blessé) treatment sg,
medical attention sg; (hygiène) care sg;
prendre ~ de to take care of, look
after; **prendre ~ de faire** to take care
to do; **les premiers ~s** first aid sg

soir [swar] nm evening; **ce ~** this evening, tonight; **demain ~** tomorrow
evening, tomorrow night; **soirée** nf
evening; (réception) party

soit [swa] vb voir être ♦ conj (à savoir)
namely; (ou): **~ ... ~** either ... or ♦ adv
so be it, very well; **~ que ... ~ que** ou
ou que whether ... or whether

soixantaine [swasɑ̃tɛn] nf: **une ~ (de)**
sixty or so, about sixty; **avoir la ~**
(âge) to be around sixty

soixante [swasɑ̃t] num sixty;
soixante-dix num seventy

soja [sɔʒa] nm soya; (graines) soya
beans pl; **germes de ~** beansprouts

sol [sɔl] nm ground; (de logement) floor;
(AGR) soil; (MUS) G; (: en chantant la
gamme) so(h)

solaire [sɔlɛr] adj (énergie etc) solar;
(crème etc) sun cpd

soldat [sɔlda] nm soldier

solde [sɔld] nf pay ♦ nm (COMM) balance; **~s** nm ou f pl (articles) sale goods;
(vente) sales; **en ~** at sale price; **solder** vt (marchandise) to sell at sale
price, sell off; **se solder par** (fig) to
end in; **article soldé (à) 10 F** item reduced to 10 F

sole [sɔl] nf sole inv (fish)

soleil [sɔlɛj] nm sun; (lumière)
sun(light); (temps ensoleillé) sun(shine),
il fait du ~ it's sunny; **au ~** in the sun

solennel, le [sɔlanɛl] adj solemn

solfège [sɔlfɛʒ] nm musical theory

solidaire [sɔlidɛr] adj: **être ~s** to show
solidarity, stand ou stick together; **être
~ de** (collègues) to stand by; **solidarité**
nf solidarity; **par solidarité (avec)** in
sympathy (with)

solide [sɔlid] *adj* solid; *(mur, maison, meuble)* solid, sturdy; *(connaissances, argument)* sound; *(personne, estomac)* robust, sturdy ♦ *nm* solid

soliste [sɔlist] *nm/f* soloist

solitaire [sɔlitɛR] *adj (sans compagnie)* solitary, lonely; *(lieu)* lonely ♦ *nm/f* (ermite) recluse; *(fig: ours)* loner

solitude [sɔlityd] *nf* loneliness; *(tranquillité)* solitude

solive [sɔliv] *nf* joist

solliciter [sɔlisite] *vt (personne)* to appeal to; *(emploi, faveur)* to seek

sollicitude [sɔlisityd] *nf* concern

soluble [sɔlybl] *adj* soluble

solution [sɔlysjɔ̃] *nf* solution; **~ de facilité** easy way out

solvable [sɔlvabl] *adj* solvent

sombre [sɔ̃bR] *adj* dark; *(fig)* gloomy; **sombrer** *vi (bateau)* to sink; **sombrer dans** *(misère, désespoir)* to sink into

sommaire [sɔmɛR] *adj (simple)* basic; *(expéditif)* summary ♦ *nm* summary

sommation [sɔmasjɔ̃] *nf (JUR)* summons *sg; (avant de faire feu)* warning

somme [sɔm] *nf (MATH)* sum; *(quantité)* amount; *(argent)* sum, amount ♦ *nm*: **faire un ~** to have a (short) nap; **en ~** all in all; **~ toute** all in all

sommeil [sɔmɛj] *nm* sleep; **avoir ~** to be sleepy; **sommeiller** *vi* to doze

sommer [sɔme] *vt*: **~ qn de faire** to command *ou* order sb to do

sommes [sɔm] *vb voir* **être**

sommet [sɔmɛ] *nm* top; *(d'une montagne)* summit, top; *(fig: de la perfection, gloire)* height

sommier [sɔmje] *nm* (bed) base

somnambule [sɔmnɑ̃byl] *nm/f* sleep-walker

somnifère [sɔmnifɛR] *nm* sleeping drug *no pl (ou* pill)

somnoler [sɔmnɔle] *vi* to doze

somptueux, -euse [sɔ̃ptɥø, øz] *adj* sumptuous

son¹, sa [sɔ̃, sa] *(pl* **ses**) *adj (antécédent humain: mâle)* his; *(: femelle)* her; *(: va-*leur indéfinie)* one's, his/her; *(antécédent non humain)* its

son² [sɔ̃] *nm* sound; *(de blé)* bran

sondage [sɔ̃daʒ] *nm*: **~ (d'opinion)** (opinion) poll

sonde [sɔ̃d] *nf (NAVIG)* lead *ou* sounding line; *(MÉD)* probe; *(TECH: de forage)* borer, driller

sonder [sɔ̃de] *vt (NAVIG)* to sound; *(TECH)* to bore, drill; *(fig: personne)* to sound out; **~ le terrain** *(fig)* to test the ground

songe [sɔ̃ʒ] *nm* dream; **songer** *vi*: **songer à** *(penser à)* to think over; *(envisager)* to consider, think of; **songer que** to think that; **songeur, -euse** *adj* pensive

sonnant, e [sɔnɑ̃, ɑ̃t] *adj*: **à 8 heures ~es** on the stroke of 8

sonné, e [sɔne] *adj (fam)* cracked; **il est midi ~** it's gone twelve

sonner [sɔne] *vi* to ring ♦ *vt (cloche)* to ring; *(glas, tocsin)* to sound; *(portier, infirmière)* to ring for; **~ faux** *(instrument)* to sound out of tune; *(rire)* to ring false

sonnerie [sɔnRi] *nf (son)* ringing; *(sonnette)* bell; **~ d'alarme** alarm bell

sonnette [sɔnɛt] *nf* bell; **~ d'alarme** alarm bell

sono [sɔno] *abr f* = **sonorisation**

sonore [sɔnɔR] *adj (voix)* sonorous, ringing; *(salle)* resonant; *(film, signal)* sound *cpd*; **sonorisation** *nf (équipement: de salle de conférences)* public address system, P.A. system; *(: de discothèque)* sound system; **sonorité** *nf (de piano, violon)* tone; *(d'une salle)* acoustics *pl*

sont [sɔ̃] *vb voir* **être**

sophistiqué, e [sɔfistike] *adj* sophisticated

sorbet [sɔRbɛ] *nm* water ice, sorbet

sorcellerie [sɔRselRi] *nf* witchcraft *no pl*

sorcier [sɔRsje] *nm* sorcerer; **sorcière** *nf* witch *ou* sorceress

sordide [sɔRdid] *adj (lieu)* squalid; *(action)* sordid

sornettes [sɔʀnɛt] *nfpl* twaddle *sg*

sort [sɔʀ] *nm* (*destinée*) fate; (*condition*) lot; (*magique*) curse, spell; **tirer au ~** to draw lots

sorte [sɔʀt] *nf* sort, kind; **de la ~** in that way; **de (telle) ~ que** so that; **en quelque ~** in a way; **faire en ~ que** to see to it that

sortie [sɔʀti] *nf* (*issue*) way out, exit; (*remarque drôle*) sally; (*promenade*) outing; (*le soir: au restaurant etc*) night out; (COMM: *d'un disque*) release; (: *d'un livre*) publication; (: *d'un modèle*) launching; **~s** *nfpl* (COMM: *somme*) items of expenditure, outgoings; **~ de bain** (*vêtement*) bathrobe; **~ de secours** emergency exit

sortilège [sɔʀtilɛʒ] *nm* (magic) spell

sortir [sɔʀtiʀ] *vi* (*gén*) to come out; (*partir, se promener, aller au spectacle*) to go out; (*numéro gagnant*) to come up ♦ *vt* (*gén*) to take out; (*produit, modèle*) to bring out; (*fam: dire*) to come out with; **~ avec qn** to be going out with sb; **s'en ~** (*malade*) to pull through; (*d'une difficulté etc*) to get through; **~ de** (*endroit*) to go (ou come) out of, leave; (*provenir de*) to come from; (*compétence*) to be outside

sosie [sɔzi] *nm* double

sot, sotte [so, sɔt] *adj* silly, foolish ♦ *nm/f* fool; **sottise** *nf* (*caractère*) silliness, foolishness; (*action*) silly *ou* foolish thing

sou [su] *nm*: **près de ses ~s** tight-fisted; **sans le ~** penniless

soubresaut [subʀəso] *nm* start; (*cahot*) jolt

souche [suʃ] *nf* (*d'arbre*) stump; (*de carnet*) counterfoil (BRIT), stub

souci [susi] *nm* (*inquiétude*) worry; (*préoccupation*) concern; (BOT) marigold; **se faire du ~** to worry; **soucier: se soucier de** *vt* to care about; **soucieux, -euse** *adj* concerned, worried

soucoupe [sukup] *nf* saucer; **~ volante** flying saucer

soudain, e [sudɛ̃, ɛn] *adj* (*douleur,*

mort) sudden ♦ *adv* suddenly, all of a sudden

soude [sud] *nf* soda

souder [sude] *vt* (*avec fil à ~*) to solder; (*par soudure autogène*) to weld; (*fig*) to bind together

soudoyer [sudwaje] (*péj*) *vt* to bribe

soudure [sudyʀ] *nf* soldering; welding; (*joint*) soldered joint; weld

souffert, e [sufɛʀ, ɛʀt] *pp de* **souffrir**

souffle [sufl] *nm* (*en expirant*) breath; (*en soufflant*) puff, blow; (*respiration*) breathing; (*d'explosion, de ventilateur*) blast; (*du vent*) blowing; **être à bout de ~** to be out of breath; **un ~ d'air** a breath of air

soufflé, e [sufle] *adj* (*fam: stupéfié*) staggered ♦ *nm* (CULIN) soufflé

souffler [sufle] *vi* (*gén*) to blow; (*haleter*) to puff (and blow) ♦ *vt* (*feu, bougie*) to blow out; (*chasser: poussière etc*) to blow away; (TECH: *verre*) to blow; (*dire*): **~ qch à qn** to whisper sth to sb; **soufflet** *nm* (*instrument*) bellows *pl*; (*gifle*) slap (in the face); **souffleur** *nm* (THÉÂTRE) prompter

souffrance [sufʀɑ̃s] *nf* suffering; **en ~** (*affaire*) pending

souffrant, e [sufʀɑ̃, ɑ̃t] *adj* unwell

souffre-douleur [sufʀədulœʀ] *nm inv* butt, underdog

souffrir [sufʀiʀ] *vi* to suffer, be in pain ♦ *vt* to suffer; endure; (*supporter*) to bear, stand; **~ de** (*maladie, froid*) to suffer from; **elle ne peut pas le ~** she can't stand *ou* bear him

soufre [sufʀ] *nm* sulphur

souhait [swɛ] *nm* wish; **tous nos ~s de** good wishes *ou* our best wishes for; **à vos ~s!** bless you!; **souhaitable** *adj* desirable

souhaiter [swete] *vt* to wish for; **~ la bonne année à qn** to wish sb a happy New Year; **~ que** to hope that

souiller [suje] *vt* to dirty, soil; (*fig: réputation etc*) to sully, tarnish

soûl, e [su, sul] *adj* drunk ♦ *nm*: **tout**

son ~ to one's heart's content

soulagement [sulaʒmɑ̃] *nm* relief

soulager [sulaʒe] *vt* to relieve

soûler [sule] *vt:* **~ qn** to get sb drunk; (*suj: boisson*) to make sb drunk; (*fig*) to make sb's head spin ou reel; **se ~** *vi* to get drunk

soulever [sul(ə)ve] *vt* to lift; (*poussière*) to send up; (*enthousiasme*) to arouse; (*question, débat*) to raise; **se ~** *vi* (*peuple*) to rise up; (*personne couchée*) to lift o.s. up

soulier [sulje] *nm* shoe

souligner [suliɲe] *vt* to underline; (*fig*) to emphasize, stress

soumettre [sumɛtʀ] *vt* (*pays*) to subject, subjugate; (*rebelle*) to put down, subdue; **se ~ (à)** to submit (to); **~ qch à qn** (*projet etc*) to submit sth to sb.

soumis, e [sumi, iz] *adj* submissive; **soumission** *nf* submission

soupape [supap] *nf* valve

soupçon [supsɔ̃] *nm* suspicion; (*petite quantité*): **un ~ de** a hint ou touch of; **soupçonner** *vt* to suspect; **soupçonneux, -euse** *adj* suspicious

soupe [sup] *nf* soup

souper [supe] *vi* to have supper ♦ *nm* supper

soupeser [supəze] *vt* to weigh in one's hand(s); (*fig*) to weigh up

soupière [supjɛʀ] *nf* (*soup*) tureen

soupir [supiʀ] *nm* sigh; **pousser un ~ de soulagement** to heave a sigh of relief

soupirail, -aux [supiʀaj, o] *nm* (small) basement window

soupirer [supiʀe] *vi* to sigh

souple [supl] *adj* supple; (*fig: règlement, caractère*) flexible; (*: démarche, taille*) lithe, supple; **souplesse** *nf* suppleness; (*de caractère*) flexibility

source [suʀs] *nf* (*point d'eau*) spring; (*d'un cours d'eau, fig*) source; **de bonne ~** on good authority

sourcil [suʀsi] *nm* (eye)brow; **sourciller** *vi:* **sans sourciller** without turning

a hair ou batting an eyelid

sourd, e [suʀ, suʀd] *adj* deaf; (*bruit*) muffled; (*douleur*) dull ♦ *nm/f* deaf person; **faire la ~e oreille** to turn a deaf ear; **sourdine** *nf* (MUS) mute; **en sourdine** softly, quietly; **sourd-muet, sourde-muette** *adj* deaf-and-dumb ♦ *nm/f* deaf-mute

souriant, e [suʀjɑ̃, jɑ̃t] *adj* cheerful

souricière [suʀisjɛʀ] *nf* mousetrap; (*fig*) trap

sourire [suʀiʀ] *nm* smile ♦ *vi* to smile; **~ à qn** to smile at sb; (*fig: plaire à*) to appeal to sb; (*suj: chance*) to smile on sb; **garder le ~** to keep smiling

souris [suʀi] *nf* mouse

sournois, e [suʀnwa, waz] *adj* deceitful, underhand

sous [su] *prép* under; **~ la pluie** in the rain; **~ terre** underground; **~ peu** shortly, before long; **sous-bois** *nm inv* undergrowth

souscrire [suskʀiʀ]: **~ à** *vt* to subscribe to

sous...: **sous-directeur, -trice** *nm/f* assistant manager(-manageress); **sous-entendre** *vt* to imply, infer; **sous-entendu, e** *adj* implied ♦ *nm* innuendo, insinuation; **sous-estimer** *vt* to underestimate; **sous-jacent, e** *adj* underlying; **sous-louer** *vt* to sublet; **sous-marin, e** *adj* (*flore, faune*) submarine; (*pêche*) underwater ♦ *nm* submarine; **sous-officier** *nm* ≈ non-commissioned officer (N.C.O.); **sous-produit** *nm* by-product; **sous-pull** *nm* thin poloneck jersey; **soussigné, e** *adj:* **je soussigné** I the undersigned; **sous-sol** *nm* basement; **sous-titre** *nm* subtitle

soustraction [sustʀaksjɔ̃] *nf* subtraction

soustraire [sustʀɛʀ] *vt* to subtract, take away; (*dérober*): **~ qch à qn** to remove sth from sb; **se ~ à** (*autorité etc*) to elude, escape from

sous...: **sous-traitant** *nm* subcontractor; **sous-traiter** *vt* to sub-contract; **sous-vêtements** *nmpl* underwear *sg*

soutane [sutan] *nf* cassock, soutane

soute [sut] *nf* hold

soutenir [sut(ə)niʀ] *vt* to support; (*assaut, choc*) to stand up to, withstand; (*intérêt, effort*) to keep up; (*assurer*): **~ que** to maintain that; **soutenu, e** *adj* (*efforts*) sustained, unflagging; (*style*) elevated

souterrain, e [suteʀɛ̃, ɛn] *adj* underground ♦ *nm* underground passage

soutien [sutjɛ̃] *nm* support; **soutien-gorge** *nm* bra

soutirer [sutiʀe] *vt*: **~ qch à qn** to squeeze *ou* get sth out of sb

souvenir [suv(ə)niʀ] *nm* memory; (*objet*) souvenir ♦ *vb*: **se ~ de** to remember; **se ~ que** to remember that; **en ~ de** in memory *ou* remembrance of

souvent [suvɑ̃] *adv* often; **peu ~** seldom, infrequently

souverain, e [suv(ə)ʀɛ̃, ɛn] *nm/f* sovereign, monarch

soyeux, -euse [swajø, øz] *adj* silky

soyons *etc* [swajɔ̃] *vb voir* **être**

spacieux, -euse [spasjø, jøz] *adj* spacious, roomy

spaghettis [spageti] *nmpl* spaghetti *sg*

sparadrap [spaʀadʀa] *nm* sticking plaster (*BRIT*), Bandaid ® (*US*)

spatial, e, -aux [spasjal, jo] *adj* (*AVIAT*) space *cpd*

speaker, ine [spikœʀ, kʀin] *nm/f* announcer

spécial, e, -aux [spesjal, jo] *adj* special; (*bizarre*) peculiar; **spécialement** *adv* especially, particularly; (*tout exprès*) specially; **spécialiser: se spécialiser** *vi* to specialize; **spécialiste** *nm/f* specialist; **spécialité** *nf* speciality; (*branche*) special field

spécifier [spesifje] *vt* to specify, state

spécimen [spesimɛn] *nm* specimen

spectacle [spektakl] *nm* (*scène*) sight; (*représentation*) show; (*industrie*) show

business; **spectaculaire** *adj* spectacular

spectateur, -trice [spektatœʀ, tʀis] *nm/f* (*CINÉMA etc*) member of the audience; (*SPORT*) spectator; (*d'un événement*) onlooker, witness

spéculer [spekyle] *vi* to speculate

spéléologie [speleɔlɔʒi] *nf* potholing

sperme [spɛʀm] *nm* semen, sperm

sphère [sfɛʀ] *nf* sphere

spirale [spiʀal] *nf* spiral

spirituel, le [spiʀitɥɛl] *adj* spiritual; (*fin, piquant*) witty

splendide [splɑ̃did] *adj* splendid

sponsoring [spɔ̃sɔʀiŋ] *nm* sponsorship

sponsoriser [spɔ̃sɔʀize] *vt* to sponsor

spontané, e [spɔ̃tane] *adj* spontaneous; **spontanéité** *nf* spontaneity

sport [spɔʀ] *nm* sport ♦ *adj inv* (*vêtement*) casual; **faire du ~** to do sport; **~s d'hiver** winter sports; **sportif, -ive** *adj* (*journal, association, épreuve*) sports *cpd*; (*allure, démarche*) athletic; (*attitude, esprit*) sporting

spot [spɔt] *nm* (*lampe*) spot(light); **~ (publicitaire)** commercial (break)

square [skwaʀ] *nm* public garden(s)

squelette [skəlɛt] *nm* skeleton; **squelettique** *adj* scrawny

stabiliser [stabilize] *vt* to stabilize

stable [stabl] *adj* stable, steady

stade [stad] *nm* (*SPORT*) stadium; (*phase, niveau*) stage; **stadier** *nm* steward (*working in a stadium*)

stage [staʒ] *nm* (*cours*) training course; **~ de formation (professionnelle)** vocational (training) course; **~ de perfectionnement** advanced training course; **stagiaire** *nm/f, adj* trainee

stagner [stagne] *vi* to stagnate

stalle [stal] *nf* stall, box

stand [stɑ̃d] *nm* (*d'exposition*) stand; (*de foire*) stall; **~ de tir** (*à la foire, SPORT*) shooting range

standard [stɑ̃daʀ] *adj inv* standard ♦ *nm* switchboard; **standardiste** *nm/f* switchboard operator

standing 266 subjectif

standing [stɑ̃diŋ] *nm* standing; **de grand ~** luxury

starter [stɑʀtɛʀ] *nm* (*AUTO*) choke

station [stasjɔ̃] *nf* station; (*de bus*) stop; (*de villégiature*) resort; **~ balnéaire** seaside resort; **~ de ski** ski resort; **~ de taxis** taxi rank (*BRIT*) *ou* stand (*US*); **stationnement** *nm* parking; **stationner** *vi* to park; **station-service** *nf* service station

statistique [statistik] *nf* (*science*) statistics *sg*; (*rapport, étude*) statistic ♦ *adj* statistical

statue [staty] *nf* statue

statu quo [statykwo] *nm* status quo

statut [staty] *nm* status; **~s** *nmpl* (*JUR, ADMIN*) statutes; **statutaire** *adj* statutory

Sté *abr* = **société**

steak [stɛk] *nm* steak; **~ haché** hamburger

sténo(dactylo) [stenodaktilo] *nf* shorthand typist (*BRIT*), stenographer (*US*)

sténo(graphie) [stenɔgʀafi] *nf* shorthand

stéréo [steʀeo] *adj* stereo

stérile [steʀil] *adj* sterile

stérilet [steʀilɛ] *nm* coil, loop

stériliser [steʀilize] *vt* to sterilize

stigmates [stigmat] *nmpl* scars, marks

stimulant [stimylɑ̃] *nm* (*fig*) stimulus, incentive; (*physique*) stimulant

stimuler [stimyle] *vt* to stimulate

stipuler [stipyle] *vt* to stipulate

stock [stɔk] *nm* stock; **stocker** *vt* to stock

stop [stɔp] *nm* (*AUTO: écriteau*) stop sign; (*: feu arrière*) brake-light; **faire du ~** (*fam*) to hitch(hike); **stopper** *vt, vi* to stop, halt

store [stɔʀ] *nm* blind; (*de magasin*) shade, awning

strabisme [strabism] *nm* squinting

strapontin [strapɔ̃tɛ̃] *nm* jump *ou* foldaway seat

stratégie [strateʒi] *nf* strategy; **straté-**

gique *adj* strategic

stress [strɛs] *nm* stress; **stressant, e** *adj* stressful; **stresser** *vt*: **stresser qn** to make sb (feel) tense

strict, e [strikt] *adj* strict; (*tenue, décor*) severe, plain; **le ~ nécessaire/minimum** the bare essentials/minimum

strident, e [stridɑ̃, ɑ̃t] *adj* shrill, strident

strophe [strɔf] *nf* verse, stanza

structure [stryktyr] *nf* structure

studieux, -euse [stydjø, jøz] *adj* studious

studio [stydjo] *nm* (*logement*) (oneroomed) flatlet (*BRIT*) *ou* apartment (*US*); (*d'artiste, TV etc*) studio

stupéfait, e [stypefɛ, ɛt] *adj* astonished

stupéfiant, e [stypefjɑ̃, jɑ̃t] *adj* (*étonnant*) stunning, astounding ♦ *nm* (*MÉD*) drug, narcotic

stupéfier [stypefje] *vt* (*étonner*) to stun, astonish

stupeur [stypœʀ] *nf* astonishment

stupide [stypid] *adj* stupid; **stupidité** *nf* stupidity; (*parole, acte*) stupid thing (to do *ou* say)

style [stil] *nm* style

stylé, e [stile] *adj* well-trained

styliste [stilist] *nm/f* designer

stylo [stilo] *nm*: **~ (à encre)** (fountain) pen; **~ (à) bille** ball-point pen; **~ feutre** felt-tip pen

su, e [sy] *pp de* **savoir** ♦ *nm*: **au ~ de** with the knowledge of

suave [sɥav] *adj* sweet

subalterne [sybaltɛʀn] *adj* (*employé, officier*) junior; (*rôle*) subordinate, subsidiary ♦ *nm/f* subordinate

subconscient [sybkɔ̃sjɑ̃] *nm* subconscious

subir [sybiʀ] *vt* (*affront, dégâts*) to suffer; (*opération, châtiment*) to undergo

subit, e [sybi, it] *adj* sudden; **subitement** *adv* suddenly, all of a sudden

subjectif, -ive [sybʒɛktif, iv] *adj* subjective

subjonctif [sybʒɔ̃ktif] *nm* subjunctive

subjuguer [sybʒyge] *vt* to captivate

submerger [sybmɛrʒe] *vt* to submerge; (*fig*) to overwhelm

subordonné, e [sybɔrdɔne] *adj, nm/f* subordinate

subrepticement [sybrɛptismɑ̃] *adv* surreptitiously

subside [sybzid] *nm* grant

subsidiaire [sybzidjɛr] *adj*: **question ~** deciding question

subsister [sybziste] *vi* (*rester*) to remain, subsist; (*survivre*) to live on

substance [sypstɑ̃s] *nf* substance

substituer [sypstitɥe] *vt*: **~ qn/qch à** to substitute sb/sth for; **se ~ à qn** (*évincer*) to substitute o.s. for sb

substitut [sypstity] *nm* (*succédané*) substitute

subterfuge [syptɛrfyʒ] *nm* subterfuge

subtil, e [syptil] *adj* subtle

subtiliser [syptilize] *vt*: **~ qch (à qn)** to spirit sth away (from sb)

subvenir [sybvənir]: **~ à** *vt* to meet

subvention [sybvɑ̃sjɔ̃] *nf* subsidy, grant; **subventionner** *vt* to subsidize

suc [syk] *nm* (*BOT*) sap; (*de viande, fruit*) juice

succédané [syksedane] *nm* substitute

succéder [syksede]: **~ à** *vt* to succeed; **se ~** *vi* (*accidents, années*) to follow one another

succès [syksɛ] *nm* success; **avoir du ~** to be a success, be successful; **à ~** successful; **~ de librairie** bestseller; **~ (féminins)** conquests

successif, -ive [syksesif, iv] *adj* successive

successeur [syksesœr] *nm* successor

succession [syksesjɔ̃] *nf* (*série, POL*) succession; (*JUR: patrimoine*) estate, inheritance

succomber [sykɔ̃be] *vi* to die, succumb; (*fig*): **~ à** to succumb to

succulent, e [sykylɑ̃, ɑ̃t] *adj* (*repas, mets*) delicious

succursale [sykyrsal] *nf* branch

sucer [syse] *vt* to suck; **sucette** *nf* (*bonbon*) lollipop; (*de bébé*) dummy (*BRIT*), pacifier (*US*)

sucre [sykr] *nm* (*substance*) sugar; (*morceau*) lump of sugar, sugar lump *ou* cube; **~ d'orge** barley sugar; **~ en morceaux/en poudre** lump/caster sugar; **~ glace/roux** icing/brown sugar; **sucré, e** *adj* (*produit alimentaire*) sweetened; (*au goût*) sweet; **sucrer** *vt* (*thé, café*) to sweeten, put sugar in; **sucreries** *nfpl* (*bonbons*) sweets, sweet things; **sucrier** *nm* (*récipient*) sugar bowl

sud [syd] *nm*: **le ~** the south ♦ *adj inv* south; (*côte*) south, southern; **au ~** (*situation*) in the south; (*direction*) to the south; **au ~ de** (to) the south of; **sud-africain, e** *adj* South African ♦ *nm/f*: **Sud-Africain, e** South African; **sud-américain, e** *adj* South American ♦ *nm/f*: **Sud-Américain, e** South American; **sud-est** *nm, adj inv* south-east; **sud-ouest** *nm, adj inv* south-west

Suède [sɥɛd] *nf*: **la ~** Sweden; **suédois, e** *adj* Swedish ♦ *nm/f*: **Suédois, e** Swede ♦ *nm* (*LING*) Swedish

suer [sɥe] *vi* to sweat; (*suinter*) to ooze; **sueur** *nf* sweat; **en sueur** sweating, in a sweat; **donner des sueurs froids à qn** to put sb in(to) a cold sweat

suffire [syfir] *vi* (*être assez*): **~ (à qn/ pour qch/pour faire)** to be enough *ou* sufficient (for sb/for sth/to do); **il suffit d'une négligence ...** it only takes one act of carelessness ...; **il suffit qu'on oublie pour que ...** one only needs to forget for ...; **ça suffit!** that's enough!

suffisamment [syfizamɑ̃] *adv* sufficiently, enough; **~ de** sufficient, enough

suffisant, e [syfizɑ̃, ɑ̃t] *adj* sufficient; (*résultats*) satisfactory; (*vaniteux*) self-important, bumptious

suffixe [syfiks] *nm* suffix

suffoquer [syfɔke] *vt* to choke, suffocate; (*stupéfier*) to stagger, astound ♦ *vi*

suffrage to choke, suffocate

suffrage [syfraʒ] *nm* (POL: *voix*) vote

suggérer [syɡʒere] *vt* to suggest; **suggestion** *nf* suggestion

suicide [sɥisid] *nm* suicide; **suicider: se suicider** *vi* to commit suicide

suie [sɥi] *nf* soot

suinter [sɥɛ̃te] *vi* to ooze

suis [sɥi] *vb voir* être; suivre

suisse [sɥis] *adj* Swiss ♦ *nm*: **S~** Swiss ♦ *nf*: **la S~** Switzerland; **la S~ romande/allemande** French-speaking/German-speaking Switzerland; **Suissesse** *nf* Swiss (woman *ou* girl)

suite [sɥit] *nf* (*continuation: d'énumération etc*) rest, remainder; (: *de feuilleton*) continuation; (: *film etc sur le même thème*) sequel; (*série*) series, succession; (*conséquence*) result; (*ordre, liaison logique*) coherence; (*appartement, MUS*) suite; (*escorte*) retinue, suite; **~s** *nfpl* (*d'une maladie etc*) effects; **prendre la ~ de** (*directeur etc*) to succeed, take over from; **donner ~ à** (*requête, projet*) to follow up; **faire ~ à** to follow; (*faisant*) **~ à votre lettre du ...:** further to your letter of the ...; **de ~** (*d'affilée*) in succession; (*immédiatement*) at once; **par la ~** afterwards, subsequently; **à la ~** one after the other; **à la ~ de** (*derrière*) behind; (*en conséquence de*) following

suivant, e [sɥivã, ɑ̃t] *adj* next, following ♦ *prép* (*selon*) according to; **au ~!** next!

suivi, e [sɥivi] *adj* (*effort, qualité*) consistent; (*cohérent*) coherent; **très/peu ~** (*cours*) well-/poorly-attended

suivre [sɥivr] *vt* (*gén*) to follow; (SCOL: *cours*) to attend; (*comprendre*) to keep up with; (COMM: *article*) to continue to stock ♦ *vi* to follow; (*élève: assimiler*) to keep up; **se ~** *vi* (*accidents etc*) to follow one after the other; **faire ~** (*lettre*) to forward; **"à ~"** "to be continued"

sujet, te [syʒɛ, ɛt] *adj*: **être ~ à** (*vertige etc*) to be liable *ou* subject to ♦

nm/f (*d'un souverain*) subject ♦ *nm* subject; **au ~ de** about; **~ de conversation** topic *ou* subject of conversation; **~ d'examen** (SCOL) examination subject

summum [sɔ(m)mɔm] *nm*: **le ~ de** the height of

super [syper] (*fam*) *adj inv* terrific, great, fantastic, super

superbe [syperb] *adj* magnificent, superb

super(carburant) [syper(karbyrɑ̃)] *nm* = 4-star petrol (BRIT), ≈ high-octane gasoline (US)

supercherie [syperʃəri] *nf* trick

supérette [syperɛt] *nf* (COMM) minimarket, superette (US)

superficie [syperfisi] *nf* (*surface*) area

superficiel, le [syperfisjɛl] *adj* superficial

superflu, e [syperfly] *adj* superfluous

supérieur, e [syperjœr] *adj* (*lèvre, étages, classes*) upper; (*plus élevé:* température, niveau, enseignement): **~ (à)** higher (than); (*meilleur: qualité, produit*): **~ (à)** superior (to); (*excellent, hautain*) superior ♦ *nm, nf* superior; **supériorité** *nf* superiority

superlatif [syperlatif] *nm* superlative

supermarché [sypermarʃe] *nm* supermarket

superposer [syperpoze] *vt* (*faire chevaucher*) to superimpose; **lits superposés** bunk beds

superproduction [syperprɔdyksjɔ̃] *nf* (*film*) spectacular

superpuissance [syperpɥisɑ̃s] *nf* super-power

superstitieux, -euse [syperstisjø, jøz] *adj* superstitious

superviser [sypervize] *vt* to supervise

supplanter [syplɑ̃te] *vt* to supplant

suppléance [sypleɑ̃s] *nf*: **faire des ~s** (*professeur*) to do supply teaching; **suppléant, e** *adj* (*professeur*) supply cpd; (*juge, fonctionnaire*) deputy cpd ♦ *nm/f* (*professeur*) supply teacher

suppléer [syplee] vt (ajouter: mot manquant etc) to supply, provide; (compenser: lacune) to fill in; ~ **à** to make up for

supplément [syplemã] nm supplement; (de frites etc) extra portion; **un ~ de travail** extra ou additional work; **payer un ~** to pay an additional charge; **le vin est en ~** wine is extra

supplémentaire adj additional, further; (train, bus) relief cpd, extra

supplications [syplikasjɔ̃] nfpl pleas, entreaties

supplice [syplis] nm torture no pl

supplier [syplije] vt to implore, beseech

support [sypɔr] nm support; (publicitaire) medium; (audio-visuel) aid

supportable [sypɔrtabl] adj (douleur) bearable

supporter¹ [sypɔrtɛr] nm supporter, fan

supporter² [sypɔrte] vt (conséquences, épreuve) to bear, endure; (défauts, personne) to put up with; (suj: chose: chaleur etc) to withstand; (: personne: chaleur, vin) to be able to take

supposer [sypoze] vt to suppose; (impliquer) to presuppose; **à ~ que** supposing (that)

suppositoire [sypozitwar] nm suppository

suppression [sypresjɔ̃] nf (voir supprimer) cancellation; removal; deletion

supprimer [syprime] vt (congés, service d'autobus etc) to cancel; (emplois, privilèges, témoin gênant) to do away with; (cloison, mot) to remove; (clause, mot) to delete

suprême [syprɛm] adj supreme

MOT-CLÉ

sur [syr] prép 1 (position) on; (pardessus) over; (au-dessus) above; **posele sur la table** put it on the table; **je n'ai pas d'argent sur moi** I haven't any money on me

2 (direction) towards; **en allant sur Paris** going towards Paris; **sur votre droite** on ou to your right

3 (à propos de) on, about; **un livre/une conférence sur Balzac** a book/lecture on ou about Balzac

4 (proportion, mesures) out of, by; **un sur 10** one in 10; (SCOL) one out of 10; **4 m sur 2** 4 m by 2

sur ce adv hereupon

sûr, e [syr] adj sure, certain; (digne de confiance) reliable; (sans danger) safe; (diagnostic, goût) reliable; **le plus ~ est de** the safest thing is to; ~ **de soi** self-confident; ~ **et certain** absolutely certain

surcharge [syrʃarʒ] nf (de passagers, marchandises) excess load; **surcharger** vt to overload

surchoix [syrʃwa] adj inv top-quality

surclasser [syrklase] vt to outclass

surcroît [syrkrwa] nm: **un ~ de** additional +nom; **par** ou **de ~** moreover; **en ~** in addition

surdité [syrdite] nf deafness

surélever [syrel(ə)ve] vt to raise, heighten

sûrement [syrmã] adv (certainement) certainly; (sans risques) safely

surenchère [syrãʃɛr] nf (aux enchères) higher bid; **surenchérir** vi to bid higher, to try and outbid each other

surent [syr] vb voir **savoir**

surestimer [syrɛstime] vt to overestimate

sûreté [syrte] nf (sécurité) safety; (exactitude: de renseignements etc) reliability; (d'un geste) steadiness; **mettre en ~** to put in a safe place; **pour plus de ~** as an extra precaution, to be on the safe side

surf [sœrf] nm surfing

surface [syrfas] nf surface; (superficie) surface area; **une grande ~** supermarket; **faire ~** to surface; **en ~** near the surface; (fig) superficially

surfait, e [syʀfɛ, ɛt] adj overrated

surfer [syʀfe] vi: ~ **sur Internet** to surf ou browse the Internet

surgelé, e [syʀʒəle] adj (deep-)frozen ♦ nm: **les ~s** (deep-)frozen food

surgir [syʀʒiʀ] vi to appear suddenly; (fig: problème, conflit) to arise

sur...: surhumain, e adj superhuman; **sur-le-champ** adv immediately; **surlendemain** nm: **le surlendemain (soir)** two days later (in the evening); **le surlendemain de** two days after; **surmenage** nm overwork(ing); **surmener: se surmener** to overwork

surmonter [syʀmɔ̃te] vt (vaincre) to overcome; (être au-dessus de) to top

surnaturel, le [syʀnatyʀɛl] adj, nm supernatural

surnom [syʀnɔ̃] nm nickname

surnombre [syʀnɔ̃bʀ] nm: **être en ~** to be too many (ou too many too many)

surpeuplé, e [syʀpœple] adj over-populated

sur-place [syʀplas] nm: **faire du ~~** to mark time

surplomber [syʀplɔ̃be] vt, vi to overhang

surplus [syʀply] nm (COMM) surplus; (reste): **~ de bois** wood left over

surprenant, e [syʀpʀənɑ̃, ɑ̃t] adj amazing

surprendre [syʀpʀɑ̃dʀ] vt (étonner) to surprise; (tomber sur: intrus etc) to catch; (entendre) to overhear

surpris, e [syʀpʀi, iz] adj: ~ **(de/que)** surprised (at/that); **surprise** nf surprise; **faire une surprise à qn** to give sb a surprise; **surprise-partie** nf party

surréservation [syʀʀezɛʀvasjɔ̃] nf double booking, overbooking

sursaut [syʀso] nm start, jump; ~ **de** (énergie, indignation) sudden fit ou burst of; **en ~** with a start; **sursauter** vi to (give) start, jump

sursis [syʀsi] nm (JUR: gén) suspended sentence; (fig) reprieve

surtaxe [syʀtaks] nf surcharge

surtout [syʀtu] adv (avant tout, d'abord) above all; (spécialement, particulièrement) especially; ~, **ne dites rien!** whatever you do don't say anything!; ~ **pas!** certainly ou definitely not!; ~ **que ...** especially as ...

surveillance [syʀvejɑ̃s] nf watch; (PO-LICE, MIL) surveillance; **sous ~ médicale** under medical supervision

surveillant, e [syʀvejɑ̃, ɑ̃t] nm/f (de prison) warder; (SCOL) monitor

surveiller [syʀveje] vt (enfant, bagages) to watch, keep an eye on; (prisonnier, suspect) to keep (a watch on; (territoire, bâtiment) to (keep) watch over; (travaux) to supervise; (SCOL: examen) to invigilate; ~ **son langage/sa ligne** to watch one's language/figure

survenir [syʀvəniʀ] vi (incident, retards) to occur, arise; (événement) to take place

survêt(ement) [syʀvɛt(mɑ̃)] nm track-suit

survie [syʀvi] nf survival; **survivant, e** nm/f survivor; **survivre** vi to survive; **survivre à** (accident etc) to survive

survoler [syʀvɔle] vt to fly over; (fig: livre) to skim through

survolté, e [syʀvɔlte] adj (fig) worked up

sus [sy(s)] : **en ~ de** prép in addition to, over and above; **en ~** in addition

susceptible [sysɛptibl] adj touchy, sensitive; ~ **de faire** liable to do

susciter [sysite] vt (admiration) to arouse; (ennuis): **(à qn)** to create (for sb)

suspect, e [syspɛ(kt), ɛkt] adj suspicious; (témoignage, opinions) suspect ♦ nm/f suspect; **suspecter** vt to suspect; (honnêteté de qn) to question, have one's suspicions about

suspendre [syspɑ̃dʀ] vt (accrocher: vêtement): ~ **qch (à)** to hang sth up (on); (interrompre, démettre) to suspend; **se ~ à** to hang from

suspendu, e [syspɑ̃dy] adj (accroché):

~ **à** hanging on (ou from); (perché): ~ **au-dessus de** suspended over

suspens [syspɑ̃]: **en** ~ adv (affaire) in abeyance; **tenir en** ~ to keep in suspense

suspense [syspɛns, syspɑ̃s] nm suspense

suspension [syspɑ̃sjɔ̃] nf suspension; (lustre) light fitting ou fitment

şut [sy] vb voir **savoir**

suture [sytyʀ] nf (MÉD): **point de** ~ stitch

svelte [svɛlt] adj slender, svelte

SVP abr (= s'il vous plaît) please

sweat-shirt [switʃœʀt] (pl ~~s) nm sweatshirt

syllabe [si(l)lab] nf syllable

symbole [sɛ̃bɔl] nm symbol; **symbolique** adj symbolic(al); (geste, offrande) token cpd; **symboliser** vt to symbolize

symétrique [simetʀik] adj symmetrical

sympa [sɛ̃pa] (fam) adj inv nice; **sois** ~, **prête-le moi** be a pal and lend it to me

sympathie [sɛ̃pati] nf (inclination) liking; (affinité) friendship; (condoléances) sympathy; **j'ai beaucoup de** ~ **pour lui** I like him a lot; **sympathique** adj nice, friendly

sympathisant, e [sɛ̃patizɑ̃, ɑ̃t] nm/f sympathizer

sympathiser [sɛ̃patize] vi (voisins etc: s'entendre) to get on (BRIT) ou along (US) (well)

symphonie [sɛ̃fɔni] nf symphony

symptôme [sɛ̃ptom] nm symptom

synagogue [sinagɔg] nf synagogue

syncope [sɛ̃kɔp] nf (MÉD) blackout; **tomber en** ~ to faint, pass out

syndic [sɛ̃dik] nm (d'immeuble) managing agent

syndical, e, -aux [sɛ̃dikal, o] adj (trade) union cpd; **syndicaliste** nm/f trade unionist

syndicat [sɛ̃dika] nm (d'ouvriers, employés) (trade) union; ~ **d'initiative** tourist office; **syndiqué, e** adj belong-

ing to a (trade) union; **syndiquer: se syndiquer** vi to form a trade union; (adhérer) to join a trade union

synonyme [sinɔnim] adj synonymous ♦ nm synonym; ~ **de** synonymous with

syntaxe [sɛ̃taks] nf syntax

synthèse [sɛ̃tɛz] nf synthesis

synthétique [sɛ̃tetik] adj synthetic

Syrie [siʀi] nf: **la** ~ Syria

systématique [sistematik] adj systematic

système [sistɛm] nm system; ~ **D** (fam) resourcefulness

T, t

t' [t] pron voir **te**

ta [ta] adj voir **ton¹**

tabac [taba] nm tobacco; (magasin) tobacconist's (shop); ~ **blond/brun** light/dark tobacco

tabagisme [tabaʒism] nm: ~ **passif** passive smoking

tabasser [tabase] (fam) vt to beat up

table [tabl] nf table; **à** ~! dinner etc is ready!; **se mettre à** ~ to sit down to eat; **mettre la** ~ to lay the table; **faire** ~ **rase de** to make a clean sweep of; ~ **à repasser** ironing board; ~ **de cuisson** (à l'électricité) hotplate; (au gaz) gas ring; ~ **de nuit** ou **de chevet** bedside table; ~ **des matières** table of contents pl; ~ **d'orientation** viewpoint indicator; ~ **roulante** trolley

tableau, x [tablo] nm (peinture) painting; (reproduction, fig) picture; (panneau) board; (schéma) table, chart; ~ **d'affichage** notice board; ~ **de bord** dashboard; (AVIAT) instrument panel; ~ **noir** blackboard

tabler [table] vi: ~ **sur** to bank on

tablette [tablɛt] nf (planche) shelf; ~ **de chocolat** bar of chocolate

tableur [tablœʀ] nm spreadsheet

tablier [tablije] nm apron

tabou [tabu] nm taboo

tabouret [tabuʀɛ] nm stool

tac [tak] nm: **il m'a répondu du ~ au ~** he answered me right back

tache [taʃ] nf (saleté) stain, mark; (ART, de couleur, lumière) spot; **~ de rousseur** freckle

tâche [taʃ] nf task

tacher [taʃe] vt to stain, mark

tâcher [taʃe] vi: **~ de faire** to try ou endeavour to do

tacheté, e [taʃte] adj spotted

tacot [tako] (péj) nm banger (BRIT), (old) heap

tact [takt] nm tact; **avoir du ~** to be tactful

tactique [taktik] adj tactical ♦ nf (technique) tactics sg; (plan) tactic

taie [tɛ] nf: **~ (d'oreiller)** pillowslip, pillowcase

taille [taj] nf cutting; (d'arbre etc) pruning; (milieu du corps) waist; (hauteur) height; (grandeur) size; **de ~ à faire** capable of doing; **de ~** sizeable; **taille-crayon(s)** nm pencil sharpener

tailler [taje] vt (pierre, diamant) to cut; (arbre, plante) to prune; (vêtement) to cut out; (crayon) to sharpen

tailleur [tajœʀ] nm (couturier) tailor; (vêtement) suit; **en ~** (assis) cross-legged

taillis [taji] nm copse

taire [tɛʀ] vi: **faire ~ qn** to make sb be quiet; **se ~** vi to be silent ou quiet

talc [talk] nm talc, talcum powder

talent [talɑ̃] nm talent

talkie-walkie [tokiwoki] nm walkie-talkie

taloche [talɔʃ] (fam) nf clout, cuff

talon [talɔ̃] nm heel; (de chèque, billet) stub, counterfoil (BRIT); **~s plats/aiguilles** flat/stiletto heels

talonner [talɔne] vt (suivre) to follow hot on the heels of; (harceler) to hound

talus [taly] nm embankment

tambour [tɑ̃buʀ] nm (MUS, aussi) drum; (musicien) drummer; (porte) revolving door(s pl); **tambourin** nm tambourine

tambouriner vi to drum; **tambouriner à/sur** to drum on

tamis [tami] nm sieve

Tamise [tamiz] nf: **la ~** the Thames

tamisé, e [tamize] adj (fig) subdued, soft

tampon [tɑ̃pɔ̃] nm (de coton, d'ouate) wad, pad; (amortisseur) buffer; (bouchon) plug, stopper; (cachet, timbre) stamp; (mémoire) (INFORM) buffer; **~ (hygiénique)** tampon; **tamponner** vt (timbres) to stamp; (heurter) to crash ou ram into; **tamponneuse** adj f: **autos tamponneuses** dodgems

tandem [tɑ̃dɛm] nm tandem

tandis [tɑ̃di]: **~ que** conj while

tanguer [tɑ̃ge] vi to pitch (and toss)

tanière [tanjɛʀ] nf lair, den

tanné, e [tane] adj weather-beaten

tanner [tane] vt to tan; (fam: harceler) to badger

tant [tɑ̃] adv so much; **~ de** (sable, eau) so much; (gens, livres) so many; **~ que** as long as; (autant que) as much as; **~ mieux** that's great; (avec une certaine réserve) so much the better; **~ pis** too bad; (conciliant) never mind

tante [tɑ̃t] nf aunt

tantôt [tɑ̃to] adv (parfois): **~ ... ~** now ... now; (cet après-midi) this afternoon

taon [tɑ̃] nm horsefly

tapage [tapaʒ] nm uproar, din

tapageur, -euse [tapaʒœʀ, øz] adj noisy; (voyant) loud, flashy

tape [tap] nf slap

tape-à-l'œil [tapalœj] adj inv flashy, showy

taper [tape] vt (porte) to bang, slam; (enfant) to slap; (dactylographier) to type (out); (fam: emprunter): **~ qn de 10 F** to touch sb for 10 F ♦ vi (soleil) to beat down; **se ~** vt (repas) to put away; (fam: corvée) to get landed with; **~ sur qn** to thump sb; (fig) to run sb down; **~ sur un clou** to hit a nail; **~ sur la table** to bang on the table; **~ à** (porte etc) to knock on; **~ dans** (se ser-

vir) to dig into; **~ des mains/pieds** to clap one's hands/stamp one's feet; **(à la machine)** to type; **se ~ un travail** (*fam*) to land o.s. a job

tapi, e [tapi] *adj* (*blotti*) crouching; (*caché*) hidden away

tapis [tapi] *nm* carpet; (*petit*) rug; **mettre sur le ~** (*fig*) to bring up for discussion; **~ de bain** bath mat; **~ de sol** (*de tente*) groundsheet; **~ de souris** (*INFORM*) mouse mat; **~ roulant** (*pour piétons*) moving walkway; (*pour bagages*) carousel

tapisser [tapise] *vt* (*avec du papier peint*) to paper; (*recouvrir*): **~ qch (de)** to cover sth (with); **tapisserie** *nf* (*tenture, broderie*) tapestry; (*papier peint*) wallpaper; **tapissier-décorateur** *nm* interior decorator

tapoter [tapɔte] *vt* (*joue, main*) to pat; (*objet*) to tap

taquin, e [takɛ̃, in] *adj* teasing; **taquiner** *vt* to tease

tarabiscoté, e [tarabiskɔte] *adj* overornate, fussy

tard [taʀ] *adv* late; **plus ~** later (on); **au plus ~** at the latest; **sur le ~** late in life

tarder [taʀde] *vi* (*chose*) to be a long time coming; (*personne*): **~ à faire** to delay doing; **il me tarde d'être** I am longing to be; **sans (plus) ~** without (further) delay

tardif, -ive [taʀdif, iv] *adj* late

taré, e [taʀe] *nm/f* cretin

tarif [taʀif] *nm*: **~ des consommations** price list; **~s postaux/douaniers** postal/customs rates; **~ des taxis** taxi fares; **~ plein/réduit** (*train*) full/reduced fare; (*téléphone*) peak/off-peak rate

tarir [taʀiʀ] *vi* to dry up, run dry

tarte [taʀt] *nf* tart; **~ aux fraises** strawberry tart; **~ Tatin** ≈ apple upside-down tart

tartine [taʀtin] *nf* slice of bread; **~ de miel** slice of bread and honey; **tarti-**

ner *vt* to spread; **fromage à tartiner** cheese spread

tartre [taʀtʀ] *nm* (*des dents*) tartar; (*de bouilloire*) fur, scale

tas [ta] *nm* heap, pile; (*fig*): **un ~ de** heaps of, lots of; **en ~** in a heap *ou* pile; **formé sur le ~** trained on the job

tasse [tas] *nf* cup; **~ à café** coffee cup

tassé, e [tase] *adj*: **bien ~** (*café etc*) strong

tasser [tase] *vt* (*terre, neige*) to pack down; (*entasser*): **~ qch dans** to cram sth into; **se ~** *vi* (*se serrer*) to squeeze up; (*s'affaisser*) to settle; (*fig*) to settle down

tata [tata] *nf* auntie

tâter [tɑte] *vt* to feel; (*fig*) to try out; **se ~** (*hésiter*) to be in two minds; **~ de** (*prison etc*) to have a taste of

tatillon, ne [tatijɔ̃, ɔn] *adj* pernickety

tâtonnement [tɑtɔnmɑ̃] *nm*: **par ~s** (*fig*) by trial and error

tâtonner [tɑtɔne] *vi* to grope one's way along

tâtons [tɑtɔ̃]: **à ~** *adv*: **chercher/avancer à ~** to grope around for/grope one's way forward

tatouage [tatwaʒ] *nm* tattoo

tatouer [tatwe] *vt* to tattoo

taudis [todi] *nm* hovel, slum

taule [tol] (*fam*) *nf* nick (*fam*), prison

taupe [top] *nf* mole

taureau, x [tɔʀo] *nm* bull; (*signe*): **le T~** Taurus

tauromachie [tɔʀɔmaʃi] *nf* bullfighting

taux [to] *nm* rate; (*d'alcool*) level; **~ de change** exchange rate; **~ d'intérêt** interest rate

taxe [taks] *nf* tax; (*douanière*) duty; **toutes ~s comprises** inclusive of tax; **la boutique hors ~s** the duty free shop; **~ à la valeur ajoutée** value added tax

taxer [takse] *vt* (*personne*) to tax; (*produit*) to put a tax on, tax

taxi [taksi] *nm* taxi; (*chauffeur: fam*) taxi

driver

Tchécoslovaquie [tʃekɔslɔvaki] *nf* Czechoslovakia; **tchèque** *adj* Czech ♦ *nm/f*: **Tchèque** Czech ♦ *nm* (LING) Czech; **la République tchèque** the Czech Republic

te, t' [tə] *pron* you; *(réfléchi)* yourself

technicien, ne [tɛknisjɛ̃, jɛn] *nm/f* technician

technico-commercial, e, -aux [tɛknikokɔmɛrsjal, jo] *adj*: **agent ~-** sales technician

technique [tɛknik] *adj* technical ♦ *nf* technique; **techniquement** *adv* technically

technologie [tɛknɔlɔʒi] *nf* technology; **technologique** *adj* technological

teck [tɛk] *nm* teak

tee-shirt [tiʃœrt] *nm* T-shirt, tee-shirt

teignais *etc* [tɛɲɛ] *vb voir* teindre

teindre [tɛ̃dr] *vt* to dye; **se ~ les cheveux** to dye one's hair; **teint, e** *adj* dyed ♦ *nm (du visage)* complexion; *(momentané)* colour ♦ *nf* shade; **grand teint** colourfast

teinté, e [tɛ̃te] *adj*: **~ de** *(fig)* tinged with

teinter [tɛ̃te] *vt (verre, papier)* to tint; *(bois)* to stain

teinture [tɛ̃tyr] *nf* dye; **~ d'iode** tincture of iodine; **teinturerie** *nf* dry cleaner's; **teinturier** *nm* dry cleaner

tel, telle [tɛl] *adj (pareil)* such; *(comme)*: **~ un/des ...** like a/like ...; *(indéfini)* such-and-such a; *(intensif)*: **un ~/de tels ... such (a)/such ...**; **rien de ~** nothing like it; **~ que** like, such as; **~ quel** as it is *(ou* tel as etc*)*; **viens ~ jour** come on such-and-such a day

télé [tele] *nf (fam)* TV

télé...: **télécabine** *nf (benne)* cable car; **télécarte** *nf* phonecard; **télécommande** *nf* remote control; **télécopie** *nf* fax; **envoyer qch par télécopie** to fax sth; **télécopieur** *nm* fax machine; **télédistribution** *nf* cable TV; **téléférique** *nm* = **téléphérique**

télégramme *nm* telegram; **télégraphier** *vt* to telegraph; cable; **téléguider** *vt* to radio-control; **télématique** *nf* telematics *sg*; **téléobjectif** *nm* telephoto lens *sg*; **télépathie** *nf* telepathy; **téléphérique** *nm* cable car

téléphone [telefɔn] *nm* telephone; **avoir le ~** to be on the (tele)phone; **au ~** on the phone; **~ mobile** mobile phone; **~ rouge** hot line; **~ sans fil** cordless (tele)phone; **~ de voiture** car phone; **téléphoner** *vi* to make a phone call; **téléphoner à** to phone, call up; **téléphonique** *adj* (tele)phone *cpd*

télescope [teleskɔp] *nm* telescope

télescoper [teleskɔpe] *vt* to smash up; **se ~** *(véhicules)* to concertina

télé...: **télescripteur** *nm* teleprinter; **télésiège** *nm* chairlift; **téléski** *nm* skitow; **téléspectateur, -trice** *nm/f* (television) viewer; **télévente** *nf* telesales; **téléviseur** *nm* television set; **télévision** *nf* television; **à la télévision** on television; **télévision numérique** digital TV

télex [teleks] *nm* telex

telle [tɛl] *adj voir* tel; **tellement** *adv (tant)* so much; *(si)* so; **tellement de** *(sable, eau)* so much; *(gens, livres)* so many; **il s'est endormi tellement il était fatigué** he was so tired (that) he fell asleep; **pas tellement** not (all) that much; not (all) that *+adjectif*

téméraire [temerɛr] *adj* reckless, rash; **témérité** *nf* recklessness, rashness

témoignage [temwaɲaʒ] *nm* (JUR: *déclaration*) testimony *no pl*, evidence *no pl*; *(rapport, récit)* account; *(fig: d'affection etc: cadeau)* token, mark; *(: geste)* expression

témoigner [temwaɲe] *vt (intérêt, gratitude)* to show ♦ *vi (JUR)* to testify, give evidence; **~ de** to bear witness to, testify to

témoin [temwɛ̃] *nm* witness ♦ *adj*: **appartement ~** show flat (BRIT); **être ~**

de to witness; **~ oculaire** eyewitness

tempe [tɑ̃p] *nf* temple

tempérament [tɑ̃peʀamɑ̃] *nm* temperament, disposition; **à ~** (*vente*) on deferred (payment) terms; (*achat*) by instalments, hire purchase *cpd*

température [tɑ̃peʀatyʀ] *nf* temperature; **avoir** *ou* **faire de la ~** to be running *ou* have a temperature

tempéré, e [tɑ̃peʀe] *adj* temperate

tempête [tɑ̃pɛt] *nf* storm; **~ de sable/neige** sand/snowstorm

temple [tɑ̃pl] *nm* temple; (*protestant*) church

temporaire [tɑ̃pɔʀɛʀ] *adj* temporary

temps [tɑ̃] *nm* (*atmosphérique*) weather; (*durée*) time; (*époque*) time, times *pl*; (*LING*) tense; (*MUS*) beat; (*TECH*) stroke; **un ~ de chien** (*fam*) rotten weather; **quel ~ fait-il?** what's the weather like?; **il fait beau/mauvais ~** the weather is fine/bad; **avoir le ~/tout son ~** to have time/plenty of time; **en ~ de paix/guerre** in peacetime/wartime; **en ~ utile** *ou* **voulu** in due time *ou* course; **ces derniers ~** lately; **dans quelque ~** in a (little) while; **de ~ en ~, de ~ à autre** from time to time; **à ~** (*partir, arriver*) in time; **à ~ complet, à plein ~** fulltime; **à ~ partiel** part-time; **dans le ~** at one time; **~ d'arrêt** pause, halt; **~ mort** (*COMM*) slack period

tenable [t(ə)nabl] *adj* bearable

tenace [tənas] *adj* persistent

tenailler [tənaje] *vt* (*fig*) to torment

tenailles [tənaj] *nfpl* pincers

tenais *etc* [t(ə)nɛ] *vb voir* **tenir**

tenancier, -ière [tənɑ̃sje] *nm/f* manager/manageress

tenant, e [tənɑ̃, ɑ̃t] *nm/f* (*SPORT*): **~ du titre** title-holder

tendance [tɑ̃dɑ̃s] *nf* (*opinions*) leanings *pl*, sympathies *pl*; (*évolution*) trend; **avoir ~ à** to have a tendency to, tend to

tendeur [tɑ̃dœʀ] *nm* (*attache*) elastic strap

tendre [tɑ̃dʀ] *adj* tender; (*bois, roche, couleur*) soft ♦ *vt* (*élastique, peau*) to stretch; (*corde*) to tighten; (*muscle*) to tense; (*fig: piège*) to set, lay; (*donner*): **~ qch à qn** to hold sth out to sb; (*offrir*) to offer sb sth; **se ~** *vi* (*corde*) to tighten; (*relations*) to become strained; **~ à qch/à faire** to tend towards sth/to do; **~ l'oreille** to prick up one's ears; **~ la main/le bras** to hold out one's hand/stretch out one's arm; **tendrement** *adv* tenderly; **tendresse** *nf* tenderness

tendu, e [tɑ̃dy] *pp de* **tendre** ♦ *adj* (*corde*) tight; (*muscles*) tensed; (*relations*) strained

ténèbres [tenɛbʀ] *nfpl* darkness *sg*

teneur [tənœʀ] *nf* content; (*d'une lettre*) terms *pl*, content

tenir [t(ə)niʀ] *vt* to hold; (*magasin, hôtel*) to run; (*promesse*) to keep ♦ *vi* to hold; (*neige, gel*) to last; **se ~** *vi* (*avoir lieu*) to be held, take place; (*être: personne*) to stand; **~ à** (*personne, objet*) to be attached to; (*réputation*) to care about; **~ à faire** to be determined to do; **~ de** (*ressembler à*) to take after; **ça ne tient qu'à lui** it is entirely up to him; **~ qn pour** to regard sb as; **~ qch de qn** (*histoire*) to have heard *ou* learnt sth from sb; (*qualité, défaut*) to have inherited *ou* got sth from sb; **~ dans** to fit into; **~ compte de qch** to take sth into account; **~ les comptes** to keep the books; **~ bon** to stand fast; **~ le coup** to hold out; **~ au chaud** to keep hot; **tiens/tenez, voilà le stylo** there's the pen!; **tiens, voilà Alain!** look, here's Alain!; **tiens?** (*surprise*) really?; **~ se ~ droit** to stand (*ou* sit) up straight; **bien se ~** to behave well; **se ~ à qch** to hold on to sth; **s'en ~ à qch** to confine o.s. to sth

tennis [tenis] *nm* tennis; (*court*) tennis court ♦ *nm ou f pl* (*aussi*: **chaussures de ~**) tennis *ou* gym shoes; **~ de table** table tennis; **tennisman** *nm* tennis

player
tension [tɑ̃sjɔ̃] nf tension; (MÉD) blood pressure; **avoir de la ~** to have high blood pressure

tentation [tɑ̃tasjɔ̃] nf temptation

tentative [tɑ̃tativ] nf attempt

tente [tɑ̃t] nf tent

tenter [tɑ̃te] vt (éprouver, attirer) to tempt; (essayer): **~ qch/de faire** to attempt ou try sth/to do; **~ sa chance** to try one's luck

tenture [tɑ̃tyr] nf hanging

tenu, e [t(ə)ny] pp de **tenir** ♦ adj (maison, comptes): **bien ~** well-kept; (obligé): **~ de faire** obliged to do ♦ nf (vêtements) clothes pl; (comportement) (good) manners pl, good behaviour; (d'une maison) upkeep; **en petite ~e** scantily dressed ou clad; **~e de route** (AUTO) road-holding; **~e de soirée** evening dress

ter [tɛr] adj: **16 ~** 16b ou B

térébenthine [terebɑ̃tin] nf: (**essence de**) **~** (oil of) turpentine

Tergal ® [tɛrgal] nm Terylene ®

terme [tɛrm] nm term; (fin) end; **à court/long ~** ♦ adj short-/long-term ♦ adv in the short/long term; (paiement) ♦ (MÉD) prematurely; **mettre un ~ à** to put an end ou a stop to; **en bons ~s** on good terms

terminaison [tɛrminɛzɔ̃] nf (LING) ending

terminal [tɛrminal, o] nm terminal; **terminale** nf (SCOL) ≈ sixth form ou year (BRIT); ≈ twelfth grade (US)

terminer [tɛrmine] vt to finish; **se ~** vi to end

terne [tɛrn] adj dull

ternir [tɛrnir] vt to dull; (fig) to sully, tarnish; **se ~** vi to become dull

terrain [tɛrɛ̃] nm (sol, fig) ground; (COMM: étendue de terre) land no pl; (parcelle) plot (of land); (à bâtir) site; **sur le ~** (fig) on the field; **~ d'aviation** airfield; **~ de camping** campsite; **~ de football/rugby** football/rugby

pitch (BRIT) ou field (US); **~ de golf** golf course; **~ de jeu** games field; (pour les petits) playground; **~ de sport** sports ground; **~ vague** waste ground no pl

terrasse [tɛras] nf terrace; **à la ~** (café) outside; **terrasser** vt (adversaire) to floor; (suj: maladie etc) to strike down

terre [tɛr] nf (gén, aussi ÉLEC) earth; (substance) soil, earth; (opposé à mer) land no pl; (contrée) land; **~s** nfpl (terrains) lands, land sg; **en ~** (pipe, poterie) clay cpd; **à ~** ou **par ~** (mettre, être, s'asseoir) on the ground (ou floor); (jeter, tomber) to the ground, down; **~ à ~** inv down-to-earth; **~ cuite** terracotta; **la ~ ferme** dry land; **~ glaise** clay

terreau [tɛro] nm compost

terre-plein [tɛrplɛ̃] nm platform; (sur chaussée) central reservation

terrer [tɛre]: **se ~** vi to hide away

terrestre [tɛrɛstr] adj (surface) earth's, of the earth; (BOT, ZOOL, MIL) land cpd; (REL) earthly

terreur [tɛrœr] nf terror no pl

terrible [tɛribl] adj terrible, dreadful; (fam) terrific; **pas ~** nothing special

terrien, ne [tɛrjɛ̃, jɛn] adj: **propriétaire ~** landowner ♦ nm/f (non martien etc) earthling

terrier [tɛrje] nm burrow, hole; (chien) terrier

terrifier [tɛrifje] vt to terrify

terrine [tɛrin] nf (récipient) terrine; (CULIN) pâté

territoire [tɛritwar] nm territory

terroir [tɛrwar] nm: **accent du ~** country accent

terroriser [tɛrɔrize] vt to terrorize

terrorisme [tɛrɔrism] nm terrorism; **terroriste** nm/f terrorist

tertiaire [tɛrsjɛr] adj tertiary ♦ nm (ÉCON) service industries pl

tertre [tɛrtr] nm hillock, mound

tes [te] adj voir **ton**¹

tesson [tesɔ̃] nm: **~ de bouteille** piece

of broken bottle

test [tɛst] *nm* test

testament [tɛstamɑ̃] *nm* (*JUR*) will; (*REL*) Testament; (*fig*) legacy

tester [tɛste] *vt* to test

testicule [tɛstikyl] *nm* testicle

têtard [tɛtaʀ] *nm* tadpole

tête [tɛt] *nf* head; (*cheveux*) hair *no pl*; (*visage*) face; **de ~** *adj* (*wagon etc*) front *cpd* ♦ *adv* (*calculer*) in one's head, mentally; **tenir ~ à qn** to stand up to sb; **la ~ en bas** with one's head down; **la ~ la première** (*tomber*) headfirst; **faire une ~** (*FOOTBALL*) to head the ball; **faire la ~** (*fig*) to sulk; **en ~** at the front; (*SPORT*) in the lead; **à la ~ de** at the head of; **à ~ reposée** in a more leisurely moment; **n'en faire qu'à sa ~** to do as one pleases; **en avoir par-dessus la ~** to be fed up with; **en ~ à ~** in private, alone together; **de la ~ aux pieds** from head to toe; **~ de lecture** (*playback*) head; **~ de liste** (*POL*) chief candidate; **~ de série** (*TENNIS*) seeded player, seed; **tête-à-queue** *nm inv*: **faire un tête-à-queue** to spin round

téter [tete] *vt*: **~ (sa mère)** to suck at one's mother's breast, feed

tétine [tetin] *nf* teat; (*sucette*) dummy (*BRIT*), pacifier (*US*)

têtu, e [tety] *adj* stubborn, pigheaded

texte [tɛkst] *nm* text; (*morceau choisi*) passage

textile [tɛkstil] *adj* textile *cpd* ♦ *nm* textile; **le ~** the textile industry

Texto ® [tɛksto] *nm* text message

texto [tɛksto] (*fam*) *adv* word for word ♦ *nm* text message

texture [tɛkstyʀ] *nf* texture

thaïlandais, e [tajlɑ̃dɛ, ɛz] *adj* Thai ♦ *nm/f*: **T~, e** Thai

Thaïlande [tajlɑ̃d] *nf* Thailand

TGV *sigle m* (= *train à grande vitesse*) high-speed train

thé [te] *nm* tea; **~ au citron** lemon tea; **~ au lait** tea with milk; **prendre le ~** to have tea; **faire le ~** to make the tea

théâtral, e, -aux [teatʀal, o] *adj* theatrical

théâtre [teatʀ] *nm* theatre; (*péj*: *simulation*) playacting; (*fig*: *lieu*): **le ~ de** the scene of; **faire du ~** to act

théière [tejɛʀ] *nf* teapot

thème [tɛm] *nm* theme; (*SCOL*: *traduction*) prose (composition)

théologie [teɔlɔʒi] *nf* theology

théorie [teɔʀi] *nf* theory; **théorique** *adj* theoretical

thérapie [teʀapi] *nf* therapy

thermal, e, -aux [tɛʀmal, o] *adj*: **station ~e** spa; **cure ~e** water cure

thermes [tɛʀm] *nmpl* thermal baths

thermomètre [tɛʀmɔmɛtʀ] *nm* thermometer

thermos ® [tɛʀmos] *nm ou nf*: **(bouteille) ~** vacuum *ou* Thermos ® flask

thèse [tɛz] *nf* thesis

thon [tɔ̃] *nm* tuna (fish)

thym [tɛ̃] *nm* thyme

tibia [tibja] *nm* shinbone, tibia; (*partie antérieure de la jambe*) shin

TIC [teise] *sigle f* (= *technologies de l'information et de la communication*) ICT

tic [tik] *nm* tic, (*nervous*) twitch; (*de langage etc*) mannerism

ticket [tikɛ] *nm* ticket; **~ de caisse** receipt; **~ de quai** platform ticket

tic-tac [tiktak] *nm* ticking; **faire ~ ~** to tick

tiède [tjɛd] *adj* lukewarm; (*vent, air*) mild, warm; **tiédir** *vi* to cool; (*se réchauffer*) to grow warmer

tien, ne [tjɛ̃, tjɛn] *pron*: **le(la) ~(ne)**, **les ~(ne)s** yours; **à la ~ne!** cheers!

tiens [tjɛ̃] *vb, excl voir* **tenir**

tierce [tjɛʀs] *adj voir* **tiers**

tiercé [tjɛʀse] *nm* system of forecast betting giving first 3 horses

tiers, tierce [tjɛʀ, tjɛʀs] *adj* third ♦ *nm* (*JUR*) third party; (*fraction*) third; **le ~ monde** the Third World

tifs [tif] (*fam*) *nmpl* hair

tige [tiʒ] *nf* stem; (*baguette*) rod

tignasse [tiɲas] (*péj*) *nf* mop of hair

tigre [tigʀ] *nm* tiger; **tigresse** *nf* tigress; **tigré, e** adj (rayé) striped; (tacheté) spotted; (chat) tabby

tilleul [tijœl] nm lime (tree), linden (tree); (boisson) lime(-blossom) tea

timbale [tɛ̃bal] nf (metal) tumbler; **~s** nfpl (MUS) timpani, kettledrums

timbre [tɛ̃bʀ] nm (tampon) stamp; (aussi: **~-poste**) (postage) stamp; (MUS: de voix, instrument) timbre, tone

timbré, e [tɛ̃bʀe] (fam) adj cracked

timide [timid] adj shy; (timoré) timid; **timidement** adv shyly; timidly; **timidité** nf shyness; timidity

tins etc [tɛ̃] vb voir **tenir**

tintamarre [tɛ̃tamaʀ] nm din, uproar

tinter [tɛ̃te] vi to ring, chime; (argent, clefs) to jingle

tique [tik] nf (parasite) tick

tir [tiʀ] nm (sport) shooting; (fait ou manière de ~) firing no pl; (rafale) fire; (stand) shooting gallery; **~ à l'arc** archery; **~ au pigeon** clay pigeon shooting

tirage [tiʀaʒ] nm (action) printing; (PHOTO) print; (de journal) circulation; (de livre: nombre d'exemplaires) (print) run; (: édition) edition; (de loterie) draw; **par ~ au sort** by drawing lots

tirailler [tiʀɑje] vt: **être tiraillé entre** to be torn between

tire [tiʀ] nf: **vol à la ~** pickpocketing

tiré, e [tiʀe] adj (traits) drawn; **~ par les cheveux** far-fetched

tire-au-flanc [tiʀoflɑ̃] (péj) nm inv skiver

tire-bouchon [tiʀbuʃɔ̃] nm corkscrew

tirelire [tiʀliʀ] nf moneybox

tirer [tiʀe] vt (gén) to pull; (extraire): **~ qch de** to take ou pull sth out of; (trait, rideau, carte, conclusion, chèque) to draw; (langue) to stick out; (en faisant feu: balle, coup) to fire; (: animal) to shoot; (journal, livre, photo) to print; (FOOTBALL: corner etc) to take ♦ vi (faire feu) to fire; (faire du ~, FOOTBALL) to shoot; **se ~** vi (fam) to push off; **s'en ~** (éviter le pire) to get off; (survivre) to

pull through; (se débrouiller) to manage; **~ sur** (corde) to pull on ou at; (faire feu sur) to shoot ou fire at; (pipe) to draw on; (approcher de: couleur) to verge ou border on; **~ qn de** (embarras etc) to help ou get sb out of; **~ à l'arc/ la carabine** to shoot with a bow and arrow/with a rifle; **~ à sa fin** to be drawing to a close; **~ qch au clair** to clear sth up; **~ au sort** to draw lots; **~ parti de** to take advantage of; **~ profit de** to profit from

tiret [tiʀɛ] nm dash

tireur [tiʀœʀ] nm gunman; **~ d'élite** marksman

tiroir [tiʀwaʀ] nm drawer; **tiroir-caisse** nm till

tisane [tizan] nf herb tea

tisonnier [tizɔnje] nm poker

tisser [tise] vt to weave; **tisserand** nm weaver

tissu [tisy] nm fabric, material, cloth no pl; (ANAT, BIO) tissue; **tissu-éponge** nm (terry) towelling no pl

titre [titʀ] nm (gén) title; (de journal) headline; (diplôme) qualification; (COMM) security; en **~** (champion) official; **à juste ~** rightly; **à quel ~?** on what grounds? **à aucun ~** on no account; **au même ~ (que)** in the same way (as); **à ~ d'information** for (your) information; **à ~ gracieux** free of charge; **à ~ d'essai** on a trial basis; **à ~ privé** in a private capacity; **~ de propriété** title deed; **~ de transport** ticket

tituber [titybe] vi to stagger (along)

titulaire [tityleʀ] adj (ADMIN) with tenure ♦ nmf (de permis) holder

toast [tost] nm slice ou piece of toast; (de bienvenue) (welcoming) toast; **porter un ~ à qn** to propose ou drink a toast to sb

toboggan [tɔbɔgɑ̃] nm slide; (AUTO) flyover

toc [tɔk] excl: **~, toc** knock knock ♦ nm: **en ~** fake

tocsin [tɔksɛ̃] nm alarm (bell)

toge [tɔʒ] nf toga; (de juge) gown

tohu-bohu [tɔybɔy] nm hubbub

toi [twa] pron you

toile [twal] nf (tableau) canvas; **de** ou **en ~** (pantalon) cotton; (sac) canvas; **~ cirée** oilcloth; **~ d'araignée** cobweb; **~ de fond** (fig) backdrop

toilette [twalɛt] nf (habits) outfit; **~s** nfpl (w.-c.) toilet sg; **faire sa ~** to have a wash, get washed; **articles de ~** toiletries

toi-même [twamɛm] pron yourself

toiser [twaze] vt to eye up and down

toison [twazɔ̃] nf (de mouton) fleece

toit [twa] nm roof; **~ ouvrant** sunroof

toiture [twatyʀ] nf roof

tôle [tol] nf (plaque) steel ou iron sheet; **~ ondulée** corrugated iron

tolérable [tɔleʀabl] adj tolerable

tolérant, e [tɔleʀɑ̃, ɑ̃t] adj tolerant

tolérer [tɔleʀe] vt to tolerate; (ADMIN: hors taxe etc) to allow

tollé [tɔ(l)le] nm outcry

tomate [tɔmat] nf tomato; **~s farcies** stuffed tomatoes

tombe [tɔ̃b] nf (sépulture) grave; (avec monument) tomb

tombeau, x [tɔ̃bo] nm tomb

tombée [tɔ̃be] nf: **à la ~ de la nuit** at nightfall

tomber [tɔ̃be] vi to fall; (fièvre, vent) to drop; **laisser ~** (objet) to drop; (personne) to let down; (activité) to give up; **laisse ~!** forget it!; **faire ~** to knock over; **~ sur** (rencontrer) to bump into; **~ de fatigue/sommeil** to drop from exhaustion/be falling asleep on one's feet; **ça tombe bien** that's come at the right time; **il est bien tombé** he's been lucky; **à l'eau** (projet) to fall through; **~ en panne** to break down

tombola [tɔ̃bɔla] nf raffle

tome [tɔm] nm volume

ton¹, ta [tɔ̃, ta] (pl **tes**) adj your

ton² [tɔ̃] nm (gén) tone; (couleur) shade, tone; **de bon ~** in good taste

tonalité [tɔnalite] nf (au téléphone) dialling tone

tondeuse [tɔ̃døz] nf (à gazon) (lawn)mower; (du coiffeur) clippers pl; (pour les moutons) shears pl

tondre [tɔ̃dʀ] vt (pelouse, herbe) to mow; (haie) to cut, clip; (mouton, toison) to shear; (cheveux) to crop

tongs [tɔ̃g] nfpl flip-flops

tonifier [tɔnifje] vt (peau, organisme) to tone up

tonique [tɔnik] adj fortifying ♦ nm tonic

tonne [tɔn] nf metric ton, tonne

tonneau, x [tɔno] nm (à vin, cidre) barrel; **faire des ~x** (voiture, avion) to roll over

tonnelle [tɔnɛl] nf bower, arbour

tonner [tɔne] vi to thunder; **il tonne** it is thundering, there's some thunder

tonnerre [tɔnɛʀ] nm thunder

tonton [tɔ̃tɔ̃] nm uncle

tonus [tɔnys] nm energy

top [tɔp] nm: **au 3ème ~** at the 3rd stroke

topinambour [tɔpinɑ̃buʀ] nm Jerusalem artichoke

topo [tɔpo] (fam) nm rundown; **c'est le même ~** it's the same old story

toque [tɔk] nf (de fourrure) fur hat; **~ de cuisinier** chef's hat; **~ de jockey/juge** jockey's/judge's cap

toqué, e [tɔke] (fam) adj cracked

torche [tɔʀʃ] nf torch

torchon [tɔʀʃɔ̃] nm cloth; (à vaisselle) tea towel ou cloth

tordre [tɔʀdʀ] vt (chiffon) to wring; (barre, fig: visage) to twist; **se ~**: **se ~ le poignet/la cheville** to twist one's wrist/ankle; **se ~ de douleur/rire** to be doubled up with pain/laughter; **tordu, e** adj bent; (fig) crazy

tornade [tɔʀnad] nf tornado

torpille [tɔʀpij] nf torpedo

torréfier [tɔʀefje] vt to roast

torrent [tɔʀɑ̃] nm mountain stream

torsade [tɔʀsad] nf: **un pull à ~s** a

cable sweater

torse [tɔʀs] *nm* chest; (*ANAT, SCULPTURE*) torso; ~ **nu** stripped to the waist

tort [tɔʀ] *nm* (*défaut*) fault; ~**s** *nmpl* (*JUR*) fault *sg*; **avoir** ~ to be wrong; **être dans son** ~ to be in the wrong; **donner** ~ **à qn** to lay the blame on sb; **causer du** ~ **à** to harm; **à** ~ wrongly; **à** ~ **et à travers** wildly

torticolis [tɔʀtikɔli] *nm* stiff neck

tortiller [tɔʀtije] *vt* to twist; (*moustache*) to twirl; **se** ~ *vi* to wriggle; (*en dansant*) to wiggle

tortionnaire [tɔʀsjɔnɛʀ] *nm* torturer

tortue [tɔʀty] *nf* tortoise; (*d'eau douce*) terrapin; (*d'eau de mer*) turtle

tortueux, -euse [tɔʀtɥø, øz] *adj* (*rue*) twisting; (*fig*) tortuous

torture [tɔʀtyʀ] *nf* torture; **torturer** *vt* to torture; (*fig*) to torment

tôt [to] *adv* early; ~ **ou tard** sooner or later; **si** ~ so early; (*déjà*) so soon; **plus** ~ earlier; **au plus** ~ at the earliest; **il eut** ~ **fait de faire** he soon did

total, e, -aux [tɔtal, o] *adj, nm* total; **au** ~ in total; (*fig*) on the whole; **faire le** ~ to work out the total; **totalement** *adv* totally; **totaliser** *vt* to total; **totalitaire** *adj* totalitarian; **totalité** *nf*: **la totalité de** (*of*); the whole +*sg*; **en totalité** entirely

toubib [tubib] (*fam*) *nm* doctor

touchant, e [tuʃɑ̃, ɑ̃t] *adj* touching

touche [tuʃ] *nf* (*de piano, de machine à écrire*) key; (*de téléphone*) button; (*PEINTURE etc*) stroke, touch; (*fig: de nostalgie*) touch; (*FOOTBALL: aussi:* **remise en** ~) throw-in; (*aussi:* **ligne de** ~) touchline

toucher [tuʃe] *nm* touch ♦ *vt* to touch; (*palper*) to feel; (*atteindre: d'un coup de feu etc*) to hit; (*concerner*) to concern, affect; (*contacter*) to reach, contact; (*recevoir: récompense*) to receive, get; (*: salaire*) to draw, get; (*: chèque*) to cash; **se** ~ (*être en contact*) to touch; **au** ~

to the touch; ~ **à** to touch; (*concerner*) to have to do with, concern; **je vais lui en** ~ **un mot** I'll have a word with him about it; ~ **à sa fin** to be drawing to a close

touffe [tuf] *nf* tuft

touffu, e [tufy] *adj* thick, dense

toujours [tuʒuʀ] *adv* always; (*encore*) still; (*constamment*) forever; ~ **plus** more and more; **pour** ~ forever; ~ **est-il que** the fact remains that; **essaie** ~ (*you can*) try anyway

toupet [tupɛ] (*fam*) *nm* cheek

toupie [tupi] *nf* (*spinning*) top

tour [tuʀ] *nf* tower; (*immeuble*) high-rise block (*BRIT*) *ou* building (*US*); (*ÉCHECS*) castle, rook ♦ *nm* (*excursion*) trip; (*à pied*) stroll, walk; (*en voiture*) run, ride; (*SPORT: aussi:* ~ **de piste**) lap; (*d'être servi ou de jouer etc*) turn; (*de roue etc*) revolution; (*POL: aussi:* ~ **de scrutin**) ballot; (*ruse, de prestidigitation*) trick; (*de potier*) wheel; (*à bois, métaux*) lathe; (*circonférence*): **de 3 m de** ~ 3 m round, with a circumference *ou* girth of 3 m; **faire le** ~ **de** to go round; (*à pied*) to walk round; **c'est au** ~ **de Renée** it's Renée's turn; **à** ~ **de rôle**, **à** ~ **in turn**; ~ **de chant** song recital; ~ **de contrôle** control tower; ~ **de garde** spell of duty; ~ **d'horizon** *nm* (*fig*) general survey; ~ **de taille/tête** *nm* waist/head measurement; **un 33** ~**s** an LP; **un 45** ~**s** a single

tourbe [tuʀb] *nf* peat

tourbillon [tuʀbijɔ̃] *nm* whirlwind; (*d'eau*) whirlpool; (*fig*) whirl, swirl; **tourbillonner** *vi* to whirl (round)

tourelle [tuʀɛl] *nf* turret

tourisme [tuʀism] *nm*: **agence de** ~ tourist agency; **faire du** ~ to go touring; (*en ville*) to go sightseeing; **touriste** *nm/f* tourist; **touristique** *adj* (*région*) touristic

tourment [tuʀmɑ̃] *nm* torment; **tourmenter** *vt* to torment; **se tourmenter** *vi* to fret, worry o.s.

tournage [turnaʒ] nm (CINÉMA) shooting

tournant [turnɑ̃] nm (de route) bend; (fig) turning point

tournebroche [turnəbrɔʃ] nm roasting spit

tourne-disque [turnədisk] nm record player

tournée [turne] nf (du facteur etc) round; (d'artiste, politicien) tour; (au café) round (of drinks)

tournemain [turnəmɛ̃]: **en un ~** adv (as) quick as a flash

tourner [turne] vt to turn; (sauce, mélange) to stir; (CINÉMA: faire les prises de vues) to shoot; (: produire) to make ♦ vi to turn; (moteur) to run; (taximètre) to tick away; (lait etc) to turn (sour); **se ~** vi to turn round; **mal ~** to go wrong; **~ autour de** to go round; (péj) to hang round; **~ à/en** to turn into; **~ à gauche/droite** to turn left/right; **~ le dos à** to turn one's back on; to have one's back to; **~ de l'œil** to pass out; **se ~ vers** to turn towards; (fig) to turn to

tournesol [turnəsɔl] nm sunflower

tournevis [turnəvis] nm screwdriver

tourniquet [turnikɛ] nm (pour arroser) sprinkler; (portillon) turnstile; (présentoir) revolving stand

tournoi [turnwa] nm tournament

tournoyer [turnwaje] vi to swirl (round)

tournure [turnyr] nf (LING) turn of phrase; (évolution): **la ~ de qch** the way sth is developing; **~ d'esprit** turn ou cast of mind; **la ~ des événements** the turn of events

tourte [turt] nf pie

tourterelle [turtərɛl] nf turtledove

tous [tu] adj, pron voir **tout**

Toussaint [tusɛ̃] nf: **la ~** All Saints' Day

La Toussaint, November 1, is a public holiday in France. People traditionally visit the graves of friends and relatives to lay wreaths of heather and chrysanthemums.

tousser [tuse] vi to cough

tout, e [tu, tut] (mpl **tous**, fpl **toutes**) adj **1** (avec article singulier) all; **tout le lait** all the milk; **toute la nuit** all night, the whole night; **tout le livre** the whole book; **tout un pain** a whole loaf; **tout le temps** all the time; the whole time; **c'est tout le contraire** it's quite the opposite

2 (avec article pluriel) every, all; **tous les livres** all the books; **toutes les nuits** every night; **toutes les fois** every time; **toutes les trois/deux semaines** every third/other ou second week, every three/two weeks; **tous les deux** both ou each of us (ou them ou you); **toutes les trois** all three of us (ou them ou you)

3 (sans article): **à tout âge** at any age; **pour toute nourriture, il avait ...** his only food was ...

♦ pron everything, all; **il a tout fait** he's done everything; **je les vois tous** I can see them all ou all of them; **nous y sommes tous allés** all of us went, we all went; **en tout** in all; **tout ce qu'il sait** all he knows

♦ nm whole; **le tout** all of it (ou them); **le tout est de ...** the main thing is to ...; **pas du tout** not at all

♦ adv **1** (très, complètement) very; **tout près** very near; **le tout premier** the very first; **tout seul** all alone; **le livre tout entier** the whole book; **tout en haut** right at the top; **tout droit** straight ahead

2: **tout en** while; **tout en travaillant** while working, as he ou works

3: **tout d'abord** first of all; **tout à coup** suddenly; **tout à fait** absolutely;

tout à l'heure a short while ago; (*futur*) in a short while, shortly; **à tout à l'heure!** see you later!; **tout de même** all the same; **tout le monde** everybody; **tout de suite** immediately, straight away; **tout terrain** *ou* **tous terrains** all-terrain

---

toutefois [tutfwa] *adv* however

toutes [tut] *adj, pron voir* **tout**

toux [tu] *nf* cough

toxicomane [tɔksikɔman] *nm/f* drug addict

toxique [tɔksik] *adj* toxic

trac [trak] *nm* (*au théâtre, en public*) stage fright; (*aux examens*) nerves *pl*; **avoir le ~** (*au théâtre, en public*) to have stage fright; (*aux examens*) to be feeling nervous

tracasser [trakase] *vt* to worry, bother; **se ~** to worry

trace [tras] *nf* (*empreintes*) tracks *pl*; (*marques, aussi fig*) mark; (*quantité infime, indice, vestige*) trace; **~s de pas** footprints

tracé [trase] *nm* (*parcours*) line; (*plan*) layout

tracer [trase] *vt* to draw; (*piste*) to open up

tract [trakt] *nm* tract, pamphlet

tractations [traktasjɔ̃] *nfpl* dealings, bargaining *sg*

tracteur [traktœr] *nm* tractor

traction [traksjɔ̃] *nf*: **~ avant/arrière** front-wheel/rear-wheel drive

tradition [tradisjɔ̃] *nf* tradition; **traditionnel, le** *adj* traditional

traducteur, -trice [tradyktœr, tris] *nm/f* translator

traduction [tradyksjɔ̃] *nf* translation

traduire [traduir] *vt* to translate; (*exprimer*) to convey; **~ qn en justice** to bring sb before the courts

trafic [trafik] *nm* traffic; **~ d'armes** arms dealing; **trafiquant, e** *nm/f* (*d'armes*) dealer; **trafiquer** (*péj*) *vt* (*vin*) to doctor; (*moteur, docu-*

ment) to tamper with

tragédie [traʒedi] *nf* tragedy; **tragique** *adj* tragic

trahir [trair] *vt* to betray; **trahison** *nf* betrayal; (*JUR*) treason

train [trɛ̃] *nm* (*RAIL*) train; (*allure*) pace; **être en ~ de faire qch** to be doing sth; **mettre qn en ~** to put sb in good spirits; **se sentir en ~** to feel in good form; **~ d'atterrissage** undercarriage; **~ de vie** style of living; **~ électrique** (*jouet*) (electric) train set; **~ autos-couchettes** car-sleeper train

traîne [trɛn] *nf* (*de robe*) train; **être à la ~** to lag behind

traîneau, x [trɛno] *nm* sleigh, sledge

traînée [trɛne] *nf* trail; (*sur un mur, dans le ciel*) streak; (*péj*) slut

traîner [trɛne] *vt* (*remorque*) to pull; (*enfant, chien*) to drag *ou* trail along ♦ *vi* (*robe, manteau*) to trail; (*être en désordre*) to lie around; (*aller lentement*) to dawdle (along); (*vagabonder, agir lentement*) to hang about; (*durer*) to drag on; **se ~** *vi* to drag o.s. along; **~ les pieds** to drag one's feet

train-train [trɛ̃trɛ̃] *nm* humdrum routine

traire [trɛr] *vt* to milk

trait [trɛ] *nm* (*ligne*) line; (*de dessin*) stroke; (*caractéristique*) feature, trait; **~s** *nmpl* (*du visage*) features; **d'un ~** (*boire*) in one gulp; **de ~** (*animal*) draught; **avoir ~ à** to concern; **d'union** hyphen

traitant, e [trɛtɑ̃, ɑ̃t] *adj* (*shampooing*) medicated; **votre médecin ~** your usual *ou* family doctor

traite [trɛt] *nf* (*COMM*) draft; (*AGR*) milking; **d'une ~** without stopping; **la ~ des noirs** the slave trade

traité [trɛte] *nm* treaty

traitement [trɛtmɑ̃] *nm* treatment; (*salaire*) salary; **~ de données** data processing; **~ de texte** word processing; (*logiciel*) word processing package

traiter [trɛte] *vt* to treat; (*qualifier*): **~**

qn d'idiot to call sb a fool ♦ vi to deal;
~ de to deal with

traiteur [tʀɛtœʀ] nm caterer

traître, -esse [tʀɛtʀ, tʀɛtʀɛs] adj (dangereux) treacherous ♦ nm traitor

trajectoire [tʀaʒɛktwaʀ] nf path

trajet [tʀaʒɛ] nm (parcours, voyage) journey; (itinéraire) route; (distance à parcourir) distance

trame [tʀam] nf (de tissu) weft; (fig) framework; usé jusqu'à la ~ threadbare

tramer [tʀame] vt: il se trame quelque chose there's something brewing

trampoline [tʀɑ̃pɔlin] nm trampoline

tramway [tʀamwɛ] nm tram(way); (voiture) tram(car) (BRIT), streetcar (US)

tranchant, e [tʀɑ̃ʃɑ̃, ɑ̃t] adj sharp; (fig) peremptory ♦ nm (d'un couteau) cutting edge; (de la main) edge; à double ~ double-edged

tranche [tʀɑ̃ʃ] nf (morceau) slice; (arête) edge; ~ d'âge/de salaires age/wage bracket

tranché, e [tʀɑ̃ʃe] adj (couleurs) distinct; (opinions) clear-cut; **tranchée** nf trench

trancher [tʀɑ̃ʃe] vt to cut, sever ♦ vi to take a decision; ~ avec to contrast sharply with

tranquille [tʀɑ̃kil] adj quiet; (rassuré) easy in one's mind, with one's mind at rest; **se tenir ~** (enfant) to be quiet; **laisse-moi/laisse-ça ~** leave me/it alone; **avoir la conscience ~** to have a clear conscience; **tranquillisant** nm tranquillizer; **tranquillité** nf peace (and quiet); (d'esprit) peace of mind

transat [tʀɑ̃zat] nm deckchair

transborder [tʀɑ̃sbɔʀde] vt to tran(s)ship

transcription [tʀɑ̃skʀipsjɔ̃] nf transcription; (copie) transcript

transférer [tʀɑ̃sfeʀe] vt to transfer; **transfert** nm transfer

transformation [tʀɑ̃sfɔʀmasjɔ̃] nf change; transformation; alteration;

(RUGBY) conversion

transformer [tʀɑ̃sfɔʀme] vt to change; (radicalement) to transform; (vêtement) to alter; (matière première, appartement, RUGBY) to convert; **(se) ~ en** to turn into

transfusion [tʀɑ̃sfyzjɔ̃] nf: ~ sanguine blood transfusion

transgresser [tʀɑ̃sgʀese] vt to contravene

transi, e [tʀɑ̃zi] adj numb (with cold), chilled to the bone

transiger [tʀɑ̃ziʒe] vi to compromise

transit [tʀɑ̃zit] nm transit; **transiter** vi to pass in transit

transitif, -ive [tʀɑ̃zitif, iv] adj transitive

transition [tʀɑ̃zisjɔ̃] nf transition; **transitoire** adj transitional

translucide [tʀɑ̃slysid] adj translucent

transmettre [tʀɑ̃smɛtʀ] vt (passer): ~ qch à qn to pass sth on to sb; (TECH, TÉL, MÉD) to transmit; (TV, RADIO: retransmettre) to broadcast; **transmission** nf transmission

transparent, e [tʀɑ̃spaʀɑ̃, ɑ̃t] adj transparent

transpercer [tʀɑ̃spɛʀse] vt (froid, pluie) to go through, pierce; (balle) to go through

transpiration [tʀɑ̃spiʀasjɔ̃] nf perspiration

transpirer [tʀɑ̃spiʀe] vi to perspire

transplanter [tʀɑ̃splɑ̃te] vt (MÉD, BOT) to transplant; **transplantation** nf (MÉD) transplant

transport [tʀɑ̃spɔʀ] nm transport; ~s en commun public transport; **transporter** vt to carry, move; (COMM) to transport, convey; **transporteur** nm haulage contractor (BRIT), trucker (US)

transvaser [tʀɑ̃svaze] vt to decant

transversal, e, -aux [tʀɑ̃svɛʀsal, o] adj (rue) which runs across; **coupe ~e** cross section

trapèze [tʀapɛz] nm (au cirque) trapeze

trappe [tʀap] nf trap door

trapu, e [tʀapy] *adj* squat, stocky

traquenard [tʀaknaʀ] *nm* trap

traquer [tʀake] *vt* to track down; (*harceler*) to hound

traumatiser [tʀomatize] *vt* to traumatize

travail, -aux [tʀavaj] *nm* (*gén*) work; (*tâche, métier*) work *no pl*, (*ÉCON, MÉD*) labour; **être sans ~** (*employé*) to be unemployed; *voir aussi* **travaux; ~ (au) noir** moonlighting

travailler [tʀavaje] *vi* to work; (*bois*) to warp ♦ *vt* (*bois, métal*) to work; (*objet d'art, discipline*) to work on; **cela le travaille** it is on his mind; **travailleur, -euse** *adj* hard-working ♦ *nm/f* worker; **travailliste** *adj* ≃ Labour *cpd*

travaux [tʀavo] *nmpl* (*de réparation, agricoles etc*) work *sg*; (*sur route*) road-works *pl*; (*de construction*) building (work); **travaux des champs** farm-work *sg*; **travaux dirigés** (*SCOL*) tutorial; **travaux forcés** hard labour *sg*; **travaux manuels** (*SCOL*) handicrafts; **travaux ménagers** housework *sg*; **travaux pratiques** (*SCOL*) practical work; (*en laboratoire*) lab work

travers [tʀavɛʀ] *nm* fault, failing; **en ~ (de)** across; **au ~ (de)/à ~** through; **de ~** (*nez, bouche*) crooked; (*chapeau*) askew; **comprendre de ~** (*fig*) to misunderstand; **regarder de ~** (*fig*) to look askance at

traverse [tʀavɛʀs] *nf* (*de voie ferrée*) sleeper; **chemin de ~** shortcut

traversée [tʀavɛʀse] *nf* crossing

traverser [tʀavɛʀse] *vt* (*gén*) to cross; (*ville, tunnel, aussi: percer, fig*) to go through; (*suj: ligne, trait*) to run across

traversin [tʀavɛʀsɛ̃] *nm* bolster

travesti [tʀavɛsti] *nm* transvestite

trébucher [tʀebyʃe] *vi:* **~ (sur)** to stumble (over), trip (against)

trèfle [tʀɛfl] *nm* (*BOT*) clover; (*CARTES: couleur*) clubs *pl*; (*: carte*) club

treille [tʀɛj] *nf* vine arbour

treillis [tʀeji] *nm* (*métallique*) wire-

mesh; (*MIL: tenue*) combat uniform; (*pantalon*) combat trousers *pl*

treize [tʀɛz] *num* thirteen; **treizième** *num* thirteenth

| treizième mois |

Le treizième mois is an end-of-year bonus roughly equal to one month's salary. For many employees it is a standard part of their salary package.

---

tréma [tʀema] *nm* diaeresis

tremblement [tʀɑ̃bləmɑ̃] *nm:* **~ de terre** earthquake

trembler [tʀɑ̃ble] *vi* to tremble, shake; **~ de** (*froid, fièvre*) to shiver *ou* tremble with; (*peur*) to shake *ou* tremble with; **~ pour qn** to fear for sb

trémousser [tʀemuse]: **se ~** *vi* to jig about, wriggle about

trempe [tʀɑ̃p] *nf* (*fig*): **de cette/sa ~** of this/his calibre

trempé, e [tʀɑ̃pe] *adj* soaking (wet), drenched; (*TECH*) tempered

tremper [tʀɑ̃pe] *vt* to soak, drench; (*aussi:* **faire ~, mettre à ~**) to soak; (*plonger*): **~ qch dans** to dip sth in(to) ♦ *vi* to soak; (*fig*): **~ dans** to be involved *ou* have a hand in; **se ~** *vi* to have a quick dip; **trempette** *nf:* **faire trempette** to go paddling

tremplin [tʀɑ̃plɛ̃] *nm* springboard; (*SKI*) ski-jump

trentaine [tʀɑ̃tɛn] *nf:* **une ~ (de)** thirty or so, about thirty; **avoir la ~** (*âge*) to be around thirty

trente [tʀɑ̃t] *num* thirty; **être sur son ~ et un** to be wearing one's Sunday best; **trentième** *num* thirtieth

trépidant, e [tʀepidɑ̃, ɑ̃t] *adj* (*fig: rythme*) pulsating; (*: vie*) hectic

trépied [tʀepje] *nm* tripod

trépigner [tʀepiɲe] *vi* to stamp (one's feet)

très [tʀɛ] *adv* very; much +*pp*, highly +*pp*

trésor [tʀezɔʀ] *nm* treasure; **T~ (pu-**

blic) public revenue; **trésorerie** *nf* (*gestion*) accounts *pl*; (*bureaux*) accounts department; **difficultés de trésorerie** cash problems, shortage of cash *ou* funds; **trésorier, -ière** *nm/f* treasurer

tressaillir [tʀesajiʀ] *vi* to shiver, shudder

tressauter [tʀesote] *vi* to start, jump

tresse [tʀes] *nf* braid, plait; **tresser** *vt* (*cheveux*) to braid, plait; (*fil, jonc*) to plait; (*corbeille*) to weave; (*corde*) to twist

tréteau, x [tʀeto] *nm* trestle

treuil [tʀœj] *nm* winch

trêve [tʀεv] *nf* (MIL, POL) truce; (*fig*) respite; **~ de ...** enough of this ...

tri [tʀi] *nm*: **faire le ~ (de)** to sort out; **le (bureau de) ~** (POSTES) the sorting office

triangle [tʀijɑ̃gl] *nm* triangle; **triangulaire** *adj* triangular

tribord [tʀibɔʀ] *nm*: **à ~** to starboard, on the starboard side

tribu [tʀiby] *nf* tribe

tribunal, -aux [tʀibynal, o] *nm* (JUR) court; (MIL) tribunal

tribune [tʀibyn] *nf* (*estrade*) platform, rostrum; (*débat*) forum; (*d'église, de tribunal*) gallery; (*de stade*) stand

tribut [tʀiby] *nm* tribute

tributaire [tʀibytɛʀ] *adj*: **être ~ de** to be dependent on

tricher [tʀiʃe] *vi* to cheat; **tricheur, -euse** *nm/f* cheat(er)

tricolore [tʀikɔlɔʀ] *adj* three-coloured; (*français*) red, white and blue

tricot [tʀiko] *nm* (*technique, ouvrage*) knitting *no pl*; (*vêtement*) jersey, sweater; **~ de peau** vest; **tricoter** *vt* to knit

trictrac [tʀiktʀak] *nm* backgammon

tricycle [tʀisikl] *nm* tricycle

triennal, e, -aux [tʀijenal, o] *adj* three-year

trier [tʀije] *vt* to sort out; (POSTES, *fruits*) to sort

trimestre [tʀimɛstʀ] *nm* (SCOL) term;

(COMM) quarter; **trimestriel, le** *adj* quarterly; (SCOL) end-of-term

tringle [tʀεgl] *nf* rod

trinquer [tʀεke] *vi* to clink glasses

triomphe [tʀijɔ̃f] *nm* triumph; **triompher** *vi* to triumph, win; **triompher de** to triumph over, overcome

tripes [tʀip] *nfpl* (CULIN) tripe *sg*

triple [tʀipl] *adj* triple ♦ *nm*: **le ~ (de)** (*comparaison*) three times as much (as); **en ~ exemplaire** in triplicate; **tripler** *vi, vt* to triple, treble

triplés, -ées [tʀiple] *nm/fpl* triplets

tripoter [tʀipɔte] *vt* to fiddle with

triste [tʀist] *adj* sad; (*couleur, temps, journée*) dreary; (*péj*): **~ personnage/affaire** sorry individual/affair; **tristesse** *nf* sadness

trivial, e, -aux [tʀivjal, jo] *adj* coarse, crude; (*commun*) mundane

troc [tʀɔk] *nm* barter

troène [tʀɔɛn] *nm* privet

trognon [tʀɔɲɔ̃] *nm* (*de fruit*) core; (*de légume*) stalk

trois [tʀwa] *num* three; **troisième** *num* third; **trois quarts** *nmpl*: **les trois quarts de** three-quarters of

trombe [tʀɔ̃b] *nf*: **des ~s d'eau** a downpour; **en ~** like a whirlwind

trombone [tʀɔ̃bɔn] *nm* (MUS) trombone; (*de bureau*) paper clip

trompe [tʀɔ̃p] *nf* (*d'éléphant*) trunk; (MUS) trumpet, horn

tromper [tʀɔ̃pe] *vt* to deceive; (*vigilance, poursuivants*) to elude; **se ~** *vi* to make a mistake, be mistaken; **se ~ de voiture/jour** to take the wrong car/get the day wrong; **se ~ de 3 cm/20 F** to be out by 3 cm/20 F; **tromperie** *nf* deception, trickery *no pl*

trompette [tʀɔ̃pɛt] *nf* trumpet; **en ~** (*nez*) turned-up

trompeur, -euse [tʀɔ̃pœʀ, øz] *adj* deceptive

tronc [tʀɔ̃] *nm* (BOT, ANAT) trunk; (*d'église*) collection box

tronçon [tʀɔ̃sɔ̃] *nm* section; **tron-**

çonner vt to saw up

trône [tʀon] nm throne

trop [tʀo] adv (+vb) too much; (+adjectif, adverbe) too; ~ **(nombreux)** too many; ~ **peu (nombreux)** too few; ~ **(souvent)** too often; ~ **(longtemps)** (for) too long; ~ **de** (nombre) too many; (quantité) too much; **de** ~, **en** ~: **des livres en** ~ a few books too many; **du lait en** ~ too much milk; **3 livres/3 F de** ~ 3 books too many/3 F too much

tropical, e, -aux [tʀopikal, o] adj tropical

tropique [tʀopik] nm tropic

trop-plein [tʀoplɛ̃] nm (tuyau) overflow ou outlet (pipe); (liquide) overflow

troquer [tʀoke] vt: ~ **qch contre** to barter ou trade sth for; (fig) to swap sth for

trot [tʀo] nm trot; **trotter** vi to trot

trotteuse [tʀotøz] nf (sweep) second hand

trottinette [tʀotinɛt] nf (child's) scooter

trottoir [tʀotwaʀ] nm pavement; **faire le** ~ (péj) to walk the streets; ~ **roulant** moving walkway, travellator

trou [tʀu] nm hole; (fig) gap; (COMM) deficit; ~ **d'air** air pocket; ~ **d'ozone** ozone hole; **le** ~ **de la serrure** the keyhole; ~ **de mémoire** blank, lapse of memory

troublant, e [tʀublɑ̃, ɑ̃t] adj disturbing

trouble [tʀubl] adj (liquide) cloudy; (image, photo) blurred; (affaire) shady, murky ♦ nm agitation; ~**s** nmpl (POL) disturbances, troubles, unrest sg; (MÉD) trouble sg, disorders; **trouble-fête** nm spoilsport

troubler [tʀuble] vt to disturb; (liquide) to make cloudy; (intriguer) to bother; **se** ~ vi (personne) to become flustered ou confused

trouer [tʀue] vt to make a hole (ou holes) in

trouille [tʀuj] (fam) nf: **avoir la** ~ to

be scared to death

troupe [tʀup] nf troop; ~ **(de théâtre)** (theatrical) company

troupeau, x [tʀupo] nm (de moutons) flock; (de vaches) herd

trousse [tʀus] nf case, kit; (d'écolier) pencil case; **aux** ~**s de** (fig) on the heels ou tail of; ~ **à outils** toolkit; ~ **de toilette** toilet bag

trousseau, x [tʀuso] nm (de mariée) trousseau; ~ **de clefs** bunch of keys

trouvaille [tʀuvaj] nf find

trouver [tʀuve] vt (rendre visite): **aller/venir** ~ **qn** to go/come and see sb; **se** ~ (être) to be; **je trouve que** I find ou think that; ~ **à boire/critiquer** to find something to drink/criticize; **se** ~ **bien** to feel well; **se** ~ **mal** to pass out

truand [tʀyɑ̃] nm gangster; **truander** vt: **se faire truander** to be swindled

truc [tʀyk] nm (astuce) way, trick; (de cinéma, prestidigitateur) trick, effect; (chose) thing, thingumajig; **avoir le** ~ to have the knack

truelle [tʀyɛl] nf trowel

truffe [tʀyf] nf truffle; (nez) nose

truffé, e [tʀyfe] adj: ~ **de** (fig) peppered with; (fautes) riddled with; (pièges) bristling with

truie [tʀɥi] nf sow

truite [tʀɥit] nf trout inv

truquage [tʀykaʒ] nm special effects

truquer [tʀyke] vt (élections, serrure, dés) to fix

TSVP sigle (= tournez svp) PTO

TTC sigle (= toutes taxes comprises) inclusive of tax

tu[1] [ty] pron you

tu[2], **e** [ty] pp de **taire**

tuba [tyba] nm (MUS) tuba; (SPORT) snorkel

tube [tyb] nm tube; (chanson) hit

tuberculose [tybɛʀkyloz] nf tuberculosis

tuer [tɥe] vt to kill; **se** ~ vi to be killed;

(*suicide*) to kill o.s.; **tuerie** *nf* slaughter *no pl*

tue-tête [tytɛt] : **à ~~** *adv* at the top of one's voice

tueur [tɥœʀ] *nm* killer; **~ à gages** hired killer

tuile [tɥil] *nf* tile; (*fam*) spot of bad luck, blow

tulipe [tylip] *nf* tulip

tuméfié, e [tymefje] *adj* puffed-up, swollen

tumeur [tymœʀ] *nf* growth, tumour

tumulte [tymylt] *nm* commotion; **tumultueux, -euse** *adj* stormy, turbulent

tunique [tynik] *nf* tunic

Tunisie [tynizi] *nf*: **la ~** Tunisia; **tunisien, ne** *adj* Tunisian ♦ *nm/f*: **Tunisien, ne** Tunisian

tunnel [tynɛl] *nm* tunnel; **le ~ sous la Manche** the Channel Tunnel

turbulences [tyʀbylɑ̃s] *nfpl* (*AVIAT*) turbulence *sg*

turbulent, e [tyʀbylɑ̃, ɑ̃t] *adj* boisterous, unruly

turc, turque [tyʀk] *adj* Turkish ♦ *nm/f*: **T~, que** Turk/Turkish woman ♦ *nm* (*LING*) Turkish

turf [tyʀf] *nm* racing; **turfiste** *nm/f* racegoer

Turquie [tyʀki] *nf*: **la ~** Turkey

turquoise [tyʀkwaz] *nf* turquoise ♦ *adj inv* turquoise

tus *etc* [ty] *vb voir* **taire**

tutelle [tytɛl] *nf* (*JUR*) guardianship; (*POL*) trusteeship; **sous la ~ de** (*fig*) under the supervision of

tuteur [tytœʀ] *nm* (*JUR*) guardian; (*de plante*) stake, support

tutoyer [tytwaje] *vt*: **~ qn** to address sb as "tu"

tuyau, x [tɥijo] *nm* pipe; (*flexible*) tube; (*fam*) tip; **~ d'arrosage** hosepipe; **~ d'échappement** exhaust pipe; **tuyauterie** *nf* piping *no pl*

TVA *sigle f* (= *taxe à la valeur ajoutée*) VAT

tympan [tɛ̃pɑ̃] *nm* (*ANAT*) eardrum

type [tip] *nm* type; (*fam*) chap, guy ♦ *adj* typical, classic

typé, e [tipe] *adj* ethnic

typique [tipik] *adj* typical

tyran [tiʀɑ̃] *nm* tyrant; **tyrannique** *adj* tyrannical

tzigane [dzigan] *adj* gipsy, tzigane

U, u

UEM *sigle f* (= *union économique et monétaire*) EMU

ulcère [ylsɛʀ] *nm* ulcer; **ulcérer** *vt* (*fig*) to sicken, appal

ultérieur, e [ylteʀjœʀ] *adj* later, subsequent; **remis à une date ~e** postponed to a later date; **ultérieurement** *adv* later, subsequently

ultime [yltim] *adj* final

ultra... [yltʀa] *préfixe*: **~moderne/ -rapide** ultra-modern/-fast

───── MOT-CLÉ ─────

un, une [œ̃, yn] *art indéf* a; (*devant voyelle*) an; **un garçon/vieillard** a boy/an old man; **une fille** a girl ♦ *pron* one; **l'un des meilleurs** one of the best; **l'un ..., l'autre** (the) one ..., the other; **les uns ..., les autres** some ..., others; **l'un et l'autre** both (of them); **l'un ou l'autre** either (of them); **l'un l'autre, les uns les autres** each other, one another; **pas un seul** not a single one; **un par un** one by one ♦ *num* one; **une pomme seulement** one apple only

unanime [ynanim] *adj* unanimous; **unanimité** *nf*: **à l'unanimité** unanimously

uni, e [yni] *adj* (*ton, tissu*) plain; (*surface*) smooth, even; (*famille*) close (-knit); (*pays*) united

unifier [ynifje] *vt* to unite, unify

uniforme [ynifɔʀm] *adj* uniform; *(surface, ton)* even ♦ *nm* uniform; **uniformiser** *vt (systèmes)* to standardize

union [ynjɔ̃] *nf* union; **~ de consommateurs** consumers' association; **U~ européenne** European Union; **U~ soviétique** Soviet Union

unique [ynik] *adj (seul)* only; *(exceptionnel)* unique; *(le même)*: **un prix/système ~** a single price/system; **fils/fille ~** only son/daughter, only child; **sens ~** one-way street; **uniquement** *adv* only, solely; *(juste)* only, merely

unir [yniʀ] *vt (nations)* to unite; *(en mariage)* to unite, join together; **s'~** to unite; *(en mariage)* to be joined together

unitaire [yniteʀ] *adj*: **prix ~** unit price

unité [ynite] *nf* unit; *(harmonie, cohésion)* unity

univers [yniveʀ] *nm* universe; **universel, le** *adj* universal

universitaire [yniveʀsiteʀ] *adj* university *cpd*; *(diplôme, études)* academic, university *cpd* ♦ *nm/f* academic

université [yniveʀsite] *nf* university

urbain, e [yʀbɛ̃, ɛn] *adj* urban, city *cpd*; **urbanisme** *nm* town planning

urgence [yʀʒɑ̃s] *nf* urgency; *(MÉD etc)* emergency; **d'~** *adj* emergency *cpd* ♦ *adv* as a matter of urgency; **(service des) ~s** casualty

urgent, e [yʀʒɑ̃, ɑ̃t] *adj* urgent

urine [yʀin] *nf* urine; **urinoir** *nm* (public) urinal

urne [yʀn] *nf (électorale)* ballot box; *(vase)* urn

urticaire [yʀtikeʀ] *nf* nettle rash

us [ys] *nmpl*: **~ et coutumes** (habits and) customs

USA *sigle mpl*: **les USA** the USA

usage [yzaʒ] *nm (emploi, utilisation)* use; *(coutume)* custom; **à l'~** with use; **à l'~ de** *(pour)* for (use of); **hors d'~** out of service; **à ~ interne** *(MÉD)* to be taken; **à ~ externe** *(MÉD)* for external

use only; **usagé, e** *adj (usé)* worn; **usager, -ère** *nm/f* user

usé, e [yze] *adj* worn; *(banal: argument etc)* hackneyed

user [yze] *vt (outil)* to wear down; *(vêtement)* to wear out; *(matière)* to wear away; *(consommer: charbon etc)* to use; **s'~** *vi (tissu, vêtement)* to wear out; **~ de** *(moyen, procédé)* to use, employ; *(droit)* to exercise

usine [yzin] *nf* factory

usité, e [yzite] *adj* common

ustensile [ystɑ̃sil] *nm* implement; **~ de cuisine** kitchen utensil

usuel, le [yzɥɛl] *adj* everyday, common

usure [yzyʀ] *nf* wear

utérus [yteʀys] *nm* uterus, womb

utile [ytil] *adj* useful

utilisation [ytilizasjɔ̃] *nf* use

utiliser [ytilize] *vt* to use

utilitaire [ytiliteʀ] *adj* utilitarian

utilité [ytilite] *nf* usefulness *no pl*; **de peu d'~** of little use *ou* help

utopie [ytɔpi] *nf* utopia

V, v

va [va] *vb voir* **aller**

vacance [vakɑ̃s] *nf (ADMIN)* vacancy; **~s** *nfpl* holiday(s *pl*), vacation *sg*; **les grandes ~s** the summer holidays; **prendre des/ses ~s** to take a holiday/one's holiday(s); **aller en ~s** to go on holiday; **vacancier, -ière** *nm/f* holiday-maker

vacant, e [vakɑ̃, ɑ̃t] *adj* vacant

vacarme [vakaʀm] *nm (bruit)* racket

vaccin [vaksɛ̃] *nm* vaccine; *(opération)* vaccination; **vaccination** *nf* vaccination; **vacciner** *vt* to vaccinate; **être vacciné contre qch** *(fam)* to be cured of sth

vache [vaʃ] *nf (ZOOL)* cow; *(cuir)* cowhide ♦ *adj (fam)* rotten, mean; **vachement** *(fam) adv (très)* really; *(pleuvoir, travailler)* a hell of a lot; **vacherie** *nf (action)* dirty trick; *(remarque)* nasty remark

vaciller [vasije] *vi* to sway, wobble; (*bougie, lumière*) to flicker; (*fig*) to be falling, falter

va-et-vient [vaevjɛ̃] *nm inv* (*de personnes, véhicules*) comings and goings *pl*, to-ings and fro-ings *pl*

vagabond [vagabɔ̃] (*rôdeur*) tramp, vagrant; (*voyageur*) wanderer; **vagabonder** *vi* to roam, wander

vagin [vaʒɛ̃] *nm* vagina

vague [vag] *nf* wave ♦ *adj* vague; (*regard*) faraway; (*manteau, robe*) loose (-fitting); (*quelconque*): **un ~ bureau/cousin** some office/cousin or other; **~ de fond** ground swell; **~ de froid** cold spell

vaillant, e [vajɑ̃, ɑ̃t] *adj* (*courageux*) gallant, valiant; (*robuste*) hale and hearty

vaille [vaj] *vb voir* **valoir**

vain, e [vɛ̃, vɛn] *adj* vain; **en ~** in vain

vaincre [vɛ̃kʀ] *vt* to defeat; (*fig*) to conquer, overcome; **vaincu, e** *nm/f* defeated party; **vainqueur** *nm* victor; (*SPORT*) winner

vais [vɛ] *vb voir* **aller**

vaisseau, x [veso] *nm* (*ANAT*) vessel; (*NAVIG*) ship, vessel; **~ spatial** spaceship

vaisselier [vesəlje] *nm* dresser

vaisselle [vesɛl] *nf* (*service*) crockery; (*plats etc à laver*) (dirty) dishes *pl*; **faire la ~** to do the washing-up (*BRIT*) ou the dishes

val [val, vo] (*pl* **vaux** *ou* **~s**) *nm* valley

valable [valabl] *adj* valid; (*acceptable*) decent, worthwhile

valent *etc* [val] *vb voir* **valoir**

valet [valɛ] *nm* manservant; (*CARTES*) jack

valeur [valœʀ] *nf* (*gén*) value; (*mérite*) worth, merit; (*COMM: titre*) security; **mettre en ~** (*détail*) to highlight; (*objet décoratif*) to show off to advantage; **avoir de la ~** to be valuable; **sans ~** worthless; **prendre de la ~** to go up ou gain in value

valide [valid] *adj* (*en bonne santé*) fit;

valions [valjɔ̃] *vb voir* **valoir**

valise [valiz] *nf* (suit)case; **faire ses ~s** to pack one's bags

vallée [vale] *nf* valley

vallon [valɔ̃] *nm* small valley; **vallonné, e** *adj* hilly

valoir [valwaʀ] *vi* (*être valable*) to hold, apply ♦ *vt* (*prix, valeur, effort*) to be worth; (*causer*): **~ qch à qn** to earn sb sth; **se ~** *vi* to be of equal merit; (*péj*) to be two of a kind; **faire ~** (*droits, prérogatives*) to assert; **faire ~ que** to point out that; **à ~ sur** to be deducted from; **vaille que vaille** somehow or other; **cela ne me dit rien qui vaille** I don't like the look of it at all; **ce climat ne me vaut rien** this climate doesn't suit me; **~ le coup** *ou* **la peine** to be worth the trouble *ou* worth it; **~ mieux: il vaut mieux se taire** it's better to say nothing; **ça ne vaut rien** it's worthless; **que vaut ce candidat?** how good is this applicant?

valse [vals] *nf* waltz

valu, e [valy] *pp de* **valoir**

vandalisme [vɑ̃dalism] *nm* vandalism

vanille [vanij] *nf* vanilla

vanité [vanite] *nf* vanity; **vaniteux, -euse** *adj* vain, conceited

vanne [van] *nf* gate; (*fig*) joke

vannerie [vanʀi] *nf* basketwork

vantard, e [vɑ̃taʀ, aʀd] *adj* boastful

vanter [vɑ̃te] *vt* to speak highly of, praise; **se ~** *vi* to boast, brag; **se ~ de** to pride o.s. on; (*péj*) to boast of

vapeur [vapœʀ] *nf* steam; (*émanation*) vapour, fumes *pl*; **~s** *nfpl* (*bouffées*) vapours; **à ~** steam-powered, steam *cpd*; **cuit à la ~** steamed; **vaporeux, -euse** *adj* (*flou*) hazy, misty; (*léger*) filmy; **vaporisateur** *nm* spray; **vaporiser** *vt* (*parfum etc*) to spray

varappe [vaʀap] *nf* rock climbing

vareuse [vaʀøz] *nf* (*blouson*) pea jacket; (*d'uniforme*) tunic

variable [vaʀjabl] *adj* variable; (*temps,*

humeur) changeable; *(divers: résultats)* varied, various

varice [varis] *nf* varicose vein

varicelle [varisɛl] *nf* chickenpox

varié, e [varje] *adj* varied; *(divers)* various

varier [varje] *vi* to vary; *(temps, humeur)* to change ♦ *vt* to vary; **variété** *nf* variety; **variétés** *nfpl:* **spectacle/émission de variétés** variety show

variole [varjɔl] *nf* smallpox

vas [va] *vb voir* **aller**

vase [vaz] *nm* vase ♦ *nf* silt, mud; **vaseux, -euse** *adj* silty, muddy; *(fig: confus)* woolly, hazy; *(: fatigué)* woozy

vasistas [vazistas] *nm* fanlight

vaste [vast] *adj* vast, immense

vaudrai *etc* [vodre] *vb voir* **valoir**

vaurien, ne [vorjɛ̃, jɛn] *nm/f* good-for-nothing

vaut [vo] *vb voir* **valoir**

vautour [votur] *nm* vulture

vautrer [votre] *vb:* **se ~ dans/sur** to wallow in/sprawl on

vaux [vo] *nmpl de* **val** ♦ *vb voir* **valoir**

va-vite [vavit]: **à la ~~** *adv* in a rush ou hurry

VDQS

VDQS *is the second highest French wine classification after AOC, indicating high-quality wine from an approved regional vineyard. It is followed by* vin de pays. Vin de table *or* vin ordinaire *is table wine of unspecified origin, often blended.*

---

veau, x [vo] *nm (ZOOL)* calf; *(CULIN)* veal; *(peau)* calfskin

vécu, e [veky] *pp de* **vivre**

vedette [vədɛt] *nf (artiste etc)* star; *(canot)* motor boat; *(police)* launch

végétal, e, -aux [veʒetal, o] *adj* vegetable ♦ *nm* vegetable, plant; **végétalien, ne** *adj, nm/f* vegan

végétarien, ne [veʒetarjɛ̃, jɛn] *adj, nm/f* vegetarian

végétation [veʒetasjɔ̃] *nf* vegetation; **~s** *nfpl (MÉD)* adenoids

véhicule [veikyl] *nm* vehicle; **~ utilitaire** commercial vehicle

veille [vɛj] *nf (état)* wakefulness; *(jour):* **la ~ (de)** the day before; **la ~ au soir** the previous evening; **à la ~ de** on the eve of; **la ~ de Noël** Christmas Eve; **la ~ du jour de l'An** New Year's Eve

veillée [veje] *nf (soirée)* evening; *(réunion)* evening gathering; **~ (funèbre)** wake

veiller [veje] *vi* to stay up ♦ *vt (malade, mort)* to watch over, sit up with; **~ à** to attend to, see to; **~ à ce que** to make sure that; **~ sur** to watch over; **veilleur** *nm:* **veilleur de nuit** night watchman; **veilleuse** *nf (lampe)* night light; *(AUTO)* sidelight; *(flamme)* pilot light

veinard, e [venar, ard] *nm/f* lucky devil

veine [vɛn] *nf (ANAT, du bois etc)* vein; *(filon)* vein, seam; *(fam: chance):* **avoir de la ~** to be lucky

véliplanchiste [veliplɑ̃ʃist] *nm/f* windsurfer

vélo [velo] *nm* bike, cycle; **faire du ~** to go cycling; **~ tout-terrain** mountain bike; **vélomoteur** *nm* moped

velours [v(ə)lur] *nm* velvet; **~ côtelé** corduroy; **velouté, e** *adj* velvety ♦ *nm:* **velouté de tomates** cream of tomato soup

velu, e [vəly] *adj* hairy

venais *etc* [vəne] *vb voir* **venir**

venaison [vənɛzɔ̃] *nf* venison

vendange [vɑ̃dɑ̃ʒ] *nf (aussi:* **~s)** grape harvest; **vendanger** *vi* to harvest the grapes

vendeur, -euse [vɑ̃dœr, øz] *nm/f* shop assistant ♦ *nm (JUR)* vendor, seller; **~ de journaux** newspaper seller

vendre [vɑ̃dr] *vt* to sell; **~ qch à qn** to sell sb sth; **"à ~"** "for sale"

vendredi [vɑ̃drədi] *nm* Friday; **V~ saint** Good Friday

vénéneux, -euse [venenø, øz] *adj* poisonous

vénérien, ne [venerjɛ̃, jɛn] *adj* venereal

vengeance [vãʒãs] *nf* vengeance *no pl*, revenge *no pl*

venger [vãʒe] *vt* to avenge; **se ~** *vi* to avenge o.s.; **se ~ de qch** to avenge o.s. for sth, take one's revenge for sth; **se ~ de qn** to take revenge on sb; **se ~ sur** to take revenge on

venimeux, -euse [vənimø, øz] *adj* poisonous, venomous; (*fig: haineux*) venomous, vicious

venin [vənɛ̃] *nm* venom, poison

venir [v(ə)niʀ] *vi* to come; **~ de** to come from; **~ de faire**: **je viens d'y aller/de le voir** I've just been there/ seen him; **s'il vient à pleuvoir** if it should rain; **j'en viens à croire que** I have come to believe that; **faire ~** (*docteur, plombier*) to call (out)

vent [vã] *nm* wind; **il y a du ~** it's windy; **c'est du ~** it's all hot air; **au ~** to windward; **sous le ~** to leeward; **avoir le ~ debout/arrière** to head into the wind/have the wind astern; **dans le ~** (*fam*) trendy

vente [vãt] *nf* sale; **la ~** (*activité*) selling; (*secteur*) sales *pl*; **mettre en ~** (*produit*) to put on sale; (*maison, objet personnel*) to put up for sale; **~ aux enchères** auction sale; **~ de charité** jumble sale

venteux, -euse [vãtø, øz] *adj* windy

ventilateur [vãtilatœʀ] *nm* fan

ventiler [vãtile] *vt* to ventilate

ventouse [vãtuz] *nf* (*de caoutchouc*) suction pad

ventre [vãtʀ] *nm* (*ANAT*) stomach; (*légèrement péj*) belly; (*utérus*) womb; **avoir mal au ~** to have stomach ache (*BRIT*) *ou* a stomach ache (*US*)

ventriloque [vãtʀilɔk] *nm/f* ventriloquist

venu, e [v(ə)ny] *pp de* **venir** ♦ *adj*: **bien ~** timely; **mal ~** out of place;

être mal ~ à *ou* **de faire** to have no grounds for doing, be in no position to do

ver [vɛʀ] *nm* worm; (*des fruits etc*) maggot; (*du bois*) woodworm *no pl*; *voir aussi* **vers**; **~ à soie** silkworm; **~ de terre** earthworm; **~ luisant** glowworm; **~ solitaire** tapeworm

verbaliser [vɛʀbalize] *vi* (*POLICE*) to book *ou* report an offender

verbe [vɛʀb] *nm* verb

verdâtre [vɛʀdɑtʀ] *adj* greenish

verdict [vɛʀdik(t)] *nm* verdict

verdir [vɛʀdiʀ] *vi, vt* to turn green; **verdure** *nf* greenery

véreux, -euse [veʀø, øz] *adj* wormeaten; (*malhonnête*) shady, corrupt

verge [vɛʀʒ] *nf* (*ANAT*) penis

verger [vɛʀʒe] *nm* orchard

verglacé, e [vɛʀglase] *adj* icy, icedover

verglas [vɛʀglɑ] *nm* (black) ice

vergogne [vɛʀgɔɲ]: **sans ~** *adv* shamelessly

véridique [veʀidik] *adj* truthful

vérification [veʀifikasjɔ̃] *nf* (*action*) checking *no pl*; (*contrôle*) check

vérifier [veʀifje] *vt* to check; (*corroborer*) to confirm, bear out

véritable [veʀitabl] *adj* real; (*ami, amour*) true

vérité [veʀite] *nf* truth; **en ~** really, actually

vermeil, le [vɛʀmɛj] *adj* ruby red

vermine [vɛʀmin] *nf* vermin *pl*

vermoulu, e [vɛʀmuly] *adj* wormeaten

verni, e [vɛʀni] *adj* (*fam*) lucky; **cuir ~** patent leather

vernir [vɛʀniʀ] *vt* (*bois, tableau, ongles*) to varnish; (*poterie*) to glaze

vernis [vɛʀni] *nm* (*enduit*) varnish; glaze; (*fig*) veneer; **~ à ongles** nail polish *ou* varnish; **vernissage** *nm* (*d'une exposition*) preview

vérole [veʀɔl] *nf* (*variole*) smallpox

verrai *etc* [veʀe] *vb voir* **voir**

verre [vɛʀ] nm glass; (de lunettes) lens sg; **boire** ou **prendre un ~** to have a drink; **~ dépoli** frosted glass; **~s de contact** contact lenses; **verrerie** nf (fabrique) glassworks sg; (activité) glass-making; (objets) glassware; **verrière** nf (paroi vitrée) glass wall; (toit vitré) glass roof

verrons etc [vɛʀɔ̃] vb voir **voir**

verrou [veʀu] nm (targette) bolt; **mettre qn sous les ~s** to put sb behind bars; **verrouillage** nm locking; **verrouillage centralisé** central locking; **verrouiller** vt (porte) to bolt; (ordinateur) to lock

verrue [veʀy] nf wart

vers [vɛʀ] nm line ♦ nmpl (poésie) verse sg ♦ prép (en direction de) toward(s); (près de) around (about); (temporel) about, around

versant [vɛʀsɑ̃] nm slopes pl, side

versatile [vɛʀsatil] adj fickle, change-able

verse [vɛʀs]: **à ~** adv: **il pleut à ~** it's pouring (with rain)

Verseau [vɛʀso] nm: **le ~** Aquarius

versement [vɛʀsəmɑ̃] nm payment; **en 3 ~s** in 3 instalments

verser [vɛʀse] vt (liquide, grains) to pour; (larmes, sang) to shed; (argent) to pay ♦ vi (véhicule) to overturn; (fig): **~ dans** to lapse into

verset [vɛʀse] nm verse

version [vɛʀsjɔ̃] nf version; (SCOL) translation (into the mother tongue); **film en ~ originale** film in the original language

verso [vɛʀso] nm back; **voir au ~** see over(leaf)

vert, e [vɛʀ, vɛʀt] adj green; (vin) young; (vigoureux) sprightly ♦ nm green

vertèbre [vɛʀtɛbʀ] nf vertebra

vertement [vɛʀtəmɑ̃] adv (réprimander) sharply

vertical, e, -aux [vɛʀtikal, o] adj vertical; **verticale** nf vertical; **à la verticale** vertically; **verticalement** adv vertically

vertige [vɛʀtiʒ] nm (peur du vide) vertigo; (étourdissement) dizzy spell; (fig) fever; **vertigineux, -euse** adj breathtaking

vertu [vɛʀty] nf virtue; **en ~ de** in accordance with; **vertueux, -euse** adj virtuous

verve [vɛʀv] nf witty eloquence; **être en ~** to be in brilliant form

verveine [vɛʀvɛn] nf (BOT) verbena, vervain; (infusion) verbena tea

vésicule [vezikyl] nf vesicle; **~ biliaire** gall-bladder

vessie [vesi] nf bladder

veste [vɛst] nf jacket; **~ droite/croisée** single-/double-breasted jacket

vestiaire [vɛstjɛʀ] nm (au théâtre etc) cloakroom; (de stade etc) changing-room (BRIT), locker-room (US)

vestibule [vɛstibyl] nm hall

vestige [vɛstiʒ] nm relic; (fig) vestige; **~s** nmpl (de ville) remains

vestimentaire [vɛstimɑ̃tɛʀ] adj (détail) of dress; (élégance) sartorial; **dépenses ~s** clothing expenditure

veston [vɛstɔ̃] nm jacket

vêtement [vɛtmɑ̃] nm garment, item of clothing; **~s** nmpl clothes

vétérinaire [veteʀinɛʀ] nm/f vet, veterinary surgeon

vêtir [vetiʀ] vt to clothe, dress

veto [veto] nm veto; **opposer un ~ à** to veto

vêtu, e [vety] pp de **vêtir**

vétuste [vetyst] adj ancient, timeworn

veuf, veuve [vœf, vœv] adj widowed ♦ nm widower

veuille [vœj] vb voir **vouloir**

veuillez [vœje] vb voir **vouloir**

veule [vøl] adj spineless

veuve [vœv] nf widow

veux [vø] vb voir **vouloir**

vexant, e [vɛksɑ̃, ɑ̃t] adj (contrariant) annoying; (blessant) hurtful

vexation [vɛksasjɔ̃] nf humiliation

vexer [vɛkse] vt: **~ qn** to hurt sb's feelings; **se ~** vi to be offended

viable [vjabl] *adj* viable; (*économie, industrie etc*) sustainable

viaduc [vjadyk] *nm* viaduct

viager, -ère [vjaʒe, ɛʀ] *adj*: **rente viagère** life annuity

viande [vjɑ̃d] *nf* meat

vibrer [vibʀe] *vi* to vibrate; (*son, voix*) to be vibrant; (*fig*) to be stirred; **faire ~** to (cause to) vibrate; (*fig*) to stir, thrill

vice [vis] *nm* vice; (*défaut*) fault ♦ *préfixe*: **~... vice-**; **~ de forme** legal flaw ou irregularity

vichy [viʃi] *nm* (*toile*) gingham

vicié, e [visje] *adj* (*air*) polluted, tainted; (*JUR*) invalidated

vicieux, -euse [visjø, jøz] *adj* (*pervers*) lecherous; (*rétif*) unruly ♦ *nm/f* lecher

vicinal, e, -aux [visinal, o] *adj*: **chemin ~** by-road, byway

victime [viktim] *nf* victim; (*d'accident*) casualty

victoire [viktwaʀ] *nf* victory

victuailles [viktɥaj] *nfpl* provisions

vidange [vidɑ̃ʒ] *nf* (*d'un fossé, réservoir*) emptying; (*AUTO*) oil change; (*de lavabo: bonde*) waste outlet; **~s** *nfpl* (*matières*) sewage *sg*; **vidanger** *vt* to empty

vide [vid] *adj* empty ♦ *nm* (*PHYSIQUE*) vacuum; (*espace*) (empty) space, gap; (*futilité, néant*) void; **avoir peur du ~** to be afraid of heights; **emballé sous ~** vacuum packed; **à ~** (*sans occupants*) empty; (*sans charge*) unladen

vidéo [video] *nf* video ♦ *adj inv*: **cassette ~** video cassette; **jeu ~** video game; **vidéoclip** *nm* music video; **vidéoclub** *nm* video shop

vide-ordures [vidɔʀdyʀ] *nm inv* (rubbish) chute

vidéothèque [videotɛk] *nf* video library

vide-poches [vidpɔʃ] *nm inv* tidy; (*AUTO*) glove compartment

vider [vide] *vt* to empty; (*CULIN: volaille, poisson*) to gut, clean out; **se ~** *vi* to empty; **~ les lieux** to quit ou vacate the premises; **videur** *nm* (*de boîte de nuit*) bouncer, doorman

vie [vi] *nf* life; **être en ~** to be alive; **sans ~** lifeless; **à ~** for life

vieil [vjɛj] *adj m voir* **vieux**; **vieillard** *nm* old man; **les vieillards** old people, the elderly; **vieille** *adj, nf voir* **vieux**; **vieilleries** *nfpl* old things; **vieillesse** *nf* old age; **vieillir** *vi* (*prendre de l'âge*) to grow old; (*population, vin*) to age; (*doctrine, auteur*) to become dated ♦ *vt* to age; **vieillissement** *nm* growing old; ageing

Vienne [vjɛn] *nf* Vienna

viens [vjɛ̃] *vb voir* **venir**

vierge [vjɛʀʒ] *adj* virgin; (*page*) clean, blank ♦ *nf* virgin; (*signe*): **la V~** Virgo

Vietnam, Viet-Nam [vjɛtnam] *nm* Vietnam; **vietnamien, ne** *adj* Vietnamese ♦ *nm/f*: **Vietnamien, ne** Vietnamese

vieux (vieil), vieille [vjø, vjɛj] *adj* old ♦ *nm/f* old man (woman) ♦ *nmpl* old people; **mon ~/ma vieille** (*fam*) old man/girl; **prendre un coup de ~** to put years on; **vieille fille** spinster; **~ garçon** bachelor; **~ jeu** *adj inv* old-fashioned

vif, vive [vif, viv] *adj* (*animé*) lively; (*alerte, brusque, aigu*) sharp; (*lumière, couleur*) bright; (*air*) crisp; (*vent, émotion*) keen; (*fort: regret, déception*) great, deep; (*vivant*): **brûlé ~** burnt alive; **de vive voix** personally; **avoir l'esprit ~** to be quick-witted; **piquer qn au ~** to cut sb to the quick; **à ~** (*plaie*) open; **avoir les nerfs à ~** to be on edge

vigne [viɲ] *nf* (*plante*) vine; (*plantation*) vineyard; **vigneron** *nm* wine grower

vignette [viɲɛt] *nf* (*ADMIN*) ≈ (road) tax disc (*BRIT*), ≈ license plate sticker (*US*); (*de médicament*) price label (*used for reimbursement*)

vignoble [viɲɔbl] *nm* (*plantation*) vineyard; (*vignes d'une région*) vineyards *pl*

vigoureux, -euse [viguʀø, øz] *adj* vigorous, robust

vigueur [vigœʀ] *nf* vigour; **entrer en ~** to come into force; **en ~** current

vil, e [vil] *adj* vile, base

vilain, e [vilɛ̃, ɛn] *adj* (laid) ugly; (affaire, blessure) nasty; (pas sage: enfant) naughty

villa [vila] *nf* (detached) house; **~ en multipropriété** time-share villa

village [vilaʒ] *nm* village; **villageois, e** *adj* village *cpd* ♦ *nm/f* villager

ville [vil] *nf* town; (importante) city; (administration): **la ~** ≈ the Corporation; ≈ the (town) council; **~ d'eaux** spa

villégiature [vi(l)leʒjatyʀ] *nf* holiday; **(lieu de) ~** (holiday) resort

vin [vɛ̃] *nm* wine; **avoir le ~ gai** to get happy after a few drinks; **~ d'honneur** reception (with wine and snacks); **~ de pays** local wine; **~ ordinaire** table wine

vinaigre [vinɛgʀ] *nm* vinegar; **vinaigrette** *nf* vinaigrette, French dressing

vindicatif, -ive [vɛ̃dikatif, iv] *adj* vindictive

vineux, -euse [vinø, øz] *adj* win(e)y

vingt [vɛ̃] *num* twenty; **vingtaine** [vɛ̃tɛn]: **une vingtaine (de)** about twenty, twenty or so; **vingtième** *num* twentieth

vinicole [vinikɔl] *adj* wine *cpd*, wine-growing

vins *etc* [vɛ̃] *vb voir* **venir**

vinyle [vinil] *nm* vinyl

viol [vjɔl] *nm* (d'une femme) rape; (d'un lieu sacré) violation

violacé, e [vjɔlase] *adj* purplish, mauvish

violemment [vjɔlamɑ̃] *adv* violently

violence [vjɔlɑ̃s] *nf* violence

violent, e [vjɔlɑ̃, ɑ̃t] *adj* violent; (remède) drastic

violer [vjɔle] *vt* (femme) to rape; (sépulture, loi, traité) to violate

violet, te [vjɔle, ɛt] *adj, nm* purple, mauve; **violette** *nf* (fleur) violet

violon [vjɔlɔ̃] *nm* violin; (fam: prison) lock-up; **~ d'Ingres** hobby; **violoncel-**

le *nm* cello; **violoniste** *nm/f* violinist

vipère [vipɛʀ] *nf* viper, adder

virage [viʀaʒ] *nm* (d'un véhicule) turn; (d'une route, piste) bend

virée [viʀe] *nf* trip; (à pied) walk; (longue) walking tour; (dans les cafés) tour

virement [viʀmɑ̃] *nm* (COMM) transfer

virent [viʀ] *vb voir* **voir**

virer [viʀe] *vt* (COMM): **~ qch (sur)** to transfer sth (into); (fam: expulser): **~ qn** to kick sb out ♦ *vi* to turn; (CHIMIE) to change colour; **~ de bord** to tack

virevolter [viʀvɔlte] *vi* to twirl around

virgule [viʀgyl] *nf* comma; (MATH) point

viril, e [viʀil] *adj* (propre à l'homme) masculine; (énergique, courageux) manly, virile

virtuel, le [viʀtɥɛl] *adj* potential; (théorique) virtual

virtuose [viʀtɥoz] *nm/f* (MUS) virtuoso; (gén) master

virus [viʀys] *nm* virus

vis¹ [vi] *vb voir* **voir; vivre**

vis² [vi] *nf* screw

visa [viza] *nm* (sceau) stamp; (validation de passeport) visa

visage [vizaʒ] *nm* face

vis-à-vis [vizavi] *prép:* **~-~-~ de qn** to(wards) sb; **en ~-~-~** facing each other

viscéral, e, -aux [viseʀal, o] *adj* (fig) deep-seated, deep-rooted

visées [vize] *nfpl* (intentions) designs

viser [vize] *vi* to aim ♦ *vt* to aim at; (concerner) to be aimed ou directed at; (apposer un visa sur) to stamp, visa; **~ à qch/faire** to aim at sth/at doing ou to do; **viseur** *nm* (d'arme) sights *pl*; (PHOTO) viewfinder

visibilité [vizibilite] *nf* visibility

visible [vizibl] *adj* visible; (disponible): **est-il ~?** can he see me?, will he see visitors?

visière [vizjɛʀ] *nf* (de casquette) peak; (qui s'attache) eyeshade

vision [vizjɔ̃] *nf* vision; (sens) (eye)sight,

vision; (fait de voir): **la ~ de** the sight of; **visionneuse** nf viewer

visite [vizit] nf visit; **~ médicale** medical examination; **~ accompagnée** ou **guidée** guided tour; **faire une ~ à qn** to call on sb, pay sb a visit; **rendre ~ à qn** to visit sb, pay sb a visit; **être en ~ (chez qn)** to be visiting (sb); **avoir de la ~** to have visitors; **heures de ~** (hôpital, prison) visiting hours

visiter [vizite] vt to visit; **visiteur, -euse** nm/f visitor

vison [viz5] nm mink

visser [vise] vt: **~ qch** (fixer, serrer) to screw sth on

visuel, le [vizɥɛl] adj visual

vit [vi] vb voir **vivre**

vital, e, -aux [vital, o] adj vital

vitamine [vitamin] nf vitamin

vite [vit] adv (rapidement) quickly, fast; (sans délai) quickly; (sous peu) soon; **~!** quick!; **faire ~** to be quick; **le temps passe ~** time flies

vitesse [vites] nf speed; (AUTO: dispositif) gear; **prendre de la ~** to pick up ou gather speed; **à toute ~** at full ou top speed; **en ~** (rapidement) quickly; (en hâte) in a hurry

viticole [vitikɔl] adj wine cpd, wine-growing; **viticulteur** nm wine grower

vitrage [vitraʒ] nm: **double ~** double glazing

vitrail, -aux [vitraj, o] nm stained-glass window

vitre [vitʀ] nf (window) pane; (de portière, voiture) window; **vitré, e** adj glass cpd; **vitrer** vt to glaze; **vitreux, -euse** adj (terne) glassy

vitrine [vitʀin] nf (shop) window; (petite armoire) display cabinet; **en ~** in the window; **~ publicitaire** display case, showcase

vivable [vivabl] adj (personne) livable-with; (maison) fit to live in

vivace [vivas] adj (arbre, plante) hardy; (fig) indestructible, inveterate

vivacité [vivasite] nf liveliness, vivacity

vivant, e [vivã, ãt] adj (qui vit) living, alive; (animé) lively; (preuve, exemple) living ♦ nm: **du ~ de qn** in sb's life-time; **les ~s** the living

vive [viv] vb voir **vif** ♦ vb voir **vivre** ♦ excl: **le roi!** long live the king!; **vivement** adv deeply ♦ excl: **vivement les vacances!** roll on the holidays!

vivier [vivje] nm (étang) fish tank; (réservoir) fishpond

vivifiant, e [vivifjã, jãt] adj invigorating

vivions [vivjɔ̃] vb voir **vivre**

vivoter [vivɔte] vi (personne) to scrape a living, get by; (fig: affaire etc) to struggle along

vivre [vivʀ] vi, vt to live; (période) to live through; **~ de** to live on; **il vit encore** he is still alive; **se laisser ~** to take life as it comes; **ne plus ~** (être anxieux) to live on one's nerves; **il a vécu** (eu une vie aventureuse) he has seen life; **être facile à ~** to be easy to get on with; **faire ~ qn** (pourvoir à sa substance) to provide (a living) for sb; **vivres** nmpl provisions, food supplies

vlan [vlã] excl wham!, bang!

VO [veo] nf: **film en ~** film in the original version; **en ~ sous-titrée** in the original version with subtitles

vocable [vɔkabl] nm term

vocabulaire [vɔkabylɛʀ] nm vocabulary

vocation [vɔkasjɔ̃] nf vocation, calling

vociférer [vɔsifeʀe] vi, vt to scream

vœu, x [vø] nm wish; (promesse) vow; **faire ~ de** to take a vow of; **tous nos ~x de bonne année, meilleurs ~x** best wishes for the New Year

vogue [vɔg] nf fashion, vogue

voguer [vɔge] vi to sail

voici [vwasi] prép (pour introduire, désigner) here is +sg, here are +pl; **et ~ que ...** and now it (ou he) ...; voir aussi **voilà**

voie [vwa] nf way; (RAIL) track, line; (AUTO) lane; **être en bonne ~** to be going well; **mettre qn sur la ~** to put sb on the right track; **pays en ~ de développement** developing country; **être en ~ d'achèvement** ou **rénovation** to be nearing completion/in the process of renovation; **par ~** buccale ou orale orally; **à ~ étroite** narrow-gauge; **~ d'eau** (NAVIG) leak; **~ de garage** (RAIL) siding; **~ ferrée** track; railway line; **la ~ publique** the public highway

voilà [vwala] prép (en désignant) there is +sg, there are +pl; **les ~** ou **voici** here ou there they are; **en ~** ou **voici** here's one, there's one; **voici mon frère et ma sœur** this is my brother and that's my sister; **~** ou **voici deux ans** two years ago; **~** ou **voici deux ans que** it's two years since; **et ~!** there we are! **~ tout** that's all; **~** ou **voici** (en offrant etc) there ou here you are; **tiens! ~ Paul** look! there's Paul

voile [vwal] nm veil; (tissu léger) net ♦ nf sail; (sport) sailing; **voiler** vt to veil; (fausser: roue) to buckle; (: bois) to warp; **se voiler** vi (lune, regard) to mist over; (voix) to become husky; (roue, disque) to buckle; (planche) to warp; **voilier** nm sailing ship; (de plaisance) sailing boat; **voilure** nf (de voilier) sails pl

voir [vwar] vi, vt to see; **se ~** vt (être visible) to show; (se fréquenter) to see each other; (se produire) to happen; **se ~ critiquer/transformer** to be criticized/transformed; **cela se voit** (c'est visible) that's obvious, it shows; **faire ~ qch à qn** to show sb sth; **en faire ~ à qn** (fig) to give sb a hard time; **ne pas pouvoir ~ qn** not to be able to stand sb; **voyons!** let's see now; (indignation etc) come on!; **avoir quelque chose à ~ avec** to have something to do with

voire [vwar] adv even

voisin, e [vwazɛ̃, in] adj (proche) neighbouring; (contigu) next; (ressemblant) connected ♦ nm/f neighbour;

voisinage [vwazinaʒ] nm (proximité) proximity; (environs) vicinity; (quartier, voisins) neighbourhood

voiture [vwatyr] nf car; (wagon) coach, carriage; **~ de course** racing car; **~ de sport** sports car

voix [vwa] nf voice; (POL) vote; **à haute ~** aloud; **à ~ basse** in a low voice; **à 2/4 ~** (MUS) in 2/4 parts; **avoir ~ au chapitre** to have a say in the matter

vol [vɔl] nm (d'oiseau, d'avion) flight; (larcin) theft; **~ régulier** scheduled flight; **à ~ d'oiseau** as the crow flies; **au ~: attraper qch au ~** to catch sth as it flies past; **en ~** in flight; **~ à main armée** armed robbery; **~ à voile** gliding; **~ libre** hang-gliding

volage [vɔlaʒ] adj fickle

volaille [vɔlaj] nf (oiseaux) poultry pl; (viande) poultry pl; (oiseau) fowl

volant, e [vɔlã, ãt] adj voir **feuille** etc ♦ nm (d'automobile) steering wheel; (de commande) wheel; (objet lancé) shuttlecock; (bande de tissu) flounce

volcan [vɔlkã] nm volcano

volée [vɔle] nf (TENNIS) volley; **à la ~: rattraper à la ~** to catch in mid-air; **à toute ~** (sonner les cloches) vigorously; (lancer un projectile) with full force; **~ de coups de flèches** volley of blows/arrows

voler [vɔle] vi (avion, oiseau, fig) to fly; (voleur) to steal ♦ vt (objet) to steal; (personne) to rob; **~ qch à qn** to steal sth from sb; **il ne l'a pas volé!** he asked for it!

volet [vɔle] nm (de fenêtre) shutter; (de feuillet, document) section

voleur, -euse [vɔlœr, øz] nm/f thief ♦ adj thieving; **"au ~!"** "stop thief!"

volière [vɔljer] nf aviary

volley [vɔle] nm volleyball

volontaire [vɔlõter] adj (acte, enrôlement, prisonnier) voluntary; (oubli) intentional; (caractère, personne: décidé) self-willed ♦ nm/f volunteer

volonté [vɔlõte] nf (faculté de vouloir)

will; (*énergie, fermeté*) will(power); (*souhait, désir*) wish; **à ~** as much as one likes; **bonne ~** goodwill, willingness; **mauvaise ~** lack of goodwill, unwillingness

volontiers [vɔlɔ̃tje] *adv* (*avec plaisir*) willingly, gladly; (*habituellement, souvent*) readily, willingly; **voulez-vous boire quelque chose? - ~!** I would like something to drink? - yes, please!

volt [vɔlt] *nm* volt

volte-face [vɔltəfas] *nf inv*: **faire ~~** to turn round

voltige [vɔltiʒ] *nf* (ÉQUITATION) trick riding; (*au cirque*) acrobatics *sg*; **voltiger** *vi* to flutter (about)

volubile [vɔlybil] *adj* voluble

volume [vɔlym] *nm* volume; (GÉOM: *solide*) solid; **volumineux, -euse** *adj* voluminous, bulky

volupté [vɔlypte] *nf* sensual delight *ou* pleasure

vomi [vɔmi] *nm* vomit; **vomir** *vi* to vomit, be sick ♦ *vt* to vomit, bring up; (*fig*) to belch out, spew out; (*exécrer*) to loathe, abhor; **vomissements** *nmpl*: **être pris de vomissements** to (suddenly) start vomiting

vont [vɔ̃] *vb voir* **aller**

vorace [vɔras] *adj* voracious

vos [vo] *adj voir* **votre**

vote [vɔt] *nm* vote; **~ par correspondance/procuration** postal/proxy vote; **voter** *vi* to vote ♦ *vt* (*projet de loi*) to vote for; (*loi, réforme*) to pass

votre [vɔtr] (*pl* **vos**) *adj* your

vôtre [votr] *pron*: **le ~, la ~, les ~s** yours; **les ~s** (*fig*) your family *ou* folks; **à la ~** (*toast*) your (good) health!

voudrai *etc* [vudre] *vb voir* **vouloir**

voué, e [vwe] *adj*: **~ à** doomed to

vouer [vwe] *vt*: **~ qch à** (*Dieu, un saint*) to dedicate sth to; **~ sa vie à** (*étude, cause etc*) to devote one's life to; **~ une amitié éternelle à qn** to vow undying friendship to sb

vouloir [vulwar] *nm*: **le bon vouloir de qn** sb's goodwill; sb's pleasure

♦ *vt* **1** (*exiger, désirer*) to want; **vouloir faire/que qn fasse** to want to do/sb to do; **voulez-vous du thé?** would you like *ou* do you want some tea?; **que me veut-il?** what does he want with me?; **sans le vouloir** (*involontairement*) without meaning to, unintentionally; **je voudrais ceci/faire** I would *ou* I'd like this/to do

2 (*consentir*): **je veux bien** (*bonne volonté*) I'll be happy to; (*concession*) fair enough, that's fine; **oui, si on veut** (*en quelque sorte*) if you like; **veuillez attendre** please wait; **veuillez agréer ...** (*formule épistolaire*) yours faithfully

3: **en vouloir à qn** to bear sb a grudge; **s'en vouloir (de)** to be annoyed with o.s. (for); **il en veut à mon argent** he's after my money

4: **vouloir de**: **l'entreprise ne veut plus de lui** the firm doesn't want him any more; **elle ne veut pas de son aide** she doesn't want his help

5: **vouloir dire** to mean

voulu, e [vuly] *adj* (*requis*) required, requisite; (*délibéré*) deliberate, intentional; *voir aussi* **vouloir**

vous [vu] *pron* you; (*objet indirect*) (to) you; (*réfléchi: sg*) yourself; (: *pl*) yourselves; (*réciproque*) each other; **~-même** yourself; **~-mêmes** yourselves

voûte [vut] *nf* vault; **voûter: se voûter** *vi* (*dos, personne*) to become stooped

vouvoyer [vuvwaje] *vt*: **~ qn** to address sb as "vous"

voyage [vwajaʒ] *nm* journey, trip; (*fait de ~*) travel(ling); **partir/être en ~** to go off/be away on a journey *ou* trip; **faire bon ~** to have a good journey; **~ d'agrément/d'affaires** pleasure/business trip; **~ de noces** honeymoon; **~ organisé** package tour

voyager [vwajaʒe] *vi* to travel; **voyageur, -euse** *nm/f* traveller; (*passager*) passenger

voyant, e [vwajɑ̃, ɑ̃t] *adj* (*couleur*) loud, gaudy ♦ *nm* (*signal*) (warning) light; **voyante** *nf* clairvoyant

voyelle [vwajɛl] *nf* vowel

voyons *etc* [vwajɔ̃] *vb voir* **voir**

voyou [vwaju] *nm* hooligan

vrac [vʀak]: **en ~** *adv* (*au détail*) loose; (*en gros*) in bulk; (*en désordre*) in a jumble

vrai, e [vʀe] *adj* (*véridique: récit, faits*) true; (*non factice, authentique*) real; **à ~ dire** to tell the truth; **vraiment** *adv* really; **vraisemblable** *adj* likely; (*excuse*) convincing; **vraisemblablement** *adj* probably; **vraisemblance** *nf* likelihood; (*romanesque*) verisimilitude

vrille [vʀij] *nf* (*de plante*) tendril; (*outil*) gimlet; (*spirale*) spiral; (*AVIAT*) spin

vrombir [vʀɔ̃biʀ] *vi* to hum

VRP *sigle m* (= *voyageur, représentant, placier*) sales rep (*fam*)

VTT *sigle m* (= *vélo tout-terrain*) mountain bike

vu, e [vy] *pp de* **voir** ♦ *adj*: **bien/mal ~** (*fig: personne*) popular/unpopular; (*: chose*) approved/disapproved of ♦ *prép* (*en raison de*) in view of; **~ que** in view of the fact that

vue [vy] *nf* (*fait de voir*): **la ~ de** the sight of; (*sens, faculté*) (eye)sight; (*panorama, image, photo*) view; **~s** *nfpl* (*idées*) views; (*dessein*) designs; **hors de ~** out of sight; **avoir en ~** to have in mind; **tirer à ~** to shoot on sight; **à ~ d'œil** visibly; **de ~** by sight; **perdre de ~** to lose sight of; **en ~** (*visible*) in sight; (*célèbre*) in the public eye; **en ~ de faire** with a view to doing

vulgaire [vylgɛʀ] *adj* (*grossier*) vulgar, coarse; (*ordinaire*) common; (*péj: quelconque*): **de ~s touristes** common tourists; (*BOT, ZOOL: non latin*) common; **vulgariser** *vt* to popularize

vulnérable [vylneʀabl] *adj* vulnerable

W, w

wagon [vagɔ̃] *nm* (*de voyageurs*) carriage; (*de marchandises*) truck, wagon; **wagon-lit** *nm* sleeper, sleeping car; **wagon-restaurant** *nm* restaurant *ou* dining car

wallon, ne [walɔ̃, ɔn] *adj* Walloon

waters [watɛʀ] *nmpl* toilet *sg*

watt [wat] *nm* watt

WC *sigle mpl* (= *water-closet(s)*) toilet

Web [wɛb] *nm inv*: **le ~** the (World Wide) Web

week-end [wikɛnd] *nm* weekend

western [wɛstɛʀn] *nm* western

whisky [wiski] (*pl* **whiskies**) *nm* whisky

X, x

xénophobe [gzenɔfɔb] *adj* xenophobic ♦ *nm/f* xenophobe

xérès [gzeʀes] *nm* sherry

xylophone [gzilɔfɔn] *nm* xylophone

Y, y

y [i] *adv* (*à cet endroit*) there; (*dessus*) on it (*ou* them); (*dedans*) in it (*ou* them) ♦ *pron* (about *ou* on *ou* of) it (*d'après le verbe employé*); **j'~ pense** I'm thinking about it; **ça ~ est!** that's it!; *voir aussi* **aller**; **avoir**

yacht [jɔt] *nm* yacht

yaourt [jauʀt] *nm* yoghourt; **~ nature/aux fruits** plain/fruit yogurt

yeux [jø] *nmpl de* **œil**

yoga [jɔga] *nm* yoga

yoghourt [jɔguʀt] *nm* = **yaourt**

yougoslave [jugɔslav] (*HISTOIRE*) *adj* Yugoslav(ian) ♦ *nm/f*: **Y~** Yugoslav

Yougoslavie [jugɔslavi] (*HISTOIRE*) *nf* Yugoslavia

Z, z

zapper [zape] *vi* to zap

zapping [zapiŋ] *nm*: **faire du ~** to flick through the channels

zèbre [zɛbʀ(ə)] *nm* (*ZOOL*) zebra; **zébré, e** *adj* striped, streaked

zèle [zɛl] *nm* zeal; **faire du ~** (*péj*) to be over-zealous; **zélé, e** *adj* zealous

zéro [zeʀo] *nm* zero, nought (*BRIT*); **au-dessous de ~** below zero (Centigrade) *ou* freezing; **partir de ~** to start from scratch; **trois (buts) à ~** 3 (goals to) nil

zeste [zɛst] *nm* peel, zest

zézayer [zezeje] *vi* to have a lisp

zigzag [zigzag] *nm* zigzag; **zigzaguer** *vi* to zigzag

zinc [zɛ̃g] *nm* (*CHIMIE*) zinc

zizanie [zizani] *nf*: **semer la ~** to stir up ill-feeling

zizi [zizi] *nm* (*langage enfantin*) willy

zodiaque [zɔdjak] *nm* zodiac

zona [zona] *nm* shingles *sg*

zone [zon] *nf* zone, area; **~ bleue** ≃ restricted parking area; **~ industrielle** industrial estate

zoo [zo(o)] *nm* zoo

zoologie [zɔɔlɔʒi] *nf* zoology; **zoologique** *adj* zoological

zut [zyt] *excl* dash (it)! (*BRIT*), nuts! (*US*)

ENGLISH – FRENCH
ANGLAIS – FRANÇAIS

A, a

A [eɪ] *n* (MUS) la *m*

a [eɪ, ə] (*before vowel or silent h: an*) *indef art* **1** un(e); **a book** un livre; **an apple** une pomme; **she's a doctor** elle est médecin

2 (*instead of the number "one"*) un(e); **a year ago** il y a un an; **a hundred/ thousand** *etc* **pounds** cent/mille *etc* livres

3 (*in expressing ratios, prices etc*): **3 a day/week** 3 par jour/semaine; **10 km an hour** 10 km à l'heure; **30p a kilo** 30p le kilo

A.A. *n abbr* = **Alcoholics Anonymous**; (BRIT: *Automobile Association*) ≈ TCF *m*

A.A.A. (US) *n abbr* (= *American Automobile Association*) ≈ TCF *m*

aback [ə'bæk] *adv*: **to be taken ~** être stupéfait(e), être décontenancé(e)

abandon [ə'bændən] *vt* abandonner

abate [ə'beɪt] *vi* s'apaiser, se calmer

abbey ['æbɪ] *n* abbaye *f*

abbot ['æbət] *n* père supérieur

abbreviation [əbriːvɪ'eɪʃən] *n* abréviation *f*

abdicate ['æbdɪkeɪt] *vt, vi* abdiquer

abdomen ['æbdəmen] *n* abdomen *m*

abduct [æb'dʌkt] *vt* enlever

aberration [æbə'reɪʃən] *n* anomalie *f*

abide [ə'baɪd] *vt*: **I can't ~ it/him** je ne peux pas le souffrir or supporter; **~ by** *vt fus* observer, respecter

ability [ə'bɪlɪtɪ] *n* compétence *f*; capacité *f*; (*skill*) talent *m*

abject ['æbdʒekt] *adj* (*poverty*) sordide; (*apology*) plat(e)

ablaze [ə'bleɪz] *adj* en feu, en flammes

able ['eɪbl] *adj* capable, compétent(e); **to be ~ to do sth** être capable de faire qch, pouvoir faire qch; **~-bodied** *adj* robuste; **ably** *adv* avec compétence or talent, habilement

abnormal [æb'nɔːməl] *adj* anormal(e)

aboard [ə'bɔːd] *adv* à bord ♦ *prep* à bord de

abode [ə'bəud] *n* (LAW): **of no fixed ~** sans domicile fixe

abolish [ə'bɒlɪʃ] *vt* abolir

aborigine [æbə'rɪdʒɪnɪ] *n* aborigène *m/f*

abort [ə'bɔːt] *vt* faire avorter; **~ion** *n* avortement *m*; **to have an ~ion** se faire avorter; **~ive** [ə'bɔːtɪv] *adj* manqué(e)

about [ə'baut] *adv* **1** (*approximately*) environ, à peu près; **about a hundred/thousand** *etc* environ cent/ mille *etc*, une centaine/un millier *etc*; **it takes about 10 hours** ça prend environ or à peu près 10 heures; **at about 2 o'clock** vers 2 heures; **I've just about finished** j'ai presque fini

2 (*referring to place*) çà et là, de côté et d'autre; **to run about** courir çà et là; **to walk about** se promener, aller et venir

3: to be about to do sth être sur le point de faire qch

♦ *prep* **1** (*relating to*) au sujet de, à propos de; **a book about London** un livre sur Londres; **what is it about?** de quoi s'agit-il?; **we talked about it** nous en avons parlé; **what or how about doing this?** et si nous faisions ceci?

2 (*referring to place*) dans; **to walk**

about the town se promener dans la ville

about-face [ə'baut'feɪs] n demi-tour m
about-turn [ə'baut'tə:n] n (MIL) demi-tour m; (fig) volte-face f
above [ə'bʌv] adv au-dessus ♦ prep au-dessus de; (more) plus de; **mentioned ~** mentionné ci-dessus; **~ all** par-dessus tout, surtout; **~board** adj franc (franche); honnête
abrasive [ə'breɪzɪv] adj abrasif(-ive); (fig) caustique, agressif(-ive)
abreast [ə'brest] adv de front; **to keep ~ of** se tenir au courant de
abroad [ə'brɔ:d] adv à l'étranger
abrupt [ə'brʌpt] adj (steep, blunt) abrupt(-e); (sudden, gruff) brusque; **~ly** adv (speak, end) brusquement
abscess ['æbsɪs] n abcès m
absence ['æbsəns] n absence f
absent ['æbsənt] adj absent(e); **~ee** [æbsən'ti:] n absent(e); (habitual) absentéiste m/f; **~-minded** adj distrait(e)
absolute ['æbsəlu:t] adj absolu(e); **~ly** [æbsə'lu:tlɪ] adv absolument
absolve [əb'zɔlv] vt: **to ~ sb (from)** (blame, responsibility, sin) absoudre qn (de)
absorb [əb'zɔ:b] vt absorber; **to be ~ed in a book** être plongé(e) dans un livre; **~ent cotton** (US) n coton m hydrophile
abstain [əb'steɪn] vi: **to ~ (from)** s'abstenir (de)
abstract ['æbstrækt] adj abstrait(e)
absurd [əb'sɜ:d] adj absurde
abundant [ə'bʌndənt] adj abondant(e)
abuse [n ə'bju:s, vb ə'bju:z] n abus m; (insults) insultes fpl, injures fpl ♦ vt (ill-treat) maltraiter; (insult) insulter; **abusive** [ə'bju:sɪv] adj grossier(-ère), injurieux(-euse)
abysmal [ə'bɪzməl] adj exécrable; (ignorance etc) sans bornes
abyss [ə'bɪs] n abîme m, gouffre m
AC abbr (= alternating current) courant

alternatif
academic [ækə'demɪk] adj universitaire; (person: scholarly) intellectuel(le); (pej: issue) oiseux(-euse), purement théorique ♦ n universitaire m; **~ year** n année f universitaire
academy [ə'kædəmɪ] n (learned body) académie f; (school) collège m; **~ of music** conservatoire m
accelerate [æk'seləreɪt] vt, vi accélérer; **accelerator** n accélérateur m
accent ['æksənt] n accent m
accept [ək'sept] vt accepter; **~able** adj acceptable; **~ance** n acceptation f
access ['æksɛs] n accès m; (LAW: in divorce) droit m de visite; **~ible** [æk'sɛsəbl] adj accessible
accessory [æk'sɛsərɪ] n accessoire m
accident ['æksɪdənt] n accident m; (chance) hasard m; **by ~** accidentellement; par hasard; **~al** [æksɪ'dɛntl] adj accidentel(le); **~ally** [æksɪ'dɛntəlɪ] adv accidentellement; **~ insurance** n assurance f accident; **~-prone** adj sujet(te) aux accidents
acclaim [ə'kleɪm] n acclamations fpl ♦ vt acclamer
accommodate [ə'kɔmədeɪt] vt loger, recevoir; (oblige, help) obliger; (car etc) contenir; **accommodating** adj obligeant(e), arrangeant(e); **accommodation** [əkɔmə'deɪʃən] n (US **accommodations**) n logement m
accompany [ə'kʌmpənɪ] vt accompagner
accomplice [ə'kʌmplɪs] n complice m/f
accomplish [ə'kʌmplɪʃ] vt accomplir; **~ment** n accomplissement m; réussite f; (skill: gen pl) talent m
accord [ə'kɔ:d] n accord m ♦ vt accorder; **of his own ~** de son plein gré; **~ance** [ə'kɔ:dəns] n: **in ~ance with** conformément à; **~ing: ~ing to** prep selon; **~ingly** adv en conséquence
accordion [ə'kɔ:dɪən] n accordéon m
account [ə'kaunt] n (COMM) compte m; (report) compte rendu; récit m; **~s** npl

diesse f

dark [dɑːk] *adj* (*night, room*) obscur(e), sombre; (*colour, complexion*) foncé(e), sombre ♦ *n*: **in the ~** dans le noir; **in the ~ about** (*fig*) ignorant tout de; **after ~** après la tombée de la nuit; **~en** *vt* obscurcir, assombrir ♦ *vi* s'obscurcir, s'assombrir; **~ glasses** *npl* lunettes noires; **~ness** *n* obscurité *f*; **~room** *n* chambre noire

darling ['dɑːlɪŋ] *adj* chéri(e) ♦ *n* chéri(e); (*favourite*): **to be the ~ of** être la coqueluche de

darn [dɑːn] *vt* repriser, raccommoder

dart [dɑːt] *n* fléchette *f*; (*sewing*) pince *f* ♦ *vi*: **to ~ towards** (*also*: **make a ~ towards**) se précipiter *or* s'élancer vers; **to ~ away/along** partir/passer comme une flèche; **~board** *n* cible *f* (de jeu de fléchettes); **~s** *n* (jeu *m* de) fléchettes *fpl*

dash [dæʃ] *n* (*sign*) tiret *m*; (*small quantity*) goutte *f*, larme *f* ♦ *vt* (*missile*) jeter *or* lancer violemment; (*hopes*) anéantir ♦ *vi*: **to ~ towards** (*also*: **make a ~ towards**) se précipiter *or* se ruer vers; **~ away** *vi* partir à toute allure; filer; **~ off** *vi* = **dash away**

dashboard ['dæʃbɔːd] *n* (*AUT*) tableau *m* de bord

dashing ['dæʃɪŋ] *adj* fringant(e)

data ['deɪtə] *npl* données *fpl*; **~base** *n* (*COMPUT*) base *f* de données; **~ processing** *n* traitement *m* de données

date [deɪt] *n* date *f*; (*with sb*) rendez-vous *m*; (*fruit*) datte *f* ♦ *vt* dater; (*person*) sortir avec; **~ of birth** date de naissance; **to ~** (*until now*) à ce jour; **out of ~** (*passport*) périmé(e); (*theory etc*) dépassé(e); (*clothes etc*) démodé(e); **up to ~** moderne; (*news*) très récent; **~d** ['deɪtɪd] *adj* démodé(e); **~ rape** *n* viol *m* (à l'issue d'un rendez-vous galant)

daub [dɔːb] *vt* barbouiller

daughter ['dɔːtə*] *n* fille *f*; **~-in-law** *n* belle-fille *f*, bru *f*

daunting ['dɔːntɪŋ] *adj* décourageant(e)

dawdle ['dɔːdl] *vi* traîner, lambiner

dawn [dɔːn] *n* aube *f*, aurore *f* ♦ *vi* (*day*) se lever; poindre; (*fig*): **it ~ed on him that ...** il lui vint à l'esprit que ...

day [deɪ] *n* jour *m*; (*as duration*) journée *f*; (*period of time, age*) époque *f*, temps *m*; **the ~ before** la veille, le jour précédent; **the ~ after, the following ~** le lendemain, le jour suivant; **the ~ after tomorrow** après-demain; **the ~ before yesterday** avant-hier; **by ~** de jour; **~break** *n* point *m* du jour; **~dream** *vi* rêver (tout éveillé); **~light** *n* (lumière *f* du) jour *m*; **~ return** (*BRIT*) *n* billet *m* d'aller-retour (valable pour la journée); **~time** *n* jour *m*, journée *f*; **~-to-~** *adj* quotidien(ne); (*event*) journalier(-ère)

daze [deɪz] *vt* (*stun*) étourdir ♦ *n*: **in a ~** étourdi(e), hébété(e)

dazzle ['dæzl] *vt* éblouir, aveugler

DC *abbr* (= *direct current*) courant continu

D-day ['diːdeɪ] *n* le jour J

dead [ded] *adj* mort(e); (*numb*) engourdi(e), insensible; (*battery*) à plat; (*telephone*): **the line is ~** la ligne est coupée ♦ *adv* absolument, complètement ♦ *npl*: **the ~** les morts; **he was shot ~** il a été tué d'un coup de revolver; **~ on time** à l'heure pile; **~ tired** éreinté(e), complètement fourbu(e); **to stop ~** s'arrêter pile *or* net; **~en** *vt* (*blow, sound*) amortir; (*pain*) calmer; **~ end** *n* impasse *f*; **~ heat** *n* (*SPORT*): **to finish in a ~ heat** terminer ex-æquo; **~line** *n* date *f or* heure *f* limite; **~lock** (*fig*) *n* impasse *f*; **~ loss** *n*: **to be a ~ loss** (*inf*: *person*) n'être bon(ne) à rien; **~ly** *adj* mortel(le); (*weapon*) meurtrier(-ère); (*accuracy*) extrême; **~pan** *adj* impassible; **D~ Sea** *n*: **the D~ Sea** la mer Morte

deaf [def] *adj* sourd(e); **~en** *vt* rendre sourd; **~ening** *adj* assourdissant(e); **~-**

mute n sourd(e)-muet(te); **~ness** n surdité f

deal [di:l] (pt, pp **dealt**) n affaire f, marché m ♦ vt (blow) porter; (cards) donner, distribuer; **a great ~ (of)** beaucoup (de); **~ in** vt fus faire le commerce de; **~ with** vt fus (person, problem) s'occuper or se charger de; (be about: book etc) traiter de; **~er** n marchand m; **~ings** npl (COMM) transactions fpl; (relations) relations fpl, rapports mpl

dean [di:n] n (REL, BRIT: SCOL) doyen m; (US: SCOL) conseiller(-ère) (principal(e)) d'éducation

dear [dɪəʳ] adj cher (chère); (expensive) cher, coûteux(-euse) ♦ n: **my ~** mon cher/ma chère; **~ me!** mon Dieu!; **D~ Sir/Madam** (in letter) Monsieur/ Madame; **D~ Mr/Mrs X** Cher Monsieur/Chère Madame; **~ly** adv (love) tendrement; (pay) cher

death [deθ] n mort f; (fatality) mort m; (ADMIN) décès m; **~ certificate** n acte m de décès; **~ly** adj de mort; **~ penalty** n peine f de mort; **~ rate** n (taux m de) mortalité f; **~ toll** n nombre m de morts

debase [dɪˈbeɪs] vt (value) déprécier, dévaloriser

debatable [dɪˈbeɪtəbl] adj discutable

debate [dɪˈbeɪt] n discussion f, débat m ♦ vt discuter, débattre

debit [ˈdebɪt] n débit m ♦ vt: **to ~ a sum to sb** or **to sb's account** porter une somme au débit de qn, débiter qn d'une somme; see also **direct**

debt [det] n dette f; **to be in ~** avoir des dettes, être endetté(e); **~or** n débiteur(-trice)

decade [ˈdekeɪd] n décennie f, décade f

decadence [ˈdekədəns] n décadence f

decaff [ˈdiːkæf] (inf) n déca m

decaffeinated [dɪˈkæfɪneɪtɪd] adj décaféiné(e)

decanter [dɪˈkæntəʳ] n carafe f

decay [dɪˈkeɪ] n (of building) délabrement m; (also: **tooth ~**) carie f (dentai-

re) ♦ vi (rot) se décomposer, pourrir; (: teeth) se carier

deceased [dɪˈsiːst] n défunt(e)

deceit [dɪˈsiːt] n tromperie f, supercherie f; **~ful** adj trompeur(-euse); **deceive** vt tromper

December [dɪˈsembəʳ] n décembre m

decent [ˈdiːsənt] adj décent(e), convenable

deception [dɪˈsepʃən] n tromperie f

deceptive [dɪˈseptɪv] adj trompeur (-euse)

decide [dɪˈsaɪd] vt (person) décider; (question, argument) trancher, régler ♦ vi se décider, décider; **to ~ to do/that** décider de faire/que; **to ~ on** décider, se décider pour; **~d** adj (resolute) résolu(e), décidé(e); (clear, definite) net(te), marqué(e); **~dly** adv résolument; (distinctly) incontestablement, nettement

deciduous [dɪˈsɪdjuəs] adj à feuilles caduques

decimal [ˈdesɪməl] adj décimal(e) ♦ n décimale f; **~ point** n ≈ virgule f

decipher [dɪˈsaɪfəʳ] vt déchiffrer

decision [dɪˈsɪʒən] n décision f

decisive [dɪˈsaɪsɪv] adj décisif(-ive); (person) décidé(e)

deck [dek] n (NAUT) pont m; (verandah) véranda f; (of bus): **top ~** impériale f; (of cards) jeu m; (record) platine f; **~chair** n chaise longue

declare [dɪˈkleəʳ] vt déclarer

decline [dɪˈklaɪn] n (decay) déclin m; (lessening) baisse f ♦ vt refuser, décliner ♦ vi décliner; (business) baisser

decoder [diːˈkəʊdəʳ] n (TV) décodeur m

decorate [ˈdekəreɪt] vt (adorn, give a medal to) décorer; (paint and paper) peindre et tapisser; **decoration** [dekəˈreɪʃən] n (medal etc, adornment) décoration f; **decorator** n peintre-décorateur m

decoy [ˈdiːkɔɪ] n piège m; (person) compère m

decrease [n ˈdiːkriːs, vb diːˈkriːs] n: **~ (in)** diminution f (de) ♦ vi, vi diminuer

decree [dɪ'kriː] n (POL, REL) décret m; (LAW) arrêt m, jugement m; ~ **nisi** [-'naɪsaɪ] n jugement m provisoire de divorce

dedicate ['dedɪkeɪt] vt consacrer; (book etc) dédier; ~**d** adj (person) dévoué(e); (COMPUT) spécialisé(e), dédié(e); **dedication** [dedɪ'keɪʃən] n (devotion) dévouement m; (in book) dédicace f

deduce [dɪ'djuːs] vt déduire, conclure

deduct [dɪ'dʌkt] vt: **to ~ sth (from)** déduire qch (de), retrancher qch (de); ~**ion** n (deducting, deducing) déduction f; (from wage etc) prélèvement m, retenue f

deed [diːd] n action f, acte m; (LAW) acte notarié, contrat m

deep [diːp] adj profond(e); (voice) grave ♦ adv: **spectators stood 20 ~** il y avait 20 rangs de spectateurs; **4 metres ~** de 4 mètres de profondeur; **~ end** (of swimming pool) grand bain; **~en** vt approfondir ♦ vi (fig) s'épaissir; **~freeze** n congélateur m; **~fry** vt faire frire (en friteuse); **~ly** adv profondément; (interested) vivement; **~sea diver** n sous-marin(e); **~sea diving** n plongée sous-marine; **~sea fishing** n grande pêche; **~seated** adj profond(e), profondément enraciné(e)

deer [dɪə'] n inv: **(red) ~** cerf m, biche f; **(fallow) ~** daim m; **(roe) ~** chevreuil m; **~skin** n daim

deface [dɪ'feɪs] vt dégrader; (notice, poster) barbouiller

default [dɪ'fɔːlt] n (COMPUT: also: **~ value**) valeur f par défaut; **by ~** (LAW) par défaut, par contumace; (SPORT) par forfait

defeat [dɪ'fiːt] n défaite f ♦ vt (team, opponents) battre

defect [n 'diːfekt, vb dɪ'fekt] n défaut m ♦ vi: **to ~ to the enemy** passer à l'ennemi; **~ive** [dɪ'fektɪv] adj défectueux(-euse)

defence [dɪ'fens] (US **defense**) n défense f; **~less** adj sans défense

defend [dɪ'fend] vt défendre; **~ant** n défendeur(-deresse); (in criminal case) accusé(e), prévenu(e); **~er** n défenseur m

defer [dɪ'fəː'] vt (postpone) différer, ajourner

defiance [dɪ'faɪəns] n défi m; **in ~ of** au mépris de; **defiant** adj provocant(e), de défi; (person) rebelle, intraitable

deficiency [dɪ'fɪʃənsɪ] n insuffisance f, déficience f; **deficient** adj (inadequate) insuffisant(e); **to be deficient in** manquer de

deficit ['defɪsɪt] n déficit m

define [dɪ'faɪn] vt définir

definite ['defɪnɪt] adj (fixed) défini(e), (bien) déterminé(e); (clear, obvious) net(te), manifeste; (certain) sûr(e); **he was ~ about it** il a été catégorique; **~ly** adv sans aucun doute

definition [defɪ'nɪʃən] n définition f; (clearness) netteté f

deflate [diː'fleɪt] vt dégonfler

deflect [dɪ'flekt] vt détourner, faire dévier

deformed [dɪ'fɔːmd] adj difforme

defraud [dɪ'frɔːd] vt frauder; **to ~ sb of sth** escroquer qch à qn

defrost [diː'frɔst] vt (fridge) dégivrer; (food) décongeler; **~er** n (US) (demister) dispositif m anti-buée inv

deft [deft] adj adroit(e), preste

defunct [dɪ'fʌŋkt] adj défunt(e)

defuse [diː'fjuːz] vt désamorcer

defy [dɪ'faɪ] vt défier; (efforts etc) résister à

degenerate [vb dɪ'dʒenəreɪt, adj dɪ'dʒenərɪt] vi dégénérer ♦ adj dégénéré(e)

degree [dɪ'griː] n degré m; (SCOL) diplôme m (universitaire); **a (first) ~ in maths** une licence en maths; **by ~s** (gradually) par degrés; **to some ~, to a certain ~** jusqu'à un certain point, dans une certaine mesure

dehydrated [diːhaɪ'dreɪtd] adj déshydraté(e); (milk, eggs) en poudre

de-ice [diːˈaɪs] vt (windscreen) dégivrer

deign [deɪn] vi: **to ~ to do** daigner faire

dejected [dɪˈdʒɛktɪd] adj abattu(e), déprimé(e)

delay [dɪˈleɪ] vt retarder ♦ vi s'attarder ♦ n délai m, retard m; **to be ~ed** être en retard

delectable [dɪˈlɛktəbl] adj délicieux (-euse)

delegate [n ˈdɛlɪgɪt, vb ˈdɛlɪgeɪt] n délégué(e) ♦ vt déléguer

delete [dɪˈliːt] vt rayer, supprimer

deliberate [adj dɪˈlɪbərɪt, vb dɪˈlɪbəreɪt] adj (intentional) délibéré(e); (slow) mesuré(e) ♦ vi délibérer, réfléchir; **~ly** [dɪˈlɪbərɪtlɪ] adv (on purpose) exprès, délibérément

delicacy [ˈdɛlɪkəsɪ] n délicatesse f; (food) mets fin or délicat, friandise f

delicate [ˈdɛlɪkɪt] adj délicat(e)

delicatessen [dɛlɪkəˈtɛsn] n épicerie fine

delicious [dɪˈlɪʃəs] adj délicieux(-euse)

delight [dɪˈlaɪt] n (grande) joie, grand plaisir ♦ vt enchanter; **to take (a) ~ in** prendre grand plaisir à; **~ed** adj: **~ed (at or with/to do)** ravi(e) (de/de faire); **~ful** adj (person) adorable; (meal, evening) merveilleux(-euse)

delinquent [dɪˈlɪŋkwənt] adj, n délinquant(e)

delirious [dɪˈlɪrɪəs] adj: **to be ~** délirer

deliver [dɪˈlɪvəʳ] vt (mail) distribuer; (goods) livrer; (message) remettre; (speech) prononcer; (MED: baby) mettre au monde; **~y** n distribution f; livraison f; (of speaker) élocution f; (MED) accouchement m; **to take ~y of** prendre livraison de

delude [dɪˈluːd] vt tromper, leurrer; **delusion** n illusion f

demand [dɪˈmɑːnd] vt réclamer, exiger ♦ n exigence f; (claim) revendication f; (ECON) demande f; **in ~** demandé(e), recherché(e); **on ~** sur demande; **~ing** adj (person) exigeant(e); (work) astreignant(e)

demean [dɪˈmiːn] vt: **to ~ o.s.** s'abaisser

demeanour [dɪˈmiːnəʳ] (US **demeanor**) n comportement m; maintien m

demented [dɪˈmɛntɪd] adj dément(e), fou (folle)

demise [dɪˈmaɪz] n mort f

demister [diːˈmɪstəʳ] (BRIT) n (AUT) dispositif m anti-buée inv

demo [ˈdɛməʊ] (inf) n abbr (= demonstration) manif f

democracy [dɪˈmɒkrəsɪ] n démocratie f; **democrat** [ˈdɛməkræt] n démocrate m/f; **democratic** [dɛməˈkrætɪk] adj démocratique

demolish [dɪˈmɒlɪʃ] vt démolir

demonstrate [ˈdɛmənstreɪt] vt montrer, prouver; (show) faire une démonstration de ♦ vi: **to ~ (for/against)** manifester (en faveur de/contre); **demonstration** [dɛmənˈstreɪʃən] n démonstration f, manifestation f; **demonstrator** n (POL) manifestant(e)

demote [dɪˈməʊt] vt rétrograder

demure [dɪˈmjʊəʳ] adj sage, réservé(e)

den [dɛn] n tanière f, antre m

denial [dɪˈnaɪəl] n démenti m; (refusal) dénégation f

denim [ˈdɛnɪm] n jean m; **~s** npl (jeans) (blue-)jean(s) m

Denmark [ˈdɛnmɑːk] n Danemark m

denomination [dɪnɒmɪˈneɪʃən] n (of money) valeur f; (REL) confession f

denounce [dɪˈnaʊns] vt dénoncer

dense [dɛns] adj dense; (stupid) obtus(e), bouché(e); **~ly** adv: **~ly populated** à forte densité de population; **density** [ˈdɛnsɪtɪ] n densité f; **double/high-density diskette** disquette f double densité/haute densité

dent [dɛnt] n bosse f ♦ vt (also: **make a ~ in**) cabosser

dental [ˈdɛntl] adj dentaire; **~ surgeon** n (chirurgien(ne)) dentiste

dentist [ˈdɛntɪst] n dentiste m/f

dentures ['dɛntʃəz] npl dentier m sg

deny [dɪ'naɪ] vt nier; (refuse) refuser

deodorant [diː'əudərənt] n déodorant m, désodorisant m

depart [dɪ'pɑːt] vi partir; **to ~ from** (fig: differ from) s'écarter de

department [dɪ'pɑːtmənt] n (COMM) rayon m; (SCOL) section f; (POL) ministère m, département m; **~ store** n grand magasin

departure [dɪ'pɑːtʃə] n départ m; **a new ~** une nouvelle voie; **~ lounge** n (at airport) salle f d'embarquement

depend [dɪ'pɛnd] vi: **to ~ on** dépendre de; (rely on) compter sur; **it ~s** cela dépend; **~ing on the result** selon le résultat; **~able** adj (person) sérieux (-euse), sûr(e); (car, watch) solide, fiable; **~ant** n personne f à charge; **~ent** adj: **to be ~ent (on)** dépendre de; **~ent** n = **dependant**

depict [dɪ'pɪkt] vt (in picture) représenter; (in words) dépeindre, décrire

depleted [dɪ'pliːtɪd] adj (considerably) réduit(e) or diminué(e)

deport [dɪ'pɔːt] vt expulser

deposit [dɪ'pɒzɪt] n (CHEM, COMM, GEO) dépôt m; (of ore, oil) gisement m; (part payment) arrhes fpl, acompte m; (on bottle etc) consigne f; (for hired goods etc) cautionnement m, garantie f ♦ vt déposer; **~ account** n compte m sur livret

depot ['dɛpəu] n dépôt m; (US: RAIL) gare f

depress [dɪ'prɛs] vt déprimer; (press down) appuyer sur, abaisser; (prices, wages) faire baisser; **~ed** adj (person) déprimé(e); (area) en déclin, touché(e) par le sous-emploi; **~ing** adj déprimant(e); **~ion** n dépression f; (hollow) creux m

deprivation [dɛprɪ'veɪʃən] n privation f; (loss) perte f

deprive [dɪ'praɪv] vt: **to ~ sb of** priver qn de; **~d** adj déshérité(e)

depth [dɛpθ] n profondeur f; **in the ~s** of despair au plus profond du désespoir; **to be out of one's ~** avoir perdu pied, nager

deputize ['dɛpjutaɪz] vi: **to ~ for** assurer l'intérim de

deputy ['dɛpjuti] adj adjoint(e) ♦ n (second in command) adjoint(e); (US: also: ~ sheriff) shérif adjoint; **~ head** directeur adjoint, sous-directeur m

derail [dɪ'reɪl] vt: **to be ~ed** dérailler

deranged [dɪ'reɪndʒd] adj: **to be (mentally) ~** avoir le cerveau dérangé

derby ['dɑːrbɪ] (US) n (bowler hat) (chapeau m) melon m

derelict ['dɛrɪlɪkt] adj abandonné(e), à l'abandon

derisory [dɪ'raɪsərɪ] adj (sum) dérisoire; (smile, person) moqueur(-euse)

derive [dɪ'raɪv] vt: **to ~ sth from** tirer qch de; (trouver qch dans ♦ vi: **to ~ from** provenir de, dériver de

derogatory [dɪ'rɒgətərɪ] adj désobligeant(e); péjoratif(-ive)

descend [dɪ'sɛnd] vt, vi descendre; **to ~ from** descendre de, être issu(e) de; **to ~ to (doing) sth** s'abaisser à (faire) qch; **descent** n descente f; (origin) origine f

describe [dɪs'kraɪb] vt décrire; **description** [dɪs'krɪpʃən] n description f; (sort) sorte f, espèce f

desecrate ['dɛsɪkreɪt] vt profaner

desert [n 'dɛzət, vb dɪ'zəːt] n désert m ♦ vt déserter, abandonner ♦ vi (MIL) déserter; **~s** npl: **to get one's just ~s** n'avoir que ce qu'on mérite; **~er** [dɪ'zəːtər] n déserteur m; **~ion** [dɪ'zəːʃən] n (MIL) désertion f; (LAW: of spouse) abandon m du domicile conjugal; **~ island** n île déserte

deserve [dɪ'zəːv] vt mériter; **deserving** adj (person) méritant(e); (action, cause) méritoire

design [dɪ'zaɪn] n (sketch) plan m, dessin m; (layout, shape) conception f, ligne f; (pattern) dessin m, motif(s) m(pl); (COMM, art) design m, stylisme m; (in-

tention) dessein m ♦ vt dessiner; élaborer; **~er** n *(TECH)* concepteur-projeteur m; *(ART)* dessinateur(-trice), designer m; *(fashion)* styliste m/f

desire [dɪˈzaɪəʳ] n désir m ♦ vt désirer

desk [desk] n *(in office)* bureau m; *(for pupil)* pupitre m; *(BRIT: in shop, restaurant)* caisse f; *(in hotel, at airport)* réception f; **~-top publishing** n publication assistée par ordinateur, PAO f

desolate [ˈdesəlɪt] adj désolé(e); *(person)* affligé(e)

despair [dɪsˈpɛəʳ] n désespoir m ♦ vi: **to ~ of** désespérer de

despatch [dɪsˈpætʃ] n, vt = **dispatch**

desperate [ˈdespərɪt] adj désespéré(e); *(criminal)* prêt(e) à tout; **to be ~ for sth/to do sth** avoir désespérément besoin de qch/de faire qch; **~ly** adv désespérément; *(very)* terriblement, extrêmement; **desperation** [despəˈreɪʃən] n désespoir m; **in (sheer) desperation** en désespoir de cause

despicable [dɪsˈpɪkəbl] adj méprisable

despise [dɪsˈpaɪz] vt mépriser

despite [dɪsˈpaɪt] prep malgré, en dépit de

despondent [dɪsˈpɔndənt] adj découragé(e), abattu(e)

dessert [dɪˈzəːt] n dessert m; **~spoon** n cuiller f à dessert

destination [destɪˈneɪʃən] n destination f

destined [ˈdestɪnd] adj: **to be ~ to do/for sth** être destiné(e) à faire/à qch

destiny [ˈdestɪnɪ] n destinée f, destin m

destitute [ˈdestɪtjuːt] adj indigent(e)

destroy [dɪsˈtrɔɪ] vt détruire; *(injured horse)* abattre; *(dog)* faire piquer; **~er** n *(NAUT)* contre-torpilleur m

destruction [dɪsˈtrʌkʃən] n destruction f

detach [dɪˈtætʃ] vt détacher; **~ed** adj *(attitude, person)* détaché(e); **~ed house** n pavillon m, maison(nette) individuelle); **~ment** n *(MIL)* détachement m; *(fig)* détachement, indifférence f

detail [ˈdiːteɪl] n détail m ♦ vt raconter en détail, énumérer; **in ~** en détail; **~ed** adj détaillé(e)

detain [dɪˈteɪn] vt retenir; *(in captivity)* détenir; *(in hospital)* hospitaliser

detect [dɪˈtekt] vt déceler, percevoir; *(MED, POLICE)* dépister; *(MIL, RADAR, TECH)* détecter; **~ion** n découverte f; **~ive** n agent m de la sûreté, policier m; **private ~ive** détective privé; **~ive story** n roman policier

detention [dɪˈtenʃən] n détention f; *(SCOL)* retenue f, consigne f

deter [dɪˈtəːʳ] vt dissuader

detergent [dɪˈtəːdʒənt] n détergent m, détersif m

deteriorate [dɪˈtɪərɪəreɪt] vi se détériorer, se dégrader

determine [dɪˈtəːmɪn] vt déterminer; **to ~ to do** résoudre de faire, se déterminer à faire; **~d** adj *(person)* déterminé(e), décidé(e)

deterrent [dɪˈterənt] n effet m de dissuasion; force f de dissuasion

detest [dɪˈtest] vt détester, avoir horreur de

detonate [ˈdetəneɪt] vt faire détoner or exploser

detour [ˈdiːtuəʳ] n détour m; *(US: AUT: diversion)* déviation f

detract [dɪˈtrækt] vt: **to ~ from** *(quality, pleasure)* diminuer; *(reputation)* porter atteinte à

detriment [ˈdetrɪmənt] n: **to the ~ of** au détriment de, au préjudice de; **~al** [detrɪˈmentl] adj: **~al to** préjudiciable or nuisible à

devaluation [diːvæljuˈeɪʃən] n dévaluation f

devastate [ˈdevəsteɪt] vt dévaster; **~d** adj *(fig)* anéanti(e); **devastating** adj dévastateur(-trice); *(news)* accablant(e)

develop [dɪˈvelɔp] vt *(gen)* développer; *(disease)* commencer à souffrir de; *(resources)* mettre en valeur, exploiter ♦ vi se développer; *(situation, disease:*

evolve) évoluer; (facts, symptoms: appear) se manifester, se produire; **~ing country** pays m en voie de développement; **the machine has ~ed a fault** un problème s'est manifesté dans cette machine; **~er** [dɪ'veləpəʳ] n (also: **property ~er**) promoteur m; **~ment** [dɪ'veləpmənt] n développement m; (of affair, case) rebondissement m, fait(s) nouveau(x)

device [dɪ'vaɪs] n (apparatus) engin m, dispositif m

devil ['dɛvl] n diable m; démon m

devious ['diːvɪəs] adj (person) sournois(e), dissimulé(e)

devise [dɪ'vaɪz] vt imaginer, concevoir

devoid [dɪ'vɔɪd] adj: **~ of** dépourvu(e) de, dénué(e) de

devolution [diːvə'luːʃən] n (POL) décentralisation f

devote [dɪ'vəut] vt: **to ~ sth to** consacrer qch à; **~d** [dɪ'vəutɪd] adj dévoué(e); **to be ~d to** (book etc) être consacré(e) à; (person) être très attaché(e) à; **~e** [dɛvəu'tiː] n (REL) adepte m/f; (MUS, SPORT) fervent(e); **devotion** n dévouement m, attachement m; (REL) dévotion f, piété f

devour [dɪ'vauəʳ] vt dévorer

devout [dɪ'vaut] adj pieux(-euse), dévot(e)

dew [djuː] n rosée f

diabetes [daɪə'biːtiːz] n diabète m; **diabetic** [daɪə'bɛtɪk] adj diabétique ♦ n diabétique m/f

diabolical [daɪə'bɔlɪkl] (inf) adj (weather) atroce; (behaviour) infernal(e)

diagnosis [daɪəg'nəusɪs] (pl diagnoses) n diagnostic m

diagonal [daɪ'ægənl] adj diagonal(e) ♦ n diagonale f

diagram ['daɪəgræm] n diagramme m, schéma m

dial ['daɪəl] n cadran m ♦ vt (number) faire, composer

dialect ['daɪəlɛkt] n dialecte m

dialling code (BRIT) n indicatif m (téléphonique)

dialling tone (BRIT) n tonalité f

dialogue ['daɪəlɔg] n dialogue m

dial tone (US) n = dialling tone

diameter [daɪ'æmɪtəʳ] n diamètre m

diamond ['daɪəmənd] n diamant m; (shape) losange m; **~s** npl (CARDS) carreau m

diaper ['daɪəpəʳ] (US) n couche f

diaphragm ['daɪəfræm] n diaphragme m

diarrhoea [daɪə'riːə] (US **diarrhea**) n diarrhée f

diary ['daɪərɪ] n (daily account) journal m; (book) agenda m

dice [daɪs] n inv dé m ♦ vt (CULIN) couper en dés ou en cubes

dictate [dɪk'teɪt] vt dicter; **dictation** n dictée f

dictator [dɪk'teɪtəʳ] n dictateur m; **~ship** n dictature f

dictionary ['dɪkʃənrɪ] n dictionnaire m

did [dɪd] pt of do; **~n't** = did not

die [daɪ] vi mourir; **to be dying for sth** avoir une envie folle de qch; **to be dying to do sth** mourir d'envie de faire qch; **~ away** vi s'éteindre; **~ down** vi se calmer, s'apaiser; **~ out** vi disparaître

diesel ['diːzl] n (vehicle) diesel m; (also: **~ oil**) carburant m diesel, gas-oil m; **~ engine** n moteur m diesel

diet ['daɪət] n alimentation f; (restricted food) régime m ♦ vi (also: **be on a ~**) suivre un régime

differ ['dɪfəʳ] vi (be different): **to ~ (from)** être différent(e) (de); (disagree): **to ~ (from sb over sth)** ne pas être d'accord (avec qn au sujet de qch); **~ence** n différence f; (quarrel) différend m, désaccord m; **~ent** adj différent(e); **~entiate** [dɪfə'rɛnʃɪeɪt] vi: **to ~entiate (between)** faire une différence (entre)

difficult ['dɪfɪkəlt] adj difficile; **~y** n difficulté f

diffident ['dɪfɪdənt] adj qui manque de

confiance or d'assurance

dig [dɪg] (*pt, pp* **dug**) *vt* (*hole*) creuser; (*garden*) bêcher ♦ *n* (*prod*) coup *m* de coude; (*fig*) coup de griffe *or* de patte; (*archeological*) fouilles *fpl*; ~ **in** *vi* (*MIL: also:* ~ **o.s. in**) se retrancher; ~ **into** *vt fus* (*savings*) puiser dans; **to** ~ **one's nails into sth** enfoncer ses ongles dans qch; ~ **up** *vt* déterrer

digest [*vb* daɪˈdʒɛst, *n* ˈdaɪdʒɛst] *vt* digérer ♦ *n* sommaire *m*, résumé *m*; **~ion** [dɪˈdʒɛstʃən] *n* digestion *f*

digit [ˈdɪdʒɪt] *n* (*number*) chiffre *m*; (*finger*) doigt *m*; **~al** *adj* digital(e), à affichage numérique *or* digital; **~al computer** calculateur *m* numérique; **~al TV** *n* télévision *f* numérique; **~al watch** montre *f* à affichage numérique

dignified [ˈdɪgnɪfaɪd] *adj* digne

dignity [ˈdɪgnɪtɪ] *n* dignité *f*

digress [daɪˈgrɛs] *vi*: **to** ~ **from** s'écarter de, s'éloigner de

digs [dɪgz] (*BRIT: inf*) *npl* piaule *f*, chambre meublée

dilapidated [dɪˈlæpɪdeɪtɪd] *adj* délabré(e)

dilemma [daɪˈlɛmə] *n* dilemme *m*

diligent [ˈdɪlɪdʒənt] *adj* appliqué(e), assidu(e)

dilute [daɪˈluːt] *vt* diluer

dim [dɪm] *adj* (*light*) faible; (*memory, outline*) vague, indécis(e); (*figure*) vague, indistinct(e); (*room*) sombre; (*stupid*) borné(e), obtus(e) ♦ *vt* (*light*) réduire, baisser; (*US: AUT*) mettre en code

dime [daɪm] (*US*) *n* = **10 cents**

dimension [daɪˈmɛnʃən] *n* dimension *f*

diminish [dɪˈmɪnɪʃ] *vt, vi* diminuer

diminutive [dɪˈmɪnjutɪv] *adj* minuscule, tout(e) petit(e)

dimmers [ˈdɪməz] (*US*) *npl* (*AUT*) phares *mpl* code *inv*; feux *mpl* de position

dimple [ˈdɪmpl] *n* fossette *f*

din [dɪn] *n* vacarme *m*

dine [daɪn] *vi* dîner; **~r** *n* (*person*) dîneur(-euse); (*US: restaurant*) petit restaurant

dinghy [ˈdɪŋgɪ] *n* youyou *m*; (*also:* **rubber ~**) canot *m* pneumatique; (*also:* **sailing ~**) voilier *m*, dériveur *m*

dingy [ˈdɪndʒɪ] *adj* miteux(-euse), minable

dining car (*BRIT*) *n* wagon-restaurant *m*

dining room *n* salle *f* à manger

dinner [ˈdɪnəʳ] *n* dîner *m*; (*lunch*) déjeuner *m*; (*public*) banquet *m*; ~ **jacket** *n* smoking *m*; ~ **party** *n* dîner *m*; ~ **time** *n* heure *f* du dîner; (*midday*) heure du déjeuner

dinosaur [ˈdaɪnəsɔːʳ] *n* dinosaure *m*

dip [dɪp] *n* déclivité *f*; (*in sea*) baignade *f*, bain *m*; (*CULIN*) ≈ sauce *f* ♦ *vt* tremper, plonger; (*BRIT: AUT: lights*) mettre en code, baisser ♦ *vi* plonger

diploma [dɪˈpləumə] *n* diplôme *m*

diplomacy [dɪˈpləuməsɪ] *n* diplomatie *f*

diplomat [ˈdɪpləmæt] *n* diplomate *m*; **~ic** [dɪpləˈmætɪk] *adj* diplomatique

dipstick [ˈdɪpstɪk] *n* (*AUT*) jauge *f* de niveau d'huile

dipswitch [ˈdɪpswɪtʃ] *n* (*AUT*) interrupteur *m* de lumière réduite

dire [daɪəʳ] *adj* terrible, extrême, affreux(-euse)

direct [dɪˈrɛkt] *adj* direct(e) ♦ *vt* diriger, orienter; (*letter, remark*) adresser; (*film, programme*) réaliser; (*play*) mettre en scène; (*order*): **to** ~ **sb to do sth** ordonner à qn de faire qch ♦ *adv* directement; **can you** ~ **me to ...?** pouvez-vous m'indiquer le chemin de ...?; ~ **debit** (*BRIT*) *n* prélèvement *m* automatique

direction [dɪˈrɛkʃən] *n* direction *f*; **~s** *npl* (*advice*) indications *fpl*; (*to a place*) indications *fpl*; **sense of** ~ sens *m* de l'orientation; **~s for use** mode *m* d'emploi

directly [dɪˈrɛktlɪ] *adv* (*in a straight line*) directement, tout droit; (*at once*) tout de suite, immédiatement

director [dɪˈrɛktəʳ] *n* directeur *m*; (*THEATRE*) metteur *m* en scène; (*CINEMA, TV*) réalisateur(-trice)

directory [dɪ'rektərɪ] n annuaire m; (COMPUT) répertoire m; **~ enquiries** (US **directory assistance**) n renseignements mpl

dirt [da:t] n saleté f; crasse f; (earth) terre f, boue f; **~-cheap** adj très bon marché inv; **~y** adj sale ♦ vt salir; **~y trick** coup tordu

disability [dɪsə'bɪlɪtɪ] n invalidité f, infirmité f

disabled [dɪs'eɪbld] adj infirme, invalide ♦ npl: **the ~** les handicapés

disadvantage [dɪsəd'vɑ:ntɪdʒ] n désavantage m, inconvénient m

disagree [dɪsə'gri:] vi (be different) ne pas concorder; (be against, think otherwise): **to ~ (with)** ne pas être d'accord (avec); **~able** adj désagréable; **~ment** n désaccord m, différend m

disallow ['dɪsə'lau] vt rejeter

disappear [dɪsə'pɪər] vi disparaître; **~ance** n disparition f

disappoint [dɪsə'pɔɪnt] vt décevoir; **~ed** adj déçu(e); **~ing** adj décevant(e); **~ment** n déception f

disapproval [dɪsə'pru:vəl] n désapprobation f

disapprove [dɪsə'pru:v] vi: **to ~ (of)** désapprouver

disarmament [dɪs'ɑ:məmənt] n désarmement m

disarray [dɪsə'reɪ] n: **in ~** (army) en déroute; (organization) en désarroi; (hair, clothes) en désordre

disaster [dɪ'zɑ:stər] n catastrophe f, désastre m; **disastrous** adj désastreux(-euse)

disband [dɪs'bænd] vt démobiliser; disperser ♦ vi se séparer; se disperser

disbelief ['dɪsbə'li:f] n incrédulité f

disc [dɪsk] n disque m; (COMPUT) = **disk**

discard [dɪs'kɑ:d] vt (old things) se débarrasser de; (fig) écarter, renoncer.à

discern [dɪ'sə:n] vt discerner, distinguer; **~ing** adj perspicace

discharge [vb dɪs'tʃɑ:dʒ, n 'dɪstʃɑ:dʒ] vt décharger; (duties) s'acquitter de; (patient) renvoyer (chez lui); (employee) congédier, licencier; (soldier) rendre à la vie civile, réformer; (defendant) relaxer, élargir ♦ n décharge f; (dismissal) renvoi m; licenciement m; élargissement m; (MED) écoulement m

discipline ['dɪsɪplɪn] n discipline f

disc jockey n disc-jockey m

disclaim [dɪs'kleɪm] vt nier

disclose [dɪs'kləuz] vt révéler, divulguer; **disclosure** n révélation f

disco ['dɪskəu] n abbr = **discotheque**

discomfort [dɪs'kʌmfət] n malaise m, gêne f; (lack of comfort) manque m de confort

disconcert [dɪskən'sə:t] vt déconcerter

disconnect [dɪskə'nekt] vt (ELEC, RADIO, pipe) débrancher; (TEL, water) couper

discontent [dɪskən'tent] n mécontentement m; **~ed** adj mécontent(e)

discontinue [dɪskən'tɪnju:] vt cesser, interrompre; **"~d"** (COMM) "fin de série"

discord ['dɪskɔ:d] n discorde f, dissension f; (MUS) dissonance f

discotheque ['dɪskəutek] n discothèque f

discount [n 'dɪskaunt, vb dɪs'kaunt] n remise f, rabais m ♦ vt (sum) faire une remise de; (fig) ne pas tenir compte de

discourage [dɪs'kʌrɪdʒ] vt décourager

discover [dɪs'kʌvər] vt découvrir; **~y** n découverte f

discredit [dɪs'kredɪt] vt (idea) mettre en doute; (person) discréditer

discreet [dɪs'kri:t] adj discret(-ète)

discrepancy [dɪs'krepənsɪ] n divergence f, contradiction f

discretion [dɪs'kreʃən] n discrétion f; **use your own ~** à vous de juger

discriminate [dɪs'krɪmɪneɪt] vi: **to ~ between** établir une distinction entre, faire la différence entre; **to ~ against** pratiquer une discrimination contre; **discriminating** adj qui a du discernement; **discrimination** [dɪskrɪmɪ'neɪʃən] n discrimination f; (judgment) discernement *m*

discuss [dɪs'kʌs] *vt* discuter de; *(debate)* discuter; **~ion** *n* discussion *f*

disdain [dɪs'deɪn] *n* dédain *m*

disease [dɪ'ziːz] *n* maladie *f*

disembark [dɪsɪm'bɑːk] *vi* débarquer

disentangle [dɪsɪn'tæŋgl] *vt (wool, wire)* démêler, débrouiller; *(from wreckage)* dégager

disfigure [dɪs'fɪgə'] *vt* défigurer

disgrace [dɪs'greɪs] *n* honte *f*; *(disfavour)* disgrâce *f* ♦ *vt* déshonorer, couvrir de honte; **~ful** *adj* scandaleux(-euse), honteux(-euse)

disgruntled [dɪs'grʌntld] *adj* mécontent(e)

disguise [dɪs'gaɪz] *n* déguisement *m* ♦ *vt* déguiser; **in ~** déguisé(e)

disgust [dɪs'gʌst] *n* dégoût *m*, aversion *f* ♦ *vt* dégoûter, écœurer; **~ing** *adj* dégoûtant(e); révoltant(e)

dish [dɪʃ] *n* plat *m*; **to do** *or* **wash the ~es** faire la vaisselle; **~ out** *vt* servir, distribuer; **~ up** *vt* servir; **~cloth** *n (for washing)* lavette *f*

dishearten [dɪs'hɑːtn] *vt* décourager

dishevelled [dɪ'ʃevəld] *(US* **disheveled)** *adj* ébouriffé(e); décoiffé(e); débraillé(e)

dishonest [dɪs'ɒnɪst] *adj* malhonnête

dishonour [dɪs'ɒnə'] *(US* **dishonor)** *n* déshonneur *m*; **~able** *adj (behaviour)* déshonorant(e); *(person)* peu honorable

dishtowel ['dɪʃtaʊəl] *(US)* *n* torchon *m*

dishwasher ['dɪʃwɒʃə'] *n* lave-vaisselle *m*

disillusion [dɪsɪ'luːʒən] *vt* désabuser, désillusionner

disinfect [dɪsɪn'fekt] *vt* désinfecter; **~ant** *n* désinfectant *m*

disintegrate [dɪs'ɪntɪgreɪt] *vi* se désintégrer

disinterested [dɪs'ɪntrəstɪd] *adj* désintéressé(e)

disjointed [dɪs'dʒɔɪntɪd] *adj* décousu(e), incohérent(e)

disk [dɪsk] *n (COMPUT)* disque *m*; (: *flop-*

py ~) disquette *f*; **single-/double-sided ~** disquette simple/double face; **~ drive** *n* lecteur *m* de disquettes; **~ette** [dɪs'ket] *n* disquette *f*, disque *m* souple

dislike [dɪs'laɪk] *n* aversion *f*, antipathie *f* ♦ *vt* ne pas aimer

dislocate ['dɪsləkeɪt] *vt* disloquer; déboiter

dislodge [dɪs'lɒdʒ] *vt* déplacer, faire bouger

disloyal [dɪs'lɔɪəl] *adj* déloyal(e)

dismal ['dɪzml] *adj* lugubre, maussade

dismantle [dɪs'mæntl] *vt* démonter

dismay [dɪs'meɪ] *n* consternation *f*

dismiss [dɪs'mɪs] *vt* congédier, renvoyer; *(soldiers)* faire rompre les rangs à; *(idea)* écarter; *(LAW):* **to ~ a case** rendre une fin de non-recevoir; **~al** *n* renvoi *m*

dismount [dɪs'maʊnt] *vi* mettre pied à terre, descendre

disobedient [dɪsə'biːdɪənt] *adj* désobéissant(e)

disobey [dɪsə'beɪ] *vt* désobéir à

disorder [dɪs'ɔːdə'] *n* désordre *m*; *(rioting)* désordres *mpl*; *(MED)* troubles *mpl*; **~ly** *adj* en désordre; désordonné(e)

disorientated [dɪs'ɔːrɪentertɪd] *adj* désorienté(e)

disown [dɪs'əʊn] *vt* renier

disparaging [dɪs'pærɪdʒɪŋ] *adj* désobligeant(e)

dispassionate [dɪs'pæʃənət] *adj* calme, froid(e); impartial(e), objectif(-ive)

dispatch [dɪs'pætʃ] *vt* expédier, envoyer ♦ *n* envoi *m*, expédition *f*; *(MIL, PRESS)* dépêche *f*

dispel [dɪs'pel] *vt* dissiper, chasser

dispense [dɪs'pens] *vt* distribuer, administrer; **~ with** *vt fus* se passer de; **~r** *n (machine)* distributeur *m*; **dispensing chemist** *(BRIT)* *n* pharmacie *f*

disperse [dɪs'pɜːs] *vt* disperser ♦ *vi* se disperser

dispirited [dɪs'pɪrɪtɪd] *adj* découragé(e), déprimé(e)

displace [dɪs'pleɪs] vt déplacer

display [dɪs'pleɪ] n étalage m; déploiement m; affichage m; (screen) écran m, visuel m; (of feeling) manifestation f ♦ vt montrer; (goods) mettre à l'étalage, exposer; (results, departure times) afficher; (pej) faire étalage de

displease [dɪs'pli:z] vt mécontenter, contrarier; **~d with** adj: **~d with** mécontent(e) de; **displeasure** [dɪs'plɛʒəʳ] n mécontentement m

disposable [dɪs'pəuzəbl] adj (pack etc) jetable, à jeter; (income) disponible; **~ nappy** (BRIT) n couche f à jeter, couche-culotte f

disposal [dɪs'pəuzl] n (of goods for sale) vente f; (of property) disposition f, cession f; (of rubbish) enlèvement m; destruction f; **at one's ~** à sa disposition

dispose [dɪs'pəuz] vt disposer; **~ of** fus (unwanted goods etc) se débarrasser de, se défaire de; (problem) expédier; **~d** adj: **to be ~d to do sth** être disposé(e) à faire qch; **disposition** [dɪspə'zɪʃən] n disposition f; (temperament) naturel m

disprove [dɪs'pru:v] vt réfuter

dispute [dɪs'pju:t] n discussion f; (also: **industrial ~**) conflit m ♦ vt contester; (matter) discuter; (victory) disputer

disqualify [dɪs'kwɔlɪfaɪ] vt (SPORT) disqualifier; **to ~ sb for sth/from doing** rendre qn inapte à qch/à faire

disquiet [dɪs'kwaɪət] n inquiétude f, trouble m

disregard [dɪsrɪ'gɑ:d] vt ne pas tenir compte de

disrepair [dɪsrɪ'pɛəʳ] n: **to fall into ~** (building) tomber en ruine

disreputable [dɪs'rɛpjutəbl] adj (person) de mauvaise réputation; (behaviour) déshonorant(e)

disrespectful [dɪsrɪ'spɛktful] adj irrespectueux(-euse)

disrupt [dɪs'rʌpt] vt (plans) déranger; (conversation) interrompre

dissatisfied [dɪs'sætɪsfaɪd] adj: **~ (with)** insatisfait(e) (de)

dissect [dɪ'sɛkt] vt disséquer

dissent [dɪ'sɛnt] n dissentiment m, différence f d'opinion

dissertation [dɪsə'teɪʃən] n mémoire m

disservice [dɪs'sə:vɪs] n: **to do sb a ~** rendre un mauvais service à qn

dissimilar [dɪ'sɪmɪləʳ] adj: **~ (to)** dissemblable (à), différent(e) (de)

dissipate ['dɪsɪpeɪt] vt dissiper; (money, efforts) disperser

dissolute ['dɪsəlu:t] adj débauché(e), dissolu(e)

dissolve [dɪ'zɔlv] vt dissoudre ♦ vi se dissoudre, fondre; **to ~ in(to) tears** fondre en larmes

distance ['dɪstns] n distance f; **in the ~** au loin

distant ['dɪstnt] adj lointain(e), éloigné(e); (manner) distant(e), froid(e)

distaste [dɪs'teɪst] n dégoût m; **~ful** adj déplaisant(e), désagréable

distended [dɪs'tɛndɪd] adj (stomach) dilaté(e)

distil [dɪs'tɪl] (US **distill**) vt distiller; **~lery** n distillerie f

distinct [dɪs'tɪŋkt] adj distinct(e); (clear) marqué(e); **as ~ from** par opposition à; **~ion** n distinction f; (in exam) mention f très bien; **~ive** adj distinctif(-ive)

distinguish [dɪs'tɪŋgwɪʃ] vt distinguer; **~ed** adj (eminent) distingué(e); **~ing** adj (feature) distinctif(-ive), caractéristique

distort [dɪs'tɔ:t] vt déformer

distract [dɪs'trækt] vt distraire, déranger; **~ed** adj (anxious) éperdu(e), égaré(e); **~ion** n distraction f; égarement m

distraught [dɪs'trɔ:t] adj éperdu(e)

distress [dɪs'trɛs] n détresse f ♦ vt affliger; **~ing** adj douloureux(-euse), pénible

distribute [dɪs'trɪbju:t] vt distribuer; **distribution** [dɪstrɪ'bju:ʃən] n distribution f; **distributor** n distributeur m

district ['dɪstrɪkt] n (of country) région f; (of town) quartier m; (ADMIN) district m; **~ attorney** (US) n ≃ procureur m de la République; **~ nurse** (BRIT) n infirmière visiteuse

distrust [dɪs'trʌst] n méfiance f ♦ vt se méfier de

disturb [dɪs'tɜːb] vt troubler; (inconvenience) déranger; **~ance** n dérangement m; (violent event, political etc) troubles mpl; **~ed** adj (worried, upset) agité(e), troublé(e); **to be emotionally ~** avoir des problèmes affectifs; **~ing** adj troublant(e), inquiétant(e)

disuse [dɪs'juːs] n: **to fall into ~** tomber en désuétude; **~d** [dɪs'juːzd] adj désaffecté(e)

ditch [dɪtʃ] n fossé m; (irrigation) rigole f ♦ vt (inf) abandonner; (person) plaquer

dither ['dɪðə*] vi hésiter

ditto ['dɪtəʊ] adv idem

dive [daɪv] n plongeon m; (of submarine) plongée f ♦ vi plonger; **to ~ into** (bag, water etc) plonger la main dans; (shop, car etc) se précipiter dans; **~r** n plongeur m

diversion [daɪ'vɜːʃən] n (BRIT: AUT) déviation f; (distraction, MIL) diversion f

divert [daɪ'vɜːt] vt (funds, BRIT: traffic) dévier; (river, attention) détourner

divide [dɪ'vaɪd] vt diviser; (separate) séparer ♦ vi se diviser; **~d highway** (US) n route f à quatre voies

dividend ['dɪvɪdend] n dividende m

divine [dɪ'vaɪn] adj divin(e)

diving ['daɪvɪŋ] n plongée f (sous-marine); **~ board** n plongeoir m

divinity [dɪ'vɪnɪtɪ] n divinité f; (SCOL) théologie f

division [dɪ'vɪʒən] n division f

divorce [dɪ'vɔːs] n divorce m ♦ vt divorcer d'avec; (dissociate) séparer; **~d** adj divorcé(e); **~e** n divorcé(e)

D.I.Y. (BRIT) n abbr = **do-it-yourself**

dizzy ['dɪzɪ] adj: **to make sb ~** donner le vertige à qn; **to feel ~** avoir la tête

qui tourne

DJ n abbr = **disc jockey**

DNA fingerprinting n technique f des empreintes génétiques

KEYWORD

do [duː] (pt **did**, pp **done**) n (inf: party etc) soirée f, fête f

♦ vb 1 (in negative constructions) non traduit; **I don't understand** je ne comprends pas

2 (to form questions) non traduit; **didn't you know?** vous ne le saviez pas?; **why didn't you come?** pourquoi n'êtes-vous pas venu?

3 (for emphasis, in polite expressions): **she does seem rather late** je trouve qu'elle est bien en retard; **do sit down/help yourself** asseyez-vous/servez-vous je vous en prie

4 (used to avoid repeating vb): **she swims better than I do** elle nage mieux que moi; **do you agree? - yes, I do/no, I don't** vous êtes d'accord? - oui/non; **she lives in Glasgow - so do I** elle habite Glasgow - moi aussi; **who broke it? - I did** qui l'a cassé? - c'est moi

5 (in question tags): **he laughed, didn't he?** il a ri, n'est-ce pas?; **I don't know him, do I?** je ne crois pas le connaître

♦ vt (gen: carry out, perform etc) faire; **what are you doing tonight?** qu'est-ce que vous faites ce soir?; **to do the cooking/washing-up** faire la cuisine/la vaisselle; **to do one's teeth/hair/nails** se brosser les dents/se coiffer/se faire les ongles; **the car was doing 100 ≃** la voiture faisait du 160 (à l'heure)

♦ vi 1 (act, behave) faire; **do as I do** faites comme moi

2 (get on, fare) marcher; **the firm is doing well** l'entreprise marche bien; **how do you do?** comment allez-vous?; (on being introduced) enchanté(e)!

3 (suit) aller; **will it do?** est-ce que ça ira?

4 (be sufficient) suffire, aller; **will £10 do?** est-ce que 10 livres suffiront?; **that'll do** ça suffit, ça ira; **that'll do!** (in annoyance) ça va or suffit comme ça!; **to make do (with)** se contenter (de)

do away with vt fus supprimer

do up vt (laces, dress) attacher; (buttons) boutonner; (zip) fermer; (renovate: room) refaire; (: house) remettre à neuf

do with vt fus (need): **I could do with a drink/some help** quelque chose à boire/un peu d'aide ne serait pas de refus; (be connected): **that has nothing to do with you** cela ne vous concerne pas; **I won't have anything to do with it** je ne veux pas m'en mêler

do without vi s'en passer ♦ vt fus se passer de

dock [dɔk] n dock m; (LAW) banc m des accusés ♦ vi se mettre à quai; (SPACE) s'arrimer; **~er** n docker m; **~yard** n chantier m de construction navale

doctor ['dɔktər] n médecin m, docteur m; (PhD etc) docteur ♦ vt (drink) frelater; **D~ of Philosophy** (degree) doctorat m; (person) Docteur m en Droit ou Lettres etc, titulaire m/f d'un doctorat

document ['dɔkjumənt] n document m; **~ary** [dɔkju'mentəri] adj documentaire ♦ n documentaire m

dodge [dɔdʒ] n truc m; combine f ♦ vt esquiver, éviter

dodgems ['dɔdʒəmz] (BRIT) npl autos tamponneuses

doe [dəu] n (deer) biche f; (rabbit) lapine f

does [dʌz] vb see **do**; **~n't** = does not

dog [dɔg] n chien(ne) ♦ vt suivre de près; poursuivre, harceler; **~ collar** n collier m de chien; (fig) faux-col m d'ecclésiastique; **~-eared** adj corné(e);

~ged ['dɔgid] adj obstiné(e), opiniâtre; **~sbody** n bonne f à tout faire, tâcheron m

doings ['duːiŋz] npl activités fpl

do-it-yourself ['duːitjɔː'self] n bricolage m

doldrums ['dɔldrəmz] npl: **to be in the ~** avoir le cafard; (business) être dans le marasme

dole [dəul] (BRIT: payment) allocation f de chômage; **on the ~** au chômage; **~ out** vt donner au compte-goutte

doll [dɔl] n poupée f

dollar ['dɔlər] n dollar m

dolled up (inf) adj: **(all) ~** sur son trente et un

dolphin ['dɔlfin] n dauphin m

dome [dəum] n dôme m

domestic [də'mestik] adj (task, appliances) ménager(-ère); (of country: trade, situation etc) intérieur(e); (animal) domestique; **~ated** adj (animal) domestiqué(e); (husband) pantouflard(e)

dominate ['dɔmineit] vt dominer

domineering [dɔmi'niəriŋ] adj dominateur(-trice), autoritaire

dominion [də'miniən] n (territory) territoire m; **to have ~ over** contrôler

domino ['dɔminəu] (pl **~es**) n domino m; **~es** n (game) dominos mpl

don [dɔn] (BRIT) n professeur m d'université

donate [də'neit] vt faire don de, donner

done [dʌn] pp of **do**

donkey ['dɔŋki] n âne m

donor ['dəunər] n (of blood etc) donneur(-euse); (to charity) donateur (-trice); **~ card** n carte f de don d'organes

don't [dəunt] vb = do not

donut ['dəunʌt] (US) n = doughnut

doodle ['duːdl] vi griffonner, gribouiller

doom [duːm] n destin m ♦ vt: **to be ~ed (to failure)** être voué(e) à l'échec

door [dɔːr] n porte f; (RAIL, car) portière f; **~bell** n sonnette f; **~handle** n poignée f de la porte; (car) poignée de portière; **~man** (irreg) n (in hotel) portier m; (in nightclub etc) videur m; **~mat** n paillasson m; **~step** n pas m de (la) porte, seuil m; **~way** n (embrasure f de la) porte f

dope [dəup] n (inf: drug) drogue f; (: person) andouille f ♦ vt (horse etc) doper

dormant ['dɔ:mənt] adj assoupi(e)

dormitory ['dɔ:mɪtrɪ] n dortoir m; (US: building) résidence f universitaire

dormouse ['dɔ:maus] (pl **dormice**) n loir m

DOS [dɒs] n abbr (= disk operating system) DOS

dose [dəus] n dose f

dosh [dɒʃ] (inf) n fric m

doss house ['dɒs-] (BRIT) n asile m de nuit

dot [dɒt] n point m; (on material) pois m ♦ vt: **~ted with** parsemé(e) de; **on the ~** à l'heure tapante or pile; **~ted line** n pointillé(s) m(pl)

double ['dʌbl] adj double ♦ adv (twice): **to cost ~** (sth) coûter le double (de qch) or deux fois plus (que qch) ♦ n double m ♦ vt doubler; (fold) plier en deux ♦ vi doubler; **~s** n (TENNIS) double m; **on** or (BRIT) **at the ~** au pas de course; **~ bass** (BRIT) n contrebasse f; **~ bed** n grand lit; **~ bend** (BRIT) n virage m en S; **~-breasted** adj croisé(e); **~-click** vi (COMPUT) double-cliquer; **~-cross** v doubler, trahir; **~-decker** n autobus m à impériale; **~ glazing** (BRIT) n double vitrage m; **~ room** n chambre f pour deux personnes; **doubly** adv doublement, deux fois plus

doubt [daut] n doute m ♦ vt douter de; **to ~ that** douter que; **~ful** adj douteux(-euse); (person) incertain(e); **~less** adv sans doute, sûrement

dough [dəu] n pâte f; **~nut** (US **donut**) n beignet m

dove [dʌv] n colombe f

Dover ['dəuvər] n Douvres

dovetail ['dʌvteɪl] vi (fig) concorder

dowdy ['daudɪ] adj démodé(e); mal fagoté(e) (inf)

down [daun] n (soft feathers) duvet m ♦ adv en bas, vers le bas; (on the ground) par terre ♦ prep en bas de; (along) le long de ♦ vt (inf: drink, food) s'envoyer; **~ with X!** à bas X!; **~and-out** n clochard(e); **~at-heel** adj éculé(e); (fig) miteux(-euse); **~cast** adj démoralisé(e); **~fall** n chute f; ruine f; **~hearted** adj découragé(e); **~hill** adv: **to go ~hill** descendre; (fig) péricliter; **~ payment** n acompte m; **~pour** n pluie torrentielle, déluge m; **~right** adj (lie etc) effronté(e); (refusal) catégorique; **~size** vt (ECON) réduire ses effectifs

Downing Street est une rue de Westminster (à Londres) où se trouve la résidence officielle du Premier ministre (numéro 10) et celle du ministre des Finances (numéro 11). Le nom "Downing Street" est souvent utilisé pour désigner le gouvernement britannique.

Down's syndrome [daunz-] n (MED) trisomie f

down: **~stairs** adv au rez-de-chaussée; à l'étage inférieur; **~stream** adv en aval; **~to-earth** adj terre à terre inv; **~town** adv en ville; **~ under** adv (in Australie/Nouvelle-Zélande; **~ward** adj, adv vers le bas; **~wards** adv vers le bas

dowry ['dauri] n dot f

doz. abbr = **dozen**

doze [dəuz] vi sommeiller; **~ off** vi s'assoupir

dozen ['dʌzn] n douzaine f; **a ~ books** une douzaine de livres; **~s of** des centaines de

Dr. abbr = **doctor**; **drive**

drab [dræb] adj terne, morne

draft [drɑ:ft] n ébauche f; (of letter, essay etc) brouillon m; (COMM) traite f;

(US: **call-up**) conscription f ♦ vt faire le brouillon or un projet de; (MIL: **send**) détacher; see also **draught**

draftsman ['drɑːftsmən] (irreg) (US) n = **draughtsman**

drag [dræg] vt traîner; (river) draguer ♦ vi traîner ♦ n (inf) casse-pieds m/f; (women's clothing): **in ~** (en) travesti; **~ on** vi s'éterniser

dragon ['drægən] n dragon m

dragonfly ['drægənflaɪ] n libellule f

drain [dreɪn] n égout m, canalisation f; (on resources) saignée f ♦ vt (land, marshes etc) drainer, assécher; (vegetables) égoutter; (glass) vider ♦ vi (water) s'écouler; **~age** n drainage m; système m d'égouts or de canalisations; **~ing board** (US **drain board**) n égouttoir m; **~pipe** n tuyau m d'écoulement

drama ['drɑːmə] n (art) théâtre m, art m dramatique; (play) pièce f (de théâtre); (event) drame m; **~tic** [drə'mætɪk] adj dramatique; spectaculaire; **~tist** ['dræmətɪst] n auteur m dramatique; **~tize** ['dræmətaɪz] vt (events) dramatiser; (adapt: for TV/cinema) adapter pour la télévision/pour l'écran

drank [dræŋk] pt of **drink**

drape [dreɪp] vt draper; **~s** (US) npl rideaux mpl

drastic ['dræstɪk] adj sévère; énergique; (change) radical(e)

draught [drɑːft] (US **draft**) n courant m d'air; (NAUT) tirant m d'eau; **on ~** (beer) à la pression; **~board** (BRIT) n damier m; **~s** (BRIT) n (jeu m de) dames fpl

draughtsman ['drɑːftsmən] (irreg) (US) n dessinateur(-trice) (industriel(le))

draw [drɔː] (pt **drew**, pp **drawn**) vt tirer; (tooth) arracher, extraire; (attract) attirer; (picture) dessiner; (line, circle) tracer; (money) retirer; (wages) toucher ♦ vi (SPORT) faire match nul ♦ n match nul; (lottery) tirage m au sort; loterie f; **to ~ near** s'approcher; approcher; **~ out** vi (lengthen) s'allonger ♦ vt (money) retirer; **~ up** vi (stop) s'arrêter ♦ vt

(chair) approcher; (document) établir, dresser; **~back** n inconvénient m, désavantage m; **~bridge** n pont-levis m

drawer [drɔːʳ] n tiroir m

drawing ['drɔːɪŋ] n dessin m; **~ board** n planche f à dessin; **~ pin** (BRIT) n punaise f; **~ room** n salon m

drawl [drɔːl] n accent traînant

drawn [drɔːn] pp of **draw**

dread [dred] n terreur f, effroi m ♦ vt redouter, appréhender; **~ful** adj affreux (-euse)

dream [driːm] (pt, pp **dreamed** or **dreamt**) n rêve m ♦ vt, vi rêver; **~y** adj rêveur(-euse); (music) langoureux (-euse)

dreary ['drɪərɪ] adj morne; monotone

dredge [dredʒ] vt draguer

dregs [dregz] npl lie f

drench [drentʃ] vt tremper

dress [dres] n robe f; (no pl: clothing) habillement m, tenue f ♦ vi s'habiller ♦ vt (wound) panser; **to get ~ed** s'habiller; **~ up** vi s'habiller; (in fancy ~) se déguiser; **~ circle** (BRIT) n (THEATRE) premier balcon; **~er** n (furniture) vaisselier m; (: US) coiffeuse f, commode f; **~ing** (MED) pansement m; (CULIN) sauce f, assaisonnement m; **~ing gown** (BRIT) n robe f de chambre; **~ing room** n (THEATRE) loge f; (SPORT) vestiaire m; **~ing table** n coiffeuse f; **~maker** n couturière f; **~ rehearsal** n (répétition) générale f

drew [druː] pt of **draw**

dribble ['drɪbl] vi (baby) baver ♦ vt (ball) dribbler

dried [draɪd] adj (fruit, beans) sec (sèche); (eggs, milk) en poudre

drier ['draɪəʳ] n = **dryer**

drift [drɪft] n (of current etc) force f, direction f; mouvement m; (of snow) rafale f; (: on ground) congère f; (general meaning) sens (général) ♦ vi (boat) aller à la dérive, dériver; (sand, snow) s'amonceler, s'entasser; **~wood** n bois flotté

drill [drɪl] n perceuse f; (~ bit) foret m, mèche f; (of dentist) roulette f, fraise f; (MIL) exercice m ♦ vt percer; (troops) entraîner ♦ vi (for oil) faire un ou des forage(s)

drink [drɪŋk] (pt **drank**, pp **drunk**) n boisson f; (alcoholic) verre m ♦ vt, vi boire; **to have a ~** boire quelque chose, boire un verre; prendre l'apéritif; a ~ **of water** un verre d'eau; **~er** n buveur(-euse); **~ing water** n eau f potable

drip [drɪp] n goutte f; (MED) goutte-à-goutte m inv, perfusion f ♦ vi tomber goutte à goutte; (tap) goutter; **~-dry** adj (shirt) sans repassage; **~ping** n graisse f de rôti

drive [draɪv] (pt **drove**, pp **driven**) n promenade f ou trajet m en voiture; (also: **~way**) allée f; (energy) dynamisme m, énergie f; (push) effort (concerté), campagne f; (also: **disk ~**) lecteur m de disquettes ♦ vt conduire; (push) chasser, pousser; (TECH: motor, wheel) faire fonctionner; entraîner; (nail, stake etc): **to ~ sth into sth** enfoncer qch dans qch ♦ vi (AUT: at controls) conduire; (: travel) aller en voiture; **left-/right-hand ~** conduite f à gauche/droite; **to ~ sb mad** rendre qn fou (folle); **to ~ sb home/to the airport** reconduire qn chez lui/conduire qn à l'aéroport; **~-by shooting** n (tentative d'assassinat par coups de feu tirés d'un voiture

drivel ['drɪvl] (inf) n idioties fpl

driver ['draɪvə'] n conducteur(-trice); (of taxi, bus) chauffeur m; **~'s license** (US) n permis m de conduire

driveway ['draɪvweɪ] n allée f

driving ['draɪvɪŋ] n conduite f; **~ instructor** n moniteur m d'auto-école; **~ lesson** n leçon f de conduite; **~ licence** (BRIT) n permis m de conduire; **~ school** n auto-école f; **~ test** n examen m du permis de conduire

drizzle ['drɪzl] n bruine f, crachin m

drool [dru:l] vi baver

droop [dru:p] vi (shoulders) tomber; (head) pencher; (flower) pencher la tête

drop [drɔp] n goutte f; (fall) baisse f; (also: **parachute ~**) saut m ♦ vt laisser tomber; (voice, eyes, price) baisser; (set down from car) déposer ♦ vi tomber; **~s** npl (MED) gouttes; **~ off** vi (sleep) s'assoupir ♦ vt (passenger) déposer; **~ out** vi (withdraw) se retirer; (student etc) abandonner, décrocher; **~out** n marginal(e); **~per** n compte-gouttes m inv; **~pings** npl crottes fpl

drought [draut] n sécheresse f

drove [drəuv] pt of **drive**

drown [draun] vt noyer ♦ vi se noyer

drowsy ['drauzɪ] adj somnolent(e)

drug [drʌg] n médicament m; (narcotic) drogue f ♦ vt droguer; **to be on ~s** se droguer; **~ addict** n toxicomane m/f, drogué(e); **~gist** (US) n pharmacien(ne)-droguiste; **~store** (US) n pharmacie-droguerie f, drugstore m

drum [drʌm] n tambour m; (for oil, petrol) bidon m; **~s** npl (kit) batterie f; **~mer** n (joueur de) tambour m

drunk [drʌŋk] pp of **drink** ♦ adj ivre, soûl(e) ♦ n (also: **~ard**) ivrogne m/f; **~en** adj (person) ivre, soûl(e); (rage, stupor) vrognè, d'ivrogne

dry [draɪ] adj sec (sèche); (day) sans pluie; (humour) pince-sans-rire inv; (lake, riverbed, well) à sec ♦ vt sécher; (clothes) faire sécher ♦ vi sécher; **~ up** vi tarir; **~-cleaner's** n teinturerie f; **~er** n séchoir m; (spin-dryer) essoreuse f; **~ness** n sécheresse f; **~ rot** n pourriture sèche (du bois)

DSS n abbr (= Department of Social Security) ≈ Sécurité sociale

DTP n abbr (= desk-top publishing) PAO f

dual ['djuəl] adj double; **~ carriageway** (BRIT) n route f à quatre voies ou à chaussées séparées; **~-purpose** adj à double usage

dubbed [dʌbd] adj (CINEMA) doublé(e)

dubious ['dju:bɪəs] adj hésitant(e), incertain(e); *(reputation, company)* douteux(-euse)

duchess ['dʌtʃɪs] n duchesse f

duck [dʌk] n canard m ♦ vi se baisser vivement, baisser subitement la tête; **~ling** ['dʌklɪŋ] n caneton m

duct [dʌkt] n conduite f, canalisation f; *(ANAT)* conduit m

dud [dʌd] n *(object, tool)*: **it's a ~** c'est de la camelote, ça ne marche pas ♦ adj: **~ cheque** *(BRIT)* chèque sans provision

due [dju:] adj dû (due); *(expected)* attendu(e); *(fitting)* qui convient ♦ n: **to give sb his** (or **her**) **~** être juste envers qn ♦ adv: **~ north** droit vers le nord; **~s** npl *(for club, union)* cotisation f; **in ~ course** en temps utile or voulu; finalement; **~ to** dû à; causé(e) par; **he's ~ to finish tomorrow** normalement il doit finir demain

duet [dju:'ɛt] n duo m

duffel bag ['dʌfl-] n sac m marin

duffel coat n duffel-coat m

dug [dʌg] pt, pp of **dig**

duke [dju:k] n duc m

dull [dʌl] adj terne, morne; *(boring)* ennuyeux(-euse); *(sound, pain)* sourd(e); *(weather, day)* gris(e), maussade ♦ vt *(pain, grief)* atténuer; *(mind, senses)* engourdir

duly ['dju:lɪ] adv *(on time)* en temps voulu; *(as expected)* comme il se doit

dumb [dʌm] adj muet(te); *(stupid)* bête; **~founded** adj sidéré(e)

dummy ['dʌmɪ] n *(tailor's model)* mannequin m; *(mock-up)* factice m, maquette f; *(BRIT: for baby)* tétine f ♦ adj faux (fausse), factice

dump [dʌmp] n *(also: **rubbish ~**)* décharge (publique); *(pej)* trou m ♦ vt *(put down)* déverser; *(get rid of)* se débarrasser de; *(COMPUT: data)* vider, transférer

dumpling ['dʌmplɪŋ] n boulette f *(de pâte)*

dumpy ['dʌmpɪ] adj boulot(te)

dunce [dʌns] n âne m, cancre m

dune [dju:n] n dune f

dung [dʌŋ] n fumier m

dungarees [dʌŋgə'ri:z] npl salopette f; bleu(s) m(pl)

dungeon ['dʌndʒən] n cachot m

duplex ['dju:plɛks] *(US)* n maison jumelée; *(apartment)* duplex m

duplicate [n 'dju:plɪkət, vb 'dju:plɪkeɪt] n double m ♦ vt faire un double de; *(on machine)* polycopier; photocopier; **in ~** en deux exemplaires

durable ['djuərəbl] adj durable; *(clothes, metal)* résistant(e), solide

duration [djuə'reɪʃən] n durée f

during ['djuərɪŋ] prep pendant, au cours de

dusk [dʌsk] n crépuscule m

dust [dʌst] n poussière f ♦ vt *(furniture)* épousseter, essuyer; *(cake etc)*: **to ~ with** saupoudrer de; **~bin** *(BRIT)* n poubelle f; **~er** n chiffon m; **~man** *(BRIT)* *(irreg)* n boueux m, éboueur m; **~y** adj poussiéreux(-euse)

Dutch [dʌtʃ] adj hollandais(e), néerlandais(e) ♦ n *(LING)* hollandais m ♦ adv *(inf)*: **to go ~** partager les frais; **the ~** npl *(people)* les Hollandais; **~man** *(irreg)* n Hollandais m; **~woman** *(irreg)* n Hollandaise f

duty ['dju:tɪ] n devoir m; *(tax)* droit m, taxe f; **on ~** de service; *(at night etc)* de garde; **off ~** libre, pas de service or de garde; **~-free** adj exempté(e) de douane, hors taxe inv

duvet ['du:veɪ] *(BRIT)* n couette f

DVD [di:vi:di:] n abbr (= digital versatile disc) DVD m

dwarf [dwɔ:f] *(pl dwarves)* n nain(e) ♦ vt écraser

dwell [dwɛl] *(pt, pp dwelt)* vi demeurer; **~ on** vt fus s'appesantir sur

dwindle ['dwɪndl] vi diminuer

dye [daɪ] n teinture f ♦ vt teindre

dying ['daɪɪŋ] adj mourant(e), agonisant(e)

dyke [daɪk] *(BRIT)* n digue f

dynamic [daɪ'næmɪk] adj dynamique

dynamite ['daɪnəmaɪt] n dynamite f
dynamo ['daɪnəməu] n dynamo f
dyslexia [dɪs'lɛksɪə] n dyslexie f

E, e

E [iː] n (MUS) mi m

each [iːtʃ] adj chaque ♦ pron chacun(e); ~ **other** l'un(e) l'autre; **they hate ~ other** ils se détestent (mutuellement); **you are jealous of ~ other** vous êtes jaloux l'un de l'autre; **they have 2 books** → ils ont 2 livres chacun

eager ['iːgəʳ] adj (keen) avide; **to be ~ to do sth** avoir très envie de faire; **to be ~ for** désirer vivement, être avide de

eagle ['iːgl] n aigle m

ear [ɪəʳ] n oreille f; (of corn) épi m; **~ache** n mal m aux oreilles; **~drum** n tympan m

earl [əːl] (BRIT) n comte m

earlier ['əːlɪəʳ] adj (date etc) plus rapproché(e); (edition, fashion etc) plus ancien(ne), antérieur(e) ♦ adv plus tôt

early ['əːlɪ] adv tôt, de bonne heure; (ahead of time) en avance; (near the beginning) au début ♦ adj qui se manifeste (or se fait) tôt or de bonne heure; (work) de jeunesse; (settler, Christian) premier(-ère); (reply) rapide; (death) prématuré(e); **to have an ~ night** se coucher tôt or de bonne heure; **in the ~ or ~ in the spring/19th century** au début du printemps/19ème siècle; **~ retirement** n: **to take ~ retirement** prendre sa retraite anticipée

earmark ['ɪəmɑːk] vt: **to ~ sth for** réserver or destiner qch à

earn [əːn] vt gagner; (COMM: yield) rapporter

earnest ['əːnɪst] adj sérieux(-euse); **in ~** ♦ adv sérieusement

earnings ['əːnɪŋz] npl salaire m; (of company) bénéfices mpl

ear: ~phones npl écouteurs mpl; **~ring** n boucle f d'oreille; **~shot** n: **within ~shot** à portée de voix

earth [əːθ] n (gen, also BRIT: ELEC) terre f ♦ vt relier à la terre; **~enware** n poterie f; faïence f; **~quake** n tremblement m de terre, séisme m; **~y** adj (vulgar: humour) truculent(e)

ease [iːz] n facilité f, aisance f; (comfort) bien-être m ♦ vt (soothe) calmer; (loosen) relâcher, détendre; **to ~ sth in/out** faire pénétrer/sortir qch délicatement or avec douceur; faciliter la pénétration/la sortie de qch; **at ~!** (MIL) repos!; **~ off** vi diminuer; (slow down) ralentir

easel ['iːzl] n chevalet m

easily ['iːzɪlɪ] adv facilement

east [iːst] n est m ♦ adj (wind) d'est; (side) est inv ♦ adv à l'est, vers l'est; **the E~** l'Orient m; les pays mpl de l'Est

Easter ['iːstəʳ] n Pâques fpl; **~ egg** n œuf m de Pâques

east: ~erly ['iːstəlɪ] adj (wind) d'est; (direction) est inv; (point) à l'est; **~ern** ['iːstən] adj de l'est, oriental(e); **~ward(s)** ['iːstwəd(z)] adv vers l'est, à l'est

easy ['iːzɪ] adj facile; (manner) aisé(e) ♦ adv: **to take it ~ or things ~** ne pas se fatiguer; (not worry) ne pas (trop) s'en faire; **~ chair** n fauteuil m; **~-going** adj accommodant(e), facile à vivre

eat [iːt] (pt **ate**, pp **eaten**) vt, vi manger; **~ away at, ~ into** vt fus ronger, attaquer; (savings) entamer

eaves [iːvz] npl avant-toit m

eavesdrop ['iːvzdrɒp] vi: **to ~ (on a conversation)** écouter (une conversation) de façon indiscrète

ebb [ɛb] n reflux m ♦ vi refluer; (fig: also: **~ away**) décliner

ebony ['ɛbənɪ] n ébène f

EC n abbr (= European Community) C.E. f

ECB n abbr (= European Central Bank) BCE f

echo ['ɛkəu] (pl **~es**) n écho m ♦ vt répéter ♦ vi résonner, faire écho

eclipse [ɪ'klɪps] n éclipse f

ecology [ɪ'kɔlədʒɪ] n écologie f

e-commerce [ˈiːkɔmɜːs] n commerce m électronique

economic [iːkə'nɔmɪk] adj économique; (business etc) rentable; **~al** adj économique; (person) économe

economics [iːkə'nɔmɪks] n économie f politique ♦ npl (of project, situation) aspect m financier

economize [ɪ'kɔnəmaɪz] vi économiser, faire des économies

economy [ɪ'kɔnəmɪ] n économie f; ~ **class** n classe f touriste; ~ **size** n format m économique

ecstasy ['ekstəsɪ] n extase f (drogue aussi); **ecstatic** [eks'tætɪk] adj extatique

ECU ['eɪkjuː] n abbr (= European Currency Unit) ECU m

eczema ['eksɪmə] n eczéma m

edge [edʒ] n bord m; (of knife etc) tranchant m, fil m ♦ vt border; **on** ~ (fig) crispé(e), tendu(e); **to** ~ **away from** s'éloigner furtivement de; **~ways** adv: **he couldn't get a word in ~ways** il ne pouvait pas placer un mot

edgy ['edʒɪ] adj crispé(e), tendu(e)

edible ['edɪbl] adj comestible

Edinburgh ['edɪnbərə] n Édimbourg

edit ['edɪt] vt (text, book) éditer; (report) préparer; (film) monter; (broadcast) réaliser; **~ion** [ɪ'dɪʃən] n édition f; **~or** n (of column) rédacteur(-trice); (of newspaper) rédacteur(-trice) en chef; (of sb's work) éditeur(-trice); **~orial** [edɪ'tɔːrɪəl] adj de la rédaction, éditorial(e) ♦ n éditorial m

educate ['edjʊkeɪt] vt (teach) instruire; (instruct) éduquer; **~d** adj (person) cultivé(e); **education** [edjʊ'keɪʃən] n éducation f; (studies) études fpl; (teaching) enseignement m, instruction f; **educational** adj (experience, toy) pédagogique; (institution) scolaire; (policy) d'éducation

eel [iːl] n anguille f

eerie ['ɪərɪ] adj inquiétant(e)

effect [ɪ'fekt] n effet m ♦ vt effectuer; **to take** ~ (law) entrer en vigueur, prendre effet; (drug) agir, faire son effet; **in** ~ en fait; **~ive** [ɪ'fektɪv] adj efficace; (actual) véritable; **~ively** adv efficacement; (in reality) effectivement; **~iveness** n efficacité f

effeminate [ɪ'femɪnɪt] adj efféminé(e)

effervescent [efə'vesnt] adj (drink) gazeux(-euse)

efficiency [ɪ'fɪʃənsɪ] n efficacité f; (of machine) rendement m

efficient [ɪ'fɪʃənt] adj efficace; (machine) qui a un bon rendement

effort ['efət] n effort m; **~less** adj (style) aisé(e); (achievement) facile

effusive [ɪ'fjuːsɪv] adj chaleureux(-euse)

e.g. adv abbr (= exempli gratia) par exemple, p. ex.

egg [eg] n œuf m; **hard-boiled/soft-boiled** ~ œuf dur/à la coque; ~ **on** vt pousser; **~cup** n coquetier m; **~plant** n (esp US) aubergine f; **~shell** n coquille f d'œuf

ego ['iːgəʊ] n (self-esteem) amour-propre m

egotism ['egəʊtɪzəm] n égotisme m

egotist ['egəʊtɪst] n égocentrique m/f

Egypt ['iːdʒɪpt] n Égypte f; **~ian** [ɪ'dʒɪpʃən] adj égyptien(ne) ♦ n Égyptien(ne)

eiderdown ['aɪdədaʊn] n édredon m

Eiffel Tower ['aɪfəl-] n tour f Eiffel

eight [eɪt] num huit; **~een** [eɪ'tiːn] num dix-huit; **~h** [eɪtθ] num huitième; **~y** ['eɪtɪ] num quatre-vingt(s)

Eire ['eərə] n République f d'Irlande

either ['aɪðər] adj l'un ou l'autre; (both, each) chaque ♦ pron: ~ (of them) l'un ou l'autre ♦ adv non plus ♦ conj: ~ **good or bad** ou bon ou mauvais, soit bon soit mauvais; **on** ~ **side** de chaque côté; **I don't like** ~ je n'aime ni l'un ni l'autre; **no, I don't** ~ moi non plus

eject [ɪ'dʒekt] vt (tenant etc) expulser;

(*object*) éjecter

elaborate [adj ɪˈlæbərɪt, vb ɪˈlæbəreɪt] adj compliqué(e), recherché(e) ♦ vt élaborer ♦ vi: **to ~ (on)** entrer dans les détails (de)

elastic [ɪˈlæstɪk] adj élastique ♦ n élastique m; **~ band** élastique m

elated [ɪˈleɪtɪd] adj transporté(e) de joie

elation [ɪˈleɪʃən] n allégresse f

elbow [ˈelbəʊ] n coude m

elder [ˈeldər] adj aîné(e) ♦ n (*tree*) sureau m; **one's ~s** ses aînés; **~ly** adj âgé(e) ♦ npl: **the ~ly** les personnes âgées

eldest [ˈeldɪst] adj, n: **the ~ (child)** l'aîné(e) (des enfants)

elect [ɪˈlekt] vt élire ♦ adj: **the president ~** le président désigné; **to ~ to do** choisir de faire; **~ion** n élection f; **~ioneering** [ɪlekʃəˈnɪərɪŋ] n propagande électorale, manœuvres électorales; **~or** n électeur(-trice); **~orate** n électorat m

electric [ɪˈlektrɪk] adj électrique; **~al** adj électrique; **~ blanket** n couverture chauffante; **~ fire** (BRIT) n radiateur m électrique; **~ian** [ɪlekˈtrɪʃən] n électricien m; **~ity** [ɪlekˈtrɪsɪtɪ] n électricité f; **electrify** [ɪˈlektrɪfaɪ] vt (RAIL, fence) électrifier; (*audience*) électriser

electronic [ɪlekˈtrɒnɪk] adj électronique; **~ mail** n courrier m électronique; **~s** n électronique f

elegant [ˈelɪgənt] adj élégant(e)

element [ˈelɪmənt] n (gen) élément m; (of heater, kettle etc) résistance f; **~ary** [elɪˈmentərɪ] adj élémentaire; (school, education) primaire

elephant [ˈelɪfənt] n éléphant m

elevation [elɪˈveɪʃən] n (raising, promotion) avancement m, promotion f; (height) hauteur f

elevator [ˈelɪveɪtər] n (in warehouse etc) élévateur m, monte-charge m inv; (US: lift) ascenseur m

eleven [ɪˈlevn] num onze; **~ses** [ɪˈlevnzɪz] npl ≈ pause-café f; **~th** num

onzième

elicit [ɪˈlɪsɪt] vt: **to ~ (from)** obtenir (de), arracher (à)

eligible [ˈelɪdʒəbl] adj: **to be ~ for** remplir les conditions requises pour; **an ~ young man/woman** un beau parti

elm [elm] n orme m

elongated [ˈiːlɒŋgeɪtɪd] adj allongé(e)

elope [ɪˈləʊp] vi (lovers) s'enfuir (ensemble)

eloquent [ˈeləkwənt] adj éloquent(e)

else [els] adv d'autre; **something ~** quelque chose d'autre, autre chose; **somewhere ~** ailleurs, autre part; **everywhere ~** partout ailleurs; **nobody ~** personne d'autre; **where ~?** à quel autre endroit?; **little ~** pas grand-chose d'autre; **~where** adv ailleurs, autre part

elude [ɪˈluːd] vt échapper à

elusive [ɪˈluːsɪv] adj insaisissable

emaciated [ɪˈmeɪsɪeɪtɪd] adj émacié(e), décharné(e)

e-mail [ˈiːmeɪl] n courrier m électronique ♦ vt (person) envoyer un message électronique à

emancipate [ɪˈmænsɪpeɪt] vt émanciper

embankment [ɪmˈbæŋkmənt] n (of road, railway) remblai m, talus m; (of river) berge f, quai m

embark [ɪmˈbɑːk] vi embarquer; **to ~ on** (journey) entreprendre; (fig) se lancer or s'embarquer dans; **~ation** [embɑːˈkeɪʃən] n embarquement m

embarrass [ɪmˈbærəs] vt embarrasser, gêner; **~ed** adj gêné(e); **~ing** adj gênant(e), embarrassant(e); **~ment** n embarras m, gêne f

embassy [ˈembəsɪ] n ambassade f

embedded [ɪmˈbedɪd] adj enfoncé(e)

embellish [ɪmˈbelɪʃ] vt orner, décorer; (fig: account) enjoliver

embers [ˈembəz] npl braise f

embezzle [ɪmˈbezl] vt détourner; **~ment** n détournement m de fonds

embitter [ɪmˈbɪtər] vt (person) aigrir;

(relations) envenimer

embody [ɪm'bɔdɪ] vt *(features)* réunir, comprendre; *(ideas)* formuler, exprimer

embossed [ɪm'bɔst] adj *(metal)* estampé(e); *(leather)* frappé(e); **~ wallpaper** papier gaufré

embrace [ɪm'breɪs] vt embrasser, étreindre; *(include)* embrasser ♦ vi s'étreindre, s'embrasser ♦ n étreinte f

embroider [ɪm'brɔɪdə^r] vt broder; **~y** n broderie f

emerald ['emərəld] n émeraude f

emerge [ɪ'mɜːdʒ] vi apparaître; *(from room, car)* surgir; *(from sleep, imprisonment)* sortir

emergency [ɪ'mɜːdʒənsɪ] n urgence f; **in an ~** en cas d'urgence; **~ cord** n sonnette f d'alarme; **~ exit** n sortie f de secours; **~ landing** n atterrissage forcé; **~ services** npl: **the ~ services** *(fire, police, ambulance)* les services mpl d'urgence

emery board ['emərɪ-] n lime f à ongles *(en carton émerisé)*

emigrate ['emɪgreɪt] vi émigrer

eminent ['emɪnənt] adj éminent(e)

emissions [ɪ'mɪʃənz] npl émissions fpl

emit [ɪ'mɪt] vt émettre

emotion [ɪ'məʊʃən] n émotion f; **~al** adj *(person)* émotif(-ive), très sensible; *(needs, exhaustion)* affectif(-ive); *(scene)* émouvant(e); *(tone, speech)* qui fait appel aux sentiments; **emotive** adj chargé(e) d'émotion; *(subject)* sensible

emperor ['empərə^r] n empereur m

emphasis ['emfəsɪs] *(pl* **-ases)** n *(stress)* accent m; *(importance)* insistance f

emphasize ['emfəsaɪz] vt *(syllable, word, point)* appuyer or insister sur; *(feature)* souligner, accentuer

emphatic [ɛm'fætɪk] adj *(strong)* énergique, vigoureux(-euse); *(unambiguous, clear)* catégorique

empire ['empaɪə^r] n empire m

employ [ɪm'plɔɪ] vt employer; **~ee** n employé(e); **~er** n employeur(-euse);

~ment n emploi m; **~ment agency** n agence f or bureau m de placement

empower [ɪm'paʊə^r] vt: **to ~ sb to do** autoriser or habiliter qn à faire

empress ['emprɪs] n impératrice f

emptiness ['emptɪnɪs] n *(of area, region)* aspect m désertique m; *(of life)* vide m, vacuité f

empty ['emptɪ] adj vide; *(threat, promise)* en l'air, vain(e) ♦ vt vider ♦ vi se vider; *(liquid)* s'écouler; **~-handed** adj les mains vides

EMU n abbr *(= economic and monetary union)* UME f

emulate ['emjʊleɪt] vt rivaliser avec, imiter

emulsion [ɪ'mʌlʃən] n émulsion f; *(also:* **~ paint)** peinture mate

enable [ɪ'neɪbl] vt: **to ~ sb to do** permettre à qn de faire

enamel [ɪ'næməl] n émail m; *(also:* **~ paint)** peinture laquée

enchant [ɪn'tʃɑːnt] vt enchanter; **~ing** adj ravissant(e), enchanteur(-teresse)

encl. abbr = **enclosed**

enclose [ɪn'kləʊz] vt *(land)* clôturer; *(space, object)* entourer; *(letter etc)*: **to ~ (with)** joindre (à); **please find ~d** veuillez trouver ci-joint; **enclosure** n enceinte f

encompass [ɪn'kʌmpəs] vt *(include)* contenir, inclure

encore [ɔŋ'kɔːr] excl bis ♦ n bis m

encounter [ɪn'kaʊntə^r] n rencontre f ♦ vt rencontrer

encourage [ɪn'kʌrɪdʒ] vt encourager; **~ment** n encouragement m

encroach [ɪn'krəʊtʃ] vi: **to ~ (up)on** empiéter sur

encyclop(a)edia [ensaɪkləʊ'piːdɪə] n encyclopédie f

end [end] n *(gen, also: aim)* fin f; *(of table, street, rope etc)* bout m, extrémité f ♦ vt terminer; *(also:* **bring to an ~, put an ~ to)** mettre fin à ♦ vi se terminer, finir; **in the ~** finalement; **on ~** *(object)* debout, dressé(e); **to stand on ~**

(hair) se dresser sur la tête; **for hours on ~** pendant des heures et des heures; **~ up** vi: to **~ up in** (condition) finir or se terminer par; (place) finir or aboutir à

endanger [ɪnˈdeɪndʒəʳ] vt mettre en danger; **an ~ed species** une espèce en voie de disparition

endearing [ɪnˈdɪərɪŋ] adj attachant(e)

endeavour [ɪnˈdɛvəʳ] (US **endeavor**) n tentative f, effort m ♦ vi: **to ~ to do** tenter or s'efforcer de faire

ending [ˈɛndɪŋ] n dénouement m, fin f; (LING) terminaison f

endive [ˈɛndaɪv] n chicorée f; (smooth) endive f

endless [ˈɛndlɪs] adj sans fin, interminable

endorse [ɪnˈdɔːs] vt (cheque) endosser; (approve) appuyer, approuver, sanctionner; **~ment** n (approval) appui m, aval m; (BRIT: on driving licence) contravention portée au permis de conduire

endure [ɪnˈdjʊəʳ] vt supporter, endurer ♦ vi durer

enemy [ˈɛnəmɪ] adj, n ennemi(e)

energetic [ɛnəˈdʒɛtɪk] adj énergique; (activity) qui fait se dépenser (physiquement)

energy [ˈɛnədʒɪ] n énergie f

enforce [ɪnˈfɔːs] vt (law) appliquer, faire respecter

engage [ɪnˈgeɪdʒ] vt engager; (attention etc) retenir ♦ vi (TECH) s'enclencher, s'engrener; **to ~ in** se lancer dans; **~d** adj (BRIT: busy, in use) occupé(e); (betrothed) fiancé(e); **to get ~d** se fiancer; **~d tone** n (TEL) tonalité f occupé inv or pas libre; **~ment** n obligation f, engagement m; rendez-vous m inv; (to marry) fiançailles fpl; **~ment ring** n bague f de fiançailles; **en·gaging** adj engageant(e), attirant(e)

engine [ˈɛndʒɪn] n (AUT) moteur m; (RAIL) locomotive f; **~ driver** n mécanicien m

engineer [ɛndʒɪˈnɪəʳ] n ingénieur n;

(BRIT: repairer) dépanneur m; (NAVY, US RAIL) mécanicien m; **~ing** n engineering m, ingénierie f; (of bridges, ships) génie m; (of machine) mécanique f

England [ˈɪŋɡlənd] n Angleterre f; **English** adj anglais(e) ♦ n (LING) anglais m; **the English** npl (people) les Anglais; **the English Channel** la Manche; **Englishman** (irreg) n Anglais; **Englishwoman** (irreg) n Anglaise f

engraving [ɪnˈɡreɪvɪŋ] n gravure f

engrossed [ɪnˈɡrəust] adj: **~ in** absorbé(e) par, plongé(e) dans

engulf [ɪnˈɡʌlf] vt engloutir

enhance [ɪnˈhɑːns] vt rehausser, mettre en valeur

enjoy [ɪnˈdʒɔɪ] vt aimer, prendre plaisir à; (have: health, fortune) jouir de; (: success) connaître; **to ~ o.s.** s'amuser; **~able** adj agréable; **~ment** n plaisir m

enlarge [ɪnˈlɑːdʒ] vt accroître; (PHOT) agrandir ♦ vi: **to ~ on** (subject) s'étendre sur; **~ment** [ɪnˈlɑːdʒmənt] n (PHOT) agrandissement m

enlighten [ɪnˈlaɪtn] vt éclairer; **~ed** adj éclairé(e); **~ment** n: **the E~ment** (HISTORY) ≃ le Siècle des lumières

enlist [ɪnˈlɪst] vt recruter; (support) s'assurer ♦ vi s'engager

enmity [ˈɛnmɪtɪ] n inimitié f

enormous [ɪˈnɔːməs] adj énorme

enough [ɪˈnʌf] adj, pron: **~ time/books** assez or suffisamment de temps/livres ♦ adv: **big ~** assez or suffisamment grand; **have you got ~?** en avez-vous assez?; **he has not worked ~** il n'a pas assez or suffisamment travaillé; **to eat ~** assez à manger; **~!** assez!, ça suffit!; **that's ~, thanks** cela suffit or c'est assez, merci; **I've had ~ of him** j'en ai assez de lui; **... which, funnily** or **oddly ~** ... qui, chose curieuse

enquire [ɪnˈkwaɪəʳ] vt, vi = **inquire**

enrage [ɪnˈreɪdʒ] vt mettre en fureur or en rage, rendre furieux(-euse)

enrol [ɪnˈrəul] (US **enroll**) vt inscrire ♦ vi s'inscrire; **~ment** n (US **enrollment**) n inscription f

en suite [ˈɒnswiːt] *adj*: **with ~ bath-room** avec salle de bains en attenante

ensure [ɪnˈʃʊəʳ] *vt* assurer; garantir; **to ~ that** s'assurer que

entail [ɪnˈteɪl] *vt* entraîner, occasionner

entangled [ɪnˈtæŋgld] *adj*: **to become ~ (in)** s'empêtrer (dans)

enter [ˈentəʳ] *vt (room)* entrer dans, pénétrer dans; *(club, army)* entrer à; *(competition)* s'inscrire à or pour; *(sb for a competition)* (faire) inscrire; *(write down)* inscrire, noter; *(COMPUT)* entrer, introduire ♦ *vi* entrer; **~ for** *vt fus* s'inscrire à, se présenter pour or à; **~ into** *vt fus (explanation)* se lancer dans; *(discussion, negotiations)* entamer; *(agreement)* conclure

enterprise [ˈentəpraɪz] *n* entreprise f; *(initiative)* (esprit m d')initiative f; **free ~** libre entreprise f; **private ~** entreprise privée; **enterprising** *adj* entreprenant(e), dynamique; *(scheme)* audacieux(-euse)

entertain [entəˈteɪn] *vt* amuser, distraire; *(invite)* recevoir (à dîner); *(idea, plan)* envisager; **~er** *n* artiste *m/f* de variétés; **~ing** *adj* amusant(e), distrayant(e); **~ment** *n (amusement)* divertissement *m*, amusement *m*; *(show)* spectacle *m*

enthralled [ɪnˈθrɔːld] *adj* captivé(e)

enthusiasm [ɪnˈθuːzɪæzəm] *n* enthousiasme *m*

enthusiast [ɪnˈθuːzɪæst] *n* enthousiaste *m/f*; **~ic** [ɪnθuːzɪˈæstɪk] *adj* enthousiaste; **to be ~ic about** être enthousiasmé(e) par

entire [ɪnˈtaɪəʳ] *adj* (tout) entier(-ère), *~ly adv* entièrement, complètement; **~ty** [ɪnˈtaɪərətɪ] *n*: **in its ~ty** dans sa totalité

entitle [ɪnˈtaɪtl] *vt*: **to ~ sb to sth** donner droit à qch à qn; **~d** [ɪnˈtaɪtld] *adj (book)* intitulé(e); **to be ~d to do** avoir le droit de or être habilité à faire

entrance [*n* ˈentrns, *vb* ɪnˈtrɑːns] *n* en-

trée f ♦ *vt* enchanter, ravir; **to gain ~ to** *(university etc)* être admis à; **~ examination** *n* examen m d'entrée; **~ fee** *n (to museum etc)* prix m d'entrée; *(to join club etc)* droit m d'inscription; **~ ramp** *(US) n (AUT)* bretelle f d'accès; **entrant** *n* participant(e); concurrent(e); *(BRIT: in exam)* candidat(e)

entrenched [enˈtrentʃt] *adj* retranché(e); *(ideas)* arrêté(e)

entrepreneur [ˈɒntrəprəˈnəːʳ] *n* entrepreneur *m*

entrust [ɪnˈtrʌst] *vt*: **to ~ sth to** confier qch à

entry [ˈentrɪ] *n* entrée f; *(in register)* inscription f; **no ~** défense d'entrer, entrée interdite; *(AUT)* sens interdit; **~ form** *n* feuille f d'inscription; **~ phone** *(BRIT) n* interphone *m*

envelop [ɪnˈvɛləp] *vt* envelopper

envelope [ˈenvələup] *n* enveloppe f

envious [ˈenvɪəs] *adj* envieux(-euse)

environment [ɪnˈvaɪərnmənt] *n* environnement *m*; *(social, moral)* milieu *m*; **~al** [ɪnvaɪərnˈmentl] *adj* écologique; du milieu; **~-friendly** *adj* écologique

envisage [ɪnˈvɪzɪdʒ] *vt (foresee)* prévoir

envoy [ˈenvɔɪ] *n (diplomat)* ministre *m* plénipotentiaire

envy [ˈenvɪ] *n* envie f ♦ *vt* envier; **to ~ sb sth** envier qch à qn

epic [ˈepɪk] *n* épopée f ♦ *adj* épique

epidemic [epɪˈdemɪk] *n* épidémie f

epilepsy [ˈepɪlepsɪ] *n* épilepsie f; **epi-leptic** *n* épileptique *m/f*

episode [ˈepɪsəud] *n* épisode *m*

epitome [ɪˈpɪtəmɪ] *n* modèle *m*; **epito-mize** *vt* incarner

equal [ˈiːkwl] *adj* égal(e) ♦ *n* égal(e) ♦ *vt* égaler; **~ to** *(task)* à la hauteur de; **~ity** [iːˈkwɒlɪtɪ] *n* égalité f; **~ize** *vi (SPORT)* égaliser; **~ly** *adv* également; *(just as)* tout aussi

equanimity [ekwəˈnɪmɪtɪ] *n* égalité f d'humeur

equate [ɪˈkweɪt] *vt*: **to ~ sth with** comparer qch à; assimiler qch à; **equa-**

tion n (MATH) équation f

equator [ı'kweıtə^r] n équateur m

equilibrium [i:kwı'lıbrıəm] n équilibre m

equip [ı'kwıp] vt: **to ~ (with)** équiper (de); **to be well ~ped** être bien équipé(e); **~ment** n équipement m; (electrical etc) appareillage m, installation f

equities ['ekwıtız] npl (BRIT) (COMM) actions cotées en Bourse

equivalent [ı'kwıvələnt] adj: **~ (to)** équivalent(e) (à) ♦ n équivalent m

era ['ıərə] n ère f, époque f

eradicate [ı'rædıkeıt] vt éliminer

erase [ı'reız] vt effacer; **~r** n gomme f

erect [ı'rekt] adj droit(e) ♦ vt construire; (monument) ériger, élever; (tent etc) dresser; **~ion** n érection f

ERM n abbr (= Exchange Rate Mechanism) MTC m

erode [ı'rəud] vt éroder; (metal) ronger

erotic [ı'rɔtık] adj érotique

errand ['erənd] n course f, commission f

erratic [ı'rætık] adj irrégulier(-ère); inconstant(e)

error ['erə^r] n erreur f

erupt [ı'rʌpt] vi entrer en éruption; (fig) éclater; **~ion** n éruption f

escalate ['eskəleıt] vi s'intensifier

escalator ['eskəleıtə^r] n escalier roulant

escapade [eskə'peıd] n (misdeed) fredaine f; (adventure) équipée f

escape [ıs'keıp] n fuite f; (from prison) évasion f ♦ vi s'échapper, fuir; (from jail) s'évader; (fig) s'en tirer; (leak) s'échapper ♦ vt échapper à; **to ~ from** (person) échapper à; (place) s'échapper de; (fig) fuir; **escapism** n (fig) évasion f

escort [n 'eskɔːt, vb ıs'kɔːt] n escorte f ♦ vt escorter

Eskimo ['eskıməu] n Esquimau(de)

especially [ıs'peʃlı] adv (particularly) particulièrement; (above all) surtout

espionage ['espıəna:ʒ] n espionnage m

Esquire [ıs'kwaıə^r] n: **J Brown, ~ Monsieur** J. Brown

essay ['eseı] n (SCOL) dissertation f; (LITERATURE) essai m

essence ['esns] n essence f

essential [ı'senʃl] adj essentiel(le); (basic) fondamental(e) ♦ n: **~s** éléments essentiels; **~ly** adv essentiellement

establish [ıs'tæblıʃ] vt établir; (business) fonder, créer; (one's power etc) asseoir, affermir; **~ed** adj bien établi(e); **~ment** n établissement m; (founding) création f

estate [ıs'teıt] n (land) domaine m, propriété f; (LAW) biens mpl, succession f; (BRIT: also: **housing ~**) lotissement m, cité f; **~ agent** n agent immobilier; **~ car** (BRIT) n break m

esteem [ıs'ti:m] n estime f

esthetic [ıs'θetık] (US) adj = **aesthetic**

estimate [n 'estımət, vb 'estımeıt] n estimation f; (COMM) devis m ♦ vt estimer; **estimation** [estı'meıʃən] n opinion f; (calculation) estimation f

estranged [ıs'treındʒd] adj séparé(e); dont on s'est séparé(e)

etc. abbr (= et cetera) etc

eternal [ı'tə:nl] adj éternel(le)

eternity [ı'tə:nıtı] n éternité f

ethical ['eθıkl] adj moral(e); **ethics** n éthique f ♦ npl moralité f

Ethiopia [i:θı'əupıə] n Éthiopie f

ethnic ['eθnık] adj ethnique; (music etc) folklorique; **~ minority** minorité f ethnique

ethos ['i:θɔs] n génie m

etiquette ['etıket] n convenances fpl, étiquette f

EU n abbr (= European Union) UE f

euro ['juərəu] n (currency) euro m

Euroland ['juərəulænd] n Euroland m

Eurocheque ['juərəutʃek] n eurochèque m

Europe ['juərəp] n Europe f; **~an** [juərə'pi:ən] adj européen(ne) ♦ n Européen(ne); **~an Community** Communauté européenne

evacuate [ɪ'vækjueɪt] vt évacuer

evade [ɪ'veɪd] vt échapper à; (question etc) éluder; (duties) se dérober à; **to ~ tax** frauder le fisc

evaporate [ɪ'væpəreɪt] vi s'évaporer; **~d milk** n lait condensé non sucré

evasion [ɪ'veɪʒən] n dérobade f; **tax ~** fraude fiscale

eve [i:v] n: **on the ~ of** à la veille de

even ['i:vn] adj (level, smooth) régulier(-ère); (equal) égal(e); (number) pair(e) ♦ adv même; **~ if** même si +indic; **~ though** alors même que +cond; **~ more** encore plus; **~ so** quand même; **not ~** pas même; **to get ~ with sb** prendre sa revanche sur qn

evening ['i:vnɪŋ] n soir m; (as duration, event) soirée f; **in the ~** le soir; **~ class** n cours m du soir; **~ dress** n tenue f de soirée

event [ɪ'vent] n événement m; (SPORT) épreuve f; **in the ~ of** en cas de; **~ful** adj mouvementé(e)

eventual [ɪ'ventʃuəl] adj final(e); **~ity** [ɪventʃu'ælɪtɪ] n possibilité f, éventualité f; **~ly** adv finalement

ever ['evə'] adv jamais; (at all times) toujours; **the best ~** le meilleur qu'on ait jamais vu; **have you ~ seen it?** l'as-tu déjà vu?, as-tu eu l'occasion or c'est-il arrivé de le voir?; **why ~ not?** mais enfin, pourquoi pas?; **~ since** adv depuis ♦ conj depuis que; **~green** n arbre m à feuilles persistantes; **~lasting** adj éternel(le)

every ['evrɪ] adj chaque; **~ day** tous les jours, chaque jour; **~ other/third day** tous les deux/trois jours; **~ other car** une voiture sur deux; **~ now and then** de temps en temps; **~body** pron tout le monde, tous pl; **~day** adj quotidien(ne), de tous les jours; **~one** pron = **everybody**; **~thing** pron tout; **~where** adv partout

evict [ɪ'vɪkt] vt expulser; **~ion** n expulsion f

evidence ['evɪdns] n (proof) preuve(s)

f(pl); (of witness) témoignage m; (sign): **to show ~** présenter des signes de; **to give ~** témoigner, déposer

evident ['evɪdnt] adj évident(e); **~ly** adv de toute évidence; (apparently) apparemment

evil ['i:vl] adj mauvais(e) ♦ n mal m

evoke [ɪ'vəuk] vt évoquer

evolution [i:və'lu:ʃən] n évolution f

evolve [ɪ'vɔlv] vt élaborer ♦ vi évoluer

ewe [ju:] n brebis f

ex- [eks] prefix ex-

exact [ɪg'zækt] adj exact(e) ♦ vt: **to ~ sth (from)** extorquer qch (à); exiger qch (de); **~ing** adj exigeant(e); (work) astreignant(e); **~ly** adv exactement

exaggerate [ɪg'zædʒəreɪt] vt, vi exagérer; **exaggeration** [ɪgzædʒə'reɪʃən] n exagération f

exalted [ɪg'zɔ:ltɪd] adj (prominent) élevé(e); (: person) haut placé(e)

exam [ɪg'zæm] n abbr (SCOL) = **examination**

examination [ɪgzæmɪ'neɪʃən] n (SCOL, MED) examen m

examine [ɪg'zæmɪn] vt (gen) examiner; (SCOL: person) interroger; **~r** n examinateur(-trice)

example [ɪg'zɑ:mpl] n exemple m; **for ~** par exemple

exasperate [ɪg'zɑ:spəreɪt] vt exaspérer; **exasperation** [ɪgzɑ:spə'reɪʃən] n exaspération f, irritation f

excavate ['ekskəveɪt] vt creuser; **excavation** [ekskə'veɪʃən] n fouilles fpl

exceed [ɪk'si:d] vt dépasser; (one's powers) outrepasser; **~ingly** adv extrêmement

excellent ['eksələnt] adj excellent(e)

except [ɪk'sept] prep (also: **~ for**, **~ing**) sauf, excepté ♦ vt excepter; **~ if/when** sauf si/quand; **~ that** sauf si, ce n'est que; **~ion** n exception f; **to take ~ion to** s'offusquer de; **~ional** adj exceptionnel(le)

excerpt ['eksə:pt] n extrait m

excess [ɪk'ses] n excès m; **~ baggage**

n excédent *m* de bagages; **~ fare** (BRIT) *n* supplément *m*; **~ive** *adj* excessif(-ive)

exchange [ɪksˈtʃeɪndʒ] *n* échange *m*; (also: **telephone ~**) central *m* ♦ *vt* (**for**) échanger (contre); **~ rate** *n* taux *m* de change

Exchequer [ɪksˈtʃɛkəʳ] (BRIT) *n*: **the ~** l'Échiquier *m*, ≃ le ministère des Finances

excise [*n* ˈɛksaɪz, *vb* ɛkˈsaɪz] *n* taxe *f* ♦ *vt* exciser

excite [ɪkˈsaɪt] *vt* exciter; **to get ~d** s'exciter; **~ment** *n* excitation *f*; **exciting** *adj* passionnant(e)

exclaim [ɪksˈkleɪm] *vi* s'exclamer; **exclamation** [ɛksklǝˈmeɪʃǝn] *n* exclamation *f*; **exclamation mark** *n* point *m* d'exclamation

exclude [ɪksˈkluːd] *vt* exclure; **exclusion zone** *n* zone interdite; **exclusive** *adj* exclusif(-ive); (*club, district*) sélect(e); (*item of news*) en exclusivité; **exclusive of VAT** TVA non comprise; **mutually exclusive** qui s'excluent l'un(e) l'autre

excruciating [ɪksˈkruːʃɪeɪtɪŋ] *adj* atroce

excursion [ɪksˈkəːʃǝn] *n* excursion *f*

excuse [*n* ɪksˈkjuːs, *vb* ɪksˈkjuːz] *n* excuse *f* ♦ *vt* excuser; **to ~ sb from** (*activity*) dispenser qn de; **~ me!** excusez-moi!, pardon!; **now if you will ~ me, ...** maintenant, si vous (le) permettez ...

ex-directory [ˈɛksdɪˈrɛktǝrɪ] (BRIT) *adj* sur la liste rouge

execute [ˈɛksɪkjuːt] *vt* exécuter; **execution** *n* exécution *f*

executive [ɪgˈzɛkjutɪv] *n* (COMM) cadre *m*; (*of organization, political party*) bureau *m* ♦ *adj* exécutif(-ive)

exemplify [ɪgˈzɛmplɪfaɪ] *vt* illustrer; (*typify*) incarner

exempt [ɪgˈzɛmpt] *adj*: **~ from** exempté(e) *or* dispensé(e) de ♦ *vt*: **to ~ sb from** exempter *or* dispenser qn de

exercise [ˈɛksǝsaɪz] *n* exercice *m* ♦ *vt* exercer; (*patience etc*) faire preuve de; (*dog*) promener ♦ *vi* prendre de l'exercice; **~ book** *n* cahier *m*

exert [ɪgˈzəːt] *vt* exercer, employer; **to ~ o.s.** se dépenser; **~ion** *n* effort *m*

exhale [ɛksˈheɪl] *vt* exhaler ♦ *vi* expirer

exhaust [ɪgˈzɔːst] *n* (also: **~ fumes**) gaz *mpl* d'échappement; (also: **~ pipe**) tuyau *m* d'échappement ♦ *vt* épuiser; **~ed** *adj* épuisé(e); **~ion** *n* épuisement *m*; **nervous ~ion** fatigue nerveuse; surmental; **~ive** *adj* très complet(-ète)

exhibit [ɪgˈzɪbɪt] *n* (ART) pièce exposée, objet exposé; (LAW) pièce à conviction ♦ *vt* exposer; (*courage, skill*) faire preuve de; **~ion** [ɛksɪˈbɪʃǝn] *n* exposition *f*; (*of ill-temper, talent etc*) démonstration *f*

exhilarating [ɪgˈzɪlǝreɪtɪŋ] *adj* grisant(e); stimulant(e)

ex-husband *n* ex-mari *m*

exile [ˈɛksaɪl] *n* exil *m*; (*person*) exilé(e) ♦ *vt* exiler

exist [ɪgˈzɪst] *vi* exister; **~ence** *n* existence *f*; **~ing** *adj* actuel(le)

exit [ˈɛksɪt] *n* sortie *f* ♦ *vi* (COMPUT, THEATRE) sortir; **~ poll** *n* sondage *m* (fait à la sortie de l'isoloir); **~ ramp** *n* (AUT) bretelle *f* d'accès

exodus [ˈɛksǝdǝs] *n* exode *m*

exonerate [ɪgˈzɔnǝreɪt] *vt*: **to ~ from** disculper de

exotic [ɪgˈzɔtɪk] *adj* exotique

expand [ɪksˈpænd] *vt* agrandir; accroître ♦ *vi* (*trade etc*) se développer, s'accroître; (*gas, metal*) se dilater

expanse [ɪksˈpæns] *n* étendue *f*

expansion [ɪksˈpænʃǝn] *n* développement *m*, accroissement *m*

expect [ɪksˈpɛkt] *vt* (*anticipate*) s'attendre à, s'attendre à ce que *+sub*; (*count on*) compter sur, escompter; (*require*) demander, exiger; (*suppose*) supposer; (*await, also baby*) attendre ♦ *vi*: **to be ~ing** être enceinte; **~ancy** *n* (*anticipation*) attente *f*; **life ~ancy** espérance *f* de vie; **~ant mother** *n* future maman; **~ation** [ɛkspɛkˈteɪʃǝn] *n* attente *f*; espérance(s) *f(pl)*

expedient [ɪksˈpiːdɪǝnt] *adj* indiqué(e),

opportun(e) ♦ *n* expédient *m*

expedition [ɛkspə'dɪʃən] *n* expédition *f*

expel [ɪks'pɛl] *vt* chasser, expulser; (SCOL) renvoyer

expend [ɪks'pɛnd] *vt* consacrer; (money) dépenser; **~iture** [ɪks'pɛndɪtʃər] *n* dépense *f*, dépenses *fpl*

expense [ɪks'pɛns] *n* dépense *f*, frais *mpl*; (high cost) coût *m*; **~s** *npl* (COMM) frais *mpl*; **at the ~ of** aux dépens de; **~ account** *n* (note *f* de) frais *mpl*; **expensive** *adj* cher (chère), coûteux (-euse); **to be expensive** coûter cher

experience [ɪks'pɪərɪəns] *n* expérience *f* ♦ *vt* connaître, faire l'expérience de; (feeling) éprouver; **~d** *adj* expérimenté(e)

experiment [ɪks'pɛrɪmənt] *n* expérience *f* ♦ *vi* faire une expérience; **to ~ with** expérimenter

expert ['ɛkspəːt] *adj* expert(e) ♦ *n* expert *m*; **~ise** [ɛkspəː'tiːz] *n* (grande) compétence *f*

expire [ɪks'paɪər] *vi* expirer; **expiry** *n* expiration *f*

explain [ɪks'pleɪn] *vt* expliquer; **explanation** [ɛksplə'neɪʃən] *n* explication *f*; **explanatory** [ɪks'plænətrɪ] *adj* explicatif(-ive)

explicit [ɪks'plɪsɪt] *adj* explicite; (definite) formel(le)

explode [ɪks'pləud] *vi* exploser

exploit [*n* 'ɛksplɔɪt, *vb* ɪks'plɔɪt] *n* exploit *m* ♦ *vt* exploiter; **~ation** [ɛksplɔɪ'teɪʃən] *n* exploitation *f*

exploratory [ɪks'plɔrətrɪ] *adj* (expedition) d'exploration; (fig: talks) préliminaire

explore [ɪks'plɔːr] *vt* explorer; (possibilities) étudier, examiner; **~r** *n* explorateur(-trice)

explosion [ɪks'pləuʒən] *n* explosion *f*; **explosive** *adj* explosif(-ive) ♦ *n* explosif *m*

exponent [ɪks'pəunənt] *n* (of school of thought etc) interprète *m*, représentant *m*

export [*vb* ɛks'pɔːt, *n* 'ɛkspɔːt] *vt* exporter ♦ *n* exportation *f* ♦ *cpd* d'exportation; **~er** *n* exportateur *m*

expose [ɪks'pəuz] *vt* exposer; (unmask) démasquer, dévoiler; **~d** *adj* (position, house) exposé(e); **exposure** *n*: exposition *f*; (publicity) couverture *f*; (PHOT) (temps *m* de) pose *f*; (: shot) pose; **to die from exposure** (MED) mourir de froid; **exposure meter** *n* posemètre *m*

express [ɪks'prɛs] *adj* (definite) formel(le), exprès(-esse); (BRIT: letter etc) exprès *inv* ♦ *n* (train) rapide *m*; (bus) car *m* express ♦ *vt* exprimer; **~ion** *n* expression *f*; **~ly** *adv* expressément, formellement; **~way** *n* (US) *n* (urban motorway) voie *f* express (à plusieurs files)

exquisite [ɛks'kwɪzɪt] *adj* exquis(e)

extend [ɪks'tɛnd] *vt* (visit, street) prolonger; (building) agrandir; (offer) présenter, offrir; (hand, arm) tendre ♦ *vi* s'étendre; **extension** *n* prolongation *f*; agrandissement *m*; (building) annexe *f*; (to wire, table) rallonge *f*; (telephone: in offices) poste *m*; (: in private house) téléphone *m* supplémentaire; **extensive** *adj* étendu(e), vaste; (damage, alterations) considérable; (inquiries) approfondi(e); **extensively** *adv*: **he's travelled extensively** il a beaucoup voyagé

extent [ɪks'tɛnt] *n* étendue *f*; **to some ~** dans une certaine mesure; **to what ~?** dans quelle mesure?, jusqu'à quel point?; **to the ~ of ...** au point de ...; **to such an ~ that ...** à tel point que ...

extenuating [ɪks'tɛnjueɪtɪŋ] *adj*: **~ circumstances** circonstances atténuantes

exterior [ɛks'tɪərɪər] *adj* extérieur(e) ♦ *n* extérieur *m*; dehors *m*

external [ɛks'təːnl] *adj* externe

extinct [ɪks'tɪŋkt] *adj* éteint(e)

extinguish [ɪks'tɪŋgwɪʃ] *vt* éteindre

extort [ɪks'tɔːt] *vt*: **to ~ sth (from)** extorquer qch (à); **~ionate** *adj* exorbitant(e)

extra ['ɛkstrə] *adj* supplémentaire, de plus ♦ *adv* (in addition) en plus ♦ *n* sup-

extract [vb ɪks'trækt, n 'ekstrækt] vt extraire; (tooth) arracher; (money, promise) soutirer ♦ n extrait m

extracurricular ['ekstrəkə'rɪkjulə*] adj parascolaire

extradite ['ekstrədaɪt] vt extrader

extra...: ~**marital** ['ekstrə'mærɪtl] adj extra-conjugal(e); ~**mural** ['ekstrə'mjuərl] adj hors faculté inv; (lecture) public(-que); ~**ordinary** [ɪks'trɔ:dnrɪ] adj extraordinaire

extravagance [ɪks'trævəgəns] n prodigalités fpl; (thing bought) folie f, dépense excessive; **extravagant** adj extravagant(e); (in spending: person) prodigue, dépensier(-ère); (: tastes) dispendieux (-euse)

extreme [ɪks'tri:m] adj extrême ♦ n extrême m; ~**ly** adv extrêmement; **extremist** adj, n extrémiste m/f

extricate ['ekstrɪkeɪt] vt: **to ~ sth (from)** dégager qch (de)

extrovert ['ekstrəvɜːt] n extraverti(e)

ex-wife n ex-femme f

eye [aɪ] n œil m (pl yeux); (of needle) trou m, chas m ♦ vt examiner; **to keep an ~ on** surveiller; ~**brow** n sourcil m; ~**drops** n gouttes fpl pour les yeux; ~**lash** n cil m; ~**lid** n paupière f; ~**liner** n eye-liner m; ~**opener** n révélation f; ~**shadow** n ombre f à paupières; ~**sight** n vue f; ~**sore** n horreur f; ~**witness** n témoin m oculaire

F, f

F [ɛf] n (MUS) fa m

fable ['feɪbl] n fable f

fabric ['fæbrɪk] n tissu m

fabulous ['fæbjuləs] adj fabuleux (-euse); (inf: super) formidable

face [feɪs] n visage m, figure f; (expression) expression f; (of clock) cadran m; (of cliff) paroi f; (of mountain) face f; (of building) façade f ♦ vt faire face à; ~**down** (person) à plat ventre; (card) face en dessous; **to lose/save** ~ perdre/sauver la face; **to make** or **pull a** ~ faire une grimace; **in the** ~ **of** (difficulties etc) face à, devant; **on the** ~ **of it** à première vue; ~ **to** ~ face à face; ~ **up to** vt fus faire face à, affronter; ~ **cloth** (BRIT) n gant m de toilette; ~ **cream** n crème f pour le visage; ~ **lift** n lifting m; (of building etc) ravalement m, retapage m; ~ **powder** n poudre f de riz; ~ **value** n (of coin) valeur nominale; **to take sth at** ~ **value** (fig) prendre qch pour argent comptant

facilities [fə'sɪlɪtɪz] npl installations fpl, équipement m; **credit** ~ **facilities** fpl de paiement

facing ['feɪsɪŋ] prep face à, en face de

facsimile [fæk'sɪmɪlɪ] n (exact replica) fac-similé m; (fax) télécopie f

fact [fækt] n fait m; **in** ~ en fait

factor ['fæktə*] n facteur m

factory ['fæktərɪ] n usine f, fabrique f

factual ['fæktjuəl] adj basé(e) sur les faits

faculty ['fækltɪ] n faculté f; (US: teaching staff) corps enseignant

fad [fæd] n (craze) engouement m

fade [feɪd] vi se décolorer, passer; (light, sound) s'affaiblir; (flower) se faner

fag [fæg] (BRIT: inf) n (cigarette) sèche f

fail [feɪl] vt (exam) échouer à; (candidate) recaler; (subj: courage, memory) faire défaut à ♦ vi échouer; (brakes) lâcher; (eyesight, health, light) baisser, s'affaiblir; **to ~ to do sth** (neglect) négliger de faire qch; (be unable) ne pas arriver or parvenir à faire qch; **without** ~ à coup sûr; sans faute; ~**ing** n défaut m ♦ prep faute de; ~**ure** n échec m; (person) raté(e); (mechanical etc) défaillance f

faint [feɪnt] adj faible; (recollection) vague; (mark) à peine visible ♦ n évanouissement m ♦ vi s'évanouir; **to feel** ~ défaillir

fair [fɛəʳ] adj équitable, juste, impartial(e); (hair) blond(e); (skin, complexion) pâle, blanc, blanc (blanche); (weather) beau (belle); (good enough) assez bon(ne); (sizeable) considérable ♦ adv: **to play ~** jouer franc-jeu ♦ n foire f; (BRIT: funfair) fête (foraine); **~ly** adv équitablement; (quite) assez; **~ness** n justice f, équité f, impartialité f

fairy ['fɛərɪ] n fée f; **~ tale** n conte m de fées

faith [feɪθ] n foi f; (trust) confiance f; (specific religion) religion f; **~ful** adj fidèle; **~fully** adv see **yours**

fake [feɪk] n (painting etc) faux m; (person) imposteur m ♦ adj faux (fausse) ♦ vt simuler; (painting) faire un faux de

falcon ['fɔːlkən] n faucon m

fall [fɔːl] (pt **fell**, pp **fallen**) n chute f; (price, temperature, dollar) baisser; **~s** npl (waterfall) chute f d'eau, cascade f; **to ~ flat** (on one's face) tomber de tout son long, s'étaler; (joke) tomber à plat; (plan) échouer; **~ back** vi reculer, se retirer; **~ back on** vt fus se rabattre sur; **~ behind** vi prendre du retard; **~ down** vi (person) tomber; (building) s'effondrer, s'écrouler; **~ for** vt fus (trick, story etc) se laisser prendre à; (person) tomber amoureux de; **~ in** vi s'effondrer; (MIL) se mettre en rangs; **~ off** vi tomber; (diminish) baisser, diminuer; **~ out** vi (hair, teeth) tomber; (MIL) rompre les rangs; (friends etc) se brouiller; **~ through** vi (plan, project) tomber à l'eau

fallacy ['fæləsɪ] n erreur f, illusion f

fallout ['fɔːlaut] n retombées (radioactives)

fallow ['fæləu] adj en jachère; en friche

false [fɔːls] adj faux (fausse); **~ alarm** n fausse alerte; **~ pretences** npl: **under ~ pretences** sous un faux prétexte; **~ teeth** (BRIT) npl fausses dents

falter ['fɔːltəʳ] vi chanceler, vaciller

fame [feɪm] n renommée f, renom m

familiar [fə'mɪlɪəʳ] adj familier(-ère); **to be ~ with** (subject) connaître

family ['fæmɪlɪ] n famille f ♦ cpd (business, doctor etc) de famille; **has he any ~?** (children) a-t-il des enfants?

famine ['fæmɪn] n famine f

famished ['fæmɪʃt] (inf) adj affamé(e)

famous ['feɪməs] adj célèbre; **~ly** adv (get on) fameusement, à merveille

fan [fæn] n (folding) éventail m; (ELEC) ventilateur m; (of person) fan m, admirateur(-trice); (of team, sport etc) supporter m/f ♦ vt éventer; (fire, quarrel) attiser

fanatic [fə'nætɪk] n fanatique m/f

fan belt n courroie f de ventilateur

fancy ['fænsɪ] n fantaisie f, envie f; imagination f ♦ adj (de) fantaisie inv ♦ vt (feel like, want) avoir envie de; (imagine, think) imaginer; **to take a ~ to** se prendre d'affection pour; **he fancies her** (inf) elle lui plaît; **~ dress** n déguisement m, travesti m; **~-dress ball** n bal masqué or costumé

fang [fæŋ] n croc m; (of snake) crochet m

fantastic [fæn'tæstɪk] adj fantastique

fantasy ['fæntəsɪ] n imagination f, fantaisie f; (dream) chimère f

far [fɑːʳ] adj lointain(e), éloigné(e) ♦ adv loin; **~ away** or **off** au loin, dans le lointain; **at the ~ side/end** à l'autre côté/bout; **~ better** beaucoup mieux; **~ from** loin de; **by ~** de loin, de beaucoup; **go as ~ as the ~m** allez jusqu'à la ferme; **as ~ as I know** pour autant que je sache; **how ~ is it to ...?** combien y a-t-il jusqu'à ...?; **how have you got?** où en êtes-vous?; **~away** ['fɑːrəweɪ] adj lointain(e); (look) distrait(e)

farce [fɑːs] n farce f

fare [fɛəʳ] n (on trains, buses) prix m du billet; (in taxi) prix de la course; (food) table f, chère f; **half ~** demi-tarif; **full ~** plein tarif

Far East n Extrême-Orient m

farewell [fɛə'wɛl] *excl* adieu ♦ *n* adieu *m*

farm [fɑːm] *n* ferme *f* ♦ *vt* cultiver; **~er** *n* fermier(-ère); cultivateur(-trice); **~hand** *n* ouvrier(-ère) agricole; **~house** *n* (maison *f* de) ferme *f*; **~ing** *n* agriculture *f*; (*of animals*) élevage *m*; **~land** *n* terres cultivées; **~ worker** *n* = farmhand; **~yard** *n* cour *f* de ferme

far-reaching [fɑː'riːtʃɪŋ] *adj* d'une grande portée

fart [fɑːt] (*inf!*) *vi* péter

farther [fɑːðəʳ] *adv* plus loin ♦ *adj* plus éloigné(e), plus lointain(e)

farthest [fɑːðɪst] *superl* of **far**

fascinate [fæsɪneɪt] *vt* fasciner; **fascinating** *adj* fascinant(e)

fascism [fæʃɪzəm] *n* fascisme *m*

fashion [fæʃən] *n* mode *f*; (*manner*) façon *f*, manière *f* ♦ *vt* façonner; **in ~** à la mode; **out of ~** démodé(e); **~able** *adj* à la mode; **~ show** *n* défilé *m* de mannequins or de mode

fast [fɑːst] *adj* rapide; (*clock*): **to be ~** avancer; (*dye, colour*) grand *or* bon teint *inv* ♦ *adv* vite, rapidement; (*stuck, held*) solidement ♦ *n* jeûne *m* ♦ *vi* jeûner; **~ asleep** profondément endormi

fasten [fɑːsn] *vt* attacher, fixer; (*coat*) attacher, fermer ♦ *vi* se fermer, s'attacher; **~er, ~ing** *n* attache *f*

fast food *n* fast food *m*, restauration *f* rapide

fastidious [fæs'tɪdɪəs] *adj* exigeant(e), difficile

fat [fæt] *adj* gros(se) ♦ *n* graisse *f*; (*on meat*) gras *m*; (*for cooking*) matière grasse

fatal [feɪtl] *adj* (*injury etc*) mortel(le); (*mistake*) fatal(e); **~ity** [fə'tælɪtɪ] *n* (*road death etc*) victime *f*, décès *m*

fate [feɪt] *n* destin *m*; (*of person*) sort *m*; **~ful** *adj* fatidique

father [fɑːðəʳ] *n* père *m*; **~-in-law** *n* beau-père *m*; **~ly** *adj* paternel(le)

fathom [fæðəm] *n* brasse *f* (= *1828 mm*) ♦ *vt* (*mystery*) sonder, pénétrer

fatigue [fə'tiːg] *n* fatigue *f*

fatten [fætn] *vt, vi* engraisser

fatty [fætɪ] *adj* (*food*) gras(se) ♦ *n* (*inf*) gros(se)

fatuous [fætjuəs] *adj* stupide

faucet [fɔːsɪt] (*US*) *n* robinet *m*

fault [fɔːlt] *n* faute *f*; (*defect*) défaut *m*; (*GEO*) faille *f* ♦ *vt* trouver des défauts à; **it's my ~** c'est de ma faute; **to find ~ with** trouver à redire or à critiquer à; **at ~** fautif(-ive), coupable; **~y** *adj* défectueux(-euse)

fauna [fɔːnə] *n* faune *f*

favour [feɪvəʳ] (*US* **favor**) *n* faveur *f*; (*help*) service *m* ♦ *vt* (*proposition*) être en faveur de; (*pupil etc*) favoriser; (*team, horse*) donner gagnant; **to do sb a ~** rendre un service à qn; **to find ~ with** trouver grâce aux yeux de; **in ~ of** en faveur de; **~able** *adj* favorable; **~ite** [feɪvrɪt] *adj, n* favori(te)

fawn [fɔːn] *n* faon *m* ♦ *adj* (*colour*) fauve ♦ *vi*: **to ~ (up)on** flatter servilement

fax [fæks] *n* (*document*) télécopie *f*, fax *m*; (*machine*) télécopieur *m* ♦ *vt* envoyer par télécopie

FBI *n abbr* (*US: Federal Bureau of Investigation*) F.B.I. *m*

fear [fɪəʳ] *n* crainte *f*, peur *f* ♦ *vt* craindre; **for ~ of** de peur que +*sub*, de peur de +*infin*; **~ful** *adj* craintif(-ive); (*sight, noise*) affreux(-euse), épouvantable; **~less** *adj* intrépide

feasible [fiːzəbl] *adj* faisable, réalisable

feast [fiːst] *n* festin *m*, banquet *m*; (*REL: also:* **~ day**) fête *f* ♦ *vi* festoyer

feat [fiːt] *n* exploit *m*, prouesse *f*

feather [fɛðəʳ] *n* plume *f*

feature [fiːtʃəʳ] *n* caractéristique *f*; (*article*) chronique *f*, rubrique *f* ♦ *vt* (*subj: film*) avoir pour vedette(s) ♦ *vi*: **to ~** figurer (en bonne place) dans; (*in film*) jouer dans; **~s** *npl* (*of face*) traits *mpl*; **~ film** *n* long métrage

February [februarɪ] *n* février *m*

fed [fɛd] *pt, pp* of **feed**

federal [fɛdərəl] *adj* fédéral(e); **~ holiday** (*US*) *n* jour *m* férié

fed up adj: **to be ~** en avoir marre, en avoir plein le dos

fee [fiː] n rémunération f; (of doctor, lawyer) honoraires mpl; (for examination) droits mpl; **school ~s** frais mpl de scolarité

feeble ['fiːbl] adj faible; (pathetic: attempt, excuse) pauvre; (: joke) piteux (-euse)

feed [fiːd] (pt, pp **fed**) n (of animal) fourrage m; pâture f; (on printer) mécanisme m d'alimentation ♦ vt (gen) nourrir; (BRIT: baby) allaiter; (: with bottle) donner le biberon à; (horse etc) donner à manger à; (machine) alimenter; (data, information) fournir qch à; **~ on** vt fus se nourrir de; **~back** n feed-back m inv

feel [fiːl] (pt, pp **felt**) n sensation f; (impression) impression f ♦ vt toucher; (explore) tâter, palper; (cold, pain) sentir; (grief, anger) ressentir, éprouver; (think, believe) trouver; **to ~ hungry/cold** avoir faim/froid; **to ~ lonely/better** se sentir seul/mieux; **I don't ~ well** je ne me sens pas bien; **it ~s soft** c'est doux (douce) au toucher; **to ~ like** (want) avoir envie de; **~ about** vi fouiller, tâtonner; **~er** n (of insect) antenne f; **~ing** n (physical) sensation f; (emotional) sentiment m

feet [fiːt] npl of **foot**

feign [feɪn] vt feindre, simuler

fell [fɛl] pt of **fall** ♦ vt (tree, person) abattre

fellow ['fɛləu] n type m; (comrade) compagnon m; (of learned societies) membre m ♦ cpd: **their ~ prisoners/students** leurs camarades prisonniers/d'étude; **~ citizen** n concitoyen(ne) m/f; **~ countryman** (irreg) n compatriote m; **~ men** npl semblables mpl; **~ship** n (society) association f; (comradeship) amitié f, camaraderie f; (grant) sorte de bourse universitaire

felony ['fɛlənɪ] n crime m, forfait m

felt [fɛlt] pt, pp of **feel** ♦ n feutre m; **~-**

tip pen n stylo-feutre m

female ['fiːmeɪl] n (ZOOL) femelle f; (pej: woman) bonne femme ♦ adj (BIO) femelle; (sex, character) féminin(e); (vote etc) des femmes

feminine ['fɛmɪnɪn] adj féminin(e)

feminist ['fɛmɪnɪst] n féministe m/f

fence [fɛns] n barrière f ♦ vt (also: ~ in) clôturer ♦ vi faire de l'escrime; **fencing** n escrime m

fend [fɛnd] vi: **to ~ for o.s.** se débrouiller (tout seul); **~ off** vt (attack etc) parer

fender ['fɛndər] n garde-feu m inv; (on boat) défense f; (US: of car) aile f

ferment [vb fə'mɛnt, n 'fɜːmɛnt] vi fermenter ♦ n agitation f, effervescence f

fern [fɜːn] n fougère f

ferocious [fə'rəuʃəs] adj féroce

ferret ['fɛrɪt] n furet m

ferry ['fɛrɪ] n (small) bac m; (large: also: ~boat) ferry(-boat) m ♦ vt transporter

fertile ['fɜːtaɪl] adj fertile; (BIO) fécond(e); **fertilizer** ['fɜːtɪlaɪzər] n engrais m

fester ['fɛstər] vi suppurer

festival ['fɛstɪvəl] n (REL) fête f; (ART, MUS) festival m

festive ['fɛstɪv] adj de fête; **the ~ season** (BRIT: Christmas) la période des fêtes; **festivities** npl réjouissances fpl

festoon [fɛs'tuːn] vt: **to ~ with** orner de

fetch [fɛtʃ] vt aller chercher; (sell for) se vendre

fête [feɪt] n fête f, kermesse f

feud [fjuːd] n dispute f, dissension f

fever ['fiːvər] n fièvre f; **~ish** adj fiévreux(-euse), fébrile

few [fjuː] adj (not many) peu de; **a ~** ♦ adj quelques ♦ pron quelques-uns (-unes); **~er** adj moins de; moins (nombreux); **~est** adj le moins de

fiancé, e [fɪ'ãːŋseɪ] n fiancé(e) m/f

fib [fɪb] n bobard m

fibre ['faɪbər] (US **fiber**) n fibre f; **~glass**

['faɪbəglɑːs] **(Fiberglass** ® US) n fibre de verre

fickle ['fɪkl] adj inconstant(e), volage, capricieux(-euse)

fiction ['fɪkʃən] n romans mpl, littérature f romanesque; (invention) fiction f; **~al** adj fictif(-ive)

fictitious adj fictif(-ive), imaginaire

fiddle ['fɪdl] n (MUS) violon m; (cheating) combine f; escroquerie f ♦ vt (BRIT: accounts) falsifier, maquiller; **~ with** vt fus tripoter

fidget ['fɪdʒɪt] vi se trémousser, remuer

field [fiːld] n champ m; (fig) domaine m, champ; (SPORT: ground) terrain m; **~work** n travaux mpl pratiques (sur le terrain)

fiend [fiːnd] n démon m

fierce [fɪəs] adj (look, animal) féroce, sauvage; (wind, attack, person) (très) violent(e); (fighting, enemy) acharné(e)

fiery ['faɪərɪ] adj ardent(e), brûlant(e); (temperament) fougueux(-euse)

fifteen [fɪf'tiːn] num quinze

fifth [fɪfθ] num cinquième

fifty ['fɪftɪ] num cinquante; **~-fifty** adj: **a ~-fifty chance** une chance etc sur deux ♦ adv moitié-moitié

fig [fɪg] n figue f

fight [faɪt] (pt, pp **fought**) n (MIL) combat m; (between persons) bagarre f; (against cancer etc) lutte f ♦ vt se battre contre; (cancer, alcoholism, emotion) combattre, lutter contre; (election) se présenter à ♦ vi se battre; **~er** n (fig) lutteur m; (plane) chasseur m; **~ing** n combats mpl; (brawl) bagarres fpl

figment ['fɪgmənt] n: **a ~ of the imagination** une invention

figurative ['fɪgjʊrətɪv] adj figuré(e)

figure ['fɪgər] n figure f; (number, cipher) chiffre m; (body, outline) silhouette f; (shape) ligne f, formes fpl ♦ vt (think: esp US) supposer ♦ vi (appear) figurer; **~ out** vt (work out) calculer; **~head** n (NAUT) figure f de proue; (pej) prête-nom m; **~ of speech** n figure f

de rhétorique

file [faɪl] n (dossier) dossier m; (folder) dossier m, chemise f; (: with hinges) classeur m; (COMPUT) fichier m; (row) file f; (tool) lime f ♦ vt (nails, wood) limer; (papers) classer; (LAW: claim) faire enregistrer; déposer ♦ vi: **to ~ in/out** entrer/sortir l'un derrière l'autre; **to ~ for divorce** faire une demande en divorce; **filing cabinet** n classeur m (meuble)

fill [fɪl] vt remplir; (need) répondre à ♦ n: **to eat one's ~** manger à sa faim; **to ~ with** remplir de; **~ in** vt (hole) boucher; (form) remplir; **~ up** vt remplir; **~ it up, please** (AUT) le plein, s'il vous plaît

fillet ['fɪlɪt] n filet m; **~ steak** n filet de bœuf, tournedos m

filling ['fɪlɪŋ] n (CULIN) garniture f, farce f; (for tooth) plombage m; **~ station** n station-service f

film [fɪlm] n film m; (PHOT) pellicule f, film; (of powder, liquid) couche f, pellicule ♦ vt (scene) filmer ♦ vi tourner; **~ star** n vedette f de cinéma

filter ['fɪltər] n filtre m ♦ vt filtrer; **~ lane** n (AUT) voie f de sortie; **~-tipped** adj à bout filtre

filth [fɪlθ] n saleté f; **~y** adj sale, dégoûtant(e); (language) ordurier(-ère)

fin [fɪn] n (of fish) nageoire f

final ['faɪnl] adj final(e); (definitive) définitif(-ive) ♦ n (SPORT) finale f; **~s** npl (SCOL) examens mpl de dernière année; **~e** [fɪ'nɑːlɪ] n finale m; **~ist** n finaliste m/f; **~ize** vt mettre au point; **~ly** adv (eventually) enfin, finalement; (lastly) en dernier lieu

finance [faɪ'næns] n finance f ♦ vt financer; **~s** npl (financial position) finances fpl; **financial** [faɪ'nænʃəl] adj financier(-ère)

find [faɪnd] (pt, pp **found**) vt trouver; (lost object) retrouver ♦ n trouvaille f, découverte f; **to ~ sb guilty** (LAW) déclarer qn coupable; **~ out** vt (truth, se-

cret) découvrir; (*person*) démasquer ♦ *vi:* **to ~ out about** (*make enquiries*) se renseigner; (*by chance*) apprendre; **~ings** (LAW) conclusions fpl, verdict *m;* (*of report*) conclusions

fine [faɪn] *adj* (*excellent*) excellent(e); (*thin, not coarse, subtle*) fin(e); (*weather*) beau (belle) ♦ *adv* (*well*) très bien ♦ *n* (LAW) amende f; contravention f ♦ *vt* (LAW) condamner à une amende; donner une contravention à; **to be ~** (*person*) aller bien; (*weather*) être beau; **~ arts** npl beaux-arts mpl; **~ry** *n* parure f

finger ['fɪŋgər] *n* doigt *m* ♦ *vt* palper, toucher; **little ~** auriculaire *m*, petit doigt; **index ~** index *m*; **~nail** *n* ongle *m* (de la main); **~print** *n* empreinte f digitale; **~tip** *n* bout *m* du doigt

finish ['fɪnɪʃ] *n* fin f; (SPORT) arrivée f; (*polish etc*) finition f ♦ *vt* finir, terminer ♦ *vi* finir, se terminer; **to ~ doing sth** finir de faire qch; **to ~ third** arriver or terminer troisième; **~ off** *vt* finir, terminer; (*kill*) achever; **~ up** *vi, vt* finir; **~ing line** *n* ligne f d'arrivée

finite ['faɪnaɪt] *adj* fini(e); (*verb*) conjugué(e)

Finland ['fɪnlənd] *n* Finlande f; **Finn** [fɪn] *n* Finlandais(e); **Finnish** *adj* finlandais(e) ♦ *n* (LING) finnois *m*

fir [fəːr] *n* sapin *m*

fire ['faɪər] *n* feu *m;* (*accidental*) incendie *m;* (*heater*) radiateur *m* ♦ *vt* (*fig: dismiss*) mettre à la porte, renvoyer; (*discharge*): **to ~ a gun** tirer un coup de feu; (*fig: shoot*) tirer, faire feu; **on ~** en feu; **~ alarm** *n* avertisseur *m* d'incendie; **~arm** *n* arme f à feu; **~ brigade** *n* (sapeurs-)pompiers mpl; **~ department** (US) *n* = **fire brigade**; **~ engine** *n* (*vehicle*) voiture f des pompiers; **~ escape** *n* escalier *m* de secours; **~ extinguisher** *n* extincteur *m;* **~man** *n* pompier *m;* **~place** *n* cheminée f; **~side** *n* foyer *m*, coin *m* du feu; **~ station** *n* caserne f

de pompiers; **~wood** *n* bois *m* de chauffage; **~works** npl feux mpl d'artifice; (*display*) feu(x) d'artifice

firing squad ['faɪərɪŋ-] *n* peloton *m* d'exécution

firm [fəːm] *adj* ferme ♦ *n* compagnie f, firme f

first [fəːst] *adj* premier(-ère) ♦ *adv* (*before all others*) le premier, la première; (*before all other things*) en premier, d'abord; (*when listing reasons etc*) en premier lieu, premièrement ♦ *n* (*person: in race*) premier(-ère); (BRIT: SCOL) mention f très bien; (AUT) première f; **at ~** au commencement, au début; **~ of all** tout d'abord, pour commencer; **~ aid** *n* premiers secours or soins; **~aid kit** *n* trousse f à pharmacie; **~-class** *adj* de première classe; (*excellent*) excellent(e), exceptionnel(le); **~-hand** *adj* de première main; **~ lady** (US) *n* femme f du président; **~ly** *adv* premièrement, en premier lieu; **~ name** *n* prénom *m;* **~-rate** *adj* excellent(e)

fish [fɪʃ] *n inv* poisson *m* ♦ *vt, vi* pêcher; **to go ~ing** aller à la pêche; **~erman** *n* pêcheur *m;* **~ farm** *n* établissement *m* piscicole; **~ fingers** (BRIT) npl bâtonnets de poisson (congelés); **~ing boat** *n* barque f or bateau *m* de pêche; **~ing line** *n* ligne f (de pêche); **~ing rod** *n* canne f à pêche; **~ing tackle** *n* attirail *m* de pêche; **~monger's (shop)** *n* poissonnerie f; **~ slice** *n* pelle f à poisson; **~ sticks** (US) npl = **fish fingers**; **~y** (*inf*) *adj* suspect(e), louche

fist [fɪst] *n* poing *m*

fit [fɪt] *adj* (*healthy*) en (bonne) forme; (*proper*) convenable; approprié(e) ♦ *vt* (*subj: clothes*) aller à; (*put in, attach*) installer, poser; adapter; (*equip*) équiper, garnir, munir; (*suit*) convenir à ♦ *vi* (*clothes*) aller; (*parts*) s'adapter; (*in space, gap*) entrer, s'adapter ♦ *n* (MED) accès *m*, crise f; (*of anger*) accès; (*of hysterics, jealousy*) crise; **~ to** en état de; **~ for** digne de; apte à; ♦

coughing quinte f de toux; **a ~ of giggles** le fou rire; **this dress is a good ~** cette robe (me) va très bien; **by ~s and starts** par à-coups; **~ in** vi s'accorder; s'adapter; **~ful** adj (sleep) agité(e); **~ment** n meuble encastré, élément m; **~ness** n (MED) forme f physique; **~ted carpet** n moquette f; **~ted kitchen** (BRIT) n cuisine équipée; **~ter** n monteur m; **~ting** adj approprié(e) ♦ n (of dress) essayage m; (of piece of equipment) pose f, installation f; **~tings** npl (in building) installations fpl; **~ting room** n cabine f d'essayage

five [faɪv] num cinq; **~r** (inf) n (BRIT) billet m de cinq livres; (US) billet de cinq dollars

fix [fɪks] vt (date, amount etc) fixer; (organize) arranger; (mend) réparer; (meal, drink) préparer ♦ n: **to be in a ~** être dans le pétrin; **~ up** vt (meeting) arranger; **to ~ sb up with sth** faire avoir qch à qn; **~ation** [fɪk'seɪʃən] n (PSYCH) fixation f; (fig) obsession f; **~ed** adj (prices etc) fixe; (smile) figé(e); **~ture** n installation f (fixée); (SPORT) rencontre f (au programme)

fizzy ['fɪzɪ] adj pétillant(e); gazeux(-euse)

flabbergasted ['flæbəgɑːstɪd] adj sidéré(e), ahuri(e)

flabby ['flæbɪ] adj mou (molle)

flag [flæg] n drapeau m; (also: **~stone**) dalle f ♦ vi faiblir; fléchir; **~ down** vt héler, faire signe (de s'arrêter) à; **~pole** n mât m; **~ship** n vaisseau m amiral; (fig) produit m vedette

flair [fleəʳ] n flair m

flak [flæk] n (MIL) tir antiaérien; (inf: criticism) critiques fpl

flake [fleɪk] n (of rust, paint) écaille f; (of snow, soap powder) flocon m ♦ vi (also: **~ off**) s'écailler

flamboyant [flæm'bɔɪənt] adj flamboyant(e), éclatant(e); (person) haut(e) en couleur

flame [fleɪm] n flamme f

flamingo [fləˈmɪŋgəʊ] n flamant m (rose)

flammable ['flæməbl] adj inflammable

flan [flæn] (BRIT) n tarte f

flank [flæŋk] n flanc m ♦ vt flanquer

flannel ['flænl] n (fabric) flanelle f; (BRIT: also: **face ~**) gant m de toilette

flap [flæp] n (of pocket, envelope) rabat m ♦ vt (wings) battre (de) ♦ vi (sail, flag) claquer; (inf: also: **be in a ~**) paniquer

flare [fleəʳ] n (signal) signal lumineux; (in skirt etc) évasement m; **~ up** vi s'embraser; (fig: person) se mettre en colère, s'emporter; (: revolt etc) éclater

flash [flæʃ] n éclair m; (also: **news ~**) flash m (d'information); (PHOT) flash m ♦ vt (light) projeter; (send: message) câbler; (look) jeter; (smile) lancer ♦ vi briller; (light) clignoter; **a ~ of lightning** un éclair; **in a ~** en un clin d'œil; **to ~ one's headlights** faire un appel de phares; **to ~ by** or **past** (person) passer (devant) comme un éclair; **~bulb** n ampoule f de flash; **~cube** n cube-flash m; **~light** n lampe f de poche; **~y** (pej) adj tape-à-l'œil inv, tapageur(-euse)

flask [flɑːsk] n flacon m, bouteille f; (also: **vacuum ~**) thermos ® m or f

flat [flæt] adj plat(e); (tyre) dégonflé(e), à plat; (beer) éventé(e); (denial) catégorique; (MUS) bémol inv; (: voice) faux (fausse); (fee, rate) fixe ♦ n (BRIT: apartment) appartement m; (AUT) crevaison f; (MUS) bémol m; **to work ~ out** travailler d'arrache-pied; **~ly** adv catégoriquement; **~ten** vt (also: **~ten out**) aplatir; (crop) coucher; (building(s)) raser

flatter ['flætəʳ] vt flatter; **~ing** adj flatteur(-euse); **~y** n flatterie f

flaunt [flɔːnt] vt faire étalage de

flavour ['fleɪvəʳ] (US **flavor**) n goût m, saveur f; (of ice cream etc) parfum m ♦ vt parfumer; **vanilla-~ed** à l'arôme de vanille, à la vanille; **~ing** n arôme m

flaw [flɔː] n défaut m; **~less** adj sans défaut

flax [flæks] n lin m

flea [fli:] n puce f

fleck [flɛk] n tacheture f; moucheture f

flee [fli:] (pt, pp **fled**) vt fuir ♦ vi fuir, s'enfuir

fleece [fli:s] n toison f ♦ vt (inf) voler, filouter

fleet [fli:t] n flotte f; (of lorries etc) parc m, convoi m

fleeting ['fli:tɪŋ] adj fugace, fugitif (-ive); (visit) très bref (brève)

Flemish ['flɛmɪʃ] adj flamand(e)

flesh [flɛʃ] n chair f; ~ **wound** n blessure superficielle

flew [flu:] pt of **fly**

flex [flɛks] n fil m or câble m électrique ♦ vt (knee) fléchir; (muscles) tendre; **~ible** adj flexible

flick [flɪk] n petite tape; chiquenaude f; (of duster) petit coup f ♦ vt donner un petit coup à; (switch) appuyer sur; ~ **through** vt fus feuilleter

flicker ['flɪkər] vi (light) vaciller; **his eyelids ~ed** il a cligné

flier ['flaɪər] n aviateur m

flight [flaɪt] n vol m; (escape) fuite f; (also: ~ **of steps**) escalier m; ~ **attendant** (US) n steward m, hôtesse f de l'air; ~ **deck** n (AVIAT) poste m de pilotage; (NAUT) pont m d'envol

flimsy ['flɪmzɪ] adj peu solide; (clothes) trop léger(-ère); (excuse) pauvre, mince

flinch [flɪntʃ] vi tressaillir; **to ~ from** se dérober à, reculer devant

fling [flɪŋ] (pt, pp **flung**) vt jeter, lancer

flint [flɪnt] n silex m; (in lighter) pierre f (à briquet)

flip [flɪp] vt (throw) lancer (d'une chiquenaude); **to ~ sth over** retourner qch

flippant ['flɪpənt] adj désinvolte, irrévérencieux(-euse)

flipper ['flɪpər] n (of seal etc) nageoire f; (for swimming) palme f

flirt [flə:t] vi flirter ♦ n flirteur(-euse) m/f

float [fləut] n flotteur m; (in procession) char m; (money) réserve f ♦ vi flotter

flock [flɔk] n troupeau m; (of birds) vol

m; (REL) ouailles fpl ♦ vi: **to ~ to** se rendre en masse à

flog [flɔg] vt fouetter

flood [flʌd] n inondation f; (of letters, refugees etc) flot m ♦ vt inonder ♦ vi (people): **to ~ into** envahir; **~ing** n inondation f; **~light** n projecteur m

floor [flɔ:r] n sol m; (storey) étage m; (of sea, valley) fond m ♦ vt (subj: question) déconcertancer; (: blow) terrasser; **on the ~** par terre; **ground ~**, (US) **first ~** rez-de-chaussée m inv; **first ~**, (US) **second ~** premier étage; **~board** n planche f (du plancher); ~ **show** n spectacle m de variétés

flop [flɔp] n fiasco m ♦ vi être un fiasco; (fall: into chair) s'affaler, s'effondrer; **~py** adj lâche, flottant(e) ♦ n (COMPUT: also: **~py disk**) disquette f

flora ['flɔ:rə] n flore f

floral ['flɔ:rl] adj (dress) à fleurs

florid ['flɔrɪd] adj (complexion) coloré(e); (style) plein(e) de fioritures

florist ['flɔrɪst] n fleuriste m/f; **~'s (shop)** n magasin m or boutique f de fleuriste

flounder ['flaundər] vi patauger ♦ n (ZOOL) flet m

flour ['flauər] n farine f

flourish ['flʌrɪʃ] vi prospérer ♦ n (gesture) moulinet m

flout [flaut] vt se moquer de, faire fi de

flow [fləu] n (ELEC, of river) courant m; (of blood in veins) circulation f; (of tide) flux m; (of orders, data) flot m ♦ vi couler; (traffic) s'écouler; (robes, hair) flotter; **the ~ of traffic** l'écoulement m de la circulation; ~ **chart** n organigramme m

flower ['flauər] n fleur f ♦ vi fleurir; ~ **bed** n plate-bande f; **~pot** n pot m (de fleurs); **~y** adj fleuri(e)

flown [fləun] pp of **fly**

flu [flu:] n grippe f

fluctuate ['flʌktjueɪt] vi varier, fluctuer

fluent ['flu:ənt] adj (speech) coulant(e), aisé(e); **he speaks ~ French, he's ~ in**

French il parle couramment le français

fluff [flʌf] *n* duvet *m*; (on jacket, carpet) peluche *f*; **~y** *adj* duveteux(-euse); (toy) en peluche

fluid ['fluːɪd] *adj* fluide ♦ *n* fluide *m*

fluke [fluːk] (*inf*) *n* (luck) coup *m* de veine

flung [flʌŋ] *pt, pp of* **fling**

fluoride ['fluəraɪd] *n* fluorure *f*; **~ toothpaste** dentifrice *m* au fluor

flurry ['flʌrɪ] *n* (of snow) rafale *f*, bourrasque *f*; **~ of activity/excitement** affairement *m*/excitation *f* soudain(e)

flush [flʌʃ] *n* (on face) rougeur *f*; (fig: of youth, beauty etc) éclat *m* ♦ *vt* nettoyer à grande eau ♦ *vi* rougir ♦ *adj*: **~ with** au ras du sol, de niveau avec; **to ~ the toilet** tirer la chasse (d'eau); **~ed** *adj* (tout)e) rouge

flustered ['flʌstəd] *adj* énervé(e)

flute [fluːt] *n* flûte *f*

flutter ['flʌtər] *n* (of panic, excitement) agitation *f*; (of wings) battement *m* ♦ *vi* (bird) battre des ailes, voleter

flux [flʌks] *n*: **in a state of ~** fluctuant sans cesse

fly [flaɪ] (*pt* **flew**, *pp* **flown**) *n* (insect) mouche *f*; (on trousers: also: **flies**) braguette *f* ♦ *vt* piloter; (passengers, cargo) transporter (par avion); (distances) parcourir ♦ *vi* voler; (passengers) aller en avion; (escape) s'enfuir, fuir; (flag) se déployer; **~ away** *vi* (bird, insect) s'envoler; **~ off** *vi* = **fly away**; **~-drive** *n* formule *f* avion plus voiture; **~ing** *n* (activity) aviation *f*; (action) vol *m* ♦ *adj*: **a ~ing visit** une visite éclair; **with ~ing colours** haut la main; **~ing saucer** *n* soucoupe volante; **~ing start** *n*: **to get off to a ~ing start** prendre un excellent départ; **~over** (BRIT) *n* (bridge) saut-de-mouton *m*; **~sheet** *n* (for tent) double toit *m*

foal [fəul] *n* poulain *m*

foam [fəum] *n* écume *f*; (on beer) mousse *f*; (also: **~ rubber**) caoutchouc mousse *m* ♦ *vi* (liquid) écumer; (soapy

water) mousser

fob [fɔb] *vt*: **to ~ sb off** se débarrasser de qn

focal point ['fəukl-] *n* (fig) point central

focus ['fəukəs] (*pl* **~es**) *n* foyer *m*; (of interest) centre *m* ♦ *vt* (field glasses etc) mettre au point ♦ *vi*: **to ~ (on)** (with camera) régler la mise au point (sur); (person) fixer son regard (sur); **out of/in ~** (picture) floue(e)/net(te); (camera) pas au point/au point

fodder ['fɔdər] *n* fourrage *m*

foe [fəu] *n* ennemi *m*

fog [fɔg] *n* brouillard *m*; **~gy** *adj*: **it's ~gy** il y a du brouillard; **~ lamp** (US **~ light**) *n* (AUT) phare *m* antibrouillard

foil [fɔɪl] *vt* déjouer, contrecarrer ♦ *n* feuille *f* de métal; (kitchen ~) papier *m* alu(minium); (complement) repoussoir *m*

fold [fəuld] *n* (bend, crease) pli *m*; (AGR) parc *m* à moutons; (fig) bercail *m* ♦ *vt* plier; (arms) croiser; **~ up** *vi* (map, table etc) se plier; (business) fermer boutique ♦ *vt* (map, clothes) plier; **~er** *n* (for papers) chemise *f*; (: with hinges) classeur *m*; (COMPUT) répertoire *m*; **~ing** *adj* (chair, bed) pliant(e)

foliage ['fəulɪɪdʒ] *n* feuillage *m*

folk [fəuk] *npl* gens *mpl* ♦ *cpd* folklorique; **~s** (*inf*) *npl* (parents) parents *mpl*; **~lore** ['fəuklɔː] *n* folklore *m*; **~ song** *n* chanson *f* folklorique

follow ['fɔləu] *vt* suivre ♦ *vi* suivre; (result) s'ensuivre; **to ~ suit** (fig) faire de même; **~ up** *vt* (letter, offer) donner suite à; (case) suivre; **~er** *n* disciple *m/f*, partisan(e); **~ing** *adj* suivant(e) ♦ *n* partisans *mpl*, disciples *mpl*

folly ['fɔlɪ] *n* inconscience *f*; folie *f*

fond [fɔnd] *adj* (memory, look) tendre; (hopes, dreams) un peu fou (folle); **to be ~ of** aimer beaucoup

fondle ['fɔndl] *vt* caresser

font [fɔnt] *n* (in church: for baptism) fonts baptismaux; (TYP) fonte *f*

food [fuːd] *n* nourriture *f*; **~ mixer** *n*

mixer m; **~ poisoning** n intoxication f alimentaire; **~ processor** n robot m de cuisine; **~stuffs** npl denrées fpl alimentaires; **~ technology** BRIT n (SCOL) technologie f des produits alimentaires

fool [fuːl] n idiot(e) f; (CULIN) mousse f de fruits ♦ vt berner, duper ♦ vi faire l'idiot or l'imbécile; **~hardy** adj téméraire, imprudent(e); **~ish** adj idiot(e), stupide; (rash) imprudent(e); insensé(e); **~proof** adj (plan etc) infaillible

foot [fut] (pl **feet**) n pied m; (of animal) patte f; (measure) pied (= 30,48 cm, 12 inches) ♦ vt (bill) payer; **on ~** à pied; **~age** n (CINEMA: length) ≃ métrage m; (: material) séquences fpl; **~ball** n ballon m (de football); (sport: BRIT) football m, foot m; (: US) football américain; **~ball player** (BRIT) n (also: **~baller**) joueur m de football; **~bridge** n passerelle f; **~hills** npl contreforts mpl; **~hold** n prise f (de pied); **~ing** n (fig) position f; **to lose one's ~ing** perdre pied; **~lights** npl rampe f; **~note** n note f (en bas de page); **~path** n sentier m; (in street) trottoir m; **~print** n trace f (de pas); **~step** n pas m; **~wear** n chaussure(s) f(pl)

---

football pools

Les football pools - ou plus familièrement les "pools" - consistent à parier sur les résultats des matches de football qui se jouent tous les samedis. L'expression consacrée en anglais est "to do the pools". Les parieurs envoient à l'avance les fiches qu'ils ont complétées à l'organisme qui gère les paris et ils attendent 17 h le samedi que les résultats soient annoncés. Les sommes gagnées se comptent parfois en milliers (ou même en millions) de livres sterling.

KEYWORD

---

for [fɔːʳ] prep **1** (indicating destination, intention, purpose) pour; **the train for London** le train pour or (à destination) de Londres; **he went for the paper** il est allé chercher le journal; **it's time for lunch** c'est l'heure du déjeuner; **what's it for?** ça sert à quoi?; **what for?** (why) pourquoi?

2 (on behalf of, representing) pour; **the MP for Hove** le député de Hove; **to work for sb/sth** travailler pour qn/qch; **G for George** G comme Georges

3 (because of) pour; **for this reason** pour cette raison; **for fear of being criticized** de peur d'être critiqué

4 (with regard to) pour; **it's cold for July** il fait froid pour juillet; **a gift for languages** un don pour les langues

5 (in exchange for): **I sold it for £5** je l'ai vendu 5 livres; **to pay 50 pence for a ticket** payer un billet 50 pence

6 (in favour of) pour; **are you for or against us?** êtes-vous pour ou contre nous?

7 (referring to distance) pendant, sur; **there are roadworks for 5 km** il y a des travaux sur 5 km; **we walked for miles** nous avons marché pendant des kilomètres

8 (referring to time) pendant; depuis; pour; **he was away for 2 years** il a été absent pendant 2 ans; **she will be away for a month** elle sera absente (pendant) un mois; **I have known her for years** je la connais depuis des années; **can you do it for tomorrow?** est-ce que tu peux le faire pour demain?

9 (with infinitive clauses): **it is not for me to decide** ce n'est pas à moi de décider; **it would be best for you to leave** le mieux serait que vous partiez; **there is still time for you to do it** vous avez encore le temps de le faire; **for this to be possible ...** pour que cela soit possible ...

10 (in spite of): **for all his work/**

efforts malgré tout son travail/tous ses efforts; **for all his complaints**, he's **very fond of her** il a beau se plaindre, il l'aime beaucoup
♦ *conj* (*since, as: rather formal*) car

forage ['fɔrɪdʒ] *vi* fourrager

foray ['fɔreɪ] *n* incursion *f*

forbid [fə'bɪd] (*pt* **forbad(e)**, *pp* **forbidden**) *vt* défendre, interdire; **to ~ sb to do** défendre or interdire à qn de faire; **~ding** *adj* sévère, sombre

force [fɔːs] *n* force *f* ♦ *vt* forcer; (*push*) pousser (de force); **the F~s** *npl* (MIL) l'armée *f*; **in ~** en vigueur; **~-feed** *vt* nourrir de force; **~ful** *adj* énergique, volontaire; **forcibly** *adv* par la force, de force; (*express*) énergiquement

ford [fɔːd] *n* gué *m*

fore [fɔːr] *n*: **to come to the ~** se faire remarquer; **~arm** *n* avant-bras *m inv*; **~boding** *n* pressentiment *m* (néfaste); **~cast** (*irreg: like* **cast**) *n* prévision *f* ♦ *vt* prévoir; **~court** *n* (*of garage*) devant *m*; **~finger** *n* index *m*; **~front** *n*: **in the ~front of** au premier rang or plan de

foregone ['fɔːgɒn] *adj*: **it's a ~ conclusion** c'est couru d'avance

foreground ['fɔːgraʊnd] *n* premier plan

forehead ['fɒrɪd] *n* front *m*

foreign ['fɒrɪn] *adj* étranger(-ère); (*trade*) extérieur(-e); **~er** *n* étranger (-ère), *m*; **~ exchange** *n* change *m*; **F~ Office** (BRIT) *n* ministère *m* des affaires étrangères; **F~ Secretary** (BRIT) *n* ministre *m* des affaires étrangères

fore: **~leg** *n* (*of cat, dog*) patte *f* de devant; (*of horse*) jambe antérieure; **~man** (*irreg*) *n* (*of factory, building site*) contremaître *m*, chef *m* d'équipe; **~most** *adj* le (la) plus en vue; premier(-ère) ♦ *adv*: **first and ~most** avant tout, tout d'abord

forensic [fə'rɛnsɪk] *adj*: **~ medicine** médecine légale; **~ scientist** médecin

m légiste

fore: **~runner** *n* précurseur *m*; **~see** (*irreg: like* **see**) *vt* prévoir; **~seeable** *adj* prévisible; **~shadow** *vt* présager, annoncer, laisser prévoir; **~sight** *n* prévoyance *f*

forest ['fɒrɪst] *n* forêt *f*; **~ry** *n* sylviculture *f*

foretaste ['fɔːteɪst] *n* avant-goût *m*

foretell [fɔː'tel] (*irreg: like* **tell**) *vt* prédire

forever [fə'rɛvər] *adv* pour toujours; (*fig*) continuellement

foreword ['fɔːwəːd] *n* avant-propos *m inv*

forfeit ['fɔːfɪt] *vt* (*lose*) perdre

forgave [fə'geɪv] *pt of* **forgive**

forge [fɔːdʒ] *n* forge *f* ♦ *vt* (*signature*) contrefaire; (*wrought iron*) forger; **to ~ money** (BRIT) fabriquer de la fausse monnaie; **~ ahead** *vi* pousser de l'avant, prendre de l'avance; **~d** *adj* faux (fausse); **~r** *n* faussaire *m*; **~ry** *n* faux *m*, contrefaçon *f*

forget [fə'get] (*pt* **forgot**, *pp* **forgotten**) *vt, vi* oublier; **~ful** *adj* distrait(e), étourdi(e); **~-me-not** *n* myosotis *m*

forgive [fə'gɪv] (*pt* **forgave**, *pp* **forgiven**) *vt* pardonner; **to ~ sb for sth/for doing sth** pardonner qch à qn/à qn de faire qch; **~ness** *n* pardon *m*

forgo [fɔː'gəu] (*pt* **forwent**, *pp* **forgone**) *vt* renoncer à

fork [fɔːk] *n* (*for eating*) fourchette *f*; (*for gardening*) fourche *f*; (*of roads*) bifurcation *f*; (*of railways*) embranchement *m* ♦ *vi* (*road*) bifurquer; **~ out** (*inf*) (*pay*) allonger; **~-lift truck** *n* chariot élévateur

forlorn [fə'lɔːn] *adj* (*deserted*) abandonné(e); (*attempt, hope*) désespéré(e)

form [fɔːm] *n* forme *f*; (SCOL) classe *f*; (*questionnaire*) formulaire *m* ♦ *vt* former; (*habit*) contracter; **in top ~** en pleine forme

formal [ˈfɔːməl] *adj* (*offer, receipt*) en bonne et due forme; (*person*) cérémonieux(-euse); (*dinner*) officiel(le); (*clothes*) de soirée; (*garden*) à la française; (*education*) à proprement parler; **~ly** *adv* officiellement; cérémonieusement

format ['fɔ:mæt] *n* format *m* ♦ *vt* (COMPUT) formater

formation [fɔ:'meɪʃən] *n* formation *f*

formative ['fɔ:mətɪv] *adj*: **~ years** années *fpl* d'apprentissage *or* de formation

former ['fɔ:mə*] *adj* ancien(ne) (*before n*), précédent(e); **the ~ ... the latter** le premier ... le second, celui-ci ... celui-là; **~ly** *adv* autrefois

formidable ['fɔ:mɪdəbl] *adj* redoutable

formula ['fɔ:mjulə] (*pl* **~e**) *n* formule *f*

forsake [fə'seɪk] (*pt* **forsook**, *pp* **forsaken**) *vt* abandonner

fort [fɔ:t] *n* fort *m*

forte ['fɔ:tɪ] *n* (point) fort *m*

forth [fɔ:θ] *adv* en avant; **to go back and ~** aller et venir; **and so ~** et ainsi de suite; **~coming** *adj* (*event*) qui va avoir lieu prochainement; (*character*) ouvert(e), communicatif(-ive); (*available*) disponible; **~right** *adj* franc (franche), direct(e); **~with** *adv* sur-le-champ

fortify ['fɔ:tɪfaɪ] *vt* fortifier

fortitude ['fɔ:tɪtju:d] *n* courage *m*

fortnight ['fɔ:tnaɪt] (BRIT) *n* quinzaine *f*, quinze jours *mpl*; **~ly** *adj* bimensuel(le) ♦ *adv* tous les quinze jours

fortunate ['fɔ:tʃənɪt] *adj* heureux (-euse); (*person*) chanceux(-euse); **it is ~ that** c'est une chance que; **~ly** *adv* heureusement

fortune ['fɔ:tʃən] *n* chance *f*; (*wealth*) fortune *f*; **~-teller** *n* diseuse *f* de bonne aventure

forty ['fɔ:tɪ] *num* quarante

forward ['fɔ:wəd] *adj* (*ahead of schedule*) en avance; (*movement, position*) en avant, vers l'avant; (*not shy*) direct(e); effronté(e) ♦ *n* (SPORT) avant *m* ♦ *vt* (*letter*) faire suivre; (*parcel, goods*) expédier; (*fig*) promouvoir, favoriser; **~(s)**

adv en avant; **to move ~** avancer

fossil ['fɔsl] *n* fossile *m*

foster ['fɔstə*] *vt* encourager, favoriser; (*child*) élever (*sans obligation d'adopter*); **~ child** *n* enfant adoptif(-ive); **~ mother** *n* mère *f* nourricière *or* adoptive

fought [fɔ:t] *pt, pp of* **fight**

foul [faul] *adj* (*weather, smell etc*) infect(e); (*language*) ordurier(-ère) ♦ *n* (SPORT) faute *f* ♦ *vt* (*dirty*) salir, encrasser; **he's got a ~ temper** il a un caractère de chien; **~ play** *n* (LAW) acte criminel

found [faund] *pt, pp of* **find** ♦ *vt* (*establish*) fonder; **~ation** [faun'deɪʃən] *n* (*act*) fondation *f*; (*base*) fondement *m*; (*also*: **~ation cream**) fond *m* de teint; **~ations** *npl* (*of building*) fondations *fpl*

founder ['faundə*] *n* fondateur *m* ♦ *vi* couler, sombrer

foundry ['faundrɪ] *n* fonderie *f*

fountain ['fauntɪn] *n* fontaine *f*; **~ pen** *n* stylo *m* (à encre)

four [fɔ:*] *num* quatre; **on all ~s** à quatre pattes; **~-poster** *n* (*also*: **~-poster bed**) lit *m* à baldaquin; **~teen** *num* quatorze; **~th** *num* quatrième

fowl [faul] *n* volaille *f*

fox [fɔks] *n* renard *m* ♦ *vt* mystifier

foyer ['fɔɪeɪ] *n* (*hotel*) hall *m*; (THEATRE) foyer *m*

fraction ['frækʃən] *n* fraction *f*

fracture ['fræktʃə*] *n* fracture *f*

fragile ['frædʒaɪl] *adj* fragile

fragment ['frægmənt] *n* fragment *m*

fragrant ['freɪgrənt] *adj* parfumé(e), odorant(e)

frail [freɪl] *adj* fragile, délicat(e)

frame [freɪm] *n* charpente *f*; (*of picture, bicycle*) cadre *m*; (*of door, window*) encadrement *m*, chambranle *m*; (*of spectacles: also*: **~s**) monture *f* ♦ *vt* encadrer; **~ of mind** disposition *f* d'esprit; **~work** *n* structure *f*

France [frɑ:ns] *n* France *f*

franchise ['fræntʃaɪz] *n* (POL) droit *m* de vote; (COMM) franchise *f*

frank [fræŋk] adj franc (franche) ♦ vt (letter) affranchir; ~ly adv franchement

frantic ['fræntɪk] adj (hectic) frénétique; (distraught) hors de soi

fraternity [frə'tɜːnɪtɪ] n (spirit) fraternité f; (club) communauté f, confrérie f

fraud [frɔːd] n supercherie f, fraude f, tromperie f; (person) imposteur m

fraught [frɔːt] adj: ~ with chargé(e) de, plein(e) de

fray [freɪ] vi s'effilocher

freak [friːk] n (also cpd) phénomène f, créature ou événement exceptionnel par sa rareté

freckle ['frekl] n tache f de rousseur

free [friː] adj libre; (gratis) gratuit(e) ♦ vt (prisoner etc) libérer; (jammed object or person) dégager; ~ (of charge), for ~ gratuitement; ~dom n liberté f; F~fone ® n numéro vert; ~-for-all n mêlée générale; ~ gift n prime f; ~hold n propriété foncière libre; ~ kick n coup franc; ~lance adj indépendant(e); ~ly adv librement; (liberally) libéralement; F~mason n franc-maçon m; F~post ® n port payé; ~range adj (hen, eggs) de ferme; ~ trade n libre-échange m; ~way n (US) autoroute f; ~ will n libre arbitre m; of one's own ~ will de son plein gré

freeze [friːz] (pt froze, pp frozen) vi geler ♦ vt geler; (food) congeler; (prices, salaries) bloquer, geler ♦ n gel m; (fig) blocage m; ~-dried adj lyophilisé(e); ~r n congélateur m; **freezing** adj: **freezing (cold)** (weather, water) glacial(e) ♦ n: **3 degrees below freezing** 3 degrés au-dessous de zéro; **freezing point** n point m de congélation

freight [freɪt] n (goods) fret m, cargaison f; (money charged) fret, prix m du transport; ~ **train** n train m de marchandises

French [frentʃ] adj français(e) ♦ n (LING) français m; the ~ npl (people) les Français; ~ **bean** n haricot vert; ~ **fried (potatoes)** (US ~ **fries**) npl (pommes

de terre fpl) frites fpl; ~ **horn** n (MUS) cor m (d'harmonie); ~ **kiss** n baiser profond; ~ **loaf** n baguette f; ~man (irreg) n Français m; ~ **window** n porte-fenêtre f; ~woman (irreg) n Française f

frenzy ['frenzɪ] n frénésie f

frequency ['friːkwənsɪ] n fréquence f

frequent [adj 'friːkwənt, vb frɪ'kwent] adj fréquent(e) ♦ vt fréquenter; ~ly adv fréquemment

fresh [freʃ] adj frais (fraîche); (new) nouveau (nouvelle); (cheeky) familier(-ère), culotté(e); ~en vi (wind, air) fraîchir; ~en up vi faire un brin de toilette; ~er n (BRIT: inf) n (SCOL) bizuth m, étudiant(e) de 1ère année; ~ly adv nouvellement, récemment; ~man (US) (irreg) n = fresher; ~ness n fraîcheur f; ~water adj (fish) d'eau douce

fret [fret] vi s'agiter, se tracasser

friar ['fraɪə] n moine m, frère m

friction ['frɪkʃən] n friction f

Friday ['fraɪdɪ] n vendredi m

fridge [frɪdʒ] n (BRIT) n frigo m, frigidaire ® m

fried [fraɪd] adj frit(e); ~ **egg** n œuf m sur le plat

friend [frend] n ami(e); ~ly adj amical(e); gentil(le); (place) accueillant(e); **they were killed by ~ly fire** ils sont morts sous les tirs de leur propre camp; ~ship n amitié f

frieze [friːz] n frise f

fright [fraɪt] n peur f, effroi m; **to take** ~ prendre peur, s'effrayer; ~en vt effrayer, faire peur à; ~ened adj: **to be** ~ened (of) avoir peur (de); ~ening adj effrayant(e); ~ful adj affreux(-euse)

frigid ['frɪdʒɪd] adj frigide

frill [frɪl] n (on dress) volant m; (on shirt) jabot m

fringe [frɪndʒ] n (BRIT: of hair) frange f; (edge: of forest etc) bordure f; ~ **benefits** npl avantages sociaux or en nature

Frisbee ® ['frɪzbɪ] n Frisbee ® m

frisk [frɪsk] vt fouiller

fritter ['frɪtə^r] n beignet m; **~ away** vt gaspiller

frivolous ['frɪvələs] adj frivole

frizzy ['frɪzɪ] adj crépu(e)

fro [frəu] adv: **to go to and ~** aller et venir

frock [frɔk] n robe f

frog [frɔg] n grenouille f; **~man** n homme-grenouille m

frolic ['frɔlɪk] vi folâtrer, batifoler

KEYWORD

from [frɔm] prep **1** (indicating starting place, origin etc) de; **where do you come from?, where are you from?** d'où venez-vous?; **from London to Paris** de Londres à Paris; **a letter from my sister** une lettre de ma sœur; **to drink from the bottle** boire à (même) la bouteille

2 (indicating time) (à partir) de; **from one o'clock to** or **until** or **till two** d'une heure à deux heures; **from January (on)** à partir de janvier

3 (indicating distance) de; **the hotel is one kilometre from the beach** l'hôtel est à un kilomètre de la plage

4 (indicating price, number etc) de; **the interest rate was increased from 9% to 10%** le taux d'intérêt est passé de 9 à 10%

5 (indicating difference) de; **he can't tell red from green** il ne peut pas distinguer le rouge du vert

6 (because of, on the basis of): **from what he says** d'après ce qu'il dit; **weak from hunger** affaibli par la faim

front [frʌnt] n (of house, dress) devant m; (of coach, train) avant m; (promenade: also: **sea ~**) bord m de mer; (MIL, METEOROLOGY) front m; (fig: appearances) contenance f, façade f ♦ adj de devant; (seat) avant inv; **in ~ (of)** devant; **~age** n (of building) façade f; **~ door** n porte f d'entrée; (of car) portière f avant; **~ier**

['frʌntɪə^r] n frontière f; **~ page** n première page; **~ room** (BRIT) n pièce f de devant, salon m; **~-wheel drive** n traction f avant

frost [frɔst] n gel m, gelée f; (also: **hoar-frost**) givre m; **~bite** n gelures fpl; **~ed** adj (glass) dépoli(e); **~y** adj (weather, welcome) glacial(e)

froth [frɔθ] n mousse f, écume f

frown [fraun] vi froncer les sourcils

froze [frəuz] pt of **freeze**

frozen ['frəuzn] pp of **freeze**

fruit [fru:t] n inv fruit m; **~erer** n fruitier m, marchand(e) de fruits; **~ful** adj (fig) fructueux(-euse); **~ion** [fru:'ɪʃən] n: **to come to** or **in** se réaliser; **~ juice** n jus m de fruit; **~ machine** (BRIT) n machine f à sous; **~ salad** n salade f de fruits

frustrate [frʌs'treɪt] vt frustrer

fry [fraɪ] (pt, pp **fried**) vt (faire) frire; see also **small**; **~ing pan** n poêle f (à frire)

ft. abbr = **foot; feet**

fudge [fʌdʒ] n (CULIN) caramel m

fuel ['fjuəl] n (for heating) combustible m; (for propelling) carburant m; **~ oil** n mazout m; **~ tank** n (in vehicle) réservoir m

fugitive ['fju:dʒɪtɪv] n fugitif(-ive)

fulfil [ful'fɪl] (US **fulfill**) vt (function, condition) remplir; (order) exécuter; (wish, desire) satisfaire, réaliser; **~ment** (US **fulfillment**) n (of wishes etc) réalisation f; (feeling) contentement m

full [ful] adj plein(e); (details, information) complet(-ète); (skirt) ample, large ♦ adv: **to know ~ well that** savoir fort bien que; **I'm ~ (up)** j'ai bien mangé; **a ~ two hours** deux bonnes heures; **at ~ speed** à toute vitesse; **in ~** (reproduce, quote) intégralement; (write) en toutes lettres; **~ employment** plein emploi; **to pay in ~** tout payer; **~-length** adj (film) long métrage; (portrait, mirror) en pied; (coat) long(ue); **~ moon** n pleine lune; **~-scale** adj (attack, war) complet(-ète), total(e); (model) grandeur nature inv; **~ stop** n point m;

time adj, adv (work) à plein temps; **~y** adv entièrement, complètement; (at least) au moins; **~y licensed** (hotel, restaurant) autorisé(e) à vendre des boissons alcoolisées; **~y-fledged** adj (barrister etc) diplômé(e); (citizen, member) à part entière

fumble ['fʌmbl] vi: **~ with** tripoter

fume [fjuːm] vi rager; **~s** npl vapeurs fpl, émanations fpl, gaz mpl

fun [fʌn] n amusement m, divertissement m; **to have ~** s'amuser; **for ~** pour rire; **to make ~ of** se moquer de

function ['fʌŋkʃən] n fonction f; (social occasion) cérémonie f, soirée officielle ♦ vi fonctionner; **~al** adj fonctionnel(le)

fund [fʌnd] n caisse f, fonds m; (source, store) source f, mine f; **~s** npl (money) fonds mpl

fundamental [fʌndə'mentl] adj fondamental(e)

funeral ['fjuːnərəl] n enterrement m, obsèques fpl; **~ parlour** n entreprise f de pompes funèbres; **~ service** n service m funèbre

funfair ['fʌnfeər] (BRIT) n fête (foraine)

fungi ['fʌŋgaɪ] npl of **fungus**

fungus ['fʌŋgəs] (pl **fungi**) n champignon m; (mould) moisissure f

funnel ['fʌnl] n entonnoir m; (of ship) cheminée f

funny ['fʌnɪ] adj amusant(e), drôle; (strange) curieux(-euse), bizarre

fur [fɜːr] n fourrure f; (BRIT: in kettle etc) (dépôt m de) tartre m

furious ['fjuərɪəs] adj furieux(-euse); (effort) acharné(e)

furlong ['fɜːlɔŋ] n = 201,17 m

furnace ['fɜːnɪs] n fourneau m

furnish ['fɜːnɪʃ] vt meubler; (supply): **to ~ sb with sth** fournir qch à qn; **~ings** npl mobilier m, ameublement m

furniture ['fɜːnɪtʃər] n meubles mpl, mobilier m; **piece of ~** meuble m

furrow ['fʌrəu] n sillon m

furry ['fɜːrɪ] adj (animal) à fourrure; (toy) en peluche

further ['fɜːðər] adj (additional) supplémentaire, autre; nouveau (nouvelle) ♦ adv plus loin; (more) davantage; (moreover) de plus ♦ vt faire avancer or progresser, promouvoir; **~ education** n enseignement m postscolaire; **~more** adv de plus, en outre

furthest ['fɜːðɪst] superl of **far**

fury ['fjuərɪ] n fureur f

fuse [fjuːz] (US **fuze**) n fusible m; (for bomb etc) amorce f, détonateur m ♦ vt, vi (metal) fondre; **to ~ the lights** (BRIT) faire sauter les plombs; **~ box** n boîte f à fusibles

fuss [fʌs] n (excitement) agitation f; (complaining) histoire(s) f(pl); **to make a ~** faire des histoires; **to make a ~ of sb** être aux petits soins pour qn; **~y** adj (person) tatillon(ne), difficile; (dress, style) tarabiscoté(e)

future ['fjuːtʃər] adj futur(e) ♦ n avenir m; (LING) futur m; **in ~** à l'avenir

fuze [fjuːz] (US) n, vt, vi = **fuse**

fuzzy ['fʌzɪ] adj (PHOT) flou(e); (hair) crépu(e)

G, g

G [dʒiː] n (MUS) sol m

G7 n abbr (= Group of 7) le groupe des 7

gabble ['gæbl] vi bredouiller

gable ['geɪbl] n pignon m

gadget ['gædʒɪt] n gadget m

Gaelic ['geɪlɪk] adj gaélique ♦ n (LING) gaélique m

gag [gæg] n (on mouth) bâillon m; (joke) gag m ♦ vt bâillonner

gaiety ['geɪɪtɪ] n gaieté f

gain [geɪn] n (improvement) gain m; (profit) gain, profit m; (increase): **~ (in)** augmentation f (de) ♦ vt gagner ♦ vi (watch) avancer; **to ~ 3 lbs (in weight)** prendre 3 livres; **to ~ on sb** (catch up) rattraper qn; **to ~ from/by** gagner de/à

gal. abbr = **gallon**

gale [geɪl] n coup m de vent

gallant ['gælənt] adj vaillant(e), brave; (towards ladies) galant

gall bladder ['gɔːl-] n vésicule f biliaire

gallery ['gælərɪ] n galerie f; (also: **art ~**) musée m; (: private) galerie

gallon ['gælən] n gallon m (BRIT: 4,5 l; US = 3,8 l)

gallop ['gæləp] n galop m ♦ vi galoper

gallows ['gæləuz] n potence f

gallstone ['gɔːlstəun] n calcul m biliaire

galore [gə'lɔːr] adv en abondance, à gogo

Gambia ['gæmbɪə] n: **(The) ~** la Gambie

gambit ['gæmbɪt] n (fig): **(opening) ~** manœuvre f stratégique

gamble ['gæmbl] n pari m, risque m calculé ♦ vt, vi jouer; **to ~ on** (fig) miser sur; **~r** n joueur m; **gambling** n jeu m

game [geɪm] n jeu m; (match) match m; (strategy, scheme) plan m; projet m; (HUNTING) gibier m ♦ adj (willing): **to be ~ (for)** être prêt(e) (à or pour); **big ~** gros gibier; **~keeper** n garde-chasse m

gammon ['gæmən] n (bacon) quartier m de lard fumé; (ham) jambon fumé

gamut ['gæmət] n gamme f

gang [gæŋ] n bande f; (of workmen) équipe f; **~ up** vi: **to ~ up on sb** se liguer contre qn; **~ster** n gangster m; **~way** ['gæŋweɪ] n passerelle f; (BRIT: of bus, plane) couloir central; (: in cinema) allée centrale

gaol [dʒeɪl] (BRIT) n = **jail**

gap [gæp] n trou m; (in time) intervalle m; (difference): **~ between** écart m entre

gape [geɪp] vi (person) être or rester bouche bée; (hole, shirt) être ouvert(e); **gaping** adj (hole) béant(e)

garage ['gærɑːʒ] n garage m

garbage ['gɑːbɪdʒ] n (US: rubbish) ordures fpl, détritus mpl; (inf: nonsense) foutaises fpl; **~ can** (US) n poubelle f, boîte f à ordures

garbled ['gɑːbld] adj (account, message) embrouillé(e)

garden ['gɑːdn] n jardin m; **~s** npl jardin public; **~er** n jardinier m; **~ing** n jardinage m

gargle ['gɑːgl] vi se gargariser

garish ['gɛərɪʃ] adj criard(e), voyant(e); (light) cru(e)

garland ['gɑːlənd] n guirlande f; couronne f

garlic ['gɑːlɪk] n ail m

garment ['gɑːmənt] n vêtement m

garrison ['gærɪsn] n garnison f

garter ['gɑːtər] n jarretière f; (US) jarretelle f

gas [gæs] n gaz m; (US: gasoline) essence f ♦ vt asphyxier; **~ cooker** (BRIT) n cuisinière f à gaz; **~ cylinder** n bouteille f de gaz; **~ fire** (BRIT) n radiateur m à gaz

gash [gæʃ] n entaille f; (on face) balafre f

gasket ['gæskɪt] n (AUT) joint m de culasse

gas mask n masque m à gaz

gas meter n compteur m à gaz

gasoline ['gæsəliːn] (US) n essence f

gasp [gɑːsp] vi haleter

gas: ~ ring n brûleur m; **~ station** (US) n station-service f; **~ tap** n bouton m (de cuisinière à gaz); (on pipe) robinet m à gaz

gastric ['gæstrɪk] adj gastrique; **~ flu** n grippe f intestinale

gate [geɪt] n (of garden) portail m; (of field) barrière f; (of building, at airport) porte f

gateau ['gætəu] n (pl **~x**) (gros) gâteau m à la crème

gatecrash vt s'introduire sans invitation dans

gateway n porte f

gather ['gæðər] vt (flowers, fruit) cueillir; (pick up) ramasser; (assemble) rassembler, réunir; recueillir; (understand) comprendre; (SEWING) froncer ♦ vi (assemble) se rassembler; **to ~ speed** prendre de la vitesse; **~ing** n rassemblement m

gaudy ['gɔːdɪ] adj voyant(e)

gauge [geɪdʒ] n (instrument) jauge f
♦ vt jauger

gaunt [gɔːnt] adj (thin) décharné(e);
(grim, desolate) désolé(e)

gauntlet ['gɔːntlɪt] n (glove) gant m

gauze [gɔːz] n gaze f

gave [geɪv] pt of **give**

gay [geɪ] adj (homosexual) homo-
sexuel(le); (cheerful) gai(e), réjoui(e);
(colour etc) gai, vif (vive)

gaze [geɪz] n regard m fixe ♦ vi: **to ~ at**
fixer du regard

gazump [gə'zʌmp] (BRIT) vi revenir sur
une promesse de vente (pour accepter une
offre plus intéressante)

GB abbr = **Great Britain**

GCE n abbr (BRIT) = **General Certificate
of Education**

GCSE n abbr (BRIT) = **General Certificate of Secondary Education**

gear [gɪə*] n matériel m, équipement m;
attirail m; (TECH) engrenage m; (AUT) vitesse f ♦ vt (fig: adapt): **to ~ sth to**
adapter qch à; **top** or (US) **high ~** quatrième (or cinquième) vitesse; **low ~**
première vitesse; **in ~** en prise; **~ box**
n boîte f de vitesses; **~ lever** (US **gear
shift**) n levier m de vitesse

geese [giːs] npl of **goose**

gel [dʒel] n gel m

gem [dʒem] n pierre précieuse

Gemini ['dʒemɪnaɪ] n les Gémeaux mpl

gender ['dʒendə*] n genre m

gene [dʒiːn] n gène m

general ['dʒenərl] n général m ♦ adj
général(e); **in ~** en général; **~ delivery** n poste restante; **~ election** n
élection(s) législative(s); **~ knowledge**
n connaissances générales; **~ly** adv généralement; **~ practitioner** n généraliste m/f

generate ['dʒenəreɪt] vt engendrer;
(electricity etc) produire; **generation** n
génération f; (of electricity etc) production f; **generator** n générateur m

generosity [dʒenə'rɒsɪtɪ] n générosité f

generous ['dʒenərəs] adj généreux
(-euse); (copious) copieux(-euse)

genetic [dʒɪ'netɪk] adj: **~ engineering**
ingénierie f génétique; **~ fingerprinting** système m d'empreinte génétique

genetically modified adj (food etc)
génétiquement modifié(e)

genetics [dʒɪ'netɪks] n génétique f

Geneva [dʒɪ'niːvə] n Genève

genial ['dʒiːnɪəl] adj cordial(e)

genitals ['dʒenɪtlz] npl organes génitaux

genius ['dʒiːnɪəs] n génie m

genteel [dʒen'tiːl] adj distingué(e)

gentle ['dʒentl] adj doux (douce)

gentleman ['dʒentlmən] n monsieur
m; (well-bred man) gentleman m

gently ['dʒentlɪ] adv doucement

gentry ['dʒentrɪ] n inv: **the ~** la petite
noblesse

gents [dʒents] n W.-C. mpl (pour hommes)

genuine ['dʒenjuɪn] adj véritable,
authentique; (person) sincère

geographical [dʒɪə'græfɪkl] adj géogra-
phique

geography [dʒɪ'ɒgrəfɪ] n géographie f

geology [dʒɪ'ɒlədʒɪ] n géologie f

geometric(al) [dʒɪə'metrɪk(l)] adj géométrique

geometry [dʒɪ'ɒmɪtrɪ] n géométrie f

geranium [dʒɪ'reɪnɪəm] n géranium m

geriatric [dʒerɪ'ætrɪk] adj gériatrique

germ [dʒɜːm] n (MED) microbe m

German ['dʒɜːmən] adj allemand(e)
♦ n Allemand(e); (LING) allemand m; **~
measles** (BRIT) n rubéole f

Germany ['dʒɜːmənɪ] n Allemagne f

gesture ['dʒestjə*] n geste m

| KEYWORD |

get [get] (pt, pp **got**, pp **gotten** (US)) vi
1 (become, be) devenir; **to get old/
tired** devenir vieux/fatigué, vieillir/se
fatiguer; **to get drunk** s'enivrer; **to get
killed** se faire tuer; **when do I get**

paid? quand est-ce que je serai payé?; **it's getting late** il se fait tard

2 (*go*): **to get to/from** aller à/de; **to get home** rentrer chez soi; **how did you get here?** comment es-tu arrivé ici?

3 (*begin*) commencer *or* se mettre à; **I'm getting to like him** je commence à l'apprécier; **let's get going** *or* **started** allons-y

4 (*modal aux vb*): **you've got to do it** il faut que vous le fassiez; **I've got to tell the police** je dois le dire à la police

♦ *vt* **1**: **to get sth done** (*do*) faire qch; (*have done*) faire faire qch; **to get one's hair cut** se faire couper les cheveux; **to get sb to do sth** faire faire qch à qn; **to get sb drunk** enivrer qn

2 (*obtain: money, permission, results*) obtenir, avoir; (*find: job, flat*) trouver; (*fetch: person, doctor, object*) aller chercher; **to get sth for sb** procurer qch à qn; **get me Mr Jones, please** (*on phone*) passez-moi Mr Jones, s'il vous plaît; **can I get you a drink?** est-ce que je peux vous servir à boire?

3 (*receive: present, letter*) recevoir, avoir; (*acquire: reputation*) avoir; (: *prize*) obtenir; **what did you get for your birthday?** qu'est-ce que tu as eu pour ton anniversaire?

4 (*catch*) prendre, saisir, attraper; (*hit: target etc*) atteindre; **to get sb by the arm/throat** prendre *or* saisir *or* attraper qn par le bras/à la gorge; **get him!** arrête-le!

5 (*take, move*) faire parvenir; **do you think we'll get it through the door?** on arrivera à le faire passer par la porte?; **I'll get you there somehow** je me débrouillerai pour t'y emmener

6 (*catch, take: plane, bus etc*) prendre

7 (*understand*) comprendre, saisir; (*hear*) entendre; **I've got it!** j'ai compris!, je saisis!; **I didn't get your name** je n'ai pas entendu votre nom

8 (*have, possess*): **to have got** avoir; **how many have you got?** vous en avez combien?

get about *vi* se déplacer; (*news*) se répandre

get along *vi* (*agree*) s'entendre; (*depart*) s'en aller; (*manage*) = **get by**

get at *vt fus* (*attack*) s'en prendre à; (*reach*) atteindre

get away *vi* partir, s'en aller; (*escape*) s'échapper

get away with *vt fus* en être quitte pour; se tirer; pardonner *or* pardonner

get back *vi* (*return*) rentrer ♦ *vt* récupérer, recouvrer

get by *vi* (*pass*) passer; (*manage*) se débrouiller

get down *vi*, *vt fus* descendre ♦ *vt* descendre; (*depress*) déprimer

get down to *vt fus* (*work*) se mettre à (faire)

get in *vi* rentrer; (*train*) arriver

get into *vt fus* entrer dans; (*car, train etc*) monter dans; (*clothes*) mettre, enfiler, endosser; **to get into bed/a rage** se mettre au lit/en colère

get off *vi* (*from train etc*) descendre; (*depart: person, car*) s'en aller; (*escape*) s'en tirer ♦ *vt* (*remove: clothes, stain*) enlever ♦ *vt fus* (*train, bus*) descendre de

get on *vi* (*at exam etc*) se débrouiller; (*agree*): **to get on (with)** s'entendre (avec) ♦ *vt fus* monter dans; (*horse*) monter sur

get out *vi* sortir; (*of vehicle*) descendre ♦ *vt* sortir

get out of *vt fus* sortir de; (*duty etc*) échapper à, se soustraire à

get over *vt fus* (*illness*) se remettre de

get round *vt fus* contourner; (*fig: person*) entortiller

get through *vi* (*TEL*) avoir la communication; **to get through to sb** atteindre qn

get together *vi* se réunir ♦ *vt* assembler

get up vi (rise) se lever ♦ vt fus monter

get up to vt fus (reach) arriver à; (prank etc) faire

getaway ['gɛtəweɪ] n (escape) fuite f

geyser ['giːzər] n (GEO) geyser m; (BRIT: water heater) chauffe-eau m inv

Ghana ['gɑːnə] n Ghana m

ghastly ['gɑːstlɪ] adj atroce, horrible; (pale) livide, blème

gherkin ['gəːkɪn] n cornichon m

ghetto blaster ['gɛtəu'blɑːstər] n stéréo f portable

ghost [gəust] n fantôme m, revenant m

giant ['dʒaɪənt] n géant(e) ♦ adj géant(e), énorme

gibberish ['dʒɪbərɪʃ] n charabia m

giblets ['dʒɪblɪts] npl abats mpl

Gibraltar [dʒɪ'brɔːltər] n Gibraltar m

giddy ['gɪdɪ] adj (dizzy): **to be** or **feel ~** avoir le vertige

gift [gɪft] n cadeau m; (donation, ability) don m; **~ed** adj doué(e); **~ shop** n boutique f de cadeaux; **~ token** n chèque-cadeau m

gigantic [dʒaɪ'gæntɪk] adj gigantesque

giggle ['gɪgl] vi pouffer (de rire), rire sottement

gill [dʒɪl] n (measure) = 0.25 pints (BRIT = 0.15 l, US = 0.12 l)

gills [gɪlz] npl (of fish) ouïes fpl, branchies fpl

gilt [gɪlt] adj doré(e) ♦ n dorure f; **~-edged** adj (COMM) de premier ordre

gimmick ['gɪmɪk] n truc m

gin [dʒɪn] n (liquor) gin m

ginger ['dʒɪndʒər] n gingembre m; **~ ale**, **~ beer** n boisson gazeuse au gingembre; **~bread** n pain m d'épices

gingerly ['dʒɪndʒəlɪ] adv avec précaution

gipsy ['dʒɪpsɪ] n = **gypsy**

giraffe [dʒɪ'rɑːf] n girafe f

girder ['gəːdər] n poutrelle f

girl [gəːl] n fille f, fillette f; (young married woman) jeune fille; (daughter) fille; **an English ~** une jeune Anglaise; **~friend** n (of girl) amie f; (of boy) petite amie f; **~ish** adj de petite or de jeune fille; (for a boy) efféminé(e)

giro ['dʒaɪrəu] n (bank) virement m bancaire; (post office ~) mandat m; (BRIT: welfare cheque) mandat m d'allocation chômage

gist [dʒɪst] n essentiel m

give [gɪv] (pt gave, pp given) vt donner ♦ vi (break) céder; (stretch: fabric) se prêter; **to ~ sb sth**, **~ sth to sb** donner qch à qn; **to ~ a cry/sigh** pousser un cri/un soupir; **~ away** vt donner; (~ free) faire cadeau de; (betray) donner, trahir; (disclose) révéler; (bride) conduire à l'autel; **~ back** vt rendre; **~ in** vi céder ♦ vt donner; **~ off** vt dégager; **~ out** vt distribuer; annoncer; **~ up** vi renoncer ♦ vt renoncer à; **to ~ up smoking** arrêter de fumer; **to ~ o.s. up** se rendre; **~ way** (BRIT) vi céder; (AUT) céder la priorité

GLA (BRIT) n abbr (= Greater London Authority) conseil municipal de Londres

glacier ['glæsɪər] n glacier m

glad [glæd] adj content(e); **~ly** adv volontiers

glamorous ['glæmərəs] adj (person) séduisant(e); (job) prestigieux(-euse)

glamour ['glæmər] n éclat m, prestige m

glance [glɑːns] n coup m d'œil ♦ vi: **to ~ at** jeter un coup d'œil à; **glancing** adj (blow) oblique

gland [glænd] n glande f

glare [glɛər] n (of anger) regard furieux; (of light) lumière éblouissante; (of publicity) feux mpl ♦ vi briller d'un éclat aveuglant; **to ~ at** lancer un regard furieux à; **glaring** adj (mistake) criant(e), qui saute aux yeux

glass [glɑːs] n verre m; **~es** npl (spectacles) lunettes fpl; **~house** (BRIT) n (for plants) serre f; **~ware** n verrerie f

glaze [gleɪz] vt (door, window) vitrer;

(*pottery*) vernir ♦ *n* (*on pottery*) vernis *m*; **~d** *adj* (*pottery*) verni(e); (*eyes*) vitreux(-euse)

glazier ['gleɪzɪəʳ] *n* vitrier *m*

gleam [gli:m] *n* lueur *f* ♦ *vi* luire, briller

glean [gli:n] *vt* (*information*) glaner

glee [gli:] *n* joie *f*

glib [glɪb] *adj* (*person*) qui a du bagou; (*response*) désinvolte, facile

glide [glaɪd] *vi* glisser; (*AVIAT, birds*) planer; **~r** *n* (*AVIAT*) planeur *m*; **gliding** *n* (*SPORT*) vol *m* à voile

glimmer ['glɪməʳ] *n* lueur *f*

glimpse [glɪmps] *n* vision passagère, aperçu *m* ♦ *vt* entrevoir, apercevoir

glint [glɪnt] *vi* étinceler

glisten ['glɪsn] *vi* briller, luire

glitter ['glɪtəʳ] *vi* scintiller, briller

gloat [gləut] *vi*: **~ (over)** jubiler (à propos de)

global ['gləubl] *adj* mondial(e); **~ warming** réchauffement *m* de la planète

globe [gləub] *n* globe *m*

gloom [glu:m] *n* obscurité *f*; (*sadness*) tristesse *f*, mélancolie *f*; **~y** *adj* sombre, triste, lugubre

glorious ['glɔ:rɪəs] *adj* glorieux(-euse); splendide

glory ['glɔ:rɪ] *n* gloire *f*; splendeur *f*

gloss [glɔs] *n* (*shine*) brillant *m*, vernis *m*; **~ over** *vt fus* glisser sur

glossary ['glɔsərɪ] *n* glossaire *m*

glossy ['glɔsɪ] *adj* brillant(e); **~ maga-zine** magazine *m* de luxe

glove [glʌv] *n* gant *m*; **~ compart-ment** *n* (*AUT*) boîte *f* à gants, vide-poches *m inv*

glow [gləu] *vi* rougeoyer; (*face*) rayonner; (*eyes*) briller

glower ['glauəʳ] *vi*: **to ~ (at)** lancer des regards mauvais (à)

glucose ['glu:kəus] *n* glucose *m*

glue [glu:] *n* colle *f* ♦ *vt* coller

glum [glʌm] *adj* sombre, morne

glut [glʌt] *n* surabondance *f*

glutton ['glʌtn] *n* glouton(ne); **a ~ for**

work un bourreau de travail; **a ~ for punishment** un masochiste (*fig*)

GM *abbr* (= *genetically modified*) génétiquement modifié(e)

gnat [næt] *n* moucheron *m*

gnaw [nɔ:] *vt* ronger

go [gəu] (*pt* **went**, *pp* **gone**, *pl* **~es**) *vi* aller; (*depart*) partir, s'en aller; (*work*) marcher; (*break etc*) céder; (*be sold*): **to ~ for £10** se vendre 10 livres; (*fit, suit*): **to ~ with** aller avec; (*become*): **to ~ pale/mouldy** pâlir/moisir ♦ *n*: **to have a ~ (at)** essayer (de faire); **to be on the ~** être en mouvement; **whose ~ is it?** à qui est-ce de jouer?; **he's ~ing to do** il va le faire, il est sur le point de faire; **to ~ for a walk** aller se promener; **to ~ dancing** aller danser; **how did it ~?** comment est-ce que ça s'est passé?; **to ~ round the back/by the shop** passer par derrière/devant le magasin; **~ about** *vi* (*rumour*) se répandre ♦ *vt fus*: **how do I ~ about this?** comment dois-je m'y prendre (pour faire ceci)?; **~ after** *vt fus* (*pursue*) poursuivre, courir après; (*job, record etc*) essayer d'obtenir; **~ ahead** *vi* (*make pro-gress*) avancer; (*get going*) y aller; **~ along** *vi* aller, avancer ♦ *vt fus* longer, parcourir; **~ away** *vi* partir, s'en aller; **~ back** *vi* rentrer; revenir; (*~ again*) retourner; **~ back on** *vt fus* (*promise*) revenir sur; **~ by** *vi* (*years, time*) passer, s'écouler ♦ *vt fus* (*se tenir à*) s'en croire; **~ down** *vi* descendre; (*ship*) couler; (*sun*) se coucher ♦ *vt fus* descendre; **~ for** *vt fus* (*fetch*) aller chercher; (*like*) aimer; (*attack*) s'en prendre à, attaquer; **~ in** *vi* entrer; **~ in for** *vt fus* (*compe-tition*) se présenter à; (*like*) aimer; **~ into** *vt fus* entrer dans; (*investigate*) étudier, examiner; (*embark on*) se lancer dans; **~ off** *vi* partir, s'en aller; (*food*) se gâter; (*explode*) sauter; (*event*) se dérouler ♦ *vt fus* ne plus aimer; **the gun went off** le coup est parti; **~ on** *vi* continuer; (*happen*) se passer; **to ~**

on doing continuer à faire; **~ out** vi sortir; (fire, light) s'éteindre; **~ over** vt fus (check) revoir, vérifier; **~ past** vt fus: **to ~ past sth** passer devant qch; **~ round** vi (circulate: news, rumour) circuler; (revolve) tourner; (suffice) suffire (pour tout le monde); **to ~ round to sb's** (visit) passer chez qn; **to ~ round (by)** (make a detour) faire un détour (par); **~ through** vt fus (town etc) traverser; **~ up** vi monter; (price) augmenter ♦ vt fus gravir; **~ with** vt fus (suit) aller avec; **~ without** vt fus se passer de

goad [gəud] vt aiguillonner

go-ahead adj dynamique, entreprenant(e) ♦ n feu vert

goal [gəul] n but m; **~keeper** n gardien m de but; **~post** n poteau m de but

goat [gəut] n chèvre f

gobble ['gɔbl] vt (also: **~ down**, **~ up**) engloutir

go-between ['gəubɪtwi:n] n intermédiaire m/f

god [gɔd] n dieu m; **G~** n Dieu m; **~child** n filleul(e); **~daughter** n filleule f; **~dess** n déesse f; **~father** n parrain m; **~forsaken** adj maudit(e); **~mother** n marraine f; **~send** n aubaine f; **~son** n filleul m

goggles ['gɔglz] npl (for skiing etc) lunettes protectrices

going ['gəuɪŋ] n (conditions) état m du terrain ♦ adj: **the ~ rate** le tarif (en vigueur)

gold [gəuld] n or m ♦ adj en or; (reserves) d'or; **~en** adj (made of gold) en or; (gold in colour) doré(e); **~fish** n poisson m rouge; **~-plated** adj plaqué(e) or inv; **~smith** n orfèvre m

golf [gɔlf] n golf m; **~ ball** n balle f de golf; (on typewriter) boule m f; **~ club** n club m de golf; (stick) club m, crosse f de golf; **~ course** n (terrain m de) golf m; **~er** n joueur(-euse) de golf

gone [gɔn] pp of **go**

gong [gɔŋ] n gong m

good [gud] adj bon(ne); (kind) gentil(le); (child) sage ♦ n bien m; **~s** npl (COMM) marchandises fpl, articles mpl; **~! bon!, très bien!; to be ~ at** être bon en; **to be ~ for** être bon pour; **would you be ~ enough to ...?** auriez-vous la bonté or l'amabilité de ...?; **a ~ deal (of)** beaucoup (de); **a ~ many** beaucoup (de); **to make ~** vi (succeed) faire son chemin, réussir ♦ vt (deficit) combler; (losses) compenser; **it's no ~ complaining** cela ne sert à rien de se plaindre; **for ~** pour de bon, une fois pour toutes; **~ morning/afternoon!** bonjour!; **~ evening!** bonsoir!; **~ night!** bonsoir!; (on going to bed) bonne nuit!; **~bye** excl au revoir!; **G~ Friday** n Vendredi saint; **~-looking** adj beau (belle), bien inv; **~-natured** adj (person) qui a un bon naturel; **~ness** n (of person) bonté f; **for ~ness sake!** je vous en prie!; **~ness gracious!** mon Dieu!; **~s train** (BRIT) n train m de marchandises; **~will** n bonne volonté

goose [gu:s] (pl **geese**) n oie f

gooseberry ['guzbərɪ] n groseille f à maquereau; **to play ~** (BRIT) tenir la chandelle

gooseflesh ['gu:sfleʃ] n, **goose pimples** npl chair f de poule

gore [gɔ:r] vt encorner ♦ n sang m

gorge [gɔ:dʒ] n gorge f ♦ vt: **to ~ o.s. (on)** se gorger (de)

gorgeous ['gɔ:dʒəs] adj splendide, superbe

gorilla [gə'rɪlə] n gorille m

gorse [gɔ:s] n ajoncs mpl

gory ['gɔ:rɪ] adj sanglant(e); (details) horrible

go-slow ['gəu'sləu] (BRIT) n grève perlée

gospel ['gɔspl] n évangile m

gossip ['gɔsɪp] n (chat) bavardages mpl; commérage m, cancans mpl; (person) commère f ♦ vi bavarder; (maliciously) cancaner, faire des commérages

got [gɔt] pt, pp of **get**; **~ten** (US) pp of

get

gout [gaut] n goutte f

govern ['gʌvən] vt gouverner; **~ess** n gouvernante f; **~ment** n gouvernement m; (BRIT: ministers) ministère m; **~or** n (of state, bank) gouverneur m; (of school, hospital) ≈ membre m du conseil d'établissement; (BRIT: of prison) directeur(-trice)

gown [gaun] n robe f; (of teacher, BRIT: of judge) toge f

GP n abbr = **general practitioner**

grab [græb] vt saisir, empoigner ♦ vi: **to ~ at** essayer de saisir

grace [greɪs] n grâce f ♦ vt honorer; (adorn) orner; **5 days' ~** cinq jours de répit; **~ful** adj gracieux(-euse), élégant(e); **gracious** ['greɪʃəs] adj bienveillant(e)

grade [greɪd] n (COMM) qualité f; (in hierarchy) catégorie f, grade m, échelon m; (SCOL) note f; (US: school class) classe f ♦ vt classer; **~ crossing** (US) n passage m à niveau; **~ school** (US) n école f primaire

gradient ['greɪdɪənt] n inclinaison f, pente f

gradual ['grædjuəl] adj graduel(le), progressif(-ive); **~ly** adv peu à peu, graduellement

graduate [n 'grædjuɪt, vb 'grædjueɪt] n diplômé(e), licencié(e); (US: of high school) bachelier(-ère) ♦ vi obtenir son diplôme; (US) obtenir son baccalauréat; **graduation** [grædju'eɪʃən] n (cérémonie f de) remise f des diplômes

graffiti [grə'fi:tɪ] npl graffiti mpl

graft [gra:ft] n (AGR, MED) greffe f; (bribery) corruption f ♦ vt greffer; **hard ~** (BRIT: inf) boulot acharné

grain [greɪn] n grain m

gram [græm] n gramme m

grammar ['græmər] n grammaire f; **~ school** (BRIT) n ≈ lycée m; **grammatical** [grə'mætɪkl] adj grammatical(e)

gramme [græm] n = **gram**

grand [grænd] adj magnifique, splendi-

de; (gesture etc) noble; **~children** npl petits-enfants mpl; **~dad** (inf) n grandpapa m; **~daughter** n petite-fille f; **~father** n grand-père m; **~ma** (inf) n grand-maman f; **~mother** n grandmère f; **~pa** (inf) n = **granddad**; **~parents** npl grands-parents mpl; **~ piano** n piano m à queue; **~son** n petit-fils m; **~stand** n (SPORT) tribune f

granite ['grænɪt] n granit m

granny ['grænɪ] n (inf) grand-maman f

grant [gra:nt] vt accorder; (a request) accéder à; (ADMIT) concéder ♦ n (SCOL) bourse f; (ADMIN) subside m, subvention f; **to take it for ~ed that** trouver tout naturel que +sub; **to take sb for ~ed** considérer qn comme faisant partie du décor

granulated sugar ['grænjuleɪtɪd-] n sucre m en poudre

grape [greɪp] n raisin m

grapefruit ['greɪpfruːt] n pamplemousse m

graph [gra:f] n graphique m; **~ic** ['græfɪk] adj graphique (account, description) vivant(e); **~ics** n arts mpl graphiques; graphisme m ♦ npl représentations fpl graphiques

grapple ['græpl] vi: **to ~ with** être aux prises avec

grasp [gra:sp] vt saisir ♦ n (grip) prise f; (understanding) compréhension f, connaissance f; **~ing** adj cupide

grass [gra:s] n herbe f; (lawn) gazon m; **~hopper** n sauterelle f; **~roots** adj de la base, du peuple

grate [greɪt] n grille f de cheminée ♦ vi grincer ♦ vt (CULIN) râper

grateful ['greɪtful] adj reconnaissant(e)

grater ['greɪtər] n râpe f

gratifying ['grætɪfaɪŋ] adj agréable

grating ['greɪtɪŋ] n (iron bars) grille f ♦ adj (noise) grinçant(e)

gratitude ['grætɪtju:d] n gratitude f

gratuity [grə'tju:ɪtɪ] n pourboire m

grave [greɪv] n tombe f ♦ adj grave, sérieux(-euse)

gravel ['grævl] n gravier m

gravestone ['greɪvstəʊn] n pierre tombale

graveyard ['greɪvjɑːd] n cimetière m

gravity ['grævɪtɪ] n (in PHYSICS) gravité f; pesanteur f; (seriousness) gravité

gravy ['greɪvɪ] n jus m (de viande); sauce f

gray [greɪ] (US) adj = **grey**

graze [greɪz] vi paître, brouter ♦ vt (touch lightly) frôler, effleurer; (scrape) écorcher ♦ n écorchure f

grease [griːs] n (fat) graisse f; (lubricant) lubrifiant m ♦ vt graisser; lubrifier; **~proof paper** (BRIT) n papier sulfurisé; **greasy** adj gras(se), graisseux(-euse)

great [greɪt] adj grand(e); (inf) formidable; **G~ Britain** n Grande-Bretagne f; **~-grandfather** n arrière-grand-père m; **~-grandmother** n arrière-grand-mère f; **~ly** adv très, grandement; (with verbs) beaucoup; **~ness** n grandeur f

Greece [griːs] n Grèce f

greed [griːd] n (also: **~iness**) avidité f; (for food) gourmandise f, gloutonnerie f; **~y** adj avide; gourmand(e), glouton(ne)

Greek [griːk] adj grec (grecque) ♦ n Grec (Grecque); (LING) grec m

green [griːn] adj vert(e); (inexperienced) (bien) jeune, naïf (naïve); (POL) vert(e), écologiste; (ecological) écologique ♦ n vert m; (stretch of grass) pelouse f; **~s** npl (vegetables) légumes verts; (POL): **the G~s** les Verts mpl; **the G~ Party** (BRIT: POL) le parti écologiste; **~ belt** n (round town) ceinture verte; **~ card** n (AUT) carte verte; (US) permis m de travail; **~ery** n verdure f; **~grocer's** (BRIT) n marchand m de fruits et légumes; **~house** n serre f; **~house effect** n effet m de serre; **~house gas** n gas m à effet de serre; **~ish** adj verdâtre

Greenland ['griːnlənd] n Groenland m

greet [griːt] vt accueillir; **~ing** n salutation f; **~ing(s) card** n carte f de vœux

gregarious [grə'gɛərɪəs] adj (person)

sociable

grenade [grə'neɪd] n grenade f

grew [gruː] pt of **grow**

grey [greɪ] (US **gray**) adj gris(e); (dismal) sombre; **~-haired** adj grisonnant(e); **~hound** n lévrier m

grid [grɪd] n grille f; (ELEC) réseau m; **~lock** n (traffic jam) embouteillage m; **~locked** adj: **to be ~locked** (roads) être bloqué par un embouteillage; (talks etc) être suspendu

grief [griːf] n chagrin m, douleur f

grievance ['griːvəns] n doléance f, grief m

grieve [griːv] vi avoir du chagrin; se désoler ♦ vt faire de la peine à, affliger; **to ~ for sb** (dead person) pleurer qn

grievous adj (LAW): **grievous bodily harm** coups mpl et blessures fpl

grill [grɪl] n (on cooker) gril m; (food: also mixed ~) grillade(s) f(pl) ♦ vt (BRIT) griller; (inf: question) cuisiner

grille [grɪl] n grille f, grillage m; (AUT) calandre f

grim [grɪm] adj sinistre, lugubre; (serious, stern) sévère

grimace [grɪ'meɪs] n grimace f ♦ vi grimacer, faire une grimace

grime [graɪm] n crasse f, saleté f

grin [grɪn] n large sourire m ♦ vi sourire

grind [graɪnd] (pt, pp **ground**) vt écraser; (coffee, pepper etc) moudre; (US: meat) hacher; (make sharp) aiguiser ♦ n (work) corvée f

grip [grɪp] n (hold) prise f, étreinte f; (control) emprise f; (grasp) connaissance f; (handle) poignée f; (holdall) sac m de voyage ♦ vt saisir, empoigner; **to come to ~s with** en venir aux prises avec; **~ping** adj prenant(e), palpitant(e)

grisly ['grɪzlɪ] adj sinistre, macabre

gristle ['grɪsl] n cartilage m

grit [grɪt] n gravillon m; (courage) cran m ♦ vt (road) sabler; **to ~ one's teeth** serrer les dents

groan [grəʊn] n (of pain) gémissement

m ♦ vi gémir

grocer ['grəʊsə^r] *n* épicier *m*; **~ies** *npl* provisions *fpl*; **~'s (shop)** *n* épicerie *f*

groin [grɔɪn] *n* aine *f*

groom [gruːm] *n* palefrenier *m*; *(also:* **bridegroom)** marié *m ♦ vt (horse)* panser; *(fig)*: **to ~ sb for** former qn pour; **well~ed** très soigné(e)

groove [gruːv] *n* rainure *f*

grope [grəʊp] *vi*: **to ~ for** chercher à tâtons

gross [grəʊs] *adj* grossier(-ère); *(COMM)* brut(e); **~ly** *adv (greatly)* très, grandement

grotto ['grɒtəʊ] *n* grotte *f*

grotty ['grɒtɪ] *(inf) adj* minable, affreux(-euse)

ground [graʊnd] *pt, pp of* **grind ♦** *n* sol *m*, terre *f*; *(land)* terrain *m*, terres *fpl*; *(SPORT)* terrain; *(US: also:* **~ wire)** terre; *(reason: gen pl)* raison *f ♦ vt (plane)* empêcher de décoller, retenir au sol; *(US: ELEC)* équiper d'une prise de terre; **~s** *npl (of coffee etc)* marc *m*; *(gardens etc)* parc *m*, domaine *m*; **on the ~, to the ~** par terre; **to gain/lose ~** gagner/perdre du terrain; **~ cloth** *(US) n* = **groundsheet**; **~ing** *n (in education)* connaissances *fpl* de base; **~less** *adj* sans fondement; **~sheet** *(BRIT) n* tapis *m* de sol; **~ staff** *n* personnel *m* au sol; **~work** *n* préparation *f*

group [gruːp] *n* groupe *m ♦ vt (also:* **~ together)** grouper *♦ vi* se grouper

grouse [graʊs] *n inv (bird)* grouse *f ♦ vi (complain)* rouspéter, râler

grove [grəʊv] *n* bosquet *m*

grovel ['grɒvl] *vi (fig)* ramper

grow [grəʊ] *(pt* **grew,** *pp* **grown)** *vi* pousser, croître; *(person)* grandir; *(increase)* augmenter, se développer; *(become)*: **to ~ rich/weak** s'enrichir/ s'affaiblir; *(develop)*: **he's ~n out of his jacket** sa veste est (devenue) trop petite pour lui *♦ vt* cultiver, faire pousser; *(beard)* laisser pousser; **he'll ~ out of it!** ça lui passera!; **~ up** *vi* grandir; **~er**

n producteur *m*; **~ing** *adj (fear, amount)* croissant(e), grandissant(e)

growl [graʊl] *vi* grogner

grown [grəʊn] *pp of* **grow**; **~-up** *n* adulte *m/f*, grande personne

growth [grəʊθ] *n* croissance *f*, développement *m*; *(what has grown)* pousse *f*, poussée *f*; *(MED)* grosseur *f*, tumeur *f*

grub [grʌb] *n* larve *f*; *(inf: food)* bouffe *f*

grubby ['grʌbɪ] *adj* crasseux(-euse)

grudge [grʌdʒ] *n* rancune *f ♦ vt*: **to ~ sb sth** *(in giving)* donner qch à qn à contre-cœur; *(resent)* reprocher qch à qn; **to bear sb a ~ (for)** garder rancune *or* en vouloir à qn (de)

gruelling ['grʊəlɪŋ] *(US* **grueling)** *adj* exténuant(e)

gruesome ['gruːsəm] *adj* horrible

gruff [grʌf] *adj* bourru(e)

grumble ['grʌmbl] *vi* rouspéter, ronchonner

grumpy ['grʌmpɪ] *adj* grincheux(-euse)

grunt [grʌnt] *vi* grogner

G-string ['dʒiːstrɪŋ] *n (garment)* cache-sexe *m inv*

guarantee [gærən'tiː] *n* garantie *f ♦ vt* garantir

guard [gɑːd] *n* garde *f*; *(one man)* garde *m*; *(BRIT: RAIL)* chef *m* de train; *(on machine)* dispositif *m* de sûreté; *(also:* **fireguard)** garde-feu *m ♦ vt* garder, surveiller; *(protect)*: **to ~ (against** *or* **from)** protéger (contre); **~ against** *vt (prevent)* empêcher, se protéger de; **~ed** *adj (fig)* prudent(e); **~ian** *n* gardien(ne); *(of minor)* tuteur(-trice); **~'s van** *(BRIT: RAIL)* fourgon *m*

guerrilla [gə'rɪlə] *n* guérillero *m*

guess [ges] *vt* deviner; *(estimate)* évaluer; *(US)* croire, penser *♦ vi* deviner *♦ n* supposition *f*, hypothèse *f*; **to take** *or* **have a ~** essayer de deviner; **~work** *n* hypothèse *f*

guest [gest] *n* invité(e); *(in hotel)* client(e); **~-house** *n* pension *f*; **~ room** *n* chambre *f* d'amis

guffaw [gʌ'fɔː] *vi* pouffer de rire

guidance ['gaɪdəns] n conseils mpl

guide [gaɪd] n (person, book etc) guide m; (BRIT: also: **girl ~**) guide f ♦ vt guider; **~book** n guide m; **~ dog** n chien m d'aveugle; **~lines** npl (fig) instructions (générales), conseils mpl

guild [gɪld] n corporation f; cercle m, association f

guillotine ['gɪlətiːn] n guillotine f

guilt [gɪlt] n culpabilité f; **~y** adj coupable

guinea pig ['gɪnɪ-] n cobaye m

guise [gaɪz] n aspect m, apparence f

guitar [gɪ'tɑːr] n guitare f

gulf [gʌlf] n golfe m; (abyss) gouffre m

gull [gʌl] n mouette f; (larger) goéland m

gullible ['gʌlɪbl] adj crédule

gully ['gʌlɪ] n ravin m; ravine f; couloir m

gulp [gʌlp] vi avaler sa salive ♦ vt (also: **~ down**) avaler

gum [gʌm] n (ANAT) gencive f; (glue) colle f; (sweet: also ~drop) boule f de gomme; (also: **chewing ~**) chewing-gum m ♦ vt coller; **~boots** (BRIT) npl bottes fpl en caoutchouc

gun [gʌn] n (small) revolver m, pistolet m; (rifle) fusil m, carabine f; (cannon) canon m; **~boat** n canonnière f; **~fire** n fusillade f; **~man** n bandit armé; **~point** n: **at ~point** sous la menace du pistolet (or fusil); **~powder** n poudre f à canon; **~shot** n coup m de feu

gurgle ['gɜːgl] vi gargouiller; (baby) gazouiller

gush [gʌʃ] vi jaillir; (fig) se répandre en effusions

gust [gʌst] n (of wind) rafale f; (of smoke) bouffée f

gusto ['gʌstəʊ] n enthousiasme m

gut [gʌt] n intestin m, boyau m; **~s** np (inf: courage) cran m

gutter ['gʌtər] n (in street) caniveau m; (of roof) gouttière f

guy [gaɪ] n (inf: man) type m; (also: **~rope**) corde f; (BRIT: figure) effigie de

Guy Fawkes (brûlée en plein air le 5 novembre)

Guy Fawkes' Night

Guy Fawkes' Night, que l'on appelle également "bonfire night", commémore l'échec du complot (le "Gunpowder Plot") contre James Ist et son parlement le 5 novembre 1605. L'un des conspirateurs, Guy Fawkes, avait été surpris dans les caves du parlement alors qu'il s'apprêtait à y mettre le feu. Chaque année pour le 5 novembre, les enfants préparent à l'avance une effigie de Guy Fawkes et ils demandent aux passants "un penny pour le guy" avec lequel ils pourront s'acheter des fusées de feu d'artifice. Beaucoup de gens font encore un feu dans leur jardin sur lequel ils brûlent le "guy".

guzzle ['gʌzl] vt avaler gloutonnement

gym [dʒɪm] n (also: **~nasium**) gymnase m; (also: **~nastics**) gym f; **~nast** n gymnaste m/f; **~nastics** [dʒɪm'næstɪks] n, npl gymnastique f; **~ shoes** npl chaussures fpl de gym; **~slip** (BRIT) n tunique f (d'écolière)

gynaecologist [gaɪnɪ'kɔlədʒɪst] (US **gynecologist**) n gynécologue m/f

gypsy ['dʒɪpsɪ] n gitan(e), bohémien(ne)

H, h

haberdashery [hæbə'dæʃərɪ] (BRIT) n mercerie f

habit ['hæbɪt] n habitude f; (REL: costume) habit m; **~ual** adj habituel(le); (drinker, liar) invétéré(e)

hack [hæk] vt hacher, tailler ♦ n (pej: writer) nègre m; **~er** n (COMPUT) pirate m (informatique); (: enthusiast) passionné(e) m/f des ordinateurs

hackneyed ['hæknɪd] adj usé(e), rebattu(e)

had [hæd] *pt, pp of* **have**

haddock ['hædək] (*pl* ~ *or* ~**s**) *n* églefin *m*; **smoked** ~ haddock *m*

hadn't ['hædnt] = **had not**

haemorrhage ['hemərɪdʒ] (*US* **hemorrhage**) *n* hémorragie *f*

haemorrhoids ['hemərɔɪdz] (*US* **hemorrhoids**) *npl* hémorroïdes *fpl*

haggle ['hægl] *vi* marchander

Hague [heɪg] *n*: **The** ~ La Haye

hail [heɪl] *n* grêle *f* ♦ *vt* (*call*) héler; (*acclaim*) acclamer ♦ *vi* grêler; ~**stone** *n* grêlon *m*

hair [heə^r] *n* cheveux *mpl*; (*of animal*) pelage *m*; (*single* ~: *on head*) cheveu *m*; (*: on body; of animal*) poil *m*; **to do one's** ~ se coiffer; ~**brush** *n* brosse *f* à cheveux; ~**cut** *n* coupe *f* (de cheveux); ~**do** *n* coiffure *f*; ~**dresser** *n* coiffeur (-euse); ~**dresser's** *n* salon *m* de coiffure, coiffeur *m*; ~ **dryer** *n* sèchecheveux *m*; ~ **gel** *n* gel *m* pour cheveux; ~**grip** *n* pince *f* à cheveux; ~**net** *n* filet *m* à cheveux; ~**piece** *n* perruque *f*; ~**pin** *n* épingle *f* à cheveux; ~**pin bend** (*US* **hairpin curve**) *n* virage *m* en épingle à cheveux; ~**-raising** *adj* à (vous) faire dresser les cheveux sur la tête; ~ **removing cream** *n* crème *f* dépilatoire; ~ **spray** *n* laque *f* (pour les cheveux); ~**style** *n* coiffure *f*; ~**y** *adj* poilu(e); (*inf: fig*) effrayant(e)

hake [heɪk] (*pl* ~ *or* ~**s**) *n* colin *m*, merlu *m*

half [hɑːf] (*pl* **halves**) *n* moitié *f*; (*of beer: also:* ~ **pint**) ≈ demi *m*; (*RAIL, bus: also:* ~ **fare**) demi-tarif *m* ♦ *adj* demi(e) ♦ *adv* à moitié, à demi; ~ **a dozen** une demi-douzaine; ~ **a pound** une demi-livre, ≈ 250 g; **two and a** ~ deux et demi; **to cut sth in** ~ couper qch en deux; ~**-caste** ['hɑːfkɑːst] *n* métis(se); ~**-hearted** *adj* tiède, peu enthousiaste; ~**-hour** *n* demi-heure *f*; ~**-mast** at ~**-mast** *adv* (*flag*) en berne; ~**penny** (*BRIT*) *n* half-penny *m*;

price *adj, adv*: **(at)** ~**-price** à moitié prix; ~ **term** (*BRIT*) *n* (*SCOL*) congé *m* de demi-trimestre; ~**-time** *n* mi-temps *f*; ~**way** *adv* à mi-chemin

hall [hɔːl] *n* salle *f*; (*entrance way*) hall *m*, entrée *f*; (*corridor*) = **corridor**

hallmark ['hɔːlmɑːk] *n* poinçon *m*; (*fig*) marque *f*

hallo [hə'ləu] *excl* = **hello**

hall of residence (*BRIT*) (*pl* **halls of residence**) *n* résidence *f* universitaire

Hallowe'en [hæləu'iːn] *n* veille *f* de la Toussaint

hallucination [həluːsɪ'neɪʃən] *n* hallucination *f*

hallway ['hɔːlweɪ] *n* vestibule *m*

halo ['heɪləu] *n* (*of saint etc*) auréole *f*

halt [hɔːlt] *n* halt *f*, arrêt *m* ♦ *vt* (*progress etc*) interrompre ♦ *vi* faire halte, s'arrêter

halve [hɑːv] *vt* (*apple etc*) partager *or* diviser en deux; (*expense*) réduire de moitié; ~**s** *npl of* **half**

ham [hæm] *n* jambon *m*

hamburger ['hæmbəgə^r] *n* hamburger *m*

hamlet ['hæmlɪt] *n* hameau *m*

hammer ['hæmə^r] *n* marteau *m* ♦ *vt* (*nail*) enfoncer; (*fig*) démolir ♦ *vi* (*on door*) frapper à coups redoublés; **to** ~ **an idea into sb** faire entrer de force une idée dans la tête de qn

hammock ['hæmək] *n* hamac *m*

hamper ['hæmpə^r] *vt* gêner ♦ *n* panier *m* (d'osier)

hamster ['hæmstə^r] *n* hamster *m*

hand [hænd] n main f; (of clock) aiguille f; (~writing) écriture f; (worker) ouvrier(-ère); (at cards) jeu ♦ vt passer, donner; **to give** or **lend sb a ~** donner un coup de main à qn; **at ~** à portée de la main; **in ~** (time) à disposition; (job, situation) en main; **to be on ~** (person) être disponible; (emergency services) être prêt(e) (à intervenir); **to ~** (information etc) sous la main, à portée de la main; **on the one ~ ..., on the other ~** d'une part ..., d'autre part; **in ~** vt remettre; **~out** vt distribuer; **~ over** vt transmettre; céder; **~bag** n sac m à main; **~book** n manuel m; **~brake** n frein m à main; **~cuffs** npl menottes fpl; **~ful** n poignée f

handicap ['hændɪkæp] n handicap m ♦ vt handicaper; **mentally/physically ~ped** handicapé(e) mentalement/physiquement

handicraft ['hændɪkrɑːft] n (travail m d')artisanat m, technique artisanale; (object) objet artisanal

handiwork ['hændɪwɜːk] n ouvrage m

handkerchief ['hæŋkətʃɪf] n mouchoir m

handle ['hændl] n (of door etc) poignée f; (of cup etc) anse f; (of knife etc) manche m; (of saucepan) queue f; (for winding) manivelle f ♦ vt toucher, manier; (deal with) s'occuper de; (treat: people) prendre; **"~ with care"** "fragile"; **to fly off the ~** s'énerver; **~bar(s)** n(pl) guidon m

hand: **~luggage** n bagages mpl à main; **~made** adj fait(e) à la main; **~out** n (from government, parents) aide f, don m; (leaflet) documentation f, prospectus m; (summary of lecture) polycopié m; **~rail** n rampe f, main courante; **~set** n (TEL) combiné m; please **replace the ~set** raccrochez s'il vous plaît; **~shake** n poignée f de main

handsome ['hænsəm] adj beau (belle); (profit, return) considérable

handwriting ['hændraɪtɪŋ] n écriture f

handy ['hændɪ] adj (person) adroit(e); (close at hand) sous la main; (convenient) pratique

hang [hæŋ] (pt, pp hung) vt accrocher; (criminal: pt, pp: ~ed) pendre ♦ vi pendre; (hair, drapery) tomber; **to get the ~ of (doing) sth** (inf) attraper le coup de; **~ about** vi traîner; **~ around** vi = hang about; **~ on** vi (wait) attendre; **~ up** vi (TEL): **to ~ up (on sb)** raccrocher (au nez de qn) ♦ vt (coat, painting etc) accrocher, suspendre

hangar ['hæŋər] n hangar m

hanger ['hæŋər] n cintre m, portemanteau m; **~-on** n parasite m

hang: **~-gliding** n deltaplane m, vol m libre; **~over** n (after drinking) gueule f de bois; **~-up** n complexe m

hanker ['hæŋkər] vi: **to ~ after** avoir envie de

hankie, hanky ['hæŋkɪ] n abbr = **handkerchief**

haphazard [hæp'hæzəd] adj fait(e) au hasard, fait(e) au petit bonheur

happen ['hæpən] vi arriver; se passer, se produire; **it so ~s that** il se trouve que; **as it ~s** justement; **~ing** n événement m

happily ['hæpɪlɪ] adv heureusement; (cheerfully) joyeusement

happiness ['hæpɪnɪs] n bonheur m

happy ['hæpɪ] adj heureux(-euse); **~ with** (arrangements etc) satisfait(e) de; **to be ~ to do** (willing) faire volontiers; **~ birthday!** bon anniversaire!; **~-go-lucky** adj insouciant(e); **~ hour** n heure pendant laquelle les consommations sont à prix réduit

harass ['hærəs] vt accabler, tourmenter; **~ment** n tracasserie fpl

harbour ['hɑːbər] (US **harbor**) n port m ♦ vt héberger, abriter; (hope, fear etc) entretenir

hard [hɑːd] adj dur(e); (question, problem) difficile, dur(e); (facts, evidence) concret(-ète) ♦ adv (work) dur; (think, *try*) sérieusement; **to look ~ at** regarder fixement; (*thing*) regarder de près; **no ~ feelings!** sans rancune!; **to be ~ of hearing** être dur(e) d'oreille; **to be ~ done by** être traité(e) injustement; **~back** *n* livre relié; **~ cash** *n* espèces *fpl*; **~ disk** *n* (COMPUT) disque dur; **~en** *vt* durcir; (*fig*) endurcir ♦ *vi* durcir; **~-headed** *adj* réaliste; décidé(e); **~ labour** *n* travaux forcés

hardly ['hɑːdlɪ] *adv* (*scarcely, no sooner*) à peine; **~ anywhere/ever** presque nulle part/jamais

hard: **~ship** *n* épreuves *fpl*; **~ shoulder** (BRIT) *n* (AUT) accotement stabilisé; **~ up** (*inf*) *adj* fauché(e); **~ware** *n* quincaillerie *f*; (COMPUT, MIL) matériel *m*; **~ware shop** *n* quincaillerie *f*; **~-wearing** *adj* solide; **~-working** *adj* travailleur(-euse)

hardy ['hɑːdɪ] *adj* robuste; (*plant*) résistant(e) au gel

hare [hɛə] *n* lièvre *m*; **~-brained** *adj* farfelu(e)

harm [hɑːm] *n* mal *m*; (*wrong*) tort *m* ♦ *vt* (*person*) faire du mal ou du tort à; (*thing*) endommager; **out of ~'s way** à l'abri du danger, en lieu sûr; **~ful** *adj* nuisible; **~less** *adj* inoffensif(-ive); sans méchanceté

harmony ['hɑːmənɪ] *n* harmonie *f*

harness ['hɑːnɪs] *n* harnais *m*; (*safety ~*) harnais de sécurité *m*; (*of horse*) harnacher; (*resources*) exploiter

harp [hɑːp] *n* harpe *f* ♦ *vi*: **to ~ on about** rabâcher

harrowing ['hærəuɪŋ] *adj* déchirant(e), très pénible

harsh [hɑːʃ] *adj* (*hard*) dur(e); (*severe*) sévère; (*unpleasant: sound*) discordant(e); (: *light*) cru(e)

harvest ['hɑːvɪst] *n* (*of corn*) moisson *f*; (*of fruit*) récolte *f*; (*of grapes*) vendange *f* ♦ *vt* moissonner; récolter; vendanger

has [hæz] *vb see* **have**

hash [hæʃ] *n* (CULIN) hachis *m*; (*fig: mess*) gâchis *m*

hasn't ['hæznt] = **has not**

hassle ['hæsl] *n* (*inf: bother*) histoires *fpl*, tracas *mpl*

haste [heɪst] *n* hâte *f*; précipitation *f*; **~n** ['heɪsn] *vt* hâter, accélérer ♦ *vi* se hâter, s'empresser; **hastily** *adv* à la hâte; précipitamment; **hasty** *adj* hâtif(-ive); précipité(e)

hat [hæt] *n* chapeau *m*

hatch [hætʃ] *n* (NAUT: *also*: **~way**) écoutille *f*; (*also*: **service ~**) passe-plats *m inv* ♦ *vi* éclore; **~back** *n* (AUT) modèle *m* avec hayon arrière

hatchet ['hætʃɪt] *n* hachette *f*

hate [heɪt] *vt* haïr, détester ♦ *n* haine *f*; **~ful** *adj* odieux(-euse), détestable; **hatred** ['heɪtrɪd] *n* haine *f*

haughty ['hɔːtɪ] *adj* hautain(e), arrogant(e)

haul [hɔːl] *vt* traîner, tirer ♦ *n* (*of fish*) prise *f*; (*of stolen goods etc*) butin *m*; **~age** *n* transport routier; (*costs*) frais *mpl* de transport; **~ier** (US **hauler**) *n* (*company*) transporteur (routier); (*driver*) camionneur *m*

haunch [hɔːntʃ] *n* hanche *f*; (*of meat*) cuissot *m*

haunt [hɔːnt] *vt* (*subj: ghost, fear*) hanter; (: *person*) fréquenter ♦ *n* repaire *m*

KEYWORD

---

have [hæv] (*pt, pp* **had**) *aux vb* **1** (*gen*) avoir; être; **to have arrived/gone** être arrivé(e)/allé(e); **to have eaten/slept** avoir mangé/dormi; **he has been promoted** il a eu une promotion

2 (*in tag questions*): **you've done it, haven't you?** vous l'avez fait, n'est-ce pas?

3 (*in short answers and questions*): **no I haven't/yes we have!** mais non!/mais si!; **so I have!** ah oui!, oui c'est vrai!; **I've been there before, have you?** j'y suis déjà allé, et vous?

♦ *modal aux vb* (*be obliged*): **to have (got) to do sth** devoir faire qch; être obligé(e) de faire qch; **she has**

to do it elle doit le faire, il faut qu'elle le fasse; **you haven't to tell her** vous ne devez pas le lui dire

♦ vt **1** (*possess, obtain*) avoir; **he has (got) blue eyes/dark hair** il a les yeux bleus/les cheveux bruns; **may I have your address?** puis-je avoir votre adresse?

2 (+*noun: take, hold etc*): **to have breakfast/a bath/a shower** prendre le petit déjeuner/un bain/une douche; **to have dinner/lunch** dîner/déjeuner; **to have a swim** nager; **to have a meeting** se réunir; **to have a party** organiser une fête

3: **to have sth done** faire faire qch; **to have one's hair cut** se faire couper les cheveux; **to have sb do sth** faire faire qch à qn

4 (*experience, suffer*) avoir; **to have a cold/flu** avoir un rhume/la grippe; **to have an operation** se faire opérer

5 (*inf: dupe*) avoir; **he's been had** il s'est fait avoir *or* rouler

have out *vt*: **to have it out with sb** (*settle a problem etc*) s'expliquer (franchement) avec qn

haven ['heɪvn] *n* port *m*; (*fig*) havre *m*

haven't ['hævnt] = **have not**

havoc ['hævək] *n* ravages *mpl*

hawk [hɔːk] *n* faucon *m*

hay [heɪ] *n* foin *m*; ~ **fever** *n* rhume *m* des foins; ~**stack** *n* meule *f* de foin

haywire (*inf*) *adj*: **to go** ~ (*machine*) se détraquer; (*plans*) mal tourner

hazard ['hæzəd] *n* (*danger*) danger *m*, risque *m* ♦ *vt* (*venture*) hasarder; ~ (**warning**) **lights** *npl* (AUT) feux *mpl* de détresse

haze [heɪz] *n* brume *f*

hazelnut ['heɪzlnʌt] *n* noisette *f*

hazy ['heɪzɪ] *adj* brumeux(-euse); (*idea*) vague

he [hiː] *pron* il; **it is** ~ **who** ... c'est lui qui ...

head [hed] *n* tête *f*; (*leader*) chef *m*; (*of*

school) directeur(-trice) ♦ *vt* (*list*) être en tête de; (*group*) être à la tête de; ~**s (or tails)** pile (ou face); ~ **first** la tête la première; ~ **over heels in love** follement *or* éperdument amoureux(-euse); **to** ~ **a ball** faire une tête; ~**ache** *n* mal *m* de tête; ~**dress** (BRIT) *n* (*of Red Indian etc*) coiffure *f*; ~**ing** *n* titre *m*; ~**lamp** (BRIT) *n* phare *m*; ~**land** promontoire *m*, cap *m*; ~**light** *n* phare *m*; ~**line** *n* titre *m*; ~**long** *adv* (*fall*) la tête la première; (*rush*) tête baissée; ~**master** *n* directeur *m*; ~**mistress** *n* directrice *f*; ~ **office** *n* bureau central, siège *m*; ~-**on** *adj* (*collision*) de plein fouet; (*confrontation*) en face à face; ~**phones** *npl* casque *m* (à écouteurs); ~**quarters** *npl* bureau *m* *or* siège central; (MIL) quartier général; ~**rest** *n* appui-tête *m*; ~**room** *n* (*in car*) hauteur *f* de plafond; (*under bridge*) hauteur limite; ~**scarf** *n* foulard *m*; ~**strong** *adj* têtu(e), entêté(e); ~ **teacher** *n* directeur(-trice); (*of secondary school*) proviseur *m*; ~ **waiter** *n* maître *m* d'hôtel; ~**way** *n*: **to make** ~**way** avancer, faire des progrès; ~**wind** *n* vent *m* contraire; (NAUT) vent debout; ~**y** *adj* capiteux(-euse); enivrant(e); (*experience*) grisant(e)

heal [hiːl] *vt, vi* guérir

health [helθ] *n* santé *f*; ~ **food** *n* aliment(s) naturel(s); ~ **food shop** *n* magasin *m* diététique; **H**~ **Service** (BRIT) *n*: **the H**~ **Service** ≈ la Sécurité sociale; ~**y** *adj* (*person*) en bonne santé; (*climate, food, attitude etc*) sain(e); bon(ne) pour la santé

heap [hiːp] *n* tas *m* ♦ *vt*: **to** ~ (**up**) entasser, amonceler; **she** ~**ed her plate with cakes** elle a chargé son assiette de gâteaux

hear [hɪə*] (*pt, pp* **heard**) *vt* entendre; (*news*) apprendre ♦ *vi* entendre; **to** ~ **about** entendre parler de; avoir des nouvelles de; **to** ~ **from sb** recevoir *or* avoir des nouvelles de qn; ~**ing** *n* (sense) ouïe f; (of witnesses) audition f; (of a case) audience f; **~ing aid** n appareil m acoustique; **~say: by ~say** adv par ouï-dire m

hearse [hɜːs] n corbillard m

heart [hɑːt] n cœur m; **~s** npl (CARDS) cœur m; **to lose/take ~** perdre/prendre courage; **at ~** au fond; **by ~** (learn, know) par cœur; **~ attack** n crise f cardiaque; **~beat** n battement m du cœur; **~breaking** adj déchirant(e), qui fend le cœur; **~broken** adj: **to be ~broken** avoir beaucoup de chagrin or le cœur brisé; **~burn** n brûlures fpl d'estomac; **~ failure** n arrêt m du cœur; **~felt** adj sincère

hearth [hɑːθ] n foyer m, cheminée f

heartily [ˈhɑːtɪlɪ] adv chaleureusement; (laugh) de bon cœur; (eat) de bon appétit; **to agree ~** être entièrement d'accord

hearty [ˈhɑːtɪ] adj chaleureux(-euse); (appetite) robuste; (dislike) cordial(e)

heat [hiːt] n chaleur f; (fig) feu m, agitation f; (SPORT: also: **qualifying ~**) éliminatoire f ♦ vt chauffer; **~ up** vi (water) chauffer; (room) se réchauffer ♦ vt réchauffer; **~ed** adj chauffé(e); (fig) passionné(e), échauffé(e); **~er** n appareil m de chauffage; radiateur m; (in car) chauffage m; (water heater) chauffe-eau m

heath [hiːθ] n (BRIT) lande f

heather [ˈheðəʳ] n bruyère f

heating [ˈhiːtɪŋ] n chauffage m

heatstroke [ˈhiːtstrəʊk] n (MED) coup m de chaleur

heat wave n vague f de chaleur

heave [hiːv] vt soulever (avec effort); (drag) traîner ♦ vi se soulever; (retch) avoir un haut-le-cœur; **to ~ a sigh** pousser un soupir

heaven [ˈhɛvn] n ciel m, paradis m; (fig) paradis; **~ly** adj céleste, divin(e)

heavily [ˈhɛvɪlɪ] adv lourdement; (drink, smoke) beaucoup; (sleep, sigh) profondément

heavy [ˈhɛvɪ] adj lourd(e); (work, sea, rain, eater) gros(se); (snow) beaucoup de; (drinker, smoker) grand(e); (breathing) bruyant(e); (schedule, week) chargé(e); **~ goods vehicle** n poids lourd; **~weight** n (SPORT) poids lourd

Hebrew [ˈhiːbruː] adj hébraïque ♦ n (LING) hébreu m

Hebrides [ˈhɛbrɪdiːz] npl: **the ~** les Hébrides fpl

heckle [ˈhɛkl] vt interpeller (un orateur)

hectic [ˈhɛktɪk] adj agité(e), trépidant(e)

he'd [hiːd] = he would; he had

hedge [hɛdʒ] n haie f ♦ vi se dérober; **to ~ one's bets** (fig) se couvrir

hedgehog [ˈhɛdʒhɔg] n hérisson m

heed [hiːd] vt (also: **take ~ of**) tenir compte de; **~less** adj insouciant(e)

heel [hiːl] n talon m ♦ vt retalonner

hefty [ˈhɛftɪ] adj (person) costaud(e); (parcel) lourd(e); (profit) gros(se)

heifer [ˈhɛfəʳ] n génisse f

height [haɪt] n (of person) taille f, grandeur f; (of object) hauteur f; (of plane, mountain) altitude f; (high ground) hauteur, éminence f; (fig: of glory) sommet m; (: of luxury, stupidity) comble m; **~en** vt (fig) augmenter

heir [ɛəʳ] n héritier m; **~ess** n héritière f; **~loom** n héritage m, meuble m (or bijou m or tableau m) de famille

held [hɛld] pt, pp of hold

helicopter [ˈhɛlɪkɔptəʳ] n hélicoptère m

hell [hɛl] n enfer m; **~!** (inf!) merde!

he'll [hiːl] = he will; he shall

hellish [ˈhɛlɪʃ] (inf) adj infernal(e)

hello [həˈləʊ] excl bonjour!; (to attract attention) hé!; (surprise) tiens!

helm [hɛlm] n (NAUT) barre f

helmet [ˈhɛlmɪt] n casque m

help [hɛlp] n aide f; (charwoman) femme f de ménage ♦ vt aider; **~!** au secours!; **~ yourself** servez-vous; he **can't ~ it** il ne peut pas s'en empêcher; **~er** n aide m/f, assistant(e); **~ful** adj serviable, obligeant(e); (useful) utile;

~ing n portion f; ~less adj impuissant(e); (defenceless) faible

hem [hɛm] n ourlet m ♦ vt ourler; ~ in vt cerner

hemorrhage ['hɛmərɪdʒ] (US) n = haemorrhage

hemorrhoids ['hɛmərɔɪdz] (US) npl = haemorrhoids

hen [hɛn] n poule f

hence [hɛns] adv (therefore) d'où, de là; 2 years ~ d'ici 2 ans, dans 2 ans; ~forth adv dorénavant

henchman ['hɛntʃmən] (irreg) n (pej) acolyte m, séïde m

her [hə:ʳ] pron (direct) la, l'; (indirect) lui; (stressed, after prep) elle ♦ adj son (sa), ses pl; see also me; my

herald ['hɛrəld] n héraut m ♦ vt annoncer; ~ry n (study) héraldique f; (coat of arms) blason m

herb [hə:b] n herbe f

herd [hə:d] n troupeau m

here [hɪəʳ] adv ici; (time) alors ♦ excl tiens!, tenez!; ~! présent!; ~ is, ~ are voici; ~ he/she is! le/la voici!; ~after adv après, plus tard; ~by adv (formal: in letter) par la présente

hereditary [hɪ'rɛdɪtrɪ] adj héréditaire

heresy ['hɛrəsɪ] n hérésie f

heritage ['hɛrɪtɪdʒ] n (of country) patrimoine m

hermit ['hə:mɪt] n ermite m

hernia ['hə:nɪə] n hernie f

hero ['hɪərəu] (pl ~es) n héros m

heroin ['hɛrəuɪn] n héroïne f

heroine ['hɛrəuɪn] n héroïne f

heron ['hɛrən] n héron m

herring ['hɛrɪŋ] n hareng m

hers [hə:z] pron le (la) sien(ne), les siens (siennes); see also mine¹

herself [hə:'sɛlf] pron (reflexive) se; (emphatic) elle-même; (after prep) elle; see also oneself

he's [hi:z] = he is; he has

hesitant ['hɛzɪtənt] adj hésitant(e), indécis(e)

hesitate ['hɛzɪteɪt] vi hésiter; hesitation [hɛzɪ'teɪʃən] n hésitation f

heterosexual ['hɛtərəu'sɛksjuəl] adj, n

hétérosexuel(le)

heyday ['heɪdeɪ] n: the ~ of l'âge m d'or de, les beaux jours de

HGV n abbr = heavy goods vehicle

hi [haɪ] excl salut!; (to attract attention) hé!

hiatus [haɪ'eɪtəs] n (gap) lacune f; (interruption) pause f

hibernate ['haɪbəneɪt] vi hiberner

hiccough, hiccup ['hɪkʌp] vi hoqueter; ~s npl hoquet m

hide [haɪd] (pt hid, pp hidden) n (skin) peau f ♦ vt cacher ♦ vi: to ~ (from sb) se cacher (de qn); ~-and-seek n cache-cache m

hideous ['hɪdɪəs] adj hideux(-euse)

hiding ['haɪdɪŋ] n (beating) correction f, volée f de coups; to be in ~ (concealed) se tenir caché(e)

hierarchy ['haɪərɑ:kɪ] n hiérarchie f

hi-fi ['haɪfaɪ] n hi-fi f inv ♦ adj hi-fi inv

high [haɪ] adj haut(e); (speed, respect, number) grand(e); (price) élevé(e); (wind) fort(e), violent(e); (voice) aigu (aiguë) ♦ adv haut; 20 m ~ haut(e) de 20 m; ~brow adj, n intellectuel(le); ~chair n (child's) chaise haute; ~er education n études supérieures; ~handed adj très autoritaire; très cavalier(-ère); ~-heeled adj à hauts talons; ~ jump n (SPORT) saut m en hauteur; ~lands npl Highlands mpl; ~light n (fig: of event) point culminant ♦ vt faire ressortir, souligner; ~lights npl (in hair) reflets mpl; ~ly adv très, fort, hautement; to speak/think ~ly of sb dire/penser beaucoup de bien de qn; ~ly paid adj très bien payé(e); ~ly strung adj nerveux(-euse), toujours tendu(e); ~ness n: Her (or His) H~ness Son Altesse f; ~-pitched adj aigu (aiguë); ~-rise adj: ~-rise block, ~-rise flats tour f (d'habitation); ~ school n lycée m; (US) établissement m d'enseignement supérieur; ~ season (BRIT) n haute saison; ~ street (BRIT) n grand-rue f; ~way n route nationale;

H~way Code (BRIT) n code m de la route

hijack ['haɪdʒæk] vt (plane) détourner; **~er** n pirate m de l'air

hike [haɪk] vi aller or faire des excursions à pied ♦ n excursion f à pied, randonnée f; **~r** n promeneur(-euse), excursionniste m/f; **hiking** n excursions fpl à pied

hilarious [hɪ'lɛərɪəs] adj (account, event) désopilant(e)

hill [hɪl] n colline f; (fairly high) montagne f; (on road) côte f; **~side** n (flanc m de) coteau m; **~-walking** n randonnée f de basse montagne; **~y** adj vallonné(e); montagneux(-euse)

hilt [hɪlt] n (of sword) garde f; **to the ~** (fig: support) à fond

him [hɪm] pron (direct) le, l'; (stressed, indirect, after prep) lui; see also **me**; **~self** pron (reflexive) se; (emphatic) lui-même; (after prep) lui; see also **oneself**

hinder ['hɪndər] vt (delay) retarder; (delay) gêner, obstacle m

hindrance ['hɪndrəns] n gêne f, obstacle m

hindsight ['haɪndsaɪt] n: **with ~** avec du recul, rétrospectivement

Hindu ['hɪnduː] adj hindou(e)

hinge [hɪndʒ] n charnière f ♦ vi (fig): **to ~ on** dépendre de

hint [hɪnt] n allusion f; (advice) conseil m ♦ vt: **to ~ that** insinuer que ♦ vi: **to ~ at** faire une allusion à

hip [hɪp] n hanche f

hippie ['hɪpɪ] n hippie m/f

hippo ['hɪpəʊ] (pl **~s**), **hippopotamus** [hɪpə'pɔtəməs] (pl **~potamuses** or **~potami**) n hippopotame m

hire ['haɪər] vt (BRIT: car, equipment) louer; (worker) embaucher, engager ♦ n location f; **for ~** à louer; (taxi) libre; **~(d) car** n voiture f de location; **~ purchase** (BRIT) n achat m (or vente f) à tempérament or crédit

his [hɪz] pron le (la) sien(ne), les siens (siennes) ♦ adj son (sa), ses pl; see also **my**; **mine**[1]

hiss [hɪs] vi siffler

historic [hɪ'stɒrɪk] adj historique; **~al** adj historique

history ['hɪstərɪ] n histoire f

hit [hɪt] (pt, pp **hit**) vt frapper; (reach: target) atteindre, toucher; (collide with: car) entrer en collision avec, heurter; (fig: affect) toucher ♦ n coup m; (success) succès m; (: song) tube m; **to ~ it off with sb** bien s'entendre avec qn; **~-and-run driver** n chauffard m (coupable du délit de fuite)

hitch [hɪtʃ] vt (fasten) accrocher, attacher; (also: **~ up**) remonter d'une saccade ♦ n (difficulty) anicroche f, contretemps m; **to ~ a lift** faire du stop; **~hike** vi faire de l'auto-stop; **~hiker** n auto-stoppeur(-euse)

hi-tech ['haɪ'tɛk] adj de pointe

hitherto [hɪðə'tuː] adv jusqu'ici

hit man n tueur m à gages

HIV n: **~-negative/-positive** adj séronégatif(-ive)/-positif(-ive)

hive [haɪv] n ruche f

HMS abbr = Her/His Majesty's Ship

hoard [hɔːd] n (of food) provisions fpl, réserves fpl; (of money) trésor m ♦ vt amasser; **~ing** (BRIT) n (for posters) panneau m d'affichage or publicitaire

hoarse [hɔːs] adj enroué(e)

hoax [həʊks] n canular m

hob [hɔb] n plaque (chauffante)

hobble ['hɔbl] vi boitiller

hobby ['hɔbɪ] n passe-temps favori

hobo ['həʊbəʊ] (US) n vagabond m

hockey ['hɔkɪ] n hockey m

hog [hɔg] n porc (châtré) ♦ vt (fig) accaparer; **to go the whole ~** aller jusqu'au bout

hoist [hɔɪst] n (apparatus) palan m ♦ vt hisser

hold [həʊld] (pt, pp **held**) vt tenir; (contain) contenir; (believe) considérer; (possess) avoir; (detain) détenir ♦ vi (withstand pressure) tenir (bon); (be valid) valoir ♦ n (also fig) prise f; (NAUT) cale f; **~ the line!** (TEL) ne quittez pas!; **to ~ one's own** (fig) (bien) se défendre; **to catch** or **get (a) ~ of** saisir; **to get ~ of** (fig) trouver; **~ back** vt retenir; (secret) taire; **~ down** vt (person) maintenir à terre; (job) occuper; **~ off** vt tenir à distance; **~ on** vi tenir bon; (wait) attendre; **~ on!** (TEL) ne quittez pas!; **~ on to** vt fus se cramponner à; (keep) conserver, garder; **~ out** vt offrir ♦ vi (resist) tenir bon; **~ up** vt (raise) lever; (support) soutenir; (delay) retarder; (rob) braquer; **~all** (BRIT) n fourre-tout m inv; **~er** n (of ticket, record) détenteur(-trice); (of office, title etc) titulaire m/f; (container) support m; **~ing** n (share) intérêts mpl; (farm) ferme f; **~up** n (robbery) hold-up m; (delay) retard m; (BRIT: in traffic) bouchon m

hole [həul] n trou m; **~-in-the-wall** n (cash dispenser) distributeur m de billets

holiday ['hɔlɪdeɪ] n vacances fpl; (day off) jour m de congé; (public) jour férié; **on ~** en congé; **~ camp** n (also: **~ centre**) camp m de vacances; **~ maker** (BRIT) n vacancier(-ère); **~ resort** n centre m de villégiature or de vacances

Holland ['hɔlənd] n Hollande f

hollow ['hɔləu] adj creux(-euse) ♦ n creux m ♦ vt: **to ~ out** creuser, évider

holly ['hɔlɪ] n houx m

holocaust ['hɔləkɔːst] n holocauste m

holster ['həulstə'] n étui m de revolver

holy ['həulɪ] adj saint(e); (bread, water) bénit(e); (ground) sacré(e); **H~ Ghost** n Saint-Esprit m

homage ['hɔmɪdʒ] n hommage m; **to pay ~ to** rendre hommage à

home [həum] n foyer m, maison f; (country) pays natal, patrie f; (institution) maison ♦ adj de famille; (ECON, POL) national(e), intérieur(e); (SPORT: game) sur leur (or notre) terrain; (team) qui reçoit ♦ adv chez soi, à la maison; au pays natal; (right in: nail etc) à fond; **at ~** chez soi, à la maison; **make yourself at ~** faites comme chez vous; **~ address** n domicile permanent;

~land n patrie f; **~less** adj sans foyer; sans abri; **~ly** adj (plain) simple, sans prétention; **~-made** adj fait(e) à la maison; **~ match** n match m à domicile; **H~ Office** (BRIT) n ministère m de l'Intérieur; **~ page** n (COMPUT) page f d'accueil; **~ rule** n autonomie f; **H~ Secretary** (BRIT) n ministre m de l'Intérieur; **~sick** adj: **to be ~sick** avoir le mal du pays; s'ennuyer de sa famille; **~ town** n ville natale; **~ward** adj (journey) du retour; **~work** n devoirs mpl

homoeopathic [həumɪəu'pæθɪk] (US **homeopathic**) adj (medicine, methods) homéopathique; (doctor) homéopathe

homogeneous [hɔmə'dʒiːnɪəs] adj homogène

homosexual [hɔmə'sɛksjuəl] adj, n homosexuel(le)

honest ['ɔnɪst] adj honnête; (sincere) franc (franche); **~ly** adv honnêtement; franchement; **~y** n honnêteté f

honey ['hʌnɪ] n miel m; **~comb** n rayon m de miel; **~moon** n lune f de miel, voyage m de noces; **~suckle** (BOT) n chèvrefeuille m

honk [hɔŋk] vi (AUT) klaxonner

honorary ['ɔnərərɪ] adj honoraire; (duty, title) honorifique

honour ['ɔnə'] (US **honor**) vt honorer ♦ n honneur m; **hono(u)rable** adj honorable; **hono(u)rs degree** n (SCOL) licence avec mention

hood [hud] n capuchon m; (of cooker) hotte f; (AUT: BRIT) capote f; (: US) capot m

hoof [huːf] (pl **hooves**) n sabot m

hook [huk] n crochet m; (on dress) agrafe f; (for fishing) hameçon m ♦ vt accrocher; (fish) prendre

hooligan ['huːlɪgən] n voyou m

hoop [huːp] n cerceau m

hooray [huː'reɪ] excl hourra

hoot [huːt] vi (AUT) klaxonner; (siren) mugir; (owl) hululer; **~er** n (BRIT: AUT) klaxon m; (NAUT, factory) sirène f

Hoover ® ['huːvə'] (BRIT) n aspirateur

m ♦ *vt:* **h~** passer l'aspirateur dans *or* sur

hooves [huːvz] *npl of* **hoof**

hop [hɔp] *vi* (*on one foot*) sauter à cloche-pied; (*bird*) sautiller

hope [həʊp] *vt, vi* espérer ♦ *n* espoir *m*; **I ~ so** je l'espère; **I ~ not** j'espère que non; **~ful** *adj* (*person*) plein(e) d'espoir; (*situation*) prometteur(-euse), encourageant(e); **~fully** *adv* (*expectantly*) avec espoir, avec optimisme; (*one hopes*) avec un peu de chance; **~less** *adj* désespéré(e); (*useless*) nul(le)

hops [hɔps] *npl* houblon *m*

horizon [həˈraɪzn] *n* horizon *m*; **~tal** [hɔrɪˈzɔntl] *adj* horizontal(e)

horn [hɔːn] *n* corne *f*; (*MUS: also:* **French ~**) cor *m*; (*AUT*) klaxon *m*

hornet [ˈhɔːnɪt] *n* frelon *m*

horoscope [ˈhɔrəskəʊp] *n* horoscope *m*

horrendous [həˈrendəs] *adj* horrible, affreux(-euse)

horrible [ˈhɔrɪbl] *adj* horrible, affreux(-euse)

horrid [ˈhɔrɪd] *adj* épouvantable

horrify [ˈhɔrɪfaɪ] *vt* horrifier

horror [ˈhɔrər] *n* horreur *f*; **~ film** *n* film *m* d'épouvante

hors d'oeuvre [ɔːˈdəːvrə] *n* (*CULIN*) hors-d'œuvre *m inv*

horse [hɔːs] *n* cheval *m*; **~back** *n*: **on ~back** à cheval; **~ chestnut** *n* (*d'Inde*): marron *m*; **~man** (*irreg*) *n* cavalier *m*; **~power** *n* puissance *f* en chevaux); **~racing** *n* courses *fpl* de chevaux; **~radish** *n* raifort *m*; **~shoe** *n* fer *m* à cheval

hose [həʊz] *n* (*also:* **~pipe**) tuyau *m*; (*also:* **garden ~**) tuyau d'arrosage

hospitable [ˈhɔspɪtəbl] *adj* hospitalier(-ère)

hospital [ˈhɔspɪtl] *n* hôpital *m*; **in ~** à l'hôpital

hospitality [hɔspɪˈtælɪtɪ] *n* hospitalité *f*

host [həʊst] *n* hôte *m*; (*TV, RADIO*) animateur(-trice); (*REL*) hostie *f*; (*large number*): **a ~ of** une foule de ♦ *vt*

(*conference, games etc*) accueillir

hostage [ˈhɔstɪdʒ] *n* otage *m*

hostel [ˈhɔstl] *n* foyer *m*; (*also:* **youth ~**) auberge *f* de jeunesse

hostess [ˈhəʊstɪs] *n* hôtesse *f*; (*TV, RADIO*) animatrice *f*

hostile [ˈhɔstaɪl] *adj* hostile; **hostility** [hɔˈstɪlɪtɪ] *n* hostilité *f*

hot [hɔt] *adj* chaud(e); (*as opposed to only warm*) très chaud; (*spicy*) fort(e); (*contest etc*) acharné(e); (*temper*) passionné(e); **to be ~** (*person*) avoir chaud; (*object*) être (très) chaud; **it is ~** (*weather*) il fait chaud; **~bed** *n* (*fig*) foyer *m*, pépinière *f*; **~ dog** *n* hot-dog *m*

hotel [həʊˈtel] *n* hôtel *m*

hot: ~house *n* serre (chaude); **~ line** *n* (*POL*) téléphone *m* rouge, ligne directe; **~ly** *adv* passionnément, violemment; **~plate** *n* (*on cooker*) plaque chauffante; **~pot** *n* (*BRIT*) *n* ragoût *m*; **~-water bottle** *n* bouillotte *f*

hound [haʊnd] *vt* poursuivre avec acharnement ♦ *n* chien courant

hour [ˈaʊər] *n* heure *f*; **~ly** *adj, adv* toutes les heures; (*rate*) horaire

house [*n* haʊs, *vb* haʊz] *n* maison *f*; (*POL*) chambre *f*; (*THEATRE*) salle *f*; auditoire *m* ♦ *vt* (*person*) loger, héberger; (*objects*) abriter; **on the ~** (*fig*) aux frais de la maison; **~ arrest** *n* assignation *f* à résidence; **~boat** *n* bateau *m* (*aménagé en habitation*); **~bound** *adj* confiné(e) chez soi; **~breaking** *n* cambriolage *m* (*avec effraction*); **~hold** *n* (*persons*) famille *f*, maisonnée *f*; (*ADMIN etc*) ménage *m*; **~keeper** *n* gouvernante *f*; **~keeping** *n* (*work*) ménage *m*; **~keeping** (*money*) argent *m* du ménage; **~warming (party)** *n* pendaison *f* de crémaillère; **~wife** (*irreg*) *n* ménagère *f*; femme *f* au foyer; **~work** *n* (*travaux mpl du*) ménage *m*

housing [ˈhaʊzɪŋ] *n* logement *m*; **~ development**, **~ estate** *n* lotissement *m*

hovel ['hɔvl] n taudis m

hover ['hɔvə*] vi planer; **~craft** n aéroglisseur m

how [hau] adv comment; **~ are you?** comment allez-vous?; **~ do you do?** bonjour; enchanté(e); **~ far is it to?** combien y a-t-il jusqu'à ...?; **~ long have you been here?** depuis combien de temps êtes-vous ici?; **~ lovely!** que or comme c'est joli!; **~ many/much?** combien?; **~ many people/much milk?** combien de gens/lait?; **~ old are you?** quel âge avez-vous?

however [hau'evə*] adv de quelque façon or manière que +subj; (+adj) quelque or si ... que +subj; (in questions) comment ♦ conj pourtant, cependant

howl [haul] vi hurler

H.P. abbr = **hire purchase**

h.p. abbr = **horsepower**

HQ abbr = **headquarters**

hub [hʌb] n (of wheel) moyeu m; (fig) centre m, foyer m; **~cap** n enjoliveur m

huddle ['hʌdl] vi: **to ~ together** se blottir les uns contre les autres

hue [hjuː] n teinte f, nuance f

huff [hʌf] n: **in a ~** fâché(e)

hug [hʌg] vt serrer dans ses bras; (shore, kerb) serrer

huge [hjuːdʒ] adj énorme, immense

hulk [hʌlk] n (ship) épave f; (car, building) carcasse f; (person) mastodonte m

hull [hʌl] n coque f

hullo [hə'ləu] excl = **hello**

hum [hʌm] vt (tune) fredonner ♦ vi fredonner; (insect) bourdonner; (plane, tool) vrombir

human ['hjuːmən] adj humain(e) ♦ n: **~ being** être humain; **~e** [hjuː'mein] adj humain(e), humanitaire; **~itarian** [hjuːmænɪ'teəriən] adj humanitaire; **~ity** [hjuː'mænɪtɪ] n humanité f

humble ['hʌmbl] adj humble, modeste ♦ vt humilier

humdrum ['hʌmdrʌm] adj monotone, banal(e)

humid ['hjuːmɪd] adj humide

humiliate [hjuː'mɪlɪeɪt] vt humilier; **humiliation** [hjuːmɪlɪ'eɪʃən] n humiliation f

humorous ['hjuːmərəs] adj humoristique; (person) plein(e) d'humour

humour ['hjuːmə*] (US **humor**) n humour m; (mood) humeur f ♦ vt (person) faire plaisir à; se prêter aux caprices de

hump [hʌmp] n bosse f

hunch [hʌntʃ] n (premonition) intuition f; **~back** n bossu(e); **~ed** adj voûté(e)

hundred ['hʌndrəd] num cent; **~s of** des centaines de; **~weight** n (BRIT) 50.8 kg, 112 lb; (US) 45.3 kg, 100 lb

hung [hʌŋ] pt, pp of **hang**

Hungary ['hʌŋgəri] n Hongrie f

hunger ['hʌŋgə*] n faim f ♦ vi: **to ~ for** avoir faim de, désirer ardemment

hungry ['hʌŋgri] adj affamé(e); (keen): **~ for** avide de; **to be ~** avoir faim

hunk [hʌŋk] n (of bread etc) gros morceau

hunt [hʌnt] vt chasser; (criminal) pourchasser ♦ vi chasser; (search): **to ~ for** chercher (partout) ♦ n chasse f; **~er** n chasseur m; **~ing** n chasse f

hurdle ['həːdl] n (in SPORT) haie f; (fig) obstacle m

hurl [həːl] vt lancer (avec violence); (abuse, insults) lancer

hurrah [hu'rɑː] excl = **hooray**

hurray [hu'rei] excl = **hooray**

hurricane ['hʌrikən] n ouragan m

hurried ['hʌrid] adj pressé(e), précipité(e); (work) fait(e) à la hâte; **~ly** adv précipitamment, à la hâte

hurry ['hʌri] (vb: also: **~ up**) n hâte f, précipitation f ♦ vi se presser, se dépêcher ♦ vt (person) faire presser, faire se dépêcher; (work) presser; **to be in a ~** être pressé(e); **to do sth in a ~** faire qch en vitesse; **to ~ in/out** entrer/sortir précipitamment

hurt [həːt] (pt, pp **hurt**) vt (cause pain to) faire mal à; (injure, fig) blesser ♦ vi faire mal ♦ adj blessé(e); **~ful** adj (remark) blessant(e)

hurtle ['hɜːtl] vi: **to ~ past** passer en trombe; **to ~ down** dégringoler
husband ['hʌzbənd] n mari m
hush [hʌʃ] n calme m, silence m ♦ vt faire taire; **~!** chut!; **~ up** vt (scandal) étouffer
husk [hʌsk] n (of wheat) balle f; (of rice, maize) enveloppe f
husky ['hʌskɪ] adj rauque ♦ n chien m esquimau or de traîneau
hustle ['hʌsl] vt pousser, bousculer ♦ n: **~ and bustle** tourbillon m (d'activité)
hut [hʌt] n hutte f; (shed) cabane f
hutch [hʌtʃ] n clapier m
hyacinth ['haɪəsɪnθ] n jacinthe f
hydrant ['haɪdrənt] n (also: **fire ~**) bouche f d'incendie
hydraulic [haɪ'drɔːlɪk] adj hydraulique
hydroelectric ['haɪdrəʊɪ'lektrɪk] adj hydro-électrique
hydrofoil ['haɪdrəfɔɪl] n hydrofoil m
hydrogen ['haɪdrədʒən] n hydrogène m
hyena [haɪ'iːnə] n hyène f
hygiene ['haɪdʒiːn] n hygiène f; **hygienic** adj hygiénique
hymn [hɪm] n hymne m; cantique m
hype [haɪp] (inf) n battage m publicitaire
hypermarket ['haɪpəmɑːkɪt] (BRIT) n hypermarché m
hypertext ['haɪpətekst] n (COMPUT) hypertexte m
hyphen ['haɪfn] n trait m d'union
hypnotize ['hɪpnətaɪz] vt hypnotiser
hypocrisy [hɪ'pɒkrɪsɪ] n hypocrisie f; **hypocrite** ['hɪpəkrɪt] n hypocrite m/f; **hypocritical** adj hypocrite
hypothesis [haɪ'pɒθɪsɪs] (pl **hypotheses**) n hypothèse f
hysterical [hɪ'sterɪkl] adj hystérique; (funny) hilarant(e); **~ laughter** fou rire m
hysterics [hɪ'sterɪks] npl: **to be in/ have ~** (anger, panic) avoir une crise de nerfs; (laughter) attraper un fou rire

I, i

I [aɪ] pron je; (before vowel) j'; (stressed) moi

ice [aɪs] n glace f; (on road) verglas m ♦ vt (cake) glacer ♦ vi (also: **~ over, ~ up**) geler; (window) se givrer; **~berg** n iceberg m; **~box** n (US) réfrigérateur m; (BRIT) compartiment m à glace; (insulated box) glacière f; **~ cream** n glace f; **~ cube** n glaçon m; **~d** adj glacé(e); **~ hockey** n hockey m sur glace; **Iceland** n Islande f; **~ lolly** (BRIT) n esquimau m (glace); **~ rink** n patinoire f; **~skating** n patinage m (sur glace)
icicle ['aɪsɪkl] n glaçon m (naturel)
icing ['aɪsɪŋ] n (CULIN) glace f; **~ sugar** (BRIT) n sucre m glace
ICT (BRIT) abbr (SCOL = Information and Communications Technology) TIC f
icy ['aɪsɪ] adj glacé(e); (road) verglacé(e); (weather, temperature) glacial(e)
I'd [aɪd] = I would; I had
idea [aɪ'dɪə] n idée f
ideal [aɪ'dɪəl] n idéal m ♦ adj idéal(e)
identical [aɪ'dentɪkl] adj identique
identification [aɪdentɪfɪ'keɪʃən] n identification f; **means of ~** pièce f d'identité
identify [aɪ'dentɪfaɪ] vt identifier
Identikit picture ® [aɪ'dentɪkɪt-] n portrait-robot m
identity [aɪ'dentɪtɪ] n identité f; **~ card** n carte f d'identité
ideology [aɪdɪ'ɒlədʒɪ] n idéologie f
idiom ['ɪdɪəm] n expression f idiomatique; (style) style m
idiosyncrasy [ɪdɪəʊ'sɪŋkrəsɪ] n (of person) particularité f, petite manie
idiot ['ɪdɪət] n idiot(e), imbécile m/f; **~ic** [ɪdɪ'ɒtɪk] adj idiot(e), bête, stupide
idle ['aɪdl] adj sans occupation, désœuvré(e); (lazy) oisif(-ive), paresseux (-euse); (unemployed) au chômage; (question, pleasures) vain(e), futile ♦ vi

(*engine*) tourner au ralenti; **to lie ~** être arrêté(e), ne pas fonctionner

idol ['aɪdl] *n* idole *f*; **~ize** *vt* idolâtrer, adorer

i.e. *adv abbr* (= *id est*) c'est-à-dire

if [ɪf] *conj* si; **~ so** si c'est le cas; **~ not** sinon; **~ only** si seulement

ignite [ɪg'naɪt] *vt* mettre le feu à, enflammer ♦ *vi* s'enflammer; **ignition** *n* (AUT) allumage *m*; **to switch on/off the ignition** mettre/couper le contact; **ignition key** *n* clé *f* de contact

ignorant ['ɪgnərənt] *adj* ignorant(e); **to be ~ of** (*subject*) ne rien connaître à; (*events*) ne pas être au courant de

ignore [ɪg'nɔː] *vt* ne tenir aucun compte de; (*person*) faire semblant de ne pas reconnaître, ignorer; (*fact*) méconnaître

ill [ɪl] *adj* (*sick*) malade; (*bad*) mauvais(e) ♦ *n* mal *m* ♦ *adv*: **to speak/think ~ of** dire/penser du mal de; **~s** *npl* (*misfortunes*) maux *mpl*, malheurs *mpl*; **to be taken ~** tomber malade; **~-advised** *adj* (*decision*) peu judicieux(-euse); (*person*) malavisé(e); **~-at-ease** *adj* mal à l'aise

I'll [aɪl] = **I will**; **I shall**

illegal [ɪ'liːgl] *adj* illégal(e)

illegible [ɪ'ledʒɪbl] *adj* illisible

illegitimate [ɪlɪ'dʒɪtɪmət] *adj* illégitime

ill-fated [ɪl'feɪtɪd] *adj* malheureux(-euse); (*day*) néfaste

ill feeling *n* ressentiment *m*, rancune *f*

illiterate [ɪ'lɪtərət] *adj* illettré(e)

ill: **~-mannered** *adj* (*child*) mal élevé(e); **~ness** *n* maladie *f*; **~-treat** *vt* maltraiter

illuminate [ɪ'luːmɪneɪt] *vt* (*room, street*) éclairer; (*for special effect*) illuminer; **illumination** [ɪluːmɪ'neɪʃən] *n* éclairage *m*; illumination *f*

illusion [ɪ'luːʒən] *n* illusion *f*

illustrate ['ɪləstreɪt] *vt* illustrer; **illustration** [ɪlə'streɪʃən] *n* illustration *f*

ill will *n* malveillance *f*

I'm [aɪm] = **I am**

image ['ɪmɪdʒ] *n* image *f*; (*public face*) image de marque; **~ry** *n* images *fpl*

imaginary [ɪ'mædʒɪnərɪ] *adj* imaginaire

imagination [ɪmædʒɪ'neɪʃən] *n* imagination *f*

imaginative [ɪ'mædʒɪnətɪv] *adj* imaginatif(-ive); (*person*) plein(e) d'imagination

imagine [ɪ'mædʒɪn] *vt* imaginer, s'imaginer; (*suppose*) imaginer, supposer

imbalance [ɪm'bæləns] *n* déséquilibre *m*

imitate ['ɪmɪteɪt] *vt* imiter; **imitation** [ɪmɪ'teɪʃən] *n* imitation *f*

immaculate [ɪ'mækjulət] *adj* impeccable; (REL) immaculé(e)

immaterial [ɪmə'tɪərɪəl] *adj* sans importance, insignifiant(e)

immature [ɪmə'tjuə] *adj* (*fruit*) (qui n'est pas mûr(e)); (*person*) qui manque de maturité

immediate [ɪ'miːdɪət] *adj* immédiat(e); **~ly** *adv* (*at once*) immédiatement; **~ly next to** juste à côté de

immense [ɪ'mens] *adj* immense; énorme

immerse [ɪ'məːs] *vt* immerger, plonger; **immersion heater** (BRIT) *n* chauffe-eau *m* électrique

immigrant ['ɪmɪgrənt] *n* immigrant(e); immigré(e); **immigration** [ɪmɪ'greɪʃən] *n* immigration *f*

imminent ['ɪmɪnənt] *adj* imminent(e)

immoral [ɪ'mɔrl] *adj* immoral(e)

immortal [ɪ'mɔːtl] *adj*, *n* immortel(le)

immune [ɪ'mjuːn] *adj*: **~ (to)** immunisé(e) (contre); (*fig*) à l'abri de; **immunity** *n* immunité *f*

impact ['ɪmpækt] *n* choc *m*, impact *m*; (*fig*) impact

impair [ɪm'peə] *vt* détériorer, diminuer

impart [ɪm'pɑːt] *vt* communiquer, transmettre; (*flavour*) donner

impartial [ɪm'pɑːʃl] *adj* impartial(e)

impassable [ɪm'pɑːsəbl] *adj* infranchissable; (*road*) impraticable

impassive [ɪm'pæsɪv] *adj* impassible

impatience [ɪm'peɪʃəns] *n* impatience *f*

impatient [ɪm'peɪʃənt] adj impatient(e); **to get** or **grow ~** s'impatienter; **~ly** adv avec impatience

impeccable [ɪm'pekəbl] adj impeccable, parfait(e)

impede [ɪm'piːd] vt gêner; **impediment** n obstacle m, gêne f; (also: **speech impediment**) défaut m d'élocution

impending [ɪm'pendɪŋ] adj imminent(e)

imperative [ɪm'perətɪv] adj (need) urgent(e), pressant(e); (tone) impérieux (-euse) ♦ n (LING) impératif m

imperfect [ɪm'pɜːfɪkt] adj imparfait(e); (goods etc) défectueux(-euse)

imperial [ɪm'pɪərɪəl] adj impérial(e); (BRIT: measure) légal(e)

impersonal [ɪm'pɜːsənl] adj impersonnel(le)

impersonate [ɪm'pɜːsəneɪt] vt se faire passer pour; (THEATRE) imiter

impertinent [ɪm'pɜːtɪnənt] adj impertinent(e), insolent(e)

impervious [ɪm'pɜːvɪəs] adj (fig): ~ **to** insensible à

impetuous [ɪm'petjuəs] adj impétueux(-euse), fougueux(-euse)

impetus ['ɪmpətəs] n impulsion f; (of runner) élan m

impinge [ɪm'pɪndʒ]: **to ~ on** vt fus (person) affecter, toucher; (rights) empiéter sur

implement [n 'ɪmplɪmənt, vb 'ɪmplɪment] n outil m, instrument m; (for cooking) ustensile m ♦ vt exécuter

implicit [ɪm'plɪsɪt] adj implicite; (complete) absolu(e), sans réserve

imply [ɪm'plaɪ] vt suggérer, laisser entendre; indiquer, supposer

impolite [ɪmpə'laɪt] adj impoli(e)

import [vb ɪm'pɔːt, n 'ɪmpɔːt] vt importer ♦ n (COMM) importation f

importance [ɪm'pɔːtns] n importance f

important [ɪm'pɔːtənt] adj important(e)

importer [ɪm'pɔːtər] n importateur(-trice)

impose [ɪm'pəuz] vt imposer ♦ vi: **to ~ on sb** abuser de la gentillesse de qn; **imposing** adj imposant(e), impressionnant(e); **imposition** [ɪmpə'zɪʃən] n (of tax etc) imposition f; **to be an imposition on** (person) abuser de la gentillesse ou la bonté de

impossible [ɪm'pɔsɪbl] adj impossible

impotent ['ɪmpətnt] adj impuissant(e)

impound [ɪm'paund] vt confisquer, saisir

impoverished [ɪm'pɔvərɪʃt] adj appauvri(e), pauvre

impractical [ɪm'præktɪkl] adj peu pratique; (person) qui manque d'esprit pratique

impregnable [ɪm'pregnəbl] adj (fortress) imprenable

impress [ɪm'pres] vt impressionner, faire impression sur; (mark) imprimer, marquer; **to ~ sth on sb** faire bien comprendre qch à qn; **~ed** adj impressionné(e)

impression [ɪm'preʃən] n impression f; (of stamp, seal) empreinte f; (imitation) imitation f; **to be under the ~ that** avoir l'impression que; **~ist** n (ART) impressionniste m/f; (entertainer) imitateur(-trice) m/f

impressive [ɪm'presɪv] adj impressionnant(e)

imprint ['ɪmprɪnt] n (outline) marque f, empreinte f

imprison [ɪm'prɪzn] vt emprisonner, mettre en prison

improbable [ɪm'prɔbəbl] adj improbable; (excuse) peu plausible

improper [ɪm'prɔpər] adj (unsuitable) déplacé(e), de mauvais goût; indécent(e); (dishonest) malhonnête

improve [ɪm'pruːv] vt améliorer ♦ vi s'améliorer; (pupil etc) faire des progrès; **~ment** n amélioration f (in de); progrès m

improvise ['ɪmprəvaɪz] vt, vi improviser

impudent ['ɪmpjudnt] adj impudent(e)

impulse ['ɪmpʌls] n impulsion f; **on ~**

impulsivement, sur un coup de tête;
impulsive *adj* impulsif(-ive)

KEYWORD

in [ɪn] *prep* **1** *(indicating place, position)*
dans; **in the house/the fridge** dans la
maison/le frigo; **in the garden** dans le
or au jardin; **in town** en ville; **in the
country** à la campagne; **in school** à
l'école; **in here/there** ici/là
2 *(with place names: of town, region,
country)*: **in London** à Londres; **in England** en Angleterre; **in Japan** au Japon;
in the United States aux États-Unis
3 *(indicating time: during)*: **in spring** au
printemps; **in summer** en été; **in
May/1992** en mai/1992; **in the afternoon** (dans) l'après-midi; **at 4 o'clock
in the afternoon** à 4 heures de
l'après-midi
4 *(indicating time: in the space of; (:
future)*: **during; I did it in 3 hours/days**
je l'ai fait en 3 heures/jours; **I'll see
you in 2 weeks** *or* **in 2 weeks' time**
je te verrai dans 2 semaines
5 *(indicating manner etc)* à; **in a loud/
soft voice** à voix haute/basse; **in pencil** au crayon; **in French** en français;
the boy in the blue shirt le garçon à
or avec la chemise bleue
6 *(indicating circumstances)*: **in the sun**
au soleil; **in the shade** à l'ombre; **in
the rain** sous la pluie
7 *(indicating mood, state)*: **in tears** en
larmes; **in anger** sous le coup de la colère; **in despair** au désespoir; **in good
condition** en bon état; **to live in luxury** vivre dans le luxe
8 *(with ratios, numbers)*: **1 in 10
(households), 1 (household) in 10** 1
(ménage) sur 10; **20 pence in the
pound** 20 pence par livre sterling;
they lined up in twos ils se mirent en
rangs (deux) par deux; **in hundreds**
par centaines
9 *(referring to people, works)* chez; **the
disease is common in children** c'est

une maladie courante chez les enfants;
in (the works of) Dickens chez
Dickens, dans (l'œuvre de) Dickens
10 *(indicating profession etc)* dans; **to
be in teaching** être dans l'enseignement
11 *(after superlative)* de; **the best pupil in the class** le meilleur élève de la
classe
12 *(with present participle)*: **in saying
this** en disant ceci
♦ *adv*: **to be in** *(person: at home, work)*
être là; *(train, ship, plane)* être arrivé(e);
(in fashion) être à la mode; **to ask sb
in** inviter qn à entrer; **to run/limp** *etc*
in entrer en courant/boitant *etc*
♦ *n*: **the ins and outs (of)** *(of proposal,
situation etc)* les tenants et aboutissants
(de).

---

in. *abbr* = **inch**

inability [ɪnə'bɪlɪtɪ] *n* incapacité *f*
inaccurate [ɪn'ækjʊrət] *adj* inexact(e);
(person) qui manque de précision
inadequate [ɪn'ædɪkwət] *adj* insuffi-
sant(e), inadéquat(e)
inadvertently [ɪnəd'vɜːtntlɪ] *adv* par
mégarde
inadvisable [ɪnəd'vaɪzəbl] *adj* (*action*)
à déconseiller
inane [ɪ'neɪn] *adj* inepte, stupide
inanimate [ɪn'ænɪmət] *adj* inanimé(e)
inappropriate [ɪnə'prəʊprɪət] *adj*
inopportun(e), mal à propos; *(word, expression)* impropre
inarticulate [ɪnɑː'tɪkjʊlət] *adj* (*person*)
qui s'exprime mal; *(speech)* indistinct(e)
inasmuch [ɪnəz'mʌtʃ-] *adv* (*insofar
as*) dans la mesure où; *(seeing that)* attendu que
inauguration [ɪnɔːgjʊ'reɪʃən] *n* inauguration *f*; *(of president)* investiture *f*
inborn [ɪn'bɔːn] *adj* (*quality*) inné(e)
inbred [ɪn'bred] *adj* inné(e), naturel(le);
(family) consanguin(e)
Inc. *abbr* = **incorporated**
incapable [ɪn'keɪpəbl] *adj* incapable

incapacitate [ɪnkəˈpæsɪteɪt] *vt*: **to ~ sb from doing** rendre qn incapable de faire

incense [*n* ˈɪnsɛns, *vb* ɪnˈsɛns] *n* encens *m* ♦ *vt* (*anger*) mettre en colère

incentive [ɪnˈsɛntɪv] *n* encouragement *m*, raison *f* de se donner de la peine

incessant [ɪnˈsɛsnt] *adj* incessant(e); **~ly** *adv* sans cesse, constamment

inch [ɪntʃ] *n* pouce *m* (= 25 mm; 12 in a foot); **within an ~ of** à deux doigts de; **he didn't give an ~** (*fig*) il n'a pas voulu céder d'un pouce

incident [ˈɪnsɪdnt] *n* incident *m*; **~al** [ɪnsɪˈdɛntl] *adj* (*additional*) accessoire; **~al to** qui accompagne; **~ally** *adv* (*by the way*) à propos

inclination [ɪnklɪˈneɪʃən] *n* (*fig*) inclination *f*

incline [*n* ˈɪnklaɪn, *vb* ɪnˈklaɪn] *n* pente *f* ♦ *vt* incliner ♦ *vi* (*surface*) s'incliner; **to be ~d to do** avoir tendance à faire

include [ɪnˈkluːd] *vt* inclure, comprendre; **including** *prep* y compris; **inclusive** *adj* inclus(e), compris(e); **inclusive of tax** *etc* taxes *etc* comprises

income [ˈɪnkʌm] *n* revenu *m*; **~ tax** *n* impôt *m* sur le revenu

incoming [ˈɪnkʌmɪŋ] *adj* qui arrive; (*president*) entrant(e); **~ mail** courrier *m* du jour; **~ tide** marée montante

incompetent [ɪnˈkɒmpɪtənt] *adj* incompétent(e), incapable

incomplete [ɪnkəmˈpliːt] *adj* incomplet(-ète)

incongruous [ɪnˈkɒŋɡruəs] *adj* incongru(e)

inconsiderate [ɪnkənˈsɪdərət] *adj* (*person*) qui manque d'égards; (*action*) inconsidéré(e)

inconsistency [ɪnkənˈsɪstənsɪ] *n* (*of actions etc*) inconséquence *f*; (*of work*) irrégularité *f*; (*of statement etc*) incohérence *f*

inconsistent [ɪnkənˈsɪstnt] *adj* inconséquent(e); irrégulier(-ère); peu cohérent(e); **~ with** incompatible avec

inconspicuous [ɪnkənˈspɪkjuəs] *adj* qui passe inaperçu(e); (*colour, dress*) discret(-ète)

inconvenience [ɪnkənˈviːnjəns] *n* inconvénient *m*; (*trouble*) dérangement *m* ♦ *vt* déranger

inconvenient [ɪnkənˈviːnjənt] *adj* (*house*) malcommode; (*time, place*) mal choisi(e), qui ne convient pas; (*visitor*) importun(e)

incorporate [ɪnˈkɔːpəreɪt] *vt* incorporer; (*contain*) contenir; **~d company** (*US*) *n* ≈ société *f* anonyme

incorrect [ɪnkəˈrɛkt] *adj* incorrect(e)

increase [*n* ˈɪnkriːs, *vb* ɪnˈkriːs] *n* augmentation *f* ♦ *vi, vt* augmenter; **increasing** *adj* (*number*) croissant(e); **increasingly** *adv* de plus en plus

incredible [ɪnˈkrɛdɪbl] *adj* incroyable

incubator [ˈɪnkjubeɪtər] *n* (*for babies*) couveuse *f*

incumbent [ɪnˈkʌmbənt] *n* (*president*) président *m* en exercice; (*REL*) titulaire *m/f* ♦ *adj*: **it is ~ on him to ...** il lui incombe or appartient de ...

incur [ɪnˈkəː] *vt* (*expenses*) encourir; (*anger, risk*) s'exposer à; (*debt*) contracter; (*loss*) subir

indebted [ɪnˈdɛtɪd] *adj*: **to be ~ to sb (for)** être redevable à qn (de)

indecent [ɪnˈdiːsnt] *adj* indécent(e), inconvenant(e); **~ assault** (*BRIT*) *n* attentat *m* à la pudeur; **~ exposure** *n* outrage *m* (public) à la pudeur

indecisive [ɪndɪˈsaɪsɪv] *adj* (*person*) indécis(e)

indeed [ɪnˈdiːd] *adv* vraiment; en effet; (*furthermore*) d'ailleurs; **yes ~!** certainement!

indefinitely [ɪnˈdɛfɪnɪtlɪ] *adv* (*wait*) indéfiniment

indemnity [ɪnˈdɛmnɪtɪ] *n* (*safeguard*) assurance *f*, garantie *f*; (*compensation*) indemnité *f*

independence [ɪndɪˈpɛndns] *n* indépendance *f*

Independence Day

*L'**Independence Day** est la fête nationale aux États-Unis, le 4 juillet. Il commémore l'adoption de la déclaration d'Indépendance, en 1776, écrite par Thomas Jefferson et proclamant la séparation des 13 colonies américaines de la Grande-Bretagne.*

independent [ɪndɪ'pɛndnt] *adj* indépendant(e); *(school)* privé(e); *(radio)* libre

index ['ɪndɛks] *n (pl: ~es: in book)* index *m*; (: *in library etc)* catalogue *m*; *(pl: indices: ratio, sign)* indice *m*; **~ card** *n* fiche *f*; **~ finger** *n* index *m*; **~-linked** *adj* indexé(e) (sur le coût de la vie *etc*)

India ['ɪndɪə] *n* Inde *f*; **~n** *adj* indien(ne); **(American)** ~n *n* Indien(ne) *f*; **(American)** ~n Indien(ne) (d'Amérique); **~n Ocean** *n* océan Indien

indicate ['ɪndɪkeɪt] *vt* indiquer; **indication** [ɪndɪ'keɪʃən] *n* indication *f*, signe *m*; **indicative** [ɪn'dɪkətɪv] *adj*: **indicative of** symptomatique de ♦ *n (LING)* indicatif *m*; **indicator** *n (sign)* indicateur *m*; *(AUT)* clignotant *m*

indices ['ɪndɪsi:z] *npl of* **index**

indictment [ɪn'daɪtmənt] *n* accusation *f*

indifferent [ɪn'dɪfrənt] *adj* indifférent(e); *(poor)* médiocre, quelconque

indigenous [ɪn'dɪdʒɪnəs] *adj* indigène

indigestion [ɪndɪ'dʒɛstʃən] *n* indigestion *f*, mauvaise digestion

indignant [ɪn'dɪɡnənt] *adj*: **~ (at sth/ with sb)** indigné(e) (de qch/contre qn)

indignity [ɪn'dɪɡnɪtɪ] *n* indignité *f*, affront *m*

indirect [ɪndɪ'rɛkt] *adj* indirect(e)

indiscreet [ɪndɪs'kri:t] *adj* indiscret (-ète); *(rash)* imprudent(e)

indiscriminate [ɪndɪs'krɪmɪnət] *adj (person)* qui manque de discernement; *(killings)* commis(e) au hasard

indisputable [ɪndɪs'pju:təbl] *adj* in

contestable, indiscutable

individual [ɪndɪ'vɪdjʊəl] *n* individu *m* ♦ *adj* individuel(le); *(characteristic)* particulier(-ère), original(e)

indoctrination [ɪndɔktrɪ'neɪʃən] *n* endoctrinement *m*

Indonesia [ɪndə'ni:zɪə] *n* Indonésie *f*

indoor ['ɪndɔ:ʳ] *adj (plant)* d'appartement; *(swimming pool)* couvert(e); *(sport, games)* pratiqué(e) en salle; **~s** *adv* à l'intérieur

induce [ɪn'dju:s] *vt (persuade)* persuader; *(bring about)* provoquer; **~ment** *n (incentive)* récompense *f*; *(pej: bribe)* pot-de-vin *m*

indulge [ɪn'dʌldʒ] *vt (whim)* céder à, satisfaire; *(child)* gâter ♦ *vi*: **to ~ in sth** *(luxury)* se permettre qch; *(fantasies etc)* se livrer à qch; **~nce** *n* fantaisie *f* (que l'on s'offre); *(leniency)* indulgence *f*; **~nt** *adj* indulgent(e)

industrial [ɪn'dʌstrɪəl] *adj* industriel(le); *(injury)* du travail; **~ action** *n* action revendicative; **~ estate** *(BRIT)* *n* zone industrielle; **~ist** *n* industriel *m*; **~ park** *(US)* *n* = **industrial estate**

industrious [ɪn'dʌstrɪəs] *adj* travailleur(-euse)

industry ['ɪndəstrɪ] *n* industrie *f*; *(diligence)* zèle *m*, application *f*

inebriated [ɪ'ni:brɪeɪtɪd] *adj* ivre

inedible [ɪn'ɛdɪbl] *adj* immangeable; *(plant etc)* non comestible

ineffective [ɪnɪ'fɛktɪv], **ineffectual** [ɪnɪ'fɛktʃʊəl] *adj* inefficace

inefficient [ɪnɪ'fɪʃənt] *adj* inefficace

inequality [ɪnɪ'kwɔlɪtɪ] *n* inégalité *f*

inescapable [ɪnɪ'skeɪpəbl] *adj* inéductable, inévitable

inevitable [ɪn'ɛvɪtəbl] *adj* inévitable; **inevitably** *adv* inévitablement

inexpensive [ɪnɪk'spɛnsɪv] *adj* bon marché *inv*

inexperienced [ɪnɪk'spɪərɪənst] *adj* inexpérimenté(e)

infallible [ɪn'fælɪbl] *adj* infaillible

infamous ['ɪnfəməs] *adj* infâme, abo

minable

infancy ['ɪnfənsɪ] n petite enfance, bas âge

infant ['ɪnfənt] n (baby) nourrisson m; (young child) petit(e) enfant; ~ **school** (BRIT) n classes fpl préparatoires (entre 5 et 7 ans)

infatuated [ɪn'fætjʊeɪtɪd] adj: ~ **with** entiché(e) de; **infatuation** [ɪnfæt-ju'eɪʃən] n engouement m

infect [ɪn'fɛkt] vt infecter, contaminer; **~ion** n infection f; (contagion) contagion f; **~ious** adj infectieux(-euse); (also fig) contagieux(-euse)

infer [ɪn'fɜː[r]] vt conclure, déduire

inferior [ɪn'fɪərɪə[r]] adj inférieur(e); (goods) de qualité inférieure ♦ n inférieur(e); (in rank) subalterne m/f; **~ity** [ɪnfɪərɪ'ɒrɪtɪ] n infériorité f

infertile [ɪn'fɜːtaɪl] adj stérile

infighting ['ɪnfaɪtɪŋ] n querelles fpl internes

infinite ['ɪnfɪnɪt] adj infini(e)

infinitive [ɪn'fɪnɪtɪv] n infinitif m

infinity [ɪn'fɪnɪtɪ] n infinité f; (also MATH) infini m

infirmary [ɪn'fɜːmərɪ] n (hospital) hôpital m

inflamed [ɪn'fleɪmd] adj enflammée(e)

inflammable [ɪn'flæməbl] (BRIT) adj inflammable

inflammation [ɪnflə'meɪʃən] n inflammation f

inflatable [ɪn'fleɪtəbl] adj gonflable

inflate [ɪn'fleɪt] vt (tyre, balloon) gonfler; (price) faire monter; **inflation** f (ECON) inflation f; **inflationary** adj inflationniste

inflict [ɪn'flɪkt] vt: **to ~ on** infliger à

influence ['ɪnfluəns] n influence f ♦ vt influencer; **under the ~ of alcohol** en état d'ébriété; **influential** [ɪnflu'ɛnʃl] adj influent(e)

influenza [ɪnflu'ɛnzə] n grippe f

influx ['ɪnflʌks] n afflux m

infomercial ['ɪnfəuməːʃl] (US) n (for product) publi-information f; (POL) émis-

sion où un candidat présente son programme électoral

inform [ɪn'fɔːm] vt: **to ~ sb (of)** informer or avertir qn (de) ♦ vi: **to ~ on sb** dénoncer qn

informal [ɪn'fɔːml] adj (person, manner, party) simple; (visit, discussion) dénué(e) de formalités; (announcement, invitation) non officiel(le); (colloquial) familier(-ère); **~ity** [ɪnfɔː'mælɪtɪ] n simplicité f, absence f de cérémonie; caractère non officiel

informant [ɪn'fɔːmənt] n informateur(-trice)

information [ɪnfə'meɪʃən] n information f; renseignements mpl; (knowledge) connaissances fpl; **a piece of ~** un renseignement; **~ desk** n accueil m; **~ office** n bureau m de renseignements

informative [ɪn'fɔːmətɪv] adj instructif(-ive)

informer [ɪn'fɔːmə[r]] n (also: **police ~**) indicateur(-trice)

infringe [ɪn'frɪndʒ] vt enfreindre ♦ vi: **to ~ on** empiéter sur; **~ment** n: **~ment (of)** infraction f (à)

infuriating [ɪn'fjuərieɪtɪŋ] adj exaspérant(e)

ingenious [ɪn'dʒiːnjəs] adj ingénieux(-euse); **ingenuity** [ɪndʒɪ'njuːɪtɪ] n ingéniosité f

ingenuous [ɪn'dʒɛnjuəs] adj naïf (naïve), ingénu(e)

ingot ['ɪŋgət] n lingot m

ingrained [ɪn'greɪnd] adj enraciné(e)

ingratiate [ɪn'greɪʃɪeɪt] vt: **to ~ o.s. with** s'insinuer dans les bonnes grâces de, se faire bien voir de

ingredient [ɪn'griːdɪənt] n ingrédient m; (fig) élément m

inhabit [ɪn'hæbɪt] vt habiter; **~ant** n habitant(e)

inhale [ɪn'heɪl] vt respirer; (smoke) avaler ♦ vi aspirer; (in smoking) avaler la fumée

inherent [ɪn'hɪərənt] adj: ~ **(in** or **to)** inhérent(e) (à)

inherit [ɪn'hɛrɪt] vt hériter (de); **~ance** n héritage m

inhibit [ɪn'hɪbɪt] vt (PSYCH) inhiber; (growth) freiner; **~ion** [ɪnhɪ'bɪʃən] n inhibition f

inhuman [ɪn'hju:mən] adj inhumain(e)

initial [ɪ'nɪʃl] adj initial(e) ♦ n initiale f ♦ vt parafer; **~s** npl (letters) initiales fpl; (as signature) parafe m; **~ly** adv initialement, au début

initiate [ɪ'nɪʃɪeɪt] vt (start) entreprendre, amorcer; (entreprise) lancer; (person) initier; **to ~ proceedings against sb** intenter une action à qn; **initiative** n initiative f

inject [ɪn'dʒɛkt] vt injecter; (person): **to ~ sb with sth** faire une piqûre de qch à qn; **~ion** n injection f, piqûre f

injure [ɪn'dʒə'] vt blesser; (reputation etc) compromettre; **~d** adj blessé(e); **injury** n blessure f; **~ time** n (SPORT) arrêts mpl de jeu

injustice [ɪn'dʒʌstɪs] n injustice f

ink [ɪŋk] n encre f

inkling ['ɪŋklɪŋ] n: **to have an/no ~ of** avoir une (vague) idée de/n'avoir aucune idée de

inlaid ['ɪnleɪd] adj incrusté(e); (table etc) marqueté(e)

inland [adj 'ɪnlənd, adv ɪn'lænd] adj intérieur(e) ♦ adv à l'intérieur, dans les terres; **Inland Revenue** (BRIT) n fisc m

in-laws ['ɪnlɔ:z] npl beaux-parents mpl, belle famille

inlet ['ɪnlɛt] n (GEO) crique f

inmate ['ɪnmeɪt] n (in prison) détenu(e); (in asylum) interné(e)

inn [ɪn] n auberge f

innate [ɪ'neɪt] adj inné(e)

inner ['ɪnə'] adj intérieur(e); **~ city** n centre m de zone urbaine; **~ tube** n (of tyre) chambre f à air

innings ['ɪnɪŋz] n (CRICKET) tour m de batte

innocent ['ɪnəsnt] adj innocent(e)

innocuous [ɪ'nɔkjuəs] adj inoffensif (-ive)

innuendo [ɪnju'ɛndəu] (pl **~es**) n insinuation f, allusion (malveillante)

innumerable [ɪ'nju:mrəbl] adj innombrable

inpatient ['ɪnpeɪʃnt] n malade hospitalisé(e)

input ['ɪnput] n (resources) ressources fpl; (COMPUT) entrée f (de données); (: data) données fpl

inquest ['ɪnkwɛst] n enquête f; (coroner's) **~** enquête judiciaire

inquire [ɪn'kwaɪə'] vi demander ♦ vt demander; **to ~ about** se renseigner sur; **~ into** vt fus faire une enquête sur; **inquiry** n demande f de renseignements; (investigation) enquête f, investigation f; **inquiries** npl: **the inquiries** (RAIL etc) les renseignements; **inquiry** or **inquiries office** (BRIT) n bureau m des renseignements

inquisitive [ɪn'kwɪzɪtɪv] adj curieux (-euse)

ins abbr = **inches**

insane [ɪn'seɪn] adj fou (folle); (MED) aliéné(e); **insanity** [ɪn'sænɪtɪ] n folie f; (MED) aliénation (mentale)

inscription [ɪn'skrɪpʃən] n inscription f; (in book) dédicace f

inscrutable [ɪn'skru:təbl] adj impénétrable; (comment) obscur(e)

insect ['ɪnsɛkt] n insecte m; **~icide** [ɪn'sɛktɪsaɪd] n insecticide m; **~ repellent** n crème f anti-insecte

insecure [ɪnsɪ'kjuə'] adj peu solide; peu sûr(e); (person) anxieux(-euse)

insensitive [ɪn'sɛnsɪtɪv] adj insensible

insert [ɪn'sə:t] vt insérer; **~ion** n insertion f

in-service ['ɪn'sə:vɪs] adj (training) continu(e), en cours d'emploi; (course) de perfectionnement; de recyclage

inshore ['ɪn'ʃɔ:'] adj côtier(-ère) ♦ adv près de la côte; (move) vers la côte

inside [ɪn'saɪd] n intérieur m ♦ adj intérieur(e) ♦ adv à l'intérieur, dedans ♦ prep à l'intérieur de; (of time): **~ 10 minutes** en moins de 10 minutes; **~s**

npl (inf) intestins *mpl;* ~ **information** *n* renseignements obtenus à la source; ~ **lane** *n (AUT: in Britain)* voie *f* de gauche; (: *in US, Europe etc*) voie *f* de droite; ~ **out** *adv* à l'envers; *(know)* à fond; ~**r dealing,** ~**r trading** *n (St Ex)* délit *m* d'initié

insight ['ɪnsaɪt] *n* perspicacité *f; (glimpse, idea)* aperçu *m*

insignificant [ɪnsɪg'nɪfɪkənt] *adj* insignifiant(e)

insincere [ɪnsɪn'sɪəʳ] *adj* hypocrite

insinuate [ɪn'sɪnjueɪt] *vt* insinuer

insist [ɪn'sɪst] *vi* insister; **to** ~ **on doing** insister pour faire; **to** ~ **on sth** exiger qch; **to** ~ **that** insister pour que; *(claim)* maintenir ou soutenir que; ~**ent** *adj* instant(e), pressant(e); *(noise, action)* ininterrompu(e)

insole ['ɪnsəʊl] *n (removable)* semelle intérieure

insolent ['ɪnsələnt] *adj* insolent(e)

insolvent [ɪn'sɔlvənt] *adj* insolvable

insomnia [ɪn'sɔmnɪə] *n* insomnie *f*

inspect [ɪn'spekt] *vt* inspecter; *(ticket)* contrôler; ~**ion** *n* inspection *f;* contrôle *m;* ~**or** *n* inspecteur(-trice); *(BRIT: on buses, trains)* contrôleur(-euse)

inspire [ɪn'spaɪəʳ] *vt* inspirer

install [ɪn'stɔːl] *vt* installer; ~**ation** [ɪnstə'leɪʃən] *n* installation *f*

instalment [ɪn'stɔːlmənt] (US **install-ment**) *n* acompte *m,* versement partiel; *(of TV serial etc)* épisode *m;* **in** ~**s** *(pay)* à tempérament; *(receive)* en plusieurs fois

instance ['ɪnstəns] *n* exemple *m;* **for** ~ par exemple; **in the first** ~ tout d'abord, en premier lieu

instant ['ɪnstənt] *n* instant *m ♦ adj* immédiat(e); *(coffee, food)* instantané(e), en poudre; ~**ly** *adv* immédiatement, tout de suite

instead [ɪn'sted] *adv* au lieu de cela; ~ **of** au lieu de; ~ **of sb** à la place de qn

instep ['ɪnstep] *n* cou-de-pied *m; (of shoe)* cambrure *f*

instigate ['ɪnstɪgeɪt] *vt (rebellion)* fo-

menter, provoquer; *(talks etc)* promouvoir

instil [ɪn'stɪl] *vt:* **to** ~ **(into)** inculquer (à); *(courage)* insuffler (à)

instinct ['ɪnstɪŋkt] *n* instinct *m*

institute ['ɪnstɪtjuːt] *n* institut *m ♦ vt* instituer, établir; *(inquiry)* ouvrir; *(proceedings)* entamer

institution [ɪnstɪ'tjuːʃən] *n* institution *f; (educational)* établissement *m* (scolaire); *(mental home)* établissement *f* (psychiatrique)

instruct [ɪn'strʌkt] *vt:* **to** ~ **sb in sth** enseigner qch à qn; **to** ~ **sb to do** charger qn ou ordonner à qn de faire; ~**ion** *n* instruction *f;* ~**ions** *npl (orders)* directives *fpl;* ~**ions (for use)** mode d'emploi; ~**or** *n* professeur *m; (for skiing, driving)* moniteur *m*

instrument ['ɪnstrumənt] *n* instrument *m;* ~**al** [ɪnstru'mentl] *adj:* **to be** ~**al in** contribuer à; ~ **panel** *n* tableau *m* de bord

insufficient [ɪnsə'fɪʃənt] *adj* insuffisant(e)

insular ['ɪnsjulə] *adj (outlook)* borné(e); *(person)* aux vues étroites

insulate ['ɪnsjuleɪt] *vt* isoler; *(against sound)* insonoriser; **insulation** [ɪnsju'leɪʃən] *n* isolation *f;* insonorisation *f*

insulin ['ɪnsjulɪn] *n* insuline *f*

insult [*n* 'ɪnsʌlt, *vb* ɪn'sʌlt] *n* insulte *f,* affront *m ♦ vt* insulter, faire affront à

insurance [ɪn'ʃuərəns] *n* assurance *f;* **fire/life** ~ assurance-incendie/-vie; ~ **policy** *n* police *f* d'assurance

insure [ɪn'ʃuəʳ] *vt* assurer; **to** ~ **(o.s.) against** *(fig)* parer à

intact [ɪn'tækt] *adj* intact(e)

intake ['ɪnteɪk] *n (of food, oxygen)* consommation *f; (BRIT: SCOL):* **an** ~ **of 200 a year** 200 admissions *fpl* par an

integral ['ɪntɪgrəl] *adj (part)* intégrant(e)

integrate ['ɪntɪgreɪt] *vt* intégrer *♦ vi* s'intégrer

intellect ['ɪntəlɛkt] n intelligence f;
~**ual** [ɪntə'lɛktjuəl] adj, n intellectuel(le)

intelligence [ɪn'tɛlɪdʒəns] n intelligence f; (MIL etc) informations fpl, renseignements mpl; ~ **service** n services secrets; **intelligent** adj intelligent(e)

intend [ɪn'tɛnd] vt (gift etc): **to ~ sth for** destiner qch à; **to ~ to do** avoir l'intention de faire

intense [ɪn'tɛns] adj intense; (person) véhément(e); ~**ly** adv intensément; profondément

intensive [ɪn'tɛnsɪv] adj intensif(-ive); ~ **care unit** n service m de réanimation

intent [ɪn'tɛnt] n intention f ♦ adj attentif(-ive); **to all ~s and purposes** en fait, pratiquement; **to be ~ on doing sth** être (bien) décidé à faire qch; ~**ion** n intention f; ~**ional** adj intentionnel(le), délibéré(e); ~**ly** adv attentivement

interact [ɪntər'ækt] vi avoir une action réciproque; (people) communiquer; ~**ive** adj (COMPUT) interactif(-ive)

interchange [n 'ɪntətʃeɪndʒ, vb ɪntə'tʃeɪndʒ] n (exchange) échange m; (on motorway) échangeur m; ~**able** adj interchangeable

intercom ['ɪntəkɔm] n interphone m

intercourse ['ɪntəkɔːs] n (sexual) rapports mpl

interest ['ɪntrɪst] n intérêt m; (pastime): **my main ~** ce qui m'intéresse le plus; (COMM) intérêts mpl ♦ vt intéresser; **to be ~ed in sth** s'intéresser à qch; **I am ~ed in going** ça m'intéresse d'y aller; ~**ing** adj intéressant(e); ~ **rate** n taux m d'intérêt

interface ['ɪntəfeɪs] n (COMPUT) interface f

interfere [ɪntə'fɪə'] vi: **to ~ in** (quarrel) s'immiscer dans; (other people's business) se mêler de; **to ~ with** (object) toucher à; (plans) contrecarrer; (duty) être en conflit avec; ~**nce** n (in affairs)

ingérance f; (RADIO, TV) parasites mpl

interim ['ɪntərɪm] adj provisoire ♦ n: **in the ~** dans l'intérim, entre-temps

interior [ɪn'tɪərɪə'] n intérieur m ♦ adj intérieur(e); (minister, department) de l'Intérieur; ~ **designer** n styliste m/f, designer m/f

interjection [ɪntə'dʒɛkʃən] n (interruption) interruption f; (LING) interjection f

interlock [ɪntə'lɔk] vi s'enclencher

interlude ['ɪntəluːd] n intervalle m; (THEATRE) intermède m

intermediate [ɪntə'miːdɪət] adj intermédiaire; (SCOL) moyen(ne)

intermission [ɪntə'mɪʃən] n pause f; (THEATRE, CINEMA) entracte m

intern [vb ɪn'təːn, n 'ɪntəːn] vt interner ♦ n (US) interne m/f

internal [ɪn'təːnl] adj interne; (politics) intérieur(e); ~**ly** adv: **"not to be taken ~ly"** "pour usage externe"; **I~ Revenue Service** (US) n fisc m

international [ɪntə'næʃənl] adj international(e)

Internet ['ɪntənɛt] n Internet m; ~ **café** cybercafé m; ~ **service provider** fournisseur m d'accès à Internet

interplay ['ɪntəpleɪ] n effet m réciproque, interaction f

interpret [ɪn'təːprɪt] vt interpréter ♦ vi servir d'interprète; ~**er** n interprète m/f

interrelated [ɪntəri'leɪtɪd] adj en corrélation, en rapport étroit

interrogate [ɪn'tɛrəugeɪt] vt interroger; (suspect etc) soumettre à un interrogatoire; **interrogation** [ɪntɛrəu'geɪʃən] n interrogatoire m

interrupt [ɪntə'rʌpt] vt, vi interrompre; ~**ion** n interruption f

intersect [ɪntə'sɛkt] vi (roads) se couper, se croiser; ~**ion** n (of roads) croisement m

intersperse [ɪntə'spəːs] vt: **to ~ with** parsemer de

intertwine [ɪntə'twaɪn] vi s'entrelacer

interval ['ɪntəvl] n intervalle m; (BRIT: THEATRE) entracte m; (: SPORT) mi-temps f; **at ~s** par intervalles

intervene [ɪntə'viːn] vi (person) intervenir; (event) survenir; (time) s'écouler (entre-temps); **intervention** n intervention f

interview ['ɪntəvjuː] n (RADIO, TV etc) interview f; (for job) entrevue f ♦ vt interviewer; avoir une entrevue avec; **~er** n (RADIO, TV) interviewer m

intestine [ɪn'testɪn] n intestin m

intimacy ['ɪntɪməsɪ] n intimité f

intimate [adj 'ɪntɪmət, vb 'ɪntɪmeɪt] adj intime; (friendship) profond(e); (knowledge) approfondi(e) ♦ vt (hint) suggérer, laisser entendre

into ['ɪntu] prep dans; **~ pieces/French** en morceaux/français

intolerant [ɪn'tɔlərnt] adj: **~ (of)** intolérant(e) (de)

intoxicated [ɪn'tɔksɪkeɪtɪd] adj (drunk) ivre

intractable [ɪn'træktəbl] adj (child) indocile, insoumis(e); (problem) insoluble

intranet ['ɪntrənet] n intranet m

intransitive [ɪn'trænsɪtɪv] adj intransitif(-ive)

intravenous [ɪntrə'viːnəs] adj intraveineux(-euse)

in-tray ['ɪntreɪ] n courrier m "arrivée"

intricate ['ɪntrɪkət] adj complexe, compliqué(e)

intrigue [ɪn'triːg] n intrigue f ♦ vt intriguer; **intriguing** adj fascinant(e)

intrinsic [ɪn'trɪnsɪk] adj intrinsèque

introduce [ɪntrə'djuːs] vt introduire; (TV show, people to each other) présenter; **to ~ sb to** (pastime, technique) initier qn à; **introduction** n introduction f; (of person) présentation f; (to new experience) initiation f; **introductory** adj préliminaire, d'introduction; **introductory offer** n (COMM) offre f de lancement

intrude [ɪn'truːd] vi (person) être importun(e); **to ~ on** (conversation etc) s'immiscer dans; **~r** n intrus(e)

intuition [ɪntjuː'ɪʃən] n intuition f

inundate ['ɪnʌndeɪt] vt: **to ~ with**

inonder de

invade [ɪn'veɪd] vt envahir

invalid [n 'ɪnvəlɪd, adj ɪn'vælɪd] n malade m/f; (with disability) invalide m/f ♦ adj (not valid) non valide or valable

invaluable [ɪn'væljuəbl] adj inestimable, inappréciable

invariably [ɪn'veərɪəblɪ] adv invariablement; toujours

invent [ɪn'vent] vt inventer; **~ion** n invention f; **~ive** adj inventif(-ive); **~or** n inventeur(-trice)

inventory ['ɪnvəntrɪ] n inventaire m

invert [ɪn'vɜːt] vt intervertir; (cup, object) retourner; **~ed commas** (BRIT) npl guillemets mpl

invest [ɪn'vest] vt investir ♦ vi: **to ~ in** sth placer son argent dans qch; (fig) s'offrir qch

investigate [ɪn'vestɪgeɪt] vt (crime etc) faire une enquête sur; **investigation** [ɪnvestɪ'geɪʃən] n (of crime) enquête f

investment [ɪn'vestmənt] n investissement m, placement m

investor [ɪn'vestə*] n investisseur m; actionnaire m/f

invigilator [ɪn'vɪdʒɪleɪtə*] n surveillant(e)

invigorating [ɪn'vɪgəreɪtɪŋ] adj vivifiant(e); (fig) stimulant(e)

invisible [ɪn'vɪzɪbl] adj invisible

invitation [ɪnvɪ'teɪʃən] n invitation f

invite [ɪn'vaɪt] vt inviter; (opinions etc) demander; **inviting** adj engageant(e), attrayant(e)

invoice ['ɪnvɔɪs] n facture f

involuntary [ɪn'vɔləntrɪ] adj involontaire

involve [ɪn'vɔlv] vt (entail) entraîner, nécessiter; (concern) concerner; (associate): **to ~ sb (in)** impliquer qn (dans), mêler qn (à); faire participer qn (à); **~d** adj (complicated) complexe; **to be ~d in** participer à; **~ment** n: **~ment (in)** participation f (à); rôle m (dans); (enthusiasm) enthousiasme m (pour)

inward ['ɪnwəd] adj (thought, feeling)

iodine 442 itch

profond(e), intime; (*movement*) vers l'intérieur; **~(s)** *adv* vers l'intérieur

iodine ['aɪədiːn] *n* iode *m*

iota [aɪ'əʊtə] *n* (*fig*) brin *m*, grain *m*

IOU *n abbr* (= *I owe you*) reconnaissance *f* de dette

IQ *n abbr* (= *intelligence quotient*) Q.I. *m*

IRA *n abbr* (= *Irish Republican Army*) IRA *f*

Iran [ɪ'rɑːn] *n* Iran *m*

Iraq [ɪ'rɑːk] *n* Irak *m*

irate [aɪ'reɪt] *adj* courroucé(e)

Ireland ['aɪələnd] *n* Irlande *f*

iris ['aɪrɪs] (*pl* **~es**) *n* iris *m*

Irish ['aɪrɪʃ] *adj* irlandais(e) ♦ *npl*: **the ~** les Irlandais; **~man** (*irreg*) *n* Irlandais *m*; **~ Sea** *n* mer d'Irlande; **~woman** (*irreg*) *n* Irlandaise *f*

iron ['aɪən] *n* fer *m*; (*for clothes*) fer m à repasser ♦ *cpd* de ou en fer; (*fig*) de fer ♦ *vt* (*clothes*) repasser; **~ out** *vt* (*fig*) aplanir; faire disparaître

ironic(al) [aɪ'rɒnɪk(l)] *adj* ironique

ironing ['aɪənɪŋ] *n* repassage *m*; **~ board** *n* planche *f* à repasser

ironmonger's (shop) ['aɪənmʌŋgəz-] *n* quincaillerie *f*

irony ['aɪrənɪ] *n* ironie *f*

irrational [ɪ'ræʃənl] *adj* irrationnel(le)

irregular [ɪ'regjulə*] *adj* irrégulier(-ère); (*surface*) inégal(e)

irrelevant [ɪ'reləvənt] *adj* sans rapport, hors de propos

irresistible [ɪrɪ'zɪstɪbl] *adj* irrésistible

irrespective [ɪrɪ'spektɪv]: **~ of** *prep* sans tenir compte de

irresponsible [ɪrɪ'spɒnsɪbl] *adj* (*act*) irréfléchi(e); (*person*) irresponsable

irrigate ['ɪrɪgeɪt] *vt* irriguer; **irrigation** [ɪrɪ'geɪʃən] *n* irrigation *f*

irritate ['ɪrɪteɪt] *vt* irriter

irritating *adj* irritant(e); **irritation** [ɪrɪ'teɪʃən] *n* irritation *f*

IRS *n abbr* = **Internal Revenue Service**

is [ɪz] *vb see* **be**

Islam ['ɪzlɑːm] *n* Islam *m*; **~ic** *adj* islamique; **~ic fundamentalists** intégris-

tes *mpl* musulmans

island ['aɪlənd] *n* île *f*; **~er** *n* habitant(e) d'une île, insulaire *m/f*

isle [aɪl] *n* île *f*

isn't ['ɪznt] = **is not**

isolate ['aɪsəleɪt] *vt* isoler; **~d** *adj* isolé(e); **isolation** [aɪsə'leɪʃən] *n* isolement *m*

ISP *n abbr* = **Internet service provider**

Israel ['ɪzreɪl] *n* Israël *m*; **~i** [ɪz'reɪlɪ] *adj* israélien(ne) ♦ *n* Israélien(ne)

issue ['ɪʃjuː] *n* question *f*, problème *m*; (*of book*) publication *f*, parution *f*; (*of banknotes etc*) émission *f*; (*of newspaper etc*) numéro *m* ♦ *vt* (*rations, equipment*) distribuer; (*statement*) publier, faire; (*banknotes etc*) émettre, mettre en circulation; **at ~** en jeu, en cause; **to take ~ with sb (over)** exprimer son désaccord avec qn (sur); **to make an ~ of sth** faire une montagne de qch

---

KEYWORD

it [ɪt] *pron* **1** (*specific: subject*) il (elle); (: *direct object*) le (la) (l'); (: *indirect object*) lui; **it's on the table** c'est ou il (ou elle) est sur la table; **about/from/of it** en; **I spoke to him about it** je lui en ai parlé; **what did you learn from it?** qu'est-ce que vous en avez tiré?; **I'm proud of it** j'en suis fier; **in/to it** y; **put the book in it** mettez-y le livre; **he agreed to it** il y a consenti; **did you go to it?** (*party, concert etc*) est-ce que vous y êtes allé(s)?

2 (*impersonal*) il; ce; **it's raining** il pleut; **it's Friday tomorrow** demain c'est vendredi *ou* nous sommes vendredi; **it's 6 o'clock** il est 6 heures; **who is it? - it's me** qui est-ce? - c'est moi

---

Italian [ɪ'tæljən] *adj* italien(ne) ♦ *n* Italien(ne); (*LING*) italien *m*

italics [ɪ'tælɪks] *npl* italiques *fpl*

Italy ['ɪtəlɪ] *n* Italie *f*

itch [ɪtʃ] *n* démangeaison *f* ♦ *vi* (*person*) éprouver des démangeaisons; (*part of*) body) démanger; **I'm ~ing to do** l'envie me démange de faire; **~y** adj qui démange; **to be ~y** avoir des démangeaisons

it'd ['ɪtd] = **it would**; **it had**

item ['aɪtəm] n article m; (on agenda) question f, point m; (also: **news ~**) nouvelle f; **~ize** vt détailler, faire une liste de

itinerary [aɪ'tɪnərərɪ] n itinéraire m

it'll ['ɪtl] = **it will**; **it shall**

its [ɪts] adj son (sa), ses pl

it's [ɪts] = **it is**; **it has**

itself [ɪt'self] pron (reflexive) se; (emphatic) lui-même (elle-même)

ITV n abbr (BRIT: Independent Television) chaîne privée

IUD n abbr (= intra-uterine device) DIU m, stérilet m

I've [aɪv] = **I have**

ivory ['aɪvərɪ] n ivoire m

ivy ['aɪvɪ] n lierre m

J, j

jab [dʒæb] vt: **to ~ sth into** enfoncer or planter qch dans ♦ n (inf: injection) piqûre f

jack [dʒæk] n (AUT) cric m; (CARDS) valet m; **~ up** vt soulever (au cric)

jackal ['dʒækl] n chacal m

jacket ['dʒækɪt] n veste f, veston m; (of book) jaquette f, couverture f; **~ potato** n pomme f de terre en robe des champs

jack: ~knife vi: **the lorry ~knifed** la remorque (du camion) s'est mise en travers; **~ plug** n (ELEC) prise jack mâle f; **~pot** n gros lot

jaded ['dʒeɪdɪd] adj éreinté(e), fatigué(e)

jagged ['dʒægɪd] adj dentelé(e)

jail [dʒeɪl] n prison f ♦ vt emprisonner, mettre en prison

jam [dʒæm] n confiture f; (also: **traffic ~**) embouteillage m ♦ vt (passage etc)

encombrer, obstruer; (mechanism, drawer etc) bloquer, coincer; (RADIO) brouiller ♦ vi se coincer, se bloquer; (gun) s'enrayer; **to be in a ~** (inf) être dans le pétrin; **to ~ sth into** entasser qch dans; enfoncer qch dans

Jamaica [dʒə'meɪkə] n Jamaïque f

jam: ~ jar n pot m à confiture; **~med** adj (window etc) coincée(e); **~-packed** adj: **~-packed (with)** bourré(e) (de)

jangle ['dʒæŋgl] vi cliqueter

janitor ['dʒænɪtə*] n concierge m

January ['dʒænjʊərɪ] n janvier m

Japan [dʒə'pæn] n Japon m; **~ese** [dʒæpə'niːz] adj japonais(e) ♦ n inv Japonais(e); (LING) japonais m

jar [dʒɑ:*] n (stone, earthenware) pot m; (glass) bocal m ♦ vi (sound discordant) produire un son grinçant or discordant; (colours etc) jurer

jargon ['dʒɑ:gən] n jargon m

jaundice ['dʒɔ:ndɪs] n jaunisse f

javelin ['dʒævlɪn] n javelot m

jaw [dʒɔ:] n mâchoire f

jay [dʒeɪ] n geai m; **~walker** n piéton indiscipliné

jazz [dʒæz] n jazz m; **~ up** vt animer, égayer

jealous ['dʒeləs] adj jaloux(-ouse); **~y** n jalousie f

jeans [dʒi:nz] npl jean m

jeer [dʒɪə*] vi: **to ~ (at)** se moquer cruellement (de), railler

Jehovah's Witness [dʒɪ'həʊvəz-] n témoin m de Jéhovah

jelly ['dʒelɪ] n gelée f; **~fish** ['dʒelɪfɪʃ] n méduse f

jeopardy ['dʒepədɪ] n: **to be in ~** être en danger or péril

jerk [dʒə:k] n secousse f; saccade f; sursaut m, spasme m; (inf: idiot) pauvre type m ♦ vt (pull) tirer brusquement ♦ vi (vehicles) cahoter

jersey ['dʒə:zɪ] n (pullover) tricot m; (fabric) jersey m

Jesus ['dʒi:zəs] n Jésus

jet [dʒet] n (gas, liquid) jet m; (AVIAT)

avion m à réaction, jet m; **~-black** adj (d'un noir) de jais; **~ engine** n moteur m à réaction; **~ lag** n (fatigue due au) décalage m horaire

jettison ['dʒɛtɪsn] vt jeter par-dessus bord

jetty ['dʒɛtɪ] n jetée f, digue f

Jew [dʒuː] n Juif m

jewel ['dʒuːəl] n bijou m, joyau m; (in watch) rubis m; **~ler** (US **jeweler**) n bijoutier(-ère), joaillier m; **~ler's (shop)** n bijouterie f, joaillerie f; **~lery** (US **jewelry**) n bijoux mpl

Jewess ['dʒuːɪs] n Juive f

Jewish ['dʒuːɪʃ] adj juif (juive)

jibe [dʒaɪb] n sarcasme m

jiffy ['dʒɪfɪ] (inf) n: **in a ~** en un clin d'œil

jigsaw ['dʒɪgsɔː] n (also: **~ puzzle**) puzzle m

jilt [dʒɪlt] vt laisser tomber, plaquer

jingle ['dʒɪŋgl] n (for advert) couplet m publicitaire ♦ vi cliqueter, tinter

jinx [dʒɪŋks] (inf) n (mauvais) sort

jitters ['dʒɪtəz] (inf) npl: **to get the ~** (inf) avoir la trouille or la frousse

job [dʒɔb] n (chore, task) travail m, tâche f; (employment) emploi m, poste m, place f; **it's a good ~ that ...** c'est heureux or c'est une chance que ...; **just the ~!** (c'est) juste or exactement ce qu'il faut!; **~ centre** (BRIT) n agence f pour l'emploi; **~less** adj sans travail, au chômage

jockey ['dʒɔkɪ] n jockey m ♦ vi: **to ~ for position** manœuvrer pour être bien placé

jog [dʒɔg] vt secouer ♦ vi (SPORT) faire du jogging; **to ~ sb's memory** rafraîchir la mémoire de qn; **~ along** vi cheminer; trotter; **~ging** n jogging m

join [dʒɔɪn] vt (put together) unir, assembler; (become member of) s'inscrire à; (meet) rejoindre, retrouver; (queue) se joindre à ♦ vi (roads, rivers) se rejoindre, se rencontrer ♦ n raccord m; **~ in** vi se mettre de la partie, participer ♦

vt fus participer à, se mêler à; **~ up** vi (meet) se rejoindre; (MIL) s'engager

joiner ['dʒɔɪnə*] (BRIT) n menuisier m

joint [dʒɔɪnt] n (TECH) jointure f; joint m; (ANAT) articulation f, jointure; (CULIN) rôti m; (inf: place) boîte f; (: of cannabis) joint m ♦ adj commun(e); **~ account** n (with bank etc) compte joint

joke [dʒəuk] n plaisanterie f; (also: **practical ~**) farce f ♦ vi plaisanter; **to play a ~ on** jouer un tour à, faire une farce à; **~r** n (CARDS) joker m

jolly ['dʒɔlɪ] adj gai(e), enjoué(e); (enjoyable) amusant(e), plaisant(e) ♦ adv (BRIT: inf) rudement, drôlement

jolt [dʒəult] n cahot m, secousse f; (shock) choc m ♦ vt cahoter, secouer

Jordan ['dʒɔːdən] n (country) Jordanie f

jostle ['dʒɔsl] vt bousculer, pousser

jot [dʒɔt] n: **not one ~** pas un brin; **~ down** vt noter; **~ter** (BRIT) n cahier m (de brouillon); (pad) bloc-notes m

journal ['dʒɜːnl] n journal m; **~ism** n journalisme m; **~ist** n journaliste m/f

journey ['dʒɜːnɪ] n voyage m; (distance covered) trajet m

joy [dʒɔɪ] n joie f; **~ful** adj joyeux (-euse); **~rider** n personne qui fait une virée dans une voiture volée; **~stick** n (AVIAT, COMPUT) manche m à balai

JP n abbr = **Justice of the Peace**

Jr abbr = **junior**

jubilant ['dʒuːbɪlnt] adj triomphant(e); réjoui(e)

judge [dʒʌdʒ] n juge m ♦ vt juger; **judg(e)ment** n jugement m

judicial [dʒuː'dɪʃl] adj judiciaire; **judiciary** n (pouvoir m) judiciaire m

judo ['dʒuːdəu] n judo m

jug [dʒʌg] n pot m, cruche f

juggernaut ['dʒʌgənɔːt] (BRIT) n (huge truck) énorme poids lourd

juggle ['dʒʌgl] vi jongler; **~r** n jongleur m

juice [dʒuːs] n jus m; **juicy** adj juteux (-euse)

jukebox ['dʒu:kbɔks] n juke-box f

July [dʒu:'laɪ] n juillet m

jumble ['dʒʌmbl] n fouillis m ♦ vt (also: ~ up) mélanger, brouiller; ~ **sale** (BRIT) n vente f de charité

---
jumble sale

Les **jumble sales** ont lieu dans les églises, salles de fêtes ou halls d'écoles, et l'on y vend des articles de toutes sortes, en général bon marché et surtout d'occasion, pour collecter des fonds pour une œuvre de charité, une école ou encore une église.

---

jumbo (jet) ['dʒʌmbəu-] n jumbo-jet m, gros porteur

jump [dʒʌmp] vi sauter, bondir; (start) sursauter; (increase) monter en flèche ♦ vt sauter, franchir ♦ n saut m, bond m; sursaut m; **to ~ the queue** (BRIT) passer avant son tour

jumper ['dʒʌmpəʳ] n (BRIT: pullover) pull-over m; (US: dress) robe-chasuble f

jumper cables (US: BRIT **jump leads**) npl câbles mpl de démarrage

jumpy ['dʒʌmpi] adj nerveux(-euse), agité(e)

Jun. abbr = **junior**

junction ['dʒʌŋkʃən] n (BRIT) (of roads) carrefour m; (of rails) embranchement m

juncture ['dʒʌŋktʃəʳ] n: **at this ~** à ce moment-là, sur ces entrefaites

June [dʒu:n] n juin m

jungle ['dʒʌŋgl] n jungle f

junior ['dʒu:nɪəʳ] adj, n: **he's ~ to me (by 2 years), he's my ~ (by 2 years)** il est mon cadet (de 2 ans), il est plus jeune que moi (de 2 ans); **he's ~ to me** (seniority) il est en dessous de moi (dans la hiérarchie), j'ai plus d'ancienneté que lui; **~ school** (BRIT) n école f primaire

junk [dʒʌŋk] n (rubbish) camelote f; (cheap goods) bric-à-brac m inv; ~ **food** n aliments mpl sans grande valeur nutri-

tive; ~ **mail** n prospectus mpl (non sollicités); ~ **shop** n (boutique f de) brocanteur m

Junr abbr = **junior**

juror ['dʒuərəʳ] n juré m

jury ['dʒuəri] n jury m

just [dʒʌst] adj juste ♦ adv: **he's ~ done it/left** il vient de le faire/partir; ~ **right/two o'clock** exactement or juste ce qu'il faut/deux heures; **she's ~ as clever as you** elle est tout aussi intelligente que vous; **it's ~ as well (that)** ... heureusement que ...; ~ **as he was leaving** au moment or à l'instant précis où il partait; ~ **before/enough/here** juste avant/assez/ici; **it's ~ me/a mistake** ce n'est que moi/(rien) qu'une erreur; ~ **missed/caught** manqué/ attrapé de justesse; ~ **listen to this!** écoutez un peu ça!

justice ['dʒʌstɪs] n justice f; (US: judge) juge m de la Cour suprême; **J~ of the Peace** n juge m de paix

justify ['dʒʌstɪfaɪ] vt justifier

jut [dʒʌt] vi (also: ~ **out**) dépasser, faire saillie

juvenile ['dʒu:vənaɪl] adj juvénile; (court, books) pour enfants ♦ n adolescent(e)

K, k

K abbr (= one thousand) K; (= kilobyte) Ko

kangaroo [kæŋgə'ru:] n kangourou m

karate [kə'rɑ:tɪ] n karaté m

kebab [kə'bæb] n kébab m

keel [ki:l] n quille f; **on an even ~** (fig) à flot

keen [ki:n] adj (eager) plein(e) d'enthousiasme; (interest, desire, competition) vif (vive); (eye, intelligence) pénétrant(e); (edge) effilé(e); **to be ~ to do or on doing sth** désirer vivement faire qch, tenir beaucoup à faire qch; **to be ~ on sth/sb** aimer beaucoup qch/qn

keep [kiːp] (pt, pp **kept**) vt (retain, preserve) garder; (detain) retenir; (shop, accounts, diary, promise) tenir; (house) avoir; (support) entretenir; (chickens, bees etc) élever ♦ vi (remain) rester; (food) se conserver ♦ n (of castle) donjon m; (food etc): **enough for his ~** assez pour (assurer) sa subsistance; (inf): **for ~s** pour de bon, pour toujours; **to ~ doing sth** ne pas arrêter de faire qch; **to ~ sb from doing** empêcher qn de faire or que qn ne fasse; **to ~ sb happy/a place tidy** faire que qn soit content/qu'un endroit reste propre; **to ~ sth to o.s.** garder qch pour soi, tenir qch secret; **to ~ sth (back) from sb** cacher qch à qn; **to ~ time** (clock) être à l'heure, ne pas retarder; **well kept** bien entretenu(e); ~ on vi: **to ~ on doing** continuer à faire; **don't ~ on about it!** arrête (d'en parler)!; ~ out vt empêcher d'entrer; **"~ out"** "défense d'entrer"; ~ up vt continuer, maintenir ♦ vi: **to ~ up with sb** (in race etc) aller aussi vite que qn; (in work etc) se maintenir au niveau de qn; **~er** n gardien(ne); **~fit** n gymnastique f d'entretien; **~ing** n (care) garde f; **in ~ing with** en accord avec, **~sake** n souvenir m

kennel ['kɛnl] n niche f; **~s** npl (boarding ~s) chenil m

kerb [kɜːb] (BRIT) n bordure f du trottoir

kernel ['kɜːnl] n (of nut) amande f, (fig) noyau m

kettle ['kɛtl] n bouilloire f; **~drum** n timbale f

key [kiː] n (gen , MUS) clé f; (of piano, typewriter) touche f ♦ cpd clé ♦ vt (also: **~ in**) saisir; **~board** n clavier m; **~ed up** adj (person) surexcité(e); **~hole** n trou m de la serrure; **~hole surgery** n chirurgie f endoscopique; **~note** n (of speech) note dominante; (MUS) tonique f; **~ ring** n porte-clés m

khaki ['kɑːkɪ] n kaki m

kick [kɪk] vt donner un coup de pied à ♦ vi (horse) ruer ♦ n coup de pied; (thrill): **he does it for ~s** il le fait parce que ça l'excite, il le fait pour le plaisir; **to ~ the habit** (inf) arrêter; **~ off** vi (SPORT) donner le coup d'envoi

kid [kɪd] n (inf: child) gamin(e), gosse m/f; (animal, leather) chevreau m ♦ vi (inf) plaisanter, blaguer

kidnap ['kɪdnæp] vt enlever, kidnapper; **~per** n ravisseur(-euse); **~ping** n enlèvement m

kidney ['kɪdnɪ] n (ANAT) rein m; (CULIN) rognon m

kill [kɪl] vt tuer ♦ n mise f à mort; **~er** n tueur(-euse); meurtrier(-ère); **~ing** n meurtre m; (of group of people) tuerie f, massacre m; **to make a ~ing** (inf) réussir un beau coup (de filet); **~joy** n rabat-joie m/f

kiln [kɪln] n four m

kilo ['kiːləʊ] n kilo m; **~byte** n (COMPUT) kilo-octet m; **~gram(me)** n kilogramme m; **~metre** (US **kilometer**) n kilomètre m; **~watt** n kilowatt m

kilt [kɪlt] n kilt m

kin [kɪn] n see **next**

kind [kaɪnd] adj gentil(le), aimable ♦ n sorte f, espèce f, genre m; (soft kind) **to be two of a ~** se ressembler; **in ~** (COMM) en nature

kindergarten ['kɪndəgɑːtn] n jardin d'enfants

kind-hearted [kaɪnd'hɑːtɪd] adj bon (bonne)

kindle ['kɪndl] vt allumer, enflammer

kindly ['kaɪndlɪ] adj bienveillant(e), plein(e) de gentillesse ♦ adv avec bonté; **will you ~ ...!** auriez-vous la bonté or l'obligeance de ...?

kindness ['kaɪndnɪs] n bonté f, gentillesse f

king [kɪŋ] n roi m; **~dom** n royaume m; **~fisher** n martin-pêcheur m; **~-size bed** n grand lit (de 1,95 m de large); **~-size(d)** adj format géant inv; (cigarettes) long (longue)

kiosk ['kiːɔsk] n kiosque m; (BRIT: TEL) cabine f (téléphonique)

kipper ['kɪpəʳ] n hareng fumé et salé

kiss [kɪs] n baiser m ♦ vt embrasser; to ~ (each other) s'embrasser; ~ of life (BRIT) n bouche à bouche m

kit [kɪt] n équipement m, matériel m; (set of tools etc) trousse f; (for assembly) kit m

kitchen ['kɪtʃɪn] n cuisine f; ~ sink n évier m

kite [kaɪt] n (toy) cerf-volant m

kitten ['kɪtn] n chaton m, petit chat

kitty ['kɪtɪ] n (money) cagnotte f

km abbr = kilometre

knack [næk] n: to have the ~ of doing avoir le coup pour faire

knapsack ['næpsæk] n musette f

knead [niːd] vt pétrir

knee [niː] n genou m; ~cap n rotule f

kneel [niːl] (pt, pp knelt) vi (also: ~ down) s'agenouiller

knew [njuː] pt of know

knickers ['nɪkəz] (BRIT) npl culotte f (de femme)

knife [naɪf] (pl knives) n couteau m ♦ vt poignarder, frapper d'un coup de couteau

knight [naɪt] n chevalier m; (CHESS) cavalier m; ~hood (BRIT) n (title): to get a ~hood être fait chevalier

knit [nɪt] vt tricoter ♦ vi tricoter; (broken bones) se ressouder; to ~ one's brows froncer les sourcils; ~ting n tricot m; ~ting needle n aiguille f à tricoter; ~wear n tricots mpl, lainages mpl

knives [naɪvz] npl of knife

knob [nɔb] n bouton m

knock [nɔk] vt frapper; (bump into) heurter; (inf) dénigrer ♦ vi (at door etc): to ~ at or on frapper à ♦ n coup m; ~ down vt renverser; ~ off vi (inf: finish) s'arrêter (de travailler) ♦ vt (from price) faire un rabais de; (inf: steal) piquer; ~ out vt assommer; (BOXING) mettre k.-o.; ~ over vt renverser, faire tomber; ~er n (on door) heurtoir

m; ~out n (BOXING) knock-out m, K.-O. m; ~out competition compétition f avec épreuves éliminatoires

knot [nɔt] n (gen) nœud m ♦ vt nouer

know [nəu] (pt knew, pp known) vt savoir; (person, place) connaître; to ~ how to do savoir (comment) faire; to ~ how to swim savoir nager; to ~ about or of sth être au courant de qch; to ~ about or of sb avoir entendu parler de qn; ~all (pej) n je-sais-tout m/f; ~how n savoir-faire m; ~ing adj (look etc) entendu(e); ~ingly adv sciemment; (smile, look) d'un air entendu

knowledge ['nɔlɪdʒ] n connaissance f; (learning) connaissances, savoir m; ~able adj bien informé(e)

knuckle ['nʌkl] n articulation f (des doigts), jointure f

Koran [kɔ'rɑːn] n Coran m

Korea [kə'rɪə] n Corée f

kosher ['kəuʃəʳ] adj kascher inv

Kosovo ['kɔsəvəu] n Kosovo m

L, l

L abbr (= lake, large) L; (= left) g; (BRIT: AUT: learner) signale un conducteur débutant

lab [læb] n abbr (= laboratory) labo m

label ['leɪbl] n étiquette f ♦ vt étiqueter

labor etc ['leɪbəʳ] (US) = **labour** etc

laboratory [lə'bɔrətərɪ] n laboratoire m

labour ['leɪbəʳ] (US labor) n (work) travail m; (workforce) main-d'œuvre f; to ~ (at) travailler dur (à), peiner (sur); in ~ (MED) en travail, en train d'accoucher; L~, the L~ party (BRIT) n parti travailliste m, les travaillistes mpl; ~ed ['leɪbəd] adj (breathing) pénible, difficile; ~er n manœuvre m; farm ~er ouvrier m agricole

lace [leɪs] n dentelle f; (of shoe etc) lacet m ♦ vt (shoe: also: ~ up) lacer

lack [læk] n manque m ♦ vt manquer

de; **through** or **for ~** faute de, par manque de; **to be ~ing** manquer, faire défaut; **to be ~ing in** manquer de

lacquer ['lækər] n laque f

lad [læd] n garçon m, gars m

ladder ['lædər] n échelle f; (BRIT: in tights) maille filée

laden ['leɪdn] adj: **~ (with)** chargé(e) (de)

ladle ['leɪdl] n louche f

lady ['leɪdɪ] n dame f; (in address): **ladies and gentlemen** Mesdames (et) Messieurs; **young ~** jeune fille f; (married) jeune femme f; **the ladies' (room)** les toilettes fpl (pour dames); **~bird**, (US **~bug**) n coccinelle f; **~like** adj distingué(e); **~ship** n: **your ~ship** Madame la comtesse/la baronne etc

lag [læg] n retard m ♦ vi (also: **~ behind**) rester en arrière, traîner; (fig) rester en traîne ♦ vt (pipes) calorifuger

lager ['lɑːgər] n bière blonde

lagoon [lə'guːn] n lagune f

laid [leɪd] pt, pp of **lay**; **~-back** (inf) adj relaxe, décontracté(e); **~ up** adj alité(e)

lain [leɪn] pp of **lie**

lake [leɪk] n lac m

lamb [læm] n agneau m; **~ chop** n côtelette f d'agneau

lame [leɪm] adj boiteux(-euse)

lament [lə'ment] n lamentation f ♦ vt pleurer, se lamenter sur

laminated ['læmɪneɪtɪd] adj laminé(e); (windscreen) (en verre) feuilleté

lamp [læmp] n lampe f; **~post** (BRIT) n réverbère m; **~shade** n abat-jour m inv

lance [lɑːns] vt (MED) inciser

land [lænd] n (as opposed to sea) terre f (ferme); (soil) terre; terrain m; (estate) terre(s), domaine(s) m(pl); (country) pays m ♦ vi (AVIAT) atterrir; (fig) (re)tomber ♦ vt (passengers, goods) débarquer; **to ~ sb with sth** (inf) coller qch à qn; **~ up** vi atterrir, (finir par se) retrouver; **~fill site** n décharge f; **~ing** n (AVIAT) atterrissage m; (of staircase)

palier m; (of troops) débarquement m; **~ing strip** n piste f d'atterrissage; **~lady** n propriétaire f, logeuse f; (of pub) patronne f; **~locked** adj sans littoral; **~lord** n propriétaire m, logeur m; (of pub etc) patron m; **~mark** n (point m de) repère m; **to be a ~mark** (fig) faire date or époque; **~owner** n propriétaire foncier or terrien; **~scape** n paysage m; **~scape gardener** n jardinier(-ère) paysagiste; **~slide** n (GEO) glissement m (de terrain); (fig: POL) raz-de-marée (électoral)

lane [leɪn] n (in country) chemin m; (AUT) voie f; file f; (in race) couloir m; **"get in ~"** (AUT) "mettez-vous dans or sur la bonne file"

language ['læŋgwɪdʒ] n langue f; (way one speaks) langage m; **bad ~** grossièretés fpl, langage grossier; **~ laboratory** n laboratoire m de langues; **~ school** n école f de langues

lank [læŋk] adj (hair) raide et terne

lanky ['læŋkɪ] adj grand(e) et maigre, efflanqué(e)

lantern ['læntən] n lanterne f

lap [læp] n (of track) tour m (de piste); (of body): **in** or **on one's ~** sur les genoux f ♦ vt (also: **~ up**) laper ♦ vi (waves) clapoter; **~ up** vt (fig) avaler, gober

lapel [lə'pel] n revers m

Lapland ['læplænd] n Laponie f

lapse [læps] n défaillance f; (in behaviour) écart m de conduite ♦ vi (LAW) cesser d'être en vigueur; (contract) expirer; **to ~ into bad habits** prendre de mauvaises habitudes; **~ of time** laps m de temps, intervalle m

laptop (computer) ['læptɒp(-)] n portable m

larceny ['lɑːsənɪ] n vol m

larch [lɑːtʃ] n mélèze m

lard [lɑːd] n saindoux m

larder ['lɑːdər] n garde-manger m inv

large [lɑːdʒ] adj grand(e); (person, animal) gros(se); **at ~** (free) en liberté; (generally) en général; see also **by**; **~ly**

adv en grande partie; *(principally)* surtout; **~scale** *adj (action)* d'envergure; *(map)* à grande échelle

lark [lɑːk] *n (bird)* alouette *f*; *(joke)* blague *f*, farce *f*

laryngitis [lærɪnˈdʒaɪtɪs] *n* laryngite *f*

laser [ˈleɪzəʳ] *n* laser *m*; **~ printer** *n* imprimante *f* laser

lash [læʃ] *n* coup *m* de fouet; *(also:* **eyelash)** cil *m* ♦ *vt* fouetter; *(tie)* attacher; **~ out** *vi:* **to ~ out at** *or* **against** attaquer violemment

lass [læs] *(BRIT)* *n (jeune)* fille *f*

lasso [læˈsuː] *n* lasso *m*

last [lɑːst] *adj* dernier(-ère) ♦ *adv* en dernier; *(finally)* finalement *m* ♦ *vi* durer; **~ week** la semaine dernière; **~ night** *(evening)* hier soir; *(night)* la nuit dernière; **at ~** enfin; **~ but one** avant-dernier(-ère); **~-ditch** *adj (attempt)* ultime, désespéré(e); **~ing** *adj* durable; **~ly** *adv* en dernier lieu, pour finir; **~-minute** *adj* de dernière minute

latch [lætʃ] *n* loquet *m*

late [leɪt] *adj (not on time)* en retard; *(far on in day etc)* tardif(-ive); *(edition, delivery)* dernier(-ère); *(former)* ancien(ne) ♦ *adv* **~ but one** *(behind time, schedule)* en retard; **of ~** dernièrement; **in ~ May** vers la fin mai; **the ~ Mr X** feu M. X; **~comer** *n* retardataire *m/f*; **~ly** *adv* récemment; **~r** *adj (date etc)* ultérieur(e); *(version etc)* plus récent(e) ♦ *adv* plus tard; **~r on** plus tard; **~st** *adj (most recent)* dernier(-ère); **at the ~st** au plus tard

lathe [leɪð] *n* tour *m*

lather [ˈlɑːðəʳ] *n* mousse *f* (de savon) ♦ *vt* savonner

Latin [ˈlætɪn] *n* latin *m* ♦ *adj* latin(e); **~ America** *n* Amérique latine; **~ American** *adj* latino-américain(e)

latitude [ˈlætɪtjuːd] *n* latitude *f*

latter [ˈlætəʳ] *adj* deuxième, dernier(-ère) ♦ *n:* **the ~** ce dernier, celui-ci; **~ly** *adv* dernièrement, récemment

laudable [ˈlɔːdəbl] *adj* louable

laugh [lɑːf] *n* rire *m* ♦ *vi* rire; **~ at** *vt fus* se moquer de; rire de; **~ off** *vt* écarter par une plaisanterie *or* par une boutade; **~able** *adj* risible, ridicule; **~ing stock** *n:* **the ~ing stock of** la risée de; **~ter** *n* rire *m*; rires *mpl*

launch [lɔːntʃ] *n* lancement *m*; *(motorboat)* vedette *f* ♦ *vt* lancer; **~ into** *vt fus* se lancer dans

Launderette ® [lɔːnˈdrɛt] *(BRIT)*, **Laundromat** ® [ˈlɔːndrəmæt] *(US)* *n* laverie *f* (automatique)

laundry [ˈlɔːndrɪ] *n (clothes)* linge *m*; *(business)* blanchisserie *f*; *(room)* buanderie *f*

laurel [ˈlɔrl] *n* laurier *m*

lava [ˈlɑːvə] *n* lave *f*

lavatory [ˈlævətərɪ] *n* toilettes *fpl*

lavender [ˈlævəndəʳ] *n* lavande *f*

lavish [ˈlævɪʃ] *adj (amount)* copieux (-euse); *(person)* avec prodigue de ♦ *vt:* **to ~ sth on sb** prodiguer qch à qn; *(money)* dépenser qch sans compter pour qn/qch

law [lɔː] *n* loi *f*; *(science)* droit *m*; **~-abiding** *adj* respectueux(-euse) des lois; **~ and order** *n* l'ordre public; **~ court** *n* tribunal *m*, cour *f* de justice; **~ful** *adj* légal(e); **~less** *adj (action)* illégal(e)

lawn [lɔːn] *n* pelouse *f*; **~mower** *n* tondeuse *f* à gazon; **~ tennis** *n* tennis *m*

law school *(US)* *n* faculté *f* de droit

lawsuit [ˈlɔːsuːt] *n* procès *m*

lawyer [ˈlɔːjəʳ] *n (consultant, with company)* juriste *m*; *(for sales, wills etc)* notaire *m*; *(partner, in court)* avocat *m*

lax [læks] *adj* relâché(e)

laxative [ˈlæksətɪv] *n* laxatif *m*

lay [leɪ] *(pt, pp* **laid)** *pt* of **lie** ♦ *adj* laïque; *(not expert)* profane ♦ *vt* poser, mettre; *(eggs)* pondre; **to ~ the table** mettre la table; **~ aside** *vt* mettre de côté; **~ by** *vt* = **lay aside**; **~ down** *vt* poser; **to ~ down the law** faire la loi; **to ~ down one's life** sacrifier sa vie; **~**

off vt (workers) licencier; **~ on** vt (provide) fournir; **~ out** vt (display) disposer, étaler; **~about** (inf) n fainéant(e); **~by** (BRIT) n aire f de stationnement (sur le bas-côté)

layer ['leɪə*] n couche f

layman ['leɪmən] (irreg) n profane m

layout ['leɪaut] n disposition f, plan m, agencement m; (PRESS) mise f en page

laze [leɪz] vi (also: **~ about**) paresser

lazy ['leɪzɪ] adj paresseux(-euse)

lb abbr = **pound** (weight)

lead¹ [li:d] (pt, pp led) n (distance, time ahead) avance f; (clue) piste f; (THEATRE) rôle principal; (ELEC) fil m; (for dog) laisse f ♦ vt mener, conduire; (be ~ of) être à la tête de ♦ vi (street etc) mener, conduire; (SPORT) mener, être en tête; **in the ~** en tête; **to ~ the way** montrer le chemin; **~ away** vt emmener; **~ back** vt: **to ~ back to** ramener à; **~ on** vt (tease) faire marcher; **~ to** vt fus mener à; conduire à; **~ up to** vt fus conduire à

lead² [lɛd] n (metal) plomb m; (in pencil) mine f; **~ed petrol** n essence f au plomb; **~en** adj (sky, sea) de plomb

leader ['li:də*] n chef m; dirigeant(e), leader m; (SPORT: in league) leader; (: in race) coureur de tête; **~ship** n direction f; (quality) qualités fpl de chef

lead-free ['lɛdfri:] adj (petrol) sans plomb

leading ['li:dɪŋ] adj principal(e); de premier plan; (in race) de tête; **~ lady** n (THEATRE) vedette (féminine); **~ light** n (person) vedette f, sommité f; **~ man** (irreg) n vedette (masculine)

lead singer [li:d-] n (in pop group) (chanteur m) vedette f

leaf [li:f] (pl **leaves**) n feuille f ♦ vi: **to ~ through** feuilleter; **to turn over a new ~** changer de conduite or d'existence

leaflet ['li:flɪt] n prospectus m, brochure f; (POL, REL) tract m

league [li:g] n ligue f; (FOOTBALL) cham-

pionnat m; **to be in ~ with** avoir partie liée avec, être de mèche avec

leak [li:k] n fuite f ♦ vi (pipe, liquid etc) fuir; (shoes) prendre l'eau; (ship) faire eau ♦ vt (information) divulguer

lean [li:n] (pt, pp leaned or leant) adj maigre ♦ vt: **to ~ sth on sth** appuyer qch sur qch ♦ vi (slope) pencher; (rest): **to ~ against** s'appuyer contre; être appuyé(e) contre; **to ~ on** s'appuyer sur; **to ~ back/forward** se pencher en arrière/avant; **~ out** vi se pencher au dehors; **~ over** vi se pencher; **~ing** n: **~ing (towards)** tendance f (à), penchant m (pour); **~t** [lɛnt] pt, pp of **lean**

leap [li:p] (pt, pp leaped or leapt) n bond m, saut m ♦ vi bondir, sauter; **~frog** n saute-mouton m; **~t** [lɛpt] pt, pp of **leap**; **~ year** n année f bissextile

learn [lɜ:n] (pt, pp learned or learnt) vt, vi apprendre; **to ~ to do sth** apprendre à faire qch; **to ~ about or of sth** (hear, read) apprendre qch; **~ed** ['lɜ:nɪd] adj érudit(e), savant(e); **~er** (BRIT) n (also: **~er driver**) (conducteur (-trice)) débutant(e); **~ing** n (knowledge) savoir m; **~t** pt, pp of **learn**

lease [li:s] n bail m ♦ vt louer à bail

leash [li:ʃ] n laisse f

least [li:st] adj: **the ~** (+noun) le (la) plus petit(e), le (la) moindre; (: smallest amount of) le moins de ♦ adv (+verb) le moins; (+adj): **the ~** le (la) moins; **at ~** au moins; (or rather) du moins; **not in the ~** pas le moins du monde

leather ['lɛðə*] n cuir m

leave [li:v] (pt, pp left) vt laisser; (go away from) quitter; (forget) oublier ♦ vi partir, s'en aller ♦ n (time off) congé m; (MIL also: consent) permission f; **to be left** rester; **there's some milk left over** il reste du lait; **on ~** en permission; **~ behind** vt (person, object) laisser; (forget) oublier; **~ out** vt oublier, omettre; **~ of absence** n congé exceptionnel; (MIL) permission spéciale

leaves [li:vz] npl of **leaf**

Lebanon ['lebanən] *n* Liban *m*

lecherous ['letʃərəs] (*pej*) *adj* lubrique

lecture ['lektʃər] *n* conférence *f*; (*SCOL*) cours *m* ♦ *vi* donner des cours; enseigner ♦ *vt* (*scold*) sermonner, réprimander; **to give a ~ on** faire une conférence sur; donner un cours sur; **~r** (*BRIT*) (*at university*) professeur *m* (d'université)

led [led] *pt, pp of* **lead¹**

ledge [ledʒ] *n* (*of window, on wall*) rebord *m*; (*of mountain*) saillie *f*, corniche *f*

ledger ['ledʒər] *n* (*COMM*) registre *m*, grand livre

leech [liːtʃ] *n* (*also fig*) sangsue *f*

leek [liːk] *n* poireau *m*

leer [lɪər] *vi*: **to ~ at sb** regarder qn d'un air mauvais *ou* concupiscent

leeway ['liːweɪ] *n* (*fig*): **to have some ~** avoir une certaine liberté d'action

left [left] *pt, pp of* **leave** ♦ *adj* (*not right*) gauche ♦ *n* gauche *f* ♦ *adv* à gauche; **on the ~, to the ~** à gauche; **the L~** (*POL*) la gauche; **~-handed** *adj* gaucher(-ère); **~-hand side** *n* gauche *f*; **~-luggage locker** *n* (casier *m* à) consigne *f* automatique; **~-luggage (office)** (*BRIT*) *n* consigne *f*; **~overs** *npl* restes *mpl*; **~-wing** *adj* (*POL*) de gauche

leg [leg] *n* jambe *f*; (*of animal*) patte *f*; (*of furniture*) pied *m*; (*CULIN: of chicken, pork*) cuisse *f*; (*: of lamb*) gigot *m*; (*of journey*) étape *f*; **1st/2nd ~** (*SPORT*) match *m* aller/retour

legacy ['legəsɪ] *n* héritage *m*, legs *m*

legal ['liːgl] *adj* légal(e); **~ holiday** (*US*) *n* jour férié; **~ tender** *n* monnaie légale

legend ['ledʒənd] *n* légende *f*

leggings ['legɪŋz] *npl* caleçon *m*

legible ['ledʒəbl] *adj* lisible

legislation [ledʒɪs'leɪʃən] *n* législation *f*; **legislature** ['ledʒɪslətʃər] *n* (corps *m*) législatif *m*

legitimate [lɪ'dʒɪtɪmət] *adj* légitime

leg-room ['legruːm] *n* place *f* pour les jambes

leisure ['leʒər] *n* loisir *m*, temps *m* libre; loisirs *mpl*; **at ~** (tout) à loisir; à tête reposée; **~ centre** *n* centre *m* de loisirs; **~ly** *adj* tranquille; fait(e) sans se presser

lemon ['lemən] *n* citron *m*; **~ade** [lemə'neɪd] *n* limonade *f*; **~ tea** *n* thé *m* au citron

lend [lend] (*pt, pp* **lent**) *vt*: **to ~ sth (to sb)** prêter qch (à qn)

length [leŋθ] *n* longueur *f*; (*section: of road, pipe etc*) morceau *m*, bout *m*; (*of time*) durée *f*; **at ~** (*at last*) enfin, à la fin; (*~ily*) longuement; **~en** *vt* allonger, prolonger ♦ *vi* s'allonger; **~ways** *adv* dans le sens de la longueur, en long; **~y** *adj* (très) long (longue)

lenient ['liːnɪənt] *adj* indulgent(e), clément(e)

lens [lenz] *n* lentille *f*; (*of spectacles*) verre *m*; (*of camera*) objectif *m*

Lent [lent] *n* carême *m*

lent [lent] *pt, pp of* **lend**

lentil ['lentɪl] *n* lentille *f*

Leo ['liːəu] *n* le Lion

leotard ['liːətɑːd] *n* maillot *m* (de danseur etc), collant *m*

leprosy ['leprəsɪ] *n* lèpre *f*

lesbian ['lezbɪən] *n* lesbienne *f*

less [les] *adj* moins de ♦ *pron, adv* moins ♦ *prep* moins; **~ than that/you** moins que cela/vous; **~ than half** moins de la moitié; **~ than ever** moins que jamais; **~ and ~** de moins en moins; **the ~ he works ...** moins il travaille ...; **~en** *vi* diminuer, s'atténuer ♦ *vt* diminuer, réduire, atténuer; **~er** *adj* moindre; **to a ~er extent** à un degré moindre

lesson ['lesn] *n* leçon *f*; **to teach sb a ~** (*fig*) donner une bonne leçon à qn

let [let] (*pt, pp* **let**) *vt* laisser; (*BRIT: lease*) louer; **to ~ sb do sth** laisser qn faire qch; **to ~ sb know sth** faire savoir qch à qn, prévenir qn de qch; **~'s go** allons-y; **~ him come** qu'il vienne; **"to ~"** "à louer"; **~ down** *vt* (*tyre*) dégonfler; (*person*) décevoir, faire faux bond à; **~ go** *vi* lâcher prise ♦ *vt* lâcher; **~ in**

vt laisser entrer; (*visitor etc*) faire entrer; ~ **off** *vt* (*culprit*) ne pas punir; (*firework etc*) faire partir; ~ **on** (*inf*) *vi* dire; ~ **out** *vt* laisser sortir; (*scream*) laisser échapper; ~ **up** *vi* diminuer; (*cease*) s'arrêter

lethal ['liːθl] *adj* mortel(le), fatal(e)

letter ['lɛtə] *n* lettre *f*; ~ **bomb** *n* lettre piégée; ~**box** (*BRIT*) *n* boîte *f* aux or à lettres; ~**ing** *n* lettres *fpl*; caractères *mpl*

lettuce ['lɛtɪs] *n* laitue *f*, salade *f*

let-up ['lɛtʌp] *n* répit *m*, arrêt *m*

leukaemia [luːˈkiːmɪə] (*US* **leukemia**) *n* leucémie *f*

level ['lɛvl] *adj* plat(e), plan(e), uni(e); horizontal(e) ♦ *n* niveau *m* ♦ *vt* niveler, aplanir; **to be ~ with** être au même niveau que; **to draw ~ with** (*person, vehicle*) arriver à la hauteur de; **"A" ~s** (*BRIT*) ≈ baccalauréat *m*; **"O" ~s** (*BRIT*) ≈ B.E.P.C.; **on the ~** (*fig: honest*) régulier(-ère); ~ **off** *vi* (*prices etc*) se stabiliser; ~ **out** *vi* = **level off**; ~ **crossing** (*BRIT*) *n* passage *m* à niveau; ~**headed** *adj* équilibré(e)

lever ['liːvə] *n* levier *m*; ~**age** *n*: ~**age** (**on** *or* **with**) prise *f* (sur)

levy ['lɛvɪ] *n* taxe *f*, impôt *m* ♦ *vt* prélever, imposer; percevoir

lewd [luːd] *adj* obscène, lubrique

liability [laɪəˈbɪlətɪ] *n* responsabilité *f*; (*handicap*) handicap *m*; **liabilities** *npl* (*on balance sheet*) passif *m*

liable ['laɪəbl] *adj* (*subject*): ~ **to** sujet(te) à; passible de; (*responsible*): ~ **(for)** responsable (de); (*likely*): ~ **to do** susceptible de faire

liaise [liːˈeɪz] *vi*: **to ~ (with)** assurer la liaison avec; **liaison** *n* liaison *f*

liar ['laɪə] *n* menteur(-euse)

libel ['laɪbl] *n* diffamation *f*; (*document*) écrit *m* diffamatoire ♦ *vt* diffamer

liberal ['lɪbərl] *adj* libéral(e); (*generous*): ~ **with** prodigue de, généreux(-euse) avec; **the L~ Democrats** (*BRIT*) le parti libéral-démocrate

liberation [lɪbəˈreɪʃən] *n* libération *f*

liberty ['lɪbətɪ] *n* liberté *f*; **to be at ~ to do** être libre de faire

Libra ['liːbrə] *n* la Balance

librarian [laɪˈbrɛərɪən] *n* bibliothécaire *m/f*

library ['laɪbrərɪ] *n* bibliothèque *f*

libretto [lɪˈbrɛtəu] *n* livret *m*

Libya ['lɪbɪə] *n* Libye *f*

lice [laɪs] *npl of* **louse**

licence ['laɪsns] (*US* **license**) *n* autorisation *f*, permis *m*; (*RADIO, TV*) redevance *f*; **driving** ~, (*US*) **driver's license** permis *m* (de conduire); ~ **number** *n* numéro *m* d'immatriculation; ~ **plate** *n* plaque *f* minéralogique

license ['laɪsns] (*US*) *n* = **licence** ♦ *vt* donner une licence à; ~**d** *adj* (*car*) muni(e) de la vignette; (*to sell alcohol*) patenté(e), qui a une licence de débit de boissons

lick [lɪk] *vt* lécher; (*inf: defeat*) écraser; **to ~ one's lips** (*fig*) se frotter les mains

licorice ['lɪkərɪs] (*US*) *n* = **liquorice**

lid [lɪd] *n* couvercle *m*; (*eyelid*) paupière *f*

lie [laɪ] (*pt* **lay**, *pp* **lain**) *vi* (*rest*) être étendu(e) or allongé(e) or couché(e); (*in grave*) être enterré(e), reposer; (*be situated*) se trouver, être; (*be untruthful: pt, pp* ~*d*) mentir ♦ *n* mensonge *m*; **to ~ low** (*fig*) se cacher; ~ **about**, ~ **around** *vi* = **lie about**; ~ **down** (*BRIT*) *n*: **to have a ~-down** s'allonger, se reposer; ~**in** (*BRIT*) *n*: **to have a ~-in** faire la grasse matinée

lieutenant [lɛfˈtɛnənt, (*US*) luːˈtɛnənt] *n* lieutenant *m*

life [laɪf] (*pl* **lives**) *n* vie *f*; **to come to ~** (*fig*) s'animer; ~ **assurance** (*BRIT*) *n* = **life insurance**; ~**belt** (*BRIT*) *n* bouée *f* de sauvetage; ~**boat** *n* canot *m* or chaloupe *f* de sauvetage; ~**buoy** *n* bouée *f* de sauvetage; ~**guard** *n* surveillant *m* de baignade; ~ **insurance** *n* assurance-vie *f*; ~ **jacket** *n* gilet *m* or ceinture *f* de sauvetage; ~**less** *adj* sans vie, inanimé(e); (*dull*) qui manque de vie or de vigueur; **~like** adj qui semble vrai(e) or vivant(e); (painting) réaliste; **~long** adj de toute une vie, de toujours; **~ preserver** (US) n = **lifebelt**; **life jacket**; **~saving** n sauvetage m; **~ sentence** n condamnation f à perpétuité; **~size(d)** adj grandeur nature inv; **~ span** n (durée f de) vie f; **~style** n style m or mode m de vie; **~support system** n (MED) respirateur artificiel; **~time** n vie f; **in his ~time** de son vivant

lift [lɪft] vt soulever, lever; (end) supprimer, lever ♦ vi (fog) se lever ♦ n (BRIT: elevator) ascenseur m; **to give sb a ~** (BRIT: AUT) emmener or prendre qn en voiture; **~off** n décollage m

light [laɪt] (pt, pp **lit**) n lumière f; (lamp) lampe f; (AUT: rear ~) feu m; (: headlight) phare m; (for cigarette etc): **have you got a ~?** avez-vous du feu?; **to come to ~** se révéler or découvert(e); **~ up** vi (face) s'éclairer ♦ vt (illuminate) éclairer, illuminer; **~ bulb** n ampoule f; **~en** vt (make less heavy) alléger; **~er** n (also: **cigarette ~er**) briquet m; **~headed** adj étourdi(e); (excited) grisé(e); **~hearted** adj gai(e), joyeux(-euse), enjoué(e); **~house** n phare m; **~ing** n (on road) éclairage m; (in theatre) éclairages mpl; **~ly** adv légèrement; **to get off ~ly** s'en tirer à bon compte; **~ness** n (in weight) légèreté f

lightning ['laɪtnɪŋ] n éclair m, foudre f; **~ conductor** (US **lightning rod**) n paratonnerre m

light pen n crayon m optique

lightweight ['laɪtweɪt] adj (suit) léger(-ère) ♦ n (BOXING) poids léger

like [laɪk] vt aimer (bien) ♦ prep comme ♦ adj semblable, pareil(le) ♦ n: **and the ~** et d'autres du même genre; **his ~s**

and dislikes ses goûts mpl or préférences fpl; **I would ~, I'd ~** je voudrais, j'aimerais; **would you ~ a coffee?** voulez-vous du café?; **to be/look ~ sb/sth** ressembler à qn/qch; **what does it look ~?** de quoi est-ce que ça a l'air?; **what does it taste ~?** quel goût est-ce que ça a?; **that's just ~ him** c'est bien de lui, ça lui ressemble; **do it ~ this** fais-le comme ceci; **it's nothing ~ ...** ce n'est pas du tout comme ...; **~able** adj sympathique, agréable

likelihood ['laɪklɪhud] n probabilité f

likely ['laɪklɪ] adj probable; plausible; **he's ~ to leave** il va sûrement partir, il risque fort de partir; **not ~!** (inf) pas de danger!

likeness ['laɪknɪs] n ressemblance f; **that's a good ~** c'est très ressemblant

likewise ['laɪkwaɪz] adv de même, pareillement

liking ['laɪkɪŋ] n (for person) affection f; (for thing) penchant m, goût m

lilac ['laɪlək] n lilas m

lily ['lɪlɪ] n lis m; **~ of the valley** n muguet m

limb [lɪm] n membre m

limber up ['lɪmbə⁻] vi se dégourdir, faire des exercices d'assouplissement

limbo ['lɪmbəu] n: **to be in ~** (fig) être tombé(e) dans l'oubli

lime [laɪm] n (tree) tilleul m; (fruit) lime f, citron vert; (GEO) chaux f

limelight ['laɪmlaɪt] n: **in the ~** (fig) en vedette, au premier plan

limerick ['lɪmərɪk] n poème m humoristique (de 5 vers)

limestone ['laɪmstəun] n pierre f à chaux; (GEO) calcaire m

limit ['lɪmɪt] n limite f ♦ vt limiter; **~ed** adj limité(e), restreint(e); **to be ~ed to** se limiter à, ne concerner que; **~ed (liability) company** (BRIT) n ≈ société f anonyme

limousine ['lɪməzi:n] n limousine f

limp [lɪmp] n: **to have a ~** boiter ♦ vi

boiter ♦ *adj* mou (molle)

limpet ['lɪmpɪt] *n* patelle *f*

line [laɪn] *n* ligne *f*; (*stroke*) trait *m*; (*wrinkle*) ride *f*; (*rope*) corde *f*; (*wire*) fil *m*; (*of poem*) vers *m*; (*row, series*) rangée *f*; (*of people*) file *f*, queue *f*; (*railway track*) voie *f*; (COMM: *series of goods*) article(s) *m(pl)*; (*work*) métier *m*, type *m* d'activité; (*attitude, policy*) position *f* ♦ *vt* (*subj: trees, crowd*) border; **in a ~** alignée(e); **in his ~ of business** dans sa partie, dans son rayon; **in ~ with** en accord avec; **to ~ (with)** (*clothes*) doubler (de); (*box*) garnir or tapisser (de); **~ up** *vi* s'aligner, se mettre en rang(s) ♦ *vt* aligner; (*event*) prévoir, préparer; **~d** *adj* (*face*) ridée(e), marqué(e); (*paper*) réglé(e)

linen ['lɪnɪn] *n* linge *m* (de maison); (*cloth*) lin *m*

liner ['laɪnə^r] *n* paquebot *m* (de ligne); (*for bin*) sac *m* à poubelle

linesman ['laɪnzmən] (*irreg*) *n* juge *m* de touche; (TENNIS) juge *m* de ligne

line-up ['laɪnʌp] *n* (US: *queue*) file *f*; (SPORT) composition *f* d'une équipe; (*row*) file *f*, rangée *f*

linger ['lɪŋgə^r] *vi* s'attarder; traîner; (*smell, tradition*) persister

linguist ['lɪŋgwɪst] *n*: **to be a good ~** être doué(e) par les langues; **~ics** [lɪŋ'gwɪstɪks] *n* linguistique *f*

lining ['laɪnɪŋ] *n* doublure *f*

link [lɪŋk] *n* lien *m*, rapport *m*; (*of a chain*) maillon *m* ♦ *vt* relier, lier, unir; **~s** *npl* (GOLF) (terrain *m* de) golf *m*; **~ up** *vt* relier ♦ *vi* se rejoindre; s'associer

lino ['laɪnəʊ] *n* = **linoleum**

linoleum [lɪ'nəʊlɪəm] *n* linoléum *m*

lion ['laɪən] *n* lion *m*; **~ess** *n* lionne *f*

lip [lɪp] *n* lèvre *f*

liposuction ['lɪpəʊsʌkʃən] *n* liposuction *f*

lip: **~-read** *vi* lire sur les lèvres; **~ salve** *n* pommade *f* rosat or pour les lèvres; **~ service** *n*: **to pay ~ service to sth** ne reconnaître le mérite de qch que pour la forme; **~stick** *n* rouge *m* à lèvres

liqueur [lɪ'kjuə^r] *n* liqueur *f*

liquid ['lɪkwɪd] *adj* liquide ♦ *n* liquide *m*; **~ize** *vt* (CULIN) passer au mixer; **~izer** *n* mixer *m*

liquor ['lɪkə^r] (US) *n* spiritueux *m*, alcool *m*

liquorice ['lɪkərɪs] (BRIT) *n* réglisse *f*

liquor store (US) *n* magasin *m* de vins et spiritueux

lisp [lɪsp] *vi* zézayer

list [lɪst] *n* liste *f* ♦ *vt* (*write down*) faire une or la liste de; (*mention*) énumérer; **~ed building** (BRIT) *n* monument classé

listen ['lɪsn] *vi* écouter; **to ~ to** écouter; **~er** *n* auditeur(-trice)

listless ['lɪstlɪs] *adj* indolent(e), apathique

lit [lɪt] *pt, pp* of **light**

liter ['liːtə^r] (US) *n* = **litre**

literacy ['lɪtərəsɪ] *n* degré *m* d'alphabétisation, fait *m* de savoir lire et écrire

literal ['lɪtərəl] *adj* littéral(e); **~ly** *adv* littéralement; (*really*) réellement

literary ['lɪtərərɪ] *adj* littéraire

literate ['lɪtərət] *adj* qui sait lire et écrire, instruit(e)

literature ['lɪtrɪtʃə^r] *n* littérature *f*; (*brochures etc*) documentation *f*

lithe [laɪð] *adj* agile, souple

litigation [lɪtɪ'geɪʃən] *n* litige *m*; contentieux *m*

litre ['liːtə^r] (US **liter**) *n* litre *m*

litter ['lɪtə^r] *n* (*rubbish*) détritus *mpl*, ordures *fpl*; (*young animals*) portée *f*; **~ bin** (BRIT) *n* boîte *f* à ordures, poubelle *f*; **~ed** *adj*: **~ed with** jonché(e) de, couvert(e) de

little ['lɪtl] *adj* (*small*) petit(e) ♦ *adv* peu; **~ milk/time** peu de lait/temps; **a ~** un peu (de); **a ~ bit** un peu; **~ by ~** petit à petit, peu à peu

live¹ [laɪv] *adj* (*animal*) vivant(e), en vie; (*wire*) sous tension; (*bullet, bomb*) non explosé(e); (*broadcast*) en direct; (*performance*) en public

live² [lɪv] *vi* vivre; (*reside*) vivre, habiter; **~ down** vt faire oublier (avec le temps); **~ on** vt fus (food, salary) vivre de; **~ together** vi vivre ensemble, cohabiter; **~ up to** vt fus se montrer à la hauteur de

livelihood ['laɪvlɪhud] n moyens mpl d'existence

lively ['laɪvlɪ] adj vif (vive), plein(e) d'entrain; (place, book) vivant(e)

liven up ['laɪvn-] vt animer ♦ vi s'animer

liver ['lɪvə^r] n foie m

lives [laɪvz] npl of **life**

livestock ['laɪvstɔk] n bétail m, cheptel m

livid ['lɪvɪd] adj livide, blafard(e); (inf: furious) furieux(-euse), furibond(e)

living ['lɪvɪŋ] adj vivant(e), en vie ♦ n: **to earn** or **make a ~** gagner sa vie; **~ conditions** npl conditions fpl de vie; **~ room** n salle f de séjour; **~ standards** npl niveau m de vie; **~ wage** n salaire m permettant de vivre (décemment)

lizard ['lɪzəd] n lézard m

load [ləud] n (weight) poids m; (thing carried) chargement m, charge f ♦ vt (also: **~ up**): **to ~ (with)** charger (de); (gun, camera) charger (avec); (COMPUT) charger; **a ~ of, ~s of** (fig) un or des tas de, des masses de; **to talk a ~ of rubbish** dire des bêtises; **~ed** adj (question) insidieux(-euse); (inf: rich) bourré(e) de fric

loaf [ləuf] (pl **loaves**) n pain m, miche f

loan [ləun] n prêt m ♦ vt prêter; **on ~** prêté(e), en prêt

loath [ləuθ] adj: **to be ~ to do** répugner à faire

loathe [ləuð] vt détester, avoir en horreur

loaves [ləuvz] npl of **loaf**

lobby ['lɔbɪ] n hall m, entrée f; (POL) groupe m de pression, lobby m ♦ vt faire pression sur

lobster ['lɔbstə^r] n homard m

local ['ləukl] adj local(e) ♦ n (BRIT: pub) pub m or café m du coin; **the ~s** npl (inhabitants) les gens mpl du pays or du coin; **~ anaesthetic** n anesthésie locale; **~ authority** n collectivité locale, municipalité f; **~ call** n communication urbaine; **~ government** n administration locale or municipale; **~ity** [ləu'kælɪtɪ] n région f, environs mpl; (position) lieu m

locate [ləu'keɪt] vt (find) trouver, repérer; (situate): **to be ~d in** être situé(e) à or en; emplacement m; **on location** (CINEMA) en extérieur

loch [lɔx] n lac m, loch m

lock [lɔk] n (of door, box) serrure f; (of canal) écluse f; (of hair) mèche f, boucle f ♦ vt (with key) fermer à clé ♦ vi (door etc) fermer à clé; (wheels) se bloquer; **~ in** vt enfermer; **~ out** vt enfermer dehors; (deliberately) mettre à la porte; **~ up** vt (person) enfermer; (house) fermer à clé ♦ vi tout fermer (à clé)

locker ['lɔkə^r] n casier m; (in station) consigne f automatique

locket ['lɔkɪt] n médaillon m

locksmith ['lɔksmɪθ] n serrurier m

lockup ['lɔkʌp] n (prison) prison f

locum ['ləukəm] n (MED) suppléant(e) (de médecin)

lodge [lɔdʒ] n pavillon m (de gardien); (hunting ~) pavillon de chasse ♦ vi (person): **to ~ (with)** être logé(e) (chez), être en pension (chez); (bullet) se loger ♦ vt: **to ~ a complaint** porter plainte; **~r** n locataire m/f; (with meals) pensionnaire m/f; **lodgings** npl chambre f, meublé m

loft [lɔft] n grenier m

lofty ['lɔftɪ] adj (noble) noble, élevé(e); (haughty) hautain(e)

log [lɔg] n (of wood) bûche f; (book) = **logbook** ♦ vt (record) noter; **~book** n (NAUT) livre m or journal m de bord; (AVIAT) carnet m de vol; (of car) ≈ carte grise

loggerheads ['lɔgəhedz] npl: **at ~ (with)** à couteaux tirés (avec)

logic ['lɔdʒɪk] n logique f; **~al** adj logique

loin [lwɛ̃] n (CULIN) filet m, longe f

loiter ['lɔɪtər] vi traîner

loll [lɔl] vi (also: ~ **about**) se prélasser, fainéanter

lollipop ['lɔlɪpɔp] n sucette f; ~ **man/lady** (BRIT: irreg) n contractuel qui fait traverser la rue aux enfants

---
lollipop men/ladies

Les lollipop men/ladies sont employés pour aider les enfants à traverser la rue à proximité des écoles à l'heure où ils entrent en classe et à la sortie. On les repère facilement à cause de leur long ciré blanc et ils portent une pancarte ronde pour faire signe aux automobilistes de s'arrêter. On les appelle ainsi car la forme circulaire de cette pancarte rappelle une sucette.

---

lolly ['lɔlɪ] (inf) n (lollipop) sucette f; (money) fric m

London ['lʌndən] n Londres m; ~**er** n Londonien(ne)

lone [ləun] adj solitaire

loneliness ['ləunlɪnɪs] n solitude f, isolement m

lonely ['ləunlɪ] adj seul(e); solitaire, isolé(e)

long [lɔŋ] adj long (longue) ♦ adv longtemps ♦ vi: **to ~ for sth** avoir très envie de qch; attendre qch avec impatience; **so or as ~ as** pourvu que; **don't be ~!** dépêchez-vous!; **how ~ is this river/course?** quelle est la longueur de ce fleuve/la durée de ce cours?; **6 metres ~** (long) de 6 mètres; **6 months ~** qui dure 6 mois, de 6 mois; **all night ~** toute la nuit; **he no ~er comes** il ne vient plus; **they're no ~er going out together** ils ne sortent plus ensemble; **I can't stand it any ~er** je ne peux plus le supporter; **~ before/after** longtemps avant/après; **before ~** (+future) avant

peu, dans peu de temps; (+past) peu (de temps) après; **at ~ last** enfin; **~distance** adj (call) interurbain(e); **~er** ['lɔŋɡər] adv see **long**; **~hand** n écriture normale ou courante; **~ing** n désir m, envie f, nostalgie f

longitude ['lɔŋgɪtjuːd] n longitude f

long: **~ jump** n saut m en longueur; **~life** adj (batteries etc) longue durée inv; (milk) longue conservation; **~lost** adj (person) perdu(e) de vue depuis longtemps; **~range** adj à longue portée; **~sighted** adj (MED) presbyte; **~standing** adj de longue date; **~suffering** adj empreint(e) d'une patience résignée; extrêmement patient(e); **~term** adj à long terme; **~wave** n grandes ondes; **~winded** adj intarissable, interminable

loo [luː] (BRIT: inf) n W.-C. mpl, petit coin

look [luk] vi regarder; (seem) sembler, paraître, avoir l'air; (building etc): **to ~ south/out) onto the sea** donner au sud/sur la mer ♦ n regard m; (appearance) air m, allure f, aspect m; **~s** npl (good ~s) physique m, beauté f; **to have a ~** regarder; **~! regardez!**; **~ (here)!** (annoyance) écoutez!; **~ after** vt fus (care for, deal with) s'occuper de; **~ at** vt fus (regard, problem etc) examiner; **~ back** vi: **to ~ back on** (event etc) évoquer, repenser à; **~ down on** vt fus (fig) regarder de haut, dédaigner; **~ for** vt fus chercher; **~ forward to** vt fus attendre avec impatience; **we ~ forward to hearing from you** (in letter) dans l'attente de vous lire; **~ into** vt fus examiner, étudier; **~ on** vi regarder (en spectateur); **~ out** vi (beware) faire attention; **~ out (for)** prendre garde (à), faire attention (à); **~ out for** vt fus être à la recherche de; guetter; **~ round** vi regarder derrière soi, se retourner; **~ to** vt fus (rely on) compter sur; **~ up** vi (lever les yeux; (improve) s'améliorer ♦ vt (word, name) chercher; **~ up to** vt fus

avoir du respect pour ♦ n poste m de
guet; (person) guetteur m; **to be on
the ~ out (for)** guetter

loom [luːm] vi (also: **~ up**) surgir; (approach: event etc) être imminent(e);
(threaten) menacer ♦ n (for weaving)
métier m à tisser

loony ['luːnɪ] (inf) adj, n timbré(e), cin-
glé(e)

loop [luːp] n boucle f; **~hole** n (fig)
porte f de sortie; échappatoire f

loose [luːs] adj (knot, screw) desserré(e);
(clothes) ample, lâche; (hair) dénoué(e),
épars(e); (not firmly fixed) pas solide;
(morals, discipline) relâché(e) ♦ n: **on
the ~** en liberté; **~ change** n petite
monnaie; **~ chippings** npl (on road)
gravillons mpl; **~ end** n: **to be at a ~
end** or (US) **at ~ ends** ne pas trop savoir quoi faire; **~ly** adv sans serrer; (im-
precisely) approximativement; **~n** vt
desserrer

loot [luːt] n (inf: money) pognon m, fric
m ♦ vt piller

lopsided ['lɒp'saɪdɪd] adj de travers,
asymétrique

lord [lɔːd] n seigneur m; **L~ Smith** lord
Smith; **the L~** le Seigneur; **good L~!**
mon Dieu!; **the (House of) L~s** (BRIT)
la Chambre des lords; **my L~** = your
Lordship; **L~ship** n: **your L~ship**
Monsieur le comte/le baron/le juge; (to
bishop) Monseigneur

lore [lɔːʳ] n tradition(s) f(pl)

lorry ['lɒrɪ] (BRIT) n camion m; **~ driver**
(BRIT) n camionneur m, routier m

lose [luːz] (pt, pp lost) vt, vi perdre; **to ~
(time)** (clock) retarder; **to get lost** vi
se perdre; **~r** n perdant(e)

loss [lɒs] n perte f; **to be at a ~** être
perplexe ou embarrassé(e)

lost [lɒst] pt, pp of **lose** ♦ adj perdu(e);
~ and found (US), **~ property** n objets trouvés

lot [lɒt] n (set) lot m; **the ~** le tout; **a
(of)** beaucoup (de); **~s of** des tas de;
to draw ~s (for sth) tirer (qch) au sort

lotion ['ləʊʃən] n lotion f

lottery ['lɒtərɪ] n loterie f

loud [laʊd] adj bruyant(e), sonore;
(voice) fort(e); (support, condemnation)
vigoureux(-euse); (gaudy) voyant(e),
tapageur(-euse) ♦ adv (speak etc) fort;
out ~ tout haut; **~hailer** (BRIT) n
porte-voix m inv; **~ly** adv fort, bruyamment; **~speaker** n haut-parleur m

lounge [laʊndʒ] n salon m; (at airport)
salle f; (BRIT: also: **~ bar**) (salle de) café
m or bar m ♦ vi (also: **~ about or
around**) se prélasser, paresser; **~ suit**
(BRIT) n complet m; (on invitation) "tenue de ville"

louse [laʊs] (pl **lice**) n pou m

lousy ['laʊzɪ] (inf) adj infect(e), moche;
I feel ~ je suis mal fichu(e)

lout [laʊt] n rustre m, butor m

lovable ['lʌvəbl] adj adorable; très sympathique

love [lʌv] n amour m ♦ vt aimer; (caring-
ly, kindly) aimer beaucoup; **~ (from)
Anne**" "affectueusement, Anne"; **I ~
chocolate** j'adore le chocolat; **to be/
fall in ~ with** être/tomber amoureux
(-euse) de; **to make ~** faire l'amour;
"15 ~" (TENNIS) "15 à rien ou zéro"; **~
affair** n liaison (amoureuse); **~ life** n
vie sentimentale

lovely ['lʌvlɪ] adj (très) joli(e), ravis-
sant(e); (delightful: person) charmant(e);
(holiday etc) (très) agréable

lover ['lʌvəʳ] n amant m; (person in
love) amoureux(-euse); (amateur): **a ~
of** un amateur de; un(e) amoureux
(-euse) de

loving ['lʌvɪŋ] adj affectueux(-euse),
tendre

low [ləʊ] adj bas (basse); (quality) mau-
vais(e), inférieur(e); (person: depressed)
déprimé(e); (: ill) bas (basse), affaibli(e)
♦ adv bas ♦ n (METEOROLOGY) dépression
f; **to be ~ on** être à court de; **to feel ~**
se sentir déprimé(e); **to reach an all-
time ~** être au plus bas; **~-alcohol** adj
peu alcoolisé(e); **~-calorie** adj hypoca-

loyal 458 **Luxembourg**

lorique; **~-cut** adj (dress) décolleté(e); **~er** inférieur(e) ♦ vt abaisser; **~er sixth** (BRIT) n (SCOL) première f; **~-fat** adj maigre; **~lands** npl (GEO) plaines fpl; **~ly** adj humble, modeste

loyal ['lɔɪəl] adj loyal(e), fidèle; **~ty** n loyauté f, fidélité f; **~ty card** n carte f de fidélité

lozenge ['lɔzɪndʒ] n (MED) pastille f

LP n abbr = **long-playing record**

LPG n abbr (AUT = liquefied petroleum gas) GPL m

L-plates ['elpleɪts] (BRIT) npl plaques fpl d'apprenti conducteur

> **L-plates**
>
> Les L-plates sont des carrés blancs portant un "L" rouge que l'on met à l'avant et à l'arrière de sa voiture pour montrer qu'on n'a pas encore son permis de conduire. Jusqu'à l'obtention du permis, l'apprenti conducteur a un permis provisoire et n'a le droit de conduire que si un conducteur qualifié est assis à côté de lui. Il est interdit aux apprentis conducteurs de circuler sur les autoroutes, même s'ils sont accompagnés.

LRP n abbr (AUT = lead replacement petrol) super m

Ltd abbr (= limited) ≃ S.A.

lubricant ['lu:brɪkənt] n lubrifiant m

lubricate ['lu:brɪkeɪt] vt lubrifier, graisser

luck [lʌk] n chance f; **bad ~** malchance f, malheur m; **bad** or **hard** or **tough ~!** pas de chance!; **good ~!** bonne chance!; **~ily** adv heureusement, par bonheur; **~y** adj (person) qui a de la chance; (coincidence, event) heureux(-euse); (object) porte-bonheur inv

ludicrous ['lu:dɪkrəs] adj ridicule, absurde

lug [lʌg] (inf) vt traîner, tirer

luggage ['lʌgɪdʒ] n bagages mpl; **~ rack** n (on car) galerie f

lukewarm ['lu:kwɔ:m] adj tiède

lull [lʌl] n accalmie f; (in conversation) pause f ♦ vt: **to ~ sb to sleep** bercer qn pour qu'il s'endorme; **to be ~ed into a false sense of security** s'endormir dans une fausse sécurité

lullaby ['lʌləbaɪ] n berceuse f

lumbago [lʌm'beɪgəu] n lumbago m

lumber ['lʌmbəʳ] n (wood) bois m de charpente; (junk) bric-à-brac m inv; **~jack** n bûcheron m

luminous ['lu:mɪnəs] adj lumineux (-euse)

lump [lʌmp] n morceau m; (swelling) grosseur f ♦ vt: **to ~ together** réunir, mettre en tas; **~ sum** n somme globale or forfaitaire; **~y** adj (sauce) avec des grumeaux; (bed) défoncé(e), peu confortable

lunar ['lu:nəʳ] adj lunaire

lunatic ['lu:nətɪk] adj fou (folle), cinglé(e) (inf)

lunch [lʌntʃ] n déjeuner m

luncheon ['lʌntʃən] n déjeuner m (chic); **~ meat** n sorte de mortadelle; **~ voucher** (BRIT) n chèque-repas m

lung [lʌŋ] n poumon m

lunge [lʌndʒ] vi (also: **~ forward**) faire un mouvement brusque en avant; **to ~ at** envoyer or assener un coup à

lurch [lɜ:tʃ] vi vaciller, tituber ♦ n écart m brusque; **to leave sb in the ~** laisser qn en plan (inf)

lure [luəʳ] n (attraction) attrait m, charme m ♦ vt attirer or persuader par la ruse

lurid ['luərɪd] adj affreux(-euse), atroce; (pej: colour, dress) criard(e)

lurk [lɜ:k] vi se tapir, se cacher

luscious ['lʌʃəs] adj succulent(e); appétissant(e)

lush [lʌʃ] adj luxuriant(e)

lust [lʌst] n (sexual) désir m; (fig): **~ for** soif f de; **~y** adj vigoureux(-euse), robuste

Luxembourg ['lʌksəmbə:g] n Luxembourg m

luxurious [lʌg'zjuəriəs] *adj* luxueux (-euse)

luxury ['lʌkʃəri] *n* luxe *m* ♦ *cpd* de luxe

lying ['laɪɪŋ] *n* mensonge(s) *m(pl)* ♦ *vb see* **lie**

lyrical ['lɪrɪkl] *adj* lyrique

lyrics ['lɪrɪks] *npl* (*of song*) paroles *fpl*

M, m

m. *abbr* = **metre**; **mile**; **million**

M.A. *abbr* = **Master of Arts**

mac [mæk] (*BRIT*) *n* imper(méable) *m*

macaroni [mækə'rəʊnɪ] *n* macaroni *mpl*

machine [mə'ʃiːn] *n* machine *f* ♦ *vt* (*TECH*) façonner à la machine; (*dress etc*) coudre à la machine; **~ gun** *n* mitrailleuse *f*; **~ language** *n* (*COMPUT*) langage-machine *m*; **~ry** *n* machinerie *f*, machines *fpl*; (*fig*) mécanisme(s) *m(pl)*

mackerel ['mækrl] *n inv* maquereau *m*

mackintosh ['mækɪntɔʃ] (*BRIT*) *n* imperméable *m*

mad [mæd] *adj* fou (folle); (*foolish*) insensé(e); (*angry*) furieux(-euse); (*keen*): **to be ~ about** être fou (folle) de

madam ['mædəm] *n* madame *f*

madden ['mædn] *vt* exaspérer

made [meɪd] *pt, pp of* **make**

Madeira [mə'dɪərə] *n* (*GEO*) Madère *f*; (*wine*) madère *m*

made-to-measure ['meɪdtə'meʒər] (*BRIT*) *adj* fait(e) sur mesure

madly ['mædlɪ] *adv* follement; **~ in love** éperdument amoureux(-euse)

madman ['mædmən] (*irreg*) *n* fou *m*

madness ['mædnɪs] *n* folie *f*

magazine [mægə'ziːn] *n* (*PRESS*) magazine *m*, revue *f*; (*RADIO, TV: also:* **~ programme**) magazine

maggot ['mægət] *n* ver *m*, asticot *m*

magic ['mædʒɪk] *n* magie *f* ♦ *adj* magique; **~al** *adj* magique; (*experience, evening*) merveilleux(-euse); **~ian** [mə'dʒɪʃən] *n* magicien(ne)

magistrate ['mædʒɪstreɪt] *n* magistrat *m*; juge *m*

magnet ['mægnɪt] *n* aimant *m*; **~ic** [mæg'netɪk] *adj* magnétique

magnificent [mæg'nɪfɪsnt] *adj* superbe, magnifique; (*splendid: robe, building*) somptueux(-euse), magnifique

magnify ['mægnɪfaɪ] *vt* grossir; (*sound*) amplifier; **~ing glass** *n* loupe *f*

magnitude ['mægnɪtjuːd] *n* ampleur *f*

magpie ['mægpaɪ] *n* pie *f*

mahogany [mə'hɔgənɪ] *n* acajou *m*

maid [meɪd] *n* bonne *f*

maiden ['meɪdn] *n* jeune fille *f* ♦ *adj* (*aunt etc*) non mariée; (*speech, voyage*) inaugural(e); **~ name** *n* nom *m* de jeune fille

mail [meɪl] *n* poste *f*; (*letters*) courrier *m* ♦ *vt* envoyer (par la poste); **~box** (*US*) *n* boîte *f* aux lettres; **~ing list** *n* liste *f* d'adresses; **~-order** *n* vente *f* or achat *m* par correspondance

maim [meɪm] *vt* mutiler

main [meɪn] *adj* principal(e) ♦ *n*: the **~(s)** *n(pl)* (*gas, water*) conduite principale, canalisation *f*; **the ~s** *npl* (*ELEC*) le secteur; **the ~ thing** l'essentiel; **in the ~** dans l'ensemble; **~frame** *n* (*COMPUT*) unité centrale; **~land** *n* continent *m*; **~ly** *adv* principalement, surtout; **~ road** *n* grand-route *f*, **~stay** *n* (*fig*) pilier *m*; **~stream** *n* courant principal

maintain [meɪn'teɪn] *vt* entretenir; (*continue*) maintenir; (*affirm*) soutenir; **maintenance** ['meɪntənəns] *n* entretien *m*; (*alimony*) pension *f* alimentaire

maize [meɪz] *n* maïs *m*

majestic [mə'dʒestɪk] *adj* majestueux (-euse)

majesty ['mædʒɪstɪ] *n* majesté *f*

major ['meɪdʒər] *n* (*MIL*) commandant *m* ♦ *adj* (*important*) important(e); (*most important*) principal(e); (*MUS*) majeur(e)

Majorca [mə'jɔːkə] *n* Majorque *f*

majority [mə'dʒɔrɪtɪ] *n* majorité *f*

make [meɪk] (*pt, pp* **made**) *vt* faire; (*manufacture*) faire, fabriquer; (*earn*)

making 460 **mania**

gagner; (cause to be): **to ~ sb sad** etc rendre qn triste etc; (force): **to ~ sb do sth** obliger qn à faire qch, faire faire qch à qn; (equal): **2 and 2 ~ 4** 2 et 2 font 4 ♦ à faire; (brand) marque f; **to ~ a fool of sb** (ridicule) ridiculiser qn; (trick) avoir or duper qn; **to ~ a profit** faire un or des bénéfice(s); **to ~ a loss** essuyer une perte; **to ~ it** (arrive) arriver; (achieve sth) parvenir à qch, réussir; **what time do you ~ it?** quelle heure avez-vous?; **to ~ do with** se contenter de; se débrouiller avec; **~ for** vt fus (place) se diriger vers; ~ **out** vt (write out: cheque) faire; (decipher) déchiffrer; (understand) comprendre; (see) distinguer; ~ **up** vt (constitute) constituer; (invent) inventer, imaginer; (parcel, bed) faire ♦ vi se réconcilier; (with cosmetics) se maquiller; ~ **up for** vt fus compenser; **~-believe** n: **it's just ~-believe** (game) c'est pour faire semblant; (invention) c'est de l'invention pure; ~**r** n fabricant m; ~**shift** adj provisoire, improvisé(e); ~**-up** n maquillage m

making ['meɪkɪŋ] n (fig): **in the ~** en formation or gestation; **to have the ~s of** (actor, athlete etc) avoir l'étoffe de

malaria [mə'lɛərɪə] n malaria f

Malaysia [mə'leɪzɪə] n Malaisie f

male [meɪl] n (BIO) mâle m ♦ adj mâle; (sex, attitude) masculin(e); (child etc) du sexe masculin

malevolent [mə'lɛvələnt] adj malveillant(e)

malfunction [mæl'fʌŋkʃən] n fonctionnement défectueux

malice ['mælɪs] n méchanceté f, malveillance f; **malicious** [mə'lɪʃəs] adj méchant(e), malveillant(e)

malignant [mə'lɪɡnənt] adj (MED) malin(-igne)

mall [mɔːl] n (also: **shopping ~**) centre commercial

mallet ['mælɪt] n maillet m

malpractice [mæl'præktɪs] n faute pro-

fessionnelle; négligence f

malt [mɔːlt] n malt m ♦ cpd (also: ~ **whisky**) pur malt

Malta ['mɔːltə] n Malte f

mammal ['mæml] n mammifère m

mammoth ['mæməθ] n mammouth m ♦ adj géant(e), monstre

man [mæn] (pl **men**) n homme m ♦ vt (NAUT: ship) garnir d'hommes; (MIL: gun) servir; (: post) être de service à; (machine) assurer le fonctionnement de; **an old ~** un vieillard; ~ **and wife** mari et femme

manage ['mænɪdʒ] vi se débrouiller ♦ vt (be in charge of) s'occuper de; (: business etc) gérer; (control: ship) manier, manœuvrer; (: person) savoir s'y prendre avec; **to ~ to do** réussir à faire; ~**able** adj (task) faisable; (number) raisonnable; ~**ment** n gestion f, administration f, direction f; ~**r** n directeur m; administrateur m; (SPORT) manager m; (of artist) impresario m; ~**ress** [mænɪdʒə'rɛs] n directrice f; gérante f; ~**rial** [mænɪ'dʒɪərɪəl] adj directorial(e); (skills) de cadre, de gestion; **managing director** n directeur général

mandarin ['mændərɪn] n (also: ~ **orange**) mandarine f; (person) mandarin m

mandatory ['mændətərɪ] adj obligatoire

mane [meɪn] n crinière f

maneuver [mə'nuːvə*] (US) vt, vi, n = **manoeuvre**

manfully ['mænfəlɪ] adv vaillamment

mangle ['mæŋɡl] vt déchiqueter; mutiler

mango ['mæŋɡəu] (pl ~**es**) n mangue f

mangy ['meɪndʒɪ] adj galeux(-euse)

man: ~**handle** vt malmener; ~**hole** n trou m d'homme; ~**hood** n âge m d'homme; virilité f; ~**-hour** n heure f de main-d'œuvre; ~**-hunt** n (POLICE) chasse f à l'homme

mania ['meɪnɪə] n manie f; ~**c** ['meɪnɪæk] n maniaque m/f; (fig) fou (folle) m/f; **manic** ['mænɪk] adj maniaque

manicure ['mænɪkjuər] n manucure f

manifest ['mænɪfɛst] vt manifester ♦ adj manifeste, évident(e); **~o** [mænɪ'fɛstəu] n manifeste m

manipulate [mə'nɪpjuleɪt] vt manipuler; (system, situation) exploiter

man: **~kind** [mæn'kaɪnd] n humanité f, genre humain; **~ly** adj viril(e); **~made** adj artificiel(le); (fibre) synthétique

manner ['mænər] n manière f, façon f; (behaviour) attitude f, comportement m; (sort): **all ~ of** toutes sortes de; **~s** npl (behaviour) manières f; **~ism** n particularité f de langage (or de comportement), tic m

manoeuvre [mə'nu:vər] (US **maneuver**) vt (move) manœuvrer; (manipulate: person) manipuler; (: situation) exploiter ♦ vi manœuvrer ♦ n manœuvre f

manor ['mænər] n (also: **~ house**) manoir m

manpower ['mænpauər] n main-d'œuvre f

mansion ['mænʃən] n château m, manoir m

manslaughter ['mænslɔ:tər] n homicide m involontaire

mantelpiece ['mæntlpi:s] n cheminée f

manual ['mænjuəl] adj manuel(le) ♦ n manuel m

manufacture [mænju'fæktʃər] vt fabriquer ♦ n fabrication f; **~r** n fabricant m

manure [mə'njuər] n fumier m

manuscript ['mænjuskrɪpt] n manuscrit m

many ['mɛnɪ] adj beaucoup de, de nombreux(-euses) ♦ pron beaucoup, un grand nombre; **a great ~** un grand nombre (de); **~ a ...** bien des ..., plus d'un(e) ...

map [mæp] n carte f; (of town) plan m; **~ out** vt tracer; (task) planifier

maple ['meɪpl] n érable m

mar [mɑ:r] vt gâcher, gâter

marathon ['mærəθən] n marathon m

marble ['mɑ:bl] n marbre m; (toy) bille f

March [mɑ:tʃ] n mars m

march [mɑ:tʃ] vi marcher au pas; (fig: protesters) défiler ♦ n marche f; (demonstration) manifestation f

mare [mɛər] n jument f

margarine [mɑ:dʒə'ri:n] n margarine f

margin ['mɑ:dʒɪn] n marge f; **~al (seat)** n (POL) siège disputé

marigold ['mærɪgəuld] n souci m

marijuana [mærɪ'wɑ:nə] n marijuana f

marina [mə'ri:nə] n (harbour) marina f

marine [mə'ri:n] adj marin(e) ♦ n fusilier marin; (US) marine

marital ['mærɪtl] adj matrimonial(e); **~ status** situation f de famille

marjoram ['mɑ:dʒərəm] n marjolaine f

mark [mɑ:k] n marque f; (of skid etc) trace f; (BRIT: SCOL) note f; (currency) mark m ♦ vt marquer; (stain) tacher; (BRIT: SCOL) noter; corriger; **to ~ time** marquer le pas; **~er** n (sign) jalon m; (bookmark) signet m

market ['mɑ:kɪt] n marché m ♦ vt (COMM) commercialiser; **~ garden** (BRIT) n jardin maraîcher; **~ing** n marketing m; **~place** n place f du marché; (COMM) marché m; **~ research** n étude f de marché

marksman ['mɑ:ksmən] (irreg) n tireur m d'élite

marmalade ['mɑ:məleɪd] n confiture f d'oranges

maroon [mə'ru:n] vt: **to be ~ed** être abandonné(e); (fig) être bloqué(e) ♦ adj bordeaux inv

marquee [mɑ:'ki:] n chapiteau m

marriage ['mærɪdʒ] n mariage m; **~ certificate** n extrait m d'acte de mariage

married ['mærɪd] adj marié(e); (life, love) conjugal(e)

marrow ['mærəu] n moelle f; (vegetable) courge f

marry ['mærɪ] vt épouser, se marier

Mars

avec; (subj: father, priest etc) marier ♦ vi
(also: **get married**) se marier

Mars [maːz] n (planet) Mars f

marsh [maːʃ] n marais m, marécage m

marshal ['maːʃl] n maréchal m; (US:
fire, police) ≃ capitaine m; (SPORT) membre m du service d'ordre ♦ vt rassembler

marshy ['maːʃɪ] adj marécageux(-euse)

martyr ['maːtər] n martyr(e); **~dom** n
martyre m

marvel ['maːvl] n merveille f ♦ vi: to ~
(at) s'émerveiller (de); **~lous** (US **mar-
velous**) adj merveilleux(-euse)

Marxist ['maːksɪst] adj marxiste ♦ n
marxiste m/f

marzipan ['maːzɪpæn] n pâte f
d'amandes

mascara [mæs'kaːrə] n mascara m

masculine ['mæskjulɪn] adj mas-
culin(e)

mash [mæʃ] vt écraser, réduire en purée; **~ed potatoes** npl purée f de
pommes de terre

mask [maːsk] n masque m ♦ vt masquer

mason ['meɪsn] n (also: **stonemason**)
maçon m; (also: **freemason**) franc-
maçon m; **~ry** n maçonnerie f

masquerade [mæskə'reɪd] vi: to ~ as
se faire passer pour

mass [mæs] n multitude f, masse f;
(PHYSICS) masse; (REL) messe f ♦ cpd
(communication) de masse; (unemployment) massif(-ive) ♦ vi se masser; **the
~es** les masses; **~es of** des tas de

massacre ['mæsəkər] n massacre m

massage ['mæsaːʒ] n massage m ♦ vt
masser

massive ['mæsɪv] adj énorme, massif
(-ive)

mass media n inv mass-media mpl

mass production n fabrication f en
série

mast [maːst] n mât m; (RADIO) pylône m

master ['maːstər] n maître m; (in secondary school) professeur m; (title for

matrix

boys): **M~ X** Monsieur X ♦ vt maîtriser;
(learn) apprendre à fond; **~ly** adj ma-
gistral(e); **~mind** n esprit supérieur ♦ vt
diriger, être le cerveau de; **M~ of
Arts/Science** n ≃ maîtrise f (en
lettres/sciences); **~piece** n chef-
d'œuvre m; **~plan** n stratégie f d'ensemble; **~y** n maîtrise f, connaissance
parfaite

mat [mæt] n petit tapis; (also: **doormat**)
paillasson m; (also: **tablemat**) napperon
m ♦ adj = **matt**

match [mætʃ] n allumette f; (game)
match m, partie f; (fig) égal(e) ♦ vt
(also: ~ **up**) assortir; (go well with) aller
bien avec, s'assortir à; (equal) égaler,
valoir ♦ vi être assorti(e); **to be a good
~** être bien assorti(e); **~box** n boîte f
d'allumettes; **~ing** adj assorti(e)

mate [meɪt] n (inf) copain (copine);
(animal) partenaire m/f, mâle/femelle;
(in merchant navy) second m ♦ vi s'accoupler

material [mə'tɪərɪəl] n (substance) matière f, matériau m; (cloth) tissu m, étoffe f; (information, data) données fpl ♦
adj matériel(le); (relevant: evidence) per-
tinent(e); **~s** npl (equipment) matériaux
mpl

maternal [mə'təːnl] adj maternel(le)

maternity [mə'təːnɪtɪ] n maternité f; **~
dress** n robe f de grossesse; **~ hospital** n maternité f

mathematical [mæθə'mætɪkl] adj mathématique

mathematics [mæθə'mætɪks] n mathématiques fpl

maths [mæθs] (US **math**) n math(s) fpl

matinée ['mætɪneɪ] n matinée f

mating call n appel m du mâle

matrices ['meɪtrɪsiːz] npl of **matrix**

matriculation [mətrɪkju'leɪʃən] n inscription f

matrimonial [mætrɪ'məunɪəl] adj ma-
trimonial(e), conjugal(e)

matrimony ['mætrɪmənɪ] n mariage m

matrix ['meɪtrɪks] (pl **matrices**) n ma-

trice f
matron ['meɪtrən] n (in hospital)
infirmière-chef f; (in school) infirmière
mat(t) [mæt] adj mat(e)
matted ['mætɪd] adj emmêlé(e)
matter ['mætəʳ] n question f; (PHYSICS)
matière f; (content) contenu m, fond m;
(MED: pus) pus m ♦ vi importer; **~s**
(affairs, situation) la situation; **it
doesn't ~** cela n'a pas d'importance;
(I don't mind) cela ne me fait rien; **what's
the ~?** qu'est-ce qu'il y a?, qu'est-ce
qui ne va pas?; **no ~ what** quoiqu'il arrive; **as a ~ of course** tout naturellement; **as a ~ of fact** en fait; **~-of-fact**
adj terre à terre; (voice) neutre
mattress ['mætrɪs] n matelas m
mature [mə'tjuəʳ] adj mûr(e); (cheese)
fait(e); (wine) arrivé(e) à maturité ♦ vi
(person) mûrir; (wine, cheese) se faire
maul [mɔːl] vt lacérer
mauve [məʊv] adj mauve
maximum ['mæksɪməm] (pl maxima)
adj maximum ♦ n maximum m
May [meɪ] n mai m; **~ Day** n le Premier
Mai; see also **mayday**
may [meɪ] (conditional **might**) vi (indicating possibility): **he ~ come** il se peut
qu'il vienne; (be allowed to): **~ I
smoke?** puis-je fumer?; (wishes): **~
God bless you!** que Dieu vous bé-
nisse!; **you ~ as well go** à votre place,
je partirais
maybe ['meɪbiː] adv peut-être; **~ he'll
...** peut-être qu'il ...
mayday ['meɪdeɪ] n SOS m
mayhem ['meɪhem] n grabuge m
mayonnaise [meɪə'neɪz] n mayonnaise
f
mayor [mɛəʳ] n maire m; **~ess** n épouse f du maire
maze [meɪz] n labyrinthe m, dédale m
M.D. n abbr (= Doctor of Medicine) titre
universitaire; = **managing director**
me [miː] pron me, m' +vowel; (stressed,
after prep) moi; **he heard ~** il m'a en-
tendu(e); **give ~ a book** donnez-moi

un livre; **after ~** après moi
meadow ['medəʊ] n prairie f, pré m
meagre ['miːgəʳ] (US **meager**) adj maigre
meal [miːl] n repas m; (flour) farine f;
~time n l'heure f du repas
mean [miːn] (pt, pp **meant**) adj (with
money) avare, radin(e); (unkind) mé-
chant(e); (shabby) misérable; (average)
moyen(ne) ♦ vt signifier, vouloir dire;
(refer to) faire allusion à, parler de; (intend): **to ~ to do** avoir l'intention de
faire ♦ n moyenne f; **~s** npl (way, money) moyens mpl; **by ~s of** par l'intermédiaire de; au moyen de; **by all ~s!**
je vous en prie!; **to be ~t for sb/sth**
être destiné(e) à qn/qch; **do you ~ it?**
vous êtes sérieux?; **what do you ~?**
que voulez-vous dire?
meander [mɪ'ændəʳ] vi faire des méan-
dres
meaning ['miːnɪŋ] n signification f,
sens m; **~ful** adj significatif(-ive); (relationship, occasion) important(e); **~less**
adj dénué(e) de sens
meanness ['miːnnɪs] n (with money)
avarice f; (unkindness) méchanceté f;
(shabbiness) médiocrité f
meant [ment] pt, pp of **mean**
meantime ['miːntaɪm] adv (also: **in the
~**) pendant ce temps
meanwhile ['miːnwaɪl] adv = **meantime**
measles ['miːzlz] n rougeole f
measure ['meʒəʳ] vt, vi mesurer ♦ n
mesure f; (ruler) règle (graduée);
~ments npl mesures fpl; **chest/hip
~ment(s)** tour m de poitrine/hanches
meat [miːt] n viande f; **~ball** n boulette
f de viande
Mecca ['mekə] n La Mecque
mechanic [mɪ'kænɪk] n mécanicien m;
~al adj mécanique; **~s** n (PHYSICS) mécanique f ♦ npl (of reading, government
etc) mécanisme m
mechanism ['mekənɪzəm] n mécanisme m

medal ['medl] n médaille f; **~lion** [mɪ'dælɪən] n médaillon m; **~list** (US **medalist**) n (SPORT) médaillé(e)

meddle ['medl] vi: to **~ in** se mêler de, s'occuper de; **to ~ with** toucher à

media ['miːdɪə] npl media mpl

mediaeval [medɪ'iːvl] adj = **medieval**

median ['miːdɪən] (US) n (also: **~ strip**) bande médiane

mediate ['miːdɪeɪt] vi servir d'intermédiaire

Medicaid ® ['medɪkeɪd] (US) n assistance médicale aux indigents

medical ['medɪkl] adj médical(e) ♦ n visite médicale

Medicare ® ['medɪkɛəʳ] (US) n assistance médicale aux personnes âgées

medication [medɪ'keɪʃən] n (drugs) médicaments mpl

medicine ['medsɪn] n médecine f; (drug) médicament m

medieval [medɪ'iːvl] adj médiéval(e)

mediocre [miːdɪ'əukəʳ] adj médiocre

meditate ['medɪteɪt] vi méditer

Mediterranean [medɪtə'reɪnɪən] adj méditerranéen(ne); **the ~ (Sea)** la (mer) Méditerranée

medium ['miːdɪəm] (pl **media**) adj moyen(ne) ♦ n (means) moyen m; (pl **~s**: person) médium m; **the happy ~** le juste milieu; **~-sized** adj de taille moyenne; **~ wave** n ondes moyennes

medley ['medlɪ] n mélange m; (MUS) pot-pourri m

meek [miːk] adj doux (douce), humble

meet [miːt] (pt, pp **met**) vt rencontrer; (by arrangement) retrouver, rejoindre; (for the first time) faire la connaissance de; (go and fetch): **I'll ~ you at the station** j'irai te chercher à la gare; (opponent, danger) faire face à; (obligations) satisfaire à ♦ vi (friends) se rencontrer, se retrouver; (in session) se réunir; (join: lines, roads) se rejoindre; **~ with** vt fus rencontrer; **~ing** n rencontre f; (session: of club etc) réunion f; (POL) meeting m; **she's at a ~ing**

mega ['mega] (inf) adv: **he's ~ rich** il est hyper-riche; **~byte** n (COMPUT) méga-octet m; **~phone** n porte-voix m inv

melancholy ['melənkəlɪ] n mélancolie f ♦ adj mélancolique

mellow ['meləu] adj velouté(e); doux (douce); (sound) mélodieux(-euse) ♦ vi (person) s'adoucir

melody ['melədɪ] n mélodie f

melon ['melən] n melon m

melt [melt] vi fondre ♦ vt faire fondre; (metal) fondre; **~ away** vi fondre complètement; **~ down** vt fondre; **~down** n fusion f (du cœur d'un réacteur nucléaire); **~ing pot** n (fig) creuset m

member ['membəʳ] n membre m; **M~ of Parliament** (BRIT) député m; **M~ of the European Parliament** Eurodéputé m; **~ship** n adhésion f; statut m de membre; (members) membres mpl, adhérents mpl; **~ship card** n carte f de membre

memento [mə'mentəu] n souvenir m

memo ['meməu] n note f (de service)

memoirs ['memwɑːz] npl mémoires mpl

memorandum [memə'rændəm] (pl **memoranda**) n note f (de service)

memorial [mɪ'mɔːrɪəl] n mémorial m ♦ adj commémoratif(-ive)

memorize ['meməraɪz] vt apprendre par cœur; retenir

memory ['memərɪ] n mémoire f; (recollection) souvenir m

men [men] npl of **man**

menace ['menɪs] n menace f; (nuisance) peste f ♦ vt menacer; **menacing** adj menaçant(e)

mend [mend] vt réparer; (darn) raccommoder, repriser ♦ n: **on the ~** en voie de guérison; **to ~ one's ways** s'amender; **~ing** n réparation f; (clothes) raccommodage m

menial ['miːnɪəl] adj subalterne

meningitis [menɪn'dʒaɪtɪs] *n* méningite *f*

menopause ['menəupɔːz] *n* ménopause *f*

menstruation [menstru'eɪʃən] *n* menstruation *f*

mental ['mentl] *adj* mental(e); **~ity** [men'tælɪtɪ] *n* mentalité *f*

mention ['menʃən] *n* mention *f* ♦ *vt* mentionner, faire mention de; **don't ~ it!** je vous en prie, il n'y a pas de quoi!

menu ['menjuː] *n* (*set ~, COMPUT*) menu *m*; (*list of dishes*) carte *f*

MEP *n abbr* = **Member of the European Parliament**

mercenary ['mɜːsɪnərɪ] *adj* intéressé(e), mercenaire ♦ *n* mercenaire *m*

merchandise ['mɜːtʃəndaɪz] *n* marchandises *fpl*

merchant ['mɜːtʃənt] *n* négociant *m*, marchand *m*; **~ bank** (*BRIT*) *n* banque *f* d'affaires; **~ navy** (*US* **merchant marine**) *n* marine marchande

merciful ['mɜːsɪful] *adj* miséricordieux(-euse), clément(e); **a ~ release** une délivrance

merciless ['mɜːsɪlɪs] *adj* impitoyable, sans pitié

mercury ['mɜːkjurɪ] *n* mercure *m*

mercy ['mɜːsɪ] *n* pitié *f*, indulgence *f*; (*REL*) miséricorde *f*; **at the ~ of** à la merci de

mere [mɪə*] *adj* simple; (*chance*) pur(e); **a ~ two hours** seulement deux heures; **~ly** *adv* simplement, purement

merge [mɜːdʒ] *vt* unir ♦ *vi* (*colours, shapes, sounds*) se mêler; (*roads*) se joindre; (*COMM*) fusionner; **~r** *n* (*COMM*) fusion *f*

meringue [mə'ræŋ] *n* meringue *f*

merit ['merɪt] *n* mérite *m*, valeur *f*

mermaid ['mɜːmeɪd] *n* sirène *f*

merry ['merɪ] *adj* gai(e); **M~ Christmas!** Joyeux Noël!; **~-go-round** *n* manège *m*

mesh [meʃ] *n* maille *f*

mesmerize ['mezməraɪz] *n* hypnotiser; fasciner

mess [mes] *n* désordre *m*, fouillis *m*, pagaille *f*; (*muddle: of situation*) gâchis *m*; (*dirt*) saleté *f*; (*MIL*) mess *m*, cantine *f*; **~ about** (*inf*) *vi* perdre son temps; **~ about with** (*inf*) *vt fus* tripoter; **~ around** (*inf*) *vi* = **mess about**; **~ around with** *vt fus* = **mess about with**; **~ up** *vt* (*dirty*) salir; (*spoil*) gâcher

message ['mesɪdʒ] *n* message *m*

messenger ['mesɪndʒə*] *n* messager *m*

Messrs ['mesəz] *abbr* (*on letters*) MM

messy ['mesɪ] *adj* sale; en désordre

met [met] *pt, pp of* **meet**

metal ['metl] *n* métal *m*; **~lic** [mɪ'tælɪk] *adj* métallique

meteorology [miːtɪə'rɒlədʒɪ] *n* météorologie *f*

meter ['miːtə*] *n* (*instrument*) compteur *m*; (*also:* **parking ~**) parcomètre *m*; (*US: unit*) = **metre**

method ['meθəd] *n* méthode *f*; **~ical** [mɪ'θɒdɪkl] *adj* méthodique; **M~ist** *n* méthodiste *m/f*

meths [meθs] (*BRIT*), **methylated spirit** ['meθɪleɪtɪd-] (*BRIT*) *n* alcool *m* à brûler

metre ['miːtə*] (*US* **meter**) *n* mètre *m*; **metric** ['metrɪk] *adj* métrique

metropolitan [metrə'pɒlɪtn] *adj* métropolitain(e); **the M~ Police** (*BRIT*) *n* police londonienne

mettle ['metl] *n*: **to be on one's ~** être d'attaque

mew [mjuː] *vi* (*cat*) miauler

mews [mjuːz] (*BRIT*) *n*: **~ cottage** cottage aménagé dans une ancienne écurie

Mexico ['meksɪkəu] *n* Mexique *m*

miaow [miːau] *vi* miauler

mice [maɪs] *npl of* **mouse**

micro ['maɪkrəu] *n* (*also:* **~computer**) micro-ordinateur *m*; **~chip** *n* puce *f*; **~phone** *n* microphone *m*; **~scope** *n* microscope *m*; **~wave** *n* (*also:* **~wave oven**) four *m* à micro-ondes

mid [mɪd] *adj:* **in ~ May** à la mi-mai; **~ afternoon** le milieu de l'après-midi; **~**

~ **air** en plein ciel; ~**day** n midi m

middle ['mɪdl] n milieu m; (waist) taille f ♦ adj du milieu; (average) moyen(ne); **in the ~ of the night** au milieu de la nuit; ~**-aged** adj d'un certain âge; **M~ Ages** npl: **the M~ Ages** le moyen âge; ~**-class** adj ≃ bourgeois(e); ~ **class(es)** n(pl): **the ~ class(es)** ≃ les classes moyennes; **M~ East** n Proche-Orient m, Moyen-Orient m; (in Iraq) n intermédiaire m; ~ **name** n deuxième nom m; ~**-of-the-road** adj (politician) modéré(e); (music) neutre; ~**weight** n (BOXING) poids moyen; **middling** adj moyen(ne)

midge [mɪdʒ] n moucheron m

midget ['mɪdʒɪt] n nain(e)

Midlands ['mɪdləndz] npl comtés du centre de l'Angleterre

midnight ['mɪdnaɪt] n minuit m

midriff ['mɪdrɪf] n estomac m, taille f

midst [mɪdst] n: **in the ~ of** au milieu de

mid [mɪd'-]: ~**summer** [mɪd'sʌmər] n milieu m de l'été; ~**way** [mɪd'weɪ] adj, adv: ~**way (between)** à mi-chemin (entre); ~**way through ...** au milieu de ..., en plein(e) ...; ~**week** [mɪd'wiːk] adj au milieu de la semaine

midwife ['mɪdwaɪf] (pl **midwives**) n sage-femme f

might [maɪt] vb see **may** ♦ n puissance f, force f; ~**y** adj puissant(e)

migraine ['miːgreɪn] n migraine f

migrant ['maɪgrənt] adj (bird) migrateur(-trice); (worker) saisonnier(-ère)

migrate [maɪ'greɪt] vi émigrer

mike [maɪk] n abbr (= microphone) micro m

mild [maɪld] adj doux (douce); (reproach, infection) léger(-ère); (illness) bénin(-igne); (interest) modéré(e); (taste) peu relevé(e) ♦ n (beer) bière légère; ~**ly** adv doucement; légèrement; **to put it ~ly** c'est le moins qu'on puisse dire

mile [maɪl] n mi(l)le m (= 1609 m); ~**age** n distance f en milles; ≃ kilométrage m; ~**ometer** [maɪ'lɒmɪtər] n compteur m (kilométrique); ~**stone** n borne f; (fig) jalon m

militant ['mɪlɪtnt] adj militant(e)

military ['mɪlɪtəri] adj militaire

militia [mɪ'lɪʃə] n milice(s) f(pl)

milk [mɪlk] n lait m ♦ vt (cow) traire; (fig: person) dépouiller, plumer; (: situation) exploiter à fond; ~ **chocolate** n chocolat m au lait; ~**man** (irreg) n laitier m; ~ **shake** n milk-shake m; ~**y** adj (drink) au lait; (colour) laiteux(-euse); **M~y Way** n voie lactée

mill [mɪl] n moulin m; (steel ~) aciérie f; (spinning ~) filature f; (flour ~) minoterie f ♦ vt moudre, broyer ♦ vi (also: ~ **about**) grouiller; ~**er** n meunier m

millennium bug [mɪ'lenɪəm-] n bogue m or bug m de l'an 2000

milligram(me) ['mɪlɪgræm] n milligramme m

millimetre ['mɪlɪmiːtər] (US **millimeter**) n millimètre m

million ['mɪljən] n million m; ~**aire** n millionnaire m

milometer [maɪ'lɒmɪtər] n compteur m kilométrique

mime [maɪm] n mime m ♦ vt, vi mimer; **mimic** ['mɪmɪk] n imitateur(-trice) m/f ♦ vt imiter, contrefaire

min. abbr = **minute(s)**; **minimum**

mince [mɪns] vt hacher ♦ n (BRIT: CULIN) viande hachée, hachis m; ~**meat** n (fruit) hachis de fruits secs utilisé en pâtisserie; (US: meat) viande hachée, hachis; ~ **pie** n (sweet) sorte de tarte aux fruits secs; ~**r** n hachoir m

mind [maɪnd] n esprit m ♦ vt (attend to, look after) s'occuper de; (be careful) faire attention à; (object to): **I don't ~ the noise** le bruit ne me dérange pas; **I don't ~** cela ne me dérange pas; **it is on my ~** cela me préoccupe; **to my ~** à mon avis or sens; **to be out of one's ~** ne plus avoir toute sa raison; **to**

keep or **bear sth in ~** tenir compte de qch; **to make up one's ~** se décider; **~ you, ...** remarquez ...; **never ~** ça ne fait rien; (don't worry) ne vous en faites pas; **"~ the step"** "attention à la marche"; **~er** n (child-minder) gardienne f; (inf: bodyguard) ange gardien (fig); **~ful** adj: **~ful of** attentif(-ive) à, soucieux(-euse) de; **~less** adj irréfléchi(e); (boring: job) idiot(e)

mine¹ [main] pron le (la) mien(ne), les miens (miennes) ♦ adj: **this book is ~** ce livre est à moi

mine² [main] n mine f ♦ vt (coal) extraire; (ship, beach) miner; **~field** n champ m de mines; (fig) situation (très délicate); **~r** n mineur m

mineral ['mɪnərəl] adj minéral(e) ♦ n minéral m; **~s** npl (BRIT: soft drinks) boissons gazeuses; **~ water** n eau minérale

mingle ['mɪŋgl] vi: **to ~ with** se mêler à

miniature ['mɪnətʃəʳ] adj (en) miniature ♦ n miniature f

minibus ['mɪnɪbʌs] n minibus m

minimal ['mɪnɪml] adj minimal(e)

minimize ['mɪnɪmaɪz] vt (reduce) réduire au minimum; (play down) minimiser

minimum ['mɪnɪməm] (pl **minima**) adj, n minimum m

mining ['maɪnɪŋ] n exploitation minière

miniskirt ['mɪnɪskɜːt] n mini-jupe f

minister ['mɪnɪstəʳ] n (BRIT: POL) ministre m; (REL) pasteur m ♦ vi: **to ~ to sb('s needs)** pourvoir aux besoins de qn; **~ial** [mɪnɪs'tɪərɪəl] (BRIT) adj (POL) ministériel(le); **ministry** n (BRIT: POL) ministère m; (REL): **to go into the ministry** devenir pasteur

mink [mɪŋk] n vison m

minor ['maɪnəʳ] adj petit(e), de peu d'importance; (MUS, poet, problem) mineur(e) ♦ n (LAW) mineur(e)

minority [maɪ'nɒrɪtɪ] n minorité f

mint [mɪnt] n (plant) menthe f; (sweet) bonbon m à la menthe ♦ vt (coins) bat-

tre; **the (Royal) M~**, (US) **the (US) M~** ≃ l'Hôtel m de la Monnaie; **in ~ condition** à l'état de neuf

minus ['maɪnəs] n (also: **~ sign**) signe m moins ♦ prep moins

minute¹ [maɪ'njuːt] adj minuscule; (detail, search) minutieux(-euse)

minute² ['mɪnɪt] n minute f; **~s** npl (official record) procès-verbal, compte rendu

miracle ['mɪrəkl] n miracle m

mirage ['mɪrɑːʒ] n mirage m

mirror ['mɪrəʳ] n miroir m, glace f; (in car) rétroviseur m

mirth [mɜːθ] n gaieté f

misadventure [mɪsəd'ventʃəʳ] n mésaventure f

misapprehension ['mɪsæprɪ'henʃən] n malentendu m, méprise f

misappropriate [mɪsə'prəuprɪeɪt] vt détourner

misbehave [mɪsbɪ'heɪv] vi mal se conduire

miscalculate [mɪs'kælkjuleɪt] vt mal calculer

miscarriage ['mɪskærɪdʒ] n (MED) fausse couche f; **~ of justice** erreur f judiciaire

miscellaneous [mɪsɪ'leɪnɪəs] adj (items) divers(es); (selection) varié(e)

mischief ['mɪstʃɪf] n (naughtiness) sottises fpl; (fun) farce f; (playfulness) espièglerie f; (maliciousness) méchanceté f; **mischievous** ['mɪstʃɪvəs] adj (playful, naughty) coquin(e), espiègle

misconception ['mɪskən'sepʃən] n idée fausse

misconduct [mɪs'kɒndʌkt] n inconduite f; **professional ~** faute professionnelle

misdemeanour [mɪsdɪ'miːnəʳ] (US **misdemeanor**) n écart m de conduite; infraction f

miser ['maɪzəʳ] n avare m/f

miserable ['mɪzərəbl] adj (person, expression) malheureux(-euse); (conditions) misérable; (weather) maussade;

(offer, donation) minable; (failure) pitoyable

miserly ['maɪzəlɪ] adj avare

misery ['mɪzərɪ] n (unhappiness) tristesse f; (pain) souffrances fpl; (wretchedness) misère f

misfire [mɪs'faɪər] vi rater

misfit ['mɪsfɪt] n (person) inadapté(e)

misfortune [mɪs'fɔːtʃən] n malchance f, malheur m

misgiving [mɪs'gɪvɪŋ] n (apprehension) craintes fpl; **to have ~s about** avoir des doutes quant à

misguided [mɪs'gaɪdɪd] adj malavisé(e)

mishandle [mɪs'hændl] vt (mismanage) mal s'y prendre pour faire ou résoudre etc

mishap ['mɪshæp] n mésaventure f

misinform [mɪsɪn'fɔːm] vt mal renseigner

misinterpret [mɪsɪn'tɜːprɪt] vt mal interpréter

misjudge [mɪs'dʒʌdʒ] vt méjuger

mislay [mɪs'leɪ] (irreg: like **lay**) vt égarer

mislead [mɪs'liːd] (irreg: like **lead**) vt induire en erreur; **~ing** adj trompeur(-euse)

mismanage [mɪs'mænɪdʒ] vt mal gérer

misplace [mɪs'pleɪs] vt égarer

misprint ['mɪsprɪnt] n faute f d'impression

Miss [mɪs] n Mademoiselle f

miss [mɪs] vt (fail to get, attend, see) manquer, rater; (regret absence of): **I ~ him/it** il/cela me manque ♦ vi manquer ♦ n (shot) coup manqué; **~ out** (BRIT) vt omettre

misshapen [mɪs'ʃeɪpən] adj difforme

missile ['mɪsaɪl] n (MIL) missile m; (object thrown) projectile m

missing ['mɪsɪŋ] adj manquant(e); (after escape, disaster: person) disparu(e); **to go ~** disparaître; **to be ~** avoir disparu

mission ['mɪʃən] n mission f; **~ary** ['mɪʃənrɪ] n missionnaire m/f; **~ statement** n déclaration f d'intention

mist [mɪst] n brume f ♦ vi (also: **~ over**: eyes) s'embuer; **~ up** vi = **mist over**

mistake [mɪs'teɪk] (irreg: like **take**) n erreur f, faute f ♦ vt (meaning, remark) mal comprendre; se méprendre sur; **to make a ~** se tromper, faire une erreur; **by ~** par erreur, par inadvertance; **to ~ for** prendre pour; **~n** pp of **mistake** ♦ adj (idea etc) erroné(e); **to be ~n** faire erreur, se tromper

mister ['mɪstər] (inf) n Monsieur m; see also **Mr**

mistletoe ['mɪsltəu] n gui m

mistook [mɪs'tuk] pt of **mistake**

mistress ['mɪstrɪs] n maîtresse f; (BRIT: in primary school) institutrice f; (: in secondary school) professeur m

mistrust [mɪs'trʌst] vt se méfier de

misty ['mɪstɪ] adj brumeux(-euse); (glasses, window) embué(e)

misunderstand [mɪsʌndə'stænd] (irreg) vt, vi mal comprendre; **~ing** n méprise f, malentendu m

misuse [n mɪs'juːs, vb mɪs'juːz] n mauvais emploi; (of power) abus m ♦ vt mal employer; abuser de; **~ of funds** détournement m de fonds

mitigate ['mɪtɪgeɪt] vt atténuer

mitt(en) ['mɪt(n)] n mitaine f; moufle f

mix [mɪks] vt mélanger; (sauce, drink etc) préparer ♦ vi se mélanger; (socialize): **he doesn't ~ well** il est peu sociable ♦ n mélange m; **~ up** vt mélanger; (confuse) confondre; **~ed** adj (feelings, reactions) contradictoire; (salad) mélangé(e); (school, marriage) mixte; **~ed grill** n assortiment m de grillades; **~ed-up** adj (confused) désorienté(e), embrouillé(e); **~er** n (for food) batteur m, mixer m; (person): **he is a good ~er** il est très liant; **~ture** n assortiment m, mélange m; (MED) préparation f; **~up** n confusion f

MLA (BRIT) n abbr (= Member of the Legislative Assembly) député m

mm abbr (= millimetre) mm

moan [məʊn] n gémissement m ♦ vi
gémir; (inf: complain): **to ~ (about)** se
plaindre (de)

moat [məʊt] n fossé m, douves fpl

mob [mɒb] n foule f; (disorderly) cohue
f ♦ vt assaillir

mobile ['məʊbaɪl] adj mobile ♦ n mobile m; **~ home** n (grande) caravane; **~
phone** n téléphone portatif

mock [mɒk] vt ridiculiser; (laugh at) se
moquer de ♦ adj faux (fausse); **~ exam**
examen blanc; **~ery** n moquerie f, raillerie f; **to make a ~ery of** tourner en
dérision; **~-up** n maquette f

mod [mɒd] adj see **convenience**

mode [məʊd] n mode m

model ['mɒdl] n modèle m; (person: for
fashion) mannequin m; (: for artist) modèle ♦ vt (with clay etc) modeler ♦ vi
travailler comme mannequin ♦ adj (railway: toy) modèle réduit inv; (child, factory) modèle; **to ~ clothes** présenter
des vêtements; **to ~ o.s. on** imiter

modem ['məʊdεm] n (COMPUT) modem
m

moderate [adj 'mɒdərət, vb 'mɒdəreɪt]
adj modéré(e); (amount, change) peu
important(e) ♦ vi se calmer ♦ vt modérer

modern ['mɒdən] adj moderne; **~ize** vt
moderniser

modest ['mɒdɪst] adj modeste; **~y** n
modestie f

modify ['mɒdɪfaɪ] vt modifier

mogul ['məʊgl] n (fig) nabab m

mohair ['məʊhεəʳ] n mohair m

moist [mɔɪst] adj humide, moite; **~en**
vt humecter, mouiller légèrement; **~ure**
n humidité f; **~urizer** n produit hydratant m

molar ['məʊləʳ] n molaire f

molasses [mə'læsɪz] n mélasse f

mold [məʊld] (US) n, vt = **mould**

mole [məʊl] n (animal, fig: spy) taupe f;
(spot) grain m de beauté

molest [mə'lεst] vt (harass) molester;
(LAW: sexually) attenter à la pudeur de

mollycoddle ['mɒlɪkɒdl] vt chouchou-
ter, couver

molt [məʊlt] (US) vi = **moult**

molten ['məʊltən] adj fondu(e); (rock)
en fusion

mom [mɒm] (US) n = **mum**

moment ['məʊmənt] n moment m,
instant m; **at the ~** en ce moment; **at
that ~** à ce moment-là; **~ary** adj mo-
mentané(e), passager(-ère); **~ous**
[məʊ'mεntəs] adj important(e), capi-
tal(e)

momentum [məʊ'mεntəm] n élan m,
vitesse acquise; (fig) dynamique f; **to
gather ~** prendre de la vitesse

mommy ['mɒmɪ] (US) n maman f

Monaco ['mɒnəkəʊ] n Monaco m

monarch ['mɒnək] n monarque m; **~y**
n monarchie f

monastery ['mɒnəstərɪ] n monastère
m

Monday ['mʌndɪ] n lundi m

monetary ['mʌnɪtərɪ] adj monétaire

money ['mʌnɪ] n argent m; **to make ~**
gagner de l'argent; **~ belt** n ceinture-
portefeuille f; **~ order** n mandat m; **~-
spinner** (inf) n mine f d'or (fig)

mongrel ['mʌŋgrəl] n (dog) bâtard m

monitor ['mɒnɪtəʳ] n (TV, COMPUT) moniteur m ♦ vt contrôler; (broadcast) être
à l'écoute de; (progress) suivre (de près)

monk [mʌŋk] n moine m

monkey ['mʌŋkɪ] n singe m; **~ nut**
(BRIT) n cacahuète f

monopoly [mə'nɒpəlɪ] n monopole m

monotone ['mɒnətəʊn] n ton m (or
voix f) monocorde; **monotonous**
[mə'nɒtənəs] adj monotone

monsoon [mɒn'suːn] n mousson f

monster ['mɒnstəʳ] n monstre m;
monstrous ['mɒnstrəs] adj
monstrueux(-euse); (huge) gigantesque

month [mʌnθ] n mois m; **~ly** adj men-
suel(le) ♦ adv mensuellement

monument ['mɒnjumənt] n monument m

moo [muː] vi meugler, beugler

mood [muːd] n humeur f, disposition f;
to be in a good/bad ~ être de
bonne/mauvaise humeur; **~y** adj (variable) d'humeur changeante, lunatique;
(sullen) morose, maussade

moon [muːn] n lune f; **~light** n clair m
de lune; **~lighting** n travail m au noir;
~lit adj: **a ~lit night** une nuit de lune

moor [muə^r] n lande f ♦ vt (ship) amarrer ♦ vi mouiller; **~land** n lande f

moose [muːs] n inv élan m

mop [mɔp] n balai m à laver; (for dishes)
lavette f (à vaisselle) ♦ vt essuyer; **~ of
hair** tignasse f; **~ up** vt éponger

mope [məup] vi avoir le cafard, se morfondre

moped ['məuped] n cyclomoteur m

moral ['mɔrl] adj moral(e) ♦ n morale f;
~s npl (attitude, behaviour) moralité f

morale [mɔ'rɑːl] n moral m

morality [mə'ræliti] n moralité f

morass [mə'ræs] n marais m, marécage
m

more [mɔː^r] adj **1** (greater in number
etc) plus (de), davantage; **more
people/work (than)** plus de gens/de
travail (que)
2 (additional) encore (de); **do you
want (some) more tea?** voulez-vous
encore du thé?; **I have no or I don't
have any more money** je n'ai plus
d'argent; **it'll take a few more weeks**
ça prendra encore quelques semaines
♦ pron plus, davantage; **more than 10**
plus de 10; **it cost more than we expected** cela a coûté plus que prévu; **I
want more** j'en veux plus or davantage; **is there any more?** est-ce qu'il en
reste?; **there's no more** il n'y en a
plus; **a little more** un peu plus;
many/much more beaucoup plus,
bien davantage
♦ adv: **more dangerous/easily (than)**
plus dangereux/facilement (que); **more
and more expensive** de plus en plus

cher; **more or less** plus ou moins;
more than ever plus que jamais

moreover [mɔː'rəuvə^r] adv de plus

morning ['mɔːnɪŋ] n matin m; matinée
f ♦ cpd matinal(e); (paper) du matin; **in
the ~** le matin; **7 o'clock in the ~** 7
heures du matin; **~ sickness** n nau-
sées matinales

Morocco [mə'rɔkəu] n Maroc m

moron ['mɔːrɔn] (inf) n idiot(e)

Morse [mɔːs] n: **~ code** code morse m

morsel ['mɔːsl] n bouchée f

mortar ['mɔːtə^r] n mortier m

mortgage ['mɔːgɪdʒ] n hypothèque f;
(loan) prêt m (or crédit m) hypothécaire
♦ vt hypothéquer; **~ company** n
société f de crédit immobilier

mortuary ['mɔːtjuəri] n morgue f

mosaic [məu'zeɪk] n mosaïque f

Moscow ['mɔskəu] n Moscou

Moslem ['mɔzləm] adj, n = **Muslim**

mosque [mɔsk] n mosquée f

mosquito [mɔs'kiːtəu] (pl **~es**) n
moustique m

moss [mɔs] n mousse f

most [məust] adj la plupart de; le plus
de ♦ pron la plupart ♦ adv le plus; (very)
très, extrêmement; **the ~** (also: + adjective) le plus; **~ of** la plus grande
partie de; **~ of them** la plupart d'entre
eux; **I saw (the) ~** j'en ai vu le plus;
at the (very) ~ au plus; **to make the ~
of** profiter au maximum de; **~ly** adv
(chiefly) surtout; (usually) généralement

MOT n abbr (BRIT: Ministry of Transport):
the MOT (test) la visite technique (annuelle) obligatoire des véhicules à moteur

motel [məu'tel] n motel m

moth [mɔθ] n papillon m de nuit; (in
clothes) mite f

mother ['mʌðə^r] n mère f ♦ vt (act as ~
to) servir de mère à; (pamper, protect)
materner; **~ country** mère patrie;
~hood n maternité f; **~-in-law** n
belle-mère f; **~ly** adj maternel(le);

of-pearl n nacre f; **M~'s Day** n fête f des Mères; **~-to-be** n future maman; **~ tongue** n langue maternelle

motion ['məʊʃən] n mouvement m; (gesture) geste m; (at meeting) motion f ♦ vt, vi: **to ~ (to) sb to do** faire signe à qn de faire; **~less** adj immobile, sans mouvement; **~ picture** n film m

motivated ['məʊtɪveɪtɪd] adj motivé(e); **motivation** [məʊtɪ'veɪʃən] n motivation f

motive ['məʊtɪv] n motif m, mobile m

motley ['mɒtlɪ] adj hétéroclite

motor ['məʊtər] n moteur m; (BRIT: inf: vehicle) auto ♦ cpd (industry, vehicle) automobile; **~bike** n moto f; **~boat** n bateau m à moteur; **~car** (BRIT) n automobile f; **~cycle** n vélomoteur m; **~cycle racing** n course f de motos; **~cyclist** n motocycliste m/f; **~ing** (BRIT) n tourisme m automobile; **~ist** n automobiliste m/f; **~ mechanic** n mécanicien m garagiste; **~ racing** (BRIT) n course f automobile; **~way** (BRIT) n autoroute f

mottled ['mɒtld] adj tacheté(e), marbré(e)

motto ['mɒtəʊ] (pl **~es**) n devise f

mould [məʊld] (US **mold**) n moule m; (mildew) moisissure f ♦ vt mouler, modeler; (fig) façonner; **mo(u)ldy** adj moisi(e); (smell) de moisi

moult [məʊlt] (US **molt**) vi muer

mound [maʊnd] n monticule m, tertre m; (heap) monceau m, tas m

mount [maʊnt] n mont m, montagne f ♦ vt monter ♦ vi (inflation, tension) augmenter; (also: **~ up:** problems etc) s'accumuler; **~ up** vi (bills, costs, savings) s'accumuler

mountain ['maʊntɪn] n montagne f ♦ cpd de montagne; **~ bike** n VTT m, vélo tout-terrain; **~eer** [maʊntɪ'nɪər] n alpiniste m/f; **~eering** n alpinisme m; **~ous** adj montagneux(-euse); **~ rescue team** n équipe f de secours en montagne; **~side** n flanc m ou versant

m de la montagne

mourn [mɔːn] vt pleurer ♦ vi: **to ~ (for)** (person) pleurer (la mort de); **~er** n parent(e) ou ami(e) du défunt; personne f en deuil; **~ing** n deuil m ♦ in **~ing** en deuil

mouse [maʊs] (pl **mice**) n (also COMPUT) souris f; **~ mat** n (COMPUT) tapis m de souris; **~trap** n souricière f

mousse [muːs] n mousse f

moustache [məs'tɑːʃ] (US **mustache**) n moustache(s) f(pl)

mousy ['maʊsɪ] adj (hair) d'un châtain terne

mouth [maʊθ] (pl **~s**) n bouche f; (of dog, cat) gueule f; (of river) embouchure f; (of hole, cave) ouverture f; **~ful** n bouchée f; **~ organ** n harmonica m; **~piece** n (of musical instrument) embouchure f; (spokesman) porte-parole m inv; **~wash** n eau f dentifrice; **~watering** adj qui met l'eau à la bouche

movable ['muːvəbl] adj mobile

move [muːv] n (~ment) mouvement m; (in game) coup m; (: turn to play) tour m; (change: of house) déménagement m; (: of job) changement m d'emploi ♦ vt déplacer, bouger; (emotionally) émouvoir; (POL: resolution etc) proposer; (in game) jouer ♦ vi (gen) bouger, remuer; (traffic) circuler; (also: ~ **house**) déménager; (situation) progresser; **that was a good ~** bien joué!; **to get a ~ on** se dépêcher, se remuer; **to ~ sb to do sth** pousser ou inciter qn à faire qch; **~ about** vi (fidget) remuer; (travel) voyager, se déplacer; (change residence, job) ne pas rester au même endroit; **~ along** vi se pousser; **~ around** vi = move about; **~ away** vi s'en aller; **~ back** vi revenir, retourner; **~ forward** vi avancer; **~ in** vi (to a house) emménager; (police, soldiers) intervenir; **~ on** vi se remettre en route; **~ out** vi (of house) déménager; **~ over** vi se pousser; **~ up** vi (pupil) passer dans la classe supérieure; (*employee*) avoir de l'avancement; **~able** *adj* = **movable**

movement ['mu:vmənt] *n* mouvement *m*

movie ['mu:vɪ] *n* film *m*; **the ~s** le cinéma

moving ['mu:vɪŋ] *adj* en mouvement; (*emotional*) émouvant(e)

mow [məʊ] (*pt* mowed, *pp* mowed *or* mown) *vt* faucher; (*lawn*) tondre; **~ down** *vt* faucher; **~er** *n* (*also:* lawn-mower) tondeuse *f* à gazon

MP *n abbr* = **Member of Parliament**

mph *abbr* = **miles per hour**

Mr ['mɪstəʳ] *n*: **~ Smith** Monsieur Smith, M. Smith

Mrs ['mɪsɪz] *n*: **~ Smith** Madame Smith, Mme Smith

Ms [mɪz] *n* (= Miss *or* Mrs): **~ Smith** Madame Smith, Mme Smith

MSc *abbr* = **Master of Science**

MSP *n abbr* = **Member of the Scottish Parliament**

much [mʌtʃ] *adj* beaucoup de ♦ *adv*, *n*, *pron* beaucoup; **how ~ is it?** combien est-ce que ça coûte?; **too ~** trop (de); **as ~ as** autant de

muck [mʌk] *n* (*dirt*) saleté *f*; **~ about** *or* **around** (*inf*) *vi* faire l'imbécile; **~ in** (*inf*) *vi* (*exam, interview*) se planter à (*fam*); **~y** *adj* (*very*) sale

mud [mʌd] *n* boue *f*

muddle ['mʌdl] *n* (*mess*) pagaille *f*, désordre *m*; (*mix-up*) confusion *f* ♦ *vt* (*also:* ~ **up**) embrouiller; **~ through** *vi* se débrouiller

muddy ['mʌdɪ] *adj* boueux(-euse)

mudguard ['mʌdgɑ:d] *n* garde-boue *m inv*

muesli ['mju:zlɪ] *n* muesli *m*

muffin ['mʌfɪn] *n* muffin *m*

muffle ['mʌfl] *vt* (*sound*) assourdir, étouffer; (*against cold*) emmitoufler; **~d** *adj* (*sound*) étouffé(e); **~r** *n* (US) (AUT) silencieux *m*

mug [mʌg] *n* (*cup*) grande tasse (*sans*

soucoupe); (: *for beer*) chope *f*; (*inf*: *face*) bouille *f*; (: *fool*) poire *f* ♦ *vt* (*assault*) agresser; **~ger** *n* agresseur *m*; **~ging** *n* agression *f*

muggy ['mʌgɪ] *adj* lourd(e), moite

mule [mju:l] *n* mule *f*

multi-level ['mʌltɪlevl] (US) *adj* = **multistorey**

multiple ['mʌltɪpl] *adj* multiple ♦ *n* multiple *m*; **~ sclerosis** [-sklɪ'rəʊsɪs] *n* sclérose *f* en plaques

multiplex cinema ['mʌltɪpleks-] *n* cinéma *m* multisalles

multiplication [mʌltɪplɪ'keɪʃən] *n* multiplication *f*; **multiply** ['mʌltɪplaɪ] *vt* multiplier ♦ *vi* se multiplier

multistorey ['mʌltɪ'stɔ:rɪ] (BRIT) *adj* (*building*) à étages; (*car park*) à étages *or* niveaux multiples ♦ *n* (*car park*) parking *m* à plusieurs étages

mum [mʌm] (BRIT: *inf*) maman *f* ♦ *adj*: **to keep ~** ne pas souffler mot

mumble ['mʌmbl] *vt, vi* marmotter, marmonner

mummy ['mʌmɪ] *n* (BRIT: *mother*) maman *f*; (*embalmed*) momie *f*

mumps [mʌmps] *n* oreillons *mpl*

munch [mʌntʃ] *vt, vi* mâcher

mundane [mʌn'deɪn] *adj* banal(e), terre à terre *inv*

municipal [mju:'nɪsɪpl] *adj* municipal(e)

murder ['mɜ:dəʳ] *n* meurtre *m*, assassinat *m* ♦ *vt* assassiner; **~er** *n* meurtrier *m*, assassin *m*; **~ous** ['mɜ:dərəs] *adj* meurtrier(-ère)

murky ['mɜ:kɪ] *adj* sombre, ténébreux(-euse); (*water*) trouble

murmur ['mɜ:məʳ] *n* murmure *m* ♦ *vt, vi* murmurer

muscle ['mʌsl] *n* muscle *m*; (*fig*) force *f*; **~ in** *vi* (*on territory*) envahir; (*on success*) exploiter; **muscular** ['mʌskjʊləʳ] *adj* musculaire; (*person, arm*) musclé(e)

muse [mju:z] *vi* méditer, songer

museum [mju:'zɪəm] *n* musée *m*

mushroom ['mʌʃrʊm] *n* champignon *m* ♦ *vi* pousser comme un champignon

music ['mju:zɪk] n musique f; **~al** adj musical(e); (person) musicien(ne) ♦ n (show) comédie musicale; **~al instrument** n instrument m de musique; **~ centre** n chaîne compacte; **~ian** [mju:'zɪʃən] n musicien(ne)

Muslim ['mʌzlɪm] adj, n musulman(e)

muslin ['mʌzlɪn] n mousseline f

mussel ['mʌsl] n moule f

must [mʌst] aux vb (obligation): **I ~ do it** je dois le faire, il faut que je le fasse; (probability): **he ~ be there by now** il doit y être maintenant, il est probablement maintenant; (suggestion, invitation): **you ~ come and see me** il faut que vous veniez me voir; (indicating sth unwelcome): **why ~ he behave so badly?** qu'est-ce qui le pousse à se conduire si mal? ♦ n nécessité f, impératif m; **it's a ~** c'est indispensable

mustache ['mʌstæʃ] (US) n = **moustache**

mustard ['mʌstəd] n moutarde f

muster ['mʌstər] vt rassembler

mustn't ['mʌsnt] = **must not**

mute [mju:t] adj muet(te); **~d** adj (colour) sourd(e); (reaction) voilé(e)

mutiny ['mju:tɪnɪ] n mutinerie f ♦ vi se mutiner

mutter ['mʌtər] vt, vi marmonner, marmotter

mutton ['mʌtn] n mouton m

mutual ['mju:tʃuəl] adj mutuel(le), réciproque; (benefit, interest) commun(e); **~ly** adv mutuellement

muzzle ['mʌzl] n museau m; (protective device) muselière f; (of gun) gueule f ♦ vt museler

my [maɪ] adj mon (ma), mes pl; **~ house/car/gloves** ma maison/mon auto/mes gants; **I've washed ~ hair/cut ~ finger** je me suis lavé les cheveux/coupé le doigt; **~self** [maɪ'self] pron (reflexive) me; (emphatic) moi-même; (after prep) moi; see also **oneself**

mysterious [mɪs'tɪərɪəs] adj mysté-

rieux(-euse)

mystery ['mɪstərɪ] n mystère m

mystify ['mɪstɪfaɪ] vt mystifier; (puzzle) ébahir

myth [mɪθ] n mythe m; **~ology** [mɪ'θɒlədʒɪ] n mythologie f

N, n

n/a abbr = **not applicable**

naff [næf] (BRIT: inf) adj nul(le)

nag [næg] vt (scold) être toujours après, reprendre sans arrêt; **~ging** adj (doubt, pain) persistant(e)

nail [neɪl] n (human) ongle m; (metal) clou m ♦ vt clouer; **to ~ sb down to a date/price** contraindre qn à accepter or donner une date/un prix; **~brush** n brosse f à ongles; **~file** n lime f à ongles; **~ polish** n vernis m à ongles; **~ polish remover** n dissolvant m; **~ scissors** npl ciseaux mpl à ongles; **~ varnish** (BRIT) n = **nail polish**

naïve [naɪ'i:v] adj naïf(-ïve)

naked ['neɪkɪd] adj nu(e)

name [neɪm] n nom m; (reputation) réputation f ♦ vt nommer; (identify: accomplice etc) citer; (price, date) fixer, donner; **by ~** par son nom; **in the ~ of** au nom de; **what's your ~?** comment vous appelez-vous?; **~less** adj sans nom; (witness, contributor) anonyme; **~ly** adv à savoir; **~sake** n homonyme m

nanny ['nænɪ] n bonne f d'enfants

nap [næp] n (sleep) (petit) somme ♦ vi: **to be caught ~ping** être pris à l'improviste or en défaut

nape [neɪp] n: **~ of the neck** nuque f

napkin ['næpkɪn] n serviette f (de table)

nappy ['næpɪ] (BRIT) n couche f (gen pl); **~ rash** n: **to have ~ rash** avoir les fesses rouges

narcissus [nɑ:'sɪsəs] (pl narcissi) n narcisse m

narcotic [nɑːˈkɔtik] n (drug) stupéfiant m; (MED) narcotique m

narrative [ˈnærətiv] n récit m

narrow [ˈnærəu] adj étroit(e); (fig) restreint(e), limité(e) ♦ vi (road) devenir plus étroit, se rétrécir; (gap, difference) se réduire; **to have a ~ escape** l'échapper belle; **to ~ sth down to** réduire qch à; **~ly** adv: **he ~ly missed injury/the tree** il a failli se blesser/ rentrer dans l'arbre; **~-minded** adj à l'esprit étroit, borné(e); (attitude) borné(e)

nasty [ˈnɑːsti] adj (person: malicious) méchant(e); (: rude) très désagréable; (smell) dégoûtant(e); (wound, situation, disease) mauvais(e)

nation [ˈneɪʃən] n nation f

national [ˈnæʃənl] adj national(e) ♦ n (abroad) ressortissant(e); (when home) national(e); **~ anthem** n hymne national; **~ dress** n costume national; **N~ Health Service** (BRIT) n service national de santé; ≈ Sécurité Sociale; **N~ Insurance** (BRIT) n ≈ Sécurité Sociale; **~ism** n nationalisme m; **~ist** adj nationaliste ♦ n nationaliste m/f; **~ity** [næʃəˈnæliti] n nationalité f; **~ize** vt nationaliser; **~ly** adv (as a nation) du point de vue national; (nationwide) dans le pays entier; **~ park** n parc national

---

National Trust

Le **National Trust** est un organisme indépendant, à but non lucratif, dont la mission est de protéger et de mettre en valeur les monuments et les sites britanniques en raison de leur intérêt historique ou de leur beauté naturelle.

---

nationwide [ˈneɪʃənwaɪd] adj s'étendant à l'ensemble du pays, (problem) à l'échelle du pays entier ♦ adv à travers or dans tout le pays

native [ˈneɪtiv] n autochtone m/f, habitant(e) du pays ♦ adj du pays, indigène; (country) natal(e); (ability) inné(e); **a ~ of Russia** une personne originaire de Russie; **a ~ speaker of French** une personne de langue maternelle française; **N~ American** n Indien(ne) d'Amérique; **~ language** n langue maternelle

NATO [ˈneɪtəu] n abbr (= North Atlantic Treaty Organization) OTAN f

natural [ˈnætʃrəl] adj naturel(le); **~ gas** n gaz naturel; **~ist** n naturaliste m/f; **~ly** adv naturellement

nature [ˈneɪtʃər] n nature f; **by ~** par tempérament, de nature

naught [nɔːt] n = **nought**

naughty [ˈnɔːti] adj (child) vilain(e), pas sage

nausea [ˈnɔːsɪə] n nausée f

naval [ˈneɪvl] adj naval(e); **~ officer** n officier m de marine

nave [neɪv] n nef f

navel [ˈneɪvl] n nombril m

navigate [ˈnævɪgeɪt] vt (steer) diriger; (plot course) naviguer ♦ vi naviguer; **navigation** [nævɪˈgeɪʃən] n navigation f

navvy [ˈnævi] (BRIT) n terrassier m

navy [ˈneɪvi] n marine f; **~(-blue)** adj bleu marine inv

Nazi [ˈnɑːtsi] n Nazi(e)

NB abbr (= nota bene) NB

near [nɪər] adj proche ♦ adv près ♦ prep (also: **~ to**) près de ♦ vt approcher de; **~by** [nɪəˈbaɪ] adj proche ♦ adv tout près, à proximité; **~ly** adv presque; **I ~ly fell** j'ai failli tomber; **~ miss** n (AVIAT) quasi-collision f; **that was a ~ miss** (gen) il s'en est fallu de peu; (of shot) c'est passé très près; **~side** n (AUT: in Britain) côté m gauche; (: in US, Europe etc) côté droit; **~-sighted** adj myope

neat [niːt] adj (person, work) soigné(e); (room etc) bien tenu(e) or rangé(e); (skilful) habile; (spirits) pur(e); **~ly** adv avec soin or ordre; habilement

necessarily [ˈnesɪsrɪli] adv nécessairement

necessary [ˈnesɪsri] adj nécessaire; **ne-**

cessity [nɪ'sɛsɪtɪ] n nécessité f; (thing needed) chose nécessaire or essentielle; **necessities** npl nécessaire m

neck [nɛk] n cou m; (of animal, garment) encolure f; (of bottle) goulot m ♦ vi (inf) se peloter; **~ and ~** à égalité; **~lace** n collier m; **~line** n encolure f; **~tie** n cravate f

need [niːd] n besoin m ♦ vt avoir besoin de; **to ~ to do** devoir faire; avoir besoin de faire; **you don't ~ to go** vous n'avez pas besoin or vous n'êtes pas obligé de partir

needle ['niːdl] n aiguille f ♦ vt asticoter, tourmenter

needless ['niːdlɪs] adj inutile

needlework ['niːdlwɜːk] n (activity) travaux mpl d'aiguille; (object(s)) ouvrage m

needn't ['niːdnt] = **need not**

needy ['niːdɪ] adj nécessiteux(-euse)

negative ['nɛgətɪv] n (PHOT, ELEC) négatif m; (LING) terme m de négation ♦ adj négatif(-ive); **~ equity** situation dans laquelle la valeur d'une maison est inférieure à celle de l'emprunt-logement contracté pour la payer

neglect [nɪ'glɛkt] vt négliger ♦ n le fait de négliger; (state of ~) abandon m; **~ed** adj négligé(e), à l'abandon

negligee ['nɛglɪʒeɪ] n déshabillé m

negotiate [nɪ'gəuʃɪeɪt] vi, vt négocier; **negotiation** [nɪgəuʃɪ'eɪʃən] n négociation f, pourparlers mpl

neigh [neɪ] vi hennir

neighbour ['neɪbər] (US **neighbor**) n voisin(e); **~hood** n (place) quartier m; (people) voisinage m; **~ing** adj voisin(e), avoisinant(e); **~ly** adj obligeant(e); (action etc) amical(e)

neither ['naɪðər] adj, pron aucun(e) (des deux), ni l'un(e) ni l'autre ♦ conj: **I didn't move and ~ did Claude** je n'ai pas bougé, Claude non plus ♦ adv: **~ good nor bad** ni bon ni mauvais; ..., **~ did I refuse ...**, (et or mais) je n'ai pas non plus refusé ...

neon ['niːɔn] n néon m; **~ light** n lampe f au néon

nephew ['nɛvjuː] n neveu m

nerve [nɜːv] n nerf m; (fig: courage) sang-froid m, courage m; (: impudence) aplomb m, toupet m; **to have a fit of ~s** avoir le trac; **~-racking** adj angoissant(e)

nervous ['nɜːvəs] adj nerveux(-euse); (anxious) inquiet(-ète), plein(e) d'appréhension; (timid) intimidé(e); **~ breakdown** n dépression nerveuse

nest [nɛst] n nid m ♦ vi (se) nicher, faire son nid; **~ egg** n (fig) bas m de laine, magot m

nestle ['nɛsl] vi se blottir

net [nɛt] n filet m; the **N~** (Internet) le Net ♦ adj net(te) ♦ vt (fish etc) prendre au filet; (profit) rapporter; **~ball** n netball m

Netherlands ['nɛðələndz] npl: the **~** les Pays-Bas mpl

nett [nɛt] adj = **net**

netting ['nɛtɪŋ] n (for fence etc) treillis m, grillage m

nettle ['nɛtl] n ortie f

network ['nɛtwɜːk] n réseau m

neurotic [njuə'rɔtɪk] adj névrosé(e)

neuter ['njuːtər] adj neutre ♦ vt (cat etc) châtrer, couper

neutral ['njuːtrəl] adj neutre ♦ n (AUT) point mort; **~ize** vt neutraliser

never ['nɛvər] adv (ne ...) jamais; **~ again** plus jamais; **~ in my life** jamais de ma vie; see also **mind**; **~-ending** adj interminable; **~theless** adv néanmoins, malgré tout

new [njuː] adj nouveau (nouvelle); (brand ~) neuf (neuve); **N~ Age** n New Age m; **~born** adj nouveau-né(e); **~comer** n nouveau venu/nouvelle venue; **~fangled** ['njuː'fæŋgld] (pej) adj ultramoderne (et farfelu(e)); **~found** adj (enthusiasm) de fraîche date; (friend) nouveau (nouvelle); **~ly** adv nouvellement, récemment; **~ly-weds** npl jeunes mariés mpl

news [njuːz] n nouvelle(s) f(pl); (RADIO, TV) informations fpl, actualités fpl; **a piece of ~** une nouvelle; **~ agency** agence f de presse; **~agent** (BRIT) n marchand de journaux; **~caster** n présentateur(-trice); **~ flash** n flash d'information; **~letter** n bulletin m; **~paper** n journal m; **~print** n papier m (de) journal; **~reader** n = newscaster; **~reel** n actualités (filmées); **~ stand** n kiosque à journaux

newt [njuːt] n triton m

New Year n Nouvel An; **~'s Day** n le jour de l'An; **~'s Eve** n la Saint-Sylvestre

New Zealand [-'ziːlənd] n la Nouvelle-Zélande; **~er** n Néo-zélandais(e)

next [nɛkst] adj (seat, room) voisin(e), d'à côté; (meeting, bus stop) suivant(e); (in time) prochain(e) ♦ adv (place) à côté; (time) la fois suivante, la prochaine fois; (afterwards) ensuite; **the ~ day** le lendemain, le jour suivant or d'après; **~ year** l'année prochaine; **~ time** la prochaine fois; **~ to** à côté de; **~ to nothing** presque rien; **~, please!** (at doctor's etc) au suivant!; **~ door** adv à côté ♦ adj d'à côté; **~-of-kin** n parent m le plus proche

NHS n abbr = **National Health Service**

nib [nɪb] n (bec m de) plume f

nibble ['nɪbl] vt grignoter

nice [naɪs] adj (pleasant, likeable) agréable; (pretty) joli(e); (kind) gentil(le); **~ly** adv agréablement; joliment; gentiment

niceties ['naɪsɪtɪz] npl subtilités fpl

nick [nɪk] n (indentation) encoche f; (wound) entaille f ♦ vt (BRIT: inf) faucher, piquer; **in the ~ of time** juste à temps

nickel ['nɪkl] n nickel m; (US) pièce f de 5 cents

nickname ['nɪkneɪm] n surnom m ♦ vt surnommer

nicotine patch ['nɪkətiːn-] n timbre m anti-tabac, patch m

niece [niːs] n nièce f

Nigeria [naɪ'dʒɪərɪə] n Nigéria m or f

niggling ['nɪglɪŋ] adj (person) tatillon(ne); (detail) insignifiant(e); (doubts, injury) persistant(e)

night [naɪt] n nuit f; (evening) soir m; **at ~** la nuit; **by ~** de nuit; **the ~ before last** avant-hier soir; **~cap** n boisson prise avant le coucher; **~ club** n boîte f de nuit; **~dress** n chemise f de nuit; **~fall** n tombée f de la nuit; **~gown** n, **~ie** ['naɪtɪ] n chemise f de nuit; **~ingale** ['naɪtɪŋgeɪl] n rossignol m; **~life** n vie f nocturne; **~ly** adj de chaque nuit or soir; (by night) nocturne ♦ adv chaque nuit or soir; **~mare** n cauchemar m; **~ porter** n gardien m de nuit, concierge m de service la nuit; **~ school** n cours mpl du soir; **~ shift** n équipe f de nuit; **~-time** n nuit f; **~ watchman** n veilleur m or gardien m de nuit

nil [nɪl] n rien m; (BRIT: SPORT) zéro m

Nile [naɪl] n: **the ~** le Nil

nimble ['nɪmbl] adj agile

nine [naɪn] num neuf m; **to call 999** (BRIT) or **911** (US) appeler les urgences; **~teen** ['naɪn'tiːn] num dix-neuf; **~ty** ['naɪntɪ] num quatre-vingt-dix; **ninth** [naɪnθ] num neuvième

nip [nɪp] vt pincer

nipple ['nɪpl] n (ANAT) mamelon m, bout m du sein

nitrogen ['naɪtrədʒən] n azote m

KEYWORD

no [nəu] (pl **noes**) adv (opposite of "yes") non; **are you coming? - no (I'm not)** est-ce que vous venez? - non; **would you like some more? - no thank you** en voulez-vous encore? - non merci

♦ adj (not any) pas de, aucun(e) (used with "ne"); **I have no money/books** je n'ai pas d'argent/de livres; **no student would have done it** aucun étudiant ne l'aurait fait; **"no smoking"** "défense de fumer"; **"no dogs"** "les

chiens ne sont pas admis"
♦ *n* non *m*

nobility [nəʊ'bɪlɪtɪ] *n* noblesse *f*
noble ['nəʊbl] *adj* noble
nobody ['nəʊbədɪ] *pron* personne
nod [nɒd] *vi* faire un signe de tête (*affirmatif ou amical*); (*sleep*) somnoler ♦ *vt*: **to ~ one's head** faire un signe de (la) tête; (*in agreement*) faire signe que oui ♦ *n* signe *m* de (la) tête; **~ off** *vi* s'assoupir
noise [nɔɪz] *n* bruit *m*; **noisy** *adj* bruyant(e)
nominal ['nɒmɪnl] *adj* symbolique
nominate ['nɒmɪneɪt] *vt* (*propose*) proposer; (*appoint*) nommer; **nominee** [nɒmɪ'niː] *n* candidat agréé; personne nommée
non... [nɒn] *prefix* non-; **~alcoholic** *adj* non-alcoolisé(e); **~committal** *adj* évasif(-ive); **~descript** *adj* quelconque, indéfinissable
none [nʌn] *pron* aucun(e); **~ of you** aucun d'entre vous, personne parmi vous; **I've ~ left** je n'en ai plus; **he's the worse for it** il ne s'en porte pas plus mal
nonentity [nɒ'nentɪtɪ] *n* personne insignifiante
nonetheless ['nʌnðə'les] *adv* néanmoins
non-existent [nɒnɪg'zɪstənt] *adj* inexistant(e)
non-fiction [nɒn'fɪkʃən] *n* littérature *f* non-romanesque
nonplussed [nɒn'plʌst] *adj* perplexe
nonsense ['nɒnsəns] *n* absurdités *fpl*, idioties *fpl*; **~!** ne dites pas d'idioties!
non-: ~smoker *n* non-fumeur *m*; **~smoking** *adj* non-fumeur; **~stick** *adj* qui n'attache pas; **~stop** *adj* direct(e), sans arrêt (*or* escale) ♦ *adv* sans arrêt
noodles ['nuːdlz] *npl* nouilles *fpl*
nook [nʊk] *n*: **~s and crannies** recoins *mpl*
noon [nuːn] *n* midi *m*

no one ['nəʊwʌn] *pron* = **nobody**
noose [nuːs] *n* nœud coulant; (*hangman's*) corde *f*
nor [nɔːʳ] *conj* = **neither** ♦ *adv* *see* neither
norm [nɔːm] *n* norme *f*
normal ['nɔːml] *adj* normal(e); **~ly** ['nɔːməlɪ] *adv* normalement
Normandy ['nɔːməndɪ] *n* Normandie *f*
north [nɔːθ] *n* nord *m* ♦ *adj* du nord, nord *inv* ♦ *adv* au *or* vers le nord; **N~ America** *n* Amérique *f* du Nord; **~east** *n* nord-est *m*; **~erly** ['nɔːðəlɪ] *adj* du nord; **~ern** ['nɔːðən] *adj* du nord, septentrional(e); **N~ern Ireland** *n* Irlande *f* du Nord; **N~ Pole** *n* pôle *m* Nord; **N~ Sea** *n* mer *f* du Nord; **~ward(s)** *adv* vers le nord; **~-west** *n* nord-ouest *m*
Norway ['nɔːweɪ] *n* Norvège *f*; **Norwegian** [nɔː'wiːdʒən] *adj* norvégien(ne) ♦ *n* Norvégien(ne); (*LING*) norvégien *m*
nose [nəʊz] *n* nez *m*; **~ about, around** *vi* fouiner *or* fureter (partout); **~bleed** *n* saignement *m* du nez; **~dive** *n* (descente *f* en) piqué *m*; **~y** (*inf*) *adj* = **nosy**
nostalgia [nɒs'tældʒɪə] *n* nostalgie *f*
nostril ['nɒstrɪl] *n* narine *f*; (*of horse*) naseau *m*
nosy ['nəʊzɪ] (*inf*) *adj* curieux(-euse)
not [nɒt] *adv* (ne ...) pas; **he is ~ or isn't here** il n'est pas ici; **you must ~ or you mustn't do that** tu ne dois pas faire ça; **it's too late, isn't it** *or* **is it ~?** c'est trop tard, n'est-ce pas?; **~ yet/now** pas encore/maintenant; **~ at all** pas du tout; *see also* **all**; only
notably ['nəʊtəblɪ] *adv* (*particularly*) en particulier; (*markedly*) spécialement
notary ['nəʊtərɪ] *n* notaire *m*
notch [nɒtʃ] *n* encoche *f*
note [nəʊt] *n* note *f*; (*letter*) mot *m*; (*banknote*) billet *m* ♦ *vt* (*also*: **~ down**) noter; (*observe*) constater; **~book** *n* carnet *m*; **~d** *adj* réputé(e); **~pad** *n*

bloc-notes *m*; **~paper** *n* papier *m* à lettres

nothing ['nʌθɪŋ] *n* rien *m*; **he does ~** il ne fait rien; **~ new** rien de nouveau; **for ~** pour rien

notice ['nəʊtɪs] *n* (*announcement, warning*) avis *m*; (*period of time*) délai *m*; (*resignation*) démission *f*; (*dismissal*) congé *m* ♦ *vt* remarquer, s'apercevoir de; **to take ~ of** prêter attention à; **to bring sth to sb's ~** porter qch à la connaissance de qn; **at short ~** dans un délai très court; **until further ~** jusqu'à nouvel ordre; **to hand in one's ~** donner sa démission, démissionner; **~able** *adj* visible; **~ board** (BRIT) *n* panneau *m* d'affichage

notify ['nəʊtɪfaɪ] *vt*: **to ~ sth to sb** notifier qch à qn; **to ~ sb (of sth)** avertir qn (de qch)

notion ['nəʊʃən] *n* idée *f*; (*concept*) notion *f*

notorious [nəʊ'tɔːrɪəs] *adj* notoire (*souvent en mal*)

nought [nɔːt] *n* zéro *m*

noun [naʊn] *n* nom *m*

nourish ['nʌrɪʃ] *vt* nourrir; **~ing** *adj* nourrissant(e); **~ment** *n* nourriture *f*

novel ['nɔvl] *n* roman *m* ♦ *adj* nouveau (nouvelle), original(e); **~ist** *n* romancier *m*; **~ty** *n* nouveauté *f*

November [nəʊ'vɛmbər] *n* novembre *m*

now [naʊ] *adv* maintenant ♦ *conj*: **~ (that)** maintenant que; **right ~** tout de suite; **by ~** à l'heure qu'il est; **just ~**: **that's the fashion just ~** c'est la mode en ce moment; **~ and then**, **~ and again** de temps en temps; **from ~ on** dorénavant; **~adays** *adv* de nos jours

nowhere ['nəʊwɛər] *adv* nulle part

nozzle ['nɔzl] *n* (*of hose etc*) ajutage *m*; (*of vacuum cleaner*) suceur *m*

nuclear ['njuːklɪər] *adj* nucléaire

nucleus ['njuːklɪəs] (*pl* **nuclei**) *n* noyau *m*

nude [njuːd] *adj* nu(e) ♦ *n* nu *m*; **in the ~** (tout(e)) nu(e)

nudge [nʌdʒ] *vt* donner un (petit) coup de coude à

nudist ['njuːdɪst] *n* nudiste *m/f*

nuisance ['njuːsns] *n*: **it's a ~** c'est (très) embêtant; **he's a ~** il est assommant *or* casse-pieds; **what a ~!** quelle barbe!

null [nʌl] *adj*: **~ and void** nul(le) et non avenu(e)

numb [nʌm] *adj* engourdi(e); (*with fear*) paralysé(e)

number ['nʌmbər] *n* nombre *m*; (*numeral*) chiffre *m*; (*of house, bank account etc*) numéro *m* ♦ *vt* numéroter; (*amount to*) compter; **a ~ of** un certain nombre de; **they were seven in ~** ils étaient (au nombre de) sept; **to be ~ed among** compter parmi; **~ plate** *n* (AUT) plaque *f* minéralogique *or* d'immatriculation

numeral ['njuːmərəl] *n* chiffre *m*

numerate ['njuːmərɪt] (BRIT) *adj*: **to be ~** avoir des notions d'arithmétique

numerical [njuː'mɛrɪkl] *adj* numérique

numerous ['njuːmərəs] *adj* nombreux(-euse)

nun [nʌn] *n* religieuse *f*, sœur *f*

nurse [nɜːs] *n* infirmière *f* ♦ *vt* (*patient, cold*) soigner

nursery ['nɜːsərɪ] *n* (*room*) nursery *f*; (*institution*) crèche *f*, pépinière *f*; (*for plants*) pépinière *f*; **~ rhyme** *n* comptine *f*, chansonnette *f* pour enfants; **~ school** *n* école maternelle; **~ slope** *n* (SKI) piste *f* pour débutants

nursing ['nɜːsɪŋ] *n* (*profession*) profession *f* d'infirmière; (*care*) soins *mpl*; **~ home** *n* clinique *f*, maison *f* de convalescence

nut [nʌt] *n* (*of metal*) écrou *m*; (*fruit*) noix *f*, noisette *f*; cacahuète *f*; **~crackers** *npl* casse-noix *m inv*, casse-noisette(s) *m*

nutmeg ['nʌtmɛg] *n* (noix *f*) muscade *f*

nutritious [njuː'trɪʃəs] *adj* nutritif(-ive),

nuts 479 **occupy**

nourrissant(e)

nuts [nʌts] (inf) adj dingue

nutshell ['nʌtʃel] n: **in a ~** en un mot

nutter ['nʌtər] (BRIT: inf) n: **he's a complete ~** il est complètement cinglé

nylon ['nailɔn] n nylon m ♦ adj de or en nylon

O, o

oak [əuk] n chêne m ♦ adj de or en (bois de) chêne

OAP (BRIT) n abbr = **old-age pensioner**

oar [ɔːr] n aviron m, rame f

oasis [əu'eisis] (pl **oases**) n oasis f

oath [əuθ] n serment m; (swear word) juron m; **under ~**, (BRIT) **on ~** sous serment

oatmeal ['əutmiːl] n flocons mpl d'avoine

oats [əuts] n avoine f

obedience [ə'biːdiəns] n obéissance f; **obedient** adj obéissant(e)

obey [ə'bei] vt obéir à; (instructions) se conformer à

obituary [ə'bitjuəri] n nécrologie f

object [n 'ɔbdʒikt, vb əb'dʒekt] n objet m; (purpose) but m, objet; (LING) complément m d'objet ♦ vi: **to ~ to** (attitude) désapprouver; (proposal) protester contre: **expense is no ~** l'argent n'est pas un problème; **he ~ed that** ... il a fait valoir or a objecté que ...; **I ~!** je proteste!; **~ion** [əb'dʒekʃən] n objection f; **~ionable** adj très désagréable; (language) choquant(e); **~ive** n objectif m ♦ adj objectif(-ive)

obligation [ɔbli'geiʃən] n obligation f, devoir m; **without ~** sans engagement; **obligatory** [ə'bligətəri] adj obligatoire

oblige [ə'blaidʒ] vt (force): **to ~ sb to do sth**forcer or obliger qn à faire; (do a favour) rendre service à, obliger; **to be ~d to sb for sth** être obligé(e) à qn de qch; **obliging** adj obligeant(e), servia-

ble

oblique [ə'bliːk] adj oblique; (allusion) indirect(e)

obliterate [ə'blitəreit] vt effacer

oblivion [ə'bliviən] n oubli m; **oblivious** adj: **oblivious of** oublieux (-euse) de

oblong ['ɔblɔŋ] adj oblong (oblongue) ♦ n rectangle m

obnoxious [əb'nɔkʃəs] adj odieux (-euse); (smell) nauséabond(e)

oboe ['əubəu] n hautbois m

obscene [əb'siːn] adj obscène

obscure [əb'skjuər] adj obscur(e) ♦ vt obscurcir; (hide: sun) cacher

observant [əb'zəːvənt] adj observateur(-trice)

observation [ɔbzə'veiʃən] n (remark) observation f; (watching) surveillance f

observatory [əb'zəːvətri] n observatoire m

observe [əb'zəːv] vt observer; (remark) faire observer or remarquer; **~r** n observateur(-trice)

obsess [əb'ses] vt obséder; **~ive** adj obsédant(e)

obsolete ['ɔbsəliːt] adj dépassé(e); démodé(e)

obstacle ['ɔbstəkl] n obstacle m; **~ race** n course f d'obstacles

obstinate ['ɔbstinət] adj obstiné(e)

obstruct [əb'strʌkt] vt (block) boucher, obstruer; (hinder) entraver

obtain [əb'tein] vt obtenir

obvious ['ɔbviəs] adj évident(e), manifeste; **~ly** adv manifestement; **~ly not!** bien sûr que non!

occasion [ə'keiʒən] n occasion f; (event) événement m; **~al** adj rare(e) or fait(e) de temps en temps; occasionnel(le); **~ally** adv de temps en temps, quelquefois

occupation [ɔkju'peiʃən] n occupation f; (job) métier m, profession f; **~al hazard** n risque m du métier

occupier ['ɔkjupaiər] n occupant(e)

occupy ['ɔkjupai] vt occuper; **to ~ o.s.**

in *or* **with doing** s'occuper à faire
occur [əˈkɔːʳ] *vi* (*event*) se produire;
(*phenomenon, error*) se rencontrer; **to
~ to sb** venir à l'esprit de qn; **~rence** *n*
(*existence*) présence *f*, existence *f*;
(*event*) cas *m*, fait *m*

ocean [ˈəuʃən] *n* océan *m*

o'clock [əˈklɔk] *adv*: **it is 5 ~** il est 5
heures

OCR *n abbr* = **optical character reader;
optical character recognition**

October [ɔkˈtəubəʳ] *n* octobre *m*

octopus [ˈɔktəpəs] *n* pieuvre *f*

odd [ɔd] *adj* (*strange*) bizarre, curieux
(-euse); (*number*) impair(e); (*not of a
set*) dépareillé(e); **60 ~** 60 et quelques;
at ~ times de temps en temps; **the ~
one out** l'exception *f*; **~ity** *n* (*person*)
excentrique *m/f*; (*thing*) curiosité *f*; **~-
job man** *n* homme à tout faire; **~
jobs** *npl* petits travaux divers; **~ly** *adv*
bizarrement, curieusement; **~ments**
npl (*COMM*) fins *fpl* de série; **~s** *npl* (*in
betting*) cote *f*; **it makes no ~s** cela n'a
pas d'importance; **at ~s** en désaccord;
~s and ends de petites choses

odour [ˈəudəʳ] (*US* **odor**) *n* odeur *f*

KEYWORD

of [ɔv, əv] *prep* **1** (*gen*) de; **a friend of
ours** un de nos amis; **a boy of 10** un
garçon de 10 ans; **that was kind of
you** c'était gentil de votre part
2 (*expressing quantity, amount, dates
etc*) de; **a kilo of flour** un kilo de farine; **how much of this do you need?**
combien vous en faut-il?; **there were 3
of them** (*people*) ils étaient 3; (*objects*)
il y en avait 3; **3 of us went** 3 d'entre
nous y sont allé(e)s; **the 5th of July** le
5 juillet
3 (*from, out of*) en, de; **a statue of
marble** une statue de *or* en marbre;
made of wood (fait) en bois

off [ɔf] *adj, adv* (*engine*) coupé(e); (*tap*)
fermé(e); (*BRIT: food: bad*) mauvais(e); (:

milk: *bad*) tourné(e); (*absent*) absent(e);
(*cancelled*) annulé(e) ♦ *prep* de; sur; **to
be ~** (*to leave*) partir, s'en aller; **to
be ~ sick** être absent pour cause de maladie; **a day ~** un jour de congé; **to
have an ~ day** n'être pas en forme; **he
had his coat ~** il avait enlevé son
manteau; **10% ~** (*COMM*) 10% de rabais; **~ the coast** au large de la côte;
I'm ~ meat je ne mange plus de viande, je n'aime plus la viande; **on the ~
chance** à tout hasard

offal [ˈɔfl] *n* (*CULIN*) abats *mpl*

off-colour [ˈɔfˈkʌləʳ] (*BRIT*) *adj* (*ill*) malade, mal fichu(e)

offence [əˈfɛns] (*US* **offense**) *n* (*crime*)
délit *m*, infraction *f*; **to take ~ at** se
vexer de, s'offenser de

offend [əˈfɛnd] *vt* (*person*) offenser,
blesser; **~er** *n* délinquant(e)

offense [əˈfɛns] (*US*) *n* = **offence**

offensive [əˈfɛnsɪv] *adj* offensant(e),
choquant(e), (*smell etc*) très déplai-
sant(e); (*weapon*) offensif(-ive) ♦ *n* (*MIL*)
offensive *f*

offer [ˈɔfəʳ] *n* offre *f*, proposition *f* ♦ *vt*
offrir, proposer; **"on ~"** (*COMM*) "en
promotion"; **~ing** *n* offrande *f*

offhand [ɔfˈhænd] *adj* désinvolte ♦ *adv*
spontanément

office [ˈɔfɪs] *n* (*place, room*) bureau *m*;
(*position*) charge *f*, fonction *f*; **doctor's
~** (*US*) cabinet (médical); **to take ~**
entrer en fonctions; **~ automation** *n*
bureautique *f*; **~ block** (*US* **office building**) *n* immeuble *m* de bureaux; **~
hours** *npl* heures *fpl* de bureau; (*US:
MED*) heures de consultation

officer [ˈɔfɪsəʳ] *n* (*MIL etc*) officier *m*;
(*also:* **police ~**) agent *m* (de police); (*of
organization*) membre *m* du bureau directeur

office worker *n* employé(e) de bureau

official [əˈfɪʃl] *adj* officiel(le) ♦ *n* officier
m; (*civil servant*) fonctionnaire *m/f*; em-
ployé(e)

officiate [əˈfɪʃɪeɪt] *vi* (*REL*) officier; **to ~**

officious

at a marriage célébrer un mariage

officious [ə'fɪʃəs] *adj* trop empressé(e)

offing [ɔfɪŋ] *n*: **in the ~** *(fig)* en perspective

off: ~-licence (BRIT) *n* (shop) débit *m* de vins et de spiritueux; **~-line** *adj, adv* (COMPUT) (en mode) autonome; (: switched off) non connecté(e); **~-peak** *adj* aux heures creuses; (electricity, heating, ticket) au tarif heures creuses; **~-putting** (BRIT) *adj* (remark) rébarbatif (-ive); (person) rebutant(e), peu engageant(e); **~-road vehicle** *n* véhicule *m* tout-terrain; **~-season** *adj, adv* hors-saison *inv*; **~set** (irreg) *vt* (counteract) contrebalancer, compenser; **~shoot** *n* (fig) ramification *f*, antenne *f*; **~shore** *adj* (breeze) de terre; (fishing) côtier (-ère); **~side** *n* (SPORT) hors jeu; (AUT: in Britain) de droite; (: in US, Europe) de gauche; **~spring** *n inv* progéniture *f*; **~stage** *adv* dans les coulisses; **~-the-peg** (US **off-the-rack**) *adv* en prêt-à-porter; **~white** *adj* blanc cassé *inv*

Un off-licence est un magasin où l'on vend de l'alcool (à emporter) aux heures où les pubs sont fermés. On peut également y acheter des boissons non alcoolisées, des cigarettes, des chips, des bonbons, des chocolats etc.

Oftel ['ɔftɛl] *n* organisme qui supervise les télécommunications

often ['ɔfn] *adv* souvent; **how ~ do you go?** vous y allez tous les combien?; **how ~ have you gone there?** vous y êtes allé combien de fois?

Ofwat ['ɔfwɔt] *n* organisme qui surveille les activités des compagnies des eaux

oh [əu] *excl* ô!, oh!, ah!

oil [ɔɪl] *n* huile *f*; (petroleum) pétrole *m*; (for central heating) mazout *m* ♦ *vt* (machine) graisser; (for storing) bidon *m* à huile;

~field *n* gisement *m* de pétrole; **~ filter** *n* (AUT) filtre *m* à huile; **~ painting** *n* peinture *f* à l'huile; **~ refinery** *n* raffinerie *f*; **~ rig** *n* derrick *m*; (at sea) plate-forme pétrolière; **~ slick** *n* nappe *f* de mazout; **~ tanker** *n* (ship) pétrolier *m*; (truck) camion-citerne *m*; **~ well** *n* puits *m* de pétrole; **~y** *adj* huileux (-euse); (food) gras(se)

ointment ['ɔɪntmənt] *n* onguent *m*

O.K., okay ['əu'keɪ] *excl* d'accord! ♦ *adj* (average) pas mal ♦ *vt* approuver; **is it ~?, are you ~?** ça va?

old [əuld] *adj* vieux (vieille); (person) vieux, âgé(e); (former) ancien(ne), vieux; **how ~ are you?** quel âge avez-vous?; **he's 10 years ~** il est âgé de 10 ans; **~er brother/sister** frère/sœur aîné(e); **~ age** *n* vieillesse *f*; **~ age pensioner** (BRIT) *n* retraité(e); **~-fashioned** *adj* démodé(e); (person) vieux jeu *inv*; **~ people's home** *n* maison *f* de retraite

olive ['ɔlɪv] *n* (fruit) olive *f*; (tree) olivier *m* ♦ *adj* (also: **~-green**) (vert) olive *inv*; **~ oil** *n* huile *f* d'olive

Olympic [əu'lɪmpɪk] *adj* olympique; **the ~ Games, the ~s** les Jeux *mpl* olympiques

omelet(te) ['ɔmlɪt] *n* omelette *f*

omen ['əumən] *n* présage *m*

ominous ['ɔmɪnəs] *adj* menaçant(e), inquiétant(e); (event) de mauvais augure

omit [əu'mɪt] *vt* omettre; **to ~ to do** omettre de faire

on [ɔn] *prep* **1** (indicating position) sur; **on the table** sur la table; **on the wall** sur le *or* au mur; **on the left** à gauche **2** (indicating means, method, condition etc): **on foot** à pied; **on the train/plane** (be) dans le train/l'avion; (go) en train/avion; **on the telephone/radio/television** au téléphone/à la radio/à la télévision; **to be on drugs** se droguer;

on holiday en vacances
3 (*referring to time*): **on Friday** vendredi; **on Fridays** le vendredi; **on June 20th** le 20 juin; **a week on Friday** vendredi en huit; **on arrival** à l'arrivée; **on seeing this** en voyant cela
4 (*about, concerning*) sur, de; **a book on Balzac/physics** un livre sur Balzac/de physique
♦ *adv* **1** (*referring to dress, covering*): **to have one's coat on** avoir (mis) son manteau; **to put one's coat on** mettre son manteau; **what's she got on?** qu'est-ce qu'elle porte?; **screw the lid on tightly** vissez bien le couvercle
2 (*further, continuously*): **to walk** *etc* **on** continuer à marcher *etc*; **on and off** de temps à autre
♦ *adj* **1** (*in operation: machine*) en marche; (: *radio, TV, light*) allumé(e); (: *tap, gas*) ouvert(e); (: *brakes*) mis(e); **is the meeting still on?** (*not cancelled*) est-ce que la réunion a bien lieu?; (*in progress*) la réunion dure-t-elle encore?; **when is this film on?** quand passe ce film?
2 (*inf*): **that's not on!** (*not acceptable*) cela ne se fait pas!; (*not possible*) pas question!

---

once [wʌns] *adv* une fois; (*formerly*) autrefois ♦ *conj* une fois que; **~ he had left/it was done** une fois qu'il fut parti/que ce fut terminé; **at ~** tout de suite, immédiatement; (*simultaneously*) à la fois; **~ a week** une fois par semaine; **~ more** encore une fois; **~ and for all** une fois pour toutes; **~ upon a time** il y avait une fois, il était une fois

oncoming ['ɔnkʌmɪŋ] *adj* (*traffic*) venant en sens inverse

KEYWORD

one [wʌn] *num* un(e); **one hundred and fifty** cent cinquante; **one day** un jour
♦ *adj* **1** (*sole*) seul(e); **the one**

book which l'unique *or* le seul livre qui; **the one man who** le seul (homme) qui
2 (*same*) même; **they came in the one car** ils sont venus dans la même voiture
♦ *pron* **1**: **this one** celui-ci (celle-ci); **that one** celui-là (celle-là); **I've already got one/a red one** j'en ai déjà un(e)/un(e) rouge; **one by one** un(e) à *or* par un(e)
2: **one another** l'un(e) l'autre; **to look at one another** se regarder
3 (*impersonal*) on; **one never knows** on ne sait jamais; **to cut one's finger** se couper le doigt

one: **~-day excursion** (*US*) *n* billet *m* d'aller-retour (valable pour la journée); **~-man** (*business*) dirigé(e) *etc* par un seul homme; **~-man band** *n* homme-orchestre *m*; **~-off** (*BRIT: inf*) *n* exemplaire *m* unique
oneself [wʌn'self] *pron* (*reflexive*) se; (*after prep*) soi(-même); (*emphatic*) soi-même; **to hurt ~** se faire mal; **to keep sth for ~** garder qch pour soi; **to talk to ~** se parler à soi-même
one: **~-sided** *adj* (*argument*) unilatéral; **~-to-~** *adj* (*relationship*) univoque; **~-way** *adj* (*street, traffic*) à sens unique
ongoing ['ɔngəʊɪŋ] *adj* en cours; (*relationship*) suivi(e)
onion ['ʌnjən] *n* oignon *m*
on-line *adj* (*also: COMPUT*) en ligne; (: *switched on*) connecté(e); **to go ~** se mettre en mode interactif
onlooker ['ɔnlʊkə*] *n* spectateur(-trice)
only ['əʊnlɪ] *adv* seulement ♦ *adj* seul(e), unique ♦ *conj* seulement, mais; **an ~ child** un enfant unique; **not ~ ...** **but also** non seulement ... (mais aussi)
onset ['ɔnsɛt] *n* début *m*; (*of winter, old age*) approche *f*
onshore ['ɔnʃɔː*] *adj* (*wind*) du large
onslaught ['ɔnslɔːt] *n* attaque *f*, assaut *m*
onto ['ɔntʊ] *prep* = **on to**

onward(s) ['ɔnwəd(z)] adv (move) en avant; **from that time ~** à partir de ce moment

ooze [uːz] vi suinter

opaque [əu'peɪk] adj opaque

OPEC ['əupɛk] n abbr (= Organization of Petroleum-Exporting Countries) O.P.E.P. f

open ['əupn] adj ouvert(e); (car) découvert(e); (road, view) dégagé(e); (meeting) public(-ique); (admiration) manifeste ♦ vt ouvrir ♦ vi (flower, eyes, door, debate) s'ouvrir; (shop, bank, museum) ouvrir; (book etc: commence) commencer, débuter; **in the ~ (air)** en plein air; **~ on to** vt fus (subj: room, door) donner sur; **~ up** vt ouvrir; (blocked road) dégager ♦ vi s'ouvrir; **~ing** n ouverture f; (opportunity) occasion f ♦ adj (remarks) préliminaires; **~ing hours** npl heures fpl d'ouverture; **~ly** adv ouvertement; **~-minded** adj à l'esprit ouvert; **~-necked** adj à col ouvert; **~-plan** adj sans cloisons

---
Open University

L'Open University a été fondée en 1969. Ce type d'enseignement comprend des cours (certaines plages horaires sont réservées à cet effet à la télévision et à la radio), des devoirs qui sont envoyés par l'étudiant à son directeur ou sa directrice d'études, et un séjour obligatoire en université d'été. Il faut couvrir un certain nombre d'unités de valeur pendant une période de temps déterminée et obtenir la moyenne à un certain nombre d'entre elles pour recevoir le diplôme visé.

---

opera ['ɔpərə] n opéra m; **~ singer** n chanteur(-euse) d'opéra

operate ['ɔpəreɪt] vt (machine) faire marcher, faire fonctionner ♦ vi fonctionner; (MED): **to ~ (on sb)** opérer (qn)

operatic [ɔpə'rætɪk] adj d'opéra

operating table n table f d'opération

operating theatre n salle f d'opération

operation [ɔpə'reɪʃən] n opération f; (of machine) fonctionnement m; **to be in ~** (system, law) être en vigueur; **to have an ~** (MED) se faire opérer

operative ['ɔpərətɪv] adj (measure) en vigueur

operator ['ɔpəreɪtə'] n (of machine) opérateur(-trice); (TEL) téléphoniste m/f

opinion [ə'pɪnjən] n opinion f, avis m; **in my ~** à mon avis; **~ated** adj aux idées bien arrêtées; **~ poll** n sondage m (d'opinion)

opponent [ə'pəunənt] n adversaire m/f

opportunity [ɔpə'tjuːnɪtɪ] n occasion f; **to take the ~ of doing** profiter de l'occasion pour faire; en profiter pour

oppose [ə'pəuz] vt s'opposer à; **~d to** opposé(e) à; **as ~d to** par opposition à; **opposing** adj (side) opposé(e)

opposite ['ɔpəzɪt] adj opposé(e); (house etc) d'en face ♦ adv en face ♦ prep en face de ♦ n opposé m, contraire m; **the ~ sex** l'autre sexe, le sexe opposé; **opposition** [ɔpə'zɪʃən] n opposition f

oppressive [ə'presɪv] adj (political regime) oppressif(-ive); (weather) lourd(e); (heat) accablant(e)

opt [ɔpt] vi: **to ~ for** opter pour; **to ~ to do** choisir de faire; **~ out** vi: **to ~ out of** choisir de ne pas participer à or de ne pas faire

optical ['ɔptɪkl] adj optique; (instrument) d'optique; **~ character recognition/reader** n lecture f/ lecteur m optique

optician [ɔp'tɪʃən] n opticien(ne)

optimist ['ɔptɪmɪst] n optimiste m/f; **~ic** [ɔptɪ'mɪstɪk] adj optimiste

option ['ɔpʃən] n choix m, option f; (SCOL) matière f à option; (COMM) option f; **~al** adj facultatif(-ive); (COMM)

or [ɔː'] conj ou; (with negative): **he hasn't seen ~ heard anything** il n'a

oral

rien vu ni entendu; ~ **else** sinon; ou bien

oral ['ɔːrəl] adj oral(e) ♦ n oral m

orange ['ɔrɪndʒ] n (fruit) orange f ♦ adj orange inv

orbit ['ɔːbɪt] n orbite f ♦ vt graviter autour de; ~**al** (motorway) n périphérique m

orchard ['ɔːtʃəd] n verger m

orchestra ['ɔːkɪstrə] n orchestre m; (US: seating) (fauteuils mpl d')orchestre

orchid ['ɔːkɪd] n orchidée f

ordain [ɔːˈdeɪn] vt (REL) ordonner

ordeal [ɔːˈdiːl] n épreuve f

order ['ɔːdər] n ordre m; (COMM) commande f ♦ vt ordonner; (COMM) commander; **in ~** en ordre; (document) en règle; **in (working) ~** en état de marche; **out of ~** (not in correct order) en désordre; (not working) en dérangement; **in ~ to do/that** pour faire/que +sub; **on ~** (COMM) en commande; **to ~ sb to do** ordonner à qn de faire; ~**form** n bon m de commande; ~**ly** n (MIL) ordonnance f; (MED) garçon m de salle ♦ adj (room) en ordre; (person) qui a de l'ordre

ordinary ['ɔːdnrɪ] adj ordinaire, normal(e); (pej) ordinaire, quelconque; **out of the ~** exceptionnel(le)

Ordnance Survey map ['ɔːdnəns-] n ≈ carte f d'État-Major

ore [ɔːr] n minerai m

organ ['ɔːgən] n organe m; (MUS) orgue m, orgues fpl; ~**ic** [ɔːˈgænɪk] adj organique; (food) biologique

organization [ˌɔːgənaɪˈzeɪʃən] n organisation f

organize ['ɔːgənaɪz] vt organiser; ~**r** n organisateur(-trice)

orgasm [ˈɔːgæzəm] n orgasme m

Orient ['ɔːrɪənt] n: **the ~** l'Orient m; **o~al** [ɔːrɪˈɛntl] adj oriental(e)

origin ['ɔrɪdʒɪn] n origine f

original [əˈrɪdʒɪnl] adj original(e); (earliest) originel(le) ♦ n original m; ~**ly** adv (at first) à l'origine

originate [əˈrɪdʒɪneɪt] vi: **to ~ from** (person) être originaire de; (suggestion) provenir de; **to ~ in** prendre naissance dans; avoir son origine dans

Orkney ['ɔːknɪ] n (also: **the ~ Islands**) les Orcades fpl

ornament ['ɔːnəmənt] n ornement m; (trinket) bibelot m; ~**al** [ɔːnəˈmɛntl] adj décoratif(-ive); (garden) d'agrément

ornate [ɔːˈneɪt] adj très orné(e)

orphan ['ɔːfn] n orphelin e

orthopaedic [ɔːθəˈpiːdɪk] (US **orthopedic**) adj orthopédique

ostensibly [ɔsˈtɛnsɪblɪ] adv en apparence

ostentatious [ɔstɛnˈteɪʃəs] adj prétentieux(-euse)

ostracize ['ɔstrəsaɪz] vt frapper d'ostracisme

ostrich ['ɔstrɪtʃ] n autruche f

other ['ʌðər] adj autre ♦ pron: **the ~ (one)** l'autre; ~**s** (~ people) d'autres; ~ **than** autrement que; à part; ~**wise** adv, conj autrement

otter ['ɔtər] n loutre f

ouch [autʃ] excl aïe!

ought [ɔːt] (pt **ought**) aux vb: **I ~ to do it** je devrais le faire, il faudrait que je le fasse; **this ~ to have been corrected** cela aurait dû être corrigé; **he ~ to win** il devrait gagner

ounce [auns] n once f (= 28.35g; 16 in a pound)

our [ˈauər] adj notre, nos pl; see also **my**; ~**s** pron le (la) nôtre, les nôtres; see also **mine**[1]; ~**selves** [auəˈsɛlvz] pron pl (reflexive, after preposition) nous; (emphatic) nous-mêmes; see also **oneself**

oust [aust] vt évincer

out [aut] adv dehors; (published, not at home etc) sorti(e); (light, fire) éteint(e); ~ **here** ici; ~ **there** là-bas; **he's ~** (absent) il est sorti; (unconscious) il est sans connaissance; **to be ~ in one's calculations** s'être trompé dans ses calculs; **to run/back** etc ~ sortir en courant/en reculant etc; ~ **loud** à haute voix; ~ **of**

(*~side*) en dehors de; (*because of: anger etc*) par; (*from among*): **~ of 10** sur 10; (*without*): **~ of petrol** sans essence, à court d'essence; **~ of order** (*machine*) en panne; (*TEL: line*) en dérangement; **~-and-** *adj* (*liar, thief etc*) véritable; **~back** *n* (*in Australia*): **the ~back** l'intérieur *m*; **~board** *n* (*also: ~board motor*) (moteur *m*) hors-bord *m*; **~break** *n* (*of war, disease*) début *m*; (*of violence*) éruption *f*; **~burst** *n* explosion *f*, accès *m*; **~cast** *n* exilé(e); (*socially*) paria *m*; **~come** *n* issue *f*, résultat *m*; **~crop** *n* (*of rock*) affleurement *m*; **~cry** *n* tollé (général); **~dated** *adj* démodé(e); **~do** (*irreg*) *vt* surpasser; **~door** *adj* de or en plein air; **~doors** *adv* dehors; au grand air

outer ['autər] *adj* extérieur(e); **~ space** *n* espace *m* cosmique

outfit ['autfit] *n* (*clothes*) tenue *f*

outing ['autɪŋ] *n* sortie *f*, excursion *f*

out: ~law *n* hors-la-loi *m inv* ♦ *vt* mettre hors-la-loi; **~lay** *n* dépenses *fpl*; (*investment*) mise *f* de fonds; **~let** *n* (*for liquid etc*) issue *f*, sortie *f*; (*US: ELEC*) prise *f* de courant; (*also: retail ~let*) point *m* de vente; **~line** *n* (*shape*) contour *m*; (*summary*) esquisse *f*, grandes lignes ♦ *vt* (*fig: theory, plan*) exposer à grands traits; **~live** *vt* survivre à; **~look** *n* perspective *f*; (*fig*) attitude *f*; **~lying** *adj* écarté(e); **~moded** *adj* démodé(e); dépassé(e); **~number** *vt* surpasser en nombre; **~of-date** (*passport*) périmé(e); (*theory etc*) dépassé(e); (*clothes etc*) démodé(e); **~-of-the-way** *adj* (*place*) loin de tout; **~patient** *n* malade *m/f* en consultation externe; **~post** *n* avant-poste *m*; **~put** *n* rendement *m*, production *f*; (*COMPUT*) sortie *f*

outrage ['autreɪdʒ] *n* (*anger*) indignation *f*; (*violent act*) atrocité *f*; (*scandal*) scandale *m* ♦ *vt* outrager; **~ous** [aut'reɪdʒəs] *adj* atroce; scandaleux(-euse)

outright [*adv* aut'raɪt, *adj* 'autraɪt] *adv* complètement; (*deny, refuse*) catégoriquement; (*ask*) carrément; (*kill*) sur le coup ♦ *adj* complet(-ète); catégorique

outset ['autset] *n* début *m*

outside [aut'saɪd] *n* extérieur *m* ♦ *adj* extérieur(e) ♦ *adv* (au) dehors, à l'extérieur ♦ *prep* hors de, à l'extérieur de; **at the ~** (*fig*) au plus or maximum; **~ lane** *n* (*AUT: in Britain*) voie *f* de droite; (*: in US, Europe*) voie de gauche; **~ line** *n* (*TEL*) ligne extérieure; **~r** *n* (*stranger*) étranger(-ère)

out: ~size ['autsaɪz] *adj* énorme; (*clothes*) grande taille *inv*; **~skirts** *npl* faubourgs *mpl*; **~spoken** *adj* très franc (franche); **~standing** *adj* remarquable, exceptionnel(le); (*unfinished*) en suspens; (*debt*) impayé(e); (*problem*) non réglé(e); **~stay** *vt*: **to ~stay one's welcome** abuser de l'hospitalité de son hôte; **~stretched** [aut'stretʃt] *adj* (*hand*) tendu(e); **~strip** [aut'strɪp] *vt* (*competitors, demand*) dépasser; **~ tray** *n* courrier *m* "départ"

outward ['autwəd] *adj* (*sign, appearances*) extérieur(e); (*journey*) (d')aller

outweigh [aut'weɪ] *vt* l'emporter sur

outwit [aut'wɪt] *vt* se montrer plus malin que

oval ['əuvl] *adj* ovale ♦ *n* ovale *m*

Oval Office

L'**Oval Office** est le bureau personnel du président des États-Unis à la Maison-Blanche, ainsi appelé du fait de sa forme ovale. Par extension, ce terme désigne la présidence elle-même.

ovary ['əuvərɪ] *n* ovaire *m*

oven ['ʌvn] *n* four *m*; **~proof** *adj* allant au four

over ['əʊvə^r] adv (par-)dessus ♦ adj (finished) fini(e), terminé(e); (too much) en plus ♦ prep sur; par-dessus; (above) au-dessus de; (on the other side of) de l'autre côté de; (more than) plus de; (during) pendant; ~ here ici; ~ there là-bas; all ~ (everywhere) partout, fini(e); ~ and ~ (again) à plusieurs reprises; ~ and above en plus de; to ask sb ~ inviter qn (à passer)

overall [adj, n 'əʊvərɔːl, adv əʊvər'ɔːl] adj (length, cost etc) total(e); (study) d'ensemble ♦ n (BRIT) blouse f ♦ adv dans l'ensemble, en général; ~s mpl bleus mpl (de travail)

over: ~awe vt impressionner; ~balance vi basculer; ~board adv (NAUT) par-dessus bord; ~book vi faire du surbooking; ~cast adj couvert(e)

overcharge [əʊvə'tʃɑːdʒ] vt: to ~ sb for sth faire payer qch trop cher à qn

overcoat ['əʊvəkəʊt] n pardessus m

overcome [əʊvə'kʌm] (irreg) vt (defeat) triompher de; (difficulty) surmonter

over: ~crowded adj bondé(e); ~do (irreg) vt exagérer; (overcook) trop cuire; to ~do it (work etc) se surmener; ~dose n dose excessive; ~draft n découvert m; ~drawn adj (account) à découvert; (person) dont le compte est à découvert; ~due adj en retard; (change, reform) qui tarde; ~estimate vt surestimer

overflow [əʊvə'fləʊ] vi déborder ♦ n (also: ~ pipe) tuyau m d'écoulement, trop-plein m

overgrown [əʊvə'grəʊn] adj (garden) envahi(e) par la végétation

overhaul [vb əʊvə'hɔːl, n 'əʊvəhɔːl] vt réviser ♦ n révision f

overhead [adv əʊvə'hɛd, adj, n 'əʊvəhɛd] adv au-dessus ♦ adj aérien(ne); (lighting) vertical(e) ♦ n (US) = **overheads**; ~s npl (expenses) frais mpl généraux; ~ projector n rétroprojecteur m

over: ~hear (irreg) vt entendre (par

hasard); ~heat vi (engine) chauffer; ~joyed adj: ~joyed (at) ravi(e) (de), enchanté(e) (de)

overland ['əʊvəlænd] adj, adv par voie de terre

overlap [əʊvə'læp] vi se chevaucher

over: ~leaf adv au verso; ~load vt surcharger; ~look vt (have view of) donner sur; (miss: by mistake) oublier; (forgive) fermer les yeux sur

overnight [adv əʊvə'naɪt, adj 'əʊvənaɪt] adv (happen) durant la nuit; (fig) soudain ♦ adj d'une (de jour) nuit; he stayed there ~ il y a passé la nuit

overpass ['əʊvəpɑːs] n pont autoroutier

overpower [əʊvə'paʊə^r] vt vaincre; (fig) accabler; ~ing adj (heat, stench) suffocant(e)

over: ~rate vt surestimer; ~ride (irreg: like ride) vt (order, objection) passer outre à; ~riding adj prépondérant(e); ~rule vt (decision) annuler; (claim) rejeter; (person) rejeter l'avis de; ~run (irreg: like run) vt (country) occuper; (time limit) dépasser

overseas [əʊvə'siːz] adv outre-mer; (abroad) à l'étranger ♦ adj (trade) extérieur(e); (visitor) étranger(-ère)

overshadow [əʊvə'ʃædəʊ] vt (fig) éclipser

oversight ['əʊvəsaɪt] n omission f, oubli m

oversleep [əʊvə'sliːp] (irreg) vi se réveiller (trop) tard

overstep [əʊvə'stɛp] vt: to ~ the mark dépasser la mesure

overt [əʊ'vɜːt] adj non dissimulé(e)

overtake [əʊvə'teɪk] (irreg) vt (AUT) dépasser, doubler

over: ~throw (irreg) vt (government) renverser; ~time n heures fpl supplémentaires; ~tone n (also: ~tones) note f, sous-entendus mpl

overture ['əʊvətʃʊə^r] n (MUS, fig) ouverture f

over: ~turn vt renverser ♦ vi se retour-

ner; **~weight** adj (person) trop
gros(se); **~whelm** vt (subj: emotion) accabler; (enemy, opponent) écraser;
~whelming adj (victory, defeat) écra-
sant(e); (desire) irrésistible

overwrought [ǝʊvǝ'rɔːt] adj excédé(e)

owe [ǝʊ] vt: **to ~ sb sth, to ~ sth to**
sb devoir qch à qn; **owing to** prep à
cause de, en raison de

owl [aʊl] n hibou m

own [ǝʊn] vt posséder ♦ adj propre; **a**
room of my ~ une chambre à moi,
ma propre chambre; **to get one's ~**
back prendre sa revanche; **on one's ~**
tout(e) seul(e); **~ up** vi avouer; **~er** n
propriétaire m/f; **~ership** n possession f

ox [ɔks] (pl **~en**) n bœuf m; **~tail** n:
~tail soup soupe f à la queue de bœuf

oxygen ['ɔksɪdʒǝn] n oxygène m

oyster ['ɔɪstǝ*] n huître f

oz. abbr = **ounce(s)**

ozone ['ǝʊzǝʊn] n: **~-friendly** adj qui
n'attaque pas or qui préserve la couche
d'ozone; **~ hole** n trou m d'ozone; **~**
layer n couche f d'ozone

P, p

p abbr = **penny**; **pence**

PA n abbr = **personal assistant**; **public
address system**

pa [pɑː] (inf) n papa m

p.a. abbr = **per annum**

pace [peɪs] n pas m; (speed) allure f; vitesse f ♦ vi: **to ~ up and down** faire les
cent pas; **to keep ~ with** aller à la
même vitesse que; **~maker** n (MED) sti-
mulateur m cardiaque; (SPORT: also:
~setter) meneur(-euse) de train

Pacific [pǝ'sɪfɪk] n: **the ~ (Ocean)** le
Pacifique, l'océan m Pacifique

pack [pæk] n (~et, US: of cigarettes) paquet m; (of hounds) meute f; (of thieves
etc) bande f; (back ~) sac m à dos; (of
cards) jeu m ♦ vt (goods) empaqueter,
emballer; (box) remplir; (cram) entasser;

to ~ one's suitcase faire sa valise; **to
~ (one's bags)** faire ses bagages; **to ~
sb off** expédier qn à qn; **~ it in!** laisse
tomber!, écrase!

package ['pækɪdʒ] n paquet m; (also: ~
deal) forfait m; **~ tour** (BRIT) n voyage
organisé

packed adj (crowded) bondé(e); **~
lunch** (BRIT) n repas froid

packet ['pækɪt] n paquet m

packing ['pækɪŋ] n emballage m; **~
case** n caisse f (d'emballage)

pact [pækt] n pacte m; traité m

pad [pæd] n bloc(-notes) m; (to prevent
friction) tampon m; (inf: home) piaule f
♦ vt rembourrer; **~ding** n rembourrage
m

paddle ['pædl] n (oar) pagaie f; (US: for
table tennis) raquette f de ping-pong
♦ vt: **to ~ a canoe** etc pagayer ♦ vi barboter, faire trempette; **paddling pool**
(BRIT) n petit bassin

paddock ['pædǝk] n enclos m; (RACING)
paddock m

padlock ['pædlɔk] n cadenas m

paediatrics [piːdɪ'ætrɪks] (US **pediatrics**) n pédiatrie f

pagan ['peɪgǝn] adj, n païen(ne)

page [peɪdʒ] n (of book) page f; (also: ~
boy) groom m, chasseur m; (at wedding) garçon m d'honneur ♦ vt (in hotel
etc) faire appeler

pageant ['pædʒǝnt] n spectacle m historique; **~ry** n apparat m, pompe f

pager ['peɪdʒǝ*] n (TEL) récepteur m
d'appels

paging device ['peɪdʒɪŋ-] n (TEL) récepteur
m d'appels

paid [peɪd] pt, pp of **pay** ♦ adj (work,
official) rémunéré(e); (holiday) payé(e);
to put a ~ to (BRIT) mettre fin à, régler

pail [peɪl] n seau m

pain [peɪn] n douleur f; **to be in ~**
souffrir, avoir mal; **to take ~s to do** se
donner du mal pour faire; **~ed** adj pei-
né(e), chagrin(e); **~ful** adj doulou-
reux(-euse); (fig) difficile, pénible;
~fully adv (fig: very) terriblement; **~-
killer** n analgésique m; **~less** adj indo-

lore; **~staking** ['peɪnzteɪkɪŋ] *adj* (person) soigneux(-euse); (work) soigné(e)

paint [peɪnt] *n* peinture *f* ♦ *vt* peindre; **to ~ the door blue** peindre la porte en bleu; **~brush** *n* pinceau *m*; **~er** *n* peintre *m*; **~ing** *n* peinture *f*; (picture) tableau *m*; **~work** *n* peinture *f*

pair [pεər] *n* (of shoes, gloves etc) paire *f*; (of people) couple *m*; **~ of scissors** (paire de) ciseaux *mpl*; **~ of trousers** pantalon *m*

pajamas [pə'dʒɑːməz] (US) *npl* pyjama(s) *m(pl)*

Pakistan [pɑːkɪ'stɑːn] *n* Pakistan *m*; **~i** *adj* pakistanais(e) ♦ *n* Pakistanais(e)

pal [pæl] (*inf*) *n* copain (copine)

palace ['pæləs] *n* palais *m*

palatable ['pælɪtəbl] *adj* bon (bonne), agréable au goût

palate ['pælɪt] *n* palais *m* (ANAT)

pale [peɪl] *adj* pâle ♦ *n*: **beyond the ~** (behaviour) inacceptable; **to grow ~** pâlir

Palestine ['pælɪstaɪn] *n* Palestine *f*; **Palestinian** [pælɪs'tɪnɪən] *adj* palestinien(ne) ♦ *n* Palestinien(ne)

palette ['pælɪt] *n* palette *f*

pall [pɔːl] *n* (of smoke) voile *m* ♦ *vi* devenir lassant(e)

pallet ['pælɪt] *n* (for goods) palette *f*

pallid ['pælɪd] *adj* blême

palm [pɑːm] *n* (of hand) paume *f*; (also: **~ tree**) palmier *m* ♦ *vt*: **to ~ sth off on sb** (*inf*) refiler qch à qn; **P~ Sunday** *n* le dimanche des Rameaux

paltry ['pɔːltrɪ] *adj* dérisoire

pamper ['pæmpər] *vt* gâter, dorloter

pamphlet ['pæmflət] *n* brochure *f*

pan [pæn] *n* (also: **saucepan**) casserole *f*; (also: **frying ~**) poêle *f*; **~cake** *n* crêpe *f*

panda ['pændə] *n* panda *m*

pandemonium [pændɪ'məʊnɪəm] *n* tohu-bohu *m*

pander ['pændər] *vi*: **to ~ to** flatter bassement; obéir servilement à

pane [peɪn] *n* carreau *m*, vitre *f*

panel ['pænl] *n* (of wood, cloth etc) panneau *m*; (RADIO, TV) experts *mpl*; (for interview, exams) jury *m*; **~ling** (US **paneling**) *n* boiseries *fpl*

pang [pæŋ] *n*: **~s of remorse/jealousy** affres *mpl* du remords/de la jalousie; **~s of hunger/conscience** tiraillements *mpl* d'estomac/de la conscience

panic ['pænɪk] *n* panique *f*, affolement *m* ♦ *vi* s'affoler, paniquer; **~ky** *adj* (person) qui panique *ou* s'affole facilement; **~-stricken** *adj* affolé(e)

pansy ['pænzɪ] *n* (BOT) pensée *f*; (*inf*: pej) tapette *f*, pédé *m*

pant [pænt] *vi* haleter

panther ['pænθər] *n* panthère *f*

panties ['pæntɪz] *npl* slip *m*

pantomime ['pæntəmaɪm] (BRIT) *n* spectacle *m* de Noël

pantomime

Une **pantomime**, *que l'on appelle également de façon familière "panto", est un genre de farce où le personnage principal est souvent un jeune garçon et où il y a toujours une* **dame**, *c'est-à-dire une vieille femme jouée par un homme, et un méchant. La plupart du temps, l'histoire est basée sur un conte de fées comme Cendrillon ou Le Chat botté, et le public est encouragé à participer en prévenant le héros d'un danger imminent. Ce genre de spectacle, qui s'adresse surtout aux enfants, vise également un public d'adultes au travers des nombreuses plaisanteries faisant allusion à des faits d'actualité.*

pantry ['pæntrɪ] *n* garde-manger *m* inv

pants [pænts] *npl* (BRIT: woman's) slip *m*; (: man's) slip, caleçon *m*; (US: trousers) pantalon *m*

pantyhose ['pæntɪhəʊz] (US) *npl* collant *m*

paper ['peɪpər] *n* papier *m*; (also: **wallpaper**) papier peint; (also: **newspaper**) journal *m*; *(academic essay)* article *m*; *(exam)* épreuve écrite ♦ *adj* en or de papier ♦ *vt* tapisser (de papier peint); **~s** *npl (also:* **identity ~s)** papiers (d'identité); **~back** *n* livre *m* de poche; livre broché or non relié; **~ bag** *n* sac *m* en papier; **~ clip** *n* trombone *m*; **~ hankie** *n* mouchoir *m* en papier; **~weight** *n* presse-papiers *m inv*; **~work** *n* papiers *mpl*; *(pej)* paperasserie *f*

par [pɑːʲ] *n* pair *m*; *(GOLF)* normale *f* du parcours; **on a ~ with** à égalité avec, au même niveau que

parachute [ˈpærəʃuːt] *n* parachute *m*

parade [pəˈreɪd] *n* défilé *m* ♦ *vt (fig)* faire étalage de ♦ *vi* défiler

paradise [ˈpærədaɪs] *n* paradis *m*

paradox [ˈpærədɔks] *n* paradoxe *m*; **~ically** [pærəˈdɔksɪklɪ] *adv* paradoxalement

paraffin [ˈpærəfɪn] *(BRIT) n (also:* **~ oil)** pétrole (lampant)

paragon [ˈpærəgən] *n* modèle *m*

paragraph [ˈpærəgrɑːf] *n* paragraphe *m*

parallel [ˈpærəlɛl] *adj* parallèle; *(fig)* semblable ♦ *n (line)* parallèle *f*; *(fig, GEO)* parallèle *m*

paralyse [ˈpærəlaɪz] *(BRIT) vt* paralyser; **paralysis** [pəˈrælɪsɪs] *n* paralysie *f*; **paralyze** *(US) vt* = **paralyse**

paramount [ˈpærəmaunt] *adj:* **of ~ importance** de la plus haute or grande importance

paranoid [ˈpærənɔɪd] *adj (PSYCH)* paranoïaque

paraphernalia [pærəfəˈneɪlɪə] *n* attirail *m*

parasol [ˈpærəsɔl] *n* ombrelle *f*; *(over table)* parasol *m*

paratrooper [ˈpærətruːpəʲ] *n* parachutiste *m (soldat)*

parcel [ˈpɑːsl] *n* paquet *m*, colis *m* ♦ *vt (also:* **~ up)** empaqueter

parchment [ˈpɑːtʃmənt] *n* parchemin *m*

pardon [ˈpɑːdn] *n* pardon *m*; grâce *f* ♦ *vt* pardonner à; **~ me!, I beg your ~!** pardon!, je suis désolé!; **(I beg your) ~?,** *(US)* **~ me?** pardon?

parent [ˈpɛərənt] *n* père *m* or mère *f*; **~s** *npl* parents *mpl*

Paris [ˈpærɪs] *n* Paris

parish [ˈpærɪʃ] *n* paroisse *f*; *(BRIT: civil)* ≃ commune *f*

Parisian [pəˈrɪzɪən] *adj* parisien(ne) ♦ *n* Parisien(ne)

park [pɑːk] *n* parc *m*, jardin public ♦ *vt* garer ♦ *vi* se garer

parking [ˈpɑːkɪŋ] *n* stationnement *m*; **"no ~"** "stationnement interdit"; **~ lot** *(US) n* parking *m*, parc *m* de stationnement; **~ meter** *n* parcomètre *m*; **~ ticket** *n* P.V. *m*

parliament [ˈpɑːləmənt] *n* parlement *m*; **~ary** [pɑːləˈmɛntərɪ] *adj* parlementaire

parlour [ˈpɑːləʲ] *(US* **parlor)** *n* salon *m*

parochial [pəˈrəukɪəl] *(pej) adj* à l'esprit de clocher

parole [pəˈrəul] *n:* **on ~** en liberté conditionnelle

parrot [ˈpærət] *n* perroquet *m*

parry [ˈpærɪ] *vt (blow)* esquiver

parsley [ˈpɑːslɪ] *n* persil *m*

parsnip [ˈpɑːsnɪp] *n* panais *m*

parson [ˈpɑːsn] *n* ecclésiastique *m*; *(Church of England)* pasteur *m*

part [pɑːt] *n* partie *f*; *(of machine)* pièce *f*; *(THEATRE etc)* rôle *m*; *(of serial)* épisode *m*; *(US: in hair)* raie *f* ♦ *adv* = **partly** ♦ *vt* séparer ♦ *vi (people)* se séparer; *(crowd)* s'ouvrir; **to take ~ in** participer à, prendre part à; **to take sth in good ~** prendre qch du bon côté; **to take sb's ~** prendre le parti de qn, prendre parti pour qn; **for my ~** en ce qui me concerne; **for the most ~** dans la plupart des cas; **~ with** *vt fus* se séparer de; **~ exchange** *(BRIT) n:* **in ~ exchange** en reprise

partial [ˈpɑːʃl] *adj (not complete)* partiel(le); **to be ~ to** avoir un faible pour

participate [pɑːˈtɪsɪpeɪt] *vi:* **to ~ in**

participer (à), prendre part (à); **participation** [pɑːtɪsɪ'peɪʃən] n participation f

participle ['pɑːtɪsɪpl] n participe m

particle ['pɑːtɪkl] n particule f

particular [pə'tɪkjʊləʳ] adj particulier (-ère); (special) spécial(e); (fussy) difficile; méticuleux(-euse); **~s** npl (details) détails mpl; (personal) nom, adresse etc; **in ~** en particulier; **~ly** adv particulièrement

parting ['pɑːtɪŋ] n séparation f; (BRIT: in hair) raie f ♦ adj d'adieu

partisan [pɑːtɪ'zæn] n partisan m ♦ adj partisan(e); de parti

partition [pɑːˈtɪʃən] n (wall) cloison f; (POL) partition f, division f

partly ['pɑːtlɪ] adv en partie, partiellement

partner ['pɑːtnəʳ] n partenaire m/f; (in marriage) conjoint(e); (boyfriend, girlfriend) ami(e); (COMM) associé(e); (at dance) cavalier(-ère); **~ship** n association f

partridge ['pɑːtrɪdʒ] n perdrix f

part-time ['pɑːt'taɪm] adj, adv à mi-temps, à temps partiel

party ['pɑːtɪ] n (POL) parti m; (group) groupe m, (LAW) partie f; (celebration) réception f, soirée f; fête f ♦ cpd (POL) de ou du parti; **~ dress** n robe habillée

pass [pɑːs] vt passer; (place) passer devant; (friend) croiser; (overtake) dépasser; (exam) être reçu(e) à, réussir; (approve) approuver, accepter ♦ vi passer; (SCOL) être reçu(e) ou admis(e), réussir ♦ n (permit) laissez-passer m inv; carte f d'accès ou d'abonnement; (in mountains) col m; (SPORT) passe f; (SCOL: also: ~ mark): **to get a ~** être reçu(e) (sans mention); **to make a ~ at sb** (inf) faire des avances à qn; **~ away** vi mourir; **~ by** vi passer ♦ vt négliger; **~ on** vt (news, object) transmettre; **~ out** vi s'évanouir; **~ up** vt (opportunity) laisser passer; **~able** adj (road) praticable; (work) acceptable

passage ['pæsɪdʒ] n (also: **~way**) couloir m; (gen, in book) passage m; (by

boat) traversée f

passbook ['pɑːsbʊk] n livret m

passenger ['pæsɪndʒəʳ] n passager (-ère)

passer-by [pɑːsə'baɪ] (pl **~s-~**) n passant(e)

passing ['pɑːsɪŋ] adj (fig) passager (-ère); **in ~** en passant; **~ place** n (AUT) aire f de croisement

passion ['pæʃən] n passion f; **~ate** adj passionné(e)

passive ['pæsɪv] adj (also LING) passif (-ive); **~ smoking** n tabagisme m passif

Passover ['pɑːsəʊvəʳ] n Pâque f (juive)

passport ['pɑːspɔːt] n passeport m; **~ control** n contrôle m des passeports; **~ office** n bureau m de délivrance des passeports

password ['pɑːswɜːd] n mot m de passe

past [pɑːst] prep (in front of) devant; (further than) au delà de, plus loin que; après; (later than) après ♦ adj passé(e); (president etc) ancien(ne) ♦ n passé m; **he's ~ forty** il a dépassé la quarantaine, il a plus de ou passé quarante ans; **for the ~ few/3 days** depuis quelques/3 jours; ces derniers/3 derniers jours; **ten/quarter ~ eight** huit heures dix/un ou et quart

pasta ['pæstə] n pâtes fpl

paste [peɪst] n pâte f; (meat ~) pâté m (à tartiner); (tomato ~) purée f, concentré m; (glue) colle f (de pâte) ♦ vt coller

pasteurized ['pæstʃəraɪzd] adj pasteurisé(e)

pastille ['pæstɪl] n pastille f

pastime ['pɑːstaɪm] n passe-temps m inv

pastry ['peɪstrɪ] n pâte f; (cake) pâtisserie f

pasture ['pɑːstʃəʳ] n pâturage m

pasty [n 'pæstɪ, adj 'peɪstɪ] n petit pâté (en croûte) ♦ adj (complexion) terreux (-euse)

pat [pæt] vt tapoter; (dog) caresser

patch [pætʃ] n (of material) pièce f; (eye

~) cache m; (spot) tache f; (on tyre) rustine f ♦ vt (clothes) rapiécer; **(to go through) a bad ~** (passer par) une période difficile; **~ up** vt réparer (grossièrement); **to ~ up a quarrel** se raccommoder; **~y** adj inégal(e); (incomplete) fragmentaire

pâté ['pæteɪ] n pâté m, terrine f

patent ['peɪtnt] n brevet m (d'invention) ♦ vt faire breveter ♦ adj patent(e), manifeste; **~ leather** n cuir verni

paternal [pə'tɜːnl] adj paternel(le)

path [pɑːθ] n chemin m, sentier m; (in garden) allée f; (trajectory) trajectoire f

pathetic [pə'θetɪk] adj (pitiful) pitoyable; (very bad) lamentable, minable

pathological [pæθə'lɔdʒɪkl] adj pathologique

pathway ['pɑːθweɪ] n sentier m, passage m

patience ['peɪʃns] n patience f; (BRIT: CARDS) réussite f

patient ['peɪʃnt] n malade m/f; (of dentist etc) patient(e) ♦ adj patient(e)

patio ['pætɪəʊ] n patio m

patriotic [pætrɪ'ɔtɪk] adj patriotique; (person) patriote

patrol [pə'trəʊl] n patrouille f ♦ vt patrouiller dans; **~ car** n voiture f de police; **~man** (irreg) (US) n agent m de police

patron ['peɪtrən] n (in shop) client(e); (of charity) patron(ne); **~ of the arts** mécène m; **~ize** ['pætrənaɪz] vt (pej) traiter avec condescendance; (shop, club) être (un) client ou un habitué de

patter ['pætər] n crépitement m, tapotement m; (sales talk) boniment m

pattern ['pætən] n (design) motif m; (SEWING) patron m

pauper ['pɔːpər] n indigent(e)

pause [pɔːz] n pause f, arrêt m ♦ vi faire une pause, s'arrêter

pave [peɪv] vt paver, daller; **to ~ the way for** ouvrir la voie à

pavement ['peɪvmənt] (BRIT) n trottoir m

~) pavillon m; tente f

paving ['peɪvɪŋ] n (material) pavé m, dalle f; **~ stone** n pavé m

paw [pɔː] n patte f

pawn [pɔːn] n (CHESS, also fig) pion m ♦ vt mettre en gage; **~broker** n prêteur m sur gages; **~shop** n mont-de-piété m

pay [peɪ] (pt, pp **paid**) n salaire m; paie f ♦ vt payer ♦ vi payer; (be profitable) être rentable; **to ~ attention (to)** prêter attention (à); **to ~ sb a visit** rendre visite à qn; **to ~ one's respects to sb** présenter ses respects à qn; **~ back** vt rembourser; **~ for** fus payer; **~ in** vt verser; **~ off** vt régler, acquitter; (person) rembourser ♦ vi (scheme, decision) se révéler payant(e); **~ up** vt (money) payer; **~able** adj: **~able to sb** (cheque) à l'ordre de qn; **~ee** [peɪˈiː] n bénéficiaire m/f; **~ envelope** (US) n = **pay packet**; **~ment** n paiement m; règlement m; **monthly ~ment** mensualité f; **~ packet** (BRIT) n paie f; **~ phone** n cabine f téléphonique, téléphone public; **~roll** n registre m du personnel; **~ slip** (BRIT) n bulletin m de paie; **~ television** n chaînes fpl payantes

PC n abbr = **personal computer**

p.c. abbr = **per cent**

pea [piː] n (petit) pois

peace [piːs] n paix f; (calm) calme m, tranquillité f; **~ful** adj paisible, calme

peach [piːtʃ] n pêche f

peacock ['piːkɔk] n paon m

peak [piːk] n (mountain) pic m, cime f; (of cap) visière f; (fig: highest level) maximum m; (: of career, fame) apogée m; **~ hours** npl heures fpl de pointe

peal [piːl] n (of bells) carillon m; **~ of laughter** éclat m de rire

peanut ['piːnʌt] n arachide f, cacahuète f; **~ butter** n beurre m de cacahuète

pear [pɛər] n poire f

pearl [pɜːl] n perle f

peasant ['pɛznt] n paysan(ne)

peat [pi:t] n tourbe f

pebble ['pɛbl] n caillou m, galet m

peck [pɛk] vt (also: ~ **at**) donner un coup de bec à ♦ n coup m de bec; (kiss) bise f; **~ing order** n ordre m des préséances; **~ish** (BRIT: inf) adj: **I feel ~ish** je mangerais bien quelque chose

peculiar [pɪ'kju:lɪə*] adj étrange, bizarre, curieux(-euse); **~ to** particulier(-ère) à

pedal ['pɛdl] n pédale f ♦ vi pédaler

pedantic [pɪ'dæntɪk] adj pédant(e)

peddler ['pɛdlə*] n (of drugs) revendeur(-euse)

pedestal ['pɛdəstl] n piédestal m

pedestrian [pɪ'dɛstrɪən] n piéton m; ~ **crossing** (BRIT) n passage clouté; **~ized** adj: **a ~ized street** une rue piétonne

pediatrics [pi:dɪ'ætrɪks] (US) n = **paediatrics**

pedigree ['pɛdɪgri:] n ascendance f; (of animal) pedigree m ♦ cpd (animal) de race

pee [pi:] (inf) vi faire pipi, pisser

peek [pi:k] vi jeter un coup d'œil (furtif)

peel [pi:l] n pelure f, épluchure f; (of orange, lemon) écorce f ♦ vt peler, éplucher ♦ vi (paint etc) s'écailler; (wallpaper) se décoller; (skin) peler

peep [pi:p] n (BRIT: look) coup d'œil furtif; (sound) pépiement m ♦ vi (look) jeter un coup d'œil (furtif); ~ **out** (BRIT) vi se montrer (furtivement); **~hole** n judas m

peer [pɪə*] vi: **to ~ at** regarder attentivement, scruter ♦ n (noble) pair m; (equal) pair, égal(e); **~age** ['pɪərɪdʒ] n pairie f

peeved [pi:vd] adj irrité(e), fâché(e)

peg [pɛg] n (for coat etc) patère f; (BRIT: also: **clothes ~**) pince f à linge

Pekin(g)ese [pi:kɪ'ni:z] n (dog) pékinois m

pelican ['pɛlɪkən] n pélican m; ~ **crossing** (BRIT) n (AUT) feu m à commande manuelle

pellet ['pɛlɪt] n boulette f; (of lead) plomb m

pelt [pɛlt] vt: **to ~ sb (with)** bombarder qn (de) ♦ vi (rain) tomber à seaux; (inf: run) courir à toutes jambes ♦ n peau f

pelvis ['pɛlvɪs] n bassin m

pen [pɛn] n (for writing) stylo m; (for sheep) parc m

penal ['pi:nl] adj pénal(e); (system, colony) pénitentiaire; **~ize** ['pi:nəlaɪz] vt pénaliser

penalty ['pɛnltɪ] n pénalité f; sanction f; (fine) amende f; (SPORT) pénalisation f; (FOOTBALL) penalty m; (RUGBY) pénalité f

penance ['pɛnəns] n pénitence f

pence [pɛns] (BRIT) npl of **penny**

pencil ['pɛnsl] n crayon m; ~ **case** n trousse f (d'écolier); ~ **sharpener** n taille-crayons m inv

pendant ['pɛndnt] n pendentif m

pending ['pɛndɪŋ] prep en attendant ♦ adj en suspens

pendulum ['pɛndjuləm] n (of clock) balancier m

penetrate ['pɛnɪtreɪt] vt pénétrer dans; pénétrer

penfriend ['pɛnfrɛnd] (BRIT) n correspondant(e)

penguin ['pɛŋgwɪn] n pingouin m

penicillin [pɛnɪ'sɪlɪn] n pénicilline f

peninsula [pə'nɪnsjulə] n péninsule f

penis ['pi:nɪs] n pénis m, verge f

penitentiary [pɛnɪ'tɛnʃərɪ] n prison f

penknife ['pɛnnaɪf] n canif m

pen name n nom m de plume, pseudonyme m

penniless ['pɛnɪlɪs] adj sans le sou

penny ['pɛnɪ] (pl **pennies** or (BRIT) **pence**) n penny m

penpal ['pɛnpæl] n correspondant(e)

pension ['pɛnʃən] n pension f; (from company) retraite f; **~er** (BRIT) n retraité(e); ~ **fund** n caisse f de pension; ~ **plan** n plan m de retraite

Pentagon

*Le **Pentagon** est le nom donné aux bureaux du ministère de la Défense américain, situés à Arlington en Virginie, à cause de la forme pentagonale du bâtiment dans lequel ils se trouvent. Par extension, ce terme est également utilisé en parlant du ministère lui-même.*

pentathlon [pɛn'tæθlən] n pentathlon m

Pentecost ['pɛntɪkɔst] n Pentecôte f

penthouse ['pɛnthaus] n appartement m (de luxe) (en attique)

pent-up ['pɛntʌp] adj (feelings) refoulé(e)

penultimate [pɛ'nʌltɪmət] adj avant-dernier(-ère)

people ['piːpl] npl gens mpl; personnes fpl; (inhabitants) population f; (POL) peuple m ♦ n (also: race) peuple m; **several** ~ **came** plusieurs personnes sont venues; ~ **say that** ... on dit que ...

pep up ['pɛp-] (inf) vt remonter

pepper ['pɛpər] n poivre m; (vegetable) poivron m ♦ vt (fig): **to** ~ **with** bombarder de; ~ **mill** n moulin m à poivre; ~**mint** n (sweet) pastille f de menthe

peptalk ['pɛptɔːk] (inf) n (petit) discours d'encouragement

per [pəː] prep par; ~ **hour** (miles etc) à l'heure; (fee) de l'heure; **kilo** etc le kilo etc; ~ **annum** par an; ~ **capita** par personne, par habitant

perceive [pə'siːv] vt percevoir; (notice) remarquer, s'apercevoir de

per cent adv pour cent; **percentage** n pourcentage m

perception [pə'sɛpʃən] n perception f; (insight) perspicacité f

perceptive [pə'sɛptɪv] adj pénétrant(e); (person) perspicace

perch [pəːtʃ] n (fish) perche f; (for bird) perchoir m ♦ vi: **to** ~ **on** se percher sur

percolator ['pəːkəleɪtər] n cafetière f (électrique)

percussion [pə'kʌʃən] n percussion f

perennial [pə'rɛnɪəl] adj perpétuel(le); (BOT) vivace

perfect [adj, n 'pəːfɪkt, vb pə'fɛkt] adj parfait(e) ♦ n (also: ~ **tense**) parfait m ♦ vt parfaire; mettre au point; ~**ly** adv parfaitement

perforate ['pəːfəreɪt] vt perforer, percer; **perforation** [pəːfə'reɪʃən] n perforation f

perform [pə'fɔːm] vt (carry out) exécuter; (concert etc) jouer, donner ♦ vi jouer; ~**ance** n représentation f, spectacle m; (of an artist) interprétation f; (SPORT) performance f; (of car, engine) fonctionnement m; (of company, economy) résultats mpl; ~**er** n artiste m/f, interprète m/f

perfume ['pəːfjuːm] n parfum m

perhaps [pə'hæps] adv peut-être

peril ['pɛrɪl] n péril m

perimeter [pə'rɪmɪtər] n périmètre m

period ['pɪərɪəd] n période f; (of history) époque f; (SCOL) cours m; (full stop) point m; (MED) règles fpl ♦ adj (costume, furniture) d'époque; ~**ic(al)** [pɪərɪ'ɔd-ɪk(l)] adj périodique; ~**ical** [pɪərɪ'ɔdɪk] n périodique m

peripheral [pə'rɪfərəl] adj périphérique ♦ n (COMPUT) périphérique m

perish ['pɛrɪʃ] vi périr; (decay) se détériorer; ~**able** adj périssable

perjury ['pəːdʒərɪ] n parjure m, faux serment

perk [pəːk] n avantage m accessoire, à-côté m; ~ **up** vi (cheer up) se ragaillardir; ~**y** adj (cheerful) guilleret(te)

perm [pəːm] n (for hair) permanente f

permanent ['pəːmənənt] adj permanent(e)

permeate ['pəːmɪeɪt] vi s'infiltrer ♦ vt s'infiltrer dans; pénétrer

permissible [pə'mɪsɪbl] adj permis(e), acceptable

permission [pə'mɪʃən] n permission f,

autorisation f

permissive [pə'mɪsɪv] adj tolérant(e), permissif(-ive)

permit [n 'pə:mɪt, vb pə'mɪt] n permis m ♦ vt permettre

perpendicular [pə:pən'dɪkjulə'] adj perpendiculaire

perplex [pə'pleks] vt (person) rendre perplexe

persecute ['pə:sɪkjuːt] vt persécuter

persevere [pə:sɪ'vɪə'] vi persévérer

Persian ['pə:ʃən] adj persan(e) ♦ n (LING) persan m; **the ~ Gulf** le golfe Persique

persist [pə'sɪst] vi: **to ~ (in doing)** persister or s'obstiner (à faire); **~ent** [pə'sɪstənt] adj persistant(e), tenace; **~ent vegetative state** état m végétatif persistant

person ['pə:sn] n personne f; **in ~** en personne; **~al** adj personnel(le); **~al assistant** n secrétaire privé(e); **~al column** n annonces personnelles; **~al computer** n ordinateur personnel; **~ality** [pə:sə'nælɪtɪ] n personnalité f; **~ally** adv personnellement; **to take sth ~ally** se sentir visé(e) (par qch); **~al organizer** n filofax m ℝ; **~al stereo** n Walkman ℝ m, baladeur m

personnel [pə:sə'nɛl] n personnel m

perspective [pə'spektɪv] n perspective f; **to get things into ~** faire la part des choses

Perspex ['pə:speks] ℝ n plexiglas ℝ m

perspiration [pə:spɪ'reɪʃən] n transpiration f

persuade [pə'sweɪd] vt: **to ~ sb to do sth** persuader qn de faire qch; **persuasion** [pə'sweɪʒən] n persuasion f; (creed) religion f

perverse [pə'və:s] adj pervers(e); (contrary) contrariant(e); **pervert** [n 'pə:və:t, vb pə'və:t] n perverti(e) ♦ vt pervertir; (words) déformer

pessimist ['pesɪmɪst] n pessimiste m/f; **~ic** [pesɪ'mɪstɪk] adj pessimiste

pest [pest] n animal m (or insecte m) nuisible; (fig) fléau m

pester ['pestə'] vt importuner, harceler

pet [pet] n animal familier ♦ cpd (favourite) favori(te) ♦ vt (stroke) caresser, câliner; **teacher's ~** chouchou m du professeur; **~ hate** bête noire

petal ['petl] n pétale m

peter out ['pi:tə-] (stream, conversation) tarir; (meeting) tourner court; (road) se perdre

petite [pə'ti:t] adj menu(e)

petition [pə'tɪʃən] n pétition f

petrified ['petrɪfaɪd] adj (fig) mort(e) de peur

petrol ['petrəl] (BRIT) n essence f; **four-star ~** super m; **~ can** n bidon m à essence

petroleum [pə'trəuliəm] n pétrole m

petrol: ~ pump (BRIT) n pompe f à essence; **~ station** (BRIT) n station-service f; **~ tank** (BRIT) n réservoir m d'essence

petticoat ['petɪkəut] n combinaison f

petty ['petɪ] adj (mean) mesquin(e); (unimportant) insignifiant(e), sans importance; **~ cash** n caisse f des dépenses courantes; **~ officer** n second-maître m

petulant ['petjulənt] adj boudeur (-euse), irritable

pew [pju:] n banc m (d'église)

pewter ['pju:tə'] n étain m

phantom ['fæntəm] n fantôme m

pharmacy ['fɑ:məsɪ] n pharmacie f

phase [feɪz] n phase f ♦ vt: **to ~ sth in/out** introduire/supprimer qch progressivement

PhD abbr = Doctor of Philosophy ♦ n abbr (title) ≃ docteur m (en droit or lettres etc.); ≃ doctorat m; (person) titulaire m/f d'un doctorat

pheasant ['feznt] n faisan m

phenomenon [fə'nɔmɪnən] (pl **phenomena**) n phénomène m

philosophical [fɪlə'sɔfɪkl] adj philosophique

philosophy [fɪ'lɔsəfɪ] n philosophie f

phobia [ˈfəubjə] n phobie f

phone [fəun] n téléphone m ♦ vt téléphoner; **to be on the ~** avoir le téléphone; *(be calling)* être au téléphone; **~ back** vt, vi rappeler; **~ up** vt téléphoner à ♦ vi téléphoner; **~ bill** n facture f de téléphone; **~ book** n annuaire m; **~ booth, ~ box** *(BRIT)* n cabine f téléphonique; **~ call** n coup m de fil or de téléphone; **~card** n carte f de téléphone; **~-in** *(BRIT)* n *(RADIO, TV)* programme m à ligne ouverte; **~ number** n numéro m de téléphone

phonetics [fəˈnɛtɪks] n phonétique f

phoney [ˈfəunɪ] adj faux (fausse), factice; *(person)* pas franc (franche), poseur(-euse)

photo [ˈfəutəu] n photo f; **~copier** n photocopieuse f; **~copy** n photocopie f ♦ vt photocopier; **~graph** n photographie f ♦ vt photographier; **~grapher** [fəˈtɔgrəfəʳ] n photographe m/f; **~graphy** [fəˈtɔgrəfɪ] n photographie f

phrase [freɪz] n expression f; *(LING)* locution f ♦ vt exprimer; **~ book** n recueil m d'expressions *(pour touristes)*

physical [ˈfɪzɪkl] adj physique; **~ education** n éducation f physique; **~ly** adv physiquement

physician [fɪˈzɪʃən] n médecin m

physicist [ˈfɪzɪsɪst] n physicien(ne)

physics [ˈfɪzɪks] n physique f

physiotherapist [fɪzɪəuˈθɛrəpɪst] n kinésithérapeute m/f

physiotherapy [fɪzɪəuˈθɛrəpɪ] n kinésithérapie f

physique [fɪˈziːk] n physique m, constitution f

pianist [ˈpiːənɪst] n pianiste m/f

piano [pɪˈænəu] n piano m

pick [pɪk] n *(tool: also: ~axe)* pic m, pioche f ♦ vt choisir; *(fruit etc)* cueillir; *(remove)* prendre; *(lock)* forcer; **take your ~** faites votre choix; **the ~ of** le *(la)* meilleur(e) de; **to ~ one's nose se mettre les doigts dans le nez; to ~ one's teeth se curer les dents; to ~ a**

quarrel with sb chercher noise à qn; **~ at** vt fus: **to ~ at one's food** manger du bout des dents, chipoter; **~ on** vt fus *(person)* harceler; **~ out** vt choisir; *(distinguish)* distinguer; **~ up** vi *(improve)* s'améliorer ♦ vt ramasser; *(collect)* passer prendre; *(AUT: give lift to)* prendre, emmener; *(learn)* apprendre; *(RADIO)* capter; **to ~ up speed** prendre de la vitesse; **to ~ o.s. up** se relever

picket [ˈpɪkɪt] n *(in strike)* piquet m de grève ♦ vt mettre un piquet de grève devant

pickle [ˈpɪkl] n *(also: ~s: as condiment)* pickles mpl; petits légumes macérés dans du vinaigre ♦ vt conserver dans du vinaigre or dans de la saumure; **to be in a ~** *(mess)* être dans le pétrin

pickpocket [ˈpɪkpɔkɪt] n pickpocket m

pick-up [ˈpɪkʌp] n *(small truck)* pick-up m inv

picnic [ˈpɪknɪk] n pique-nique m

picture [ˈpɪktʃəʳ] n image f; *(painting)* peinture f, tableau m; *(etching)* gravure f; *(photograph)* photo(graphie) f; *(drawing)* dessin m; *(film)* film m; *(fig)* description f; tableau m ♦ vt se représenter; **the ~s** *(BRIT: inf)* le cinéma; **~ book** n livre m d'images

picturesque [pɪktʃəˈrɛsk] adj pittoresque

pie [paɪ] n *(of fruit)* tarte f; *(of meat)* pâté m en croûte

piece [piːs] n morceau m; *(item)*: **a ~ of furniture/advice** un meuble/conseil ♦ vt: **to ~ together** rassembler; **to take to ~s** démonter; **~meal** adv *(irregularly)* au coup par coup; *(bit by bit)* par bouts; **~work** n travail m aux pièces

pie chart n graphique m circulaire, camembert m

pier [pɪəʳ] n jetée f

pierce [pɪəs] vt percer, transpercer; **~d** adj *(ears etc)* percé(e)

pig [pɪg] n cochon m, porc m

pigeon [ˈpɪdʒən] n pigeon m; **~hole** n casier m

piggy bank ['pɪgɪ-] n tirelire f
pig: **~headed** adj entêté(e), têtu(e);
~let n porcelet m, petit cochon; **~skin**
n peau m de porc; **~sty** n porcherie f;
~tail n natte f, tresse f
pike [paɪk] n (fish) brochet m
pilchard ['pɪltʃəd] n pilchard m (sorte
de sardine)
pile [paɪl] n (pillar, of books) pile f;
(heap) tas m; (of carpet) poils mpl ♦ vt
(also: ~ **up**) empiler, entasser ♦ vi (also:
~ **up**) s'entasser, s'accumuler; **to ~ into**
(car) s'entasser dans; **~s** npl hémorroïdes fpl; **~-up** n (AUT) télescopage m,
collision f en série
pilfering ['pɪlfərɪŋ] n chapardage m
pilgrim ['pɪlgrɪm] n pèlerin m
pill [pɪl] n pilule f
pillage ['pɪlɪdʒ] vt piller
pillar ['pɪlə*] n pilier m; **~ box** (BRIT) n
boîte f aux lettres (publique)
pillion ['pɪljən] n: **to ride ~** (on motorcycle) monter derrière
pillow ['pɪləʊ] n oreiller m; **~case** n
taie f d'oreiller
pilot ['paɪlət] n pilote m ♦ cpd (scheme
etc) pilote, expérimental(e) ♦ vt piloter;
~ light n veilleuse f
pimp [pɪmp] n souteneur m, maquereau m
pimple ['pɪmpl] n bouton m
pin [pɪn] n épingle f; (TECH) cheville f ♦
vt épingler; **~s and needles** fourmis
fpl; **to ~ sb down** (fig) obliger qn à répondre; **to ~ sth on sb** (fig) mettre
qch sur le dos de qn
PIN [pɪn] n abbr (= personal identification
number) numéro m d'identification personnel
pinafore ['pɪnəfɔː*] n tablier m
pinball ['pɪnbɔːl] n flipper m
pincers ['pɪnsəz] npl tenailles fpl; (of
crab etc) pinces fpl
pinch [pɪntʃ] n (of salt etc) pincée f ♦ vt
pincer; (inf: steal) piquer, chiper; **at a ~**
à la rigueur
pincushion ['pɪnkʊʃən] n pelote f à

épingles
pine [paɪn] n (also: ~ **tree**) pin m ♦ vi:
to ~ for s'ennuyer de, désirer ardemment; ~ **away** vi dépérir
pineapple ['paɪnæpl] n ananas m
ping [pɪŋ] n (noise) tintement m; **~-
pong** ® n ping-pong ® m
pink [pɪŋk] n (colour) rose m;
(BOT) œillet m, mignardise f
PIN (number) ['pɪn(-)] n code m confidentiel
pinpoint ['pɪnpɔɪnt] vt indiquer or localiser (avec précision); (problem) mettre
le doigt sur
pint [paɪnt] n pinte f (BRIT = 0.57l; US =
0.47l); (BRIT: inf) ≈ demi m
pioneer [paɪə'nɪə*] n pionnier m
pious ['paɪəs] adj pieux(-euse)
pip [pɪp] n (seed) pépin m; **the ~s** npl
(BRIT: time signal on radio) le(s) top(s)
sonore(s)
pipe [paɪp] n tuyau m, conduite f; (for
smoking) pipe f ♦ vt amener par tuyau;
~s npl (also: **bagpipes**) cornemuse f; ~
cleaner n cure-pipe m; ~ **dream** n
chimère f, château m en Espagne;
~line n pipe-line m; **~r** n joueur(-euse)
de cornemuse
piping ['paɪpɪŋ] adv: ~ **hot** très
chaud(e)
pique [piːk] n dépit m
pirate ['paɪrət] n pirate m; **~d** adj pira-
té(e)
Pisces ['paɪsiːz] n les Poissons mpl
piss [pɪs] (inf!) vi pisser; **~ed** adj (inf!)
(drunk) bourré(e)
pistol ['pɪstl] n pistolet m
piston ['pɪstən] n piston m
pit [pɪt] n trou m, fosse f; (also: **coal ~**)
puits m de mine; (quarry) carrière f ♦ vt:
to ~ one's wits against sb se mesurer à qn; **~s** npl (AUT) aire f de service
pitch [pɪtʃ] n (MUS) ton m; (BRIT: SPORT)
terrain m; (tar) poix f; (fig) degré m;
point m ♦ vt (throw) lancer ♦ vi (fall)
tomber; **to ~ a tent** dresser une tente;
~-black adj noir(e) (comme du cirage);

~ed battle n bataille rangée

pitfall ['pɪtfɔːl] n piège m

pith [pɪθ] n (of orange etc) intérieur m de l'écorce; **~y** adj piquant(e)

pitiful ['pɪtɪful] adj (touching) pitoyable

pitiless ['pɪtɪlɪs] adj impitoyable

pittance ['pɪtns] n salaire m de misère

pity ['pɪtɪ] n pitié f ♦ vt plaindre; **what a ~!** quel dommage!

pizza ['piːtsə] n pizza f

placard ['plækɑːd] n affiche f; (in march) pancarte f

placate [plə'keɪt] vt apaiser, calmer

place [pleɪs] n endroit m, lieu m; (proper position, job, rank, seat) place f; (home): **at/to his ~** chez lui ♦ vt (object) placer; (identify) situer; reconnaître; **to take ~** avoir lieu; **out of ~** (not suitable) déplacé(e), inopportun(e); **to change ~s with sb** changer de place avec qn; **in the first ~** d'abord, en premier

plague [pleɪg] n fléau m; (MED) peste f ♦ vt (fig) tourmenter

plaice [pleɪs] n inv carrelet m

plaid [plæd] n tissu écossais

plain [pleɪn] adj (in one colour) uni(e); (simple) simple; (clear) clair(e), évident(e); (not handsome) quelconque, ordinaire ♦ n plaine f; **~ chocolate** n chocolat m à croquer; **~ clothes** adj (police officer) en civil; **~ly** adv clairement; (frankly) carrément, sans détours

plaintiff ['pleɪntɪf] n plaignant(e)

plait [plæt] n tresse f, natte f

plan [plæn] n (scheme) projet m ♦ vt (think in advance) projeter; (prepare) organiser; (house) dresser les plans de, concevoir ♦ vi faire des projets; **to ~ to do** prévoir de faire

plane [pleɪn] n (AVIAT) avion m; (ART, MATH etc) plan m; (fig) niveau m, plan m; (tool) rabot m; (also: ~ **tree**) platane m ♦ vt raboter

planet ['plænɪt] n planète f

plank [plæŋk] n planche f

planner ['plænər] n planificateur(-trice); (town ~) urbaniste m/f

planning ['plænɪŋ] n planification f; **family ~** planning familial; **~ permission** n permis m de construire

plant [plɑːnt] n plante f; (machinery) matériel m; (factory) usine f ♦ vt planter; (bomb) poser; (microphone, incriminating evidence) cacher

plaster ['plɑːstər] n plâtre m; (also: **~ of Paris**) plâtre à mouler; (BRIT: also: **sticking ~**) pansement adhésif; **~ cast** (MED) plâtre; (cover): **to ~ with** couvrir de; **~ed** (inf) adj soûl(e)

plastic ['plæstɪk] n plastique m ♦ adj (made of ~) en plastique; **~ bag** n sac m en plastique

Plasticine ® ['plæstɪsiːn] n pâte f à modeler

plastic surgery n chirurgie f esthétique

plate [pleɪt] n (dish) assiette f; (in book) gravure f, planche f; (dental ~) dentier m

plateau ['plætəu] (pl **~s** or **~x**) n plateau m

plate glass n verre m (de vitrine)

platform ['plætfɔːm] n plate-forme f; (at meeting) tribune f; (stage) estrade f; (RAIL) quai m

platinum ['plætɪnəm] n platine m

platter ['plætər] n plat m

plausible ['plɔːzɪbl] adj plausible; (person) convaincant(e)

play [pleɪ] n (THEATRE) pièce f (de théâtre) ♦ n (game) jouer à; (team, opponent) jouer contre; (instrument) jouer de; (part, piece of music, note) jouer; (record etc) passer ♦ vi jouer; **to ~ safe** ne prendre aucun risque; **~ down** vt minimiser; **~ up** vi (cause trouble) faire des siennes; **~boy** n playboy m; **~er** n joueur(-euse); (THEATRE) acteur(-trice); (MUS) musicien(ne); **~ful** adj enjoué(e); **~ground** n cour f de récréation; (in park) aire f de jeux; **~group** n garderie f; **~ing card** n carte f à jouer; **~ing**

field n terrain m de sport; **~mate** n camarade m/f, copain (copine) f; **~off** n (SPORT) belle f; **~ park** n terrain de jeu; **~pen** n parc m (pour bébé); **~thing** n jouet m; **~time** n récréation f; **~wright** n dramaturge m

plc abbr (= public limited company) SARL f

plea [pli:] n (request) appel m; (LAW) défense f

plead [pli:d] vt plaider; (give as excuse) invoquer ♦ vi (LAW) plaider; (beg): **to ~ with sb** implorer qn

pleasant ['plɛznt] adj agréable; **~ries** npl (polite remarks) civilités fpl

please [pli:z] excl s'il te (or vous) plaît ♦ vt plaire à ♦ vi plaire; (think fit): **do as you ~** faites comme il vous plaira; **~ yourself!** à ta (or votre) guise!; **~d** adj: **~d** (with) content(e) (de); **~d to meet you** enchanté (de faire votre connaissance); **pleasing** adj plaisant(e), qui fait plaisir

pleasure ['plɛʒəʳ] n plaisir m; "**it's a ~**" "je vous en prie"

pleat [pli:t] n pli m

pledge [plɛdʒ] n (promise) promesse f ♦ vt engager; promettre

plentiful ['plɛntɪful] adj abondant(e), copieux(-euse)

plenty ['plɛntɪ] n: **~ of** beaucoup de; (bien) assez de

pliable ['plaɪəbl] adj flexible; (person) malléable

pliers ['plaɪəz] npl pinces fpl

plight [plaɪt] n situation f critique

plimsolls ['plɪmsəlz] (BRIT) npl chaussures fpl de tennis, tennis mpl

plinth [plɪnθ] n (of statue) socle m

P.L.O. n abbr (= Palestine Liberation Organization) OLP f

plod [plɔd] vi avancer péniblement; (fig) peiner

plonk [plɔŋk] (inf) n (BRIT: wine) pinard m, piquette f ♦ vt: **to ~ sth down** poser brusquement qch

plot [plɔt] n complot m, conspiration f;

(of story, play) intrigue f; (of land) lot m de terrain, lopin m ♦ vt (sb's downfall) comploter; (mark out) pointer; relever, déterminer ♦ vi comploter

plough [plau] (US **plow**) n charrue f ♦ vt (earth) labourer; **to ~ money into** investir dans; **~ through** vt fus (snow etc) avancer péniblement dans; **~man's lunch** (BRIT) n assiette froide avec du pain, du fromage et des pickles

ploy [plɔɪ] n stratagème m

pluck [plʌk] vt (fruit) cueillir; (musical instrument) pincer; (bird) plumer; (eyebrow) épiler ♦ n courage m, cran m; **to ~ up courage** prendre son courage à deux mains

plug [plʌg] n (ELEC) prise f de courant; (stopper) bouchon m, bonde f; (AUT: also: **spark(ing)** ~) bougie f ♦ vt (hole) boucher; (inf: advertise) faire de la battage pour; **~ in** (ELEC) brancher

plum [plʌm] n (fruit) prune f ♦ cpd: **~ job** (inf) travail m en or

plumb [plʌm] vt: **to ~ the depths** (fig) toucher le fond (du désespoir)

plumber ['plʌməʳ] n plombier m

plumbing ['plʌmɪŋ] n (trade) plomberie f; (piping) tuyauterie f

plummet ['plʌmɪt] vi: **to ~ (down)** plonger, dégringoler

plump [plʌmp] adj rondelet(te), dodu(e), bien en chair ♦ vi: **to ~ for** (inf: choose) se décider pour

plunder ['plʌndəʳ] n pillage m; (loot) butin m ♦ vt piller

plunge [plʌndʒ] n plongeon m; (fig) chute f ♦ vt plonger ♦ vi (dive) plonger; (fall) tomber, dégringoler; **to take the ~** se jeter à l'eau; **plunging** ['plʌndʒɪŋ] adj: **plunging neckline** décolleté plongeant

pluperfect [plu:'pə:fɪkt] n plus-que-parfait m

plural ['pluərl] adj pluriel(le) ♦ n pluriel m

plus [plʌs] n (also: **~ sign**) signe m plus ♦ prep plus; **ten/twenty ~** plus de dix/vingt

plush [plʌʃ] *adj* somptueux(-euse)

ply [plaɪ] *vt* (*a trade*) exercer ♦ *vi* (*ship*) faire la navette ♦ *n* (*of wool, rope*) fil *m*, brin *m*; **to ~ sb with drink** donner continuellement à boire à qn; **to ~ sb with questions** presser qn de questions; **~wood** *n* contre-plaqué *m*

PM *abbr* = **Prime Minister**

p.m. *adv abbr* (= *post meridiem*) de l'après-midi

pneumatic drill [nju:'mætɪk-] *n* marteau-piqueur *m*

pneumonia [nju:'məunɪə] *n* pneumonie *f*

poach [pəutʃ] *vt* (*cook*) pocher; (*steal*) pêcher (*or* chasser) sans permis ♦ *vi* braconner; **~ed egg** *n* œuf poché; **~er** *n* braconnier *m*

P.O. box *n abbr* = **post office box**

pocket ['pɔkɪt] *n* poche *f* ♦ *vt* empocher; **to be out of ~** (*BRIT*) en être de sa poche; **~book** *n* (*US*) *n* (*wallet*) portefeuille *m*; **~ calculator** *n* calculette *f*; **~ knife** *n* canif *m*; **~ money** *n* argent *m* de poche

pod [pɔd] *n* cosse *f*

podgy ['pɔdʒɪ] *adj* rondelet(te)

podiatrist [pɔ'di:ətrɪst] (*US*) *n* pédicure *m/f*, podologue *m/f*

poem ['pəuɪm] *n* poème *m*

poet ['pəuɪt] *n* poète *m*; **~ic** [pəu'etɪk] *adj* poétique; **~ry** ['pəuɪtrɪ] *n* poésie *f*

poignant ['pɔɪnjənt] *adj* poignant(e); (*sharp*) vif (vive)

point [pɔɪnt] *n* point *m*; (*tip*) pointe *f*; (*in time*) moment *m*; (*in space*) endroit *m*; (*subject, idea*) point, sujet *m*; (*purpose*) sens *m*; (*ELEC*) prise *f*; (*also*: **decimal ~**): **2 ~ 3 (2.3)** 2 virgule 3 (2,3) ♦ *vt* (*show*) indiquer; (*gun etc*): **to ~ sth at** braquer *or* diriger qch sur ♦ *vi*: **to ~ at** montrer du doigt; **~s** *npl* (*AUT*) vis platinées; (*RAIL*) aiguillage *m*; **to be on the ~ of doing sth** être sur le point de faire qch; **to make a ~ of doing** ne pas manquer de faire; **to get the ~** comprendre, saisir; **to miss the ~** ne

pas comprendre; **to come to the ~** en venir au fait; **there's no ~ (in doing)** cela ne sert à rien (de faire); **~ out** *vt* faire remarquer, souligner; **~ to** *vt fus* (*fig*) indiquer; **~-blank** *adv* (*fig*) catégoriquement; (*also*: **at ~-blank range**) à bout portant; **~ed** *adj* (*shape*) pointu(e); (*remark*) plein(e) de sous-entendus; **~er** *n* (*needle*) aiguille *f*; (*piece of advice*) conseil *m*; (*clue*) indice *m*; **~less** *adj* inutile, vain(e); **~ of view** *n* point de vue

poise [pɔɪz] *n* (*composure*) calme *m*

poison ['pɔɪzn] *n* poison *m* ♦ *vt* empoisonner; **~ous** *adj* (*snake*) venimeux (-euse); (*plant*) vénéneux(-euse); (*fumes etc*) toxique

poke [pəuk] *vt* (*fire*) tisonner; (*jab with finger, stick etc*) piquer; pousser du coude; (*put*): **to ~ sth in(to)** fourrer *or* enfoncer qch dans; **~ about** *vi* fureter; **~r** *n* tisonnier *m*; (*CARDS*) poker *m*

Poland ['pəulənd] *n* Pologne *f*

polar ['pəulə'] *adj* polaire; **~ bear** *n* ours blanc

Pole [pəul] *n* Polonais(e)

pole [pəul] *n* poteau *m*; (*of wood*) mât *m*, perche *f*; (*GEO*) pôle *m*; **~ bean** (*US*) *n* haricot *m* (à rames); **~ vault** *n* saut à la perche

police [pə'li:s] *npl* police *f* ♦ *vt* maintenir l'ordre dans; **~ car** *n* voiture *f* de police; **~man** (*irreg*) *n* agent *m* de police, policier *m*; **~ station** *n* commissariat *m* de police; **~woman** (*irreg*) *n* femme-agent *f*

policy ['pɔlɪsɪ] *n* politique *f*; (*also*: **insurance ~**) police *f* (d'assurance)

polio ['pəulɪəu] *n* polio *f*

Polish ['pəulɪʃ] *adj* polonais(e) ♦ *n* (*LING*) polonais *m*

polish ['pɔlɪʃ] *n* (*for shoes*) cirage *m*; (*for floor*) cire *f*, encaustique *f*; (*shine*) éclat *m*, poli *m*; (*fig*: *refinement*) raffinement *m* ♦ *vt* (*put* ~ *on shoes, wood*) cirer; (*make shiny*) astiquer, faire briller; **~**

off (inf) vt (food) liquider; **~ed** adj (fig) raffiné(e)

polite [pə'laɪt] adj poli(e); **in ~ society** dans la bonne société; **~ly** adv poliment; **~ness** n politesse f

political [pə'lɪtɪkl] adj politique; **~ly correct** adj politiquement correct(e)

politician [pɔlɪ'tɪʃən] n homme m/femme f politique

politics ['pɔlɪtɪks] npl politique f

poll [pəul] n scrutin m, vote m; (also: **opinion ~**) sondage m (d'opinion) ♦ vt obtenir

pollen ['pɔlən] n pollen m

polling day ['pəulɪŋ-] (BRIT) n jour m des élections

polling station (BRIT) n bureau m de vote

pollute [pə'lu:t] vt polluer; **pollution** n pollution f

polo ['pəuləu] n polo m; **~-necked** adj à col roulé; **~ shirt** n polo m

polyester [pɔlɪ'estə*] n polyester m

polystyrene [pɔlɪ'staɪri:n] n polystyrène m

polythene ['pɔlɪθi:n] n polyéthylène m; **~ bag** n sac m en plastique

pomegranate ['pɔmɪɡrænɪt] n grenade f

pomp [pɔmp] n pompe f, faste m, apparat m; **~ous** adj pompeux(-euse)

pond [pɔnd] n étang m, mare f

ponder ['pɔndə*] vt considérer, peser; **~ous** adj pesant(e), lourd(e)

pong [pɔŋ] (BRIT: inf) n puanteur f

pony ['pəunɪ] n poney m; **~tail** n queue f de cheval; **~ trekking** (BRIT) n randonnée f à cheval

poodle ['pu:dl] n caniche m

pool [pu:l] n (of rain) flaque f; (pond) mare f; (also: **swimming ~**) piscine f; (billiards) poule f ♦ vt mettre en commun; **~s** npl (football ~s) ≈ loto sportif

poor [puə*] adj pauvre; (mediocre) médiocre, faible, mauvais(e) ♦ npl: **the ~** les pauvres mpl; **~ly** adj souffrant(e),

malade ♦ adv mal; médiocrement

pop [pɔp] n (MUS) musique f pop; (drink) boisson gazeuse; (US: inf: father) papa m; (noise) bruit sec ♦ vt (put) mettre (rapidement) ♦ vi éclater; (cork) sauter; **~ in** vi entrer en passant; **~ out** vi sortir (brièvement); **~ up** vi apparaître, surgir; **~corn** n pop-corn m

pope [pəup] n pape m

poplar ['pɔplə*] n peuplier m

popper ['pɔpə*] (BRIT: inf) n bouton-pression m

poppy ['pɔpɪ] n coquelicot m; pavot m

Popsicle ® ['pɔpsɪkl] (US) n esquimau m (glace)

popular ['pɔpjulə*] adj populaire; (fashionable) à la mode

population [pɔpju'leɪʃən] n population f

porcelain ['pɔːslɪn] n porcelaine f

porch [pɔːtʃ] n porche m; (US) véranda f

porcupine ['pɔːkjupaɪn] n porc-épic m

pore [pɔː*] n pore m ♦ vi: **to ~ over** s'absorber dans, être plongé(e) dans

pork [pɔːk] n porc m

porn [pɔːn] (inf) adj, n porno m

pornographic [pɔːnə'ɡræfɪk] adj pornographique

pornography [pɔː'nɔɡrəfɪ] n pornographie f

porpoise ['pɔːpəs] n marsouin m

porridge ['pɔrɪdʒ] n porridge m

port [pɔːt] n (harbour) port m; (NAUT: left side) bâbord m; (wine) porto m; **~ of call** escale f

portable ['pɔːtəbl] adj portatif(-ive)

porter ['pɔːtə*] n (for luggage) porteur m; (doorkeeper) gardien(ne); portier m

portfolio [pɔːt'fəulɪəu] n portefeuille m; (of artist) portfolio m

porthole ['pɔːthəul] n hublot m

portion ['pɔːʃən] n portion f, part f

portrait ['pɔːtreɪt] n portrait m

portray [pɔː'treɪ] vt faire le portrait de; (in writing) dépeindre, représenter; (subj: actor) jouer

Portugal ['pɔːtjuɡl] n Portugal m; Por-

tuguese [pɔːtjuˈgiːz] adj portugais(e) ♦ n inv Portugais(e); (LING) portugais m

pose [pəuz] n pose f ♦ vi (pretend): **to ~ as** se poser en ♦ vt poser; (problem) créer

posh [pɔʃ] (inf) adj chic inv

position [pəˈzɪʃən] n position f; (job) situation f ♦ vt placer

positive [ˈpɔzɪtɪv] adj positif(-ive); (certain) sûr(e), certain(e); (definite) formel(le), catégorique

possess [pəˈzɛs] vt posséder; **~ion** n possession f

possibility [pɔsɪˈbɪlɪtɪ] n possibilité f; éventualité f

possible [ˈpɔsɪbl] adj possible; **as big as ~** aussi gros que possible; **possibly** adv (perhaps) peut-être; **if you possibly can** si cela vous est possible; **I cannot possibly come** il m'est impossible de venir

post [pəust] n poste f; (BRIT: letters, delivery) courrier m; (job, situation, MIL) poste m; (pole) poteau m ♦ vt (BRIT: send by ~) poster; (: appoint): **to ~** affecter à; **~age** n tarifs mpl d'affranchissement; **~al order** n mandat(-poste) m; **~box** (BRIT) n boîte f aux lettres; **~card** n carte postale; **~code** (BRIT) n code postal

poster [ˈpəustər] n affiche f

poste restante [pəustˈrɛstɑ̃ːnt] (BRIT) n poste restante

postgraduate [pəustˈgrædjuət] n ≈ étudiant(e) de troisième cycle

posthumous [ˈpɔstjuməs] adj posthume

postman [ˈpəustmən] (irreg) n facteur m

postmark [ˈpəustmɑːk] n cachet m (de la poste)

postmortem [pəustˈmɔːtəm] n autopsie f

post office n (building) poste f; (organization): **the P~ O~** les Postes; **~ ~ box** n boîte postale

postpone [pəusˈpəun] vt remettre (à

plus tard)

posture [ˈpɔstʃər] n posture f; (fig) attitude f

postwar [pəustˈwɔːr] adj d'après-guerre

postwoman n factrice f

posy [ˈpəuzɪ] n petit bouquet

pot [pɔt] n pot m; (for cooking) marmite f; casserole f; (teapot) théière f; (coffeepot) cafetière f; (inf: marijuana) herbe f ♦ vt (plant) mettre en pot; **to go to ~** (inf: work, performance) aller à vau-l'eau

potato [pəˈteɪtəu] (pl **~es**) n pomme f de terre; **~ peeler** n épluche-légumes m inv

potent [ˈpəutnt] adj puissant(e); (drink) fort(e), très alcoolisé(e); (man) viril

potential [pəˈtɛnʃl] adj potentiel(le) ♦ n potentiel m

pothole [ˈpɔthəul] n (in road) nid m de poule; (BRIT: underground) gouffre m, caverne f; **potholing** (BRIT) n: **to go potholing** faire de la spéléologie

potluck [pɔtˈlʌk] n: **to take ~** tenter sa chance

pot plant n plante f d'appartement

potted [ˈpɔtɪd] adj (food) en conserve; (plant) en pot; (abbreviated) abrégé(e)

potter [ˈpɔtər] n potier m ♦ vi: **to ~ around**, **~ about** (BRIT) bricoler; **~y** n poterie f

potty [ˈpɔtɪ] adj (inf: mad) dingue ♦ n (child's) pot m

pouch [pautʃ] n (ZOOL) poche f; (for tobacco) blague f; (for money) bourse f

poultry [ˈpəultrɪ] n volaille f

pounce [pauns] vi: **to ~ (on)** bondir (sur), sauter (sur)

pound [paund] n (unit of money) livre f; (unit of weight) livre f ♦ vt (beat) bourrer de coups, marteler; (crush) piler, pulvériser ♦ vi (heart) battre violemment, taper

pour [pɔːr] vt verser ♦ vi couler à flots; **to ~ (with rain)** pleuvoir à verse; **to ~ sb a drink** verser or servir à boire à qn; **~ away** vt vider; **~ in** vi (people) affluer, se précipiter; (news, letters etc) arriver en masse; **~ off** vt = **pour away**; **~ out** vi (people) sortir en masse ♦ vt vider; (fig) déverser; (serve: a drink) verser; **~ing** ['pɔːrɪŋ] adj: **~ing rain** pluie f torrentielle

pout [paut] vi faire la moue

poverty ['pɔvətɪ] n pauvreté f, misère f; **~-stricken** adj pauvre, déshérité(e)

powder ['paudər] n poudre f ♦ vt: **to ~ one's face** se poudrer; **~ compact** n poudrier m; **~ed milk** n lait m en poudre; **~ room** n toilettes fpl (pour dames)

power ['pauər] n (strength) puissance f, force f; (ability, authority) pouvoir m; (of speech, thought) faculté f; (ELEC) courant m; **to be in ~** (POL etc) être au pouvoir; **~ cut** n coupure f de courant; **~ed** adj: **~ed by** actionné(e) par, fonctionnant à; **~ failure** n panne f de courant; **~ful** adj puissant(e); **~less** adj impuissant(e); **~ point** n (BRIT) prise f de courant; **~ station** n centrale f électrique; **~ struggle** n lutte f pour le pouvoir

p.p. abbr (= per procurationem): **p.p. J. Smith** pour M. J. Smith

PR n abbr = **public relations**

practical ['præktɪkl] adj pratique; **~ity** [præktɪ'kælɪtɪ] (no pl) n (of person) sens m pratique; **~ities** npl (of situation) aspect m pratique; **~ joke** n farce f; **~ly** adv (almost) pratiquement

practice ['præktɪs] n pratique f; (of profession) exercice m; (at football etc) entraînement m; (business) cabinet m ♦ vt, vi (US) = **practise**; **in ~** (in reality) en pratique; **out of ~** rouillé(e)

practise ['præktɪs] (US **practice**) vt (musical instrument) travailler; (train for: sport) s'entraîner à; (a lawyer, religion) pratiquer; (profession) exercer ♦ vi s'exercer, travailler; (train) s'entraîner; (lawyer, doctor) exercer; **practising** adj (Christian etc) pratiquant(e); (lawyer) en exercice

practitioner [præk'tɪʃənər] n prati-

cien(ne)

prairie ['prɛərɪ] n steppe f, prairie f

praise [preɪz] n éloge(s) m(pl), louange(s) f(pl) ♦ vt louer, faire l'éloge de; **~worthy** adj digne d'éloges

pram [præm] (BRIT) n landau m, voiture f d'enfant

prance [prɑːns] vi (also: **~ about**: person) se pavaner

prank [præŋk] n farce f

prawn [prɔːn] n crevette f (rose); **~ cocktail** n cocktail m de crevettes

pray [preɪ] vi prier; **~er** [prɛər] n prière f

preach [priːtʃ] vt, vi prêcher

precaution [prɪ'kɔːʃən] n précaution f

precede [prɪ'siːd] vt précéder

precedent ['prɛsɪdənt] n précédent m

preceding adj qui précède/précédait m

precinct ['priːsɪŋkt] n (US) circonscription f, arrondissement m; **~s** npl (neighbourhood) alentours mpl, environs mpl; **pedestrian ~** (BRIT) zone piétonnière or piétonne; **shopping ~** (BRIT) centre commercial

precious ['prɛʃəs] adj précieux(-euse)

precipitate [prɪ'sɪpɪteɪt] vt précipiter

precise [prɪ'saɪs] adj précis(e); **~ly** adv précisément

precocious [prɪ'kəuʃəs] adj précoce

precondition ['priːkən'dɪʃən] n condition f nécessaire

predecessor ['priːdɪsɛsər] n prédécesseur m

predicament [prɪ'dɪkəmənt] n situation f difficile

predict [prɪ'dɪkt] vt prédire; **~able** adj prévisible

predominantly [prɪ'dɔmɪnəntlɪ] adv en majeure partie; surtout

pre-empt [priː'ɛmt] vt anticiper, devancer

preen [priːn] vt: **to ~ itself** (bird) se lisser les plumes; **to ~ o.s.** s'admirer

prefab ['priːfæb] n bâtiment m préfabriqué

preface ['prɛfəs] n préface f

prefect ['pri:fekt] (BRIT) n (in school) élève chargé(e) de certaines fonctions de discipline

prefer [prɪ'fəːʳ] vt préférer; **~ably** ['prefrəblɪ] adv de préférence; **~ence** ['prefrəns] n préférence f; **~ential** [prefə'renʃəl] adj: **~ential treatment** traitement m de faveur or préférentiel

prefix ['pri:fɪks] n préfixe m

pregnancy ['prɛgnənsɪ] n grossesse f

pregnant ['prɛgnənt] adj enceinte; (animal) pleine

prehistoric ['pri:hɪs'tɔrɪk] adj préhistorique

prejudice ['prɛdʒudɪs] n préjugé m; **~d** adj (person) plein(e) de préjugés; (in a matter) partial(e)

premarital ['pri:'mærɪtl] adj avant le mariage

premature ['prɛmətʃuəʳ] adj prématuré(e)

premenstrual syndrome [priː'mɛnstruəl-] n syndrome prémenstruel

premier ['prɛmɪəʳ] adj premier(-ère), principal(e) ♦ n (POL) Premier ministre

première ['prɛmɪɛəʳ] n première f

Premier League n première division

premise ['prɛmɪs] n prémisse f; **~s** npl (building) locaux mpl; **on the ~s** sur les lieux; sur place

premium ['pri:mɪəm] n prime f; **to be at a ~** faire prime; **~ bond** (BRIT) n bon m à lot, obligation f à prime

premonition [prɛmə'nɪʃən] n prémonition f

preoccupied [pri:'ɔkjupaɪd] adj préoccupé(e)

prep [prɛp] n (SCOL) étude f

prepaid ['pri:'peɪd] adj payé(e) d'avance

preparation [prɛpə'reɪʃən] n préparation f; **~s** npl (for trip, war) préparatifs mpl

preparatory [prɪ'pærətərɪ] adj préliminaire; **~ school** (BRIT) n école primaire privée

prepare [prɪ'pɛəʳ] vt préparer ♦ vi: **to ~ for** se préparer à; **~d to** prêt(e) à

preposition [prɛpə'zɪʃən] n préposition f

preposterous [prɪ'pɔstərəs] adj absurde

prep school n = preparatory school

prerequisite [priː'rɛkwɪzɪt] n condition f préalable

Presbyterian [prɛzbɪ'tɪərɪən] adj, n presbytérien(ne)

prescribe [prɪ'skraɪb] vt prescrire; **prescription** [prɪ'skrɪpʃən] n (MED) ordonnance f; (: medicine) médicament (obtenu sur ordonnance)

presence ['prɛzns] n présence f; **~ of mind** présence d'esprit

present [adj, n 'prɛznt, vb prɪ'zɛnt] adj présent(e) ♦ n (gift) cadeau m; (actuality) présent m ♦ vt présenter; (prize, medal) remettre; (give): **to ~ sb with sth** or **sth to sb** offrir qch à qn; **to give sb a ~** offrir un cadeau à qn; **at ~** en ce moment; **~ation** [prɛzn'teɪʃən] n présentation f; (ceremony) remise f du cadeau (or de la médaille etc); **~-day** adj contemporain(e), actuel(le); **~er** n (RADIO, TV) présentateur(-trice); **~ly** adv (with verb in future) tout à l'heure, bientôt; (soon) tout à l'heure, bientôt; (at present) en ce moment

preservative [prɪ'zəːvətɪv] n agent m de conservation

preserve [prɪ'zəːv] vt (keep safe) préserver, protéger; (maintain) conserver, garder; (food) mettre en conserve ♦ n (often pl: jam) confiture f

president ['prɛzɪdənt] n président(e); **~ial** [prɛzɪ'dɛnʃl] adj présidentiel(le)

press [prɛs] n presse f; (for wine) pressoir m ♦ vt (squeeze) presser, serrer; (push) appuyer sur; (clothes: iron) repasser; (put ~ure on) faire pression sur; (insist): **to ~ sth on sb** presser qn d'accepter qch ♦ vi appuyer, peser; **to ~ for sth** faire pression pour obtenir qch; **we are ~ed for time/money** le

temps/l'argent nous manque; **~ on** *vi*
continuer; **~ conference** *n* conférence
f de presse; **~ing** *adj* urgent(e), pressant(e); **~ stud** (*BRIT*) *n* bouton-pression
m; **~-up** (*BRIT*) *n* traction *f*

pressure ['preʃər] *n* pression *f*; (*stress*)
tension *f*; **to put ~ on sb (to do)** faire
pression sur qn (pour qu'il/elle fasse); **~
cooker** *n* cocotte-minute *f*; **~ gauge** *n*
manomètre *m*; **~ group** *n* groupe *m* de
pression

prestige [pres'ti:ʒ] *n* prestige *m*; **prestigious** [pres'tɪdʒəs] *adj* prestigieux(-euse)

presumably [prɪ'zju:məblɪ] *adv* vraisemblablement

presume [prɪ'zju:m] *vt* présumer, supposer

pretence [prɪ'tens] (*US* **pretense**) *n*
(*claim*) prétention *f*; **under false ~s**
sous des prétextes fallacieux

pretend [prɪ'tend] *vt* (*feign*) feindre, simuler ♦ *vi* faire semblant

pretext ['pri:tekst] *n* prétexte *m*

pretty ['prɪtɪ] *adj* joli(e) ♦ *adv* assez

prevail [prɪ'veɪl] *vi* (*be usual*) avoir
cours; (*win*) l'emporter, prévaloir; **~ing**
adj dominant(e); **prevalent**
['prevələnt] *adj* répandu(e), courant(e)

prevent [prɪ'vent] *vt*: **to ~ (from
doing)** empêcher (de faire); **~ative**
[prɪ'ventətɪv], **~ive** [prɪ'ventɪv] *adj*
préventif(-ive)

preview ['pri:vju:] *n* (*of film etc*)
avant-première *f*

previous ['pri:vɪəs] *adj* précédent(e);
antérieur(e); **~ly** *adv* précédemment,
auparavant

prewar [pri:'wɔ:r] *adj* d'avant-guerre

prey [preɪ] *n* proie *f* ♦ *vi*: **to ~ on** s'attaquer à; **it was ~ing on his mind** cela
le travaillait

price [praɪs] *n* prix *m* ♦ *vt* (*goods*) fixer
le prix de; **~less** *adj* sans prix, inestimable; **~ list** *n* liste *f* des prix, tarif *m*

prick [prɪk] *n* piqûre *f* ♦ *vt* piquer; **to ~
up one's ears** dresser *or* tendre l'oreille

prickle ['prɪkl] *n* (*of plant*) épine *f*; (*sensation*) picotement *m*; **prickly** *adj* piquant(e), épineux(-euse); **prickly heat**
n fièvre *f* miliaire

pride [praɪd] *n* orgueil *m*; fierté *f* ♦ *vt*:
to ~ o.s. on se flatter de; s'enorgueillir
de

priest [pri:st] *n* prêtre *m*; **~hood** *n*
prêtrise *f*, sacerdoce *m*

prim [prɪm] *adj* collet monté *inv*, guindé(e)

primarily ['praɪmərɪlɪ] *adv* principalement, essentiellement

primary ['praɪmərɪ] *adj* (*first in importance*) premier(-ère), primordial(e),
principal(e) ♦ *n* (*US*: *election*) (élection *f*)
primaire *f*; **~ school** (*BRIT*) *n* école *f*
primaire *f*

prime [praɪm] *adj* primordial(e), fondamental(e); (*excellent*) excellent(e) ♦ *n*:
in the ~ of life dans la fleur de l'âge ♦
vt (*wood*) apprêter; (*fig*) mettre au courant; **P~ Minister** *n* Premier ministre
m

primeval [praɪ'mi:vəl] *adj* primitif(-ive);
~ forest *n* forêt *f* vierge

primitive ['prɪmɪtɪv] *adj* primitif(-ive)

primrose ['prɪmrəuz] *n* primevère *f*

primus (stove) ® ['praɪməs] (*BRIT*) *n*
réchaud *m* de camping

prince [prɪns] *n* prince *m*

princess [prɪn'ses] *n* princesse *f*

principal ['prɪnsɪpl] *adj* principal(e) ♦ *n*
(*headmaster*) directeur(-trice), principal
m

principle ['prɪnsɪpl] *n* principe *m*; **in/
on ~** en/par principe

print [prɪnt] *n* (*mark*) empreinte *f*; (*letters*) caractères *mpl*; (*ART*) gravure *f*, estampe *f*; (*: photograph*) photo *f* ♦ *vt* imprimer; (*publish*) publier; (*write in block
letters*) écrire en caractères d'imprimerie; **out of ~** épuisé(e); **~ed matter** *n*
imprimé(s) *m(pl)*; **~er** *n* imprimeur *m*;
(*machine*) imprimante *f*; **~ing** *n* impression *f*; **~-out** *n* copie *f* papier

prior ['praɪər] *adj* antérieur(e), précédent(e); (more important) prioritaire ♦ adv: **~ to doing** avant de faire; **~ity** [praɪˈɔrɪtɪ] n priorité f

prise [praɪz] vt: **to ~ open** forcer

prison [ˈprɪzn] n prison f ♦ cpd pénitentiaire; **~er** n prisonnier(-ère)

pristine [ˈprɪstiːn] adj parfait(e)

privacy [ˈprɪvəsɪ] n intimité f, solitude f

private [ˈpraɪvɪt] adj (personal) personnel(le); (house, lesson) particulier(-ère); (quiet: place) tranquille; (reserved: person) secret(-ète) ♦ n soldat m de deuxième classe; **"~"** (on envelope) "personnelle"; **in ~** en privé; **~ detective** n détective privé; **~ enterprise** n l'entreprise privée; **~ property** n propriété privée; **privatize** vt privatiser

privet [ˈprɪvɪt] n troène m

privilege [ˈprɪvɪlɪdʒ] n privilège m

privy [ˈprɪvɪ] adj: **to be ~ to** être au courant de

prize [praɪz] n prix m ♦ adj (example, idiot) parfait(e); (bull, novel) primé(e) ♦ vt priser, faire grand cas de; **~-giving** n distribution f des prix; **~winner** n gagnant(e)

pro [prəʊ] n (SPORT) professionnel(le); **the ~s and cons** le pour et le contre

probability [prɒbəˈbɪlɪtɪ] n probabilité f

probable [ˈprɒbəbl] adj probable; **probably** adv probablement

probation [prəˈbeɪʃən] n: **on ~** (LAW) en liberté surveillée, en sursis; (employee) à l'essai

probe [prəʊb] n (MED, SPACE) sonde f; (enquiry) enquête f, investigation f ♦ vt sonder, explorer

problem [ˈprɒbləm] n problème m

procedure [prəˈsiːdʒə'] n (ADMIN, LAW) procédure f; (method) marche f à suivre, façon f de procéder

proceed [prəˈsiːd] vi (go forward) avancer; **to ~ (with)** continuer, poursuivre; **to ~ to do sth** se mettre à faire; **~ings** npl (LAW) poursuites fpl; (meeting) réunion f, séance f ♦

['prəʊsiːdz] npl produit m, recette f

process [ˈprəʊses] n processus m; (method) procédé m ♦ vt traiter; **~ing** n (PHOT) développement m; **~ion** [prəˈseʃən] n défilé m, cortège m; (REL) procession f; **funeral ~ion** (on foot) cortège m funèbre; (in cars) convoi m mortuaire

proclaim [prəˈkleɪm] vt déclarer, proclamer

procrastinate [prəʊˈkræstɪneɪt] vi faire traîner les choses, vouloir tout remettre au lendemain

procure [prəˈkjʊə'] vt obtenir

prod [prɒd] vt pousser

prodigal [ˈprɒdɪgl] adj prodigue

prodigy [ˈprɒdɪdʒɪ] n prodige m

produce [n ˈprɒdjuːs, vb prəˈdjuːs] n (AGR) produits mpl ♦ vt produire; (to show) présenter; (cause) provoquer, causer; (THEATRE) monter, mettre en scène; **~r** n producteur m; (THEATRE) metteur m en scène

product [ˈprɒdʌkt] n produit m

production [prəˈdʌkʃən] n production f; (THEATRE) mise f en scène; **~ line** n chaîne f (de fabrication)

productivity [prɒdʌkˈtɪvɪtɪ] n productivité f

profession [prəˈfeʃən] n profession f; **~al** n professionnel(le) ♦ adj professionnel(le); (work) de professionnel; **~ally** adv professionnellement; (SPORT: play) en professionnel; **she sings ~ally** c'est une chanteuse professionnelle; **I only know him ~ally** je n'ai avec lui que des relations de travail

professor [prəˈfesə'] n professeur m (titulaire d'une chaire)

proficiency [prəˈfɪʃənsɪ] n compétence f, aptitude f

profile [ˈprəʊfaɪl] n profil m

profit [ˈprɒfɪt] n bénéfice m; profit m ♦ vi: **to ~ (by or from)** profiter (de); **~able** adj lucratif(-ive), rentable

profound [prəˈfaʊnd] adj profond(e)

profusely [prəˈfjuːslɪ] adv abondamment; avec effusion

prognosis [prɒg'nəʊsɪs] (pl **prognoses**) n pronostic m

programme ['prəʊgræm] (US **program**) n programme m; (RADIO, TV) émission f ♦ vt programmer; **~r** (US **programer**) n programmeur(-euse) f; **programming** (US **programing**) n programmation f

progress [n 'prəʊgres, vb prə'gres] n progrès m(pl) ♦ vi progresser, avancer; **in ~** en cours; **~ive** [prə'gresɪv] adj progressif(-ive); (person) progressiste

prohibit [prə'hɪbɪt] vt interdire, défendre

project [n 'prɒdʒekt, vb prə'dʒekt] n (plan) projet m, plan m; (venture) opération f, entreprise f; (research) étude f, dossier m ♦ vt projeter ♦ vi faire saillie, s'avancer; **~ion** n projection f; (overhang) saillie f; **~or** n projecteur m

prolong [prə'lɒŋ] vt prolonger

prom [prɒm] n abbr = **promenade**; (US: ball) bal m d'étudiants

promenade [prɒmə'nɑːd] n (by sea) esplanade f, promenade f; **~ concert** (BRIT) n concert m populaire (de musique classique)

---

promenade concert

En Grande-Bretagne, un **promenade concert** (ou **prom**) est un concert de musique classique, ainsi appelé car, à l'origine, le public restait debout et se promenait au lieu de rester assis. De nos jours, une partie du public reste debout, mais il y a également des places assises (plus chères). Les Proms les plus connus sont les Proms londoniens. La dernière séance (the Last Night of the Proms) est un grand événement médiatique où se jouent des airs traditionnels et patriotiques. Aux États-Unis et au Canada, le **prom** ou **promenade** est un bal organisé par le lycée.

---

prominent ['prɒmɪnənt] adj (standing out) proéminent(e); (important) important(e)

promiscuous [prə'mɪskjʊəs] adj (sexually) de mœurs légères

promise ['prɒmɪs] n promesse f ♦ vt, vi promettre; **promising** adj prometteur(-euse)

promote [prə'məʊt] vt promouvoir; (new product) faire la promotion de; **~r** n (of event) organisateur(-trice); (of cause, idea) promoteur(-trice); **promotion** n promotion f

prompt [prɒmpt] adj rapide ♦ adv (punctually) à l'heure ♦ n (COMPUT) message m (de guidage) ♦ vt provoquer; (person) inciter, pousser; (THEATRE) souffler (son rôle ou ses répliques) à; **~ly** adv rapidement, sans délai; ponctuellement

prone [prəʊn] adj (lying) couché(e) (face contre terre); **~ to** enclin(e) à

prong [prɒŋ] n (of fork) dent f

pronoun ['prəʊnaʊn] n pronom m

pronounce [prə'naʊns] vt prononcer; **pronunciation** [prənʌnsɪ'eɪʃən] n prononciation f

proof [pruːf] n preuve f; (TYP) épreuve f ♦ adj: **~ against** à l'épreuve de

prop [prɒp] n support m, étai m; (fig) soutien m ♦ vt (also: **~ up**) étayer, soutenir; (lean): **to ~ sth against** appuyer qch contre or à

propaganda [prɒpə'gændə] n propagande f

propel [prə'pel] vt propulser, faire avancer; **~ler** n hélice f

propensity [prə'pensɪtɪ] n: **a ~ for** or **to/to do** une propension à/à faire

proper ['prɒpər] adj (suited, right) approprié(e), bon (bonne); (seemly) correct(e), convenable; (authentic) vrai(e), véritable; (referring to place): **the village ~** le village proprement dit; **~ly** adv correctement, convenablement; **~ noun** n nom m propre

property ['prɒpətɪ] n propriété f;

(*things owned*) biens *mpl*; propriété(s) *f(pl)*; (*land*) terres *fpl*

prophecy ['prɒfɪsɪ] *n* prophétie *f*

prophesy ['prɒfɪsaɪ] *vt* prédire

prophet ['prɒfɪt] *n* prophète *m*

proportion [prə'pɔːʃən] *n* proportion *f*; (*share*) part *f*; partie *f*; **~al**, **~ate** *adj* proportionnel(le)

proposal [prə'pəuzl] *n* proposition *f*, offre *f*; (*plan*) projet *m*; (*of marriage*) demande *f* en mariage

propose [prə'pəuz] *vt* proposer, suggérer ♦ *vi* faire sa demande en mariage; **to ~ to do** avoir l'intention de faire; **proposition** [prɒpə'zɪʃən] *n* proposition *f*

proprietor [prə'praɪətə'] *n* propriétaire *m/f*

propriety [prə'praɪətɪ] *n* (*seemliness*) bienséance *f*, convenance *f*

prose [prəuz] *n* (*not poetry*) prose *f*

prosecute ['prɒsɪkjuːt] *vt* poursuivre; **prosecution** [prɒsɪ'kjuːʃən] *n* poursuites *fpl* judiciaires; (*accusing side*) partie plaignante; **prosecutor** *n* (*US: plaintiff*) plaignant(e); (*also*: **public prosecutor**) procureur *m*, ministère public

prospect [*n* 'prɒspɛkt, *vb* prə'spɛkt] *n* perspective *f* ♦ *vt*, *vi* prospecter; **~s** *npl* (*for work etc*) possibilités *fpl* d'avenir, débouchés *mpl*; **~ing** *n* (*for gold, oil etc*) prospection *f*; **~ive** *adj* (*possible*) éventuel(le); (*future*) futur(e)

prospectus [prə'spɛktəs] *n* prospectus *m*

prosperity [prɒ'spɛrɪtɪ] *n* prospérité *f*

prostitute ['prɒstɪtjuːt] *n* prostitué(e)

protect [prə'tɛkt] *vt* protéger; **~ion** *n* protection *f*; **~ive** *adj* protecteur(-trice); (*clothing*) de protection

protein ['prəutiːn] *n* protéine *f*

protest [*n* 'prəutɛst, *vb* prə'tɛst] *n* protestation *f* ♦ *vi*, *vt*: **to ~ (that)** protester (que)

Protestant ['prɒtɪstənt] *adj*, *n* protestant(e)

protester [prə'tɛstə'] *n* manifestant(e)

protracted [prə'træktɪd] *adj* prolongé(e)

protrude [prə'truːd] *vi* avancer, dépasser

proud [praud] *adj* fier(-ère); (*pej*) orgueilleux(-euse)

prove [pruːv] *vt* prouver, démontrer ♦ *vi*: **to ~ (to be) correct** *etc* s'avérer juste *etc*; **to ~ o.s.** montrer ce dont on est capable

proverb ['prɒvɜːb] *n* proverbe *m*

provide [prə'vaɪd] *vt* fournir; **to ~ sb with sth** fournir qch à qn; **~ for** *vt fus* (*person*) subvenir aux besoins de; (*future event*) prévoir; **~d (that)** *conj* à condition que +*sub*; **providing** *conj*: **providing (that)** à condition que +*sub*

province ['prɒvɪns] *n* province *f*; (*fig*) domaine *m*; **provincial** [prə'vɪnʃəl] *adj* provincial(e)

provision [prə'vɪʒən] *n* (*supplying*) fourniture *f*; approvisionnement *m*; (*stipulation*) disposition *f*; **~s** *npl* (*food*) provisions *fpl*; **~al** *adj* provisoire

proviso [prə'vaɪzəu] *n* condition *f*

provocative [prə'vɒkətɪv] *adj* provocateur(-trice), provocant(e)

provoke [prə'vəuk] *vt* provoquer

prowess ['prauɪs] *n* prouesse *f*

prowl [praul] *vi* (*also*: **~ about**, **~ around**) rôder ♦ *n*: **on the ~** à l'affût; **~er** *n* rôdeur(-euse)

proxy ['prɒksɪ] *n* procuration *f*

prudent ['pruːdnt] *adj* prudent(e)

prune [pruːn] *n* pruneau *m* ♦ *vt* élaguer

pry [praɪ] *vi*: **to ~ into** fourrer son nez dans

PS *n abbr* (= *postscript*) p.s.

psalm [sɑːm] *n* psaume *m*

pseudonym ['sjuːdənɪm] *n* pseudonyme *m*

psyche ['saɪkɪ] *n* psychisme *m*

psychiatrist [saɪ'kaɪətrɪst] *n* psychiatre *m/f*

psychic ['saɪkɪk] *adj* (*also*: **~al**) (*métal*)psychique; (*person*) doué(e) d'un sixième sens

psychoanalyst [saɪkəʊˈænəlɪst] n psychanalyste m/f

psychological [saɪkəˈlɒdʒɪkl] adj psychologique

psychologist [saɪˈkɒlədʒɪst] n psychologue m/f

psychology [saɪˈkɒlədʒɪ] n psychologie f

PTO abbr (= please turn over) T.S.V.P.

pub [pʌb] n (public house) pub m

---

pub

Un *pub* comprend en général deux salles: l'une ("the lounge") est plutôt confortable, avec des fauteuils et des bancs capitonnés, tandis que l'autre ("the public bar") est simplement un bar où les consommations sont en général moins chères. Cette dernière est souvent aussi une salle de jeux, les jeux les plus courants étant les fléchettes, les dominos et le billard. Il y a parfois aussi une petite arrière-salle douillette appelée "the snug". Beaucoup de pubs servent maintenant des repas, surtout à l'heure du déjeuner, et c'est alors le seul moment où les enfants sont acceptés, à condition d'être accompagnés. Les pubs sont en général ouverts de 11 h à 23 h, mais cela peut varier selon leur licence; certains pubs ferment l'après-midi.

---

public [ˈpʌblɪk] adj public(-ique) ♦ n public m; **in ~** en public; **to make ~** rendre public; **~ address system** n (système m de) sonorisation f; haut-parleurs mpl

publican [ˈpʌblɪkən] n patron m de pub

public: ~ company n société f anonyme (cotée en Bourse); **~ convenience** (BRIT) n toilettes fpl; **~ holiday** n jour férié; **~ house** (BRIT) n pub m

publicity [pʌbˈlɪsɪtɪ] n publicité f

publicize [ˈpʌblɪsaɪz] vt faire connaître, rendre public(-ique)

public: ~ opinion n opinion publique; **~ relations** n relations publiques; **~ school** n (BRIT) école (secondaire) privée; (US) école publique; **~-spirited** adj qui fait preuve de civisme; **~ transport** n transports mpl en commun

publish [ˈpʌblɪʃ] vt publier; **~er** n éditeur m; **~ing** n édition f

pub lunch n repas m de bistrot

pucker [ˈpʌkə⁺] vt plisser

pudding [ˈpʊdɪŋ] n pudding m; (BRIT: sweet) dessert m, entremets m; **black ~**, (US) **blood ~** boudin m (noir)

puddle [ˈpʌdl] n flaque f (d'eau)

puff [pʌf] n bouffée f ♦ vt: **to ~ one's pipe** tirer sur sa pipe ♦ vi (pant) haleter; **~ out** vt (fill with air) gonfler; **~ pastry** (US **puff paste**) n pâte feuilletée; **~y** adj bouffi(e)f, boursouflé(e)

pull [pʊl] n (tug): **to give sth a ~** tirer sur qch ♦ vt tirer; (trigger) presser ♦ vi tirer; **to ~ to pieces** mettre en morceaux; **to ~ one's punches** ménager son adversaire; **to ~ one's weight** faire sa part (du travail); **to ~ o.s. together** se ressaisir; **to ~ sb's leg** (fig) faire marcher qn; **~ apart** vt (break) mettre en pièces, démantibuler; **~ down** vt (house) démolir; **~ in** vi (AUT) entrer; (RAIL) entrer en gare; **~ off** vt enlever, ôter; (deal etc) mener à bien, conclure; **~ out** vi démarrer, partir ♦ vt sortir; arracher; **~ over** vi (AUT) se ranger; **~ through** vi s'en sortir; **~ up** vi (stop) s'arrêter ♦ vt remonter; (uproot) déraciner, arracher

pulley [ˈpʊlɪ] n poulie f

pullover [ˈpʊləʊvə⁺] n pull(-over) m, tricot m

pulp [pʌlp] n (of fruit) pulpe f

pulpit [ˈpʊlpɪt] n chaire f

pulsate [pʌlˈseɪt] vi battre, palpiter; (music) vibrer

pulse [pʌls] n (of blood) pouls m; (of heart) battement m; (of music, engine) vibrations fpl; (BOT, CULIN) légume sec

pump [pʌmp] n pompe f; (shoe) escarpin m ♦ vt pomper; ~ **up** vt gonfler

pumpkin ['pʌmpkɪn] n potiron m, citrouille f

pun [pʌn] n jeu de mots, calembour m

punch [pʌntʃ] n (blow) coup m de poing; (tool) poinçon m; (drink) punch m ♦ vt (hit): **to ~ sb/sth** donner un coup de poing à qn/sur qch; **~line** n (of joke) conclusion f; **~-up** (BRIT: inf) n bagarre f

punctual ['pʌŋktjuəl] adj ponctuel(le)

punctuation [pʌŋktju'eɪʃən] n ponctuation f

puncture ['pʌŋktʃəʳ] n crevaison f

pundit ['pʌndɪt] n individu m qui pontifie, pontife m

pungent ['pʌndʒənt] adj piquant(e), âcre

punish ['pʌnɪʃ] vt punir; **~ment** n punition f, châtiment m

punk [pʌŋk] n (also: ~ rocker) punk m/f; (also: ~ **rock**) le punk rock; (US: inf: hoodlum) voyou m

punt [pʌnt] n (boat) bachot m

punter ['pʌntəʳ] n (BRIT) (gambler) parieur(-euse); (inf): **the ~s** le public

puny ['pjuːnɪ] adj chétif(-ive); (effort) piteux(-euse)

pup [pʌp] n chiot m

pupil ['pjuːpl] n (SCOL) élève m/f; (of eye) pupille f

puppet ['pʌpɪt] n marionnette f, pantin m

puppy ['pʌpɪ] n chiot m, jeune chien(ne)

purchase ['pəːtʃɪs] n achat m ♦ vt acheter; **~r** n acheteur(-euse)

pure [pjuəʳ] adj pur(e); **~ly** adv purement

purge [pəːdʒ] n purge f ♦ vt purger

purple ['pəːpl] adj violet(te); (face) cramoisi(e)

purpose ['pəːpəs] n intention f, but m; **on ~** exprès; **~ful** adj déterminé(e), résolu(e)

purr [pəːʳ] vi ronronner

purse [pəːs] n (BRIT: for money) portemonnaie m; (US: handbag) sac m à main ♦ vt serrer, pincer

purser [n (NAUT) commissaire m du bord

pursue [pə'sjuː] vt poursuivre; **pursuit** [pə'sjuːt] n poursuite f; (occupation) occupation f, activité f

push [puʃ] n poussée f ♦ vt pousser; (button) appuyer sur; (product) faire de la publicité pour; (thrust): **to ~ sth (into)** enfoncer qch (dans) ♦ vi pousser; (demand): **to ~ for** exiger, demander avec insistance; **~ aside** vt écarter; **~ off** (inf) vi filer, ficher le camp; **~ on** vi (continue) continuer; **~ through** vi se frayer un chemin ♦ vt (measure) faire accepter; **~ up** vt (total, prices) faire monter; **~chair** (BRIT) n poussette f; **~er** n (drug pusher) revendeur(-euse) (de drogue), ravitailleur(-euse) (en drogue); **~over** (inf) n: **it's a ~over** c'est un jeu d'enfant; **~-up** (US) n traction f; **~y** (pej) adj arriviste

puss [pus], **pussy (cat)** ['pusɪ(kæt)] (inf) n minet m

put [put] (pt, pp **put**) vt mettre, poser, placer; (say) dire, exprimer; (a question) poser; (case, view) exposer, présenter; (estimate) estimer; **~ about** vt (rumour) faire courir; **~ across** vt (ideas etc) communiquer; **~ away** vt (store) ranger; **~ back** vt (replace) remettre, replacer; (postpone) remettre; (delay) retarder; **~ by** vt (money) mettre de côté, économiser; **~ down** vt (parcel etc) poser, déposer; (in writing) mettre par écrit, inscrire; (suppress: revolt etc) réprimer, faire cesser; (animal) abattre; (dog, cat) faire piquer; (attribute) attribuer; **~ forward** vt (ideas) avancer; **~ in** vt (gas, electricity) installer; (application, complaint) soumettre; (time, effort) consacrer; **~ off** vt (light etc) éteindre; (postpone) remettre à plus tard, ajourner; (discourage) dissuader; **~ on** vt (clothes, lipstick, record) mettre; (light etc) allumer; (play etc) monter; (food:

cook) mettre à cuire *or* à chauffer; (*gain*): **to ~ on weight** prendre du poids, grossir; **to ~ the brakes on** freiner; **to ~ the kettle on** mettre l'eau à chauffer; **~ out** *vt* (*take out*) mettre dehors; (*one's hand*) tendre; (*light etc*) éteindre; (*person: inconvenience*) déranger, gêner; **~ through** *vt* (TEL: *call*) passer; (: *person*) mettre en communication; (*plan*) faire accepter; **~ up** *vt* (*raise*) lever, relever, remonter; (*pin up*) afficher; (*hang*) accrocher; (*build*) construire, ériger; (*tent*) monter; (*umbrella*) ouvrir; (*increase*) augmenter; (*accommodate*) loger; **~ up with** *vt fus* supporter

putt [pʌt] *n* coup roulé; **~ing green** *n* green *m*

putty ['pʌti] *n* mastic *m*

put-up ['putʌp] (BRIT) *adj*: **~-~ job** coup monté

puzzle ['pʌzl] *n* énigme *f*, mystère *m*; (*jigsaw*) puzzle *m* ♦ *vt* intriguer, rendre perplexe ♦ *vi* se creuser la tête; **~d** *adj* perplexe; **puzzling** *adj* déconcertant(e)

pyjamas [pə'dʒɑːməz] (BRIT) *npl* pyjama(s) *m(pl)*

pylon ['pailən] *n* pylône *m*

pyramid ['pirəmid] *n* pyramide *f*

Pyrenees [pirə'niːz] *npl*: **the ~** les Pyrénées *fpl*

Q, q

quack [kwæk] *n* (*of duck*) coin-coin *m inv*; (*pej: doctor*) charlatan *m*

quad [kwɔd] *n abbr* = **quadrangle**; **quadruplet**

quadrangle ['kwɔdræŋgl] *n* (*courtyard*) cour *f*

quadruple [kwɔ'druːpl] *vt, vi* quadrupler; **~ts** *npl* quadruplés

quail [kweil] *n* (ZOOL) caille *f* ♦ *vi*: **to ~ at** *or* **before** reculer devant

quaint [kweint] *adj* bizarre; (*house, village*) au charme vieillot, pittoresque

quake [kweik] *vi* trembler

qualification [kwɔlifi'keiʃən] *n* (*often pl: degree etc*) diplôme *m*; (*training*) qualification(s) *f(pl)*, expérience *f*; (*ability*) compétence(s) *f(pl)*; (*limitation*) réserve *f*, restriction *f*

qualified ['kwɔlifaid] *adj* (*trained*) qualifié(e); (*professionally*) diplômé(e); (*fit, competent*) compétent(e), qualifié(e); (*limited*) conditionnel(le)

qualify ['kwɔlifai] *vt* qualifier; (*modify*) atténuer, nuancer ♦ *vi*: **to ~ (as)** obtenir son diplôme (de); **to ~ (for)** remplir les conditions requises (pour); (SPORT) se qualifier (pour)

quality ['kwɔliti] *n* qualité *f*; **~ time** *n* moments privilégiés

---

quality (news)papers

Les **quality (news)papers** (*ou la* **quality press**) englobent les journaux sérieux, quotidiens ou hebdomadaires, par opposition aux journaux populaires (**tabloid press**). Ces journaux visent un public qui souhaite des informations détaillées sur un éventail très vaste de sujets et qui est prêt à consacrer beaucoup de temps à leur lecture. Les **quality newspapers** sont en général de grand format.

---

qualm [kwɑːm] *n* doute *m*; scrupule *m*

quandary ['kwɔndri] *n*: **in a ~** devant un dilemme, dans l'embarras

quantity ['kwɔntiti] *n* quantité *f*; **~ surveyor** *n* métreur *m* vérificateur

quarantine ['kwɔrəntiːn] *n* quarantaine *f*

quarrel ['kwɔrl] *n* querelle *f*, dispute *f* ♦ *vi* se disputer, se quereller

quarry ['kwɔri] *n* (*for stone*) carrière *f*; (*animal*) proie *f*, gibier *m*

quart [kwɔːt] *n* ≈ litre *m*

quarter ['kwɔːtər] *n* quart *m*; (US: *coin: 25 cents*) quart de dollar; (*of year*) trimestre *m*; (*district*) quartier *m* ♦ *vt* (*divide*) partager en quartiers *or* en quatre;

~s npl (living ~) logement m; (MIL) quartiers mpl, cantonnement m; **a ~ of an hour** un quart d'heure; **~ final** n quart m de finale; **~ly** adj trimestriel(le) ♦ adv tous les trois mois

quartet(te) [kwɔː'tɛt] n quatuor m; (jazz players) quartette m

quartz [kwɔːts] n quartz m

quash [kwɔʃ] vt (verdict) annuler

quaver ['kweɪvə*] vi trembler

quay [kiː] n (also: **~side**) quai m

queasy ['kwiːzɪ] adj: **to feel ~** avoir mal au cœur

queen [kwiːn] n reine f; (CARDS etc) dame f; **~ mother** n reine mère f

queer [kwɪə*] adj étrange, curieux (-euse); (suspicious) louche ♦ n (inf!) homosexuel m

quell [kwɛl] vt réprimer, étouffer

quench [kwɛntʃ] vt: **to ~ one's thirst** se désaltérer

query ['kwɪərɪ] n question f ♦ vt remettre en question, mettre en doute

quest [kwɛst] n recherche f, quête f

question ['kwɛstʃən] n question f ♦ vt (person) interroger; (plan, idea) remettre en question, mettre en doute; **beyond ~** sans aucun doute; **out of the ~** hors de question; **~able** adj discutable; **~ mark** n point m d'interrogation; **~naire** [kwɛstʃə'nɛə*] n questionnaire m

queue [kjuː] (BRIT) n queue f, file f ♦ vi (also: **~ up**) faire la queue

quibble ['kwɪbl] vi: **~ (about)** or **(over)** or **(with sth)** ergoter (sur qch)

quick [kwɪk] adj rapide; (agile) agile, vif (vive) ♦ n: **cut to the ~** (fig) touché(e) au vif; **be ~!** dépêche-toi!; **~en** vt accélérer, presser ♦ vi s'accélérer, devenir plus rapide; **~ly** adv vite, rapidement; **~sand** n sables mouvants; **~-witted** adj à l'esprit vif

quid [kwɪd] (BRIT: inf) n, pl inv livre f

quiet ['kwaɪət] adj tranquille, calme; (voice) bas(se); (ceremony, colour) discret(-ète) ♦ n tranquillité f, calme m;

(silence) silence m ♦ vt, vi (US) = **quieten**; **keep ~!** tais-toi!; **~en** vi (also: **~en down**) se calmer, s'apaiser ♦ vt calmer, apaiser; **~ly** adv tranquillement, calmement; (silently) silencieusement; **~ness** n tranquillité f, calme m; (silence) silence m

quilt [kwɪlt] n édredon m; (continental ~) couette f

quin [kwɪn] n abbr = **quintuplet**

quintuplets [kwɪn'tjuːplɪts] npl quintuplé(e)s

quip [kwɪp] n remarque piquante or spirituelle, pointe f

quirk [kwəːk] n bizarrerie f

quit [kwɪt] (pt, pp quit or quitted) vt quitter; (smoking, grumbling) arrêter de ♦ vi (give up) abandonner, renoncer; (resign) démissionner

quite [kwaɪt] adv (rather) assez, plutôt; (entirely) complètement, tout à fait; (following a negative = almost): **that's not ~ big enough** ce n'est pas tout à fait assez grand; **I ~ understand** je comprends très bien; **~ a few of them** un assez grand nombre d'entre eux; **~ (so)!** exactement!

quits [kwɪts] adj: **~ (with)** quitte (envers); **let's call it ~** restons-en là

quiver ['kwɪvə*] vi trembler, frémir

quiz [kwɪz] n (game) jeu-concours m ♦ vt interroger; **~zical** adj narquois(e)

quota ['kwəʊtə] n quota m

quotation [kwəʊ'teɪʃən] n citation f; (estimate) devis m; **~ marks** npl guillemets mpl

quote [kwəʊt] n citation f; (estimate) devis m ♦ vt citer; (price) indiquer; **~s** npl guillemets mpl

R, r

rabbi ['ræbaɪ] n rabbin m

rabbit ['ræbɪt] n lapin m; **~ hutch** n clapier m

rabble ['ræbl] (pej) n populace f

rabies ['reɪbi:z] n rage f

RAC n abbr (BRIT) = Royal Automobile Club

rac(c)oon [rə'ku:n] n raton laveur

race [reɪs] n (species) race f; (competition, rush) course f ♦ vt (horse) faire courir ♦ vi (compete) faire la course, courir; (hurry) aller à toute vitesse, courir; (engine) s'emballer; (pulse) augmenter; **~ car** (US) n = **racing car**; **~ car driver** n (US) = **racing driver**; **~course** n champ m de courses; **~horse** n cheval m de course; **~r** n (bike) vélo m de course; **~track** n piste f

racial ['reɪʃl] adj racial(e)

racing ['reɪsɪŋ] n courses fpl; **~ car** (BRIT) n voiture f de course; **~ driver** (BRIT) n pilote m de course

racism ['reɪsɪzəm] n racisme m; **racist** adj raciste ♦ n raciste m/f

rack [ræk] n (for guns, tools) râtelier m; (also: luggage ~) porte-bagages m inv, filet m à bagages; (also: roof ~) galerie f; (dish ~) égouttoir m ♦ vt tourmenter; **to ~ one's brains** se creuser la cervelle

racket ['rækɪt] n (for tennis) raquette f; (noise) tapage m, vacarme m; (swindle) escroquerie f

racquet ['rækɪt] n raquette f

racy ['reɪsɪ] adj plein(e) de verve; (slightly indecent) osé(e)

radar ['reɪdɑ:ʳ] n radar m

radial ['reɪdɪəl] adj (also: ~-ply) à carcasse radiale

radiant ['reɪdɪənt] adj rayonnant(e)

radiate ['reɪdɪeɪt] vt (heat) émettre, dégager; (emotion) rayonner de ♦ vi (lines) rayonner; **radiation** [reɪdɪ'eɪʃən] n rayonnement m; (radioactive) radia-

tion f; **radiator** ['reɪdɪeɪtəʳ] n radiateur m

radical ['rædɪkl] adj radical(e)

radii ['reɪdɪaɪ] npl of **radius**

radio ['reɪdɪəʊ] n radio f ♦ vt appeler par radio; **on the ~** à la radio; **~active** ['reɪdɪəʊ'æktɪv] adj radioactif(-ive); **~ cassette** n radiocassette m; **~-controlled** adj téléguidé(e); **~ station** n station f de radio

radish ['rædɪʃ] n radis m

radius ['reɪdɪəs] (pl **radii**) n rayon m

RAF n abbr = Royal Air Force

raffle ['ræfl] n tombola f

raft [rɑ:ft] n (craft; also: life ~) radeau m

rafter ['rɑ:ftəʳ] n chevron m

rag [ræg] n chiffon m; (pej: newspaper) feuille f de chou, torchon m; (student ~) attractions organisées au profit d'œuvres de charité; **~s** npl (torn clothes etc) haillons mpl; **~ doll** n poupée f de chiffon

rage [reɪdʒ] n (fury) rage f, fureur f ♦ vi (person) être fou (folle) de rage; (storm) faire rage, être déchaîné(e); **it's all the ~** cela fait fureur

ragged ['rægɪd] adj (edge) inégal(e); (clothes) en loques; (appearance) déguenillé(e)

raid [reɪd] n (attack, also: MIL) raid m; (criminal) hold-up m inv; (by police) descente f, rafle f ♦ vt faire un raid sur ou un hold-up ou une descente dans

rail [reɪl] n (on stairs) rampe f; (on bridge, balcony) balustrade f; (of ship) bastingage m; **~s** npl (track) rails mpl, voie ferrée; **by ~** par chemin de fer, en train; **~ing(s)** n(pl) grille f; **~road** (US), **~way** (BRIT) n (track) voie ferrée; (company) chemin m de fer; **~way line** (BRIT) n ligne f de chemin de fer; **~wayman** (BRIT) (irreg) n cheminot m; **~way station** (BRIT) n gare f

rain [reɪn] n pluie f ♦ vi pleuvoir; **in the ~** sous la pluie; **it's ~ing** il pleut; **~bow** n arc-en-ciel m; **~coat** n imperméable m; **~drop** n goutte f de pluie; **~fall** n chute f de pluie; (measurement)

hauteur f des précipitations; **~forest** n
forêt f tropicale humide; **~y** adj
pluvieux(-euse)

raise [reɪz] n augmentation f ♦ vt (lift)
lever; hausser; (increase) augmenter;
(morale) remonter; (standards) rehausser;
(question, doubt) provoquer, soulever; (cattle, family) élever; (crop) faire
pousser; (funds) rassembler; (loan) obtenir; (army) lever; **to ~ one's voice**
élever la voix

raisin ['reɪzn] n raisin sec

rake [reɪk] n (tool) râteau n ♦ vt (garden, leaves) ratisser

rally ['rælɪ] n (POL etc) meeting m, rassemblement m; (AUT) rallye m; (TENNIS)
échange m ♦ vt (support) gagner ♦ vi
(sick person) aller mieux; (Stock Exchange) reprendre; **~ round** vt fus venir
en aide à

RAM [ræm] n abbr (= random access memory) mémoire vive

ram [ræm] n bélier m ♦ vt enfoncer;
(crash into) emboutir; percuter

ramble ['ræmbl] n randonnée f ♦ vi
(walk) se promener, faire une randonnée; (talk: also: **~ on**) discourir, pérorer;
~r n promeneur(-euse), randonneur
(-euse); (BOT) rosier grimpant; **rambling** adj (speech) décousu(e); (house)
plein(e) de coins et de recoins; (BOT)
grimpant(e)

ramp [ræmp] n (incline) rampe f; dénivellation f; **on ~, off ~** (US: AUT) bretelle f d'accès

rampage [ræm'peɪdʒ] n: **to be on the
~** se déchaîner

rampant ['ræmpənt] adj (disease etc)
qui sévit

ram raiding [-reɪdɪŋ] n pillage d'un magasin en enfonçant la vitrine avec une voiture

ramshackle ['ræmʃækl] adj (house) délabré(e); (car etc) déglingué(e)

ran [ræn] pt of **run**

ranch [rɑːntʃ] n ranch m; **~er** n propriétaire m de ranch

rancid ['rænsɪd] adj rance

rancour ['ræŋkəʳ] (US **rancor**) n rancune f

random ['rændəm] adj fait(e) ou établi(e) au hasard; (MATH) aléatoire ♦ n:
at ~ au hasard; **~ access** n (COMPUT)
accès sélectif

randy ['rændɪ] (BRIT: inf) adj excité(e);
lubrique

rang [ræŋ] pt of **ring**

range [reɪndʒ] n (of mountains) chaîne
f; (of missile, voice) portée f; (of products) choix m, gamme f; (MIL: also:
shooting ~) champ m de tir; (indoor)
stand m de tir; (also: **kitchen ~**) fourneau m (de cuisine) ♦ vt (place in a line)
mettre en rang, ranger ♦ vi: **to ~ over**
(extend) couvrir; **to ~ from ... to ...** aller
de ... à; **a ~ of** (series: of proposals etc)
divers(e)

ranger ['reɪndʒəʳ] n garde forestier

rank [ræŋk] n rang m; (MIL) grade m;
(BRIT: also: **taxi ~**) station f de taxis ♦ vi:
to ~ among compter ou se classer parmi ♦ adj (stinking) fétide, puant(e); **the
~ and file** (fig) la masse, la base

ransack ['rænsæk] vt fouiller (à fond);
(plunder) piller

ransom ['rænsəm] n rançon f; **to hold
to ~** (fig) exercer un chantage sur

rant [rænt] vi fulminer

rap [ræp] vt frapper sur ou à; taper sur
♦ n: **~ music** rap m

rape [reɪp] n viol m; (BOT) colza m ♦ vt
violer; **~(seed) oil** n huile f de colza

rapid ['ræpɪd] adj rapide; **~s** npl (GEO)
rapides mpl

rapist ['reɪpɪst] n violeur m

rapport [ræ'pɔːʳ] n entente f

rapturous ['ræptʃərəs] adj enthousiaste, frénétique

rare [reəʳ] adj rare; (CULIN: steak) saignant(e)

raring ['reərɪŋ] adj: **~ to go** (inf) très
impatient(e) de commencer

rascal ['rɑːskl] n vaurien m

rash [ræʃ] adj imprudent(e), irréfléchi(e)

♦ n (MED) rougeur f, éruption f; (spate: of events) série (noire)

rasher ['ræʃə*] n fine tranche f (de lard)

raspberry ['rɑːzbərɪ] n framboise f; ~ **bush** n framboisier m

rasping ['rɑːspɪŋ] adj: ~ **noise** grincement m

rat [ræt] n rat m

rate [reɪt] n taux m; (speed) vitesse f, rythme m; (price) tarif m ♦ vt classer; évaluer; ~s npl (BRIT: tax) impôts locaux; (fees) tarifs mpl; **to ~ sb/sth as** considérer qn/qch comme; **~able value** (BRIT) n valeur locative imposable; **~payer** ['reɪtpeɪə*] n (BRIT) contribuable m/f (payant les impôts locaux)

rather ['rɑːðə*] adv plutôt; **it's ~ expensive** c'est assez cher; (too much) c'est un peu cher; **there's ~ a lot** il y en a beaucoup; **I would** or **I'd ~ go** j'aimerais mieux or je préférerais partir

rating ['reɪtɪŋ] n (assessment) évaluation f; (score) classement m; ~s npl (RADIO, TV) indice m d'écoute

ratio ['reɪʃɪəʊ] n proportion f

ration ['ræʃən] n (gen pl) ration(s) f(pl)

rational ['ræʃənl] adj raisonnable, sensé(e); (solution, reasoning) logique; **~e** [ræʃə'nɑːl] n raisonnement m; **~ize** ['ræʃənaɪz] vt (conduct) essayer d'expliquer or de motiver

rat race n foire f d'empoigne

rattle ['rætl] n (of door, window) battement m; (of coins, chain) cliquetis m; (of train, engine) bruit m de ferraille; (object: for baby) hochet m ♦ vi cliqueter; (car, bus): **to ~ along** rouler dans un bruit de ferraille ♦ vt agiter (bruyamment); (unnerve) déconcerter; **~snake** n serpent m à sonnettes

raucous ['rɔːkəs] adj rauque; (noisy) bruyant(e), tapageur(-euse)

rave [reɪv] vi (in anger) s'emporter; (with enthusiasm) s'extasier; (MED) délirer ♦ n (BRIT: inf: party) rave f, soirée f techno

raven ['reɪvən] n corbeau m

ravenous ['rævənəs] adj affamé(e)

ravine [rə'viːn] n ravin m

raving ['reɪvɪŋ] adj: ~ **lunatic** ♦ n fou (folle) furieux(-euse)

ravishing ['rævɪʃɪŋ] adj enchanteur(-eresse)

raw [rɔː] adj (uncooked) cru(e); (not processed) brut(e); (sore) à vif, irrité(e); (inexperienced) inexpérimenté(e); (weather, day) froid(e) et humide; ~ **deal** (inf) n sale coup m; ~ **material** n matière première

ray [reɪ] n rayon m; ~ **of hope** lueur f d'espoir

raze [reɪz] vt (also: ~ **to the ground**) raser, détruire

razor ['reɪzə*] n rasoir m; ~ **blade** n lame f de rasoir

Rd abbr = **road**

RE n abbr = **religious education**

re [riː] prep concernant

reach [riːtʃ] n portée f, atteinte f; (of river etc) étendue f ♦ vt atteindre; (conclusion, decision) parvenir à ♦ vi s'étendre, étendre le bras; **out of/within ~** hors de/à portée; **within ~ of the shops** pas trop loin des or à proximité des magasins; ~ **out** vt tendre ♦ vi: **to ~ out (for)** allonger le bras (pour prendre)

react [riː'ækt] vi réagir; **~ion** n réaction f

reactor [riː'æktə*] n réacteur m

read [riːd, pt, pp red] (pt, pp **read**) vi lire ♦ vt lire; (understand) comprendre; (interpret) interpréter; (study) étudier; (meter) relever; ~ **out** vt lire à haute voix; **~able** adj facile or agréable à lire; (writing) lisible; **~er** n lecteur(-trice); (BRIT: at university) chargé(e) d'enseignement; **~ership** n (of paper etc) (nombre m de) lecteurs mpl

readily ['redɪlɪ] adv volontiers, avec empressement; (easily) facilement

readiness ['redɪnɪs] n empressement m; **in ~** (prepared) prêt(e)

reading ['riːdɪŋ] n lecture f; (understanding) interprétation f; (on instrument) indications fpl

ready ['rɛdɪ] adj prêt(e); (willing) prêt, disposé(e); (available) disponible ♦ n: **at the ~** (MIL) prêt à faire feu; **to get ~** se préparer ♦ vt préparer; **~-made** adj tout(e) fait(e); **~-to-wear** adj prêt(e) à porter

real [rɪəl] adj véritable; réel(le); **in terms** dans la réalité; **~ estate** n biens fonciers or immobiliers; **~istic** [rɪə'lɪstɪk] adj réaliste; **~ity** [rɪː'ælɪtɪ] n réalité f

realization [rɪəlaɪ'zeɪʃən] n (awareness) prise f de conscience; (fulfilment; also: of asset) réalisation f

realize ['rɪəlaɪz] vt (understand) se rendre compte de; (a project, COMM: asset) réaliser

really ['rɪəlɪ] adv vraiment; **~?** vraiment?, c'est vrai?

realm [rɛlm] n royaume m; (fig) domaine m

realtor ® ['rɪəltɔːʳ] (US) n agent immobilier

reap [riːp] vt moissonner; (fig) récolter

reappear [rɪːə'pɪəʳ] vi réapparaître, reparaître

rear [rɪəʳ] adj de derrière, arrière (in AUT: wheel etc) arrière ♦ n arrière m ♦ vt (cattle, family) élever ♦ vi (also: ~ up: animal) se cabrer; **~guard** n (MIL) arrière-garde f; **~-view mirror** n (AUT) rétroviseur m

reason ['riːzn] n raison f ♦ vi: **to ~ with sb** raisonner qn, faire entendre raison à qn; **to have ~ to think** avoir lieu de penser; **it stands to ~ that** il va sans dire que; **~able** adj raisonnable; (not bad) acceptable; **~ably** adv raisonnablement, à peu près; **~ing** n raisonnement m

reassurance [rɪːə'ʃuərəns] n réconfort m; (factual) assurance f, garantie f

reassure [rɪːə'ʃuəʳ] vt rassurer

rebate ['riːbeɪt] n (on tax etc) dégrèvement m

rebel [n 'rɛbl, vb rɪ'bɛl] n rebelle m/f ♦ vi se rebeller, se révolter; **~lious** [rɪ'bɛljəs] adj rebelle

rebound [vb rɪ'baund, n 'riːbaund] vi (ball) rebondir ♦ n rebond m; **to marry on the ~** se marier immédiatement après une déception amoureuse

rebuff [rɪ'bʌf] n rebuffade f

rebuke [rɪ'bjuːk] vt réprimander

rebut [rɪ'bʌt] vt réfuter

recall [vb rɪ'kɔːl, n 'riːkɔl] vt rappeler; (remember) se rappeler, se souvenir de ♦ n rappel m; (ability to remember) mémoire f

recant [rɪ'kænt] vi se rétracter; (REL) abjurer

recap ['riːkæp], **recapitulate** [riːkə'pɪtjuleɪt] vi, vt récapituler

rec'd abbr = **received**

recede [rɪ'siːd] vi (tide) descendre; (disappear) disparaître peu à peu; (memory, hope) s'estomper; **receding** adj (chin) fuyant(e); **receding hairline** front dégarni

receipt [rɪ'siːt] n (document) reçu m; (for parcel etc) accusé m de réception; (act of receiving) réception f; **~s** npl (COMM) recettes fpl

receive [rɪ'siːv] vt recevoir; **~r** n (TEL) récepteur m, combiné m; (RADIO) récepteur m; (of stolen goods) receleur m; (LAW) administrateur m judiciaire

recent ['riːsnt] adj récent(e); **~ly** adv récemment

receptacle [rɪ'sɛptɪkl] n récipient m

reception [rɪ'sɛpʃən] n réception f; (welcome) accueil m, réception f; **~ desk** n réception f; **~ist** n réceptionniste m/f

recess [rɪ'sɛs] n (in room) renfoncement m, alcôve f; (secret place) recoin m; (POL etc: holiday) vacances fpl

recession [rɪ'sɛʃən] n récession f

recipe ['rɛsɪpɪ] n recette f

recipient [rɪ'sɪpɪənt] n (of payment) bénéficiaire m/f; (of letter) destinataire m/f

recital [rɪ'saɪtl] n récital m

recite [rɪ'saɪt] vt (poem) réciter

reckless ['rekləs] *adj* (*driver etc*) imprudent(e)

reckon ['rekən] *vt* (*count*) calculer, compter; (*think*): **I ~ that ...** je pense que ...; **~ on** *vt fus* compter sur, s'attendre à; **~ing** *n* compte *m*, calcul *m*; estimation *f*

reclaim [rɪ'kleɪm] *vt* (*demand back*) réclamer (le remboursement or la restitution de); (*land: from sea*) assécher; (*waste materials*) récupérer

recline [rɪ'klaɪn] *vi* être allongé(e) or étendu(e); **reclining** *adj* (*seat*) à dossier réglable

recluse [rɪ'kluːs] *n* reclus(e), ermite *m*

recognition [rekəg'nɪʃən] *n* reconnaissance *f*; **to gain ~** être reconnu(e); **transformed beyond ~** méconnaissable

recognizable ['rekəgnaɪzəbl] *adj*: **~ (by)** reconnaissable (à)

recognize ['rekəgnaɪz] *vt*: **to ~ (by/as)** reconnaître (à/comme étant)

recoil [*vb* rɪ'kɔɪl, *n* 'riːkɔɪl] *vi* (*person*): **to ~ (from sth/doing sth)** reculer (devant qch/l'idée de faire qch) ♦ *n* (*of gun*) recul *m*

recollect [rekə'lekt] *vt* se rappeler, se souvenir de; **~ion** *n* souvenir *m*

recommend [rekə'mend] *vt* recommander

reconcile ['rekənsaɪl] *vt* (*two people*) réconcilier; (*two facts*) concilier, accorder; **to ~ o.s. to** se résigner à

recondition [riːkən'dɪʃən] *vt* remettre à neuf; réviser entièrement

reconnoitre [rekə'nɔɪtər] (*US* **reconnoiter**) *vt* (*MIL*) reconnaître

reconsider [riːkən'sɪdər] *vt* reconsidérer

reconstruct [riːkən'strʌkt] *vt* (*building*) reconstruire; (*crime, policy, system*) reconstituer

record [*n* 'rekɔːd, *vb* rɪ'kɔːd] *n* rapport *m*, récit *m*; (*of meeting etc*) procès-verbal *m*; (*register*) registre *m*; (*file*) dossier *m*; (*also*: **criminal ~**) casier *m* judi-

ciaire; (*MUS: disc*) disque *m*; (*SPORT*) record *m*; (*COMPUT*) article *m* ♦ *vt* (*set down*) noter; (*MUS: song etc*) enregistrer; **in ~ time** en un temps record *inv*; **off the ~** ♦ *adj* officieux(-euse) ♦ *adv* officieusement; **~ card** *n* fiche *f*; **~ed delivery** *etc* lettre *etc* recommandée; **~ed delivery letter** *etc* (*BRIT: POST*): **~ed delivery letter** *etc* lettre *etc* recommandée; **~er** *n* (*MUS*) flûte *f* à bec; **~ holder** *n* (*SPORT*) détenteur(-trice) du record; **~ing** *n* (*MUS*) enregistrement *m*; **~ player** *n* tourne-disque *m*

recount [rɪ'kaunt] *vt* raconter

re-count ['riːkaunt] *n* (*POL: of votes*) deuxième compte *m*

recoup [rɪ'kuːp] *vt*: **to ~ one's losses** récupérer ce qu'on a perdu, se refaire

recourse [rɪ'kɔːs] *n*: **to have ~ to** avoir recours à

recover [rɪ'kʌvər] *vt* récupérer ♦ *vi*: **to ~ (from)** (*illness*) se rétablir (de); (*from shock*) se remettre (de); **~y** *n* récupération *f*; rétablissement *m*; (*ECON*) redressement *m*

recreation [rekrɪ'eɪʃən] *n* récréation *f*, détente *f*; **~al** *adj* pour la détente, récréatif(-ive)

recruit [rɪ'kruːt] *n* recrue *f* ♦ *vt* recruter

rectangle ['rektæŋgl] *n* rectangle *m*; **rectangular** [rek'tæŋgjulər] *adj* rectangulaire

rectify ['rektɪfaɪ] *vt* (*error*) rectifier, corriger

rector ['rektər] *n* (*REL*) pasteur *m*

recuperate [rɪ'kjuːpəreɪt] *vi* récupérer; (*from illness*) se rétablir

recur [rɪ'kɔː*r*] *vi* se reproduire; (*symptoms*) réapparaître; **~rence** *n* répétition *f*; réapparition *f*; **~rent** *adj* périodique, fréquent(e)

recycle [riː'saɪkl] *vt* recycler; **recycling** *n* recyclage *m*

red [red] *n* rouge *m*; (*POL: pej*) rouge *m/f* ♦ *adj* rouge; (*hair*) roux (rousse) ♦ *adj*; **in the ~** (*account*) à découvert; (*business*) en déficit; **~ carpet treatment** *n* réception *f* en grande pompe; **R~ Cross** *n*

Croix-Rouge f; **~currant** n groseille f (rouge); **~den** vt, vi rougir

redecorate [riː'dekəreɪt] vi (with wallpaper) retapisser; (with paint) refaire les peintures

redeem [rɪ'diːm] vt (debt) rembourser; (sth in pawn) dégager; (fig, also REL) racheter; **~ing** adj (feature) qui sauve, qui rachète (le reste)

redeploy [riːdɪ'plɔɪ] vt (resources) réorganiser

red: **~-haired** adj roux (rousse); **~-handed** adj: **to be caught ~-handed** être pris(e) en flagrant délit or la main dans le sac; **~head** n roux (rousse); **~ herring** n (fig) diversion f, fausse piste; **~-hot** adj chauffé(e) au rouge, brûlant(e)

redirect [riːdaɪ'rekt] vt (mail) faire suivre

red light n: **to go through a ~** (AUT) brûler un feu rouge; **red-light district** n quartier m des prostituées

redo [riː'duː] (irreg) vt refaire

redress [rɪ'dres] n réparation f ♦ vt redresser

red: **R~ Sea** n mer Rouge f; **~skin** n Peau-Rouge m/f; **~ tape** n (fig) paperasserie f (administrative)

reduce [rɪ'djuːs] vt réduire; (lower) abaisser; **"~ speed now"** (AUT) "ralentir"; **reduction** [rɪ'dʌkʃən] n réduction f; (discount) rabais m

redundancy [rɪ'dʌndənsɪ] n (BRIT) n licenciement m, mise f au chômage

redundant [rɪ'dʌndnt] adj (BRIT: worker) mis(e) au chômage, licencié(e); (detail, object) superflu(e); **to be made ~** être licencié(e), être mis(e) au chômage

reed [riːd] n (BOT) roseau m; (MUS: of clarinet etc) hanche f

reef [riːf] n (of sea) récif m, écueil m

reek [riːk] vi: **to ~ (of)** puer, empester

reel [riːl] n bobine f; (FISHING) moulinet m; (CINEMA) bande f; (dance) quadrille écossais ♦ vi (sway) chanceler; **~ in** vt

(fish, line) ramener

ref [ref] (inf) n abbr (= referee) arbitre m

refectory [rɪ'fektərɪ] n réfectoire m

refer [rɪ'fɜː] vt: **to ~ sb to** (inquirer: for information, patient: to specialist) adresser qn à; (reader: to text) renvoyer qn à; (dispute, decision): **to ~ sth to** soumettre qch à ♦ vi: **~ to** (allude to) parler de, faire allusion à; (consult) se reporter à

referee [refə'riː] n arbitre m; (BRIT: for job application) répondant(e)

reference ['refrəns] n référence f, renvoi m; (mention) allusion f, mention f; (for job application: letter) références f, lettre f de recommandation; **with ~ to** (COMM: in letter) me référant à, suite à; **~ book** n ouvrage m de référence

refill [vb riː'fɪl, n 'riːfɪl] vt remplir à nouveau; (pen, lighter etc) recharger ♦ n (for pen etc) recharge f

refine [rɪ'faɪn] vt (sugar, oil) raffiner; (taste) affiner; (theory, idea) fignoler (inf); **~d** adj (person, taste) raffiné(e); **~ry** n raffinerie f

reflect [rɪ'flekt] vt (light, image) réfléchir, refléter; (fig) refléter ♦ vi (think) réfléchir, méditer; **it ~s badly on him** cela le discrédite; **it ~s well on him** c'est tout à son honneur; **~ion** n réflexion f; (image) reflet m; (criticism): **~ion on** critique f de; atteinte f à; **on ~ion** réflexion faite

reflex ['riːfleks] adj réflexe ♦ n réflexe m; **~ive** [rɪ'fleksɪv] adj (LING) réfléchi(e)

reform [rɪ'fɔːm] n réforme f ♦ vt réformer; **~atory** [rɪ'fɔːmətən] (US) n centre m d'éducation surveillée

refrain [rɪ'freɪn] vi: **to ~ from doing** s'abstenir de faire ♦ n refrain m

refresh [rɪ'freʃ] vt rafraîchir; (subj: sleep) reposer; **~er course** (BRIT) n cours m de recyclage; **~ing** adj (drink) rafraîchissant(e); (sleep) réparateur(-trice); **~ments** npl rafraîchissements mpl

refrigerator [rɪ'frɪdʒəreɪtə] n réfrigérateur m, frigidaire ® m

refuel [ri:'fjuəl] *vi* se ravitailler en carburant

refuge ['refju:dʒ] *n* refuge *m*; **to take ~ in** se réfugier dans; **~e** [refju'dʒi:] *n* réfugié(e)

refund [*n* 'ri:fʌnd, *vb* ri'fʌnd] *n* remboursement *m* ♦ *vt* rembourser

refurbish [ri:'fɜ:biʃ] *vt* remettre à neuf

refusal [ri'fju:zəl] *n* refus *m*; **to have first ~ on** avoir droit de préemption sur

refuse[1] [ri'fju:z] *vt*, *vi* refuser

refuse[2] ['refju:s] *n* ordures *fpl*, détritus *mpl*; **~ collection** *n* ramassage *m* d'ordures

regain [ri'geɪn] *vt* regagner; retrouver

regal ['ri:gl] *adj* royal(e)

regard [ri'gɑːd] *n* respect *m*, estime *f*, considération *f* ♦ *vt* considérer; **to give one's ~s to** faire ses amitiés à; **"with kindest ~s"** "bien amicalement"; **as ~s, with ~ to = regarding**; **~ing** *prep* en ce qui concerne; **~less** *adv* quand même; **~less of** sans se soucier de

régime [rei'ʒi:m] *n* régime *m*

regiment ['redʒimənt] *n* régiment *m*; **~al** [redʒi'mentl] *adj* d'un ou du régiment

region ['ri:dʒən] *n* région *f*; **in the ~ of** (*fig*) aux alentours de; **~al** *adj* régional(e)

register ['redʒistə*r*] *n* registre *m*; (*also:* **electoral ~**) liste électorale ♦ *vt* enregistrer; (*birth, death*) déclarer; (*vehicle*) immatriculer; (*POST: letter*) envoyer en recommandé; (*subj: instrument*) marquer ♦ *vi* s'inscrire; (*at hotel*) signer le registre; (*make impression*) être (bien) compris(e); **~ed** *adj* (*letter, parcel*) recommandé(e); **~ed trademark** *n* marque déposée; **registrar** ['redʒistrɑː*r*] *n* officier *m* de l'état civil; **registration** [redʒis'treiʃən] *n* enregistrement *m*, (*BRIT: AUT: also:* **registration number**) numéro d'immatriculation

registry ['redʒistri] *n* bureau *m* de l'enregistrement; **~ office** (*BRIT*) *n* bureau

m de l'état civil; **to get married in a ~ office** ≈ se marier à la mairie

regret [ri'gret] *n* regret *m* ♦ *vt* regretter; **~fully** *adv* à or avec regret

regular ['regjulə*r*] *adj* régulier(-ère), (*usual*) habituel(le); (*soldier*) de métier ♦ *n* (*client etc*) habitué(e); **~ly** *adv* régulièrement

regulate ['regjuleɪt] *vt* régler; **regulation** [regju'leɪʃən] *n* (*rule*) règlement *m*; (*adjustment*) réglage *m*

rehabilitation ['ri:əbili'teiʃən] *n* (*of offender*) réinsertion *f*; (*of addict*) réadaptation *f*

rehearsal [ri'hɜ:səl] *n* répétition *f*

rehearse [ri'hɜ:s] *vt* répéter

reign [rein] *n* règne *m* ♦ *vi* régner

reimburse [ri:ɪm'bɜ:s] *vt* rembourser

rein [rein] *n* (*for horse*) rêne *f*

reindeer ['reindiə*r*] *n, pl inv* renne *m*

reinforce [ri:ɪn'fɔːs] *vt* renforcer; **~d concrete** *n* béton armé; **~ments** *npl* (*MIL*) renfort(s) *m(pl)*

reinstate [ri:ɪn'steit] *vt* rétablir, réintégrer

reject [*n* 'ri:dʒɛkt, *vb* ri'dʒɛkt] *n* (*COMM*) article *m* de rebut ♦ *vt* refuser; (*idea*) rejeter; **~ion** *n* rejet *m*, refus *m*

rejoice [ri'dʒɔis] *vi*: **to ~ (at or over)** se réjouir (de)

rejuvenate [ri'dʒu:vəneit] *vt* rajeunir

relapse [ri'læps] *n* (*MED*) rechute *f*

relate [ri'leit] *vt* (*tell*) raconter; (*connect*) établir un rapport entre ♦ *vi*: **this ~s to** cela se rapporte à; **to ~ to sb** entretenir des rapports avec qn; **~d** *adj* apparenté(e); **relating to** *prep* concernant

relation [ri'leiʃən] *n* (*person*) parent(e); (*link*) rapport *m*, lien *m*; **~ship** *n* rapport *m*, lien *m*; (*personal ties*) relations *fpl*, rapports; (*also:* **family ~ship**) lien de parenté

relative ['relətiv] *n* parent(e) ♦ *adj* relatif(-ive); **all her ~s** toute sa famille; **~ly** *adv* relativement

relax [ri'læks] *vi* (*muscle*) se relâcher;

(person: unwind) se détendre ♦ vt relâcher; (mind, person) détendre; **~ation** [riːlækˈseɪʃən] n relâchement m; (of mind) détente f, relaxation f; (recreation) détente f, délassement m; **~ed** adj détendu(e); **~ing** adj délassant(e)

relay [n ˈriːleɪ, vb rɪˈleɪ] n (SPORT) course f de relais ♦ vt (message) retransmettre, relayer

release [rɪˈliːs] n (from prison, obligation) libération f; (of gas etc) émission f; (of film etc) sortie f; (new recording) disque m ♦ vt (prisoner) libérer; (gas etc) émettre, dégager; (free: from wreckage etc) dégager; (TECH: catch, spring etc) faire jouer; (book, film) sortir; (report, news) rendre public, publier

relegate [ˈrelɪgeɪt] vt reléguer; (BRIT: SPORT): **to be ~d** descendre dans une division inférieure

relent [rɪˈlent] vi se laisser fléchir; **~less** adj implacable; (unceasing) continuel(le)

relevant [ˈreləvənt] adj (question) pertinent(e); (fact) significatif(-ive); (information) utile; **~ to** ayant rapport à, approprié à

reliable [rɪˈlaɪəbl] adj (person, firm) sérieux(-euse), fiable; (method, machine) fiable; (news, information) sûr(e); **reliably** adv: **to be reliably informed** savoir de source sûre

reliance [rɪˈlaɪəns] n: **~ (on)** (person) confiance f (en); (drugs, promises) besoin m (de), dépendance f (de)

relic [ˈrelɪk] n (REL) relique f; (of the past) vestige m

relief [rɪˈliːf] n (from pain, anxiety etc) soulagement m; (help, supplies) secours m(pl); (ART, GEO) relief m

relieve [rɪˈliːv] vt (pain, patient) soulager; (fear, worry) dissiper; (bring help) secourir; (take over from: gen) relayer; (: guard) relever; **to ~ sb of sth** débarrasser qn de qch; **to ~ o.s.** se soulager

religion [rɪˈlɪdʒən] n religion f; **religious** adj religieux(-euse); (book) de piété

relinquish [rɪˈlɪŋkwɪʃ] vt abandonner; (plan, habit) renoncer à

relish [ˈrelɪʃ] n (CULIN) condiment m; (enjoyment) délectation f ♦ vt (food etc) savourer; **to ~ doing** se délecter à faire

relocate [riːləʊˈkeɪt] vt installer ailleurs ♦ vi déménager, s'installer ailleurs

reluctance [rɪˈlʌktəns] n répugnance f

reluctant [rɪˈlʌktənt] adj peu disposé(e), qui hésite; **~ly** adv à contrecœur

rely on [rɪˈlaɪ-] vt fus (be dependent) dépendre de; (trust) compter sur

remain [rɪˈmeɪn] vi rester; **~der** n reste m; **~ing** adj qui reste; **~s** npl restes mpl

remake [ˈriːmeɪk] n (CINEMA) remake m

remand [rɪˈmɑːnd] n: **on ~** en détention préventive ♦ vt: **to be ~ed in custody** être placé(e) en détention préventive

remark [rɪˈmɑːk] n remarque f, observation f ♦ vt (faire) remarquer, dire; **~able** adj remarquable; **~ably** adv remarquablement

remarry [riːˈmærɪ] vi se remarier

remedial [rɪˈmiːdɪəl] adj (tuition, classes) de rattrapage; **~ exercises** gymnastique corrective

remedy [ˈremədɪ] n: **~ (for)** remède m (contre or à) ♦ vt remédier à

remember [rɪˈmembər] vt se rappeler, se souvenir de; (send greetings): **~ me to him** saluez-le de ma part; **remembrance** n souvenir m; mémoire f; **Remembrance Day** n le jour de l'Armistice

---

Remembrance Sunday

Remembrance Sunday ou **Remembrance Day** est le dimanche le plus proche du 11 novembre, jour où la Première Guerre mondiale a officiellement pris fin, et rend hommage aux victimes des deux guerres mondiales. À cette occasion, un silence de deux minutes est observé à 11 h, heure de la signature de l'armistice avec l'Alle-

*magne en 1918; certains membres de
la famille royale et du gouvernement
déposent des gerbes de coquelicots au
cénotaphe de Whitehall, et des cou-
ronnes sont placées sur les monuments aux morts dans toute la
Grande-Bretagne; par ailleurs, les gens
portent des coquelicots artificiels fabri-
qués et vendus par des membres de la
légion britannique blessés au combat,
au profit des blessés de guerre et de
leur famille.*

remind [rɪ'maɪnd] *vt*: **to ~ sb of** rappeler à qn; **to ~ sb to do** faire penser
à qn à faire, rappeler à qn qu'il doit faire; **~er** *n* (*souvenir*) souvenir *m*; (*letter*)
rappel *m*

reminisce [remɪ'nɪs] *vi*: **to ~** (**about**)
évoquer ses souvenirs (de); **~nt** *adj*: **to
be ~nt of** rappeler, faire penser à

remiss [rɪ'mɪs] *adj* négligent(e); **~ion**
n (*of illness, sins*) rémission *f*; (*of debt,
prison sentence*) remise *f*

remit [rɪ'mɪt] *vt* (*send: money*) envoyer;
~tance *n* paiement *m*

remnant ['remnənt] *n* reste *m*, restant
m; (*of cloth*) coupon *m*; **~s** *npl* (COMM)
fins *fpl* de série

remorse [rɪ'mɔːs] *n* remords *m*; **~ful**
adj plein(e) de remords; **~less** *adj* (fig)
impitoyable

remote [rɪ'məʊt] *adj* éloigné(e), loin-
tain(e); (*person*) distant(e); (*possibility*)
vague; **~ control** *n* télécommande *f*;
~ly *adv* au loin; (*slightly*) très vaguement

remould ['riːməʊld] (BRIT) *n* (*tyre*) pneu
rechapé

removable [rɪ'muːvəbl] *adj* (*detachable*) amovible

removal [rɪ'muːvəl] *n* (*taking away*)
enlèvement *m*; suppression *f*; (BRIT: from
house) déménagement *m*; (*from office:
dismissal*) renvoi *m*; (*of stain*) nettoyage
m; (MED) ablation *f*; **~ van** (BRIT) *n* camion *m* de déménagement

remove [rɪ'muːv] *vt* enlever, retirer;
(*employee*) renvoyer; (*stain*) faire partir;
(*abuse*) supprimer; (*doubt*) chasser

render ['rendəʳ] *vt* rendre; **~ing** *n* (MUS
etc) interprétation *f*

rendezvous ['rɒndɪvuː] *n* rendez-vous
m inv

renew [rɪ'njuː] *vt* renouveler; (*negotiations*) reprendre; (*acquaintance*) renouer; **~able** *adj* (*energy*) renouvelable;
~al *n* renouvellement *m*; reprise *f*

renounce [rɪ'naʊns] *vt* renoncer à

renovate ['renəveɪt] *vt* rénover; (*art
work*) restaurer

renown [rɪ'naʊn] *n* renommée *f*; **~ed**
adj renommé(e)

rent [rent] *n* loyer *m* ♦ *vt* louer; **~al** *n*
(*for television, car*) (prix *m* de) location *f*

reorganize [riː'ɔːgənaɪz] *vt* réorganiser

rep [rep] *n abbr* = **representative**; **repertory**

repair [rɪ'peəʳ] *n* réparation *f* ♦ *vt* réparer; **in good/bad ~** en bon/mauvais
état; **~ kit** *n* trousse *f* de réparation

repatriate [riː'pætrɪeɪt] *vt* rapatrier

repay [riː'peɪ] (*irreg*) *vt* (*money, creditor*)
rembourser; (*sb's efforts*) récompenser;
~ment *n* remboursement *m*

repeal [rɪ'piːl] *n* (*of law*) abrogation *f*
♦ *vt* (*law*) abroger

repeat [rɪ'piːt] *n* (RADIO, TV) reprise *f* ♦ *vt*
répéter; (COMM: order) renouveler;
(SCOL: a class) redoubler ♦ *vi* répéter;
~edly *adv* souvent, à plusieurs reprises

repel [rɪ'pel] *vt* repousser; **~lent** *adj* re-
poussant(e) ♦ *n*: **insect ~lent** insectifu-
ge *m*

repent [rɪ'pent] *vi*: **to ~** (**of**) se repentir
(de); **~ance** *n* repentir *m*

repertory ['repətərɪ] *n* (*also: ~ theatre*)
théâtre *m* de répertoire

repetition [repɪ'tɪʃən] *n* répétition *f*

repetitive [rɪ'petɪtɪv] *adj* (*movement,
work*) répétitif(-ive); (*speech*) plein(e) de
redites

replace [rɪ'pleɪs] *vt* (*put back*) remettre,
replacer; (*take the place of*) remplacer;

~ment n (substitution) remplacement m; (person) remplaçant(e)

replay ['riːpleɪ] n (of match) match rejoué; (of tape, film) répétition f

replenish [rɪ'plenɪʃ] vt (glass) remplir (de nouveau); (stock etc) réapprovisionner

replica ['replɪkə] n réplique f, copie exacte

reply [rɪ'plaɪ] n réponse f ♦ vi répondre

report [rɪ'pɔːt] n rapport m; (PRESS etc) reportage m; (BRIT: also: **school ~**) bulletin m (scolaire); (of gun) détonation f ♦ vt rapporter, faire un compte rendu de; (PRESS etc) faire un reportage sur; (bring to notice: occurrence) signaler ♦ vi (make a ~) faire un rapport (or un reportage); (present o.s.): **to ~ (to sb)** se présenter (chez qn); (be responsible to): **to ~ to sb** être sous les ordres de qn; **~ card** (US, SCOTTISH) n bulletin m scolaire; **~edly** adv: **she is ~edly living in** ... elle habiterait ...; **he ~edly told them to** ... il leur aurait ordonné de ...; **~er** n reporter m

repose [rɪ'pəʊz] n: **in ~** en ou au repos

represent [reprɪ'zent] vt représenter; (view, belief) présenter, expliquer; (describe): **to ~ sth as** présenter or décrire qch comme; **~ation** [reprɪzen'teɪʃən] n représentation f; **~ations** npl (protest) démarche f; **~ative** [reprɪ'zentətɪv] n représentant(e); (US: POL) député m ♦ adj représentatif(-ive), caractéristique

repress [rɪ'pres] vt réprimer; **~ion** n répression f

reprieve [rɪ'priːv] n (LAW) grâce f; (fig) sursis m, délai m

reprisal [rɪ'praɪzl] n: **~s** ♦ npl représailles fpl

reproach [rɪ'prəʊtʃ] vt: **to ~ sb with sth** reprocher qch à qn; **~ful** adj de reproche

reproduce [riːprə'djuːs] vt reproduire ♦ vi se reproduire; **reproduction** [riːprə'dʌkʃən] n reproduction f

reproof [rɪ'pruːf] n reproche m

reptile ['reptaɪl] n reptile m

republic [rɪ'pʌblɪk] n république f; **~an** adj républicain(e)

repudiate [rɪ'pjuːdɪeɪt] vt répudier, rejeter

repulsive [rɪ'pʌlsɪv] adj repoussant(e), répulsif(-ive)

reputable ['repjutəbl] adj de bonne réputation; (occupation) honorable

reputation [repju'teɪʃən] n réputation f

reputed [rɪ'pjuːtɪd] adj (supposed) supposé(e); **~ly** adv d'après ce qu'on dit

request [rɪ'kwest] n demande f; (formal) requête f ♦ vt: **to ~ (of** or **from sb)** demander (à qn); **~ stop** (BRIT) n (for bus) arrêt facultatif

require [rɪ'kwaɪə'] vt (need: subj: person) avoir besoin de; (: thing, situation) demander; (want) exiger; (order): **to ~ sb to do sth/sth of sb** exiger que qn fasse qch/qch de qn; **~ment** n exigence f; besoin m; condition requise

requisition [rekwɪ'zɪʃən] n: **~ (for)** demande f (de) ♦ vt (MIL) réquisitionner

rescue ['reskjuː] n (from accident) sauvetage m; (help) secours mpl ♦ vt sauver; **~ party** n équipe f de sauvetage; **~r** n sauveteur m

research [rɪ'səːtʃ] n recherche(s) f(pl) ♦ vt faire des recherches sur

resemblance [rɪ'zembləns] n ressemblance f

resemble [rɪ'zembl] vt ressembler à

resent [rɪ'zent] vt être contrarié(e) par; **~ful** adj irrité(e), plein(e) de ressentiment; **~ment** n ressentiment m

reservation [rezə'veɪʃən] n (booking) réservation f; (doubt) réserve f; (for tribe) réserve f; **to make a ~ (in a hotel/a restaurant/on a plane)** réserver or retenir une chambre/une table/une place

reserve [rɪ'zəːv] n réserve f; (SPORT) remplaçant(e) ♦ vt (seats etc) réserver, retenir; **~s** npl (MIL) réservistes mpl; **in ~** en réserve; **~d** adj réservé(e)

reshuffle [riː'ʃʌfl] n: Cabinet ~ (POL) remaniement ministériel

residence ['rezidəns] n résidence f; ~ **permit** (BRIT) n permis m de séjour

resident ['rezidənt] n résident(e) ♦ adj résidant(e); **~ial** [rezi'denʃəl] adj résidentiel(le); (course) avec hébergement sur place; **~ial school** n internat m

residue ['rezidjuː] n reste m; (CHEM, PHYSICS) résidu m

resign [ri'zaɪn] vt (one's post) démissionner de ♦ vi démissionner; **to ~ o.s. to** se résigner à; **~ation** [rezig'neɪʃən] n (of post) démission f; (state of mind) résignation f; **~ed** adj résigné(e)

resilient [ri'ziliənt] adj (material) élastique; (person) qui réagit, qui a du ressort

resist [ri'zist] vt résister à; **~ance** n résistance f

resit [riː'sit] vt (exam) repasser ♦ n deuxième session f (d'un examen)

resolution [rezə'luːʃən] n résolution f

resolve [ri'zɒlv] n résolution f ♦ vi (problem) résoudre ♦ vi: **to ~ to do** résoudre or décider de faire

resort [ri'zɔːt] n (seaside town) station f balnéaire; (ski ~) station de ski; (recourse) recours m ♦ vi: **to ~ to** avoir recours à; **in the last ~** en dernier ressort

resounding [ri'zaundiŋ] adj retentissant(e)

resource [ri'sɔːs] n ressource f; **~s** npl (supplies, wealth etc) ressources; **~ful** adj ingénieux(-euse), débrouillard(e)

respect [ris'pekt] n respect m ♦ vt respecter; **~s** npl (compliments) respects, hommages mpl; **with ~ to** en ce qui concerne; **in this ~** à cet égard; **~able** adj respectable; **~ful** adj respectueux (-euse); **~ively** adv respectivement

respite ['respait] n répit m

respond [ris'pɒnd] vi répondre; (react) réagir; **response** n réponse f; réaction f

responsibility [rispɒnsi'biliti] n responsabilité f

responsible [ris'pɒnsibl] adj (liable): ~ **(for)** responsable (de); (person) digne de confiance; (job) qui comporte des responsabilités

responsive [ris'pɒnsiv] adj qui réagit; (person) qui n'est pas réservé(e) or indifférent(e)

rest [rest] n repos m; (stop) arrêt m, pause f; (MUS) silence m; (support) support m, appui m; (remainder) reste m, restant m ♦ vi se reposer; (be supported): **to ~ on** appuyer or reposer sur; (remain) rester ♦ vt (lean): **to ~ sth on/against** appuyer qch sur/contre; **the ~ of them** les autres; **it ~s with him to ...** c'est à lui de ...

restaurant ['restərɒn] n restaurant m; ~ **car** (BRIT) n wagon-restaurant m

restful ['restful] adj reposant(e)

restive ['restiv] adj agité(e), impatient(e); (horse) rétif(-ive)

restless ['restlis] adj agité(e)

restoration [restə'reɪʃən] n restauration f; restitution f; rétablissement m

restore [ri'stɔːr] vt (building) restaurer; (sth stolen) restituer; (peace, health) rétablir; **to ~ to** (former state) ramener à

restrain [ris'treɪn] vt contenir; (person): **to ~ (from doing)** retenir (de faire); **~ed** adj (style) sobre; (manner) mesuré(e); **~t** n (restriction) contrainte f; (moderation) retenue f

restrict [ris'trikt] vt restreindre, limiter; **~ion** n restriction f, limitation f

rest room (US) n toilettes fpl

result [ri'zʌlt] n résultat m ♦ vi: **to ~ in** aboutir à, se terminer par; **as a ~ of** à la suite de

resume [ri'zjuːm] vt, vi (work, journey) reprendre

résumé ['reizjuːmeɪ] n résumé m; (US) curriculum vitae m

resumption [ri'zʌmpʃən] n reprise f

resurgence [ri'sɜːdʒəns] n (of energy, activity) regain m

resurrection [rezə'rekʃən] n résurrection f

resuscitate [rɪ'sʌsɪteɪt] vt (MED) réanimer

retail ['riːteɪl] adj de ou au détail ♦ adv au détail; **~er** n détaillant(e); **~ price** n prix m de détail

retain [rɪ'teɪn] vt (keep) garder, conserver; **~er** n (fee) acompte m, provision f

retaliate [rɪ'tælɪeɪt] vi: **to ~ (against)** se venger (de); **retaliation** [rɪtælɪ'eɪʃən] n représailles fpl, vengeance f

retarded [rɪ'tɑːdɪd] adj retardé(e)

retch [retʃ] vi avoir des haut-le-cœur

retentive [rɪ'tentɪv] adj: **~ memory** excellente mémoire

retina ['retɪnə] n rétine f

retire [rɪ'taɪə*] vi (give up work) prendre sa retraite; (withdraw) se retirer, partir; (go to bed) (aller) se coucher; **~d** adj (person) retraité(e); **~ment** n retraite f; **retiring** adj (shy) réservé(e); (leaving) sortant(e)

retort [rɪ'tɔːt] vi riposter

retrace [riː'treɪs] vt: **to ~ one's steps** revenir sur ses pas

retract [rɪ'trækt] vt (statement, claws) rétracter; (undercarriage, aerial) rentrer, escamoter

retrain [riː'treɪn] vt (worker) recycler

retread ['riːtred] n (tyre) pneu rechapé

retreat [rɪ'triːt] n retraite f ♦ vi battre en retraite

retribution [retrɪ'bjuːʃən] n châtiment m

retrieval [rɪ'triːvəl] n (see vb) récupération f; réparation f

retrieve [rɪ'triːv] vt (sth lost) récupérer; (situation, honour) sauver; (error, loss) réparer; **~r** n chien m d'arrêt

retrospect ['retrəspekt] n: **in ~** rétrospectivement, après coup; **~ive** [retrə'spektɪv] adj rétrospectif(-ive); (law) rétroactif(-ive)

return [rɪ'tɜːn] n (going or coming back) retour m; (of sth stolen) restitution f; (FINANCE: from land, shares) rendement m, rapport m ♦ cpd (journey) de retour;

(BRIT: ticket) aller et retour; (match) retour ♦ vi (come back) revenir; (go back) retourner ♦ vt rendre; (bring back) rapporter; (send back; also: ball) renvoyer; (put back) remettre; (POL: candidate) élire; **~s** npl (COMM) recettes fpl; **in ~ (for)** en échange (de); **by ~ of post** par retour (du courrier); **many happy ~s (of the day)!** bon anniversaire!

reunion [riː'juːnɪən] n réunion f

reunite [riːjuː'naɪt] vt réunir

reuse [riː'juːz] vt réutiliser

rev [rev] n abbr (AUT: = revolution) tour m ♦ vt (also: **rev up**) emballer

revamp [riː'væmp] vt (firm, system etc) réorganiser

reveal [rɪ'viːl] vt (make known) révéler; (display) laisser voir; **~ing** adj révélateur(-trice); (dress) au décolleté généreux ou suggestif

revel ['revl] vi: **to ~ in sth/in doing** se délecter de qch/à faire

revenge [rɪ'vendʒ] n vengeance f; **to take ~ on** (enemy) se venger sur

revenue ['revənjuː] n revenu m

reverberate [rɪ'vɜːbəreɪt] vi (sound) retentir, se répercuter; (fig: shock etc) se propager

reverence ['revərəns] n vénération f, révérence f

Reverend ['revərənd] adj (in titles): **the ~ John Smith** (Anglican) le révérend John Smith; (Catholic) l'abbé (John) Smith; (Protestant) le pasteur (John) Smith

reversal [rɪ'vɜːsl] n (of opinion) revirement m; (of order) renversement m; (of direction) changement m

reverse [rɪ'vɜːs] n contraire m, opposé m; (back) dos m, envers m; (of paper) verso m; (of coin; also: setback) revers m; (AUT: also: **~ gear**) marche f arrière ♦ adj (order, direction) opposé(e), inverse ♦ vt (order, position) changer, inverser; (direction, policy) changer complètement de; (decision) annuler; (roles) renverser; (car) faire marche arrière avec ♦ vi (BRIT: AUT) faire marche arrière; **he ~d (the car) into a wall** il a embouti un mur en marche arrière; **~d charge call** (BRIT) n (TEL) communication f en PCV; **reversing lights** (BRIT) npl (AUT) feux mpl de marche arrière or de recul

revert [rɪ'vɜːt] vi: **to ~ to** revenir à, retourner à

review [rɪ'vjuː] n revue f; (of book, film) critique f, compte rendu; (of situation, policy) examen m, bilan m ♦ vt passer en revue; faire la critique de; examiner; **~er** n critique m

revise [rɪ'vaɪz] vt réviser, modifier; (manuscript) revoir, corriger ♦ vi (study) réviser; **revision** [rɪ'vɪʒən] n révision f

revival [rɪ'vaɪvəl] n reprise f; (recovery) rétablissement m; (of faith) renouveau m

revive [rɪ'vaɪv] vt (person) ranimer; (custom) rétablir; (economy) relancer; (hope, courage) raviver, faire renaître; (play) reprendre ♦ vi (person) reprendre connaissance; (: from ill health) se rétablir; (hope etc) renaître; (activity) reprendre

revoke [rɪ'vəʊk] vt révoquer; (law) abroger

revolt [rɪ'vəʊlt] n révolte f ♦ vi se révolter, se rebeller ♦ vt révolter, dégoûter; **~ing** adj dégoûtant(e)

revolution [revə'luːʃən] n révolution f; (of wheel etc) tour m, révolution; **~ary** adj révolutionnaire ♦ n révolutionnaire m/f

revolve [rɪ'vɒlv] vi tourner

revolver [rɪ'vɒlvər] n revolver m

revolving [rɪ'vɒlvɪŋ] adj tournant(e); (chair) pivotant(e); **~ door** n (porte f à) tambour m

revulsion [rɪ'vʌlʃən] n dégoût m, répugnance f

reward [rɪ'wɔːd] n récompense f ♦ vt: **to ~ (for)** récompenser (de); **~ing** adj (fig) qui (en) vaut la peine, gratifiant(e)

rewind [riː'waɪnd] (irreg) vt (tape) rembobiner

rewire [riː'waɪər] vt (house) refaire l'installation électrique de

rheumatism ['ruːmətɪzəm] n rhumatisme m

Rhine [raɪn] n Rhin m

rhinoceros [raɪ'nɒsərəs] n rhinocéros m

Rhone [rəʊn] n Rhône m

rhubarb ['ruːbɑːb] n rhubarbe f

rhyme [raɪm] n rime f; (verse) vers mpl

rhythm ['rɪðm] n rythme m

rib [rɪb] n (ANAT) côte f

ribbon ['rɪbən] n ruban m; **in ~s** (torn) en lambeaux

rice [raɪs] n riz m; **~ pudding** n riz au lait

rich [rɪtʃ] adj riche; (gift, clothes) somptueux(-euse) ♦ npl: **the ~** les riches mpl; **~es** npl richesses fpl; **~ly** adv richement; (deserved, earned) largement

rickets ['rɪkɪts] n rachitisme m

rid [rɪd] (pt, pp rid) vt: **to ~ sb of** débarrasser qn de; **to get ~ of** se débarrasser de

riddle ['rɪdl] n (puzzle) énigme f ♦ vt: **to be ~d with** être criblé(e) de; (fig: guilt, corruption, doubts) être en proie à

ride [raɪd] (pt rode, pp ridden) n (in car) promenade f, tour m; (distance covered) trajet m ♦ vi (as sport) monter (à cheval), faire du cheval; (go somewhere: on horse, bicycle) aller (à cheval or bicyclette etc); (journey: on bicycle, motorcycle, bus) rouler ♦ vt (a certain horse) monter; (distance) parcourir, faire; **to take sb for a ~** (fig) faire marcher qn; **to ~ a horse/bicycle** monter à cheval/à bicyclette; **~r** n cavalier(-ère); (in race) jockey m; (on bicycle) cycliste m/f; (on motorcycle) motocycliste m/f

ridge [rɪdʒ] n (of roof, mountain) arête f; (of hill) faîte m; (on object) strie f

ridicule ['rɪdɪkjuːl] n ridicule m; dérision f

ridiculous [rɪ'dɪkjuləs] adj ridicule

riding ['raɪdɪŋ] n équitation f;

school n manège m, école f d'équitation

rife [raɪf] adj répandu(e); **~ with** abondant(e) en, plein(e) de

riffraff ['rɪfræf] n racaille f

rifle ['raɪfl] n fusil m (à canon rayé) ♦ vt vider, dévaliser; **~ through** vt (belongings) fouiller; (papers) feuilleter; **~ range** n champ m de tir; (at fair) stand m de tir

rift [rɪft] n fente f, fissure f; (fig: disagreement) désaccord m

rig [rɪg] n (also: **oil ~**: at sea) plateforme pétrolière ♦ vt (election etc) truquer; **~ out** (BRIT) vt: **to ~ out as/in** habiller en/de; **~ up** vt arranger, faire avec des moyens de fortune; **~ging** n (NAUT) gréement m

right [raɪt] adj (correctly chosen: answer, road etc) bon (bonne); (true) juste, exact(e); (suitable) approprié(e), convenable; (just) juste, équitable; (morally good) bien adv (not left) droit(e) ♦ n (what is morally ~) bien m; (title, claim) droit m; (not left) droite f ♦ adv (answer) correctement, juste; (treat) bien, comme il faut; (not on the left) à droite ♦ vt redresser ♦ excl bon!; **to be ~** (person) avoir raison; (answer) être juste or correct(e); (clock) être à l'heure (juste); **by ~s** en toute justice; **on the ~** à droite; **to be in the ~** avoir raison; **~ now** en ce moment même; tout de suite; **~ in the middle** en plein milieu; **~ away** immédiatement; **~ angle** n (MATH) angle droit; **~eous** ['raɪtʃəs] adj droit(e), vertueux(-euse); (anger) justifié(e); **~ful** adj légitime; **~-handed** adj (person) droitier(-ère); **~-hand man** n bras droit (fig); **~-hand side** n la droite; **~ly** adv (with reason) à juste titre; **~ of way** n droit m de passage; (AUT) priorité f; **~-wing** adj (POL) de droite

rigid ['rɪdʒɪd] adj rigide; (principle, control) strict(e)

rigmarole ['rɪgmərəʊl] n comédie f

rigorous ['rɪgərəs] adj rigoureux(-euse)

rile [raɪl] vt agacer

rim [rɪm] n bord m; (of spectacles) monture f; (of wheel) jante f

rind [raɪnd] n (of bacon) couenne f; (of lemon etc) écorce f, zeste m; (of cheese) croûte f

ring [rɪŋ] (pt rang, pp rung) n anneau m; (on finger) bague f; (also: **wedding ~**) alliance f; (of people, objects) cercle m; (of spies) réseau m; (of smoke etc) rond m; (arena) piste f, arène f; (for boxing) ring m; (sound of bell) sonnerie f ♦ vi (telephone, bell) sonner; (person: by telephone) téléphoner; (also: **~ out**: voice, words) retentir; (ears) bourdonner ♦ vt (BRIT: TEL: also: **~ up**) téléphoner à, appeler; (bell) faire sonner; **to ~ the bell** sonner; **to give sb a ~** (BRIT: TEL) appeler qn; **~ back** (BRIT) vt, vi (TEL) rappeler; **~ off** (BRIT) vi (TEL) raccrocher; **~ up** (BRIT) vt (TEL) appeler; **~ binder** n classeur m à anneaux; **~ing** ['rɪŋɪŋ] n (of telephone) sonnerie f; (of bell) tintement m; (in ears) bourdonnement m; **~ing tone** (BRIT) n (TEL) sonnerie f; **~leader** n (of gang) chef m, meneur m; **~lets** npl anglaises fpl; **~ road** (BRIT) n route f de ceinture; (motorway) périphérique m

rink [rɪŋk] n (also: **ice ~**) patinoire f

rinse [rɪns] vt rincer

riot ['raɪət] n émeute f; (of flowers, colour) profusion f ♦ vi faire une émeute, manifester avec violence; **to run ~** se déchaîner; **~ous** adj (mob, assembly) séditieux(-euse), déchaîné(e); (living, behaviour) débauché(e); (party) très animé(e); (welcome) délirant(e)

rip [rɪp] n déchirure f ♦ vt déchirer ♦ vi se déchirer; **~cord** n poignée f d'ouverture

ripe [raɪp] adj (fruit) mûr(e); (cheese) fait(e); **~n** vt mûrir ♦ vi mûrir

rip-off (inf) n: **it's a ~~!** c'est de l'arnaque!

ripple ['rɪpl] n ondulation f; (of applause, laughter) cascade f ♦ vi onduler

rise [raɪz] (pt **rose**, pp **risen**) n (slope) côte f, pente f; (hill) hauteur f; (increase: in wages: BRIT) augmentation f; (: in prices, temperature) hausse f, augmentation f; (fig: to power etc) ascension f ♦ vi s'élever, monter; (prices, numbers) augmenter; (waters) monter; (sun; person: from chair, bed) se lever; (also: ~ up: tower, building) s'élever; (: rebel) se révolter; (in rank) s'élever; **to give ~ to** donner lieu à; **to ~ to the occasion** se montrer à la hauteur; **~r** n: **to be an early ~r** être matinal(e); **rising** adj (number, prices) en hausse; (tide) montant(e); (sun, moon) levant(e)

risk [rɪsk] n risque m ♦ vt risquer; **at ~** en danger; **at one's own ~** à ses risques et périls; **~y** adj risqué(e)

rissole ['rɪsəul] n croquette f

rite [raɪt] n rite m; **last ~s** derniers sacrements

ritual ['rɪtjuəl] adj rituel(le) ♦ n rituel m

rival ['raɪvl] adj, n rival(e); (in business) concurrent(e) ♦ vt (match) égaler; **~ry** ['raɪvlrɪ] n rivalité f, concurrence f

river ['rɪvə'] n rivière f; (major, also fig) fleuve m ♦ cpd (port, traffic) fluvial(e); **up/down~** en amont/aval; **~bank** n rive f, berge f; **~bed** n lit m (de rivière or de fleuve)

rivet ['rɪvɪt] n rivet m ♦ vt (fig) river, fixer

Riviera [rɪvɪ'ɛərə] n: **the (French) ~** la Côte d'Azur; **the Italian ~** la Riviera (italienne)

road [rəud] n route f; (in town) rue f; (fig) chemin, voie f; **major/minor ~** route principale or à priorité/voie secondaire; **~ accident** n accident m de la circulation; **~block** n barrage routier; **~hog** n chauffard m; **~ map** n carte routière; **~ rage** n comportement très agressif de certains usagers de la route; **~ safety** n sécurité routière; **~side** n bord m de la route, bas-côté m; **~ sign** n panneau m de signalisation; **~way** n chaussée f; **~ works** npl travaux mpl

(de réfection des routes); **~worthy** adj en bon état de marche

roam [rəum] vi errer, vagabonder

roar [rɔː'] n rugissement m; (of crowd) hurlements mpl; (of vehicle, thunder, storm) grondement m ♦ vi rugir; hurler; gronder; **to ~ with laughter** éclater de rire; **to do a ~ing trade** faire des affaires d'or

roast [rəust] n rôti m ♦ vt (faire) rôtir; (coffee) griller, torréfier; **~ beef** n rôti m de bœuf, rosbif m

rob [rɔb] vt (person) voler; (bank) dévaliser; **to ~ sb of sth** voler or dérober qch à qn; (fig: deprive) priver qn de qch; **~ber** n bandit m, voleur m; **~bery** n vol m

robe [rəub] n (for ceremony etc) robe f; (also: **bathrobe**) peignoir m; (US) couverture f

robin ['rɔbɪn] n rouge-gorge m

robot ['rəubɔt] n robot m

robust [rəu'bʌst] adj robuste; (material, appetite) solide

rock [rɔk] n (substance) roche f, roc m; (boulder) rocher m; (US: small stone) caillou m; (BRIT: sweet) = sucre m d'orge f ♦ vt (swing gently: cradle) balancer; (: child) bercer; (shake) ébranler, secouer ♦ vi (swing gently) se balancer; (: child) se balancer; être ébranlé(e) or secoué(e); **on the ~s** (drink) avec des glaçons; (marriage etc) en train de craquer; **~ and roll** n rock (and roll) m, rock'n'roll m; **~-bottom** adj (fig: prices) sacrifié(e); **~ery** n (jardin m de) rocaille f

rocket ['rɔkɪt] n fusée f; (MIL) fusée, roquette f; (CULIN) roquette f

rocking chair n fauteuil m à bascule

rocking horse n cheval m à bascule

rocky ['rɔkɪ] adj (hill) rocheux(-euse); (path) rocailleux(-euse)

rod [rɔd] n (wooden) baguette f; (metallic) tringle f; (TECH) tige f; (also: **fishing ~**) canne f à pêche

rode [rəud] pt of **ride**

rodent ['rəudnt] n rongeur m

rodeo ['rəʊdɪəʊ] (*US*) *n* rodéo *m*

roe [rəʊ] *n* (*species: also:* **~ deer**) chevreuil *m*; (*of fish: also:* **hard ~**) œufs *mpl* de poisson; **soft ~** laitance *f*

rogue [rəʊg] *n* coquin *m*

role [rəʊl] *n* rôle *m*; **~ play** *n* jeu *m* de rôle

roll [rəʊl] *n* rouleau *m*; (*of banknotes*) liasse *f*; (*also:* **bread ~**) petit pain; (*register*) liste *f*; (*sound: of drums etc*) roulement *m* ♦ *vt* rouler; (*also:* **~ up**) enrouler; (*: sleeves*) retrousser; (*also:* **~ out**: *pastry*) étendre au rouleau, abaisser ♦ *vi* rouler; **~ about** *vi* rouler ça et là; (*person*) se rouler par terre; **~ around** *vi* = **roll about**; **~ by** *vi* (*time*) s'écouler, passer; **~ over** *vi* se retourner; **~ up** *vi* (*inf: arrive*) arriver, s'amener ♦ *vt* rouler; **~ call** *n* appel *m*; **~er** *n* rouleau *m*; (*wheel*) roulette *f*; (*for road*) rouleau compresseur; **~er blade** *n* patin *m* en ligne; **~er coaster** *n* montagnes *fpl* russes; **~er skates** *npl* patins *mpl* à roulettes; **~er skating** *n* patin *m* à roulettes; **~ing** *adj* (*landscape*) onduleux(-euse); **~ing pin** *n* rouleau *m* à pâtisserie; **~ing stock** *n* (*RAIL*) matériel roulant

ROM [rɔm] *n abbr* (= *read only memory*) mémoire morte

Roman ['rəʊmən] *adj* romain(e); **~ Catholic** *adj*, *n* catholique *m/f*

romance [rə'mæns] *n* (*love affair*) idylle *f*; (*charm*) poésie *f*; (*novel*) roman *m* à l'eau de rose

Romania [rəʊ'meɪnɪə] *n* Roumanie *f*; **~n** *adj* roumain(e) ♦ *n* Roumain(e); (*LING*) roumain *m*

Roman numeral *n* chiffre romain

romantic [rə'mæntɪk] *adj* romantique; sentimental(e)

Rome [rəʊm] *n* Rome

romp [rɔmp] *n* jeux bruyants ♦ *vi* (*also:* **~ about**) s'ébattre, jouer bruyamment; **~ers** *npl* barboteuse *f*

roof [ruːf] (*pl* **~s**) *n* toit *m* ♦ *vt* couvrir (d'un toit); **the ~ of the mouth** la

voûte du palais; **~ing** *n* toiture *f*; **~ rack** *n* (*AUT*) galerie *f*

rook [rʊk] *n* (*bird*) freux *m*; (*CHESS*) tour *f*

room [ruːm] *n* (*in house*) pièce *f*; (*also:* **bedroom**) chambre *f* (à coucher); (*in school etc*) salle *f*; (*space*) place *f*; (*lodging*) meublé *m*; **"~s to let"** (*BRIT*) or **"~s for rent"** (*US*) "chambres à louer"; **single/double ~** chambre pour une personne/deux personnes; **there is ~ for improvement** cela laisse à désirer; **~ing house** (*US*) *n* maison *f* or immeuble *m* de rapport; **~mate** *n* camarade *m/f* de chambre; **~ service** *n* service *m* des chambres (*dans un hôtel*); **~y** *adj* spacieux(-euse); (*garment*) ample

roost [ruːst] *vi* se jucher

rooster ['ruːstə*r*] *n* (*esp US*) coq *m*

root [ruːt] *n* (*BOT, MATH*) racine *f*; (*fig: of problem*) origine *f*, fond *m* ♦ *vi* (*plant*) s'enraciner; **~ about** *vi* (*fig*) fouiller; **~ for** *vt fus* encourager, applaudir; **~ out** *vt* (*find*) dénicher

rope [rəʊp] *n* corde *f*; (*NAUT*) cordage *m* ♦ *vt* (*tie up* or *together*) attacher; (*climbers: also:* **~ together**) encorder; (*area:* **~ off**) interdire l'accès de; (*: divide off*) séparer (*à l'aide d'une corde*); **to know the ~s** (*fig*) être au courant, connaître les ficelles; **~ in** *vt* (*fig: person*) embringuer

rosary ['rəʊzərɪ] *n* chapelet *m*

rose [rəʊz] *pt of* **rise** ♦ *n* rose *f*; (*also:* **~bush**) rosier *m*; (*on watering can*) pomme *f*

rosé ['rəʊzeɪ] *n* rosé *m*

rosebud ['rəʊzbʌd] *n* bouton *m* de rose

rosemary ['rəʊzmərɪ] *n* romarin *m*

roster ['rɔstə*r*] *n*: **duty ~** tableau *m* de service

rostrum ['rɔstrəm] *n* tribune *f* (*pour un orateur etc*)

rosy ['rəʊzɪ] *adj* rose; **a ~ future** un bel avenir

rot [rɔt] *n* (*decay*) pourriture *f*; (*fig: pej*)

idioties fpl ♦ vt, vi pourrir

rota ['rəʊtə] n liste f, tableau m de service; **on a ~ basis** par roulement

rotary ['rəʊtərɪ] adj rotatif(-ive)

rotate [rəʊ'teɪt] vt (revolve) faire tourner; (change round: jobs) faire à tour de rôle ♦ vi (revolve) tourner; **rotating** adj (movement) tournant(e).

rotten ['rɔtn] adj (decayed) pourri(e); (dishonest) corrompu(e); (inf: bad) mauvais(e), moche; **to feel ~** (ill) être mal fichu(e)

rotund [rəʊ'tʌnd] adj (person) rondelet(te)

rough [rʌf] adj (cloth, skin) rêche, rugueux(-euse); (terrain) accidenté(e); (path) rocailleux(-euse); (voice) rauque, rude; (person, manner: coarse) rude, fruste; (: violent) brutal(e); (district, weather) mauvais(e); (sea) hou leux(-euse); (plan etc) ébauché(e); (guess) approximatif(-ive) ♦ n (GOLF) rough m ♦ vt: **to ~ it** vivre à la dure; **to sleep ~** (BRIT) coucher à la dure; **~age** n fibres fpl alimentaires; **~-and-ready** adj rudimentaire; **~ copy**, **~ draft** n brouillon m; **~ly** adv (handle) rudement, brutalement; (speak) avec brusquerie; (make) grossièrement; (approximately) à peu près, en gros

roulette [ruː'let] n roulette f

Roumania [ruː'meɪnɪə] n = **Romania**

round [raʊnd] adj rond(e) ♦ n (BRIT: of toast) tranche f; (duty: of policeman, milkman etc) tournée f; (: of doctor) visites fpl; (game: of cards, in competition) partie f; (BOXING) round m; (of talks) série f ♦ vt (corner) tourner ♦ prep autour de ♦ adv: **all ~** tout autour; **the long way ~** (par) le chemin le plus long; **all the year ~** toute l'année; **it's just ~ the corner** (fig) c'est tout près; **the clock** 24 heures sur 24; **to go ~ to sb's (house)** passer chez qn; **go ~ the back** passez par derrière; **enough to go ~** assez pour tout le monde; **~ of ammunition** cartouche f; **~ of ap-**

plause ban m, applaudissements mpl; **~ of drinks** tournée f; **~ of sandwiches** sandwich m; **~ off** vt (speech etc) terminer; **~ up** vt rassembler; (criminals) effectuer une rafle de; (price, figure) arrondir (au chiffre supérieur); **~about** n (BRIT: AUT) rond-point m (à sens giratoire); (: at fair) manège m (de chevaux de bois) ♦ adj (route, means) détourné(e); **~ers** n (game) sorte de baseball; **~ly** adv (fig) tout net, carrément; **~ trip** n (voyage m) aller et retour m; **~up** n rassemblement m; (of criminals) rafle f

rouse [raʊz] vt (wake up) réveiller; (stir up) susciter; provoquer; éveiller; **rousing** adj (welcome) enthousiaste

route [ruːt] n itinéraire m; (of bus) parcours m; (of trade, shipping) route f

routine [ruː'tiːn] adj (work) ordinaire, courant(e); (procedure) d'usage ♦ n (habits) habitudes fpl; (pej) train-train m; (THEATRE) numéro m

rove [rəʊv] vt (area, streets) errer dans

row[1] [rəʊ] n (line) rangée f; (of people, seats, KNITTING) rang m; (behind one another: of cars, people) file f ♦ vi (in boat) ramer; (as sport) faire de l'aviron ♦ vt (boat) faire aller à la rame or à l'aviron; **in a ~** (fig) d'affilée

row[2] [raʊ] n (noise) vacarme m; (dispute) dispute f, querelle f; (scolding) réprimande f, savon m ♦ vi se disputer, se quereller

rowboat ['rəʊbəʊt] (US) n canot m (à rames)

rowdy ['raʊdɪ] adj chahuteur(-euse); (occasion) tapageur(-euse)

rowing ['rəʊɪŋ] n canotage m; (as sport) aviron m; **~ boat** (BRIT) n canot m (à rames)

royal ['rɔɪəl] adj royal(e); **R~ Air Force** (BRIT) n armée de l'air britannique; **~ty** n (royal persons) (membres mpl de la) famille royale; (payment: to author) droits mpl d'auteur; (: to inventor) royalties fpl

rpm abbr (AUT) (= revolutions per minute)

tr/mn

RSVP *abbr* (= *répondez s'il vous plaît*) R.S.V.P.

Rt Hon. *abbr* (BRIT: *Right Honourable*) titre donné aux députés de la Chambre des communes

rub [rʌb] *vt* frotter; frictionner; (hands) se frotter ♦ *n* (with cloth) coup *m* chiffon *or* de torchon; **to give sth a ~** donner un coup de chiffon *or* de torchon à; **to ~ sb up** (BRIT) *or* **~ sb** (US) **the wrong way** prendre qn à rebrousse-poil; **~ off** *vi* partir; **~ off on** *vt fus* déteindre sur; **~ out** *vt* effacer

rubber ['rʌbə*] *n* caoutchouc *m*; (BRIT: *eraser*) gomme *f* (à effacer); **~ band** élastique *m*; **~ plant** caoutchouc *m* (plante *verte*)

rubbish ['rʌbɪʃ] *n* (from household) ordures *fpl*; (fig: *pej*) camelote *f*; (non-sense) bêtises *fpl*, idioties *fpl*; **~ bin** (BRIT) *n* poubelle *f*; **~ dump** *n* décharge publique, dépotoir *m*

rubble ['rʌbl] *n* décombres *mpl*; (smaller) gravats *mpl*; (CONSTR) blocage *m*

ruby ['ru:bɪ] *n* rubis *m*

rucksack ['rʌksæk] *n* sac *m* à dos

rudder ['rʌdə*] *n* gouvernail *m*

ruddy ['rʌdɪ] *adj* (face) coloré(e); (inf: *damned*) sacré(e), fichu(e)

rude [ru:d] *adj* (impolite) impoli(e); (coarse) grossier(-ère); (shocking) indécent(e), inconvenant(e)

ruffle ['rʌfl] *vt* (hair) ébouriffer; (clothes) chiffonner; (fig: *person*): **to get ~d** s'énerver

rug [rʌg] *n* petit tapis; (BRIT: *blanket*) couverture *f*

rugby ['rʌgbɪ] *n* (also: **~ football**) rugby *m*

rugged ['rʌgɪd] *adj* (landscape) accidenté(e); (features, *character*) rude

ruin ['ru:ɪn] *n* ruine *f* ♦ *vt* ruiner; (spoil, *clothes*) abîmer; (event) gâcher; **~s** *npl* (of building) ruine(s)

rule [ru:l] *n* règle *f*; (regulation) règlement *m*; (government) autorité *f*,

gouvernement *m* ♦ *vt* (country) gouverner; (person) dominer ♦ *vi* commander; (LAW) statuer; **as a ~** normalement, en règle générale; **~ out** *vt* exclure; **~d** *adj* (paper) réglé(e); **~r** *n* (sovereign) souverain(e); (for *measuring*) règle *f*; **ruling** *adj* (party) au pouvoir; (class) dirigeant(e) ♦ *n* (LAW) décision *f*

rum [rʌm] *n* rhum *m*

Rumania [ru:'meɪnɪə] *n* = **Romania**

rumble ['rʌmbl] *vi* gronder; (stomach, *pipe*) gargouiller

rummage ['rʌmɪdʒ] *vi* fouiller

rumour ['ru:mə*] (US **rumor**) *n* rumeur *f*, bruit *m* (qui court) ♦ *vt*: **it is ~ed that** le bruit court que

rump [rʌmp] *n* (of animal) croupe *f*; (inf: *of person*) postérieur *m*; **~ steak** *n* rumsteck *m*

rumpus ['rʌmpəs] (inf) *n* tapage *m*, chahut *m*

run [rʌn] (*pt* **ran**, *pp* **run**) *n* (fast pace) (pas *m* de) course *f*; (outing) tour *m* *or* promenade *f* (en voiture); (distance *travelled*) parcours *m*, trajet *m*; (series) suite *f*, série *f*; (THEATRE) série de représentations; (SKI) piste *f*; (CRICKET, BASEBALL) point *m*; (in tights, *stockings*) maille filée, échelle *f* ♦ *vt* (operate: *business*) diriger; (: competition, *course*) organiser; (: hotel, *house*) tenir; (race) participer à; (COMPUT) exécuter; (: to pass: hand, *finger*) passer; (water, *bath*) faire couler; (PRESS: *feature*) publier ♦ *vi* courir; (flee) s'enfuir; (work: machine, *factory*) marcher; (bus, *train*) circuler; (continue: play) se jouer; (: contract) être valide; (flow: river, bath; *nose*) couler; (colours, *washing*) déteindre; (in *election*) être candidat, se présenter; **to go for a ~** faire un peu de course à pied; **there was a ~ on ...** (meat, *tickets*) les gens se sont rués sur ...; **in the long ~** à longue échéance; à la longue; en fin de compte; **on the ~** en fuite; **I'll ~ you to the station** je vais vous emmener *or* conduire à la gare; **to ~ a risk** courir un risque; **~ about** vi (children) courir çà et là; **~ across** vt fus (find) trouver par hasard; **~ around** vi = run about; **~ away** vi s'enfuir; **~ down** vt (production) réduire progressivement de; (factory) réduire progressivement la production de; (AUT) renverser; (criticize) critiquer, dénigrer; **to be ~ down** (person: tired) être fatigué(e) or à plat; **~ in** (BRIT) vt (car) roder; **~ into** vt fus (meet: person) rencontrer par hasard; (trouble) se heurter à; (collide with) heurter; **~ off** vi s'enfuir ♦ vt (water) laisser s'écouler; (copies) tirer; **~ out** vi (person) sortir en courant; (liquid) couler; (lease) expirer; (money) être épuisé(e); **~ out of** vt fus se trouver à court de; **~ over** vt (AUT) écraser ♦ vt fus (revise) revoir, reprendre; (play) répéter; **~ through** vt fus (recapitulate) parcourir; **~ up** vt (make) confectionner; **to ~ up against** (difficulties) se heurter à; **to ~ up a debt** s'endetter; **~away** adj (horse) emballé(e); (truck) fou (folle); (person) fugitif(-ive); (teenager) fugueur(-euse)

rung [rʌŋ] pp of ring ♦ n (of ladder) barreau m

runner ['rʌnəʳ] n (in race: person) coureur(-euse); (: horse) partant m; (on sledge) patin m; (for drawer etc) coulisseau m; **~ bean** (BRIT) n haricot m (à rames); **~-up** n second(e)

running ['rʌnɪŋ] n course f; (of business, organization) gestion f, direction f ♦ adj (water) courant(e); **to be in/out of the ~ for sth** être/ne pas être sur les rangs pour qch; **6 days ~** 6 jours de suite; **~ commentary** n commentaire détaillé; **~ costs** npl frais mpl d'exploitation

runny ['rʌnɪ] adj qui coule

run-of-the-mill ['rʌnəvðə'mɪl] adj ordinaire, banal(e)

runt [rʌnt] n avorton m

run-up ['rʌnʌp] n: **~~ to sth** (election etc) période f précédant qch

runway ['rʌnweɪ] n (AVIAT) piste f

rupture ['rʌptʃəʳ] n (MED) hernie f

rural ['rʊərl] adj rural(e)

rush [rʌʃ] n (hurry) hâte f, précipitation f; (of crowd, COMM: sudden demand) ruée f; (current) flot m; (of emotion) vague f; (BOT) jonc m ♦ vt (hurry) transporter or envoyer d'urgence ♦ vi se précipiter; **~ hour** n heures fpl de pointe

rusk [rʌsk] n biscotte f

Russia ['rʌʃə] n Russie f; **~n** adj russe ♦ n Russe m/f; (LING) russe m

rust [rʌst] n rouille f ♦ vi rouiller

rustic ['rʌstɪk] adj rustique

rustle ['rʌsl] vi bruire, produire un bruissement ♦ vt froisser

rustproof ['rʌstpru:f] adj inoxydable

rusty ['rʌstɪ] adj rouillé(e)

rut [rʌt] n (track) rut m; (ZOOL) rut m; **to be in a ~** suivre l'ornière, s'encroûter

ruthless ['ru:θlɪs] adj sans pitié, impitoyable

rye [raɪ] n seigle m

S, s

Sabbath ['sæbəθ] n (Jewish) sabbat m; (Christian) dimanche m

sabotage ['sæbɑtɑ:ʒ] n sabotage m ♦ vt saboter

saccharin(e) ['sækərɪn] n saccharine f

sachet ['sæʃeɪ] n sachet m

sack [sæk] n (bag) sac m ♦ vt (dismiss) renvoyer, mettre à la porte; (plunder) piller, mettre à sac; **to get the ~** être renvoyé(e), être mis(e) à la porte; **~ing** n (material) toile f à sac; (dismissal) renvoi m

sacrament ['sækrəmənt] n sacrement m

sacred ['seɪkrɪd] adj sacré(e)

sacrifice ['sækrɪfaɪs] n sacrifice m ♦ vt sacrifier

sad [sæd] adj triste; (deplorable) triste, fâcheux(-euse)

saddle ['sædl] n selle f ♦ vt (horse) seller; **to be ~d with sth** (inf) avoir qch sur les bras; **~bag** n sacoche f

sadistic [sə'dɪstɪk] adj sadique

sadly ['sædlɪ] adv tristement; (unfortunately) malheureusement; (seriously) fort

sadness ['sædnɪs] n tristesse f

s.a.e. n abbr = stamped addressed envelope

safe [seɪf] adj (out of danger) hors de danger, en sécurité; (not dangerous) sans danger; (cautious) prudent(e); (sure: bet etc) assuré(e) ♦ n coffre-fort m; **~ from** à l'abri de; **~ and sound** sain(e) et sauf (sauve); **(just) to be on the ~ side** pour plus de sûreté, par précaution; **~ journey!** bon voyage!; **~conduct** n sauf-conduit m; **~deposit** n (vault) dépôt m de coffres-forts; (box) coffre-fort m; **~guard** n sauvegarde f, protection f ♦ vt sauvegarder, protéger; **~keeping** n bonne garde; **~ly** adv (assume, say) sans risque d'erreur; (drive, arrive) sans accident; **~ sex** n rapports mpl sexuels sans risque

safety ['seɪftɪ] n sécurité f; **~ belt** n ceinture f de sécurité; **~ pin** n épingle f de sûreté or de nourrice; **~ valve** n soupape f de sûreté

sag [sæg] vi s'affaisser; (hem, breasts) pendre

sage [seɪdʒ] n (herb) sauge f; (person) sage m

Sagittarius [sædʒɪ'tɛərɪəs] n le Sagittaire

Sahara [sə'hɑːrə] n: **the ~ (Desert)** le (désert du) Sahara

said [sɛd] pt, pp of **say**

sail [seɪl] n (on boat) voile f; (trip): **to go for a ~** faire un tour en bateau ♦ vt (boat) manœuvrer, piloter ♦ vi (travel: ship) avancer, naviguer; (set off) partir, prendre la mer; (SPORT) faire de la voile; **they ~ed into Le Havre** ils sont entrés dans le port du Havre; **~ through** vi, vt fus (fig) réussir haut la main; **~boat** n (US) n bateau m à voiles, voilier m; **~ing** n (SPORT) voile f; **to go ~ing** faire de la

voile; **~ing boat** n bateau m à voiles, voilier m; **~ing ship** n grand voilier; **~or** n marin m, matelot m

saint [seɪnt] n saint(e)

sake [seɪk] n: **for the ~ of** pour (l'amour de), dans l'intérêt de; **par égard pour**

salad ['sæləd] n salade f; **~ bowl** n saladier m; **~ cream** (BRIT) n (sorte f de) mayonnaise f; **~ dressing** n vinaigrette f

salami [sə'lɑːmɪ] n salami m

salary ['sælərɪ] n salaire m

sale [seɪl] n vente f; (at reduced prices) soldes mpl; **"for ~"** "à vendre"; **on ~** en vente; **on ~ or return** vendu(e) avec faculté de retour; **~room** n salle f des ventes; **~s assistant** (US **sales clerk**) n vendeur(-euse); **~sman** (irreg) n vendeur m; (representative) représentant m; **~s rep** n (COMM) représentant(e) m/f; (representative) représentante f; **~swoman** (irreg) n vendeuse f; (representative) représentante f

salmon ['sæmən] n inv saumon m

salon ['sælɔn] n salon m

saloon [sə'luːn] n (US) bar m; (BRIT: AUT) berline f; (ship's lounge) salon m

salt [sɔːlt] n sel m ♦ vt saler; **~ cellar** n salière f; **~water** adj de mer; **~y** adj salé(e)

salute [sə'luːt] n salut m ♦ vt saluer

salvage ['sælvɪdʒ] n (saving) sauvetage m; (things saved) biens sauvés or récupérés ♦ vt sauver, récupérer

salvation [sæl'veɪʃən] n salut m; **S~ Army** n armée f du Salut

same [seɪm] adj même ♦ pron: **the ~** le (la) même, les mêmes; **the ~ book as** le même livre que; **at the ~ time** en même temps; **all or just the ~** tout de même, quand même; **to do the ~** faire de même, en faire autant; **to do the ~ as sb** faire comme qn; **the ~ to you!** à vous de même!; (after insult) toi-même!

sample ['sɑːmpl] n échantillon m; (blood) prélèvement m ♦ vt (food, wine) goûter

sanction ['sæŋkʃən] n approbation f, sanction f

sanctity ['sæŋktɪtɪ] n sainteté f, caractère sacré

sanctuary ['sæŋktjuərɪ] n (holy place) sanctuaire m; (refuge) asile m; (for wild life) réserve f

sand [sænd] n sable m ♦ vt (furniture: also: ~ **down**) poncer

sandal ['sændl] n sandale f

sand: ~**box** (US) n tas m de sable; ~**castle** n château m de sable; ~**paper** n papier m de verre; ~**pit** (BRIT) n (for children) tas m de sable; ~**stone** n grès m

sandwich ['sændwɪtʃ] n sandwich m; **cheese/ham** ~ n sandwich au fromage/jambon; ~ **course** (BRIT) n cours m de formation professionnelle

sandy ['sændɪ] adj sablonneux(-euse); (colour) sable inv, blond roux inv

sane [seɪn] adj (person) sain(e) d'esprit; (outlook) sensé(e), sain(e)

sang [sæŋ] pt of **sing**

sanitary ['sænɪtərɪ] adj (system, arrangements) sanitaire; (clean) hygiénique; ~ **towel** (US **sanitary napkin**) n serviette f hygiénique

sanitation [sænɪ'teɪʃən] n (in house) installations fpl sanitaires; (in town) système m sanitaire; ~ **department** (US) n service m de voirie

sanity ['sænɪtɪ] n santé mentale; (common sense) bon sens

sank [sæŋk] pt of **sink**

Santa Claus [sæntə'klɔːz] n le père Noël

sap [sæp] n (of plants) sève f ♦ vt (strength) saper, miner

sapling ['sæplɪŋ] n jeune arbre m

sapphire ['sæfaɪər] n saphir m

sarcasm ['sɑːkæzm] n sarcasme m, raillerie f; **sarcastic** [sɑː'kæstɪk] adj sarcastique

sardine [sɑː'diːn] n sardine f

Sardinia [sɑː'dɪnɪə] n Sardaigne f

sash [sæʃ] n écharpe f

sat [sæt] pt, pp of **sit**

satchel ['sætʃl] n cartable m

satellite ['sætəlaɪt] n satellite m; ~ **dish** n antenne f parabolique; ~ **television** n télévision f par câble

satin ['sætɪn] n satin m ♦ adj en or de satin, satiné(e)

satire ['sætaɪər] n satire f

satisfaction [sætɪs'fækʃən] n satisfaction f

satisfactory [sætɪs'fæktərɪ] adj satisfaisant(e)

satisfied ['sætɪsfaɪd] adj satisfait(e)

satisfy ['sætɪsfaɪ] vt satisfaire, contenter; (convince) convaincre, persuader; ~**ing** adj satisfaisant(e)

Saturday ['sætədɪ] n samedi m

sauce [sɔːs] n sauce f; ~**pan** n casserole f

saucer ['sɔːsər] n soucoupe f

Saudi ['saudɪ-]: ~ **Arabia** n Arabie Saoudite; ~ **(Arabian)** adj saoudien(ne)

sauna ['sɔːnə] n sauna m

saunter ['sɔːntər] vi: **to** ~ **along/in/out** etc marcher/entrer/sortir etc d'un pas nonchalant

sausage ['sɒsɪdʒ] n saucisse f; (cold meat) saucisson m; ~ **roll** n friand m

savage ['sævɪdʒ] adj (cruel, fierce) brutal(e), féroce; (primitive) primitif(-ive), sauvage ♦ n sauvage m/f

save [seɪv] vt (person, belongings) sauver; (money) mettre de côté, économiser; (time) (faire) gagner; (keep) garder; (COMPUT) sauvegarder; (SPORT: stop) arrêter; (avoid: trouble) éviter ♦ vi (also: ~ **up**) mettre de l'argent de côté ♦ n (SPORT) arrêt m (du ballon) ♦ prep sauf, à l'exception de

saving ['seɪvɪŋ] n économie f ♦ adj: **the** ~ **grace of sth** ce qui rachète qch; ~**s** npl (money saved) économies fpl; ~**s account** n compte m d'épargne; ~**s bank** n caisse f d'épargne

saviour ['seɪvjər] (US **savior**) n sauveur m

savour ['seɪvə'] (US **savor**) vt savourer; **~y** (US **savory**) adj (dish: not sweet) salé(e)

saw [sɔ:] (pt **sawed**, pp **sawed** or **sawn**) vt scier ♦ n (tool) scie f ♦ pt of **see**; **~dust** n sciure f; **~mill** n scierie f; **~-off** adj: **~-off shotgun** carabine f à canon scié

sax [sæks] (inf) n saxo m

saxophone ['sæksəfəʊn] n saxophone m

say [seɪ] (pt, pp **said**) n: **to have one's ~** dire ce qu'on a à dire ♦ vt dire; **to have a** or **some ~ in sth** avoir voix au chapitre; **could you ~ that again?** pourriez-vous répéter ce que vous venez de dire?; **that goes without ~ing** cela va sans dire, cela va de soi; **~ing** n dicton m, proverbe m

scab [skæb] n croûte f; (pej) jaune m

scaffold ['skæfəld] n échafaud m; **~ing** n échafaudage m

scald [skɔ:ld] n brûlure f ♦ vt ébouillanter

scale [skeɪl] n (of fish) écaille f; (MUS) gamme f; (of ruler, thermometer etc) graduation f, échelle (graduée); (of salaries, fees etc) barème m; (of map, also size, extent) échelle ♦ vt (mountain) escalader; **~s** npl (for weighing) balance f; (also: **bathroom ~**) pèse-personne m inv; **on a large ~** sur une grande échelle, en grand; **~ of charges** tableau m des tarifs; **~ down** vt réduire

scallop ['skɔləp] n coquille f Saint-Jacques; (SEWING) feston m

scalp [skælp] n cuir chevelu ♦ vt scalper

scampi ['skæmpɪ] npl langoustines (frites), scampi mpl

scan [skæn] vt scruter, examiner; (glance at quickly) parcourir; (TV, RADAR) balayer ♦ n (MED) scanographie f

scandal ['skændl] n scandale m; (gossip) ragots mpl

Scandinavia [skændɪ'neɪvɪə] n Scandinavie f; **~n** adj scandinave

scant [skænt] adj insuffisant(e); ['skæntɪ] adj peu abondant(e), insuffisant(e); (underwear) minuscule

scapegoat ['skeɪpgəʊt] n bouc m émissaire

scar [skɑ:] n cicatrice f ♦ vt marquer (d'une cicatrice)

scarce [skeəs] adj rare, peu abondant(e); **to make o.s. ~** (inf) se sauver; **~ly** adv à peine; **scarcity** n manque m, pénurie f

scare [skeə'] n peur f, panique f ♦ vt effrayer, faire peur à; **to ~ sb stiff** faire une peur bleue à qn; **bomb ~** alerte f à la bombe; **~ away; ~ off** vt = **scare away**; **~crow** n épouvantail m; **~d** adj: **to be ~d** avoir peur

scarf [skɑ:f] (pl **~s** or **scarves**) n (long) écharpe f; (square) foulard m

scarlet ['skɑ:lɪt] adj écarlate; **~ fever** n scarlatine f

scary ['skeərɪ] (inf) adj effrayant(e)

scathing ['skeɪðɪŋ] adj cinglant(e), acerbe

scatter ['skætə'] vt éparpiller, répandre; (crowd) disperser ♦ vi se disperser; **~brained** adj écervelé(e), étourdi(e)

scavenger ['skævəndʒə'] n (person: in bins etc) pilleur m de poubelles

scene [si:n] n scène f; (of crime, accident) lieu(x) m(pl); (sight, view) spectacle m, vue f; (THEATRE) décor(s) m(pl); (landscape) paysage m; **~ry** ['si:nərɪ] n (THEATRE) décor(s) m(pl); (landscape) paysage m; **scenic** adj (picturesque) offrant de beaux paysages ou panoramas

scent [sent] n parfum m, odeur f; (track) piste f

sceptical ['skeptɪkl] (US **skeptical**) adj sceptique

schedule ['ʃedju:l, (US) 'skedju:l] n programme m, plan m; (of trains) horaire m; (of prices etc) barème m, tarif m ♦ vt prévoir; **on ~** à l'heure (prévue); to be ahead of/behind ~ avoir de l'avance/du retard; **~d flight** n vol régulier

scheme [ski:m] n plan m, projet m,

(dishonest plan, plot) complot *m*, combine *f*; *(arrangement)* arrangement *m*, classification *f*; *(pension ~ etc)* régime *m* ♦ *vi* comploter, manigancer; **scheming** *adj* rusé(e), intrigant(e) ♦ *n* manigances *fpl*, intrigues *fpl*

scholar ['skɔlə'] *n* érudit(e); *(pupil)* boursier(-ère); **~ship** *n* *(knowledge)* érudition *f*; *(grant)* bourse *f* (d'études)

school [sku:l] *n* école *f*; *(secondary ~)* collège *m*, lycée *m*; *(US: university)* université *f*; *(in university)* faculté *f* ♦ *cpd* scolaire; **~book** *n* livre *m* scolaire or de classe; **~boy** *n* écolier *m*; collégien *m*, lycéen *m*; **~children** *npl* écoliers *mpl*; collégiens *mpl*, lycéens *mpl*; **~girl** *n* écolière *f*; collégienne *f*, lycéenne *f*; **~ing** *n* instruction *f*, études *fpl*; **~master** *n* professeur *m*; **~mistress** *n* professeur *m*; **~teacher** *n* instituteur(-trice); professeur *m*

science ['saɪəns] *n* science *f*; **~ fiction** *n* science-fiction *f*; **scientific** [saɪən'tɪfɪk] *adj* scientifique; **scientist** *n* scientifique *m/f*; *(eminent)* savant *m*

scissors ['sɪzəz] *npl* ciseaux *mpl*

scoff [skɔf] *vt* *(BRIT: inf)* avaler, bouffer ♦ *vi*: **to ~ (at)** *(mock)* se moquer (de)

scold [skəuld] *vt* gronder

scone [skɔn] *n* sorte de petit pain rond au lait

scoop [sku:p] *n* pelle *f* (à main); *(for ice cream)* boule *f* à glace; *(PRESS)* scoop *m*; **~ out** *vt* évider, creuser; **~ up** *vt* ramasser

scooter ['sku:tə'] *n* *(also: motor ~)* scooter *m*; *(toy)* trottinette *f*

scope [skəup] *n* *(capacity: of plan, undertaking)* portée *f*, envergure *f*; *(: of person)* compétence *f*, capacités *fpl*; *(opportunity)* possibilités *fpl*; **within the ~ of** dans les limites de

scorch [skɔtʃ] *vt* *(clothes)* brûler (légèrement), roussir; *(earth, grass)* dessécher, brûler

score [skɔ:'] *n* score *m*, décompte *m*

des points; *(MUS)* partition *f*; *(twenty)* vingt ♦ *vt* *(goal, point)* marquer; *(success)* remporter ♦ *vi* marquer des points; *(FOOTBALL)* marquer un but; *(keep ~)* compter les points; **~s of** *(very many)* beaucoup de, un tas de *(fam)*; **on that ~** sur ce chapitre, à cet égard; **to ~ 6 out of 10** obtenir 6 sur 10; **~ out** *vt* rayer, barrer, biffer; **~board** *n* tableau *m*

scorn [skɔ:n] *n* mépris *m*, dédain *m*

Scorpio ['skɔ:pɪəu] *n* le Scorpion

Scot [skɔt] *n* Écossais(e)

Scotch [skɔtʃ] *n* whisky *m*, scotch *m*

scot-free ['skɔt'fri:] *adv*: **to get off ~~** s'en tirer sans être puni(e)

Scotland ['skɔtlənd] *n* Écosse *f*; **Scots** *adj* écossais(e); **Scotsman** *(irreg)* *n* Écossais *m*; **Scotswoman** *(irreg)* *n* Écossaise *f*; **Scottish** *adj* écossais(e); **Scottish Parliament** *n* Parlement *m* écossais

scoundrel ['skaundrl] *n* vaurien *m*

scour ['skauə'] *vt* *(search)* battre, parcourir

scout [skaut] *n* *(MIL)* éclaireur *m*; *(also: boy ~)* scout *m*; **girl ~** *(US)* guide *f*; **~ around** *vi* explorer, chercher

scowl [skaul] *vi* avoir l'air maussade; **to ~ at** regarder de travers

scrabble ['skræbl] *vi* *(also: ~ around, ~ search)* chercher à tâtons; *(claw)*: **to ~ (at)** gratter ♦ *n*: **S~** ® Scrabble ® *m*

scram [skræm] *(inf)* *vi* ficher le camp

scramble ['skræmbl] *n* *(rush)* bousculade *f*, ruée *f* ♦ *vi*: **to ~ up/down** grimper/descendre tant bien que mal; **to ~ out** sortir or descendre à toute vitesse; **to ~ through** se frayer un passage (à travers); **to ~ for** se bousculer or se disputer pour (avoir); **~d eggs** *npl* œufs brouillés

scrap [skræp] *n* bout *m*, morceau *m*; *(fight)* bagarre *f*; *(also: ~ iron)* ferraille *f* ♦ *vt* jeter, mettre au rebut; *(fig)* abandonner, laisser tomber ♦ *vi* *(fight)* se bagarrer; **~s** *npl* *(waste)* déchets *mpl*;

~ album m; **~ dealer** n marchand m de ferraille

scrape [skreɪp] vt, vi gratter, racler ♦ n: **to get into a ~** s'attirer des ennuis; **to ~ through** réussir de justesse; **~ together** vt (money) racler ses fonds de tiroir pour réunir

scrap: **~ heap** n: **on the ~ heap** (fig) au rancart or rebut; **~ merchant** (BRIT) n marchand m de ferraille; **~ paper** n papier m brouillon

scratch [skrætʃ] n égratignure f, rayure f; éraflure f (from claw) coup m de griffe ♦ cpd: **~ team** équipe f de fortune or improvisée ♦ vt (rub) (se) gratter; (record) rayer; (paint etc) érafler; (with claw, nail) griffer ♦ vi (se) gratter; **to start from ~** partir de zéro; **to be up to ~** être à la hauteur

scrawl [skrɔːl] vi gribouiller

scrawny [ˈskrɔːnɪ] adj décharné(e)

scream [skriːm] n cri perçant, hurlement m ♦ vi crier, hurler

screech [skriːtʃ] vi hurler; (tyres) crisser; (brakes) grincer

screen [skriːn] n écran m; (in room) paravent m; (fig) écran, rideau m ♦ vt (conceal) masquer, cacher; (from the wind etc) abriter, protéger; (film) projeter; (candidates etc) filtrer; **~ing** n (MED) test m (or tests) de dépistage; **~play** n scénario m; **~ saver** n (COMPUT) économiseur m d'écran

screw [skruː] n vis f ♦ vt (also: **~ in**) visser; **~ up** vt (paper etc) froisser; **to ~ up one's eyes** plisser les yeux; **~driver** n tournevis m

scribble [ˈskrɪbl] vt, vi gribouiller, griffonner

script [skrɪpt] n (CINEMA etc) scénario m, texte m; (writing) (écriture f) script m

Scripture(s) [ˈskrɪptʃə(r)(-əz)] n(pl) (Christian) Écriture sainte; (other religions) écritures saintes

scroll [skrəʊl] n rouleau m

scrounge [skraʊndʒ] (inf) vt: **to ~ sth off or from sb** taper qn de qch; **~r**

(inf) n parasite m

scrub [skrʌb] n (land) broussailles fpl ♦ vt (floor) nettoyer à la brosse; (pan) récurer; (washing) frotter; (inf: cancel) annuler

scruff [skrʌf] n: **by the ~ of the neck** par la peau du cou

scruffy [ˈskrʌfɪ] adj débraillé(e)

scrum(mage) [ˈskrʌm(ɪdʒ)] n (RUGBY) mêlée f

scruple [ˈskruːpl] n scrupule m

scrutiny [ˈskruːtɪnɪ] n examen minutieux

scuff [skʌf] vt érafler

scuffle [ˈskʌfl] n échauffourée f, rixe f

sculptor [ˈskʌlptə*] n sculpteur m

sculpture [ˈskʌlptʃə*] n sculpture f

scum [skʌm] n écume f, mousse f; (pej: people) rebut m, lie f

scurry [ˈskʌrɪ] vi filer à toute allure; **to ~ off** détaler, se sauver

scuttle [ˈskʌtl] n (also: **coal ~**) seau m (à charbon) ♦ vt (ship) saborder ♦ vi (scamper): **to ~ away or off** détaler

scythe [saɪð] n faux f

SDP n abbr (= Social Democratic Party)

sea [siː] n mer f ♦ cpd marin(e), de (la) mer; **by ~** (travel) par mer, en bateau; **on the ~** (boat) en mer; (town) au bord de la mer; **to be all at ~** (fig) nager complètement; **out to ~** au large; (out) at ~ en mer; **~board** n côte f; **~food** n fruits mpl de mer; **~front** n bord m de mer; **~going** adj (ship) de mer; **~gull** n mouette f

seal [siːl] n (animal) phoque m; (stamp) sceau m, cachet m ♦ vt sceller; (envelope) coller; (: with ~) cacheter; **~ off** vt (forbid entry to) interdire l'accès de

sea level n niveau m de la mer

sea lion n otarie f

seam [siːm] n couture f; (of coal) veine f, filon m

seaman [ˈsiːmən] (irreg) n marin m

seance [ˈseɪɒns] n séance f de spiritisme

seaplane ['si:pleɪn] n hydravion m

search [sə:tʃ] n (for person, thing, COMPUT) recherche(s) f(pl); (LAW: at sb's home) perquisition f ♦ vt fouiller; (examine) examiner minutieusement; scruter ♦ vi: to ~ for chercher; in ~ of à la recherche de; ~ through vt fus fouiller; ~ing adj pénétrant(e); ~light n projecteur m; ~ party n expédition f de secours; ~ warrant n mandat m de perquisition

sea: ~shore n rivage m, plage f, bord m de la (la) mer; ~sick adj: to be ~sick avoir le mal de mer; ~side n bord de la mer; ~side resort n station f balnéaire

season ['si:zn] n saison f ♦ vt assaisonner, relever; to be in/out of ~ être/ne pas être en saison; ~al adj (work) saisonnier(-ère); ~ed adj (fig) aguerri(e); ~ ticket n carte f d'abonnement

seat [si:t] n siège m; (in bus, train: place) place f; (buttocks) postérieur m; (of trousers) fond m ♦ vt faire asseoir, placer; (have room for) avoir des places assises pour, pouvoir accueillir; ~ belt n ceinture f de sécurité

sea: ~ water n eau f de mer; ~weed n algues fpl; ~worthy adj en état de naviguer

sec. abbr = **second(s)**

secluded [sɪ'klu:dɪd] adj retiré(e), à l'écart

seclusion [sɪ'klu:ʒən] n solitude f

second[1] ['sɛkənd] (BRIT) vt (employee) affecter provisoirement

second[2] ['sɛkənd] adj deuxième, second(e) ♦ adv (in race etc) en seconde position ♦ n (unit of time) seconde f; (AUT: ~ gear) seconde; (COMM: imperfect) article m de second choix; (BRIT: UNIV) licence f avec mention ♦ vt (motion) appuyer; ~ary adj secondaire; ~ary school n collège m, lycée m; ~-class adj de deuxième classe; (RAIL) de seconde (classe); (POST) au tarif réduit;

(pej) de qualité inférieure ♦ adv (RAIL) en seconde; (POST) au tarif réduit; ~hand adj d'occasion; de seconde main; ~ hand n (on clock) trotteuse f; ~ly adv deuxièmement; ~ment [sɪ'kɔndmənt] (BRIT) n détachement m; ~rate adj de deuxième ordre, de qualité inférieure; ~ thoughts npl doutes mpl; on ~ thoughts or (US) thought à la réflexion

secrecy ['si:krəsɪ] n secret m

secret ['si:krɪt] adj secret(-ète) ♦ n secret m; in ~ en secret, secrètement, en cachette

secretary ['sɛkrətərɪ] n secrétaire m/f; (COMM) secrétaire général; S~ of State (for) (BRIT: POL) ministre m (de)

secretive ['si:krətɪv] adj dissimulé(e)

secretly ['si:krɪtlɪ] adv en secret, secrètement

sectarian [sɛk'tɛərɪən] adj sectaire

section ['sɛkʃən] n section f; (of document) section, article m, paragraphe m; (cut) coupe f

sector ['sɛktəʳ] n secteur m

secular ['sɛkjuləʳ] adj profane, laïque, séculier(-ère)

secure [sɪ'kjuəʳ] adj (free from anxiety) sans inquiétude, sécurisé(e); (firmly fixed) solide, bien attaché(e) or fermé(e) etc); (in safe place) en lieu sûr, en sûreté ♦ vt (fix) fixer, attacher; (get) obtenir, se procurer

security [sɪ'kjuərɪtɪ] n sécurité f, mesures fpl de sécurité; (for loan) caution f, garantie f; ~ guard n garde chargé de la sécurité; (when transporting money) convoyeur m de fonds

sedate [sɪ'deɪt] adj calme, posé(e) ♦ vt (MED) donner des sédatifs à

sedative ['sɛdɪtɪv] n calmant m, sédatif m

seduce [sɪ'dju:s] vt séduire; **seduction** [sɪ'dʌkʃən] n séduction f; **seductive** adj séduisant(e); (smile) séducteur (-trice); (fig: offer) alléchant(e)

see [si:] (pt saw, pp seen) vt voir; (accompany): to ~ sb to the door reconduire *or* raccompagner qn jusqu'à la porte ♦ *vi* voir ♦ *n* évêché *m*; **to ~ that** (*ensure*) veiller à ce que +*sub*, faire en sorte que +*sub*, s'assurer que; **~ you soon!** à bientôt!; **~ about** *vt fus* s'occuper de; **~ off** *vt* accompagner (à la gare *or* à l'aéroport *etc*); **~ through** *vt* mener à bonne fin ♦ *vt fus* voir clair dans; **~ to** *vt fus* s'occuper de, se charger de

seed [siːd] *n* graine *f*; (*fig*) germe *m*; (*TENNIS etc*) tête *f* de série; **to go to ~** monter en graine; (*fig*) se laisser aller; **~ling** *n* jeune plant *m*, semis *m*; **~y** *adj* (*shabby*) minable, miteux/-euse

seeing ['siːɪŋ] *conj*: **~ (that)** vu que, étant donné que

seek [siːk] (*pt, pp* **sought**) *vt* chercher, rechercher

seem [siːm] *vi* sembler, paraître; **there ~s to be** ... il semble qu'il y a ...; on dirait qu'il y a ...; **~ingly** *adv* apparemment

seen [siːn] *pp of* **see**

seep [siːp] *vi* suinter, filtrer

seesaw ['siːsɔː] *n* (jeu *m* de) bascule *f*

seethe [siːð] *vi* être en effervescence; **to ~ with anger** bouillir de colère

see-through ['siːθruː] *adj* transparent(e)

segment ['sɛgmənt] *n* segment *m*; (*of orange*) quartier *m*

segregate ['sɛɡrɪgeɪt] *vt* séparer, isoler

seize [siːz] *vt* saisir, attraper; (*take possession of*) s'emparer de; (*opportunity*) saisir; **~ up** *vi* (*TECH*) se gripper; **~ (up)on** *vt fus* saisir, sauter sur

seizure ['siːʒəʳ] *n* (*MED*) crise *f*, attaque *f*; (*of power*) prise *f*

seldom ['sɛldəm] *adv* rarement

select [sɪˈlɛkt] *adj* choisi(e), d'élite ♦ *vt* sélectionner, choisir; **~ion** *n* sélection *f*, choix *m*

self [sɛlf] (*pl* **selves**) *n*: **the ~** le moi *inv* ♦ *prefix* auto-; **~-assured** *adj* sûr(e) de soi; **~-catering** (*BRIT*) *adj* avec cuisine, où l'on peut faire sa cuisine; **~-centred** (*US* **self-centered**) *adj* égocentrique; **~-confidence** *n* confiance *f* en soi; **~-conscious** *adj* timide, qui manque d'assurance; **~-contained** (*BRIT*) *adj* (*flat*) avec entrée particulière, indépendant(e); **~-control** *n* maîtrise *f* de soi; **~-defence** (*US* **self-defense**) *n* autodéfense *f*; (*LAW*) légitime défense *f*; **~-discipline** *n* discipline personnelle; **~-employed** *adj* qui travaille à son compte; **~-evident** *adj*: **to be ~-evident** être évident(e), aller de soi; **~-governing** *adj* autonome; **~-indulgent** *adj* qui ne se refuse rien; **~-interest** *n* intérêt personnel; **~-ish** *adj* égoïste; **~-ishness** *n* égoïsme *m*; **~-less** *adj* désintéressé(e); **~-pity** *n* apitoiement *m* sur soi-même; **~-possessed** *adj* assuré(e); **~-preservation** *n* instinct *m* de conservation; **~-respect** *n* respect *m* de soi, amour-propre *m*; **~-righteous** *adj* suffisant(e); **~-sacrifice** *n* abnégation *f*; **~-satisfied** *adj* content(e) de soi, suffisant(e); **~-service** *adj* libre-service, self-service; **~-sufficient** *adj* autosuffisant(e); (*person: independent*) indépendant(e); **~-taught** *adj* (*artist, pianist*) qui a appris par lui-même

sell [sɛl] (*pt, pp* **sold**) *vt* vendre ♦ *vi* se vendre; **to ~ at** *or* **for 10 F** se vendre 10 F; **~ off** *vt* liquider; **~ out** *vi*: **to ~ out (of sth)** (*use up stock*) vendre tout son stock (de qch); **the tickets are all sold out** il ne reste plus de billets; **~-by date** *n* date *f* limite de vente; **~er** *n* vendeur(-euse), marchand(e); **~ing price** *n* prix *m* de vente

Sellotape ® ['sɛləʊteɪp] (*BRIT*) *n* papier *m* collant, scotch ® *m*

selves [sɛlvz] *npl of* **self**

semblance ['sɛmbləns] *n* semblant *m*

semen ['siːmən] *n* sperme *m*

semester [sɪˈmɛstəʳ] *n* (*esp US*) semestre *m*

semi ['sɛmɪ] *prefix* semi-, demi-; à demi,

à moitié; **~circle** n demi-cercle m; **~co-lon** n point-virgule m; **~detached (house)** (BRIT) n maison jumelée (-melle; **~final** n demi-finale f

seminar ['semɪnɑːʳ] n séminaire m; **~y** n (REL: for priests) séminaire m

semiskilled [semɪ'skɪld] adj: **~ worker** ouvrier(-ère) spécialisé(e)

semi-skimmed milk [semɪ'skɪmd-] n lait m demi-écrémé

senate ['senɪt] n sénat m; **senator** n sénateur m

send [send] (pt, pp sent) vt envoyer; **~ away** vt (letter, goods) envoyer, expédier; (unwelcome visitor) renvoyer; **~ away for** vt fus commander par correspondance, se faire envoyer; **~ back** vt renvoyer; **~ for** vt fus envoyer chercher; faire venir; **~ off** vt (goods) envoyer, expédier; (BRIT: SPORT: player) expulser ou renvoyer du terrain; **~ out** vt (invitation) envoyer (par la poste); (light, heat, signal) émettre; **~ up** vt faire monter; (BRIT: parody) mettre en boîte, parodier; **~er** n expéditeur (-trice); **~-off** n: **a good ~-off** les adieux chaleureux

senior ['siːnɪəʳ] adj (high-ranking) de haut niveau; (of higher rank): **to be ~ to sb** être le supérieur de qn ♦ n (older): **she is 15 years his ~** elle est son aînée de 15 ans, elle est plus âgée que lui de 15 ans; **~ citizen** n personne âgée; **~ity** [siːnɪ'ɔrɪtɪ] n (in service) ancienneté f

sensation [sen'seɪʃən] n sensation f; **~al** adj qui fait sensation; (marvellous) sensationnel(le)

sense [sens] n sens m; (feeling) sentiment m; (meaning) sens m, signification f; (wisdom) bon sens ♦ vt sentir, pressentir; **it makes ~** c'est logique; **~less** adj insensé(e), stupide; (unconscious) sans connaissance

sensible ['sensɪbl] adj sensé(e), raisonnable; sage

sensitive ['sensɪtɪv] adj sensible

sensual ['sensjuəl] adj sensuel(le)

sensuous ['sensjuəs] adj voluptueux (-euse), sensuel(le)

sent [sent] pt, pp de send

sentence ['sentns] n (LING) phrase f; (LAW: judgment) condamnation f, sentence f; (: punishment) peine f ♦ vt: **to ~ sb to death/to 5 years in prison** condamner qn à mort/à 5 ans de prison

sentiment ['sentɪmənt] n sentiment m; (opinion) opinion f, avis m; **~al** [sentɪ'mentl] adj sentimental(e)

sentry ['sentrɪ] n sentinelle f

separate [adj 'seprɪt, vb 'sepəreɪt] adj séparé(e), indépendant(e), différent(e) ♦ vt séparer; (make a distinction between) distinguer ♦ vi se séparer; **~ly** adv séparément; **~s** npl (clothes) coordonnés mpl; **separation** [sepə'reɪʃən] n séparation f

September [sep'tembəʳ] n septembre m

septic ['septɪk] adj (wound) infecté(e); **~ tank** n fosse f septique

sequel ['siːkwl] n conséquence f; séquelles fpl; (of story) suite f

sequence ['siːkwəns] n ordre m, suite f; (film ~) séquence f; (dance ~) numéro m

sequin ['siːkwɪn] n paillette f

Serbia ['səːbɪə] n Serbie f

serene [sɪ'riːn] adj serein(e), calme, paisible

sergeant ['sɑːdʒənt] n sergent m; (POLICE) brigadier m

serial ['sɪərɪəl] n feuilleton m; **~ killer** n meurtrier m tuant en série; **~ number** n numéro m de série

series ['sɪərɪz] n inv série f; (PUBLISHING) collection f

serious ['sɪərɪəs] adj sérieux(-euse); (illness) grave; **~ly** adv sérieusement; (hurt) gravement

sermon ['səːmən] n sermon m

serrated [sɪ'reɪtɪd] adj en dents de scie

servant ['səːvənt] n domestique m/f;

(fig) serviteur/servante

serve [səːv] *vt (employer etc)* servir, être au service de; *(purpose)* servir à; *(customer, food, meal)* servir; *(subj: train)* desservir; *(apprenticeship)* faire, accomplir; *(prison term)* purger; ♦ *vt (be useful)*: **to ~ as/for/to do** servir de/à/à faire ♦ *n (TENNIS)* service *m*; **it ~s him right** c'est bien fait pour lui; **~ out, ~ up** *vt (food)* servir

service ['səːvɪs] *n* service *m*; *(AUT: maintenance)* révision *f* ♦ *vt (car, washing machine)* réviser; **the S~s** les forces armées; **to be of ~ to sb** rendre service à qn; **15% ~ included** service 15% compris; **~ not included** service non compris; **~able** *adj* pratique, commode; **~ area** *n (on motorway)* aire *f* de services; **~ charge** *(BRIT)* *n* service *m*; **~man** *(irreg)* *n* militaire *m*; **~ station** *n* station-service *f*

serviette [səːvɪˈet] *(BRIT)* *n* serviette *f* (de table)

session ['seʃən] *n* séance *f*

set [set] *(pt, pp* **set)** *n* série *f*, assortiment *m*; *(of tools etc)* jeu *m*; *(RADIO, TV)* poste *m*; *(TENNIS)* set *m*; *(group of people)* cercle *m*, milieu *m*; *(THEATRE: stage)* scène *f*; (: *scenery)* décor *m*; *(MATH)* ensemble *m*; *(HAIRDRESSING)* mise *f* en plis ♦ *adj (fixed)* fixe, déterminé(e); *(ready)* prêt(e) ♦ *vt (place)* poser, placer; *(fix, establish)* fixer; (: *record)* établir; *(adjust)* régler; *(decide: rules etc)* fixer, choisir; *(task)* donner; *(exam)* composer ♦ *vi (sun)* se coucher; *(jam, jelly, concrete)* prendre; *(bone)* se ressouder; **to be ~ on doing** être résolu à faire; **to ~ the table** mettre la table; **to ~ (to music)** mettre en musique; **to ~ on fire** mettre le feu à; **to ~ free** libérer; **to ~ sth going** déclencher qch; **to ~ sail** prendre la mer; **~ about** *vt fus (task)* entreprendre, se mettre à; **~ aside** *vt* mettre de côté; *(time)* garder; **~ back** *vt (in time)*: **to ~ back (by)** retarder (de); *(cost)*: **to ~ sb back £5** coûter 5 livres

à qn; **~ off** *vi* se mettre en route, partir ♦ *vt (bomb)* faire exploser; *(cause to start)* déclencher; *(show up well)* mettre en valeur, faire valoir; **~ out** *vi* se mettre en route, partir ♦ *vt (arrange)* disposer; *(arguments)* présenter, exposer; **to ~ out to do** entreprendre de faire, avoir pour but or intention de faire; **~ up** *vt (organization)* fonder, créer; **~back** *n (hitch)* revers *m*, contretemps *m*; **~ menu** *n* menu *m*

settee [seˈtiː] *n* canapé *m*

setting ['setɪŋ] *n* cadre *m*; *(of jewel)* monture *f*; *(position: of controls)* réglage *m*

settle ['setl] *vt (argument, matter, account)* régler; *(problem)* résoudre; *(MED: calm)* calmer ♦ *vi (bird, dust etc)* se poser; *(also: ~ down)* s'installer, se fixer; *(calm down)* se calmer; **to ~ for sth** accepter qch, se contenter de qch; **to ~ on sth** opter or se décider pour qch; **~ in** *vi* s'installer; **~ up** *vi*: **to ~ up with sb** régler (ce que l'on doit à) qn; **~ment** *n (payment)* règlement *m*; *(agreement)* accord *m*; *(village etc)* établissement *m*, hameau *m*; **~r** *n* colon *m*

setup ['setʌp] *n (arrangement)* manière *f* dont les choses sont organisées; *(situation)* situation *f*

seven ['sevn] *num* sept; **~teen** *num* dix-sept; **~th** *num* septième; **~ty** *num* soixante-dix

sever ['sevər] *vt* couper, trancher; *(relations)* rompre

several ['sevrəl] *adj, pron* plusieurs *m/fpl*; **~ of us** plusieurs d'entre nous

severance ['sevərəns] *n (of relations)* rupture *f*; **~ pay** *n* indemnité *f* de licenciement

severe [sɪˈvɪər] *adj (stern)* sévère, strict(e); *(serious)* grave, sérieux(-euse); *(plain)* sévère, austère; **severity** [sɪˈverɪtɪ] *n* sévérité *f*; gravité *f*; rigueur *f*

sew [səu] *(pt* **sewed**, *pp* **sewn)** *vt, vi* coudre; **~ up** *vt* (re)coudre

sewage ['su:idʒ] n vidange(s) f(pl)

sewer ['su:ə'] n égout m

sewing ['səuɪŋ] n couture f; (item(s)) ouvrage m; ~ **machine** n machine f à coudre

sewn [səun] pp of **sew**

sex [seks] n sexe m; **to have ~ with** avoir des rapports (sexuels) avec; ~**ism** n sexisme m; ~**ist** adj sexiste; ~**ual** ['seksjuəl] adj sexuel(le); ~**uality** [seksjuˈælɪtɪ] n sexualité f; ~**y** adj sexy inv

shabby ['ʃæbɪ] adj miteux(-euse); (behaviour) mesquin(e), méprisable

shack [ʃæk] n cabane f, hutte f

shackles ['ʃæklz] npl chaînes fpl, entraves fpl

shade [ʃeɪd] n ombre f; (for lamp) abat-jour m inv; (of colour) nuance f, ton m ♦ vt abriter du soleil, ombrager; **in the ~** à l'ombre; **a ~ too large/more** un tout petit peu trop grand(e)/plus

shadow ['ʃædəu] n ombre f ♦ vt (follow) filer; ~ **cabinet** (BRIT) n (POL) cabinet parallèle formé par l'Opposition; ~**y** adj ombragé(e); (dim) vague, indistinct(e)

shady ['ʃeɪdɪ] adj ombragé(e); (fig: dishonest) louche, véreux(-euse)

shaft [ʃɑːft] n (of arrow, spear) hampe f; (AUT, TECH) arbre m; (of mine) puits m; (of lift) cage f; (of light) rayon m, trait m

shaggy ['ʃægɪ] adj hirsute; en broussaille

shake [ʃeɪk] (pt **shook**, pp **shaken**) vt secouer; (bottle, cocktail) agiter; (house, confidence) ébranler ♦ vi trembler; **to ~ one's head** (in refusal) dire ou faire non de la tête; (in dismay) secouer la tête; **to ~ hands with sb** serrer la main à qn; ~ **off** vt secouer; (pursuer) se débarrasser de; ~ **up** vt secouer; ~**n** pp of **shake**; **shaky** adj (hand, voice) tremblant(e); (building) branlant(e), peu solide

shall [ʃæl] aux vb: **I ~ go** j'irai; ~ **I open the door?** j'ouvre la porte?; **I'll get**

the coffee, ~ **I?** je vais chercher le café, d'accord?

shallow ['ʃæləu] adj peu profond(e); (fig) superficiel(le)

sham [ʃæm] n frime f ♦ vt simuler

shambles ['ʃæmblz] n (muddle) confusion f, pagaie f, fouillis m

shame [ʃeɪm] n honte f ♦ vt faire honte à; **it is a ~ (that/to do)** c'est dommage (que +sub/de faire); **what a ~!** quel dommage!; ~**ful** adj honteux(-euse); ~**less** adj éhonté(e), effronté(e)

shampoo [ʃæmˈpuː] n shampooing m ♦ vt faire un shampooing à; ~ **and set** n shampooing m (et) mise f en plis

shamrock ['ʃæmrɔk] n trèfle m (emblème de l'Irlande)

shandy ['ʃændɪ] n bière panachée

shan't [ʃɑːnt] = **shall not**

shanty town ['ʃæntɪ-] n bidonville m

shape [ʃeɪp] n forme f ♦ vt façonner, modeler; (sb's ideas) former; (sb's life) déterminer ♦ vi (also: ~ **up**: events) prendre tournure; (: person) faire des progrès, s'en sortir; **to take ~** prendre forme ou tournure; ~**d** suffix: **heart-~d** en forme de cœur; ~**less** adj informe, sans forme; ~**ly** adj bien proportionné(e), beau (belle)

share [ʃeə'] n part f; (COMM) action f ♦ vt partager; (have in common) avoir en commun; ~ **out** vi partager; ~**holder** n actionnaire m/f

shark [ʃɑːk] n requin m

sharp [ʃɑːp] adj (razor, knife) tranchant(e), bien aiguisé(e); (point, voice) aigu(-guë); (nose, chin) pointu(e); (outline, increase) net(te); (cold, pain) vif (vive); (taste) piquant(e), âcre; (MUS) dièse; (person: quick-witted) vif (vive), éveillé(e); (: unscrupulous) malhonnête ♦ adv (MUS) dièse m ♦ adv (precisely): **at 2 o'clock** à 2 heures pile ou précises; ~**en** vt aiguiser; (pencil) tailler; ~**ener** n (also: **pencil ~ener**) taille-crayon(s) m inv; ~**-eyed** adj à qui rien n'échappe;

~ly adv (turn, stop) brusquement; (stand out) nettement; (criticize, retort) sèchement, vertement

shatter ['ʃætə^r] vt briser; (fig: upset) bouleverser; (: ruin) briser, ruiner ♦ vi voler en éclats, se briser

shave [ʃeɪv] vt raser ♦ vi se raser n: to have a ~ se raser; ~r n (also: **electric ~r**) rasoir m électrique

shaving ['ʃeɪvɪŋ] (action) rasage m; ~s npl (of wood etc) copeaux mpl; ~ **brush** n blaireau m; ~ **cream** n crème f à raser; ~ **foam** n mousse f à raser

shawl [ʃɔːl] n châle m

she [ʃiː] pron elle ♦ prefix: ~**-cat** chatte f; ~**-elephant** éléphant m femelle

sheaf [ʃiːf] (pl **sheaves**) n gerbe f; (of papers) liasse f

shear [ʃɪə^r] (pt **sheared**, pp **shorn**) vt (sheep) tondre; ~s npl (for hedge) cisaille(s) f(pl)

sheath [ʃiːθ] n gaine f, fourreau m, étui m; (contraceptive) préservatif m

shed [ʃed] (pt, pp **shed**) n remise f, resserre f ♦ vt perdre; (tears) verser, répandre; (workers) congédier

she'd [ʃiːd] = she had; she would

sheen [ʃiːn] n lustre m

sheep [ʃiːp] n inv mouton m; ~**dog** n chien m de berger; ~**skin** n peau f de mouton

sheer [ʃɪə^r] adj (utter) pur(e), pur et simple; (steep) à pic, abrupt(e); (almost transparent) extrêmement fin(e) ♦ adv à pic, abruptement

sheet [ʃiːt] n (on bed) drap m; (of paper) feuille f; (of glass, metal etc) feuille, plaque f

sheik(h) [ʃeɪk] n cheik m

shelf [ʃelf] (pl **shelves**) n étagère f, rayon m

shell [ʃel] n (on beach) coquillage m; (of egg, nut etc) coquille f; (explosive) obus m; (of building) carcasse f ♦ vt (peas) écosser; (MIL) bombarder d'obus

she'll [ʃiːl] = she will; she shall

shellfish ['ʃelfɪʃ] n inv (crab etc) crustacé m; (scallop etc) coquillage m ♦ (as food) fruits mpl de mer

shell suit n survêtement m (en synthétique froissé)

shelter ['ʃeltə^r] n abri m, refuge m ♦ vt abriter, protéger; (give lodging to) donner asile à ♦ vi s'abriter, se mettre à l'abri; ~**ed housing** n foyers mpl (pour personnes âgées ou handicapées)

shelve [ʃelv] vt (fig) mettre en suspens or en sommeil; ~s npl of **shelf**

shepherd ['ʃepəd] n berger m ♦ vt (guide) guider, escorter; ~'s **pie** (BRIT) ≃ hachis m Parmentier

sheriff ['ʃerɪf] (US) n shérif m

sherry ['ʃerɪ] n xérès m, sherry m

she's [ʃiːz] = she is; she has

Shetland ['ʃetlənd] n (also: **the ~ Islands**) les îles fpl Shetland

shield [ʃiːld] n bouclier m; (protection) écran m de protection ♦ vt: **to ~ (from)** protéger (de or contre)

shift [ʃɪft] n (change) changement m; (work period) période f de travail; (of workers) équipe f, poste m ♦ vt déplacer, changer de place; (remove) enlever ♦ vi changer de place, bouger; ~ **work** n travail m en équipe or par relais or par roulement; ~y adj sournois(e); (eyes) fuyant(e)

shimmer ['ʃɪmə^r] vi miroiter, chatoyer

shin [ʃɪn] n tibia m

shine [ʃaɪn] (pt, pp **shone**) n éclat m, brillant m ♦ vi briller ♦ vt (torch etc): **to ~ on** braquer sur; (polish: pt, pp ~d) faire briller or reluire

shingle ['ʃɪŋgl] n (on beach) galets mpl; ~s n (MED) zona m

shiny ['ʃaɪnɪ] adj brillant(e)

ship [ʃɪp] n bateau m; (large) navire m ♦ vt transporter (par mer); (send) expédier (par mer); ~**building** n construction navale; ~**ment** n cargaison f, chargement m; ~**ping** n (ships) navires mpl; (the industry) industrie navale; (transport) transport m; ~**wreck** n (ship) épave f; (event) naufrage m ♦ vt: **to be**

~**wrecked** faire naufrage; ~**yard** n chantier naval

shire ['ʃaɪəʳ] (BRIT) n comté m

shirt [ʃəːt] n (man's) chemise f; (woman's) chemisier m; **in (one's) ~ sleeves** en bras de chemise

shit [ʃɪt] (inf!) n, excl merde f (!)

shiver ['ʃɪvəʳ] n frisson ♦ vi frissonner

shoal [ʃəul] n (of fish) banc m; (fig: also: ~s) masse f, foule f

shock [ʃɔk] n choc m, (ELEC) secousse f; (MED) commotion f, choc ♦ vt (offend) choquer, scandaliser; (upset) bouleverser; ~ **absorber** n amortisseur m; ~**ing** adj (scandalizing) choquant(e), scandaleux(-euse); (appalling) épouvantable

shoddy ['ʃɔdɪ] adj de mauvaise qualité, mal fait(e)

shoe [ʃuː] (pt, pp shod) n chaussure f, soulier m; (also: **horseshoe**) fer m à cheval; (of horse) ferrer; ~**lace** n lacet m (de soulier); ~ **polish** n cirage m; ~ **shop** n magasin m de chaussures; ~**string** n (fig): **on a ~string** avec un budget dérisoire

shone [ʃɔn] pt, pp of **shine**

shook [ʃuk] pt of **shake**

shoot [ʃuːt] (pt, pp shot) n (on branch, seedling) pousse f ♦ vt (game) chasser; tirer; abattre; (person) blesser or tuer d'un coup de fusil (or de revolver); (execute) fusiller; (arrow) tirer; (gun) tirer un coup de (film) tourner ♦ vi (with gun, bow): **to ~ (at)** tirer (sur); (FOOTBALL) shooter, tirer; ~ **down** vt (plane) abattre; ~ **in** vi entrer comme une flèche; ~ **out** vi sortir comme une flèche; ~ **up** vi (fig) monter en flèche; ~**ing** n (shots) coups mpl de feu, fusillade f; (HUNTING) chasse f; ~**ing star** n étoile filante

shop [ʃɔp] n magasin m; (workshop) atelier m ♦ vi (also: **go ~ping**) faire ses courses or ses achats, faire des courses; ~ **assistant** (BRIT) n vendeur(-euse); ~ **floor** (BRIT) n (INDUSTRY: fig) ouvriers mpl; ~**keeper** n

commerçant(e); ~**lifting** n vol m à l'étalage; ~**per** n personne f qui fait ses courses, acheteur(-euse); ~**ping** n (goods) achats mpl, provisions fpl; ~**ping bag** n sac m à provisions); ~**ping centre** (US **shopping center**) n centre commercial; ~**soiled** adj défraîchi(e), qui a fait la vitrine; ~ **steward** (BRIT) n (INDUSTRY) délégué(e) syndical(e); ~ **window** n vitrine f

shore [ʃɔːʳ] n (of sea, lake) rivage m, rive f ♦ vt: **to ~ (up)** étayer; **on ~** à terre

shorn [ʃɔːn] pp of **shear**

short [ʃɔːt] adj (not long) court(e); (soon finished) court(e), bref (brève); (person, step) petit(e); (curt) brusque, sec (sèche); (insufficient) insuffisant(e); **to be/run ~ of sth** être à court de or manquer de qch; **in ~** bref; en bref; ~ **of doing** ... à moins que ... + sub; **everything ~ of** tout sauf; **it is ~ for** c'est l'abréviation or le diminutif de; **to cut ~** (speech, visit) abréger, écourter; **to fall ~ of** ne pas être à la hauteur de; **to run ~ of** arriver à court de, venir à manquer de; **to stop ~** s'arrêter net; **to stop ~ of** ne pas aller jusqu'à; ~**age** n manque m, pénurie f; ~**bread** n ≈ sablé m; ~**change** vt ne pas rendre assez à; ~**circuit** n court-circuit m; ~**coming** n défaut m; ~**(crust) pastry** (BRIT) n pâte brisée; ~**cut** n raccourci m; ~**en** vt raccourcir; (text, visit) abréger; ~**fall** n déficit m; ~**hand** (BRIT) n sténo(graphie) f; ~**hand typist** (BRIT) n sténodactylo m/f; ~**list** (BRIT) n (for job) liste f des candidats sélectionnés; ~**ly** adv bientôt, sous peu; ~ **notice** n: **at ~ notice** au dernier moment; ~**s** npl: **(a pair of)** ~**s** un short; ~**sighted** adj (BRIT) myope; (fig) qui manque de clairvoyance; ~**staffed** adj à court de personnel; ~**stay** adj (car park) de courte durée; ~ **story** n nouvelle f; ~**tempered** adj qui s'emporte facilement; ~**term** adj (effect) à court terme; ~ **wave** n (RADIO) ondes courtes

shot [ʃɔt] *pt, pp of* **shoot** ♦ *n* coup *m* (de feu); *(try)* coup, essai *m*; *(injection)* piqûre *f*; *(PHOT)* photo *f*; **I** tire bien/mal; **like a good/ poor ~** il tire bien/mal; *(very readily)* sans hésiter; **~gun** *n* fusil *m* de chasse

should [ʃud] *aux vb*: **I ~ go now** je devrais partir maintenant; **he ~ be there now** il devrait être arrivé maintenant; **I ~ go if I were you** si j'étais vous, j'irais; **I ~ like to** j'aimerais bien, volontiers

shoulder ['ʃəuldər] *n* épaule *f* ♦ *vt* (fig) endosser, se charger de; **~ bag** *n* sac *m* à bandoulière; **~ blade** *n* omoplate *f*

shouldn't ['ʃudnt] = **should not**

shout [ʃaut] *n* cri *m* ♦ *vt* crier ♦ *vi* (also: **~ out**) crier, pousser des cris; **~ down** *vt* huer; **~ing** *n* cris *mpl*

shove [ʃʌv] *vt* pousser; *(inf: put)*: **to ~ sth in** fourrer *ou* ficher qch dans; **~ off** *vi* (inf) ficher le camp

shovel ['ʃʌvl] *n* pelle *f*

show [ʃəu] *(pt* **showed**, *pp* **shown**) *n* (of emotion) manifestation *f*, démonstration *f*; (semblance) semblant *m*, apparence *f*; (exhibition) exposition *f*, salon *m*; (THEATRE, TV) spectacle *m* ♦ *vt* montrer; (film) donner; (courage) etc faire preuve de, manifester; (exhibit) exposer ♦ *vi* se voir, être visible; **for ~** pour l'effet; **on ~** (exhibits etc) exposé(e); **~ in** *vt* (person) faire entrer; **~ off** *vi* (pej) crâner ♦ *vt* (display) faire valoir; **~ out** *vt* (person) reconduire (jusqu'à la porte); **~ up** *vi* (stand out) ressortir; (inf: turn up) se montrer ♦ *vt* (flaw) faire ressortir; **~ business** *n* le monde du spectacle; **~down** *n* épreuve *f* de force

shower ['ʃauər] *n* (rain) averse *f*; (of stones etc) pluie *f*, grêle *f*; (~bath) douche *f* ♦ *vi* prendre une douche, se doucher ♦ *vt*: **to ~ sb with** (gifts etc) combler qn de; **to have** *ou* **take a ~** prendre une douche; **~ gel** *n* gel *m* douche; **~proof** *adj* imperméabilisé(e)

showing ['ʃəuiŋ] *n* (of film) projection *f*

show jumping *n* concours *m* hippique

shown [ʃəun] *pp of* **show**

show: ~-off (inf) *n* (person) crâneur (-euse), m'as-tu-vu(e); **~piece** *n* (of exhibition) trésor *m*; **~room** *n* magasin *m* *ou* salle *f* d'exposition

shrank [ʃræŋk] *pt of* **shrink**

shrapnel ['ʃræpnl] *n* éclats *mpl* d'obus

shred [ʃred] *n* (gen pl) lambeau *m*, petit morceau *m* ♦ *vt* mettre en lambeaux, déchirer; (CULIN: grate) râper; (: lettuce etc) couper en lanières; **~der** *n* (for vegetables) râpeur *m*; (for documents) déchiqueteuse *f*

shrewd [ʃruːd] *adj* astucieux(-euse), perspicace; (businessman) habile

shriek [ʃriːk] *n* hurler, crier

shrill [ʃril] *adj* perçant(e), aigu(-guë), strident(e)

shrimp [ʃrimp] *n* crevette *f*

shrine [ʃrain] *n* (place) lieu *m* de pèlerinage

shrink [ʃriŋk] *(pt* **shrank**, *pp* **shrunk**) *vi* rétrécir; (fig) se réduire, diminuer; (move: also: **~ away**) reculer ♦ *vt* (wool) (faire) rétrécir ♦ *n* (inf: pej) psychiatre *m/f*, psy *m/f*; **to ~ from (doing) sth** reculer devant (la pensée de faire) qch; **~wrap** *vt* emballer sous film plastique

shrivel ['ʃrivl] *vt* (also: **~ up**) ratatiner, flétrir ♦ *vi* se ratatiner, se flétrir

shroud [ʃraud] *n* linceul *m* ♦ *vt*: **~ed in mystery** enveloppé(e) de mystère

Shrove Tuesday ['ʃrəuv-] *n* (le) Mardi gras

shrub [ʃrʌb] *n* arbuste *m*; **~bery** *n* massif *m* d'arbustes

shrug [ʃrʌg] *vt, vi*: **to ~ (one's shoulders)** hausser les épaules; **~ off** *vt* faire fi de

shrunk [ʃrʌŋk] *pp of* **shrink**

shudder ['ʃʌdər] *vi* frissonner, frémir

shuffle ['ʃʌfl] *vt* (cards) battre; **to ~ (one's feet)** traîner les pieds

shun [ʃʌn] *vt* éviter, fuir

shunt [ʃʌnt] *vt* (RAIL) aiguiller

shut [ʃʌt] *(pt, pp* **shut**) *vt* fermer ♦

(se) fermer; **~ down** vt, vi fermer définitivement; **~ off** vt couper, arrêter; **~ up** vi (inf: keep quiet) se taire ♦ vt (close) fermer; (silence) faire taire ♦ **~ter** n volet m; (PHOT) obturateur m

shuttle ['ʃʌtl] n navette f (also: **~ service**) (service m de) navette f; **~cock** n volant m (de badminton); **~ diplomacy** n navettes fpl diplomatiques

shy [ʃaɪ] adj timide

Siberia [saɪ'bɪərɪə] n Sibérie f

Sicily ['sɪsɪlɪ] n Sicile f

sick [sɪk] adj malade; (vomiting): **to be ~** vomir; (humour) noir(e), macabre; **to feel ~** avoir envie de vomir, avoir mal au cœur; **to be ~ of** (fig) en avoir assez de; **~ bay** n infirmerie f; **~en** vt écœurer; **~ening** adj (fig) écœurant(e), dégoûtant(e)

sickle ['sɪkl] n faucille f

sick: ~ leave n congé m de maladie; **~ly** adj maladif(-ive), souffreteux(-euse); (causing nausea) écœurant(e); **~ness** n maladie f; (vomiting) vomissement(s) m(pl); **~ note** n (from parents) mot m d'absence; (from doctor) certificat médical; **~ pay** n indemnité f de maladie

side [saɪd] n côté m; (of lake, road) bord m; (team) camp m, équipe f ♦ adj (door, entrance) latéral(e) ♦ vi: **to ~ with sb** prendre le parti de qn, se ranger du côté de qn; **by the ~ of** au bord de; **by ~** côte à côte; **from ~ to ~** d'un côté à l'autre; **to take ~s (with)** prendre parti (pour); **~board** n buffet m; **~boards** (BRIT), **~burns** npl (whiskers) pattes fpl; **~ drum** n tambour plat; **~ effect** n effet m secondaire; **~light** n (AUT) veilleuse f; **~line** n (SPORT) (ligne f de) touche f; (fig) travail m secondaire; **~long** adj oblique; **~show** n attraction f; **~step** vt (fig) éluder; éviter; **~ street** n (petite) rue transversale; **~track** vt (fig) faire dévier de son sujet; **~walk** n (US) n trottoir m; **~ways** adv de côté

siding ['saɪdɪŋ] n (RAIL) voie f de garage

siege [siːdʒ] n siège m

sieve [sɪv] n tamis m, passoire f

sift [sɪft] vt (fig: also: **~ through**) passer en revue; (lit: flour etc) passer au tamis

sigh [saɪ] n soupir m ♦ vi soupirer, pousser un soupir

sight [saɪt] n (faculty) vue f; (spectacle) spectacle m; (on gun) mire f ♦ vt apercevoir; **in ~** visible; **out of ~** hors de vue; **~seeing** n tourisme m; **to go ~seeing** faire du tourisme

sign [saɪn] n signe m; (with hand etc) signe, geste m; (notice) panneau m, écriteau m ♦ vt signer; **~ on** vi (as unemployed) s'inscrire au chômage; (for course) s'inscrire ♦ vt (employee) embaucher; **~ over** vt: **to ~ sth over to sb** céder qch par écrit à qn; **~ up** vt engager ♦ vi (MIL) s'engager; (for course) s'inscrire

signal ['sɪgnl] n signal m ♦ vi (AUT) mettre son clignotant ♦ vt (person) faire signe à; (message) communiquer par signaux; **~man** (irreg) n (RAIL) aiguilleur m

signature ['sɪgnətʃəʳ] n signature f; **~ tune** n indicatif musical

signet ring ['sɪgnət-] n chevalière f

significance [sɪg'nɪfɪkəns] n signification f; importance f

significant [sɪg'nɪfɪkənt] adj significatif(-ive); (important) important(e), considérable

sign language n langage m par signes

signpost n poteau indicateur

silence ['saɪləns] n silence m ♦ vt faire taire, réduire au silence; **~r** n (on gun, BRIT: AUT) silencieux m

silent ['saɪlənt] adj silencieux(-euse); (film) muet(te); **to remain ~** garder le silence, ne rien dire; **~ partner** n (COMM) bailleur m de fonds, commanditaire m

silhouette [sɪluː'et] n silhouette f

silicon chip ['sɪlɪkən-] n puce f électronique

silk [sɪlk] n soie f ♦ cpd de or en soie; **~y**

adj soyeux(-euse)

silly ['sɪlɪ] *adj* stupide, sot(te), bête

silt [sɪlt] *n* vase *f*; limon *m*

silver ['sɪlvər] *n* argent *m*; (*money*) monnaie *f* (en pièces d'argent); (*also:* ~ware) argenterie *f* ♦ *adj* d'argent, en argent; ~ **paper** (BRIT) *n* papier *m* d'argent *or* d'étain; ~**plated** *adj* plaqué(e) argent *inv*; ~**smith** *n* orfèvre *m/f*; ~**y** *adj* argenté(e)

similar ['sɪmɪlər] *adj*: ~ (**to**) semblable (à); ~**ly** *adv* de la même façon, de même

simmer ['sɪmər] *vi* cuire à feu doux, mijoter

simple ['sɪmpl] *adj* simple; **simplicity** [sɪm'plɪsɪtɪ] *n* simplicité *f*; **simply** *adv* (*without fuss*) avec simplicité

simultaneous [sɪməl'teɪnɪəs] *adj* simultané(e)

sin [sɪn] *n* péché *m* ♦ *vi* pécher

since [sɪns] *adv*, *prep* depuis ♦ *conj* (*time*) depuis que; (*because*) puisque, étant donné que; (*as*), comme; ~ **then**, ever ~ depuis ce moment-là

sincere [sɪn'sɪər] *adj* sincère; ~**ly** *adv* *see* **yours**; **sincerity** [sɪn'serɪtɪ] *n* sincérité *f*

sinew ['sɪnjuː] *n* tendon *m*

sing [sɪŋ] (*pt* **sang**, *pp* **sung**) *vt*, *vi* chanter

Singapore [sɪŋgə'pɔːr] *n* Singapour *m*

singe [sɪndʒ] *vt* brûler légèrement; (*clothes*) roussir

singer ['sɪŋər] *n* chanteur(-euse)

singing ['sɪŋɪŋ] *n* chant *m*

single ['sɪŋgl] *adj* seul(e), unique; (*unmarried*) célibataire; (*not double*) simple ♦ *n* (BRIT: *also:* ~ **ticket**) aller *m* (simple); (*record*) 45 tours *m*; ~ **out** *vt* choisir; (*distinguish*) distinguer; ~ **bed** *n* lit *m* d'une personne; ~**breasted** *adj* droit(e); ~ **file** *n*: **in** ~ **file** en file indienne; ~**handed** *adv* tout(e) seul(e), sans (aucune) aide; ~**minded** *adj* résolu(e), tenace; ~ **parent** *n* parent *m* unique; ~ **room** *n* chambre *f* à un lit *or*

pour une personne; ~**s** *n* (TENNIS) simple *m*; ~**track road** *n* route *f* à voie unique; **singly** *adv* séparément

singular ['sɪŋgjulər] *adj* singulier(-ère), étrange; (*outstanding*) remarquable; (LING) (au) singulier, du singulier ♦ *n* singulier *m*

sinister ['sɪnɪstər] *adj* sinistre

sink [sɪŋk] (*pt* **sank**, *pp* **sunk**) *n* évier *m* ♦ *vt* (*ship*) (faire) couler, faire sombrer; (*foundations*) creuser ♦ *vi* couler, sombrer; (*ground level*) s'affaisser; (*also:* ~ **back**, ~ **down**) s'affaisser, se laisser retomber; **to** ~ **sth into** enfoncer qch dans; **my heart sank** j'ai complètement perdu courage; ~ **in** *vi* (*fig*) pénétrer, être compris(e)

sinner ['sɪnər] *n* pécheur(-eresse)

sinus ['saɪnəs] *n* sinus *m inv*

sip [sɪp] *n* gorgée *f* ♦ *vt* boire à petites gorgées

siphon ['saɪfən] *n* siphon *m*; ~ **off** *vt* siphonner; (*money: illegally*) détourner

sir [sər] *n* monsieur *m*; **S~ John Smith** sir John Smith; **yes** ~ oui, Monsieur

siren ['saɪərn] *n* sirène *f*

sirloin ['səːlɔɪn] *n* (*also:* ~ **steak**) aloyau *m*

sissy ['sɪsɪ] (*inf*) *n* (*coward*) poule mouillée

sister ['sɪstər] *n* sœur *f*; (*nun*) religieuse *f*, sœur; (BRIT: *also:* ~ **nurse**) infirmière *f* en chef; ~**in-law** *n* belle-sœur *f*

sit [sɪt] (*pt*, *pp* **sat**) *vi* s'asseoir; (*be ~ting*) être assis(e); (*assembly*) être en séance, siéger; (*for painter*) poser ♦ *vt* (*exam*) passer, se présenter à; ~ **down** *vi* s'asseoir; ~ **in on** *vt fus* assister à; ~ **up** *vi* s'asseoir; (*straight*) se redresser; (*not go to bed*) rester debout, ne pas se coucher

sitcom ['sɪtkɔm] *n abbr* (= *situation comedy*) comédie *f* de situation

site [saɪt] *n* emplacement *m*, site *m*; (*also:* **building** ~) chantier *m* ♦ *vt* placer

sit-in ['sɪtɪn] *n* (*demonstration*) sit-in *m inv*, occupation *f* (de locaux)

sitting ['sɪtɪŋ] n (of assembly etc) séance f; (in canteen) service m; ~ **room** n salon m

situated ['sɪtjueɪtɪd] adj situé(e)

situation [sɪtju'eɪʃən] n situation f; "~s **vacant**" (BRIT) "offres d'emploi"

six [sɪks] num six; ~**teen** num seize; ~**th** num sixième; ~**ty** num soixante

size [saɪz] n taille f; dimensions fpl; (of clothing) taille; (of shoes) pointure f; (fig) ampleur f; (glue) colle f; ~ **up** vt juger, jauger; ~**able** adj assez grand(e); assez important(e)

sizzle ['sɪzl] vi grésiller

skate [skeɪt] n patin m; (fish: pl inv) raie f ♦ vi patiner; ~**board** n skateboard m, planche f à roulettes; ~**boarding** n skateboard m; ~**r** n patineur(-euse); **skating** n patinage m; **skating rink** n patinoire f

skeleton ['skɛlɪtn] n squelette m; (outline) schéma m; ~ **staff** n effectifs réduits

skeptical ['skɛptɪkl] (US) adj = **sceptical**

sketch [skɛtʃ] n (drawing) croquis m, esquisse f; (THEATRE) sketch m, saynète f ♦ vt esquisser, faire un croquis or une esquisse de; ~ **book** n carnet m à dessin; ~**y** adj incomplet(-ète), fragmentaire

skewer ['skju:ə'] n brochette f

ski [ski:] n ski m ♦ vi skier, faire du ski; ~ **boot** n chaussure f de ski

skid [skɪd] vi déraper

ski: ~**er** n skieur(-euse); ~**ing** n ski m; ~ **jump** n saut m à skis

skilful ['skɪlful] (US **skillful**) adj habile, adroit(e)

ski lift n remonte-pente m inv

skill [skɪl] n habileté f, adresse f, talent m; (requiring training: gen pl) compétences fpl; ~**ed** adj habile, adroit(e); (worker) qualifié(e)

skim [skɪm] vt (milk) écrémer; (glide over) raser, effleurer ♦ vi: to ~ **through** (fig) parcourir; ~**med milk** n lait écré-

mé

skimp [skɪmp] vt (also: ~ **on**: work) bâcler, faire à la va-vite; (: cloth etc) lésiner sur; ~**y** adj (skirt) étriqué(e)

skin [skɪn] n peau f ♦ vt (fruit etc) éplucher; (animal) écorcher; ~ **cancer** n cancer m de la peau; ~**-deep** adj superficiel(le); ~**-diving** n plongée sousmarine; ~**head** n skinhead m/f; ~**ny** adj maigre, maigrichon(ne); ~**tight** adj (jeans etc) moulant(e), ajusté(e)

skip [skɪp] n petit bond or saut m; (BRIT: container) benne f ♦ vi gambader, sautiller; (with rope) sauter à la corde ♦ vt sauter

ski pass n forfait-skieur(s) m

ski pole n bâton m de ski

skipper ['skɪpə'] n capitaine m; (in race) skipper m

skipping rope ['skɪpɪŋ-] (BRIT) n corde f à sauter

skirmish ['skə:mɪʃ] n escarmouche f, accrochage m

skirt [skə:t] n jupe f ♦ vt longer, contourner; ~**ing board** (BRIT) n plinthe f

ski: ~ **slope** n piste f de ski; ~ **suit** n combinaison f (de ski); ~ **tow** n remonte-pente m inv

skittle ['skɪtl] n quille f; ~**s** n (game) (jeu m de) quilles fpl

skive [skaɪv] (BRIT: inf) vi tirer au flanc

skull [skʌl] n crâne m

skunk [skʌŋk] n mouffette f

sky [skaɪ] n ciel m; ~**light** n lucarne f; ~**scraper** n gratte-ciel m inv

slab [slæb] n (of stone) dalle f; (of food) grosse tranche

slack [slæk] adj (loose) lâche, desserré(e); (slow) stagnant(e); (careless) négligent(e), peu sérieux(-euse) or consciencieux(-euse); ~**s** npl (trousers) pantalon m; ~**en** vi ralentir, diminuer ♦ vt (speed) réduire; (grip) relâcher; (clothing) desserrer

slag heap n crassier m

slag off (BRIT: inf) vt dire du mal de

slam [slæm] vt (door) (faire) claquer; (throw) jeter violemment, flanquer (fam); (criticize) démolir ♦ vi claquer

slander ['slɑːndə^r] n calomnie f; diffamation f

slang [slæŋ] n argot m

slant [slɑːnt] n inclinaison f; (fig) angle m, point m de vue; **~ed** adj = **slanting**; **~ing** adj en pente, incliné(e); **~ing eyes** yeux bridés

slap [slæp] n claque f, gifle f, tape f ♦ vt donner une claque or une gifle or une tape à; (paint) appliquer rapidement ♦ adv (directly) tout droit, en plein; **~dash** adj fait(e) sans soin or à la vavite; (person) insouciant(e), négligent(e); **~stick** n (comedy) grosse farce, style m tarte à la crème; **~-up** (BRIT) adj: **a ~-up meal** un repas extra or fameux

slash [slæʃ] vt entailler, taillader; (fig: prices) casser

slat [slæt] n latte f, lame f

slate [sleɪt] n ardoise f ♦ vt (fig: criticize) éreinter, démolir

slaughter ['slɔːtə^r] n carnage m, massacre m ♦ vt (animal) abattre; (people) massacrer; **~house** n abattoir m

slave [sleɪv] n esclave m/f ♦ vi (also: **~ away**) trimer, travailler comme un forçat; **~ry** n esclavage m

slay [sleɪ] (pt **slew**, pp **slain**) vt tuer

sleazy ['sliːzɪ] adj miteux(-euse), minable

sledge [slɛdʒ] n luge f ♦ vi: **to go sledging** faire de la luge

sledgehammer n marteau m de forgeron

sleek [sliːk] adj (hair, fur etc) brillant(e), lisse; (car, boat etc) aux lignes pures or élégantes

sleep [sliːp] (pt, pp **slept**) n sommeil m ♦ vi dormir; (spend night) coucher, dormir; **to go to ~** s'endormir; **~ around** vi coucher à droite et à gauche; **~ in** vi (oversleep) se réveiller trop tard; **~er** n (BRIT) (RAIL: train) train-

couchettes m; (: berth) couchette f; **~ing bag** n sac m de couchage; **~ing car** n (RAIL) wagon-lit m, voiture-lit f; **~ing partner** n (BRIT) = **silent partner**; **~ing pill** n somnifère m; **~less** adj: **a ~less night** une nuit blanche; **~walker** n somnambule m/f; **~y** adj qui a sommeil; (fig) endormi(e)

sleet [sliːt] n neige fondue

sleeve [sliːv] n manche f; (of record) pochette f

sleigh [sleɪ] n traîneau m

sleight [slaɪt] n: **~ of hand** tour m de passe-passe

slender ['slɛndə^r] adj svelte, mince; (fig) faible, ténu(e)

slept [slɛpt] pt, pp of **sleep**

slew [sluː] vi (also: **~ around**) virer, pivoter ♦ pt of **slay**

slice [slaɪs] n tranche f; (round) rondelle f; (utensil) spatule f, truelle f ♦ vt couper en tranches (or en rondelles)

slick [slɪk] adj (skilful) brillant(e) (en apparence); (salesman) qui a du bagout ♦ n (also: **oil ~**) nappe f de pétrole, marée noire

slide [slaɪd] (pt, pp **slid**) n (in playground) toboggan m; (PHOT) diapositive f; (BRIT: also: **hair ~**) barrette f; (in prices) chute f, baisse f ♦ vt (faire) glisser ♦ vi glisser; **sliding** adj (door) coulissant(e); **sliding scale** n échelle f mobile

slight [slaɪt] adj (slim) mince, menu(e); (frail) frêle; (trivial) faible, insignifiant(e); (small) petit(e), léger(-ère) (before n) ♦ n offense f, affront m; **not in the ~est** pas le moins du monde, pas du tout; **~ly** adv légèrement, un peu

slim [slɪm] adj mince ♦ vi maigrir; (diet) suivre un régime amaigrissant

slime [slaɪm] n (mud) vase f; (other substance) substance visqueuse

slimming ['slɪmɪŋ] adj (diet, pills) amaigrissant(e); (foodstuff) qui ne fait pas grossir

sling [slɪŋ] (pt, pp **slung**) n (MED) écharpe f; (for baby) porte-bébé m; (weapon) fronde f, lance-pierre m ♦ vt lancer, jeter

slip [slɪp] n faux pas m; (mistake) erreur f, étourderie f; bévue f; (underskirt) combinaison f; (of paper) petite feuille, fiche f ♦ vt (slide) glisser ♦ vi glisser; (decline) baisser; (move smoothly): **to ~ into/out of** se glisser or se faufiler dans/hors de; **to ~ sth on/off** enfiler/enlever qch; **to give sb the ~** fausser compagnie à qn; **a ~ of the tongue** un lapsus; **~ away** vi s'esquiver; **~ in** vt glisser ♦ vi (errors) s'y glisser; **~ out** vi sortir; **~ up** vi faire une erreur, gaffer; **~ped disc** n déplacement m de vertèbre

slipper ['slɪpə'] n pantoufle f

slippery ['slɪpərɪ] adj glissant(e)

slip: **~ road** (BRIT) n (to motorway) bretelle f d'accès; **~up** n bévue f; **~way** n cale f (de construction or de lancement)

slit [slɪt] (pt, pp **slit**) n fente f; (cut) incision f ♦ vt fendre; couper; inciser

slither ['slɪðə'] vi (of glass, wood) éclat m; (of cheese etc) petit morceau, fine tranche

slob [slɔb] (inf) n rustaud(e)

slog [slɔg] (BRIT) vi travailler très dur ♦ n gros effort; tâche fastidieuse

slogan ['slɒugən] n slogan m

slope [sləup] n pente f, côte f; (side of mountain) versant m, (slant) inclinaison f ♦ vi: **to ~ down** être or descendre en pente; **to ~ up** monter; **sloping** adj en pente; (writing) penché(e)

sloppy ['slɔpɪ] adj (work) peu soigné(e), bâclé(e); (appearance) négligé(e), débraillé(e)

slot [slɔt] n fente f ♦ vt: **to ~ sth into** encastrer or insérer qch dans

sloth [sləuθ] n (laziness) paresse f

slouch [slautʃ] vi avoir le dos rond, être voûté(e)

slovenly ['slʌvənlɪ] adj sale, débrail-

lé(e); (work) négligé(e)

slow [sləu] adj lent(e); (watch): **to be ~** retarder ♦ adv lentement ♦ vt, vi (also: **~ down, ~ up**) ralentir; "~" (road sign) "ralentir"; **~ly** adv lentement; **~ motion** n: **in ~ motion** au ralenti

sludge [slʌdʒ] n boue f

slug [slʌg] n limace f; (bullet) balle f

sluggish ['slʌgɪʃ] adj (person) mou (molle), lent(e); (stream, engine, trading) lent

sluice [sluːs] n (also: **~ gate**) vanne f

slum [slʌm] n (house) taudis m

slump [slʌmp] n baisse soudaine, effondrement m; (ECON) crise f ♦ vi s'effondrer, s'affaisser

slung [slʌŋ] pt, pp of **sling**

slur [slɜː'] n (fig: smear): **to ~ (on)** atteinte f (à); insinuation f (contre) ♦ vt mal articuler

slush [slʌʃ] n neige fondue

slut [slʌt] (pej) n souillon f

sly [slaɪ] adj (smile, expression, remark) sournois(e); (clever) rusé(e); (person)

smack [smæk] n (slap) tape f; (on face) gifle f ♦ vt donner une tape à; (on face) gifler; (on bottom) donner la fessée à ♦ vi: **to ~ of** avoir des relents de, sentir

small [smɔːl] adj petit(e); **~ ads** npl petites annonces; **~ change** n petite or menue monnaie; **~holder** (BRIT) n petit cultivateur; **~ hours** npl: **in the ~ hours** au petit matin; **~pox** n variole f; **~ talk** n menus propos

smart [smɑːt] adj (neat, fashionable) élégant(e), chic inv; (clever) intelligent(e), astucieux(-euse), futé(e); (quick) rapide, vif (vive), prompt(e) ♦ vi faire mal, brûler; (fig) être piqué(e) au vif; **~ card** n carte f à puce; **~en up** vi devenir plus élégant(e), se faire beau (belle) ♦ vt rendre plus élégant(e)

smash [smæʃ] n (also: **~up**) collision f, accident m; (also: **~ hit**) succès foudroyant ♦ vt casser, briser, fracasser; (opponent) écraser; (SPORT: record) pulvériser ♦ vi se briser, se fracasser; s'écraser; **~ing** (inf) adj formidable

smattering ['smætərɪŋ] n: **a ~ of** quelques notions de

smear [smɪəʳ] n tache f, salissure f; trace f; (MED) frottis m ♦ vt enduire; (make dirty) salir; **~ campaign** n campagne f de diffamation

smell [smɛl] (pt, pp **smelt** or **smelled**) n odeur f; (sense) odorat m ♦ vt sentir ♦ vi (food etc): **to ~ (of)** sentir (de); (pej) sentir mauvais; **~y** adj qui sent mauvais, malodorant(e)

smile [smaɪl] n sourire m ♦ vi sourire

smirk [smɜːk] n petit sourire suffisant or affecté

smock [smɔk] n blouse f

smog [smɔg] n brouillard mêlé de fumée, smog m

smoke [sməʊk] n fumée f ♦ vt, vi fumer; **~d** adj (bacon, glass) fumé(e); **~r** n (person) fumeur(-euse); (RAIL) wagon m fumeurs; **~ screen** n rideau m or écran m de fumée; (fig) paravent m; **smoking** n tabagisme m; **"no smoking"** (sign) "défense de fumer"; **to give up smoking** arrêter de fumer; **smoking compartment** (US **smoking car**) n wagon m fumeurs; **smoky** adj enfumé(e); (taste) fumé(e)

smolder ['sməʊldəʳ] (US) vi = smoulder

smooth [smuːð] adj lisse; (sauce) onctueux(-euse); (flavour, whisky) moelleux(-euse); (movement) régulier(-ère), sans à-coups or heurts; (pej: person) doucereux(-euse), mielleux(-euse) ♦ vt (also: **~ out:** skirt, paper) lisser, défroisser; (: creases, difficulties) faire disparaître

smother ['smʌðəʳ] vt étouffer

smoulder ['sməʊldəʳ] (US **smolder**) vi couver

smudge [smʌdʒ] n tache f, bavure f ♦ vt salir, maculer

smug [smʌg] adj suffisant(e)

smuggle ['smʌgl] vt passer en contrebande or en fraude; **~r** n

contrebandier(-ère); **smuggling** n contrebande f

smutty ['smʌtɪ] adj (fig) grossier(-ère), obscène

snack [snæk] n casse-croûte m inv; **~ bar** n snack(-bar) m

snag [snæg] n inconvénient m, difficulté f

snail [sneɪl] n escargot m

snake [sneɪk] n serpent m

snap [snæp] n (sound) claquement m, bruit sec; (photograph) photo f, instantané m ♦ adj subit(e); fait(e) sans réfléchir ♦ vt (break) casser net; (fingers) faire claquer ♦ vi se casser net or avec un bruit sec; (speak sharply) parler d'un ton brusque; **to ~ shut** se refermer brusquement; **~ at** vt fus (subj: dog) essayer de mordre; **~ off** vi (break) casser net; **~ up** vt sauter sur, saisir; **~py** (inf) adj prompt(e); (slogan) qui a du punch; **make it ~py!** grouille-toi, fait(e) que ça saute!; **~shot** n photo f, instantané m

snare [snɛəʳ] n piège m

snarl [snɑːl] vi gronder

snatch [snætʃ] n (small amount): **~es of** des fragments mpl or bribes fpl de ♦ vt saisir (d'un geste vif); (steal) voler

sneak [sniːk] vi: **to ~ in/out** entrer/sortir furtivement or à la dérobée ♦ n (inf: pej: informer) faux jeton; **to ~ up on sb** s'approcher de qn sans faire de bruit; **~ers** npl tennis mpl, baskets mpl

sneer [snɪəʳ] vi ricaner; **to ~ at** traiter avec mépris

sneeze [sniːz] vi éternuer

sniff [snɪf] vi renifler ♦ vt renifler, flairer; (glue, drugs) sniffer, respirer

snigger ['snɪgəʳ] vi ricaner; pouffer de rire

snip [snɪp] n (cut) petit coup; (BRIT: inf: bargain) (bonne) occasion or affaire f ♦ vt couper

sniper ['snaɪpəʳ] n tireur embusqué

snippet ['snɪpɪt] n bribe(s) f(pl)

snob [snɔb] n snob m/f; **~bish** adj snob inv

snooker ['snu:kə^r] n sorte de jeu de billard

snoop [snu:p] vi: to ~ about fureter

snooze [snu:z] n petit somme ♦ vi faire un petit somme

snore [snɔ:^r] vi ronfler

snorkel ['snɔ:kl] n (of swimmer) tuba m

snort [snɔ:t] vi grogner; (horse) renâcler

snout [snaut] n museau m

snow [snəu] n neige f ♦ vi neiger; ~ball n boule f de neige; ~bound adj enneigé(e), bloqué(e) par la neige; ~drift n congère f; ~drop n perceneige m inv f; ~fall n chute f de neige; ~flake n flocon m de neige; ~man (irreg) n bonhomme m de neige; ~plough (US ~plow) n chasseneige m inv; ~shoe n raquette f (pour la neige); ~storm n tempête f de neige

snub [snʌb] vt repousser, snober ♦ n rebuffade f; ~-nosed adj au nez retroussé

snuff [snʌf] n tabac m à priser

snug [snʌg] adj douillet(te), confortable; (person) bien au chaud

snuggle ['snʌgl] vi: to ~ up to sb se serrer ou se blottir contre qn

---

so [səu] adv **1** (thus, likewise) ainsi; **if so** si oui; **so do** ou **have I** moi aussi; **it's 5 o'clock – so it is!** il est 5 heures – en effet! ou c'est vrai; **I hope/think so** je l'espère/le crois; **so far** jusqu'ici, jusqu'à maintenant; (in past) jusque-là

2 (in comparisons etc: to such a degree) si, tellement; **so big (that)** si ou tellement grand (que); **she's not so clever as her brother** elle n'est pas aussi intelligente que son frère

3: so much
♦ adj, adv tant (de); **I've got so much work** j'ai tant de travail; **I love you so much** je vous aime tant; **so many** tant (de)

4 (phrases): **10 or so** à peu près ou environ 10; **so long!** (inf: goodbye) au revoir!, à un de ces jours!

♦ conj **1** (expressing purpose): **so as to do** pour faire, afin de faire; **so (that)** pour que ou afin que +sub

2 (expressing result) donc, par conséquent; **so that** si bien que, de (telle) sorte que

---

soak [səuk] vt faire tremper; (drench) tremper ♦ vi tremper; ~ **in** vi être absorbé(e); ~ **up** vt absorber; ~**ing** adj trempé(e)

soap [səup] n savon m; ~**flakes** npl paillettes fpl de savon; ~ **opera** n feuilleton télévisé; ~ **powder** n lessive f; ~**y** adj savonneux(-euse)

soar [sɔ:^r] vi monter (en flèche), s'élancer; (building) s'élancer

sob [sɔb] n sanglot m ♦ vi sangloter

sober ['səubə^r] adj qui n'est pas (or plus) ivre; (serious) sérieux(-euse), sensé(e); (colour, style) sobre, discret(-ète); ~ **up** vt dessoûler (inf) ♦ vi dessoûler (inf)

so-called ['səu'kɔ:ld] adj soi-disant inv

soccer ['sɔkə^r] n football m

social ['səuʃl] adj social(e); (sociable) sociable ♦ n (petite) fête; ~ **club** n amicale f, foyer m; ~**ism** n socialisme m; ~**ist** adj socialiste ♦ n socialiste m/f; ~**ize** vi: to ~**ize** (with) lier connaissance (avec); parler (avec); ~ **security** (BRIT) n aide sociale; ~ **work** n assistance sociale, travail social; ~ **worker** n assistant(e) social(e)

society [sə'saɪətɪ] n société f; (club) société, association f; (also: **high** ~) (haute) société, grand monde

sociology [səusɪ'ɔlədʒɪ] n sociologie f

sock [sɔk] n chaussette f

socket ['sɔkɪt] n cavité f; (BRIT: ELEC: also: **wall** ~) prise f de courant

sod [sɔd] n (of earth) motte f; (BRIT: inf!) con m (!); salaud m (!)

soda ['səudə] n (CHEM) soude f; (also: ~ **water**) eau f de Seltz; (US: also: ~ **pop**) soda m

sofa ['səʊfə] n sofa m, canapé m

soft [sɒft] adj (not rough) doux (douce);
(not hard) doux; mou (molle); (not
loud) doux, léger(-ère); (kind) doux,
gentil(le); ~ **drink** n boisson non alcoolisée; **~en** vt (r)amollir; (fig) adoucir; atténuer ♦ vi se ramollir; s'adoucir; s'atténuer; **~ly** adv doucement; gentiment;
~ness n douceur f; **~ware** n (COMPUT)
logiciel m, software m

soggy ['sɒgɪ] adj trempé(e); détrem-
pé(e)

soil [sɔɪl] n (earth) sol m, terre f ♦ vt salir; (fig) souiller

solar ['səʊlər] adj solaire; ~ **panel** n
panneau m solaire; ~ **power** n énergie
solaire

sold [səʊld] pt, pp of **sell**

solder ['səʊldər] vt souder (au fil à souder) ♦ n soudure f

soldier ['səʊldʒər] n soldat m, militaire
m

sole [səʊl] n (of foot) plante f; (of shoe)
semelle f; (fish: pl inv) sole f ♦ adj
seul(e), unique

solemn ['sɒləm] adj solennel(le); (person) sérieux(-euse), grave

sole trader n (COMM) chef m d'entreprise individuelle

solicit [sə'lɪsɪt] vt (request) solliciter ♦ vi
(prostitute) racoler

solicitor [sə'lɪsɪtər] n (for wills etc) ≈
notaire m; (in court) ≈ avocat m

solid ['sɒlɪd] adj solide; (not hollow)
plein(e), compact(e), massif(-ive); (entire): **3 ~ hours** 3 heures entières ♦ n
solide m

solidarity [sɒlɪ'dærɪtɪ] n solidarité f

solitary ['sɒlɪtərɪ] adj solitaire; ~ **confinement** n (LAW) isolement m

solo ['səʊləʊ] n solo m ♦ adv (fly) en solitaire; **~ist** n soliste m/f

soluble ['sɒljʊbl] adj soluble

solution [sə'luːʃən] n solution f

solve [sɒlv] vt résoudre

solvent ['sɒlvənt] adj (COMM) solvable
♦ n (CHEM) (dis)solvant m

KEYWORD

some [sʌm] adj 1 (a certain amount or
number of): **some tea/water/ice
cream** du thé/de l'eau/de la glace;
some children/apples des enfants/
pommes

2 (certain: in contrasts): **some people
say that ...** il y a des gens qui disent
que ...; **some films were excellent,
but most ...** certains films étaient ex-
cellents, mais la plupart ...

3 (unspecified): **some woman was
asking for you** il y avait une dame qui
vous demandait; **he was asking for
some book (or other)** il demandait un
livre quelconque; **some day** un de ces
jours; **some day next week** un jour la
semaine prochaine

♦ pron 1 (a certain number) quelques-
un(e)s, certain(e)s; **I've got some
(books etc)** j'en ai (quelques-uns);
some (of them) have been sold certains ont été vendus

2 (a certain amount) un peu; **I've got
some (money, milk)** j'en ai (un peu)

♦ adv: **some 10 people** quelque 10
personnes, 10 personnes environ

some: ~body ['sʌmbədɪ] pron = **someone**; **~how** adv d'une façon ou
d'une autre; (for some reason) pour une
raison ou une autre; **~one** pron quelqu'un; **~place** (US) adv = **somewhere**

somersault ['sʌməsɔːlt] n culbute f,
saut périlleux ♦ vi faire la culbute or un
saut périlleux; (car) faire un tonneau

some: ~thing pron quelque chose;
~thing interesting quelque chose
d'intéressant; **~time** adv (in future) un
de ces jours, un jour ou l'autre; (in
past): **~time last month** au cours du
mois dernier; **~times** adv quelquefois,
parfois; **~what** adv quelque peu, un
peu; **~where** adv quelque part

son [sʌn] n fils m

song [sɒŋ] n chanson f; (of bird) chant

m

son-in-law *n* gendre *m*, beaux-fils *m*

soon [su:n] *adv* bientôt; (*early*) tôt; ~ **afterwards** peu après; *see also* **as**; ~ **er** *adv* (*time*) plus tôt; (*preference*): **I would ~er do** j'aimerais autant or je préférerais faire; **~er or later** tôt ou tard

soot [sut] *n* suie *f*

soothe [su:ð] *vt* calmer, apaiser

sophisticated [sə'fıstıkeıtıd] *adj* raffiné(e); (*sophistiqué*); (*machinery*) hautement perfectionné(e), très complexe

sophomore ['sɔfəmɔ:ʳ] *n* (*US*) étudiant(e) de seconde année

sopping ['sɔpıŋ] *adj* (*also*: ~ **wet**) complètement trempé(e)

soppy ['sɔpı] (*pej*) *adj* sentimental(e)

soprano [sə'prɑ:nəu] *n* (*singer*) soprano *m/f*

sorcerer ['sɔ:sərəʳ] *n* sorcier *m*

sore [sɔ:ʳ] *adj* (*painful*) douloureux (-euse), sensible ♦ *n* plaie *f*; **~ly** ['sɔ:lı] *adv* (*tempted*) fortement

sorrow ['sɔrəu] *n* peine *f*, chagrin *m*

sorry ['sɔrı] *adj* désolé(e); (*condition, excuse*) triste, déplorable; ~! pardon!, excusez-moi!; ~? pardon?; **to feel ~ for sb** plaindre qn

sort [sɔ:t] *n* genre *m*, espèce *f*, sorte *f* ♦ *vt* (*also*: ~ **out**) trier; classer; ranger; (: *problems*) résoudre, régler; **~ing office** ['sɔ:tıŋ-] *n* bureau *m* de tri

SOS *n* S.O.S. *m*

so-so ['səusəu] *adv* comme ci comme ça

sought [sɔ:t] *pt, pp of* **seek**

soul [səul] *n* âme *f*; **~ful** ['səulful] *adj* sentimental(e); (*eyes*) expressif(-ive)

sound [saund] *adj* (*healthy*) en bonne santé, sain(e); (*safe, not damaged*) solide, en bon état; (*reliable, not superficial*) sérieux(-euse), valable; (*sensible*) sensé(e) ♦ *adv*: ~ **asleep** profondément endormi(e) ♦ *n* son *m*; bruit *m*; (*GEO*) détroit *m*, bras *m* de mer ♦ *vt* (*alarm*) sonner ♦ *vi* sonner, retentir; (*fig: seem*) sembler

(*être*); **to ~ like** ressembler à; ~ **out** *vt* sonder; ~ **barrier** *n* mur *m* du son; ~ **bite** *n* phrase *f* toute faite (*pour être citée dans les médias*); ~ **effects** *npl* bruitage *m*; **~ly** *adv* (*sleep*) profondément; (*beat*) complètement, à plate couture; **~proof** *adj* insonorisé(e); **~track** *n* (*of film*) bande *f* sonore

soup [su:p] *n* soupe *f*, potage *m*; ~ **plate** *n* assiette creuse or à soupe; ~ **spoon** *n* cuiller *f* à soupe

sour ['sauəʳ] *adj* aigre; **it's ~ grapes** (*fig*) c'est du dépit

source [sɔ:s] *n* source *f*

south [sauθ] *n* sud *m* ♦ *adj* sud *inv*, du sud ♦ *adv* au sud, vers le sud; **S~ Africa** *n* Afrique *f* du Sud; **S~ African** *adj* sud-africain(e) ♦ *n* Sud-Africain(e); **S~ America** *n* Amérique *f* du Sud; **S~ American** *adj* sud-américain(e) ♦ *n* Sud-Américain(e); **~-east** *n* sud-est *m*; **~erly** ['sʌðəlı] *adj* du sud; au sud; **~ern** ['sʌðən] *adj* (*du*) sud; méridional(e); **S~ Pole** *n* Pôle *m* Sud; **S~ Wales** *n* sud *m* du Pays de Galles; **~ward(s)** *adv* vers le sud; **~-west** *n* sud-ouest *m*

souvenir [su:və'nıəʳ] *n* (*objet*) souvenir *m*

sovereign ['sɔvrın] *n* souverain(e)

soviet ['səuvıət] *adj* soviétique; **the S~ Union** l'Union *f* soviétique

sow¹ [sau] *n* truie *f*

sow² [səu] (*pt* **sowed**, *pp* **sown**) *vt* semer

sown [səun] *pp of* **sow²**

soya ['sɔıə] (*US* **soy**) *n*: ~ **bean** graine *f* de soja; **soy(a) sauce** sauce *f* au soja

spa [spɑ:] *n* (*town*) station thermale; (*US: also*: **health ~**) établissement *m* de cure de rajeunissement *etc*

space [speıs] *n* espace *m*; (*room*) place *f*; espace; (*length of time*) laps *m* de temps ♦ *cpd* spatial(e) ♦ *vt* (*also*: ~ **out**) espacer; **~craft** *n* engin spatial; **~man** (*irreg*) *n* astronaute *m*, cosmonaute *m*; **~ship** *n* = **spacecraft**; **spacing** *n* espacement *m*; **spacious** ['speɪʃəs] *adj* spacieux(-euse), grand(e)

spade [speɪd] *n* (*tool*) bêche *f*, pelle *f*; (*child's*) pelle *f*; **~s** *npl* (CARDS) pique *m*

Spain [speɪn] *n* Espagne *f*

span [spæn] *n* (*of bird, plane*) envergure *f*; (*of arch*) portée *f*; (*in time*) espace *m* de temps, durée *f* ♦ *vt* enjamber, franchir; (*fig*) couvrir, embrasser

Spaniard ['spænjəd] *n* Espagnol(e)

spaniel ['spænjəl] *n* épagneul *m*

Spanish ['spænɪʃ] *adj* espagnol(e) ♦ *n* (LING) espagnol *m*; **the ~** *npl* les Espagnols *mpl*

spank [spæŋk] *vt* donner une fessée à

spanner ['spænər] *n* (BRIT) clé *f* (de mécanicien)

spare [spɛər] *adj* de réserve, de rechange; (*surplus*) de or en trop, de reste ♦ *n* (*part*) = **spare part** ♦ *vt* (*do. without*) se passer de; (*afford to give*) donner, accorder; (*refrain from hurting*) épargner; **to ~** (*surplus*) en surplus, de trop; **~ part** *n* pièce *f* de rechange, pièce détachée; **~ time** *n* moments *mpl* de loisir, temps *m* libre; **~ wheel** *n* (AUT) roue *f* de secours; **sparingly** *adv* avec modération

spark [spɑːk] *n* étincelle *f*; **~(ing) plug** *n* bougie *f*

sparkle ['spɑːkl] *n* scintillement *m*, éclat *m* ♦ *vi* étinceler, scintiller; **sparkling** *adj* (*wine*) mousseux(-euse), pétillant(e); (*water*) pétillant(e); (*fig: conversation, performance*) étincelant(e), pétillant(e)

sparrow ['spærəu] *n* moineau *m*

sparse [spɑːs] *adj* clairsemé(e)

spartan ['spɑːtən] *adj* (*fig*) spartiate

spasm ['spæzəm] *n* (MED) spasme *m*; **~odic** [spæz'mɔdɪk] *adj* (*fig*) intermittent(e)

spastic ['spæstɪk] *n* handicapé(e) moteur

spat [spæt] *pt, pp of* **spit**

spate [speɪt] *n* (*fig*): **a ~ of** une avalanche *or* un torrent de

spawn [spɔːn] *vi* frayer ♦ *n* frai *m*

speak [spiːk] (*pt* **spoke**, *pp* **spoken**) *vt* parler; (*truth*) dire ♦ *vi* parler; (*make a speech*) prendre la parole; **to ~ to sb/of** *or* **about sth** parler à qn/de qch; **~ up!** parle plus fort!; **~er** *n* (*in public*) orateur *m*; (*also:* **loudspeaker**) haut-parleur *m*; **the S~er** (BRIT: POL) le président de la chambre des Communes; (US: POL) le président de la chambre des Représentants

spear [spɪər] *n* lance *f* ♦ *vt* transpercer; **~head** *vt* (*attack etc*) mener

spec [spek] (*inf*) *n*: **on ~** à tout hasard

special ['speʃl] *adj* spécial(e); **~ist** *n* spécialiste *m/f*; **~ity** [speʃɪ'ælɪtɪ] *n* spécialité *f*; **~ize** *vi*: **to ~ize (in)** se spécialiser (dans); **~ly** *adv* spécialement, particulièrement; **~ty** (*esp US*) *n* = **speciality**

species ['spiːʃiːz] *n inv* espèce *f*

specific [spə'sɪfɪk] *adj* précis(e); particulier(-ère); (BOT, CHEM *etc*) spécifique; **~ally** *adv* expressément, explicitement; **~ation** [spesɪfɪ'keɪʃən] *n* (TECH) spécification *f*; (*requirement*) stipulation *f*

specimen ['spesɪmən] *n* spécimen *m*, échantillon *m*; (*of blood*) prélèvement *m*

speck [spek] *n* petite tache, petit point; (*particle*) grain *m*

speckled ['spekld] *adj* tacheté(e), moucheté(e)

specs [speks] (*inf*) *npl* lunettes *fpl*

spectacle ['spektəkl] *n* spectacle *m*; **~s** *npl* (*glasses*) lunettes *fpl*; **spectacular** [spek'tækjulər] *adj* spectaculaire

spectator [spek'teɪtər] *n* spectateur (-trice)

spectrum ['spektrəm] (*pl* **spectra**) *n* spectre *m*

speculation [spekju'leɪʃən] *n* spéculation *f*

speech [spiːtʃ] *n* (*faculty*) parole *f*; (*manner of speaking*) façon *f* de parler, langage *m*; (*enunciation*) élocution *f*; **~less**

muet(te)

speed [spiːd] n vitesse f; (promptness) rapidité f ♦ vi: **to ~ along/past** etc aller/passer etc à toute vitesse or allure; **at full** or **top ~** à toute vitesse or allure; **~ up** vi aller plus vite, accélérer ♦ vt accélérer; **~boat** n vedette f, hors-bord m inv; **~ily** adv rapidement, promptement; **~ing** n (AUT) excès m de vitesse; **~ limit** n limitation f de vitesse, vitesse maximale permise; **~ometer** [spɪˈdɔmɪtə^r] n compteur m (de vitesse); **~way** n (SPORT: also: **~way racing**) épreuve(s) f(pl) de vitesse de motos; **~y** adj rapide, prompt(e)

spell [spel] n (pt, pp spelt or spelled) n (also: **magic ~**) sortilège m, charme m; (period of time) (courte) période f ♦ vt (in writing) écrire, orthographier; (aloud) épeler; (fig) signifier; **to cast a ~ on sb** jeter un sort à qn; **he can't ~** il fait des fautes d'orthographe; **~bound** adj envoûté(e), subjugué(e); **~ing** n orthographe f

spend [spend] (pt, pp spent) vt (money) dépenser; (time, life) passer; consacrer; **~thrift** n dépensier(-ère)

sperm [spəːm] n sperme m

sphere [sfɪə^r] n sphère f

spice [spaɪs] n épice f; **spicy** adj épicé(e), relevé(e); (fig) piquant(e)

spider [ˈspaɪdə^r] n araignée f

spike [spaɪk] n pointe f; (BOT) épi m

spill [spɪl] (pt, pp spilt or spilled) vt renverser; répandre ♦ vi se répandre; **~ over** vi déborder

spin [spɪn] (pt spun or span, pp spun) n (revolution of wheel) tour m; (AVIAT) (chute f en) vrille f; (trip in car) petit tour, balade f ♦ vt (wool etc) filer; (wheel) faire tourner ♦ vi filer; (turn) tourner, tournoyer

spinach [ˈspɪnɪtʃ] n épinard m; (as food) épinards

spinal [ˈspaɪnl] adj vertébral(e), spinal(e); **~ cord** n moelle épinière

spin doctor n personne employée pour présenter un parti politique sous un jour favorable

spin-dryer [spɪnˈdraɪə^r] (BRIT) n essoreuse f

spine [spaɪn] n colonne vertébrale; (thorn) épine f; **~less** adj (fig) mou (molle)

spinning [ˈspɪnɪŋ] n (of thread) filature f; **~ top** n toupie f

spin-off [ˈspɪnɔf] n avantage inattendu; sous-produit m

spinster [ˈspɪnstə^r] n célibataire f; vieille fille (péj)

spiral [ˈspaɪərl] n spirale f ♦ vi (fig) monter en flèche; **~ staircase** n escalier m en colimaçon

spire [spaɪə^r] n flèche f, aiguille f

spirit [ˈspɪrɪt] n esprit m; (mood) état m d'esprit; (courage) courage m, énergie f; **~s** npl (drink) spiritueux mpl, alcool m; **in good ~s** de bonne humeur; **~ed** adj vif (vive), fougueux(-euse), plein(e) d'allant; **~ual** adj spirituel(le); (religious) religieux(-euse)

spit [spɪt] (pt, pp spat) n (for roasting) broche f; (saliva) salive f ♦ vi cracher; (sound) crépiter

spite [spaɪt] n rancune f, dépit m ♦ vt contrarier, vexer; **in ~ of** en dépit de, malgré; **~ful** adj méchant(e), malveillant(e)

spittle [ˈspɪtl] n salive f; (of animal) bave f; (spat out) crachat m

splash [splæʃ] n (sound) plouf m; (of colour) tache f ♦ vt éclabousser ♦ vi (also: **~ about**) barboter, patauger

spleen [spliːn] n (ANAT) rate f

splendid [ˈsplendɪd] adj splendide, superbe, magnifique

splint [splɪnt] n attelle f, éclisse f

splinter [ˈsplɪntə^r] n (wood) écharde f; (glass) éclat m ♦ vi se briser, se fendre

split [splɪt] (pt, pp split) n fente f, déchirure f; (fig: POL) scission f ♦ vt diviser; (work, profits) partager, répartir ♦ vi (divide) se diviser; **~ up** vi (couple) se séparer, rompre; (meeting) se disperser

spoil [spɔɪl] (*pt, pp* **spoilt** *or* **spoiled**) *vt* (*damage*) abîmer; (*mar*) gâcher; (*child*) gâter; **~s** *npl* butin *m*, (*fig: profits*) bénéfices *npl*; **~sport** *n* trouble-fête *m*, rabat-joie *m*

spoke [spəuk] *pt of* **speak** ♦ *n* (*of wheel*) rayon *m*

spoken ['spəukn] *pp of* **speak**

spokesman ['spəuksmən], **spokeswoman** ['spəukswumən] (*irreg*) *n* porte-parole *m inv*

sponge [spʌndʒ] *n* éponge *f*; (*also: ~ cake*) ≃ biscuit *m* de Savoie ♦ *vt* éponger ♦ *vi*: **to ~ off** *or* **on** vivre aux crochets de; **~ bag** (*BRIT*) *n* trousse *f* de toilette

sponsor ['spɒnsə*r*] *n* (*RADIO, TV, SPORT*) sponsor *m*; (*for application*) parrain *m*, marraine *f*; (*BRIT: for fund-raising event*) donateur(-trice) ♦ *vt* sponsoriser; parrainer; faire un don à; **~ship** *n* sponsoring *m*; parrainage *m*; dons *mpl*

spontaneous [spɒn'teɪnɪəs] *adj* spontané(e)

spooky ['spu:kɪ] (*inf*) *adj* qui donne la chair de poule

spool [spu:l] *n* bobine *f*

spoon [spu:n] *n* cuiller *f*; **~-feed** *vt* nourrir à la cuiller; (*fig*) mâcher le travail à; **~ful** *n* cuillerée *f*

sport [spɔ:t] *n* sport *m*; (*person*) chic type *m* (*fille* *f*) ♦ *vt* arborer; **~ing** *adj* sportif(-ive); **to give sb a ~ing chance** donner sa chance à qn; **~ jacket** (*US*) *n* = **sports jacket**; **~s car** *n* voiture *f* de sport; **~s jacket** (*BRIT*) *n* veste *f* de sport; **~sman** (*irreg*) *n* sportif *m*; **~smanship** *n* esprit sportif, sportivité *f*; **~swear** *n* vêtements *mpl* de sport; **~swoman** (*irreg*) *n* sportive *f*; **~y** *adj* sportif(-ive)

spot [spɒt] *n* tache *f*; (*dot: on pattern*) pois *m*; (*pimple*) bouton *m*; (*place*) endroit *m*, coin *m*; (*RADIO, TV: in programme: for person*) numéro *m*; (: *for activity*) rubrique *f*; (*small amount*): **a ~ of** un peu de ♦ *vt* (*notice*) apercevoir,

repérer; **on the ~** sur place, sur les lieux; (*immediately*) sur-le-champ; (*in difficulty*) dans l'embarras; **~ check** *n* sondage *m*, vérification ponctuelle; **~less** *adj* immaculé(e); **~light** *n* projecteur *m*; **~ted** *adj* (*fabric*) à pois; **~ty** *adj* (*face, person*) boutonneux(-euse)

spouse [spaus] *n* époux (épouse)

spout [spaut] *n* (*of jug*) bec *m*; (*of pipe*) orifice *m* ♦ *vi* jaillir

sprain [spreɪn] *n* entorse *f*, foulure *f* ♦ *vt*: **to ~ one's ankle** *etc* se fouler or se tordre la cheville *etc*

sprang [spræŋ] *pt of* **spring**

sprawl [sprɔ:l] *vi* s'étaler

spray [spreɪ] *n* jet *m* (en fines gouttelettes); (*from sea*) embruns *mpl*, vaporisateur *m*; (*for garden*) pulvérisateur *m*; (*aerosol*) bombe *f*; (*of flowers*) petit bouquet ♦ *vt* vaporiser, pulvériser; (*crops*) traiter

spread [spred] (*pt, pp* **spread**) *n* (*distribution*) répartition *f*; (*CULIN*) pâte *f* à tartiner; (*inf: meal*) festin *m* ♦ *vt* étendre, étaler; répandre; (*wealth, workload*) distribuer ♦ *vi* (*disease, news*) se propager; (*also: ~ out: stain*) s'étaler; **~ out** *vi* (*people*) se disperser; **~-eagled** *adj* étendu(e) bras et jambes écartés; **~sheet** *n* (*COMPUT*) tableur *m*

spree [spri:] *n*: **to go on a ~** faire la fête

sprightly ['spraɪtlɪ] *adj* alerte

spring [sprɪŋ] (*pt* **sprang**, *pp* **sprung**) *n* (*leap*) bond *m*, saut *m*; (*coiled metal*) ressort *m*; (*season*) printemps *m*; (*of water*) source *f* ♦ *vi* (*leap*) bondir, sauter; **in ~** au printemps; **to ~ from** provenir de; **~ up** *vi* (*problem*) se présenter, surgir; (*plant, buildings*) surgir de terre; **~board** *n* tremplin *m*; **~-clean(ing)** *n* grand nettoyage de printemps; **~time** *n* printemps *m*

sprinkle ['sprɪŋkl] *vt*: **to ~ water** *etc* **on, ~ with water** *etc* asperger d'eau *etc*; **to ~ sugar** *etc* **on, ~ with sugar** *etc* saupoudrer de sucre *etc*; **~r** *n* (for lawn) arroseur m; (to put out fire) diffuseur m d'extincteur automatique d'incendie

sprint [sprint] n sprint m ♦ vi courir à toute vitesse; (SPORT) sprinter; **~er** n sprinteur(-euse)

sprout [spraut] vi germer, pousser; **~s** npl (also: **Brussels ~s**) choux mpl de Bruxelles

spruce [spruːs] n inv épicéa m ♦ adj net(te), pimpant(e)

sprung [sprʌŋ] pp of **spring**

spun [spʌn] pt, pp of **spin**

spur [spəː] n éperon m; (fig) aiguillon m ♦ vt (also: **~ on**) éperonner; aiguillonner; **on the ~ of the moment** sous l'impulsion du moment

spurious ['spjuəriəs] adj faux (fausse)

spurn [spəːn] vt repousser avec mépris

spurt [spəːt] n (of blood) jaillissement m; (of energy) regain m, sursaut m ♦ vi jaillir, gicler

spy [spai] n espion(ne) ♦ vi: **to ~ on** espionner, épier; (see) apercevoir; **~ing** n espionnage m

sq. abbr = **square**

squabble ['skwɔbl] vi se chamailler

squad [skwɔd] n (MIL, POLICE) escouade f, groupe m; (FOOTBALL) contingent m

squadron ['skwɔdrn] n (MIL) escadron m; (AVIAT, NAUT) escadrille f

squalid ['skwɔlid] adj sordide

squall [skwɔːl] n rafale f, bourrasque f

squalor ['skwɔlə] n conditions fpl sordides

squander ['skwɔndə] vt gaspiller, dilapider

square [skweə] n carré m; (in town) place f ♦ adj carré(e); (inf: ideas, tastes) vieux jeu inv ♦ vt (arrange) régler; arranger; (MATH) élever au carré ♦ vi (reconcile) concilier; **all ~** quitte, à égalité; **a ~ meal** un repas convenable; **2 metres ~** (de) 2 mètres sur 2; **2 ~ metres** 2 mètres carrés; **~ly** adv carrément

squash [skwɔʃ] n (BRIT: drink): **lemon/**

orange ~ citronnade f/orangeade f; (US: marrow) courge f; (SPORT) squash m ♦ vt écraser

squat [skwɔt] adj petit(e) et épais(se), ramassé(e) ♦ vi (also: **~ down**) s'accroupir; **~ter** n squatter m

squeak [skwiːk] vi grincer, crier; (mouse) pousser un petit cri

squeal [skwiːl] vi pousser un or des cri(s) aigu(s) or perçant(s); (brakes) grincer

squeamish ['skwiːmiʃ] adj facilement dégoûté(e)

squeeze [skwiːz] n pression f; (ECON) restrictions fpl de crédit ♦ vt presser; (hand, arm) serrer; **~ out** vt exprimer

squelch [skwɛltʃ] vi faire un bruit de succion

squid [skwid] n calmar m

squiggle ['skwigl] n gribouillis m

squint [skwint] vi loucher ♦ n: **he has a ~** il louche, il souffre de strabisme

squirm [skwəːm] vi se tortiller

squirrel ['skwirl] n écureuil m

squirt [skwəːt] vi jaillir, gicler

Sr abbr = **senior**

St abbr = **saint; street**

stab [stæb] n (with knife etc) coup m (de couteau etc); (of pain) lancée f; (inf: try): **to have a ~ at (doing) sth** s'essayer à (faire) qch ♦ vt poignarder

stable ['steibl] n écurie f ♦ adj stable

stack [stæk] n tas m, pile f ♦ vt (also: **~ up**) empiler, entasser

stadium ['steidiəm] (pl **stadia** or **~s**) n stade m

staff [stɑːf] n (workforce) personnel m; (BRIT: SCOL) professeurs mpl ♦ vt pourvoir en personnel

stag [stæg] n cerf m

stage [steidʒ] n scène f; (platform) estrade f; (point) étape f, stade m; (profession): **the ~** le théâtre ♦ vt (play) monter, mettre en scène; (demonstration) organiser; **in ~s** par étapes, par degrés; **~coach** n diligence f; **~ manager** n régisseur m

stagger ['stægər] *vi* chanceler, tituber ♦ *vt* (*person: amaze*) stupéfier; (*hours, holidays*) étaler, échelonner; **~ing** *adj* (*amazing*) stupéfiant(e), renversant(e)

stagnate [stæg'neɪt] *vi* stagner, croupir

stag party *n* enterrement *m* de vie de garçon

staid [steɪd] *adj* posé(e), rassis(e)

stain [steɪn] *n* tache *f*; (*colouring*) colorant *m* ♦ *vt* tacher; (*wood*) teindre; **~ed glass window** *n* vitrail *m*; **~less** (*steel*) acier *m* inoxydable, inox *m*; **~ remover** *n* détachant *m*

stair [steər] *n* (*step*) marche *f*; **~s** *npl* (*flight of steps*) escalier *m*; **~case, ~way** *n* escalier *m*

stake [steɪk] *n* pieu *m*, poteau *m*; (*BETTING*) enjeu *m*; (*COMM: interest*) intérêts *mpl* ♦ *vt* risquer, jouer; **to be at ~** être en jeu; **to ~ one's claim (to)** revendiquer

stale [steɪl] *adj* (*bread*) rassis(e), pas frais (fraîche); (*food*) éventé(e); (*beer*) éventé(e); (*smell*) de renfermé; (*air*) confiné(e)

stalemate ['steɪlmeɪt] *n* (*CHESS*) pat *m*; (*fig*) impasse *f*

stalk [stɔːk] *n* tige *f* ♦ *vt* traquer ♦ *vi*: **to ~ out/off** sortir/partir d'un air digne

stall [stɔːl] *n* (*BRIT: in street, market etc*) éventaire *m*, étal *m*; (*in stable*) stalle *f* ♦ *vt* (*AUT*) caler; (*delay*) retarder ♦ *vi* (*AUT*) caler; (*fig*) essayer de gagner du temps; **~s** *npl* (*BRIT: in cinema, theatre*) orchestre *m*

stallion ['stæljən] *n* étalon *m* (*cheval*)

stamina ['stæmɪnə] *n* résistance *f*, endurance *f*

stammer ['stæmər] *n* bégaiement *m* ♦ *vi* bégayer

stamp [stæmp] *n* timbre *m*; (*rubber ~*) tampon *m*; (*mark, also fig*) empreinte *f* ♦ *vi* (*also*: **~ one's foot**) taper du pied ♦ *vt* (*letter*) timbrer; (*with rubber ~*) tamponner; **~ album** *n* album *m* de timbres(-poste); **~ collecting** *n* philatélie *f*

stampede [stæm'piːd] *n* ruée *f*

stance [stæns] *n* position *f*

stand [stænd] (*pt, pp* **stood**) *n* (*position*) position *f*; (*for taxis*) station *f* (de taxis); (*music ~*) pupitre *m* à musique; (*COMM*) étalage *m*, stand *m*; (*SPORT: also*: **~s**) tribune *f* ♦ *vi* être or se tenir (debout); (*rise*) se lever, se mettre debout; (*be placed*) se trouver; (*remain: offer etc*) rester valable; (*BRIT: in election*) être candidat(e), se présenter ♦ *vt* (*place*) mettre, poser; (*tolerate, withstand*) supporter; (*treat, invite to*) offrir, payer; **to make** *or* **take a ~** prendre position; **to ~ at** (*score, value etc*) être de; **to ~ for parliament** (*BRIT*) se présenter aux élections législatives; **~ by** *vi* (*be ready*) se tenir prêt(e) ♦ *vt fus* (*opinion*) s'en tenir à; (*person*) ne pas abandonner, soutenir; **~ down** *vi* (*withdraw*) se retirer; **~ for** *vt fus* (*signify*) représenter, signifier; (*tolerate*) supporter, tolérer; **~ in for** *vt fus* remplacer; **~ out** *vi* (*be prominent*) ressortir; **~ up** *vi* (*rise*) se lever, se mettre debout; **~ up for** *vt fus* défendre; **~ up to** *vt fus* tenir tête à, résister à

standard ['stændəd] *n* (*level*) niveau (voulu); (*norm*) norme *f*, étalon *m*; (*criterion*) critère *m*; (*flag*) étendard *m* ♦ *adj* (*size etc*) ordinaire, normal(e); courant(e); (*text*) de base; **~s** *npl* (*morals*) morale *f*, principes *mpl*; **~ lamp** *n* lampadaire *m*; **~ of living** *n* niveau *m* de vie

stand-by ['stændbaɪ] *n* remplaçant *m*; **to be on ~~** se tenir prêt(e) (à intervenir); être de garde; **~~ ticket** *n* (*AVIAT*) billet *m* stand-by

stand-in ['stændɪn] *n* remplaçant(e)

standing ['stændɪŋ] *adj* debout *inv*; (*permanent*) permanent(e) ♦ *n* réputation *f*, rang *m*, standing *m*; **of many years'** qui dure or existe depuis longtemps; **~ joke** *n* sujet de plaisanterie; **~ order** (*BRIT*) *n* (*at bank*) virement *m* automatique, prélèvement *m* bancaire; **~ room** *n* places *fpl* debout

standpoint ['stændpɔint] n point m de vue

standstill ['stændstil] n: **at a ~** paralysé(e); **to come to a ~** s'immobiliser, s'arrêter

stank [stæŋk] pt of **stink**

staple ['steipl] n (for papers) agrafe f ♦ adj (food etc) de base ♦ vt agrafer; **~r** n agrafeuse f

star [stɑ:r] n étoile f; (celebrity) vedette f ♦ vi: **to ~ (in)** être la vedette (de) ♦ vt (CINEMA etc) avoir pour vedette; **the ~s** npl l'horoscope m

starboard ['stɑ:bɔ:d] n tribord m

starch [stɑ:tʃ] n amidon m; (in food) fécule f

stardom ['stɑ:dəm] n célébrité f

stare [stɛər] n regard m fixe ♦ vi: **to ~ at** regarder fixement

starfish ['stɑ:fiʃ] n étoile f de mer

stark [stɑ:k] adj (bleak) désolé(e), morne ♦ adv: **~ naked** complètement nu(e)

starling ['stɑ:liŋ] n étourneau m

starry ['stɑ:ri] adj étoilé(e); **~-eyed** adj (innocent) ingénu(e)

start [stɑ:t] n commencement m, début m; (of race) départ m; (sudden movement) sursaut m; (advantage) avance f, avantage m ♦ vt commencer; (found) créer; (engine) mettre en marche ♦ vi partir, se mettre en route; (jump) sursauter; **to ~ doing** or **to do sth** se mettre à faire qch; **~ off** vi commencer; (leave) partir; **~ up** vi commencer; (car) démarrer ♦ vt (business) créer; (car) mettre en marche; **~er** n (AUT) démarreur m; (SPORT: official) starter m; (BRIT: CULIN) entrée f; **~ing point** n point m de départ

startle ['stɑ:tl] vt faire sursauter; donner un choc à; **startling** adj (news) surprenant(e)

starvation [stɑ:'veiʃən] n faim f, famine f

starve [stɑ:v] vi mourir de faim; être affamé(e) ♦ vt affamer

state [steit] n état m; (POL) État m ♦ vt dé-

clarer, affirmer; **the S~s** npl (America) les États-Unis mpl; **to be in a ~** être dans tous ses états; **~ly** adj majestueux(-euse), imposant(e); **~ly home** n château m; **~ment** n déclaration f; **~sman** (irreg) n homme m d'État

static ['stætik] n (RADIO, TV) parasites mpl ♦ adj statique

station ['steiʃən] n gare f; (police ~) poste m de police ♦ vt placer, poster

stationary ['steiʃnəri] adj à l'arrêt, immobile

stationer ['steiʃənər] n papetier-(ère); **~'s (shop)** n papeterie f; **~y** n papier m à lettres, petit matériel de bureau

stationmaster ['steiʃənmɑːstər] n (RAIL) chef m de gare

station wagon (US) n break m

statistic n statistique f; **~s** [stə'tistiks] n (science) statistique f

statue ['stætju:] n statue f

status ['steitəs] n position f, situation f; (official) statut m; (prestige) prestige m; **~ symbol** n signe extérieur de richesse

statute ['stætjuːt] n loi f, statut m; **statutory** ['stætjutri] adj statutaire, prévu(e) par un article de loi

staunch [stɔ:ntʃ] adj sûr(e), loyal(e)

stay [stei] n (period of time) séjour m ♦ vi rester; (reside) loger; (spend some time) séjourner; **to ~ put** ne pas bouger; **to ~ with friends** loger chez des amis; **to ~ the night** passer la nuit; **~ behind** vi rester en arrière; **~ in** vi (at home) rester à la maison; **~ on** vi rester; **~ out** vi (of house) ne pas rentrer; **~ up** vi (at night) ne pas se coucher; **~ing power** n endurance f

stead [sted] n: **in sb's ~** à la place de qn; **to stand sb in good ~** être très utile à qn

steadfast ['stedfɑ:st] adj ferme, résolu(e)

steadily ['stedili] adv (regularly) progressivement; (firmly) fermement; (: walk) d'un pas ferme; (fixedly: look) sans détourner les yeux

steady ['stɛdɪ] adj stable, solide, ferme; (regular) constant(e), régulier(-ère); (person) calme, pondéré(e) ♦ vt stabiliser; (nerves) calmer; **a ~ boyfriend** un petit ami

steak [steɪk] n (beef) bifteck m, steak m; (fish, pork) tranche f

steal [sti:l] (pt **stole**, pp **stolen**) vt voler ♦ vi voler; (move secretly) se faufiler, se déplacer furtivement

stealth [stɛlθ] n: **by ~** furtivement

steam [sti:m] n vapeur f ♦ vt (CULIN) cuire à la vapeur ♦ vi fumer; **~ engine** n locomotive f à vapeur; **~er** n (boat) (bateau m à) vapeur m; (CULIN) = **steamer**; **~y** adj embué(e), humide

steel [sti:l] n acier m ♦ adj d'acier; **~works** n aciérie f

steep [sti:p] adj raide, escarpé(e); (price) excessif(-ive)

steeple ['sti:pl] n clocher m

steer [stɪə*] vt diriger; (boat) gouverner; (person) guider, conduire ♦ vi tenir le gouvernail; **~ing** n (AUT) conduite f; **~ing wheel** n volant m

stem [stɛm] n (of plant) tige f; (of glass) pied m ♦ vt contenir, arrêter, juguler; **~ from** vt fus provenir de, découler de

stench [stɛntʃ] n puanteur f

stencil ['stɛnsl] n stencil m; (pattern used) pochoir m ♦ vt polycopier

stenographer [stɛ'nɔɡrəfə*] n (US) sténographe m/f

step [stɛp] n pas m; (stair) marche f; (action) mesure f, disposition f ♦ vi: **to ~ forward/back** faire un pas en avant/arrière, avancer/reculer; **~s** npl (BRIT) = **stepladder**; **to be in/out of ~ (with)** aller dans le sens (de)/être déphasé(e) (par rapport à); **~ down** vi (fig) se retirer, se désister; **~ up** vt augmenter; intensifier; **~brother** n demi-frère m; **~daughter** n belle-fille f; **~father** n beau-père m; **~ladder** (BRIT) n escabeau m; **~mother** n belle-mère f; **~ping stone** n pierre f de gué; tremplin m; **~sister** n demi-sœur f;

~son n beau-fils m

stereo ['stɛrɪəʊ] n (sound) stéréo f; (hi-fi) chaîne f stéréo inv ♦ adj (also: **~phonic**) stéréo(phonique)

sterile ['stɛraɪl] adj stérile; **sterilize** ['stɛrɪlaɪz] vt stériliser

sterling ['stɜ:lɪŋ] adj (silver) de bon aloi, fin(e) ♦ n (ECON) livres fpl sterling inv; **a pound ~** une livre sterling

stern [stɜ:n] adj sévère ♦ n (NAUT) arrière m, poupe f

stew [stju:] n ragoût m ♦ vt, vi cuire (à la casserole)

steward ['stjuːəd] n (on ship, plane, train) steward m; **~ess** n hôtesse f (de l'air)

stick [stɪk] (pt, pp **stuck**) n bâton m; (walking ~) canne f ♦ vt (glue) coller; (inf: put) mettre, fourrer; (: tolerate) supporter; (thrust): **to ~ sth into** planter or enfoncer qch dans ♦ vi (become attached) rester collé(e) or fixé(e); (be unmoveable: wheels etc) se bloquer; (remain) rester; **~ out** vi dépasser, sortir; **~ up** vi = stick out; **~ up for** vt fus défendre; **~er** n auto-collant m; **~ing plaster** n sparadrap m, pansement adhésif

stick-up ['stɪkʌp] (inf) n braquage m, hold-up m inv

sticky ['stɪkɪ] adj poisseux(-euse); (label) adhésif(-ive); (situation) délicat(e)

stiff [stɪf] adj raide; rigide; dur(e); (difficult) difficile, ardu(e); (cold) froid(e), distant(e); (strong, high) fort(e), élevé(e) ♦ adv: **to be bored/scared/frozen** s'ennuyer à mort/être mort(e) de peur/froid; **~en** vi se raidir; **~ neck** n torticolis m

stifle ['staɪfl] vt étouffer, réprimer

stigma ['stɪɡmə] n stigmate m

stile [staɪl] n échalier m

stiletto [stɪ'lɛtəʊ] (BRIT) n (also: **~ heel**) talon m aiguille

still [stɪl] adj immobile ♦ adv (up to this time) encore, toujours; (even) encore; (nonetheless) quand même, tout de même; **~born** adj mort-né(e); **~ life** n nature morte

stilt [stɪlt] n (for walking on) échasse f; (pile) pilotis m

stilted ['stɪltɪd] adj guindé(e), emprunté(e)

stimulate ['stɪmjʊleɪt] vt stimuler

stimuli ['stɪmjʊlaɪ] npl of **stimulus**

stimulus ['stɪmjʊləs] (pl **stimuli**) n stimulant m; (BIOL, PSYCH) stimulus m

sting [stɪŋ] (pt, pp **stung**) n piqûre f; (organ) dard m ♦ vt, vi piquer

stingy ['stɪndʒɪ] adj avare, pingre

stink [stɪŋk] (pt **stank**, pp **stunk**) n puanteur f ♦ vi puer, empester; **~ing** (inf) adj (fig) infect(e), vache; **a ~ing** ... un(e) foutu(e) ...

stint [stɪnt] n part f de travail ♦ vi: **to ~ on** lésiner sur, être chiche de

stir [stəːʳ] n agitation f, sensation f ♦ vt remuer ♦ vi remuer, bouger; **~ up** vt (trouble) fomenter, provoquer

stirrup ['stɪrəp] n étrier m

stitch [stɪtʃ] n (SEWING) point m; (KNITTING) maille f; (MED) point de suture; (pain) point de côté ♦ vt coudre, piquer; (MED) suturer

stoat [stəʊt] n hermine f (avec son pelage d'été)

stock [stɔk] n réserve f, provision f; (COMM) stock m; (AGR) cheptel m, bétail m; (CULIN) bouillon m; (descent, origin) souche f; (FINANCE) valeurs fpl, titres mpl ♦ adj (fig: reply etc) classique ♦ vt (have in ~) avoir, vendre; **~s and shares** valeurs (mobilières), titres; **in/out of ~** en stock or en magasin/épuisé(e); **to take ~ of** (fig) faire le point de; **~ up** vi: **to ~ up (with)** s'approvisionner (en); **~broker** n agent m de change; **~ cube** n bouillon-cube m; **~ exchange** n Bourse f

stocking ['stɔkɪŋ] n bas m

stock: ~ market n Bourse f, marché financier; **~pile** n stock m, réserve f ♦ vt stocker, accumuler; **~taking** (BRIT) n (COMM) inventaire m

stocky ['stɔkɪ] adj trapu(e), râblé(e)

stodgy ['stɔdʒɪ] adj bourratif(-ive), lourd(e)

stoke [stəʊk] vt (fire) garnir, entretenir; (boiler) chauffer

stole [stəʊl] pt of **steal** ♦ n étole f

stolen ['stəʊln] pp of **steal**

stomach ['stʌmək] n estomac m; (abdomen) ventre m ♦ vt digérer, supporter; **~ache** n mal à l'estomac or au ventre

stone [stəʊn] n pierre f; (pebble) caillou m, galet m; (in fruit) noyau m; (MED) calcul m; (BRIT: weight) 6,348 kg ♦ adj de or en pierre ♦ vt (person) lancer des pierres sur, lapider; **~-cold** adj complètement froid(e); **~-deaf** adj sourd(e) comme un pot; **~work** n maçonnerie f

stood [stʊd] pt, pp of **stand**

stool [stuːl] n tabouret m

stoop [stuːp] vi (also: **have a ~**) être voûté(e); (also: **~ down**: bend) se baisser

stop [stɔp] n arrêt m; halte f; (in punctuation: also: **full ~**) point m ♦ vt arrêter, bloquer; (break off) interrompre; (also: **put a ~ to**) mettre fin à ♦ vi s'arrêter; (rain, noise etc) cesser, s'arrêter; **to ~ doing sth** cesser or arrêter de faire qch; **~ dead** vi s'arrêter net; **~ off** vi faire une courte halte; **~ up** vt (hole) boucher; **~gap** n (person) bouche-trou m; (measure) mesure f intérimaire; **~over** n halte f; (AVIAT) escale f; **~page** n (strike) arrêt de travail; (blockage) obstruction f; **~per** n bouchon m; **~ press** n nouvelles fpl de dernière heure; **~watch** n chronomètre m

storage ['stɔːrɪdʒ] n entreposage m; **~ heater** n radiateur m électrique par accumulation

store [stɔːʳ] n (stock) provision f, réserve f; (depot) entrepôt m; (BRIT: large shop) grand magasin; (US) magasin m ♦ vt emmagasiner; (information) enregistrer; **~s** npl (food) provisions; **in ~** en réserve; **~ up** vt mettre en réserve; accumuler; **~room** n réserve f, magasin m

storey ['stɔːrɪ] n (US story) étage m

stork [stɔːk] n cigogne f

storm [stɔːm] n tempête f; (thunderstorm) orage m ♦ vi (fig) fulminer ♦ vt prendre d'assaut; **~y** adj orageux(-euse)

story ['stɔːrɪ] n histoire f, récit m; (US) = **storey**; **~book** n livre m d'histoires ou de contes

stout [staut] adj solide; (fat) gros(se), corpulent(e) ♦ n bière brune

stove [stəuv] n (for cooking) fourneau m; (: small) réchaud m; (for heating) poêle m

stow [stəu] vt (also: **~ away**) ranger; **~away** n passager(-ère) clandestin(e)

straddle ['strædl] vt enjamber, être à cheval sur

straggle ['strægl] vi être (or marcher) en désordre

straight [streɪt] adj droit(e); (hair) raide; (frank) honnête, franc (franche); (simple) simple ♦ adv (tout) droit; (drink) sec, sans eau; **to put** or **get** (fig) mettre au clair; **~ away**, **~ off** (at once) tout de suite; **~en** vt ajuster; (bed) arranger; **~en out** vt (fig) débrouiller; **~-faced** adj impassible; **~forward** adj simple; (honest) honnête, direct(e)

strain [streɪn] n tension f; pression f; (physical) effort m; (mental tension nerveuse); (breed) race f ♦ vt (stretch: resources etc) mettre à rude épreuve, grever; (hurt: back etc) se faire mal à; (vegetables) égoutter; **~s** npl (MUS) accords mpl, accents mpl; **back ~** tour m de rein; **~ed** adj (muscle) froissé(e); (laugh etc) forcé(e), contraint(e); (relations) tendu(e); **~er** n passoire f

strait [streɪt] n (GEO) détroit m; **~s** npl: **to be in dire ~s** avoir de sérieux ennuis (d'argent); **~jacket** n camisole f de force; **~-laced** adj collet monté m

strand [strænd] n (of thread) fil m, brin m; (of rope) toron m; (of hair) mèche f;

~ed adj en rade, en plan

strange [streɪndʒ] adj (not known) inconnu(e); (odd) étrange, bizarre; **~ly** adv étrangement, bizarrement; see also **enough**; **~r** n inconnu(e); (from another area) étranger(-ère)

strangle ['stræŋgl] vt étrangler; **~hold** n (fig) emprise totale, mainmise f

strap [stræp] n lanière f, courroie f, sangle f; (of slip, dress) bretelle f; **~py** adj (dress) à bretelles; (sandals) à lanières

strategy ['strætɪdʒɪ] n stratégie f

straw [strɔː] n paille f; **that's the last ~!** ça, c'est le comble!

strawberry ['strɔːbərɪ] n fraise f

stray [streɪ] adj (animal) perdu(e), errant(e); (scattered) isolé(e) ♦ vi s'égarer; **~ bullet** n balle perdue

streak [striːk] n bande f, filet m; (in hair) raie f ♦ vt zébrer, strier ♦ vi: **to ~ past** passer à toute allure

stream [striːm] n (brook) ruisseau m; (current) courant m, flot m; (of people) défilé ininterrompu, flot ♦ vt (SCOL) répartir par niveau ♦ vi ruisseler; **to ~ in/ out** entrer/sortir à flots

streamer ['striːmər] n serpentin m; (banner) banderole f

streamlined ['striːmlaɪnd] adj aérodynamique; (fig) rationalisé(e)

street [striːt] n rue f; **~car** (US) n tramway m; **~ lamp** n réverbère m; **~ plan** n plan m (des rues); **~wise** (inf) adj futé(e), réaliste

strength [streŋθ] n force f; (of girder, knot etc) solidité f; **~en** vt (muscle etc) fortifier; (nation, case etc) renforcer; (building, ECON) consolider

strenuous ['strɛnjuəs] adj vigoureux(-euse), énergique

stress [strɛs] n (force, pressure) pression f; (mental strain) tension (nerveuse), stress m; (accent) accent m ♦ vt insister sur, souligner

stretch [stretʃ] n (of sand etc) étendue f ♦ vi s'étirer; (extend): **to ~ to** or **as far**

as s'étendre jusqu'à ♦ vt tendre, étirer; (fig) pousser (au maximum); **~ out** vi s'étendre ♦ vt (arm etc) allonger, tendre; (spread) étendre

stretcher ['strɛtʃər] n brancard m, civière f

stretchy ['strɛtʃɪ] adj élastique

strewn [struːn] adj: **~ with** jonché(e) de

stricken ['strɪkən] adj (person) très éprouvé(e); (city, industry etc) dévasté(e); **~ with** (disease etc) frappé(e) or atteint(e) de

strict [strɪkt] adj strict(e)

stride [straɪd] (pt **strode**, pp **stridden**) n grand pas, enjambée f ♦ vi marcher à grands pas

strife [straɪf] n conflit m, dissensions fpl

strike [straɪk] (pt, pp **struck**) n grève f, (of oil etc) découverte f; (attack) raid m ♦ vt frapper; (oil etc) trouver, découvrir; (deal) conclure ♦ vi faire grève; (attack) attaquer; (clock) sonner; **on ~** (workers) en grève; **to ~ a match** frotter une allumette; **~ down** vt terrasser; **~ up** vt (MUS) se mettre à jouer; **to ~ up a friendship** se lier d'amitié avec; **to ~ up a conversation (with)** engager une conversation (avec); **~r** n gréviste m/f; (SPORT) buteur m; **striking** adj frappant(e), saisissant(e); (attractive) éblouissant(e)

string [strɪŋ] (pt, pp **strung**) n ficelle f, (row: of beads) rang m; (: of onions) chapelet m; (MUS) corde f ♦ vt: **to ~ out** échelonner; **the ~s** npl (MUS) les instruments mpl à cordes; **to ~ together** enchaîner; **to pull ~s** (fig) faire jouer le piston; **~(ed) instrument** n (MUS) instrument m à cordes

stringent ['strɪndʒənt] adj rigoureux (-euse)

strip [strɪp] n bande f ♦ vt (undress) déshabiller; (paint) décaper; (also: **~ down:** machine) démonter ♦ vi se déshabiller; **~ cartoon** n bande dessinée

stripe [straɪp] n raie f, rayure f; (MIL) ga-

lon m; **~d** adj rayé(e), à rayures

strip: ~ lighting (BRIT) n éclairage m au néon or fluorescent; **~per** n stripteaseur(-euse) f; **~ search** n fouille corporelle (en faisant se déshabiller la personne) ♦ vt: **he was ~ searched** on l'a fait se déshabiller et soumis à une fouille corporelle

stripy ['straɪpɪ] adj rayé(e)

strive [straɪv] (pt **strove**, pp **striven**) vi: **to ~ to do/for sth** s'efforcer de faire/ d'obtenir qch

strode [strəʊd] pt of **stride**

stroke [strəʊk] n coup m; (SWIMMING) nage f; (MED) attaque f ♦ vt caresser; **at a ~** d'un (seul) coup

stroll [strəʊl] n petite promenade ♦ vi flâner, se promener nonchalamment; **~er** (US) n (pushchair) poussette f

strong [strɒŋ] adj fort(e); vigoureux (-euse); (heart, nerves) solide; **they are 50 ~** ils sont au nombre de 50; **~hold** n bastion m; **~ly** adv fortement, avec force; vigoureusement; **~room** n chambre forte

strove [strəʊv] pt of **strive**

struck [strʌk] pt, pp of **strike**

structural ['strʌktʃrəl] adj structural(e); (CONSTR: defect) de construction; (damage) affectant les parties portantes

structure ['strʌktʃər] n structure f; (building) construction f

struggle ['strʌgl] n lutte f ♦ vi lutter, se battre

strum [strʌm] vt (guitar) jouer (en sourdine) de

strung [strʌŋ] pt, pp of **string**

strut [strʌt] n étai m, support m ♦ vi se pavaner

stub [stʌb] n (of cigarette) bout m, mégot m; (of cheque etc) talon m ♦ vt: **to ~ one's toe** se cogner le doigt de pied; **~ out** vt écraser

stubble ['stʌbl] n chaume m; (on chin) barbe f de plusieurs jours

stubborn ['stʌbən] adj têtu(e), obstiné(e), opiniâtre

stuck [stʌk] pt, pp of **stick** ♦ adj (jammed) bloqué(e), coincé(e); **~-up** (inf) adj prétentieux(-euse)

stud [stʌd] n (on boots etc) clou m; (on collar) bouton m de col; (earring) petite boucle d'oreille; (of horses: also: ~ **farm**) écurie f, haras m; (also: ~ **animal**) étalon m ♦ vt (fig): **~ded with** parsemé(e) or criblé(e) de

student ['stju:dənt] n étudiant(e) ♦ adj estudiantin(e); d'étudiant; ~ **driver** (US) n (conducteur-trice) débutant(e)

studio ['stju:diəu] n studio m, atelier m; (TV etc) studio

studious ['stju:diəs] adj studieux (-euse), appliqué(e); (attention) soutenu(e); **~ly** adv (carefully) soigneusement

study ['stʌdi] n étude f; (room) bureau m ♦ vt étudier; (examine) examiner ♦ vi étudier, faire ses études

stuff [stʌf] n chose(s) f(pl); (substance) substance f ♦ vt rembourrer; (CULIN) farcir; (inf: push) fourrer; **~ing** n bourre f, rembourrage m; (CULIN) farce f; **~y** adj (room) mal ventilé(e) or aéré(e); (ideas) vieux jeu inv

stumble ['stʌmbl] vi trébucher; **to ~ across** or **on** (fig) tomber sur; **stumbling block** n pierre f d'achoppement

stump [stʌmp] n souche f; (of limb) moignon m ♦ vt: **to be ~ed** sécher, ne pas savoir que répondre

stun [stʌn] vt étourdir; (fig) abasourdir

stung [stʌŋ] pt, pp of **sting**

stunk [stʌŋk] pp of **stink**

stunned [stʌnd] adj sidéré(e)

stunning ['stʌniŋ] adj (news etc) stupéfiant(e); (girl etc) éblouissant(e)

stunt [stʌnt] n (in film) cascade f, acrobatie f; (publicity) ~) truc m publicitaire ♦ vt retarder, arrêter; **~man** ['stʌntmæn] (irreg) n cascadeur m

stupendous [stju:'pendəs] adj prodigieux(-euse), fantastique

stupid ['stju:pid] adj stupide, bête; **~ity** [stju:'piditi] n stupidité f, bêtise f

sturdy ['stə:di] adj robuste; solide

stutter ['stʌtər] vi bégayer

sty [stai] n (for pigs) porcherie f

stye [stai] n (MED) orgelet m

style [stail] n style m; (distinction) allure f, cachet m, style; **stylish** adj élégant(e), chic inv

stylus ['stailəs] (pl **styli** or **~es**) n (of record player) pointe f de lecture

suave [swa:v] adj doucereux(-euse), onctueux(-euse)

sub... [sʌb] prefix sub..., sous-; **~conscious** adj subconscient(e); **~contract** vt sous-traiter

subdue [səb'dju:] vt subjuguer, soumettre; **~d** adj (light) tamisé(e); (person) qui a perdu de son entrain

subject [n 'sʌbdʒikt, vb səb'dʒekt] n sujet m; (SCOL) matière f ♦ vt: **to ~ to** soumettre à; exposer à; **to be ~ to** (law) être soumis(e) à; (disease) être sujet(te) à; **~ive** [səb'dʒektiv] adj subjectif(-ive); ~ **matter** n (content) contenu m

sublet [sʌb'let] vt sous-louer

submarine [sʌbmə'ri:n] n sous-marin m

submerge [səb'mə:dʒ] vt submerger ♦ vi plonger

submission [səb'miʃən] n soumission f; **submissive** adj soumis(e)

submit [səb'mit] vt soumettre ♦ vi se soumettre

subnormal [sʌb'nɔ:ml] adj au-dessous de la normale

subordinate [sə'bɔ:dinət] adj subalterne ♦ n subordonné(e)

subpoena [səb'pi:nə] n (LAW) citation f, assignation f

subscribe [səb'skraib] vi cotiser; **to ~ to** (opinion, fund) souscrire à; (newspaper) s'abonner à; être abonné(e) à; **~r** n (to periodical, telephone) abonné(e); **subscription** [səb'skripʃən] n (to magazine etc) abonnement m

subsequent ['sʌbsikwənt] adj ultérieur(e), suivant(e); consécutif(-ive); **~ly** adv

adv par la suite

subside [səb'said] *vi* (*flood*) baisser; (*wind, feelings*) tomber; **~nce** [səb'saidns] *n* affaissement *m*

subsidiary [səb'sidiəri] *adj* subsidiaire; accessoire ♦ *n* filiale *f*

subsidize ['sʌbsidaiz] *vt* subventionner; **subsidy** ['sʌbsidi] *n* subvention *f*

substance ['sʌbstəns] *n* substance *f*

substantial [səb'stænʃl] *adj* substantiel(le); (*fig*) important(e); **~ly** *adv* considérablement; (*in essence*) en grande partie

substantiate [səb'stænʃieit] *vt* étayer, fournir des preuves à l'appui de

substitute ['sʌbstitju:t] *n* (*person*) remplaçant(e); (*thing*) succédané *m* ♦ *vt*: **to ~ sth/sb** for substituer qch/qn à, remplacer par qch/qn

subterranean [sʌbtə'reiniən] *adj* souterrain(e)

subtitle ['sʌbtaitl] *n* (*CINEMA, TV*) sous-titre *m*; **~d** *adj* sous-titré(e)

subtle ['sʌtl] *adj* subtil(e)

subtotal [sʌb'təutl] *n* total partiel

subtract [səb'trækt] *vt* soustraire, retrancher; **~ion** *n* soustraction *f*

suburb ['sʌbə:b] *n* faubourg *m*; **the ~s** *npl* la banlieue; **~an** [sə'bə:bən] *adj* de banlieue, suburbain(e); **~ia** [sə'bə:biə] *n* la banlieue

subway ['sʌbwei] *n* (*US: railway*) métro *m*; (*BRIT: underpass*) passage souterrain *m*

succeed [sək'si:d] *vi* réussir ♦ *vt* succéder à; **to ~ in doing** réussir à faire; **~ing** *adj* (*following*) suivant(e)

success [sək'ses] *n* succès *m*, réussite *f*; **~ful** (*venture*) couronné(e) de succès; **to be ~ful (in doing)** réussir (à faire); **~fully** *adv* avec succès

succession [sək'seʃən] *n* succession *f*; **3 days in ~** 3 jours de suite

successive [sək'sesiv] *adj* successif (-ive), consécutif(-ive)

such [sʌtʃ] *adj* tel (telle); (*of that kind*): **~ a book** un livre de ce genre, un livre pareil, un tel livre; (*so much*): **~ cour-**

age un tel courage ♦ *adv* si; **~ books** des livres de ce genre, des livres pareils, de tels livres; **~ a long trip** un si long voyage; **~ a lot of** tellement *or* tant de; **~ as** (*like*) tel que, comme; **as ~** en tant que tel, à proprement parler; **~- and-~** *adj* tel ou tel

suck [sʌk] *vt* sucer; (*breast, bottle*) téter; **~er** *n* ventouse *f*; (*inf*) poire *f*

suction ['sʌkʃən] *n* succion *f*

sudden ['sʌdn] *adj* soudain(e), subit(e); **all of a ~** soudain, tout à coup; **~ly** *adv* brusquement, tout à coup, soudain

suds [sʌdz] *npl* eau savonneuse

sue [su:] *vt* poursuivre en justice, intenter un procès à

suede [sweid] *n* daim *m*

suet ['suit] *n* graisse *f* de rognon

suffer ['sʌfə*] *vt* souffrir, subir; (*bear*) tolérer, supporter ♦ *vi* souffrir; **~er** *n* (*MED*) malade *m/f*; **~ing** *n* souffrance(s) *f(pl)*

sufficient [sə'fiʃənt] *adj* suffisant(e); **~ money** suffisamment d'argent; **~ly** *adv* suffisamment, assez

suffocate ['sʌfəkeit] *vi* suffoquer, étouffer

sugar ['ʃugə*] *n* sucre *m* ♦ *vt* sucrer; **~ beet** *n* betterave sucrière; **~ cane** *n* canne *f* à sucre

suggest [sə'dʒest] *vt* suggérer, proposer; (*indicate*) dénoter; **~ion** *n* suggestion *f*

suicide ['suisaid] *n* suicide *m*; *see also* **commit**

suit [su:t] *n* (*man's*) costume *m*, complet *m*; (*woman's*) tailleur *m*, ensemble *m*; (*LAW*) poursuite *f(pl)*, procès *m*; (*CARDS*) couleur *f* ♦ *vt* aller à; convenir à; (*adapt*): **to ~ sth to** adapter *or* approprier qch à; **well ~ed** (*well matched*) faits l'un pour l'autre, très bien assortis; **~able** *adj* qui convient; approprié(e); **~ably** *adv* comme il se doit (*or se devait etc*), convenablement

suitcase ['su:tkeis] *n* valise *f*

suite [swi:t] *n* (*of rooms, also MUS*) suite

f; (*furniture*): **bedroom/dining room ~** (ensemble *m* de) chambre *f* à coucher/ salle *f* à manger

suitor ['suːtər] *n* soupirant *m*, prétendant *m*

sulfur ['sʌlfər] (*US*) *n* = **sulphur**

sulk [sʌlk] *vi* bouder; **~y** *adj* boudeur (-euse), maussade

sullen ['sʌlən] *adj* renfrogné(e), maussade

sulphur ['sʌlfər] (*US* **sulfur**) *n* soufre *m*

sultana [sʌl'tɑːnə] *n* (*CULIN*) raisin (sec) de Smyrne

sultry ['sʌltrɪ] *adj* étouffant(e)

sum [sʌm] *n* somme *f*; (*SCOL etc*) calcul *m*; **~ up** *vt*, *vi* résumer

summarize ['sʌməraɪz] *vt* résumer

summary ['sʌmərɪ] *n* résumé *m*

summer ['sʌmər] *n* été *m* ♦ *adj* d'été, estival(e); **~house** *n* (*in garden*) pavillon *m*; **~time** *n* été *m*; **~ time** *n* (*by clock*) heure *f* d'été

summit ['sʌmɪt] *n* sommet *m*

summon ['sʌmən] *vt* appeler, convoquer; **~ up** *vt* rassembler, faire appel à; **~s** *n* citation *f*, assignation *f*

sun [sʌn] *n* soleil *m*; **in the ~** au soleil; **~bathe** *vi* prendre un bain de soleil; **~block** *n* écran *m* total; **~burn** *n* coup *m* de soleil; **~burned**, **~burnt** *adj* (*tanned*) bronzé(e)

Sunday ['sʌndɪ] *n* dimanche *m*; **~ school** *n* ≃ catéchisme *m*

sundial ['sʌndaɪəl] *n* cadran solaire

sundown ['sʌndaʊn] *n* coucher *m* du (*or* de) soleil

sundries ['sʌndrɪz] *npl* articles divers

sundry ['sʌndrɪ] *adj* divers(e), différent(e) ♦ *n*: **all and ~** tout le monde, n'importe qui

sunflower ['sʌnflaʊər] *n* tournesol *m*

sung [sʌŋ] *pp of* **sing**

sunglasses ['sʌnglɑːsɪz] *npl* lunettes *fpl* de soleil

sunk [sʌŋk] *pp of* **sink**

sun: **~light** (lumière *f* du) soleil *m*; **~lit** *adj* ensoleillé(e); **~ny** *adj* ensoleil-

lé(e); **~rise** *n* lever *m* du (*or* de) soleil; **~ roof** *n* (*AUT*) toit ouvrant; **~screen** *n* crème *f* solaire; **~set** *n* coucher *m* du (*or* de) soleil; **~shade** *n* (*over table*) parasol *m*; **~shine** (lumière *f* du) soleil *m*; **~stroke** *n* insolation *f*; **~tan** *n* bronzage *m*; **~tan lotion** *n* lotion *f* or lait *m* solaire; **~tan oil** *n* huile *f* solaire

super ['suːpər] (*inf*) *adj* formidable

superannuation [suːpərænjʊ'eɪʃən] *n* (*contribution*) cotisations *fpl* pour la pension

superb [suː'pəːb] *adj* superbe, magnifique

supercilious [suːpə'sɪlɪəs] *adj* hautain(e), dédaigneux(-euse)

superficial [suːpə'fɪʃl] *adj* superficiel(le)

superimpose ['suːpərɪm'pəʊz] *vt* superposer

superintendent [suːpərɪn'tɛndənt] *n* directeur(-trice); (*POLICE*) ≃ commissaire *m*

superior [suː'pɪərɪər] *adj*, *n* supérieur(e); **~ity** [sʊpɪərɪ'ɔrɪtɪ] *n* supériorité *f*

superlative [suː'pəːlətɪv] *n* (*LING*) superlatif *m*

superman ['suːpəmæn] (*irreg*) *n* surhomme *m*

supermarket ['suːpəmɑːkɪt] *n* supermarché *m*

supernatural [suːpə'nætʃərəl] *adj* surnaturel(le)

superpower ['suːpəpaʊər] *n* (*POL*) superpuissance *f*

supersede [suːpə'siːd] *vt* remplacer, supplanter

superstitious [suːpə'stɪʃəs] *adj* superstitieux(-euse)

supervise ['suːpəvaɪz] *vt* surveiller; diriger; **supervision** [suːpə'vɪʒən] *n* surveillance *f*; contrôle *m*; **supervisor** *n* surveillant(e); (*in shop*) chef *m* de rayon

supper ['sʌpər] *n* dîner *m*; (*late*) souper *m*

supple ['sʌpl] *adj* souple

supplement [*n* 'sʌplɪmənt, *vb*

sʌpli'mənt] *n* supplément *m* ♦ *vt*
compléter; **~ary** [sʌpli'mɛntəri] *adj*
supplémentaire; **~ary benefit** (BRIT)
n allocation *f* (supplémentaire) d'aide sociale

supplier [sə'plaɪə^r] *n* fournisseur *m*

supply [sə'plaɪ] *vt* (provide) fournir;
(equip): **to ~ (with)** approvisionner or
ravitailler (en); fournir (en) ♦ *n* provision *f*, réserve *f*; (~ing) approvisionnement *m*; **supplies** *npl* (food) vivres *mpl*;
(MIL) subsistances *fpl*; **~ teacher** (BRIT)
n suppléant(e)

support [sə'pɔːt] *n* (moral, financial etc)
soutien *m*, appui *m*; (TECH) support *m*,
soutien *m* ♦ *vt* soutenir, supporter; (finan-
cially) subvenir aux besoins de; (uphold)
être pour, être partisan de, appuyer;
~er *n* (POL etc) partisan(e); (SPORT) supporter *m*

suppose [sə'pəʊz] *vt* supposer; imaginer; **to be ~d to do** être censé(e) faire;
~dly [sə'pəʊzɪdlɪ] *adv* soi-disant; **supposing** *conj* si, à supposer que +*sub*

suppress [sə'prɛs] *vt* (revolt) réprimer;
(information) supprimer; (yawn) étouffer; (feelings) refouler

supreme [su'priːm] *adj* suprême

surcharge ['sɜːtʃɑːdʒ] *n* surcharge *f*

sure [ʃʊə^r] *adj* sûr(e); (definite, con-
vinced) sûr, certain(e); **~!** (of course) bien
sûr!; **~ enough** effectivement; **to make
~ of sth** s'assurer de or vérifier qch;
to make ~ that s'assurer or vérifier
que; **~ly** *adv* sûrement; certainement

surf [sɜːf] *n* (waves) ressac *m*

surface ['sɜːfɪs] *n* surface *f* ♦ *vt* (road)
poser un revêtement sur ♦ *vi* remonter
à la surface; faire surface; **~ mail** *n*
courrier *m* par voie de terre (or maritime)

surfboard ['sɜːfbɔːd] *n* planche *f* de
surf

surfeit ['sɜːfɪt] *n*: **a ~ of** un excès de;
une indigestion de

surfing ['sɜːfɪŋ] *n* surf *m*

surge [sɜːdʒ] *n* vague *f*, montée *f* ♦ *vi*
déferler

surgeon ['sɜːdʒən] *n* chirurgien *m*

surgery ['sɜːdʒərɪ] *n* chirurgie *f*; (BRIT:
room) cabinet *m* (de consultation);
(: also: **~ hours**) heures *fpl* de consultation

surgical ['sɜːdʒɪkl] *adj* chirurgical(e); **~
spirit** (BRIT) *n* alcool *m* à 90º

surname ['sɜːneɪm] *n* nom *m* de famille

surplus ['sɜːpləs] *n* surplus *m*, excédent
m ♦ *adj* en surplus, de trop; (COMM) ex-
cédentaire

surprise [sə'praɪz] *n* surprise *f*; (astonishment) étonnement *m* ♦ *vt* surprendre; (astonish) étonner; **surprising** *adj*
surprenant(e), étonnant(e); **surpris-
ingly** *adv* (easy, helpful) étonnamment

surrender [sə'rɛndə^r] *n* reddition *f*, ca-
pitulation *f* ♦ *vi* se rendre, capituler

surreptitious [sʌrəp'tɪʃəs] *adj* subrepti-
ce, furtif(-ive)

surrogate ['sʌrəgɪt] *n* substitut *m*; **~
mother** *n* mère porteuse or de substitution

surround [sə'raʊnd] *vt* entourer; (MIL
etc) encercler; **~ing** *adj* environnant(e);
~ings *npl* environs *mpl*, alentours *mpl*

surveillance [sɜː'veɪləns] *n* surveillance
f

survey [*n* 'sɜːveɪ, *vb* sɜː'veɪ] *n* enquête
f, étude *f*; (in housebuying etc) inspection *f*, (rapport *m* d')expertise *f*; (of
land) levé *m* ♦ *vt* enquêter sur; inspecter; (look at) embrasser du regard; **~or**
n (of house) expert *m*; (of land) (arpenteur *m*) géomètre *m*

survival [sə'vaɪvl] *n* survie *f*; (relic) vestige *m*

survive [sə'vaɪv] *vi* survivre; (custom
etc) subsister ♦ *vt* survivre à; **survivor**
n survivant(e); (fig) battant(e)

susceptible [sə'sɛptəbl] *adj*: **~ (to)**
sensible (à); (disease) prédisposé(e) à

suspect [*adj*, *n* 'sʌspɛkt, *vb* səs'pɛkt]
adj, *n* suspect(e) ♦ *vt* soupçonner, suspecter

suspend [səs'pɛnd] vt suspendre; **~ed sentence** n condamnation f avec sursis; **~er belt** n porte-jarretelles m inv; **~ers** npl (BRIT) jarretelles fpl; (US) bretelles fpl

suspense [səs'pɛns] n attente f, incertitude f; (in film etc) suspense m

suspension [səs'pɛnʃən] n suspension f; (of driving licence) retrait m provisoire; **~ bridge** n pont suspendu

suspicion [səs'pɪʃən] n soupçon(s) m(pl); **suspicious** adj (suspecting) soupçonneux(-euse), méfiant(e); (causing suspicion) suspect(e)

sustain [səs'teɪn] vt soutenir; (food etc) nourrir, donner des forces à; (suffer) subir; recevoir; **~able** adj (development, growth etc) viable; **~ed** adj (effort) soutenu(e), prolongé(e); **sustenance** ['sʌstɪnəns] n nourriture f; (money) moyens mpl de subsistance

swab [swɔb] n (MED) tampon m

swagger ['swægəʳ] vi plastronner

swallow ['swɔləu] n (bird) hirondelle f ♦ vt avaler; **~ up** vt engloutir

swam [swæm] pt of **swim**

swamp [swɔmp] n marais m, marécage m ♦ vt submerger

swan [swɔn] n cygne m

swap [swɔp] vt: **to ~ (for)** échanger (contre), troquer (contre)

swarm [swɔ:m] n essaim m ♦ vi fourmiller, grouiller

swastika ['swɔstɪkə] n croix gammée

swat [swɔt] vt écraser

sway [sweɪ] vi se balancer, osciller ♦ vt (influence) influencer

swear [sweəʳ] (pt **swore**, pp **sworn**) vt, vi jurer; **~word** n juron m, gros mot

sweat [swɛt] n sueur f, transpiration f ♦ vi suer

sweater ['swɛtəʳ] n tricot m, pull m

sweaty ['swɛtɪ] adj en sueur, moite or mouillé(e) de sueur

Swede [swi:d] n Suédois(e)

Swede [swi:d] (BRIT) n rutabaga m

Sweden ['swi:dn] n Suède f; **Swedish**

adj suédois(e) ♦ n (LING) suédois m

sweep [swi:p] (pt, pp **swept**) n (also: chimney ~) ramoneur m ♦ vt balayer; (subj: current) emporter; entraîner; ♦ vi avancer majestueusement or rapidement; **~ away** vt balayer; entraîner; emporter; **~ past** vi passer majestueusement or rapidement; **~ up** vt, vi balayer; **~ing** adj (gesture) large; circulaire; **a ~ing statement** une généralisation hâtive

sweet [swi:t] n (candy) bonbon m; (BRIT: pudding) dessert m ♦ adj doux (douce); (not savoury) sucré(e); (fig: kind) gentil(le); (baby) mignon(ne); **~corn** ['swi:tkɔ:n] n maïs m; **~en** vt adoucir; (with sugar) sucrer; **~heart** n amoureux(-euse); **~ness** n goût sucré; douceur f; **~ pea** n pois m de senteur

swell [swɛl] (pt **swelled**, pp **swollen** or **swelled**) n (of sea) houle f ♦ adj (US: inf: excellent) chouette ♦ vi grossir, augmenter; (sound) s'enfler; ♦ vt enfler; **~ing** n (MED) enflure f; (lump) grosseur f

sweltering ['swɛltərɪŋ] adj étouffant(e), oppressant(e)

swept [swɛpt] pt, pp of **sweep**

swerve [swə:v] vi faire une embardée or un écart; dévier

swift [swɪft] n (bird) martinet m ♦ adj rapide, prompt(e)

swig [swɪg] (inf) n (drink) lampée f

swill [swɪl] n (also: **~ out**, **~ down**) laver à grande eau

swim [swɪm] (pt **swam**, pp **swum**) n: **to go for a ~** aller nager or se baigner ♦ vi nager; (SPORT) faire de la natation; (head, room) tourner ♦ vt traverser (à la nage); (a length) faire (à la nage); **~mer** n nageur(-euse); **~ming** n natation f; **~ming cap** n bonnet m de bain; **~ming costume** (BRIT) n maillot m (de bain); **~ming pool** n piscine f; **~ming trunks** npl caleçon m or slip m de bain; **~suit** n maillot m (de bain)

swindle ['swɪndl] n escroquerie f

swine [swaɪn] (inf!) n inv salaud m (!)

swing [swɪŋ] n (pt, pp **swung**) n balançoire f; (movement) balancement m, oscillations fpl; (change: in opinion etc) revirement m ♦ vt balancer, faire osciller; (also: ~ round) balancer; ♦ vi se balancer, osciller; (also: ~ round) virer, tourner; **to be in full ~** battre son plein; **~ bridge** n pont tournant; **~ door** (US **swinging door**) n porte battante

swingeing ['swɪndʒɪŋ] (BRIT) adj écrasant(e); (cuts etc) considérable

swipe [swaɪp] (inf) vt (steal) piquer

swirl [swəːl] vi tourbillonner, tournoyer

Swiss [swɪs] adj suisse ♦ n inv Suisse m/f

switch [swɪtʃ] n (for light, radio etc) bouton m; (for change) changement m, revirement m ♦ vt changer; **~ off** vt éteindre; (engine) arrêter; **~ on** vt allumer; (engine, machine) mettre en marche; **~board** n (TEL) standard m

Switzerland ['swɪtsələnd] n Suisse f

swivel ['swɪvl] vi (also: ~ round) pivoter, tourner

swollen ['swəʊlən] pp of **swell**

swoon [swuːn] vi se pâmer

swoop [swuːp] n (by police) descente f ♦ vi (also: ~ down) descendre en piqué, piquer

swop [swɒp] vt = swap

sword [sɔːd] n épée f; **~fish** n espadon m

swore [swɔːʳ] pt of **swear**

sworn [swɔːn] pp of **swear** ♦ adj (statement, evidence) donné(e) sous serment

swot [swɒt] vi bûcher, potasser

swum [swʌm] pp of **swim**

swung [swʌŋ] pt, pp of **swing**

syllable ['sɪləbl] n syllabe f

syllabus ['sɪləbəs] n programme m

symbol ['sɪmbl] n symbole m

symmetry ['sɪmɪtrɪ] n symétrie f

sympathetic [sɪmpə'θetɪk] adj compatissant(e); bienveillant(e), compréhensif(-ive); (likeable) sympathique; **~ towards** bien disposé(e) envers

sympathize ['sɪmpəθaɪz] vi: **to ~ with sb** plaindre qn; (in grief) s'associer à la

douleur de qn; **to ~ with sth** comprendre qch; **~r** n (POL) sympathisant(e)

sympathy ['sɪmpəθɪ] n (pity) compassion f; **sympathies** npl (support) soutien m; **left-wing etc sympathies** penchants mpl à gauche etc; **in ~ with** (strike) en or par solidarité avec; **with our deepest ~** en vous priant d'accepter nos sincères condoléances

symphony ['sɪmfənɪ] n symphonie f

symptom ['sɪmptəm] n symptôme m; indice m

syndicate ['sɪndɪkɪt] n syndicat m, coopérative f

synopsis [sɪ'nɒpsɪs] (pl **synopses**) n résumé m

synthetic [sɪn'θetɪk] adj synthétique

syphon ['saɪfən] n, vb = **siphon**

Syria ['sɪrɪə] n Syrie f

syringe [sɪ'rɪndʒ] n seringue f

syrup ['sɪrəp] n sirop m; (also: **golden ~**) mélasse raffinée

system ['sɪstəm] n système m; (ANAT) organisme m; **~atic** [sɪstə'mætɪk] adj systématique; méthodique; **~ disk** n (COMPUT) disque m système; **~s analyst** n analyste fonctionnel(le)

T, t

ta [tɑː] (BRIT: inf) excl merci!

tab [tæb] n (label) étiquette f; (on drinks can etc) languette f; **to keep ~s on** (fig) surveiller

tabby ['tæbɪ] n (also: ~ **cat**) chat(te) tigré(e)

table ['teɪbl] n table f ♦ vt (BRIT: motion etc) présenter; **to lay** or **set the ~** mettre le couvert or la table; **~cloth** n nappe f; **~ d'hôte** [tɑːbl'dəʊt] adj (meal) à prix fixe; **~ lamp** n lampe f de table; **~mat** n (for plate) napperon m, set m; (for hot dish) dessous-de-plat m inv; **~ of contents** n table f des matières; **~spoon** n cuiller f de service;

*(also: ~***spoonful***: as measurement)* cuillerée *f* à soupe

tablet ['tæblɪt] *n (MED)* comprimé *m*

table tennis *n* ping-pong ® *m*, tennis *m* de table

table wine *n* vin *m* de table

tabloid ['tæblɔɪd] *n* quotidien *m* populaire

---
tabloid press

Le terme **tabloid press** désigne les journaux populaires de demi-format où l'on trouve beaucoup de photos et qui adoptent un style très concis. Ce type de journaux vise des lecteurs s'intéressant plus aux faits divers ayant un parfum de scandale; voir **quality (news)papers**.

---

tack [tæk] *n (nail)* petit clou ♦ *vt* clouer; *(fig)* direction *f*; *(BRIT: stitch)* faufiler ♦ *vi* tirer un *or* des bord(s)

tackle ['tækl] *n* matériel *m*, équipement *m*; *(for lifting)* appareil *m* de levage; *(RUGBY)* plaquage *m* ♦ *vt (difficulty, animal, burglar etc)* s'attaquer à; *(person: challenge)* s'expliquer avec; *(RUGBY)* plaquer

tacky ['tækɪ] *adj* collant(e); *(pej: of poor quality)* miteux(-euse)

tact [tækt] *n* tact *m*; **~ful** *adj* plein(e) de tact

tactical ['tæktɪkl] *adj* tactique

tactics ['tæktɪks] *npl* tactique *f*

tactless ['tæktlɪs] *adj* qui manque de tact

tadpole ['tædpəʊl] *n* têtard *m*

tag [tæg] *n* étiquette *f*; **~ along** *vi* suivre

tail [teɪl] *n* queue *f*; *(of shirt)* pan *m* ♦ *vt (follow)* suivre, filer; **~s** *npl* habit *m*; **~ away**, **~ off** *vi (in size, quality etc)* baisser peu à peu; **~back** *(BRIT) n (AUT)* bouchon *m*; **~ end** *n* bout *m*, fin *f*; **~gate** *n (AUT)* hayon *m* arrière

tailor ['teɪlə*] *n* tailleur *m*; **~ing** *n (cut)* coupe *f*; **~-made** *adj* fait(e) sur mesure;

(fig) conçu(e) spécialement

tailwind ['teɪlwɪnd] *n* vent *m* arrière *inv*

tainted ['teɪntɪd] *adj (food)* gâté(e); *(water, air)* infecté(e); *(fig)* souillé(e)

take [teɪk] *(pt* **took***, pp* **taken***) vt* prendre; *(gain: prize)* remporter; *(require: effort, courage)* demander; *(tolerate)* accepter, supporter; *(hold: passengers etc)* contenir; *(accompany)* emmener, accompagner; *(bring, carry)* apporter, emporter; *(exam)* passer, se présenter à; **to ~ sth from** *(drawer etc)* prendre qch dans; *(person)* prendre qch à; **I ~ it that** ... je suppose que ...; **~ after** *vt fus* ressembler à; **~ apart** *vt* démonter; **~ away** *vt* enlever; *(carry off)* emporter; **~ back** *vt (return)* rendre, rapporter; *(one's words)* retirer; **~ down** *vt (building)* démolir; *(letter etc)* prendre, écrire; **~ in** *vt (deceive)* tromper, rouler; *(understand)* comprendre, saisir; *(include)* comprendre, inclure; *(lodger)* prendre; **~ off** *vi (AVIAT)* décoller ♦ *vt (remove)* enlever; **~ on** *vt (work)* accepter, se charger de; *(employee)* prendre, embaucher; *(opponent)* accepter de se battre contre; **~ out** *vt (invite)* emmener, sortir; *(remove)* enlever; **to ~ sth out of sth** *(drawer, pocket etc)* prendre qch dans qch; **~ over** *vt (business)* reprendre ♦ *vi*: **to ~ over from sb** prendre la relève de qn; **~ to** *vt fus (person)* se prendre d'amitié pour; *(thing)* prendre goût à; **~ up** *vt (activity)* se mettre à; *(dress)* raccourcir; *(occupy: time, space)* prendre, occuper; **to ~ sb up on an offer** accepter la proposition de qn; **~away** *(BRIT) adj (food)* à emporter ♦ *n (shop, restaurant)* café *m* qui vend des plats à emporter; **~off** *n (AVIAT)* décollage *m*; **~over** *n (COMM)* rachat *m*; **takings** *npl (COMM)* recette *f*

talc [tælk] *n (also:* **~um powder***)* talc *m*

tale [teɪl] *n (story)* conte *m*, histoire *f*; *(account)* récit *m*; **to tell ~s** *(fig)* rapporter

talent ['tælnt] *n* talent *m*, don *m*; **~ed**

adj doué(e), plein(e) de talent

talk [tɔːk] *n* (*a speech*) causerie *f*, exposé *m*; (*conversation*) discussion *f*, entretien *m*; (*gossip*) racontars *mpl* ♦ *vi* parler; **~s** *npl* (POL *etc*) entretiens *mpl*; **to ~ about** parler de; **to ~ sb into/out of doing** persuader qn de faire/ne pas faire; **to ~ shop** parler métier *or* affaires; **~ over** *vt* discuter (de); **~ative** *adj* bavard(e); **~ show** *n* causerie (télévisée *or* radiodiffusée

tall [tɔːl] *adj* (*person*) grand(e); (*building, tree*) haut(e); **to be 6 feet ~** ≃ mesurer 1 mètre 80; **~ story** *n* histoire *f* invraisemblable

tally ['tælɪ] *n* compte *m* ♦ *vi*: **to ~ (with)** correspondre (à)

talon ['tælən] *n* griffe *f*; (*of eagle*) serre *f*

tame [teɪm] *adj* apprivoisé(e); (*fig: story, style*) insipide

tamper ['tæmpər] *vi*: **to ~ with** toucher à

tampon ['tæmpɔn] *n* tampon *m* (hygiénique *or* périodique)

tan [tæn] *n* (*also*: **suntan**) bronzage *m* ♦ *vt, vi* bronzer ♦ *adj* (*colour*) brun clair

tang [tæŋ] *n* odeur *or* saveur piquante

tangent ['tændʒənt] *n* (MATH) tangente *f*; **to go off at a ~** (fig) changer de sujet

tangerine [tændʒə'riːn] *n* mandarine *f*

tangle ['tæŋgl] *n* enchevêtrement *m*; **to get in(to) a ~** s'embrouiller

tank [tæŋk] *n* (*water ~*) réservoir *m*; (*for fish*) aquarium *m*; (MIL) char *m* d'assaut

tanker ['tæŋkər] *n* (*ship*) pétrolier *m*, tanker *m*; (*truck*) camion-citerne *m*

tantalizing ['tæntəlaɪzɪŋ] *adj* (*smell*) extrêmement appétissant(e); (*offer*) terriblement tentant(e)

tantamount ['tæntəmaunt] *adj*: **~ to** qui équivaut à

tantrum ['tæntrəm] *n* accès *m* de colère

Taoiseach ['tiːʃəx] *n* Premier ministre *m* irlandais

tap [tæp] *n* (*on sink etc*) robinet *m*; (*gentle blow*) petite tape *f* ♦ *vt* frapper *or* taper légèrement; (*resources*) exploiter, utiliser; (*telephone*) mettre sur écoute; **on ~** (fig: resources) disponible; **~-dancing** *n* claquettes *fpl*

tape [teɪp] *n* ruban *m*; (*also*: **magnetic ~**) bande *f* (magnétique); (*cassette*) cassette *f*; (*sticky*) scotch *m* ♦ *vt* (*record*) enregistrer; (*stick with ~*) coller avec du scotch; **~ deck** *n* platine *f* d'enregistrement; **~ measure** *n* mètre *m* à ruban

taper ['teɪpər] *vi* s'effiler

tape recorder *n* magnétophone *m*

tapestry ['tæpɪstrɪ] *n* tapisserie *f*

tar [tɑː] *n* goudron *m*

target ['tɑːgɪt] *n* cible *f*; (fig) objectif *m*

tariff ['tærɪf] *n* (COMM) tarif *m*; (*taxes*) tarif douanier

tarmac ['tɑːmæk] *n* (BRIT: on road) macadam *m*; (AVIAT) piste *f*

tarnish ['tɑːnɪʃ] *vt* ternir

tarpaulin [tɑː'pɔːlɪn] *n* bâche (goudronnée)

tarragon ['tærəgən] *n* estragon *m*

tart [tɑːt] *n* (CULIN) tarte *f*; (BRIT: inf: prostitute) putain *f* ♦ *adj* (*flavour*) âpre, aigrelet(te); **~ up** (BRIT: inf) *vt* (*object*) retaper; **~ o.s. up** se faire beau (belle), s'attifer (pej)

tartan ['tɑːtn] *n* tartan *m* ♦ *adj* écossais(e)

tartar ['tɑːtər] *n* (*on teeth*) tartre *m*; **~(e) sauce** *n* sauce *f* tartare

task [tɑːsk] *n* tâche *f*; **to take sb to ~** prendre qn à partie; **~ force** *n* (MIL, POLICE) détachement spécial

tassel ['tæsl] *n* gland *m*; pompon *m*

taste [teɪst] *n* goût *m*; (fig: glimpse, idea) idée *f*, aperçu *m* ♦ *vt* goûter ♦ *vi*: **to ~ of** *or* **like** (fish etc) avoir le *or* un goût de; **you can ~ the garlic (in it)** on sent bien l'ail, ça a un goût d'ail; **can I have a ~ of this wine?** puis-je goûter un peu de ce vin?; **in good/bad ~** de bon/mauvais goût; **~ful** *adj* de bon goût; **~less** *adj* (food) fade; (*remark*) de mauvais goût;

tasty adj savoureux(-euse), délicieux (-euse)

tatters ['tætəz] npl: **in ~** en lambeaux

tattoo [tə'tuː] n tatouage m; (spectacle) parade f militaire ♦ vt tatouer

tatty ['tætɪ] (BRIT: inf) adj (clothes) frippé(e); (shop, area) délabré(e)

taught [tɔːt] pt, pp of **teach**

taunt [tɔːnt] n raillerie f ♦ vt railler

Taurus ['tɔːrəs] n le Taureau

taut [tɔːt] adj tendu(e)

tax [tæks] n (on goods etc) taxe f; (on income) impôts mpl, contributions fpl ♦ vt taxer; imposer; (fig: patience etc) mettre à l'épreuve; **~able** adj (income) imposable; **~ation** [tæk'seɪʃən] n taxation f; impôts mpl, contributions fpl; **~ avoidance** n dégrèvement fiscal; **~ disc** (BRIT) n (AUT) vignette f (automobile); **~ evasion** n fraude fiscale; **~-free** adj exempt(e) d'impôts

taxi ['tæksɪ] n taxi m ♦ vi (AVIAT) rouler (lentement) au sol; **~ driver** n chauffeur m de taxi; **~ rank** (BRIT) n station f de taxis; **~ stand** n = taxi rank

tax: **~ payer** n contribuable m/f; **~ relief** n dégrèvement fiscal; **~ return** n déclaration f d'impôts ou de revenus

TB n abbr = **tuberculosis**

tea [tiː] n thé m; (BRIT: snack: for children) goûter m; **high ~** collation combinant goûter et dîner; **~ bag** n sachet m de thé; **~ break** (BRIT) n pause-thé f

teach [tiːtʃ] (pt, pp **taught**) vt: **to ~ sb sth, ~ sth to sb** apprendre qch à qn; (in school etc) enseigner qch à qn ♦ vi enseigner; **~er** n (in secondary school) professeur m; (in primary school) instituteur(-trice); **~ing** n enseignement m

tea: **~ cloth** n torchon m; **~ cosy** n cloche f à thé; **~ cup** n tasse f à thé

teak [tiːk] n teck m

tea leaves npl feuilles fpl de thé

team [tiːm] n équipe f; (of animals) attelage m; **~work** n travail m d'équipe

teapot ['tiːpɔt] n théière f

tear¹ [tɛəʳ] (pt **tore**, pp **torn**) n déchirure f ♦ vt déchirer ♦ vi se déchirer; **~ along** vi (rush) aller à toute vitesse; **~ up** vt (sheet of paper etc) déchirer, mettre en morceaux ou pièces

tear² [tɪəʳ] n larme f; **in ~s** en larmes; **~ful** adj larmoyant(e); **~ gas** n gaz m lacrymogène

tearoom ['tiːruːm] n salon m de thé

tease [tiːz] vt taquiner; (unkindly) tourmenter

tea set n service m à thé

teaspoon ['tiːspuːn] n petite cuiller; (also: **~ful:** as measurement) ≈ cuillerée f à café

teat [tiːt] n tétine f

teatime ['tiːtaɪm] n l'heure f du thé

tea towel (BRIT) n torchon m (à vaisselle)

technical ['teknɪkl] adj technique; **~ity** [teknɪ'kælɪtɪ] n (detail) détail m technique; (point of law) vice m de forme; **~ly** adv techniquement; (strictly speaking) en théorie

technician [tek'nɪʃən] n technicien(ne)

technique [tek'niːk] n technique f

techno ['teknəu] n (music) techno f

technological [teknə'lɔdʒɪkl] adj technologique

technology [tek'nɔlədʒɪ] n technologie f

teddy (bear) ['tedɪ(-)] n ours m en peluche

tedious ['tiːdɪəs] adj fastidieux(-euse)

tee [tiː] n (GOLF) tee m

teem [tiːm] vi: **to ~ (with)** grouiller (de); **it is ~ing (with rain)** il pleut à torrents

teenage ['tiːneɪdʒ] adj (fashions etc) pour jeunes, pour adolescents; (children) adolescent(e); **~r** n adolescent(e)

teens [tiːnz] npl: **to be in one's ~** être adolescent(e)

tee-shirt ['tiːʃəːt] n = **T-shirt**

teeter ['tiːtəʳ] vi chanceler, vaciller

teeth [tiːθ] npl of **tooth**

teethe [tiːð] vi percer ses dents

teething troubles npl (fig) difficultés initiales

teetotal ['tiː'təutl] adj (person) qui ne boit jamais d'alcool

tele: ~communications npl télécommunications fpl; **~conferencing** n téléconférence(s) f(pl); **~gram** n télégramme m; **~graph** m télégraphe m; **~graph pole** n poteau m télégraphique

telephone ['tɛlɪfəun] n téléphone m ♦ vt (person) téléphoner à ♦ (message) téléphoner; **on the ~** au téléphone; **to be on the ~** (BRIT: have a ~) avoir le téléphone; **~ booth**, **~ box** (BRIT) n cabine f téléphonique; **~ call** n coup de téléphone, appel m téléphonique; **~ directory** n annuaire m (du téléphone); **~ number** n numéro m de téléphone; **telephonist** [tə'lɛfənɪst] (BRIT) n téléphoniste m/f

telesales ['tɛlɪseɪlz] n télévente f

telescope ['tɛlɪskəup] n télescope m

television ['tɛlɪvɪʒən] n télévision f; **on ~** à la télévision; **~ set** n (poste f de) télévision m

telex ['tɛlɛks] n télex m

tell [tɛl] (pt, pp **told**) vt dire; (relate: story) raconter; (distinguish): **to ~ sth from** distinguer qch de ♦ vi (talk): **to ~ (of)** parler (de); (have effect) se faire sentir, se voir; **to ~ sb to do** dire à qn de faire; **~ off** vt réprimander, gronder; **~er** n (in bank) caissier(-ère); **~ing** adj (remark, detail) révélateur(-trice); **~tale** adj (sign) éloquent(e), révélateur(-trice)

telly ['tɛlɪ] (BRIT: inf) n abbr (= television) télé f

temp [tɛmp] n abbr (= temporary) (secrétaire f) intérimaire f

temper ['tɛmpər] n (nature) caractère m; (mood) humeur f; (fit of anger) colère f ♦ vt (moderate) tempérer, adoucir; **to be in a ~** être en colère; **to lose one's ~** se mettre en colère

temperament ['tɛmprəmənt] n (nature) tempérament m; **~al** [tɛmprə'mɛntl] adj capricieux(-euse)

temperate ['tɛmprət] adj (climate, country) tempéré(e)

temperature ['tɛmprətʃər] n température f; **to have** or **run a ~** avoir de la fièvre

temple ['tɛmpl] n (building) temple m; (ANAT) tempe f

temporary ['tɛmpərəri] adj temporaire, provisoire; (job, worker) temporaire

tempt [tɛmpt] vt tenter; **to ~ sb into doing** persuader qn de faire; **~ation** [tɛmp'teɪʃən] n tentation f; **~ing** adj tentant(e)

ten [tɛn] num dix

tenacity [tə'næsɪtɪ] n ténacité f

tenancy ['tɛnənsɪ] n location f; état m de locataire

tenant ['tɛnənt] n locataire m/f

tend [tɛnd] vt s'occuper de ♦ vi: **to ~ to do** avoir tendance à faire; **~ency** ['tɛndənsɪ] n tendance f

tender ['tɛndər] adj tendre; (delicate) délicat(e); (sore) sensible ♦ n (COMM: offer) soumission f ♦ vt offrir

tenement ['tɛnəmənt] n immeuble m

tennis ['tɛnɪs] n tennis m; **~ ball** n balle f de tennis; **~ court** n (court m de) tennis; **~ player** n joueur(-euse) de tennis; **~ racket** n raquette f de tennis; **~ shoes** npl (chaussures fpl de) tennis mpl

tenor ['tɛnər] n (MUS) ténor m

tenpin bowling ['tɛnpɪn-] (BRIT) n bowling m (à dix quilles)

tense [tɛns] adj tendu(e) ♦ n (LING) temps m

tension ['tɛnʃən] n tension f

tent [tɛnt] n tente f

tentative ['tɛntətɪv] adj timide, hésitant(e); (conclusion) provisoire

tenterhooks ['tɛntəhuks] npl: **on ~** sur des charbons ardents

tenth [tɛnθ] num dixième

tent peg n piquet m de tente

tent pole n montant m de tente

tenuous ['tɛnjuəs] adj ténu(e)

tenure ['tɛnjuər] n (of property) bail m;

(*of job*) période f de jouissance

tepid ['tepɪd] *adj* tiède

term [tɜːm] *n* terme m; (SCOL) trimestre m ♦ *vt* appeler; **~s** npl (*conditions*) conditions fpl; (COMM) tarif m; **in the short/long ~** à court/long terme; **to come to ~s with** (*problem*) faire face à

terminal ['tɜːmɪnl] *adj* (*disease*) dans sa phase terminale; (*patient*) incurable ♦ *n* (ELEC) borne f; (*for oil, ore etc,* COMPUT) terminal m; (*also:* **air ~**) aérogare f; (BRIT: *also:* **coach ~**) gare routière; **~ly** *adv*: **to be ~ly ill** être condamné(e)

terminate ['tɜːmɪneɪt] *vt* mettre fin à; (*pregnancy*) interrompre

terminus ['tɜːmɪnəs] (*pl* **termini**) *n* terminus m

terrace ['terəs] *n* terrasse f; (BRIT: *row of houses*) rangée f de maisons (*attenantes*); **the ~s** npl (BRIT: SPORT) les gradins mpl; **~d** *adj* (*garden*) en terrasses

terracotta ['terə'kɔtə] *n* terre cuite

terrain [te'reɪn] *n* terrain m (*sol*)

terrible ['terɪbl] *adj* terrible, atroce; (*weather, conditions*) affreux(-euse), épouvantable; (*very badly*) affreusement; **terribly** *adv* terriblement; (*very badly*) affreusement mal

terrier ['terɪər] *n* terrier m (*chien*)

terrific [tə'rɪfɪk] *adj* fantastique, incroyable, terrible; (*wonderful*) formidable, sensationnel(le)

terrify ['terɪfaɪ] *vt* terrifier

territory ['terɪtərɪ] *n* territoire m

terror ['terər] *n* terreur f; **~ism** *n* terrorisme m; **~ist** *n* terroriste m/f

test [test] *n* (*trial, check*) essai m; (*of courage etc*) épreuve f; (MED) examen m; (CHEM) analyse f; (SCOL) interrogation f; (*also:* **driving ~**) (examen du) permis m de conduire ♦ *vt* essayer, mettre à l'épreuve; examiner; analyser; faire subir une interrogation à

testament ['testəmənt] *n* testament m; **the Old/New T~** l'Ancien/le Nouveau Testament

testicle ['testɪkl] *n* testicule m

testify ['testɪfaɪ] *vi* (LAW) témoigner, déposer; **to ~ to sth** attester qch

testimony ['testɪmənɪ] *n* témoignage m; (*clear proof*): **to be (a) ~ to** être la preuve de

test match *n* (CRICKET, RUGBY) match international

test tube *n* éprouvette f

tetanus ['tetənəs] *n* tétanos m

tether ['teðər] *vt* attacher ♦ *n*: **at the end of one's ~** à bout (de patience)

text [tekst] *n* texte m ♦ *vt* envoyer un texto à; **~book** *n* manuel m; **~ message** *n* texto m

textile ['tekstaɪl] *n* textile m

texture ['tekstʃər] *n* texture f; (*of skin, paper etc*) grain m

Thailand ['taɪlænd] *n* Thaïlande f

Thames [temz] *n*: **the ~** la Tamise

than [ðæn, ðən] *conj* que; (*with numerals*): **more ~ 10/once** plus de 10/d'une fois; **I have more/less ~ you** j'en ai plus/moins que toi; **she has more apples ~ pears** elle a plus de pommes que de poires

thank [θæŋk] *vt* remercier, dire merci à; **~s** npl (*gratitude*) remerciements mpl ♦ *excl* merci!; **~ you (very much)** merci (beaucoup); **~s to** grâce à; **~ God!** Dieu merci!; **~ful** *adj*: **~ful (for)** reconnaissant(e) (de); **~less** *adj* ingrat(e); **T~sgiving (Day)** *n* jour m d'action de grâce (*fête américaine*)

Thanksgiving Day

Thanksgiving Day *est un jour de congé aux États-Unis, le quatrième jeudi du mois de novembre, commémorant la bonne récolte que les Pèlerins venus de Grande-Bretagne ont eue en 1621; traditionnellement, c'est un jour où l'on remerciait Dieu et où l'on organisait un grand festin. Une fête semblable a lieu au Canada le deuxième lundi d'octobre.*

KEYWORD

that [ðæt] *adj* (*demonstrative*: *pl* those) ce, cet +*vowel or h mute*, cette *f*; (*not "this"*) ce/cet homme-là/cette femme-là ce livre; (*not "this"*) ce/cet homme-là/cette femme-là/ce livre-là; **that one** celui-là (celle-là)

♦ *pron* **1** (*demonstrative*: *pl* those) ce; (*not "this one"*) cela, ça; **who's that?** qui est-ce?; **what's that?** qu'est-ce que c'est?; **is that you?** c'est toi?; **I prefer this to that** je préfère ceci à cela *or* ça; **that's what he said** c'est *or* voilà ce qu'il a dit; **that is (to say)** c'est-à-dire, à savoir

2 (*relative*: *subject*) qui; (: *object*) que; (: *indirect*) lequel (laquelle), lesquels (lesquelles) *pl*; **the book that I read** le livre que j'ai lu; **the books that are in the library** les livres qui sont dans la bibliothèque; **all that I have** tout ce que j'ai; **the box that I put it in** la boîte dans laquelle je l'ai mis; **the people that I spoke to** les gens auxquels *or* à qui j'ai parlé

3 (*relative*: *of time*) où; **the day that he came** le jour où il est venu

♦ *conj* que; **he thought that I was ill** il pensait que j'étais malade

♦ *adv* (*demonstrative*): **I can't work that much** je ne peux pas travailler autant que cela; **I didn't know it was that bad** je ne savais pas que c'était si *or* aussi mauvais; **it's about that high** c'est à peu près de cette hauteur

thatched [θætʃt] *adj* (*roof*) de chaume; **~ cottage** chaumière *f*

thaw [θɔ:] *n* dégel *m* ♦ *vi* (*ice*) fondre; (*food*) dégeler ♦ *vt* (*food*: *also*: **~ out**) (faire) dégeler

KEYWORD

the [ði:, ðə] *def art* **1** (*gen*) le, la *f*, l' +*vowel or h mute*, les *pl*; **the boy/girl/ink** le garçon/la fille/l'encre; **the child-**

ren les enfants; **the history of the world** l'histoire du monde; **give it to the postman** donne-le au facteur; **to play the piano/flute** jouer de /piano/ de la flûte; **the rich and the poor** les riches et les pauvres

2 (*in titles*): **Elizabeth the First** Elisabeth première; **Peter the Great** Pierre le Grand

3 (*in comparisons*): **the more he works, the more he earns** plus il travaille, plus il gagne de l'argent

theatre ['θɪətə*] *n* théâtre *m*; (*also*: **lecture ~**) amphi(théâtre) *m*; (MED: *also*: **operating ~**) salle *f* d'opération; **~ goer** *n* habitué(e) du théâtre; **theatrical** [θɪ'ætrɪkl] *adj* théâtral(e)

theft [θeft] *n* vol *m* (*larcin*)

their [ðɛə*] *adj* (*pl*) leurs; *see also* **my**; **~s** *pron* le (la) leur; (*pl*) les leurs; *see also* **mine**[1]

them [ðɛm, ðəm] *pron* (*direct*) les; (*indirect*) leur; (*stressed, after prep*) eux (elles); *see also* **me**

theme [θi:m] *n* thème *m*; **~ park** *n* parc *m* (d'attraction) à thème; **~ song** *n* chanson principale

themselves [ðəm'selvz] *pron* (*reflexive*) se; (*emphatic, after prep*) eux-mêmes (elles-mêmes); *see also* **oneself**

then [ðɛn] *adv* (*at that time*) alors, à ce moment-là; (*next*) puis, ensuite; (*and also*) et puis ♦ *conj* (*therefore*) alors, dans ce cas ♦ *adj*: **the ~ president** le président d'alors *or* de l'époque; **by ~** (*past*) à ce moment-là; (*future*) d'ici là; **from ~ on** dès lors

theology [θɪ'ɔlədʒɪ] *n* théologie *f*

theoretical [θɪə'rɛtɪkl] *adj* théorique

theory ['θɪərɪ] *n* théorie *f*

therapy ['θɛrəpɪ] *n* thérapie *f*

KEYWORD

there [ðɛə*] *adv* **1**: **there is, there are** il y a; **there are 3 of them** (*people, things*) il y en a 3; **there has been an**

accident il y a eu un accident
2 (referring to place) là, là-bas; **it's there** c'est là(-bas); **in/on/up/down there** là-dedans/là-dessus/là-haut/en bas; **he went there on Friday** il y est allé vendredi; **I want that book there** je veux ce livre-là; **there he is!** le voilà!
3: **there, there** (esp to child) allons, allons!

there: **~abouts** adv (place) par là, près de là; (amount) environ, à peu près; **~after** adv par la suite; **~by** adv ainsi; **~fore** adv donc, par conséquent; **~'s** = **there is**; **there has**

thermal ['θəːml] adj (springs) thermal(e); (underwear) en thermolactyl ®; (COMPUT: paper) thermosensible; (: printer) thermique

thermometer [θə'mɒmɪtər] n thermomètre m

Thermos ® ['θəːməs] n (also: **~ flask**) thermos ® m or f inv

thermostat ['θəːməustæt] n thermostat m

thesaurus [θɪ'sɔːrəs] n dictionnaire m des synonymes

these [ðiːz] pl adj ces; (not "those"): **~ books** ces livres-ci ♦ pl pron ceux-ci (celles-ci)

thesis ['θiːsɪs] (pl **theses**) n thèse f

they [ðeɪ] pl pron ils (elles); (stressed) eux (elles); **~ say that ...** (it is said that) on dit que ...; **~'d** = **they had**; **they would**; **~'ll** = **they shall**; **they will**; **~'re** = **they are**; **~'ve** = **they have**

thick [θɪk] adj épais(se); (stupid) bête, borné(e) ♦ n: **in the ~ of** au beau milieu de, en plein cœur de; **it's 20 cm ~** il/elle a 20 cm d'épaisseur; **~en** vi s'épaissir ♦ vt (sauce etc) épaissir; **~ness** n épaisseur f; **~set** adj trapu(e), costaud(e)

thief [θiːf] (pl **thieves**) n voleur(-euse)

thigh [θaɪ] n cuisse f

thimble ['θɪmbl] n dé m (à coudre)

thin [θɪn] adj mince; (skinny) maigre;

(soup, sauce) peu épais(se), clair(e); (hair, crowd) clairsemé(e) ♦ vt: **to ~ (down)** (sauce, paint) délayer

thing [θɪŋ] n chose f; (object) objet m; (contraption) truc m; (mania): **to have a ~ about** être obsédé(e) par; **~s** npl (belongings) affaires fpl; (anything) affaires fpl; **poor ~!** le (la) pauvre!; **the best ~ would be to** le mieux serait de; **how are ~s?** comment ça va?

think [θɪŋk] (pt, pp **thought**) vi penser, réfléchir ♦ vt (believe) penser ♦ vt (imagine) imaginer; **what did you ~ of them?** qu'avez-vous pensé d'eux?; **to ~ about sth/sb** penser à qch/qn; **I'll ~ about it** je vais y réfléchir; **to ~ of doing** avoir l'idée de faire; **I ~ so/not** je crois que oui/non; **to ~ well of** avoir une haute opinion de; **~ over** vt bien réfléchir à; **~ up** vt inventer, trouver; **~ tank** n groupe m de réflexion

thinly ['θɪnlɪ] adv (cut) en fines tranches; (spread) en une couche mince

third [θəːd] num troisième ♦ n (fraction) tiers m; (AUT) troisième (vitesse) f; (BRIT: SCOL: degree) ≈ licence f sans mention; **~ly** adv troisièmement; **~ party insurance** (BRIT) n assurance f au tiers; **~rate** adj de qualité médiocre; **the T~ World** n le tiers monde

thirst [θəːst] n soif f; **~y** adj (person) qui a soif, assoiffé(e); (work) qui donne soif; **to be ~y** avoir soif

thirteen [θəː'tiːn] num treize

thirty ['θəːtɪ] num trente

KEYWORD

---

this [ðɪs] adj (demonstrative: pl **these**) ce, cet +vowel or h mute, cette f; **this man/woman/book** cet homme/cette femme/ce livre; (not "that") cet homme-ci/cette femme-ci/ce livre-ci; **this one** celui-ci (celle-ci)
♦ pron (demonstrative: pl **these**) ce; (not "that one") celui-ci (celle-ci), ceci; **who's this?** qui est-ce?; **what's this?** qu'est-ce que c'est?; **I prefer this to**

that je préfère ceci à cela; **this is what he said** voici ce qu'il a dit; **this is Mr Brown** (in introductions) je vous présente Mr Brown; (in photo) c'est Mr Brown; (on telephone) ici Mr Brown
♦ adv (demonstrative): **it was about this big** c'était à peu près de cette grandeur or grand comme ça; **I didn't know it was this bad** je ne savais pas que c'était si or aussi mauvais

thistle ['θɪsl] n chardon m

thorn [θɔːn] n épine f

thorough ['θʌrə] adj (search) minutieux(-euse); (knowledge, research) approfondi(e); (work, person) consciencieux(-euse); (cleaning) à fond; **~bred** n (horse) pur-sang m inv; **~fare** n route f; **"no ~fare"** "passage interdit"; **~ly** adv minutieusement; en profondeur; à fond; (very) tout à fait

those [ðəuz] pl adj ces; (not "these"): ~ **books** ces livres-là ♦ pl pron ceux-là (celles-là)

though [ðəu] conj bien que +sub, quoique +sub ♦ adv pourtant

thought [θɔːt] pt, pp of **think** ♦ n pensée f; (idea) idée f; (opinion) avis m; **~ful** adj (deep in thought) pensif(-ive); (serious) réfléchi(e); (considerate) prévenant(e); **~less** adj étourdi(e); qui manque de considération

thousand ['θauzənd] num mille; **two ~** deux mille; **~s of** des milliers de; **~th** num millième

thrash [θræʃ] vt rouer de coups; donner une correction à; (defeat) battre à plate couture; ~ **about**, ~ **around** vi se débattre; ~ **out** vt débattre de

thread [θred] n fil m; (TECH) pas m, filetage m ♦ vt (needle) enfiler; **~bare** adj râpé(e), élimé(e)

threat [θret] n menace f; **~en** vi menacer ♦ vt: **to ~en sb with sth/to do** menacer qn de qch/de faire

three [θriː] num trois; **~-dimensional** adj à trois dimensions; **~-piece suit** n

complet m (avec gilet); **~-piece suite** n salon m comprenant un canapé et deux fauteuils assortis; **~-ply** adj (wool) trois fils inv

threshold ['θreʃhəuld] n seuil m

threw [θruː] pt of **throw**

thrifty ['θrɪftɪ] adj économe

thrill [θrɪl] n (excitement) émotion f, sensation forte; (shudder) frisson m ♦ vt (audience) électriser; **to be ~ed** (with gift etc) être ravi(e); **~er** n film m (or roman m or pièce f) à suspense; **~ing** adj saisissant(e), palpitant(e)

thrive [θraɪv] (pt, pp thrived) vi pousser, se développer; (business) prospérer; **he ~s on it** cela lui réussit; **thriving** adj (business, community) prospère

throat [θrəut] n gorge f; **to have a sore ~** avoir mal à la gorge

throb [θrɒb] vi (heart) palpiter; (engine) vibrer; **my head is ~bing** j'ai des élancements dans la tête

throes [θrəuz] npl: **in the ~ of** au beau milieu de

throne [θrəun] n trône m

throng ['θrɒŋ] n foule f ♦ vt se presser dans

throttle ['θrɒtl] n (AUT) accélérateur m ♦ vt étrangler

through [θruː] prep à travers; (time) pendant, durant; (by means of) par, par l'intermédiaire de; (owing to) à cause de ♦ adj (ticket, train, passage) direct(e) ♦ adv à travers; **to put sb ~ to** (BRIT: TEL) passer qn à qn; **to be ~** (BRIT: TEL) avoir la communication; (esp US: have finished) avoir fini; **to be ~ with sb** (relationship) avoir rompu avec qn; **"no ~ road"** (BRIT) "impasse"; **~out** prep (place) partout dans; (time) durant tout(e) le (la) ♦ adv partout

throw [θrəu] (pt threw, pp thrown) n jet m; (SPORT) lancer m ♦ vt lancer, jeter; (SPORT) lancer; (rider) désarçonner; (fig) décontenancer; **to ~ a party** donner une réception; ~ **away** vt jeter; ~ **off** vt se débarrasser de; ~ **out** vt jeter ject) rejeter; (person) mettre à la porte; **~ up** vi vomir; **~away** adj à jeter; (remark) fait(e) en passant; **~-in** (SPORT) remise f en jeu

thru [θruː] (US) = **through**

thrush [θrʌʃ] n (bird) grive f

thrust [θrʌst] (pt, pp **thrust**) n (TECH) poussée f ♦ vt pousser brusquement; (push in) enfoncer

thud [θʌd] n bruit sourd

thug [θʌg] n voyou m

thumb [θʌm] n (ANAT) pouce m ♦ vt: **to ~ a lift** faire de l'auto-stop, arrêter une voiture; **~ through** n (book) feuilleter; **~tack** (US) n punaise f (clou)

thump [θʌmp] n grand coup; (sound) bruit sourd ♦ vt cogner sur ♦ vi cogner, battre fort

thunder [ˈθʌndər] n tonnerre m ♦ vi tonner; (train etc): **to ~ past** passer dans un grondement or un bruit de tonnerre; **~bolt** n foudre f; **~clap** n coup m de tonnerre; **~storm** n orage m; **~y** adj orageux(-euse)

Thursday [ˈθəːzdɪ] n jeudi m

thus [ðʌs] adv ainsi

thwart [θwɔːt] vt contrecarrer

thyme [taɪm] n thym m

tiara [tɪˈɑːrə] n diadème m

tick [tɪk] n (sound: of clock) tic-tac m; (mark) coche f; (ZOOL) tique f; (BRIT: inf): **in a ~** dans une seconde ♦ vi faire tic-tac ♦ vt (item on list) cocher; **~ off** vt (item on list) cocher; (person) réprimander, attraper; **~ over** vi (engine) tourner au ralenti; (fig) aller or marcher doucettement

ticket [ˈtɪkɪt] n billet m; (for bus, tube) ticket m; (in shop: on goods) étiquette f; (for library) carte f; (parking ~) papillon m, p.-v. m; **~ collector** n inspecteur n contrôleur(-euse); **~ office** n guichet m, bureau m de vente des billets

tickle [ˈtɪkl] vt, vi chatouiller; **ticklish** adj (person) chatouilleux(-euse); (problem) épineux(-euse)

tidal [ˈtaɪdl] adj (force) de la marée; (estuary) à marée; **~ wave** n raz-de-marée m inv

tidbit [ˈtɪdbɪt] (US) = **titbit**

tiddlywinks [ˈtɪdlɪwɪŋks] n jeu m de puce

tide [taɪd] n marée f; (fig: of events) cours m ♦ vt: **to ~ sb over** dépanner qn; **high/low ~** marée haute/basse

tidy [ˈtaɪdɪ] adj (room) bien rangé(e); (dress, work) net(te), soigné(e); (person) ordonné(e), qui a de l'ordre ♦ vt (also: **~ up**) ranger

tie [taɪ] n (string etc) cordon m; (BRIT: also: **necktie**) cravate f; (fig: link) lien m; (SPORT: draw) égalité f de points; match nul ♦ vt attacher; (ribbon, shoelaces) nouer ♦ vi (SPORT) faire match nul; finir à égalité de points; **to ~ sth in a bow** faire un nœud à; **to ~ a knot in sth** faire un nœud à qch; **~ down** vt (fig): **to ~ sb down** (to) contraindre qn (à accepter); **to be ~d down** (by relationship) se fixer; **~ up** vt (parcel) ficeler; (dog, boat) attacher; (prisoner) ligoter; (arrangements) conclure; **to be ~d up** (busy) être pris(e) ou occupé(e)

tier [tɪər] n gradin m; (of cake) étage m

tiger [ˈtaɪgər] n tigre m

tight [taɪt] adj (rope) tendu(e), raide; (clothes) étroit(e), très juste; (budget, programme, bend) serré(e); (control) strict(e), sévère; (inf: drunk) ivre, rond(e) ♦ adv (squeeze) très fort; (shut) hermétiquement, bien; **~en** vt (rope) tendre; (screw) resserrer; (control) renforcer ♦ vi se tendre, se resserrer; **~fisted** adj avare; **~ly** adv (grasp) bien, très fort; **~rope** n corde f raide; **~s** (BRIT) npl collant m

tile [taɪl] n (on roof) tuile f; (on wall or floor) carreau m; **~d** adj en tuiles; carrelé(e)

till [tɪl] n caisse (enregistreuse) ♦ vt (land) cultiver ♦ prep, conj = **until**

tiller [ˈtɪlər] n (NAUT) barre f (du gouvernail)

tilt [tɪlt] *vt* pencher, incliner ♦ *vi* pencher, être incliné(e)

timber ['tɪmbə'] *n* (*material*) bois *m* (de construction); (*trees*) arbres *mpl*

time [taɪm] *n* temps *m*; (*epoch: often pl*) époque *f*, temps; (*by clock*) heure *f*; (*moment*) moment *m*; (*occasion, also* MATH) fois *f*; (*MUS*) mesure *f* ♦ *vt* (*race*) chronométrer; (*programme*) minuter; (*visit*) fixer; (*remark etc*) choisir le moment de; **a long ~** un long moment, longtemps; **for the ~ being** pour le moment; **4 at a ~** 4 à la fois; **from ~ to ~** de temps en temps; **at ~s** parfois; **in ~** (*soon enough*) à temps; (*after some ~*) avec le temps, à la longue; (*MUS*) en mesure; **in a week's ~** dans une semaine; **in no ~** en un rien de temps; **any ~** n'importe quand; **on ~** à l'heure; **5 ~s 5** 5 fois 5; **what ~ is it?** quelle heure est-il?; **to have a good ~** bien s'amuser; **~ bomb** *n* bombe *f* à retardement; **~ lag** (*BRIT*) *n* décalage *m*; (*in travel*) décalage horaire; **~less** *adj* éternel(le); **~ly** *adj* opportun(e); **~ off** *n* temps *m* libre; **~r** *n* (*TECH*) minuteur *m*; (*in kitchen*) compte-minutes *m inv*; **~scale** *n* délais *mpl*; **~share** *n* maison *f*/appartement *m* en multipropriété; **~ switch** (*BRIT*) *n* minuteur *m*; (*for lighting*) minuterie *f*; **~table** *n* (*RAIL*) (indicateur *m*) horaire *m*; (*SCOL*) emploi *m* du temps; **~ zone** *n* fuseau *m* horaire

timid ['tɪmɪd] *adj* timide; (*easily scared*) peureux(-euse)

timing ['taɪmɪŋ] *n* minutage *m*; chronométrage *m*; **the ~ of his resignation** le moment choisi pour sa démission

timpani ['tɪmpənɪ] *npl* timbales *fpl*

tin [tɪn] *n* étain *m*; (*also: ~ plate*) fer-blanc *m*; (*BRIT: can*) boîte *f* (de conserve); (*for storage*) boîte *f*; **~foil** *n* papier *m* d'étain *ou* aluminium

tinge [tɪndʒ] *n* nuance *f* ♦ *vt*: **~d with** teinté(e) de

tingle ['tɪŋgl] *vi* picoter; (*person*) avoir des picotements

tinker ['tɪŋkə'] *n* (*gipsy*) romanichel *m*; **~ with** *vt fus* bricoler, rafistoler

tinkle ['tɪŋkl] *vi* tinter

tinned [tɪnd] (*BRIT*) *adj* (*food*) en boîte, en conserve

tin opener (*BRIT*) *n* ouvre-boîte(s) *m*

tinsel ['tɪnsl] *n* guirlandes *fpl* de Noël (argentées)

tint [tɪnt] *n* teinte *f*; (*for hair*) shampooing colorant; **~ed** *adj* (*hair*) teint(e); (*spectacles, glass*) teinté(e)

tiny ['taɪnɪ] *adj* minuscule

tip [tɪp] *n* (*end*) bout *m*; (*gratuity*) pourboire *m*; (*BRIT: for rubbish*) décharge *f*; (*advice*) tuyau *m* ♦ *vt* (*waiter*) donner un pourboire à; (*tilt*) incliner; (*overturn: also: ~ over*) renverser; (*empty: also: ~ out*) déverser; **~-off** *n* (*hint*) tuyau *m*; **~ped** (*BRIT*) *adj* (*cigarette*) (à bout) filtre *inv*

tipsy ['tɪpsɪ] (*inf*) *adj* un peu ivre, éméché(e)

tiptoe ['tɪptəu] *n*: **on ~** sur la pointe des pieds

tiptop [tɪp'tɒp] *adj*: **in ~ condition** en excellent état

tire ['taɪə'] *n* (*US*) = **tyre** ♦ *vt* fatiguer ♦ *vi* se fatiguer; **~d** *adj* fatigué(e); **to be ~d of** en avoir assez de, être las (lasse) de; **~less** *adj* (*person*) infatigable; (*efforts*) inlassable; **~some** *adj* ennuyeux(-euse); **tiring** *adj* fatigant(e)

tissue ['tɪʃu:] *n* tissu *m*; (*paper handkerchief*) mouchoir *m* en papier, kleenex ® *m*; **~ paper** *n* papier *m* de soie

tit [tɪt] *n* (*bird*) mésange *f*; **to give ~ for tat** rendre la pareille

titbit ['tɪtbɪt] *n* (*food*) friandise *f*; (*news*) potin *m*

title ['taɪtl] *n* titre *m*; **~ deed** *n* (*LAW*) titre (constitutif) de propriété; **~ role** *n* rôle principal

TM *abbr* = **trademark**

to [tu:, tə] *prep* 1 (*direction*) à; **to go to**

France/Portugal/London/school aller en France/au Portugal/à Londres/à l'école; **to go to Claude's/the doctor's** aller chez Claude/le docteur; **the road to Edinburgh** la route d'Édimbourg

2 (*as far as*) (jusqu'à); **to count to 10** compter jusqu'à 10; **from 40 to 50 people** de 40 à 50 personnes

3 (*with expressions of time*): **a quarter to 5** 5 heures moins le quart; **it's twenty to 3** il est 3 heures moins vingt

4 (*for, of*) de; **the key to the front door** la clé de la porte d'entrée; **a letter to his wife** une lettre (adressée) à sa femme

5 (*expressing indirect object*) à; **to give sth to sb** donner qch à qn; **to talk to sb** parler à qn

6 (*in relation to*) à; **3 goals to 2** 3 (buts) à 2; **30 miles to the gallon** 9,4 litres aux cent (km)

7 (*purpose, result*): **to come to sb's aid** venir au secours de qn, porter secours à qn; **to sentence sb to death** condamner qn à mort; **to my surprise** à ma grande surprise

♦ *with vb* **1** (*simple infinitive*): **to go/eat** aller/manger

2 (*following another vb*): **to want/try/start to do** vouloir/essayer de/commencer à faire

3 (*with vb omitted*): **I don't want to** je ne veux pas

4 (*purpose, result*): **I did it to help you** je l'ai fait pour vous aider

5 (*equivalent to relative clause*): **I have things to do** j'ai des choses à faire; **the main thing is to try** l'important est d'essayer

6 (*after adjective etc*): **ready to go** prêt(e) à partir; **too old/young to ...** trop vieux/jeune pour ...

♦ *adv*: **push/pull the door to** tirez/poussez la porte

toad [təud] *n* crapaud *m*

toadstool ['təudstu:l] *n* champignon (vénéneux)

toast [təust] *n* (*CULIN*) pain grillé, toast *m*; (*drink, speech*) toast ♦ *vt* (*CULIN*) faire griller; (*drink to*) porter un toast à; **~er** *n* grille-pain *m inv*

tobacco [tə'bækəu] *n* tabac *m*; **~nist** *n* marchand(e) de tabac; **~nist's (shop)** *n* (bureau *m* de) tabac *m*

toboggan [tə'bɔgən] *n* toboggan *m*; (*child's*) luge *f* ♦ *vi*: **to go ~ing** faire de la luge

today [tə'dei] *adv* (*also fig*) aujourd'hui ♦ *n* aujourd'hui *m*

toddler ['tɔdlə*] *n* enfant *m/f* qui commence à marcher, bambin *m*

toe [təu] *n* doigt *m* de pied, orteil *m*; (*of shoe*) bout *m* ♦ *vt*: **to ~ the line** (*fig*) obéir, se conformer; **~nail** *n* ongle *m* du pied

toffee ['tɔfi] *n* caramel *m*; **~ apple** (*BRIT*) *n* pomme caramélisée

together [tə'geðə*] *adv* ensemble; (*at same time*) en même temps; **~ with** avec

toil [tɔil] *n* dur travail, labeur *m* ♦ *vi* peiner

toilet ['tɔilət] *n* (*BRIT: lavatory*) toilettes *fpl* ♦ *cpd* (*accessories etc*) de toilette; **~ bag** *n* nécessaire *m* de toilette; **~ paper** *n* papier *m* hygiénique; **~ries** *npl* articles *mpl* de toilette; **~ roll** *n* rouleau *m* de papier hygiénique

token ['təukən] *n* (*sign*) marque *f*, témoignage *m*; (*metal disc*) jeton *m* ♦ *adj* (*strike, payment etc*) symbolique; **book/record ~** (*BRIT*) chèque-livre/-disque *m*; **gift ~** *n* bon-cadeau *m*

told [təuld] *pt, pp of* **tell**

tolerable ['tɔlərəbl] *adj* (*bearable*) tolérable; (*fairly good*) passable

tolerant ['tɔlərnt] *adj*: **~ (of)** tolérant(e) (à l'égard de)

tolerate ['tɔləreit] *vt* supporter, tolérer

toll [təul] *n* (*tax, charge*) péage *m* ♦ *vi* (*bell*) sonner; **the accident ~ on the**

roads le nombre des victimes de la route

tomato [tə'mɑːtəu] (pl **~es**) n tomate f

tomb [tuːm] n tombe f

tomboy ['tɒmbɔɪ] n garçon manqué

tombstone ['tuːmstəun] n pierre tombale

tomcat ['tɒmkæt] n matou m

tomorrow [tə'mɒrəu] adv (also fig) demain ♦ n demain m; **the day after ~** après-demain; **~ morning** demain matin

ton [tʌn] n tonne f (BRIT = 1016kg; US = 907kg); (metric) tonne (= 1000 kg); **~s of** (inf) des tas de

tone [təun] n ton m ♦ vi (also: **~ in**) s'harmoniser; **~ down** vt (colour, criticism) adoucir; (sound) baisser; **~ up** vt (muscles) tonifier; **~-deaf** adj qui n'a pas d'oreille

tongs [tɒŋz] npl (for coal) pincettes fpl; (for hair) fer m à friser

tongue [tʌŋ] n langue f; **~ in cheek** ironiquement; **~-tied** adj (fig) muet(te); **~ twister** n phrase f très difficile à prononcer

tonic ['tɒnɪk] n (MED) tonique m; (also: **~ water**) tonic m, Schweppes ® m

tonight [tə'naɪt] adv, n cette nuit; (this evening) ce soir

tonsil ['tɒnsl] n amygdale f; **~litis** [tɒnsɪ'laɪtɪs] n angine f

too [tuː] adv (excessively) trop; (also) aussi; **~ much** adv trop ♦ adj trop de; **~ many** trop de; **~ bad!** tant pis!

took [tuk] pt of **take**

tool [tuːl] n (of car horn) coup m de klaxon; (of whistle) coup m de sifflet ♦ vi (with car horn) klaxonner

tooth [tuːθ] (pl **teeth**) n (ANAT, TECH) dent f; **~ache** n mal m de dent; **~brush** n brosse f à dents; **~paste** n (pâte f) dentifrice m; **~pick** n cure-dent m

top [tɒp] n (of mountain, head) sommet m; (of page, ladder, garment) haut m; (of box, cupboard, table) dessus m; (lid: of box, jar) couvercle m; (: of bottle) bouchon m; (toy) toupie f ♦ adj du haut; (in rank) premier(-ère); (best) meilleur(e) ♦ vt (exceed) dépasser; (be first in) être en tête de; **on ~ of** sur; (in addition to) en plus de; **from ~ to bottom** de fond en comble; **~ up** (US **~ off**) vt (bottle) remplir; (salary) compléter; **~ floor** n dernier étage; **~ hat** n haut-de-forme m; **~-heavy** adj (object) trop lourd(e) du haut

topic ['tɒpɪk] n sujet m, thème m; **~al** adj d'actualité

top: **~less** adj (bather etc) aux seins nus; **~-level** adj (talks) au plus haut niveau; **~most** adj (le) la plus haut(e)

topple ['tɒpl] vt renverser, faire tomber ♦ vi basculer; tomber

top-secret ['tɒp'siːkrɪt] adj top secret (-ète)

topsy-turvy ['tɒpsɪ'tɜːvɪ] adj, adv sens dessus dessous

torch [tɔːtʃ] n torche f; (BRIT: electric) lampe f de poche

tore [tɔːʳ] pt of **tear**[1]

torment [n 'tɔːment, vb tɔː'ment] n tourment m ♦ vt tourmenter; (fig: annoy) harceler

torn [tɔːn] pp of **tear**[1]

tornado [tɔː'neɪdəu] (pl **~es**) n tornade f

torpedo [tɔː'piːdəu] (pl **~es**) n torpille f

torrent ['tɒrənt] n torrent m; **~ial** [tɔ'renʃl] adj torrentiel(le)

tortoise ['tɔːtəs] n tortue f; **~shell** adj en écaille

torture ['tɔːtʃəʳ] n torture f ♦ vt torturer

Tory ['tɔːrɪ] (BRIT: POL) adj, n tory (m/f), conservateur(-trice)

toss [tɒs] vt lancer, jeter; (pancake) faire sauter; (head) rejeter en arrière; **to ~ a coin** jouer à pile ou face; **to ~ up for sth** jouer qch à pile ou face; **to ~ and turn** (in bed) se tourner et se retourner

tot [tɒt] n (BRIT: drink) petit verre; (child)

bambin *m*

total ['təʊtl] *adj* total(e) ♦ *n* total *m* ♦ *vt* (*add up*) faire le total de, additionner; (*amount to*) s'élever à; **~ly** *adv* totalement

totter ['tɒtə'] *vi* chanceler

touch [tʌtʃ] *n* contact *m*, toucher *m*; (*sense, also skill: of pianist etc*) toucher ♦ *vt* toucher; (*tamper with*) toucher à; **a ~ of** (*fig*) un petit peu de; une touche de; **to get in ~ with** prendre contact avec; **to lose ~** (*friends*) se perdre de vue; **~ on** *vt fus* (*topic*) effleurer, aborder; **~ up** *vt* (*paint*) retoucher; **~-and-go** *adj* incertain(e); **~down** *n* atterrissage *m*; (*on sea*) amerrissage *m*; (*US: FOOTBALL*) touché-en-but *m*; **~ed** *adj* (*moved*) touché(e); **~ing** *adj* touchant(e), attendrissant(e); **~line** *n* (*SPORT*) ligne *f* de touche; **~y** *adj* (*person*) susceptible

tough [tʌf] *adj* dur(e); (*resistant*) résistant(e), solide; (*meat*) dur, coriace; (*firm*) inflexible; (*task*) dur, pénible; **~en** *vt* (*character*) endurcir; (*glass etc*) renforcer

toupee ['tu:peɪ] *n* postiche *m*

tour ['tʊə'] *n* voyage *m*; (*also: package ~*) voyage organisé; (*of town, museum*) tour *m*, visite *f*; (*by artist*) tournée *f* ♦ *vt* visiter; **~ guide** *n* (*person*) guide *m/f*

tourism ['tʊərɪzm] *n* tourisme *m*

tourist ['tʊərɪst] *n* touriste *m/f* ♦ *cpd* touristique; **~ office** *n* syndicat *m* d'initiative

tournament ['tʊənəmənt] *n* tournoi *m*

tousled ['taʊzld] *adj* (*hair*) ébouriffé(e)

tout [taʊt] *vi:* **to ~ for** essayer de racrocher, racoler ♦ *n* (*also:* **ticket ~**) revendeur *m* de billets

tow [təʊ] *vt* remorquer; (*caravan, trailer*) tracter; **"on ~"** (*BRIT*) or **"in ~"** (*US*) (*AUT*) "véhicule en remorque"

toward(s) [tə'wɔːd(z)] *prep* vers; (*of attitude*) envers, à l'égard de; (*of purpose*) pour

towel ['taʊəl] *n* serviette *f* (de toilette);

~ling *n* (*fabric*) tissu éponge *m*; **~ rail** (*US* **towel rack**) *n* porte-serviettes *m*

tower ['taʊə'] *n* tour *f*; **~ block** (*BRIT*) *n* tour *f* (d'habitation); **~ing** *adj* très haut(e), imposant(e)

town [taʊn] *n* ville *f*; **to go to ~** aller en ville; (*fig*) y mettre le paquet; **~ centre** *n* centre *m* de la ville, centre-ville *m*; **~ council** *n* conseil municipal; **~ hall** *n* ≈ mairie *f*; **~ plan** *n* plan *m* de ville; **~ planning** *n* urbanisme *m*

towrope ['təʊrəʊp] *n* (câble *m* de) remorque *f*

tow truck (*US*) *n* dépanneuse *f*

toy [tɔɪ] *n* jouet *m*; **~ with** *vt fus* jouer avec; (*idea*) caresser

trace [treɪs] *n* trace *f* ♦ *vt* (*draw*) tracer, dessiner; (*follow*) suivre la trace de; (*locate*) retrouver; **tracing paper** *n* papier-calque *m*

track [træk] *n* (*mark*) trace *f*; (*path: gen*) chemin *m*, piste *f*; (*: of bullet etc*) trajectoire *f*; (*: of suspect, animal*) piste *f*; (*RAIL*) voie ferrée, rails *mpl*; (*on tape, SPORT*) piste; (*on record*) plage *f* ♦ *vt* suivre la trace or la piste de; **to keep ~ of** suivre; **~ down** *vt* (*prey*) trouver et capturer; (*sth lost*) finir par retrouver; **~suit** *n* survêtement *m*

tract [trækt] *n* (*of land*) étendue *f*

traction ['trækʃən] *n* traction *f*; (*MED*): **in ~** en extension

tractor ['træktə'] *n* tracteur *m*

trade [treɪd] *n* commerce *m*; (*skill, job*) métier *m* ♦ *vi* faire du commerce ♦ *vt* (*exchange*): **to ~ sth (for sth)** échanger qch (contre qch); **~ in** *vt* (*old car etc*) faire reprendre; **~ fair** *n* foire-(exposition) commerciale; **~-in price** *n* prix *m* à la reprise; **~mark** *n* marque *f* de fabrique; **~ name** *n* nom *m* de marque; **~r** *n* commerçant(e), négociant(e); **~sman** (*irreg*) *n* (*shopkeeper*) commerçant; **~ union** *n* syndicat *m*; **~ unionist** *n* syndicaliste *m/f*

tradition [trə'dɪʃən] *n* tradition *f*; **~al** *adj* traditionnel(le)

traffic ['træfɪk] n trafic m; (cars) circulation f ♦ vi: **to ~ in** (pej: liquor, drugs) faire le trafic de; **~ calming** n ralentissement m de la circulation; **~ circle** (US) n rond-point m; **~ jam** n embouteillage m; **~ lights** npl feux mpl (de signalisation); **~ warden** n contractuel(le)

tragedy ['trædʒədɪ] n tragédie f

tragic ['trædʒɪk] adj tragique

trail [treɪl] n (tracks) trace f, piste f; (path) chemin m, piste; (of smoke etc) traînée f ♦ vt traîner, tirer; (follow) suivre ♦ vi traîner; (in game, contest) être en retard; **~ behind** vi traîner, être à la traîne; **~er** n (AUT) remorque f; (US) caravane f; (CINEMA) bande-annonce f; **~er truck** (US) n (camion m à) semi-remorque m

train [treɪn] n train m; (in underground) rame f; (of dress) traîne f ♦ vt (apprentice, doctor etc) former; (sportsman) entraîner; (dog) dresser; (memory) exercer; (point: gun etc): **to ~ sth on** braquer qch sur ♦ vi suivre une formation; (SPORT) s'entraîner; **one's ~ of thought** le fil de sa pensée; **~ed** adj qualifié(e), qui a reçu une formation; (animal) dressé(e); **~ee** [treɪ'niː] n stagiaire m/f; (in trade) apprenti(e); **~er** n (SPORT: coach) entraîneur(-euse); (: shoe) chaussure f de sport; (of dogs etc) dresseur(-euse); **~ing** n formation f; entraînement m; in **~ing** (SPORT) en entraînement; (fit) en forme; **~ing college** n école professionnelle; (for teachers) ≈ école normale; **~ing shoes** npl chaussures fpl de sport

trait [treɪt] n trait m (de caractère)

traitor ['treɪtəʳ] n traître m

tram [træm] (BRIT) n (also: **~car**) tram(way) m

tramp [træmp] n (person) vagabond(e), clochard(e); (inf: pej: woman): **to be a ~** être coureuse ♦ vi marcher d'un pas lourd

trample ['træmpl] vt: **to ~ (underfoot)**

piétiner

trampoline ['træmpəliːn] n trampoline m

tranquil ['træŋkwɪl] adj tranquille; **~lizer** (US **tranquilizer**) n (MED) tranquillisant m

transact [træn'zækt] vt (business) traiter; **~ion** n transaction f

transatlantic ['trænzət'læntɪk] adj transatlantique

transfer [n 'trænsfəʳ, vb træns'fəːʳ] n (gen, also SPORT) transfert m; (POL: of power) passation f; (picture, design) décalcomanie f; (: stick-on) autocollant m ♦ vt transférer; passer; **to ~ the charges** (BRIT: TEL) téléphoner en P.C.V.; **~ desk** n (AVIAT) guichet m de transit

transform [træns'fɔːm] vt transformer

transfusion [træns'fjuːʒən] n transfusion f

transient ['trænzɪənt] adj transitoire, éphémère

transistor [træn'zɪstəʳ] n (~ radio) transistor m

transit ['trænzɪt] n: **in ~** en transit

transitive ['trænzɪtɪv] adj (LING) transitif(-ive)

transit lounge n salle f de transit

translate [trænz'leɪt] vt traduire; **translation** n traduction f; **translator** n traducteur(-trice)

transmission [trænz'mɪʃən] n transmission f

transmit [trænz'mɪt] vt transmettre; (RADIO, TV) émettre

transparency [træns'pɛərnsɪ] n (of glass etc) transparence f; (BRIT: PHOT) diapositive f

transparent [træns'pærnt] adj transparent(e)

transpire [træns'paɪəʳ] vi (turn out): **it ~d that ...** on a appris que ...; (happen) arriver

transplant [vb træns'plɑːnt, n 'trænsplɑːnt] vt transplanter; (seedlings) repiquer ♦ n (MED) transplantation f

transport [n 'trænspɔːt, vb træns'pɔːt]

n transport *m*; (*car*) moyen *m* de transport, voiture *f* ♦ *vt* transporter; **~ation** [ˌtrænspɔː'teɪʃən] *n* transport *m*; (*means of transportation*) moyen *m* de transport; **~ café** (*BRIT*) *n* ≈ restaurant *m* de routiers

trap [træp] *n* (*snare, trick*) piège *m*; (*carriage*) cabriolet *m* ♦ *vt* prendre au piège; (*confine*) coincer; **~ door** *n* trappe *f*

trapeze [trə'piːz] *n* trapèze *m*

trappings ['træpɪŋz] *npl* ornements *mpl*; attributs *mpl*

trash [træʃ] (*pej*) *n* (*goods*) camelote *f*; (*nonsense*) sottises *fpl*; **~ can** (*US*) *n* poubelle *f*; **~y** (*inf*) *adj* de camelote; (*novel*) de quatre sous

trauma ['trɔːmə] *n* traumatisme *m*; **~tic** [trɔː'mætɪk] *adj* traumatisant(e)

travel ['trævl] *n* voyage(s) *m(pl)* ♦ *vi* voyager; (*news, sound*) circuler, se propager ♦ *vt* (*distance*) parcourir; **~ agency** *n* agence *f* de voyages; **~ agent** *n* agent *m* de voyages; **~ler** (*US* **traveler**) *n* voyageur(-euse); **~ler's cheque** (*US* **traveler's check**) *n* chèque *m* de voyage; **~ling** (*US* **traveling**) *n* voyage(s) *m(pl)*; **~ sickness** *n* mal *m* de la route (or de mer or de l'air)

trawler ['trɔːlər] *n* chalutier *m*

tray [treɪ] *n* (*for carrying*) plateau *m*; (*on desk*) corbeille *f*

treacherous ['trɛtʃərəs] *adj*. (*person, look*) traître(-esse); (*ground, tide*) dont il faut se méfier

treacle ['triːkl] *n* mélasse *f*

tread [trɛd] (*pt* **trod**, *pp* **trodden**) *n* pas *m*; (*sound*) bruit *m* de pas; (*of tyre*) chape *f*, bande *f* de roulement ♦ *vi* marcher; **~ on** *vt fus* marcher sur

treason ['triːzn] *n* trahison *f*

treasure ['trɛʒər] *n* trésor *m* ♦ *vt* (*value*) tenir beaucoup à; **~r** *n* trésorier(-ère); **treasury** *n*: **the Treasury**, (*US*) **the Treasury Department** le ministère des Finances

treat [triːt] *n* petit cadeau, petite surpri-

se ♦ *vt* traiter; **to ~ sb to sth** offrir qch à qn

treatment *n* traitement *m*

treaty ['triːtɪ] *n* traité *m*

treble ['trɛbl] *adj* triple ♦ *vt*, *vi* tripler; **~ clef** *n* (*MUS*) clé *f* de sol

tree [triː] *n* arbre *m*

trek [trɛk] *n* (*long*) voyage; (*on foot*) (longue) marche, tirée *f*

tremble ['trɛmbl] *vi* trembler

tremendous [trɪ'mɛndəs] *adj* (*enormous*) énorme, fantastique; (*excellent*) formidable

tremor ['trɛmər] *n* tremblement *m*; (*also*: **earth ~**) secousse *f* sismique

trench [trɛntʃ] *n* tranchée *f*

trend [trɛnd] *n* (*tendency*) tendance *f*; (*of events*) cours *m*; (*fashion*) mode *f*; **~y** *adj* (*idea, person*) dans le vent; (*clothes*) dernier cri *inv*

trespass ['trɛspəs] *vi*: **to ~ on** s'introduire sans permission dans; **"no ~ing"** "propriété privée", "défense d'entrer"

trestle ['trɛsl] *n* tréteau *m*

trial ['traɪəl] *n* (*LAW*) procès *m*, jugement *m*; (*test: of machine etc*) essai *m*; **~s** *npl* (*unpleasant experiences*) épreuves *fpl*; **to be on ~** (*LAW*) passer en jugement; **by ~ and error** par tâtonnements; **~ period** *n* période d'essai

triangle ['traɪæŋgl] *n* (*MATH, MUS*) triangle *m*; **triangular** [traɪ'æŋgjulər] *adj* triangulaire

tribe [traɪb] *n* tribu *f*; **~sman** (*irreg*) *n* membre d'une tribu

tribunal [traɪ'bjuːnl] *n* tribunal *m*

tributary ['trɪbjutərɪ] *n* (*river*) affluent *m*

tribute ['trɪbjuːt] *n* tribut *m*, hommage *m*; **to ρay ~ to** rendre hommage à

trick [trɪk] *n* (*magic ~*) tour *m*; (*joke, prank*) tour, farce *f*; (*skill, knack*) astuce *f*, truc *m*; (*CARDS*) levée *f* ♦ *vt* attraper, rouler; **to play a ~ on sb** jouer un tour à qn; **that should do the ~** ça devrait faire l'affaire; **~ery** *n* ruse *f*

trickle ['trɪkl] *n* (*of water etc*) filet *m*

♦ *vi* couler en un filet *or* goutte à goutte

tricky ['trɪkɪ] *adj* difficile, délicat(e)

tricycle ['traɪsɪkl] *n* tricycle *m*

trifle ['traɪfl] *n* bagatelle *f*; (CULIN) ≈ diplomate *m* ♦ *adv*: **a ~ long** un peu long; **trifling** *adj* insignifiant(e)

trigger ['trɪgə'] *n* (of gun) gâchette *f*; **~ off** *vt* déclencher

trim [trɪm] *adj* (house, garden) bien tenu(e); (figure) svelte ♦ *n* (haircut etc) légère coupe; (on car) garnitures *fpl* ♦ *vt* (cut) couper légèrement; (NAUT: a sail) gréer; (decorate): **to ~ (with)** décorer (de); **~mings** *npl* (CULIN) garniture *f*

trinket ['trɪŋkɪt] *n* bibelot *m*; (piece of jewellery) colifichet *m*

trip [trɪp] *n* voyage *m*; (excursion) excursion *f*; (stumble) faux pas ♦ *vi* faire un faux pas, trébucher; **on a ~** en voyage; **~ up** *vi* trébucher ♦ *vt* faire un croc-en-jambe à

tripe [traɪp] *n* (CULIN) tripes *fpl*; (pej: rubbish) idioties *fpl*

triple ['trɪpl] *adj* triple; **~ts** *npl* triplés (-ées); **triplicate** ['trɪplɪkət] *n*: **in triplicate** en trois exemplaires

tripod ['traɪpɔd] *n* trépied *m*

trite [traɪt] *adj* (pej) usé(e) banal(e)

triumph ['traɪʌmf] *n* triomphe *m* ♦ *vi*: **to ~ (over)** triompher (de)

trivia ['trɪvɪə] (pej) futilités *fpl*; **~l** *adj* insignifiant(e); (commonplace) banal(e)

trod [trɔd] *pt* of **tread**; **~den** *pp* of **tread**

trolley ['trɔlɪ] *n* chariot *m*

trombone [trɔm'bəun] *n* trombone *m*

troop [tru:p] *n* bande, groupe *m* ♦ *vi*: **~ in/out** entrer/sortir en groupe; **~s** *npl* (MIL) troupes *fpl*; (: men) hommes *mpl*, soldats *mpl*; **~ing the colour** (BRIT) *n* le salut au drapeau

trophy ['trəufɪ] *n* trophée *m*

tropic ['trɔpɪk] *n* tropique *m*; **~al** *adj* tropical(e)

trot [trɔt] *n* trot *m* ♦ *vi* trotter; **on the ~** (BRIT: fig) d'affilée

trouble ['trʌbl] *n* difficulté(s) *f(pl)*, problème(s) *m(pl)*; (worry) ennuis *mpl*, soucis *mpl*; (bother, effort) peine *f*; (POL) troubles *mpl*; (MED): **stomach etc ~** troubles gastriques etc ♦ *vt* (disturb) déranger, gêner; (worry) inquiéter ♦ *vi*: **to ~ to do** prendre la peine de faire; **~s** *npl* (POL etc) troubles *mpl*; (personal) ennuis, soucis; **to be in ~** avoir des ennuis; (ship, climber etc) être en difficulté; **what's the ~?** qu'est-ce qui ne va pas?; **~d** *adj* (person) inquiet(-iète); (epoch, life) agité(e); **~maker** *n* élément perturbateur, fauteur de troubles; **~shooter** *n* (in conflict) médiateur *m*; **~some** *adj* (child) fatigant(e), difficile; (cough etc) gênant(e)

trough [trɔf] *n* (also: **drinking ~**) abreuvoir *m*; (also: **feeding ~**) auge *f*; (depression) creux *m*

trousers ['trauzəz] *npl* pantalon *m*; **short ~** culottes courtes

trout [traut] *n* inv truite *f*

trowel ['trauəl] *n* truelle *f*; (garden tool) déplantoir *m*

truant ['truənt] (BRIT) *n*: **to play ~** faire l'école buissonnière

truce [tru:s] *n* trêve *f*

truck [trʌk] *n* camion *m*; (RAIL) wagon *m* à plate-forme; **~ driver** *n* camionneur *m*; **~ farm** (US) *n* jardin maraîcher

true [tru:] *adj* vrai(e); (accurate) exact(e); (genuine) vrai, véritable; (faithful) fidèle; **to come ~** se réaliser

truffle ['trʌfl] *n* truffe *f*

truly ['tru:lɪ] *adv* vraiment, réellement; (truthfully) sans mentir; see also **yours**

trump [trʌmp] *n* (also: **~ card**) atout *m*

trumpet ['trʌmpɪt] *n* trompette *f*

truncheon ['trʌntʃən] (BRIT) *n* bâton *m* (d'agent de police); matraque *f*

trundle ['trʌndl] *vt*, *vi*: **to ~ along** rouler lentement et bruyamment

trunk [trʌŋk] *n* (of tree, person) tronc *m*; (of elephant) trompe *f*; (case) malle *f*; (US: AUT) coffre *m*; **~s** *npl* (also: **swimming ~s**) maillot *m* or slip *m* de bain

truss [trʌs] vt: **to ~ (up)** ligoter

trust [trʌst] n confiance f; (*responsibility*) charge f; (LAW) fidéicommis m ♦ vt (*rely on*) avoir confiance en; (*hope*) espérer; (*entrust*): **to ~ sth to sb** confier qch à qn; **to take sth on ~** accepter qch les yeux fermés; **on ~** ce que l'on a en confiance; **~ee** [trʌs'ti:] n (LAW) fidéicommissaire m/f; (*of school etc*) administrateur(-trice); **~ful, ~ing** adj confiant(e); **~worthy** adj digne de confiance

truth [tru:θ] n vérité f; **~ful** adj (*person*) qui dit la vérité; (*answer*) sincère

try [traɪ] n essai m, tentative f; (RUGBY) essai m ♦ vt (*attempt*) essayer, tenter; (*test: sth new*: also: ~ **out**) essayer, tester; (LAW: *person*) juger; (*strain*) éprouver ♦ vi essayer; **to have a ~** essayer; **to ~ to do** essayer de faire; (*seek*) chercher à faire; ~ **on** vt (*clothes*) essayer; **~ing** adj pénible

T-shirt ['ti:ʃə:t] n tee-shirt m

T-square ['ti:skweə'] n équerre f en T, té m

tub [tʌb] n cuve f; (*for washing clothes*) baquet m; (*bath*) baignoire f

tubby ['tʌbɪ] adj rondelet(te)

tube [tju:b] n tube m; (BRIT: *underground*) métro m; (*for tyre*) chambre f à air

tuberculosis [tjubə:kju'ləʊsɪs] n tuberculose f

TUC n abbr (BRIT: *Trades Union Congress*) confédération des syndicats britanniques

tuck [tʌk] vt (*put*) mettre; ~ **away** vt cacher, ranger; ~ **in** vt rentrer; (*child*) border ♦ vi (*eat*) manger (de bon appétit); ~ **up** vt (*child*) border; ~ **shop** (BRIT) n boutique f à provisions (*dans une école*)

Tuesday ['tju:zdɪ] n mardi m

tuft [tʌft] n touffe f

tug [tʌg] n (*ship*) remorqueur m ♦ vt tirer (sur); **~-of-war** n lutte f à la corde; (*fig*) lutte acharnée

tuition [tju:'ɪʃən] n (BRIT: (:

private ~) cours particuliers; (US: *school fees*) frais mpl de scolarité

tulip ['tju:lɪp] n tulipe f

tumble ['tʌmbl] n (*fall*) chute f, culbute f ♦ vi tomber, dégringoler; **to ~ to sth** (*inf*) réaliser qch; **~down** adj délabré(e); ~ **dryer** (BRIT) n séchoir m à air chaud

tumbler ['tʌmblə'] n (*glass*) verre (droit), gobelet m

tummy ['tʌmɪ] n (*inf*) ventre m; ~ **upset** n maux mpl de ventre

tumour ['tju:mə'] (US **tumor**) n tumeur f

tuna ['tju:nə] n inv (*also*: ~ **fish**) thon m

tune [tju:n] n (*melody*) air m ♦ vt (*also*: ~ **up**) (MUS) accorder; (RADIO, TV, AUT) régler; **to be in/out of ~** (*instrument*) être accordé/désaccordé; (*singer*) chanter juste/faux; **to be in/out of ~ with** (*fig*) être en accord/désaccord avec; ~ **in** vi (RADIO, TV): **to ~ in (to)** se mettre à l'écoute (de); ~ **up** vi (*musician*) accorder son instrument; **~ful** adj mélodieux(-euse); **~r** n: **piano ~r** accordeur m (de pianos)

tunic ['tju:nɪk] n tunique f

Tunisia [tju:'nɪzɪə] n Tunisie f

tunnel ['tʌnl] n tunnel m; (*in mine*) galerie f ♦ vi percer un tunnel

turbulence ['tə:bjuləns] n (AVIAT) turbulence f

tureen [tə'ri:n] n (*for soup*) soupière f; (*for vegetables*) légumier m

turf [tə:f] n gazon m; (*clod*) motte f (de gazon) ♦ vt gazonner; ~ **out** (*inf*) vt (*person*) jeter dehors

Turk [tə:k] n Turc (Turque)

Turkey ['tə:kɪ] n Turquie f

turkey ['tə:kɪ] n dinde f, dindon m

Turkish ['tə:kɪʃ] adj turc (turque) ♦ n (LING) turc m

turmoil ['tə:mɔɪl] n trouble m, bouleversement m; **in ~** en émoi, en effervescence

turn [tə:n] n tour m; (*in road*) tournant m; (*of mind, events*) tournure f; (*performance*) numéro m; (MED) crise f, attaque *f* ♦ *vt* tourner; (*collar, steak*) retourner; (*change*): **to ~ sth into** changer qch en ♦ *vi* (*object, wind, milk*) tourner; (*person: look back*) se (re)tourner; (*in reverse direction*) faire demi-tour; (*become*) devenir; (*age*) atteindre; **to ~ into** se changer en; **a good ~** un service; **it gave me quite a ~** ça m'a fait un coup; **"no left ~"** (AUT) "défense de tourner à gauche"; **it's your ~** c'est (à) votre tour; **in ~** à son tour; **to ~ a tour de rôle; **to take ~s (at)** se relayer (pour *or* à); **~ away** *vi* se détourner ♦ *vt* (*applicants*) refuser; **~ back** *vi* revenir, faire demi-tour ♦ *vt* (*person, vehicle*) faire faire demi-tour à; (*clock*) reculer; **~ down** *vt* (*refuse*) rejeter, refuser; (*reduce*) baisser; (*fold*) rabattre; **~ in** *vi* (*inf: go to bed*) aller se coucher ♦ *vt* (*fold inwards*) rentrer; **~ off** *vi* (*from road*) tourner ♦ *vt* (*light, radio etc*) éteindre; (*tap*) fermer; (*engine*) arrêter; **~ on** *vt* (*light, radio etc*) allumer; (*tap*) ouvrir; (*engine*) mettre en marche; **~ out** *vt* (*light, gas*) éteindre; (*produce*) produire ♦ *vi* (*voters, troops etc*) se présenter; **to ~ out to be ...** s'avérer ..., se révéler ...; **~ over** *vi* (*person*) se retourner ♦ *vt* (*object*) retourner; (*page*) tourner; **~ round** *vi* faire demi-tour (*rotate*) tourner; **~ up** *vi* (*person*) arriver, se pointer (*inf*); (*lost object*) être retrouvé(e) ♦ *vt* (*collar*) remonter; (*radio, heater*) mettre plus fort; **~ing** *n* (*in road*) tournant *m*; **~ing point** *n* (*fig*) tournant *m*, moment décisif

turnip ['tə:nɪp] *n* navet *m*

turn: **~out** *n* (*of voters*) taux *m* de participation; **~over** *n* (COMM: *of money*) chiffre *m* d'affaires; (: *of goods*) roulement *m*; (*of staff*) renouvellement *m*, changement *m*; **~pike** (US) *n* autoroute *f* à péage; **~stile** *n* tourniquet *m* (*d'entrée*); **~table** *n* (*on record player*) platine *f*; **~up** (BRIT) *n* (*on trousers*) revers *m*

turpentine ['tə:pəntaɪn] *n* (*also:* **turps**)

(*essence f de*) térébenthine *f*

turquoise ['tə:kwɔɪz] *n* (*stone*) turquoise *f* ♦ *adj* turquoise *inv*

turret ['tʌrɪt] *n* tourelle *f*

turtle ['tə:tl] *n* tortue marine *or* d'eau douce; **~neck (sweater)** *n* (BRIT) pullover *m* à col montant; (US) pullover *m* à col roulé

tusk [tʌsk] *n* défense *f*

tutor ['tju:təʳ] *n* (*in college*) directeur (-trice) d'études; (*private teacher*) précepteur(-trice); **~ial** [tju:'tɔ:rɪəl] *n* (SCOL) (séance *f* de) travaux *mpl* pratiques

tuxedo [tʌk'si:dəu] (US) *n* smoking *m*

TV *n abbr* (= *television*) télé *f*

twang [twæŋ] *n* (*of instrument*) son vibrant; (*of voice*) ton nasillard

tweed [twi:d] *n* tweed *m*

tweezers ['twi:zəz] *npl* pince *f* à épiler

twelfth [twelfθ] *num* douzième

twelve [twelv] *num* douze; **at ~ (o'clock)** à midi; (*midnight*) à minuit

twentieth ['twentɪθ] *num* vingtième

twenty ['twentɪ] *num* vingt

twice [twaɪs] *adv* deux fois; **~ as much** deux fois plus

twiddle ['twɪdl] *vt, vi*: **to ~ (with) sth** tripoter qch; **to ~ one's thumbs** (*fig*) se tourner les pouces

twig [twɪg] *n* brindille *f* ♦ *vi* (*inf*) piger

twilight ['twaɪlaɪt] *n* crépuscule *m*

twin [twɪn] *adj, n* jumeau(-elle) ♦ *vt* jumeler; **~(-bedded) room** *n* chambre *f* à deux lits; **~ beds** *npl* lits jumeaux

twine [twaɪn] *n* ficelle *f* ♦ *vi* (*plant*) s'enrouler

twinge [twɪndʒ] *n* (*of pain*) élancement *m*; **a ~ of conscience** un certain remords; **a ~ of regret** un pincement au cœur

twinkle ['twɪŋkl] *vi* scintiller; (*eyes*) pétiller

twirl [twə:l] *vt* faire tournoyer ♦ *vi* tournoyer

twist [twɪst] *n* torsion *f*, tour *m*; (*in road*) virage *m*; (*in wire, flex*) tortillon m; (in story) coup m de théâtre ♦ vt tordre; (weave) entortiller; (roll around) enrouler; (fig) déformer ♦ vi (road, river) serpenter

twit [twɪt] (inf) n crétin(e)

twitch [twɪtʃ] n (pull) coup sec, saccade f; (nervous) tic m ♦ vi se convulser; avoir un tic

two [tu:] num deux; **to put ~ and ~ together** (fig) faire le rapprochement; **~-door** adj (AUT) à deux portes; **~-faced** (pej) adj (person) faux (fausse); **~-fold** adv: **to increase ~fold** doubler; **~-piece** (suit) n (man's) costume m (deux-pièces) m (woman's) (tailleur m) deux-pièces m inv; **~-piece** (swimsuit) n (maillot m de bain) deux-pièces m inv; **~-some** n (people) couple m; **~-way** adj (traffic) dans les deux sens

tycoon [taɪ'ku:n] n: **(business) ~** gros homme d'affaires

type [taɪp] n (category) type m, genre m, espèce f; (model, example) type m, modèle m; (TYP) type, caractère m ♦ vt (letter etc) taper (à la machine); **~-cast** adj (actor) condamné(e) à toujours jouer le même rôle; **~-face** n (TYP) œil m de caractère; **~-script** n texte dactylographié; **~-writer** n machine f à écrire; **~-written** adj dactylographié(e)

typhoid ['taɪfɔɪd] n typhoïde f

typical ['tɪpɪkl] adj typique, caractéristique

typing ['taɪpɪŋ] n dactylo(graphie) f

typist ['taɪpɪst] n dactylo m/f

tyrant ['taɪərənt] n tyran m

tyre ['taɪə'] (US **tire**) n pneu m; **~ pressure** n pression f (de gonflage)

U, u

U-bend ['ju:bɛnd] n (in pipe) coude m

ubiquitous [ju:'bɪkwɪtəs] adj omniprésent(e)

udder ['ʌdə'] n pis m, mamelle f

UFO ['ju:fəʊ] n abbr (= unidentified flying object) OVNI m

Uganda [ju:'gændə] n Ouganda m

ugh [ə:h] excl pouah!

ugly ['ʌglɪ] adj laid(e), vilain(e); (situation) inquiétant(e)

UHT abbr (= ultra heat treated): **UHT milk** lait m UHT or longue conservation

UK n abbr = **United Kingdom**

ulcer ['ʌlsə'] n ulcère m; (also: **mouth ~**) aphte f

Ulster ['ʌlstə'] n Ulster m; (inf: Northern Ireland) Irlande f du Nord

ulterior [ʌl'tɪərɪə'] adj: **~ motive** arrière-pensée f

ultimate ['ʌltɪmət] adj ultime, final(e); (authority) suprême; **~ly** adv (at last) en fin de compte; (fundamentally) finalement

ultrasound ['ʌltrəsaund] n ultrason m

umbilical cord [ʌm'bɪlɪkl-] n cordon ombilical

umbrella [ʌm'brɛlə] n parapluie m; (for sun) parasol m

umpire ['ʌmpaɪə'] n arbitre m

umpteen [ʌmp'ti:n] adj je ne sais combien de; **~th** adj: **for the ~th time** pour la nième fois

UN n abbr = **United Nations**

unable [ʌn'eɪbl] adj: **to be ~ to** ne pas pouvoir, être dans l'impossibilité de; (incapable) être incapable de

unacceptable [ʌnək'sɛptəbl] adj (behaviour) inadmissible; (price, proposal) inacceptable

unaccompanied [ʌnə'kʌmpənɪd] adj (child, lady) non accompagné(e); (song) sans accompagnement

unaccustomed [ʌnə'kʌstəmd] adj: **to be ~ to sth** ne pas avoir l'habitude de qch

unanimous [ju:'nænɪməs] adj unanime; **~ly** adv à l'unanimité

unarmed [ʌn'ɑ:md] adj (without a weapon) non armé(e); (combat) sans armes

unattached [ʌnə'tætʃt] adj libre, sans attaches; (part) non attaché(e), indépendant(e)

unattended [ʌnə'tɛndɪd] adj (car, child, luggage) sans surveillance

unattractive [ʌnə'træktɪv] adj peu attrayant(e); (character) peu sympathique

unauthorized [ʌn'ɔ:θəraɪzd] adj non autorisé(e), sans autorisation

unavoidable [ʌnə'vɔɪdəbl] adj inévitable

unaware [ʌnə'wɛəʳ] adj: **to be ~ of** ignorer, être inconscient(e) de; **~s** adv à l'improviste, au dépourvu

unbalanced [ʌn'bælənst] adj déséquilibré(e); (report) peu objectif(-ive)

unbearable [ʌn'bɛərəbl] adj insupportable

unbeatable [ʌn'bi:təbl] adj imbattable

unbeknown(st) [ʌnbɪ'nəun(st)] adv: **~ to me/Peter** à mon insu/à l'insu de Peter

unbelievable [ʌnbɪ'li:vəbl] adj incroyable

unbend [ʌn'bɛnd] (irreg) vi se détendre
♦ vt (wire) redresser, détordre

unbiased [ʌn'baɪəst] adj impartial(e)

unborn [ʌn'bɔ:n] adj à naître, qui n'est pas encore né(e)

unbreakable [ʌn'breɪkəbl] adj incassable

unbroken [ʌn'brəukən] adj intact(e); (fig) continu(e), ininterrompu(e)

unbutton [ʌn'bʌtn] vt déboutonner

uncalled-for [ʌn'kɔ:ldfɔ:ʳ] adj déplacé(e), injustifié(e)

uncanny [ʌn'kænɪ] adj étrange, troublant(e)

unceremonious [ʌnsɛrɪ'məunɪəs] adj (abrupt, rude) brusque

uncertain [ʌn'sə:tn] adj incertain(e); (hesitant) hésitant(e); **in no ~ terms** sans équivoque possible; **~ty** n incertitude f, doute(s) m(pl)

uncivilized [ʌn'sɪvɪlaɪzd] adj (gen) non civilisé(e); (fig: behaviour etc) barbare; (hour) indu(e)

uncle ['ʌŋkl] n oncle m

uncomfortable [ʌn'kʌmfətəbl] adj in-

comfortable, peu confortable; (uneasy) mal à l'aise, gêné(e); (situation) désagréable

uncommon [ʌn'kɔmən] adj rare, singulier(-ère), peu commun(e)

uncompromising [ʌn'kɔmprəmaɪzɪŋ] adj intransigeant(e), inflexible

unconcerned [ʌnkən'sə:nd] adj: **to be ~ (about)** ne pas s'inquiéter (de)

unconditional [ʌnkən'dɪʃənl] adj sans conditions

unconscious [ʌn'kɔnʃəs] adj sans connaissance, évanoui(e); (unaware): **~ of** inconscient(e) de; **the n: ~** l'inconscient m; **~ly** adv inconsciemment

uncontrollable [ʌnkən'trəuləbl] adj indiscipliné(e); (temper, laughter) irrépressible

unconventional [ʌnkən'vɛnʃənl] adj peu conventionnel(le)

uncouth [ʌn'ku:θ] adj grossier(-ère), fruste

uncover [ʌn'kʌvəʳ] vt découvrir

undecided [ʌndɪ'saɪdɪd] adj indécis(e), irrésolu(e)

under ['ʌndəʳ] prep sous; (less than) (de) moins de; au-dessous de; (according to) selon, en vertu de ♦ adv au-dessous; en dessous; **~ there** là-dessous; **~ repair** en cours de réparation; **~age** adj (person) qui n'a pas l'âge réglementaire; **~carriage** n (AVIAT) train m d'atterrissage; **~charge** vt ne pas faire payer assez à; **~coat** n (paint) couche f de fond; **~cover** adj secret(-ète), clandestin(e); **~current** n courant ou sentiment sous-jacent; **~cut** (irreg) vt vendre moins cher que; **~dog** n opprimé m; **~done** adj (CULIN) saignant(e); (pej) pas assez cuit(e); **~estimate** vt sous-estimer; **~fed** adj sous-alimenté(e); **~foot** adv sous les pieds; **~go** (irreg) vt subir; (treatment) suivre; **~graduate** n étudiant(e) (qui prépare la licence); **~ground** n (BRIT: railway) métro m; (POL) clandestinité f ♦ adj souterrain(e); (fig) clandestin(e) ♦ adv dans la clandestinité, clandestinement; **~growth** n broussailles fpl, sous-bois m; **~hand(ed)** adj (fig: behaviour, method etc) en dessous; **~lie** (irreg) vt être à la base de; **~line** vt souligner; **~mine** vt saper, miner; **~neath** adv (en dessous ♦ prep sous, au-dessous de; **~paid** adj sous-payé(e); **~pants** npl caleçon m, slip m; **~pass** (BRIT) n passage souterrain; (on motorway) passage inférieur; **~privileged** adj défavorisé(e), économiquement faible; **~rate** vt sous-estimer; **~shirt** (US) n tricot m de corps; **~shorts** (US) npl caleçon m, slip m; **~side** n dessous m; **~skirt** (BRIT) n jupon m

understand [ʌndə'stænd] (irreg: like stand) vt je comprendre; **I ~ that ...** je me suis laissé dire que ...; je crois comprendre que ...; **~able** adj compréhensible; **~ing** adj compréhensif(-ive) ♦ n compréhension f; (agreement) accord m

understatement ['ʌndəsteitmənt] n: **that's an ~** c'est (bien) peu dire, le terme est faible

understood [ʌndə'stud] pt, pp of **understand** ♦ adj entendu(e); (implied) sous-entendu(e)

understudy ['ʌndəstʌdɪ] n doublure f

undertake [ʌndə'teik] (irreg) vt entreprendre; se charger de; **to ~ to do sth** s'engager à faire qch

undertaker [ʌndə'teikə*r*] n entrepreneur m des pompes funèbres, croquemort m

undertaking ['ʌndəteikɪŋ] n entreprise f; (promise) promesse f

under: **~tone** n: **in an ~tone** à mivoix; **~water** adv sous l'eau ♦ adj sous-marin(e); **~wear** n sousvêtements mpl; (women's only) dessous mpl; **~world** n (of crime) milieu m, pègre f; **~write** n (INSURANCE) assureur m

undies ['ʌndiz] (inf) npl dessous mpl, lingerie f

undiplomatic ['ʌndiplə'mætɪk] adj peu diplomatique

undo [ʌn'du:] (irreg) vt défaire; **~ing** n ruine f, perte f

undoubted [ʌn'dautid] adj indubitable, certain(e); **~ly** adv sans aucun doute

undress [ʌn'drɛs] vi se déshabiller

undue [ʌn'dju:] adj indu(e), excessif (-ive)

undulating ['ʌndjuleitiŋ] adj ondoyant(e), onduleux(-euse)

unduly [ʌn'dju:li] adv trop, excessivement

unearth [ʌn'ə:θ] vt déterrer; (fig) dénicher

unearthly [ʌn'ə:θli] adj (hour) indu(e), impossible

uneasy [ʌn'i:zi] adj mal à l'aise, gêné(e); (worried) inquiet(-ète); (feeling) désagréable; (peace, truce) fragile

uneconomic(al) ['ʌni:kə'nɔmɪk(l)] adj peu économique

uneducated [ʌn'edjukeitid] adj (person) sans instruction

unemployed [ʌnim'plɔid] adj sans travail, en or au chômage ♦ n: **the ~** les chômeurs mpl; **unemployment** n chômage m

unending [ʌn'endiŋ] adj interminable, sans fin

unerring [ʌn'ə:rɪŋ] adj infaillible, sûr(e)

uneven [ʌn'i:vn] adj inégal(e); (quality, work) irrégulier(-ère)

unexpected [ʌniks'pektid] adj inattendu(e), imprévu(e); **~ly** [ʌniks'pektidli] adv (arrive) à l'improviste; (succeed) contre toute attente

unfailing [ʌn'feiliŋ] adj inépuisable; (remedy) infaillible

unfair [ʌn'fɛə*r*] adj: **~ (to)** injuste (envers)

unfaithful [ʌn'feiθful] adj infidèle

unfamiliar [ʌnfə'miliə*r*] adj étrange, inconnu(e); **to be ~ with** mal connaître

unfashionable [ʌn'fæʃnəbl] adj

(clothes) démodé(e); *(place)* peu chic *inv*

unfasten [ʌn'fɑːsn] *vt* défaire; détacher; *(open)* ouvrir

unfavourable [ʌn'feɪvrəbl] *(US* **unfavorable)** *adj* défavorable

unfeeling [ʌn'fiːlɪŋ] *adj.* insensible, dur(e)

unfinished [ʌn'fɪnɪʃt] *adj* inachevé(e)

unfit [ʌn'fɪt] *adj* en mauvaise santé; pas en forme; *(incompetent)*: ~ **(for)** impropre (à); *(work, service)* inapte (à)

unfold [ʌn'fəʊld] *vt* déplier ♦ *vi* se dérouler

unforeseen [ʌnfɔː'siːn] *adj* imprévu(e)

unforgettable [ʌnfə'getəbl] *adj* inoubliable

unfortunate [ʌn'fɔːtʃənət] *adj* malheureux(-euse); *(event, remark)* malencontreux(-euse); **~ly** *adv* malheureusement

unfounded [ʌn'faʊndɪd] *adj* sans fondement

unfriendly [ʌn'frendlɪ] *adj* inamical(e), peu aimable

ungainly [ʌn'geɪnlɪ] *adj* gauche, dégingandé(e)

ungodly [ʌn'gɒdlɪ] *adj (hour)* indu(e)

ungrateful [ʌn'greɪtfʊl] *adj* ingrat(e)

unhappiness [ʌn'hæpɪnɪs] *n* tristesse *f*, peine *f*

unhappy [ʌn'hæpɪ] *adj.* triste, malheureux(-euse); ~ **about** *or* **with** *(arrangements etc)* mécontent(e) de, peu satisfait(e) de

unharmed [ʌn'hɑːmd] *adj.* indemne, sain(e) et sauf (sauve)

UNHCR *n abbr* (= *United Nations High Commission for refugees)* HCR *m*

unhealthy [ʌn'helθɪ] *adj* malsain(e); *(person)* maladif(-ive)

unheard-of [ʌn'hɜːdɒv] *adj* inouï(e), sans précédent

unhurt [ʌn'hɜːt] *adj* indemne

unidentified [ʌnaɪ'dentɪfaɪd] *adj* non identifié(e); *see also* **UFO**

uniform ['juːnɪfɔːm] *n* uniforme *m* ♦ *adj* uniforme

uninhabited [ʌnɪn'hæbɪtɪd] *adj* inhabité(e)

unintentional [ʌnɪn'tenʃənəl] *adj* involontaire

union ['juːnjən] *n* union *f*; *(also:* **trade ~)** syndicat *m* ♦ *cpd* du syndicat, syndical(e); **U~ Jack** *n* drapeau du *Royaume-Uni*

unique [juː'niːk] *adj* unique

UNISON ['juːnɪsn] *n* grand syndicat des services publics en Grande-Bretagne

unison ['juːnɪsn] *n:* **in** ~ *(sing)* à l'unisson; *(say)* en chœur

unit ['juːnɪt] *n* unité *f*; *(section: of furniture etc)* élément *m*, bloc *m*; **kitchen** ~ élément de cuisine

unite [juː'naɪt] *vt* unir ♦ *vi* s'unir; **~d** *adj* uni(e); unifié(e); *(effort)* conjugué(e); **U~d Kingdom** *n* Royaume-Uni *m*; **U~d Nations (Organization)** *n* (Organisation *f* des) Nations unies; **U~d States (of America)** *n* États-Unis *mpl*

unit trust *(BRIT)* *n* fonds commun de placement

unity ['juːnɪtɪ] *n* unité *f*

universal [juːnɪ'vɜːsl] *adj* universel(le)

universe ['juːnɪvɜːs] *n* univers *m*

university [juːnɪ'vɜːsɪtɪ] *n* université *f*

unjust [ʌn'dʒʌst] *adj* injuste

unkempt [ʌn'kempt] *adj* négligé(e), débraillé(e); *(hair)* mal peigné(e)

unkind [ʌn'kaɪnd] *adj* peu gentil(le), méchant(e)

unknown [ʌn'nəʊn] *adj* inconnu(e)

unlawful [ʌn'lɔːfʊl] *adj* illégal(e)

unleaded ['ʌn'ledɪd] *adj (petrol, fuel)* sans plomb

unleash [ʌn'liːʃ] *vt (fig)* déchaîner, déclencher

unless [ʌn'les] *conj:* ~ **he leaves** à moins qu'il ne parte

unlike [ʌn'laɪk] *adj* dissemblable, différent(e) ♦ *prep* contrairement à

unlikely [ʌn'laɪklɪ] *adj (happening)* improbable; *(explanation)* invraisemblable

unlimited [ʌn'lɪmɪtɪd] *adj* illimité(e)

unlisted ['ʌn'lɪstɪd] *(US) adj (TEL)* sur la

liste rouge
unload [ʌn'ləud] vt décharger
unlock [ʌn'lɔk] vt ouvrir
unlucky [ʌn'lʌkɪ] adj (person) malchanceux(-euse); (object, number) qui porte malheur; **to be ~** (person) ne pas avoir de chance
unmarried [ʌn'mærɪd] adj célibataire
unmistak(e)able [ʌnmɪs'teɪkəbl] adj indubitable; qu'on ne peut pas ne pas reconnaître
unmitigated [ʌn'mɪtɪgeɪtɪd] adj non mitigé(e), absolu(e), pur(e)
unnatural [ʌn'nætʃrəl] adj non naturel(le); (habit) contre nature
unnecessary [ʌn'nesəsərɪ] adj inutile, superflu(e)
unnoticed [ʌn'nəutɪst] adj: **(to go** or **pass) ~** (passer) inaperçu(e)
UNO n abbr = **United Nations Organization**
unobtainable [ʌnəb'teɪnəbl] adj impossible à obtenir
unobtrusive [ʌnəb'tru:sɪv] adj discret(-ète)
unofficial [ʌnə'fɪʃl] adj (news) officieux(-euse); (strike) sauvage
unorthodox [ʌn'ɔːθədɔks] adj peu orthodoxe; (REL) hétérodoxe
unpack [ʌn'pæk] vi défaire sa valise ♦ vt (suitcase) défaire; (belongings) déballer
unpalatable [ʌn'pælətəbl] adj (meal) mauvais(e); (truth) désagréable à entendre)
unparalleled [ʌn'pærəleld] adj incomparable, sans égal
unpleasant [ʌn'pleznt] adj déplaisant(e), désagréable
unplug [ʌn'plʌg] vt débrancher
unpopular [ʌn'pɔpjulər] adj impopulaire
unprecedented [ʌn'presɪdentɪd] adj sans précédent
unpredictable [ʌnprɪ'dɪktəbl] adj imprévisible
unprofessional [ʌnprə'feʃənl] adj: ~

conduct manquement m aux devoirs de la profession
UNPROFOR n abbr (= United Nations Protection Force) FORPRONU f
unqualified [ʌn'kwɔlɪfaɪd] adj (teacher) non diplômé(e), sans titres; (success, disaster) sans réserve, total(e)
unquestionably [ʌn'kwestʃənəblɪ] adv incontestablement
unravel [ʌn'rævl] vt démêler
unreal [ʌn'rɪəl] adj irréel(le); (extraordinary) incroyable
unrealistic ['ʌnrɪə'lɪstɪk] adj irréaliste; peu réaliste
unreasonable [ʌn'ri:znəbl] adj qui n'est pas raisonnable
unrelated [ʌnrɪ'leɪtɪd] adj sans rapport; sans lien de parenté
unreliable [ʌnrɪ'laɪəbl] adj sur qui (or quoi) on ne peut pas compter, peu fiable
unremitting [ʌnrɪ'mɪtɪŋ] adj inlassable, infatigable, acharné(e)
unreservedly [ʌnrɪ'zɜːvɪdlɪ] adv sans réserve
unrest [ʌn'rest] n agitation f, troubles mpl
unroll [ʌn'rəul] vt dérouler
unruly [ʌn'ru:lɪ] adj indiscipliné(e)
unsafe [ʌn'seɪf] adj (in danger) en danger; (journey, car) dangereux(-euse)
unsaid [ʌn'sed] adj: **to leave sth ~** passer qch sous silence
unsatisfactory ['ʌnsætɪs'fæktərɪ] adj peu satisfaisant(e)
unsavoury [ʌn'seɪvərɪ] (US **unsavory**) adj (fig) peu recommandable
unscathed [ʌn'skeɪðd] adj indemne
unscrew [ʌn'skruː] vt dévisser
unscrupulous [ʌn'skru:pjuləs] adj sans scrupules
unsettled [ʌn'setld] adj perturbé(e); instable
unshaven [ʌn'ʃeɪvn] adj non or mal rasé(e)
unsightly [ʌn'saɪtlɪ] adj disgracieux(-euse), laid(e)

unskilled [ʌn'skɪld] adj: ~ worker manœuvre m

unspeakable [ʌn'spi:kəbl] adj indicible; (awful) innommable

unstable [ʌn'steɪbl] adj instable

unsteady [ʌn'stedɪ] adj mal assuré(e), chancelant(e), instable

unstuck [ʌn'stʌk] adj: **to come ~** se décoller; (plan) tomber à l'eau

unsuccessful [ʌnsək'sesful] adj (attempt) infructueux(-euse), vain(e); (writer, proposal) qui n'a pas de succès; **to be ~** (in attempting sth) ne pas réussir; ne pas avoir de succès; (application) ne pas être retenu(e)

unsuitable [ʌn'su:təbl] adj qui ne convient pas, peu approprié(e); inopportun(e)

unsure [ʌn'ʃuəʳ] adj pas sûr(e); **to be ~ of o.s.** manquer de confiance en soi

unsuspecting [ʌnsəs'pektɪŋ] adj qui ne se doute de rien

unsympathetic ['ʌnsɪmpə'θetɪk] adj (person) antipathique; (attitude) peu compatissant(e)

untapped [ʌn'tæpt] adj (resources) inexploité(e)

unthinkable [ʌn'θɪŋkəbl] adj impensable, inconcevable

untidy [ʌn'taɪdɪ] adj (room) en désordre; (appearance, person) débraillé(e); (person: in character) sans ordre, désordonné

untie [ʌn'taɪ] vt (knot, parcel) défaire; (prisoner, dog) détacher

until [ən'tɪl] prep jusqu'à; (after negative) avant ♦ conj jusqu'à ce que +sub; (in past, after negative) avant que +sub; **~ he comes** jusqu'à ce qu'il vienne, jusqu'à son arrivée; **~ now** jusqu'à présent, jusqu'ici; **~ then** jusque-là

untimely [ʌn'taɪmlɪ] adj inopportun(e); (death) prématuré(e)

untold [ʌn'təʊld] adj (story) jamais raconté(e); (wealth) incalculable; (joy, suffering) indescriptible

untoward [ʌntə'wɔːd] adj fâcheux

(-euse), malencontreux(-euse)

unused¹ [ʌn'ju:zd] adj (clothes) neuf (neuve)

unused² [ʌn'ju:st] adj: **to be ~ to sth/to doing sth** ne pas avoir l'habitude de qch/de faire qch

unusual [ʌn'ju:ʒuəl] adj insolite, exceptionnel(le), rare

unveil [ʌn'veɪl] vt dévoiler

unwanted [ʌn'wɔntɪd] adj (child, pregnancy) non désiré(e); (clothes etc) à donner

unwelcome [ʌn'welkəm] adj importun(e); (news) fâcheux(-euse)

unwell [ʌn'wel] adj souffrant(e); **to feel ~** ne pas se sentir bien

unwieldy [ʌn'wi:ldɪ] adj (object) difficile à manier; (system) lourd(e)

unwilling [ʌn'wɪlɪŋ] adj: **to be ~ to do** ne pas vouloir faire; **~ly** adv à contrecœur, contre son gré

unwind [ʌn'waɪnd] (irreg) vt dérouler ♦ vi (relax) se détendre

unwise [ʌn'waɪz] adj irréfléchi(e), imprudent(e)

unwitting [ʌn'wɪtɪŋ] adj involontaire

unworkable [ʌn'wə:kəbl] adj (plan) impraticable

unworthy [ʌn'wə:ðɪ] adj indigne

unwrap [ʌn'ræp] vt défaire; ouvrir

unwritten [ʌn'rɪtn] adj (agreement) tacite

KEYWORD

---

up [ʌp] prep: **he went up the stairs/the hill** il a monté l'escalier/la colline; **the cat was up a tree** le chat était dans un arbre; **they live further up the street** ils habitent plus haut dans la rue

♦ adv **1** (upwards, higher): **up in the sky/the mountains** (là-haut) dans le ciel/les montagnes; **put it a bit higher up** mettez-le un peu plus haut; **up there** là-haut; **up above** au-dessus

2: to be up (out of bed) être levé(e); (prices) avoir augmenté or monté

3: up to (as far as) jusqu'à; **up to now** jusqu'à présent

4: to be up to (depending on): **it's up to you** c'est à vous de décider; (equal to): **he's not up to it** (job, task etc) il n'en est pas capable; (inf: be doing): **what is he up to?** qu'est-ce qu'il peut bien faire?

♦ n: **ups and downs** hauts et bas mpl

up-and-coming [ˈʌpəndˈkʌmɪŋ] adj plein(e) d'avenir or de promesses

upbringing [ˈʌpbrɪŋɪŋ] n éducation f

update [ʌpˈdeɪt] vt mettre à jour

upgrade [ʌpˈgreɪd] vt (house) moderniser; (job) revaloriser; (employee) promouvoir

upheaval [ʌpˈhiːvl] n bouleversement m; branle-bas m

uphill [ˈʌpˈhɪl] adj qui monte; (fig: task) difficile, pénible ♦ adv (face, look) en amont; **to go** ~ monter

uphold [ʌpˈhəuld] (irreg) vt (law, decision) maintenir

upholstery [ʌpˈhəulstəri] n rembourrage m; (cover) tissu m d'ameublement; (of car) garniture f

upkeep [ˈʌpkiːp] n entretien m

upon [əˈpɔn] prep sur

upper [ˈʌpə*] adj supérieur(e); du dessus ♦ n (of shoe) empeigne f; ~-**class** adj de la haute société, aristocratique; ~ **hand** n: **to have the** ~ **hand** avoir le dessus; **what was** ~**most in my mind** ce à quoi je pensais surtout; ~ **sixth** n terminale f

upright [ˈʌpraɪt] adj droit(e); vertical(e); (fig) droit, honnête

uprising [ˈʌpraɪzɪŋ] n soulèvement m, insurrection f

uproar [ˈʌprɔː*] n tumulte m; (protests) tempête f de protestations

uproot [ʌpˈruːt] vt déraciner

upset [n ˈʌpset, vb, adj ʌpˈset] (irreg: like **set**) n bouleversement m; (stomach ~) indigestion f ♦ vt (glass etc) renverser;

(plan) déranger; (person: offend) contrarier; (: grieve) faire de la peine à; bouleverser ♦ adj contrarié(e); peiné(e); (stomach) dérangé(e)

upshot [ˈʌpʃɔt] n résultat m

upside-down [ˈʌpsaɪdˈdaun] adv à l'envers; **to turn** ~ mettre sens dessus dessous

upstairs [ʌpˈstɛəz] adv en haut ♦ adj (room) du dessus, d'en haut ♦ n: **the** ~ l'étage m

upstart [ˈʌpstɑːt] (pej) n parvenu(e)

upstream [ʌpˈstriːm] adv en amont

uptake [ˈʌpteɪk] n: **to be quick/slow on the** ~ comprendre vite/être lent à comprendre

uptight [ʌpˈtaɪt] (inf) adj très tendu(e), crispé(e)

up-to-date [ˈʌptəˈdeɪt] adj moderne; (information) très récent(e)

upturn [ˈʌptəːn] n (in luck) retournement m; (COMM: in market) hausse f

upward [ˈʌpwəd] adj ascendant(e); vers le haut; ~(**s**) adv vers le haut; ~(**s**) **of 200** 200 et plus

urban [ˈəːbən] adj urbain(e); ~ **clearway** n rue f à stationnement interdit

urbane [əːˈbeɪn] adj urbain(e), courtois(e)

urchin [ˈəːtʃɪn] n polisson m

urge [əːdʒ] n besoin m; envie f; forte envie, désir m ♦ vt: **to** ~ **sb to do** exhorter qn à faire, pousser qn à faire; recommander vivement à qn de faire

urgency [ˈəːdʒənsɪ] n urgence f; (of tone) insistance f

urgent [ˈəːdʒənt] adj urgent(e); (tone) insistant(e), pressant(e)

urinal [ˈjuərɪnl] n urinoir m

urine [ˈjuərɪn] n urine f

urn [əːn] n urne f; (also: **tea** ~) fontaine f à thé

US n abbr = **United States**

us [ʌs] pron nous; see also **me**

USA n abbr = **United States of America**

use [n juːs, vb juːz] n emploi m, utilisa-

tion f; usage m; (~fulness) utilité f ♦ vt
se servir de, utiliser, employer; **in ~** en
usage; **out of ~** hors d'usage; **to be**
of ~ servir, être utile; **it's no ~** ça ne
sert à rien; **she ~d to do it** elle le faisait (autrefois), elle avait coutume de le
faire; **~d to: to be ~d to** avoir l'habitude
de de, être habitué(e) à; **~ up** vt finir,
épuiser; consommer; **~d** [juːzd] adj
(car) d'occasion; **~ful** ['juːsful] adj utile; **~fulness** n utilité f; **~less** ['juːslɪs]
adj inutile; (person: hopeless) nul(le); **~r**
['juːzər] n utilisateur(-trice), usager m;
~r-friendly adj (computer) convivial(e),
facile d'emploi

usher ['ʌʃər] n (at wedding ceremony)
placeur m; **~ette** [ʌʃə'rɛt] n (in cinema)
ouvreuse f

usual ['juːʒuəl] adj habituel(le); **as ~**
comme d'habitude; **~ly** ['juːʒuəlɪ] adv
d'habitude, d'ordinaire

utensil [juː'tɛnsl] n ustensile m

uterus ['juːtərəs] n utérus m

utility [juː'tɪlɪtɪ] n utilité f; (also: **public**
~) service public; **~ room** n buanderie
f

utmost ['ʌtməust] adj extrême; le (la)
plus grand(e) ♦ n: **to do one's ~** faire
tout son possible

utter ['ʌtər] adj total(e), complet(-ète)
♦ vt (words) prononcer, proférer;
(sounds) émettre; **~ance** n paroles fpl;
~ly adv complètement, totalement

U-turn ['juː'təːn] n demi-tour m

V, v

v. abbr = **verse**; **versus**; **volt**; (= vide)
voir

vacancy ['veɪkənsɪ] n (BRIT: job) poste
vacant; (room) chambre f disponible;
"no vacancies" "complet"

vacant ['veɪkənt] adj (seat etc) libre,
disponible; (expression) distrait(e)

vacate [və'keɪt] vt quitter

vacation [və'keɪʃən] n vacances fpl

vaccinate ['væksɪneɪt] vt vacciner

vacuum ['vækjum] n vide m; **~ clean-**
er n aspirateur m; **~-packed** adj em-
ballé(e) sous vide

vagina [və'dʒaɪnə] n vagin m

vagrant ['veɪgrənt] n vagabond(e)

vague [veɪg] adj vague, imprécis(e);
(blurred: photo, outline) flou(e); **~ly** adv
vaguement

vain [veɪn] adj (useless) vain(e); (conceited) vaniteux(-euse); **in ~** en vain

valentine ['væləntaɪn] n (also: ~ **card**)
carte f de la Saint-Valentin; (person)
bien-aimé(e) (le jour de la Saint-
Valentin); **V~'s day** n Saint-Valentin f

valiant ['vælɪənt] adj vaillant(e)

valid ['vælɪd] adj valable; (document)
valable, valide

valley ['vælɪ] n vallée f

valour ['vælər] (US **valor**) n courage m

valuable ['væljuəbl] adj (jewel) de valeur; (time, help) précieux(-euse); **~s** npl
objets mpl de valeur

valuation [vælju'eɪʃən] n (price) estimation f; (quality) appréciation f

value ['væljuː] n valeur f ♦ vt (fix price)
évaluer, expertiser; (appreciate) apprécier;
~ added tax (BRIT) n taxe f à la
valeur ajoutée; **~d** adj (person) esti-
mé(e); (advice) précieux(-euse)

valve [vælv] n (in machine) soupape f,
valve f; (MED) valve, valvule f

van [væn] n (AUT) camionnette f

vandal ['vændl] n vandale m/f; **~ism** n
vandalisme m; **~ize** vt saccager

vanguard ['væŋgɑːd] n (fig): **in the ~**
of à l'avant-garde de

vanilla [və'nɪlə] n vanille f

vanish ['vænɪʃ] vi disparaître

vanity ['vænɪtɪ] n vanité f

vantage point ['vɑːntɪdʒ-] n bonne
position

vapour ['veɪpər] (US **vapor**) n vapeur f;
(on window) buée f

variable ['vɛərɪəbl] adj variable; (mood)
changeant(e)

variance ['vɛərɪəns] n: **to be at ~**

(with) être en désaccord (avec); *(facts)* être en contradiction (avec)

varicose ['værɪkəʊs] *adj*: **~ veins** varices *fpl*

varied ['veərɪd] *adj* varié(e), divers(e)

variety [və'raɪətɪ] *n* variété *f*; *(quantity)* nombre *m*, quantité *f*; **~ show** *n* (spectacle *m* de) variétés *fpl*

various ['veərɪəs] *adj* divers(e), différent(e); *(several)* divers, plusieurs

varnish ['vɑːnɪʃ] *n* vernis *m* ♦ *vt* vernir

vary ['veərɪ] *vt, vi* varier, changer

vase [vɑːz] *n* vase *m*

Vaseline ® ['væsɪliːn] *n* vaseline *f*

vast [vɑːst] *adj* vaste, immense; *(amount, success)* énorme

VAT [væt] *n abbr* (= value added tax) TVA *f*

vat [væt] *n* cuve *f*

vault [vɔːlt] *n* (of roof) voûte *f*; (tomb) caveau *m*; (in bank) salle *f* des coffres; chambre *f* forte ♦ *vt* (also: **~ over**) sauter (d'un bond)

vaunted ['vɔːntɪd] *adj*: **much-~** tant vanté(e)

VCR *n abbr* = **video cassette recorder**

VD *n abbr* = **venereal disease**

VDU *n abbr* = **visual display unit**

veal [viːl] *n* veau *m*

veer [vɪə*r*] *vi* tourner; virer

vegan ['viːgən] *n* végétalien(ne)

vegeburger ['vedʒɪbɜːgə*r*] *n* burger végétarien

vegetable ['vedʒtəbl] *n* légume *m* ♦ *adj* végétal(e)

vegetarian [vedʒɪ'teərɪən] *adj, n* végétarien(ne)

vehement ['viːɪmənt] *adj* violent(e), impétueux(-euse); *(impassioned)* ardent(e)

vehicle ['viːɪkl] *n* véhicule *m*

veil [veɪl] *n* voile *m*

vein [veɪn] *n* veine *f*; (on leaf) nervure *f*

velocity [vɪ'lɒsɪtɪ] *n* vitesse *f*

velvet ['velvɪt] *n* velours *m*

vending machine ['vendɪŋ-] *n* distributeur *m* automatique

veneer [və'nɪə*r*] *n* (on furniture) placage *m*; (fig) vernis *m*

venereal [vɪ'nɪərɪəl] *adj*: **~ disease** maladie vénérienne

Venetian blind [vɪ'niːʃən-] *n* store vénitien

vengeance ['vendʒəns] *n* vengeance *f*; **with a ~** (fig) vraiment, pour de bon

venison ['venɪsn] *n* venaison *f*

venom ['venəm] *n* venin *m*

vent [vent] *n* conduit *m* d'aération; (in dress, jacket) fente *f* ♦ *vt* (fig: one's feelings) donner libre cours à

ventilator ['ventɪleɪtə*r*] *n* ventilateur *m*

ventriloquist [ven'trɪləkwɪst] *n* ventriloque *m/f*

venture ['ventʃə*r*] *n* entreprise *f* ♦ *vt* risquer, hasarder ♦ *vi* s'aventurer, se risquer

venue ['venjuː] *n* lieu *m*

verb [vɜːb] *n* verbe *m*; **~al** *adj* verbal(e); (translation) littéral(e)

verbatim [vɜː'beɪtɪm] *adj, adv* mot pour mot

verdict ['vɜːdɪkt] *n* verdict *m*

verge [vɜːdʒ] *n* (BRIT) bord *m*, bas-côté *m*; **"soft ~s"** (BRIT: AUT) "accotement non stabilisé"; **on the ~ of doing** sur le point de faire; **~ on** *vt fus* approcher de

verify ['verɪfaɪ] *vt* vérifier; (confirm) confirmer

vermin ['vɜːmɪn] *npl* animaux *mpl* nuisibles; (insects) vermine *f*

vermouth ['vɜːməθ] *n* vermouth *m*

versatile ['vɜːsətaɪl] *adj* polyvalent(e)

verse [vɜːs] *n* (poetry) vers *mpl*; (stanza) strophe *f*; (in Bible) verset *m*

version ['vɜːʃən] *n* version *f*

versus ['vɜːsəs] *prep* contre

vertical ['vɜːtɪkl] *adj* vertical(e) ♦ *n* verticale *f*

vertigo ['vɜːtɪgəʊ] *n* vertige *m*

verve [vɜːv] *n* brio *m*, enthousiasme *m*

very ['verɪ] *adv* très ♦ *adj*: **the ~ book which** le livre même que; **the ~ last** le tout dernier; **at the ~ least** tout au moins; ~ **much** beaucoup

vessel ['vɛsl] n (ANAT, NAUT) vaisseau m; (container) récipient m

vest [vɛst] n (BRIT) tricot m de corps; (US: waistcoat) gilet m

vested interest n (COMM) droits acquis

vet [vɛt] n abbr (BRIT: veterinary surgeon) vétérinaire m/f ♦ vt examiner soigneusement

veteran ['vɛtərn] n vétéran m; (also: war ~) ancien combattant

veterinary surgeon ['vɛtrɪnərɪ] (BRIT), **veterinarian** [vɛtrɪ'nɛərɪən] (US) n vétérinaire m/f

veto ['viːtəu] (pl ~es) n veto m ♦ vt opposer son veto à

vex [vɛks] vt fâcher, contrarier; ~**ed** adj (question) controversé(e)

via ['vaɪə] prep par, via

viable ['vaɪəbl] adj viable

vibrate [vaɪ'breɪt] vi vibrer

vicar ['vɪkəʳ] n pasteur m (de l'Église anglicane); ~**age** n presbytère m

vicarious [vɪ'kɛərɪəs] adj indirect(e)

vice [vaɪs] n (evil) vice m; (TECH) étau m

vice- [vaɪs] prefix vice-

vice squad n ≈ brigade mondaine

vice versa ['vaɪsɪ'vɜːsə] adv vice versa

vicinity [vɪ'sɪnɪtɪ] n environs mpl, alentours mpl

vicious ['vɪʃəs] adj (remark) cruel(le), méchant(e); (blow) brutal(e); (dog) méchant(e), dangereux(-euse); (horse) vicieux(-euse); ~ **circle** n cercle vicieux

victim ['vɪktɪm] n victime f

victor ['vɪktəʳ] n vainqueur m

Victorian [vɪk'tɔːrɪən] adj victorien(ne)

victory ['vɪktərɪ] n victoire f

video ['vɪdɪəu] cpd vidéo inv ♦ n (~ film) vidéo f; (also: ~ **cassette**) vidéocassette f; (also: ~ **cassette recorder**) magnétoscope m; ~ **tape** n bande f vidéo inv; (cassette) vidéocassette f; ~ **wall** n mur m d'images vidéo

vie [vaɪ] vi: **to ~ with** rivaliser avec

Vienna [vɪ'ɛnə] n Vienne f

Vietnam ['vjɛt'næm] n Viêt-Nam m,

Vietnam m; ~**ese** [vjɛtnə'miːz] adj vietnamien(ne) ♦ n inv Vietnamien(ne); (LING) vietnamien m

view [vjuː] n vue f; (opinion) avis m, vue f ♦ vt voir, regarder; (situation) considérer; (house) visiter; **in full ~ of** sous les yeux de; **in ~ of the weather/the fact that** étant donné le temps/que; **in my ~** à mon avis; ~**er** n (TV) téléspectateur(-trice); ~**finder** n viseur m; ~**point** n point m de vue

vigorous ['vɪgərəs] adj vigoureux(-euse)

vile [vaɪl] adj (action) vil(e); (smell, food) abominable; (temper) massacrant(e)

villa ['vɪlə] n villa f

village ['vɪlɪdʒ] n village m; ~**r** n villageois(e)

villain ['vɪlən] n (scoundrel) scélérat m; (BRIT: criminal) bandit m; (in novel etc) traître m

vindicate ['vɪndɪkeɪt] vt (person) innocenter; (action) justifier

vindictive [vɪn'dɪktɪv] adj vindicatif(-ive), rancunier(-ère)

vine [vaɪn] n vigne f; (climbing plant) plante grimpante

vinegar ['vɪnɪgəʳ] n vinaigre m

vineyard ['vɪnjɑːd] n vignoble m

vintage ['vɪntɪdʒ] n (year) année f, millésime m; ~ **car** n voiture f d'époque; ~ **wine** n vin m de grand cru

viola [vɪ'əulə] n (MUS) alto m

violate ['vaɪəleɪt] vt violer

violence ['vaɪələns] n violence f

violent ['vaɪələnt] adj violent(e)

violet ['vaɪələt] adj violet(te) ♦ n (colour) violet m; (plant) violette f

violin [vaɪə'lɪn] n violon m; ~**ist** [vaɪə'lɪnɪst] n violoniste m/f

VIP n abbr (= very important person) V.I.P. f

virgin ['vɜːdʒɪn] n vierge f ♦ adj vierge

Virgo ['vɜːgəu] n la Vierge

virile ['vɪraɪl] adj viril(e)

virtually ['vɜːtjuəlɪ] adv (almost) pratiquement

virtual reality ['vəːtjuəl-] n (COMPUT) réalité virtuelle

virtue ['vəːtjuː] n vertu f; (advantage) mérite m, avantage m; **by ~ of** en vertu or en raison de; **virtuous** adj vertueux(-euse)

virus ['vaɪərəs] n (COMPUT) virus m

visa ['viːzə] n visa m

visibility [vɪzɪ'bɪlɪtɪ] n visibilité f

visible ['vɪzəbl] adj visible

vision ['vɪʒən] n (sight) vue f, vision f; (foresight, in dream) vision f

visit ['vɪzɪt] n visite f; (stay) séjour m ♦ vt (person) rendre visite à; (place) visiter; **~ing hours** npl (in hospital etc) heures fpl de visite; **~or** n visiteur(-euse); (to one's house) visite f, invité(e); **~or centre** n hall m or centre m d'accueil

visor ['vaɪzə*] n visière f

vista ['vɪstə] n vue f

visual ['vɪzjuəl] adj visuel(le); **~ aid** n support visuel; **~ display unit** n console f de visualisation, visuel m; **~ize** vt se représenter, s'imaginer; **~ly-impaired** adj malvoyant(e)

vital ['vaɪtl] adj vital(e); (person) plein(e) d'entrain; **~ly** adv (important) absolument; **~ statistics** npl (fig) mensurations fpl

vitamin ['vɪtəmɪn] n vitamine f

vivacious [vɪ'veɪʃəs] adj animé(e), qui a de la vivacité

vivid ['vɪvɪd] adj (account) vivant(e); (light, imagination) vif (vive); **~ly** adv (describe) d'une manière vivante; (remember) de façon précise

V-neck ['viːnɛk] n décolleté m en V

vocabulary [vəu'kæbjuları] n vocabulaire m

vocal ['vəukl] adj vocal(e); (articulate) qui sait s'exprimer; **~ cords** npl cordes vocales

vocation [vəu'keɪʃən] n vocation f; **~al** adj professionnel(le)

vociferous [və'sɪfərəs] adj bruyant(e)

vodka ['vɔdkə] n vodka f

vogue [vəug] n: **in ~** en vogue f

voice [vɔɪs] n voix f ♦ vt (opinion) exprimer, formuler; **~ mail** n (system) messagerie f vocale; (device) boîte f vocale

void [vɔɪd] n vide m ♦ adj nul(le); **~ of** vide de, dépourvu(e) de

volatile ['vɔlətaɪl] adj volatil(e); (person) versatile; (situation) explosif(-ive)

volcano [vɔl'keɪnəu] (pl **~es**) n volcan m

volition [və'lɪʃən] n: **of one's own ~** de son propre gré

volley ['vɔlɪ] n (of gunfire) salve f; (of stones etc) grêle f, volée f; (of questions) multitude f, série f; (TENNIS etc) volée f; **~ball** n volley(-ball) m

volt [vəult] n volt m; **~age** n tension f, voltage m

volume ['vɔljuːm] n volume m

voluntarily ['vɔləntrɪlɪ] adv volontairement

voluntary ['vɔləntəri] adj volontaire; (unpaid) bénévole

volunteer [vɔlən'tɪə*] n volontaire m/f ♦ vi (MIL) s'engager comme volontaire; **to ~ to do** se proposer pour faire

vomit ['vɔmɪt] n vomi m, vi vomir

vote [vəut] n vote m, suffrage m; (cast) voix f, vote; (franchise) droit m de vote ♦ vt (elect): **to be ~d chairman** etc être élu président etc; (propose): **to ~ that** proposer que ♦ vi voter; **~ of thanks** n discours m de remerciement; **~r** n électeur(-trice); **voting** n scrutin m, vote m

voucher ['vautʃə*] n (for meal, petrol, gift) bon m

vouch for ['vautʃ-] vt fus se porter garant de

vow [vau] n vœu m, serment m ♦ vi jurer

vowel ['vauəl] n voyelle f

voyage ['vɔɪɪdʒ] n voyage m par mer, traversée f; (by spacecraft) voyage

vulgar ['vʌlgə*] adj vulgaire

vulnerable ['vʌlnərəbl] adj vulnérable

vulture ['vʌltʃə*] n vautour m

W, w

wad [wɔd] n (of cotton wool, paper) tampon m; (of banknotes etc) liasse f
waddle ['wɔdl] vi se dandiner
wade [weɪd] vi: **to ~ through** marcher dans, patauger dans; (fig: book) s'évertuer à lire
wafer ['weɪfəʳ] n (CULIN) gaufrette f
waffle ['wɔfl] n (CULIN) gaufre f; (inf) verbiage m, remplissage m ♦ vi parler pour ne rien dire, faire du remplissage
waft [wɔft] vt porter ♦ vi flotter
wag [wæg] vt agiter, remuer ♦ vi remuer
wage [weɪdʒ] n (also: **~s**) salaire m, paye f ♦ vt: **to ~ war** faire la guerre; **~ earner** n salarié(e); **~ packet** n (enveloppe f de) paye f
wager ['weɪdʒəʳ] n pari m
wag(g)on ['wægən] n (horse-drawn) chariot m; (BRIT: RAIL) wagon m (de marchandises)
wail [weɪl] n gémir; (siren) hurler
waist [weɪst] n taille f; **~coat** (BRIT) n gilet m; **~line** n (tour m de) taille f
wait [weɪt] n attente f ♦ vi attendre; **to keep sb ~ing** faire attendre qn; **to ~ for** attendre; **I can't ~ to ...** (fig) je meurs d'envie de ...; **~ behind** vi rester (à attendre); **~ on** vt fus servir; **~er** n garçon m (de café), serveur m; **~ing** n: **"no ~ing"** (BRIT: AUT) "stationnement interdit"; **~ing list** n liste f d'attente; **~ing room** n salle f d'attente; **~ress** n serveuse f
waive [weɪv] vt renoncer à, abandonner
wake [weɪk] (pt **woke, waked**, pp **woken, waked**) vt (also: **~ up**) réveiller ♦ vi (also: **~ up**) se réveiller ♦ n (for dead person) veillée f mortuaire; (NAUT) sillage m
Wales [weɪlz] n pays m de Galles; **the Prince of ~** le prince de Galles

walk [wɔːk] n promenade f; (short) petit tour; (gait) démarche f; (path) chemin m; (in park etc) allée f ♦ vi marcher; (for pleasure, exercise) se promener ♦ vt (distance) faire à pied; (dog) promener; **10 minutes'** **~ from** à 10 minutes à pied de; **from all ~s of life** de toutes conditions sociales; **~ out** vi (audience) sortir, quitter la salle; (workers) se mettre en grève; **~ out on** (inf) vt fus quitter; **~er** n (person) marcheur (-euse); **~ie-talkie** n talkie-walkie m; **~ing** n marche f à pied; **~ing shoes** npl chaussures fpl de marche; **~ing stick** n canne f; **W~man ®** n Walkman ® m; **~out** n (of workers) grève-surprise f; **~over** (inf) n victoire f or examen etc facile; **~way** n promenade f
wall [wɔːl] n mur m; (of tunnel, cave etc) paroi f; **~ed** adj (city) fortifié(e); (garden) entouré(e) d'un mur, clos(e)
wallet ['wɔlɪt] n portefeuille m
wallflower ['wɔːlflauəʳ] n giroflée f; **to be a ~** (fig) faire tapisserie
wallow ['wɔləu] vi se vautrer
wallpaper ['wɔːlpeɪpəʳ] n papier peint ♦ vt tapisser
walnut ['wɔːlnʌt] n noix f; (tree, wood) noyer m
walrus ['wɔːlrəs] (pl **~** or **~es**) n morse m
waltz [wɔːlts] n valse f ♦ vi valser
wand [wɔnd] n (also: **magic ~**) baguette f (magique)
wander ['wɔndəʳ] vi (person) errer; (thoughts) vagabonder, errer ♦ vt errer dans
wane [weɪn] vi (moon) décroître; (reputation) décliner
wangle ['wæŋgl] (BRIT: inf) vt se débrouiller pour avoir; carotter
want [wɔnt] vt (wish for) désirer; (need) avoir besoin de ♦ n: **for ~ of** par manque de, faute de; **~s** npl (needs) besoins mpl; **to ~ to do** vouloir faire; **to ~ sb to do** vouloir que qn fasse; **~ed** adj (criminal)

recherché(e) par la police; **"cook ~ed"** "on recherche un cuisinier"; **~ing** *adj:* **to be found ~ing** ne pas être à la hauteur

war [wɔːⁱ] *n* guerre *f;* **to make ~ (on)** faire la guerre (à)

ward [wɔːd] *n (in hospital)* salle *f;* (POL) canton *m;* (LAW: *child)* pupille *m/f;* **~ off** *vt (attack, enemy)* repousser, éviter

warden ['wɔːdn] *n (of institution)* directeur(-trice); (: *also:* **traffic ~)** contractuel(le); *(of youth hostel)* père *m* ou mère *f* aubergiste

warder ['wɔːdəⁱ] (BRIT) *n* gardien *m* de prison

wardrobe ['wɔːdrəub] *n (cupboard)* armoire *f;* (*clothes)* garde-robe *f;* (THEATRE) costumes *mpl*

warehouse ['wɛəhaus] *n* entrepôt *m*

wares [wɛəz] *npl* marchandises *fpl*

warfare ['wɔːfɛəⁱ] *n* guerre *f*

warhead ['wɔːhɛd] *n* (MIL) ogive *f*

warily ['wɛərɪlɪ] *adv* avec prudence

warm [wɔːm] *adj* chaud(e); *(thanks, welcome, applause, person)* chaleureux(-euse); **it's ~** il fait chaud; **I'm ~** j'ai chaud; **~ up** *vi (person, room)* se réchauffer; *(water)* chauffer; *(athlete)* s'échauffer ♦ *vt (food)* (faire) réchauffer; *(water)* (faire) chauffer; *(engine)* faire chauffer; **~-hearted** *adj* affectueux(-euse); **~ly** *adv* chaudement; chaleureusement; **~th** *n* chaleur *f*

warn [wɔːn] *vt* avertir, prévenir; **to ~ sb (not) to do** conseiller à qn de (ne pas) faire; **~ing** *n* avertissement *m;* *(notice)* avis *m;* *(signal)* avertisseur *m;* **~ing light** *n* avertisseur lumineux; **~ing triangle** *n* (AUT) triangle *m* de présignalisation

warp [wɔːp] *vi (wood)* travailler, se déformer ♦ *vt (fig: character)* pervertir

warrant ['wɔrnt] *n (guarantee)* garantie *f;* (LAW: *to arrest)* mandat *m* d'arrêt; (: *to search)* mandat de perquisition; **~y** *n* garantie *f*

warren ['wɔrən] *n (of rabbits)* terrier *m;*

(fig: of streets etc) dédale *m*

warrior ['wɔrɪəⁱ] *n* guerrier(-ère)

Warsaw ['wɔːsɔː] *n* Varsovie

warship ['wɔːʃɪp] *n* navire *m* de guerre

wart [wɔːt] *n* verrue *f*

wartime ['wɔːtaɪm] *n:* **in ~** en temps de guerre

wary ['wɛərɪ] *adj* prudent(e)

was [wɔz] *pt of* **be**

wash [wɔʃ] *vt* laver ♦ *vi* se laver; *(sea):* **to ~ over/against sth** inonder/ baigner qch ♦ *n (clothes)* lessive *f;* (*~ing programme)* lavage *m;* *(of ship)* sillage *m;* **to have a ~** se laver, faire sa toilette; **to give sth a ~** laver qch; **~ away** *vt (stain)* enlever au lavage; *(subj: river etc)* emporter; **~ off** *vi* partir au lavage; **~ up** *vi* (BRIT) faire la vaisselle; (US) se débarbouiller; **~able** *adj* lavable; **~basin** (US **washbowl**) *n* lavabo *m;* **~cloth** (US) *n* gant *m* de toilette; **~er** *n* (TECH) rondelle *f,* joint *m;* **~ing** *n (dirty)* linge *m;* *(clean)* lessive *f;* **~ing machine** *n* machine à laver; **~ing powder** (BRIT) *n* lessive *f* (en poudre); **~ing-up** *n* vaisselle *f;* **~ing-up liquid** *n* produit *m* pour la vaisselle; **~-out** (inf) *n* désastre *m;* **~room** (US) *n* toilettes *fpl*

wasn't ['wɔznt] = **was not**

wasp [wɔsp] *n* guêpe *f*

wastage ['weistɪdʒ] *n* gaspillage *m;* *(in manufacturing, transport etc)* pertes *fpl,* déchets *mpl;* **natural ~** départs naturels

waste [weist] *n* gaspillage *m;* *(of time)* perte *f;* *(rubbish)* déchets *mpl;* *(also:* **household ~)** ordures *fpl* ♦ *adj (land, ground: in city)* à l'abandon; *(leftover):* **~ material** déchets *mpl* ♦ *vt (squander):* *(time, opportunity)* perdre; **~s** *npl (area)* étendue *f* désertique; **~ away** *vi* dépérir; **~ disposal unit** (BRIT) *n* broyeur *m* d'ordures; **~ful** *adj* gaspilleur(-euse); *(process)* peu économique; **~ ground** (BRIT) *n* terrain *m* vague; **~paper basket** *n* corbeille *f* à papier

watch [wɔtʃ] *n* montre *f;* *(act of ~ing)*

surveillance f; guet m; (MIL: *guards*) garde f; (NAUT: *guards, spell of duty*) quart m ♦ vt (*look at*) observer; (: *match, programme, TV*) regarder; (*spy on, guard*) surveiller; (*be careful with*) faire attention à ♦ vi regarder; (*keep guard*) monter la garde; **~ out** vi faire attention; **~dog** n chien m de garde; (*fig*) gardien(ne); **~ful** adj attentif(-ive), vigilant(e); **~ maker** n horloger(-ère); **~man** (*irreg*) n see **night**; **~strap** n bracelet m de montre

water ['wɔːtə^r] n eau f ♦ vt (*plant, garden*) arroser ♦ vi (*eyes*) larmoyer; (*mouth*): **it makes my mouth ~** j'en ai l'eau à la bouche; **in British ~s** dans les eaux territoriales britanniques; **~ down** vt (*milk*) couper d'eau; (*fig: story*) édulcorer; **~colour** (US **watercolor**) n aquarelle f; **~cress** n cresson m (de fontaine); **~fall** n chute f d'eau; **~ heater** n chauffe-eau m; **~ing can** n arrosoir m; **~ lily** n nénuphar m; **~line** n (NAUT) ligne f de flottaison; **~logged** adj (*ground*) détrempé(e); **~ main** n canalisation f d'eau; **~melon** n (GEO) ligne f de partage des eaux; (*fig*) moment m critique, point décisif; **~ skiing** n ski m nautique; **~tight** adj étanche; **~works** n (*building*) station f hydraulique; **~y** adj (*coffee, soup*) trop faible; (*eyes*) humide, larmoyant(e)

watt [wɔt] n watt m

wave [weɪv] n vague f; (*of hand*) geste m, signe m; (RADIO) onde f; (*in hair*) ondulation f ♦ vi (*flag*) faire signe de la main; (*grass*) ondoyer ♦ vt (*handkerchief*) agiter; (*stick*) brandir; **~length** n longueur f d'ondes

waver ['weɪvə^r] vi vaciller; (*voice*) trembler; (*person*) hésiter

wavy ['weɪvɪ] adj (*hair, surface*) ondulé(e); (*line*) onduleux(-euse)

wax [wæks] n cire f; (*for skis*) fart m ♦ vt cirer; (*car*) lustrer; (*skis*) farter ♦ vi (*moon*) croître; **~works** npl personnages mpl de cire ♦ n musée m de cire

way [weɪ] n chemin m, voie f; (*distance*) distance f; (*direction*) chemin m, direction f; (*manner*) façon f, manière f; (*habit*) habitude f, façon f; **which ~? - this - that** par où? - par ici; **on the ~** (*en route*) en route; **to be on one's ~** être en route; **to go out of one's ~ to do** se donner du mal pour faire; **to be in the ~** bloquer le passage; (*fig*) gêner; **to lose one's ~** perdre son chemin; **under ~** en cours; **in a ~** dans un sens; **in some ~s** à certains égards; **no ~!** (*inf*) pas question!; **by the ~ ...** à propos ...; **"~ in"** (BRIT) "entrée"; **"~ out"** (BRIT) "sortie"; **the ~ back** le chemin du retour; **"give ~"** (BRIT: AUT) "cédez le passage"; **~lay** (*irreg*) vt attaquer

wayward ['weɪwəd] adj capricieux (-euse), entêté(e)

W.C. n abbr w.c. mpl, waters mpl

we [wiː] pl pron nous

weak [wiːk] adj faible; (*health*) fragile; (*beam etc*) peu solide; **~en** vi faiblir, décliner ♦ vt affaiblir; **~ling** n (*physically*) gringalet m; (*morally etc*) faible m/f; **~ness** n faiblesse f; (*fault*) point m faible; **to have a ~ness for** avoir un faible pour

wealth [welθ] n (*money, resources*) richesse(s) f(pl); (*of details*) profusion f; **~y** adj riche

wean [wiːn] vt sevrer

weapon ['wepən] n arme f

wear [weə^r] (*pt* **wore**, *pp* **worn**) n (*use*) usage m; (*deterioration through use*) usure f; (*clothing*): **sports/babywear** vêtements mpl de sport/pour bébés ♦ vt (*clothes*) porter; (*put on*) mettre; (*damage: through use*) user ♦ vi (*last*) faire de l'usage; (*rub: become thin*) s'user; **town/evening ~** tenue f de ville/ soirée; **~ away** vt user, ronger ♦ vi s'effacer; **~ down** vt user; (*strength, person*) épuiser; **~ off** vi disparaître; **~ out** vt user; (*person, strength*) épuiser; **~ and tear** n usure f

weary ['wɪərɪ] adj (tired) épuisé(e); (dispirited) las (lasse), abattu(e) ♦ vi: **to ~ of** se lasser de

weasel ['wi:zl] n (ZOOL) belette f

weather ['weðər] n temps m ♦ vt (tempest, crisis) essuyer, réchapper à; survivre à; **under the ~** (fig: ill) mal fichu(e); **~-beaten** adj (person) hâlé(e); (building) dégradé(e) par les intempéries; **~cock** n girouette f; **~ forecast** n prévisions fpl météorologiques, météo f; **~ man** (irreg) (inf) n météorologue m; **~ vane** n = **weathercock**

weave [wi:v] (pt **wove**, pp **woven**) vt (cloth) tisser; (basket) tresser; **~r** n tisserand(e)

web [web] n (of spider) toile f; (on foot) palmure f; (fabric, also fig) tissu m; **the (World Wide) W~** le Web

website ['websaɪt] n (COMPUT) site m Web

wed [wed] (pt, pp **wedded**) vt épouser ♦ vi se marier

we'd [wi:d] = **we had**; **we would**

wedding [wedɪŋ] n mariage m; **silver/ golden ~ (anniversary)** noces fpl d'argent/d'or; **~ day** n jour m du mariage; **~ dress** n robe f de mariée; **~ ring** n alliance f

wedge [wedʒ] n (of wood etc) coin m, cale f; (of cake) part f ♦ vt (fix) caler; (pack tightly) enfoncer

Wednesday ['wɛnzdɪ] n mercredi m

wee [wi:] (SCOTTISH) adj (tout(e)) petit(e)

weed [wi:d] n mauvaise herbe f ♦ vt désherber; **~killer** n désherbant m; **~y** adj (man) gringalet

week [wi:k] n semaine f; **a ~ today/on Friday** aujourd'hui/vendredi en huit; **~day** n jour m de semaine; (COMM) jour ouvrable; **~end** n week-end m; **~ly** adv une fois par semaine, chaque semaine ♦ adj hebdomadaire

weep [wi:p] (pt, pp **wept**) vi (person) pleurer; **~ing willow** n saule pleureur

weigh [weɪ] vt, vi peser; **to ~ anchor** lever l'ancre; **~ down** vt (person, animal) écraser; (fig: with worry) accabler; **~ up** vt examiner

weight [weɪt] n poids m; **to lose/put on ~** maigrir/grossir; **~ing** (allowance) n indemnité f, allocation f; **~lifter** n haltérophile m; **~lifting** n haltérophilie f; **~y** adj lourd(e); (important) de poids, important(e)

weir [wɪər] n barrage m

weird [wɪəd] adj bizarre

welcome ['wɛlkəm] adj bienvenu(e) ♦ n accueil m ♦ vt accueillir; (also: **bid ~**) souhaiter la bienvenue à; (be glad of) se réjouir de; **thank you - you're ~!** merci - de rien or il n'y a pas de quoi!

welder ['wɛldər] n soudeur(-euse)

welfare ['wɛlfɛər] n (wellbeing) bien-être m; (social aid) assistance sociale; **~ state** n État-providence m

well [wel] n puits m ♦ adv bien ♦ adj: **to be ~** aller bien ♦ excl eh bien!; (relief also) bon!; (resignation) enfin!; **as ~** aussi, également; **as ~ as** en plus de; **~ done!** bravo!; **get ~ soon** remets-toi vite!; **to do ~** bien réussir; (business) prospérer; **~ up** vi monter

we'll [wi:l] = **we will**; **we shall**

well: ~-behaved adj sage, obéissant(e); **~-being** n bien-être m; **~-built** adj (person) bien bâti(e); **~-deserved** adj (bien) mérité(e); **~-dressed** adj bien habillé(e); **~-heeled** (inf) adj (wealthy) nanti(e)

wellingtons ['wɛlɪŋtənz] npl (also: **wellington boots**) bottes fpl de caoutchouc

well: ~-known adj (person) bien connu(e); **~-mannered** adj bien élevé(e); **~-meaning** adj bien intentionné(e); **~-off** adj aisé(e), riche; **~-read** adj cultivé(e); **~-to-do** adj aisé(e); **~-wishers** npl amis mpl et admirateurs mpl; (friends) amis mpl

Welsh [welʃ] adj gallois(e) ♦ n (LING) gallois m; **the ~** npl (people) les Gallois mpl; **~ Assembly** n Parlement m gallois; **~man** (irreg) n Gallois m;

~woman (irreg) n Galloise f

went [wɛnt] pt of **go**

wept [wɛpt] pt, pp of **weep**

were [wəːʳ] pt of **be**

we're [wɪəʳ] = **we are**

weren't [wəːnt] = **were not**

west [wɛst] n ouest m ♦ adj ouest inv, de or à l'ouest ♦ adv à or vers l'ouest; **the W~** l'Occident m, l'Ouest; **the W~ Country** (BRIT) ♦ n le sud-ouest de l'Angleterre; **~erly** adj (wind) d'ouest; (point) à l'ouest; **~ern** adj occidental(e), de or à l'ouest ♦ n (CINEMA) western m; **W~ Indian** adj antillais(e) ♦ n Antillais(e); **W~ Indies** npl Antilles fpl; **~ward(s)** adv vers l'ouest

wet [wɛt] adj mouillé(e); (damp) humide; (soaked) trempé(e); (rainy) pluvieux(-euse) ♦ n (BRIT: POL) modéré m du parti conservateur; **to get ~** se mouiller; "**~ paint**" "attention peinture fraîche"; **~ suit** n combinaison f de plongée

we've [wiːv] = **we have**

whack [wæk] vt donner un grand coup à

whale [weɪl] n (ZOOL) baleine f

wharf [wɔːf] (pl **wharves**) n quai m

KEYWORD

what [wɔt] adj quel(le); **what size is he?** quelle taille fait-il?; **what colour is it?** de quelle couleur est-ce?; **what books do you want?** quels livres vous faut-il?; **what a mess!** quel désordre!

♦ pron 1 (interrogative) que, prep +quoi; **what are you doing?** que faites-vous?; **what's happening?** qu'est-ce que vous faites?; **what is happening?** qu'est-ce qui se passe?, que se passe-t-il?; **what are you talking about?** de quoi parlez-vous?; **what is it called?** comment est-ce que ça s'appelle?; **what about me?** et moi?; **what about doing ...?** et si on faisait ...?

2 (relative: subject) ce qui; (: direct object) ce que; (: indirect object) ce +prep

+quoi, ce dont; **I saw what you did/was on the table** j'ai vu ce que vous avez fait/ce qui était sur le table; **tell me what you remember** dites-moi ce dont vous vous souvenez

♦ excl (disbelieving) quoi, comment!

whatever [wɔt'ɛvəʳ] adj: **~ book** quel que soit le livre que (or qui) +sub; n'importe quel livre ♦ pron: **do ~ is necessary** faites (tout) ce qui est nécessaire; **~ happens** quoi qu'il arrive; **no reason ~** pas la moindre raison; **nothing ~** rien du tout

whatsoever [wɔtsəu'ɛvəʳ] adj = **whatever**

wheat [wiːt] n blé m, froment m

wheedle [wiːdl] vt: **to ~ sb into doing sth** cajoler or enjôler qn pour qu'il fasse qch; **to ~ sth out of sb** obtenir qch de qn par des cajoleries

wheel [wiːl] n roue f; (also: steering **~**) volant m; (NAUT) gouvernail m ♦ vt (pram etc) pousser ♦ vi (birds) tournoyer; (also: **~ round**: person) virevolter; **~barrow** n brouette f; **~chair** n fauteuil roulant; **~ clamp** n (AUT) sabot m (de Denver)

wheeze [wiːz] vi respirer bruyamment

KEYWORD

when [wɛn] adv quand; **when did he go?** quand est-ce qu'il est parti?

♦ conj 1 (at, during, after the time that) quand, lorsque; **she was reading when I came in** elle lisait quand or lorsque je suis entré

2 (on, at which): **on the day when I met him** le jour où je l'ai rencontré

3 (whereas) alors que; **I thought I was wrong when in fact I was right** j'ai cru que j'avais tort alors qu'en fait j'avais raison

whenever [wɛn'ɛvəʳ] adv quand donc ♦ conj quand; (every time that) chaque fois que

where [wɛəʳ] *adv, conj* où; **this is ~** c'est là que; **~abouts** ['wɛərəbaʊts] *adv* où donc ♦ *n*: **nobody knows his ~abouts** personne ne sait où il se trouve; **~as** [wɛər'æz] *conj* alors que; **~by** *adv* par lequel (or laquelle *etc*); **~ever** [wɛər'ɛvəʳ] *adv* où donc ♦ *conj* où que +*sub*; **~withal** ['wɛəwɪðɔːl] *n* moyens *mpl*

whether ['wɛðəʳ] *conj* si; **I don't know ~ to accept or not** je ne sais pas si je dois accepter ou non; **it's doubtful ~** il est peu probable que +*sub*; **~ you go or not** que vous y alliez ou non

---
KEYWORD
---

which [wɪtʃ] *adj* (*interrogative: direct, indirect*) quel(le); **which picture do you want?** quel tableau voulez-vous?; **which one?** lequel (laquelle)?; **in which case** auquel cas
♦ *pron* **1** (*interrogative*) lequel (laquelle), lesquels (lesquelles) *pl*; **I don't mind which** peu importe lequel; **which (of these) are yours?** lesquels sont à vous?; **tell me which you want** dites-moi lequel or ceux que vous voulez

2 (*relative: subject*) qui; (: *object*) que, *prep* +lequel (laquelle); **the apple which you ate/which is on the table** la pomme que vous avez mangée/qui est sur la table; **the chair on which you are sitting** la chaise sur laquelle vous êtes assis; **the book of which you spoke** le livre dont vous avez parlé; **he knew, which is true/I feared it** le savait, ce qui est vrai/ce que je craignais; **after which** après quoi

whichever [wɪtʃ'ɛvəʳ] *adj*: **take ~ book you prefer** prenez le livre que vous préférez, peu importe lequel; **~ book you take** quel que soit le livre que vous preniez

while [waɪl] *n* moment *m* ♦ *conj* pendant que; (*as long as*) tant que;

(*whereas*) alors que; bien que +*sub*; **for a ~** pendant quelque temps; **~ away** *vt* (*time*) (faire) passer

whim [wɪm] *n* caprice *m*

whimper ['wɪmpəʳ] *vi* geindre

whimsical ['wɪmzɪkl] *adj* (*person*) capricieux(-euse); (*look, story*) étrange

whine [waɪn] *vi* gémir, geindre

whip [wɪp] *n* fouet *m*; (*for riding*) cravache *f*; (POL: *person*) chef de file assurant la discipline dans son groupe parlementaire ♦ *vt* fouetter; (*eggs*) battre; **~ped cream** *n* crème fouettée; **~round** (BRIT) *n* collecte *f*

whirl [wəːl] *vi* tournoyer; (*dancers*) tournoyer ♦ *vt* faire tournoyer; faire tournoyer; **~pool** *n* tourbillon *m*; **~wind** *n* tornade *f*

whirr [wəːʳ] *vi* (*motor etc*) ronronner; (: *louder*) vrombir

whisk [wɪsk] *n* (CULIN) fouet *m* ♦ *vt* fouetter; (*eggs*) battre; **to ~ sb away** or **off** emmener qn rapidement

whiskers ['wɪskəz] *npl* (*of animal*) moustaches *fpl*; (*of man*) favoris *mpl*

whisky ['wɪskɪ] (IRELAND, US **whiskey**) *n* whisky *m*

whisper ['wɪspəʳ] *vt, vi* chuchoter

whistle ['wɪsl] *n* (*sound*) sifflement *m*; (*object*) sifflet *m* ♦ *vi* siffler

white [waɪt] *adj* blanc (blanche); (*with fear*) blême ♦ *n* blanc *m*; (*person*) blanc (blanche); **~ coffee** (BRIT) *n* café *m* au lait, (café) crème *m*; **~-collar worker** *n* employé(e) de bureau; **~ elephant** (*fig*) objet dispendieux et superflu; **~ lie** *n* pieux mensonge; **W~ Pages** (US) *npl* (TEL) pages *fpl* blanches; **~ paper** *n* (POL) livre blanc; **~wash** *vt* blanchir à la chaux; (*fig*) blanchir ♦ *n* (*paint*) blanc *m* de chaux

whiting ['waɪtɪŋ] *n inv* (*fish*) merlan *m*

Whitsun ['wɪtsn] *n* la Pentecôte

whizz [wɪz] *vi*: **to ~ past** or **by** passer à toute vitesse; **~ kid** (*inf*) *n* petit prodige

who [huː] *pron* qui; **~dunit** [huː'dʌnɪt] (*inf*) *n* roman policier

whoever [huːˈɛvəʳ] *pron*: ~ **finds it** celui (celle) qui le trouve(, qui que ce soit), quiconque le trouve; **ask ~ you like** demandez à qui vous voulez; ~ **he marries** quelle que soit la personne qu'il épouse; ~ **told you that?** qui a bien pu vous dire ça?

whole [həul] *adj* (*complete*) entier(-ère), tout(e); (*not broken*) intact(e), complet(-ète) ♦ *n* (*all*): **the ~ of** la totalité de, tout(e) le (la); (*entire unit*) tout *m*; **the ~ of the town** la ville tout entière; **on the ~, as a ~** dans l'ensemble; **~food**s *n(pl)* aliments complets; **~hearted** *adj* sans réserve(s); **~meal** (*BRIT*) *adj* (*bread, flour*) complet(-ète); **~sale** *n* (*vente f en*) gros *m* ♦ *adj* (*price*) de gros; (*destruction*) systématique ♦ *adv* en gros; **~saler** *n* grossiste *m/f*; **~some** *adj* sain(e); **~wheat** *adj* = **wholemeal**; **wholly** ['həulɪ] *adv* entièrement, tout à fait

KEYWORD

whom [huːm] *pron* 1 (*interrogative*) qui; **whom did you see?** qui avez-vous vu?; **to whom did you give it?** à qui l'avez-vous donné?
2 (*relative*) que, *prep* +qui; **the man whom I saw/to whom I spoke** l'homme que j'ai vu/à qui j'ai parlé

whooping cough ['huːpɪŋ-] *n* coqueluche *f*

whore [hɔːʳ] *n* (*inf: pej*) putain *f*

KEYWORD

whose [huːz] *adj* 1 (*possessive: interrogative*): **whose book is this?** à qui est ce livre?; **whose pencil have you taken?** à qui est le crayon que vous avez pris?, c'est le crayon de qui que vous avez pris?; **whose daughter are you?** de qui êtes-vous la fille?
2 (*possessive: relative*): **the man whose son you rescued** l'homme dont or de qui vous avez sauvé le fils; **the girl**

whose sister you were speaking to la fille à la sœur de qui or à laquelle vous parliez; **the woman whose car was stolen** la femme dont la voiture a été volée
♦ *pron* à qui; **whose is this?** à qui est ceci?; **I know whose it is** je sais à qui c'est

why [waɪ] *adv* pourquoi ♦ *excl* eh bien!, tiens!; **the reason ~** la raison pour laquelle; **tell me ~** dites-moi pourquoi; ~ **not?** pourquoi pas?

wicked ['wɪkɪd] *adj* mauvais(e), méchant(e); (*crime*) pervers(e); (*mischievous*) malicieux(-euse)

wicket ['wɪkɪt] *n* (*CRICKET*) guichet *m*; terrain *m* (*entre les deux guichets*)

wide [waɪd] *adj* large; (*area, knowledge*) vaste, très étendu(e); (*choice*) grand(e) ♦ *adv*: **to open ~** ouvrir tout grand; **to shoot ~** tirer à côté; **~-awake** *adj* bien éveillé(e); **~ly** *adv* (*differing*) radicalement; (*spaced*) sur une grande étendue; (*believed*) généralement; (*travel*) beaucoup; **~n** *vt* élargir ♦ *vi* s'élargir; ~ **open** *adj* grand(e) ouvert(e); **~spread** *adj* (*belief etc*) très répandu(e)

widow ['wɪdəu] *n* veuve *f*; **~ed** *adj* veuf (veuve); **~er** *n* veuf *m*

width [wɪdθ] *n* largeur *f*

wield [wiːld] *vt* (*power*) exercer

wife [waɪf] (*pl* **wives**) *n* femme *f*, épouse *f*

wig [wɪg] *n* perruque *f*

wiggle ['wɪgl] *vt* agiter, remuer

wild [waɪld] *adj* sauvage; (*sea*) déchaîné(e); (*idea, life*) fou (folle); (*behaviour*) extravagant(e), déchaîné(e); **to make a ~ guess** émettre une hypothèse à tout hasard; **~card** *n* (*COMPUT*) (caractère *m*) joker *m*; **~erness** ['wɪldənɪs] *n* désert *m*, région *f* sauvage; **~life** *n* (*animals*) faune *f*; **~ly** *adv* (*behave*) de manière déchaînée; (*applaud*) frénétiquement; (*hit, guess*) au hasard; (*happy*) follement; **~s** *npl* (*re-*

mote area) régions *fpl* sauvages

wilful ['wilful] (*US* **willful**) *adj* (*person*) obstiné(e); (*action*) délibéré(e)

KEYWORD
---

will [wil] (*vt: pt, pp* **willed**) *aux vb* **1** (*forming future tense*): **I will finish it tomorrow** je le finirai demain; **I will have finished it by tomorrow** je l'aurai fini d'ici demain; **will you do it? - yes I will/no I won't** le ferez-vous? - oui/non

2 (*in conjectures, predictions*): **he will** *or* **he'll be there by now** il doit être arrivé à l'heure qu'il est; **that will be the postman** ça doit être le facteur

3 (*in commands, requests, offers*): **will you be quiet!** voulez-vous bien vous taire!; **will you help me?** est-ce que vous pouvez m'aider?; **will you have a cup of tea?** voulez-vous une tasse de thé?; **I won't put up with it!** je ne le tolérerai pas!

♦ *vt*: **to will sb to do** souhaiter ardemment que qn fasse; **he willed himself to go on** par un suprême effort de volonté, il continua

♦ *n* volonté *f*; testament *m*

willing ['wiliŋ] *adj* de bonne volonté, serviable; **he's ~ to do it** il est disposé à le faire, il veut bien le faire; **~ly** *adv* volontiers; **~ness** *n* bonne volonté

willow ['wiləu] *n* saule *m*

willpower ['wil'pauə'] *n* volonté *f*

willy-nilly ['wili'nili] *adv* bon gré mal gré

wilt [wilt] *vi* dépérir; (*flower*) se faner

win [win] (*pt, pp* **won**) *n* (*in sports etc*) victoire *f* ♦ *vt* gagner; (*prize*) remporter; (*popularity*) acquérir ♦ *vi* gagner; **~ over** *vt* convaincre; **~ round** (*BRIT*) *vt* = **win over**

wince [wins] *vi* tressaillir

winch [wintʃ] *n* treuil *m*

wind¹ [wind] *n* (*also MED*) vent *m*; (*breath*) souffle *m* ♦ *vt* (*take breath*)

couper le souffle à

wind² [waind] (*pt, pp* **wound**) *vt* enrouler; (*wrap*) envelopper; (*clock, toy*) remonter ♦ *vi* (*road, river*) serpenter; **~ up** *vt* (*clock*) remonter; (*debate*) terminer, clôturer

windfall ['windfɔ:l] *n* coup *m* de chance

winding ['waindiŋ] *adj* (*road*) sinueux(-euse); (*staircase*) tournant(e)

wind instrument ['wind-] *n* (*MUS*) instrument *m* à vent

windmill ['windmil] *n* moulin *m* à vent

window ['windəu] *n* fenêtre *f*; (*in car, train, also:* **~ pane**) vitre *f*; (*in shop etc*) vitrine *f*; **~ box** *n* jardinière *f*; **~ cleaner** *n* (*person*) laveur(-euse) de vitres; **~ ledge** *n* rebord *m* de la fenêtre; **~ pane** *n* vitre *f*, carreau *m*; **~shopping** *n*: **to go ~shopping** faire du lèche-vitrines; **~sill** ['windəusil] *n* (*inside*) appui *m* de la fenêtre; (*outside*) rebord *m* de la fenêtre

windpipe ['windpaip] *n* trachée *f*

wind power ['wind-] *n* énergie éolienne

windscreen ['windskri:n] *n* pare-brise *m inv*; **~ washer** *n* lave-glace *m inv*; **~ wiper** *n* essuie-glace *m inv*

windshield ['windʃi:ld] (*US*) *n* = **windscreen**

windswept ['windswept] *adj* balayé(e) par le vent; (*person*) ébouriffé(e)

windy ['windi] *adj* venteux(-euse); **it's ~** il y a du vent

wine [wain] *n* vin *m*; **~ bar** *n* bar *m* à vin; **~ cellar** *n* cave *f* à vin; **~ glass** *n* verre *m* à vin; **~ list** *n* carte *f* des vins; **~ waiter** *n* sommelier *m*

wing [wiŋ] *n* aile *f*; **~s** *npl* (*THEATRE*) coulisses *fpl*; **~er** *n* (*SPORT*) ailier *m*

wink [wiŋk] *n* clin *m* d'œil ♦ *vi* faire un clin d'œil; (*blink*) cligner des yeux

winner ['winə'] *n* gagnant(e)

winning ['winiŋ] *adj* (*team*) gagnant(e); (*goal*) décisif(-ive); **~s** *npl* gains *mpl*

winter ['wɪntə^r] n hiver m; **in ~** en hiver; **~ sports** npl sports mpl d'hiver; **wintry** adj hivernal(e)

wipe [waɪp] vt: **to give sth a ~** donner un coup de torchon/de chiffon/d'éponge à qch ♦ vt essuyer; (erase: tape) effacer; **~ off** vt enlever; **~ out** vt (debt) éteindre, amortir; (memory) effacer; (destroy) anéantir; **~ up** vt essuyer

wire ['waɪə^r] n fil m (de fer); (ELEC) fil électrique; (TEL) télégramme m ♦ vt (house) faire l'installation électrique de; (also: **~ up**) brancher; (person: send telegram to) télégraphier à; **~less** n (BRIT) poste m de radio; **wiring** n installation f électrique; wiry adj noueux(-euse), nerveux(-euse); (hair) dru(e)

wisdom ['wɪzdəm] n sagesse f; (of action) prudence f; **~ tooth** n dent f de sagesse

wise [waɪz] adj sage, prudent(e); (remark) judicieux(-euse) ♦ suffix: **...wise**: **timewise** etc en ce qui concerne le temps etc

wish [wɪʃ] n (desire) désir m; (specific desire) souhait m, vœu m ♦ vt souhaiter, désirer, vouloir; **best ~es** (on birthday etc) meilleurs vœux; **with best ~es** (in letter) bien amicalement; **to ~ sb goodbye** dire au revoir à qn; **he ~ed me well** il m'a souhaité bonne chance; **to ~ to do/sb to do** désirer or vouloir faire/que qn fasse; **to ~ for** souhaiter; **~ful** adj: **it's ~ful thinking** c'est prendre ses désirs pour des réalités

wistful ['wɪstful] adj mélancolique

wit [wɪt] n (gen pl) intelligence f, esprit m; (presence of mind) présence f d'esprit; (wittiness) esprit; (person) homme/femme d'esprit

witch [wɪtʃ] n sorcière f; **~craft** n sorcellerie f

KEYWORD

with [wɪð, wɪθ] prep 1 (in the company of) avec; (at the home of) chez; **we stayed with friends** nous avons logé chez des amis; **I'll be with you in a minute** je suis à vous dans un instant

2 (descriptive): **a room with a view** une chambre avec vue; **the man with the grey hat/blue eyes** l'homme au chapeau gris/aux yeux bleus

3 (indicating manner, means, cause): **with tears in her eyes** les larmes aux yeux; **to walk with a stick** marcher avec une canne; **red with anger** rouge de colère; **to shake with fear** trembler de peur; **to fill sth with water** remplir qch d'eau

4: **I'm with you** (I understand) je vous suis; **to be with it** (inf: up-to-date) être dans le vent

withdraw [wɪð'drɔː] (irreg) vt retirer ♦ vi se retirer; **~al** n retrait m; **~al symptoms** npl (MED): **to have ~al symptoms** être en état de manque; **~n** adj (person) renfermé(e)

wither ['wɪðə^r] vi (plant) se faner

withhold [wɪθ'həuld] (irreg) vt (money) retenir; (to ~ from) (information) cacher (à); (permission) refuser (à)

within [wɪð'ɪn] prep à l'intérieur de ♦ adv à l'intérieur; **~ his reach** à sa portée; **~ sight of** en vue de; **~ a kilometre of** à moins d'un kilomètre de; **~ the week** avant la fin de la semaine

without [wɪð'aut] prep sans; **~ a coat** sans manteau; **~ speaking** sans parler; **to go ~ sth** se passer de qch

withstand [wɪθ'stænd] (irreg) vt résister à

witness ['wɪtnɪs] n (person) témoin m ♦ vt (event) être témoin de; (document) attester l'authenticité de; **to bear ~ (to)** (fig) attester; **~ box** (US **witness stand**) n barre f des témoins

witty ['wɪtɪ] adj spirituel(le), plein(e) d'esprit

wives [waɪvz] npl of **wife**

wizard ['wɪzəd] n magicien m

wk abbr = **week**

wobble ['wɔbl] vi trembler; (chair)

branler

woe [wəu] n malheur m

woke [wəuk] pt of **wake**; **~n** pp of **wake**

wolf [wulf] (pl **wolves**) n loup m

woman [ˈwumən] (pl **women**) n femme f; **~ doctor** n femme f médecin; **~ly** adj féminin(e)

womb [wu:m] n (ANAT) utérus m

women [ˈwimin] npl of **woman**; **~'s lib** (inf) n MLF m; **W~'s (Liberation) Movement** n mouvement m de libération de la femme

won [wʌn] pt, pp of **win**

wonder [ˈwʌndəʳ] n merveille f, miracle m; (feeling) émerveillement m ♦ vi: **to ~ whether/why** se demander si/pourquoi; **to ~ at** (marvel) s'émerveiller de; **to ~ about** songer à; **it's no ~ (that)** il n'est pas étonnant (que +sub); **~ful** adj merveilleux(-euse)

won't [wəunt] = **will not**

wood [wud] n (timber, forest) bois m; **~ed** adj boisé(e); **~en** adj en bois; (fig) raide; inexpressif(-ive); **~pecker** n pic m (oiseau); **~wind** n (MUS): **the ~wind** les bois mpl; **~work** n menuiserie f; **~worm** n ver m du bois

wool [wul] n laine f; **to pull the ~ over sb's eyes** (fig) en faire accroire à qn; **~len** (US **woolen**) adj de or en laine; (industry) lainier(-ère); **~lens** npl (clothes) lainages mpl; **~ly** (US **wooly**) adj laineux(-euse); (fig: ideas) confus(e)

word [wə:d] n mot m; (promise) parole f; (news) nouvelles fpl ♦ vt rédiger, formuler; **in other ~s** d'autres termes; **to break/keep one's ~** manquer à sa parole/tenir parole; **~ing** n termes mpl; libellé m; **~ processing** n traitement m de texte; **~ processor** n machine f de traitement de texte

wore [wɔ:ʳ] pt of **wear**

work [wə:k] n travail m; (ART, LITERATURE) œuvre f ♦ vi travailler; (mechanism) marcher, fonctionner; (plan etc) marcher; (medicine) agir ♦ vt (clay, wood

etc) travailler; (mine etc) exploiter; (machine) faire marcher or fonctionner; (miracles, wonders etc) faire; **to be out of ~** être sans emploi; **to ~ loose** se défaire, se desserrer; **~ on** vt fus travailler à; (influence) (essayer d')influencer; **~ out** vi (plans etc) marcher ♦ vt (problem) résoudre; (plan) élaborer; **it ~s out at £100** ça fait 100 livres; **~ up** vt: **to get ~ed up** se mettre dans tous ses états; **~able** adj (solution) réalisable; **~aholic** [wə:kəˈhɔlɪk] n bourreau m de travail; **~er** n travailleur(-euse), ouvrier(-ère); **~ experience** n stage m; **~force** n main-d'œuvre f; **~ing class** n classe ouvrière; **~ing-class** adj ouvrier(-ère); **~ing order** n: **in ~ing order** en état de marche; **~man** (irreg) n ouvrier m; **~manship** (skill) n métier m, habileté f; **~s** n (BRIT: factory) usine f ♦ npl (of clock, machine) mécanisme m; **~ sheet** n (for pupil) fiche f d'exercices; (COMPUT) feuille f de programmation; **~shop** n atelier m; **~ station** n poste m de travail; **~-to-rule** (BRIT) n grève f du zèle

world [wə:ld] n monde m ♦ cpd (champion) du monde; (power, war) mondial(e); **to think the ~ of sb** (fig) ne jurer que par qn; **~ly** adj de ce monde; (knowledgeable) qui a l'expérience du monde; **~wide** adj universel(le); **W~ Wide Web** n Web m

worm [wə:m] n ver m

worn [wɔ:n] pp of **wear** ♦ adj usé(e); **~out** adj (object) complètement usé(e); (person) épuisé(e)

worried [ˈwʌrɪd] adj inquiet(-ète)

worry [ˈwʌrɪ] n souci m ♦ vt inquiéter ♦ vi s'inquiéter, se faire du souci

worse [wə:s] adj pire, plus mauvais(e) ♦ adv plus mal ♦ n pire m; **a change for the ~** une détérioration; **~n** vt empirer; **~ off** adj moins à l'aise financièrement; (fig): **you'll be ~ off this way** ça ira moins bien de cette façon

worship [ˈwə:ʃɪp] n culte m (of God)

worst rendre un culte à; (person) adorer; **Your W~** (BRIT: to mayor) Monsieur le maire; (: to judge) Monsieur le juge

worst [wəːst] adj le (la) pire, le (la) plus mauvais(e) ♦ adv le plus mal ♦ n pire m; **at ~** au pis aller

worth [wəːθ] n valeur f ♦ adj: **to be ~** valoir; **it's ~ it** cela en vaut la peine, ça vaut la peine; **it is ~ one's while (to do)** on gagne (à faire); **~less** adj qui ne vaut rien; **~while** adj (activity, cause) utile, louable

worthy [wəːði] adj (person) digne; (motive) louable; **~ of** digne de

would [wud] aux vb **1** (conditional tense): **if you asked him he would do it** si vous le lui demandiez, il le ferait; **if you had asked him he would have done it** si vous le lui aviez demandé, il l'aurait fait
2 (in offers, invitations, requests): **would you like a biscuit?** voulez-vous un biscuit?; **would you close the door please?** voulez-vous fermer la porte, s'il vous plaît?
3 (in indirect speech): **I said I would do it** j'ai dit que je le ferais
4 (emphatic): **it WOULD have to snow today!** naturellement il neige aujourd'hui! or il fallait qu'il neige aujourd'hui!
5 (insistence): **she wouldn't do it** elle n'a pas voulu or elle a refusé de le faire
6 (conjecture): **it would have been midnight** il devait être minuit
7 (indicating habit): **he would go there on Mondays** il y allait le lundi

would-be ['wudbiː] (pej) adj soi-disant
wouldn't ['wudnt] = **would not**
wound¹ [wuːnd] n blessure f ♦ vt blesser
wound² [waund] pt, pp of **wind²**
wove [wəuv] pt of **weave**; **~n** pp of **weave**

wrap [ræp] vt (also: **~ up**) envelopper, emballer; (wind) enrouler; **~per** n (BRIT: of book) couverture f; (on chocolate) emballage m, papier m; **~ping paper** n papier m d'emballage; (for gift) papier cadeau

wreak [riːk] vt: **to ~ havoc (on)** avoir un effet désastreux (sur)

wreath [riːθ] (pl **~s**) n couronne f

wreck [rek] n (ship) épave f; (vehicle) véhicule accidenté; (pej: person) loque humaine ♦ vt démolir; (fig) briser, ruiner; **~age** n débris mpl; (of building) décombres mpl; (of ship) épave f

wren [ren] n (ZOOL) roitelet m

wrench [rentʃ] n (TECH) clé f (à écrous); (tug) violent mouvement de torsion; (fig) déchirement m ♦ vt tirer violemment sur, tordre; **to ~ sth from** arracher qch à or de

wrestle ['resl] vi: **to ~ (with sb)** lutter (avec qn); **~r** n lutteur(-euse); **wrestling** n lutte f; (also: **all-in wrestling**) catch m, lutte f libre

wretched ['retʃid] adj misérable; (inf) maudit(e)

wriggle ['rigl] vi (also: **~ about**) se tortiller

wring [riŋ] (pt, pp **wrung**) vt tordre; (wet clothes) essorer; (fig): **to ~ sth out of sb** arracher qch à qn

wrinkle ['riŋkl] n (on skin) ride f; (on paper etc) pli m ♦ vt plisser ♦ vi se plisser; **~d** adj (skin, face) ridé(e)

wrist [rist] n poignet m; **~watch** n montre-bracelet f

writ [rit] n acte m judiciaire

write [rait] (pt **wrote**, pp **written**) vt, vi écrire; (prescription) rédiger; **~ down** vt noter; (put in writing) mettre par écrit; **~ off** vt (debt) passer aux profits et pertes; (project) mettre une croix sur; **~ out** vt écrire; **~ up** vt rédiger; **~-off** n perte totale; **~r** n auteur m, écrivain m

writhe [raið] vi se tordre

writing ['raitiŋ] n écriture f; (of author) œuvres fpl; **in ~** par écrit; **~ paper** n papier m

papier *m* à lettres

wrong [rɒŋ] *adj* (*incorrect*) faux (fausse); (*morally*) mauvais(e); (*wicked*) mal; (*unfair*) injuste ♦ *adv* mal ♦ *n* tort *m* ♦ *vt* faire du tort à, léser; **you are ~ to do it** tu as tort de le faire; **you are ~ about that, you've got it ~** tu te trompes; **what's ~?** qu'est-ce qui ne va pas?; **you've got the ~ number** vous vous êtes trompé de numéro; **to go ~** (*person*) se tromper; (*plan*) mal tourner; (*machine*) tomber en panne; **to be in the ~** avoir tort; **~ful** *adj* injustifié(e); **~ly** *adv* mal, incorrectement; **~ side** *n* (*of material*) envers *m*

wrote [rəut] *pt of* **write**

wrought iron [rɔːt] *n* fer forgé

wrung [rʌŋ] *pt, pp of* **wring**

wt. *abbr* = **weight**

WWW *n abbr* (= *World Wide Web*): **the ~** le Web

X, x

Xmas ['eksməs] *n abbr* = **Christmas**

X-ray ['eksreɪ] *n* (*ray*) rayon *m* X; (*photo*) radio(graphie) *f*

xylophone ['zaɪləfəun] *n* xylophone *m*

Y, y

Y2K *abbr* (= *year 2000*) l'an *m* 2000

yacht [jɒt] *n* yacht *m*; voilier *m*; **~ing** *n* yachting *m*, navigation *f* de plaisance; **~sman** (*irreg*) *n* plaisancier *m*

Yank [jæŋk], **Yankee** ['jæŋkɪ] (*pej*) *n* Amerloque *m/f*

yap [jæp] *vi* (*dog*) japper

yard [jɑːd] *n* (*of house etc*) cour *f*; (*measure*) yard *m* (= 91,4 *cm*); **~stick** *n* (*fig*) mesure *f*, critères *mpl*

yarn [jɑːn] *n* fil *m*; (*tale*) longue histoire

yawn [jɔːn] *n* bâillement *m* ♦ *vi* bâiller; **~ing** *adj* (*gap*) béant(e)

yd. *abbr* = **yard(s)**

yeah [jeə] (*inf*) *adv* ouais

year [jɪə] *n* an *m*, année *f*; **to be 8 ~s old** avoir 8 ans; **an eight-~-old child** un enfant de huit ans; **~ly** *adj* annuel(le) ♦ *adv* annuellement

yearn [jəːn] *vi*: **to ~ for sth** aspirer à qch, languir après qch

yeast [jiːst] *n* levure *f*

yell [jel] *vi* hurler

yellow ['jeləu] *adj* jaune; **Y~ Pages** ® (*BRIT*) *npl* (*TEL*) *fpl* pages *fpl* jaunes

yelp [jelp] *vi* japper; glapir

yes [jes] *adv* oui; (*answering negative question*) si ♦ *n* oui *m*; **to say/answer ~** dire/répondre oui

yesterday ['jestədɪ] *adv* hier ♦ *n* hier *m*; **~ morning/evening** hier matin/soir; **all day ~** toute la journée d'hier

yet [jet] *adv* encore; déjà ♦ *conj* pourtant, néanmoins; **it is not finished ~** ce n'est pas encore fini *or* toujours pas fini; **the best ~** le meilleur jusqu'ici *or* jusque-là; **as ~** jusqu'ici, encore

yew [juː] *n* if *m*

yield [jiːld] *n* production *f*, rendement *m*; rapport *m* ♦ *vt* produire, rendre, rapporter; (*surrender*) céder ♦ *vi* céder; (*US: AUT*) céder la priorité

YMCA *n abbr* (= *Young Men's Christian Association*) YMCA *m*

yob [jɒb] (*BRIT: inf*) *n* loubar(d) *m*

yog(h)urt ['jəugət] *n* yaourt *m*

yoke [jəuk] *n* joug *m*

yolk [jəuk] *n* jaune *m* (d'œuf)

KEYWORD

you [juː] *pron* **1** (*subject*) tu; (*polite form*) vous; (*plural*) vous; **you French enjoy your food** vous autres Français, vous aimez bien manger; **you and I will go** toi et moi *or* vous et moi, nous irons

2 (*object: direct, indirect*) te, t' +*vowel*, vous; **I know you** je te *or* vous connais; **I gave it to you** je vous l'ai donné, je te l'ai donné

3 (*stressed*) toi; vous; **I told YOU to do it** c'est à toi *or* vous que j'ai dit de le faire

4 (after prep, in comparisons) toi; vous; **it's for you** c'est pour toi or vous; **she's younger than you** elle est plus jeune que toi or vous

5 (impersonal: one) on; **fresh air does you good** l'air frais fait du bien; **you never know** on ne sait jamais

you'd [juːd] = **you had**; **you would**
you'll [juːl] = **you will**; **you shall**

young [jʌŋ] adj jeune ♦ npl (of animal) petits mpl; (people): **the ~** les jeunes, la jeunesse; **~er** [jʌŋɡəʳ] adj (brother etc) cadet(te); **~ster** n jeune m (garçon m); (child) enfant m/f

your [jɔːʳ] adj ton (ta), tes pl; (polite form, pl) votre, vos pl; see also **my**

you're [juəʳ] = **you are**

yours [jɔːz] pron le (la) tien(ne), les tiens (tiennes); (polite form, pl) le (la) vôtre, les vôtres; **~ sincerely/faithfully/truly** veuillez agréer l'expression de mes sentiments les meilleurs; see also **mine¹**

yourself [jɔːˈsɛlf] pron (reflexive) te; (: polite form) vous; (after prep) toi; vous; (emphatic) toi-même; vous-même; see also **oneself**; **yourselves** pl pron vous; (emphatic) vous-mêmes

youth [juːθ] n jeunesse f; (young man: pl ~s) jeune homme m; **~ club** n centre m de jeunes; **~ful** adj jeune; (enthusiasm) de jeunesse, juvénile; **~ hostel** n auberge f de jeunesse

you've [juːv] = **you have**

YTS n abbr (BRIT: Youth Training Scheme) ≈ TUC m

Yugoslav [ˈjuːɡəʊslɑːv] adj yougoslave ♦ n Yougoslave m/f

Yugoslavia [ˈjuːɡəʊˈslɑːvɪə] n Yougoslavie f

yuppie [ˈjʌpɪ] (inf) n yuppie m/f

YWCA n abbr (= Young Women's Christian Association) YWCA m

Z, z

zany [ˈzeɪnɪ] adj farfelu(e), loufoque

zap [zæp] vt (COMPUT) effacer

zeal [ziːl] n zèle m, ferveur f; empressement m

zebra [ˈziːbrə] n zèbre m; **~ crossing** (BRIT) n passage clouté or pour piétons

zero [ˈzɪərəʊ] n zéro m

zest [zɛst] n entrain m, élan m; (of orange) zeste m

zigzag [ˈzɪɡzæɡ] n zigzag m

Zimbabwe [zɪmˈbɑːbwɪ] n Zimbabwe m

Zimmer frame [ˈzɪmə-] n déambulateur m

zinc [zɪŋk] n zinc m

zip [zɪp] n fermeture f éclair ® ♦ vt (also: ~ up) fermer avec une fermeture éclair ®; **~ code** (US) n code postal; **~per** (US) n = **zip**

zit [zɪt] (inf) n bouton m

zodiac [ˈzəʊdɪæk] n zodiaque m

zone [zəʊn] n zone f

zoo [zuː] n zoo m

zoom [zuːm] vi: **to ~ past** passer en trombe; **~ lens** n zoom m

zucchini [zuːˈkiːnɪ] (US) n(pl) courgette(s) f(pl)

VERB TABLES

1 Participe présent *2* Participe passé *3* Présent *4* Imparfait *5* Futur *6* Conditionnel *7* Subjonctif présent

acquérir *1* acquérant *2* acquis *3* acquiers, acquérons, acquièrent *4* acquérais *5* acquerrai *7* acquière

ALLER *1* allant *2* allé *3* vais, vas, va, allons, allez, vont *4* allais *5* irai *6* irais *7* aille

asseoir *1* asseyant *2* assis *3* assieds, asseyons, asseyez, asseyent *4* asseyais *5* assiérai *7* asseye

atteindre *1* atteignant *2* atteint *3* atteins, atteignons *4* atteignais *7* atteigne

AVOIR *1* ayant *2* eu *3* ai, as, a, avons, avez, ont *4* avais *5* aurai *6* aurais *7* aie, aies, ait, ayons, ayez, aient

battre *1* battant *2* battu *3* bats, bat, battons *4* battais *7* batte

boire *1* buvant *2* bu *3* bois, buvons, boivent *4* buvais *7* boive

bouillir *1* bouillant *2* bouilli *3* bous, bouillons *4* bouillais *7* bouille

conclure *1* concluant *2* conclu *3* conclus, concluons, concluais *7* conclue

conduire *1* conduisant *2* conduit *3* conduis, conduisons *4* conduisais *7* conduise

connaître *1* connaissant *2* connu *3* connais, connaît, connaissons *4* connaissais *7* connaisse

coudre *1* cousant *2* cousu *3* couds, cousons, cousez, cousent *4* cousais *7* couse

courir *1* courant *2* couru *3* cours, courons *4* courais *5* courrai *7* coure

couvrir *1* couvrant *2* couvert *3* couvre, couvrons *4* couvrais *7* couvre

craindre *1* craignant *2* craint *3* crains, craignons *4* craignais *7* craigne

croire *1* croyant *2* cru *3* crois, croyons, croient *4* croyais *7* croie

croître *1* croissant *2* crû, crue, crus, crues *3* croîs, croissons *4* croissais *7* croisse

cueillir *1* cueillant *2* cueilli *3* cueille, cueillons *4* cueillais *5* cueillerai *7* cueille

devoir *1* devant *2* dû, due, dus, dues *3* dois, devons, doivent *4* devais *5* devrai *7* doive

dire *1* disant *2* dit *3* dis, disons, dites, disent *4* disais *7* dise

dormir *1* dormant *2* dormi *3* dors, dormons *4* dormais *7* dorme

écrire *1* écrivant *2* écrit *3* écris, écrivons *4* écrivais *7* écrive

ÊTRE *1* étant *2* été *3* suis, es, est, sommes, êtes, sont *4* étais *5* serai *6* serais *7* sois, sois, soit, soyons, soyez, soient

FAIRE *1* faisant *2* fait *3* fais, fais, fait, faisons, faites, font *4* faisais *5* ferai *6* ferais *7* fasse

falloir *1* fallu *3* faut *4* fallait *5* faudra *7* faille

FINIR *1* finissant *2* fini *3* finis, finis, finit, finissons, finissez, finissent *4* finissais *5* finirai *6* finirais *7* finisse

fuir *1* fuyant *2* fui *3* fuis, fuyons, fuient *4* fuyais *7* fuie

joindre *1* joignant *2* joint *3* joins, joignons *4* joignais *7* joigne

lire *1* lisant *2* lu *3* lis, lisons *4* lisais *7* lise

luire *1* luisant *2* lui *3* luis, luisons *4* luisais *7* luise

maudire *1* maudissant *2* maudit *3*

maudis, maudissons 4 maudissait 7 maudisse

mentir 1 mentant 2 menti 3 mens, mentons 4 mentais 7 mente

mettre 1 mettant 2 mis 3 mets, mettons 4 mettais 7 mette

mourir 1 mourant 2 mort 3 meurs, mourons, meurent 4 mourais 5 mourrai 7 meure

naître 1 naissant 2 né 3 nais, naissons 4 naissais 7 naisse

offrir 1 offrant 2 offert 3 offre, offrons 4 offrais 7 offre

PARLER 1 parlant 2 parlé 3 parle, parles, parle, parlons, parlez, parlent 4 parlais, parlais, parlait, parlions, parliez, parlaient 5 parlerai, parleras, parlera, parlerons, parlerez, parleront 6 parlerais, parlerais, parlerait, parlerions, parleriez, parleraient 7 parle, parles, parle, parlions, parliez, parlent *impératif* parle! parlez!

partir 1 partant 2 parti 3 pars, partons 4 partais 7 parte

plaire 1 plaisant 2 plu 3 plais, plaît, plaisons 4 plaisais 7 plaise

pleuvoir 1 pleuvant 2 plu 3 pleut, pleuvent 4 pleuvait 5 pleuvra 7 pleuve

pourvoir 1 pourvoyant 2 pourvu 3 pourvois, pourvoyons, pourvoient 4 pourvoyais 7 pourvoie

pouvoir 1 pouvant 2 pu 3 peux, peut, pouvons, peuvent 4 pouvais 5 pourrai 7 puisse

prendre 1 prenant 2 pris 3 prends, prenons, prennent 4 prenais 7 prenne

prévoir *like* **voir** 5 prévoirai

RECEVOIR 1 recevant 2 reçu 3 reçois, reçois, reçoit, recevons, recevez, reçoivent 4 recevais 5 recevrai 6 recevrais 7 reçoive

RENDRE 1 rendant 2 rendu 3 rends, rends, rend, rendons, rendez, rendent 4 rendais 5 rendrai 6 rendrais 7 rende

résoudre 1 résolvant 2 résolu 3 résous, résolvons 4 résolvais 7 résolve

rire 1 riant 2 ri 3 ris, rions 4 riais 7 rie

savoir 1 sachant 2 su 3 sais, savons, savent 4 savais 5 saurai 7 sache *impératif* sache, sachons, sachez

servir 1 servant 2 servi 3 sers, servons 4 servais 7 serve

sortir 1 sortant 2 sorti 3 sors, sortons 4 sortais 7 sorte

souffrir 1 souffrant 2 souffert 3 souffre, souffrons 4 souffrais 7 souffre

suffire 1 suffisant 2 suffi 3 suffis, suffisons 4 suffisais 7 suffise

suivre 1 suivant 2 suivi 3 suis, suivons 4 suivais 7 suive

taire 1 taisant 2 tu 3 tais, taisons 4 taisais 7 taise

tenir 1 tenant 2 tenu 3 tiens, tenons, tiennent 4 tenais 5 tiendrai 7 tienne

vaincre 1 vainquant 2 vaincu 3 vaincs, vainc, vainquons 4 vainquais 7 vainque

valoir 1 valant 2 valu 3 vaux, vaut, valons 4 valais 5 vaudrai 7 vaille

venir 1 venant 2 venu 3 viens, venons, viennent 4 venais 5 viendrai 7 vienne

vivre 1 vivant 2 vécu 3 vis, vivons 4 vivais 7 vive

voir 1 voyant 2 vu 3 vois, voyons, voient 4 voyais 5 verrai 7 voie

vouloir 1 voulant 2 voulu 3 veux, veut, voulons, veulent 4 voulais 5 voudrai 7 veuille *impératif* veuillez

VERBES IRRÉGULIERS

present	pt	pp	present	pt	pp
arise	arose	arisen	**draw**	drew	drawn
awake	awoke	awaked	**dream**	dreamed,	dreamed,
be (am, is,	was, were	been		dreamt	dreamt
are; being)			**drink**	drank	drunk
bear	bore	born(e)	**drive**	drove	driven
beat	beat	beaten	**dwell**	dwelt	dwelt
become	became	become	**eat**	ate	eaten
begin	began	begun	**fall**	fell	fallen
behold	beheld	beheld	**feed**	fed	fed
bend	bent	bent	**feel**	felt	felt
beset	beset	beset	**fight**	fought	fought
bet	bet,	bet,	**find**	found	found
	betted	betted	**flee**	fled	fled
bid	bid, bade	bid,	**fling**	flung	flung
		bidden	**fly** (flies)	flew	flown
bind	bound	bound	**forbid**	forbade	for-
bite	bit	bitten			bidden
bleed	bled	bled	**forecast**	forecast	forecast
blow	blew	blown	**forget**	forgot	forgotten
break	broke	broken	**forgive**	forgave	forgiven
breed	bred	bred	**forsake**	forsook	forsaken
bring	brought	brought	**freeze**	froze	frozen
build	built	built	**get**	got	got, (US)
burn	burnt,	burnt,			gotten
	burned	burned	**give**	gave	given
burst	burst	burst	**go** (goes)	went	gone
buy	bought	bought	**grind**	ground	ground
can	could	(been	**grow**	grew	grown
		able)	**hang**	hung,	hung,
cast	cast	cast		hanged	hanged
catch	caught	caught	**have** (has;	had	had
choose	chose	chosen	having)		
cling	clung	clung	**hear**	heard	heard
come	came	come	**hide**	hid	hidden
cost	cost	cost	**hit**	hit	hit
creep	crept	crept	**hold**	held	held
cut	cut	cut	**hurt**	hurt	hurt
deal	dealt	dealt	**keep**	kept	kept
dig	dug	dug	**kneel**	knelt,	knelt,
do (3rd	did	done		kneeled	kneeled
person;			**know**	knew	known
he/she/it/			**lay**	laid	laid
does)			**lead**	led	led

614

present	pt	pp	present	pt	pp
lean	leant, leaned	leant, leaned	shine	shone	shone
leap	leapt, leaped	leapt, leaped	shoot	shot	shot
learn	learnt, learned	learnt, learned	show	showed	shown
			shrink	shrank	shrunk
leave	left	left	shut	shut	shut
lend	lent	lent	sing	sang	sung
let	let	let	sink	sank	sunk
lie (lying)	lay	lain	sit	sat	sat
light	lit, lighted	lit, lighted	slay	slew	slain
			sleep	slept	slept
			slide	slid	slid
lose	lost	lost	sling	slung	slung
make	made	made	slit	slit	slit
may	might	—	smell	smelt, smelled	smelt, smelled
mean	meant	meant			
meet	met	met	sow	sowed	sown, sowed
mistake	mistook	mistaken			
mow	mowed	mown, mowed	speak	spoke	spoken
			speed	sped, speeded	sped, speeded
must	(had to)	(had to)	spell	spelt, spelled	spelt, spelled
pay	paid	paid			
put	put	put	spend	spent	spent
quit	quit, quitted	quit, quitted	spill	spilt, spilled	spilt, spilled
read	read	read	spin	spun	spun
rid	rid	rid	spit	spat	spat
ride	rode	ridden	split	split	split
ring	rang	rung	spoil	spoiled, spoilt	spoiled, spoilt
rise	rose	risen			
run	ran	run	spread	spread	spread
saw	sawed	sawn	spring	sprang	sprung
say	said	said	stand	stood	stood
see	saw	seen	steal	stole	stolen
seek	sought	sought	stick	stuck	stuck
sell	sold	sold	sting	stung	stung
send	sent	sent	stink	stank	stunk
set	set	set	stride	strode	stridden
shake	shook	shaken	strike	struck	struck, stricken
shall	should	—			
shear	sheared	shorn, sheared	strive	strove	striven
			swear	swore	sworn
shed	shed	shed	sweep	swept	swept

615

present	pt	pp	present	pt	pp
swell	swelled	swollen, swelled	wake	woke, waked	woken, waked
swim	swam	swum	wear	wore	worn
swing	swung	swung	weave	wove, weaved	woven, weaved
take	took	taken			
teach	taught	taught	wed	wedded, wed	wedded, wed
tear	tore	torn			
tell	told	told	weep	wept	wept
think	thought	thought	win	won	won
throw	threw	thrown	wind	wound	wound
thrust	thrust	thrust	wring	wrung	wrung
tread	trod	trodden	write	wrote	written

LES NOMBRES

NUMBERS

un(une)	1	one
deux	2	two
trois	3	three
quatre	4	four
cinq	5	five
six	6	six
sept	7	seven
huit	8	eight
neuf	9	nine
dix	10	ten
onze	11	eleven
douze	12	twelve
treize	13	thirteen
quatorze	14	fourteen
quinze	15	fifteen
seize	16	sixteen
dix-sept	17	seventeen
dix-huit	18	eighteen
dix-neuf	19	nineteen
vingt	20	twenty
vingt et un(une)	21	twenty-one
vingt-deux	22	twenty-two
trente	30	thirty
quarante	40	forty
cinquante	50	fifty
soixante	60	sixty
soixante-dix	70	seventy
soixante et onze	71	seventy-one
soixante-douze	72	seventy-two
quatre-vingts	80	eighty
quatre-vingt-un(-une)	81	eighty-one
quatre-vingt-dix	90	ninety
quatre-vingt-onze	91	ninety-one
cent	100	a hundred
cent un(une)	101	a hundred and one
trois cents	300	three hundred
trois cent un(une)	301	three hundred and one
mille	1 000	a thousand
un million	1 000 000	a million

premier(première), 1er	first, 1st
deuxième, 2e or 2ème	second, 2nd
troisième, 3e or 3ème	third, 3rd
quatrième	fourth, 4th
cinquième	fifth, 5th
sixième	sixth, 6th

LES NOMBRES

septième
huitième
neuvième
dixième
onzième
douzième
treizième
quatorzième
quinzième
seizième
dix-septième
dix-huitième
dix-neuvième
vingtième
vingt-et-unième
vingt-deuxième
trentième
centième
cent-unième
millième

Les Fractions etc

un demi
un tiers
deux tiers
un quart
un cinquième
zéro virgule cinq, 0,5
trois virgule quatre, 3,4
dix pour cent
cent pour cent

Examples

il habite au dix
c'est au chapitre sept
à la page sept
il habite au septième (étage)
il est arrivé (le) septième
une part d'un septième
échelle au vingt-cinq millième

NUMBERS

seventh
eighth
ninth
tenth
eleventh
twelfth
thirteenth
fourteenth
fifteenth
sixteenth
seventeenth
eighteenth
nineteenth
twentieth
twenty-first
twenty-second
thirtieth
hundredth
hundred-and-first
thousandth

Fractions etc

a half
a third
two thirds
a quarter
a fifth
(nought) point five, 0.5
three point four, 3.4
ten per cent
a hundred per cent

Examples

he lives at number 10
it's in chapter 7
on page 7
he lives on the 7th floor
he came in 7th
a share of one seventh
scale one to twenty-five thousand

L'HEURE

quelle heure est-il?

il est ...

minuit
une heure (du matin)

une heure cinq
une heure dix
une heure et quart
une heure vingt-cinq

une heure et demie, une heure
trente
une heure trente-cinq, deux heures moins vingt-cinq
deux heures moins vingt, une
heure quarante
deux heures moins le quart, une
heure quarante-cinq
deux heures moins dix, une heure cinquante
midi
deux heures (de l'après-midi)

sept heures (du soir)

à quelle heure?

à minuit
à sept heures

dans vingt minutes
il y a quinze minutes

THE TIME

what time is it?

it's ...

midnight, twelve p.m.
one o'clock (in the morning),
one (a.m.)

five past one
ten past one
a quarter past one, one fifteen
twenty-five past one, one
twenty-five
half past one, one thirty

twenty-five to two, one thirty-
five
twenty to two, one forty

a quarter to two, one forty-five

ten to two, one fifty

twelve o'clock, midday, noon
two o'clock (in the afternoon),
two (p.m.)
seven o'clock (in the evening),
seven (p.m.)

at what time?

at midnight
at seven o'clock

in twenty minutes
fifteen minutes ago